Economics:

in terms of
The Good, The Bad and The Economist

Second edition

Matt McGee

Library Catalogue:

McGee, M.

1. Economics, 2. International Baccalaureate.

Series Title: International.

2. International Baccalaureate.

Series Title: International Baccalaureate in Detail.

ISBN-13: 978-1-876659-22-6

ISBN-10: 1-876659-10-6

IBID Press would like to sincerely thank the International Baccalaureate Organisation for permission to reproduce its intellectual property.

This material has been developed independently by the publisher and the content is in no way connected with nor endorsed by the International Baccalaureate Organisation.

Acknowledgements

While every care has been taken to trace and acknowledge copyright, the publishers tender their apologies for any accidental infringement where copyright has proved untraceable. They would be pleased to come to a suitable arrangement with the rightful owner in each case.

The publisher and author would like to thank the following individuals and organisations for their kind permission to reproduce personal and copyright material:

Pages: 47 Chengdu: Melinda Lancashire; 87 media.artdiamondblog.com; 524 Muhammad Yunus, Grameen Bank: Nobel Committee.

Rather than indicating every occurrence of a trademarked name as such, this book uses the names only in an editorial manner and to the benefit of the trademark owner with no intention of infringement of the trademark. Trademarks used in this book are the property of their respective owners.

Cover design by Adcore Creative.

Published by IBID Press, 36 Quail Crescent, Melton 3337, Victoria, Australia.

Printed by Trojan Press, Victoria, Australia.

DEDICATION

Writing this book would have been a nightmare without the existence of the people below. I will not live long enough to repay my debt to them.

Top of the Thank You List must of course go to Rob the Housey. In the two years we've shared a house here on Expat Street you have shown yourself to be a man of exceptional honesty, incredible consideration, infinite kindness, unthinking generosity and off-the-grid humour. You never made an issue of giving me as much writing time as possible by way of doing the shopping, taking care of food and making sure the bills were paid on time. Not once have we had the slightest form of altercation. Never have the following phrases been uttered in our house: 'Em, could you clean up your mess?' (= the maid will do it, ultimately); 'Isn't it your turn to do the dishes?' (= there are some clean ones left, I can wait for the maid); 'Em, could you clean up your room since my girlfriend is coming over?' (= 'Hey mate, I closed your bedroom door, OK?'). These have been two of the best years of my life – and I have a lot more years than you to compare with! Perhaps the only irritant is that you can still arm-curl a lot more weight than I.

To Arianna – friend, colleague and saviour: don't ever leave! Basically, remain in school every day doing all the things I get paid to do but in fact wind up on your desk. We both know I'd be lost without you … but I don't think John and Susan need know this. Seriously, I love you Kid.

To Toni, Paty, Jacki and Amelie: Thank you for taking care of me and making sure I don't do the wrong thing in the wrong place with the wrong person. Mexico is not the place to go off experimenting. You gave me a home here.

To my wonderful students: thank you for being the wonderful people you are. You made sure I survived here in Mexico. Your kindnesses (cigars, tequila and parties) and wonderful sense of humour (yes, I know that 'jugo con pulpa' is not octopus juice) kept me going. I apologise beforehand for all the stories about you I've included here. No, wait, I don't apologise at all – you deserve it! To the ladies; don't marry rich! To the gentlemen; a Windsor knot is the only tie-knot worth tying!

To the gang here on Expat Street: Thank you John and Lizzie for taking pity on me and making sure I got a hot meal now and then – and for the speed with which your tequila bottle comes out. Thank you Nikki and Graham for top notch TV ('Massive!') together with the very occasional (and very small) jelly bean – and for helpful hints into the female psyche. Thank you Dom for tea and help with photos – and for being the only person with less hair than I. Thank you Kim and Steve for hospitality and midday sandwiches, and for letting me go running rather than wake-boarding. Thank you Marc and Hang for wonderful food and for keeping track of when Rob gets home at night. Thank you Skinny-Chick and Naomi for wine and relaxation – not to mention about 45,856 stories that will go into the next edition.

Thank you Clarissa for my desks, shelves and copies – and for not firing me. Thank you John for your humour and wonderful laissez faire attitude towards your teachers – and for not firing me. Thank you Susan for prompt delivery of *The Financial Times* and access to school whenever – and for not firing me.

To Marcia the Intrepid Editor: you got thrown to the dogs by way of me landing on your to-do table. Sorry. Heart felt thanks for your patience, diligence and skill. I owe you.

Matt McGee

Mexico City, 19 May 2009

Author and blue marlin

PREFACE

Dear Student,

It won't take you many pages of reading this book to realise that I am a very happy man. I get to do what I love, and I love what I do, which is warp young innocent minds with economics. It's a bit like the 1950s film *Invasion of the Body Snatchers*; I take a normal young person and replace him/her with an identical external copy – but who secretly has become an economist.

This book has been written for you, not your teacher. The theory content is mainstream economics and in accordance with the IB syllabus, but the style of writing is uniquely mine, and will naturally differ from other teachers in general and your teacher in particular. It is most important that you realise this, and that this book – like so many others – doesn't contain the 'truth' in any way, but merely one of many possible versions of what we call reality. You and your teachers will both agree and disagree with some of the content here, and that is exactly as it should be! From disagreement comes discussion and debate. From debate comes argumentation. And from argumentation comes learning – to both sides hopefully.

Life is fun and so is economics. In fact, I cannot separate the two any longer – much to the irritation of anyone who tries to hold a serious conversation with me. I urge you not to regard economics as a subject confined to classrooms and complex diagrams, but as an outlook on life and things happening around you. That is why I have put so many personal little stories in here; to convince you that economics is just a way of putting words to events and concepts thereby providing a little order and structure.

Dear Colleague,

Virtually every economics colleague I meet is either better educated, more experienced, or a better teacher than I. I have realised this for some time and therefore know that they could have written a book as good – or better – than this one. The difference between them and me is that I did, and they didn't. You are thus not holding what is a book on economics – nor is it the book on economics. It is my book on economics, which means – for better or worse – that the examples and stories are all done from a personal vantage point, and laced with my own rather pithy sense of humour. The personal outlook is intentional, as I wish to show our students that life indeed is applied economics. The stories, jokes and shoot-from-the-hip comments are unfortunately inevitable – I simply don't find anything really worth taking that seriously. Especially myself.

I sincerely hope you are not put off by the personal style of writing and come to realise that while there is lots of nonsense interspaced in the text, there is also a good deal of rather sensible and accessible economics. My reasoning is simple; a spoonful of sugar helps the medicine go down. I have always found that if one is able to hook new and sometimes intimidating concepts onto scenarios or events which people are familiar with, or can see humour in, learning becomes easier. Economics is not boring or other-worldly, so why should economics texts be that way? It is always easier to pull a piece of string across a table than push it.

Winston Churchill once said; 'Criticism may not be agreeable, but it is necessary. It fulfils the same function as pain in the human body. It calls attention to an unhealthy state of things'. The editors and proofreaders at IBID have spent countless hours seeking out errors, omissions and mistakes, yet I alone am ultimately responsible. There will naturally be mistakes in the text – either due to oversight or plain ignorance on my part. You and your students would be of invaluable assistance to me if you bring to my attention any and all errors in the text – and/or comment on the book in general. Write to me and the errors will be immediately commented on in the 'Errata' section of the Economics homepage at http://www.ibid.com.au. I will answer all serious correspondence.

With my penchant towards rather pedantic academia coupled with shoot-from-the-hip Irish blarney; with humility, anticipation and dread in equal portions; I am

Yours, Matt (matt.ibid@hotmail.com)

USING THIS BOOK

The structure of the book

This book follows the IB syllabus to the letter – in fact, the headings used herein are the same as the IB syllabus. Main syllabus headings are in blue and smaller IB syllabus headings are clearly marked with '©IBO 2003'. It is definitely not necessary to follow the syllabus order (in fact, many teachers don't), yet I would recommend doing Section 1 and 2.1 initially, since the concepts therein are the basis for much of economic theory.

Section 1 deals with the economic basics, such as opportunity costs and the basic economic problems arising in societies. While this section might be considered a bit long, the intention is to give new students a breadth of examples and illustrations to make the initial meeting with economics as easy as possible.

Section 2 goes into microeconomics, and again, I have taken care to extensively exemplify and illustrate the use of perhaps the most important economic model: supply and demand. Having a solid understanding of how to use and apply the basic supply and demand model makes it easier to learn higher order concepts in later chapters.

Section 3 deals with macroeconomics, and at this stage I have assumed students to be comfortable with basic economic concepts, so I have limited the extent of explanatory text and increased the use of case studies and applied economics.

Section 4 focuses on trade issues, and is strongly linked to both micro/macro issues and development. I have put great effort into finding examples and statistics of recent date, and to use as many contextual examples as could fit.

Section 5 is development economics and builds heavily on concepts introduced in all other syllabus sections. The 'spread' of development issues throughout the syllabus is intentional, as IB economics puts major focus on development issues and emphasizes this by relating development to a number of issues throughout the syllabus.

Throughout the book

Numerous *Pop quizzes* have been included in every section and sub-section. These are of 'test your understanding of the issues above' type, and the answers are included at the back of the book.

Outside the box is where I have put non-syllabus concepts, theories and models. *A little depth* means that a certain syllabus concept/theory is examined further and/or applied in greater depth. *Case studies* bring up current and historical events pertaining to economics. *Applied economics* looks at specific scenarios from an economic vantage point. All of these are really just 'flesh on the bones' of the core IB syllabus content, and are included merely to tweak interest and further illustrate the linkage between our complex world and economic thought. *Storytime* is mostly nonsense that I simply couldn't resist including. All of the content under the captions above is clearly delineated from the core body of text.

At the end of all sections – and many sub-sections – I have included a number of short answer and extended response questions. While short answer questions are not really intended for SL, I have deliberately included short answer questions that are applicable to SL content. Data response questions have been left out completely, as I felt it better to cover a wide range of issues in as little space as possible – this is easier to do using short answer and extended response questions. Most schools have a battery of data response questions to use in practice tests.

All of the answers to the short answer and essay questions are to found at http://www.ibid.com.au. They may be downloaded, printed and copied for use within your own institution at your discretion.

Contents

SECTION 2   MICROECONOMICS   49

INTRODUCTION TO ECONOMICS

1

Economics is the study of us. As economists we are basically studying what we are, how we have created societies and what drives us. In studying this we are gathering information in order to outline possible solutions to very real problems.

Introduction to economics

1.1

CONTENTS

INTRODUCTION TO ECONOMICS

Definitions of social science and economics ©IBO 2003

Every year I introduce this wonderful subject to IB1s whose initial interest in economics varies from 'keen' to 'I'd rather be cleaning my room!' I spend my first hours with the uninitiated trying to impress upon them two main points. The first is that economics is the study of *us*; as economists we are basically studying what we are, how we have created societies and what drives us. In studying this we are gathering information in order to outline possible solutions to very real problems and my key point here is that economics is not an abstract study (= purely theoretical or hypothetical) of 'numbers and money' but an *applied science*. We look at reality with the intention of using information gathered in order to construct models and theories useful in real life, for example issues such as how to increase the production of food and goods without causing irreparable damage to the environment. My second point to young economists is that economics is not a 'dismal science'[1] but in fact a rather *optimistic* science. The basic facts are that in many respects humankind is increasingly better off: we live longer and healthier lives and have immensely increased the opportunities, choices and abilities to lead better lives – of course that there are some notable and distressing exceptions and that the future is by no means certain.

Social science

Social science is an umbrella concept, i.e. a concept which covers any number of things – here, a number of sub-disciplines. A dry and somewhat uninspiring definition is that social science is the study of human society and of the relationships between people and organisations/institutions over time. Social science seeks thus to address the fundamental questions that follow the existence of humankind and its civilisations, spanning from Hammurabi's Laws (the oldest known written laws of man, circa 1775 BC, Mesopotamia) to the present debate on cloning human beings. In between you can find such earth shattering issues as 'Who is the most efficient singer in AC/DC, Bon Scott or Brian Johnson?'[2] Naturally, such a span of study must be broken down into more manageable

components and this gives us a lengthy list of disciplines under the collective 'umbrella'. More specific social sciences can be used to study a particular phase or aspect in the myriad societal events within the boundaries of human endeavour. This gives us the sub-disciplines commonly included in social studies, such as the scientific disciplines history, sociology, psychology, anthropology, political science and economics.

> Social science: A science which studies the institutions, functions, relationships and organisation of human society.

Social science = weak science?

A fundamental weakness in the field of social science is the lack of absolute answers – social sciences do not deal with the (relative) certainties of mathematics and natural sciences and therefore is full of diverse and conflicting claims and conclusions. It can be considered 'weak' as a science, since it is quite possible – some even say probable – that different scientists will arrive at different answers to the same question, while being scientifically correct. In other words, two social scientists could use the exact same set of data but approach it from different models or theories and arrive at entirely different conclusions.

In any given social science it is clear that there are countless unknown and quite unpredictable variables which can influence outcomes any which way. Trying to construct a model which correctly predicts changes in societal behaviour – say changes in *consumption* – as a result of changes in an associated variable – say *income* – will be full of faults since so many other (often unknown) influences on consumption patterns exist. The way forward is to arrive at a conclusion by looking at a *select few* well-defined variables – here, income and consumption – while assuming that any *other possible influences do not change* or impact on consumption. (This is 'keeping all else constant' and has a central role in economic theory – see "Ceteris paribus" on page 13.)

This is the main reason why models, theories and ultimately the resulting predictions in the social sciences are so rife with *assumptions*. In putting together a study on the impact of changing incomes on

---

1. A quote commonly attributed to 19th century author Thomas Carlyle who was referring to the economists Thomas Malthus and David Ricardo.
2. You think I'm making this up? Check out University of Calgary archives at http://mpra.ub.uni-muenchen.de/3196/.

the level of consumption in society, the social scientist will have to keep a number of variables constant in the model – such as price level, social benefits, tax levels and anything which has been shown to have an impact on consumption. This is the only way in which the scientist can arrive at a clear and answerable question or *hypothesis* (which is basically a question posed as a statement) that can be proved or disproved.

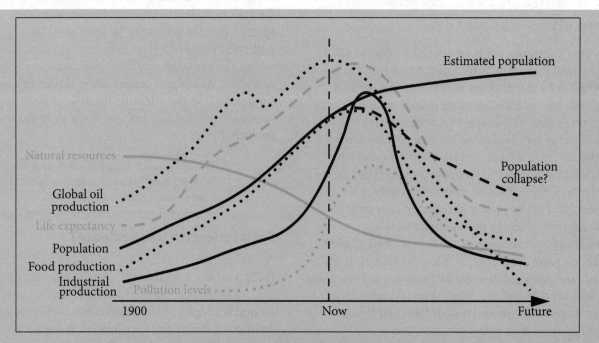

(Source: adapted from Meadows 1992, p.133, *World oil*. Duncan & Youngquist 1998)

Figure 1.1.1 *Then ... now and when?*

Figure 1.1.1 is an attempt to illustrate what is indeed the title of this book: *The Good* – rising food and industrial production has more than kept pace with population growth (in fact, food output *per person* today is greater than ever!) and life expectancy has increased dramatically; *the Bad* – decreasing natural resources together with increasing population; *and the Economist* – the core question of how the ongoing depletion of natural resources and rising populations can be met by increased efficiency in the production of food and the development of alternative energy sources. The future scenarios are most uncertain but, as one single example, economists take into consideration the prospect of a production peak for oil (it already has according to the Energy Watch Group![a]) and that decreasing oil production together with the depletion of natural resources might result in *falling* food and industrial production. Noticeably missing in Figure 1.1.1 are many other issues facing our world such as global warming, HIV/AIDS, poverty levels, fresh water supplies, and so forth. What we do in economics is study these issues from the point of view of how societies' wants and needs can be met now and in the future.

---

a. 'Steep decline in oil production brings risk of war and unrest, says new study', *The Guardian*, 22 October 2007.

Scientific method

Using the variables consumption and income as an example, the basic three-step methodology of the social scientist is the following:[4]

1. The first step is to organise reality in a rational manner by observation and subsequent gathering of data[5]. It is most important to define the concepts that are being systematised. If we are studying income and the effects on consumption then it is imperative to clearly outline whether we are looking at gross or net income, including social benefits or not, what time period, which population, etc.

---

4.   This is loosely based on the work of Karl Popper – to whom your TOK teacher will most assuredly introduce you!

5.   It should be noted that many a cynical social scientist has observed that 'data is the plural of anecdote ... if the anecdotes have been selected systematically'.

2. Next is to spotlighting aspects of the data in order to see whether any patterns emerge. Any and all models and/or theories which emerge will inevitably be limited in applicability but the basic strategy is to find correlation (= a relationship or correspondence) between the variables being studied. We might see that consumption increases as net incomes rise (e.g. positive correlation).

3. Finally, one formulates a hypothesis based on any patterns, for example, 'increased income results in an increase in consumption' and then tests this by applying the model to other sets of data (such as the income and consumption figures over a longer time period or for another country) in order to see whether the model has more general applicability, i.e. to test whether the results are generally consistent with the theory being formulated.

It has been put to me by a number of my colleagues – independently of each other – in the 'hard-core' sciences such as mathematics and physics that pure mathematics is the only 'real' and 'dependable' science. All the rest are invented by us and thus subject to continuous re-examination and rebuilding. As the world around us is increasingly dynamic and inconsistent, the life expectancy of any given social model of human interaction will necessarily be limited and will have to be modified intermittently. One *must*, in fact, teach old dogs new tricks in the social sciences.

POP QUIZ 1.1.1   ON SOCIAL SCIENCE

1 'The social sciences are generally "weaker" than the natural sciences'. Comment on the accuracy of this statement.

2 What is the purpose of including assumptions in scientific models?

3 You are collecting data to be used in an essay on cruelty to animals. You are using official company data on animal usage by large pharmaceutical firms. Comment on the reliability of these figures.

Economics

John Maynard Keynes, perhaps the most famous of all modern economists, claimed that economics was the most difficult of sciences, as one needed to be a mathematician, philosopher, politician and psychologist[6]. A standard textbook definition would be along the lines of 'economics is about utilising and allocating scarce economic resources to achieve optimum output and/or utility', and most of my colleagues would agree that three key concepts are at the heart of economics, namely *scarcity, resource allocation* and *incentives*[7]. The first two concepts deal with how societies use scarce resources to produce the endless needs and wants in society. The third issue is that of how people, firms and institutions will act in accordance with these needs and wants; the willingness and ability of households to save, work and start businesses; the willingness of firms to invest, produce and innovate, and the *willingness* and *ability* of institutions to regulate such transactions and provide safety nets.

Right, who wants something?!

My own personal favourite (which I stole from someone, naturally) is that *economics is about incentives* – everything else is a footnote. I also make sure that my bright-eyed and bushy-tailed younger students get to hear me – at least once during the first week – that 'you're born, live through an endless series of trade-offs, and then you die'.

Economics looks at the systems created by society which exist to serve us in order to improve the system and thus societal wellbeing. The economist takes care to define 'beneficial to society' in as measurable terms as possible. 'Beneficial' can mean 'the highest possible quantity of goods for the lowest possible consumption of resources' – but also 'inflicting the lowest possible costs on society in producing goods'[8]. However

---

6. Keynes' exact words were: '... the master economist must possess a rare combination of gifts ... He must be a mathematician, historian, statesman [and] philosopher – in some degree. He must understand symbols and speak in words ... He must study the present in the light of the past for the purposes of the future. No part of man's nature or his institutions must lie entirely outside his regard.' (See *Essays in Biography. The Collected Writings of John Maynard Keynes*, Vol.X, Royal Economic Society. Published by MacMillan Press Ltd 1972.)
7. Allocation is central to economic terminology. It means roughly, 'placement', or 'the placing of'.

pompous this might sound, we are basically dealing with optimising production methods, increasing the quantity of goods, enhancing the quality and choice of goods – and increasing everyone's accessibility to the goods.

> Economics: The study (= weighing of options) of **society's** (= individuals, organisations, institutions) **optimal use** (= best allocation in terms of alternative possible uses) of **scant resources** (land, labour, capital). Economics is a social science focused primarily on the analysis of the societal systems of production, distribution, and consumption of goods and services.

The methodology of the economist means using a specific set of well-defined terms and concepts and applying them to the complexities of reality. In doing this, he/she must by and large disregard individual behaviour in favour of group behaviour. It is virtually impossible to predict how a single individual will act but quite possible to give general predictions on the behaviour of a group. In the manner outlined in the social science introduction above, an economist uses previous observations to formulate a theory of behaviour and build a model, e.g. that rising incomes will in all probability cause consumption to increase on a general level. By basing forecasts and predictions on oft-observed patterns put into a model, predicting the 'behaviour of the herd', as I am fond of saying, is far more accurate than pinpointing the actions of an individual wildebeest (= gnu).

A little depth:
Correlation vs causality

It is important to note that correlation is *not* the same as causality! Consider three variables: income, consumption and birth rate. Standard economic theory shows that an increase in general incomes in a country will lead to higher consumption rates as any given percentage of income going towards consumption will necessarily mean higher consumption as incomes grow. We have **positive correlation** between the variables income and consumption. Studies also show that as incomes grow (on a national level) the birth rate markedly falls – this means that there is **negative correlation** between income and birth rates. Hence, a collection of data on birth rates and consumption might show how birth

rates fall when consumption in households rises – this would in all likelihood be an example of 'spurious' or nonsense correlation.

Thus, while there is correlation in all three cases above, one would be on thin ice indeed in claiming that there is also causality in all pairs. In the case of income and consumption most economists would agree that the increase in income causes an increase in general consumption – a relatively clear example of cause and effect. Most studies would also show that increasing incomes over time leads to a drop in birth rates (often measured as live births per 1,000 women) as higher tax revenues provide social welfare systems and pension funds which in turn enable couples not to have to rely on having a good many children to take care of them in times of need and old age. Rising incomes will cause lower birth rates. In other words, there is also a causal flow (causality) in regards to changes in income and subsequent changes in consumption and birth rates.

The point to be made now is that if we were to study the variables consumption and birth rates we might well find that there would be negative correlation: as total consumption rises over a period of years, birth rates fall! This is where a good, sceptical outlook on the use of statistics is absolutely vital. It is pretty obvious that increased consumption does not cause lower birth rates or vice versa, but that the two are in causal contact with a common underlying variable – income. Figure 1.1.2 illustrates the difference between the variables that are correlated and the variables which show causal links.

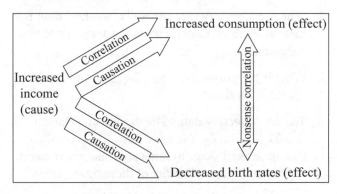

Figure 1.1.2 *Nonsense correlation*

Correlation without causality is spurious (= fake, false) or nonsense correlation. There are some pretty far-out examples of studies which – in varying degrees of self-seriousness – find strong correlation between a number of variables. One classic study in 1875 by the famous economist William Jevons found correlation

---

8. For a most illustrative illustration on the challenges and issues dealt with by the science of economics, I recommend the list of global priorities put together by the Copenhagen Consensus at www.copenhagenconsensus.com.

between sun-spots and the business cycle (see http://cepa.newschool.edu/het/profiles/jevons) while more recent (jesting?) studies show positive correlation between the amount of churches and violent crime (see http://www.selu.edu/Academics/Education)! My personal favourite, however, is the classic study from 1950 showing an astoundingly strong (positive) correlation between the number of people classified as 'mental defectives' and the number of radios in households during the 1930s and 1940s (see http://www.sommestad.com/text/essay). (They must have been listening to an early version of rap music. Proto-rap, maybe.)

In these three examples, the answer to seeming correlation can be found in underlying, common variables. Sun spots might cause changes in weather patterns and thus crops which ultimately could lead to increased harvests and falling grain prices and, in turn, trigger a crisis. Churches are more frequent in highly populated areas and this often means cities – which have higher crime rates than the countryside. As for radios and correlation to mental illness, the study was carried out during a period of rapid societal change which would lead to the radio becoming a common household item and vast improvements in diagnosing mental illness. Thus, in all three cases, seeming correlation must in fact be explained by entirely different data.

Final note: As any number of my colleagues delight in pointing out, it is a mainstay of the failings of the dismal science of economics that it is often impossible to actually definitely prove causality. Too often there are so many underlying and parallel variables involved that it becomes impossible to attribute (or even show) causality between a pair of variables. There are simply too many other possible influences to attribute a degree of causality to any one variable. I strongly recommend Chapter 4 'Where have all the criminals gone?' in the book *Freakonomics*[9], where the authors claim that the remarkable decrease in crime rates in the US during the 1990s had little or nothing to do with a 'roaring economy', harsher gun laws, increased use of the death penalty or new police strategies but was clearly linked to the famous US abortion law (Roe v. Wade) from 1973! The authors make a case that mothers who are socially disadvantaged – single parents with low income – are strongly correlated with having children turning to crime. The dramatic increase in abortions during the 1970s meant fewer births in the very social groups where children were at worst risk in becoming

criminals. The effect of this was that by the time the early 1990s rolled around, there were far fewer early teens with the propensity to become criminals and the crime rate began to fall. I hasten to point out that the authors very quickly question their own results by stating the 'likeliest first objection', namely that there might NOT be causality but simply correlation. They then use several statistical methods to test their findings and indeed find causality.

Definitions of microeconomics and macroeconomics ©IBO 2003

Microeconomics centres on the forces working at the individual level, e.g. the behavioural patterns and decision making processes of individual firms and consumers (often bunched together in households) . Here economics focuses on the needs, desires and buying habits of the individual consumer in conjunction with the output capabilities of firms for particular products. In short, microeconomics looks at firms' output and pricing decisions and consumers' purchasing decisions, for example studying how firms react to increasing costs of production by raising the price and subsequently how consumer/household spending is adjusted when the price rises.

> **Microeconomics**: Microeconomics is the field of economics dealing with the **relationships between individual components** in the economy: firms, industries and consumers (households). This interplay is the basis for individual markets.

Withdrawing from the study of individual market participants in order to study the broad interaction of the aggregate (= sum, combined, cumulative) of separate (micro) parts is the venue of **macroeconomics**. The four main issues here are aggregate *output* (and thus economic growth), *price level* (and thus inflation), *labour* markets (e.g. unemployment), and finally *foreign sector* dealings (such as the balance of trade and exchange rates). Central to the study of macroeconomics is the business cycle (also known as the trade cycle), which shows total output in the economy over time – this is often put into the context of variations in economic activity (recessions and expansions) and the links to macroeconomic policy.

---

9.   Steven D. Levit & Stephen J. Dubner, *Freakonomics*, 2005.

> **Macroeconomics**: The sum total of all micro parts, the **aggregate of individuals' and firms' behaviour**. The four main areas of study are:
> 1. growth (increase in total output)
> 2. price level (inflation)
> 3. labour market (unemployment)
> 4. the balance in the foreign sector (exports/imports, exchange rates).

Let us compare the two using a few examples. Looking at how a firm reacts to increased demand for its product is a micro-issue while studying the effects on all firms in the economy due to a general increase in demand is a macro-issue; the decision of a worker to work less due to lower wages is micro while total hours of labour (and unemployment) is macro; the effects on an industry (= group of firms producing similar goods) due to higher labour taxes is micro while the effect on total production in the economy due to taxes is macro; government legislation aimed at monopolies is micro but government legislation aimed at increasing taxes on profits for all firms is macro.

The distinction between the two areas is admittedly blurred, somewhat contrived and ultimately none-too-useful. I often find the two areas overlapping and would be hard put to draw a concrete line between them in many real-life situations. Basically the difference isn't vitally important unless an exam question addresses the issue … which is just the sort of statement designed to get me into a hefty argument with some of my colleagues[10].

POP QUIZ 1.1.2   ECONOMICS AS A SCIENCE

1   Would the study of a price war between rival firms be a microeconomic or macroeconomic issue?

2   What are the main issues in macroeconomics? Are there any other issues one could include? Explain your answer.

3   Explain the main difference between micro and macro using the term 'aggregate'.

Growth, development, sustainable development ©IBO 2003

Economists are heavily preoccupied – obsessed some might say – with the concept of economic growth. At the heart of almost any discussion in macroeconomics there will be references to growth and its link to other economic variables, say unemployment and/or inflation.

Growth

Growth is when an economy expands, e.g. there is an increase in the quantity of goods and services produced in an economy. In general usage, national output is the sum of all goods and services produced by an economy during a given period of time – usually one year. This is called Gross Domestic Product (GDP) or Gross National Product (GNP) the distinction of which will be made clear in Section 3.1. Growth, or more correctly *economic growth*, measures the total increase in goods and services produced within an economy (i.e. GDP) compared to a previous time period. GDP is put into money values and often put into real terms, i.e. adjusted for inflation.

> **Growth**: Growth is the increase in national output (GDP – gross domestic product) within an economy (country or region) during a time period – usually 12 months. This is put in *percentage terms* to show the annual percentage increase in output compared to a previous time period. It is measured in money terms and *adjusted for inflation* to show *real* growth, i.e. to show what has actually been produced by disregarding the amount by which goods and services have increased in price. Growth is therefore the **increase in real GDP during one year**.

In my childhood home in a place called Åkers Styckebruk[11], Sweden, there is a well-scribbled and well-hacked doorpost where countless children, grandchildren, friends, and neighbourhood kids have marked their height during the past 30 years. Careful scrutiny yields the name of my oldest friend, Guy, several times and more recently Amanda – his daughter. *Tempus fugit*, and all that[12]. Amanda's marks on the doorpost are shown in Figure 1.1.3.

---

10. I answer all correspondence. Please write to me at matt.ibid@hotmail.com.
11. Not pronounced 'Acres of Stickybricks'.
12. 'Time flies' (and, according to my mother, gravity sucks).

We see four specific points in time in Figure 1.1.3 and Amanda's height at each specific time. The change in height between the four points in time is, of course, growth. The rate of change per time period is illustrated in the simple table.

What this simple example illustrates is that growth is a dynamic concept and can really only be measured by looking at the change between time periods. Amanda's growth rate can only be measured by 'taking stock' of her actual height on two occasions. (Note that the 'growth rate' for Amanda increases during both Period 2 and Period 3 – something her parents no doubt loved as she grew out of all her clothing at an even quicker rate.)

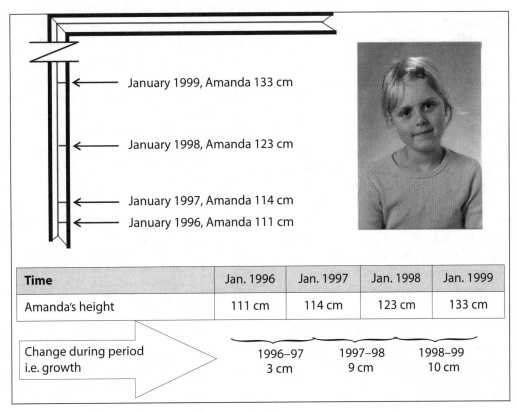

Time	Jan. 1996	Jan. 1997	Jan. 1998	Jan. 1999
Amanda's height	111 cm	114 cm	123 cm	133 cm

Change during period i.e. growth	1996–97 3 cm	1997–98 9 cm	1998–99 10 cm

January 1999, Amanda 133 cm

January 1998, Amanda 123 cm

January 1997, Amanda 114 cm
January 1996, Amanda 111 cm

Figure 1.1.3 *Amanda's growth 1996 to 1999*

Table 1.1.1 *Using Sweden's GDP figures for the same period**

Year	1996	1997	1998	1999
Real GDP for Sweden (SEK = Swedish crowns)	1,958 Billion SEK	2,002 Billion SEK	2,070 Billion SEK	2,143 Billion SEK

Economic growth rates for Sweden

e.g. period 1:

$$\frac{2,002 - 1,958}{1,958} \times 100 = 2.24\%$$

Period 1 (1996–97) 2.24%	Period 2 (1997–98) 3.4%	Period 3 (1998–99) 3.5%

* Swedish Bureau of statistics, at http://www.scb.se/templates/tableOrChart____26651.asp

Just like Amanda, the rate of growth of Sweden is increasing during the time period from 2.24% per year to 3.5% per year[13] (see Table 1.1.1). Often the term 'national *income*' is used when referring to total output in an economy. This is actually identical to output, the reason being that the total money value of all output is

13. But when the 'Dotcom bubble' burst in early 2000 the rate of growth slowed to just over 1%.

in fact the income of firms – which are owned by people. Just picture a fish shop in Åkers Styckebruk selling a tin of surströmming[14]; the price paid by the consumer is the same as the money received by the owner. The value of output (tin of rotten fish) is the same as income (the price paid for the tin), hence output and income are identical.

A little depth:
Stock and flow concepts

It helps to understand the two basic concepts of **stock** and **flow**. A stock concept is a quantity or amount at a given point in time – a snapshot picture – for example, amount of savings in the bank. If one has US$100 in the bank in January and US$250 in February, then one has increased the flow of savings into the bank account by US$150. This saving (note no 's'!) shows the change (flow) in savings (with an 's'!) per time period, which is a flow. Savings is thus a stock concept and savings is a flow concept. Another common stock and flow 'pair' is, respectively, the price level and inflation. Inflation is the change (flow concept) in the general price level (a stock concept which has been indexed – see Section 3.1) between two points in time.

In Table 1.1.2, the value of each variable is given at a specific point in time – t_0 is the starting point in time and t_1 is the next – and this gives the flow values, i.e. the change over the time period.

Table 1.1.2 *Stock and flow*

Variables (stock/flow)	Stock at t_0	Stock at t_1	Change (= flow)
Savings & saving	Savings = US$100 in the bank in Jan	Savings = USD250 in the bank in Dec	Saving of US$150
Price level & inflation	Price level = 100 in Jan	Price level = 105 in Dec	5% inflation

National income is in fact a flow concept, as we are measuring the total amount of expenditure (spending) on goods and services during a period of time. Growth is a statement of how much this flow changes from one period to another. This is examined in greater detail in Section 3.1 on national income accounting.

Development

One of the central questions you will have to deal with in the IB course is the distinction between growth and **development**. While defining growth is relatively straightforward, the concept of development is notoriously tricky to define. Where growth is a matter of accounting for increases in the quantity of output, development is highly subjective and in many cases is very broadly defined. There are many weaknesses and difficulties involved in comparing the GDP and growth of different countries, as mentioned above, and arriving at a reasonable way to compare development levels in different countries is even more complex for the simple reason that development is a **qualitative** measurement rather than growth which is a **quantitative** measurement.

> **Development**: The concept of development is a qualitative variable and thus far broader than any of the variables aimed at describing it. A short definition would be 'an increase in the standard of living across a broad section of the general population'. Development is therefore often put in terms of goal attainment such as access to basic necessities such as food, water and shelter; availability of employment, education and culture, and having social choices and basic freedoms such as freedom of speech and democratic elections. An often used indicator of development is the **Human Development Index** (HDI) which measures attainment levels for education, life expectancy and GDP per capita (see Section 3.2). Note that this definition is somewhat lacking, as 'It does not, for example, include important indicators such as respect for human rights, democracy and inequality'. (Human Development Report, 2006, p. 263).

Development as a goal

So what is it that wealthy countries have that poor countries don't, aside from wealth? Why is that 'some places prosper and thrive while others just do not?' in the words of the very cynical humorist P. J. O'Rourke[15]. The answer to this lies in the definition of development, which is notoriously difficult to define and differs greatly between economists. I would follow Michael Todaro[16], one of the leading economists on the subject, in outlining three main focal areas which frame *development as a goal*:

---

14. Surströmming is raw herring sealed in a can and left to rot for a year. The smell … The Swedes could sell this stuff to the bio-weapons division of any major military industry and beat Volvo's exports hands down. Wait– this wouldn't be allowed by the Geneva Convention!
15. *Eat the rich*, O'Rourke P.J., Picador, 1999, p.1.

1. Increase the availability and widen the distribution of **basic necessities** such as food, water, shelter, health and physical protection

2. Raise **living standards**, employment, education and cultural activity

3. Provide economic and **social choice** for people by freeing them from servitude and dependence.

Since development clearly is a qualitative variable it is difficult to determine and measure. It is similar to attempting to set down criteria for 'beautiful' or 'love'. These terms vary greatly in meaning from person to person, society to society (not to mention historically) and are thus highly *normative and subjective* in nature. Having said that, just ponder the following brief comparisons instead and think a bit …

- Turning on the tap and having a drink of water … OR … walking 15 kilometres with a 25 litre drum to have it filled at the community well, which is laced with arsenic.[17] [Bangladesh]

- Getting on the school bus with your sister hoping that the teacher won't pick you in class as you haven't done your homework … OR … running 25 kilometres to school after spending three days in the mountains chasing cattle thieves armed with AK47 assault rifles. [Kenya]

- Having a croissant and a cup of coffee on the way to the office … OR … getting your daily ration of coca leaves (to stave off hunger and exhaustion) from the work leader as you clamber into the mine shaft, pickaxe in hand, to hack out US$2 worth of tin ore in the next 12 hours. [Peru]

One can say that development is about having choices: economic choice; political choice; the choice of schools; health care, and the choice of government. It is also about having opportunities: for education; for work; for public office; for private ownership; for leisure. Finally it is about freedom: freedom of opinion and speech; freedom from dependence and servitude; freedom of movement and leisure time, and freedom from arbitrary governance and random applicability of the law. If you, unlike I, live in a more developed

country (MDC) then you probably take most of the above for granted – or at least find them unsurprisingly obvious. Yet I always stop here and ask my students how many countries in the world fulfilled the above development criteria 100 years ago. (The answer is in the footnote below.[18])

Sustainable development ©IBO 2003

The concept of sustainable development was coined in a 1987 report headed by Gro Harlem Brundtland, ex-prime minister of Norway and director general of WHO 1998–2003. 'Our Common Future' or 'The Brundtland Report' states that a sustainable development path is one that ensures that growth in the future is not diminished by the manner in which we attain growth now. The concept basically centres on responsible use of our limited resources today so that sufficient resources are available for future generations.

> Sustainable development: Sustainable development is 'development that meets the needs of the present without compromising the ability of future generations to meet their own needs'[19].

There is still ongoing debate as to the precise meaning of this phrase and what it means in a practical respect. Most economists would say that it is highly doubtful that economic activity (and thus growth) could be possible and still have zero impact on the environment, thus indeed compromising future wellbeing due to pollution, depletion of natural resources and so on. Others point to sustainable growth as being an ambition or aspiration rather than a target comprised of quantifiable and measurable objectives. The World Bank has defined sustainable growth as 'growth that lasts' which basically means that growth is within long-term carrying capacity of the environment with respect to population and use of resources.

16. *Economic Development*, Michael P. Todaro, & Stephen C. Smith, Pearson Education Limited, 2006, p. 22.
17. I'm not making this up. Seepage of arsenic into drinking water in Bangladesh is a serious problem and is slowly killing hundreds of thousands of people.
18. None. Zero. Zip. This was, quite often, because women did not have voting rights. New Zealand was the first to grant women general voting rights in 1893. There is limited choice, freedom and independence when half the population is unable to participate in electing those who will govern.
19. World Commission on Environment and Development (WCED) 1987, *Our common future*, Oxford University Press, p. 43.

Correlation and causality revisited – growth and environment

The tricky issue of correlation and causality comes to light within the debate on growth, development and environment/sustainability. There has been a degree of polarisation in later years between 'deep ecology' groups who view economic growth as inherently dangerous and linked to consumerism, large corporations and an increasingly global marketplace. To put this particular reasoning rather bluntly, environmental damage is caused by growth. Growth entails increasing output and incomes which in turn will increase consumption, etc. The classic example is 'What would happen to the earth if the Chinese and Indians had the same number of cars per capita as the West?'[20] The opposing view is that yes, there is correlation, but it could well be that it is the other way around; growth creates the means by which human development can take place and increasing wealth means that there are sufficient resources to improve the method of production and lower pollution levels, use less material and overall make more goods with less impact on resources. Thus environmental damage is quite often the result of a lack of growth. This view takes into account the enormous advances in technology and the vast improvements in production and the benefits this has proven to have for the environment.

The debate also rages on as to whether or not a good many developing countries in South America, Africa and Southeast Asia are suffering from severe 'short-termism' in terms of development. For example, by chopping down virgin rain forests in order to earn the foreign currency necessary to buy imported goods, these LDCs are doing away with invaluable finite resources and endangering the livelihood of future generations. A counter-argument – often put forward by officials in countries with rain forests – is that many European countries did the same, albeit some four to five hundred years ago. England used vast tracts of forest during the initial phase of the industrial revolution and increasing populations quickly encroached upon the remainder in order to plant wheat and corn. The use of these resources resulted in an incredible surge in population and also in an incredible increase in living standards and reduction of poverty. The price was the environment – and let's face it, the Sherwood Forest of the legendary Robin Hood is not quite what it used to be.[21]

I suppose you've noticed that I've not provided you with any real answers but rather only questions. The reason is simple; I don't have the answers. Nor, it would seem, does anyone else. There are countless expert studies on the issues of the links between poverty, environment, growth rates, political system, economic system, etc. yet it is very difficult to find absolute answers. We will return to all these issues in Section 5, where I will once again pose the questions and attempt to address them.

Positive and normative concepts

Positive and normative statements

Positive statements have nothing to do with positive attitude or such. A positive statement is one which does not contain subjective or opinionated elements but is based on facts that can be proved or disproved. Examples of positive statements are 'Socrates is a man' (see my economic syllogism in the section on opportunity costs); 'He was sentenced to death'; 'Socrates was a convicted thief' or perhaps even 'Socrates was a woman'. Note that nothing value-laden is included. It's just stating facts – or ridiculous assertions as the last two are intended to show – that can be tested be looking at data and facts as far as they are known. Therefore 'positive' in no way means 'good', but rather that there is no value judgement involved. So if I were to say 'There are very few repeat-offenders amongst those who have been executed' I am actually using a positive statement.

However, stating that 'The death penalty is abhorrent (= objectionable) to a modern democratic country' is a normative statement, just as if one – like those who convicted him – were to say 'Socrates was immoral'. The reason is that one would be standing on a platform of *evaluation*. Often this type of statement is

---

20. Twenty of the thirty most air-polluted cities in the world are now in China. There is food for thought here.
21. I've been there. Sherwood Forest would be considered a 'nice park' by the Swedes and a 'nice garden' by the Finns.

referred to as being value-laden, i.e. being burdened with moral/ethical values. One is using a certain standpoint – religious, cultural or philosophical – to express the value of something that cannot be refuted by logic or objective reasoning. One is using a *normative* vantage point to express opinion.[22]

> **Positive and normative statements**: **Positive statements** are based on facts or evidence, free from value-laden and subjective standpoints. They can be proven or disproved using a scientific approach. **Normative statements** are based on norms, thus they are subjective and biased – they can not be proven or disproved. 'Man evolved from apes …' a Darwinist proposition, is a positive statement while 'Man was created by God' is clearly a normative statement.[24]

The aim of economic theory is to provide a basis for analyses which is as unburdened by normative statements as is possible. Generally speaking, scientific research should be confined to positive questions, i.e. questions or hypotheses which can be either *verified* or *refuted* by looking at real-life observations and data. The stricter we are in our use of definitions, assumptions and consequent models, the more we can weed out the more emotional aspects of economic conclusions. Economics as a science attempts to outline 'good' and 'bad' without resorting to subjective views. An economist aims to pose questions that can be stated positively by defining 'good' and 'bad' in economic terms rather than moral terms and then answering the questions by examining facts and evidence.

Ceteris paribus ©IBO 2003

In scientific research in general and economic models in particular, one builds a model knowing that there are many possible influences on the relationships one is looking at. In using a model which studies the effects of increased household income, for example that an increase in income will lead to an increase in consumption, we would assume that a number of other influences on consumption would be kept constant. Consumption would be correlated to income, yes, but so too would consumption and the general price level, consumption and household debt, consumption and the price of housing, etc. Assuming that the price level,

household debt and price of housing remain unchanged, we are able to simply *one* causal relationship – consumption and income – and explain clearly what the effects of a rise in income would be.

The assumption of ceteris paribus – all else equal – is almost always present in our economic models. It is virtually impossible to leave out of our models as it raises the level of scientific trustworthiness by creating a more rigid framework of deductive reasoning, e.g. that a change in *X* will lead to a predictable change in *Y* as long as the situation is not muddied by an infinite number of other possible influences. One of the most prominent uses of the *ceteris paribus* assumption is within the standard supply and demand model which will be done in greater depth in Section 2.1.

> **Ceteris paribus**: *Ceteris paribus* is Latin and means 'all else remaining equal' or 'all other things remaining the same'. This essential assumption allows economic models to predict outcomes and relationships with a degree of certainty and conviction simply by *assuming that variables not addressed in the model are kept constant.*

POP QUIZ 1.1.3   POSITIVE, NORMATIVE, CETERIS PARIBUS

1 Discuss the statement 'GNP causes a change in the level of development'.

2 'Governments should raise taxes on the wealthy in order to create a more equal society!' Is this a positive or normative statement?

3 Assume I was to say 'My students think that development economics should be a larger part of the IB syllabus'. Is this a positive or normative statement? Be careful on this one!

Scarcity ©IBO 2003

In outlining the factors of production (land, labour, capital and the entrepreneur) available to the economic system, we inevitably come upon the issue of scarcity which has a rather specific meaning in economics as it goes to the very heart of what economics is all about, namely the optimal use of resources. **Scarcity** means that all societies face the common problem of limited

---

22. A norm is a rule or guideline arising from within the evolved standards of a society, e.g. 'Socrates should be punished by being forced to drink poison!'

23. There is a rather remarkable example of the difference in philosophical outlook between the US and Britain. The US dollar notes have 'In God we trust' on them while the British pound notes have Darwin and, more recently, Adam Smith on them!

resources and how to best allocate these resources to provide for our endless wants. Scarcity is a universal problem, but does *not* necessarily mean that all peoples in all economies lack the same things! A most valuable resource is water, which the Swedes have in abundance in Sweden but has to be shipped in by tanker every day to the Greek island of Hydra where I lived as a child. On the other hand, on Hydra there is no lack of master stone-masons and marble, enabling marble sinks, counter-tops, tiles – we actually had a toilet seat made out of marble! When I think of it now, the amount of marble we had there could have funded my university studies.

This is my point: scarcity is an issue for all nations and has been for all time. It's simply a matter of what is scarce and the reasons for this relative scarcity. Scarcity is defined by availability of resources, true, but also by our wants and desires, which are infinite. No matter what need is fulfilled, there is always another lurking in the background and this is true in all people. Naturally all these needs cannot be satisfied as there are limits to society's ability to satisfy them, the reason being that while our needs are seemingly *endless* the resources (land, labour, capital, etc.) used in satisfying them are quite definitely *finite*, or limited. Scarcity is what one might call a triumph of harsh reality of the inborn wants of man; all societies during all ages will have wrestled with the abundance of human wants, the inability of the economic system to supply all wants, and the resulting choices resulting from scarcity of available resources.

> **Scarcity**: The excess of wants resulting from having limited resources (land, labour, capital and entrepreneurs) – scarcity arises in satisfying the *endless wants* of people using *limited resources*. Scarcity is a universal problem for all economies – it is not limited to poor countries.

Factors of production: land, labour, capital and management/entrepreneurship

We use the term 'resources' a great deal in economics, and traditionally assign all economic resources four headings; land, labour, capital and entrepreneurial spirit. These four groups constitute the **factors of production** used, to one extent or anther, in the production of all goods.

> **Resources/factors of production**: The factors of production are commonly divided into **land**, **labour**, **capital** and **entrepreneurial drive**. These are the resources necessary to create/supply goods and services in an economy.

Land is used in a wider sense, and covers not only the use of land for farming and space for factories, but to a wide variety of natural resources such as oil, water, timber and ore. One often uses the term 'raw material' for these natural resources. Land is also agricultural goods such as rapeseed and fish from the sea. All of the aforementioned resources are often referred to as **primary goods**, (or **primary commodities**) and I often tell my students is that 'If you can dig it up, chop it down or pluck it, it's a primary good'.

Labour is pretty much self-explanatory but it is worthwhile to note that it is often the element of labour that adds value to all basic natural resources and transforms basic (simple) goods such as silicon and oil into higher value goods such as silicon chips and plastic casing used in the computer I am using to write this.

Capital is any *man-made* factor of production, such as a factory or machine.[24] Yet the term is more far-reaching, as it can also mean the whiteboard pen I use to fill the board when I am using it to produce education. Capital, as a term, is specific in that the item must be used in the production of goods and not in simple consumption. One could say that capital is defined more by usage than anything else. A guitar in my hands is simply a consumer good (and a mistake) while in the hands of Marilyn Manson it is a capital offence … sorry, that's 'capital'.

The **entrepreneur** is the person who brings the other three together and creates goods to fulfil wants and needs in society. From Edison's light bulb to Picasso's painting *Guernica* all production necessitates the idea, drive and ambition of an entrepreneur to put land, labour and capital together and create something. As a personal addendum, I would add education, training and experience to the four production factors above – this is commonly referred to as **human capital**.

---

24. Be very careful in using the term 'capital' in economics! Very often the term is confused with 'money' – which is *not* a factor of production. (Money is just a representation of goods or resources – just try to build a boat on a deserted island with a stack of yen!) 'Capital' is one of many terms with subject-specific meaning which also has other, wider, meanings outside of economics. In its purest usage in economics capital is a man-made factor of production, yet in a wider more general way we use it to connote financial or physical assets which can generate income, such as property or shares in a company.

Human capital is frequently considered of increasing importance in modern production, as manufacturing methods become more complex.

Payments to factors of production: rent, wages, interest, profit ©IBO 2003

Having just stated that resources are scarce, shouldn't they then be rather dear? In other words, seeing as how resources are scarce, there must be a reward to those who have control (ownership) of these factors of production? And finally, shouldn't there be some sort of reward involved when an entrepreneur gives up his/her time in order to satisfy some of the infinite wants in society?

Answer 'yes' to all the above. As most economists would agree, the system of production in society is inevitably based on some form of self-interest and *incentives*. An incentive is an inducement or promise of reward. My ultimate incentive for spending a few thousand hours rewriting this book is the reward of royalty payments, e.g. a percentage of the profit. This is no different from a businessman spending a weekend looking at ways to increase sales in order to increase profit. All resources are provided because ultimately the provider receives payment for their provision. These **payments** are grouped into **rent**, **wages**, **interest** and **profit** and are easiest explained using the **circular flow model** shown in Figure 1.1.4.

> **Payments to factors of production:**
> The factors of production – land, labour, capital and the entrepreneur – receive, respectively, **rent**, **wages**, **interest** and **profit** for providing these resources.

Figure 1.1.4 portrays a simplified economy where all activity flows to and from two sectors: *households* and *firms*. Households contain people and it is these people who control resources. People in households own the land, supply the labour and own the firms – either directly or indirectly via shares. The other sector is the productive sector, e.g. firms, which in turn will need the resources owned by the households. This circular flow is shown by the blue flow arrows in the figure: households provide factors of production and receive payments from firms for them. In fact, our model shows a mirror image of the factors of production in terms of the equivalent compensation for them.

Table 1.1.3 is rather simplified for two reasons. It does not take into account that there is any number of possible combinations, for example, the self-employed

would not only receive profit but also wages, rent and interest from their firm. (The self-employed are sitting on two chairs at once – they are both providers and buyers of production factors!) The other simplification is that interest is not 'money received for keeping funds in the bank' but is an imputed (= assigned) compensation for the ownership of capital. (We will return to this in Section 3.1.)

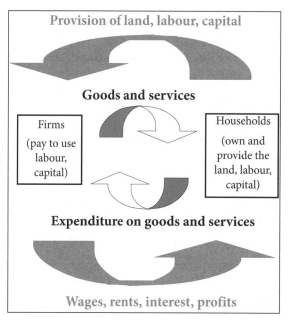

Figure 1.1.4 *The The circular flow model (simplified version – no government, financial or foreign sector)*

Table 1.1.3 *Factors of production*

Factor of production	Use	Compensation (payment)
Land	Households let (= rent out) to firms	Households receive **rent**
Labour	Households provide labour	Households receive **wages**
Capital	Households own the capital	Households receive **interest**
Entrepreneur	Households provide risk & ideas	Households receive **profit**

The blue arrows in Figure 1.1.4 show how households provide factors of production and are compensated for this provision. The grey arrows show the flow of expenditure (= spending) from households to firms, and the subsequent flow of goods and services to households. In brief, households provide the factors of production for compensation which gives rise to *factor markets*. Firms supply goods and services demanded by households with the result that we now have a *market for goods and services* in our economic system, which is of course total output in the economy, or GDP. We will return to national income in the circular flow model in Section 3.1 and enhance it to show government, financial sector and foreign sector.

POP QUIZ 1.1.4   FACTORS OF PRODUCTION

1 Classic question: Why is money not a factor of production?

2 Which two market types are evident in the circular flow model?

3 'Scarcity is a problem commonly associated with poor countries.' Comment on this from the viewpoint of an economist.

Choice ©IBO 2003

Every day households face any number of choices, from the daily shopping to moving house. The personal choices of households ultimately rest on the economic concepts of **utility** and **opportunity costs**.[25]

Utility

Utility refers to the *usefulness perceived* and *satisfaction derived* from the consumption/use of a good. The perception of a good's utility forms our preferences. The term springs from the Latin *utilitas*, meaning usefulness or applicability.[26] Just think of utensils!

> Utility: The benefit/satisfaction/usefulness one gets from the consumption of a good. The concept is quite obviously highly normative as people's preferences vary greatly. My perceived usefulness will not be the same as yours. Thus utility is a value-laden concept and basically impossible to measure.

Utility is one of the classic abstract concepts, right up there with quality and happiness. (In fact, I once bet one of my students USD100 that he could not define quality and he never got back to me and he has now graduated from the London School of Economics!) It

simply defies any form of enumerative measurement and appraisal, just like love – try grading your love for your boyfriend/girlfriend on a curve!

The same goes for utility: one simply cannot put the satisfaction one might feel, say, from the consumption of chocolate into numerical values. Picture yourself standing in front of long row of shop windows filled to the brim with goods. You are standing in front of a certain shop window – and other people are standing in front of other windows. Why isn't everybody at the same shop front?

Simple, utility differs between prospective customers and this steers preferences and therefore selective perception. While perhaps you are fogging up the window of the Italian shoe shop, your friend might have his nose pressed against the armoured glass of a Swiss watch shop.[27]

Utility is at the heart of economic reasoning when it comes to analysing people's wants and purchasing habits. As we shall see, utility explains why we buy a good in the first place – but the concept does an even better job of explaining why we buy goods in the second place! What – second place? Well, stop and think; have you in fact bought many single goods in your lifetime? Are we not, in fact, constantly buying more goods, i.e. another good rather than a good? If so, then it should be of far greater interest for the social scientist to explain why we buy an additional unit of a good rather than the first one, seeing as how recurrent purchasing is far more common than a 'virgin' purchase. Point in fact: I wasn't buying a watch (see "Storytime: Watch out for un-watched heathen!" on page 17) but another watch. Thus we need a concept which addresses the addition to utility caused by consuming one more unit of the good. This is **marginal utility**.

---

25. I just heard my housemate Rob ask one of the hung-over rugby players occupying the downstairs if he wanted cereal or bacon and eggs for breakfast … the time was 15:30! The answer – in a very hoarse voice – was 'water and aspirin!'

26. This translation was provided years ago by Pia Birgander, my incredible IB co-ordinator in Sweden. She knows about 18 languages, Latin being but one. Now, having her around is utility – talk about useful!

27. Take it from an old person: don't shop in pairs! The opportunity cost of looking at things which bore you out of your skull quickly becomes unbearable when you realise that you are giving up your own valuable shopping time.

Storytime: Watch out for un-watched heathen!

'You did what?!'

This was voiced loudly and almost in concert by a group of colleagues who had gathered for evening grape juice (= wine) and yummies at one of the houses along Expat Street here in Mexico close to the school we all work in. Word had apparently spread that I'd bought a new watch for some ungodly sum and Marc – being a stout Yorkshire lad with no inhibitions whatsoever – handed me my wine, glanced at my watch and said, 'Ay, looks good! I used to see those all over the place in the black markets in Vietnam'.

'You most certainly did not', I growled. 'This isn't a back-alley copy but the real thing – proudly manufactured in Geneva by the Little Swiss Watch Gnomes.'

By this time my friends in the know were all grinning like possums eating the core out of a Mexican cactus, waiting for Marc's look when he found out how much it cost. I can't quote him in print, but basically he said, 'You're crazy!' It took about 3.4 seconds for this to become the consensus view and if their looks had taken on physical action I would have left the party in a straitjacket. Virtually everyone had different views on 'the insane waste of money' and 'what one could have gotten instead'. The alternatives ranged from a new car to 4 weeks at a good hotel in Cancun or Acapulco. What they also all agreed on was that I shouldn't wear it anywhere risky – which in Mexico means anywhere outside the house and/or near the police.

The point of this story is that the satisfaction I feel from wearing (e.g. consuming) the watch is different from what the others would feel. I derive such pleasure in owning fine mechanical timepieces that I am prepared to pay a great deal for them – and thus give up numerous other goods. In economic language, I am spending my income in such a way that I get maximum pleasure from the goods I spend my money on – I am maximising my utility. *Any other option would have added less to my overall sense of satisfaction. By allocating my income towards the consumption of a (-nother) watch, I added to my happiness the most. This is marginal utility, dealt with next.*

Marginal utility ('living on the edge')

Economists are infatuated with concepts which incorporate the concept of 'marginal'. We have 'marginal efficiency', 'marginal costs' and 'marginal revenue', to name but a few. **Marginal utility** is the increase in total utility received from consuming one more unit of a particular good.

> **Marginal utility**: The addition to total utility (i.e. total benefit/satisfaction/ usefulness or wellbeing) resulting from the consumption of one more unit of a good. Ultimately choices are based on the perceived marginal utility of one more unit of a good.

So much of human choice – and economic behaviour in general – takes place 'on the margin'. In dealing with watches or vacation we are basing our ultimate decision on which option will add the most to our overall wellbeing – I personally feel that a Rolex GMT Master II is worth giving up 4 weeks in Cancun. I maximise my total utility (i.e. sense of overall satisfaction) by having a hand-made Swiss timepiece and am willing to forgo a certain amount of sun, sand and surf. Marginal utility explains my choice. While I indeed desire both a new watches and a vacation my limited financial resources mean that I will have to choose. In choosing the Rolex I've stated that the marginal utility of the watch exceeds the marginal utility of the vacation. I have to forfeit (= give up) a certain amount of something else in obtaining the watch, which in fact the measures my marginal utility, e.g. how much of a Good Y we are willing to give up in the consumption of a Good X.[28] (At the time of writing, everyone I know is in Cancun for mid-term break and I am waiting for delivery of yet another very nice Swiss watch, a Breitling Chrono Avenger in titanium which, like the Rolex, is outrageously expensive – not to mention huge.[29] Utility maximisation indeed.)

A beer in the desert

My favourite example of marginal utility – and one which lends itself to immediate recognition and knowing laughter by every student I've had – is the 'cold beer in the desert' allegory (= comparison). Picture yourself marooned in the Kalahari with nothing but the clothes on your back and your trusty credit card securely tucked away in a Velcro pocket. You set off on foot towards what you hope will be the nearest town. It's 45°C in the shade – which would be fine if there was any shade[30]. But you are walking in the midday sun, which is hot enough to fry the niblets off a bronze elephant[31]. Walk, walk, walk. Sweat, sweat, sweat.[32]

Suddenly, through the shimmering heat waves and consequent mirages, you see a large parasol in the distance. You do a high-speed shuffle towards it and coming closer discover that it is real – you also see the painted sign with the legend 'Mabogunje's Finest Kind Cold Refreshments! All major credit cards accepted!' There are a number of bar stools set out in front of a bar counter. You set yourself down on one of the stools in front of the smiling Mabogunje, slap your credit card on the bar and order a beer. Mabogunje pulls the draft-lever a few times and sets an ice-cold pint of beer in front of you.

You start slow and end fast – just like a good opera. Indeed, quaffing away there, you actually hear blissful choirs and feel like the injured Tristan being cured by Isolde. What sweet satisfaction! 'It ain't over 'til the Fat Lady sings', you think and order another beer …

Whap! Mabogunje slaps another cold one on the counter and whips your card through the register. Your initial thirst having been satisfied, you drink the next one with a bit more ease. It too is incredibly tasty – though it doesn't quite give you the lust-filled experience of the initial stein. Still, it's satisfying enough for you to want a third … which is, again, very tasty but not quite in the same satisfaction league as the previous. You feel better and better after each additional beer – but not at the same rate. This continues through the fourth, fifth and sixth beer. Each additional beer will add to your overall satisfaction – and inebriation – up to the seventh beer.[33] Putting this little story into the traditional illustrative method of the economist, we get tables and diagrams.

Quantity	Total utility	Marginal utility
0	0	
		100
1	100	
		70
2	170	
		45
3	215	
		27
4	242	
		15
5	257	
		5
6	262	
		−3
7	259	

Figure 1.1.5 *Total and marginal utility of drinking beer in the desert*

Figure 1.1.5 shows how total utility increases – but that each additional beer adds to total utility less than the previous beer. Shakespeare was well aware of marginal utility when he wrote, 'Can one desire too much of a good thing?' The first beer renders total utility of 100, the second beer renders total utility of 170 – thus there is *diminishing marginal utility* since the second beer adds to total utility by 70 rather than an additional 100 units of utility. Note that one shows 'movement', i.e. rate of change, by putting any marginal values *between* the absolute values. For example, the second beer increases total utility from 100 to 170 which is shown in Figure 1.1.5 and Figure 1.1.6 on page 19 as a marginal utility value of 70 between the

---

28. Sharp-eyed colleagues might object to some corner-cutting here, since the correct term would be the marginal rate of substitution.

29. I mean HUGE: it might be the only man-made object visible from the moon. It comes complete with a sling to rest your arm.

30. The correct term for '°C' is degrees Celsius – not centigrade. The scale was invented by the Swedish scientist Anders Celsius in 1742 (source: http://www.astro.uu.se).

31. I dare not go into the subject of niblets. You are much too young and innocent.

32. Or 'Perspire, perspire, perspire' if you are being polite.

33. This is when you inadvertently start crawling in the sand violently sick or fall into a drunken stupor. Or both, in that order.

total utility for beers number one and beer number 2. The diagram shows how total utility increases at a decreasing rate, i.e. diminishing marginal utility, up to the seventh beer. Swigging the seventh beer confers *negative utility*, i.e. *disutility*, and you wind up

grovelling in the sand, proposing marriage to a cactus or picking fights with claw-equipped nocturnal animals. Basically you'd be prepared to pay someone to drink the seventh beer!

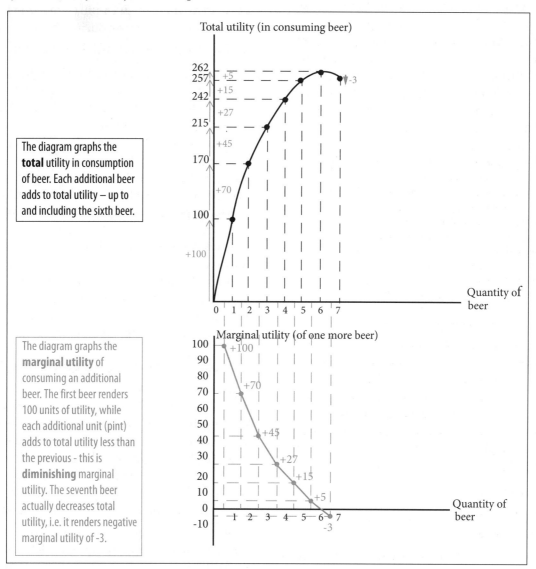

Figure 1.1.6 *Total and marginal utility of drinking beer in the desert*

Marginal utility has wide applicability in the study of demand patterns. It helps to explain consumption habits and patterns and also why goods such as diamonds – which are in no way necessities – are very dear, while water – which is an essential of life – is nowhere near as expensive as diamonds.

POP QUIZ 1.1.5   UTILITY

1   As total utility increases at an ever slower pace, marginal utility will … Finish the sentence!

2   What do you think would affect the beer drinker in the example above the most in terms of marginal utility – drinking a second pint or spilling the third?

3   What do you think is the connection between a person's marginal utility in the consumption of Good X and that person's willingness to pay for Good X?

Opportunity cost ©IBO 2003

Resources are scarce and society's wants are endless; this means making a choice which in turn means giving something up. An opportunity cost arises as soon as one alternative means giving up the next best available alternative. For example if my preference ranking (in descending order) in spending USD10,000 is 1) a Blancpain watch; 2) 4 weeks vacation in Cancun; 3) a new car, then in choosing the Blancpain my opportunity cost is 4 weeks vacation – not the new car, because my opportunity cost is the highest ranking, e.g. second-best alternative I give up.

> Opportunity cost: Opportunity cost is the option foregone in making a choice of 'Alternative A' over 'Alternative B'. Assuming that all possible choices have been ranked in order of preference, the opportunity cost is the relinquishing of the second-best possible alternative, i.e. the foregone opportunity of obtaining the highest ranked of all possible alternatives. The concept is fundamental in all subsequent economic concepts.

The issue of what/how/whom is naturally one of choices. In some way, one has to choose between options. Let us use the learning tool of choice for Aristotle, the **syllogism**. A syllogism is a set of factual statements ordered in a state of natural progression which all lead to an (inescapable?) logical conclusion. The classical syllogism is one where Aristotle referred to his teacher Socrates:

1. Man is mortal.
2. Socrates is a man.
3. Socrates will die.

The economic syllogism is somewhat less dramatic:

1. People's (or society's) wants are infinite.
2. Resources are finite.
3. Choices must be made.

We'd best comment on the above, primarily in order to explain and perhaps defend the premises therein[34]. Most people would ultimately agree that no matter what one has attained, one always has an additional want. Mick Jagger couldn't get no satisfaction (and knew you can't always get what you want) – and he was a drop-out from the London School of Economics! Fulfilling one's desire for a new watch doesn't mean that one wouldn't want a vacation in Cancun and a new car to drive there in. Even Bill Gates, who has earned millions in interest alone during the time it has taken me to write this section, will have unfulfilled wants[35].

The premise of endless wants and thus hard choices holds as true for society as for the individual. A municipality (= local government) might face the decision of allocating funds towards new computers for the local public school or an all-expenses-paid fact-finding mission to Monaco for municipal councilmen and spouses. National government might have a choice between 15 new fighter jets and a new cancer research centre. To phrase it in economic terminology, there are simply too few resources (e.g. land, labour and capital) available to enable all wants to be taken care of. We are thus presented with interminable *trade-offs* at personal, municipal and national level: the Blancpain or vacation; school computers or vaca … em … fact-finding mission; fighter jets or health care. These trade-offs mean an opportunity foregone.

The concept of cost on a global level

If we were to look at somewhat wider issues as an illustration we could also exemplify the difficulties in ranking the alternatives. Let's look at the cost of putting a satellite into orbit around earth (see Figure 1.1.7 on page 21). It costs roughly USD20,000 dollars per kilo of orbital transmitters, which is enough to provide 4,000 primary school years or 500 people with health care (including cost of fighting AIDS) in a less developed country (LDC).[36] Simple mathematics (and the assumption that costs are constant) tells us that the opportunity cost of a kilo of satellite is 4,000 much-needed school years.

Now the issue arises of the merit of the above *ranking*. Remember, the opportunity cost is the next best alternative – out of any number of alternatives. Who is to say that primary education is the top contender for resources presently going to global communications networks?! The answer is, I do! In

---

34. We will be using the term 'premise' rather often. A premise (pl. premises) is a basic assumption, often in a line of reasoning or argumentation where the premise must be included at the outset in order for subsequent conclusions to hold true. For example, my premise in writing this is that my students are adequately versed in English.

35. Detractors may say that world domination comes the closest.

36. See http://radhome.gsfc.nasa.gov/radhome/papers/slideshow9/sld018.htm and www.unicef.org/programme/education/costs_ed.htm; *Business Week* at http://www.businessweek.com/magazine/content/02_02/b3765071.htm , 'For Developing Countries, Health Is Wealth'; Also, basic education is considered the most powerful development tool available: every extra school year in very poor countries can increase earnings by an average of 10% to 20%. *International Herald Tribune*, 2 July 2002, p.7.

other words, the ranking here is my own. In my world, education is one of the most critically needed goods for the betterment of mankind – the construction of a satellite means that I have thus foregone education, which is the opportunity cost. Others (economists or normal people) will have other rankings based on their assessment of societal needs.

To drive the point home, try to rank the following alternatives, i.e. the preferential use of the resources it takes to put 50 kg of satellite in orbit (at a cost of USD1 million):

- 200,000 primary school years in a less developed country (LDC)

- One year's health care for 25,000 people in a more developed country (MDC)
- One smart bomb dropped on an alleged Al- Qaeda stronghold in Afghanistan
- Additional fencing around the few remaining sea turtle nesting areas on beaches along the Mexican coast
- Posting bail money for Paris Hilton.

In short, the opportunity cost of putting a satellite in orbit is the foregone second-best alternative in the list above. All one has to do is rank the alternatives.

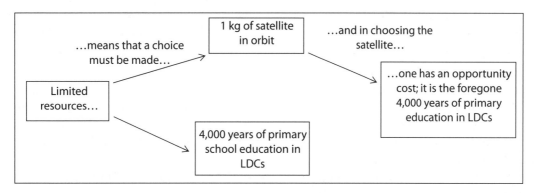

Figure 1.1.7 *Ranking opportunity cost*

It's not that simple, is it? And although you and I are not directly in a position to exert influence over the oversimplified (and ridiculous, in the case of the last two) alternatives above, you may rest assured that it is precisely along these lines that societal decision-making moves. It is the nature of the decision-making process that varies, not the nature of the decisions themselves.

> **Free and economic goods**: A **free good is infinitely abundant** and thus does not incur any opportunity costs in its production, i.e. the resources involved can be used without foregoing the production of alternative goods. An **economic good is a good which uses scarce resources** in being provided and thus there is an opportunity cost of the alternative goods foregone.

Free and economic goods ©IBO 2003

Any resource used in the production of goods and services which has alternative uses has an opportunity cost attached, so in producing a given amount of health care society will trade-off a given amount of, say, roads. These goods are economic goods, since they use scarce resources in production. If, however, a resource were so abundant that no opportunity cost arose in the production of a good, it would be a free good. The basic distinction is that goods which are scarce (e.g. based upon the use of scarce resources) are economic goods while goods in perfect abundance (e.g. use resources which are unlimited) are free goods.

The cost of everything – economic resources

I come from a long line of caustic and less-than-politically-correct Irish-Americans. My paternal grandfather takes the prize though, having been formatted by raising a family in a tough time and place – depression and the Second War World in St Louis, Missouri. This uneducated rough-neck managed to become a successful and quite wealthy man ultimately but never passed up the opportunity to pass on a few baubles of hard-earned wisdom to my father and me. Top of the list was 'There ain't no free meals'.[37]

I live in Mexico now and have never met a more hospitable, kind, happy and generous people. And

---

37. Very little of his remaining pithy (= terse) commentary is printable, unfortunately.

while meals are not free, whenever I stop for curb-side dining, e.g. food prepared on the sidewalk, I am always offered very generous free-testing of whatever exotic dish happens to be being prepared.[38] When I visit my cigar manufacturer, Ramirez, in Vera Cruz and buy loads of cigars I always get a big bag of specially made robustos. My question to you is, are these freebies in fact free? No, of course not. Someone planted, culled, cut and packed the avocados and tobacco. Land, fertilizer, hoes and machines were used in the process. All of these freebies used resources – *economic resources* – in production and these resources had alternative uses. Therefore there was indeed an opportunity cost involved in putting 15 cigars in my gift bag. In economic reasoning, any good that uses resources which could have been put to use producing something else is an economic good.

Get used to this axiom (= truism, proverb). Any good supplied which has used a limited resource can never be a free good as it has disenabled the production of something else. As soon as a good is produced an opportunity cost is incurred, as the factors of production used could be used for something else. Shakespeare in the park is not free since the unemployed actor/artiste/hippie could be used for … uh … well … hmmm … OK, Shakespeare in the park is a free good. But everything else uses resources that could be reapplied elsewhere and thus any production using these resources means that there is an economic cost.

Are there any free goods?

I wax philosophical in class at times and put to my people the proposition that nothing is, in fact, free. I posit that not only economic goods, i.e. goods produced by using scant resources but virtually everything has some sort of opportunity cost attached. I suggest that not a single undertaking is possible without there being an opportunity cost lurking somewhere in the background. After baiting my students for a while I often get two suggestions of things which have no opportunity cost – love and air[39].

A free sunset?

Taking the hard line, I argue that love indeed carries considerable opportunity costs, such as clarity of thought, discipline and focus on anything other than the object of our love[40]. (Also, one usually has to maintain a certain level of time-consuming personal hygiene.) Living in Mexico City, I further maintain that air – at least the breathable type – means foregoing the bright lights and action of the inner city. Not being able to have both suggests opportunity costs are involved.

In any case, as an economist, never make the mistake of thinking that something is free simply because no payment is involved. I might go so far as to say that 'free good' is an example of a contradiction in terms, such as 'military intelligence' or printing 'batteries not included' on a pack of batteries.

POP QUIZ 1.1.6   OPPORTUNITY COSTS

1   What might the opportunity costs of getting an education be?

2   Why is it necessary to rank all the possible alternatives in order to arrive at the opportunity cost?

3   Can free goods have opportunity costs attached?

4   Can economic goods have zero opportunity costs?

Production possibility curves

©IBO 2003

One of my common sayings in class is that a good shortcut to understanding economic jargon is to 'taste the term', meaning that many economic terms can be readily understood using a sound grasp of language and some logic. A case in point is the **production possibility frontier,** or PPF. Just taste: 'production' must mean output of goods and services; 'possibility' is

---

38. Such as ant eggs, grasshoppers, beetles, armadillo, iguana (which is illegal) and of course goat. I am trying to find a restaurant serving Xoloitzcuintle (indigenous dog - pronounced cho-le-squint-le), an ancient Aztec delicacy, but since there are only a few thousand of these dogs left I calculate that dinner would run about USD2,000. Goat will do.

39. 'Love is in the air' is a perfectly ghastly, lugubrious (= miserable) song from the 1970s. Anyone involved in it should have been sent to forced re-education camp.

40. As soon as new students in my classes find boyfriends and/or girlfriends the test results fall. Some day I am going to graph this in a diagram and start a pre-IB dating service to increase my grade average.

maximum attainable amount, and 'frontier' means border or boundary. Taken together the concept is self-explanatory: the PPF shows the boundary of what is possible to produce and is used as an illustration in economics to show the choices facing all countries in producing goods which use limited factors of production. IB grades is a PPF.

> **Production possibility frontier (PPF)**: The PPF is a diagrammatical illustration of total attainable output based on the limits of available resources. It is drawn grouping all output into two goods or groups. The PPF line shows the limits of all possible output combinations for an economy assuming all possible resources are fully/efficiently employed.

Diagrams showing opportunity cost, actual and potential output

©IBO 2003

Now we move into the realm of macroeconomics and put the PPF to use in showing the limits of production and the opportunity costs facing economies. Again, these limits arise due to *limited resources*. Figure 1.1.8 on page 24 shows the production possibility frontier, PPF, of a fictitious village, Mirageville. Like all models and diagrams you will encounter, the PPF is based on several assumptions, and is highly (even trivially) simplified – yet ultimately a useful conceptual tool.[41]

Warning!
'Proving' and 'Illustrating'

One of my cheekier students once walked by my desk and asked me what time it was. Before I could look up – and much less answer – she quipped, 'Wait, I'll get you a whiteboard pen!' Apart from histrionics, she had a most viable point: economists do it with diagrams.

It must immediately be noted by the neophyte (= beginner) economist, that we use countless pictures, illustrations, diagrams and flowcharts in getting our message across. Yes, a picture does say more than a thousand words – at least between two economists. Yet I always warn the student never to confuse an

illustration with its subject, i.e. a picture of Hitler is, thankfully, not actually Hitler, but merely a few million pixels showing his image and perhaps conjuring up all the horrific emotions associated with him. The same goes for the emotions generated by a modern icon such as Paris Hilton. And thus it is in economics: a diagram is not the market, nor does moving a curve prove that prices and/or quantity on the market will change. The diagram illustrates certain points – keeping in mind any number of assumptions, limitations and other constraints.

This is a common error on the part of young economists, using diagrams to prove a point but referring to the diagram as if the illustration is the proof unto itself! The diagram shows and illustrates – it does not prove. I ask you therefore to take heed and *never replace cogent, articulate thought and clarity of writing with illustrations*. Once again, the diagram serves to underline, illustrate and clarify your line of thought and can never replace written or spoken language.

Opportunity cost using a PPF

All economies face the same issues outlined in the basic economic questions of 'what to produce, how and for whom', and all economies face infinite wants and limited resources.

A simple PPF

Assume a small economy, Mirageville, and the following:

1. The economy only has the resources to produce two goods, guns and roses.

2. There is a *known maximum output* and the economy can attain this level, i.e. there is no unemployment or idle factors of production.

3. There is *no trade* with other villages, thus production equals consumption (much more on this in Section 4).

4. That any given quantity of resources transferred from one sector to another are *equally productive*, (or reapplicable) resulting in the trade-off being constant all along the PPF (this assumption will be changed in later PPFs).

---

41. When the Nazis sent the SS to war, the rule was 'When in doubt, kill'. When economists start a harangue (= ranting lecture), the rule of thumb is 'When in doubt, assume'. For example, in answering how many economists it takes to change a light bulb the answer is 'Well, it depends. Now, assume one ladder …' Seriously, all use of models and examples must inevitably be firmly anchored in assumptions and/or premises.

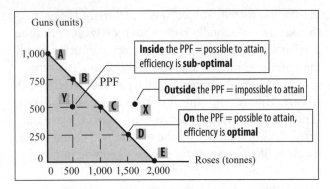

Figure 1.1.8 *A simple PPF for Mirageville*

There are three relatively straightforward conclusions and one slightly more elaborate to be drawn from this illustration of Mirageville's productive capacity.

1. There are **infinite output combinations** of the two goods – but only within the boundaries of the PPF. Our fictitious village can *maximally* produce 1,000 units of guns or 2,000 tonnes of roses, but it can also produce any possible combination of goods, for example, 500 units of guns plus 1,000 tonnes of roses at point **C**. The blue area fences in the virtually infinite number of output combinations of guns and roses; point **Y** is possible as it is within the PPF, while point **X** is impossible as it lies outside the PPF. Anywhere on the PPF shows maximum efficiency in the use of resources, while anywhere within the PPF shows idle resources.

2. The concept of **opportunity cost arises only when the village is on the PPF**. At any point within the PPF it is possible to increase one good while keeping output of the other constant – or even increasing it. This is intuitive, as any economy not using all possible resources to the fullest may well increase the output of all goods – which thus does not entail giving up any goods. Mirageville could move from point **Y** to point **C** for example.

3. The **opportunity cost is constant**. Assuming that Mirageville is actually on the PPF, i.e. that there is no unemployment or idle machinery, then moving from point **B** to **C** increases output of roses by 500 tonnes but results in 250 fewer units of guns.

Moving from point **B** to **C** has the same result – an increase in rose output of 500 tonnes and a decrease in guns by 250 units. The PPF shows the trade-off moving from one given combination of output to another. As the PPF is a straight line the trade-off will be constant.

4. In keeping with the thrid conclusion, it follows that **all factors of production are equally reapplicable** in both sectors of the economy. This is the elaborate conclusion and is explained further on.

POP QUIZ 1.1.7   MORE OPPORTUNITY COSTS

1 What is the opportunity cost of the increased output of roses in moving from point C to point E?

2 What would happen to the level of unemployment in moving from point C to E?

3 Why is point X impossible to attain?

Opportunity cost and factor applicability

Looking at Mirageville's PPF in greater detail in Figure 1.1.9 on page 25 we can see the opportunity costs of Mirageville moving from the production of guns to roses.

Assuming that Mirageville puts all its resources into the production of guns the village's output point would be at point **A** in Figure 1.1.9, and put total output at 1,000 units of guns and zero roses – which probably doesn't do wonders for romanticism in the community. Anyhow, assuming the advent of a slightly more harmonious (and perhaps amorous) village council, the decision is taken to produce (I think they plant them, or something) 200 tonnes of roses. As the village is producing on the frontier it is impossible for production of roses to take place unless resources (factors of production) are taken from the munitions factories and put to work in the horticultural sector. This will reallocate resources in our little economy. The villagers, in reallocating resources from guns to roses will have to forego an amount of guns in order to produce roses, and thus the opportunity cost of roses is the amount of foregone guns.

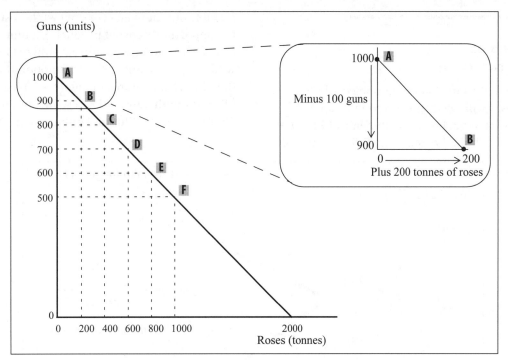

Figure 1.1.9 *Detail of Mirageville's opportunity costs*

The opportunity cost of roses: The village was initially producing at point **A**, which rendered 1,000 units of guns, no roses, and an indeterminate amount of love-sickness. As resources are reallocated to the production of roses, people, machines and land are taken from the munitions factories and put to work producing roses. Mirageville is now producing at point **B**; 900 units of guns and 200 tonnes of roses. The opportunity cost of those 200 tonnes of roses is the loss of 100 units of guns, e.g. *each unit of roses means foregoing a half tonne of guns*. It bears restating: resources are finite and thus one has to make a choice in what to produce – this incurs opportunity costs.

The remaining points, **C** through **F** show that when the increasingly beautifying villagers increase the output of roses, total output of guns falls, and that the *rate* at which the output of guns falls per increase in roses is *constant*. The opportunity cost of 200 tonnes of roses is 100 units of guns, a ratio that is constant all along the PPF. In moving from point *A* to **B**, from **B** to **C** or from **E** to **F**, the opportunity cost of one tonne of roses is constantly one half a unit of guns.[42]

The opportunity cost of guns: One can also see the cost of guns. Posit that more hawkish members of the peaceful economy take over and reverse the trend at point **F**, where total output consists of 500 units of guns and 1,000 tonnes of roses. Reallocating resources and moving back to point **E** on the PPF means that while 100 more units of guns are produced, there are 200

fewer tonnes of roses with which to adorn rifle muzzles. Correct, the opportunity cost of each additional batch of 100 guns will carry the opportunity cost of 200 tonnes of roses. We now know the cost of roses – *a tonne of roses costs half a unit of guns* and vice versa, each unit of guns costs (200/100) 2 tonnes of roses.

Factor applicability: In going from point *A* (1,000 units of guns and 0 tonnes of roses) to **B** (900 units of guns and 200 tonnes of roses), the amount of land/labour/machines reallocated to produce 200 tonnes of roses meant an opportunity cost of 100 units of guns. The cost does not change when the economy moves from point **E** (600 units of guns and 800 tonnes of roses) to point **F** (500 units of guns and 1,000 tonnes of roses). The production factors must therefore be equally reapplicable no matter where the village is producing (moving along) the PPF. Having constant opportunity costs means that production factors are *perfectly reapplicable* at any level of output.

A few colleagues have asked me to point out that my somewhat flippant (joking) example, using guns and roses, is an updated version of the example that has long been part of the staple diet of economics – the 'guns or butter' problem which portrays the dilemma facing society in choosing between more armaments or more food. Simply replace roses with foodstuffs and ask yourself if a shipment of AK47s is worth one year's supply of maize (corn) for 20,000 people.

---

42. When production reaches an output of 500 guns and 1,000 roses the villagers might decide to start a rock band.

Outside the box:
PPFs and cost ratios

There is no end of confusion on the subject of PPFs and cost ratios. I will say this now and in Chapter 4.1 on trade and Chapter 5.4 on development: a PPF is *not* the same as a cost ratio diagram. The PPF shows total possible output in an economy while cost ratios show the opportunity cost of producing a unit of Good X in terms of foregoing a certain amount of Good Y – all the while operating under the assumption that one is on the PPF. The diagrams in Figure 1.1.10 show the cost ratios for both guns and roses; one unit of guns costs 2 units of roses – thus one unit of roses costs 0.5 guns.

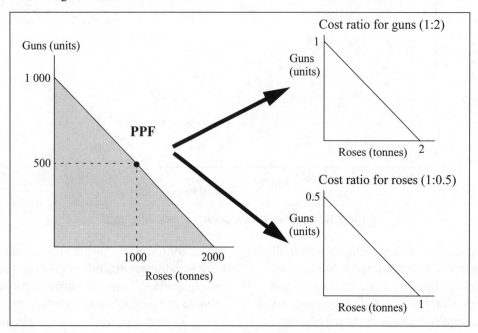

Figure 1.1.10 *PPFs and cost ratios*

A more realistic PPF

The PPF rests on the assumptions of an economy producing only two goods, that there is a known and attainable output maximum, and that no trade is done with other economies. I agree, this is unrealistic and in all likelihood non-existent. Yet the simple trade-off line clearly illustrates the larger, very real, questions facing all countries, namely those of whether society wishes to use limited societal resources in the production of *X* rather than in *Y*. The PPF serves mores as an illustration in clearly outlining opportunity cost thinking. In any event, let us at least approach a more realistic illustration of an economy using a PPF, and then apply it to the central issues of growth and development.

An island economy: Sifnos

Let's apply the PPF to an island economy, namely my little island in the Aegean, Sifnos. The island geography consists of some 35 square kilometres of basalt rock, marble, parched mountains, terraced fields, and 90 kilometres of coastline. Flora consists primarily of low-lying shrubs, diminutive pine trees and the traditional Greek agricultural items such as fig and olive trees. There are 2,000 year-round inhabitants, 1,000 migrant labourers (mostly from Albania) and 5,000 sheep[43]. The main source of income is from a flourishing pottery industry and the tens of thousands of tourists that visit during the period May to October. That was the outline, now let us assume – as done earlier – that the island's total output can be divided into two distinct categories, tourism and pottery, that the economy is maximally efficient (i.e. on the PPF), and that the island is not trading with the mainland or other islands. However, let us now assume that while the factors of production are reapplicable, *some factors are better than others* in the production of tourism service or pottery production.

---

43. Yes, all my old students knew I was going to fit some sheep in here somewhere!

Increasing opportunity costs: Figure 1.1.11 is the PPF for Sifnos. Output ranges from 600,000 hours of tourism and zero pottery to 4,000 tonnes of pottery and zero hours of tourism. Let us say that Sifnos is at point **A**, where the Sifnians are producing 600,000 hours of tourism and nothing else. Moving to point **B** to produce the initial 1,000 tonnes of pottery entails giving up 2,000 hours of tourism service, which is thus the opportunity cost of the first tonne of pottery. The striking difference for the Sifnians will occur when

they increase output of pottery further, from point **B** to point **C** along the PPF. It is immediately obvious that the cost ratio has changed – the second 1,000 tonnes of pottery entails giving up the production of 6,000 hours of tourism service. In other words, the opportunity cost of the second batch of pottery is 6,000 tourism hours – three times the cost of the first batch. Moving from point **C** to **D** we see how the opportunity cost of pottery production rises to 12,000 hours of tourism per tonne of pottery.

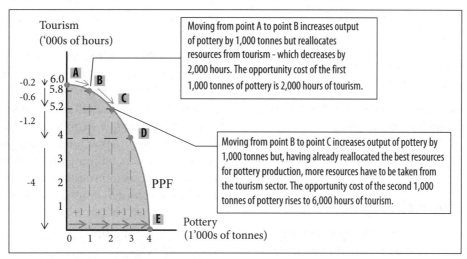

Figure 1.1.11 *PPF for Sifnos – increasing opportunity costs*

This increasing cost ratio is heavily exaggerated and accentuated by the time we reach points **D** to **E**; the final possible tonne of pottery means that the Syfnians give up 40,000 hours of tourism service, i.e. producing the final tonne would entail giving up two-thirds of total possible tourism service.

Reasons for rising opportunity costs: It appears that in moving from the production of tourism to the production of pottery we run into reallocation issues which seem to raise the costs as we divert more and more resources into pottery production. The factors of production are evidently *not* perfectly reapplicable!

Welcome to reality. Put yourself into the shoes of the islanders and consider the issue of resource allocation. All available resources are being used optimally in the production of tourism and a decision is made to also produce some pottery.

Which land should be used for the kiln? Which of the people in restaurants, hotels and transportation should become potters? Which tennis courts should give way for the production of clay? The answer to these questions is rather simple: use the resources which would mean giving up the least amount of tourism output! That is, use the factors of production which are best suited to produce pottery – taking into account

that these resources should naturally not be vital for tourism production. The combination renders a relatively low loss of tourism service (i.e. a low opportunity cost) in providing a given initial quantity of pottery.

Niko does both – entertains tourists AND produces pottery!

So, using the *best* land, labour and capital suited for pottery – and hopefully also the least necessary in tourism output – the Syfnians start an initial production plant. Yannis, Maria, Georgios and Andonis have all had prior experience in pottery and loathe the loudmouthed tourists so they quit waiting on tables and go about finding suitable land and factory sites. Maikis the shepherd has vast knowledge of clay marls and fresh water basins and is sick and tired of the stench of sheep – which incidentally are terrified of him! The Dionysos nightclub no longer attracts the crowds as before and can thus be easily transformed into a car rental service, etc. All of this ultimately renders a relatively high initial output of pottery per unit of tourism hours given up. Yet when other

Syfnians (encouraged by the success) turn to pottery production, they will discover that the best resources are already taken. The second group of potters will have to make do with the second-best cluster of resources; the rate of return simply cannot be as high for the copy-cats as they do not have equally suitable factors of production at their disposal. Producing the final tonne of pottery might mean taking the banking people, the ferry people, the bus drivers, the hoteliers, and hey presto – no more tourism service or tourists.

POP QUIZ 1.1.8   PPFS

1   Why is an 'outward-bending' or convex PPF more realistic than a straight-line PPF?

2   What does the 'outward-bending' PPF show us? Use 'costs' and 'allocation' in your answer.

3   How can a PPF illustrate the opportunity cost issues all countries face?

Actual and potential output

What economies basically want is to somehow have more of everything. Using the PPF we can illustrate how economies wish to move as close as possible to the boundary set by production possibilities – and also the economy will want to increase in total size – illustrated by a *shift* in the PPF 'outwards' (i.e. away from the origin). It is vital at the outset that you do not misunderstand – nor misinterpret – the difference between 'increasing production' and 'extending the PPF'. The former is increasing output within the boundaries set by the PPF while the latter is a hypothetical or theoretical case where a country increases its *potential* output. A shift in the PPF does not *necessarily* entail an increase in actual output! This is one of the most common fallacies amongst my students in using PPFs.

Once again, we set the parameters. Assume an economy capable of producing all of the millions of goods we can find in a modern economy. The previous assumptions (no trade and factors of production are not equally well reallocated) hold true here too and others will be added piecemeal. Let us now classify all

of these goods into two distinct groups in order to be able to use the simplicity of a dual-axis model, the PPF. There is any number of groupings commonly used as examples here but I will limit myself to the following three; consumer goods and capital goods, military and non-military goods, and public/merit goods[44] and 'all other goods'.

Increasing actual output, i.e. economic growth

In diagram I of Figure 1.1.12 on page 29, the economy shows *growth* since *actual output* has expanded from point *A* to *B*.[45] Our model economy has just increased the production of both capital and consumer goods while the PPF remains in place. This example of growth illustrates that unused resources have been put into use, for example firms start utilising unused machines and hire previously unemployed labourers. Note that we are assuming that the quantity and/or quality of factors of production remain the same so the PPF has not shifted. Points **A** to **B** could illustrate an economy recovering from recession.

Remember, the PPF is a purely hypothetical construct. We have already taken into account all possible production circumstances such as technology, labour skills and quality of raw materials in drawing the curve – that is why more or better use of existing available resources illustrates growth in the PPF without an associated shift in the PPF in diagram I of Figure 1.1.12. Diagram II illustrates the effects on both potential output (the PPF shifts outwards) and actual output/growth (point **A'** to **B'**). The increase in productive potential and subsequent actual growth is the result of more and/or improved resources being put to use.

Changing the quality of the factors of production

An increase in the *quality of labour*, such as education, training, and experience, will inevitably result in the ability of labourers to produce more goods during any given period of time.[46] The *quality of land* can entail new farming methods, high-yielding crop types or purer iron ore for making steel. Improved *capital*, such as production technology could render more widgets

---

44. I take the liberty of bundling public and merit goods together at this stage. Examples of public goods are roads, judicial systems and defence, while merit goods are schools, health care, pension systems and social security. They are often – but by no means always – provided and/or paid for by government. See Chapter 3.2.

45. Note that 'point to point' movements in PPF diagrams are grossly exaggerated. In diagram I Figure 1.1.12 on page 29, it appears as if both consumer and capital goods have increased by 25%. Again, keep in mind that the diagram is only a description and not a scaled representation of reality.

46. Yet anyone having spent a summer working on an assembly line, as I have, knows that one uses one's experience and skill to have longer breaks – not produce more! I gleefully note that the firm in question went bankrupt.

per hour and possibly also use less raw material to produce the same amount of widgets[47], and innovation in the production of capital goods, in turn, means improved machines for consumer goods.

Changing the quantity of the factors of production

If there are *more* factors of production available, then potential output has increased. Using available *capital* in the manufacture of more capital increases potential output; adding more land (as the Dutch have done for hundreds of years by way of building dikes) adds to potential arable land, and an increase in the *labour* force (for example, a 'baby-boom' generation exiting school or increased immigration) all mean that potential output has increased – and that *actual output* increases when these resources are employed.

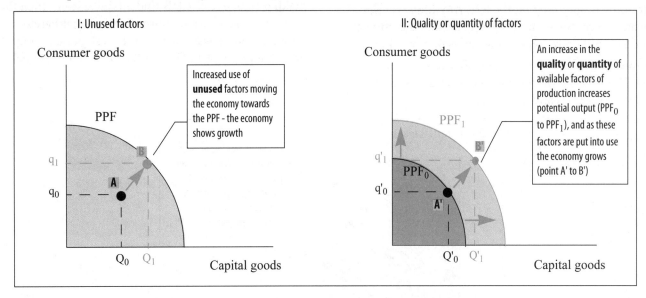

Figure 1.1.12 *An increase in actual output – two possible versions*

Increasing potential output, i.e. potential economic growth

As noted above, there are basically two ways in which the PPF might shift: changes in the *quality* and/or *quantity* of the factors of production. In Figure 1.1.13, the economy is at point *A*. An increase in *potential output* is shown by an outward shift from PPF_0 to PPF_1, but *actual* output remains the same: the economy remains at point **A**. The actual output is unchanged but the conditions for increasing future actual output have improved. In short, there is an increase in the quality and/or quantity of factors of production but these factors are as yet *unutilised* – the economy has in other words incurred more favourable conditions for the creation of goods and services in the future.

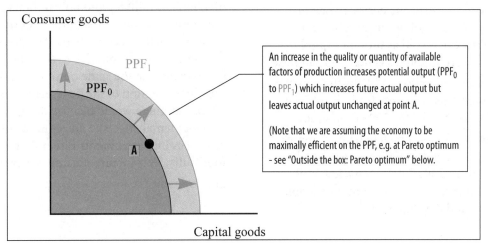

Figure 1.1.13 *An increase in potential output*

---

47. A 'widget' is a fictitious/hypothetical product or thing. Economists use the term 'widget' to make up for a sad lack of fantasy and imagination in trying to conjure up good real-life products in textbook examples.

Outside the box:
Pareto optimum

The concept of social efficiency in an economy was pioneered by the Italian/French social-economist Wifredo Pareto (1848–1923) and can be illustrated using a PPF. Social efficiency is maximised when the economy is operating on the PPF. Anything else would mean that resources are not being used to the utmost. The PPF in Figure 1.1.14 shows an economy where output is divided into goods for IB teachers[48] (such as TOK books and comfortable shoes) and IB students (Nintendo games and marshmallows).

At point **A**, the economy is *maximally efficient* and it is impossible to increase the output of teachers' goods without decreasing output of students' goods and vice versa. Therefore, anywhere along the PPF, the economy can be said to be optimally socially efficient. This is referred to as a **Pareto optimum**. The condition is put as a conditional phrase: 'If it is impossible to increase the wellbeing of one person [here IB teachers] without making someone else [IB students] worse off, then the economy is at a Pareto optimum.' Note that Pareto optimality in no way suggests the 'best' point of output, only that points **A** to **D** fulfil the criteria for optimal efficiency.

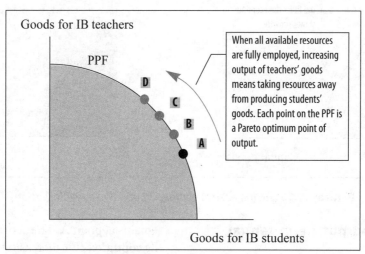

Figure 1.1.14 *Pareto optimum*

Growth and development

'Another issue where **inter-temporal trade-offs** are of central importance concerns the desirable rate of capital formation. By foregoing consumption for investment in **physical as well as human capital** (education and research), today's generation can raise the welfare of future generations.'[49] Why the quotation marks here? Simple, this is a quote from the official Nobel Prize press release for the 2006 economics award[50] to Edmund Phelps. I merely wish to impress upon you, yet again, that economics is an applied science in concluding this section with a few PPF diagrams that address the issue of – and distinction between – growth and development.

Growth versus development using a PPF

In Figure 1.1.15 on page 31 diagram I, total output is divided into military and non-military goods, and public/merit goods and all other goods. Diagram I illustrates that an economy has increased total output for military goods, point *A* to *B*, while non-military goods remain at the same output level. With the possible exception of the generals running Burma/ Myanmar, there would be little debate as to the developmental effects to an economy of putting scarce resources into armaments rather than schools and foodstuffs. This picture illustrates growth, yes, but not development.[51]

---

48. There are so many things I'd love to put here … but my editor won't let me. Feel free to write to me with suggestions!

49. See the original quote at the Official Nobel website, http://nobelprize.org/nobel_prizes/economics/laureates/2006/press.html.

50. Technically, there is no Nobel Prize in economics but 'The Swedish National Bank's Prize in Economic Sciences in Memory of Alfred Nobel'.

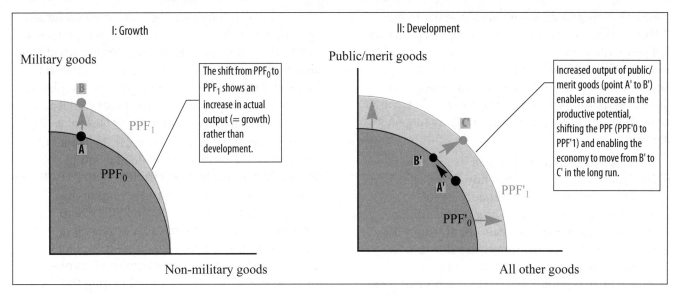

Figure 1.1.15 *Growth and development*

It is important to keep growth and development separate – they are not synonymous. However, most economists would agree that development is strongly linked to economic growth, i.e. there is positive correlation. In Figure 1.1.15 diagram II, diverting resources from 'all other goods' towards public/merit goods (point A' to B') such as schooling, health care and public roads has short-run and long-run effects. In the short run there is an inter-temporal opportunity cost of foregone 'other good' in the reallocation of resources from 'other goods' to public/merit goods. (See "A little depth: Inter-temporal opportunity costs".) This is inter-temporal as the investment in *physical capital* (for example, roads) and *human capital* (such as the availability of education and improvements in health care) all serve to enhance the productive capacity of factors of production, thus enabling increased *future* output. This is shown by a shift of the PPF outwards from PPF'$_0$ to PPF'$_1$. This utilisation of improved factors renders *economic growth*; the economy moves from point B' to point C'. Increased actual output further enables an increase in the standard of living and also increased government tax revenues – which in turn can provide more public/merit goods. This pro-developmental cycle will be brought up in greater depth in Section 5.3.

A little depth:
Inter-temporal opportunity costs

My grandmother was big on 'saving for a rainy day' – a proverb I didn't really figure out until I was about 19.[52] What she meant was that one should have a buffer in case of future need. She also took me to the local bank when I was about six to show me 'my' money. I was actually so insistent on seeing specifically my money that the kindly bank manager took us into the vault and pointed to a pile of dollars lying on a shelf, saying 'There you are Mr McGee. That's your pile in the middle. And you just leave it right there and we'll make it grow.' Faaaaaaar out! I don't know what impressed me the most, seeing my stack of dollars or being called Mr McGee. Neither has happened since, incidentally.

It wasn't until later that I started to reflect on the '…we'll make it grow' part of the bank manager's statement. I know now that he was referring to interest, i.e. the return one gets for putting money in a bank[53]. Let's assume that I had USD100 in the bank back in 1968 and that I could have received an average of 5% yearly interest up to today; I'd have USD670 in the bank now![54] Now we have an inter-temporal issue of

---

51. World military expenditure in 2001 was estimated at $839 billion (in current dollars), accounting for 2.6 % of world gross domestic product (GDP) and a world average of $137 per capita. (Source: *The Economist*, 18 July 2002; the Stockholm International Peace Research Institute at http://editors.sipri.se/pubs/yb02/ch06.html.) I put it to you that the opportunity costs of using scant resources to buy arms rather than building schools is rather considerable in LDCs.

52. I mean, come on!? We lived in Jamaica at the time, where the rainy season lasted three months – and I still wasn't supposed to use my savings!?

53. The bank then lends this to house-buyers helping to create the ongoing (2009) 'sub-prime' crisis which you will have as a case study in university. The case study will be titled 'Insane overconfidence'.

choice that my grandmother could have put to me: 'Matt, do you want two pairs of cowboy boots now or ten pairs when you're forty?' The answer, of course, is neither – I'd much rather have a box of Cohiba cigars and a bottle of Hennessey Cognac, but it clearly illustrates the concept of opportunity costs in terms of now versus the future. (It also illustrates taking on bad habits.)

One hundred US dollars now or five hundred US dollars later? Two pairs of boots now or ten pairs later? Which is preferable? The *opportunity cost* of consuming two pairs of boots now is the additional eight I could have later. Alternatively, the future 10 pairs mean that I can't consume two pairs now. Drawing a parallel to an imaginary economy, let us assume that an economy can produce consumer goods and capital goods and are maximally efficient. Look upon the trade-off issue our economy faces, putting resources into producing consumer goods or producing capital goods. Is this not pretty much the same as in the example above, where we could consume 2 units now or 10 units later? Remember, capital is used in the production of all goods. This means that any current consumption that is forfeited will liberate resources which can be used in the production of capital – which could subsequently be used in the production of even greater amounts of consumer goods in the future. Put in opportunity cost terms, *the cost of present consumption is greater future consumption.*

Figure 1.1.16 illustrates the present versus future opportunity costs. In accordance with our previous assumptions, the economy is maximally efficient and thus on the initial PPF (PPF_0) at point A. Altering emphasis to the production of capital goods (physical capital) moves the economy from point A to B along PPF_0, rendering present opportunity costs of A–B of consumer goods in order to increase the output of capital goods. This increases potential output, ultimately resulting in a shift from PPF_0 to PPF_1. In due course, as the economy takes advantage of the increased availability of capital, output of both categories of goods will increase, i.e. there is growth, shown by the movement from point B to point C. In the final reckoning, the movement from point A to C indicates economic growth resulting from the initial investment in capital.

The economy has thus chosen to forego an amount of *present* consumption in order to consume more in the *future* – not at all unlike putting aside your income as savings in order to be able to buy more in the future. This was what grandma was trying to get across to me: the opportunity cost of *present* consumption is the possibility of greater *future* consumption. By now you should have no difficulty in tossing the issue around in order to consequently state that **the opportunity cost of investment in capital is present consumption**.

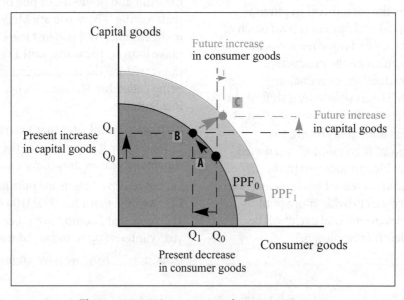

Figure 1.1.16 *Inter-temporal opportunity costs*

54. There is an interest-upon-interest effect, known as compounded interest. After the first year I would have USD100 × 1.05 = USD105.00. In year two I would have USD105 × 1.05 = USD110.25. The 39 years between 1968 and 2007, would yield USD100 × 1.0539 = USD607.50. Albert Einstein called compounded interest 'the most powerful force in the universe'.

You know, I never did get that pile of dollars. But I did get … Manta Ray boots.

Dealing with exam questions

There are five common errors in using PPFs:

1 Not having points along the PPF and values along the axes when illustrating opportunity costs. Referring to values on the axes allows the examiner to see (a) what the opportunity costs are and perhaps (b) that opportunity costs are increasing.

2 Trying to show opportunity costs by putting two points *within* the PPF. Opportunity costs are illustrated in moving along the PPF, not within the PPF.

3 Trying to show rising opportunity costs by putting only two points on the PPF. Opportunity costs arise in moving along the PPF and *three* points are needed to show that the opportunity cost of the 5th unit of, say, guns, is greater than the cost of the 4th unit of guns. (See Figure 1.1.10 on page 26.)

4 Not including relevant assumptions. For example, if you are illustrating opportunity costs then the assumption is that the economy is 'on the PPF' – which means you are assuming the economy is maximally efficient (Pareto efficient). Another weighty assumption is whether the factors of production are equally reapplicable from the production of one good to the other, as this determines the shape of the PPF.

5 Not using relevant 'bundles' of goods. You must try to link the PPF clearly to the question at hand and this almost always means dividing the economy into two groups of goods – 'bundles'. So, rather than 'Good *X* and Good *Y*', use, for example, 'Public/merit goods and military goods' to show development and 'Capital and consumer goods' to illustrate potential growth.

A personal note on development

I know a good many nasty words. Most of my students will happily attest to this as will all of my ex-bosses who may at some point have been on the receiving end of my temper. The nastiest word I know is 'waste'. This is the dread of economists as it represents resources being squandered, in other words a loss that could be avoided.

That is why I feel so strongly about poverty and the lack of development in some two-thirds of the world: it is so incredibly wasteful. I am not the 'touchy-feely, save-the-rainforest-at-all-cost' type of person as you no doubt have already surmised. I try not to use emotional or moral arguments in speaking of development issues. I ultimately look at development from the point of self-interest; how many Einsteins, Edisons, and da Vincis have been lost to poverty, lack of opportunity, disease and famine. Inevitably I tell my students: 'This is wasteful. This is economically appalling. This is damaging us all. This is wrong.'

It is awkward to round off this introductory section on development so abruptly. The issues herein make up such a vitally significant section that it is very easy to become fixated on the many topics that are of such immediate importance – and I am speaking of life, not the syllabus. Look at the picture. I took it in November 2002 in Ovamboland, northern Namibia, while on a project for the Swedish International Development Co-operation Agency (SIDA). We were crossing the street in Oshakati when I saw this tiny lad desperately trying to follow what I assumed was his older brother, who was also carrying a large bag. On impulse I held up my camera and raised my eyebrows. He just looked at me. Then he nodded in a non-committed way and put down his load which probably weighed as much as he did. I took his picture and for a month afterwards I kept having a recurring vision of him standing there with his bag of maize meal. I couldn't figure out why this image seemed to leave such an impression. It didn't dawn on me until I saw the photograph: he looks absolutely lifeless and dejected as if he had no hope whatsoever. Namibia was a tremendous journey, yet this is my most vivid memory of it.

I implore you – study hard. Listen well but keep an open and critical mind as you plough through your course in economics. Question your reading matter (especially this textbook!) and teachers to develop your argumentative skills and insight. Try to keep in mind that learning from books and teachers is only part of the job – it is up to you to put that learning to use by being inquisitive to the happenings around the world. Should you live in a wealthy country, I beg you to keep half an eye on the news, between zapping from MTV to 'Paris Hilton and friends': If you happen to see a news sequence of a desperate young boy trying to earn a few pesos by cleaning windshields in traffic gridlock in smog-filled downtown Mexico City, you might have somewhere in the back of your mind that 'There but for the grace of God go I'.

POP QUIZ 1.1.9   PPFS, GROWTH AND DEVELOPMENT

1 How would you think that information technology has affected potential output for the global economy? Illustrate this with a PPF.

2 The average pension age has fallen significantly during the past 30 years. How might this affect the PPF?

3 Increasing globalisation (= integration of world markets via trade and investment) has increased the degree of specialisation in many countries. Show the likely results of this using PPFs.

4 Draw a PPF showing that both actual and potential output has increased.

Rationing systems   ©IBO 2003

The central issues of opportunity costs and scarcity lead to choice, which in turn leads to the man-made solution to the question of how these choices are made – *economic systems*. The purpose of the system is to fulfil wants by using factors of production, which by their nature of scarcity mean that all wants cannot be satisfied. Somehow the goods must be *rationed*, i.e. 'who gets how much of what'.

Basic economic questions   ©IBO 2003

The **basic economic questions** that economics seeks to answer have permeated all societies throughout history:

- What to produce?
- How to produce?
- For whom to produce?

The first issue, 'what', deals with the allocation of resources to make the goods that society wants. The issue can be as trivial as 'red shoes or blue shoes' or as broad as the classic 'guns or butter' question we shall look at in just a moment. The issue of 'how' deals with production methodology, organisation and technology. The final issue, 'who', is the wider issue of distribution, i.e. to whom the spoils of production go. All societies have to deal with these issues, from the Aztec society which created the lookout tower up the hill here on Expat Street in Mexico City, to the centrally planned economy of Cuba which made the excellent cigars I – but not my housemate Rob – enjoy.

> **The basic economic questions**: The enduring central issue of economics; how all human societies, throughout time, are forced to deal with the questions of what to produce, how to produce it and for whom to produce.

Economic systems – and ultimately – politics

From caveman to spaceman, the basic economic problem must be solved and dealt with via some form of societal system. The two of most relevance today are the *free* or *competitive market* system and the *planned economy* (sometimes called a **command economy**). Both have failings and advantages in the production and/or distribution of goods which may help to explain the fact that there has in fact never been a pure version of either. All economic systems are in fact *mixed economies*: it is simply the degree to which markets and government planning address the basic economic question. A good deal of the mix is the result of ideology and politics. I would be lax not to point out that it is most assuredly *not* the task of economic science to advocate one economic system or another, but to provide objective and rational options as the basis of decisions. It is the curse of economics as a science that the line between objective alternatives and politics is so often fuzzy.

The traditional (or subsistence) economic system

Once upon a time, not too long after (well, OK, a few million years) the first *Australopithecus* stood up on quivering legs on the savannah and shielded her eyes against the sun, an economic system would be comprised of people living in small, close-knit communities relying primarily on hunting, agriculture and the barter (trading) of goods with one another. There was little specialisation and most of the output was produced and consumed within the family or extended family unit. Needless to say, per capita output was very low by today's standards, but basic needs and wants were provided for. This subsistence level economy was non-monetary and based more on co-operation and survival than organised labour based on ownership and property rights. This laughably archaic system only survived for about 30,000 years (and still does in a number of places).

The market system

Established markets have followed human civilizations hand in glove from the outset of written history. The generic term 'market' is exactly what it sounds like: buyers and sellers interacting in a market place. Trade started to flourish and the relative scarcity or abundance of goods established the price, i.e. the trade ratios, since in many instances goods would be brought to market and simply traded for other goods which was *bartering*. One piglet for one barrel of mead (i.e. warm, flat, sour beer – much like the British still drink), for example.

Eventually, the system was *monetized*. Carrying all those piglets around to buy drinks with was a real bother. Money also made smaller transactions possible: how would one go about spending a piglet when you only wanted a cup of mead rather than a barrel?! How would you get small change on trading a full-grown swine for the cup of mead?! (Tipping was a real mess – what did you do, leave a snout or an ear?) Monetising the economy also enabled saving, lending, and a system for both, banks and other financial institutions.[55]

While a supply and demand function (see Section 2.1) was always built into the barter market system of economic transaction, money made things immeasurably easier. One could sell the piglet, get coins instead of mead, and store the coins as wealth. One could then go out and buy a round of mead or get the barrel of mead after a few months – and not have had to feed the piglet in the interim! Money meant that one could buy the goods one needed, and in any incremental quantities. This facilitated increasing specialisation, as households no longer needed to produce virtually everything but could use money to buy goods from specialised producers on the market. By the middle of the 16th century, there were banks functioning along modern lines (notably Italy and Germany), where deposited money would earn interest and also be lent to investors for a higher interest rate.

By the time the 19th century rolled around, all the necessary conditions for a competitive – and capitalist – market economy were in place. The industrial revolution with its roots in the 18th century provided technology that enhanced productivity and increased output many times over. The necessary funding for the capital was provided by the banks. Liberalism provided the ideological reasoning and justification for abandoning the closed mercantilist system and embracing the laissez faire[56] economic reasoning of Adam Smith and others. Shifts in power away from the aristocrats and fledgling democracies provided a legal system steeped in the sanctity of private ownership and property rights – which primarily empowered the burgeoning bourgeois class. Finally, the incredible increase in agricultural productivity created abundant labour to work in the factories. (The disempowered class of people which Karl Marx called the 'proletariat' at the time.) The system is basically survives to this day, and, while far from perfect (like so much else in the world) it does work.

Planned (or command) economies

The planned economy is in stark contrast to the above. Planned economies imply strong centralised government and ditto planning of output. In the planned, or command, economies, markets had far less to do with output decisions as these were primarily in the hands of centralized government bureaucrats. The production factors are owned and/or allocated by the state and complex planning mechanisms are formalized in the hierarchical architecture of the state, such as committees assessing demand, assigning output, setting production targets/quotas and subsequent pricing of the goods.

> **Centrally planned economy or command economy economy**: An economic system relying on centralized government ownership/planning and control to solve the basic economic problem of 'what, how, for whom'.

Planning was largely implemented in communist countries, most notably in the former Central and Eastern European countries and the Soviet Union, and still is in varying degrees in Cuba, China and a handful of other countries. However, do not make the error of linking planned economies to the left or right of the political spectrum, as is all too often done. Some of the most notoriously right-wing periods in history have shown centralized, planned economies: Hitler's totalitarian capitalism in Germany in the 1930s and 1940s and Mussolini's corporativism of the 1920s to 1940s are notable examples.[57]

---

55. Looking at the ongoing sub-prime credit crisis (2009), we probably should have stuck to pigonomics.
56. Roughly, 'let us do'. This was something of a battle-cry for the liberals in matters pertaining to production, and referred to the state not intervening in the market via taxes, subsidies and other measures.
57. D. Dillard, *Västeuropas och Förenta staternas ekonomiska historia*, Liber Förlag 1985, p. 462.

Mixed economies ©IBO 2003

Economies are for the most part comprised of both private and public ownership/control of resources, which is to say mixed economies, since – to put it bluntly – none of the two systems outlined above has ever existed in *pure* form. They are both extremes as far as reality goes. The planned economies were always forced to overlook the ideologically objectionable fact that a great deal of private consumption was supplied by illegal private enterprises. At the same time, there has never been a completely free market economy as such: lighthouses and roads are for the most part planned and provided by governments, and one would encounter considerable difficulties in the most liberal of economies in starting a private police force or openly selling cocaine outside school zones.

> **Mixed economy**: An economic system where the fundamental economic question of 'who, what, for whom' is solved by a *mixture of government ownership/ intervention/planning and the dynamics of (free) market forces*. All economies are in fact mixed economies.

Economic systems are man-made and all are virtually a mixture of markets and planning. Getting the system to work is a practical problem rather than a theoretical exercise. Market economies' governments also intervene on competitive markets via legislation on monopolies, barriers to free trade, subsidies in agriculture and the public provision of goods such as health care and education. Also, planning encompasses taking population censuses every 10 years or so in most market economies which then lay the basis for planning roads, hospitals, schools and the like. Almost all economic systems are mixed economies, and from this follows the distinction between *public* and *private ownership*.

Public ownership ©IBO 2003

My home country, Sweden, has one of the highest standards of living in the world. It also has a government sector spending ratio of 54.8% of GDP – also one of the highest in the world.[58] I cannot claim that the majority of Swedes support a large government sector but, according to surveys, the majority of Swedes enjoy the benefits. Being a most open and democratic society, the Swedes have had an intense debate for

decades about limiting the size and scope of the public sector and public ownership.

The public sector comprises state, regional, local, and municipal governments. This includes the judicial system, military and civil defence, tax authorities, road workers, health care, schools, nurseries … and anything funded by monies from state/regional/ municipal government. The largest portion of the money being spent by the public sector comes from *taxes*. Yes, Sweden also has one of the highest **total tax-ratios** in the world – 51.1% of GDP. And this is where the debate starts, when citizens start to ask whether they are receiving benefits in proportion to tax burdens. This debate is mirrored in every industrialised country in the world, safe to say.[59]

> **Public sector and public ownership**: The public sector is broadly defined as the government-funded provision of goods and services. Public ownership means government ownership and operation of enterprises providing goods and services at local, regional and national levels.

Public ownership overlaps most of the activities within the public sector but often has more specific meaning. Public ownership is when government has ownership or control of firms. One of the forms of public ownership is in the form of *nationalized* industries, i.e. government ownership of certain industries. In Europe there was a marked drive after the Second World War towards a far larger share of industries being owned and operated by government, main examples being gas works, electricity, steel works, mining operations and telecommunications. This turned around during the late 1970s – notably in Reagan's USA and Thatcher's Great Britain – when the political tide turned in favour of *privatisation*, i.e. selling off government owned/controlled industries to the private sector.

Private ownership ©IBO 2003

The concept of private ownership is one of the key foundations of market-based economic systems and basically means that private individuals have the right to own factors of production, e.g. capital and land. Most free market democracies have the rule of *property rights* codified in written law – and many have it written into the constitution.

---

58. See http://finans.regeringen.se (official government site).
59. Possible exceptions are Hong Kong and Singapore, which have very low tax rates internationally speaking.

> **Private ownership**: Private ownership is the ownership of factors of production by private individuals.

Many economists put the right of private ownership of factors of production under the rule of law as the most important element in a successful market system, as it enables the owner to act in accordance with self-interest, e.g. profit.

There are numerous economic agents in our environment: households, firms, and interest groups (to name but a few) and are all active and interactive members of society operating under various forms of *self-interest*. Economic theory suggests that in the course of market interaction, these economic agents will act to maximise, respectively, gains such as utility, profit or influence. Thus, consumers buy either guns or tickets to Guns 'n' Roses – or both if it's a Ramones

concert[60] – to maximise marginal utility. Firms use factor inputs and pass on the output, guns or concert tickets, to maximise profit. Political interest groups such as the Moral Majority and the National Rifle Association (NRA) lobbyists in America wine and dine congressmen to ban certain concerts but allow card-carrying NRA members in Missouri to buy semi-automatic Uzis to hunt squirrels.

Silliness aside, self-interest lies in the centre of a core economic term, without which economics would walk like a wounded Missouri squirrel, namely *incentives*. An incentive is a lure/reward or promise of something positive which entices us to act in a certain manner in order to obtain the reward. Private ownership of resources means that individuals have the incentive to put resources into enterprises from which profit can be had, and this is the very basis of a free market economy.

 CELEBRITY BUBBLE: ADAM SMITH (1723–90)

Often referred to as the 'Father of economics', Adam Smith can indeed be considered one of the most influential writers in the history of mankind – putting him right next to Newton, Einstein and Dr. Seuss*. Born in County Fife, Scotland, Smith studied at Oxford and ultimately came to teach at the University of Glasgow. He was quite the eccentric – incredibly absent-minded and always immersed in thought, he was much loved by his students – in spite of them sometimes having to search for him as he distractedly wandered the moors in his night-shirt in the evening!

In 1776 the world was rocked by the publication of his magnum opus, 'The Wealth of Nations'. This rambling work was built on the work of others but was unique in compiling the brunt of economic knowledge at the time and putting forth insights that to this day are staples in economics. This book became one of the main pillars of liberalism during the next century. His basic principle was that the combined self-interest of individuals striving within the framework of economic freedom would lead to the best possible outcome for society as a whole.

His two most famous contributions are probably the dissertation on the division of labour and his concept of the 'invisible hand'. The former focuses on the issue of productivity, and the latter refers to how the price function of supply and demand creates optimal societal benefits when these two forces are allowed free rein. Both concepts are used to explain how countries become wealthy.

(Source: 'The Worldly Philosophers', Robert L. Heilbroner, pp. 46–74)

(*Joke! Dr Seuss is the author of a series of brilliant and incredibly successful children's books .)

---

60. Yes, I know Johnny Ramone is dead, but I can't think of any other rock star so intimately linked to guns. Suggestions?

Outside the box:

'Private or public' – the view of a famous free-market advocate

One of the world's leading economists advocating pro-market/non-government intervention, the late Milton Friedman, said that there are four ways to spend money (in a famous book *Free to Choose* written together with Rose Friedman, his wife).

1. One can spend it on oneself.
2. One can spend one's own money on others.
3. One can spend other people's money on oneself.
4. One can spend other people's money on others.

Spending on oneself is most efficient, as one is inclined to search for the goods yielding the highest utility for money spent. Spending one's own money on others might still mean searching for good value but one runs the risk of buying something the other person doesn't want. Spending other people's money oneself means that the inclination is low to shop around for the best deal and to be frugal in one's purchases. Finally, spending other people's money on others …

Question: How would this support a viewpoint of limited government involvement and control of resources?

The benevolence of the butcher

> *Give me that which I want, and you shall have this which you want, is the meaning of every such offer; and it is in this manner that we obtain from one another the far greater part of those good offices which we stand in need of. It is not from the benevolence of the butcher, the brewer, or the baker that we expect our dinner, but from their regard to their own interest. We address ourselves, not to their humanity but to their self-love, and never talk to them of our own necessities but of their advantages. Nobody but a beggar chooses to depend chiefly upon the benevolence of his fellow citizens.*[61]

This was written by the 'father of economics', Adam Smith, over two centuries ago. Goods are produced out of self-interest, i.e. the private *profit motive* of the owners of firms. Goods are purchased for the same self-serving reason: the consumer receives the benefit of the good and as he/she is willing to give up a certain amount of other goods to obtain it then it must be in his/her self-interest. Smith was also taking for granted that the butcher, brewer and baker all had *private ownership* of the land and capital that went into production and that these property rights were well established in the code of law.

Central planning versus free market economies ©IBO 2003

The centrally planned system allocates resources primarily via central planning and free market economies rely primarily on markets. In differentiating between the two systems let's look at how output is decided, the underlying value system (e.g. philosophy) and the question of property rights and ownership.

Central planning: demand assessment and production targets

Generally, the system was based on a centralized system of three stages: 1) assessment of demand by central planning committees; 2) setting of production targets; 3) doing an input/output analysis in order to determine the amount of resources necessary to produce the target quantity of goods. In addition to this, prices on output were set at central level, which for the most part meant that the price of goods never matched the corresponding use of factors of production.

This economic system entailed central planners deciding what goods were to be produced and how resources would be allocated to produce them. The founding ideological base of socialism was one of equality and the good of the collective rather than the individual. This meant that every citizen had the right to employment: many prices were set very low in order for everyone to afford the goods; wages were set centrally rather than by industries; goods such as health care and education were freely available to all and housing was provided by the state. Property rights in terms of production resources did not exist to any noticeable extent as ownership was centralised under the state.

---

61. Adam Smith, *Wealth of Nations*, book one, chapter II.

Storytime: The problem of output targets

However politically incorrect, I can't help but give a few hilarious examples of failures resulting from the difficulties in output targeting in the planned economic system.

One of the main problems in the Soviet-style system of central planning was how to set output targets that were well defined and attainable. For example, in setting targets for furniture, would one use the measure of 'X quantity of tables and chairs'; 'weight of total furniture' or perhaps 'total surface area of furniture'? This problem was persistent in all production sectors. Here are a few stories:

A shoe factory was given an output target of 'X quantity of shoes'. The factory promptly produced 10,000 children's shoes as this was the easiest possible way to meet the target. It also saved on material.

A bed factory was given a target of 'X tonnes of beds'. Solution: make cast-iron beds.

A transportation sector for road transports was to produce 'X kilometres of transport per year'. Solution: have all vehicles take the longest road possible between A and B.

These stories of the failings of the system were sometimes openly admitted to by the party apparatus. Nikita Khrushchev himself complained of chandeliers so heavy 'that they pull the ceilings down on our heads' (qtd. in Roberts and LaFollette 1990, p. 8). There was also a very famous cartoon showing a plant manager for a nail factory receiving a medal for surpassing his output target of the month. In the background there are two giant cranes holding up one enormous nail.

The Soviet Union had a system whereby drilling crews for oil were rewarded based on the number of feet drilled. Since it is easier to drill numerous shallow wells than fewer deep wells, billions of roubles were wasted on pointless shallow wells – in spite of the fact that geologists pointed out that these holes couldn't possibly reach oil depths.

Source. (http://ingrimayne.com/econ/IndividualGroup/CentralPlanning.html)

Problems in the planned system

The majority of the planned systems came to a screeching halt during the latter part of the 20th century. The Soviet Union and Central and Eastern European economies collapsed – both from within and due to external pressure – in the late 1980s. A number of built-in weaknesses of the system became irrepressible it would seem: co-ordination failed in supplying materials to industries; output targets were notoriously exaggerated and inflated – as were the reports showing that targets had been met; military spending was grossly understated – an estimated 15% to 17% of GNP went into the production of military goods in the Soviet Union by the mid-1980s[62] ; the lack of incentives such as wages based on quality and quantity of work meant that labour productivity was very low; the right to employment meant that many production sites were padded with an excess of labour which in fact was simply hidden unemployment; the absence of profits meant that resources were abysmally wasted – and the environment suffered accordingly; and the setting of low prices to enable all basic goods affordable led to excess demand and thus interminable queues and rationing of goods such as sugar, butter and meat. Compounding all this was the 'GDP race' against the West during most of the 1950s and 1960s encouraging central planners to focus on the production of capital goods rather than consumer goods, as this added most to national output.

To compound all this, political momentum – notably in the guise of Mikhail Gorbachev's *perestroika* (restructuring) and *glasnost* (openness) in the Soviet Union – set the ball in motion by allowing a freer flow of information both within the country and towards the West. It became evident that as soon as the degree of political freedom increased, andd oppression and suppression decreased, there was no stopping it. By 1992 the planned economies of Eastern Europe were in the *transitional* stage of becoming market economies.

---

62. See http://www.globalsecurity.org/military/world/russia/mo-budget.htm.

Free markets: the price mechanism

In the competitive market system, entrepreneurs formulate business ideas in accordance with a profit incentive and offer their goods on the open market. The cost or scarcity of resources utilised in production determine supply, while the preferences of consumers set demand – one could say that consumers vote for goods[63], creating consumer sovereignty (= consumer power). The interaction between the two forces sets market price. This is the price mechanism so central to a market system. The market price acts as a signal to suppliers since higher demand higher demand forces up prices creating an incentive for suppliers to put more of the good on the market. Consequently, lower demand means downward pressure on the price and suppliers will decrease output and put their efforts into producing other goods. This is the **incentives function** of the price mechanism.

The other function of prices is that it also decides who will get the goods; this is the **rationing function** of price. Higher prices serve to remove consumers unwilling/unable to pay the price and the quantity purchased will decrease. Falling prices consequently mean that more people can and want to buy the good – more quantity will be sold. The competition between firms for our votes will force them to become as efficient as possible to match market prices, whereby firms using less efficient means of production (i.e. cannot produce at the market price) will be forced to leave the market. This is how prices determine how society will use its resources and how the competitive market system solves the basic economic questions. Consumers' demands and suppliers' ability to meet that demand decides *what* is produced, the price decides *who* gets the good, and competition in production decides *how* it will be produced (e.g. the most efficient manner).

There are additional advantages of the market system other than efficient resource allocation, for example competition gives us new and better products. Price competition motivates firms to improve production methods in order to lower costs, which in the long run increases the ability of more consumers to buy more goods. A market system is fair in that it allows anyone to enter the market and compete with other producers, spreading the availability of income and wealth.

The list can be made longer but the basic issues are those above. Consumer sovereignty decides what to produce in conjunction with a firm's ability to produce it. Both parties look to satisfy their self-interest – utility

and profit – while operating under the safety of private ownership rights. The resulting system, the market, is an efficient way of organising production as it enables producers and consumers to interact via 'signalling' rather than centralised planning.

> **Price mechanism:** The price mechanism in a free market acts as a signal for suppliers to increase or decrease the quantity supplied, i.e. the **incentives function** of price. The price mechanism also tells consumers whether to increase or decrease their purchases of a good, which is the **rationing function** of the price. In this way, prices act as a mechanism to correctly allocate productive resources (land, labour and capital) to different sectors in the economy.

Problems in the market system

Taken as a whole, private ownership maintains the system of reciprocal self-interest in the production of goods and services and serves the purpose of taking care of our individual wants. Yet no system is perfect. A main criticism of the market system is in the distribution of goods and services, e.g. that the accumulation of capital and thus wealth seems to be an inevitable by-product of the (capitalist) free-market system with noticeable **income inequalities** as a result. Other fundamental criticisms are that markets often result in negative social effects such as pollution, overproduction of goods with *harmful* effects to society such as alcohol and tobacco, *underprovision* of public and merit goods, and that many markets show a tendency to gain power at the expense of consumers, for example, monopolies. These examples of market failures are the subject of Section 2.4.

POP QUIZ 1.1.10   MARKETS AND THEIR MERITS

1 Explain the difference between how a market economy and a planned economy solve the basic economic problem.

2 Explain how 'the price reflects scarcity'.

3 For which reasons do all countries have a degree of public ownership and public control? Give a few specific examples.

4 Why would education be an example of a good which would be underprovided by the private sector?

5 Why are property rights so important for the competitive market system to function?

---

63. An allegory used by Nobel laureate Paul Samuelson.

Planned versus market economies – summing up

Both systems (and thus supporting ideologies) have their share of successes and failures. The market economy has been far more successful in *producing* goods but perhaps been less successful in the *distribution* of goods – an oft-cited media example being how homeless American veterans of the Vietnam War have been found frozen to death not 200 metres from the White House. Another harsh observer might point out that the centralised economies of former Eastern Europe indeed had excellent income and wealth distribution. There were almost no rich people – virtually everybody suffered the same level of relative poverty.

You surely recognize the free market or planned economy arguments in the political right or left debate. The core discussion here is the fundamental issue of extent the creation and distribution of the fruits of economic activity should be left to the private and government sector. The discussion takes place somewhere in between 'Planning is for society's best' and 'Markets rule'.

The brief for-and-against list in Table 1.1.4 is rather exaggerated – in both directions – and serves mainly as a starting point for one of the central questions in economics – how to best increase living standards in our society. Both in skimming through the 12 points above and in your continued studies in economics, I urge you to reflect and look things up on your own rather than solely taking the word of an economics book and/or teacher. Wisdom is not the by-product of sitting at someone's feet. Use your own feet.

Table 1.1.4 *Planned versus market economies*

Planning is for society's best!	Markets rule!
• Planning is better for society than private profit. • People are motivated by societal good. • There is less waste of resources in the planned society – primarily labour. • A centralized economy creates a wider spread of income and wealth. • Markets lead to the empowerment of firms over citizens. • Markets induce harsh competition and profits are the only reward. The weak are left behind.	• Markets assure that the right goods are produced. • Self-interest and competition see to it that the best goods are produced. • There is less waste in a market economy. • The planned economy is poor in addressing the demands of people. • A competitive market system is superior in creating income and wealth. • Good markets mean less environmental impact.

Storytime: '-isms'

A few classic definitions pinned to our student lodge kitchen door when I was at university.

SOCIALISM: You have two cows. The state takes one and gives it to someone else.

COMMUNISM: You have two cows. The state takes both of them and gives you milk.

FASCISM: You have two cows. The state takes both of them and sells you milk.

NAZISM: You have two cows. The state takes both of them and shoots you.

BUREAUCRACY: You have two cows. The state takes both of them, kills one and spills the milk in the sewer.

CAPITALISM: You have two cows. You sell one and buy a bull.

EXTREME CAPITALISM: You have two cows. You sell one and force the remaining cow to produce the milk of four cows. You are shocked when the cow dies.

POP QUIZ 1.1.11 PRICES, RATIONING AND ALLOCATION

1 What is the function of money in an economic system? Why is it economically superior to bartering?

2 Picture yourself standing in line to buy concert tickets. It's you – and 150,000 other people. There are 40,000 tickets available. Assuming that the price is not set (i.e. a free market), explain how the price mechanism will ration available tickets.

3 What if only 10,000 people were waiting in line and the producers of the concert therefore decided to get a different group to perform. This would be an example of ….?

Economies in transition ©IBO 2003

During the writing of the first edition, in 2003–04, I had collected numerous articles taken from various publications over the previous five or six years. I scanned all the articles dealing with former planned economies of Central and Eastern Europe and the Former Soviet Union (CEEFSU), and ran a search on the scanned articles for various versions of the phrase 'committed to the rubbish heap of history'. I found some 15 references.

Former Central and Eastern Europe and former Soviet Union (CEEFSU)

Being a bit versed in history, I would be careful in putting forward this as the end of the story as history has a propensity (= tendency) to repeat itself. Yet let us look at the simple facts, which are that when the citizens of the planned economies were able to, they voted with their feet and fled, and when the planned systems started to fall apart in the late 1980s it took less than three years to see total meltdown of the Central and Eastern European planned economies.

So what happened in the following decade? A most painful transition in many cases. The time period between 1990 and 2000 put a large part of the CEEFSU[64] region on the level of LDC economies (see Table 1.1.5 on page 43). For example, the Russian economy GDP shrank by 40% between 1990 and 1999, and by 2000 had an estimated output of only 63% of its 1990 level.[65] The south-eastern European and Baltic states took eight years to return to 1990 levels. There were some notable exceptions however, such as Poland, where the economy actually grew by some 40% during this time. *Unemployment* increased dramatically as inefficient state-owned firms were *privatised* and subjected to competitive market forces making thousands of workers redundant. Even one of the most successful transition economies, Poland, had unemployment of 17% as late as in 2001.[66] Another problem was *inflation*, which became an issue as soon as prices were set free. During the early years of transition inflation averaged around 450% in Central and Eastern European countries. The combination of falling income and increased inflation increased the level of *poverty* (living on less than USD2.15 a day according to one definition by the World Bank) in the CEEFSU countries from one person in twenty-five to one in five, according to the World Bank[67].

Table 1.1.5 on page 43 shows the dramatic fall in national income (adjusted for inflation, i.e. real values) and the equally striking levels of inflation. Only two countries, Poland and Hungary, managed to recoup 1990 GDP in the ten-year period and all of the countries had double-digit average inflation rates of over the time period.

Finally, *exchange rates* plummeted as the artificially high rates previously set by central government now were subjected to market forces. What basically happened was that previous illegal (black market) exchange rates became the official rates. Then many of the currencies continued to fall for the first few years and some have not stabilised even now. Case in point, the Russian currency depreciated (= fell in value) by over 90% from 1990 to 2001, as shown in Figure 1.1.17. The fall in the exchange rate had severe repercussions for the Russian economy since all imported goods became more expensive and also scared off desperately needed foreign investors.

---

64. The CEEFSU is comprised of the former Soviet Union, Poland, Czechoslovakia, East Germany (DDR), Romania, Bulgaria, Hungary, Estonia, Latvia and Lithuania.

65. Take these figures with a *large* grain of salt! GDP figures during the Soviet era were highly inflated to show impressive growth rates. Now, GDP is grossly underestimated as so much of the economic activity is black market activity or simply is not accounted for in order to avoid taxes. It is in fact most unlikely that GDP is lower now than 12 years ago.

66. *Transition: The First Ten Years. Analysis and Lessons for Eastern Europe and the Former Soviet Union* The World Bank, Washington, D.C. © 2002.

67. The CIA *World Factbook* put the poverty level at 40% of the population. Again, figures are at best estimates.

Table 1.1.5 *Real GDP and average inflation in CEEFSU economies 1990–2000*

Country	Real GDP in 2000 (1990 = 100)	Average Inflation (1991–2000)
CSB average	*106*	*41*
Czech Republic	99	13
Hungary	109	20
Lithuania	68	88
Poland	147	26
Romania	83	102
CIS average	*62*	*185*
Belarus	89	344
Georgia	30	257
Kazakhstan	65	163
Russian Federation	66	163
Ukraine	43	244
Uzbekistan	97	182

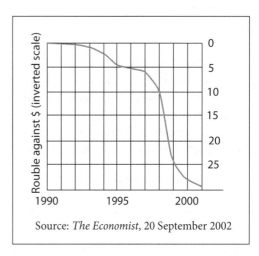
Source: *The Economist*, 20 September 2002

Figure 1.1.17 *The rouble turns to rubble*

(CSB = Countries of South-Eastern Europe and the Baltics.
CIS = Commonwealth of Independent States)

Case study: **In real life – Effects of inflation in Russia after 1991**

One of my many amazing students is Miss Anna Semenikhina, from Russia. She was kind enough to interview her mother and grandparents for this little / on the effects of rampant inflation. Here's her mother's story word for word.

'Inflation happened really suddenly. It had not been "announced" on TV, but things happening around you made you think of what had happened. Due to the situation in my family, related to my husband's sickness and then death, I moved to the evening department of the University and began working at one of the very first Russian "co-operatives", which was a small privately owned company, with free commercial prices to its products. It was hardly possible to call it "products", as there were not much to sell in the country. The company was selling those things, which had been forbidden, haunted to some degree, and lacked all sort of information about them. Wushu, yoga and Maharishi Aurveda with Transcendental Meditation as its part. I was one of those rare ones, whose income was correspondent to the prices in the grocery shops with free prices and co-operative shops, where you could buy everything. I believe in July 1990 my salary went up to 2000 roubles, at the same time most of the salaries varied from 90 to 200 roubles. One could buy a new "Zhiguli" (LADA) car for 4000 roubles (with the right connections, of course). This is just an idea about how much money it was at that time.

In real life, the whole population became divided into governmentally owned workers and "kooperativshiki" (co-operativshiks), people with money. The government didn't really understand how much money some people were making at that time, as all that had been going on for 3 to 5 months; and all those people "up there" couldn't react to that and were not used to reacting. The first co-operative restaurant, which opened in Moscow, attracted the attention of the authorities and made them look at the situation differently due to the following.

The man, who owned the restaurant, was a Communist party member, and being an honest member of the party he paid party dues every month. I can't remember exact figures, but one month he paid dues equivalent to thousands of dollars. I will try to recall the prices in his restaurant. I believe I could eat there for 40 roubles. The governmental rate to a dollar was 0.35 (?) kopecks, (only used for non-currency operations for the diplomats and such), but black market rate was 13–16 roubles for a dollar. So it's not hard to calculate the real equivalent cost of food there.

The black market: the only real market in the country. To put it in two phrases, everyone in the whole country had certain connections to the people, which were selling stuff. The black market penetrated all spheres of life and existed as a parallel reality. It was very powerful. I can say it was a parallel economic system in the country. One of the most prestigious professions was a seller in a food store. All actual sales happened through the back door, while the counters offered matches, salt and canned fish. That was not risky at all. The real dangerous black market business was selling and buying hard currency. Article 88 of Russia's Criminal Code. Up to 8 years in prison.

Pensioners: My father served in the army, it paid rather well to be in the army, and by the time of default he had about 20,000 roubles on his account, with which he could buy several cars or live trouble-free for the rest of his life. I had a friend, who was deeply into black market and he started to advise my parents to take cash from the bank and start buying everything "hard". Gold, dollars, cars, whatever, things he could sell a bit later. My father, who served for his country all his life, wanted to believe that the country would not leave him in trouble and was waiting for the compensation to the last moment. He had never recovered from the betrayal. At the moment he died he was absolutely poor – with a pension equivalent to about 50–100 dollars per month.'

Overview of transition problems

During the past 15 years' transition towards market-based systems and democracy in most of the former planned economies the speed and depth of change has of course varied. However, there are a number of points frequently observed in the majority of the ex-planned economies:

- All the transition economies in Central and Eastern Europe and the former Soviet Union have experienced **falling output** and in many cases prolonged falling output, i.e. shrinking economies.
- **Corruption** has been ever-present in most former command economies, as governments and institutions collapsed leaving a judicial vacuum. The EBRD Transition Report from 1997 said former Soviet (Russia and Ukraine amongst others) corruption levels were the highest in the world.

- Lack of **legal institutions** has meant difficulties in both setting and collecting taxes and affirming ownership, both of which impaired the creation of viable companies to replace defunct government run enterprises.
- Lack of **financial institutions** (e.g. banks) and capital markets often meant that good businesses collapsed due to lack of loanable funds, and that start-up companies could not get initial loans.
- This problem was exacerbated (= enhanced, exaggerated) by people simply being unaccustomed to a market economy with the ensuing **competition**. It sounds perhaps simplistic, but has had a very real impact on these countries' ability to adapt.

- High **inflation** rates resulted from prices being set free which helped cause falling exchange rates. The net effect was a redistribution of incomes at best – and at worst an obliteration of years of saving. Those on fixed incomes fared particularly ill, e.g. pensioners.

- Entrenched former party officials were often able to use connections to enrich themselves in the 'cowboy capitalism' prevalent in cases where the fall of the command system came swiftly. This added to already increasing differences in income and wealth. The result was often highly **unequal income distribution**.

- Rampant inflation often led to **falling exchange rates**. This created a chaotic situation where the combination of the two effectively made domestic currencies worthless creating a decline in trade. (Point in fact: Russia came very close to adopting the US dollar as its currency.)

- As the monetary economy in some cases ceased to function, barter economies (= simple trading) took over sizable portions of economic activity. This is a most wasteful and time-consuming system when applied across a large portion of the economy.

- As an elongation of all the above, **black markets** and **organised crime** gained a foothold in many former planned economies. Estimates of the black market share of total economic activity in Russia in the late 1990s varied form one-quarter to one-third.

- Illegal gains, high inflation and increasingly worthless currencies all aided and abetted massive **capital flight**, i.e. monies were sent to other countries. This also led to a vicious circle in terms of the economies lacking necessary funds for domestic investment.

- Finally, most of the former planned economies saw increased **unemployment**. State-owned firms declined as they were subjected to competitive forces, letting workers go. Hidden unemployment became very apparent. At the same time, demand for domestic goods was falling which further lowered demand for labour which in turn lowered incomes. Few of the countries involved had sound social safety nets to deal with the problem.

Other transitional economies

The five remaining (ex-?) planned economies are China, Vietnam, North Korea, Laos and Cuba. All five countries have seen monumental changes in economic structure over the past 20 years but show distinct differences. Let us look at the wealthiest of the five – China.

One of the first hard-line communist countries to push forward with large scale reforms was China during the late 1970s. 'To get rich is glorious' proclaimed former Premier Deng Xiaoping in the early 1980s.[68] Since then, there has been a marked revamping of the collectivized industries via controlled privatisation and so-called economic zones where privatisation and thus competitive markets are allowed to function within certain limits. All in all, the basic elements of a market economy increasingly became a pillar of the world's largest planned economy – or indeed the world's third-largest economy after the USA and Germany by 2005.[69]

China has had phenomenal growth rates during the past 25 years. GDP per capita grew at an average yearly rate of around 8% from 1982 to 2002 and over 9% from 2002 to 2006.[70] Hazy property rights were dealt with during the mid-1990s enabling factors to be owned, rented and prices according to costs rather than central decree. The economy became increasingly open, joining the **World Trade Organisation (WTO)** in 2001 and attracting some US$72 billion in foreign investment in 2005 – up from US$2 billion in 1986.[71] It has even established business links and direct flights to its long-time rival, Taiwan.

It appears that China has been more successful than the CEEFSU countries in moving towards a market-based system. Three reasons stand out:

1. China has consistently pursued a 'two-track' economic system, where market forces have gradually been let in to determine prices. The planned and market system has been on two tracks which have been allowed to gradually converge, reducing inflationary shocks in going from centrally set prices to market prices. This is in stark contrast to the 'big bang' approach by many of the CEEFSU countries.

68. *Star Tribune,* 17 June 2001.
69. Ted Fishman, 'China Inc', 2005, p. 16.
70. 'To each according to his needs', *The Economist,* 31May 2002; and http://www.chinability.com/GDP.htm. Once again, these growth figures are dubiously fuzzy and in all probability too high. Noted economist Paul Krugman estimates that at least the official figures are roughly two percentage points too high (Krugman, *International Economics,* p. 269).
71. 'Uncertain Times for Foreign Investment in China', *Wall Street Journal* on 24 June 2002; and http://www.chinability.com/GDP.htm.

2.   Central planning was never as deep as in the CEEFSU area. The insanity of the Great Leap Forward (a period of mass-industrialisation from 1958–62) caused widespread famine leaving an estimated 20 to 30 million people dead and the Cultural Revolution (1966–76) wiped out over half of the party officials. This left a mark on society of diminished confidence in centralised planning, resulting in the share of planning in total industrial output falling from over 90% in 1978 to 5% in 1993.[72]

3.   Increasing openness to trade and foreign investment has had an incredible impact on industrialisation and export industries. China's focus on gaining entrance to the WTO has given it some of the lowest import tax barriers amongst LDCs.[73]

There is, of course, a flip-side to the coin. China's main problems are linked to the market changes of the past 25 years. As the jump from a primarily agricultural economy to an industrial economy has taken place, *income inequalities* rose by close to 50% between 1981 and 2006.[74] This did not come as any great shock to the Chinese leadership, in fact, the Chinese leader Deng Xiao Ping said at the outset: 'Let some people get rich first.' This indeed has happened, to the point where the richest 20% of the population accounted for 42% of income and the poorest 20% accounted for 6.5% of income by the year 2001.[75] *Unemployment* is an increasing problem which is more and more frequently admitted to by the Chinese government. Official figures published by the UN agency **International Labour Organisation (ILO)** claim that unemployment was 3.6% in 2001, but the World Bank believes the figure to be closer to 20% if disguised, hidden and underemployment is taken into account.[76] Rapid economic growth created considerable inflation in the early 1990s, hitting 21% by 1994. Finally, the rampant growth rate of the past 25 years has led to some of the highest *pollution* levels in the world. Only one per cent of the 560 million people in cities have air quality that would pass safety norms in the European Union and pollution is now the number one cause of death according to the Ministry of Health.[77]

---

72. 'Transition Report', World Bank 1996, http://www.worldbank.org.
73. 'A dragon out of puff', *The Economist*, 13 June 2002.
74. Measured by the Gini index. See World Bank at http://web.worldbank.org under 'China Quick Facts'.
75. 'To each according to his abilities', *The Economist*, 31 May 2001.
76. See www.laborst.ilo.org.
77. 'As China Roars, Pollution Reaches Deadly Extremes', *New York Times* (Asia Pacific), 26 August 2007.

The market price? Air pollution in Chengdu, Sichuan Province, China

POP QUIZ 1.1.12   TRANSITIONAL ECONOMIES

1 Which groups in society stand to be hurt the most by high levels of inflation?

2 What is one of the main weaknesses in claiming that national income fell drastically in Russia after it abandoned the planned system?

3 What is the role of financial institutions in laying a base for a (capitalist) market economy?

Preparing for exams

Short answer questions (10 marks each)

1 Use a PPF to explain the trade-offs that all economies face.

2 A country's choice between the production of education and nuclear submarines is an issue of opportunity cost. Explain the issue using a PPF.

3 Why is the concept of 'scarcity' relevant to both LDCs and MDCs?

4 Explain opportunity costs using a PPF where 'investment goods' is on one axis and 'consumption goods' on the other.

5 Explain whether or not GDP is a good measurement of development.

6 Use a PPF to explain the difference between actual and potential growth.

7 How might one assess whether or not a country is experiencing both growth and development?

8 What is the role of profits in a market economy?

Extended response questions (25 marks each)

1 a 'Planning is something that planned economies need – not market economies.' Comment on this from the viewpoint of an economist. (10 marks)

   b What problems might a planned (command) economy encounter in moving towards a market system? (15 marks)

2 a Distinguish between development and growth. (10 marks)

   b Why and how are economists attempting to create more accurate measurements of development? (15 marks)

3 a How would you go about comparing the welfare of citizens in different countries? (10 marks)

   b Assess whether market economies have been more successful than planned economies in providing welfare for citizens. (15 marks)

MICROECONOMICS

2

The section on microeconomics deals with how markets attempt to solve the basic economic problem. Wants are paired-off with firms' ability to satisfy those wants, creating the keystone of economic analysis: the supply and demand model.

Higher level students will then go into greater depth concerning the decision-making process within firms, where costs, profit and market demand facing the firm decide output and price.

In the final part of this section the issue of the limits and failings of markets will be looked at, together with attempts to solve them.

Markets

2.1

CONTENTS

MARKETS ©IBO 2003

Definition of markets

Pick up the morning paper and flip to the classified advertisements. 'Used bicycle – call Adam.' 'Baby-sitter urgently needed! Call the Svenssons!' 'Kittens! Call Sandy.' 'Change money at Sami's – no commission!' All of these fictitious ads are examples of markets in action. In each and every case, there is something being offered or asked for. Any replies will thus show the flip side of the coin – someone who wants the good or someone who can supply the good.

Let us revise the circular flow model from the introduction. In Figure 2.1.1 the two sectors, households and firms, interact and thereby create two markets; a factor market and a goods and services market. Households are the actual owners of the factors of production (land, labour and capital) and these are sold/rented to firms giving rise to the income - payments for factors - shown by the blue arrow. The black arrow shows the factor inputs. These transactions create the factor market.

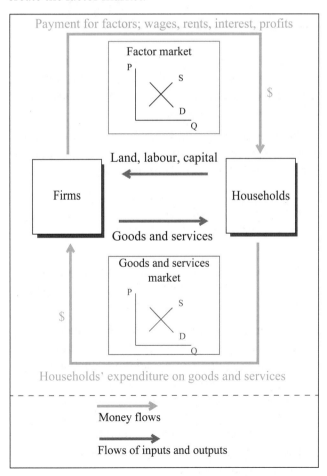

Figure 2.1.1 *The circular flow model – how markets arise*

Households then use this income to purchase the goods and services created by firms; the expenditure (= spending) on goods and services are shown by another blue arrow going from households to firms, and a corresponding black arrow showing firms' outputs of goods and services. The little diagrams in the boxes are supply and demand models; the *factor market* shows firms' demand for land, labour and capital while the *goods and services market* shows households' demand for goods and services.

Markets are well-established institutions and operate at all levels of human interaction. When one thinks of 'markets', one often envisions stalls in an open square where goods are put out for sale and potential customers meander looking and perhaps buying. This traditional market place is a brilliant example, as all the necessary prerequisites are in place; there are numerous buyers (or customers) and numerous sellers (suppliers). Many of the stalls will have similar goods and similar prices yet many people will still circulate in the market, perhaps foregoing the wares offered at one stall in order to look at the same goods at another. Is that haggling I hear?! '… one dinar for this?! How about two dinars for three?!'

Cut to an air-conditioned office equipped with wall to wall computer screens and phones. Thirty young men and women are glued to the screens – all the while talking in to multiple phones and feverishly taking notes. Cyber-dating? Nope. Just another day in the life of ('blip' and AUD$250,000 were just transferred to Tokyo) a foreign currency exchange office.

Market place at Chichen Itza, Mexico. Maya-Toltec style, 900-1200 AD

> **Markets**: A market is a situation where potential buyers are in contact with potential sellers. It enables the needs and wants of both parties to be fulfilled whilst establishing a price and allowing an exchange to take place.

You get the picture. An example could be from yesterday or from the Vikings celebrating their successful invasion of York in 866: 'Yah, Sven, plenty women to kill and cattle to rape! I'm hungry – I'll trade you one ox for two women.'[1] A more recent example is from any modern financial institution dealing with international buying and selling of currencies on the Forex (foreign exchange) market. The only real difference between the two markets' structures is that the buyers and sellers of currencies are not in physical contact with each other – and also that the Australian dollar is not bought at the business end of a 4.5 kilogram broadsword.

Storytime: Open market in Northern Namibia

Out of Africa: open market somewhere in Namibia, November 2002.

We had stopped in a town in Ovamboland in northern Namibia to have a look at the local market. I, of course, wanted to know the prices of various produce and immediately created no end of confusion and not a little amusement when I asked the man in the picture what the price per kilo was. Our wonderful guide and interpreter, John Shamhula, patiently explained that meat was sold per piece – by measuring from fingertips to halfway to elbow. I suggested we find a butcher with longer arms.

Market types ©IBO 2003

In the description of markets above it is implied that there are a number of firms competing on the market for goods and services. While this is often enough the case, there are a number of instances where the degree of competition is considerably lower, for a number of reasons. The competitive market has many firms and a high degree of competition, whereas a monopoly is at the other extreme; a single powerful firm and no competition. In between there is a 'large fuzzy grey area' where we find markets characterised by a few large firms – oligopoly – and high profile firms characterised by heavy advertising and brand-imaging – monopolistic competition. Figure 2.1.2 on page 53 arranges these four market structures according to four sets of criteria. (For greater depth on market structures – even for the ambitious SL student! I recommend Section 2.3, theory of the firm.)

The four criteria in Figure 2.1.2 are in fact used as assumptions, as we are defining the market structure by assuming that certain traits are fulfilled. The *size and number of firms* has a powerful influence on the level of competition and price, and therefore the power of the firm relative to the consumer. Many firms will mean more competition and vice versa. The more firms that compete, the less power any individual firm will have over market prices.

Barriers to entry mean that it is difficult/costly for potential newcomers (firms) to enter the market. High barriers to entry are mainly of three types:

1. **Legalistic** – for example, the restrictions and regulations governing banks and airlines, or not having certain patent rights necessary for production;

2. **Financial** – including difficulties in getting the funding together to start a railroad company, or not having access to raw materials);

3. **Economic** – newcomers would be producing small amounts which will mean high cost per unit whereas existing firms would have much lower costs. The various forms of entry barriers compound the question of competition, as high barriers to entry will allow existing firms to act without giving too much consideration to the possibility of firms entering the market and increasing competition.

---

1. Or something to that effect. They weren't too brainy those Vikings. Too much salted herring.

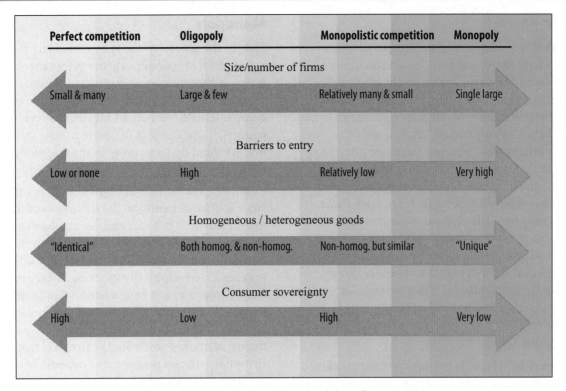

Perfect competition	Oligopoly	Monopolistic competition	Monopoly
Size/number of firms			
Small & many	Large & few	Relatively many & small	Single large
Barriers to entry			
Low or none	High	Relatively low	Very high
Homogeneous / heterogeneous goods			
"Identical"	Both homog. & non-homog.	Non-homog. but similar	"Unique"
Consumer sovereignty			
High	Low	High	Very low

Figure 2.1.2 *Market structures and their characteristics*

The degree of ***homogeneity*** and ***heterogeneity*** defines the composition or make-up of the good. Homogeneous means 'same' or 'identical' and in economics signifies whether a good has any number of identical (or close) substitutes or not; potatoes is an oft-cited example. Heterogeneous is of course the opposite; a good which is differentiated (= set apart) from possible substitutes. It is relevant to note that goods do not actually have to be physically different – it is sufficient for us to perceive that goods are different – there are many taco restaurants but only one Mama Rosita's! (See "Monopolistic competition" on page 54.)

Finally, there is a question of the relative bargaining power of consumers and firms. If consumers have a good deal of influence on prices and output, then ***consumer sovereignty*** is high. One would indeed expect to find this in competitive markets where there are many firms. If, however, there is only one firm (supplier) then there are no substitutes available and consumer sovereignty will be low. Regarding the empowerment of consumers as the ability to 'cast votes' on goods, then a competitive market will empower consumers more than non-competitive markets.

The shading in Figure 2.1.2 is not by accident. If you look at the characteristics of the perfectly competitive market and monopoly, you will see that they are each others' opposites, being basically two extremes. Oligopolies and monopolistically competitive firms, on the other hand, portray very little correspondence in terms of neatly following the arrows separating the two extremes. This 'fuzzy grey area' is the most difficult to characterise accurately and unfortunately this is the area most of the real world winds up in. Also, don't be fooled by the neat figure; in reality there is a great deal of overlapping, where an oligopoly is monopolistically competitive and could also have elements of monopoly markets embedded. Examples would be Microsoft, Macintosh and Linux operating systems.

Perfect competition ©IBO 2003

A perfectly competitive market is characterised by many buyers and many sellers, all interacting in such a way so as to provide the highest possible quantity at the lowest possible price. As the goods are assumed to be 100% homogeneous, the only competitive element is price-competition, which in turn empowers consumers and the market is demand-driven. In providing this outcome there is no waste – all goods are produced in order to fulfil market demand. This optimum outcome in terms of resource allocation is what is 'perfect' about the market structure. **Agricultural goods** like tomatoes and coffee and **basic commodities** such as iron and copper could be considered perfectly competitive market goods. The remaining three market structures are commonly referred to as 'imperfect competition'.

Oligopoly ©IBO 2003

The main defining elements of an oligopoly are 'few' and 'large', where there could well be several hundred firms but four or five firms dominate the market. The dominant firms in an oligopolistic market structure might have access to limited raw materials, such as bauxite (for aluminium) and oil, creating **entry barriers** for other potential firms. Firms are often large because of the necessity to produce very large quantities of goods to cover high costs of production and research and developments (R & D). Such firms are said to enjoy **benefits of scale** (scale means size) where the cost per unit of output falls as the firm increases in size. Examples of such oligopolies are pharmaceutical and car companies. There is also an incentive for firms to **collude** (= co-operate), for example by agreeing to set identical prices or by dividing the market up geographically so as to avoid head-on competition.

This type of behaviour is harshly frowned upon in most industrialised countries and severe legal penalties are often set for collusive behaviour.

Monopolistic competition ©IBO 2003

This is an increasingly common market structure where there are a large number of firms producing similar goods which are **differentiated**. The defining elements of monopolistic competition are taken from perfect competition and monopoly – hence the name. The market is **competitive** as entry barriers are low and potential firms will have access to attractive markets. The market is also **monopolistic**, as goods are highly profiled – firms put a great deal of resources into marketing in order to convince us that while there are many possible substitutes, there is only one 'Brand X'. This is known as **branding** and serves to create in the mind of the beholder that a particular good or service is in some way different, e.g. superior, to others. Standard textbook examples of monopolistically competitive firms are restaurants, hotels, car repair services and bakeries.

One also often finds a number of markets which are largely monopolistically competitive but where there are a few large, dominant firms; the markets for sports shoes and soft drinks are notable examples. In reality therefore, the line between monopolistic competition and oligopoly is often blurred.

Monopoly ©IBO 2003

Finally, the far end of the spectrum. Here the assumption in economic theory is that there is one firm only – a pure monopoly. Examples of pure monopoly markets are postal services, state television and even oil companies (Pemex here in Mexico) as seen in many countries. The concept of a pure private monopoly doesn't stand up to scrutiny in the real world particularly well and I'd be hard put to find a specific example.[2] The definition of monopoly is a tricky one since it often depends on the definition of the market in terms of both product and geographical area. Hence, de Beers might be considered a monopoly in the supply of raw diamonds but not in the market for diamond jewellery. Geographically speaking, local gas, water and cable companies can have a regional monopoly but not on all gas, water and TV/Internet services in the country. The definition becomes a question of the degree of market power for the firm, i.e. that monopoly firms have market power at the expense of consumers as there are no close substitutes and thus scant competition.

Firms have the power to set output and price without taking competitive forces into consideration. In the final analysis, consumer sovereignty in a pure monopoly situation is a bit like voting in the former Soviet Union; everyone could vote freely but there was only one party.

Price as a signal and an incentive

©IBO 2003

In explaining and outlining the competitive market system previously, the price acted as a signal to suppliers as to how much of the good should be put on the market.

The price mechanism and resource allocation (revisited)

Assume a competitive market for two goods: red and green whiteboard pens. Let us say that green becomes so popular that the market supply cannot match demand. There will be a shortage of green pens which will drive up the price. This is an incentive for the pen factories to increase output of green pens. Keeping in mind the short-run constraints in simply increasing output of green pens, resources will be taken from the

---

2. Diamonds are a possible example, where De Beers has for over 70 years controlled some 70% to 90% of the total market for raw diamonds – and the European Union, threatening a fine of up to 10% of De Beers global sales, prohibited the company's method of controlling the market via intervention purchasing in 2006. (*International Herald Tribune*, 22 February 2006, 'De Beers loosens grip on diamond market'). Much of the definitional difficulty here arises due to the complexity of defining the market. HL will return to this issue in Section 2.3.

manufacturing of red pens and put into making green pens. Assuming that consumers have a degree of sovereignty, the increase in demand for green pens will cause suppliers to allocate (= roughly 'place' or 'assign') resources to the Green Pen Factories.

However, assume that too many green pens were made, i.e. that there was a green pen glut (= surplus). This would mean unsold green pens on the shelves.

The excess of green pens would put downward pressure on the price, which in turn would cause the manufacturers to scale back production of green pens until, once again, the equilibrium point was achieved where supply equals demand. In summary, the price mechanism allocates scarce resources to their best possible use. (See "A little depth: The price as a signal" on page 83.)

THE USE OF SYMBOLS IN ECONOMICS

Economists often use symbols as shortcuts in explanations. It's a kind of shorthand which enables us to quickly convey ideas and concepts without being too sociable. The resource allocation in the red and green pen example above would be put as follows:

$\rightarrow$: leads to $\uparrow$: rises $\downarrow$: falls   D: demand   S: supply   P: price

$$D_{green\ pens} \uparrow \rightarrow D_{green\ pens} > S_{green\ pens} \rightarrow P_{green\ pens} \uparrow \rightarrow S_{green\ pens} \uparrow \rightarrow \sum S_{green\ pens} = D_{green\ pens}$$

The above reads:

'Demand for green pens rises and outpaces supply, leading to an increase in the price of green pens. This is an incentive for suppliers to increase supply of green pens, which will ultimately lead to market equilibrium.'

How would you use symbols to illustrate the falling production of red pens due to reallocation?

Demand ©IBO 2003

Part of the economic problem is that people have endless wants. However, simply wanting or desiring a good does not constitute demand. Demand is more an activity than a state of mind, e.g. when you are actually willing to purchase a good at a certain price. Demand in market terms is the quantity consumers are **willing** and **able** to buy at a given price, not what they would like to have. I would most assuredly want a Patek Phillipe wristwatch but I am not in the market for one (yet if you bought this book I'm getting there). This distinction is most important within the context of market clearing further on.

Definition of demand ©IBO 2003

Recall the 'Beer in the desert' example I used to show utility and marginal utility (see Section 1). Let us assume that 100 people pulled up to the desert bar in air-conditioned Desert Cruisers to have a 'cold one' before going off to see the lions and giraffes in the national park. What if the barman had just dipped his head in his own wares, gone raucous (= wild), and

subsequently decided to have a wild 'Half-price Party' just as the group entered the scene?! Would he have sold more beer, seeing as how the price of beer was effectively halved? Another way of putting the question is whether there is some sort of relationship between the price of a good (here, beer) and the quantity sold on the market.

The answer is yes. There would be a negative relationship between the variables price and quantity: when the price of beer falls the quantity of beer purchased will increase. This is another example of correlation, and one which is at the heart of the supply and demand models in economics which plot out the relationship between price and quantity. It is quite common for the correlation to be either purely positive or purely negative. For example, correlating 'IB grades' with 'Quantity recreational drugs consumed per week' will most assuredly be negative all along the length of the x-axis and I challenge anyone to find a positive relationship between these two variables.[3] Correlation between price and consumer demand is always negative – with one or two highly hypothetical exceptions which we will come to.

---

3. A legendary story from my university tells about a young man studying medicine and being fully unprepared two weeks before exams. Having the keys to the medicine cabinet at the institution he 'prescribed' himself a large quantity of amphetamine in order to be able to study for two weeks in a row. He did so and basically stayed up and studied until his eyes bled. On the day of the exams, with eyes like tea plates, he sat down in the exam hall and got the exam papers – and wrote 'I KNOW THIS!' on every single question. After 15 minutes he handed in his answers, fully confident that he had passed in flying colours. He didn't.

Theory of demand

The starting point for our model of demand is positing (= proposing) that a rise in the price of a good will lead to lower quantity demanded for the good – keeping all other variables constant. This is the law of demand, which states that 'Ceteris paribus, a change in price will lead to a change in the quantity demanded'.

> **Law of demand**: Ceteris paribus, a fall in the price for good X will result in an increase in the quantity demanded for good X. An increase in the price of X will result in a decrease of quantity demanded.
>
> The law of demand states that as long as all other variables (income, price of other goods, preferences) remain unchanged, then a fall in the price of a good will lead to an increase in the quantity demanded. This means that the demand curve is downward sloping and thus that quantity demanded is negatively correlated with price.

Let's look at this law more closely. *Ceteris paribus* means that all else remains the same – incomes don't change, the prices of other goods don't change, preferences don't change, etc. This is most important. We must assume all else to be unchanged in order to be able to map out the effect that a change in price would have on the quantity demanded. In the coming model, a fundamental premise is that the demand curve is drawn using the assumption that all other determinants of demand are held constant.

There are two reasons for an increase in quantity demanded when the price of a good falls; the *income effect* and the *substitution effect*.

- **Income effect**: A fall in price means that people who have a demand for the good are now richer in real terms, i.e. their income can buy more of the good. If your income remains the same but prices fall you have increased your real income (your income allows you to buy more goods) and would have the propensity (= tendency) to increase your purchases.
- **Substitution effect**: Secondly, a fall in the price of a good means that relatively speaking the price of alternative goods has increased. People change their purchasing behaviour and switch to the relatively less pricey good. In simple terms, consumers will substitute other goods with the lower priced good. If the price of good X increases the quantity demanded for goods X will fall since goods Y and Z (substitutes) are now relatively cheaper.

Law of demand with diagrammatic analysis ©IBO 2003

In essence, we are painting a picture of the pattern of demand for a good, where all possible prices are coupled to the quantities demanded. This gives us any number of possible combinations of price and quantity, as seen in Figure 2.1.3, where I have mapped the demand for cinema tickets in a most cost-conscious town called 'Econopolis'. (They use the euro = €.) It is worth stressing once again that demand does not plot out 'what people would like to have', but rather the ability and willingness of consumers to buy the good at a given price, e.g. effective demand. Also, it goes without saying that the market demand curve for a certain good is nothing else but an aggregate (= entire sum) of all the individual demand curves of individual consumers.

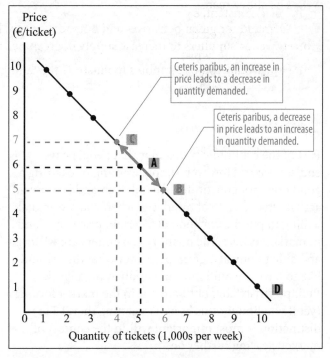

Figure 2.1.3 *The demand schedule for cinema tickets in Econopolis*

In Figure 2.1.3, assume that the initial price is €6 and thus that quantity demanded per week is 5,000 tickets. If the price is lowered to €5, the quantity demanded increases to 6,000 tickets per week. This is shown by a movement along the demand curve, from A to B, which means, using correct economic terminology, that 'the quantity demanded increases from 5,000 tickets to 6,000 tickets per week.' If the price were instead raised to €7, then the quantity demanded would fall from 5,000 tickets per week to 4,000. The demand curve extends or contracts, i.e. any movement along the demand curve can be referred to as an extension/contraction of demand. The curve is actually created by all the combined points of price and quantity demanded.

A few comments on the simple relationship in Figure 2.1.3 on page 56:

1. Plotting out the demand of the townsfolk for cinema tickets has rendered a demand schedule; the **downward sloping demand curve**.[4] We are assuming that prices can be anywhere between whole numbers, e.g. '€6.39'[5].

2. The relationship between price and quantity demanded is negative; any downward sloping curve shows that an increase in one variable (price) leads to a decrease in the other variable (quantity) which is entirely in keeping with the law of demand. Note once again that in 'moving along' the demand curve we are assuming that all other influences on demand are held constant, e.g. the ceteris paribus condition.

3. Have you noticed that we have put the independent variable on the 'wrong' axis?![6] The norm is to put the independent variable on the x-axis and the dependent variable on the y-axis. As quantity is undoubtedly the dependent variable, we have 'switched places' in our model.

It is most important to keep firmly in mind that there is a time frame involved, here '1,000 tickets per week'. Economists are notoriously sloppy and lazy for some reason when it comes to including this rather important premise, and I urge you to include the time element in your own diagrams. Not having a time frame (i.e. a time limit) would basically mean that the demand curve is set in stone for all eternity! It is not; the demand curve is most dynamic over time as we shall see.

Exam tip: Using the language of an economist

Ever wondered about the language that language teachers insist upon using? Me neither. Rather than saying 'do-words' they say 'verbs'; rather than 'thing-words' they say 'nouns'. They have an entire menagerie (= collection) of terms that could just as soon be said in Martian as far as I'm concerned. Unfortunately, economists are no different - something I will never admit to the face of a language teacher. We have an immense array of very subject-specific terms, concepts. The successful economics student must incorporate them into his/ her active vocabulary. Distinguishing carefully between 'change in the quantity demanded' and 'change in demand' is an excellent place to start.

Any change in the price will result in an extension (= increase) or contraction (= decrease) in the quantity demanded. An increase or decrease in price means a **movement along** the demand curve. This is referred to as a **change in quantity demanded**.

- changing the *price* does not change demand but the *quantity demanded*
- a change in the quantity demanded is a *movement along* the demand curve.

A few assumptions of our model

Any model must be based on assumptions and limitations, as stated in Section 1. The supply and demand model is no different. We have already been through the basic assumption that there is no change in any other variable when drawing our pattern of demand, i.e. the ceteris paribus condition.

There are other assumptions baked into the model.

- One is that we are operating in a competitive environment, which means that there are a great number of suppliers where no single supplier can set the price.

- Another assumption is that the goods offered on a particular market illustrated in a diagram are homogeneous, i.e. that there is no qualitative difference between goods supplied by different suppliers. This must mean that consumers' marginal utility will remain the same regardless of from whom they purchase the good.

- Finally, consumers are assumed to have perfect knowledge of market conditions – prices, quality, etc. and are thus able to maximise their utility by purchasing the good at the lowest possible price.

---

4. Yes, I know that a 'linear curve' is a contradiction in terms. However, in economics all supply and demand schedules are referred to as 'curves' regardless of whether they are non-linear or linear. You'll get used to it.

5. This is known as a 'continuous variable'. Temperature and speed are other examples.

6. This is the fault of one of the most influential textbook authors in economics, Alfred Marshall (1842–1924). The story has it that he simply made an error – which has stuck with us ever since!

Warning!
One hand clapping

Hard-earned experience dictates that I include a few words on using demand in analytical iterations. Far too often I have seen students building an entire argument or analysis of markets around a solitary demand curve. This is the equivalent of holding an archery competition and providing bows but no arrows. The winner is then crowned and the audience applauds by clapping with one hand only (no co-operation allowed!).

The demand curve simply does not work in explaining market dynamics without its soul-mate, the supply curve. Just as Romeo would look ridiculous standing on a balustrade singing a lusty song to an empty balcony above, the demand curve is pitifully incomplete without a corresponding supply curve.* I go through each curve singularly – like separate instruments – in order to make each one clear. Then I put them together and rock 'n' roll.

*Actually, he looked pretty silly anyhow. Those tights! Sheesh!

Determinants of demand ©IBO 2003

In the coming model, a fundamental premise is that **quantity demanded** is a **function** of many different variables, the main determinant being the price of the good. All others are **non-price determinants** of demand which will *shift* the demand curve, the main ones being:

1. **income** of consumers

2. **price of other goods** (substitutes and complements – more on this later)

3. changes in consumers' **tastes**/preferences

4. changes in consumers' **expectations**/hopes

5. **population** changes – both in terms of size and structure

6. **derived demand** – e.g. where the demand for cars creates demand for steel.

This book doesn't permit going into the other 1,800 possible influences on demand. Let us look at the above six non-price determinants of demand and put them into context, i.e. how these determinants would lead to a shift in the demand curve.

> **The demand function:** '$Q_{Dx} = \int Px; Py; Y;...n$'
> The demand function reads: 'The demand for good X is a function of:
> 1. the **price** of good X;
> 2. the price of good Y (substitute or complement);
> 3. **income** (Y);
> 4. **n** – being tastes, population, etc.'
> Our diagrammatic analysis links the price to quantity.

Shifting the demand curve

As mentioned above, there are a great many influences on demand. These 'other variables', as encapsulated by our ceteris paribus assumption, are known non-price determinants of demand. Any change in non-price variables will shift the demand curve. Note that in using the demand model, actual quantities and prices are seldom used. The diagrams serve as illustrations rather than real-life depictions of actual data.

> **Non-price determinants of demand:** Any variable that changes the pattern of demand other than price is a non-price determinant of demand. Changes in income, price of substitutes, price of complements, tastes, expectations, population and derived demand will all have an effect on demand for goods. A change in a non-price determinant shifts the demand curve.

Income

It cannot come as a surprise that an increase in income would increase demand for a good. Just recall that our wants are endless! Thus, any furthering of the ability to satisfy those wants will mean that people will have an increased tendency to do. When demand increases for a good due to an increase in income, economists commonly refer to such goods as 'normal' goods. (See income elasticity in Section 2.2.)

I do two weeks of teaching at the Oxford Study Courses in England every Easter.[7] The first time I did this I flew via Stanstead Airport, which is a small and somewhat basic airport unlike the larger Heathrow or Gatwick airports. On returning home I told my then wife[8] that we were lucky that I flew via Stanstead, as the wages I'd been paid were burning a hole in my pocket;

---

7. Basically, I'm greedy – and Blancpain watches aren't given away.

8. I seem to collect not only wrist watches but ex-wives. One of my cheekier students plotted out my marriage habits and then correlated my ups and downs with the business cycle. She found correlation – the regression coefficient was 0.35! Maybe you should write me and ask about my marital status before buying any shares or property…

had I flown via Heathrow I probably would have spent the entire week's wages at the Tax Free shop on a new watch. Sad but true. So, did I then save my increase in income? Nope. I was surfing the Internet for Blancpain watches that very evening.

What might cause an increase in general incomes in an economy? Perhaps a decrease in income taxes leaves people with higher disposable incomes. Or general increasing prosperity gives the people in an economy higher wages and thus incomes. In any event, an increase in disposable income, (= income after taxes and including any welfare benefits and such), will increase the demand for normal goods. In the example of Swiss watches, this will cause a shift in the demand curve to the right, from D_0 to D_1 in Figure 2.1.4, i.e. more watches are demanded at all prices. (SFR = Swiss francs.)

This is a general pattern for households. Demand increases due to an increase in income – and decreases when income falls. This is a very powerful force in buying behaviour. An increase in income allows households to satisfy more of their endless wants, resulting in an increase in demand. An increase in general income, say wage increases for an entire economy, would, *ceteris paribus* (!), result in a general rise in demand for goods and services.

I'd best add a brief note on 'abnormal' behaviour within the context of the income effect. The goods exemplified above are **normal goods** as the norm (= custom) is for demand to increase when income rises. However, it is possible that demand for some goods might actually fall when incomes rise simply because a rise in income will change households' preferences – increased income could cause households to substitute certain goods with other, more preferred goods. Such goods are called **inferior goods**, possible examples of which are public transport and potatoes. We return to this issue in Section 2.2.

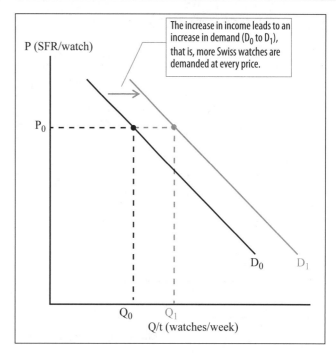

Figure 2.1.4 *Demand for Swiss watches*

Price of other goods

Substitute goods: When two goods are in *competitive* demand they are said to be substitutes – and thus a rise in the price of one good would cause an increase in demand for a substitute.

For example, there are a number of new formats for recording and viewing movies at home, the most recent are the formats Blu-ray and HD DVD which look to compete with the standard DVD system.[9]

When one looks at these products, they are obviously competitors for my money. Should the price of Blu-ray players fall (P_0 to P_1 in diagram I of Figure 2.1.5 on page 60) there will be an increase in quantity demanded for Blu-ray players (Q_0 to Q_1) and one can expect demand for standard DVD players to decrease (D_0 to D_1 in Figure 2.1.5 diagram I), e.g. fewer DVD players are demanded at the price of P_0 and all other prices. Note that, once again, we are assuming all else equal, i.e. there is no change in the quality or function of either good. Consumers are simply substituting one good with another.

---

9. I actually wonder if Blu-ray will take off – the picture is *too* good! A goodly number of my students agree that the picture sharpness is a bit staggering. I think my initial comment was something like 'It's too real … like viewing the world sober. I'm not sure I need more reality.'

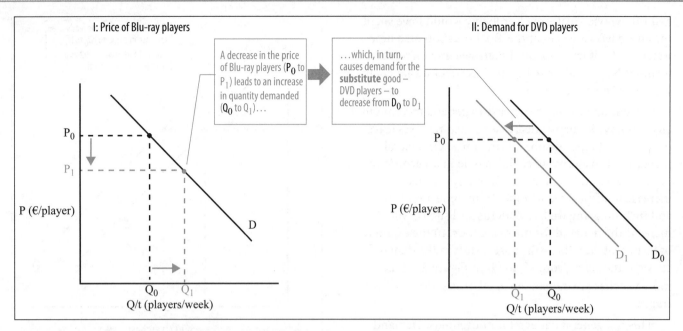

Figure 2.1.5 *Price of Blu-ray players and demand for DVD players*

Other examples of substitute goods are rail travel and bus travel, apples and pears, or, to be most product specific, Pepsi® and Coke®[10]. (Many textbooks give tea and coffee as examples, which I find to be utter nonsense, but then I am heavily addicted to coffee. Nothing substitutes for coffee in my book.)

Complement goods: Now, how would one go about buying one of the DVD or Blu-ray players? Being an economist, you would look at the total ('bundle') price of usage, in other words the price of the player *and* the disks – either for recording or playing. These two goods are in **joint demand**, commonly referred to as **complement goods**. The two are a 'package deal' basically, as one is useless without the other. Being complementary to each other, a change in price of one good will affect demand for the other. Should the new standard, Blu-ray, take hold of the market by decreasing substantially in price, one can expect demand for Blu-ray disks to increase. Consequently, a rise in the price of Blu-ray players will cause demand for Blu-ray disks to fall. Diagram I in Figure 2.1.6 on page 61 shows how a decrease in the price of Blu-ray

players (P_0 to P_1) leads to an increase in the quantity demanded (Q_0 to Q_1). Subsequently, the demand for Blu-ray disks increases (D_0 to D_1 in Figure 2.1.6 diagram I), which means that more disks are demanded at the price of P_0 and indeed at all prices.

Other standard examples of complement goods are tennis balls and tennis racquets, film and cameras, and staples and staplers.[11] Note that all complement goods are often not as 'joined at the hip' as in my example, but are as often as not quite weakly connected via preferences and habits. I often give the examples of cognac and cigars, strawberries and cream, and mustard and pea soup. I bet that last one caught your attention. Yes, in Sweden one customarily puts a dollop of mustard in one's bowl of pea soup. I added this example to illustrate the cultural dimension of many complement goods – just think of French fries with ketchup (USA), French fries with vinegar (England) and French fries with mayonnaise (Belgium). Here in Mexico, lime juice is a complement to … well, anything in the way of food![12] Oh, so is chilli![13]

---

10. My students disagree with me most adamantly here! Me, I failed the 'Pepsi Challenge™'.

11. Here in Mexico, a money clip holding one's driving licence and a 100 peso note (approximately US$9) are complement goods. If you need to show your licence to one of Mexico's finest you'll also need a '*mordida*', i.e. a 'donation' to get you on your way. Commonly, the licence and the bill are handed over together. Also, drinking and driving are not substitutes but complements. This is the sort of comment that apparently caused my colleagues to start betting on my life expectancy here. Nobody has me down for more than four years. When the colleagues say goodbye to me on Fridays, they say it with depth and *mean* it.

12. I wonder if I can get away with including my favourite drink recipe: 'Take a dark beer (not the English stuff – real beer) and pour into a large mug with two limes worth of juice and chilli. Coat the rim of the mug with salt and chilli. Now you have a delicious "*michelada cubana*"!' Salud!

13. I love putting forth absolutely insane business ideas. One of these, which unfortunately came to me in an energy-drink induced vision blazed across the whiteboard while teaching and subsequently was worded out loud, was 'chilli flavoured condoms'. After the shrieks died down, one of the young ladies, with a look of complete seriousness, asked: 'Em, Matt, flavoured on the inside or outside?' God I'm old.

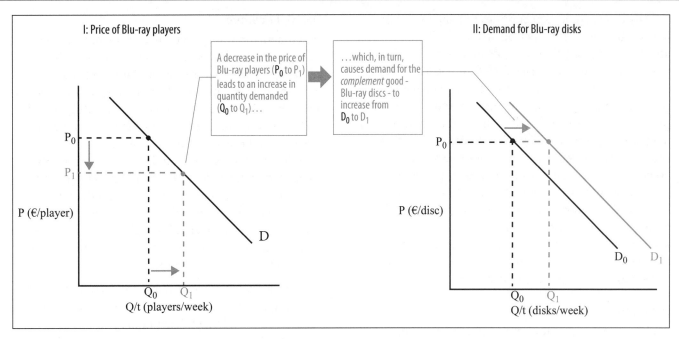

I: Price of Blu-ray players

A decrease in the price of Blu-ray players (P_0 to P_1) leads to an increase in quantity demanded (Q_0 to Q_1)...

...which, in turn, causes demand for the *complement* good - Blu-ray discs - to increase from D_0 to D_1

II: Demand for Blu-ray disks

Figure 2.1.6 *Price of Blu-ray players and demand for Blu-ray disks*

Tastes and preferences

The Atkins diet was a nightmare for the consumer, but also for us. – Guido Barilla, chairman of Barilla Pasta, *The Economist*, 20 January 2007

Looking around at my students I sometimes feel caught in a time warp. They are dressed almost exactly as I was some 30 years ago: snug T-shirts, tight bell-bottomed pants with soprano-inducing waistlines, etc. Most of my generation would rather forget the 1970s (ask your parents!) but we are right back there again – demand for circulation-cutting pants came back. Thank you MTV. Thank you Madonna and other pop icons.

As for the effects of advertising, let us say that the amazing life expectancy of the Greeks is used by an olive oil firm. The advertisement shows how the Greeks have one of the highest average lifespans in Europe – in spite of having one of the highest European proportions of smokers in the population and one of the lowest levels of physical exercise! The answer, according to research, lies in the use of healthy olive oil. A successful advertising campaign would increase demand for olive oil, shifting the demand curve to the right. Our tastes can also change as the result of intellect rather than emotions: cigarette smoking is declining in a good many countries as the health issues become better known.

Expectations

The strength of expectations is difficult to overestimate. So much of our behaviour is directly related to what we hope/expect/want to happen. Just imagine how house buyers would react if a major highway were to be built right through the neighbourhood they were looking at. Demand for the houses would drop like a paralysed parakeet due to the expectation of falling future property prices.[14]

Please note that expectation is one of many possible variables which will have an impact on demand. **Expectations** are noteworthy in the light of current stock markets bottoming out (November 2008). It doesn't require a degree in rocket surgery to understand that when people expect certain things to happen in the future, it can well affect their demand in the present. As house buyers have seed prices fall they have held off on new house purchases – which leads to a decrease in demand. This has led to a *self-fulfilling prophecy*. As housing prices have fallen, people expect this to continue. As consumers wait for a further fall in prices they actually hold off on new housing. This means that demand falls … and that prices fall as an effect! This self-reinforcing negative feedback loop has proven immensely powerful for overall demand in the US economy since so much of household wealth is tied to property. As (perceived) wealth of home-owners declines, so too will demand for goods.[15]

---

14. This example of a 'self-fulfilling prophecy' is a notable element in speculative behaviour and *possibly* resulting in an upward sloping demand curve – which is a HL concept. I should mention that the ongoing liquidity/credit/housing/stock market crisis (2008) is strongly linked to *speculative buying* on the housing market during the early 2000s.

Any time people expect things to happen within a foreseeable future time period, demand will be affected. If future prices are expected to rise, people's present demand might rise; if the future value of shares on the stock market is expected to rise, speculators' present demand for shares might rise; and if taxes on property are expected to fall in the future, present demand for property might rise. A recent example of speculatively driven demand is the price of oil during 2008, where expectations of ever higher prices led speculators to buy up contracts for future delivery of oil (so called 'futures') at a rather frenzied rate. From January to July the price of oil went from US$S100 to just under USD150 and economic observers estimate that some 50% to 60% of this increase in price was indeed driven by speculative demand.

Population

An increase in population causing an increase in demand should be relatively plain. Yet there are also demand changes caused by a change in the *structure* of the population. For example, increased immigration will change the demand for certain types of food; age structure will change the demand for goods such as baby food or pensioners homes; income and wealth redistribution in a country will affect demand for income sensitive goods, and so on.

Derived demand

When demand for a good, say cars, increases then factor inputs such as steel will see an increase in demand. We say that the demand for steel is **derived** from the demand for cars. Derived means 'to be based on' or 'have its source in'. The concept is rather useful in understanding the interrelationship between goods that don't fall precisely into the category of complement goods. Derived demand is commonly associated with production, where firms using any number of products as inputs will affect demand for said inputs. Continuing with the example, car manufacturers use steel, rubber, plastic, glass, etc. A fall in the demand for cars will affect car manufacturers' demand for all of these inputs.

One of my favourite examples of derived demand is currency, say the Namibian dollar, the demand for which is derived from the demand for tourism in Namibia, demand for Namibian exports, and the demand for investment in Namibia. Note that the causal flows can be reversed! Here in Mexico we receive a great deal of American tourists and when the US dollar appreciates (= increases in value compared to the Mexican peso) American tourists get more pesos for their dollar. Consequently, the US demand for hotels in holiday resorts such as Acapulco increases.

Putting the pieces together: Oil and silicon

During 2007 and 2008, several economic commentators noticed how the increase in oil prices led to an increase in demand for silicon. Confused? It's really quite simple and deals with some of the issues outlined above, namely *substitutes* and *derived demand*.

As the price of oil increased dramatically households started to look to possible substitutes.

Oil is used in many industries, one of which is energy. As energy costs for households rose, possible substitutes became more and more economically viable (= possible).

One of the substitutes for oil in the field of energy is solar power. Thus, demand for solar panels increased drastically ...

... and since silicon is used in the manufacturing of solar panels, the derived demand for silicon rose and led to a tenfold price increase during 2007–08.

On a personal note, I saw the writing on the wall early on in 2007 and bought shares in Vesta, a Danish company manufacturing wind power generators. Sometimes you win.

---

15. This is known as the 'wealth effect' and has a very powerful influence on the macro environment.

POP QUIZ 2.1.1 NON-PRICE DETERMINANTS OF DEMAND

1 SARS (severe acute respiratory syndrome), created quite a scare during 2003. This lethal and airborne virus killed a number of people around the world, starting in China. How do you think this affected tourism and airline industries around the world?

2 Now use the price function to explain why the number of flights leaving from major airports fell during the SARS scare.

3 Let us say that a major story in the media this week is that people are getting sick after eating salmonella tainted chicken. How might this affect demand for fish and beef?

4 Audi is now in the process of increasing the number of cars made from aluminium. What will the effect be on demand for bauxite? (Look up bauxite.)

5 'The demand for euros is derived from the demand for tourism in Europe, not the other way around!' Comment on this statement.

'Movement along' versus 'shift' of the demand curve ©IBO 2003

Note the outcome of the shifts in Figure 2.1.7. It is not a change in price that causes a change in how much is demanded but one of the non-price variables. One says that the quantity demanded has changed at all price levels – which is NOT a 'movement along' the curve (or extension/contraction) but a *shift* in the demand curve showing how demand has changed at *all* prices.

The basic rules are:

- A change in price leads (*ceteris paribus*) to a change in the quantity demanded – see points **A** and **B** in Figure 2.1.7:

$$\Delta P \rightarrow \Delta Qd$$
for example:
$$\uparrow P \rightarrow \downarrow Qd \text{ (point A in Figure 2.1.7)}$$

- A change in any other demand determinant (e.g. non-price determinant) leads to a change in demand – see D_0 and D_1 in Figure 2.1.7

$$\text{non-P determinant} \rightarrow \Delta D$$
for example:
$$\uparrow \text{income} \rightarrow \uparrow D \quad (\mathbf{D_1} \text{ in Figure 2.1.7})$$

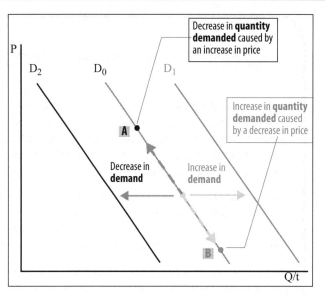

Figure 2.1.7 *Change in demand and change in quantity demanded*

POP QUIZ 2.1.2 'QUANTITY DEMANDED' VERSUS 'DEMAND'

1 Explain why the demand curve slopes downward for normal goods.

2 Any change in a non-price determinant of demand will …

3 What will happen to the demand for oil if:

a cars become more efficient

b the price of oil falls

c public transport becomes cheaper

d solar power becomes more and more common.

Storytime: The New York smoking ban

In December, 2002 New York governor Mike Bloomberg put through legislation banning all smoking in public places such as pubs, bars and restaurants. The purpose was to provide smoke-free environments for the many thousands of people working as waiters and bartenders. Some 14,000 bar, restaurants, clubs and other handful of cigar bars and bars that have enclosed, ventilated rooms for smokers. The law went into effect in April 2003 and the effects thus far have been mixed.

The most noticeable effect thus far is that visitors to restaurants and pubs have gone down. Revenue in bars has dropped by 20% since the imposition of the ban and bar workers run the risk of redundancy and lay-offs. There has been a marked drop in demand for beer and other forms of alcohol. One of the world's largest brewers, Heineken, has noticed a distinct drop in sales to the US, citing the ban on smoking.

It would appear that cigarettes and alcohol are in strong joint demand. So strong, in fact, that one of the major problems has been to keep people indoors with their drinks. The sidewalks and streets outside of popular bars and nightclubs are now often full of people smoking and drinking (illegally). Most of the complaints come from people living in surrounding apartments who suffer from noise and raucous behaviour.

HIGHER LEVEL EXTENSION TOPICS

Is there a possibility that some goods actually behave in a manner inconsistent with that of the demand curve? Well, according to textbook theory, yes. That is, it is *possible* – albeit not particularly likely. I close this chapter with a few musings on the possibility of an **upward-sloping demand curve**. Welcome to 'Mermaidomics'.[16]

Little Mermaid,
Copenhagen

Exceptions to the law of demand (the upward-sloping demand curve) ©IBO 2003

Caliope and grand-daughter Caliope the younger, Sifnos

When I lived in the 'Old World' (= Europe) I used to sit at the Zacharoplasteio (roughly, café) in Appolonia on Sifnos, Greece. It was run by the most marvellous lady, Caliope. Caliope was nobody's fool, and while she had no formal education in economics she was as sharp as a fox when it comes to the business of running a café.

When I commented on how her place was always filled with local people rather than the tourist crowd, she said 'Yes. The Greek tourists don't want to have coffee here because the price is too low. They want to be in the fancy places. I keep my prices as they are so as not to lose my long-standing customers.'

---

16. In other words, an area where mermaids, unicorns, honest Mexican cops and other fairy tale figures play in Make-Believe Land.

What Caliope said, in effect, is that there is *positive correlation* between price and demand! She was well aware of how the upward climbing and very socially conscious Greek tourists are prone to sit and be seen in the upmarket cafés – which are really not *that* different from her café apart from the higher prices. This Ray Ban crowd, as I call them, have a marked preference for goods which are ostentatiously more expensive; basically, they demand more café services as the price rises!

This is an example of a possible upward-sloping demand curve, as shown in Figure 2.1.8. As the price rises, the quantity demanded rises. Economics identifies three possible reasons for this; ostentatious

goods (Veblen goods), speculative (expectations-based) goods and Giffen goods.

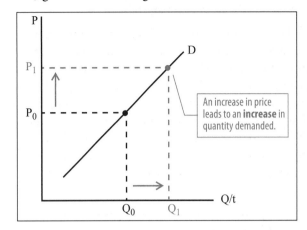

Figure 2.1.8 *Upward-sloping demand curve*

 CELEBRITY BUBBLE: THORSTEIN VEBLEN (1857–1929)

In a world of strange and aloof economists, Veblen must undoubtedly take the prize. Born in Minnesota, USA, of Norwegian immigrants, he grew up on a farm in a community of hard-working and prudent Scandinavians. In spite of these solid and reasonably prosperous surroundings, he was forever to feel apart from the society around him.

He studied at Yale and Cornell universities and went on to teach at a number of universities, notably at Chicago and Stanford. Voracious reading and a razor-sharp mind soon gave him something of a reputation as an academic. He was noted for his scathing criticism of classical economic theory and also for his contempt for his students – he was so unpopular amongst the students that his class hours at one university went from three hours a week to 'Mondays: 10 to 10:05' (Heilbroner, p. 227). He was also notorious for getting a bit too close to other men's wives – one story tells of his response to the president of Yale who was concerned that Veblen's presence might lead the professors to worry about their wives, to which Veblen is to have responded: 'They need not worry; I have seen their wives.' (Galbraith, p. 171).

His animosity towards societal norms and distanced dislike of society around him coloured his writing, needless to say. He was fascinated by the immense wealth of the upper class in American society created in the late 19th century. His most notable work, *The theory of the leisure class*, brought him fame. In it he attacked the rich and affluent in society, the 'leisure class' as he put it, for being occupied with little else than conspicuous consumption. In short, Veblen claimed that the only possible way for members of this 'class' to outdo each other was by buying very expensive items and flaunting them, thereby clearly demonstrating their wealth and ability to consume.

Such goods became known as 'Veblen goods'.

Sources: *The Worldly Philosophers*, by Robert Heilbroner, pp. 218–48; and *A History of Economics* by John Kenneth Galbraith, pp. 170–77.

Ostentatious (Veblen) goods ©IBO 2003

Ever wonder about those people who spend $2 apiece on those little bottles of Evian water? Try spelling Evian backward. – George Carlin, comedian

The first reason deals with the basic need of people to distinguish and differentiate themselves by being seen to consume goods which are known to be expensive.

Caliope's café apparently didn't fulfil this need for those people who need to be seen at places considered to be upmarket. This is basically a type of conspicuous and ostentatious (= showy, flamboyant) pattern of consumption. Such goods are referred to as **Veblen goods**, after the economist Thorstein Veblen who coined the term 'ostentatious' or 'conspicuous' consumption, quote: *'Conspicuous consumption of* *valuable goods is a means of reputability to the gentleman of leisure.'* (See "Celebrity bubble: Thorstein Veblen (1857–1929)" on page 65.)

The reasoning behind this upward sloping demand curve is the following: Posit that you and everyone around you are well aware of the price of a good and that the good is considered to confer a certain status on the owner. Now, assuming that everyone keeps tabs on changes in the price of the good, an increase in the price could make the good more desirable since viewers will know that you can afford it at an even higher price. This might mean that a price increase actually could increase the quantity demanded – leading to an upward-sloping demand curve. Goods which might be considered Veblen goods are goods with 'snob appeal', such as Lacoste shirts, Rolex watches and Rolls Royce automobiles.

Don't kill yourself looking for examples of Veblen goods in real life. In actual fact, claiming an upward slope on the demand curve is rather contrived and there are few, if any, real-life examples of this type of inverted demand.[17]

Storytime: Crocs and 'gators.

In Athens, in 2000, a shady businessman was charged with large-scale plagiarism of the famous Lacoste tennis shirts. He was caught red-handed by the police with boxes full of shirts with the well-known logotype of a crocodile on the breast. He was charged with illegal copying and brand infringement and box-loads of the phoney shirts were presented as evidence. He pleaded innocent at the trial, however. Referring to the logo on the shirts, his defence was: 'That's not a crocodile – it's an alligator.' He was convicted in spite of this brilliant defence.

Role of expectations ©IBO 2003

When people expect something to happen and act firmly upon their beliefs, it is possible that they create the very thing they expected to happen. This is the self-reinforcing feedback loop referred to earlier in the context of housing or share prices; people expect prices to continue to fall and thus demand falls in the present time period causing future prices to fall.

What if prices were expected to rise? Same phenomenon, different direction of prices. Expectations of future price increases could increase demand at present, leading to higher prices. This force of expectations could also work on individual goods that are not only purchased for personal use or consumption but for **speculative** purposes. Say that the market price for gold has gone up over a period of time, and a number of speculators believe that this will continue so they buy gold. This demand causes the price of gold to increase and then … we now have a self-reinforcing feedback loop.

17. However reluctant I am to admit it, academic honesty forces me to comment on the surprising results obtained in an extended essay by one of my people, Enrique. His father is president of one of the larger chains of department stores in Mexico and kindly did something of an experiment for us by increasing the prices on several 'snobbish goods'. When Enrique compiled the sales figures after the price increases, it was clear that sales had actually *increased*. However, I repeat that one should be careful in drawing extensive conclusions since many other variables have influence on demand other than price.

For example, during the studied period (September to November 2008) the UD dollar appreciated (= increased in price compared to the Mexican peso) by some 30%, leading many high income Mexican shoppers to shop at home rather than go to the US and buy clothing. I believe that it was *expectations* of a continued falling peso that drove up demand. High income people here in Mexico keep a sharp eye on the peso exchange rate and there was widespread belief that the peso would continue to fall thus making imported luxury goods even more expensive in the future. Wise Veblenites simply brought forward their purchases to the present rather than paying more in the future.

A little depth:
Cause and effect in price versus demand

Note that an upward-sloping demand curve due to speculation is firmly denied by a good many economists, yours truly included. In many of my colleagues' opinions, the upward-sloping demand curve does exactly what we try to hammer into our students not to do – it confuses cause and effect and hence does not distinguish between 'movement along' and 'shift' in the demand curve.

Simply put, for an upward sloping demand curve to exist, there must be direct causality between price and quantity demanded, e.g. a change in price leads to increased quantity demanded for the good. However, it is more than likely that previous or ongoing increases in price lead to – cause – an increase in demand. In

other words, expectations of higher prices for goods subject to speculation (houses, gold and shares) lead to an increase in demand! It is this increase in demand that subsequently drives up the price of the good.

In summary: it is not necessarily a price increase which causes an increase in demanded quantity but quite probably the reverse, i.e. an increase in demand (due to expectations) leads to an increase in price. Price is determined by demand – not the other way around.

(Yes colleagues, you can reach me at matt.ibid@hotmail.com)

Two common examples of speculative goods are shares and property. Shares have seen any number of speculative surges, resulting 'bubbles' and consequent collapses in the stock markets. When these bubbles burst it is often due to negative expectations of *falling* prices and speculators start leaving the market in droves thus driving down demand (and in fact increasing supply). Two recent examples are the 'Dot Com' bubble and crash of 1999–2001 and the 2007–08 stock market implosion when share prices around the world fell from all-time highs which had been caused by speculation to a large extent. Property prices often go hand-in-glove with stock market collapse: Ireland showed distinct signs of speculation, as house prices increased by over 200% between 1995 and 2002 and at the time of writing (November 2008) prices have dropped by over 15% since the peak in March 2007.[18]

Giffen goods ©IBO 2003

A Giffen good is a rather peculiar type of *inferior* good. It was posited by Sir Robert Giffen in the 19th century that a rise in the price of bread would actually increase the quantity demanded. The reasoning was that bread was a vital element of consumption for the extreme poor, and claimed a very large portion of their income, and that their diet would be seen to by buying bread first. Any money left over might buy a piece of cheese or meat as a tasty, but not absolutely vital, supplement. Thus, a rise in price of bread left little room for the consumption of any 'extras', so families substituted the foregone cheese or meat with more bread. If the price of bread fell, subsistence quantity could be had by spending less on bread and substituting it with a bit of meat.

Most of my colleagues and I look upon the possibility of a Giffen good as highly unlikely. It is more of an historical curio (= novelty) than a viable economic concept. The concept simply seems to have dug its teeth into textbooks during the late 19th century and like a dog with a Frisbee it has never let go. Economic textbooks often point out that such goods are 'most unusual' – my way of putting it is that the first person to prove the existence of a Giffen good will be on the short list for a Nobel Prize in economics.[19]

18. *The Economist*, 6 March 2003, 'Betting the house', http://www.finfacts.com/irishfinancenews/article_1013768.shtml and http://uk.reuters.com/article/propertyNews/idUKNOA74357620080327
19. A mermaid will give the Nobel speech and a leprechaun will hand over the prize. Incorruptible Mexican police will stand guard.

HIGHER LEVEL

Story from history: Tulipmania in 1637

The world's first proper stock market was founded in the early 17th century in Amsterdam. It didn't take too long before there was rash speculation, a commodity boom and ensuing crash – all within the time frame of less than four years.

Tulips arrived in Holland in the mid 16th century from Eastern Mediterranean countries, most likely from Turkey, where they grew in the wild. They were greatly appreciated and horticulturists set about breeding many new varieties of tulips. Many of these new types were rare and thus most coveted by the rich of Holland. They became symbols of status and sophistication in the upper class.

It didn't take long before enterprising merchants, dock workers, captains of ships, farmers and citizens from every walk of life started to speculate in an endless ascension of the value of tulips. Tulip speculation was based on the selling of bulbs (by weight). They came to be sold, speculated and used as collateral for loans. Also, due to being highly seasonal, much of this was while the tulip bulbs were still in the ground – and nobody had actually seen the flowers as yet! Talk about a bubble – this trade actually was referred to as 'wind trade'.

Rare bulbs fetched preposterous prices as speculative euphoria and mass psychosis reached its pinnacle in 1636–37. A bulb of the Semper Augustus type worth 1,000 guilders in 1623 was sold for 5,500 guilders in 1637 – more than USD55,000 at today's prices. Traders in tulips could earn 5,000 guilders in a month where the average income at the time was 150 guilders.

This mania came to a screeching halt during 1637 when some of the more cautious and perhaps far-sighted speculators started to leave the market by selling off their stock without replenishing it. A chain reaction set off where falling prices ultimately saw everyone trying to sell their stock before prices fell even further. The bottom fell out of the market and prices went down to under 10% of peak market values. A great many formerly wealthy people lost their fortunes to speculation as they stood after the crash with enormous debt and only tulip bulbs – now deemed worthless – as security for this debt.

Sources: M. Dash, Tulipomania: The Story of the World's Most Coveted Flower & The Extraordinary Passions it Aroused. *Crown Publ., 1999. J.K. Galbraith,* A short history of financial euphoria, *1993, Penguin Books.*

Supply ©IBO 2003

The supply curve – adding a hand to clap against.

One of the hippie credos of my troubled childhood was the T-shirt legend, 'What if they gave a war and nobody came?' This is like saying that a good has been provided but there is no demand for it whatsoever. There is no such thing. In order to be able to refer to a market, there has to be both willing buyers and willing sellers. This is the 'two hands clapping' in our basic market model, i.e. *supply and demand*.

Definition of supply ©IBO 2003

The supply curve operates along the exact same parameters as demand. A *change in price* will – ceteris paribus – result in a *change in the quantity supplied*. As in the pattern of demand, there is clear correlation as

long as other influencing factors remain the same. This is the law of supply, and differs from demand in having *positive correlation* – when the price rises, *ceteris paribus*, the quantity supplied increases and vice versa.

> **Law of supply:** *Ceteris paribus*, a rise in the price for good X will result in an increase in the quantity supplied of good X. A fall in the price of X will result in a decrease of quantity supplied.
>
> The law of supply states that as long as all other variables (the cost, availability and quality of factors of production) remain unchanged, then a rise in the price of a good will lead to an increase in the quantity supplied.

As so many issues in economics, this is intuitively obvious. An increase in the market price (for whatever reason) increases the propensity of suppliers to put the good on the market. There are a few simple reasons for this – all of which deal (once again) with the **willingness, ability,** and **propensity** of suppliers to put goods on the market. Just as was done in the section on the demand curve, it is necessary to clarify that supply is not the amount that suppliers would *like* to supply, but rather the quantity they *intend* to sell (= are willing and able to sell) during a given time period.

Unwilling seller!

Law of supply with diagrammatic analysis ©IBO 2003

Let us return to the market for movies in the fictitious town of Econopolis. In Figure 2.1.9, if the price rises from €5 to €6, the quantity supplied increases from 5,000 cinema tickets to 6,000 per week. This is in accordance with the law of supply: a higher price creates an incentive – the possibility of higher profit – for producers/suppliers to put more of the good (service, actually, in this example) on the market. We once again use the ceteris paribus assumption when drawing the supply curve. However, it is not incomes, preferences and other goods' prices that are kept constant (as we did in drawing the demand curve) but the **price, availability** and **quality of production factors** which we assume to be constant. (There are also various forms of government intervention which affect supply. More later.)

The supply curve in Figure 2.1.9 shows the market supply for cinema tickets (seats) in Econopolis, i.e. the sum of all movie theatres' supply on the market. Let's look more closely at the issue of the upward slope of the supply curve for movies in Econopolis. It is almost intuitive that higher prices would cause existing theatres increasing output. There are two reasons for this *positive correlation*.

- The first is that a higher ticket price might add to firms' *revenue* (price times quantity), and perhaps also additional to *profit* (total revenue minus total costs – more in later chapters). Thus, if the market price rises suppliers will have an **incentive** to put more of the good on the market. In the case of movie theatres, more seat rows could be added and films could be shown more often.

- The other reason why an additional quantity is supplied at a higher price deals with the **costs** of producers. (A key issue here are *rising marginal costs*, a HL concept in Section 2.3, theory of the firm.) It is easy to understand that different suppliers have different cost levels. If the market price for movies is €5 per ticket and the cost to a theatre of providing another seat is €5.50 … then basically the movie theatre would lose 50 cents for each additional seat and it would not be provided. Now, if the market price rises to €6 per seat, then the theatre would be *able* and *willing* to provide the additional seat. This goes for all the other theatres where the cost of providing an additional seat is less or equal to €6.

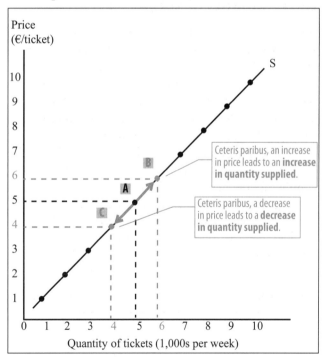

Figure 2.1.9 *The supply of cinema tickets in Econopolis*

The increase in price has caused an increase in the quantity supplied simply because suppliers want more revenue/profit and need a higher price to cover increased costs of supplying the goods. The increase in price causes an increase in the quantity supplied simply because suppliers want more revenue/profit and need a higher price to cover increased costs of supplying the good.

Warning!
Law of supply

Important note: 'Supply' is NOT the same as 'quantity in existence'. It is most important that you understand at an early stage that having 200 tonnes of cheese in a storage room is not the same as 200 tonnes being on the market. You see, if the producer of the cheese in question is simply storing the cheese then it is not actually offered on the market. It is not part of supply. It will become part of supply if the market price of this cheese increases to the level where the producer decides that it is not worth storing any more and offers it for sale.

Thus, oil in an oilfield is NOT part of supply; oil in a cistern which is offered to a petroleum company IS part of supply. Schools of tuna fish are NOT part of supply; when tins of tuna held in a warehouse are offered to the supermarkets they ARE part of supply.

Determinants of supply ©IBO 2003

Just as in demand, there are 'other variables' affecting supply within the ceteris paribus assumption. These are non-price determinants of supply. Any change in a **non-price determinant of supply** means that the pattern of supply changes, shown by a *shift* of the supply curve. Profit incentive and covering increasing (marginal) costs explain why the supply curve is upward-sloping and, just as in the pattern of demand, there are a number of non-price determinants of supply, all of which will *shift the supply curve*.

> **Non-price determinants of supply**: Any variable that changes the pattern of supply other than price is a non-price determinant of supply. Changes in the price, availability, quality and quantity of factors of production will all have an effect on the supply of goods.

Shifting the supply curve

I have divided the non-price determinants of supply into three main categories:

1. Changes in relevant **market factors**: these are costs of factors of production; price of related goods (producer substitutes); firms' expectations; and market entry/exit.

2. Changes in availability/**scarcity of factors** of production: these include reserves of natural resources; weather and climate changes; natural disasters.

3. Changes in the **quality/quantity of factors** of production: factor inputs improve over time due to improved production methods; technological advances, and advances in materials.

A change in relevant market factors

Cost of factors of production: Any increase in costs to suppliers will mean that the cost of producing goods will increase. This lowers the ability and willingness of suppliers to put the goods on the market (since they cannot influence the market price) and producers will respond by *decreasing* output. Decreased raw material prices, lower labour costs and lower rents would all cause production costs to decrease and supply to increase. Thus, if wages or salaries rise, then the workers used in production become more costly whereupon producers will decrease output, e.g. the supply curve shifts left. Figure 2.1.10 illustrates how an increase in labour costs for Swiss watch manufacturers will cause a *shift* in the supply curve to the left, from S_0 to S_1, i.e. fewer watches are supplied at P_0 and at *all* prices.[20]

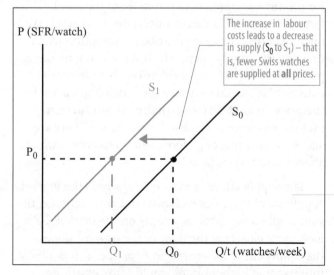

Figure 2.1.10 *A decrease in supply: less quantity supplied at every price (Swiss watches)*

- *Price of related goods:* Producers will have any number of possible *producer substitutes* (not to be confused with consumer substitutes!) such as DVDs and Blu-ray disks. An increase in demand/price for Blu-ray disks might cause suppliers to reallocate (= shift) resources from the production of DVDs to Blu-ray disks, causing the supply of (the producer substitute) DVDs to decrease from S_0 to S_1 as shown in diagram I of Figure 2.1.11.

Another possibility is that producers have goods that are in *joint supply*. An example would be gold and copper which are often found in the same geological veins and pockets. An increase in the price of gold would lead to an increase in the supply of gold – and also of copper, this is illustrated by the shift to the right in supply (S'_0 to S'_1) in diagram II of Figure 2.1.11. In a similar vein (pun intended), a decrease in demand (and hence price) of beef would also decrease the supply of leather.

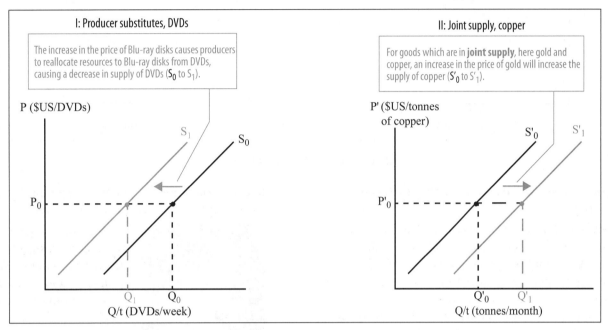

Figure 2.1.11 *Producer substitutes, DVDs and Joint supply, copper*

- *The expectations of firms:* If firms expect a surge in demand, such as seasonal demand for tourism, they might actually increase supply of, say, rental cars in order to build a sizable stock for the coming increase in demand.

Diagram I of Figure 2.1.12 on page 72 shows how anticipation of the tourist season in Cancun, Mexico, leads suppliers of rental cars to increase supply from S_0 to S_1. (MXN = Mexican pesos.)

- *Market entry/exit:* If existing firms on a market are making a profit, newcomers might be attracted. As firms enter the market, total supply of goods will increase. This is often the case for new products, where the success of the iPhone resulted in a rapid increase in 'copycat' (= similar, copied) products. In the same way, if an industry becomes less profitable then firms will leave the market, decreasing supply, for example the decline in the Swedish ship-building industry in the 1980s caused by far more competitive ship-builders in Korea. (SEK = Swedish crowns). This is illustrated in diagram II of Figure 2.1.12 on page 72.

---

20. I did not use labour costs as an example randomly. Raw material costs, even such precious metals as gold and platinum, represent a fraction of the final value of a good Swiss watch. Perhaps the most complicated watch in the world, 'Calibre 89' made by Patek Philippe for its 150th anniversary in 1989, contains 1,728 parts, and had four people working on it for nine years, measured from initial research/design to final completion. When I get the required USD6 million together from book sales I'm going to get one.

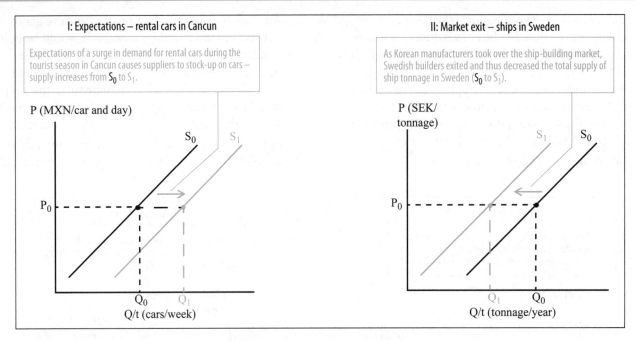

Figure 2.1.12 *Rental cars in Cancun*

A change in the availability/scarcity of factors of production

- *Availability and scarcity of factors*: Any and all factors used in production are subject to relative scarcity. Should factors become more available or abundant, then the same market laws will apply to them, i.e. scarcity will *raise the price* of any given factor of production. Studies show that during the end of the decade, teachers in Sweden will be retiring at a rate far beyond the rate of replenishment via teacher colleges. This will decrease the supply of teachers – and hopefully raise the salaries of those of us who remain in the profession. As for tangible (= physical) goods, suppose that the existing diamond mines in Botswana, Namibia, South Africa and Russia start to peter out (= diminish). This would mean that there would be less diamonds available no matter what we are willing to pay for them. While there is a nifty Swedish firm selling jewellery made from elk faeces, I don't envision this being a viable substitute in the context of weddings.

- Force majeure, *unexpected events:* Disruptions such as earthquakes, fires, floods and other natural disasters can have significant effects on the supply of goods – not only agricultural goods but all goods needing transport. Look at the frequent disruptions to oil supply; every time there is a terrorist attack (Iraq: blown-up pipelines), flood (Mexico: workers can't get to the offshore wells) or hurricane (Texas:

destroyed oil refineries) there is a resulting decrease in the supply of oil and petroleum products.

In the same mode, an increase in the supply of factors will both increase availability and lower the costs for producers. Just imagine how the discovery of new oil fields would help suppliers all around the world by lowering the dependency on the oil cartel, OPEC. Another thing mentionable in this context is the effect of weather conditions on agricultural output. During 2008, tens of thousands of people in Ethiopia once again faced starvation according to the FAO[21] due to lower than normal rains and poor harvests.

A change in the quality/efficiency of factors of production

- *The quality of factors of production:* Anything which enables a producer/supplier to put more on the market without increasing costs means that supply increases, i.e. the supply curve shifts to the right. Better production methods and/or a more educated and well-trained labour force would increase output during any given time period. This is an increase in the efficiency in use of factors and enables the subsequent increase in productivity. *Production techniques* (division of labour for example),

---

21. Food and agricultural organisation of the United Nations.

advancing technology (computer assisted design and computer assisted manufacturing – CAD/CAM to name but one), new and *improved materials* in production (any number of ceramics), and of course anything dealing with increasing *knowledge*, research and development (R & D), education, training, etc.

- *Technology:* Better tools, production processes, materials, computer assisted design and computer assisted manufacturing – CAD/CAM, etc. are all elements of advancing technology which increase output per unit of time which is the same as increasing supply. For example, it now takes General Motors in the US an average of 24.4 hours to assemble a vehicle – 6.4% shorter time than the year before.[22]

'Movement along' versus 'shift' of the supply curve ©IBO 2003

Just as in the issue of shifting the demand curve, it is not a change in price that causes a change in how much is supplied but instead, one of the non-price variables. The basic rules are still:

- A change in price leads (*ceteris paribus*) to a change in the quantity supplied – see points A and B in Figure 2.1.13

  $\Delta P \rightarrow Qs$, for example:
  $\uparrow P \rightarrow \uparrow Qs$ (point B in Figure 2.1.13)

- A change in any other supply determinant (e.g. non-price determinant) leads to a change in supply – see S_0 and S_1 in Figure 2.1.13

  Δnon-P determinant $\rightarrow \Delta S$, for example: $\uparrow$labour costs $\rightarrow \downarrow S$ (S2 in Figure 2.1.13)

Once again, I beg you to take heed of the outcome of the above shifts. The price has not changed yet more of the good is supplied … at *all* prices. One says that the quantity supplied has changed at all price levels – which is NOT a 'movement along' the curve (or extension/contraction) but a change in supply. The entire supply curve shifts and shows how at any given price, supply has changed.

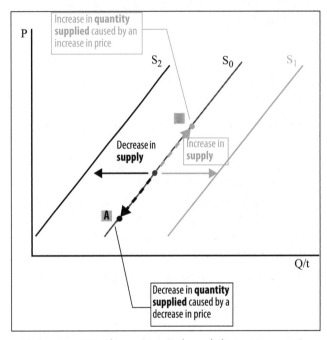

Figure 2.1.13 *Change in supply and change in quantity supplied*

22. 'US carmakers' efficiency rises', *Business Week*, 30 June 2003.

Outside the box:
Mermaidonics revisited – backward-bending 'S-curve'

(With help from http://web.mit.edu/krugman/www/opec.html.)

During the speculative oil price shock of 2007–08, several economic commentators observed that oil suppliers in fact had an incentive to *decrease* output of oil as the price rose. This seemingly contradicts economic theory, yet in fact it can be explained quite logically.

In Figure 2.1.14, the price of oil is at P_0 and rises to P_1 and the quantity supplied of oil increases to Q_1. Now, assume that:

- Oil production starts to reach maximum (short-run) output potential.
- Oil producers have a level of target revenue, i.e. an aimed-for level of oil revenue.

Two forces kick in which in fact might cause oil suppliers to decrease the quantity supplied: *expectations* of higher future oil prices and limited *investment alternatives*.

Expectations: Assume that suppliers are satisfied with the oil revenues at P_1. This is the area given by $P_1 \times Q_1$. A rise in price to P_2 means that suppliers can in fact decrease quantity supplied on the oil market (Q_2) while retaining the target revenue. (The loss of revenue – the grey area – is equal to the gain in revenue shown by the blue area.) If suppliers expect oil prices to remain high or continue upwards, they have an incentive to hold of on increasing capacity and supplies

– they can sell less and still make at least the same revenue in the future.

Investment alternatives: Oil is a finite resource. Any oil left in the ground is a form of investment. Basically, by leaving the oil in the ground and – in line with the expectations-based argument above – betting on permanently higher oil prices, producers have 'invested' in future oil revenues. As suppliers are reaching maximum short-run output levels at P_1, increasing costs of extraction above P_1 simply might lead suppliers to hold off on production increases.

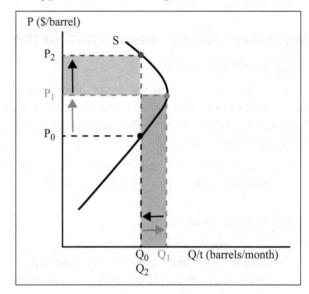

Figure 2.1.14 *Supply of oil*

Effect of taxes and subsidies on supply

©IBO 2003

In addition to the forces arising from within the market itself, there are also forces which can be said to be imposed from without, i.e. market intervention by government. Two common ways for governments to intervene are by imposing an indirect tax[23] on goods or subsidising goods. An **indirect tax** on goods sold – an expenditure tax – such as *value-added tax* (VAT) on goods sold is a percentage increase of the sales price of the good and will in effect be an increase in costs for producers, thus decreasing supply (see Figure 2.1.15). A **subsidy** is the opposite, a payment to producers (often per unit of output, for example per tonne of wheat) which lowers producers' costs (HL: marginal costs) and also acts as an incentive to produce more. This increases supply. More to come in Section 2.2.

It is also worth noting that in many instances market forces are not a major factor in determining the supply of goods. Many goods provided by governments, e.g. public and merit goods, are provided 'at cost' or even at a loss. This is the subject of Section 2.4.

Summary of supply curve shifts

By now you should be accustomed to the methodology I use in explaining concepts. I try to follow a 'define – exemplify – context' formula, which I realise is both time consuming and frequently tiresome.

Therefore I shall simplify the iteration of changes in supply by using the nine additional examples given in Table 2.1.1 on page 76 and labelling them accordingly in Figure 2.1.16.

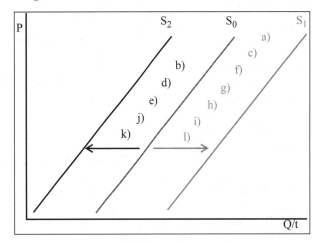

Figure 2.1.16 *Summary of supply curve shifts*

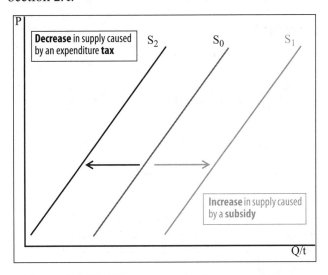

Figure 2.1.15 *Effects on supply of an expenditure tax and subsidy*

Indirect tax and subsidy: An **indirect tax** such as an expenditure tax is added to the price of the good and causes suppliers to increase the price at all levels of supply. The supply curve shifts left.

A **subsidy** is a payment or money grant to suppliers. This works as an incentive to produce more and also lowers (marginal) costs of production. The supply curve shifts right.

---

23. Indirect taxes are taxes which indirectly go to government, since VAT is paid to the suppliers who then in turn transfer the taxes to government. A direct tax is income and profit (corporate) tax, since this goes directly to government. We get shafted either way.

Table 2.1.1 *Summary of supply curve shifts*

Example:	Effect:	Supply will:	In:
1. A change in the relevant market factors			
a) wages for road workers fall	cost of making roads falls	supply curve for roads shifts right	S_0 to S_1
b) price of steel rises	cost of making cars rises	supply curve for cars shifts left	S_0 to S_2
c) price of flour falls	cost of making bread falls	supply curve for bread shifts right	S_0 to S_1
2. A change in the availability/scarcity of factors of production			
d) fewer study medicine	fewer doctors in hospitals	supply curve for health care shifts left	S_0 to S_2
e) pilots go on strike	fewer flights available	supply curve for air travel shifts left	S_0 to S_2
f) new copper deposits found	more copper available	supply curve for electrical wire shifts right	S_0 to S_1
3. A change in the quality/efficiency of factors of production			
g) increased use of robots	industrial production is faster	industrial supply curve shifts right	S_0 to S_1
h) better basic education	all labourers more efficient	supply curve for most goods shifts right	S_0 to S_1
i) IT revolution	most production more efficient	supply curve for most goods shifts right	S_0 to S_1
4. Non-market variables, i.e. intervention			
j) increased restrictions on cigarette sales	fewer sales outlets for cigarettes	Supply curve shifts to the left	S_0 to S_2
k) taxes on gasoline are increased	firms must pay a portion of sales revenue to government	Supply curve shifts to the left	S_0 to S_2
l) a subsidy is granted for the production of milk	milk producers have an incentive to produce more milk and production costs decrease	Supply curve shifts to the right	S_0 to S_1

What we now need to do is put the supply and demand curves together in the same diagram, in order to be able to analyse market behaviour. It bears repeating: nothing done so far has equipped you with the necessary tools to do a market analysis! For this you need supply and demand working together, not the separate (explanatory) graphs done thus far. Let's put it all together.

Putting the pieces together: Wage negotiations (part 1)

A few years ago I had a horrendous row with my (then) boss.[24] What the issue boiled down to was my unwillingness to accept more teaching hours and more students without a substantial rise in my salary.[25] Being me, I used a great deal of harsh language – most of it in print – and started to pack my bags and empty my computer. I was simply not prepared to give up any more of my increasingly valuable (i.e. scarce!) free time without increased remuneration (= payment). One could say that my opportunity costs of teaching additional classes were increasing and that I wanted my income to match this increased cost. This would render Figure 2.1.17. (We are assuming that my supply curve would be 'normal', i.e. I would supply more labour at a higher salary.)

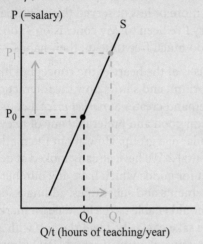

P (=salary)

Figure 2.1.17 *Matt's supply of teaching hours*

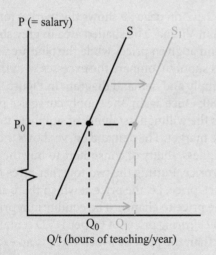

P (= salary)

Figure 2.1.18 *Matt's supply of teaching hours*

The row ended equitably (= fairly) for both parties: I got my money and the school got additional teaching hours. (It's amazing what one can accomplish simply by leaving school mid-lesson to sit on the balcony and drink beer – and one's students go on support-strike! They joined me on the balcony and brought six-packs supplied by parents. True story.) You should recognize this by now – the quantity supplied (here, teaching hours) increased due to an increase in the price (here, salary). This is the standard 'movement along the supply-curve' shown above as price increasing from P_0 to P_1 and quantity increasing from Q_0 to Q_1. Yet one cannot help wondering if a similar outcome could not have been achieved without it costing the municipality more in terms of salaries paid.

Of course it is possible! My school could entice me to supply more teaching hours without paying me more, i.e. change my overall willingness, ability and propensity to supply teaching hours. Any suggestions? Perhaps giving me my own office, preferably equipped with a hot computer, cold bar, colour TV, sofa and view. Or alleviating me from attending mind –numbing teachers meetings in the study hall?![26] Or extending all my vacations?! Or giving me complete and utter power over all the language teachers at school?!

You get the drift. This would mean **more hours taught at all price levels**. This is shown in Figure 2.1.18. If, for example, I accepted a better office rather than an increase in pay, I would provide additional teaching service at the same price thus increasing my supply from S_0 to S_1. As the price hasn't changed, and the amount of teaching hours supplied has increased, supply has increased I have increased my willingness to supply teaching hours at all prices.

---

24. I have in fact more ex-bosses than ex-wives.

25. A wage means 'x dollars per hour', i.e. an amount of money per labour hour. A salary is not based on an hourly rate but is a fixed sum per month. Auto-workers get wages, teachers get salaries.

26. No wait – I didn't attend those anyhow. Oh well.

Interaction of demand and supply

©IBO 2003

If it's not part of the solution ...

... then it's part of the problem. The simple function of a market is to put both parties – customers and suppliers – in touch with other. The rest follows: any given want of a potential buyer will result in search behaviour, and the opportunity costs of that search are lowest where a great many items may be seen and compared in the shortest amount of time. The lower opportunity cost is thus; the potential buyer can compare a great many similar goods in short order and perhaps bargain the way towards the highest satisfaction. This is far more efficient than gallivanting around the countryside in search of 20 different items. The market is simply a very efficient method of displaying the merchandise.

The same holds for providers of goods, as the demand is a signal to suppliers as to what goods should be provided and what the going price is. If the price is attractive and/or the demand is high then rest assured that the supplier will be back the next time with more goods for sale! Should there be too many similar goods for sale, then one can assume that a number of suppliers will put effort into finding other or better goods to sell – or other places to sell them. If the going market price is too low for a supplier to be able to sell his/her wares, then there is a strong incentive for the supplier to increase efficiency in order to lower costs – and thus compete on the market.

The market thus functions as a mechanism to fulfil both customers' and suppliers' wants. The market system also addresses the issue of excess and quality: any superfluous goods are simply not sold at the existing price. Market dynamics have thus solved the basic economic problem of what, how and for whom: consumers' demand decides what is to be produced; basic competition between suppliers addresses the issue of how to produce (as inefficient producers are forced to leave the market), and the price decides who gets the goods.

As long as we are all good comparison shoppers and firms operate from within competitive forces, the system will provide the 'right amount of goods' at the 'correct price'. In theory, that is. Unfortunately, as we shall see, for the tooth fairy to deliver, one has to knock out a few teeth.

Equilibrium market clearing price and quantity ©IBO 2003

Both hands clapping – putting supply and demand together

In class, I often bring up the open markets I've visited. I describe them in some detail in terms of the time spent putting shoddy goods out for sale. I still claim that many of them obey only half the law of supply/demand; if something 'sucks' there's always plenty of it. I have more or less observed this in virtually every country I've been to. My conclusion – too many people have too much free time on their hands.

This is at the heart of the concept of market equilibrium, and shows how the interaction of supply and demand creates a *market price*. Let us use a common good and preferably one of relevance to your particular age group. How about the market for DVD film rentals? We have already looked at demand on the market for goods which have any number of complements and substitutes, adding a supply curve now should enable us to elucidate on market dynamics. For the sake of clarity, I will start off with a simple table showing the quantity of rental DVD films demanded and supplied in a fictitious town, Vidina, at a number of different prices.

Table 2.1.2 on page 79 shows the market for DVD rental in Vidina. The shaded area in grey shows excess demand at given prices while the blue area shows excess supply. Compare the excesses with the curves in the supply and demand diagram in Figure 2.1.19 on page 80. Once again, the supply curve is a pattern that shows the willingness/ability of suppliers to put a good on the market. The demand curve shows the equivalent willingness/ability of consumers to buy the good at a given price. Putting the two together gives rise to the 'correct' price, i.e. the price at which there are no forces for the price to change. The equilibrium price, (or *market clearing* price) of €6 per DVD rental, is nothing other than the price at which there is no excess in either quantity demanded or quantity supplied – all goods that are put on the market are bought.

Storytime: Something for nothing

 *I simply have to tell the story of my father's experience at an open market in Mexico City in the mid-1960s. An old lady had a large blanket spread out on the zócalo (= main plaza or square) with a largish pile of limes on it. My father, of course, needed limes for the evening cocktail party with the expatriate crowd. He asked "how much" and got a price quote per kilo and then asked "How much for the entire pile?" expecting a better deal. The old lady doubled the price! My utterly confused old man stammered out a question as to why the price was higher since he was prepared to buy them all. The answer: 'Ah, señor. If I sell you all my limes I will have nothing to do for the rest of the day and I will go home. Then I won't be able to see all my friends here at the zócalo.' I love the answer, for two reasons. One, it shows the limits of 'market clearing theory', and two, there are people for whom there are things more important than profit. There's hope.*

Table 2.1.2 *Market clearing for DVDs in Vidina*

Price (€)	Quantity supplied (1,000s)	Quantity demanded (1,000s)	Excess supply
11	10	0	10 (excess quantity supplied)
10	9	1	8 (excess quantity supplied)
9	8	2	6 (excess quantity supplied)
8	7	3	4 (excess quantity supplied)
7	6	4	2 (excess quantity supplied)
6	**5 ....**	**5 ....**	**0 (market clearing price!)**

Price (€)	Quantity supplied (1,000s)	Quantity demanded (1,000s)	Excess demand
5	4	6	2 (excess quantity demanded)
4	3	7	4 (excess quantity demanded)
3	2	8	6 (excess quantity demanded)
2	1	9	8 (excess quantity demanded)
1	0	10	10 (excess quantity demanded)
0	-	11	11 (excess quantity demanded)

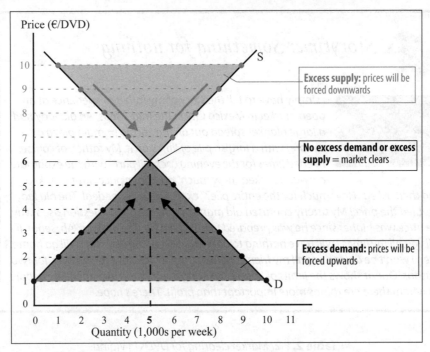

Figure 2.1.19 *Market equilibrium for DVDs (market clearing)*

Figure 2.1.19 shows how at *any price above* €€6 suppliers have an *incentive* to put too much on the market. The high price acts as a signal to suppliers to put more of the good on the market. However, consumer demand at prices above €6 is less than the amount suppliers would put on the market, there is *excess supply* (or surplus). Firms supplying DVDs will soon discover that they are stocking too many DVD films and will act to cut this amount. This market glut will therefore cause a downward movement in price as suppliers begin to lower prices and cut excess films on their shelves. (It is worthy of revising the concept of opportunity cost here. Just imagine how costly it is for a supplier of DVD films to have purchased or rented 50 copies of Britney Spears's latest epic drama only to discover that 49 of them sit on the shelf week after week.[27] The shelf space could be used for other items – other DVD films or complement goods such as potato chips – and the supplier's cost of obtaining the films means that these resources could have been put to better use.)

In the same manner, if the *price is set below* €€6, consumers will demand more DVDs than will be supplied during the week. This excess demand will mean that suppliers have empty shelves and full queues of customers. The price is evidently too low so they will raise the price. This will act as a stimulus and incentive for suppliers to restock the shelves quicker in answer to the excess demand. More DVD films will be made available. An increasing market and the resulting increase in quantity supplied means that the excess demand will decrease as price moves towards equilibrium at €6 per DVD.

The above illustrates the price mechanism at work. Another way of looking at the dynamics of supply, demand and price is that suppliers will want to charge as much as possible and consumers will want to pay as little as possible. It is in this arena that the bargaining process will play out. I often find it useful to think of the supply and demand interplay as a form of auction.

There are a given number of goods at an offered price and it is now up to consumers' demand to arrive at a price whereby the proffered goods are sold. Highly demanded goods will be 'bid up' in price while unsold goods will be auctioned off at lower prices.

---

27. I wonder if a stretch of prison for poor Britney would in fact have increased demand for her films.

POP QUIZ 2.1.3 MARKET EQUILIBRIUM

1 Below are some figures for the supply of wheat during a three month period. What is the equilibrium price per tonne? (Q_d = quantity demanded, Q_s = quantity supplied, P = price)

P ($)	Q_s (tonnes)	Q_d (tonnes)
3	2	20
4	4	16
5	6	12
6	8	8
7	10	4
8	12	0

2 What would be a possible effect on the market in question **1** if the quantity demanded was higher than the quantity supplied and the price was fixed by law?

An increase in demand and the effects on price/quantity

The saga (= story) continues. Recall that our so-called equilibrium price is in actual fact the price at which the market clears **within a given period of time**. What if a non-price determinant of demand were to change within the given time frame? For example, what if Swedish consumers' preferences changed in favour of more environmentally friendly modes of transportation, for example, bicycles? This would shift the demand curve for bicycles from D_0 to D_1, as shown in Figure 2.1.20. At the new level of demand, there would be more willing buyers than supply on the market (e.g. excess demand) at P_0 and this would force prices upwards from P_0 to P_1 causing suppliers to increase the quantity supplied (Q_0 to Q_1). This is the same as saying that the increase in demand (= shift of demand curve) has caused upward pressure on the (equilibrium) price and an increase in quantity supplied.

In economic shorthand:
$$\uparrow D_{bicycles} \rightarrow Q_D > Q_S \rightarrow \uparrow P_{bicycles} \rightarrow \uparrow Q_S$$
$$\rightarrow QS = QD \text{ at } P1$$

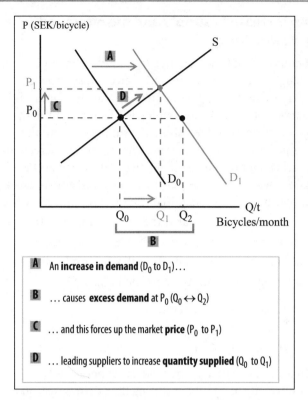

A An **increase in demand** (D_0 to D_1)...

B ... causes **excess demand** at P_0 ($Q_0 \leftrightarrow Q_2$)

C ... and this forces up the market **price** (P_0 to P_1)

D ... leading suppliers to increase **quantity supplied** (Q_0 to Q_1)

Figure 2.1.20 *Market for bicycles – increased demand*

This is perhaps the most important conclusion so far within our market model: *a change in demand is price-determining* – while a change in quantity demanded is price-*determined*! Once again, when demand changes, for example, due to a change in preferences, then the entire demand curve will shift, *causing* the price to change and a *movement along* the supply curve. This is an important lesson in what economists call causality, i.e. the forces of cause and effect.

POP QUIZ 2.1.4 EFFECT OF CHANGES IN DEMAND

1 How would demand for bicycles (see Figure 2.1.20 above) be affected if the price of gasoline fell?

2 What other variable could affect demand as illustrated in Figure 2.1.20?

An increase in supply and the effects on price/quantity

Let us look at how a change in supply results in a change in price. In Figure 2.1.21 we can see how an increase in the supply of coffee, say due to a bountiful harvest of coffee beans (which is a factor input in the production of coffee), shifts the supply curve to the right. This is intuitively self-explanatory: an increase in market supply will create relative abundance of the good (within the time period in question) and an *excess supply* of coffee at the initial price P_0 and thus force the price downwards towards the new equilibrium (at P_1). The increase in supply (S_0 to S_1) has caused the equilibrium price to fall (P_0 to P_1), in turn leading to an increase in quantity demanded (Q_0 to Q_1).

In economic shorthand:

$\uparrow S_{coffee} \rightarrow Q_S > Q_D \rightarrow \downarrow P_{coffee} \rightarrow \uparrow Q_D$
$\rightarrow Q_S = Q_D$ at P_1

In a similar vein, anyone who has experienced abnormally bad weather during the growing season for any number of vegetables and fruits can instinctively predict how the price of coffee would be forced upwards due to detrimental growing conditions and the ensuing hit to supply of green coffee.

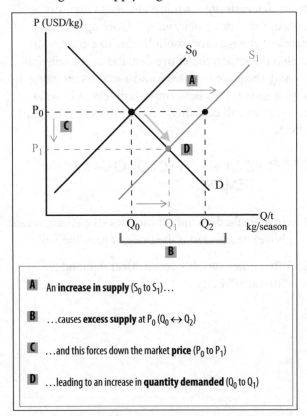

A An **increase in supply** (S_0 to S_1)...

B ...causes **excess supply** at P_0 ($Q_0 \leftrightarrow Q_2$)

C ...and this forces down the market **price** (P_0 to P_1)

D ...leading to an increase in **quantity demanded** (Q_0 to Q_1)

Figure 2.1.21 *Market for coffee – increased supply*

Warning!
Increase in demand, increase in supply

One of the most common errors of my fresh students is in insisting on shifting the supply curve in order to show how suppliers react to changes in demand. The second common error is in insisting on shifting the demand curve to show how consumers react to a shift in supply. Both are technically erroneous, absolutely superfluous and just plain wrong!

Any shift of the demand curve already SHOWS how suppliers will react (e.g. a change in supplied quantity) without any further assistance from the supply curve. In a similar mode, shifting the supply curve shows how consumers will react (change in quantity demanded) and no shift in the demand curve is necessary. Offered to the supermarkets they ARE part of supply.

POP QUIZ 2.1.5   EFFECT OF CHANGES IN SUPPLY

1 How might the increase in supply of coffee shown in Figure 2.1.21 affect the market for cocoa?

2 How might cocoa producers act if they knew in advance that the supply of coffee was going to increase?

Decreasing supply and demand

We're cooking now, right? So, how hard can it be to make a logical jump over to the outcome of a decrease in supply or demand? In diagram I of Figure 2.1.22 on page 83, we see how supply has decreased from S'_0 to S'_1 (for example, due to increasing labour costs), and how the price has adjusted upwards from P'_0 to P'_1 and quantity demanded has consequently decreased from Q'_0 to Q'_1. In Figure 2.1.22 diagram II, demand has decreased from D_0 to D_1 (say due to a fall in the price of a substitute) forcing the equilibrium price downwards from P_0 to P_1, decreasing quantity supplied from Q_0 to Q_1.

- In economic shorthand (diagram I):
  $\downarrow S' \rightarrow Q'_S < Q'_D \rightarrow \uparrow P' \rightarrow \downarrow Q'_D \rightarrow Q'_S = Q'_D$ at P'_1

- In economic shorthand (diagram II):
  $\downarrow D \rightarrow Q_D < Q_S \rightarrow \downarrow P \rightarrow \downarrow Q_S \rightarrow Q_S = Q_D$ at P_1

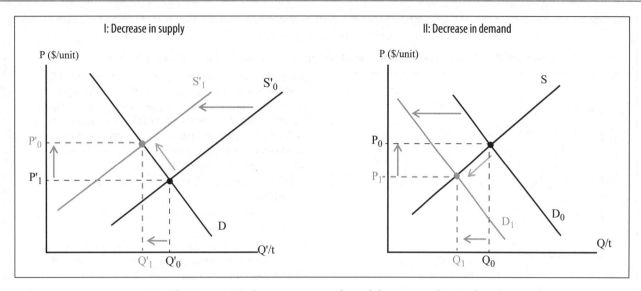

Figure 2.1.22 *Decrease in supply and decrease in demand*

POP QUIZ 2.1.6   EFFECT OF A CHANGE IN SUPPLY
FOR ONE GOOD ON THE PRICE OF ANOTHER

1   Assuming that the two goods in Figure 2.1.22 diagrams I and II above are *related* in some way, what might these two goods be?

A little depth:
The price as a signal

The interaction of the supply and demand curves in Figures 2.1.23 to 2.1.25 on page 84 illustrate how the flexibility of competitive markets leads to market dynamism. Prices change, ultimately, in accordance with the forces of supply and demand. Economists often refer to the market model's dynamism in terms of three separate functions of the price mechanism:

• the signalling function
• the incentives function
• the rationing function.

Any change in market price is a ***signal*** to suppliers to either increase or decrease output. This is perhaps one of the great successes in the market system – and shows the dismal failure of a centrally planned system. An increase in price due, for example, to an increase in demand means that there is the possibility of increased revenue (or profit) to be made. This is the ***incentives*** function of the producers on the market; more will be provided if there is a demand for it, owing to the driving force of self-interest. Finally, scarce goods mean, per definition, that there is an excess of demand which

means that available goods need to be ***rationed*** in some way. We could construct a queuing system or allot a given quantity per consumer – but in a market system this would be unnecessary, as the excess demand will drive up prices and thereby ration consumers' ability to purchase the good.

A tricky question in our market model deals with the speed at which the market clears – or whether the market indeed clears at all! This is highly dependant on the market characteristics. An immediate shock to the market for any number of goods might lead to excess demand or supply for an indeterminate period. For example, it is highly unlikely that a decrease in the supply of beef would *immediately* cause an increase in the price of hamburgers – even in the most open and responsive economic systems. However, our model and subsequent analysis indicates that in the longer term, market disequilibrium cannot exist and that prices will indeed move in order to balance relative scarcities or excesses. The price tends to *move towards* market equilibrium.

Dealing with exam questions

Sample: Red pens – illustrating and explaining 'reallocation' and the 'price mechanism'

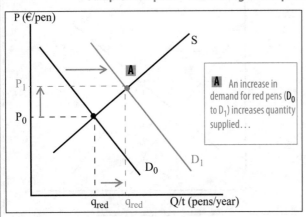

A An increase in demand for red pens (D_0 to D_1) increases quantity supplied...

Figure 2.1.23 *Red pens*

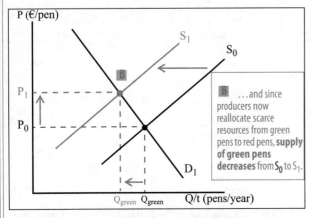

B ...and since producers now reallocate scarce resources from green pens to red pens, **supply of green pens decreases** from S_0 to S_1.

Figure 2.1.24 *Green pens*

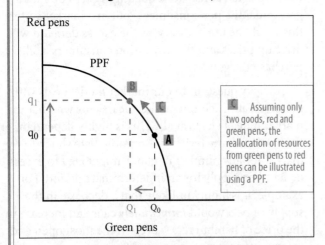

C Assuming only two goods, red and green pens, the reallocation of resources from green pens to red pens can be illustrated using a PPF.

Figure 2.1.25 *PPF*

One of the more common exam questions posed in IB economics is somehow also one of the most sloppily addressed, namely the basic issue of the function of prices in competitive markets. Variants of this question are along the lines of '… explain how the price mechanism allocates resources in a market economy …' and ask that you address three fundamental issues:

1 The basic issue of scarcity and the basic economic problem

2 How the price acts as a mechanism to allocate resources

3 Use supply and demand analysis to illustrate how prices act as signals to producers (*incentives function*) and consumers (*rationing function*).

Assume two goods, for example, red and green pens, and optimum efficiency (Pareto optimum) in an economy. Outline the basic issue of scarcity and endless wants and how markets solve the basic economic problem via the signalling function of prices. Use supply and demand diagrams to illustrate the market mechanism.

Figure 2.1.23 illustrates an increase in demand for red pens which drives up the price and signals suppliers (*incentive function* of price!) to increase the quantity supplied of red pens (q_{red} to q_{red}).

As resources used in the manufacturing of green pens become more scarce, the supply for green pens decreases from S_0 to S_1 (see Figure 2.1.24). The increase in price (P_0 to P_1) signals consumers to decrease their consumption (*rationing function* of price!) of green pens – quantity demanded for green pens decreases from Q_{green} to Q_{green}.

Since the economy is operating at Pareto optimum (point A, Figure 2.1.25), pen suppliers must reallocate resources from green pens to red pens (points A to B).

Supply and demand analysis

My father had firm views on child rearing.[28] Basically, his methodology might be termed 'Darwinistic Nurturing' – or, today, 'child abuse'. Learning how to swim was on a 'sink-or-swim' basis, where I got the basic techniques in the Sheraton Hotel pool and gained hard-earned experience by getting tossed into the sea from the boat. 'We'll pull ashore on the little island over there, Matthew. Keep your chin up.' This, incidentally, in the Caribbean Sea where one could be accompanied at any time by barracudas, sharks, highly poisonous jellyfish – and where the seabed was littered with sea urchins sporting six-inch spikes. A few added flotation incentives, you might say.

And that is how a good deal of your own applications of economics will be played out in the remaining examples. It is impossible to give extensive examples of the virtually endless uses of the supply and demand model – you will mostly learn by doing. However, I conclude this chapter with two basic examples of market interaction, using the basic tools of supply and demand and linking to previous concepts. Then I leave it to you to learn how to reapply economic illustrations to whatever real-life scenarios you need to deal with in exams or internal assessment. Sink or swim people.

S & D (plus reallocation) analysis number one: 'Oh Lord, won't you buy me, a Mercedes-Benz?'[29]

Dodge Charger

The father of Nico, one of my IB1 kids, is one of the largest retailers of cars in Mexico – something he no doubt regrets since I've had him put me on the short list of 'Favoured Customers' for a new 425 horse-power Dodge Charger.[30] I started looking for the Charger with my pal Toni last year, who basically has said 'Mateo, for crying on a crutch –just get it! You can afford it … give up a new wristwatch or two.' I patiently explained that I am waiting for prices to fall like a paralysed parakeet; 'Toni, by the time I'm ready to buy, Nico's dad is going to *pay me* to get it off

the parking lot and have two of the cute salesgirls go with me!' Am I as crazy as my colleagues say I am? Well, not in economics at least – let me explain.

The high cost of gasoline (during what will probably become known as the 'Speculative oil crisis of 2008') is changing consumers' behaviour. Gasoline and cars are very close complements. As the price of gasoline surged during 2007 and 2008, households increasingly switched from large to small 'Econo-cars', i.e. demand has decreased considerably for large gas-guzzling cars, shown in diagram I of Figure 2.1.26 on page 86 (D_0 to D_1). This is associated with the increase in demand for available substitutes, in this case more fuel-efficient cars. This is shown by the increase in demand from D'_0 to D'_1 for fuel-efficient cars in Figure 2.1.26 diagram I.

Now, I know what you're thinking. Didn't I – in both diagrams I and II – just break the rule of 'not shifting supply due to a shift in demand'?!

No – because there's more to the above story. You see, automobile manufacturers are presently preparing for the current surge in demand by taking factors of production no longer needed in Gas-guzzlers and putting them to work in the Econo-car production plants. Resources are being ***reallocated*** to the production of fuel efficient cars in order to increase output during the ongoing 'switch-over period'. This is shown in diagram I by the decrease in supply of Gas-guzzlers (S_0 to S_1) resulting in a further decrease in the quantity of SUVs purchased on the market (Q_2) and an equilibrium price of P_2. In diagram II, the increase in supply from S'_0 to S'_1 for Econo-cars is the result of resources being reallocated to small fuel efficient cars. I have shown – rather speculatively, it should be noted – how the equilibrium price for Gas-guzzlers goes down since the decrease in demand for them outstrips (= exceeds) the decrease in supply and results in a lower price.[31] Equally speculatively, the price of Econo-cars increases since the increase in demand outstrips the increase in supply.

---

28. 'Don't have any!'

29. This is the title of an absolutely incredible song by Janis Joplin.

30. For reasons unknown to me, my students at some point always want to know what type of car I drive and invariably expect the answer to be either a Mercedes-Benz or a BMW. I assume it's because I wear a suit and tie but they'll probably give 'machismo' as their answer. There might be something in it. In sensible Sweden I drove very sensible cars – VW Polos and Toyota Corollas. Here in Mexico I went for speed, power and mass. Anything to intimidate, escape from and/or turn into purée the robo-cops (play on words; 'robo' is 'robbery' in Spanish) and wild dogs – both of which clutter up the highways when I'm enjoying complement goods. Life expectancy: T *plus* 2 years and counting.

31. Several of my students have gleefully pointed out that the Mexican police are in the process of changing all their old cars for new Chargers – which in fact might *increase* the price of this particular model. Our ~~bribe~~…em, *tax* money in action.

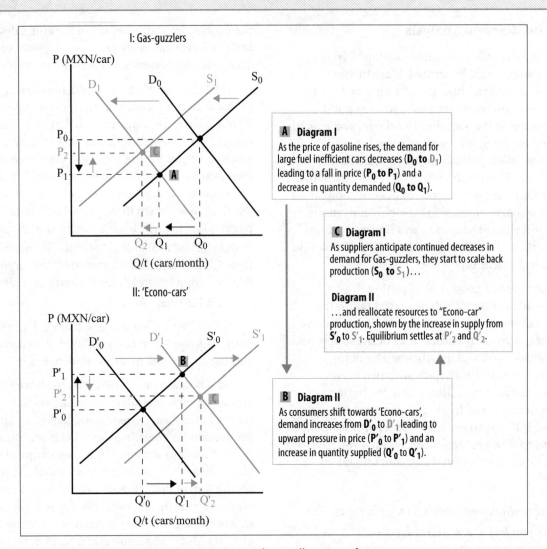

Figure 2.1.26 *Car market: reallocation of resources*

- In economic shorthand:
  $\uparrow P_{gas} \rightarrow \downarrow D_{SUVs} > \downarrow S_{SUVS} \rightarrow \downarrow P_{SUVs}$
  - $\uparrow D_{econo\text{-}cars} > \uparrow S_{econo\text{-}cars} \rightarrow \uparrow P_{econo\text{-}cars}$

Basically what oil and gasoline prices are doing are reallocating resources via the laws of supply and demand. There is an enormous incentive for car makers to *divert resources* from high fuel-consuming cars to more efficient cars. This is an example of the process of reallocation.

Putting the pieces together: Wage negotiations (part 2)

I now return to the story of my wage negotiations and the (thus far) happy ending. Sitting there with my prospective boss, discussing the terms of my possible employment, I had drawn what I considered to be a supply curve which represented the 'uniqueness' on the market for IB teachers in Skåne (Swedish geographical region), S in Figure 2.1.27. I claimed that being bilingual, experienced, accredited in many subjects, etc. made me uniquely qualified for the post of economics teacher to the extent that there were no real alternatives. I then proceeded to itemize what I had taken care to investigate prior to wage discussions: how the demand for an IB education was increasing due to a number of factors, three in particular.

Number one, the increasing openness of the European Union was giving incredible opportunities to young people to study abroad, which increased the need for language and a competitive edge in getting into university. It became increasingly obvious that an IB education would be an invaluable asset for young people wanting to see other pastures.

This was accentuated, number two, by a change in Swedish legislation allowing far easier switching and choice of school. This created a great increase in demand for alternatives to the traditional municipal school, the IB being one of these substitutes.

And finally, though this is not going to endear me to some of my Swedish colleagues, the increase in demand was a direct response to pressures on the quality of Swedish upper secondary education –parents have been empowered via school vouchers to vote with their feet and are staying away in droves from a good many municipal schools. Taken as a whole, demand for an IB education was – and is – increasing. I put this proposition forward, drew the figure here (see Figure 2.1.27), shifted demand from D_0 to D_1, leaned back and waited for the reaction.

The basic situation shown in Figure 2.1.27 is one where the market for IB economics teachers is in disequilibrium, or using alternative economic terminology, where the market has not cleared. Now, let's assume that my boss had told me to take a short step off a high cliff, i.e. refused any negotiating of salary above the level set by the teacher union and the municipal council – P_0. Economic theory, not to mention simple common sense, says that the excess in demand would have forced the market price upwards. At a price of P_0, the quantity demanded is far in excess of the quantity supplied, shown by the distance from point **A** to point **B**.

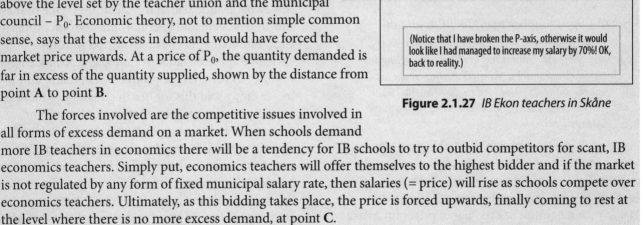

(Notice that I have broken the P-axis, otherwise it would look like I had managed to increase my salary by 70%! OK, back to reality.)

Figure 2.1.27 *IB Ekon teachers in Skåne*

The forces involved are the competitive issues involved in all forms of excess demand on a market. When schools demand more IB teachers in economics there will be a tendency for IB schools to try to outbid competitors for scant, IB economics teachers. Simply put, economics teachers will offer themselves to the highest bidder and if the market is not regulated by any form of fixed municipal salary rate, then salaries (= price) will rise as schools compete over economics teachers. Ultimately, as this bidding takes place, the price is forced upwards, finally coming to rest at the level where there is no more excess demand, at point **C**.

So what happened? Well, I was able to increase both the quantity and the quality of my cigars, watches and vacation experiences. Go figure. Yet one does wonder what would have happened if my then boss had refused to grant me an increase in salary, referring perhaps to general union agreements and municipal salary tariffs. The answer is that the school might have been without an economics teacher for an indeterminate period. I should point out that one can easily criticise my use of the supply and demand model! It is in fact highly unlikely that the supply curve would be completely vertical ('completely inelastic' in correct terminology) since there are many highly qualified teachers who might be willing to put themselves on the market at higher salary levels, i.e. there would be positive correlation between salary levels and the quantity of economics teachers offering their services. We would in reality have an upward sloping supply curve rather than a vertical.

S & D analysis number two: 'Tortillas and oil'

While many worry about filling their gas tanks, many others around the world are struggling to fill their stomachs. And it's getting more and more difficult every day. – World Bank President, Robert Zoellick, *The Guardian*, 30 April 2008)

It was applied economics in the making; we watched, week by week, how oil prices wreaked havoc (= chaos) on poor families in Mexico. No, not because of rising gasoline prices – gasoline is heavily subsidized in Mexico – but because of ever higher prices for maize and maize tortillas. World food prices – according to the International Monetary Fund (IMF) – rose by some

45% between the end of 2006 and April 2008. In Mexico, for the 50% of the country's 106 million citizens living on less than five US dollars a day, the staple (= basic, essential) food is the tortilla – a flat bread made of maize meal (corn flour). When the price of maize skyrocketed during 2007–08 the effect was to cause the price of tortillas to increase from around 7 Mexican pesos (MXN) to over MXN10.[32] I didn't notice the price increase – but I don't live on US$5 a day as millions of Mexicans do.[33] However, as shown in Figure 2.1.28, I did notice the thousands of protesters in Mexico City banging empty pots against the walls of government buildings.

Figure 2.1.28 *Protesters in Mexico City demonstrate over the rising price of food staples*

(Source: http://media.artdiamondblog.com)

So what caused the rise in the price of tortillas? A number of things – all related. The main cause was the surge in oil and gasoline prices which caused a somewhat frantic search for substitutes. One of these substitutes is ethanol (alcohol) made from, primarily, sugar and maize. US farmers started shifting agricultural land (standard example of reallocation of resources!) towards the production of maize and increasingly sold this for use in ethanol production. Hence, as maize meal for tortillas and maize for ethanol are in joint supply, an increase in demand for ethanol in the US served to decrease the available supply of maize for foodstuffs. How could this affect Mexico which supplies most of the maize for its domestic market? Three causes stand out: *competition laws*, higher *import prices* and *speculation* – but not necessarily in that order of occurrence or importance.

---

32. The exchange rate then was between MXN10.5 to MXN11 for USD1.

33. The official minimum wage in Mexico (at the current exchange rate of USD1 = MXN13.5) is just over USD4. It rather makes sense why my Mexican ex-lady friend refused to get in the car with me if I was wearing one of my watches. Basically, my Rolex GMT Master II represents about 6 years minimum wage and she didn't want to be a collateral victim of highway robbers due to my nonchalant habit of letting my left arm hang out the car window during traffic. Affectionate parents who invite me to parties inevitably send a car and driver for me since I refuse to wear a cheapo watch. Maybe they figure I need both hands to do term reports.

Let me do a brief point-by-point explanation:

1. Mexico has allowed imports of maize since 1994[34] but has *limited* these imports to protect domestic farmers from the very efficient and heavily subsidised American farms. However, 80% of imported maize in Mexico comes from the US. As fuel prices in the US soared and ethanol demand subsequently increased (recall that an increase in the price of a good will increase demand for substitutes) more and more US maize was diverted towards ethanol, creating a surge in maize prices.

2. This decreased the US supply of maize for exports and increased the price of imported maize to Mexico.

3. The main maize suppliers for tortillas in Mexico are, somewhat notoriously, operating in an oligopoly market. There is ample evidence that domestic Mexican suppliers withheld maize in speculative anticipation of higher future prices.

The causal flows (oil → maize → tortillas) are illustrated in Figure 2.1.29 on page 90.

- Demand for oil increased (diagram I) during 2006 – 2008 due to increasing demand from oil hungry countries – primarily India and China – and speculation of higher prices. While suppliers attempted to increase production of oil, demand far outstripped supply. This caused gasoline prices to double in the US during the time period and consequently caused a search for substitutes – primarily ethanol.

- This in turn caused an increase in demand for maize to produce ethanol. It also caused maize growers to step up maize production to meet ethanol demand. This is illustrated in diagram II by the increase in demand from D'_0 to D'_1 and the increase in supply from S'_0 to S'_1. Since more US maize was now going to the production of ethanol, the available supply of maize for the Mexican market decreased and Mexican import prices for maize shot up.

- This resulted in higher production costs for Mexican tortilla producers, shown by decrease in supply (S^*_0 to S^*_1) in diagram III. When maize producers in Mexico acted upon *expectations* of higher world market prices for maize, they started to hoard supplies, e.g. they held off on releasing enough maize to meet current demand in speculation of higher future prices.

- This further increased production costs for tortilla producers, decreasing supply (S^*_1 to S^*_2) and drove up the price of tortillas by some 200% during the first months of 2007.[35]

In economic shorthand:

$\uparrow P_{oil} \rightarrow \uparrow D_{ethanol\ US} \rightarrow \uparrow D_{maize\ US} > \uparrow S_{maize\ US} \rightarrow \downarrow S_{export\ maize\ US} \rightarrow \downarrow S_{import\ maize\ Mex} \rightarrow \uparrow P_{import\ maize\ Mex}$ + speculative hoarding of maize in Mexico $\rightarrow \downarrow S_{maize\ Mex} \rightarrow \uparrow P_{maize\ Mex} \rightarrow \downarrow S_{tortillas} \rightarrow \uparrow P_{tortillas}$

Here it was my intention to continue with the secondary and tertiary effects on the markets for solar power, silicon and computers. But I'm tired, so I shall instead turn to the trusted method of didactic (= educational) laziness etched in stone tablets by countless generations of teachers since the days of ivy-covered castles all around, hi-ho. Yes, you guessed it: I will pose questions.

---

34. When the North American Free Trade Agreement came into effect.

35. See http://www.nytimes.com/2007/01/19/world/americas/19tortillas.html, http://www.reuters.com/article/GCA-Agflation/idUSN1451427920080514 and http://news.bbc.co.uk/2/hi/americas/7432164.stm.

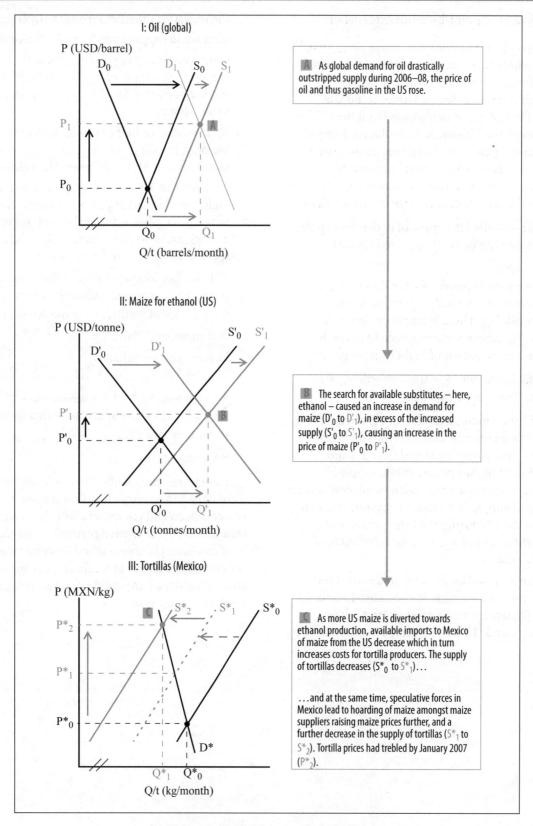

I: Oil (global)

A As global demand for oil drastically outstripped supply during 2006–08, the price of oil and thus gasoline in the US rose.

II: Maize for ethanol (US)

B The search for available substitutes – here, ethanol – caused an increase in demand for maize (D'_0 to D'_1), in excess of the increased supply (S'_0 to S'_1), causing an increase in the price of maize (P'_0 to P'_1).

III: Tortillas (Mexico)

C As more US maize is diverted towards ethanol production, available imports to Mexico of maize from the US decrease which in turn increases costs for tortilla producers. The supply of tortillas decreases (S^*_0 to S^*_1)...

...and at the same time, speculative forces in Mexico lead to hoarding of maize amongst maize suppliers raising maize prices further, and a further decrease in the supply of tortillas (S^*_1 to S^*_2). Tortilla prices had trebled by January 2007 (P^*_2).

Figure 2.1.29 *Oil, maize and tortillas*

POP QUIZ 2.1.7 SUPPLY AND DEMAND

Refer to Figure 2.1.29 "Oil, maize and tortillas" on page 90 to answer Questions 1 to 3.

1 How might the price of oil have affected the price of solar panels in the US?

2 How might the price of oil have affected the price of silicon? (This is a continuation of Question **1**. Hint: look up 'photovoltaic cells' and 'silicates'.)

3 How might the price of oil have affected the supply of computers? (This is a continuation of Question **2** above. Did you look things up?)

4 'In some countries the price of houses rises while the demand for houses rises.' Using supply and demand analysis, explain why this statement does not contradict the law of demand.

5 Briefly state what is meant by the 'productivity of a factor'. For what reasons might the productivity of agricultural land change over time?

6 Using supply and demand diagrams, explain how the price of seasonal goods would be prone to fluctuate during a year.

7 You believe that property prices will soon plummet (= fall drastically). Being a property speculator, you act on this belief. Illustrate the possible outcome of this situation using supply and demand curves. Assume that other speculators will follow your lead.

Price controls ©IBO 2003

Throughout the market iteration thus far, we have operated under the assumption of competitive markets, i.e. markets where only the forces of supply and demand set equilibrium price and quantity. In reality things are far more complex, as there are a number of elements which can offset and negate (= work against) freely operating market forces. Market intervention via controlling prices will have the effect of non-clearing markets with either an excess of supply or an excess demand as a result. Governments can set *maximum* and *minimum prices*, while *buffer stock schemes* and *commodity agreements* are the result of government agreements or co-operative arrangements between suppliers (firms). We now look at each of these in turn.

Maximum price: causes and consequences ©IBO 2003

A maximum price – also known as a ceiling price – is when the price is set under the market clearing price level. This is a mechanism imposed by government primarily in order to increase availability – perhaps hereby increasing equality in society by permitting more people to afford the good. Notable examples have been war-time centralised prices, extreme measures in times of high inflation and when prices are set centrally in planned economies. In all cases there are two major side-effects. The first effect is an **excess of demand** which in turn will create *queues* and second-hand selling, i.e. *parallel markets*.

Let us assume that a government wishes to set a limit on the rents of inner-city housing – something my home country, Sweden, does in the case of apartments in Stockholm.[36] The free market supply and demand result in the price P_{mkt} and the quantity Q_{mkt} in Figure 2.1.30 on page 92 (SEK in the figures means 'Swedish crowns'.) As quantity demanded is in excess of quantity supplied at P_{max}, there will be a good portion of pent-up demand amongst consumers. If no limit is set on the amount of housing one can rent, there is an incentive to rent more apartments than one can use in order to rent out the rest on a parallel (black) market. The black market price – called sub-letting rent – would be at a price of up to $P_{B.M.}$ since this is what consumers would be willing to pay for the quantity of Q_S according to the demand curve. The grey quadrant between the minimum reselling price (the official maximum price of P_{max}) and the black market price ($P_{B.M.}$) is the possible *black market*. Note that the black-market price of $P_{B.M.}$ is based on the assumption that *all* of Q_S housing hits the parallel market!

> Maximum price: A maximum price – also ceiling price – is a price set down in law that the price may not be set above a certain level. Such intervention often leads to shortages and black markets.

The consequences of imposing maximum prices are the queues and resulting black markets. This is something that the government will have to deal with and the most common form of solution has been to limit the quantity per person by either a rationing

---

36. The queue system works something like this: After giving birth, the happy mother takes the infant down to the official registrar for apartments and puts the toddler in the queue. Twenty to twenty-five years later, the young man/lady might get an apartment. I've had numerous 18-year-old students who had been in the queue all their lives. Very patient people, the Swedes. Maybe that's why they drive Volvos.

system, or a queuing system. Rationing is achieved by setting a limit to purchases and such instruments as coupons for coffee and meat, while a queue system is basically done by instituting a 'first come – first served' system often found on markets for rent-controlled inner-city apartments.

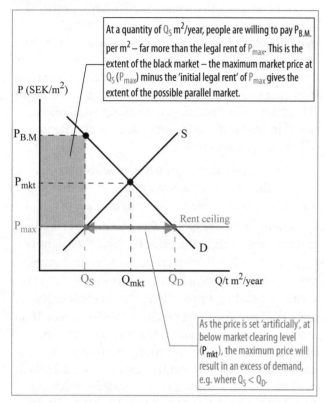

At a quantity of Q_S m²/year, people are willing to pay $P_{B.M.}$ per m² – far more than the legal rent of P_{max}. This is the extent of the black market – the maximum market price at Q_S (P_{max}) minus the 'initial legal rent' of P_{max} gives the extent of the possible parallel market.

As the price is set 'artificially', at below market clearing level (P_{mkt}), the maximum price will result in an excess of demand, e.g. where $Q_S < Q_D$.

Figure 2.1.30 *Maximum price on inner city rents, Stockholm*

Questions

Refer to Figure 2.1.30.

1. What would happen to the market clearing price (P_{mkt}) if the maximum price were to be set *above* P_{mkt}?

2. Fill in the blanks.
    Assume that government implements a maximum price on meat. One can expect that those with the _____ opportunity costs of standing in line will try to buy as _____ as possible and then to sell what they don't need to others – who will probably have _____ opportunity costs of standing in line and thus be prepared to pay _____ than the original buyer.

3. Explain, using a suitable diagram, what would happen if the government removed an existing maximum price.

Additional possible government responses in maximum prices[37]

There is also the possibility of using market forces to move back to equilibrium. Let us look at two general possibilities – shifting supply or demand for inner-city Stockholm housing where a maximum price has been set. In diagrams I and II of Figure 2.1.31, the maximum price creates an *excess demand* of $Q_S \Leftrightarrow Q_d$, shown by the double-ended arrow.

The government could *subsidise* cheap inner-city housing by offering low cost loans to building companies or by offering incentives for city councils to increase the amount of apartments. This would shift the supply curve from S_0 to $S_{+subsidy}$ in Figure 2.1.31

diagram I), which would do away with the shortage of housing – and the black market.

Alternatively, government could offer any number of *incentives* for people to forego inner-city living by enhancing the alternative (= outer city areas), which would lower demand for city housing. For example, increased/improved transportation to outer city areas, tax benefits for those who commute, or even by increasing certain inner-city specific taxes – say parking fees and traffic fees – which are all ways for government to change citizens' living preferences. This is illustrated in diagram II), where the decrease in demand (D_0 to D_1) lowers the black-market price to the official maximum price, thereby obliterating the excess demand for inner-city housing.

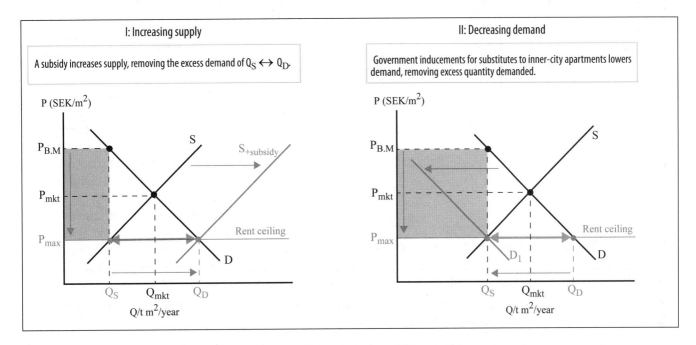

Figure 2.1.31 *Possible solutions to the housing shortage*

---

37. In 301 AD, the Roman emperor Diocletian instituted price controls to curb rampant inflation. The penalty for selling at a price above minimum price was death. This somewhat extreme measure didn't stop either an excess demand due to sellers hoarding their goods nor a parallel market.

Putting the pieces together: Born again in the USA

No, the title is not a reference to the Republican vice-presidential candidate in USA 2008, but to one of Bruce Springsteen's most famous songs.

Bruce Springsteen released a new album in 2002, the first with his original E-Street Band since 1987. Basically, his latest album was in commemoration of the 11 September attacks in New York in 2001 and came out on the anniversary. The hype was of such magnitude that Springsteen's 2003 tour was virtually sold out in a matter of hours. In Göteborg Sweden (on 4 November 2002), all 50,000 tickets for the concert on the 21 June 2003 were sold within 40 minutes and the queues snaked around the entire city block! This was quickly resolved by organising another Springsteen concert for the 22 June.

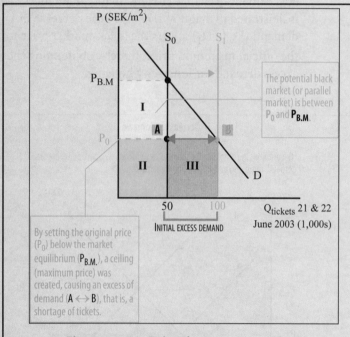

The potential black market (or parallel market) is between P_0 and $P_{B.M.}$

By setting the original price (P_0) below the market equilibrium ($P_{B.M.}$), a ceiling (maximum price) was created, causing an excess of demand ($A \leftrightarrow B$), that is, a shortage of tickets.

Figure 2.1.32 *Tickets for Springsteen concert*

This was, of course, not entirely due to Springsteen's undying devotion to his fans. Two reasons were put forward by the organisers. The first was that one wished to avoid the chaos of scalpers (= black-market ticket sellers) and black market tickets by trying to accommodate demand. Secondly, more tickets simply meant more revenue! 'Bums on seats' and all that. This scenario is shown in Figure 2.1.32.

The initial supply curve is S_0 and is perfectly vertical (= supply is completely price inelastic in correct economic jargon) at 50,000 seats. At the set price, there would be a possible black market created by the excess demand ($A \leftrightarrow B$) and the high demand is an incentive for reselling tickets on the 'second-hand' market. This is shown by the shaded area I, which is given by the intersection of the original supply curve and the demand curve. One can say that anyone fortunate to get hold of a (first hand) ticket would be able to resell it at the black market price of $P_{B.M.}$. (Note that this is the possible black market price and not necessarily an equilibrium price. Anyone reselling a ticket would need good luck or some degree of searching in order to get this price.)

By holding an additional concert, the organisers increased the supply of tickets from S_0 to S_1. This resulted in a new market equilibrium price of P_0, destroying the potential black market. One can also see how the total revenue (price times quantity) increases from area II to area II + III. One might say that this move swept the market out from under the ticket scalpers' feet.

Minimum price: causes and consequences

©IBO 2003 Another example of government intervention on markets is the establishing of minimum prices. While this has sometimes been applied generally to all goods in an economy, it is far more common for specific markets to be targeted, perhaps the most obvious being agricultural goods and labour markets. A minimum price sets a 'floor' under which the market price is not allowed to go. The intention of minimum price is to protect and aid certain suppliers. A minimum price on agricultural goods will guarantee farmers what government considers an acceptable income, while minimum prices on labour, i.e. minimum wage, would benefit those supplying their labour. In setting the minimum price on a good, the government is attempting to benefit society – an outcome that is often not the case.

> Minimum price: A minimum price – also floor price – is a price set down in law that the price may not be set below a certain level. Often governments must guarantee the price by purchasing the excess supply.

Minimum (floor) price on an agricultural good

Government intervention on agricultural markets is often motivated by wanting to preserve a landscape or a traditional way of life by aiding farmers in keeping an equitable (= fair) standard of living, e.g. similar to that in other sectors in society. By setting minimum prices on agricultural goods, governments can even-out income differentials (= differences) by guaranteeing that farmers will receive a certain price for their goods. In doing this, the government puts the market function out of order – in essence by guaranteeing that farmers will get a minimum price for their goods.

Figure 2.1.33 shows the effects of a minimum price on grain in the European Union. Setting a minimum price at P_{min} decreases the quantity demand from Q_{mkt} to Q_D but has the effect of increasing the quantity supplied, from Q_{mkt} to Q_S. The outcome is an *excess of supply*, or surplus, of grain. For the minimum price scheme to function, this excess grain cannot be allowed on the market as this would serve to lower the price and the system would break down. Therefore any minimum price scheme must be accompanied by a method of dealing with the excess supply – a *price support scheme* (or government repurchasing scheme).

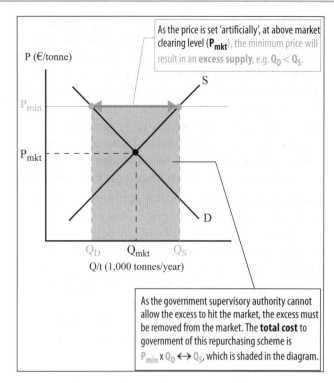

As the price is set 'artificially', at above market clearing level (**P_{mkt}**), the minimum price will result in an **excess supply**, e.g. $Q_D < Q_S$.

As the government supervisory authority cannot allow the excess to hit the market, the excess must be removed from the market. The **total cost** to government of this repurchasing scheme is $P_{min} \times Q_D \leftrightarrow Q_S$, which is shaded in the diagram.

Figure 2.1.33 *Minimum price on grain*

Questions

Refer to Figure 2.1.33.

1. What if the government sold the entire excess to another country at P_{mkt}? What would the total cost to government be?

2. What would the effects of removing the minimum price be on consumers, producers and government?

3. What other methods could be used by government to keep the price above market equilibrium price?

4. 'Consumers pay twice for minimum price schemes!' Explain what this statement refers to.

A price support scheme simply means that the government agrees to purchase the excess at the agreed minimum price. In Figure 2.1.33, the total excess amount of grain is $Q_1 \Leftrightarrow Q_2$, which the government would have to buy at a price of P_{min}. Total government expenditure is thus the grey square. One should mention that other costs linked to the minimum price scheme will arise, such as administrative costs, storage costs, and transportation costs – an estimated 60% of the total cost of the European Union's (EU) Common Agricultural Policy (CAP) paid by taxpayers went to storage and administrative costs.[38] Anyhow, the government portrayed in our example now has a few hundred thousand tonnes of grain to deal with. Now what?

---

38. *The Wall Street Journal*, 'A rotten harvest', by Richard Howarth, 29 June 2000.

Often agricultural surpluses have simply been stored in warehouses, resulting in 'grain heaps', 'beef mountains' and 'wine lakes' which nobody seems quite sure what to do with. In many cases the surplus has been burnt, sold on other markets (see 'dumping'), or even sold back to farmers at a fraction of the minimum price – which was then often used as cattle feed to produce more butter and beef … I have to be careful here. My students tell me I have a tendency to get very loud and froth at the mouth when I get to government involvement in agricultural output.[39] Suffice it to say that many of the minimum price schemes used in agricultural policies have historically been very wasteful, since suppliers have often produced too much, consumers have paid unnecessarily high prices and developing countries have seen their markets disrupted by excess produce dumped on their countries. We will return to the highly inflammatory debate on agricultural policies in Sections 4.2, 4.3 and 5.3.

Minimum price on labour – minimum wage

Many countries' governments impose a **minimum wage** via legislation, while many other countries have a de facto (= actual) minimum wage through the influence of strong unions and centralised wage agreements with employer organisations. The reasoning behind minimum wages is that weaker members of society (e.g. workforce) need support such as unskilled labourers, young people entering the labour market, people with little job experience, minority groups, etc. There is also, once again, an element of attempting to even-out income differentials in society. Whatever the case, the market for labour is similar to the market for goods and services, which can be seen in Figure 2.1.34, and shows the effects of a minimum wage.

The supply of labour (S_L) shows the propensity of the labour force to accept jobs at given wage rates, while the demand for labour (D_L) shows the willingness of firms to hire at given wage rates. Equilibrium wage on a perfectly free market would be P_{L_0} and the amount of people employed would be Q_{L_0}. A minimum wage above the market equilibrium means that more people offer themselves on the labour market, shown by the increase from Q_{L_0} to Q_{L_S}. At the set minimum wage of $P_{L_{min}}$, firms' demand for labour decreases from Q_{L_0} to Q_{L_D}. This strongly resembles the

outcome in the previous example; there is a *surplus of labour*, otherwise known as an increase in **unemployment**, shown in the diagram as the distance from Q_{L_D} to Q_{L_S}.

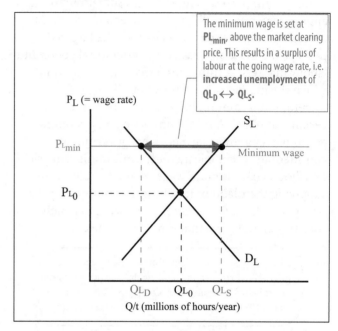

The minimum wage is set at PL_{min}, above the market clearing price. This results in a surplus of labour at the going wage rate, i.e. **increased unemployment** of $QL_D \leftrightarrow QL_S$.

Figure 2.1.34 *Minimum wage*

Questions

Refer to Figure 2.1.34.

1. What would happen to the wage rate if the demand for labour increased so that the demand curve intersected the supply curve somewhere below $P_{L_{min}}$?

2. Same scenario as in question **1**: what would happen to the level of unemployment?

3. What would happen on the labour market if the minimum wage rate were lowered?

4. What would happen on the labour market if demand for goods and services in the economy increased? (Hint: 'derived demand'.)

The effects of minimum wages are the subject of a very hot political debate. Defendants of minimum wages argue that many labourers would otherwise be powerless on the labour market since firms could set wages at close to existence minimum for weak labour groups. Opponents argue that minimum wages add to unemployment and lead to inefficient labour markets, resulting in sub-optimal resource allocation. We will look into this in greater depth in Section 3.5.

---

39. Just this week my IB2's banned me from using any type of energy drink during school hours – and received strong support from colleagues in adjacent rooms. I fear coffee and sugar are next. That leaves only my tequila shelf. Oh well.

The basic order of progression in analysing the effects of a minimum price is the following (refer to Figure 2.1.33 on page 95):

1 Initial outcome: excess supply ($\mathbf{Q_D} \Leftrightarrow \mathbf{Q_S}$).

2 Initial possible government response: repurchasing scheme to get rid of excess supply.

3 Winners and losers I: higher prices for consumers but increased revenue for suppliers. The cost of the repurchasing and storage all come from taxpayer monies.

4 Secondary possible government responses: the excess must be dealt with, e.g. via storage, destruction or dumping.

5 Long-run scenarios (winners and losers II): the government earns revenue which can recover some of the costs of repurchasing and storage. The excess is dumped on a developing country which cannot compete with the dumping price. This destroys livelihoods in the developing country.

POP QUIZ 2.1.8   MAXIMUM AND MINIMUM PRICES

1 Using diagrams, explain what happens to resource allocation when a minimum or maximum price is put on a good.

2 Explain why a government cannot put a maximum price on a good without other measures. Illustrate your answer with an appropriate diagram.

3 In the same diagram as in Question **2**, show total government costs of the minimum price scheme.

4 A government institutes a minimum price scheme for agricultural goods. What are the likely effects on farmers' incomes? Use a diagram and show total income for farmers.

Price support/buffer stock schemes

©IBO 2003

The concept of a price support mechanism, or scheme, was illustrated above in the example of minimum prices on agricultural goods. A minimum price leads to a surplus of goods which has to be removed from the market in order to keep the minimum price level. By buying the surplus, market supply is lowered and the price is kept above market equilibrium.

Another form of market intervention is to use the market forces more directly, by regulating the supply of the good. (It would do you well to recall that supply is defined as the amount allowed on the market by suppliers rather than the amount in existence.) By regulating the supply, one can adjust the market price in the long run. This is an example of a price support scheme which aims at keeping prices stable over time, and is referred to as a buffer stock scheme – buffer meaning 'safeguard' or 'just in case'. Buffer stocks can be managed by governments and by co-operative agreement between suppliers. The buffering mechanism is characterised by three main points:

1. The good has to be storable since it runs the risk of being stored for an indeterminate period.

2. The good is often a commodity, i.e. a primary good such as rubber, sugar, coffee and grain.

3. There are considerable price fluctuations on the market.

The purpose of a buffer stock scheme is to stabilise and uphold a certain price. The mechanism is simple enough: when there is a tendency for the price of the commodity to fall, an amount of the good is taken off the market, decreasing supply and also acting as a buffer in case of an upward tendency in price – which is met by releasing an amount of the good from stocks. Figure 2.1.35 on page 98 illustrates a buffer stock scheme on the market for wheat.

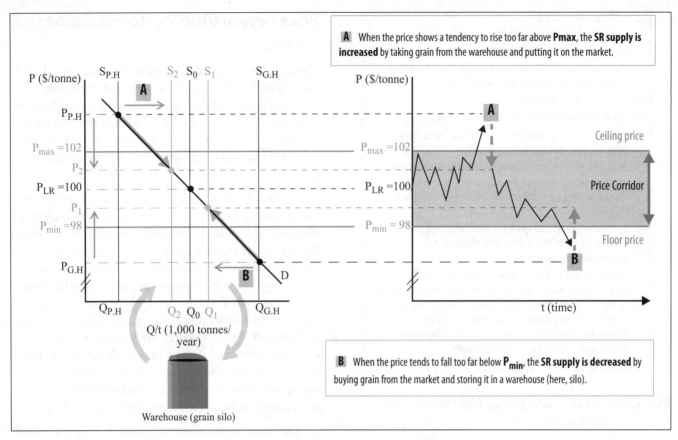

A When the price shows a tendency to rise too far above **Pmax**, the **SR supply is increased** by taking grain from the warehouse and putting it on the market.

B When the price tends to fall too far below **P$_{min}$**, the **SR supply is decreased** by buying grain from the market and storing it in a warehouse (here, silo).

Warehouse (grain silo)

Figure 2.1.35 *Buffer stock scheme for wheat*

Prices of many commodities tend to fluctuate a great deal, often due to the stark element of seasonality involved in their production. A buffer stock scheme is an attempt to reduce the price fluctuations. Assume a long-run target price of $100 and that the scheme allows price fluctuations of +/- 2%.

- **Above the ceiling**: If market prices show tendencies to rise above $102 (point A) due to a poor harvest ($S_{P.H.}$ = poor harvest), grain is taken from the warehouse (grain silo) and put on the market, increasing the short-run (SR) supply from $S_{P.H.}$ to S_2, thereby increasing the quantity on the market from $Q_{P.H.}$ to Q_2. This lowers the market prices to P_2 – within the established ceiling price, P_{max}, aimed at by the scheme.

- **Below the floor**: The reverse takes place when there is pressure on the market price to fall below the floor of the price-corridor (point **B**) due to a good harvest ($S_{G.H.}$ = good harvest). Grain is removed (e.g. bought) from the market and warehoused, whereby supply decreases from $S_{G.H.}$ to S_1 and P_1 is attained at a level above the floor price. My reason for illustrating the LR price as a 'corridor' is simply to impress upon you that it is virtually impossible to

keep market prices absolutely constant over any length of time.

There is an addendum worthy of comment in regard to buffer stocks. Many countries keep strategic reserves of certain goods, which would be used in emergencies such as trade embargos, severe supply disturbances and all-out war. The USA is a notable example here, in the context of the 570 million barrel Strategic Petroleum Reserve (SPR) kept in underground oil tanks. In September of 2000, the US government released 30 million barrels of oil to force petrol prices down. This was the first use of the SPR since the Gulf war in 1990[40]. The attempt to force the oil price down was due to fears that the recessionary pressure at the time would be further exacerbated by high oil prices, which would increase the cost of living and lower overall demand in the American economy.

Just as in minimum price schemes and intervention purchasing, there are numerous costs associated with keeping the system in place, e.g. administration, storage and the money needed to buy excess supply and remove it from the market. It is clear that buffer stocks have had limited success in later years. During the 1980s and 1990s, many buffer stocks simply collapsed.

---

40. Reuters 25/09/2000, via ITN.

Commodity agreements ©IBO 2003

There are a number of international commodity agreements (ICAs) in place. An ICA is an agreement amongst producers serving to create price stability and often to keep prices from falling as they historically have been prone to do since the 1960s. ICAs are administrative and co-operative entities which are able to use buffer stocks to influence world prices. There is often a large portion of government involvement in the agreement, and many of the goods are highly regulated in terms of ownership, pricing policies and access to markets. ICOs are under the overseeing of the United Nations Conference for Trade and Development, UNCTAD.

There are ICAs for rubber, cocoa, coffee, tin, zinc and lead, cotton, sugar, tropical timber, jute, olive oil, grains, and ... wait for it ... the moment you've all been waiting for – OIL. The Organisation of Petroleum Exporting Countries – better known as OPEC – is by far the most well known of all the ICAs and has had a major influence on the global economy since the early 1970s.

The International Coffee Organisation

Let us briefly touch one of the world's most traded commodities, *coffee*, which is grown in over 60 countries, ranging from South America to South East Asia. The International Coffee Organisation (ICO) came into being in 1963 with the help of the United Nations. Coffee sales total over USD70 billion per year whereof 97% of it is under the umbrella of the ICO. The organisation works closely with governments to co-ordinates policies and output plans but also in research and marketing.

The ICO has a strong export developing leaning, focused on improving the terms of trade for many of the countries which are highly dependent on exporting coffee – comprising upwards of 75% of export earnings in some cases. One of the main aims of the ICO is to halt the falling price of coffee on the international market and to stabilise the price over periods of time using buffer stocks. This has met with limited success. In fact, the commodity agreement for coffee collapsed in 1985 and coffee prices have fallen to the lowest levels in the past 30 years – or the past 100 years in real prices, leading to a joint World Bank/ICO address in April 2003 of the 'coffee crisis'.[41] The endeavour of the ICO is ostensibly (= seemingly) a development issue at heart.[42] The aim is to maintain a price level which will allow coffee growers to live on their income.

However, there are some criticisms of commodity agreements. Many economists will question whether large-scale intervention actually creates price stability, claiming instead that open and transparent bidding on commodities would better harmonise market clearing. It has also been questioned whether gains from elevated prices actually benefit the farmers at the bottom of the chain. Oxfam, a non-government organisation (NGO), puts it quite succinctly:

Many developing nations depend on coffee as their chief export, and their entire economies are collapsing with the market. In Ethiopia, the government has lost twice as much revenue to the coffee market as it has received through debt relief. The repercussions of this crisis will last for decades, holding back efforts around the world to help developing countries move out of poverty.[43]

POP QUIZ 2.1.9   PRICE SUPPORT/BUFFER STOCK SCHEMES

1   Show in a S/D figure how government purchasing of goods to stockpile (= store, for example in the case of war or disaster) would affect the market price.

2   What are the costs involved in instituting price-support schemes?

---

41. See http://web.worldbank.org/WBSITE/EXTERNAL/NEWS.
42. See http://www.ico.org.
43. See http://www.oxfamamerica.org/campaigncoffee.

Preparing for exams

Short answer questions (10 marks each)

1 What actions could a government take in order to keep the price above market equilibrium?

2 A government attempts to alleviate a lack of housing by putting a ceiling on rents. Use a diagram to explain the possible outcome of this action.

3 How might governments use buffer stocks to stabilise prices?

4 Use a supply and demand diagram to help explain how a city council might decrease traffic congestion in the city during weekends.

5 Show the possible outcome of setting a minimum wage for under-eighteens.

6 Why would the weekly price of rental scooters in a holiday resort vary over the course of a year?

7 Explain the factors which would affect the price of a good.

8 Explain 'consumer sovereignty' and why it might not be that extensive in real life.

9 A major sporting event sets the price of tickets such that a great number of people are not able to get hold of tickets. What might the outcome of this be? Use a diagram to support your answer.

10 Government raises the taxes on car ownership. Explain possible market outcomes of such a decision.

Extended response questions (25 marks each)

1 a What do economists mean by 'markets'? (10 marks)

  b Are markets the best way of solving the basic economic problem? Justify your answer. (15 marks)

2 a How would the price mechanism decide resource allocation in a competitive (free) market? (10 marks)

  b Examine how the above would apply to non-renewable resources such as oil. (15 marks)

[HL Only]

3 a Explain how a government might use buffer stocks to even-out price fluctuations. (10 marks)

  b What are the costs and difficulties of such an operation? (15 marks)

Elasticities

2.2

CONTENTS

ELASTICITIES ©IBO 2003

This section deals with the responsiveness in quantity supplied or demanded for goods due to changes in variables which influence them, such as price and income. Looking at these relationships allows us to decipher the choices and actions of the major players, firms, households and governments.

Price elasticity of demand (PED)

©IBO 2003

You have no doubt already reflected upon how different goods must have different patterns of demand, i.e. different demand curves. For example one's demand for, say, food should be different from that for wrist watches.[1] It can easily be portrayed diagrammatically.

Different patterns of demand

Let us look at a few different untitled demand curves in Figure 2.2.1 and see if you can set correct captions to them. Choose between drugs, DVD films and cars. Send me $5 for correct answers.[2]

It makes sense doesn't it? The demand curve will be very 'steep' for some goods – i.e. our quantity demanded will not decrease a great deal when the price of the good increases. (Note: using the term 'steep' in reference to a change in quantity demanded resulting from a change in price is faulty use of economic terminology. The correct term is *price elasticity of demand* as shall be seen.) Other goods will show a marked decrease in quantity demanded should the price rise; a rise in the price of DVDs will decrease quantity demanded quite considerably. At the same time, a massive increase in the price of my asthma medicine will probably have little effect on my quantity demanded. The common denominator is often the availability of goods which we could buy instead within a given period of time – *substitute goods*. The more available substitutes there are (and the closer they are) the easier it is to switch to another good. The increase in the price of DVDs leads to a larger relative (percentage) decrease in the quantity demanded. Conversely, a rise in the price of asthma medicine, which has few substitutes, would mean that quantity demanded would not fall significantly.

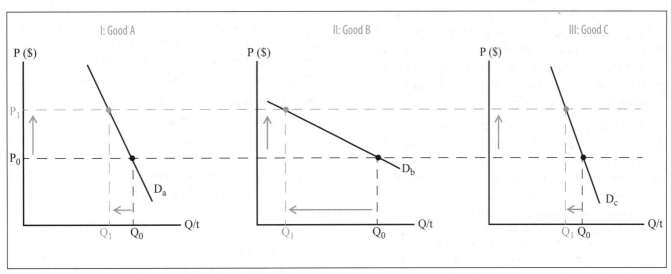

Figure 2.2.1 *Demand curves of different goods*

---

1. But again, people are *not* the same in their preferences! I remember living on oatmeal for six months as a poor student so I could by a USD2,000 Baume & Mercier watch. It bears repeating that the demand curve is the *aggregate* of individual demand.
2. No, you'd better not. The answers are: Figure a = cars, figure b = DVDs, figure c = drugs. Note that drugs can be pharmaceuticals as well as the ~~Mexic~~…that's, illegal variety.

Formula $\%\Delta Q_d / \%\Delta P$

The correct term for the measure of price sensitivity in the demand for goods is **price elasticity of demand** (PED). In short, we are looking at how responsive demand is to an increase or decrease in the price of a good, which can be put as: 'What is the *relative* change in quantity demanded due to a *relative* change in the price?'

Putting the quote above in formulaic language, we get:

$$\frac{\%\Delta \text{ in Qd}}{\%\Delta \text{ in price}}$$

Exam tip:
Referring to elasticities in exam answers

When either using elasticities or defining them, always include the basic formulaic expression – just to make sure. Your definition should include the term relative, e.g. 'the relative change in quantity demanded due to the relative change in price'. Also, remember 'Quantity rules!' or 'Quantity on top!' No matter which measure of elasticity you are using, quantity is always the numerator ('on top' in the formula).

Note the key word here, 'relative'. An increase in price of €5 simply does not mean the same thing when talking about a Jaguar car or a bag of crisps. Similarly, a decrease in quantity demanded of 500 units per week doesn't mean the same for Jags as for bags of crisps. We must put the change into relative terms by using *percentage* increase/decrease.

By dividing 'percentage change in quantity demanded with percentage change in price' we get a value of the price elasticity of demand. If the price of margarine **rises** by 10% and households respond by decreasing their quantity demanded by 20% we get:

Price elasticity of demand (PED): The price elasticity of demand is a measure of the responsiveness of the quantity demanded for a good with respect to a change in the price of the good. It is the relative change in quantity demanded (Q_d) due to a relative change in price (P). As the demand curve is downward sloping, PED will have a negative value. The formula is:

Price elasticity of demand (PED) =

$$\frac{\%\Delta \text{ in } Q_d}{\%\Delta \text{ P}}$$

Price elasticity of demand (PED)

$$= \frac{\%\Delta \text{ in Qd}}{\%\Delta \text{ in price}} \rightarrow \frac{-20\%}{+10\%} = -2$$

Note the *negative value*; any downward sloping curve will have a negative slope, which means that virtually all demand curves will have a negative value of price elasticity of demand. This is why economists seldom bother in actually saying 'price elasticity of demand is minus 2' but simply 'price elasticity of demand is two'.[3] However, do NOT confuse the values above with 'slope'. The value of –2 is just the value of price elasticity of demand along a given section of the demand curve (or, more commonly, at a given *point* on the demand curve), nothing else. Nor do price elasticity values have any sort of relativistic meaning, such as kilograms and centimetres might have. What I mean by this is that while two kilos is twice as heavy as one kilogram, a price elasticity of 2 is not 'twice as elastic' as a price elasticity of 1.

A little depth:
Percentage change

Using percentages as a measurement of an increase or decrease can be a bit confusing. If my income goes from £100 to £125 (+ £25) then I have increased my income by 25%. If my income falls from £125 to £100 (- £25) then my income has decreased by 20%. A percentage change is arrived at by dividing the change with the original value. In formula:

Increasing from 100 to 125

Percentage change in income (y) =

$$\frac{y_1 - y_0}{y_0} \times 100 \rightarrow \frac{125 - 100}{100} \times 100 = +25\%$$

Decreasing from 125 to 100

Percentage change in income (y) =

$$\frac{y_1 - y_0}{y_0} \times 100 \rightarrow \frac{100 - 125}{125} \times 100 = -20\%$$

In all formulae I will use, all variables using the lower '0', signify the starting value and '1' the next value. You have already seen this in supply and demand curves. In the formulae above, y_0 is the starting value: £100 pounds in the first case which increases to £125. In the second case, y_0 is 125 and y_1 is 100 as we have lowered income. As long as one is consistent in the use of the starting values in this formula it is impossible to go wrong.

---

3. The mathematically inclined will realise that we are simply referring to PED as an absolute value, i.e. |2|.

Warning!
Elasticities

Once again I should warn you. An all-too-often made mistake in using the concept of elasticity is to confuse the value of elasticity with the slope of the curve. Any straight-line curve will have a slope that is constant – while the value of PED along the same slope will vary.

I also strongly advise against the use of any alternative formula. There are a number of ways to rewrite the basic formula of 'percentage change in quantity over percentage change in price'. The exam halls are littered with the bodies of students who have tried to use these alternatives and monumentally failed.

Definition ©IBO 2003

Calculating price elasticities is no more complex than calculating a percentage increase in income; it is simply a matter of being stringent and consistent. Calculate the percentage change of quantity and divide this by the percentage change in price. Just remember to be consistent in your use of starting values.

Possible range of values ©IBO 2003

Let us use three different goods, imaginatively reusing the goods from Table 2.2.1 – cars, DVDs and pharmaceutical drugs. The original quantity demanded is 100 for each good and all three have an initial price of 10. (Using different currency units in order to be a bit realistic.) Now *we raise the price to 12*, an increase in price of 20%, causing the quantity demanded to fall by a certain amount for each good.

Here's a simple table of the outcomes in terms of quantity demanded when the price is raised from 10 to 12, and the calculated PED for each good.

Table 2.2.1 *Effect on demand and PED when price increases*

Good	$P_0 \rightarrow P_1$	P	%P	$Q_0 \rightarrow Q_1$	Q_d	%Q_d	PED
Cars	€10,000 → €12,000	+ €2,000	+20%	100 → 80	-20	-20%	- 1.0
DVDs	$10 → $12	+ $2	+20%	100,000 → 40,000	-60,000	-60%	-3
Drugs	£10 → £12	+ £2	+20%	100,000 → 90,000	-10,000	-10%	-0.5

The PED values at the far right were calculated by using the formula $\frac{\%Qd}{\%P}$.

Here is the PED calculation for cars:

$$\text{PED}_{cars} = \frac{\%\Delta \text{ in Qd}}{\%\Delta \text{ in price}} \rightarrow \frac{\frac{Q_1 - Q_0}{Q_0} \times 100}{\frac{P_1 - P_0}{P_0} \times 100} = \frac{\frac{80 - 100}{100} \times 100}{\frac{12 - 10}{10} \times 100} \rightarrow \frac{-20\%}{+20\%} = -1.0$$

In the example, the prices of all three goods were raised by the same *relative* amount, +20%. The percentage decrease in quantity demanded for each good was different: –20% for cars; –60% for DVDs and –10% for pharmaceutical drugs. The least price sensitive (*price inelastic*) good is drugs, where a 20% increase in price resulted in a modest 10% decrease in quantity demanded, e.g. PED = –0.5. The most price sensitive (*price elastic*) good is DVDs, where the same 20% increase in price led to a 60% fall in quantity demanded: PED = –3. Car sales fell by the same proportional amount (*unit elastic*) as the rise in price: PED = –1.[4] Please notice that throughout the discussion on elasticities the subject of *absolute* changes in price or quantity demanded is largely

---

4. In reality, the estimated PED for cars is closer to -2.

irrelevant – we are only interested in the *relative* changes.

> **Range of PED values**: A price elasticity of demand of less than 1 is called *inelastic* demand; PED that is equal to one is *unit elastic*; PED that is higher than 1 is *elastic*.
> (Note that I have dropped the minus sign, e.g. used absolute values. |x|)
>
> PED < |1|: inelastic
> PED = |1|: unit elastic
> PED > |1|: elastic

Diagrams illustrating the range of values of elasticity ©IBO 2003

Here's where it gets a bit hairy (= difficult) so look sharp. It is necessary to use a number of diagrams in order to explain the intricacies involved in price elasticity of demand and I will start by showing the PED values from the previous example in a diagram. Each of the goods in Figure 2.2.2 start at the same price and quantity for ease of comparison.

The three demand curves for cars, DVDs and pharmaceutical drugs all show how the exact same percentage increase in price (+20%) leads to entirely different outcomes in terms of percentage decrease in the quantity demanded. The PED values are: a) cars = 1; b) DVDs = 3; c) drugs = 0.5. Yet please read the next section carefully, as you must not think that any given demand curve has the same PED all along the curve, i.e. do not confuse the value of price elasticity of demand with the slope of a curve.

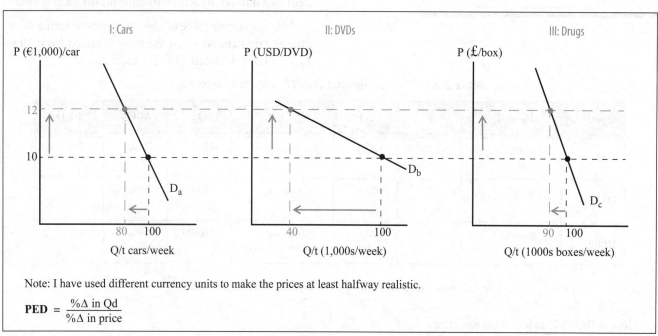

Note: I have used different currency units to make the prices at least halfway realistic.

$$PED = \frac{\%\Delta \text{ in Qd}}{\%\Delta \text{ in price}}$$

Figure 2.2.2 *PED for cars, DVDs and pharmaceuticals*

Varying elasticity along a straight-line D-curve ©IBO 2003

Remember how an economist always begins an answer? 'It depends …' or 'Assume that …' This is unfortunately true even in the case of calculating price elasticities. In moving along the curve and plotting out the points, one will get two different values, depending on whether the price falls or rises.

Computational problems with PED

In Figure 2.2.3 on page 107, the detail of the PED for DVDs is shown. In raising the price from $10 to $12, the quantity demanded fell from 100,000 to 40,000, giving a price elasticity of demand of 3. (Note that I have dropped the minus sign now.)

However, if the initial price is at $12 and it *falls* by $2 to $10, we get:

$$PED_{DVDs} = \frac{\%\Delta \text{ in Qd}}{\%\Delta \text{ in price}} \rightarrow \frac{\frac{Q_1 - Q_0}{Q_0} \times 100}{\frac{P_1 - P_0}{P_0} \times 100} = \frac{\frac{100 - 40}{40} \times 100}{\frac{10 - 12}{12} \times 100} \rightarrow \frac{+150\%}{-16.7\%} = \mathbf{8.98}$$

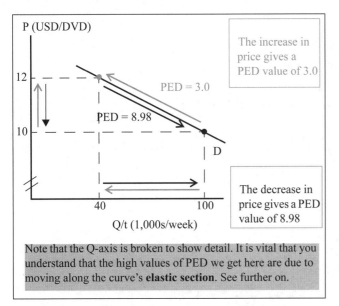

Figure 2.2.3 *Detail of differing PED for DVDs*

In lowering the price we got a higher value of PED – even though we used the same figures. This is the *arc* elasticity of demand which shows the value of PED over the arc of two points. The way to countermand this problem is to calculate a *mid-point value* by using average values of price and quantity, which is done in "Outside the box: Calculation of PED using the mid-point formula " below as it is not directly part of the syllabus. (Do not be alarmed by the seeming

complexity of the formula as you will never be required to use it in actual calculations.)

Now what would go well with this? How much cheese can one get for $2?

I have deliberated long and hard as to the best way of showing price elasticity values and have finally arrived at the following: all references to PED will be based on the values at a *single point* unless otherwise stated.[5] Feel free to skip the next 'Outside the box' and simply move on to the section on elasticity along the entire demand curve. Just keep in mind that PED values used in this book are in fact based upon the mid-point formula unless clearly stated or otherwise shown.

Outside the box:

Calculation of PED using the mid-point formula

The computational paradox of using the arc PED formula can be solved by using *average* changes in the price and quantity. This is the mid-point method, which gives us a value of PED that is in between the

two different values we would get by using the arc formula given earlier.

The values we got before were:

Raising the price from 10 to 12:

$$\frac{\frac{40-100}{100} \times 100}{\frac{12-10}{10} \times 100} \rightarrow \frac{-60\%}{+20\%} = 3.0$$

Lowering the price from 12 to 10:

$$\frac{\frac{100-40}{40} \times 100}{\frac{10-12}{12} \times 100} \rightarrow \frac{+150\%}{-16.7\%} = 8.98$$

The **mid-point formula** uses the same proportionate change in price and quantity – but uses an **average value as the denominator**. Thus we get the same PED no matter whether we are moving up or down the demand curve (see Figure 2.2.4 on page 108).

---

5. I went crying to my friend and colleague, Joe the math teacher. He simply said, 'This elasticity stuff is a bunch of nonsense'.

Raising the price from 10 to 12:

$$\frac{\left(\dfrac{Q_1 - Q_0}{\left(\dfrac{Q_0 + Q_1}{2}\right)}\right) \times 100}{\left(\dfrac{P_1 - P_0}{\left(\dfrac{P_0 + P_1}{2}\right)}\right) \times 100} \rightarrow \frac{\left(\dfrac{40 - 100}{\left(\dfrac{100 + 40}{2}\right)}\right) \times 100}{\left(\dfrac{12 - 10}{\left(\dfrac{10 + 12}{2}\right)}\right) \times 100} \rightarrow \frac{-85\%}{+18.2\%} = \mathbf{4.71}$$

Lowering the price from 12 to 10:

$$\frac{\left(\dfrac{Q_1 - Q_0}{\left(\dfrac{Q_0 + Q_1}{2}\right)}\right) \times 100}{\left(\dfrac{P_1 - P_0}{\left(\dfrac{P_0 + P_1}{2}\right)}\right) \times 100} \rightarrow \frac{\left(\dfrac{100 - 40}{\left(\dfrac{40 + 100}{2}\right)}\right) \times 100}{\left(\dfrac{10 - 12}{\left(\dfrac{10 + 12}{2}\right)}\right) \times 100} \rightarrow \frac{+85.7\%}{-18.2\%} = \mathbf{4.71}$$

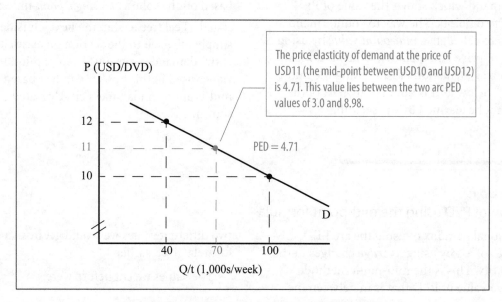

The price elasticity of demand at the price of USD11 (the mid-point between USD10 and USD12) is 4.71. This value lies between the two arc PED values of 3.0 and 8.98.

PED = 4.71

Figure 2.2.4 *Mid-point calculation of PED for DVDs*

Calculating elasticity along an entire demand curve

Elasticity varies not only between different goods, but also along the demand curve for any specific good portrayed using a straight-line demand curve. A good 'law' to keep in mind when dealing with PED for straight-line demand curves is that the **price elasticity of demand will go from infinity to zero with unit elasticity in the middle.**

I now return to the fictitious town of Vidina and the demand for DVD rentals. The demand curve in Figure 2.2.5 on page 109 shows the quantity demanded for rentals in thousands of films per week at specific points along the curve. I have used these values to calculate the (point) PED values (blue dots) along the curve – and since all demand curves are downward sloping, we can disregard the minus sign. The diagram illustrates how PED values change along the slope of a straight-line curve.

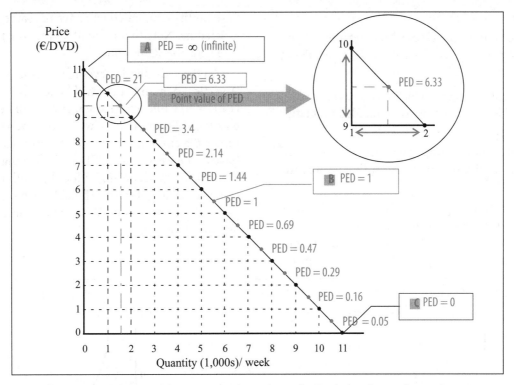

Figure 2.2.5 *Demand for DVD rentals – values of PED along a linear demand curve*

There are three notable points along the demand curve in Figure 2.2.5.

- The first shows that the value of **PED on the P-axis is infinity** ('A' in the figure.) Pure mathematics says that anytime one tries to divide a value by zero the result is undefined (or, less correctly, infinite). At point A we would be dividing a change in quantity with an average price change of *zero*, thus we have a PED of infinity, the sign for which is.

- Moving downwards from the point of infinite elasticity, PED falls consistently until a point right in the middle of the curve, point B, at a price of 5.5 and 5,500 in quantity demanded. Here the **PED is 1**, or **unitary**. Unitary PED means that the quantity demanded changes by the same proportion as price, for example an increase in price of 10% would decrease quantity demanded by 10%. At any point below the price at unit elasticity, PED is lower than 1.

- At point C where the demand curve intercepts the Q-axis we have **zero price elasticity of demand**. PED is zero here as the numerator in the formula for PED is zero, since the average percentage change in quantity is zero and whatever denominator will result in an elasticity of zero, no matter what the change in price. All three points are in Figure 2.2.6.

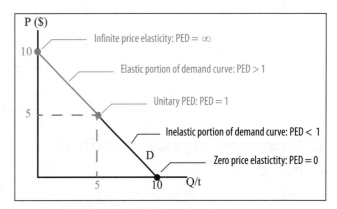

Figure 2.2.6 *PED along a linear curve*

POP QUIZ 2.2.1   PED AND SLOPE

1 Look at the two curves below; one is called 'Price inelastic' and the other 'Price elastic'. Given that the value of PED goes from infinity to zero in a straight-line demand curve, how can one refer to a curve as 'elastic' or 'inelastic'? (Answer is in "Outside the box: PED and the missing link" on page 112.)

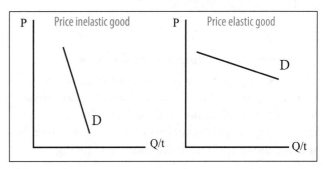

Three 'extremes' of PED

There are three additional cases which together cover all three 'extremes' of price elasticity of demand. These are shown in Figure 2.2.7 diagrams I–III.

- Diagram I shows a good which has *zero elasticity*, i.e. where the same quantity is demanded no matter what the price.

- Diagram II shows the opposite: quantity demanded is *infinite* at a price of four or below (but zero at any price above $4).

- Diagram III shows a good which will have the same proportional response to any change in price – demand is *unit elastic* at all price levels. No matter what the price level and percentage change in price,

quantity demanded will have the same proportional change. Note that no matter what the price, P × Q yields the same value.

All three demand curves have a single value of PED. A vertical demand curve will be totally inelastic (PED = 0) while a horizontal curve will be infinitely elastic (PED =). A curve which has the same area under the curve no matter what point one is on, will have unitary elasticity (PED = 1) all along the curve. (Such a curve, according to Joe the math teacher, is called a 'rectangular hyperbola'. Now go and win a game of Trivial Pursuit. Who makes these names up, anyhow?! *Rectangle?!*)

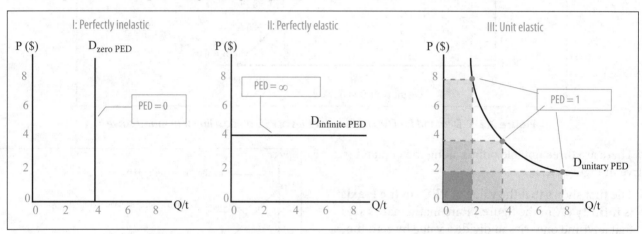

Figure 2.2.7 *Constant elasticity along a curve*

Determinants of price elasticity of demand ©IBO 2003

There are any number of factors that will have an influence on the price elasticity of demand, all of which deal directly or indirectly with the strength of consumers' preferences and their ability to find/accept other goods instead. One realises intuitively that the elasticity of demand for medicines will differ from that of luxury cruises in the Caribbean. The determinants of price elasticity of demand can be outlined in three headings:

1. The availability/closeness of *substitutes*.

2. The *time span* involved.

3. The *proportion of income* spent on the good.

1. Availability and closeness of substitutes

PED basically measures how responsive consumers are to a change in the price of a good, and the closeness/availability of substitutes is doubtlessly the main determinant of price elasticity of demand. Just like the moving along a PPF induces choice and giving

something up, so too does switching from one good to a comparable good. The choice is based on the **ability** and **willingness** of consumers to give up Good X for Good Y – both of which are determined by whether there is in fact a substitute in the first place and secondly whether there is a high degree of perceived similarity, or closeness in the two goods. The rule of thumb is that the closer the perceived substitute, the higher the value of PED, i.e. *high substitutability* leads to *greater price elasticity* of demand.

Notice that I use 'perceived' closeness. This is not by accident. While milk and cream are chemically quite similar, I know of few people who would substitute milk with cream as a refreshing drink – and I certainly wouldn't want to have a seat next to them on an aeroplane. At the same time, Rolls Royce cars and yachts are highly dissimilar, but are in fact relatively close substitutes! Beauty is in the eye of the beholder, and so too is substitutability. The *propensity* and *willingness* of people to substitute one good for another defines whether goods are close or not.

Many goods are conceivably not substitutable at all. My asthma medicine, cigars and compressed air for scuba diving would be considered highly inelastic goods … by ME … and, OK, by most others too.[6] Again, it is the aggregate of individual choice that builds market demand and therefore price elasticity. Alcohol, tobacco and other mind-altering substances would all have low values of PED as they would be non-substitutable for many people's habits or addictions.

It all comes down to the perception of people and how one defines markets. The wider the definition of goods, the lower the value of elasticity – as the wider definition would include any possible substitutes. For example, my addiction to coffee is shared by a good number of people; coffee has an estimated PED of 0.25 (highly inelastic) but if we include a number of coffee substitutes in our definition of the market – say tea and cocoa – and call the market 'hot beverages' then elasticity would fall even further. In including possible substitutes in the grouping, we further limit the scope of possible substitution.

Highly substitutable goods would have many examples within the rubric (= heading) of *brands*. In Greece I always buy the local beer, Mithos, instead of the locally brewed Amstel/Heineken. Is it a preference? No, I couldn't tell the difference to save my life. However, Mithos is always a little cheaper and as they are perfect substitutes … Perhaps now it makes sense that what advertising and marketing does is to help convince us that Brand X is superior to Brand Y. Beauty is in the eye of the beholder – but values change and perhaps can be changed for us.

2. Time span

Demand tends to be more price inelastic in the short run than in the long run. When I bring this subject up in class, I always ask my people if anyone took a taxi during the weekend. I always get a few raised hands and it inevitably turns out that they were at a party and took a cab home at 03:00 in the morning.[7] Taxis are notoriously expensive – plus the fact that the night rate is higher – yet none of the kids even considered alternatives to the taxi. This is an example of how a short time span will lead to low elasticity of demand;

there are simply fewer viable options within a short span of time than within a longer period.

When the first oil crisis hit in 1973/74 and the price of oil quadrupled, the demand for oil was virtually perfectly price inelastic in northern countries, as sub-zero temperatures were the case during the crisis and there simply were no credible alternatives in the time span of those first winter months. Come spring, the first thing people did was to increase insulation, install double-glazed windows, build wood-burning fire places, and install thermal energy pumps … everything to decrease dependency on oil. This meant that over a longer period of time, the PED for oil increased as people had time to set up viable options and adjust.

There are also a goodly number of goods which one can postpone the purchase of, such as sofas and interior decorations, while other goods are considered necessities, such as electricity and, em, well, cigars.[8] I often say that there is, in fact, only one determinant of demand – the availability of substitutes. 'Time' is just another way of saying that one will have the incentive, opportunity and propensity to search for viable substitutes. Short time-span → lack of adjustment and search time for substitutes → inelastic demand.

3. Proportion of income spent on the good

'How many of you bought paper clips this week? None? How about rubber bands? No? How many of you have *never* bought paper clips or rubber bands?' Every hand in the class goes up. What do you think the PED is for a good which represents a fraction of a fraction of one's income?! Yes, highly inelastic. The overall effect is negligible which means that even if the price were to double, the overall effect on total consumption capability will be so low that one would buy the good anyhow. In line with this argument, goods which account for a major proportion of income will be more elastic as an increase in the price would force household to cut back on outlays to make ends meet. Food and clothing are standard examples of such goods. Keep in mind though, that different income groups will have different price elasticities. High income groups and high income countries will spend proportionately less of income on housing and clothing and therefore have lower PED for these goods than low income groups and low income countries.

---

6. It just struck me: I have asthma, smoke cigars, run Marathons, scuba dive … and live at 2,200 metres in one of the most air-polluted cities in the world, Mexico City. Man, my lungs WORK for a living. There must be an opportunity cost issue in here somewhere.
7. Yeah, I tried this in my IB2 in Mexico. The ladies looked at me with utter disbelief: 'A *taxi*?! At 03:00? Are you out of your cotton-pickin' Swedish mind?!' It turns out that every single female student is banned by parents from taking taxis at night. It's simply too dangerous.
8. It's my book and I'll define things as I see 'em.

Real-life elasticities

Let's finish this discourse on price elasticities by looking at a few real-world examples of PED and putting them into the context of the above three determinants of elasticity. Table 2.2.2 gives the elasticity of demand for a number of goods. The figures seem to conform to what has been said about the prime

determinants of price elasticity. I have number-coded the goods according to the three determinants above. Note that many of the goods overlap in terms of which determinants shape PED. For example, salt is price inelastic due to both lack of substitutes and percentage of income spent, giving it 1 and 3.

Table 2.2.2 *Elasticity of demand for a number of goods*

Goods	Estimated Price Elasticity of Demand	Determinant (s)
Inelastic		
Salt	0.1	1 & 3
Gasoline, short-run	0.2	1 & 2
Gasoline, long-run	0.7	1
Coffee	0.25	1
Tobacco products, short-run	0.45	1 & 2
Approximately Unitary Elasticity		
Movies	0.9	1) & 2)
Private education	1.1	1) & 2)
Oysters, consumed at home	1.1	1)
Elastic		
Restaurant meals	2.3	1)
Foreign travel, long-run	4	1) & 2)
Airline travel, long-run	2.4	1) & 2)

(Source: *Economics: Private and Public Choice*, James D. Gwartney and Richard L. Stroup, 8th edition 1997, 7th edition 1995.)

Outside the box:
PED and the missing link

My students are on the ball. When dealing with PED and the issue of not confusing the value of PED with the slope of a straight line, I am often asked how one is able to refer to a straight line demand curve as being 'elastic' or 'inelastic', seeing as how the PED will go from infinity where it cuts the *y*-axis to zero where it cuts the *x*-axis.

The answer is given in the series below. If the entire range of any given (straight-line) demand curve is portrayed in the diagram, PED will indeed vary from infinity to zero. However, when illustrating a good for which demand is highly inelastic or highly elastic, the diagram will often only show the significant portion of the demand curve. I have broken these portions out in the two diagrams in Figure 2.2.8.

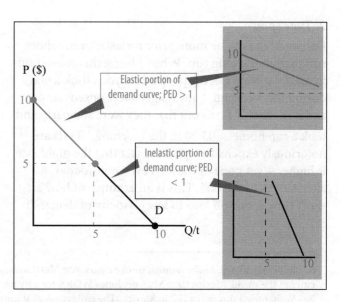

Figure 2.2.8 *Elastic and inelastic curves*

Cross-price elasticity of demand

©IBO 2003

Recall that many goods reveal that they have relationships with other goods. CD players and CDs are in joint demand while DVD players are in competitive demand with Blu-Ray players. This section looks at how sensitive these goods might be in terms of the price of one good affecting the demand for another. This is cross-elasticity, or as will be used here, cross-price elasticity of demand (abbreviated CPED).

> **Cross-price elasticity of demand**: The cross-price elasticity of demand – CPED – measures the relative sensitivity of a change in the quantity demanded of Good X with respect to a change in the price of Good Y. Cross-price elasticity measures the closeness of substitutes and the relevance of complements.

Definition ©IBO 2003

Cross-price elasticity is basically addressing the question 'If the price of Blu-ray players falls, what will be the extent of change in: a) the demand for DVD players, or b) the demand for Blu-ray discs?' Cross price elasticity is a proportional measure of the sensitivity of demand for a good with respect to a change in price of another good. In the question above, we can expect the demand for DVD players to fall because the two goods are *substitutes*. As for Blu-ray discs, demand would increase as the two goods are *complements*.

The definition of cross-price elasticity of demand is very similar to PED. All we are doing is calculating the sensitivity of Good X with respect to *another* good, Good Y. Dividing the percentage change in quantity demanded for Good X by the percentage change in the price of Good Y gives us a value of the cross-price sensitivity of the two goods.

Formula ©IBO 2003

Assume that the price of Good Y increases by 10% which causes the quantity demanded for Good X to fall by 20%. To calculate cross-price elasticity for Good Y, we divide the percentage change in the quantity demanded of Good X (remember, 'quantity on top') with the percentage change in the price of Good Y. The value of cross-price elasticity will tell us whether the goods are closely related – and whether they are complements or substitutes.

$$PED_{x,y} = \frac{\%\Delta \text{ in Qd for X}}{\%\Delta \text{ in price of Y}} \rightarrow \frac{\frac{Q_{X_1} - Q_{X_0}}{Q_{X_0}} \times 100}{\frac{P_{Y_1} - P_{Y_0}}{P_{Y_0}} \times 100}$$

Significance of sign with respect to complements and substitutes ©IBO 2003

Complements

Complement goods are goods where the consumption of one good leads to the consumption of another good, such as the classic 'tennis balls and tennis racquets', which is a singularly uninspiring example. I will instead vent my spleen (= express my feelings strongly) using a particular pair of products that has long yanked my chain (= irritated me), namely printers and printer ink cartridges.

When looking at printers, one will of course look at the total cost picture: a printer needs ink cartridges. Say that the price of ink cartridges fell from €15 to €13.5 (–10%) and that subsequently demand for printers increased from 10,000 units per week to 12,000 (+20%). The cross-price elasticity (X = printers; Y = ink cartridges) of printers with regard to cartridges would be:

$$\frac{\frac{Q_{X_1} - Q_{X_0}}{Q_{X_0}} \times 100}{\frac{P_{Y_1} - P_{Y_0}}{P_{Y_0}} \times 100} \rightarrow \frac{\frac{12000 - 10000}{10000} \times 100}{\frac{135 - 150}{150} \times 100} \rightarrow \frac{+20\%}{-10\%} = -2$$

Notice the appropriate signs in the formula and answer. Take heed; it is most important to assign these signs correctly to cross price elasticity values. The *minus sign* tells us that we are dealing with complement goods; as the goods are complementary a decrease in the price of one good will cause an increase in the quantity demanded of the other. Any positive value divided by a negative value – or vice versa – will render a negative value. The value of minus 2 also tells us that printers and ink cartridges are highly complementary, known as *strong complements*. The higher the value of CPED (in absolute terms, i.e. disregarding the minus sign) the stronger is the joint demand. Note that even when the price of one good rises and causes the quantity demanded for another to fall, we will get a negative value.

113

Substitutes

Let us continue with the example of DVD players and Blu-ray players. Assume that the price of Blu-ray players falls. This would most certainly have an effect on the demand for DVD players as the two goods would seem to be highly substitutable. Say that the price of Blu-ray players went from USD200 to USD180 and that the quantity demanded of DVD players decreased from 10,000 units to 9,500 units during a given time period. Our cross-price elasticity (X =DVD players; Y = Blu-ray players) would be:

$$\frac{\dfrac{Q_{X_1} - Q_{X_0}}{Q_{X_0}} \times 100}{\dfrac{P_{Y_1} - P_{Y_0}}{P_{Y_0}} \times 100} \rightarrow \frac{\dfrac{9500 - 10000}{10000} \times 100}{\dfrac{180 - 200}{200} \times 100} \rightarrow \frac{-5\%}{-10\%} = +0.5$$

A **positive value** of 0.5 tells us that the goods are **substitutes** – but a value of less than one tells us that they are relatively weak substitutes. A lower price of Blu-ray players led to a decrease in quantity demanded for the substitute, DVD players. As no surprise, if the

price of one had risen, the quantity demanded of the other would have increased which means that the cross-price elasticity would still be positive.

Accept no substitutes!
(On the road in the Yucatan, Mexico,
July 2007)

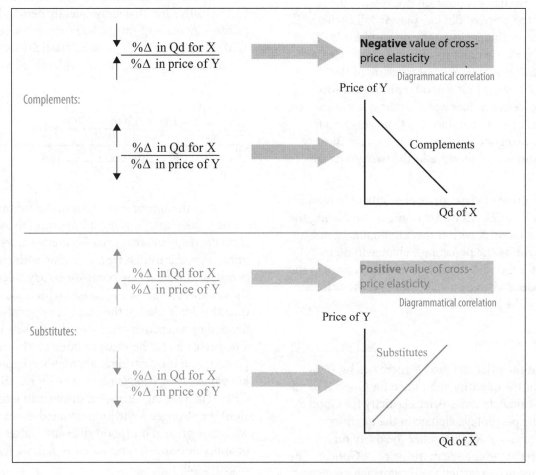

Figure 2.2.9 *Summary of cross-price elasticities*

Diagrammatic analysis of substitutes and complements

You must be able to use diagrams in economic analysis and cross-price elasticity is no exception. Here are two examples of how we could use supply and demand analysis to show the relationship between complementary goods and substitute goods.

Complement goods

I continue with the two complementary goods, printers and ink cartridges. In Figure 2.2.10 diagram I, the supply of printers increases, say due to increased productivity at the firms producing the players. This lowers the market price of printers and increases demand for the ink cartridges used in the printers, Figure 2.2.10 diagram II.

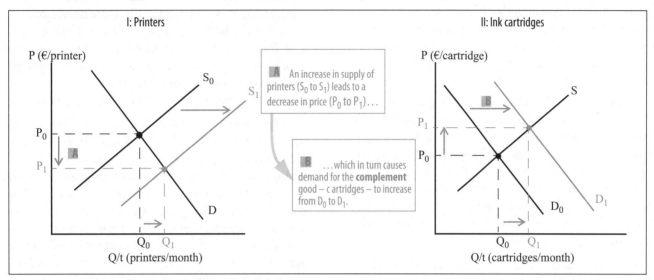

Figure 2.2.10 *Complement goods*

Substitute goods

As for substitute goods, DVD players and Blu-ray players are of course in competitive demand. In Figure 2.2.11 diagrams I and II, the supply of Blu-ray players has increased, say due to lower production costs in manufacturing. This lowers the market price of Blu-ray players and decreases demand for DVD players which are substitutes.

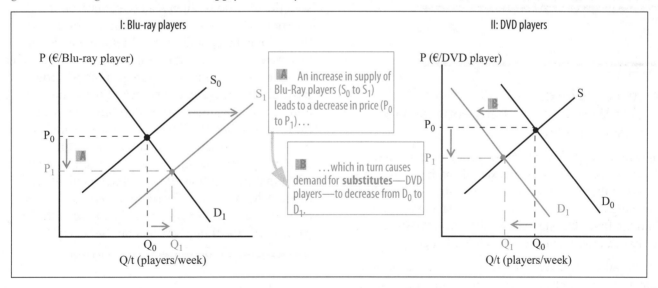

Figure 2.2.11 *Substitute goods*

Warning!
CPED and 'ΔQd' versus 'ΔD'

One of my economics colleagues at the Oxford Study Courses took issue (in a very polite British manner) with my illustrations of the correlation between the change in price of Y and the change in quantity demanded of X shown in Figure 2.2.9 on page 114. Stephen is a super, modest, unpretentious bloke (and commands great respect from his students who invariably call him 'Mr Holroyd') so I shan't name him.

Stephen pointed out that using a diagram with 'Price of Y' on the y-axis and 'Quantity demanded of X' on the x-axis would be 'invariably confusing and borderline erroneous' since a change in price of a good for which there is a complement or substitute good will shift demand for said complement/substitute. Yes, this is correct. My defence in using the correlative diagrams $(P_Y \Leftrightarrow Qd_X)$ is simply to illustrate what the formula is based on: $\%\Delta P_Y \rightarrow \%\Delta Qd_X$.

I recommend that you do as Stephen says. Don't use the explanatory diagrams in Figure 2.2.9 but the ones further on (see Figure 2.2.10 on page 115 and Figure 2.2.11). I don't want to make trouble with a 195 cm man who outweighs me by some 30 kilograms and spends his free time hauling 10 kg honey pots – the man has muscles in his teeth!

Outside the box:
A little rumination ... Harry Potter and the Economist's Stone

The much-hyped return of the young necromancer Harry Potter is an excellent example of the relationship between different goods offered on a market. The J.K. Rowling's series of books has been a fabulous success and the first film released in 2001 was a smash hit. Let us have a look at some of the market issues.

Recall how the demand for a good is influenced by the price, availability and demand for other goods;

substitutes and complements. A substitute is a good which is in competitive demand with another, while a complement good is in dual demand with another good. Let us go through the possible substitutes and complements.

December is the period for 'Big Movies'. It was therefore no accident that the second Harry Potter movie hit the market at this time during 2002. Yet another Big Movie opened at the same time; none other that the latest instalment of *Lord of The Rings*, 'The Two Towers'. The relationship between these two goods is that of substitute goods – though I might get some severe disagreement from my students as to whether they both appeal to the same age groups.

A few thoughts on the subject. Many of my students are avid fans of the *Lord of The Rings* trilogy. We have had many a discussion on the subject of the relationship between books and films based on books. We have arrived at some sort of consensus, as we have agreed that these two goods are in fact both substitutes and complements. Our argument goes something like this: if one has read a book and really enjoyed it then chances are one would want to see the film in order to see whether the film is true to the book. These two goods would thus be in joint demand – they are in fact complement goods.

Having said this, one can also make a strong case for saying that they are substitute goods! How often have we seen a film but not read the book? And having seen the film, do we then read the book? Good question! There is an impulse to think, 'Naaah. Been there, done that, got the t-shirt.' Yet there is also an incentive to find out if the book is better – as is so often the case – so one might want to get hold of a copy. Basically, the question is whether a film made from a book will complement the book by creating demand for it, or whether the film can act as a substitute for the book. A most unscientific inquiry amongst my students paints a picture of a stronger complement effect that substitution effect – which incidentally might help to explain why so many recent editions of both the Harry Potter books and The Lord of the Rings trilogy have the film characters on the cover!

POP QUIZ 2.2.2   PED AND CROSS-PRICE ELASTICITY

1   Explain how a change in the price of Good X can cause both price and quantity to increase for complement good Y.

2   A certain product has very few substitutes and a very small proportion of consumer income is spent on the product. What would the PED be like?

3   The price of municipal bus fare rises from 80 pence to 90 pence and quantity demanded falls by 10%. What is the value of price elasticity of demand?

4   Assume that apples and oranges have a positive cross-elasticity of demand whilst oranges and orange peelers have a negative cross elasticity. How would you define the two separate 'pairs' using economic terminology?

5   Letters and email have a cross price elasticity of 3. If the price of postage rises from 4 DKK (Danish Crowns) to 6 DKK, how much will demand for email change?

Income elasticity of demand

©IBO 2003

The concepts income and demand are inextricably linked, just like having a good day on the stock markets and celebrating with a nice cigar and bottle of champagne. One is unlikely to celebrate by going out and splurging on, say … potatoes![9] This is what income elasticity looks at: the propensity to change one's consumption of certain goods due to a change in income. **Income elasticity of demand** measures how responsive quantity demanded is to a change in income.

Definition   ©IBO 2003

The issue at hand is to relate a change in quantity demanded with an increase in income, i.e. the *percentage change in quantity demanded over the percentage change in income*. Most goods will behave normally, which is, the quantity demanded will increase as income increases. However, some goods will actually behave in an opposite manner; quantity demanded will fall when income rises. Therefore, just as in cross-price elasticity, we are interested not only in the *value* of elasticity, but also the *sign*.

> **Income elasticity of demand**: Income elasticity of demand – yED – measures the responsiveness of demand, i.e. the relative (percentage) change in the quantity demanded for a good due to a relative (percentage) change in income. (The lower case 'y' signifies personal income, since upper case 'Y' is reserved for national income.)

Formula   ©IBO 2003

The formula for income elasticity is nothing new – we simply replace 'relative change in price' with 'relative change in income'. (Note that the lowercase 'y' is used to represent *personal* income rather than national income.) 'yED' is pronounced 'income elasticity of demand'.

$$yED = \frac{\% \Delta \text{ in Qd}}{\% \Delta \text{ in y}} \rightarrow \frac{\dfrac{Q_1 - Q_0}{Q_0} \times 100}{\dfrac{y_1 - y_0}{y_0} \times 100}$$

Normal goods   ©IBO 2003

The last time I almost resigned (or was almost fired – these seem to be complement goods in my case) I stormed home and told my then wife that a number of planned expenditures would have to be dropped. The mere whiff of less income caused a change in purchasing behaviour. As soon as I was rehired (with the mediator help of Joe Cool, the Irish math teacher) my household's buying plans went right back on track. This is how consumers are prone to act – and all the goods whose quantity demanded fell and rose in concert with my income are normal goods. The definition of a **normal good** is that it is positively related to income. Most goods are normal goods, but there are a few possible exceptions.[10]

> **Normal good**: A normal good is positively correlated to income, i.e yED is positive. A rise in income increases demand for normal goods. A fall in income decreases demand for normal goods.

An *income-elastic* good is a good for which quantity demanded rises proportionately more than an increase in income, i.e. income elasticity is greater than +1. High-end market goods such as vintage wines and luxury goods are income elastic, as are services and tourism. At the other end of the spectrum are goods

---

9.   Unless you're Swedish or Irish.
10.   This goes for school headmasters also.

where the increase in quantity demanded is proportionately less than the increase in income; *income inelastic* goods, which have values of income elasticity less than +1. Commonly referred-to examples are clothing and cigarettes.

I figure you are all big boys and girls now, so I shall forgo all the formulaic usage and confine myself to examples based on percentages. Let us assume that income for a specified group of consumers rises by 10%, which is a bit unrealistic but makes the calculations easier. If quantity demanded for vintage wines from Bordeaux increases by 20% we get a yED of +2; an increase of vegetable consumption by 2% renders a yED of +0.1.

Quite naturally, income elasticities will vary between high and low income groups and more significantly perhaps, between high and low income countries. Food, for example, has an income elasticity of between +0.5 and +0.6 in LDCs while most MDCs hover between +0.2 and +0.5.[11] What might be considered a luxury good in rural China, a bicycle for example, would have a correspondingly high income elasticity of demand whereas a MDC would most assuredly have a lower income elasticity of demand for such a good. In line with this, development and accompanying higher incomes will change the pattern of income elasticities away from basic commodities towards manufactured goods and services.

Inferior goods ©IBO 2003

A good where quantity demanded falls as income rises is known as an **inferior good**, the term being used not as a descriptor of the good per se, but rather as a descriptor of our relative consumption preferences at higher income levels. Potatoes are not 'inferior' to pasta yet when incomes rise evidence suggests that our relative preferences will cause us to actually lower our consumption of potatoes and substitute the good with something preferable. Potatoes might thus have a *negative* income elasticity of demand, as an increase in income is correlated to decreased quantity demanded.

Inferior good: An inferior good is negatively correlated to income, i.e. the yED is negative. A rise in income decreases demand for inferior goods. A fall in income increases demand for inferior goods.

It is worth commenting on the possibility that many goods are in fact normal up to certain incomes and thereafter inferior. At low levels of income, any addition to income might mean increased quantity demanded for basic goods such as food and clothing. However, at some point at higher level income, the quantity demanded for such goods would surely not proportionally match an increase in income. Just imagine how the yED values for economics students at university would change upon getting a good job in London City after graduation.

An oft-cited concept within the context of inferior goods is the aforementioned Giffen good, i.e. a good where quantity demanded is positively correlated to price. This would be a type of inferior good … but I've just decided that it would be a waste of time explaining this, as Giffen goods invariably wind up in the same category as mermaids, goblins and UFOs. I hereby declare an international boycott against the use of the term 'Giffen Good'. Sue me.

POP QUIZ 2.2.3   INCOME ELASTICITY

1   How will demand for inferior goods in an economy be affected if:

    a   incomes rise

    b   unemployment decreases

    c   the general price level rises?

    Treat each as a separate case.

2   You read in the newspaper about a good with 'an elasticity of –2'. Explain why you need more information about the type of elasticity since '–2' can actually be referring to two entirely different goods!

3   Must income elasticity of demand be solely positive or solely negative? Illustrate your answer with a diagram.

---

11. *International Evidence on Consumption Patterns 1989*, Greenwich, Connecticut JAI Press Inc.

Price elasticity of supply ©IBO 2003

This chapter addresses the issue of the *ability* and *willingness* of suppliers to put a good on the market. Compare the three goods in Figure 2.2.12 on page 119. Why would a supply curve be 'steep' or 'shallow'? Try to fit the correct good to each diagram; blank DVDs, the Olympic boxing finals and the supply of IB economics hours in a public school (answer in footnote)[12]. It is rather self-evident that the supply curves indicate the willingness/ability of firms to increase output of a good within a given period of time. The measurement of this is the **price elasticity of supply**.

Definition ©IBO 2003

The diagram series above pretty much says it all. The price has increased by 50% in all three cases (from 100 to 150) but the percentage increase in quantity supplied varies from 100% to zero. We have just defined price elasticity of supply (PES); it is the *relative increase in quantity supplied* due to a *relative increase in price*. The price elasticity of supply (PES) for Good A is 100/50; PES = 2: Good B is 20/50; PES = 0.4. Good C is 0/50; PES = 0.

> **Price elasticity of supply (PES)**: The price elasticity of supply (PES) is a measure of the responsiveness of firms in increasing the quantity supplied on the market due to a change in price. The supply curve is upward sloping, i.e. PES will be positively correlated to price, with few exceptions.

Formula ©IBO 2003

By now you should recognise the formula methodology. The only difference between the formula for PES and PED is that we replace Qd (quantity demanded) with Qs (quantity supplied).

$$PES = \frac{\%\Delta \text{ in Qs}}{\%\Delta \text{ in price}} \rightarrow \frac{\frac{Q_1 - Q_0}{Q_0} \times 100}{\frac{P_1 - P_0}{P_0} \times 100}$$

Possible range of values ©IBO 2003

Just as demand elasticity will have an endless range, so will supply elasticities. The main difference is that elasticity of supply will not have a range of infinity to zero along a single curve. Yet the *definition* of what is elastic remains the same.

> **Range of PES values**: A price elasticity of supply of less than 1 is called *inelastic supply*; PES that is equal to one is *unit elastic*; PES that is higher than 1 is *elastic*.
>
> PES < 1; inelastic
> PES = 1; unit elastic
> PES > 1; elastic

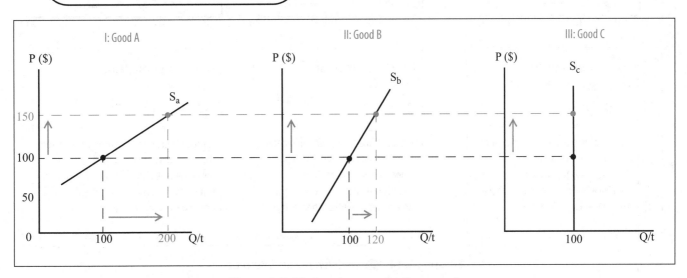

Figure 2.2.12 *Supply curves for three goods*

12. The answers are: diagram I = blank DVDs, diagram II = supply of IB economics, diagram III = supply of tickets to the Olympic boxing finals. You may still send me $5.

Diagrams illustrating the range of values of elasticity ©IBO 2003

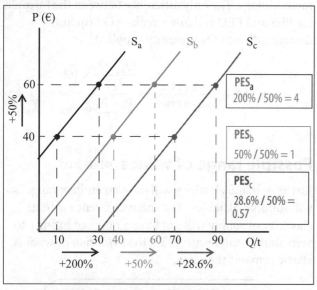

Figure 2.2.13 *PES for three goods*

Supply curves S_a, S_b and S_c in Figure 2.2.13 show the differences in price elasticities of supply for the three goods. As in PED, the values of PES will vary along the curves, yet depending on whether the curve intercepts the P-axis, Q-axis, or origin, there is a boundary to the values.

Any straight-line supply curve which starts on the P-axis will have a PES of **more** than one. A straight-line curve starting at the origin will have a PES **equal** to 1 and in full logical consequence; a straight-line originating from the Q-axis will have a PES of **less** than 1.

Note that this rule is valid no matter what the slope of a (straight-line) supply curve is. This is illustrated in Figure 2.2.14 on page 120, where the changes in quantity and price have been marked out along the axis for comparison.

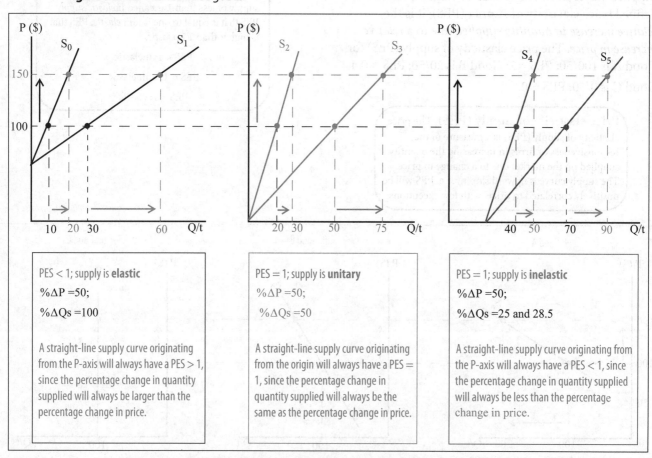

Figure 2.2.14 *PES for different axis-intercepts*

There are two extreme cases of price elasticity of supply. One is where the quantity supplied remains the same no matter what the price, i.e. *perfectly inelastic* supply. The other case is when quantity supplied is infinite at one specific price, i.e. *perfectly elastic* supply. In both cases, there is actually no correlation between price and quantity supplied. Figure 2.2.15 illustrates this.

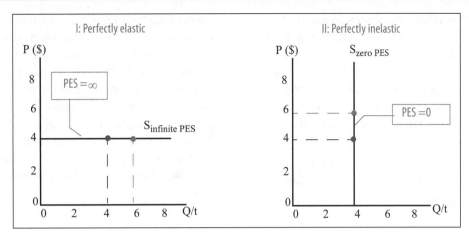

Figure 2.2.15 *Extreme cases of PES*

When supply is *perfectly elastic*, suppliers are able/willing to supply any amount at a price of $4, while a change in price will have no effect on a good which has a *perfectly inelastic* supply curve. It bears mentioning that while equivalent extreme forms of PED are most difficult to find in the real world, there are several

examples of both perfectly inelastic and perfectly elastic supply. A valid example of the former would be concert tickets ("Putting the pieces together: Born again in the USA" on page 94) and of the latter the world supply curve for a good in an importing country (See Figure 4.2.1 on page 409.)

Outside the box:
A special S-curve

I have taken care to use the term 'straight-line' supply curve in explaining how the PES will be limited depending on where the curve originates. The reason is illustrated in Figure 2.2.16, where a curve with an increasing slope shows that point values of PES along the curve change. In the case here, following the tangential points from S_1 through S_5, PES goes from infinity to zero. This shape of the supply-curve has relevance for the total output curve (= aggregate supply curve) in Section 3.3.

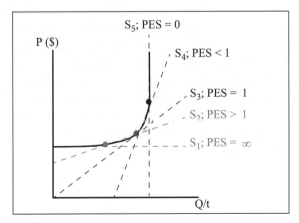

Figure 2.2.16 *Changing PES along the curve*

Determinants of price elasticity of supply ©IBO 2003

The price elasticity of supply is determined by the flexibility, ease and speed with which suppliers can increase output. The major determinants can be divided into two main categories of determinants of price elasticity of supply; the issue of **time** and/or the availability of **producer substitutes**.

Time as a determinant of PES

The ability to increase output is intimately hinged on the **time span** in question; the shorter the time period, the lower the PES. The quantity supplied of fresh tomatoes is difficult to increase in a two week period while a period of six months gives entirely different supply elasticity. So would canned tomatoes – part of the time issue is whether a good is **storable** or not. (Recall that supply is defined as the amount suppliers are willing and able to put to market, not the 'quantity in existence'.) It is far quicker to furnish the market from a warehouse. Non-storable goods will render an inelastic supply-curve, an example of which would be frozen oysters. Fresh oysters are an excellent example of a good which cannot be stored for any length of time.

In a similar vein, time is an issue for producers who are at the limits of **output capacity**. The availability of excess capacity, say available machines, labour and factory space, will have a major impact on the ability to increase supply within a given time frame. In the short run it can be difficult to get hold of scarce factors and to expand the size of production plants. Over longer time-periods it is easier to plan and target output by increasing bulk-buying of material and increasing the amount of capital used.

This makes sense when one thinks about how the difficulties in increasing the supply would be alleviated over time. Increasing the quantity of beef supplied per month is far more difficult that increasing the supply over a two year period. The producers will have time to come up with better cross-breeding methods and expand herds. All this would increase producers'/suppliers' ability to increase the quantity supplied within the time period. Figure 2.2.17 on page 122 shows how supply would differ over time. The diagram also serves as an introduction to the concept of how the short-run supply inelasticity of *primary goods* such as agricultural produce, iron ore, and oil will affect prices in the short run.

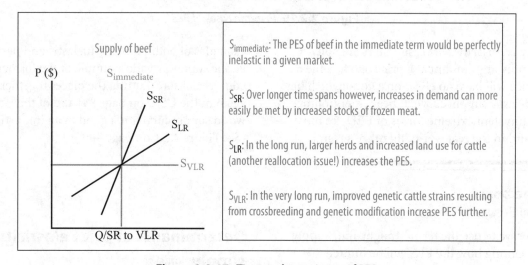

Figure 2.2.17 *Time as determinant of PES*

Producer substitutes as a determinant of PES

Closely related to the issue of the time involved in increasing quantity supplied within a given period, is the ability (and cost!) incurred by producers in switching from the production of one good to another. A producer substitute is a good which suppliers can switch to as an alternative – not to be confused with consumer substitutes. The ease or difficulty any given supplier experiences in moving productive resources from one good to another will be a major factor in determining supply elasticity. A common classroom example is whiteboard pens and permanent markers being very close producer substitutes. Switching from whiteboard pens to permanent markers[13] would involve very little in the way of tool readjustment, machine modifications, new material and knowledge and so forth. Supply would be very elastic. Switching from compact cars to mid-sized cars is also fairly supply elastic.

Many *primary goods* such as iron ore, teak wood and agricultural goods will be highly inelastic, as the ability to switch to such goods in the short run is very limited. The basic premise here is that once suppliers have a large amount of resources sunk in a certain sector, the reapplicability of these resources is the key to increasing supply of other goods. Just consider commodities such as iron and copper; if you have a copper mine and demand for iron increases it's going to be a bit difficult to switch production to iron. I mean, you have a *copper* mine …

---

13. A favourite classroom prank known to all my students, incidentally.

Storytime: Flexible manufacturing – automobiles after 1991

One of the ongoing efforts to increase the speed of market reaction – called 'lead time' in the industry jargon – is to create systems where manufacturing is highly flexible. The automobile industry leads the way in many respects.

The auto industry is increasingly integrated; six large groups control 75% of the global market for automobiles. The 13 largest manufacturers are increasingly co-operative ventures, where the major firms merge (= join together) in certain manufacturing areas, form joint ventures in production process design and share production plants, engines, parts and design centres.

Honda has gone very far in adjusting its production to react quickly to market demand; all of the factories around the world are now capable of making multiple models, and while American auto manufacturers might spend 4 to 6 weeks to adjust production lines for a different car model, Honda can do it overnight. (The Economist, 21 February 2002) Honda itself claims that its new production line at the Sayama Plant, Japan, has reduced investment by half for any new model. (http://world.honda.com/news)

Looking at the broader market, the industry as a whole suffers from chronic overcapacity. It is estimated that in 1997/98, car producers were operating at between 50 and 75% of total capacity.

Taken together, increasing flexibility renders increasing supplier substitutability, while excess capacity accentuates supply potential; price elasticity of supply is increasing in the automotive industry. This would go a long way in explaining how average real prices of cars continue to fall.

APPLIED ECONOMICS:
We're on a highway to hell!

One day Joe the math teacher came down to my office to ask me 'what the heck I was doing' in my IB1 class 'and would I please stop doing it'. Apparently, I had made the claim that we would never run out of oil. Ever. Joe wanted to take issue with this statement. I explained that I was not making any claim that oil was 'infinite' as a resource but that market forces would make sure that as long as there was a need for oil, there would be a supply. The Stone Age did not end because we ran out of stones.

What happened in November of 1973, was that OPEC – for political reasons – decreased supply. As demand was highly inelastic in the short run the price of oil went from USD3 per barrel to short-run equilibrium of USD11 during 1974, a 260% increase in price. The next 'oil crisis' in 1979/80 was caused primarily by the ripple-effects of negative expectations as the Iran–Iraq war broke out. The price rose even further, but not the shock level of 1973/1974 as the PED of oil had increased.

We have been running out of oil since my grandfather drove buses in St. Louis during the depression. We have been running out of oil since World War Two, since the 1960s, since the first and second oil crises in 1973–74 and 1979–80 … you get the picture. In 1940 there was an estimated 10 years of consumption left, in 1980 over 25 years, and in 2000

there was 40 years! The real price of a barrel of oil in 2000 was the same as in 1920. The Bronze Age did not end because we ran out of copper and tin.

This is a classic example of the 'horse manure theorem'. I read somewhere that had computers existed in the mid-19th century, they would have predicted that by the end of the 21st century the world would be covered in six feet of horse manure. This is the danger of extrapolation; basing a prediction on past and current facts/happenings. What has happened, of course, is that we have moved on to other forms of transportation. Just like stones, horses, and the original Donkey Kong games, we have moved on. Yes, we are running out of oil. We would run out of oil ultimately even if we only used 10 litres per year – that is the definition of 'finite resource'. Yet the fact remains: oil supply is not a question of physics but of economics. The Iron Age did not end for a lack of iron.

We are not running out of oil for three reasons:

1. The price and incentives function of supply and demand has made sure that when oil prices have skyrocketed, there has been a major incentive to find new fields and to use the old fields more efficiently by developing technology. The simple fact is that previously costly oil resources became economically viable when the oil price rose. Enormous fields were found in the 1980s and 1990s;

As price increases, there is an incentive to find new fields and get oil out of previously non-economically viable oil wells and oil fields. These include the North Sea, Russia, Indonesia, Mexico, Canada, Alaska, to name a few.

The high price of oil has also led to previously unprofitable shale oil deposits (oil locked in sand) becoming increasingly interesting. Estimates of the amount of oil held in shale deposits in Canada alone could increase total known reserves by 50% – the problem being that it is more expensive to extract, about USD30 per barrel rather than USD8–15 in Alaska and Saudi Arabia. If the price of oil increases enough, then it becomes economically viable to extract the shale oil. Estimates of total reserves of shale oil would take care of the world's TOTAL energy needs (at present rate of consumption) for the next 5,000 years.

2. 'Oil crisis' never meant that there wasn't enough oil, but that supply had fallen. Scarcity does not mean 'not enough oil' but 'dear oil'. As oil became expensive during the 1970s and 1980s oil crises, the rationing function and substitution effects kicked in. The rationing effect meant that quantity demanded fell and the substitution effect meant that people started to find substitutes and ways to become less dependent on oil.

3. The reasons outlined above have led to far greater efficiency in both the extraction and use of oil. We are simply getting better in production and use. In 1973, 38% of the world's oil came from the Middle East – now it's below 30%, in spite of a 25% increase in demand. Technology in oil production means that when previously 20% of the oil in a field could be withdrawn we can now withdraw over 30%. Estimates show that America's 10 largest oil fields held over 60% of their oil when the fields were closed down. These 'known reserves' increase by the year – the increase in known reserves is about 900% since 1950 and by close to 50% since the mid

1970s. The cost of extracting the aforementioned shale oil in Canada has dropped from USD30 a barrel in the 1970s to less than USD12 a barrel in 2002. On the users side, cars have increased efficiency by over 50% since mid-1970s, houses are better insulated and we have become much better at recycling plastics and other materials which use oil in their production.

In summary: the supply of oil has been increasing monumentally while our demand, although increasing, has become more elastic as we have started to seriously look at substitutes, such as natural gas and also renewable resources such as geothermal energy, wind and solar power, etc. Again, we started to look for substitutes as soon as renewable energy options became competitive with oil. Twenty-five years after the first oil crisis, the price of oil was marginally higher in 2000 than it was in 1973. The present Information Age will not end because we run out of information.

Oil is not going to become scarce. It is going to become uninteresting.

During the 1980s and 1990s, demand for oil continued to rise and supply was able to not only keep up but outstrip demand increases to the extent that the price of a barrel of oil dropped to the historic low of USD10 a barrel during 1997/98, when the real price of oil was the lowest ever.

Addendum to this edition: during the spring of 2008, a couple of colleagues were sniggering over the fact that this 'Applied economics' box would have to be scrapped – or severely redone. The underlying reasoning was a mixture of 'we've passed 'peak oil production', 'oil prices are at a permanently high level', etc. I continued to argue that there will *always* be enough oil – or in fact, *too* much oil, given CO_2 issues – and that this box would be kept in the next edition. In December 2008, I looked at the diagram in Figure 2.2.18. You tell me: did I do the right thing?

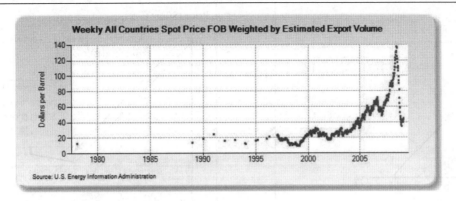

Weekly All Countries Spot Price FOB Weighted by Estimated Export Volume

Source: U.S. Energy Information Administration

(Source: http://
tonto.eia.doe.gov/dnav/pet/hist/wtotworldw.htm)

Most of the figures and statistical data have been taken from a truly astounding book, *The Skeptical Environmentalist*, Björn Lomborg, pp. 118–38. Additional figures on shale deposits have been taken from *The Economist*, 'There's oil in them thar sands!', 26 June 2003.

Figure 2.2.18 *Oil demand and oil price*

Highly theoretical question to keep you awake at night: Assume that we have 100 years' consumption of oil left – at the present consumption rate. Now, if we increase our consumption by 1% per year yet manage to increase our efficiency in oil usage by 2% each year, how long before we run out of oil? Send me some oil futures for the answer … no, it's in the footnote below.[14]

POP QUIZ 2.2.4   PRICE ELASTICITY OF SUPPLY

1   Draw three straight line S-curves showing, respectively: PES = 1, PES > 1, PES < 1.

2   How would faster-growing wheat strains affect the PES of wheat?

3   What is the likely price elasticity of supply for a good which has large price fluctuations due to changes in demand?

Applications of concepts of elasticity ©IBO 2003

This section looks at how the concept of elasticity can be applied to real-life scenarios. Price elasticities can provide firms with decision-making data on price and output, and governments with information on the effects of subsidies and taxes. On the international arena, PED and yED will have major implications within trade and development.

PED and business decisions: the effect of price changes on total revenue

©IBO 2003

First off is the effect that sales of goods have on firms; revenue. Any child running a lemonade stand on the corner will quickly realise that sales bring in money – this is more accurately known as *revenue*. At the end of the day, when our budding entrepreneur counts total cash, i.e. total $Q_{lemonade}$ sold times the $P_{lemonade}$, he/she will have counted the *total revenue*, **TR**.

> **Revenue and total revenue (TR)**: Revenue is money earned by a firm's business activity. The total income from business activity during a time period, price times quantity sold, is the total revenue, TR. (Warning: revenue is NOT the same as profit! Profit is defined as total revenue minus total costs.)

Total revenue is easily shown in a diagram. It is the area under any specific point on the demand curve given by the price times quantity.

Figure 2.2.19 shows total revenue at three different prices. Each rectangle represents total revenue; price times quantity. Notice that a rise in price from $1 to $1 would lead to an increase in TR, while an increase in price from $2 to $3 would lead to a decrease in TR. While tempting to assume that this is because of the slope of the demand curves, the answer lies elsewhere.

14. The answer is: Never! (But I'm still bribable. It's the only thing I have in common with Mexican cops.)

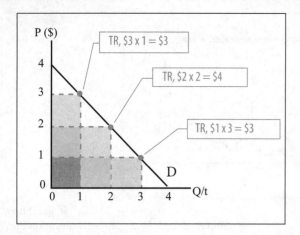

Figure 2.2.19 *Total revenue (TR) along a demand curve*

Price and total revenue

So, Lina sets up her lemonade stand – having done her homework. No, not geography or history – she has done a market survey in order to find out demand for lemonade. Her street corner is busy enough to have the demand curve you see in Figure 2.2.20 on page 126. She is interested in maximising her revenue, and plotting out all the various prices and quantity demanded, she soon arrives at a price of $1.25 per 25 cl glass = $5 per litre. (Not having finished Econ 101, she disregards any notion of profit – as will you for the time being!) At any other price, her total revenue will fall.[15]

Diagram I in Figure 2.2.20 is the standard-issue S&D diagram, showing a price level from $10 to zero and a quantity from zero to 10 litres. At every given price the total revenue (TR) is shown in the total revenue diagram (diagram II). At $10 per litre, quantity demanded is zero. By lowering the price quantity, demand increases as does TR – up to the price of $5. Below the price of $5 TR starts to fall, becoming zero again when the price is zero and the quantity demanded is (perhaps somewhat unrealistically) ten litres.

The conclusion is that *total revenue is maximised* at the point where *PED is unitary*. In other words, no matter what the initial price is, moving towards unitary PED will increase TR. One can formulate a rule for maximising TR as 'Lowering the price for a price *elastic* good will increase TR, while raising the price for a price *inelastic* good will increase TR'.

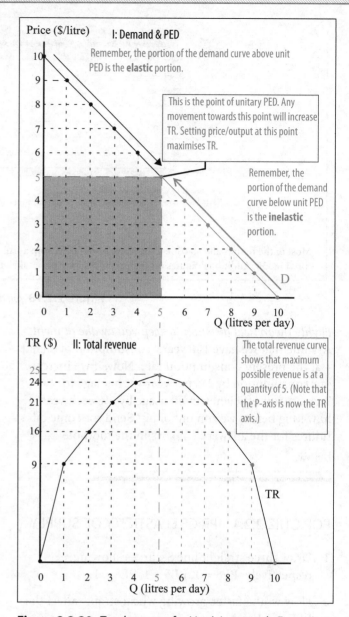

Figure 2.2.20 *Total revenue for Lina's Lemonade Emporium*

TR and PED – increasing supply

Let's look at a two different demand curves in order to illustrate the change in TR when supply increases. Figure 2.2.21 shows that in increasing supply and lowering the price of a demand-inelastic good, the loss of revenue is greater than the increase. Total revenue falls. An increase in the supply of a demand-elastic good will not lower the price to the same degree as the increase in revenue – thereby increasing total revenue. Another conclusion is that when demand is inelastic, changes in supply will create large price fluctuations, while changes in supply for demand-elastic goods will cause quantity fluctuations.

---

15. When she adds gin, demand shifts to the right.

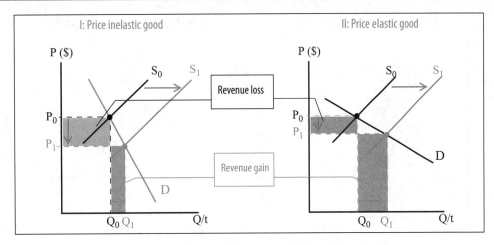

Figure 2.2.21 *Effect on TR due to a shift in the supply curve*

TR and unitary PED

Now, what if a business was to lower or raise the price and TR remained the same? How would the demand curve look? You have actually already dealt with such a curve, so stop right here and think before you read on. A demand curve with the same revenue is only possible if the sum of P × Q is the same at all price levels so that the area under the demand curve at any point along it must be the same. This is the unit elastic demand curve done previously. Figure 2.2.22 illustrates TR for a rectangular hyperbola.

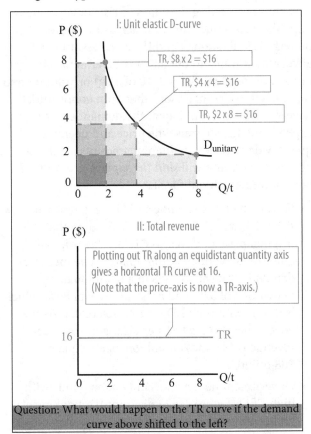

Figure 2.2.22 *Unit inelastic D-curve and Total revenue curve*

APPLIED ECONOMICS:
Commodity price fluctuations

One of the clearer uses of price elasticities is in showing how massive price fluctuations are caused on markets where both the PED and PES are very low. Diagram II in Figure 2.2.23 on page 128 shows the price fluctuation on the market for commodities – the industrial price index of *The Economist* of 2000. Prices have fluctuated wildly over the past 160 years yet with a distinct downward trend. Figure 2.2.23 shows how low PED for these goods together with low PES causes these extreme price fluctuations.

The supply and demand curves are shown in a rather exaggerated way, but for good reason. Any good which has inelastic supply and demand will fluctuate in price more than goods which are elastic in demand. Recall from Section 2.1 how buffer stock schemes attempt to stabilise these price fluctuations. The shifts in supply for industrial commodities could be the result of seasonal variations, changes in labour and productivity, supply disruptions such as numerous wars during the period, etc. Demand for industrial commodities will be highly linked to efficiency and economic activity in the firms/countries using these commodities.

It has been the case for many years that most of the users of commodities are what we now call more developed countries (MDCs) while many of the suppliers are less developed countries (LDCs). We will revisit this subject in Section 5.3.

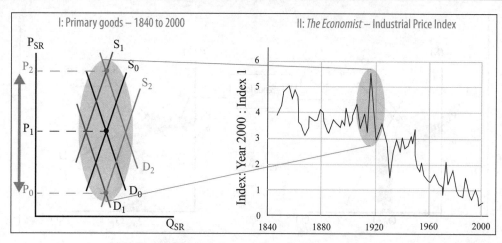

I: Primary goods – 1840 to 2000   II: *The Economist* – Industrial Price Index

Figure 2.2.23 *Commodity price fluctuations*

PED and taxation ©IBO 2003

What this country needs is a good five-cent cigar. – Thomas Riley Marshall, US Vice President 1913–21

When I introduce this section in class, I often refer to myself as 'The World's Best Tax-Payer'. It's not that I don't try to avoid tax as much as the next person, I just happen to be a consumer of the type of goods favoured by governments for expenditure tax. On my desk here in my office there is a box of cigars (Cuban – thanks Ana!), a wide variety of alcohol (thanks Shota, Ji In and Daniel!) and assorted fruits and nuts (which is not my IB1 class but bananas, almonds and raisins – which I actually bought myself). OK, most of these are gifts – maybe I'm not such a great taxpayer. Anyhow, while I pour myself a drink and disconnect the school's smoke detector so I can light up, spot the heavily taxed goods.[16]

Yes, I know; it isn't exactly rocket surgery. Governments tax alcohol and cigars far more than almonds. Why? There are two reasons:

1. Perhaps the initial, somewhat intuitive answer is that smoking and drinking is harmful to me and by extension, to society in general. My use of tobacco/alcohol not only damages *my* health but affects society by inflicting economic and social costs on my fellow citizens. Increased sick days, increased health care, and a possible serious case of premature death will all have a negative effect on my contribution to and burden on society. Therefore, government imposes a *disincentive* on certain goods such as tobacco and alcohol by raising the price of such goods via expenditure taxes.

2. There is, however, an additional answer to why we tax tobacco/alcohol and not almonds; the difference in *government tax revenue* will be much higher for goods which have low price elasticities of demand than for goods with high PED.

   I am now skirting the edges of HL concepts, but I hope the basic issue will come across in Figure 2.2.24 on page 129 diagrams I and II. Let us assume that government wants to put a $1 tax on either each cigar or each hectogram ('hg' = 1/10 of a kg) of almonds and (for the sake of comparison) that both goods initially have the same price and quantity demanded. An expenditure tax will raise the price and decrease quantity demanded by different amounts. (Putting a tax on expenditure will *shift the supply curve to the left*, but I am leaving it out for SL.)

   - Government tax revenue and tax on goods with low PED (Figure 2.2.24 diagram I): Assume that the original price of a cigar is $1, and the original quantity demanded is 100 million. The inelastic demand for cigars results in a fall in quantity demanded of 32% and a rise in price of 80%, which is in line with the PED for tobacco of 0.4. As the government will get $1 per cigar sold, total tax revenue is $1 times 68 million cigars equals $68 million.

   - Government tax revenue and tax on goods with high PED (Figure 2.2.24 diagram II): Looking at taxing almond consumption, quantity demanded

16. Anyone who thinks I'm actually serious here should be sent to forced re-education clown camp.

has fallen by 50% and the price has risen by 10%, which is in line with a PED for dried fruits of 4.6. Total tax revenue to government is $50 million – $18 million less than cigars would give.

Taxation of goods is fairly comprehensible. Goods which are either highly addictive, habit-forming or totally lacking in close substitutes are highly price inelastic and will most likely be targeted for taxation. Goods which have all three attributes will have statues erected in their honour at head tax offices.

Allow me to put forward a slice of personal rumination on what increasing numbers of economist are starting to question on the expenditure tax issue. One of the basic arguments for taxing tobacco is the health argument brought up above. Recent studies point to smokers actually paying a great deal more in tax than the actual cost of extra health care needed by smokers. In addition to this, a good many recent studies point out 'junk food' and obesity as a far greater health issue and economic cost to society that tobacco. Obesity related costs in America are in the area of $46 billion per year. The cost adds an estimated 36% to spending on patients and a 77% increase in medication – compared to the additional costs of smoking which are estimated at 21% and 28% increases.[17]

Similarly, obesity-related costs in Britain are in the area of £2.1 billion per year.[18] This is becoming ever more of an issue as rich countries around the world start to compare costs. Apart from the Norwegian government which was seriously considering raising indirect taxes on high-sugar and high-fat foods in 2007, to date, no 'obesity tax' has been levied on junk foods or high fat foods in general.

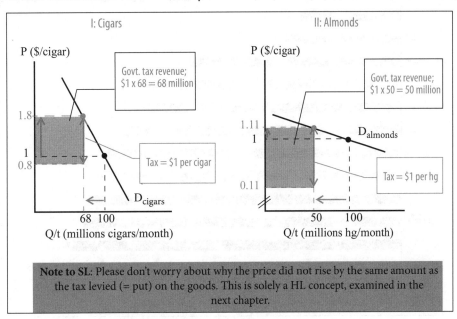

Note to SL: Please don't worry about why the price did not rise by the same amount as the tax levied (= put) on the goods. This is solely a HL concept, examined in the next chapter.

Figure 2.2.24 *Expenditure tax on cigars and almonds*

Sorting out the terms: different forms of taxation

Life is tax and then you die – and pay funeral tax![19] Tax revenues account for the brunt of government income and there are a number of different ways to base taxes. Taxes are mostly based on different types of economic activity and are commonly divided into two main groups.

1. *Direct taxes*: A direct tax is clearly visible to whomever is paying it; an 'in your face' tax, if you will. *Income tax* is the slice taken out of your wages/ salary – for the most part it is removed before you get your pay check. Firms pay a number of taxes, the most obvious being *profit taxes* (or corporate taxes) on any profits made. Finally, both firms and individuals will pay taxes on any gains resulting from bank interest and profits made selling shares

---

17. See http://www.who.int/bulletin; *The Economist,* 'Don't just sit there', 9 May 2003; 'Obesity Tops Smoking for Medical Costs', study compiled by Rhonda L. Rundles, staff reporter for *The Wall Street Journal*, 1998.

18. National Audit Office of Great Britain, taken from '*The "fat tax": Economic Incentives to Reduce Obesity*', Institute for Fiscal Studies; http://www.ifs.org.uk/bns/bn49.pdf.

19. No, I'm not joking. The funeral tax in my country, Sweden, is 0.3% of gross income. This means that an average Swedish income earner over a life time will pay approximately SEK70,000 (around USD8600 in December 2008) for the Final Service. No wonder we have one of the highest suicide rates in the world – it's another way to avoid tax! (I wonder how one could measure the PED for this service.)

or property. These are collectively known as *capital gains taxes*.

2. *Indirect taxes*: Taxes that are 'hidden' or at least not as obvious are called indirect taxes, as they are paid to government indirectly. *Import taxes* (commonly called tariffs), *specific taxes* on petrol, tobacco and alcohol – known as excise duties – and *value-added taxes* (VAT) are all examples of indirect taxation. Note that specific taxes are often set per unit, for example £2 tax per bottle of wine, whereas value-added taxes are a percentage tax based on the selling price, for example 25% on all sporting goods or 12% on foodstuffs. A percentage tax is referred to as an *ad valorem tax*.

Figure 2.2.25 (WHO data) shows the total tax weight (which includes both specific taxes and VAT) on a pack of cigarettes in selected countries. The percentage of tax constitutes between 25% and 85% of the price. As smoking still seems to be commonplace in these countries, one can well imagine how government coffers are padded by these taxes. (See also "'Case (of stupidity) study: Tobacco tax in Sweden 1997/98" on page 131.)

It is estimated that a 10% increase in the price of tobacco would result in a 4% decrease in quantity demanded in MDCs and around 8% in LDCs.[20] This gives a PED of between 0.4 and 0.8, (Table 2.2.2 on page 112 gives 0.45.) which is quite price inelastic and no surprise whatsoever.

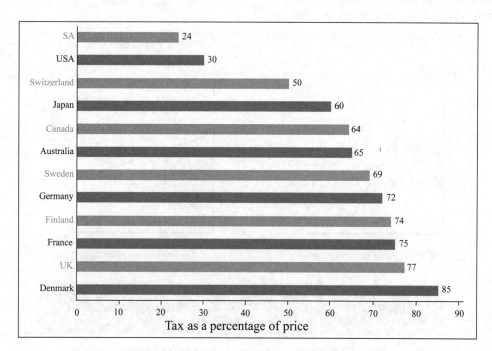

(Source: World Health Organisation. *Tobacco Alert: The Tobacco Epidemic: A Global Public Health Emergency*, May 1996, WHO: Geneva)

Figure 2.2.25 *Tax as a percentage of price – selected countries*

---

20. *The Economist*, 28 February 2002.

Case (of stupidity) study: **Tobacco tax in Sweden 1997/98**

Some movies should be obligatory viewing for politicians. The Swedish government would have done well to watch *The Untouchables* (about the infamous Al Capone and organised crime's rise to power during the ban on alcohol in America in the 1930s) prior to increasing tobacco taxes in 1997. Here's what happened.

In August of 1997, the Swedish government raised the tax on tobacco by 18% as part of a health drive and possibly to increase tax revenue. Nobody actually seems to know. In any case, cigarette consumption plummeted by 20% which would seem to belie the 0.45 PED for tobacco in Table 2.2.1 on page 105.

What the Swedish government did not seem to realise, yet every single one of my IB1 students did, was that there were indeed any number of substitutes available for cigarettes, which would explain the massive 20% fall in consumption, pointing to a PED of 1.1. It turned out that the Baltic states, Russia and Poland had an abundance of cheap black market cigarettes and also a number of budding capitalists who saw an opportunity to make a good deal of money. 'Duh!' said all my IB1 students who snidely predicted exactly what was to happen!

Figure 2.2.26 diagram I: The increase in tax lowered the legal quantity demanded from Q'97 to Q'98 while the official market (O.M.) price of cigarettes rose from P97 (point A) to P98 (point A). (Note that I once again leave the supply curve out.)

Figure 2.2.26 diagram II: An immediate surge in demand for black market cigarettes was the result, where demand rose from DB.M.97 to DB.M.98 and quantity went from Q'97 to Q'98 (point B').

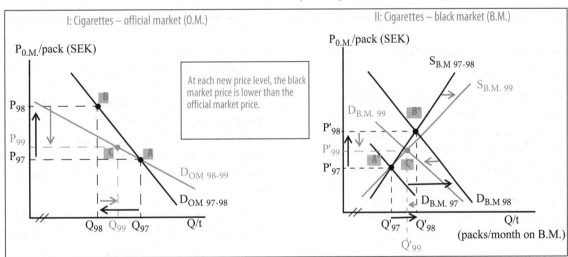

Figure 2.2.26 *Cigarettes – official market and black market*

Secondary effects: During the period of 1997/98, demand for official market cigarettes had become more elastic, due to the availability of substitutes. By the time the tax on cigarettes was lowered, demand had shifted/revolved to DOM 98-99, which meant that quantity demanded didn't return to the previous level, but only to Q99 (point C). The reason for this was that the supply of black market cigarettes had increased markedly, from SB.M.97/98 to SB.M.99. PES increased also, since by this time the black marketer s' supply chains and stocks had been firmly established. The lower tax did have an effect on demand for illegal cigarettes, as shown by the shift of DB.M. 98 to DB.M. 99, yet the black market equilibrium did not return to the previous level (point B') but was established at point C'. Throughout the period, the black market price was kept firmly below the official price level, making it possible for black marketers to remain entrenched (= established) on the market.

In other words, the decrease in consumption on the official market was substituted by an increase in black market consumption – more than made up for by some estimates. Within 12 months, the extent of smuggling and accompanying mafia-like organised criminals and violence had reached the pain threshold of government and the tax was removed in late 1998. However, the availability of substitutes at lower prices than the official enabled cigarette smugglers to remain on the market.

The final results can be seen today. Black market cigarettes are abundantly available at about half the official price (according to my students, who keep track of such things); highly organised criminal gangs have established themselves in Sweden and have expanded operations to other areas such as prostitution and protection racketeering; government tax revenues from cigarettes have fallen; and smoking is actually on the increase amongst young people, who find it easier and cheaper to buy on the black market than in shops where there is an age limit of 16 years of age to buy tobacco.

Basically, calling the increase in tobacco tax a mistake is being too kind – and the Swedish government learning curve looks to be horizontal, since taxes on tobacco increased by some 150% between 2006 and 2008. In October 2006, the head of Swedish Criminal Intelligence (that's SCI, not CSI), Thord Modin, confirmed most level-headed worries about organised crime: 'Higher taxes on tobacco are something organised crime is simply waiting for. These gangs already have established channels to work with.'

(Source: *Svenska Dagbladet*, 16 October 2006 at http://www.svd.se/nyheter/inrikes/artikel_361708.svd)

Cross-elasticity of demand: relevance for firms ©IBO 2003

The sensitivity of quantity demanded in relation to a change in the price of related goods will have a major impact on pricing and output decisions of firms. The example of DVD players and DVDs used earlier illustrates how suppliers of discs will have to be well aware of changes in the market price of players in order to compensate output and/or prices of discs. Knowledge of the cross-price elasticity of these *complement goods* will enable the disc firm to plan ahead.

The same is true for *substitute goods*. If a competitive good, say Blu-ray players, fall in price then suppliers of both DVD players and Blu-ray discs will need to know how their own good will be affected and by how much. Again, producers will want to plan for eventual production changes by increasing or decreasing factor inputs, e.g. labour and capital. A main element in knowing the effect on demand is being able to budget the operation correctly. Both revenue and profit will be affected by any change in demand, so firms put a great deal of effort into correctly estimating future demand. Many firms will in fact have entire divisions whose purpose is to analyse

potential opportunities and threats to their product. Threats might be the new revolutionary product of a rival firm which would threaten own sales. Opportunities might be being able to purchase the patent rights, production rights, licence rights or entire rival company. This is the case very often in the highly competitive market for hand-held computers, where rivals often buy the license to use software or simply merge.

Cross-price elasticity of demand also helps to understand the increasing importance of the ongoing process of *international integration*. Improved ease of cross-border trade has increased the proportion of exports far faster than GDP (gross domestic product – e.g. national income) in most of the industrialised countries. Many firms rely increasingly on exports for the brunt of their sales. As home country exports are competing with many other countries, the cross-price elasticity between domestic and foreign goods will be that of substitutes – positive. High cross-price elasticity for a country's domestic goods vis-à-vis imports means that if domestic inflation is higher than foreign countries' inflation rates, there will be a proportionately larger increase in demand for imported goods (see Section 4.7).

Significance of income elasticity for sectoral change (primary/secondary/ tertiary) as economic growth occurs

©IBO 2003

Income elasticities play an important roll in illuminating the problems of developing counties caught in producing primary goods. A solid grasp of how income affects consumption preferences is central to understanding how economic growth influences trade and development.

Primary, secondary and tertiary goods

Primary goods have been brought up previously. They are goods which are 'raw' as in not being highly processed, i.e. have low value-added. Natural resources such as timber, iron ore and Greek marble provide raw materials for industries. Other primary goods are agricultural goods such as coffee and wheat. Many of these goods make up what is known as the commodities market.

Secondary goods are basically manufactured goods, i.e. the result of processing primary goods into consumer goods and capital, to use the widest possible collective terms. Secondary goods add value to primary goods by taking primary inputs and using labour and capital to create something more.

Tertiary goods are intangible (= non-touchable) goods, i.e. services. When you get charged a commission for changing currencies at the foreign exchange office, you are in fact buying a service. Doctors, teachers, cleaning personnel, used car salesmen and TV newscasters all provide services, i.e. tertiary goods.

What has been happening over the past 50 or so years, is that primary products have become ever cheaper in real terms (and in many cases even in nominal terms) and also an increasingly smaller part of total output. For example, the 24 major raw materials accounting for over 95% of total global output of raw materials, only accounts for 1% of global GDP.[21] Agriculture accounts for 3% of GDP in developed countries and 14% in less developed countries.

PED/PES/yED and primary/secondary/ tertiary goods

Just as price elasticity of demand is low for primary goods, income elasticity is lower for primary goods than for secondary and tertiary goods. Let's first look at two ways of how PED and PES are linked to primary goods.

Low PED/PES and falling prices for primary goods/ commodities

- *Low PED* means that a given increase in supply of primary goods – often due to increased specialisation and improved technology – results in a greater percentage decrease in prices. This decreases revenue for any given quantity of primary products sold.

- *Low PES* also contributes to falling prices for primary goods. Many primary goods have been shown to be highly substitutable due to technological change – jute (very strong natural fibre) used to make sacks became increasingly substituted by cheap plastic and fibre-optic cables largely replaced copper telecom wires. A fall in demand for goods with low PES will lead to a proportionately larger decrease in price.

Implications for development

Countries which rely to a great extent on exporting commodities will be at the mercy of international commodity markets. National income in MDCs has been growing at an average of around 2% to 2.5% yearly for the past 20 years. This has not been the trend in LDCs and income elasticities help to explain why; large scale dependency on the production of primary goods which are income, supply and demand inelastic.

Low yED and terms of trade

LDCs are highly dependent on the production of primary commodities. 71% of non-Asian LDC exports are made up of primary goods.[22] Yet the same countries account for just 12% of total world trade and 17% of total world GDP (1998 figures).[23] Summing this up paints a picture of a group of counties whose output is exported mainly to rich countries, and where the demand for these primary goods is highly dependent on growth rates in high-income countries.

- As average global incomes increase, demand for goods with high yED (secondary and tertiary goods) will rise faster than for goods with low yED (primary goods).

- This paints an important picture of *relative* prices; the price of secondary goods will rise faster than prices of primary goods. In economic lingo, primary goods become *relatively* cheaper than secondary goods.

---

21. Lomborg, p. 139.
22. Todaro, p 68.
23. *The World Economy, A millennial perspective*, OECD, table 3-1c, p. 127.

- Economies specialising in primary goods will now see that increasing quantities of, say, coffee must be exported in order to import any given amount of machinery. The price of exports relative to the price of imports is known as the *terms of trade*. As export prices fall in relation to import prices, the terms of trade worsen for primary goods specialists.

Low PED/PES and changes in growth rates

- Low yED for primary goods meant that the high growth rates in more developed countries (MDCs) during the 1980s and 1990s has not yielded more than modest growth of exports in commodities in less developed countries (LDCs) which are specialised in primary goods.

- Fluctuations in economic activity in MDCs, e.g. importers of primary goods, lead to fluctuations in the (derived) demand for primary goods used in production. Low PES helps to explain why/how the price of primary goods fluctuates so wildly, as changes in demand for primary goods will cause price volatility along an inelastic supply curve.

A little depth:
What is an index?

An index is a simple and rather clever way of comparing things. An index is made by assigning a certain numerical value to something and then comparing this with the relative values of other things. One assigns a base value to a variable, for example, 'the price level in 1980' or 'GDP in 1990' and then compares changes over time. Indexes are normally based on decimal systemisation, i.e. the base value can be 1, 10, 100, or 1,000.

One can construct an index to compare virtually anything. An index of Amanda's growth (see page 9) could show how much she grew over the time period. She grew from 111 centimetres to 133 centimetres. This gives a change of 22 centimetres, which is 19.8%.

Our index would show this as an increase from 1 to 1.198 … or … 10 to 11.98 … or … 100 to 119.8 … or

… 1000 to 1198. Each index version shows the same relative change, i.e. an increase of 19.8%.

Perhaps the most common index in economics is used to show changes in GDP, where the base of 100 is commonly used.

Let's construct a simple index for the GDP figures of New Zealand.

Our index is of course comprised of stock values and show how national income in New Zealand fell for two years before increasing. Each index value is compared to the value in the base year. In 2002 the value of GDP exceeded that of 1999 by 3.6%, which is total growth for the time period. By indexing national incomes for different countries, one can compare growth rates for economies of vastly different sizes, e.g. Japan and Iceland. (Source: OECD, 2003)

	1999	2000	2001	2002
GDP (Billion US$, in 2001 values)	55.9	51	50.5	57.9
Index (base year = 1999)	100	$\frac{51}{55.9} \times 100 = 91.2*$	$\frac{50.5}{55.9} \times 100 = 90.3*$	$\frac{57.9}{55.9} \times 100 = 103.6*$

(* The formula for each new indexed value is: GDP for the relevant year divided by the base year value times 100.)

POP QUIZ 2.2.5   ELASTICITIES

1 Draw a D-curve that gives the supplier the same revenue no matter what the price.

2 Use two different D-curves to show which goods the government should tax in order to earn the most revenue.

3 'We sold more units – and made less money!?' Does this statement make sense? Explain.

4 Fill in the blanks: 'Along a unit elastic demand curve, when the price is lowered the loss of revenue is _____ as the increase in revenue. Therefore, the *net* increase in revenue is _____!'

5 Assume that you are a wine connoisseur (= enthusiast) and only go for high quality vintages rather than low-quality plonk[24]. What type of tax would you rather have on wine – ad valorem or unit tax?

6 Why would the PES of *dried* cod be higher than that of *fresh* cod? Use a diagram.

Putting the pieces together: Rent controls on inner city apartments – a study of PES over time

One thing I make sure my students know is that I am training them not to by my equal but to be my superior, and I always succeed. I encourage them to go off to university after graduation and return to straighten me out. Many of them do. One young lady, Sara, came for a visit to discuss how price elasticities can explain the limited supply of inner-city housing. This is HER story.

'When a maximum (ceiling) price is put on desirable inner-city housing, there will be an excess of market demand, Q_S to Q_D in the diagram', explained Sara. 'Right?' [See Figure 2.2.27.]

'Yup', I said, 'but what's with the new supply curve?'

'Well, it is foreseeable that landowners over time simply don't feel that the rent is worth it, and would take rooms and areas off the housing market, decreasing supply to S_1.'

'For what?! I mean, better to at least get something for it!'

'Ah, but you are forgetting the opportunity costs! These rooms, attics and other space might be better used for other things: office space, ateliers, gyms or simple storage. The maximum price governs living area, not other activities!'

'Hmmm, OK, I'm with you on the "shift" part, but what's the "swivel" and thus increase in PES?'

'Simple', said Sara with that special smile young women reserve for old men who aren't quite with it. 'As the owners have converted some of the available floor area into other uses, there are now an increased amount of producer substitutes available! Should the price ceiling be lifted, suppliers will be able to quickly convert floor space back into living areas for rent. We assume that demand is the same, which means that full-out supply of rooms would be as before; at P_{mkt} and Q_{mkt}.'

I thought this was a pretty cool use of PES. Thanks Sara. Incidentally, all of you may feel perfectly free to excel beyond my level and thereupon come and educate me! Welcome.

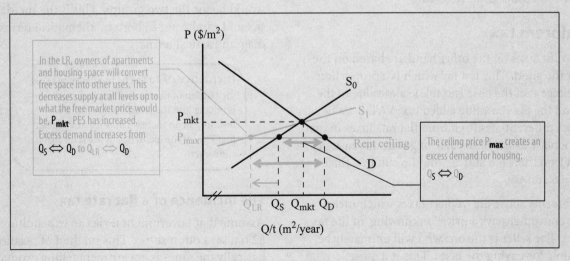

In the LR, owners of apartments and housing space will convert free space into other uses. This decreases supply at all levels up to what the free market price would be, P_{mkt}. PES has increased. Excess demand increases from $Q_S \Leftrightarrow Q_D$ to $Q_{LR} \Leftrightarrow Q_D$.

The ceiling price P_{max} creates an excess demand for housing; $Q_S \Leftrightarrow Q_D$

Figure 2.2.27 *Rent Controls – LR effects*

---

24. Alcohol, booze.

HIGHER LEVEL EXTENSION TOPICS

The art of taxation consists in so plucking the goose as to obtain the largest possible amount of feathers with the smallest possible amount of hissing. – Jean-Baptist Colbert, controller general of finance under King Louis XIV

This section delves a bit deeper into the effects of market intervention in the forms of taxes and subsidies. The issue at hand is who bears the greatest **burden of an expenditure tax** and who gets the largest **benefits from subsidies**. The answer, of course, is that it depends ...

Flat rate and ad valorem taxes

©IBO 2003

There are three certainties in life: death, taxes and car trouble.

Flat rate tax

Start off by tasting the term. **Flat rate** can only mean that the rate of tax per unit is independent of quantity or price. A flat rate tax on expenditure is a tax on *each unit* consumed – which is why such taxes are often referred to as *unit taxes*. The most common unit taxes are taxes on petrol (euros € per litre), on alcohol (€ per litre) and tobacco (€ per kilo). Import taxes are also frequently unit taxes, such as € per tonne/automobile/cubic metre. Flat rate refers to the tax being the same on each unit. A €2 unit tax a bottle of wine is the same tax on both a €5 bottle of Cote du Rhône as on a €50 bottle of 1964 Rioja Gran Reserva.

Ad valorem tax

Ad valorem taxes on the other hand are based on the value of the good. This is a tax which is a proportion – a percentage – of the base (taxable) sales value of the good, and the tax is a value added tax, VAT. A value added tax differentiates itself from flat rate taxes in that it will increase as the base value of goods increase. A 20% VAT on the wine above, would result in a final price of €6 and €60.

Both forms above are *indirect* taxes which means that the consumer pays a price 'unknowing' of the tax involved. The seller is the one who will ultimately be responsible for paying the taxes. This is a most important part of the model of how taxes will affect the price: an indirect tax on goods is basically a tax on each unit sold, i.e. a tax where suppliers will decide what proportion of the tax is passed on to consumers.

> **Flat rate and Ad valorem taxes**: A flat rate tax is the same amount on each unit sold, such as an amount per litre or kilo. It is therefore often called a unit tax. An ad valorem tax (value added tax) is based on the base value (price) of a good sold, and as it is a percentage the amount of tax will increase as the base value increases.

Incidence of indirect taxes and subsidies on the producer and consumer ©IBO 2003

Taxes and subsidies are common methods of market intervention by governments. The reasons vary, but apart from simply using taxes as a method of tax collection, taxes are also commonly levied on goods in order to decrease the output/consumption of goods which have negative effects on society. Subsidies are used to increase output/consumption of certain goods which are considered beneficial to society in some way. In both cases, these forms of government intervention serve to reallocate resources.

The incidence (here, burden) of indirect taxes

How then would a tax on the consumption of a good, an expenditure tax, affect consumers and producers? Another way of putting it is what the *burden* of a tax would be for the two groups. This is the incidence of tax and can be put in both mathematical terms and diagrammatical terms.

> **Incidence of tax**: The incidence of tax is the burden of the expenditure tax on the producer and the consumer. A tax of $4 resulting in an increase in price of $3 means that 75% of the incidence of tax is on the consumer.

The incidence of a flat rate tax

Assume that government levies an expenditure tax of €2 on, say cotton shirts. This method of taxation is basically the same as government telling producers that at whatever price they sell the shirts, for each unit sold they have to send €2 to the tax authorities. Assume that the original retail price (= final consumer price) of an Alligator Shirt is €10 and that the seller buys the shirts for €5. Now, the question is, the suppliers know that however many shirts they sell, each one represents a 'tax debt' to the government – so by how much do they raise the price in order to pay this coming debt?!

Theoretically, producers could still sell the shirts at €10 and simply be satisfied with a gain (gross profit in accounting-speak) of €3 per shirt rather than the previous €5. Or, they could raise the price by the same amount as the tax, to €12, in order to keep the same profit margin. In the first case, the incidence of tax is entirely on the producer and in the second case the incidence of tax is entirely on the consumer. The main issue here is how consumers react, e.g. their sensitivity to an increase in price. The responsibility of the final price is in the hands of the producer, which is basically the producer thinking 'How much of the tax dare I levy on the consumer?!'

Figure 2.2.28 shows how the €2 expenditure tax causes the price to increase by €1 which is a 50% tax burden on the consumer. The other €1 comes out of the pocket of the producer, the remaining 50% of total tax incidence. As the tax is basically an increase in costs for producers, supply decreases (S_0 to S_{+tax}) by the amount of the unit tax.

The original price of the shirts was €10, and a tax of €2 was levied on each shirt. The tax shifts the supply curve to the left raising the price per shirt by €1 at a market equilibrium price of €11. The tax can be seen by the vertical distance between S_0 and S_{+tax} – at every level, the difference between them is €2. The total incidence of the €2 tax on consumers is the upper shaded rectangle, the incidence on producers the lower grey rectangle. Together they make up total government tax revenue for the shirts.

Put in a formula, Incidence of tax on the consumer

$$= \frac{\Delta \text{ in P}}{T}$$

… where P is the price to the consumer and T is the unit tax on the good.

There are additional effects of a tax, namely the decrease in producers' revenue and the increase in consumers' consumption and spending:

- *Producer revenue* decreases from €1 million (€10 × 100,000) to €720,000 (€9 × 80,000) per month
- *Consumption* decreases by 20,000 shirts per month and consumer spending goes from €1 million (€10 × 100,000) to €880,000 (€11 × 80,000).

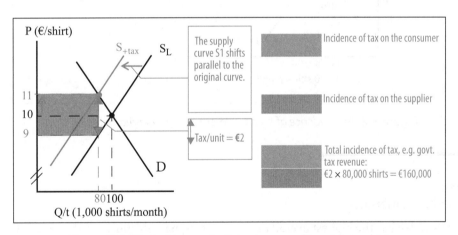

Figure 2.2.28 *Incidence of a flat rate expenditure tax on shirts*

Exam tip: Clarity in diagrams

Note in Figure 2.2.28 above how I 'break out' the tax arrow and refer to it clearly as 'Tax/unit'. When we add in additional economic concepts, such as dead-weight loss (see Section 2.3), you will make your examiner's life easier by keeping all points, arrows and distances clearly distinguishable. Basically, as I tell all my students: 'Do you want to yank the chain of the person grading your exams?' (yank someone's chain = harass someone)

I recommend that you do the "break-out the tax arrow" (or something like it) in all your diagrams and basically make it a 'knee-jerk' (= natural) reaction. During exams you will be stressed out and that's when you get messy/unclear – and lose marks as a result. One of my karate teachers, Kawasoe sensei, was very clear that what you practice in the dojo (= karate gym) is what you do in a stressful situation (= getting attacked[25]). He was right. I am asking you to make neat and clear diagrams a part of your 'econ karate nature' so that when the exam questions assault you, your neatness-reaction is second nature.

137

A value added tax (VAT)

A tax based on the taxable, or base, value of a good is just like any percentage-based tax. For example, a 30% income tax means you pay £30 on an income of £100, £60 on an income of £200 and so forth. The same effect is evident when levying an ad valorem tax (value-added tax or VAT); the tax per unit will increase as the price of the good rises. Figure 2.2.29 shows the effect of VAT on our Alligator shirts. Assume that a VAT of 20% is imposed at an equilibrium price of €11 and a quantity of 80,000. The supply curve shifts *disproportionally*, from S_0 to S_{+vat}, since the higher the price, the larger the price increase of the 20% VAT.

At higher prices the ad valorem tax shifts the supply curve higher, increasing the distance between S_0 and S_{+vat}. At the new equilibrium price of €12, the 20% VAT renders a €2 tax per unit.

A brief footnote on my examples (Figure 2.2.28 on page 137 and Figure 2.2.29). Many of you are probably wondering what lunacy possessed me to put first a unit tax – and then a value added tax on top of that! The example of 'taxing a tax' looks absolutely bizarre, silly and impractical. Quite naturally, this is exactly what is done in many countries. Petrol prices in Europe, for example, will be comprised of around 80% tax. Say that the base price of a litre of petrol is €0.2 to which a €0.6 unit tax (per litre) is added, and then topped off by a 25% VAT. This brings the final price to €0.8 + 25% = €1. There are some very heavy economic arguments upholding the high rate of expenditure taxes on certain goods, and we will get to them in Section 2.4. [25]

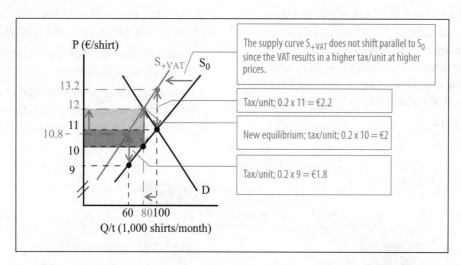

Figure 2.2.29 *Incidence of an ad valorem (VAT) expenditure tax on shirts*

Outside the box:
Income tax and black markets

My home country of Sweden has the highest overall tax pressure in the world. Income tax is a major part of government revenue and of course a burden on households. My Swedish students were well aware of the incentive for parents to hire black market labour in, say, redoing the kitchen or adding on to the garage. Several asked during the first edition of this book that I include in the next edition what I did on the board in class, namely illustrate the incentive for me to join the black market for labour during a summer when I was a poor student. [26] (Note that while I am using the Figure 2.2.30 on page 139 to illustrate a *personal* story, it is equally reapplicable to the *aggregate*, i.e. the labour market as a whole.)

---

25. You think I'm making this up? Listen, I live on coffee, sugar, nicotine and stress. Basically I'm pretty wired. When I'm out running in 'bad areas' here in Mexico I am frequently attacked by wild dogs – carrying any number of diseases which are probably not even in the books. To date I've palm-smacked and front-kicked at least three dogs into the brush. I send a mental note of thanks to Kawasoe sensei every time. Oh, lately, fearing getting some nasty disease via physical contact with the mutts, I had the workers in school make me a nice pair of nunchuks. I get more exercise swinging the nunchuks at dogs than from the actual running.
26. To anybody in the Swedish tax dictatorship bureaucracy who happens to see this; we are well past the statute of limitations! Just give me my pension fund and I'll be on my way.

Basically what happened was that a friend of mine who ran a large retail store needed help one summer stocking goods on shelves and packaging goods for customers. (SEK = Swedish crowns – and I don't remember the wages so I've indexed the values.) 'Look Matt, if I pay you officially, then I'll be subject to labour taxes and social security payments. Your wage of SEK100 per hour will cost me an additional SEK30. On the SEK100 you will pay 30% in income tax. In other words; your net wage of SEK70 will cost me SEK130.

Now, what if we split the difference and cut out the "middleman" in the government tax office.'

It didn't take a degree in rocket surgery to figure out that by avoiding the taxman, my employer could save SEK30 and I could increase my wage by SEK30. I would be willing to work more hours (Q_{L0}) and he would be willing to pay for it. Everybody wins, except, of course, the tax office; oh, and the people who benefit from public and merit goods – 9 million Swedes.

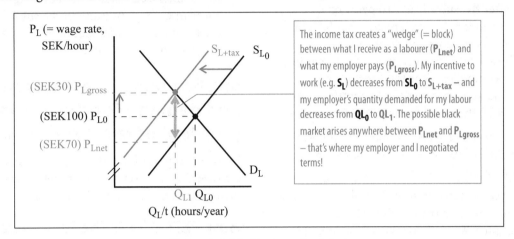

Figure 2.2.30 *Black market labour*

The incidence (= benefit) of a subsidy

The interesting thing about economics is the almost endless array of seeming contradictions. Recall the 'guns or butter' opportunity cost issue I brought up in Section 1. Now, which of these two goods do you think governments are inclined to subsidise?! The answer is 'Both'. Governments consider military defence a priority and often render grants to private military contractors for R&D. As for butter, rural development and traditional values often lead to farm subsidies so that farmers can attain what is considered reasonable income levels. In any case, a **subsidy** is a money payment to producers in order to increase the supply of the good and lower the price.

> **Subsidy**: A subsidy is a money gift/grant from government which acts as a a) an incentive to producers to produce more; and b)lowers the (marginal) costs of production. Both of these forces serve to increase supply.

The European Union's Common Agricultural Policy (CAP) spends some USD50 billion a year on agricultural subsidies. The effect has thus been periodic oversupply. Figure 2.2.31 on page 140 shows an example of how a subsidy on wheat would affect wheat output. Market equilibrium is at a price of €100 per metric tonne and a quantity of €50 million tonnes. When a subsidy of €10 per tonne of wheat is granted, supply increases, S_0 to $S_{subsidy}$, and a new equilibrium price of €95 is reached. The amount supplied on the market has increased to 60 million tonnes. The total incidence of the subsidy is €10 per tonne times 60 million tonnes; €600 million. (Please compare the total incidence of the subsidy in Figure 2.2.31 with the total incidence of a tax done in Figure 2.2.28 on page 137 (effect of a flat rate tax). Don't mix the two up – it's a common error.[27])

---

27. In dealing with total incidences of either tax or subsidy, I always tell my people the following trick: 'Find the new equilibrium point (where S_1 = D), draw a line straight up/down till you hit the old supply curve. Then go 'home' – to the P-axis – from both points that you have on the two supply curves. This **square horse-shoe shape** is total incidence of tax or subsidy.'

> **Incidence of a subsidy**: The incidence of a subsidy is basically the 'weight' of the benefit received by producers and consumers. If a unit subsidy of €4 lowers the price by €1 then the incidence of the subsidy on consumers is 25% and for producers 75%.

Who gains from the subsidy? Again, be very careful here because the incidences have 'switched places' compared to the incidence of taxes. The initial price was €100 and after the subsidy of €10 per tonne, consumers are paying €95, which means that 50% of the subsidy benefits the consumer – this is the incidence of the subsidy on consumers. The remaining incidence goes to suppliers. The total cost of the subsidy is the unit subsidy times total quantity produced; €10 × 60 thousand tonnes = €600 thousand.

There are additional effects of a subsidy, namely the increase in producers' revenue and the change in consumers' consumption and spending:

- *Producer revenue* increases from €5 million (€100 × 50,000) to €6,3 million (€10 × 60,000 from government plus €95 × 60,000 from consumers) per year
- *Consumer spending* goes from €5 million (€100 × 50,000) to €5.7 million and consumption increases by 10,000 tonnes per year.

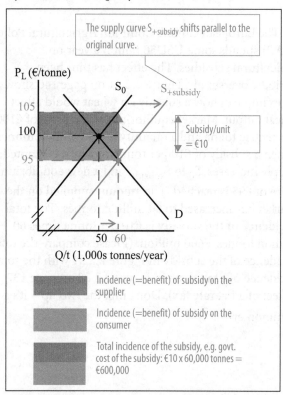

Figure 2.2.31 *Incidence of a subsidy on wheat*

Questions

Refer to Figure 2.2.31.

1. Who would benefit the most if demand were more inelastic?

2. What would total government expenditure be if the government set a minimum price of 105 *instead* of the subsidy and implemented a repurchasing scheme?

3. Assume that market equilibrium is where $S_{subsidy}$ and D intersect. What will happen to price, government expenditure on the subsidy, and market quantity if demand increases? Assume ceteris paribus, of course.

Implication of elasticity of supply and demand for the incidence (burden) of taxation ©IBO 2003

In this final part of Section 2.2, we look at how we can utilise elasticities together with the concept of incidence of tax in economic analysis.

How PED affects the incidence of tax

Let us compare two goods, one with low PED and one with high PED: petrol and oranges. This time, we extend the analysis to how consumers and producers will be affected by the tax. Figure 2.2.32 on page 141 shows supply and demand for the two goods, and we assume rather unrealistically both goods to have an initial price of ¥100 (Japanese yen) and quantity of 100 (basically, I am indexing prices and quantity). A flat rate tax of ¥50 is put on both goods,[28] raising the price of both goods – but the comparison pretty much ends there.

Both goods' demand curves will have a marked effect on whom the main incidence of tax will fall; the lower the PED, the higher the increase in price due to the expenditure tax.

- The tax on petrol (see Figure 2.2.32 diagram I) has caused a far higher price hike than for oranges. The brunt of the petrol tax will of course be paid for by the consumer who has no real substitutes; the major incidence of tax, 80%, is a burden on the consumer. This makes intuitive sense, for as soon as consumers lack viable alternatives they will be willing to pay a great deal of a price increase, something that firms are well aware of.

- Oranges, (see Figure 2.2.32 diagram II) on the other hand, have many possible substitutes – and hence a high PED – and this shows inasmuch as consumers only bear 20% of the total tax burden. As for the question of which good would be more suitable for taxation, I leave that to you to figure out.

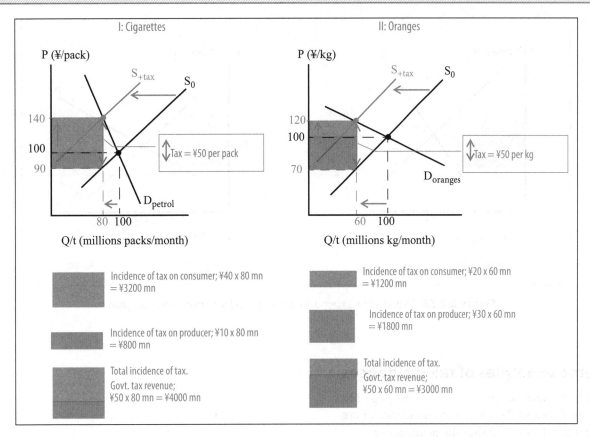

Figure 2.2.32 *Expenditure tax on cigarettes and oranges*

How PES affects the incidence of tax

We now look at the incidences of indirect taxation in relation to different *supply* curves. Let me be a trifle provocative in the choice of goods with which to exemplify this. I will use nuclear energy as one good and coal as the other. Let's put in a few assumptions:

1. Nuclear power and coal are the only two available sources of electricity.

2. Both are perfect consumer substitutes with identical PED values.

3. Both industries are operating close to maximum output.

4. Increasing nuclear power is far more supply inelastic than increasing coal powered electricity, as it takes a great deal more time to install additional nuclear reactors than coal furnaces.

Once again, we assume that the original price and quantity are the same for both goods. Government now

looks at the possibility of levying a 'green tax' on one of the two alternatives. (I forego using actual figures now as you are assumed to be online.)

- Diagram I of Figure 2.2.33 on page 142 shows how an environment tax on nuclear power which has low PES will put most of the tax burden on producers; the shift from S_0 to S_1 raises the price far less than the total amount of tax. This puts the main incidence on producers, as shown by the grey rectangle.

- The alternative, coal-fired energy in Figure 2.2.33 diagram II, lowers quantity far more and puts the main tax burden on consumers. The choice boils down, once again, to 'who should pay the most' and also which of the two alternatives government wishes to dissuade use of. It is also clearly evident that supplied quantity is more affected when PES is high.

---

28. I will limit myself to flat rate taxes in showing incidences of tax. There is simply no real benefit in using an ad valorem tax to show the burden of tax.

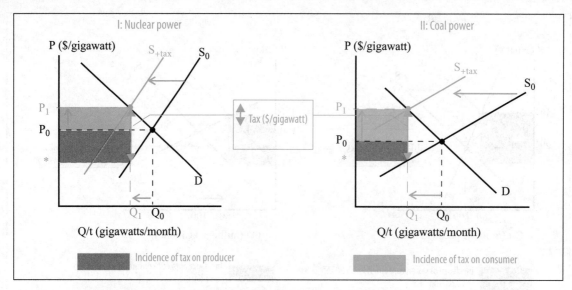

Figure 2.2.33 *Effects of an expenditure tax on nuclear power and coal power*

Extreme examples of tax incidences

The four examples in Figure 2.2.34 on page 143 show how PES and PED affect the incidence of tax such that it is 100% on either the producer or consumer.

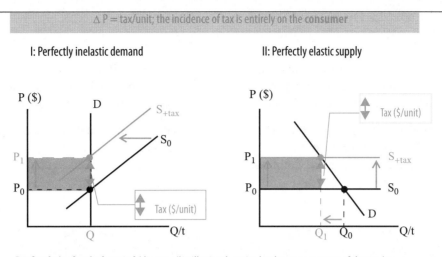

Δ P = tax/unit; the incidence of tax is entirely on the **consumer**

I: Perfectly inelastic demand

II: Perfectly elastic supply

Perfectly inelastic demand (diagram I) will raise the price by the same amount of the tax (no change in Qd), as will **perfectly elastic supply** (diagram II). The entire incidence of tax thereby falls on the consumer.

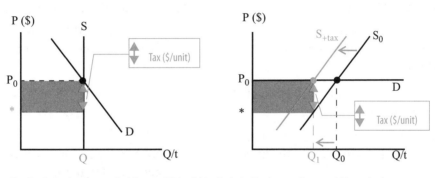

No Δ P due to tax; the incidence of tax is entirely on the **producer**

III: Perfectly inelastic supply

IV: Perfectly elastic demand

Perfectly inelastic supply (diagram III) is trickier. Technically, the supply curve shifts up by the amount of the unit tax, i.e. stays in place. There is no change in quantity demanded – any tax will have to come out of producers' pockets.

A **perfectly elastic demand curve** (diagram IV) means that demand is constant at a given price. Any movement along the demand means the price remains the same, so the entire incidence of tax is levied on the producer.

Hint: Don't try to commit the above to memory. I still haven't! All one needs to do is remember that if a tax is levied and the price changes by the same amount as the tax, the consumer will bear the entire tax burden. In a case where the price doesn't change, the producer will bear the entire incidence of tax.

Figure 2.2.34 *Four extreme cases of the incidence of tax*

HIGHER LEVEL

POP QUIZ 2.2.6   INCIDENCE OF TAXES AND SUBSIDIES

1 Draw S/D curves that show how the incidence of a subsidy benefits mainly the consumer. What type of good might this be? Why might it be subsidised?

2 Draw a S/D diagram showing how a government subsidy on a good affects the revenue of the supplying firms. Point out total revenue. Point out total government expenditure.

3 How do indirect taxes and subsidies affect resource allocation? In which cases would the reallocation of resources due to a subsidy or tax be the greatest?

4 What are the benefits of taxing goods such as cigarettes and alcohol?

Preparing for exams

Short answer questions (10 marks each)

1 How do economists use the theory of income elasticity of demand to distinguish between different types of goods?

2 What determines whether the supply of a product is price elastic or price inelastic?

3 A business person believes that halving her prices will double her revenue. Explain why this might not happen.

4 [HL Only] A government imposes an indirect tax on the supply of a good with zero price elasticity of demand. Using a diagram, explain why consumers, not producers, could in the end pay this tax.

5 [HL Only] If the coefficient of PES is lower than the coefficient of PED, upon whom will the largest incidence of a producer tax fall? Use diagrams to aid your explanation.

6 Explain why both the PES and PED tend to be inelastic in the short run for primary goods.

Essay questions (25 marks each)

1 a Using commodities as an example, explain the factors influencing the PES for such goods. (10 marks)

   b How does the PED and PES of commodities affect producers in developing countries? (15 marks)

2 a Explain the factors influencing the value of PED and yED. (10 marks)

   b Evaluate the importance of knowing PES and yED in firms' decision-making process. (15 marks)

Theory of the firm

2.3

HIGHER LEVEL

THEORY OF THE FIRM ©IBO 2003

Fatherly advice to the student!

The theory of the firm is centred on the cost picture of firms and the surrounding environment of competitive, co-operative and interventionist forces. Most of what will be done here will involve a great many diagrams to illustrate and support the narrative. I strongly urge you to do likewise when you address questions and write your Internal Assessment commentaries. The rule in theory of the firm is IF IT CAN BE DONE VIA DIAGRAMS – DO IT!

Types of costs: fixed and variable

©IBO 2003

In economics, one has the tendency to look upon the firm as an entity (= being) that has a mind of its own. This is, of course, not true; decisions and actions are taken by people within the firms rather than by the firms themselves. A firm is simply an entity which organises and rationalises productive resources in order to supply a market. The firm's (e.g. owner's) goal is – ultimately – profit. We start by looking at the payments for the use of production factors which are the costs firms meet.

Fixed costs

All costs are commonly divided into *fixed costs* and *variable costs*. Using the production of the book you are holding as an example, let's say that I did not only all the writing of this book, but also the typesetting, printing, marketing, sales and shipment. Within all the activities herein, there would be a number of costs which would not change – whether I ultimately sold one book or one thousand.

For example, there would be rent for office space and copying machines; maintenance and cleaning costs; insurance costs; and the depreciation (see box below) on the printing machines, computers and other capital purchased to run the firm. All of these are examples of fixed costs, i.e. costs which do not change with the quantity of books sold.

Depreciation: It is important to have a basic understanding of one of the most critical fixed costs to firms – the cost of buying machines and increasing plant size. If a firm expands capacity by buying more capital or building additional buildings, the fixed cost is the depreciation of the capital, or the consumption rate of capital. The cost can be estimated by dividing the market price of the capital with the expected lifespan of it. For example, a firm buys a new machine for $100,000 and expects to have to replace it in 10 years when it is worn out. This capital is therefore 'consumed' at a rate of 1/10 per year. The fixed cost of the machine is then $10,000 per year ($100,000/10 years).

Naturally, most machines and buildings, etc. simply don't go 'poof' after 10 years. There is a residual value, i.e. a market value when the machine or building is sold second hand. If the firm in my example sold the machine for $20,000 at the end of its lifespan, then the cost of capital consumption – depreciation – is $80,000 divided by 10 years ($8,000 per year). (I am disregarding any effects of inflation, interest paid on loans made in order to buy the machine, and the opportunity cost of not using the $100,000 for something else!)

Don't make the mistake of thinking that the costs of machinery, buildings and other forms of capital are fixed only. There are many variable costs that enter into the picture, such as maintenance, repairs, spare parts, etc. All of these additional costs will increase as utilisation of the additional capital increases, which means they are per definition variable costs.

Variable costs

Conversely, variable costs vary with the quantity produced – hence the name. In actually producing the first book, a number of additional costs would arise in direct consequence: ink/paper and other raw material costs, additional labour, advertising, and increased wear and tear on capital, i.e. higher rate of depreciation (please see box on depreciation above once more). The distinction is quite simple: fixed costs do not change with output levels while variable costs do[1].

---

1. Labour is notoriously tricky to define in terms of 'fixed or variable'. In an industry such as apple-picking where additional labour is often and quickly added then we must regard it as variable. However, in a school, labour would be considered a fixed factor as more pupils do not immediately entail more staff. We will initially assume labour to be a variable factor.

> **Fixed and variable costs:**
> *Fixed costs* are not linked to the quantity of output produced. They are constant since they are incurred whether the firm produces or not.
> *Variable costs* are linked to quantity of output and are sometimes called 'operating costs'. Variable costs increase as quantity produced increases.

> **Short run and long run:**
> *The short run* is defined as the time period during which one or more factors of production are fixed, i.e. there is at least one fixed cost.
> *The long run* is when all factors are variable, i.e. all costs are variable.

Short run and long run

It would be impossible to use absolute time, as in days/weeks/months, to define the short and long run. Any such usage would be rather arbitrary in fact. However, as there is always a time element involved in the speed with which firms can increase output, there is a difference between costs of increasing output. We use this as a device to aid in the definition of short run and long run. For example, it's far easier for a firm to use more electricity and raw material than to increase the size of the production plant – variable factors can and are changed far quicker than fixed factors of production. This is how we can differentiate the short run from the long run:

- The short run is defined as the time period where one or more factors of production are fixed, i.e. the period of time within which the firm cannot increase a fixed factor of production.

- As soon as the time period extends to the ability of a firm to increase all factors of production, then the long run has been defined. Quite naturally, in the long run all factors and thus all costs are variable.

How long is the long run? Well, how long should a person's legs be?! ('Long enough to reach the ground' – it depends on how tall the person is.[2]) The long run varies immensely depending on the activity of the firm. A nuclear energy firm might have to define the long run as 10 years, which is the time it takes to build a new reactor core and get it up and running. The long run for a pizzeria might be a few months, the time it takes to increase the size of the kitchen and install new ovens. In other words, we don't use the concept of short run as measure of time, but as a definitional period of the length of time needed for a given firm or industry to increase fixed factors of production.

Total, average and marginal costs

©IBO 2003

Total fixed costs (TFC) and total variable costs (TVC)

Adding all the fixed costs of a firm renders total *fixed* costs (**TFC**), and doing likewise with all the variable costs gives the total *variable* costs (**TVC**). The sum of total fixed and total variable costs gives us *total* costs (**TC**).

Here are a few standard formulaic expressions:

$$\text{TC} = \text{TFC} + \text{TVC} \quad \rightarrow \quad \text{TFC} = \text{TC} - \text{TVC} \quad \rightarrow$$
$$\text{TVC} = \text{TC} - \text{TFC}$$

One of the easier ways to become confused in the beginning of this section is to not properly understand the highly important distinction between total and per unit. A firm which has total costs (TC) of £1,000 and produces 100 widgets means that the cost per widget is £10, i.e. £1,000 divided by 100 units. Just think 'cost per unit' in mathematical terms and you get 'cost/unit' – no stranger than taking total costs and dividing them by total number of units produced. Thus, total costs divided by total output gives us average total costs (ATC).

Average fixed costs (AFC), average variable costs (AVC) and average total costs (ATC)

Just like total costs are comprised of total variable and total fixed costs, average total costs are comprised of average fixed costs (AFC) and average variable costs (AVC). Neither concept is any more complicated than anything done previously; simply take total fixed costs or total variable costs and divide by quantity of output. In another series of formulae:

$$\text{TFC} \ldots\ldots + \ldots\ldots \text{TVC} \ldots\ldots = \ldots\ldots \text{TC}$$

$$\frac{\text{TFC}}{\text{Q}} = \text{AFC} \qquad \frac{\text{TVC}}{\text{Q}} = \text{AVC} \qquad \frac{\text{TC}}{\text{Q}} = \text{ATC}$$

---

2. Classic answer by Abraham Lincoln.

Marginal cost (MC)

It takes a bit more to arrive at marginal cost (MC). Go back to the PPFs and/or "A beer in the desert" on page 18 and revise the concept of marginal. The outward-bending PPF shows increasing costs of one more unit, which is in fact the same as marginal cost. In the case of utility, marginal utility was the addition to total utility in the consumption of one more beer. It's quite the same here; marginal cost is the *addition to total costs in producing one more unit* of output. If the Widget factory above produced one more unit, i.e. 101 units, and total costs went from 1,000 to $1,020 then the marginal cost of that last unit is $20.

The formula for *marginal cost*[3] is: $MC = \frac{\Delta TC}{\Delta Q}$.

Note that all the costs thus far have been short-run costs, which means that the Widget factory will ultimately have increasing difficulties in putting ever more widgets into the market, and marginal costs will rise. Putting the above into a highly simplistic and abridged (= shortened) Table 2.3.1:

Table 2.3.1 *Total, average and marginal cost*

Total output (Q of Widgets)	Total Costs (TC)	Average Cost (AC) TC/Q	Marginal cost (MC) $\Delta TC/\Delta Q$
100	$1,000	$10	
			$20
101	$1,020	10.1	
			$25
102	$1,045	$10.24	

An in-class example (literally) of 'marginal'

Note that average costs are increasing at a far slower rate than marginal costs. This is pretty commonsensical, if one stops to think about it. I often use my students in class as an example. See Table 2.3.2. I start with an extremely small person, say Sofia (151 cm) who I think started smoking and drinking at far too early an age, and move my way up via Anna (155 cm), Myggan (158 cm), Charlie (168 cm), and finally Axel (196 cm) who I am going to drug-test for possible illegal growth substance abuse. Constructing a table for height, we get:

Table 2.3.2 *Total, average and marginal height in class*

Student's height	Total height	Average height	Marginal height
Sofia = 151	151	151	
			155
Anna = 155	306	153	
			158
Myggan = 158	464	154.6	
			168
Charlie = 168	642	160.5	
			196
Axel = 196	840	168	

---

3. Or, if the change in quantity is always just one more, the formula is: $MC = TC_n - TC_{n-1}$. (It can be read as 'The MC of the 101st unit is the TC of producing 101 units minus the TC of producing 100 units'. 'n' means 'referred-to amount'.)

HIGHER LEVEL

(Note: Average height is the total height of all the students divided by the number of students. The second average value is thus $\frac{151 + 155}{2} = 153$ and the last average value is $\frac{840}{5} = 168$. Marginal height is of course the height of each additional student.)

By the time I've lined them all up they're all giggling so it's hard to measure them – much less get them to pretend that they are standing on each others heads! – but it soon becomes clear that average values do not increase as fast as marginal values. The addition to the total is simply spread out over increasing numbers so in fact an average value cannot increase faster than a marginal value. Anna's addition of 155 centimetres increases the average from 151 to 153 $\frac{151 + 155}{2} = 153$ which is less than the 155 cm she brought with her as a marginal contribution. As shall soon be seen, this is the same way that costs in firms behave; marginal costs increase at a faster rate than average costs.

> **Total, average and marginal costs**:
>
> *Total costs* (TC) are total fixed costs (TFC) plus total variable costs (TVC).
>
> *Average costs* are total costs divided by quantity:
>
> - TFC / Q = AFC
> - TVC / Q = AVC
> - TC / Q = ATC
>
> *Marginal cost* is the addition to total cost in producing one more unit (?TC/?Q), or the cost of the last unit produced.

Accounting cost + opportunity cost = economic cost ©IBO 2003

I once spent a weekend chopping down oak trees on my grandfather's land in Missouri to sell as firewood. Two days of backbreaking, callused-hand-inducing hard labour. I sold four cords (a silly measurement used for firewood – about $1.5 \times 0.5 \times 3$ metres) of wood for $140. After subtracting costs of petrol for the pickup truck and chainsaw, two new axe handles, leather gloves, and a respectable quantity of bandages and iodine (well, I couldn't use the first aid kit at home and let my grandmother know I cut through my foot with the chainsaw) I was left with $110. My costs were thus $30, right?

Wrong. The concept of cost has been used a great deal and now comes the time to more carefully define the term, which unfortunately is from the 'One-plus-one-equals-three' school of mathematics. Costs, according to economists, are simply not a straightforward addition of numbers – that is called accounting cost. Instead, costs in economics take into account the *opportunity costs* involved – we *impute* (= assign) *values* to costs which in fact have had no money outlay. See Figure 2.3.1 on page 151. Spending the weekend chopping wood meant not being able to work at a local Pimple-Palace (= hamburger restaurant) where I had been offered a job; I was forgoing 18 hours at $3.50 an hour. This $63 in foregone income must be factored-in to the equation of an economist. In addition to this, I could have put the $30 I spent on factor inputs (axe handles, etc.) into something that gave me a rate of return – shares in Apple Computing for example. Let's say that Apple shares bought on Friday for $30 could have been sold on Monday for $31. Finally, there is a risk involved that I would not be able to sell the wood. That risk has a price tag too, which is the minimum return I would require to be in the wood-chopping business in the first place – this is my normal profit, basically the profit I would be satisfied with. Let's impute normal profit at $40. Here's a summary of the costs.

By adding on the foregone opportunities, which are implicit (= implied) in all economic activity, we get entirely different costs. The opportunity costs together with the accounting costs give us economic costs. I didn't make a profit of $140 minus $30, i.e. $110. According to the reasoning of an economist, I made an economic profit of $140 minus $134, i.e. $6. This silly example is really no different from the way all costs are accounted for by economists. All firms will have alternative uses for land, labour and capital just as in the above example. By using economic costs rather than the more straightforward accounting costs, we are able to assess whether the overall use of resources is optimal or sub-optimal. We will return to the concept of economic cost and economic profit and expound upon them in the chapter on profit. Just keep in mind that all costs used in economics, fixed or variable, average or marginal, implicitly have economic costs baked in to them.

> **Accounting cost and economic cost**:
>
> *Accounting costs* are visible and/or directly quantifiable costs such as the cost of raw material and labour.
>
> *Economic costs* are estimated by adding onto accounting costs the (imputed, e.g. costs where no payment is made) opportunity costs of using factors of production, plus the 'risk premium' of required minimum profit called normal profit.

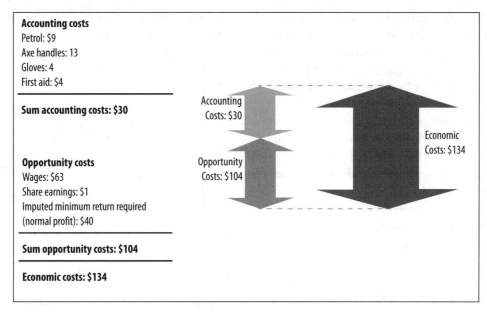

Figure 2.3.1 *Accounting and economic costs for McGee's chop 'til you drop*

Do you understand the following joke?

Q: What's the difference between a degree in accounting and a degree in economics?

A: Opportunity cost!

POP QUIZ 2.3.1   COST THEORY

1   'Labour is a fixed cost!' 'Labour is a variable cost!' Discuss the seeming contradiction between these two statements.

2   Explain, using cost concepts, why the economist's definition of the short run is not determined by an absolute measure of time.

3   A firm has an AVC of £10 at an output of 100,000 units. TFC are £1,500,000. What is the ATC?

4   Why are economists so careful to differentiate economic costs from (pure) accounting costs?

Short run ©IBO 2003

In virtually every scenario analysed within the theory of the firm, the time span is carefully expressed in the assumptions. This is because different time spans often render different aims and different assessments of opportunity costs and profit.

Law of diminishing returns ©IBO 2003

When I was feverishly trying to get my final paper together for my Master's Degree, my supervisor and I stole a credo (probably from a bumper sticker) to put on the wall of the economics and business institution:

'The first 90% of the job takes 90% of the time. The remaining 10% of the job also takes 90% of the time.' I thought this very funny until it turned out to be true. It became funny again when I realised that it irritated a good many math teacher.

In adding one more unit of any given variable factor of production, the rate at which output increases will start to decrease – assuming that there is one or more *fixed factors* of production that the firm cannot increase in the given time period. I give you the Diminishing returns Doctrine: 'Diminishing returns ultimately set in if one, or more, factors of production is/are fixed'. Now, how did we previously use 'if one or more factors are fixed'? Think about this while you read on.

> **Law of diminishing returns**: Diminishing returns or *the law of variable proportions* means that the output per additional unit of variable factor input will ultimately fall. These diminishing returns will always set in if one or more factors of production are fixed.

Total product, average product, marginal product ©IBO 2003

Consider the following experiment I've done in class a number of times. Each of my 28 students was instructed on how to fold a specific type of paper aeroplane which required 12 separate folding movements. The class was then divided in two, 14 students in each group. To make a short story shorter, one group simply made aeroplanes as individuals, i.e. started and finished each individual aeroplane by himself/herself. The other group was asked to divide the labour, where each student would be given one or two folding tasks, pass the paper on to the next student and do the same operation(s) again with a new paper. Each group was given a stack of paper and 5 minutes of production time. The result was overwhelmingly in favour of the divided labour group. I believe the output was four times higher! A helpful way of rephrasing this is that each individual student produced, on average, four times as many units – which basically meant that productivity was 300% higher. Broadly speaking, the fewer the tasks and actual movements involved per labourer, the higher the productivity is as a whole.

So, if the first student could fold 40 aeroplanes per hour, adding the second student would mean a total output of 80. The third would bring output to 120, the fourth to 160 and so forth. Right? Nope. This would be to totally disregard the gains to output derived from the division of labour. Two people working and co-operating together create more final output than the sum of two people working separately. Just imagine the time saved – in the paper aeroplane example – when everyone is fully occupied with a narrow range of simple moves and tasks. No dead or wasted time arises by stooping to pick up another box of paper or leaving the production table to stack aeroplanes on the shelf. These tasks are already assigned. Output would at first increase at an increasing rate, and then output would increase at a slower rate (diminishing returns sets in) since more and more students are crowding around the same table. The table is a fixed factor of production.

Total and marginal product

What would output look like in a factory where at least one factor of production is fixed? Let us build an example of a small factory making sturdy work-pants. Total product (i.e. total output) is measured per week and we assume labour to be a variable factor while a quantity of capital (here the number of riveting machines) is fixed. This first labourer could produce 40 Sturdy-Pants within the week … and the second could produce 50, bringing total product (TP) to 90. Figure 2.3.2 plots out the figures given in Table 2.3.3 on page 153, and shows how total product increases by 50 units when adding labourer number 2, i.e. this labourer 'brought with him/her' an additional 50 units. Each additional labourer adds to the total output – this is marginal product (MP). Or, in our example, the correct term would be the marginal output of labour. As tasks are more finely divided and tuned and there is less time wasted, the addition of another unit of labour increases total output more than the previous unit of

labour. Each additional labourer 'brings with him/her' more than the previous.

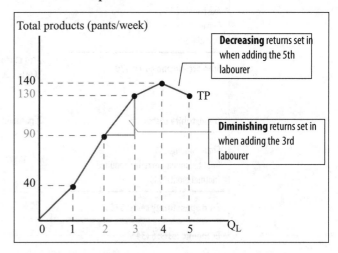

Figure 2.3.2 *Total product (= output) at Sturdy-Pants*

> **Marginal product (output):** The addition to total output caused by adding one more unit of a variable factor (here; labour) is the marginal product (output).

Something happens when the third labourer is added. Total product still increases, from 90 pairs of pants per week to 130 per week, but the *rate of increase falls* – labourer number 2 increased total output by 50 pairs but labourer number 3 increases total product by 40 pairs. It seems that the rate at which total product increases is falling – and labourer number 5 actually decreases total output by 10. (Note: it is always simpler, in concocting tables and diagrams, to put anything 'marginal' [increase or decrease] in *between* the two total values. I have tried to make this clear by using brackets in Table 2.3.3 on page 153 and then shifting the marginal values down half a step.)

The graph in Figure 2.3.3 on page 154 illustrates the 'classic' diminishing return curve. While the first two labourers increase the rate increase of total product, the third labourer lowers – not total product – but the rate of *increase* in total product. An additional increase in labour reinforces this: output continues to increase but at an increasingly slower rate. The return on each additional unit of labour is falling – we have **diminishing returns.** The fourth labourer increases total product by 10 while the fifth labourer actually lowers total output by 10, in other words, he/she yields negative returns! So too will any additional labourers.

So what is the issue? Do IQs suddenly drop drastically after the first two labourers? Are labourers number 3 and beyond incredibly inept, maladroit fumblers – the fifth labourer probably not being smart enough to find his/her gluteus maximus with both hands in back pockets? No, the answer is that we are operating under the conditions where there are one (or more) factors of production that is fixed. Our premise was that there was a certain amount of *fixed capital*; the riveting machine used to put rivets in stress seams in the pants. As more and more labourers crowd around the machine, at some point they are simply not able to be as efficient in their use of the machine as the

previous labourer – thus the machine will not be able to keep up with the relative increase in labour. The machine's capacity remains the same while more and more labourers try to pile around it, each additional labourer beyond number 3 will simply not be able to utilise the machine to the same extent as previous labourers.

Table 2.3.3 *Total, average and marginal product (output) at Sturdy-Pants*

$$AP = TP / Q_L$$

$$MP = \Delta TP / \Delta Q_L$$

Quantity of labour (Q_L)	Total product (TP)	Average product (AP)	Marginal product (MP)
0	0	–	
			→ 40
1	40	40	
			→ 50
2	90	45	
			→ 40
3	130	43.3	
			→ 10
4	140	40	
			→ –10
5	130	–10	

We move on to plotting out marginal and average output in a diagram. The values in Figure 2.3.3 on page 154 give the following two curves:

- *Average product*: Total product (TP) divided by the quantity of labour (Q_L) will render the average product per labourer; this is the grey AP-curve in the diagram II in Figure 2.3.3.

- *Marginal product*: The change in TP by adding additional labours is the marginal product (MP); the grey curve in the diagram II in Figure 2.3.3. Note that the MP curve is drawn 'in-between' the values for Q_L in order to show 'change in' or 'addition to' quantity of labour.

There are a few important conclusions to be seen in Figure 2.3.3.

1. The first is that when the rate of increase in TP ('speed of change') *decreases* then *MP falls*. The third labourer adds less to TP than the previous labourer; MP falls.

2. The second conclusion deals with the divergence of the AP and MP curves. MP will start to fall while AP continues to rise, and …

3. … third, when the *AP is at its peak, it will cut the falling MP curve*. Therefore, if AP is falling then MP must also be falling. The shapes of both the marginal and average product curves show that diminishing returns will set in eventually. Diminishing marginal returns set in at the third unit of labour which means that average returns will ultimately also fall. I beg you to take note of this very important point, as it is central to the models used in theory of the firm.

4. When TP is maximised at four labour units, MP is zero. This makes intuitive sense: any additional unit of labour after four will lower TP and of course 'bring with it' a negative value in terms of additional output, e.g. negative MP.

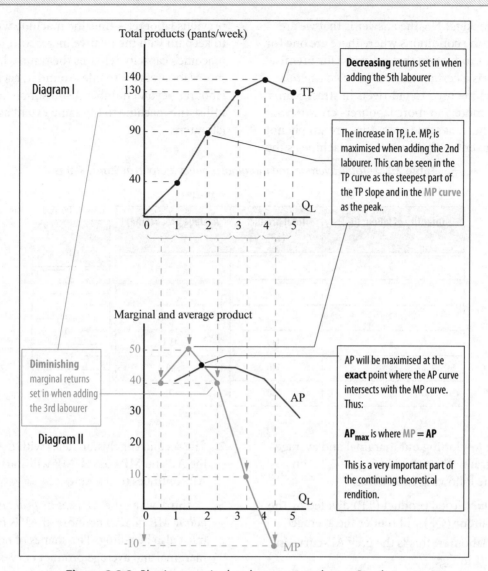

Figure 2.3.3 *Plotting marginal and average product at Sturdy-pants*

A little depth:
Labour productivity

As an important reminder, any measurement of productivity is simply the quantity of output (or yield), divided by the quantity of input (or production factors). Labour productivity is no different. It means the total quantity of widgets produced divided by the amount of labourers or labour hours. For example, imagine two firms. One large firm in Japan with 2,000 labourers working 40 hours per week and producing a total of 10,000 widgets per week. Another firm, in France, has 4,000 employees working 35 hours a week producing 20,000 widgets per week. Which firm has the highest productivity of labour?!

OK, you spotted it. Yes, I'm being nasty. The answer is that it depends on which measure of productivity we use! If we use the measurement 'widgets per labourer',

then the score is one-one, as the French firm has an output of 5 widgets per labourer $\left(\frac{20000}{4000}\right)$ while the Japanese firm also has 5 widgets per labourer $\left(\frac{10000}{2000}\right)$.

However, if we add in the additional variable of actual amount of time used in production, the labour hours utilised, the score becomes 2 to 1 to the French. The French firm produces the 20,000 widgets using 140,000 labour hours ($35 \times 4,000$), and thus produces widgets at a rate of 7 labour hours per unit $\left(\frac{140000}{20000}\right)$. The equivalent rate of labour productivity for Japan is 8 hours per widget $\left(\frac{2000 \times 40}{10000}\right)$.

Storytime: Productive timing

I probably shouldn't but I can't help telling the following story. On one occasion in class, after having spent fully 45 minutes going through the TP, AP and MP curves, I was going to use the final 15 minutes to revise everything by firing a few questions at my students. Unfortunately, I directed the first question at a young man who evidently had left his body in class but had astro-projected his mind to the Mother Ship, hovering around the vicinity of Pluto. My question to him was: 'What does point 'B' in the diagram on total product represent?', point 'B' being where total product peaked and subsequently fell. His answer is now enshrouded in the mists of legend; 'Em, that's where the producer starts to eat what he has produced!'

In my career as a teacher, I have ended a handful of classes abruptly. This was one of them. I shan't name the poor man, as he is a very sweet person and normally a bright guy. He's also done rather specialised military service and I want no quarrel with a man trained in the use of AK47s and flamethrowers.

Short-run cost curves ©IBO 2003

The iteration so far has dealt with output as a function of the use of factors in the short run. Firms' output decisions will be based on translating factor usage into short-run costs figures. We commonly use two 'pictures', i.e. diagrams, to illustrate the costs, the total cost picture and the unit cost picture.

The total cost picture

A firm's *total cost picture* is given by taking total fixed costs (**TFC**) and adding the total variable costs (**TVC**). This gives us total costs (**TC**).

$$TC = TFC + TVC$$

It is often easier to see the different costs in a table and diagram. Table 2.3.4 shows output and total costs for the Sturdy-Pants Company as used earlier. The

quantity is based on the same weekly output figures for the firm. Note that for me to be able to continue with this example, we must make two assumptions:

- We will assume that only labour costs are variable. Each unit of labour costs $500 per week.

- All other factors are fixed, e.g. everything else is part of the $1,000 'fixed cost package'. (This would mean that raw material, transport, electricity, etc. would be fixed, which would most certainly not be the case in a real firm!) Let me once again clarify that examples are often used to help you to understand concepts rather than depict reality.

Total fixed costs are $1,000 per week and labourers have a wage of $500 per unit and week while quantity is at the same output rate as in the previous example. Putting these values into the table gives us the firm's total cost picture.

Table 2.3.4 *Output and total costs for the Sturdy-Pants Company*

Q of labour (Q$_L$)	Total output (Q)	Total Fixed Costs (TFC)	Total Variable Costs (TVC)	Total Costs (TC)
0	0	$1,000	$0	$1000
1	40	1,000	500	1,500
2	90	1,000	1,000	2,000
3	130	1,000	1,500	2,500
4	140	1,000	2,000	3,000
5	130	1,000	2,500	3,500

Guess what we do now? Yes. Another diagram. This time, however, the object is to show costs, not output. The y-axis becomes the cost axis while the x-axis is the output axis.

The total cost curve is just a way of showing the cost of total output at different quantities of pants per week in Figure 2.3.4. Notice that total variable costs (**TVC**) and thus total costs (**TC**) increase at an even slower rate at first but then at an increasing rate. This is in complete correspondence with the law of diminishing returns. We have put a price tag on the use of each unit of labour, and as the marginal output per given unit of labour starts to fall, then of course the cost of the additional output has to increase. Think of it this way:

- If labourer number 2 is getting $500 and adds 50 pairs of pants to total output, then the marginal cost of each of those pants is $500 ÷ 50; **$10** per pair.

- The next labourer adds 40 – but gets the *same wage* – increasing the marginal cost to $500 ÷ 40: **$12.5**.

The unit cost picture

The above is easier to see in a *unit-cost picture*. Moving from the total cost picture to the unit cost picture is no more of an intellectual jump than moving from total milk consumption in a household to the average quantity per person in the household – and how much milk consumption changes when a friend stays overnight. Here are the formulae to help you make the jump:

$$\text{TFC} \ldots\ldots + \ldots\ldots \text{TVC} \ldots\ldots = \ldots\ldots \text{TC}$$

$$\frac{\text{TFC}}{\text{Q}} = \text{AFC} \qquad \frac{\text{TVC}}{\text{Q}} = \text{AVC} \qquad \frac{\text{TC}}{\text{Q}} = \text{ATC}$$

In moving to the unit-cost picture, we divide the totals to arrive at averages. Marginal values are calculated as

$$\text{MC} = \frac{\Delta \text{TC}}{\Delta \text{Q}}.$$

Table 2.3.4 on page 155 is relatively uncomplicated, yet one point is worthy of comment. That is that it would be most difficult indeed to calculate MC as 'the cost of the last unit produced', which is why calculations are most often based on an average of the last batch, say the final 10 units produced in our example. The first 40 units have in fact an 'average' marginal cost of $500/40 = **$12.5**, e.g. TC / Q. All the marginal cost values have been calculated like this.

Once again, 'diminishing returns' is another way of saying 'increasing marginal costs'.

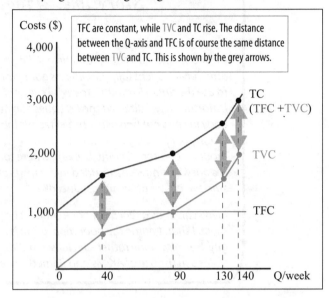

Figure 2.3.4 *Total cost picture at Sturdy-pants*

Putting the figures from Table 2.3.5 into diagrammatic form results in Figure 2.3.5 on page 157. Note the connection between the MC curve and both the AVC and ATC curves; the MC curve intersects both the average curves' lowest points, i.e. **AVC_min** and **ATC_min**. We will return to this later as it is an important point in our definition of efficiency. Let us now briefly look at each cost curve in Figure 2.3.5:

- *Average fixed costs*: I often compare TFC with spreading butter on a piece of bread: the more bread you spread a given amount of butter across, the thinner the layer. AFC falls continuously as we are spreading the fixed factor cost of $1,000 across increasing output. At an output of 40 units the AFC is $25 – at output of 140 units, ATC is $7.10.

- *Average variable costs:* The AVC curve falls and then rises as diminishing average returns set in. Unit costs rise because increasing the use of variable factors while fixed factors remain constant decreases the rate at which output increases. Average costs rise.

- *Average total costs:* Adding AFC to AVC we get the ATC curve, which also clearly portrays diminishing returns.

- *Marginal costs:* (MC) fall until around 70 units of output and then rise – diminishing marginal returns set in.

Table 2.3.5 *Total and unit costs for Sturdy-pants*

Total output (Q)	TFC	TVC	TC	AFC (TFC/Q)	AVC (TVC/Q)	ATC (TC/Q)	MC (TC/Q)
0	$1,000	$0	$1000	-	-	-	
							12.5
40	1,000	500	1,500	$25	$12.5	$37.5	
							10
90	1,000	1,000	2,000	11.1	11.1	22.2	
							12.5
130	1,000	1,500	2,500	7.7	11.5	19.2	
							50
140	1,000	2,000	3,000	7.1	14.3	21.4	

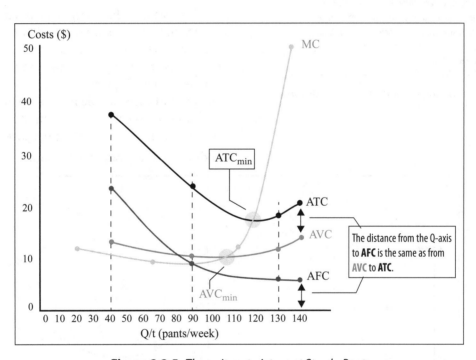

Figure 2.3.5 *The unit cost picture at Sturdy-Pants*

Diminishing returns revisited

We are now back where we started – with diagrams showing how diminishing returns will arise in the short run. The comparison in Figure 2.3.6 on page 158 illustrates how falling marginal output is the same as rising marginal costs by comparing average and marginal product curves with ditto cost curves.

Falling marginal and average output rates and the U-shaped cost curves tell us that diminishing returns

are present. Once again, diminishing returns are only possible in the short run – and the short run is defined by the time period during which one or more factors of production are fixed. In the next chapter, we un-fix them … eh, we move into the long run where all factors are variable. Before we get to that, it is necessary to elaborate on the difference between a change in *fixed* costs and a change in *variable* costs.

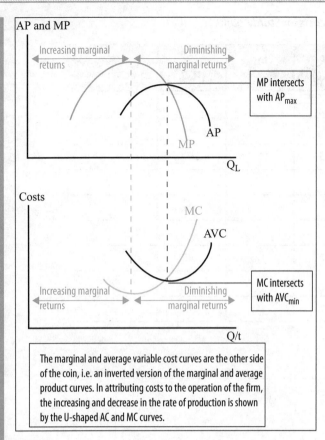

Figure 2.3.6 *Comparing product curves to cost curves*

A change in fixed costs in the short run

Assume that total fixed costs are at first $300,000 and double to £600,000. This means that the average fixed cost per unit goes from $30 at an output of 10,000 units to an AFC of $60. Of course this means that the AFC at 30,000 units goes from $10 to $20.

Figure 2.3.7 shows that ATC 'rolls' up the MC curve – the increase in fixed costs causes the AFC curve to shift considerably more at low levels of output than at high ones. An increase in fixed costs – say increased rent – causes the AFC curve to shift upwards. The shift is 'uneven' as fixed costs per unit at low levels will change far more than fixed costs at high levels of output. Therefore, in order for ATC to always intersect with the MC curve when AC is at the lowest point, the ATC curve will 'roll' up the MC curve as shown in the diagram on the left. This is something many students find confusing when confronted with for the first time: why *MC is unaffected by an increase in fixed costs.*

The reason is that marginal costs measure the change in total costs when an additional unit is produced. The rate of increase remains the same when total costs change by the same amount at all levels. A simple example is given in Table 2.3.6 on page 159, where fixed costs double from $100 to $200. This increases total costs at every output level by $100 yet the rate of change – the marginal cost of producing an additional unit – remains the same.[4]

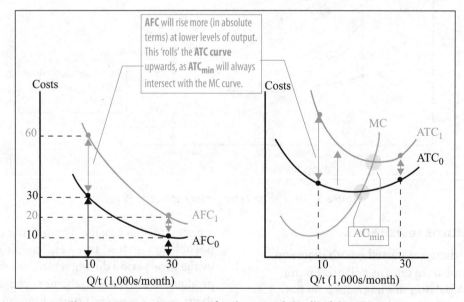

Figure 2.3.7 *An increase in fixed costs – the 'roll' of the ATC curve*

---

4. Favourite in-class trick: Take three students ranging from small to large, line them up in front of the class and put their heights on the board, e.g. '156 cm → 166 cm → 180 cm'. What's the 'marginal rate of increase in height'? It is 10 cm and 14 cm. 'Now guys, stand on your toes … and now stand on a chair … did the marginal values change? Would they change if you were on Mt Everest?' It drives home the point that marginal costs do not change due to a change in fixed costs (disregarding the long run).

Table 2.3.6 *Marginal cost of producing an additional unit*

Total output (Q)	TC0 (FC = $100)	MC0 (ΔTC / ΔQ)		Total output (Q)	TC1 (FC = $200)	MC1 (ΔTC / ΔQ)
0	$100			0	$200	
		10				10
1	110			1	210	
		8				8
2	118			2	218	
		9				9
3	127			3	227	
		12				12
4	139			4	239	

A change in variable costs in the short run

A change in variable costs has the effect of shifting the MC curve. If the cost of, say, raw material falls then the cost of producing each additional unit will fall. The result is that the MC curve will shift downwards as in Figure 2.3.8. At every output level the cost of producing an additional unit decreases, shifting the MC curve from MC_0 to MC_1. (Note that in keeping with the axiom that AC_{min} will always intersect with the MC curve, the AC curve will also shift downwards.)

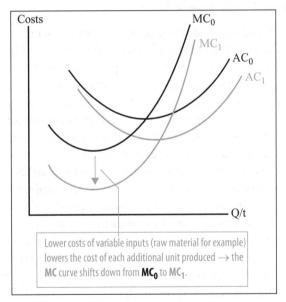

Lower costs of variable inputs (raw material for example) lowers the cost of each additional unit produced → the **MC** curve shifts down from MC_0 to MC_1.

Figure 2.3.8 *A decrease in variable costs*

Question: What else could cause the MC curve to shift, other than a change in the cost of variable factor inputs?

To summarise, a change in fixed costs will 'roll' the AC curve up or down along the MC curve – always keeping the AC_{min} point at MC – while a change in variable costs will shift the MC curve (and ATC curve). It is worth repeating that we have only dealt with the short run, i.e. one or more factors are fixed.

POP QUIZ 2.3.2   SHORT RUN AND THE FIRM

1   Assuming a firm where one or more factors of production are fixed and labour is the only variable factor, explain why total product (TP) will ultimately increase at a slower rate.

2   Continuing on question 1 above, what is the connection between TP and MP_{max}? Use diagrams in your explanation.

3   Fill in the blanks: 'When MP turns negative, TP will _____.'

4   Why do marginal and average costs ultimately rise? Would this be equally certain in both the long run and short run?

5   In increasing output from 5,000 units to 5,500 units, TC goes from £100,000 to £130,000. What is the MC per unit of the additional 500 units?

6   Why does a falling marginal product curve show the same thing as a rising marginal cost curve?

7   'A rise in FC results in a disproportional increase in ATC!' Explain.

8   Explain the effect on MC and AC when FC is tripled. Illustrate with a diagram.

9   Assume that the cost of variable inputs rises for a firm. How will this affect the unit-cost picture of the firm?

Long run ©IBO 2003

An American firm was once approached by a Swedish firm proposing a business venture. The American firm politely wrote back asking for references as a guarantee that the Swedish firm had a solid and reputable historical standing and therefore a good credit rating. The Swedish CEO (chief executive officer) promptly wrote back that their credit rating had been excellent during the entire time the firm had been a shareholding company – which started some 40 years before Columbus set off on his voyage to 'India' in 1492. One might say that this is somewhat beyond the boundaries of the short run.

The **long run** is simply defined in economics; it is the time period where a firm can increase any and all factors of production, i.e. *all factors are variable*. Over time, firms will institute changes to factory size, machines, and any other type of fixed factor. Being able to adjust overall factor inputs in proportion to output needs, firms will be able to lower the unit costs as the scale of operations increases.

> **Long run**: The long run (LR) is defined as the period within which all factors of production are variable. This lowers the average cost since firms will optimise the mixture of fixed and variable factors.

Economies of scale ©IBO 2003

A firm which increases its use of fixed factors of production will naturally incur higher costs. However, as long as the additional costs are spread over increasing units of output, the unit costs will go down (as long as the proportional increase in unit costs are lower than the increase in output). Say that a firm is producing 50 thousand units and has total costs of $500 thousand; the average cost per unit is $10. Now, if the firm increases its use of capital, say a new machine in the production line, by a (fixed) cost of $10 thousand and thereby is able to increase output by 5 thousand units, then average cost per unit drops to $9.27 ($510 thousand / 55 thousand units = $9.27 per unit). This fall in long-run costs (long-run *average* costs; LRAC) is the result of economies of scale, or the *benefits of scale*. Note that 'scale' in the case of firms' operations means *size* and nothing else.

> **Economies of scale**: Scale economies are said to exist when a firm increases output and increases both variable and fixed factors, whereby output increases at a proportionately higher rate than the increase in costs per unit. Thus average costs fall as firms achieves increased output per unit of input. This is also known as benefits of scale.

As soon as one has grasped the central issue of how increasing costs are spread ever thinner over increasing quantity of output, it's quite easy to think of real-life examples when scale economies would be apparent; industries which have large fixed costs and/ or where there are obvious advantages to being large. Possible scale benefits are often grouped into internal and external economies of scale.

Internal economies of scale

Internal means that the benefits of being large arise within the firm itself. The increasing scale of operations allows the firm to reap benefits of its own growth – regardless of the overall growth of the industry the firm is in. There are five major sources of internal economies of scale:

1. *Technical economies of scale:* These arise when a firm can take better advantage of its fixed capital. Using machines at 90% of capacity rather than 80% of capacity means that fixed costs per unit produced will fall, since the fixed costs are spread over increasing units. Therefore, buying additional machines and other capital goods serve to lower average costs when the new capital is used to its capacity. This is an example of how **indivisibilities** of production add to the merits of economies of scale; the machine can not be divided in order for the firm to use it on only four out of five days (= 80%). The machine will cost the firm just as much in fixed costs on the fifth day, so by utilising the available machine time more fully, the firm will be able to lower costs per unit.

In addition to production capabilities, increasing size give firms the ability to fully utilise transport availability. If goods are being shipped by truck, train or cargo ship, the firm will lower transport costs per unit by filling all available shipping space. Another example of decreasing costs of transportation is the *container principle*, which shows that an increase in the surface area of a tanker or other cylindrical container[5] will render a

---

5. The volume of a container is given by $\pi r^2 \times h$. If the radius of a cylindrical container measuring 1 metre times 8 metres increases by 50%, the area of the container increases by 58% but the volume increases by 125%.

far greater increase in the volume of the container. The increase in available transport volume far exceeds the cost of the increased container size.

2. *Managerial economies of scale*: arise when firms can enhance productivity and output in all areas by increasing specialisation in all areas of production; increasing scale will allow the firm to break tasks down into smaller parts and increase productivity. There are also possible '**synergy**' ('synchronised' plus 'energies') effects; development of new production methods, new materials, etc. in one area of production can be used across the board in other areas, for example, a new plastic manufacturing method in the consumer electronics division could be reapplied to the automotive division.

3. *Purchasing economies of scale*: The larger the firm, the more likely it is to be able to negotiate good contracts for the *bulk-buying* of materials, components and such. Such *purchasing economies* of scale are most noticeable in manufacturing firms which use large amounts of basic commodities. Yet increasingly one finds purchasing economies of scale in firms which actually don't produce any goods themselves; Nike in sports goods and IKEA in furniture are good examples of firms which do not actually produce goods but instead design prototypes and subsequently have manufacturing firms submit lowest-cost tenders for the production of the goods. IKEA basically asks firms to submit 'bids' for the production of a few hundred thousand bookshelves – the lowest bid wins! You can just imagine that IKEA is able to play production companies against each other and get a far lower price per bookshelf than Mom & Pop's Furniture Store up the street.

4. *Marketing economies of scale*: Anyone who's seen TV commercials for large multinational companies in different countries soon notices that the advertisements are often the same no matter where you are. In fact, the commercials are often made without the actors speaking, as this makes it easier to do a voice-over in the background in the local language. Thus, Coke, Honda, Ericsson and Adidas can make one commercial and have it aired all over the world without making 170 different versions. This is an example of *marketing economies* of scale,

and also includes such things as having widespread brand recognition, and creating barriers to other firms which do not have the advertising budget of incumbent (= already existing) firms and which are trying to enter the market.

5. *Financial economies of scale*: Getting funds for investment is one of the major issues for firms and the interest payments on loans are a sizable portion of a firm's total costs. Larger firms will often have much more in the way of assets to use as security for loans and therefore can negotiate better terms of interest and repayment than smaller firms. These *financial economies* of scale will give large firms a distinct cost advantage over small firms[6].

In addition to the above, there are distinct possibilities of larger firms being able to *spread risks* by diversifying (= broadening) the range of output into other areas. Many Japanese and Korean firms are notable examples of this type of extension. These are often referred to as conglomerates; large firms which produce a vast array of goods – sometimes with no discernable connection between them but often with a good many products which partially overlap in markets. For example, the Korean conglomerate Daewoo International Corporation produces steel, automobiles, media, electronics, textiles, commodities and energy. It has subsidiary companies in over 50 countries and branch offices in most of them. This breadth in terms of both markets and products enables the company to buffer its risks over time and ride out downfalls in regional business activity – the business cycle – and also changes in market demand for products. By having a wide product and sales base, the firm can afford short-term losses in one sector by making it up in another.

External economies of scale

When there are benefits to scale arising outside the realm of the firm, one speaks of external benefits of scale. This is the overall growth in an industry which creates benefits by which all firms operating on the market will benefit. Increasing the size of an industry will result in more and better trained labour; more efficient sub-contractors providing parts and components; an infrastructure which benefits all firms in the industry; and a general rise in the knowledge

---

6. I often have some fun with the many inventive and often provocative T-shirts worn by my students. I pick someone wearing, say, a red T-shirt emblazoned with the image of Che Guevarra and the old Soviet flag and ask that we go down to the bank (separately) and negotiate a loan. The object is to see who gets the most favourable terms of finance; the Suit and Tie Man (me) or the Provocative T-shirt Person. The issue being dealt with is the perceived risk of the bank in lending money – the lower the lender's perceived risk, the better the terms for the borrower. I believe that lax dress standards helped create the 2007/08 liquidity crisis – you simply should not lend money to a guy wearing flip-flops and a grain store cap.

and technology base needed to increase productivity. The Swiss watch industry is a good example, as this very important industry for the Swiss economy has benefited enormously from being concentrated to a limited geographical area, as this has led to a good many external benefits such as a long tradition of schools for watch-making, small parts manufacturing and high quality instruments.

The lure of economies of scale

Scale economies are most valuable in helping to explain a number of events in the global economy during the past 30 to 40 years. Perhaps the most obvious is the increasing concentration of firms, where industries have become increasingly oligopolistic, as firms force out rivals, merge or are bought up by rivals. In the beginning of the 1900s there were over 1,000 automobile manufacturers in the USA, whereas now there are basically three. Mergers and take-overs have been an increasingly strong presence during the 1980s and 1990s, and the motives were growth; new markets; attaining new technology and know-how; risk-spreading; and of course to enjoy benefits of scale. This has been most pronounced, perhaps, in the pharmaceutical business, where soaring costs of producing ever-more complicated and research intensive medicines necessitated consolidation in the industry in order to achieve scale benefits. For example, the merging of Glaxo, SmithKline and Wellcome PLC became what is now the 16th largest company in the world, Glaxo-SmithKline[7].

Merging in the Pharmaceutical industry: Old names and new (global 2002 market share in parentheses)

- Astra AB and Zeneca Group plc … became … AstraZeneca (4.6%)
- Hoechst AG and Rhône-Poulenc SA … became … Aventis (3.5%)
- Pharmacia & Upjohn and Monsanto … became … Pharmacia (3.4%)
- Pfizer and Warner-Lambert … became … Pfizer (7.5%)
- Glaxo, Wellcome and SmithKline Beecham … became … Glaxo SmithKline (7.0%)[8]

Going hand-in-glove with 'merger-mania' (as somewhat hyperbolically inclined magazines put it) is the increasing integration of regional markets on a global scale. The rationale is that a small country will have a small market, too small for a firm to get to the level where scale benefits are to be found. The answer is often found in looking to markets outside the country, i.e. exports. Many of the largest multinational companies (MNCs) can be found in very small countries; Holland's Phillips, Finland's Nokia, Switzerland's Nestlé, and Sweden's IKEA to name but a few. It is often argued in today's world of lower barriers to trade and an increasingly integrated global economy that large companies which can receive benefits of scale are the only way to remain competitive. We will look at this further in Section 4.1.

Diseconomies of scale ©IBO 2003

Economic theory allows for the possibility of increasing costs in the long run, i.e. where costs per unit increase proportionately more than the increase in output. Such **diseconomies of scale** could result from a number of factors. For example, as organisations and firms become larger, the complexities of management might increase and together with an increasing span of control for middle-management, might result in more time involved in decision making and implementation. This adds to total costs proportionately more than to output. There might also arise something called '*organisational slack*', whereby the firm becomes so large that it seemingly lacks real competitors and complacency (= self-satisfaction) sets in, with lower productivity and higher costs as a result.

Please note that I have been most careful to use adjectives such as 'might' and 'could' above. Few studies have shown conclusive evidence for the existence of diseconomies of scale, and I personally file diseconomies of scale under 'Mermaids' or 'Giffen goods'. In reality, firms that might 'outgrow' themselves in terms of factor use versus productivity ultimately scale back on production or cut costs in other ways, thereby avoiding diseconomies of scale.

> **Diseconomies of scale**: Diseconomies of scale occur when there is a rise in long-run average costs – due perhaps to communications problems and lack of control in an increasingly complex organisation.

Long-run cost curves ©IBO 2003

The central theme in short-run costs is productive efficiency, which is defined as how efficiently the firm

---

7. 'The Global 1000', *Business Week*, 14 July 2003.
8. Sources: http://www.imshealth.com/ims/portal/front/indexC/0,2605,6025_1825,00.htm and OECD http://www.oecd.org/std/nahome.htm, August 2002, Office for National Statistics.

is using all factors of production – fixed and variable – in producing a given amount of output. This is of course shown by average costs, which fall at first and then rise in accordance with diminishing returns. Optimum productive efficiency exists when the total cost per unit of output is at its lowest. Thus, whereas in the short run AC_{min} would be the measure of efficiency, in the long run we can adjust all factors of production and increase output at a proportionately higher rate than costs. A firm will act in accordance with market demand and estimate whether to increase fixed factors in order to increase output. Figure 2.3.9 looks at the possibility for a firm to lower average costs by increasing fixed factors such as machinery or additional production area.

If the firm is producing Q_0 then it would be productively efficient in the short run, since short-run

average costs (SRAC) are minimised at AC_0. If, however, the firm anticipates that it could indeed sell the quantity Q_1, then it would experience significant increases in average costs as diminishing returns set in, the constraint being the fixed production factors. Therefore the firm assesses options to expand output by increasing certain fixed factors. The estimated average cost of increasing fixed factors is shown by the new short-run average cost curve, $SRAC_1$. It is clear that the increased use of fixed factors – new machinery or factory area – adds to average costs at the *present* level of output (Q_0), by 50%, i.e. from AC_0 to AC^*_0. The firm must move to Q_{min} in order to have the same initial cost per unit of AC_0 – and can lower average costs by one third by producing at Q_1, which is the new optimal point of output along the new short-run average cost curve, $SRAC_1$.

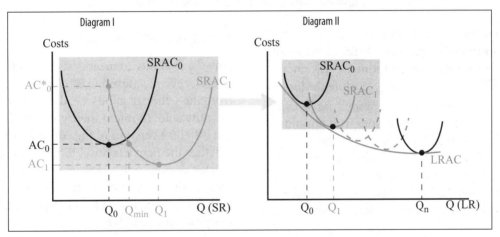

Figure 2.3.9 *Increasing fixed factors – the enveloping effect of average costs in LR*

The SRAC curves show how additional (fixed) factors lift the constraints of the short run, and assuming that any and all additional capital and other fixed factors are variable in the long run, we get an infinite array of SRAC curves, shown in diagram II in Figure 2.3.9. The short-run curves are *enveloped* by the long-run curve, or rather, the long-run average cost curve is made up of the tangential points of an infinite array of SRAC curves. Note that the assumption of endless SRAC curves means that fixed factors can be increased by minute incremental amounts. Also, any point on the LRAC curve will be equal to or lower than all tangential points on the SRAC curves. The SRAC curves never cross any part of the LRAC as this would mean two possible points on the SRAC curve being equal to the LRAC.

The enveloping effect of the LRAC in Figure 2.3.10 on page 164 will form an L-shaped or U-shaped LRAC curve.

- If increased use of fixed factors results in a lower SRAC curve, there are *economies of scale* – or increasing benefits of scale.

- When additional expansion results in same-level SRAC then costs are optimised yielding *constant benefits of scale*. This is the LR optimum scale.

- If SRAC increase this would of mean that average costs are increasing due to the scale of the operation. The firm experiences *diseconomies of scale*. I always show the upward-sloping portion of the LRAC curve as a dotted line to convey the pronounced uncertainty as to the existence of diseconomies of scale. A rather large body of research points to LRAC curves being L-shaped (from Q_0 to Q_1 in Figure 2.3.10, diagram I) rather than U-shaped (Q_1 to Q_2) since diseconomies of scale simply are not sufficiently proven.

HIGHER LEVEL

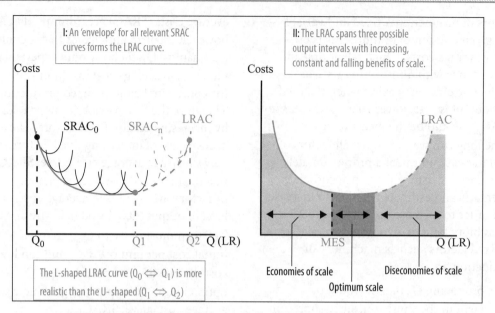

Figure 2.3.10 *LRAC and economies of scale*

On a final 'outside the box' note, Figure 2.3.10 shows the **minimum efficient scale (MES)** at the point where SRAC curves bottom out. Optimum efficiency in the short run is shown by $SRAC_{min}$, while the long-run cost curve has a potential range of *constant benefits of scale*, i.e. many possible points of long-run optimum efficiency levels of output. The MES shows the minimum level of output that is possible in order to obtain long-run lowest costs in production. I will return to this 'outside the box' concept in Section 5.3 when we deal with trade barriers in developing countries.

POP QUIZ 2.3.3   LONG RUN AND THE FIRM

1   For what reasons might (internal) economies of scale exist?

2   How might the existence of economies of scale be linked to the following?

   a   the increasing size of firms

   b   mergers

   c   oligopolies

   d   increasing trade and globalisation.

3   Using diagrams, explain carefully the difference between diminishing returns and diseconomies of scale.

4   Why is AC used as a measure of productive efficiency? Why not MC?!

Revenues ©IBO 2003

Any firm's ability to meet costs depends on its ability to earn revenue. Revenue is the money going to a firm from the selling of goods, i.e. the product of price times quantity sold. In micro theory, one finds it useful to use different versions of the concept, depending on whether the firm has the ability to set the price on the market or not. In this chapter we will compare a competitive market firm with a monopoly firm and look at total revenue (**TR**), average revenue (**AR**) and marginal revenue (**MR**).

Total revenue ©IBO 2003

Total revenue (TR) is the price of the good times the amount sold: $\mathbf{P \times Q = TR}$, as defined earlier in Section 2.2. Note that the total revenue curve shown earlier was for the *market* as a whole and that the TR curve was defined by the boundary of the demand curve. Let's revise this by assuming that the market demand is supplied in total by a single firm, a monopoly.

TR for a monopoly firm

As we are assuming that only one firm supplies the market, market demand will be the same for the monopoly firm. The firm can set any price and the pattern of demand will determine output. In Figure 2.3.11 on page 165 total revenue will peak at $2,000, when the price is $10. This is in accordance with the earlier rule which states that revenue maximum is where price is set at unitary price elasticity of demand. At any other price, TR will be lower.

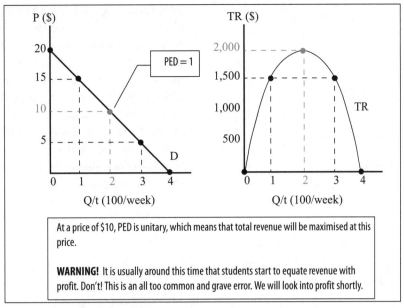

At a price of $10, PED is unitary, which means that total revenue will be maximised at this price.

WARNING! It is usually around this time that students start to equate revenue with profit. Don't! This is an all too common and grave error. We will look into profit shortly.

Figure 2.3.11 *Total revenue (TR) for a monopoly*

TR for a competitive firm

Assume that the market for widgets is instead a perfectly competitive market, and we turn our attention to one single firm in the market. Assume that there are 1,000 firms supplying the widget market and none of them are big enough to influence supply – or price. The firm is thus a *price taker* and has simply to accept a market price. Now, a little bit of syllogistic logic (see 'syllogism' Section 1) says that if the firm is too small to influence supply, and if the firm simply accepts the market price, then the firm can sell all it produces at the going market price.

Figure 2.3.12 shows the total revenue curve for a firm operating under perfectly competitive market conditions. Assuming that the market price is $10, total revenue is a matter of multiplying quantity of output with price. TR must of course be an *upward sloping* curve; as the firm sells each additional unit of output at the same price, revenue increases.

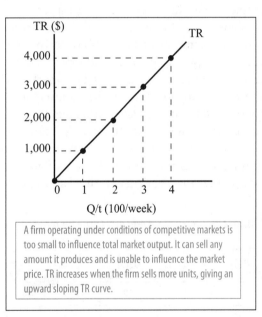

A firm operating under conditions of competitive markets is too small to influence total market output. It can sell any amount it produces and is unable to influence the market price. TR increases when the firm sells more units, giving an upward sloping TR curve.

Figure 2.3.12 *Total revenue (TR) for a firm operating on a perfectly competitive market*

Marginal revenue ©IBO 2003

MR for a competitive firm

Recall that the definition of marginal cost is the change in total cost over the change in output. Marginal revenue is the same; it is the addition to total revenue over the change in quantity sold. We often put this in terms of the revenue gained in selling one more unit, or, but formulaically speaking we get: MR = TR/Q. Figure 2.3.13 on page 166 shows that a price of $10 per unit adds to marginal revenue by the same amount as the price. The rule is summarised as 'P = MR for a perfectly competitive firm'.

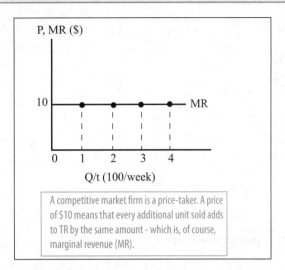

A competitive market firm is a price-taker. A price of $10 means that every additional unit sold adds to TR by the same amount - which is, of course, marginal revenue (MR).

Figure 2.3.13 *Marginal revenue (MR) for a firm operating on a perfectly competitive market*

MR for a monopoly firm

As simple as marginal revenue is to grasp, as incomprehensible at first sight is the concept when applied to a monopoly firm. Let us lay down the relevant assumptions again; the monopoly firm is alone in the market and is able to set the market price – therefore the market demand is the same as the monopoly's demand. We also assume that the monopoly sets a single price (the relevance of this assumption will become clear in the chapter on price discrimination). Using the same ballpark figures as for the competitive market firm described above gives Table 2.3.7.

Table 2.3.7 *Marginal revenue table for a monopoly*

P ($)	Q	TR ($)	MR ($)
20	0	$0	
15	1	15	15
10	2	20	5
5	3	15	– 5
0	4	0	– 15

Two things stand out immediately:

1) Firstly, MR is always lower than AR (or the price).

2) MR is continuously decreasing throughout the span of the demand curve.

This gives us Figure 2.3.14, which plots the MR of the monopoly. As the market is the same as the firm, basically, the firm will sell more by lowering the price. Starting at a price of $20 and moving to a price of $15,

total revenue goes from $0 to $15; MR = **$15**. This is plotted out in the diagram as the point halfway between zero and 1 on the quantity axis. In lowering the price further, from $15 to $10, quantity demanded increases by one unit; the revenue gained is the additional $10. However, as the firm is a single-price monopolist (more on this further on), it must sell both the first and second unit for $10, bringing TR up to $20. This is a $5 increase over the previous $15, leading to a MR of $5, shown by the second point between 1 and 2 on the quantity axis.

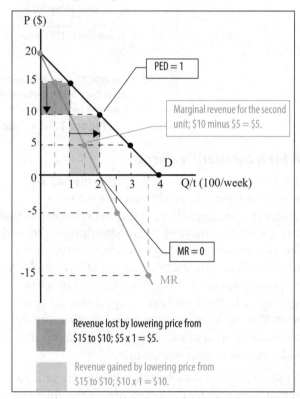

Figure 2.3.14 *Marginal revenue diagram for a price-setting firm (monopoly)*

Perhaps a simpler way of looking at MR for a monopolist is to look at the *areas* of revenue gain and revenue loss. Going, once again, from a price of $15 to $10, the revenue gain is the blue area in Figure 2.3.14. The subsequent loss of revenue is the light grey area; the difference is MR. Doing the same all along the demand curve renders the MR curve for the monopolist – it is 'halfway' between the demand curve and the price axis.

Now, fill in the following blanks below as you wait with baited breath for greater depth in the chapter on monopoly:

I) 'When PED is unitary, the MR is _____!'

II) 'TR is maximised when MR is _____!'

III) 'As TR increases, MR is _____!'

Average revenue ©IBO 2003

The last version of revenue is the revenue per unit; average revenue, or AR. As in average cost, the AR is total revenue divided by quantity sold: AR = TR/Q. This is the same in both a competitive and monopoly firm.

Average revenue for a competitive firm

Just as MR was equal to price for a price-taking firm, the AR is equal to price. This can be shown by breaking down the formula for AR.

$$AR = \frac{TR}{Q} \rightarrow \frac{P \times Q}{Q} \rightarrow \frac{P \times \cancel{Q}}{\cancel{Q}} \rightarrow AR = P$$

In the example used earlier, when the firm was facing a market price of $10 and sold a quantity of four widgets, TR would be $40. Dividing this by the quantity of 4 gives an AR of $10. Therefore, in a price-taking firm, P = MR = AR.

Average revenue for a monopoly firm

The above holds perfectly true for a monopoly, yet there is an additional link to the monopoly's unit cost picture, namely that the average revenue curve will be the same as the market demand curve. Figure 2.3.15 shows that even though TR rises and then falls, AR will follow the same path as the demand curve. The conclusion is that **in a monopoly firm, P = AR = D**.

By now it is quite easy to have forgotten or confused everything done above in terms of revenues! Don't worry, we're going to do it all again in the chapters on perfectly competitive markets and monopolies.

P	Q	TR ($)	AR ($)
20	0	0	-
15	1	15	15
10	2	20	10
5	3	15	5
0	4	0	0

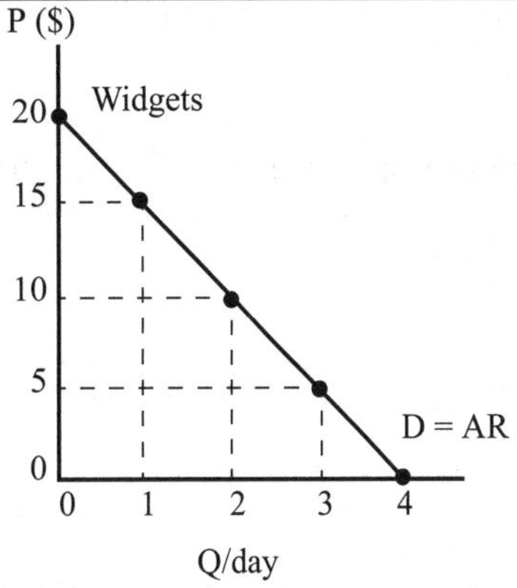

Figure 2.3.15 *Average revenue (AR) for a monopoly*

POP QUIZ 2.3.4 REVENUE

1 When does the maxim 'P = MR' hold true?

2 Show, using diagrams, the difference between the marginal revenue of a competitive firm and a monopoly.

3 What happens to TR in a monopoly as MR values turn negative?

Profit ©IBO 2003

At a basic level, profit is total revenue minus total costs. However, it is most important, as an economist, that you understand the monumental difference between accounting profit done in business studies and the concept of economic profit. We have dealt with the concept of economic costs using the basic concept of opportunity cost and now we take it one step further by adding on revenue and profit.

Distinction between normal (zero) and supernormal (abnormal) profit

©IBO 2003

Basically, normal profit is when a business or enterprise uses resources and receives an amount of revenue or income that gives him/her a rate of return that is no different from the next best alternative. If the

venture gives a rate of return that is higher, we speak of economic/abnormal/ supernormal profits.

> **Normal and supernormal profit:** *Normal profit* is the profit earned by the firm which covers all costs – both accounting and opportunity costs – and hence TC = TR. Thus there is no incentive for the firm to leave the market as the second best alternative cannot increase profits. This profit enables/incentivises the firm to keep resources in their present use.
>
> Any profit above and beyond normal profit is *supernormal profit* (or economic, abnormal, excess profit). This creates incentives for market entry by other firms.

Let's say I finally manage to get myself severely, unalterably and definitively fired, and then pursue my passion for Swiss watches by starting a fine watch shop. Below in Figure 2.3.16 I give you the accountant's version and the economist's version of the same figures.

The accounting method	The economist's method
TR = £500 000	TR = £500 000
Costs:	Costs:
- Wholesale cost of watches = £300,000	- Wholesale cost of watches = £300,000
- Utilities, services, insurance = £40,000	- Utilities, services, insurance = £40 000
- Wages = £40,000	- Wages = £40,000
- Depreciation = £30,000	- Depreciation = £30,000
- Interest paid on bank loans = £20,000	- Interest paid on bank loans = £20,000
	1) - **Fall in market value of assets** = £15,000 [See 1) below]
	2) - **My foregone wages (implicit)** = £25,000 [See 2) below]
	3) - **Foregone interest revenue of my money invested in firm** = £15,000 [See 3) below]
	4) - **My 'risk premium' for being in the business, i.e. the normal profit** = £10,000 [See 4) below]
Total costs = £430,000	Total economic costs = £495,000
Profit = £70,000	**Supernormal profit = £5,000**
	(or economic/abnormal/excess profit)

Figure 2.3.16 *Accounting is in the eye of the beholder!*

Comments on the additional costs in the economist's version:

1. **Cost of keeping a stock of watches:** There is an estimated opportunity cost of £15 000 in keeping a supply of watches in stock as that money could have been used otherwise.

2. **Foregone wages (implicit):** I could have made £25 000 in my next best option available and therefore there is an imputed opportunity cost of that income foregone.

3. **Foregone interest revenue of my own money invested in firm:** I invested £300 000 in the firm and current interest would yield 5% per annum: $0.05 \times £300\,000 = £15\,000$.

4. My '**risk premium**': There is always a risk of losing everything by being in business for oneself. The amount that I estimate the risk at is £10 000, which is to say that my estimate of the lower limit of profit in undertaking the watch enterprise is £10 000 – my normal profit. Simply put, I estimate that the opportunity costs of taking the risk at £10,000.

In summary, whenever we in the future talk about 'profit', we are inferring that both the opportunity cost issues and imputed risk premium – normal profits – have in some way been implicitly baked into the cost picture of the firm. Profit is anything above and beyond covering opportunity costs and risk premiums, i.e. 'abnormal/supernormal profit' unless otherwise specified.

Profit maximisation: total revenue and total costs, marginal revenue and marginal cost ©IBO 2003

Every year when I get to this point in the syllabus, I have threatened to have a set of T-shirts made for my people with the legend '**MC = MR Rules OK!**' emblazoned on the front – and maybe 'Mr McGee Rules Too!' on the back. That would wake the local school board up in the morning. What does the legend mean? It means that profit is maximised at the point where marginal cost is equal to marginal revenue (but

only when MCs are rising, see following). This is the short-run **profitmax condition** facing firms in the short run.

> **MC = MR profitmax condition**: Profit will be maximised when the cost of the last unit equals the revenue of the last unit. This point of output is where MC = MR.

Profit maximisation using the total cost picture: TR and TC

Let's use a scale which is a bit more realistic. Assume a Widget firm (widget = 'manufactured thing') which is operating on a competitive market and cannot influence market price or market output – it will produce the quantity which maximises profit as we assume that the firm is a short-run profit maximiser. The **total** cost picture and equivalent **unit-cost** picture are given in Figure 2.3.17 on page 170. The total cost picture shows increasing TR as more units are sold at the market price of $5, while the TC curve portrays the standard diminishing return curvature. At zero output, the firm would make a loss of $5,000, as the fixed costs would not be covered by any revenue. As output increases and revenue does too, total costs increase at a slower rate giving the firm a *break-even point* (where TR = TC) at 1,500 units. This would give the firm a *normal profit*.

The area shaded in blue shows the supernormal profit (remember, opportunity costs are included in TC!) attainable at output levels between 1,500 and 4,000 widgets per day. Supernormal profit is maximised, i.e. the difference between TR and TC is the greatest, when the firm is producing 3,000 units a day. At this output level the TR is $15,000 and TC is $10,000, yielding a supernormal profit of $5,000 per day. It is worthy of notice that should the firm decide to forgo profit maximisation, perhaps in order to expand its sphere to new markets, it could produce an additional 1,000 units and set output level at 4,000 units where, once again, TC is equal to TR.

HIGHER LEVEL

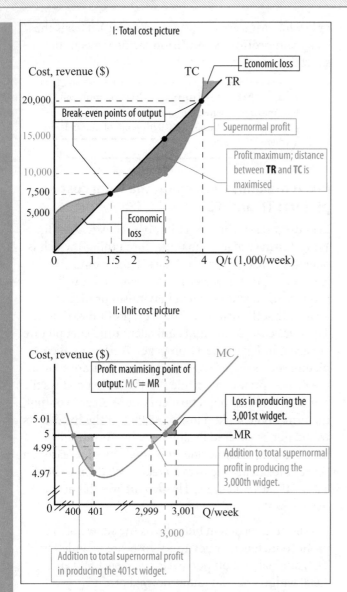

Figure 2.3.17 *Profit maximisation using TR/TC and MR/MC curves*

Profit maximisation using the unit cost picture: MR and MC

Economic theory predicts (as does common sense, as soon as the concepts are understood) that if the price one can get for the sale of an additional unit (MR) is higher than the cost of producing that unit (MC), then it will be produced. This is a somewhat simplistic way of introducing the **MC = MR maxim** (= saying, proverb), but it is a common sense argument readily understood. The unit-cost diagram in Figure 2.3.17 shows an 'abbreviated' (and grossly exaggerated!) MC curve in order to be able to fit the profitmax level of output in conjunction with the total-cost picture

above. (Note that the Q-axis is not equidistant to the total-cost picture.)

The curves in the unit cost picture show that the first 399 units will cost more to produce than the firm can sell them for at the market price of $5. Producing the 401st unit would add to total costs by $4.97 and add $5 towards total revenue, giving $0.03 towards profit. Note that this is NOT profit but a *contribution* to making up for the initial loss making production of the first units. Subsequent units will have lower marginal costs (MC) than the market price of $5, i.e. each unit will have a MR of $5 and even after diminishing marginal returns kick in and the contributions to total profit become ever-smaller, the firm still stands to gain by producing them. This is why the 3,000th Widget is produced; it adds one cent in contributing to total profits. (Note that I have broken the P-axis in several places.) Producing the 3,001st widget would cost $5.01 but still only fetch the market price of $5, which would remove 1 cent from overall profit.

We now have the basis for the profitmax condition facing a short-run profit maximising firm. A firm will expand output beyond initial loss-making levels as marginal costs fall to below market price. The profit-maximising firm will **increase output to the quantity where MC = MR**[9] but **decrease output if MC > MR**. This sets the profit maximising level of output at the point where marginal costs are equal to marginal revenue.

> **Profitmax condition of MC=MR**: When MC < MR a profit maximising firm will increase output. If MC > MR (and MC is rising), then output will be decreased. The profit maximising level of output is when MC = MR (and MC is rising).

Criticism and defence of the profitmax condition

Note that the model of marginal cost pricing is a purely theoretical rendition of how to optimise profits. Firms will in fact use other methods to set price, for example a **cost-plus price** strategy, where price is set at estimated average cost per unit whereupon a profit element is added on. Another method – increasingly common in, for example, the car industry – is to set a maximum price at the initial design stage of the product and then **build the product to conform to the**

---

9. Note that there are in fact *two points where MC = MR*, so one should add the qualification that profitmax output is where MC = MR when *marginal costs are rising*.

costs. Neither method corresponds to the MC = MR criteria and methodology outlined in this chapter, which makes it easy to criticize both the premises and predictive quality of the model as being unrealistic and abstract.

However, the model is not a 'blueprint' or 'roadmap' for firms to arrive at the best possible output level, but a scientific method of clarifying the concept of maximum possible profit. It is in fact more the reverse that must be true; if a firm is maximising profits, then it must be pricing at MC = MR! Our models in the theory of the firm are attempts to put into theoretical context what firms in all likelihood are doing. We are in effect trying to explain rather than prescribe. My friend Mats, the school's amazing biologist, once tried to explain to me how incredibly efficient ants are in their use of energy. He used any number of weird terms and models to prove his point and I was finally so confused that I tried to joke it off by asking, 'Yes, but do the ants know this?!'

'Probably not. But I don't explain it to them – I explain it to the students!'

Profit maximisation ©IBO 2003

Profit maximisation: assumed to be the main goal of firms but other goals exist (sales volume maximisation, revenue maximisation, environmental concerns)

©IBO 2003

We will often assume the firm to be a SR profit maximiser in our models. However, firms often behave quite differently in reality and forego SR profit for several reasons:

- One reason is that the firm might want to capture a larger share of the market and thus sets a relatively low price. Strategic **market entry pricing** is designed to maximise sales volume and attract and hopefully keep a loyal customer base over time, which could enable the firm to work up to economies of scale perhaps and thus ultimately make a profit. '**Predatory pricing**' is a type herein, where the (large!) firm tries to 'kill off' competition by setting a price that most competitors cannot match – the large firm can bear losses for a much longer period of time than small(-er) firms. This has been quite common in the market for air travel, where existing airlines have basically set loss-making prices to evict rivals from lucrative routes.

- Many times firms will act as '**good corporate citizens**' in price-setting. Pharmaceutical companies have been forced by some very strong public opinion to forgo excessive profits in order to fend off possible negative advertising effects and even boycotts. Firms must also increasingly act in accordance with *environmental concerns* and legislation; higher demands on firms via both consumers and interest groups can for example force firms to lower output and/or increase marginal costs to decrease pollutants.

- Firms will often try to **keep prices stable** over time. Consumers do not like the insecurity and lack of predictability in not being able to plan future expenditure. Thus, increasing costs, changing exchange rates, or tax levies – to name but a few – would in many cases not affect a firms output level, in spite of a change in the MC = MR point.

- Selling at break-even price or even at a loss and still making an overall profit is quite possible when the use/application/upkeep of the good has a number of pricey complement goods in the future which are the sole proprietorship of the firm. Such **strategic pricing** is common for such goods as computer hardware which would need accompanying software or cars and service or spare parts. One of the more noticeable consumer goods of late to use this method is printers and ink cartridges, where manufacturers often sell the printer at below cost but then recoup losses on the sales of cartridges – which are increasingly protected by copyright laws in order to prohibit less costly version produced by other companies. This has gone so far that producers have built in 'smart-chips' in order to hinder consumers from simply buying their own ink and refilling the cartridges. This has resulted in a series of complaints by consumer groups to the European Union which is currently investigating the case as being potentially harmful to competition.

- Finally, as we will cover later, the firm might want to **maximise revenue** instead of profit – this will give a different price and/or output than that of profit maximising.

The cynic in me has to add that no matter what the pricing strategy allegedly is, firms exist to make a profit. End of story. All the various goals listed above are simply ways for a firm to increase future profits.

POP QUIZ 2.3.5   MORE REVENUE

1   Assume a profit maximising firm operating on a competitive market and producing at MC = MR. How would the firm react to an increase in MC? How would in react to an increase in MR?

2   Two competing soft-drink firms, Cepsi and Poke, are entering a new market where neither has been sold before. What type of pricing strategy would these firms consider?

Perfect competition   ©IBO 2003

If a man write a better book, preach a better sermon, or make a better mousetrap than his neighbour, tho' he build his house in the woods, the world will make a beaten path to his door.
– credited to Ralph Waldo Emerson (1803–82)

Assumptions of the model   ©IBO 2003

Recall that a poor model is one which does not do a good job of explaining or predicting reality. I would add that a good model is also one which is based upon realistic assumptions, meaning that the model is not too removed from reality by the time all the model's assumptions are in place. As we shall see, many of our models within this section turn out to be fraught with assumptions and stipulations which weaken their explanatory and predictive links to reality. Yet one should be careful in being distracted from the value of micro economic models that are abstractions of reality – they do indeed offer insight into most of the essential real-world features of economic activity in firms. The model of perfect competition is at one end of the extreme while monopoly is to be found at the other. We will go through them both, black and white, in order to mix a potpourri of grey – where in fact 99% of reality is to be found.

The model of perfect competition operates within the confines of five basic assumptions:

1.   There are a **large number of firms** competing in the market: A single firm is powerless to influence total market output and/or price. Therefore the firm is a price-taker.

2.   The firms are producing **homogeneous** (identical)

goods: Firm A's Widgets will in no way be differentiated from those of Firm B. This results in price competition.

3.   Each firm is a **short-run profit maximiser**: Firms operate under the profitmax condition of setting output at MC = MR.

4.   There is **perfect knowledge/information** amongst both firms and consumers: Firms will have total knowledge of any improvements in technology and manufacturing processes, while consumers will be fully aware of all firms' prices.

5.   There are **no barriers to entry**: Nothing hinders firms from entering the market in order to compete with existing producers. Such barriers could be insurmountably high initial (start-up) costs, lack of access to key technology or raw materials, and legal barriers such as not having necessary patent rights.

Comments on the assumptions

I would be lax in not commenting on the implicit (= underlying) necessity of having a legal framework and the rule of law for firms to operate within. This is one of the major obstacles in many developing countries, as the right to private ownership (often called property rights) and protection of these rights under a (democratic?) rule of law is often lacking. It has been duly noted for several years that Russia is in more dire need of lawyers than economists.

I would also be remiss in not offering some basic criticism of the assumptions. As a whole, I cannot think of one single industry or market that comes even close to fulfilling all of them. Very few goods are in fact homogeneous – even water is branded and sold at ridiculous prices.[10]

The closest one comes to homogeneous goods are probably to be found in basic commodities such as copper and potatoes. And looking at perfect knowledge, well, how many times have you bought something in a shop and then seen the same good in another at a lower price?![11] All the assumptions above remove us from real life, yes, but again, our model serves us well as an approximation of real life. 'Perfect' does not mean 'best' or 'optimal' in any normative sense of the word but rather a situation where all factors of production can freely flow to the best possible use.

---

10.   I just saw a report on TV from a wealthy area in the US where the price of bottled water at a rather upmarket store was far higher than the price of petrol.

11.   It's embarrassing, but I must tell this story. For five years I had been going into the school's student café for my daily dose of chocolate. One day a student of mine asked me why I didn't buy the chocolate from the vending machine which for five years had been parked right outside the entrance to the café and had the same chocolate bars at a 20% lower price. I think this was the most embarrassing event in my life which didn't involve a woman or a head waiter.

Demand curve facing the industry and the firm in perfect competition

©IBO 2003

I often fall for the temptation to have a little fun in class here. I start out by drawing two identical supply and demand diagrams on the board and then I ask if they can spot the difference. Unfortunately they know me too well by then and I get a lot of smart-ass answers. Then I say that the one on the right shows the increase in market supply when one of the firms on the market doubles its output. 'Ahhhhh!', goes the class, as assumption number one (firm is a price-taker) occurs to them. So, if the firm cannot influence supply, yet is able to sell all its output at the given market price, what would market demand look like from the firm's point of view? You guessed it; demand facing the firm would be infinite.

The market for potatoes (see Figure 2.3.18) shows that market supply and demand forces create an equilibrium price of 10 Danish Crowns (DKK). The firm cannot influence this on its own, and thus simply accepts that it is facing a fixed price. The demand curve for the firm is infinitely elastic, since the market can soak up any amount produced by any one supplier. This is the perfectly competitive market firm's demand curve, which looks confusingly like the average revenue (AR) and marginal revenue (MR) curve – which is because it is one and the same.

In summing up so far, we arrive at the following identity for the perfectly competitive market firm; the price will be the same as a horizontal demand curve, which is also the average and marginal revenue. Here's another credo for your presentation T-shirt to your economics teacher: 'Price equals murder!' Spelt '**P = MR, D, AR**'. Get it?

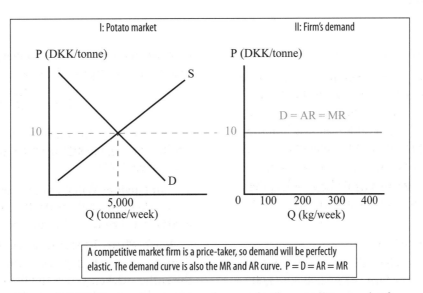

Figure 2.3.18 *Demand and revenue for a perfectly competitive market firm*

What about the supply curve for the firm? Well, consider that the firm will always set output where marginal costs equal marginal revenue and that the demand curve is given by market supply and demand. A change in, say, demand, would shift the demand curve for the firm also – and the MC = MR point would change. Figure 2.3.19 shows that when market demand increases from D_0 to D_1 and decreases to D_2, the demand curve (which is also the MR and AR curve) for the firm shifts upwards, *along* the upward-sloping MC curve! Any change in MR will change the profitmax intersection of MC = MR. The MC curve is thus the firm's supply curve and is the ultimate reason why market supply curves are upward sloping.

HIGHER LEVEL

173

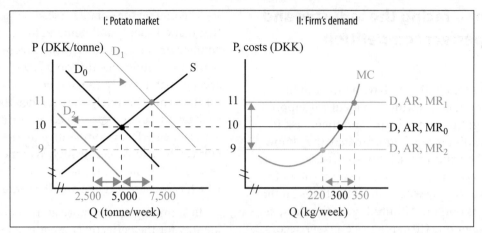

Figure 2.3.19 *The PCM firm's supply curve*

I will elaborate on the short-run and long-run supply curve for the firm in the chapter on break-even and shut-down points further on. I introduce the concept at this stage in order for you to be able to adequately follow the examples on increasing and decreasing output levels in a firm.

A little depth:
PED seen from a firm

Perfectly competitive firm as price-taker

Consider the following: Perfo-Firm is one out of 4,000 competing firms in a market for widgets; PED is 1; total output is 60 million units; the market price of a widget is 10 Swedish Crowns (SEK); and each of the 4,000 firms has an equal share of the market.

How would the market be affected by a **100% increase in output by Perfo-Firm**?! Lets look at the market change first and then try to show why Perfo-Firm is a price taker.

Here are the main figures:

Total market output = 60 million. Average output of a single firm, e.g. Perfo-Firm => 60,000,000/4,000 = 15,000 units. Market price = 10 SEK. PED = –1. Percentage increase in total market output due to 100% increase by Perfo-Firm => 15 000/60 000 000 = 0.00025%.

Total impact on market: (remember, we know the PED of widgets, and that

$$PED = \frac{\% \, \Delta Q_d}{\% \, \Delta P}$$

How would the market price be affected by Perfo-Firm's doubling of output? As we know the PED and increase in quantity of the widgets on the market, it's a matter of working out the change in price:

$$-1 = \frac{+0.00025}{P}.$$

We would see the market price fall by 0.00025%, or 1 SEK × (1 – 0.0000025), which gives a new market price of 9.999975.

Conclusion: When a single firm doubles its output, the market price falls by 0.000025 SEK! (About 0.003125 US cents at the current exchange rate.)

Perfo-Firm's PED; this individual firm faces a demand curve which gives a different PED than that of the entire market. When the firm raised output by 100%, the price changed by -0.00025%.

$$PED = \frac{\% \, \Delta Q_d}{\% \, \Delta P} \Rightarrow \text{PED for Perfo-Firm is } \frac{+100}{-0.00025} = -400,000!$$

Conclusion: The single firm faces a PED that is 400,000, or the functional equivalent of infinity. That is why the D-curve for the firm is horizontal for the firm operation on a perfectly competitive market – the firm cannot affect the market price and is thus a price taker.

Profit maximising level of output and price in the short run and long run

©IBO 2003

Short-run price and output

The perfectly competitive market firm ('PCM firm' henceforth) is basically left with two decisions in the short run; whether to produce and how much to produce. We will start by assuming that the firm has answered 'Yes' to the former and is now regarding the latter. In line with our assumption of profitmax, the PCM firm will set output at the point where MC equals MR. Being a price-taker, the price is set by market forces (supply and demand) and the firm will have three possible outcomes in the short run, as shown in Figure 2.3.20 on page 175. (Note: AC is used for average *total* costs unless otherwise stated.)

Recall that profit is the result of subtracting total costs from total revenue, which in the unit-cost picture corresponds to subtracting average costs from average revenue. Figure 2.3.20 shows three possibilities:

- *Normal profit:* When the market price equals the AC of the PCM firm, the firm will *break-even*, i.e. it will enjoy normal profits. This is shown in diagram I, as the MR = MC point coincides with average costs. As AR = AC there is a normal profit.

- *Abnormal/supernormal profit*: Diagram II illustrates a situation where the market price (and thus the MR curve) is above the lowest average cost (AC_{min}). The firm sets output at Q_{-max} and earns an *abnormal profit*, shown by the blue area.

- *Loss*: Finally, when the price is below any point on the AC-curve, the firm will operate at a loss, as profitmax output (Q_{-max} – which is the same as the loss minimising level of output; $Q_{loss-min}$ in the diagram) results in an AR below AC. The loss is shown by the grey area in diagram III.[12]

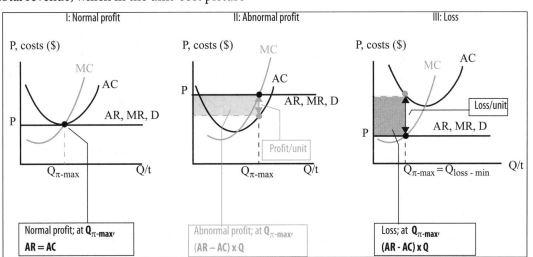

Figure 2.3.20 *Short-run possibilities in a PCM firm*

The possibility of abnormal profits/ losses in the short run and normal profits in the long run ©IBO 2003

An invasion of armies can be resisted but not an idea whose time has come. – Victor Hugo[13]

A firm in a perfectly competitive environment can only enjoy abnormal profits in the short run. The same holds for losses, which makes intuitive sense as no firm will be willing/able to uphold long-term losses.[14] The market mechanism together with the assumptions will act to create long-run equilibrium where the PCM firm will earn normal profits only. We look at both scenarios in turn.

---

12. Students often ask why the firm continues to set output at MC = MR even when average costs are higher than the price. The answer is that this point is also the *loss minimising* point of output, i.e. the firm would make an even greater loss by setting output at any other level than the MC = MR point.

13. I simply must point out that Hugo knew the value of a good timepiece. He was a premier customer of Breguet watches and even mentioned the watches in his stories.

14. Possible exceptions: US car manufacturers. I'm reading about the USD14 billion dollar US government bailout of GM and Chrysler as I write this.

Short-run abnormal profit

I originally wanted at least two colours for this book, one of them being red. The blue area of abnormal profit in Figure 2.3.21 on page 176 would have been done as a bullfighter's cape, in brilliant scarlet red. You see, a firm which is making a profit above and beyond possible alternatives, an abnormal profit, would be to other firms what the cape is to the bull – a signal to charge in. The firm depicted in diagram I has an AC curve where the AC_{min} point is below the market price, P_0. The firm sets output at the profitmax point of MC = MR and thus has an average revenue which is above average cost. This is the abnormal profit per unit, shown by the double-edged arrow, and this times the

quantity shows the total abnormal profit for the PCM firm – the blue rectangle.

What then happens, keeping in mind the assumptions of 1) *free market entry* and 2) *perfect knowledge/information*, is that new firms will be attracted and of course enter the market. This increases supply from S_0 to S_1 causing the price to fall from P_0 to P_1. Falling market price will lower AR for the single PCM firm, creating a long-run equilibrium where once again AR = AC. The firm's short-run profit is thus eroded in the long run by market entry.

Question: How is it possible that the individual firm in Figure 2.3.21 is producing less, while market output has evidently increased?!

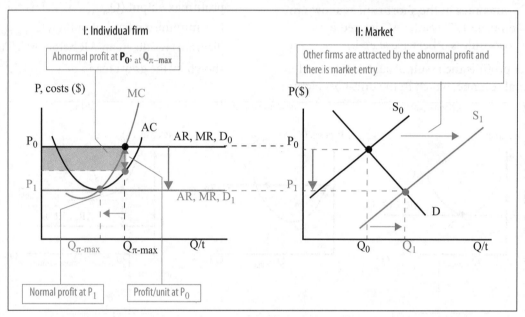

Figure 2.3.21 *Short-run profit in a perfectly competitive market (PCM) firm*

Short-run loss

Assume that firms which have been attracted to the market (as outlined in the example above) increased market output to the extent where the increase in supply lowered the market price to a level where individual firms made losses. This is the situation shown in Figure 2.3.22 on page 177 for a loss-making firm. At a market price of P_0, the firm's AR is below AC. The firm will still produce at MC = MR ('loss-

minimising' point in this case) and will run at a loss, shown by the double-ended arrow. Total loss is the grey rectangle. As firms begin to exit the market over time – switching to more attractive producer substitutes – the market supply curve will shift to the left. Firms, such as the one in our example, which have managed to 'ride out the storm', will see how the price once again rises to a level where a normal profit can be made; AR = AC.

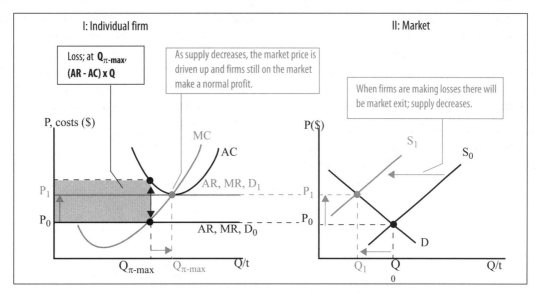

I: Individual firm   II: Market

Loss; at $Q_{\pi\text{-max}}$, **(AR - AC) x Q**

As supply decreases, the market price is driven up and firms still on the market make a normal profit.

When firms are making losses there will be market exit; supply decreases.

Figure 2.3.22 *Short-run loss in a PCM firm*

The firm makes a SR loss shown by the grey area in diagram I; loss is when AR < AC. At the market price of P_0 this firm, and in all likelihood other firms, will run at a loss. In the LR, firms will exit the market and market supply will decrease – shown by the shift from S_0 to S_1 in the market diagram II. As the market price rises, the firm's AR rises and when AR = AC once again, there is **LR equilibrium** and normal profits.

As you no doubt already suspect, firms will not simply sit with crossed arms and wait for better times. As a PCM firm is a price taker, not much can be done to influence the AR side of the coin, so firms are focused on lowering costs. A firm running at a loss will have to find ways to become more efficient (i.e. lower MC) and/or decrease costs in general. One of the most common methods used to decrease costs is to decrease the amount of labour used in production and to try to use remaining labour more efficiently. This is a major part of the issue of unemployment and the business cycle dealt with in Section 3.5.

Conclusions

- The PCM firm can make abnormal profits in the short run, but will make a *normal profit in the long run* as lack of entry barriers allows new firms to enter the market and increase supply and lower the market price.

- The firm cannot run at a loss in the long run either since firms will leave the market and supply will convene on a long-run equilibrium which allows the (surviving) firm a normal profit once again.

- The *LR equilibrium level of output* is thus:
  $P = AC_{min} = MC = AR = MR.$

Shut-down price, break-even price

©IBO 2003

*I'll be here 'til the end of time, So you gotta let me know, **Should I stay or should I go?** –* Awesome song by The Clash, from 'Combat Rock', 1981

When a firm is earning normal profit, output is at the point where AR = AC; this is the break-even point of output. What then, is the point where a firm will leave the market? Simple, the shut-down point is the output level where it is equally costly for the firm to continue producing as it is for the firm to leave the market. If the firm can cover all of the variable costs and at least some of the fixed costs then it has an incentive to remain on the market. If the price falls below the AVC then the firm will not even cover the variable costs – and leave the market. Hence, the point where the firm must decide whether to remain on the market or leave is when AR = AVC. This is the shut-down point.

> **Break-even price and shut-down price**:
> When a firm is selling at a price where total revenue is equal to total costs one speaks of the *break-even price*. In the unit cost picture this is when **P (AR) = AC**.
>
> When a firm is operating at a price level where the price only covers average variable costs and none of the average fixed costs, then the firm must make a decision whether to remain on the market or exit. This *shut-down price* is defined as **P = AVC**.
>
> PED > |1|; elastic

I will use figures to show this, as my experience is that it is easier to comprehend actual numbers rather than using 'points A, B and C'. The firm depicted in

Figure 2.3.23 shows a firm subjected to ever-lower market price. Assume that the original demand on the market gives a market price of €10, which is the firm's AR. This is the long-run equilibrium and also the break-even point, as the firm covers all its costs – even opportunity costs – earning it a normal profit.

Say that for some reason (either increasing supply or decreasing demand) the market price starts to fall and subsequently the firm's AR, MR, D-curve falls to a price level of €6. Being a profit maximiser, the firm sets output where MC = MR, which is now at 80 units rather that 100. At this output level the firm cannot cover all its costs; ATC at an output of 80 is €11. The firm loses €5 on each unit produced, giving an overall loss of €400 (€5 × 80 units) shown by the 'narrowest' grey area and double-ended arrow **A** in the Figure 2.3.23 on page 178.

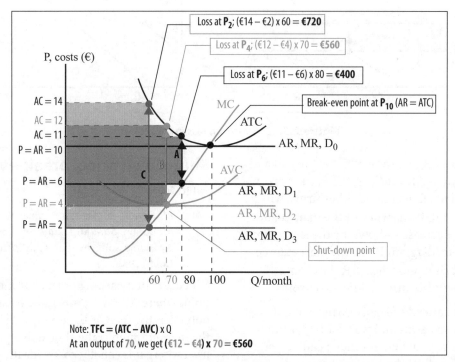

Figure 2.3.23 *Short-run loss in a perfectly competitive market firm*

Why doesn't the firm leave the market at a price level of €6? Consider the choices facing the firm:

1. Stay in the business and make a loss of €400

2. Leave the business and make a loss of €560, which is the total fixed cost (see TFC calculation in Figure 2.3.23).

This is not much of a choice, rather a lack of options. The firm will have a strong incentive to stay on the market during the short run, hoping perhaps that either market price will increase or that increased efficiency and/or cost-cutting can lower MC and AC to a normal profit level again. If, however, the market price falls even further, to €4, then the options become:

1. Stay in the business and make a loss of €560.

2. Leave the business and make a loss of €560.

This is what my grandmother called 'choosing between sleeping on a rock or a hard place', i.e. not much of a choice. The firm's TR (€4 × 70 = €280) will be identical to the TVC – which means that there is no contribution towards covering the fixed costs. The firm is making a loss of €560 by staying in the business and would make the same loss by leaving it. The point where P (AR) = AVC *is therefore the shut-down* point for the firm. The firm will not produce at a lower price level – just consider the options at a price of €2. The firm's TR would be €120 (€2 × 60) and TC would be €720 (€12 × 60) leading to a loss of €600. The reason is that at a price (e.g. AR) of €2 the firm would not even be covering all its variable costs so total costs would be greater than total fixed costs alone. At any price below AVC, the firm will leave the market.

Conclusion: As long as the firm has an AR above AVC, the firm covers variable costs and at least some of the fixed costs – therefore there is an incentive to stay in the business in the short run. **The shut-down point is when P (AR) = AVC.**[15]

SR and LR supply curves for the firm

At any price (AR) above €4, the AR received will help to cover at least some of the fixed costs. This contribution to covering total costs would enable the firm to stay in the business during the short run, as any price which is above AVC will mean less loss to the firm than shutting down and still having to pay the total fixed costs.

- The PCM firm's supply curve in the *short run* is thus the portion of the MC curve which is *above the AVC curve*.
- The *long-run* supply would be the portion of the MC curve *above ATC* as no firm could withstand indefinite losses and would ultimately have to leave the market if it did not cover all costs.

Back to basics: explaining the supply curve

I finish this chapter by 'circling around' and connecting the firm's supply curve to the market supply curve. Building on the proposition that firms will supply at any possible level above the average variable cost curve in the short run, the market supply can be derived from this. Figure 2.3.24 assumes a market of three firms (it wouldn't matter if I used 35,000 firms, but my editor has told me to save space) which all have different marginal and average costs. Only the portion of the MC-curve above AVC is of interest in this case, and summing the individual firms' output at various prices yields the short-run industry/market supply curve; 5,000 units per month at a price of €5 up to 25,000 units per month at a price of €12.

This is when most of my students have something of an 'Ah-ha!' experience. The concept of increasing marginal costs coupled to the profitmax condition of MC = MR renders each individual firm's supply curve, and the aggregate thereof is market supply. It helps in understanding that when firms' marginal costs are affected by technology, production improvements, lower costs of labour and raw material, etc. the total market supply will change as a result.

Definitions of allocative and productive (technical) efficiency

©IBO 2003

I had this brilliant idea once for 'Floor-laying Instructions For Complete Morons'. I suggested to Glenn, my friend in the house-renovation business, that we could market easy-do-it-yourself kits for people redoing their bathrooms. On the bottom of each floor tile we would print 'If you can read this, you are doing it wrong!' There are two versions of efficiency for economists: **productive efficiency** and **allocative efficiency**. Productive efficiency means 'doing things right', while allocative efficiency means 'doing the right things'. Putting the tiles in with the least amount of resource use, i.e. doing it correctly, is productively efficient. Putting in the kind of tiles that your better half (= wife or husband) likes the most is allocatively efficient. Hmmm, I suppose I should be a bit more technical …

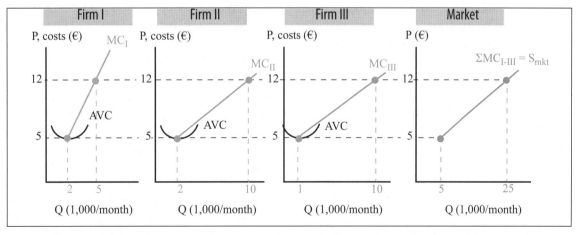

Figure 2.3.24 *Foundation of market supply; ΣMC_PCM firms = market supply*

Productive efficiency – doing things right

A firm is *productively* efficient when total use of resources (factor inputs) results in the lowest possible cost per unit of output. This would be the point where average total cost is minimised. Any other level of average costs would be sub-optimal. A perfectly competitive industry is characterised by forever attempting to implement production methods and technology that increases efficiency – see the LRAC curve.

> **Productive efficiency**: Productive efficiency occurs when goods are produced at the lowest possible cost per unit, taking into account all costs arising. For a firm, this is when output level is at ACmin.

Allocative (economic) efficiency – doing the right things

If the market is producing 1,000 red pens at the lowest possible average cost, but market demand enables it to sell only 800 then the firm is utilising resources wrongly. There is waste since the resources used in the production of the excess 200 units could be better allocated. Firms could use the resources to produce goods which are in higher demand, say green pens. Thus, on a market level, optimal *allocative* efficiency (also known as economic efficiency) occurs when supply equals demand on the market.

In regards to individual firms, the definition of allocative efficiency is that the individual firm is producing the correct quantity of the right goods – 'doing the right things'. In stating that the correct quantity is produced we are in fact saying that since the last unit produced costs exactly what the consumer is willing to pay, resources have been optimally allocated. As consumers buy 'on the margin' (see Section 2.2) then the price paid reflects the value placed on the good. Resources have been optimally allocated when there is no waste, i.e. when the price equals marginal cost of the last unit produced. This occurs when the output level is where P (AR) = MC for the firm. When all firms fulfil this criterion then supply equals demand on the market.

> **Allocative (economic) efficiency**: When there is no waste in resources in the production of goods, allocative efficiency is optimised. This point is reached when there is zero excess supply or demand on the market and the marginal revenue is equal to the firm's marginal cost. S = D...and... P (AR) = MC.

Consumer and supplier surplus (not part of syllabus)

A most useful concept within the context of market theory, utility and allocative efficiency is *consumer surplus*. Imagine walking by a store window on your way to school every day, and seeing a really nice jacket that you just must have. It's expensive, €180, so you save for a few months. One day you walk in with your wad of money to buy the jacket, and it turns out that you have just hit the sales! The jacket 'only' costs €150. You buy it and enjoy the additional pleasure of having been prepared to pay €180 but not having to do so. You get a 'surplus' valued at €30, i.e. an enjoyment above and beyond what you paid for. You got €180 worth of marginal utility for €150.

Consumer surplus

Assume that you did pay the full price, i.e. €180. *You* might not receive a surplus, but others would – say those willing to pay €190 or even €200. Let's assume a local market for jackets and that each potential customer only wants one jacket and that demand is zero at a price of €210. Figure 2.3.25 on page 181 illustrates how consumer surplus is summed up.

- *Areas A to E*: Let's say that 100 people walk in to buy a jacket and are prepared to pay a price of €200 and the market price is €150. This 'group' gets a marginal utility of areas A, B, C, D and E; 100 units time €50.

- *Areas F to I*: If 200 people buy a jacket each, the first group of 100 people (Group A to E) will receive a surplus benefit (i.e. pay a price below the value they place on the item) of €50 each. The second group is prepared to pay €190 and also pay the market price of €150. Group F to I receive a surplus of €40 each.

At the market price of €150, total consumer surplus is shown by the fifteen shaded squares. And as prices in fact do not move in increments of €10, but can theoretically move 'one cent at a time', total consumer surplus in the entire shaded triangle above the market price, shown in the diagram on the right. Conclusion: At a market price of €150, a possible 599 people are getting 'more than they pay for', i.e. receive consumer satisfaction valued at more than the market price. The concept of consumer surplus tells us that all economic transactions are of value to participants – otherwise they would not take place. Any action on a market which diminishes consumer surplus has a negative effect on both consumers and allocative efficiency.

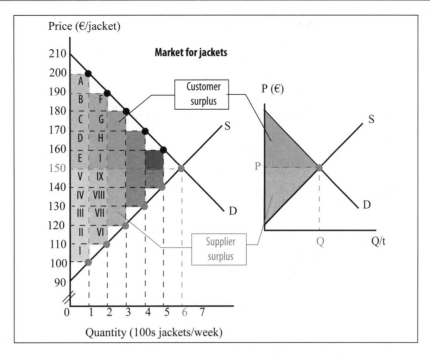

Figure 2.3.25 *Consumer and supplier surplus*[16]

Supplier surplus

Suppliers providing goods at the market price also receive a surplus; the price which is above and beyond the price at which certain suppliers would be willing (and able) to provide the good at.

- *Areas I to V*: The supply curve in Figure 2.3.25 shows that suppliers would be willing/able to put 100 jackets on the market at a price of €100. At a market price of €150 the average revenue received is €50 above the marginal cost of producing these 100 jackets. Areas I, II, III, IV and V show the **supplier surplus**, i.e. the total additional marginal revenue above and beyond what suppliers would be willing/able to put on the market for the first 100 jackets.

- *Areas VI to X*: At an even higher price of €110, producers add an additional €40 of surplus, areas VI to IX … and so on up to the market clearing price of €150, At a market price of €150, producers receive a total supplier surplus of the grey triangle in the diagram on the right.

In summary: As with consumer surplus, if the transaction takes place, then there is a marginal benefit for the supplier. The perfectly competitive market at equilibrium price will maximise both consumer and supplier surplus, leading to an **optimal allocation of resources**. Any action which reduces this surplus renders an allocatively sub-optimal outcome. (See for example, "Monopoly " on page 185.)

Efficiency in perfect competition

©IBO 2003

The firm operating within a perfectly competitive market will be both productively and allocatively efficient in the long run. It has been shown that the firm cannot have an abnormal profit in the long run due to the entry of new firms whereby the subsequent increase in supply and lower market price will dissolve any such profits. Nor can the firm survive endless losses. Figure 2.3.26 on page 182 shows the LR equilibrium for a PCM firm; output is at $P = AC_{min} = MC = AR = MR$.

- **Productive efficiency**: The LR equilibrium for the perfectly competitive market shows that $AR = AC_{min}$. The firm is *productively efficient*.

- **Allocative efficiency**: The horizontal demand curve will set output along the upward sloping MC curve, inevitably forcing the firm to produce where the marginal revenue equals the marginal cost. In LR equilibrium, $P (AR) = MC$. The firm is *allocatively efficiency*.

---

16. Now think; why are post-Christmas sales so enjoyable?!

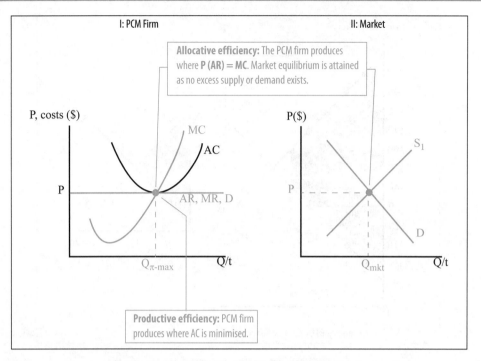

Figure 2.3.26 *Short-run loss in a perfectly competitive market firm*

In summarising the issues in perfect competition and efficiency, we must conclude that the PCM firm in the long run produces at an output level where $P = AC_{min} = MC = AR = MR$. This identity fulfils the criteria for both productive and allocative efficiency, i.e. the model shows that the perfectly competitive firm (and market) is both productively and allocatively efficient in the long run. Yet, as we shall see in Section 2.4, there are a good many 'howevers' involved in the real world.

Summary of how to 'interpret' cost curves

The curves used in *theory of the firm* tell us different things about the state of the firm's environment and possible choices. The main ones are:

Profitmax output: Firm's output is where $MC = MR$

Profit: $TR - TC$ and $AR - AC$ (note that opportunity costs are included)

Productive efficiency: Firm's output is at AC_{min} (or where $AC = MC$)

Allocative efficiency: Firm's output is where $P (AR) = MC$ (also when $S = D$ on the competitive market)

A little depth:
New technology and the perfectly competitive market

An estimate shows that global GDP per capita (in constant purchasing power dollars, 1990s) was around $400 for most of the last 2,000 years. In 1800 this jumped to around $700 and by the year 2000, global GDP per capita was over $6,000. During the same period, England's GDP/capita increased 20-fold and the USA's 36-fold. It doesn't take an intellectual quantum-leap to understand why this enormous increase in productivity occurred during the end of the 1800s; the industrial/technological revolution.

A central point in any competitive environment is the ability to make better use of resources. A firm

which comes up with a better method of production or implements new technology at an early stage will be able to increase output per unit of factor use. This is equivalent to saying that the cost per widget falls. Diagram I in Figure 2.3.27 on page 183 portrays a firm which has implemented new technology, for example, a computer-assisted manufacturing system. This lowers the marginal cost (from MC_0 to MC_1) and also average costs (AC_0 to AC_1) – which is in line with previous diagrams of increased capital use lowering AC in the long run. The firm will increase output to Q_1 in line with the MC = MR condition of profitmax. (Note that the firm is producing beyond AC_{min}.) The firm's increase in output does not influence market output or price at P_0 and Q'_1. The firm is now able to enjoy an abnormal profit (the blue area) as AR is higher than AC.

As the firm is operating in a competitive market, two key assumptions of the perfectly competitive market come in to play and cause market forces to react and increase market output:

1. *Perfect knowledge/information* – other firms on the market will know about the new technology and start to adopt it;

2. *No barriers to entry* – there will be an incentive for other firms to enter the market as abnormal profits are being made.

Taken together, market output will increase, shown in diagram II by the shift of S_0 to S_1. As more firms

adopt/enter causing an increase in supply, output increases from Q'_0 to Q_1 and the market price falls from P_0 to P_1.

The lower market price accordingly shifts the **AR, MR, D** curve downwards to **AR, MR, D_1**, in diagram II. This will lower the firm's output as MR moves along the MC curve to where long-run equilibrium is attained at Q_2. Once again, at P_1 and Q_2, the PCM firm is making a normal profit, as abnormal profits have been eaten away by existing firms' technology adoption and additional firms entering the market.

Conclusion: The 'path' of output increase in the long run here is in total accordance with the LRAC curve.[17]

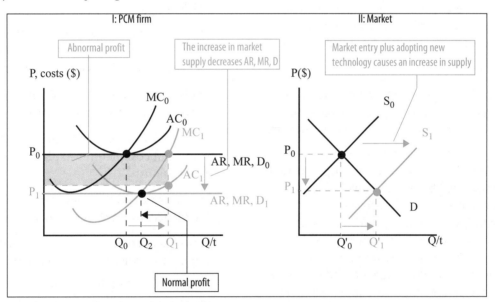

Figure 2.3.27 *New technology and SR abnormal profit*

A little rumination … 'perfect'…

A perfectly competitive market could easily be considered a dream world stretch of the imagination - 'Mermaidomics' to coin a phrase. There *are* barriers to entry such as high initial costs and legislative barriers; there is *no such thing* as perfect knowledge/information since no one person could possible amass all prices for example[18]; many markets have only a *few*

suppliers; and many firms *do* have the power to set price and/or quantity.

However, our model will be broadly in tune with reality as many firms will in fact be reaching for solutions that increase profit – they will act to lower costs, enhance efficiency and increase output. The competitive forces on a market do create a dynamic over time where firms tend towards efficient solutions in order to reap profits.

17. Delong, J. Bradford, 2000a, 'Estimating world GDP, One million B.C. – present', www://econ161.berkely.edu/tceh/2000/world_gdp/estimatina_world_gdp.html.

18. Yes colleagues, this is debatable. Currency markets might be considered to be perfectly symmetric in terms of available information. Yet I always ask myself why there are willing sellers of, say, US dollars no matter what…

HIGHER LEVEL

In the long run, it is empirically (= practically observable) apparent that many firms will be struggling to make the most of scarce factors; this is a competitive outcome leading to efficiency. The theory of the competitive market can help us to understand this.

... and how Churchill would have loved the Internet!

Winston Churchill apparently smoked between 10 and 15 rather sizeable cigars each day. Throughout the Second World War he managed to bring in boxes of his favourite Cuban cigars, Romeo e Julieta. While I am nowhere near his rate of consumption, I do enjoy an evening puff and being rather economically-minded, I have done my consumer research.

It turns out that Spain, for historic reasons, is the world's largest consumer and importer of Cuban cigars. Over 50% of total Cuban output goes to Spain, and is purchased by a government run monopoly which also sets the prices. This has two results which benefit cigar consumers: 1) The purchasing monopoly has enormous bulk-buying benefits, and 2) this is shown in the maximum prices set by government. The result is that Cuban cigars are anywhere from 50 to 75% cheaper in Spain than in other European markets.

Here's where the Internet comes in, by lowering the entry costs for firms in purveying to a far larger market and by providing incredibly low-cost mail order service, since firms can compete by lowering profit margins and selling a far greater quantity, it is quite possible for firms to enjoy benefits of scale. Consumers will be able to benefit greatly, as search costs are reduced, knowledge of markets increase, and prices are lowered as competition increases and more firms are able to cut profit margins yet still make a larger profit. It also becomes far more difficult for firms to price discriminate on the basis of geography since local prices will be increasingly easily compared with the prices of thousands (literally) of other purveyors in other countries. This will increase price transparency on markets.

The Internet has thus brought markets closer to the 'perfect' solution of many small firms, zero abnormal profits, perfect knowledge and information, etc. In the long run, one can hope/expect the increase in competition to force traditional suppliers to cut prices in order to compete. Conscientious shoppers are becoming increasingly aware of price differentials. For example, how many people walk into a store in order to try out shoes – only to go on-line and order them from an Internet firm for a lower price?! Or, walk back to the store and use Internet prices to bargain for a better deal?!

I therefore ordered my cigars from Spain when I was living in Europe. Tabacos Garcia has a most user-friendly site, where I simply click on the cigars and give my customer number. The price is debited my credit card and I get an immediate confirmation and tracking number from a most helpful gentleman, Mr Jesus Alzola. Four days later I picked them up at the post office. It was always fun to pick them up since the people at the post office invariable brought out my package with a big smile; 'Another gift from Jesus!'

POP QUIZ 2.3.6   PERFECT COMPETITION

1 Illustrate and explain the concept of allocative and productive efficiency in a perfectly competitive market.

2 Why does our assumption of each individual firm being too small to influence the market have such an effect on the firm's demand curve?

3 Explain why the sum of individual firms' MC curves is the market supply curve.

4 How would increased labour costs affect the PCM firm's unit cost picture? Explain. Use appropriate assumptions!

5 Why can a PCM firm only make a normal profit in the LR according to our model?

6 A firm is operating at a loss. Explain why the firm might stay rather than exit the market.

7 Assume a total of three firms operating all operating in *equilibrium* on a perfectly competitive market. AR = €8. Firm A can produce a quantity of 6,000 at a MC of €8; Firm B can produce 4,000 at MC = €8; Firm C can produce 2,000 at AC_{min}. What is total market demand?

8 Using diagrams, explain the probable effects of a permanent increase in demand on a perfectly competitive market. Might the price actually decrease ultimately?

9 Tricky one (and outside the syllabus!): How would a lump-sum tax (which is a one-off or 'once only' tax – for example, if all firms had to pay £1,000 pounds as a 'one-only environmental fee') affect MC and AC?

Monopoly ©IBO 2003

And now for something completely different: (the larch[19]) … that's monopolies. The perfectly competitive market model is one theoretical extreme of non-pricing and non-output power. Monopoly firms are quite the opposite.

Assumptions of the model ©IBO 2003

The assumptions of the monopoly market model are markedly different from the competitive model:

1. There is *one firm* supplying the market.
2. There are *barriers to entry*.

   One assumption, however, remains the same:

3. The firm is a short-run *profit maximiser*, just like the PCM firm.

Sources of monopoly power/barriers to entry ©IBO 2003

In fulfilling the assumptions above, a monopoly firm will have a great deal of power on the market, often at the expense of the consumer. A single monopoly firm is able to choose to produce at any point along the market demand curve. Therefore the firm is a *price-setter*. This power is a consequence of the lack of available consumer substitutes. A monopoly must – per definition – be supplying a good which is quite unique in terms of perceived utility, and therefore cannot be replaced. Postal service has long been an example of monopoly power, but (as seems to be the case in the long run) this power has been eroded over time as private delivery firms and email increasingly encroach this market.

Barriers to entry

Firms attempting to enter a market could experience **technical barriers**, where the monopoly firm enjoys decreasing marginal costs over the span of market demand (see "Natural monopoly" on page 186), for example, special techniques and production methods involved in production, or ownership of unique factors of production (e.g. raw material). An example of the former would be Pilkington Glass of England which in the early 1950s invented a revolutionary process for producing sheet glass used in windows and then licensed the technology to firms around the world. As for controlling a vital factor input, ALCOA (Aluminum Company of America) of USA controlled most of the world's bauxite (from which aluminium is produced) until the 1940s.

There could also be **legal barriers to entry**, for example intellectual property rights such as patents and copyrights. The firm could also enjoy government-granted production rights in public utilities such as postal service and telecommunication. Microsoft Corporation has a monopoly on both DOS and Windows and many countries will have legislation in place governing which companies are allowed to supply electrical power and telecom cables to the market.[20]

Finally, it is quite common – even likely, according to some studies – that firms which are able to will attempt to **create barriers** in the aims of constructing a monopoly-like market situation. The monopoly firm's activities on the market could dissuade other firms from entering the market. For example, a monopoly firm could aim to control the supply on the market by buying up the output of other firms in order to control end-user supply. The diamond merchant De Beers previously controlled – via a **cartel** – some 70% of the market for diamonds (depending, once again, on how the market is defined) which it has consistently tried to uphold by controlling not only the mines but also the wholesaling chain via purchasing and stockpiling diamonds from mines not under company control.

Control of monopolies

Most countries will have legislation which severely limits both the creation and activities of monopolies and other restrictive competition practices. As we shall see in the chapter on oligopolies, when the few act as one there is a monopoly, i.e. when oligopolistic firms act in concert – by perhaps forming a cartel – the result is basically a monopoly. These anti-trust laws are in place to limit and regulate such collusive (= co-operative) and harmful behaviour. The anti-trust laws in America are amongst the harshest in the world, and make it illegal for a firm to have monopoly power at all (!), whereby firms that are judged to be monopolies can be forcibly broken into parts by order of law. The most famous example perhaps is when Standard Oil, created by John D. Rockefeller, was forced in 1911 to divest (= sell) itself of holdings in many other companies – one of which became today's ExxonMobile. This is also what happened to the aforementioned ALCOA in 1945 and AT&T in 1983; both were considered to have too large a market share

---

19. This refers to the hilarious 'Larch-intervals' by the magnificent *Monty Python* gang.
20. Have you noticed that all Microsoft product names are accepted by the automatic spell-checker in Word?! Just try writing 'MS Word' and then 'MS Nerd'!

and were forced to break up into smaller competing firms. As a comparison, the European Union's charter does not explicitly forbid monopoly creation per se, but the 'abuse of the dominant position of a company which negatively affects the trade between Member States'[21].

Natural monopoly ©IBO 2003

A natural monopoly has nothing to do with 'organic', in case any of you neo-hippies were wondering. A natural monopoly is when the barriers to other firms entering the market are in some way built-in to the environment, infrastructure or the nature of the good itself. In this, the single firm will have very large **benefits of scale** which competing firms could never acquire – this enables the incumbent (= 'sitting', 'current') monopoly firm to continuously undercut potential rivals and (intentionally or unintentionally) prohibit them from entering the market.

On one of my trips through Ireland in the mid-eighties, I visited a far-northern town called Glencolombcille. It soon became apparent that getting there involved taking a series of buses – which were mostly provided by non-competing bus companies which had local monopolies for a number of town-to-town routes. It also became apparent that there was no co-operation between the companies since arriving buses invariably arrived ten minutes after connecting buses had departed![22] Bus services have high fixed costs since it basically costs the same to drive an empty bus from point **A** to point **B** as a bus full of inebriated Irish fiddle-players and confused tourists. The route I was travelling simply could not have supported competing bus lines, and it would be ludicrous to think that competitive forces could have lowered the market price while firms still covered their costs.

Part of the network of gas pipelines in the Australian outback

Natural monopolies do tend to occur where fixed costs are very high, giving potential economies of scale only to firms which can exploit sheer size to some extent and spread the fixed costs over large output; one firm can satisfy market demand at a lower cost than competing firms. The markets for cable TV, water/gas/ electrical utilities, railroad tracks and local bus services all have strong elements of natural monopoly. Just imagine how inefficient it would be to have several hundred competing gas pipes to each household or fifteen firms each laying down competing railroad tracks! The Öresund bridge connecting Sweden to Denmark is also a natural ~~disaster~~ monopoly[23] … and *two* bridges would basically be a monument to financial stupidity – and that might explain why politicians at this very moment are planning yet another connection via a tunnel[24].

---

21. See http://europa.eu.int/comm/competition/antitrust/legislation/entente3_en.html.

22. I strongly suspect collusion between the bus companies and local pubs – which were always right next to the bus stations. It was all very Irish and very fun; we'd all get off one bus, tumble into the pub for a few pints, singing, joke-telling and fiddle-playing, and off we'd go on the next bus. I spent more in the pubs than on the bus tickets.

23. The bridge has been a monumental failure in terms of recouping the immense initial costs of building it. It has run at a loss since its inauguration in July 2000 – in part because of the high price for those in the vehicles that use it. I will return to this example on price discrimination in "Outside the box: Turning loss into profit" on page 217.

24. I am not making this up!

Demand curve facing monopolist

©IBO 2003

Picture the market demand curve. Now cross out 'Market demand' and replace the title with 'Monopoly demand'. You're finished; the demand curve for the market is the demand curve facing the monopolist, as there are no other providers of the good. The main difference compared to a PCM firm, as shown in the chapter on marginal revenue, is the marginal revenue curve for the monopolist firm. Figure 2.3.28 returns to the demand, average and marginal revenue curves for a monopoly firm.

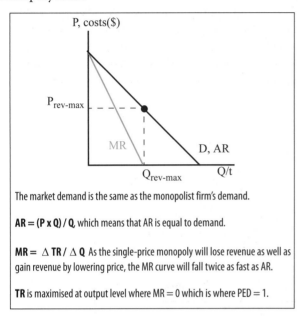

The market demand is the same as the monopolist firm's demand.

AR = (P x Q) / Q, which means that AR is equal to demand.

MR = $\triangle$ TR / $\triangle$ Q As the single-price monopoly will lose revenue as well as gain revenue by lowering price, the MR curve will fall twice as fast as AR.

TR is maximised at output level where MR = 0 which is where PED = 1.

Figure 2.3.28 *Demand, AR and MR for a monopoly*

Profit-maximising level of output

©IBO 2003

Paraphrasing an incredibly silly and insipid (= dull) song from the 1930s: 'Yes, we have no supply curve'.[25] As the monopoly firm faces a market where no other goods are substitutes, the market demand will be satisfied by the monopoly firm. And since we retain the assumption of the firm being a short-run profit maximiser, the firm will produce where MC equals MR. By drawing the marginal cost curve of the monopoly firm we get the profit-maximising level of output seen in Figure 2.3.29. The single-price monopolist sets output at the profitmax point (MC = MR) which is shown by $Q_{P\text{-max}}$ in the diagram. The price can of course be set anywhere below the demand curve at the profitmax point of output, but the monopoly will set the maximum price – denoted by the boundary of demand at $Q_{P\text{-max}}$, which is at $P_{P\text{-max}}$.

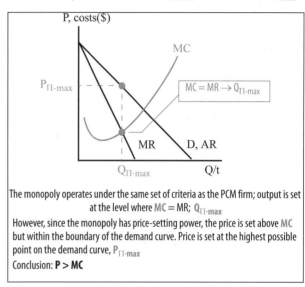

The monopoly operates under the same set of criteria as the PCM firm; output is set at the level where MC = MR; $Q_{\Pi\text{-max}}$

However, since the monopoly has price-setting power, the price is set above MC but within the boundary of the demand curve. Price is set at the highest possible point on the demand curve, $P_{\Pi\text{-max}}$

Conclusion: **P > MC**

Figure 2.3.29 *Profit-maximising level of output in a monopoly*

Question: How well does the monopoly firm illustrated above fulfil the criteria for *allocative efficiency*?

The unit-cost picture and the market picture meld (= join) in the case of monopolies. The demand curve is a 'given' but since there is only one supplier, the assumption of profitmax and the entailing MC = MR condition turns the monopoly firm's MC curve into the market supply curve. I actually recommend avoiding the use of 'supply curve' in conjunction with monopoly output.

---

25. The title of the song was 'Yes, We Have No Bananas!' Soon a cover by Britney Spears if she's not in jail.

Warning!
Drawing the monopoly diagram

The two most common mistakes in dealing with monopoly diagrams are:

1. Drawing faulty MR curves, and

2. Confusing revenue maximum with the point where the MC curve intersects with the demand curve.

Faulty MR curves: Diagram I in Figure 2.3.30 illustrates the first problem. As the MR must lie 'halfway' between the demand curve and the price-axis, all the MR curves in blue are incorrect! Only the black MR curve is correct. It is amazing how many times one sees this mistake in both economic literature and official exam papers. It's the sort of mistake that, when done by a student, is taken to show sloppiness,

lack of understanding, or both. Like drugs, just don't do it.

The other common mistake is to arrive at the conclusion that the unit elastic point on the demand curve is where the MC curve will intersect. Diagram II shows that while this is possible, shown by the blue MC curve, any number of MC curves are also possible which do not intersect the D-curve at the point where PED equals 1. I recommend drawing diagrams that distinctly show that you have not confused this by making sure that your MC curve passes through the demand curve above or below unit elasticity of demand.

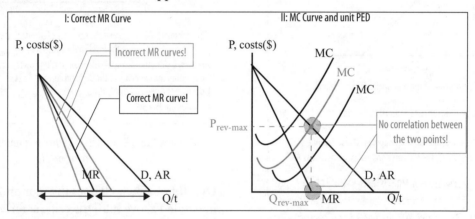

Figure 2.3.30 *Diagrams to illustrate monopolies*

The benefits of being single on the market

While the profit maximising decision for a monopolist is not different from that of the competitive firm, the pricing decision leads to a higher price than marginal cost, as explained above. In many – but far from all – cases, the monopoly firm will have an average cost level that is below the price, as shown in Figure 2.3.31 on page 189, giving the firm an abnormal profit (shaded area).

Since a basic assumption is that there are no competitors, i.e. there are no substitute goods, and that market entry is severely limited, the firm will be able to enjoy abnormal profits in the long run in addition to short-run profits. Firms will be attracted to the market but will be unable to overcome the entry barriers, allowing the existing monopoly to continue to reap abnormal profits.

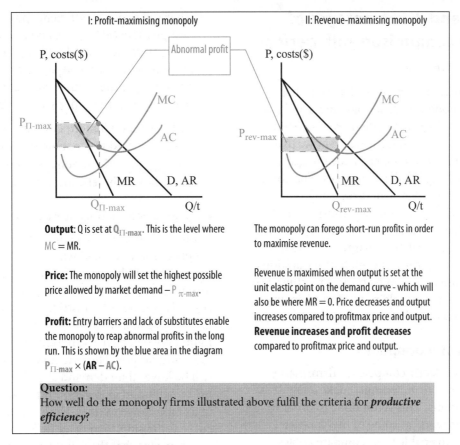

Figure 2.3.31 *Abnormal profits and LR in monopoly*

Normal profits and loss in a monopoly

It is possible that the monopoly firm faces market demand that yields less than abnormal profits. Figure 2.3.32 shows two possibilities. In the case where the AC curve is tangential to the demand curve (AC_0) the monopoly will make a normal profit, as AR equals AC. If average costs are pictured by AC_1, then the total cost per unit is higher than total revenue per unit; the firm will run at a total loss represented by the grey area in the diagram. In keeping with the truism of profitmax and loss-min, the firm with an average cost curve of AC_1 cannot set the price at any other level in order to lower losses; MC = MR will render the lowest possible loss to the firm.

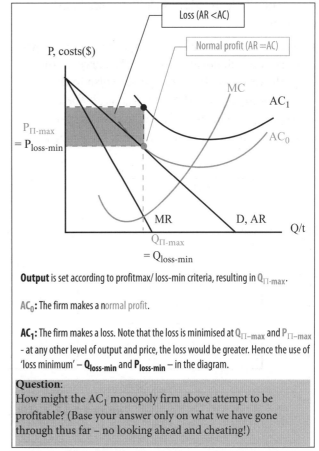

Output is set according to profitmax/ loss-min criteria, resulting in $Q_{\Pi\text{-max}}$.

AC_0: The firm makes a normal profit.

AC_1: The firm makes a loss. Note that the loss is minimised at $Q_{\Pi\text{-max}}$ and $P_{\Pi\text{-max}}$ - at any other level of output and price, the loss would be greater. Hence the use of 'loss minimum' – $Q_{loss\text{-min}}$ and $P_{loss\text{-min}}$ – in the diagram.

Question:
How might the AC_1 monopoly firm above attempt to be profitable? (Base your answer only on what we have gone through thus far – no looking ahead and cheating!)

Figure 2.3.32 *Normal profit and loss in monopoly*

Advantages and disadvantages of monopoly in comparison with perfect competition ©IBO 2003

It's fairly safe to say that monopolies have a rather poor reputation amongst both us consumers and also the political entities we elect to safeguard our interests. But the full story, as so often is the case, shows that monopolies in fact have a number of advantages – sometimes outweighing the disadvantages. The ability to compare different market structures using economic jargon and diagrammatical illustrations is the MOST important component of theory of the firm. Simply committing a number of diagrams to memory will not enable you to address the analytical questions posed in the IB exams – you must be able to utilise the concepts and diagrams to explain, assess and analyse the world around you. Study this section carefully.

Disadvantages of monopolies

In comparing the perfectly competitive firm/market with the monopolistic firm, we must make a few additional assumptions. This is not done in order to 'make the diagrams work' as some of my 'snottier' students claim, but to enable us to compare apples with apples, rather than apples with oranges. We make two assumptions in addition to those previously outlined:

1. The sum of the perfectly competitive market's MC curves are identical to the supply-curve on the perfectly competitive market and also to the **monopoly's MC curve: MC$_{\text{PCM firms}}$ = S$_{\text{PCM}}$** = MC$_{\text{monopoly}}$. This is not as outlandish as first sight might indicate. Consider a competitive market

where all firms are efficient and operating along the best possible MC curves and that one large firm buys up all the individual firms. The large monopoly runs each separate firm as a plant belonging to the mother company – the MC remains the same, since we also assume that…

2. …there are **no benefits of scale** involved. If there were, we could not assume that MC$_{\text{PCM firms}}$ = MC$_{\text{monopoly}}$, as the monopoly would gain scale benefits and thereby lower both AC and MC.

Higher price and lower output

It follows common sense that a firm which can affect supply but not demand will set a price which will optimise profit by way of increasing the margin (= distance) between the market price and the firm's costs. This is done by restricting output and setting the price above marginal cost. Figure 2.3.33 shows that a monopoly will have a different outcome in terms of price and output. The MR curve for the monopolist will be lower than demand at all levels which sets the MC = MR point at lower output than would be the case in a competitive market. Note that the monopoly MC curve is the sum total of all PCM firms' MC curves, which means that the supply curve for both the competitive market and the MC curve for the monopoly are one and the same.

As the monopoly restricts market output and raises the price, the producer gains at the expense of the consumers. This loss of *consumer sovereignty* is the most noticeable negative effect of monopoly market situations; consumers 'pay more for less'. See "Outside the box: Monopolies and deadweight loss" on page 191.

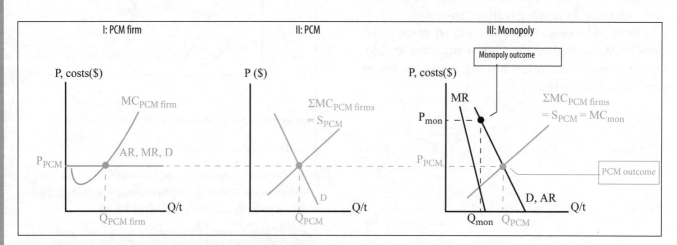

Figure 2.3.33 *The PCM firm compared to a monopoly*

Outside the box:
Monopolies and deadweight loss

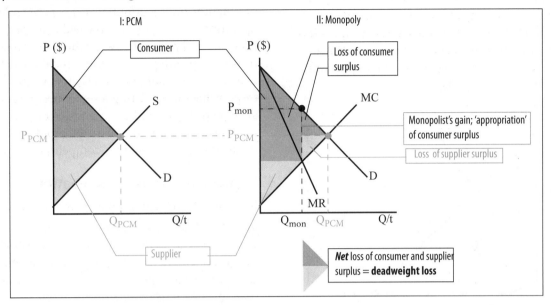

Figure 2.3.34 *Deadweight loss in a monopoly*

I apologise if the additional theory in these boxes weighs you down by adding to your already considerable workload. My justification is that I am trying to provide you with a set of tools which will enable you to better address the questions you will face in the field of economics. Being able to use the concept of consumer/supplier surplus to show *dead-weight loss* is quite valuable.

Recall that the PCM will result in optimal allocative efficiency since total consumer and supplier surplus will be maximised. The diagrams in Figure 2.3.34 illustrate what happens when a monopoly supplies the market rather than competitive firms. (Note the assumption of PCM supply = monopoly's MC curve!) Diagram II shows that when the PCM provides the good at P_{PCM} and Q_{PCM}, consumer and supplier surplus

are maximised – any other price would lower total surplus.

Diagram I illustrates what happens. When a monopoly provides the good, the price rises to P_{mon} and market quantity falls to Q_{mon} whereby the monopoly firm 'appropriates' a portion of consumer surplus (dark blue area). Furthermore, both the supplier and consumers lose a portion of their surplus (grey and blue triangles). These triangles show that at each level of output lost, the potential benefits (shown by the D-curve) outweigh any increase in cost (shown by the MC curve). This is a welfare loss to society commonly termed a **deadweight loss**.

The PCM has no deadweight loss and is therefore allocatively efficient. The monopoly's deadweight loss illustrates that it is not allocatively efficient.

Predatory pricing

One way to create and/or uphold a monopoly is simply to get rid of rivals and dissuade (= discourage) potential entrants to the market. A monopoly has the market power to price at a lower level than potential entrants can set. This pricing policy is short run, as it is intended to kill off rivals (hence the term '*predatory pricing*') so that the monopoly can maintain profitmax pricing and abnormal profits.

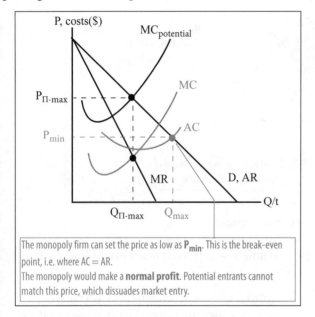

The monopoly firm can set the price as low as P_{min}. This is the break-even point, i.e. where AC = AR.
The monopoly would make a **normal profit**. Potential entrants cannot match this price, which dissuades market entry.

Figure 2.3.35 *Predatory pricing in monopoly*

Suppose that the most efficient *potential* competitor(s) could attain a marginal cost of $MC_{potential}$, shown in Figure 2.3.35. This would be competitive with the monopolist's profitmax price of $P_{\Pi\text{-}max}$. The monopoly might therefore lower its price and accept a lower abnormal profit margin. Indeed, it is quite possible for the monopoly to set the price where AC = AR, i.e. the break-even point of output. It is worthy of mentioning that many countries' anti-trust laws strictly forbid any type of predatory pricing.

Limiting competition

A monopoly can protect its captive market from possible entry in a number of ways. It can refuse to sell monopolised parts to potential competitors, which is what Microsoft did in the late 1990s when the company refused to sell Windows to computer manufacturers which did not also accept the web

browser Microsoft Internet Explorer, which ultimately cost the leading browser at the time, Netscape, most of its market share. In essence, a monopoly can seek to block/hinder rivals' access to supply-chains in production and retail/outlet chains at the sales end of operations. Monopolies also wield considerable financial and political power, which can create a 'cosy' relationship with governments which not only are consumers of monopoly goods, but are also responsible for regulating monopolies. Monopolies are also interested in setting the end-user price (i.e. the retail price) and can therefore attempt to force retailers to set prices which are non-competitive.

Higher costs and less innovation

It is possible that a monopoly firm may choose 'the quiet life'[26], i.e. be satisfied with a comfortable level of abnormal profit rather than putting effort into increasing efficiency. The outcome would be suboptimal, since productivity increases would be less than in a perfectly competitive market.

Advantages of monopolies

Life is seldom so simple as to neatly divide reality into good or bad[27]. Monopoly power is no exception and as the following headings encapsulate, there are three main areas where the monopoly can prove itself superior to the perfectly competitive firm: 1) economies of scale; 2) natural monopolies; and 3) government run monopolies. Additional possible benefits of monopolies are increased profits for research and development (R&D), 'creative destruction' and the reduction of negative externalities.

Economies of scale

When there are very large fixed/initial costs and a very large potential for economies of scale based on technological gains, a monopoly might well have a profitmax point which renders a lower price and higher output than a perfectly competitive market. We now relax our earlier two assumptions added-on in comparing a monopoly with a perfectly competitive market. The sum of the MC curves for PCM firms are *not* the MC curve for the monopoly; and there are indeed economies of scale to be had.

---

26. Description of monopoly by Nobel laureate J. R. Hicks. web.mala.bc.ca/econ/quotes.htm.
27. That is why we have divorce.

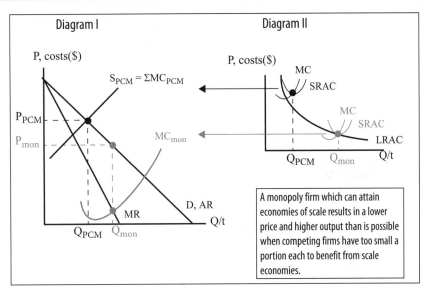

Figure 2.3.36 *Economies of scale in a monopoly*

Figure 2.3.36 illustrates the outcome when a monopoly can enjoy economies of scale. The supply curve for the perfectly competitive market (diagram I) is the sum of the MC curves shown in the LRAC diagram II. Scale economies allow the monopoly to move along the LRAC (diagram II), allowing the monopoly to decrease MC and AC. The monopoly can produce a higher quantity and lower price – **Q_mon** and **P_mon** – than the perfectly competitive market. Simply put, a large quantity of (smaller) competing firms could not attain large enough scale to be able to compete with a single monopoly firm.

Natural monopolies

The concept of a natural monopoly is an extension of the scale benefit model done above. However, a natural monopoly will have such large scale benefits, that no single firm can fully exploit them. 'Natural' in usage here means that the economies of scale make it more efficient for one firm to produce the good than for any other constellation in the industry.[28] Easily understandable examples of natural monopolies are gas networks for households, water lines, electricity, telecommunications and cable TV – imagine the costs in having each individual gas or electricity company having their own lines into each house! My favourite example is railways; imagine having two competing companies with their own tracks – side by side – running between two cities.

There are of course very high barriers to entry in industries characterised by natural monopolies. This is due to two common characteristics of natural monopolies:

1. Extremely high fixed costs and low variable costs
2. High initial (start-up) costs – often infrastructural.

This is illustrated by the continuously falling AC curve in Figure 2.3.37 on page 194. As average costs fall throughout the entire boundary of market demand, MC too continues to fall. This renders three possible pricing outcomes – all of which are lower than for a PCM:

1. **Profitmax pricing**; where the monopoly sets price according to the MC = MR condition. This creates an output of **Q_-max** and a price of **P_-max**. The firm makes an abnormal profit of the dark grey area. Examples include private telecoms companies and gas companies.

2. **Average cost pricing**; is when the monopoly sets the price at the break-even point of AC = AR.

3. **Marginal cost pricing**; at an output of **Q_MC**, the monopolist would incur a loss of the light grey shaded area. Marginal cost pricing is commonly done in order to achieve social benefits – for example, providing water – and often involve public ownership or government funding via subsidies.

---

28. It is noteworthy that the term natural monopoly does not in fact refer to the dominant *firm* but rather to the *industry* itself. There can be many competing firms in a natural monopoly situation and in using the term natural monopoly we are claiming that one firm would increase efficiency in the industry. This is a common political argument put forward in favour of nationalising water works, electricity and train services.

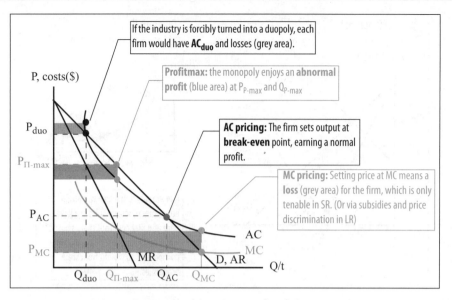

Figure 2.3.37 *Natural monopoly*

What would happen if the natural monopoly was broken up in order to establish a competitive market? Assume an existing monopoly at the profitmax price of **P-max**. If government forced the firm to break up into two parts – a **duopoly** – each firm would have a far higher AC than the monopoly; the two firms would have an average cost of **AC_duo** and an output of **Q_duo**. This is clearly economically impractical. (Note the suboptimal *productive efficiency* in all three pricing scenarios, and the suboptimal *allocative efficiency* in all cases but MC pricing.)

Public and merit goods

Goods provided and/or produced by government monies, i.e. **public and merit goods** such as roads and health care are often priced at AC or MC. Societal welfare is deemed to benefit so much by the provision of such goods that the profitmax condition is not considered applicable. Instead, the good is priced at cost or – via subsidies – at below marginal cost.

Whether public/merit goods warrant government support or provision or not is subject to very heated debate. The trend over the past 20 years has been increasingly in favour of market openness and privatisation, where a number of traditionally government-controlled markets have been sold off or otherwise subjected to open market competition. State-owned telecom companies, electricity and railroads are notable examples. In certain cases the results have been rather dismaying, for example England's privatisation of British Rail, completed in 1997, was called a 'Disaster' by *Time* Magazine[29]; over 100 different competing rail-service providers saw how costs spiralled upwards continuously leading to fewer departures and lower levels of service. There are increasingly loud cries for re-nationalisation. A very similar debate raged in California during 2002, as overloaded private electricity companies led to daily blackouts. You can just imagine how popular sudden power interruptions were to the programmers in Silicon Valley.

Profits for R&D (innovation and new products)

There is also the possibility of monopolies having far greater research and development (R&D) capabilities as a direct result of being able to earn abnormal profits. Ploughing profits back into product enhancements and innovative new products could increase consumer choice and benefits to society in the longer term. PCM firms could never have the LR profits available to monopolies, and would thus not be able to fund R&D to the same extent as monopoly firms.

---

29. *Time* Magazine, 14 July 2003, pp. 54–57.

HIGHER LEVEL

Other possible advantages of monopoly

A rather interesting possibility was put forward by noted economist Joseph Schumpeter, who theorised that there is an ongoing process of **creative destruction**. While it sounds distastefully 'socio-Darwinist', Schumpeter posited that over time sheer monopoly power would force potential entrants to develop outstandingly new/superior substitute goods in order to compete in some way, rather than the incremental (= 'little at a time') improvements of competitive markets. The new and major new product would effectively destroy the market for the 'old' product while creating a new market. These 'leaps' of innovation and invention effectively terminate markets – creative destruction – in providing superior substitutes. This is posited as being more beneficial in the long run than competitive markets.

Finally there is the distinct possibility that the monopolist outcome of higher prices and lower output actually benefits society! This would be the case in the production and consumption of goods which are harmful to society, called **negative externalities**. For example, the production of certain plastics is highly harmful to the environment, as numerous carcinogenic toxins (= cancer-causing poisons) are released into the air. A monopoly firm might well produce less of the good and thereby have less negative impact on society than would a perfectly competitive market. We will look into this issue in greater depth in Section 2.4.

Efficiency in monopoly ©IBO 2003

We now re-insert the assumption that the sum of PCM firms' marginal costs equals PCM market supply and also the MC curve of a monopoly. Figure 2.3.38 on page 196 summarises the cost pictures for a firm operating on a competitive market and a monopoly market.

- *PCM firm*: Recall that the long-run equilibrium of the competitive market is when each PCM firm is operating at the lowest possible average cost (AC_{min}) and where the price of the last unit is equal to the cost of the last unit (P [MR] = MC). The PCM firm is therefore both *productively* and *allocatively efficient*.

- *Monopoly*: The monopoly firm is in stark contrast, since the price is higher than marginal cost; the monopoly is *not allocatively efficient*. Nor will the monopoly firm necessarily be productively efficient, as the output level which has been determined by the MC = MR condition means that the monopolist might well produce where AC_{min} is not attained.

Monopoly versus PCM – a summary

It has been shown that, under the assumption that the PCM supply curve is identical to the monopolist's MC curve, the monopoly will:

- enjoy *abnormal profits* in both short and long runs

- be *allocatively inefficient* (P[AR] > MC), and in all likelihood *productively inefficient* ($Q \neq AC_{min}$)

- produce a lower level of output at a higher price – this leads to a net loss of consumer and supplier surplus called *deadweight loss* [not part of syllabus – see "Outside the box: Monopolies and deadweight loss" on page 191].

In relaxing the assumption of $S_{PCM} = MC_{mon}$, there is a mixed bag of both disadvantages and advantages. A monopoly could:

- raise existing *entry barriers* and indulge in *predatory pricing* to dissuade entrants

- idle along at low productivity levels, resulting in *suboptimality* in productivity gains

- enjoy *economies of scale* and *natural monopoly*, lowering price and increasing output compared to the PCM

- be *more innovative* that competitive firms, since abnormal profits are available for *R&D*

HIGHER LEVEL

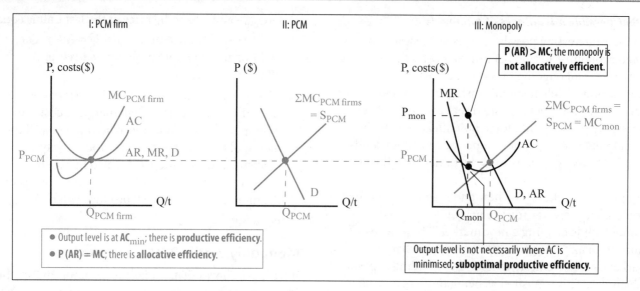

Figure 2.3.38 *Efficiency in a monopoly*

POP QUIZ 2.3.7   MONOPOLY

1   Explain why a monopoly can earn a supernormal profit even in the LR.

2   Explain why the profit maximising monopolist will always set output along the elastic portion of the demand curve. Use a diagram to illustrate your answer.

3   Explain how/why a monopoly which aims to maximise revenue will have a higher level of output than when it is profit maximising.

4   If, at a certain output, the MC is greater than MR, what should a profit maximising monopolist do?

5   Is it always the case that a monopoly leads to a higher market price and lower output than a perfectly competitive market or are there exceptions?

6   Explain how a natural monopoly's price would differ from that of competitive firms on the same market.

Monopolistic competition   ©IBO 2003

We have now covered the two extremes of perfect competition and monopoly. While many markets have strong elements of these market types, most goods will be provided by firms which have elements of both. The result is **imperfect competition**, since most goods are in fact not homogeneous and are sold using arguments which are not based on the price of the good. These forces of *non-price competition* provide the foundation for **monopolistic competition**, which is a mixture of elements from both the competitive and monopoly markets. I often draw a Venn diagram on the board – to groans of weariness from my poor students – with one circle as a monopoly and the other as a competitive market.[30]

The market structure in monopolistic competition can, once again, be 'tasted'; the term monopolistic entails the firm being alone in providing the product while competition implies that the firm still has to take into consideration the possibility of *substitutes*. Consider running shoes; there are many competing brand names such as Adidas, Brookes and Asics, but only one Airmax – produced by Nike. There are many hamburgers – but only one Big Mac; many taco restaurants but only one Mama Rosita's; many wristwatches but only one Fortis B-42, and so on.

Assumptions of the model   ©IBO 2003

The assumptions of a monopolistically competitive market are almost identical to those outlined in the model of perfect competition; many sellers; no entry barriers; the firm is a short-run profit maximiser; and the market actors have perfect knowledge. There is one important change, namely that the good is **non-homogeneous** or **differentiated**.

> **Monopolistic competition:** A market where numerous sellers provide goods which are non-homogeneous/differentiated is a monopolistically competitive market.

---

30. Heads hit the tables when I add on a third circle; oligopoly.

Characteristics of monopolistic competition

The simple examples above together with the added assumption of non-homogeneous goods outline the three main characteristics of monopolistic competition:

1. There are a **large number of providers** of the good on a most competitive market. While the PCM will have a large number of suppliers and the monopoly only one, the monopolistic market will have a range of suppliers depending on the good. The main point is that the firms are independent competitors with relatively small market share, therefore firms will largely disregard the actions of other firms and the incentive to collude is quite small.

2. **Products are differentiated** by way of marketing and advertising. While there might not be any tangible (= substantial) difference between a pair of Reeboks and a pair of Nikes, the marketing efforts behind these goods seek to convince the consumer that there is a real difference between the brands. Beauty is in the eye of the beholder, and by strengthening a brand name and image, the firm attempts to create a difference in the perceived benefits of its product. (See "Product differentiation" on page 198.)

3. The firm has a **certain degree of market power**. As the firm has the monopoly (or proprietary) rights to the product, or brand, a degree of brand loyalty can be created by careful profiling of the product/brand image, which serves to separate the product from substitutes. The firm is therefore not a pure price-taker but a price-giver to a certain degree.

It turns out that there are in fact few market constellations which live up to the above characteristics and create *pure* monopolistic competition. Most of the examples, upon closer examination, show a very high concentration ratio; the four to five largest firms on the market have a controlling share of the total market. This is in fact an **oligopoly** market, dealt with in the next chapter. To remain strictly within the definition of monopolistic competition, one often winds up with local goods and service providers. Pubs, restaurants, corner stores, car repair shops and hotels can be considered purely monopolistically competitive.

Short-run and long-run equilibrium

©IBO 2003

As the firm sells a differentiated product, it will face a downward sloping demand curve rather than a perfectly elastic one like the PCM firm. However, the element of *substitutability* will have strong impact on the price elasticity of demand for the firm. Recall that the closer the (perceived!) substitute, the more elastic demand tends to be. A defining element regarding short and long run for the monopolistically competitive firm is to what extent consumers regard a good as substitutable.

- *Innovative stage*: Assume that a firm hits the market with a product which is indeed markedly innovative and has no close substitutes, giving the producer a monopoly market. This is shown in Figure 2.3.39 on page 198, where the innovative firm enjoys an abnormal profit, owing to the fact that other firms have not yet entered the market with their own versions of the good.

- *Close-follower stage*: Ultimately, since we are assuming perfect knowledge/information and no entry barriers, other firms see the abnormal profits and start to produce copy-cat products which are close enough substitutes to steal market share away from the innovative firm. These 'close-followers', in providing substitutes, will cause a decrease in demand for the innovative firm, shown by the shift from D, AR_0 to D, AR_1 in the next diagram. The price elasticity of demand increases since there are now substitutes available on the market. The innovative firm has been forced to lower the price from P_0 to P_1, but has still lost customers to the degree where it is making a loss, shown by the grey area.

- *Long run*: In the long run, as other firms also accrue losses and leave, and potential entrants are dissuaded by losses or scant profits, the innovative firm will see an increase in demand and decreasing PED. Over time, monopolistically competitive firms will produce where the AC curve is tangential to the AR curve, the result being that in the long run, the monopolistically competitive firm will make a normal profit only, just as the PCM firm.

Be careful in ascribing too large a degree of static equilibrium to the model! It is highly unlikely in the real world that the innovative firm will simply stand by and watch how its market share is eroded by competitors. The firm will strive to stay ahead by marketing its product and by continuously looking at ways to improve the good – superficially if nothing else. What the model shows, is that there will be a tendency towards the LR equilibrium point of zero abnormal profits.

HIGHER LEVEL

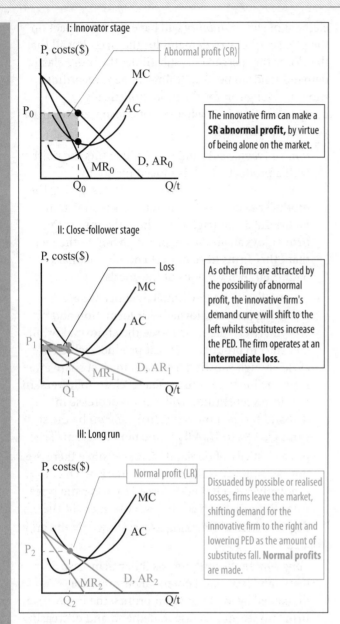

I: Innovator stage

Abnormal profit (SR)

The innovative firm can make a **SR abnormal profit,** by virtue of being alone on the market.

II: Close-follower stage

Loss

As other firms are attracted by the possibility of abnormal profit, the innovative firm's demand curve will shift to the left whilst substitutes increase the PED. The firm operates at an **intermediate loss.**

III: Long run

Normal profit (LR)

Dissuaded by possible or realised losses, firms leave the market, shifting demand for the innovative firm to the right and lowering PED as the amount of substitutes fall. **Normal profits** are made.

Figure 2.3.39 *Monopolistic competition – SR to LR*

Product differentiation ©IBO 2003

I have always been a sucker for new, cool consumer electronics. When Sony came out with the *Walkman*[31] in 1978–79, I was first in line. It cost me $280 in 2003 prices and exchange rates, which is a bit pricey. Within a year of my buying it, numerous other electronics firms came out with similar products. Sony reacted in true monopolistically competitive style; by differentiating the product. Sony set about making many different styles and models, all equipped with new features different from other brands. Ten years

later, Sony had over 200 models of Walkmans. The 1990s saw Sony extend the brand to portable CDs (Discman) and then the Minidisc. MP3 players and iPods are the latest. Each product creates an array of 'me-too' products vying for a share of the market.

> **Product differentiation**: When firms on a monopolistically competitive market enhance product heterogeneity by changing the good (physically) and/or using advertising to create an image and uphold/enhance a brand, one speaks of product differentiation.

Differentiating a product is seldom as hands-on and tangible as adding new gizmos and dials to the product. Often as not it is a matter of simply changing the packaging or colour. How many times have you seen a 'new' product advertised by some phrase like 'Now in an all-new Mango-Ice-Fire colour!' or other such nonsense?![32] In any case, the adding-on of tangible and/or intangible features allows the firm to pass its product off as differentiated in its marketing drive.

Monopolistic competition is like an endless game of catch-up; as there are no barriers to entry, successful products will immediately have a following of copy-cat products which will steal market share from the original manufacturing firm. The response is to differentiate the product as much as possible. Just follow the ongoing battle between iPod and the myriad (= numerous) close-followers in the electronics industry – which is changing so quickly I'm not even going to bother with examples.

In the final analysis, the more consumers feel a product to be substantially different, the more successful the firm will be. I often claim that the standard catch-phrase of TV commercials 'New and improved!' would actually be a bit of an overkill if the firm actually meant it. It is quite sufficient for the firm simply to *convince* consumers that the product is different. One example rather close to us is the market for economics textbooks in the IB, where the first tailor-made textbook was by Alan Glanville, the second by me and the latest is the official IB version by Dorton and Blink. While these are indeed close competitors, there are distinct differences between them as we all seek to differentiate our books from the others. [33]

---

31. *Walkman* is an example of brand degradation, which is when a brand name becomes a generic term for any similar good. *Hoover, Aspirin* and *Thermos* are other notable examples.

32. I just have to tell this one! Here in Mexico, I happened to pick up a plastic bottle of soda which had the proud legend blazed across the label: 'Same drink! Different label!' Wow. Sign me up for some bulk-buying.

A little depth:
Monopolistic competition in the watch industry

My friend Toni took the photograph below from a sample out of the McGee watch collection – amidst snotty remarks from both him and his wife Pati that I should sell a few and buy a house (and get a ~~wife~~ life) instead. From left to right you see: Sinn (model Flieger 356 II) for USD1,500; Fortis (model B-42) for USD2,500; Breitling (model Chrono Avenger) for USD3,500; a Panerai (Luminor GMT PAM88) for USD7,000; and a Chronoswiss (model Lunar Chrono) for USD12,500. All are waterproof to between 50 and 300 metres. All are automatic (= self-winding). All have sapphire crystal glass. All are well within official chronometer limits (a maximum of +6 to -4 seconds deviation per day). Why are they here in the section of monopolistic competition? Simple; they all contain the exact same mechanical movement ('ebauch' in watch-speak), namely the ETA-Valjoux 7750.

ETA is the largest manufacturer of Swiss watch movements in the world, and is owned by the Swatch Group. It supplies movements for the brands owned by Swatch (Omega, Tissot, Longines, Swatch to name but a few) and also sells to at *least* 100 other watch manufacturers – five of which are pictured. Watch manufacturers making some of the most expensive mechanical watches in the world (IWC for example) to some of the cheapest (Aristo) all use the same movements from ETA. What differs is the price, obviously, but also the way the products are *differentiated*.

So what does the USD 3,500 Breitling do that the USD1,000 Sinn doesn't? Well, not much, I shamefacedly admit. Here's how the manufacturers of the five watches above sell their wares:

- Sinn: '… company started by legendary pilot Helmut Sinn … noted for advanced technology … advanced water-proofing using argon-filled chambers and copper-sulfate anti-humidity capsules … used by German special forces …'
- Fortis: '… aeronautical watches used by air forces … official watch of the European Space Station and Russian Cosmonauts …'
- Breitling: '… Instruments for professionals … officially certified by the Official Swiss Chronometer Testing Institute …' (Advertisements run with John Travolta standing in front of an aircraft, caption: 'Profession: pilot. Career: actor.')
- Panerai: '… originally made for the Italian navy commandos … unique patented crown lock system … highly limited editions … official suppliers to the 2006 North Pole Expedition by Mike Horn …'
- Chronoswiss: '… fascination of watch-making … classic timepieces … limited production of 7,000 pieces per year … still manufactured by the founder, Gerd Lang …'

So does the differentiation work? Well, I have one of each, you tell me. Am I the only sucker (= easy target) out there?

HIGHER LEVEL

---

33. Since Glanville has basically been in the business since the 1990s and helped write several IB syllabuses, his book might be considered the Yoda of IB econ literature. Dorton & Blink have the official version, e.g. Luke Skywalker. Mine? Probably Jar Jar Binks.

Efficiency in monopolistic competition

©IBO 2003

Just as the PCM firm, the monopolistically competitive firm receives normal profits in the long run. However, as soon as one compares the two markets in terms of efficiency, the similarities end.

Diagram I of Figure 2.3.40 shows that a firm operating in monopolistic competition with other firms, will set price *above marginal cost* (leading to suboptimal allocative efficiency) and produce at an average cost *above AC_{min}* (meaning that the firm is not productively efficient).

The monopolistically competitive firm will produce at an output level **where neither allocative nor productive efficiency criteria are met**, i.e. the firm will not produce where P (AR) = MC, or at AC_{min}. [Outside the syllabus: Note that sub-optimal resource allocation can be seen in the deadweight loss, the grey triangle in the diagram II.]

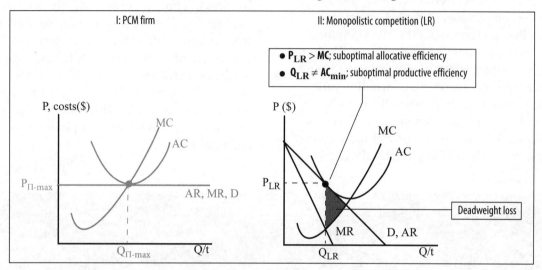

Figure 2.3.40 *Efficiency in monopolistic competition – a comparison to the PCM*

A degree of consumer sovereignty in the end

It would be far too simplistic – not to mention incorrect – to say that monopolistic competition is closer to a pure monopoly in terms of efficiency, or that market power enhances suppliers' power at the expense of consumers'. On the contrary, one may well argue that by continuously augmenting (= adding to) and differentiating products, the market creates a wide variety of goods and therefore enhances consumer choice far more than in a perfectly competitive market. Who's to say that the suboptimal allocative and productive efficiency is not worth this added choice? It is evident that the vast array of new products is quite often the result of non-price competition, which often takes place in monopolistically competitive firms.

POP QUIZ 2.3.8 MONOPOLISTIC COMPETITION

1 What is 'imperfect' about monopolistic competition?

2 Explain how/why monopolistically competitive firms in LR must earn normal profits.

3 Using the concept product differentiation, explain how a monopolistically competitive firm might earn an abnormal profit.

4 What, if any, are the advantages of monopolistic competition over perfect competition?

5 Examine the level of efficiency in the long run in monopolistic competition.

Oligopoly ©IBO 2003

The final market version to be found lying in-between the extremes of perfect competition and monopoly is another form of non-price competition – **oligopoly**, meaning 'few sellers'. The defining line between monopolistic competition and oligopoly can be very thin, and many of the markets have in fact elements of both. Oligopoly markets are increasingly common in the real world – and perhaps the most important market structure to study. Unfortunately it has perhaps the weakest theoretical base as there is no single model which is able to conclusively describe it.

Assumptions of the model ©IBO 2003

An oligopoly has some key defining characteristics, namely that the market is dominated by a few large firms and that potential entrants face high barriers to entry – the latter being a key difference to the monopolistically competitive market. Furthermore, products can be both homogeneous and differentiated. With these outlining assumptions in place the oligopolistic market takes on a number of rather unique features which subsequently define the market.

Size and number of firms

Standard economic theory defines an oligopolistic market as one where the four or five largest firms control a major share of the market. This is the market **concentration ratio**, and is most frequently calculated as the total sales of an individual firm divided by total market sales. The rule of thumb is that when the four largest firms have over 40% of the market, an oligopoly situation is at hand. Note that while a highly concentrated oligopoly of four firms might account for 90% of sales, the remaining 10% could be in the hands of hundreds of small firms.

Oligopolies are found in all markets, from primary goods (oil, cement, aluminium), secondary goods (pharmaceuticals, automobiles, soft drinks), to tertiary goods (banking, telecommunications, air travel). Table 2.3.8 looks at a selection of four-firm concentration ratios in the US in 1997.

Table 2.3.8 *Four-firm concentration ratios for various industries*

Industry	Four-firm concentration ratio
Gypsum	68.4%
Aluminium	48.0%
Breakfast cereals	84%
Hobby/toy stores	70.3%
Credit card issuing	53.8%

(Source: *Official US census figures*, see: www.census.gov/epcd/www/econ97.html)

One final statistic shows the extent of oligopolistic concentration on a global scale. The three largest soft drink manufacturers, Coke, Pepsi and Cadbury Schweppes, in 95 countries (which comprise 90% of the world's population) account for 79% of the market.[34]

Benefits of scale

A common denominator in oligopolistic markets is that there are very high barriers to entry, with well-established firms being able to heighten these barriers by using extensive advertising and branding to dissuade potential entrants. This is accentuated by the sheer size of many oligopoly firms, which are able to move along the LRAC curve and enjoy benefits of scale. This helps explain why many highly efficient firms in due course are left with few competitors, since firms which do not attain such scale benefits will be competed out of the market – or be forced to merge with another firm.

Mergers

In the last decades of the 20th century, many large firms increased competitiveness by *merging*, which is the joining of two or more companies into a single firm. This furthered their ability to enjoy economic benefits of scale in advertising, bulk-buying, etc. The merger process resulted in further consolidation (= bringing together, strengthening) of oligopolies, in that the 'few and large' controlled increasing portions of the market. There are three main types of mergers: (Note that mergers do not, per definition, necessarily create actual oligopolies!)

---

34. See http://www.beverage-digest.com.

1. *Horizontal mergers*, where firms selling similar products join forces, for example the oil companies Esso, Exxon and Mobile became Exxon Mobil.

2. *Vertical mergers*, where two or more firms along the supply chain integrate in order to have control over more phases of production. For example, in Mexico the steel producer Accelor Mittal has acquired several iron mines.

3. *Conglomerate mergers*, when firms with little common ground in terms of products) group under one owner. The Korean 'chaebol' such as Hyundai Group, Samsung and LG are conglomerates of this type, producing an array of products ranging from foodstuffs to ocean liners.

Interdependence

Having only a few *main* rivals to take into consideration, one would think that an individual oligopolist might be able to largely disregard them. Wrong. In fact, quite the contrary; any action taken by one major firm will have immediate repercussion on the others. As a single firm will not have total control of the market but still be large enough to affect output and price, firms will be acutely aware of each other and will make it their business to have a great deal of knowledge about the others. This leads to a large degree of *interdependence* as each firm knows that any action on its part will cause some form of reciprocal (= 'in return') action or reaction, 'What goes around, comes around'. This makes it very difficult to predict price and output outcomes, as we shall see.

Collusive and non-collusive oligopoly

©IBO 2003

'*There are two paths you can go by, but in the long run …*' This is an excerpt from a classic Led Zeppelin song, and is relevant (for once, you probable say) in the context of oligopoly choice. Firms will know full well how 'tit-for-tat' competitiveness is potentially damaging to all firms, the extreme scenario being a full-blown price war where everyone – but the consumer! – loses. For example, consider a *duopoly* (two firms controlling the market) of two airlines operating on the same routes, which is rather common in many countries. Here are some of the strategic issues facing the two airlines:

- If one airline lowers ticket prices then the other might be forced to compete and lower its price … and both firms stand to lose revenue and profit.

- If one airline runs an advertising blitz to 'steal customers' from the other it might succeed – but the other airline might answer in kind to get its customers back. Both firms could spend money on costly advertising and ultimately wind up back where they started.

- One airline might enhance flight quality by offering preflight snacks, better onboard meals or TV screens at every seat. The other airline would have to counter…

- The two airlines could collude by setting the price of tickets or by dividing the market up so they never met in head-on competition on the same routes.

> **Collusive and non-collusive oligopolies**: A collusive oligopoly is when firms in an oligopoly market collude (co-operate) on prices, output or sales venues in order to maximise profits. If oligopoly firms instead compete independently one speaks of a non-collusive oligopoly.

The two paths the firms in the example can go by are basically to *collude* or *compete*. (They could also simply do nothing! This is not as silly as it might sound.) In the long run, either of the options will lead to a degree of *price rigidity*. Let us look at each option in turn.

Collusive oligopolies

When I was living in Sweden and had clean air, I ran marathons. Every year or so I had to get a new pair of running shoes and I would actually put it off since I knew how angry the process would make me. You see, the sport shoe retail outlet business in Sweden consists of a three-firm oligopoly which I am convinced are colluding. I base my suspicion on the fact that while the large brand names such as Nike and Adidas might be sold in all three outlets, I was never able to find the same model of shoes in all three places. This makes comparison shopping impossible – which is probably exactly the point![35] Retailers can avoid price competition by not competing with identical products – here, simply by not carrying the same models.[36] *Collusion* takes on several forms:

---

35. My latest ex-wife daintily avoided coming with me as I would inevitably vent my spleen (= unleash my anger) on the poor sales people. It was not a pretty sight.

36. This is going to get censored but I'm still going to include it. I once compared oligopolies with men in cultures where virginity is highly prized: 'both seek to enhance their own competitiveness by avoiding good comparison shoppers'.

1. *Overt collusion*: If the main actors on the oligopoly instead have a *formal* agreement as to price and/or output, then collusion is *overt* (= open). (This is basically a cartel and will be dealt with below.)

2. *Covert collusion*: Most forms of collusion will in any case be *covert* (= secret) rather than overt (= open) since most countries have strict regulations against this type of competition-limiting behaviour; basically collusion is illegal.[37] (See "Unhealthy cartel" on page 205.)

3. *Tacit collusion*: There could be *tacit* (= unspoken) collusion where there is a price leader that the rest follow, or firms could follow benchmark prices such as recommended prices set down (legally!) by a producer organisation. Firms which have similar cost pictures could use the same mark-up (as in cost-plus pricing) and arrive at the same price level.

In any shape or form, collusion tends to move the market towards a monopoly outcome with very little price fluctuation as the price is more a result of agreement than market forces.

Ways of collusion

Firms have quite a few options when it comes to colluding, the most common forms being:

- Setting the *price* is perhaps the most common method, yet there are many other ways to lower the competitive forces which harm oligopolist's profit. (Pharmaceutical companies)

- *Dividing the market* into regions basically creates regional monopolies. (Glass companies in the EU)

- Agreeing on *quotas* will limit supply and drive up the market price. (OPEC)

Collusive agreements seldom last for long and there is a simple explanation. Any type of collusion requires a manageable number of firms controlling the market and continuous co-ordination and openness between firms in order for all members to 'walk in step' and not break the agreement. There is also very little honour amongst thieves! Since the agreement is illegal, there is no way for members to exert pressure on anyone who does not follow set prices or quotas. It is possible – even probable – that a member 'cheats' on the agreement in order to earn an even greater profit at the expense of members who stick to the agreement. All it takes is for one firm to sell above set quota or below set price for the collusive agreement to break down and the oligopoly to become competitive. Price will then tend towards a quasi-market solution with, again, little tendency for price change.

Non-collusive oligopolies

Business is a good game – lots of competition and a minimum of rules. You keep score with money.[38]

An increasingly important part of the economics tool chest is game theory[39], which can clarify the options and outcomes available to players (firms) based on certain rules. The classic example is that of two people who commit a crime and are given an offer they can't (?) refuse.

A beautiful bind – the prisoner's dilemma[40]

Jack and Jill decide that carrying water up and down the hill is a waste of resources and decide to resort to the old-fashioned method of theft [41]. They illegally siphon water from a nearby reservoir and ultimately the 'leakage' is noticed. The police arrest them on charges of grand-theft but have only enough evidence to convict them of stealing a hose. The two are put into separate holding cells, all the while pleading their innocence to the crime of water-siphoning, but admitting to the crime of stealing hoses. The hose theft carries a two year jail sentence, and the interrogator knows that the prosecutor needs a confession to convict them of the greater crime of water-siphoning. The two accused are unable to communicate.

The crafty interrogator makes the following offer – separately – to Jack and Jill: 'We have evidence enough to convict you for the theft of the hose, and put you each in jail for two years. However, we also know that you are also guilty of siphoning water. If I get confessions from both of you, we will give you each two years in a soft, minimum security prison. If one of you confesses while the other denies, the confessor will get one year but the other will get a 10-year penalty where you will spend your days with rapists, murderers, Britney Spears fans and hardened criminals.'

---

37. There is some seriously scary reading available at http://ec.europa.eu/competition/cartels/cases/cases.html.
38. Statement by *Nolan Bushnell*, founder of Atari. Taken from *Perloff*, p. 419.
39. Game theory was developed by the Hungarian-born American mathematician John von Neumann and Oskar Morgenstern, a German-born American economist, to solve problems in economics. *The Theory of Games and Economic Behavior* was published in 1944. One of the first applications was, however, in the deceptions that preceded the D-Day invasion.
40. This is a play on words, referring to the wonderful film *A Beautiful Mind*, about John Nash, Nobel laureate and game theorist.
41. I am alluding to a childhood nursery rhyme; 'Jack and Jill went up the hill to fetch a pail of water...' and I forget the rest.

HIGHER LEVEL

He then leaves the both of them to think over their options, which are:

1. Co-operate and stick to denial! This will result in two years in prison for each of them.

2. Confess and get a maximum of three years in prison.

As both Jack and Jill have two options each, there are four possible outcomes. Note that Jill's decision will affect Jack's outcome and vice versa! That is, the two are *interdependent*. Figure 2.3.41 shows the four possible outcomes in a payoff matrix.

Each one ponders away in his/her cell. The dilemma facing each of them is not knowing what the other will do! Let's look at Jill's options. If she sticks to her denial, she can hope to have a maximum of two years in prison – IF Jack also denies. Jill's temptation to confess comes with the realisation that Jack too is thinking the same way. Thus, if Jill denies she runs the risk that Jack confesses, which lands Jill in prison for 10 years! The question both are asking themselves is 'I don't know what the other is going to do! Do I dare deny and put my hopes in the other also denying?!'

Collusion, i.e. both denying, would produce the optimum total outcome of two years each, but the problem is that Jack and Jill are not allowed to communicate. The best outcome for one of them is confessing – cheating on each other – while the other denies. If both decide to minimise the impact of not knowing what the other will do, then both will confess. The dilemma creates a movement towards the grey box in the pay-off matrix above, an outcome known as a *Nash equilibrium*, where each player has adopted a strategy giving him/her the *best possible outcome given the expected action of the other*.

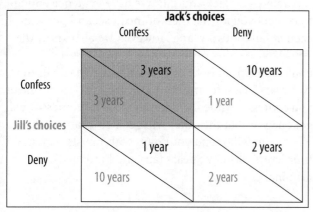

Figure 2.3.41 *Pay-off matrix for Prisoner's Dilemma*

The oligopolist's dilemma

The line of thinking illustrated in the prisoner's dilemma can be applied to oligopoly strategy. Consider two oligopoly firms which have 100% of the market together, a duopoly. Posit that each firm initially is making a normal profit. Each firm wants to increase its profit and looks at the options. By raising the price in concert (collusion) both firms might make an abnormal profit as they would be acting as a monopoly. However, Firm A could stand to lose customers and profit if Firm B keeps the same price. If Firm A lowers the price it could make an abnormal profit – or the action could force Firm B to also lower the price and both lose! The final uncertainty of the other's action could force each firm into doing nothing – which would then be the best decision taking into account the expected action of the other – there would be a Nash equilibrium.

I have taken great artistic license and grossly oversimplified the use of game theory in the preceding example, and I am bending the syllabus boundaries as it is. There are many possible outcomes in a 'duopoly game', since the game would not be a 'one shot only' game such as portrayed in the prisoner's dilemma. Firm A will face the knowledge that firm B could retaliate A's price by lowering their price, leading to retaliation again by A … and a price war results which is harmful to both firms. The outcome is most uncertain. Non-collusive oligopoly is often characterised by brief spells of competitive flurries yet broad price rigidity.

Cartels ©IBO 2003

Thou shall not steal; an empty feat, When it's so lucrative to cheat. – Arthur Hugh Clough, 1819–61

A collusive agreement taken to the extreme results in a **cartel**. A cartel acts to increase profits by setting/controlling output, or price, by dividing the market up between firms. The most famous cartels today are De Beers diamond cartel and the Organisation of Petroleum Exporting Countries – better known as OPEC. The aim is to avoid competition and act as one – a monopoly outcome is the end result. For this reason, cartels are illegal in virtually all industrialised countries. De Beers and OPEC are not subject to this restriction as they both to a large extent are based on an arrangement between governments and producers where governments have controlling interests. Also, the international aspect of these cartels transcends (= goes beyond) national law.

Cartels are notoriously difficult to uphold and maintain. The primary reason has been given earlier; the temptation for members to cheat, knowing that the arrangement is illegal in the first place and in the second place that one can earn additional profits at the expense of the others.[42] It is also hard to get all members to agree to a common set of quotas and/or prices, as these will be set with the common good in mind rather than that of an individual firm.

Case study: **Unhealthy cartel**

In 2001, the European Commission fined eight companies ¤855 million for taking part in a cartel for vitamins and related products. The cartel had been operating since 1989 and had several distinct components; a market-sharing component where members were allotted certain products and a pure price-fixing cartel for vitamin products. The Swiss company Hoffman-La Roche was at the head of the cartel and as such received the highest fine: €462 million.

The Competition Commissioner for the EU, Mario Monti, called the cartel '... the most damaging series of cartels the Commission had ever investigated ...'. The commission found that 13 companies from Europe and abroad participated in the attempt to eliminate competition in the vitamin market, amongst them Hoffman-La Roche (Switzerland), BASF (Germany), Aventis (France) and Solvay Pharmaceuticals (Netherlands).

The EU commission found that the cartel was established high up in the hierarchies of the companies, pointing to a long-term strategic plan of dominating the global market for vitamins. The cartel had regular meetings and a formal structure of management to exchange information on sales and production volumes. Output and revenue was carefully monitored in order for members to comply with quotas set by the cartel management. Amazingly enough, the same players had pleaded guilty to identical illegal collusion in the US in 1999! La Roche paid $500 million and BASF paid $225 million in fines.

As a striking footnote, the last year during which the cartel for vitamin C was in place brought total revenues of €250 million. Three years later – with the vitamin C cartel broken up – revenues were down to €120 million. This illustrates the lure of cartels quite clearly.

I also have to comment on the size of the fines. However difficult it is to estimate the gains of collusion, one can look at the total revenue to get some idea of the severity of the fine. Hoffman-La Roche had sales of €10.8 billion in 2001, which means that the €462 million fine was just under 4.3% of sales. The EU commission can set fines of up to 10% of sales.

(Source: http://www.health.fgov.be/WHI3 , www.roche.com & www.eu-oplysningen.dk/euidag)

---

42. Basically you need to be some kind of stupid to take notes of meetings, keep logs and put to paper/email all the activities and agreements involved in keeping up an illegal cartel. This is gleefully enough exactly what happened in 2007, when the European Commission found brewers Heineken, InBev, Grolsch and Bavaria guilty of running an illegal cartel for beer in The Netherlands during the period 1996–99. Ample evidence of hand-written notes from meetings provided the basis for the verdict – and a rather hefty fine of €273 million (approximately USD360 million) for the brewers. I wonder if the brewers were perhaps … inebriated.

Kinked demand curve as one model to describe interdependent behaviour

©IBO 2003

Another way to illustrate the aforementioned outcome of price rigidity in non-collusive oligopoly situations is the **kinked demand curve**[43]. Consider a firm operating in an oligopolistic market, where a non-collusive price is (somehow) arrived at, P_{EQ} in Figure 2.3.42. Just as in the prisoner's dilemma, the firm is in a highly interdependent situation, where a change in price will certainly lead to a reaction from other firms in the oligopoly. The model suggests the individual firm will arrive at the following; 'If I raise my price nobody will follow since they will expect to steal my customers. If I lower my price everybody will follow in order to hinder me from stealing their customers!' Plotting this out in Figure 2.3.42:

- A *higher* price will cause a proportionally larger decrease in revenue for the firm and thus the demand curve will be *elastic* above the starting equilibrium price of P_{EQ}. The firm would lose market share to other firms by raising the price.

- In *lowering* the price, a firm would quickly be followed by competitors who themselves would fear losing sales to the price-lowering firm. Therefore any decrease in price below P_{EQ} would mean a more *inelastic* demand curve and a decrease in revenue.

The demand curve will be 'kinked' at the point of equilibrium price and output, and as the MR curve is dependent on the shape of the demand curve, the MR curve is discontinued.[44]

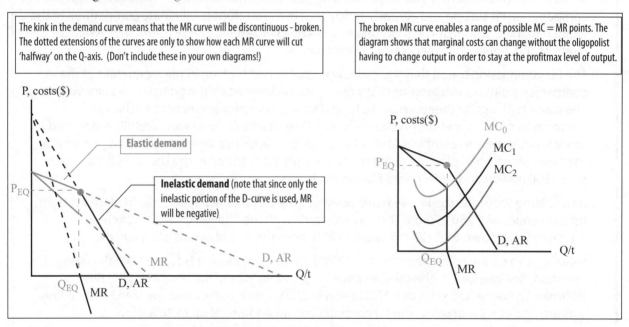

Figure 2.3.42 *Kinked demand curve*

We are assuming the firm to be a short-run profit maximiser, and the discontinuous MR curve gives a range of possible profitmax points for the MC curve to pass through. This doesn't mean that output has a range, but that the firm has a number of possible MC curves anywhere between MC_0 and MC_2, enabling absorption of any additional costs without the output level being affected. In other words, an increase in marginal costs would not necessarily have any effect on output or price since the firm could remain at Q_{EQ}

and simply accept a lower profit margin.

The model of the kinked demand curve helps to explain two key characteristics of oligopolistic markets:

1. Why oligopolies have a tendency towards *price rigidity*. The 'kink' in the demand curve is the same situation as in the prisoner's dilemma; a Nash equilibrium, where each firm's decision to leave the price untouched is actually the best outcome for the firm – as long as all the other firms act the same!

---

43. Not 'kinky' but kinked, meaning 'bent'.

44. The issue of what the MR curve should look like in the kinked demand curve is subject to heated discussion. When the first edition came out, my friend Alan 'Gandalf' Hobson immediately took issue with the fact that I'd left a portion of the lower part of the MR curve *above* the Q-axis – while claiming that the relevant portion of the demand curve was *inelastic*. Alan, I've thought it through. You are right.

2. Why oligopolies so often do not compete in price but rather resort to various forms of *non-price competition*. (See "Importance of non-price competition" below.)

It bears mentioning that there are conspicuous *weaknesses* in the model:

- Firstly, it doesn't explain how the *equilibrium price* is arrived at in the first place.
- Secondly, dynamic market effects – supply and demand changes – resulting from *non-price competition* are not explained.
- Thirdly, the model does not allow for any *other interpretation* of the demand curve and how firms would act if their view of the demand curve turns out to be incorrect.

Importance of non-price competition

Price competition is evidently something that is not a major factor in the competitive processes of oligopoly markets, but rather a situation to be avoided. Firms will instead seek to enhance their products by differentiating and profiling their product in other ways than via price, thereby avoiding head-on competition. Here are a few examples of how an oligopolistic firm can compete other than via price.

Quality and innovation

In an argument similar to that in the monopoly model, large oligopoly firms could well have large abnormal profits available for R&D, quality enhancement and innovative new products. Using, once again, my passion for wristwatches as a starting point, Rolex has a long history of innovation; patenting of the perpetual motion mechanism (a self-winding watch mechanism); the famous 'Oyster case' was made in 1926 thereby creating the world's first truly water-proof watch; a date was added in 1945, resulting in the Date-just watch (virtually unchanged today it is probably the most recognised watch in the world); the Submariner watch became the first diving watch in the late 1950s and so forth. The latest version of the Rolex

Sea-Dweller ('Deep Sea') is waterproof to … wait for it – *3,900 metres*[45]!

'Inventing a better mousetrap' is indeed an incentive for the firm as this will serve to *differentiate* the product from others on the market. For example, auto manufacturers will put inordinate effort into quality control and will continuously strive to increase fuel efficiency, performance and safety. Retail chains can present higher (perceived) quality by offering longer opening hours, delivery service, on-line ordering, and advantageous credit purchases. Oligopolistic producers often seek to create a number of different versions of a product for different market segments, e.g. Toyota, which produces economy cars under the Toyota label and luxury cars under the Lexus brand – in order to make demand as inelastic as possible for each single product.

Enhancing perceived value

One of the world's most famous marketers, Philip Kotler, uses a model of 'Core, tangible and augmented product' to explain how firms can develop a product's profile[46]. A firm in non-price competition will seek to add to the perceived value in consuming the good by focusing on many possible intangible aspects – the 'feel' of the good.

The 'core' of the product is about what the consumer is looking for in the product. It is the basic perception of utility that the firm tries to create; a car is not 'transportation' but a 'driving experience' for a BMW owner and 'sophisticated comfort' for a Cadillac owner. The core product must be backed up by any number of 'tangible' (= concrete or physical) qualities such as packaging, styling and design, brand image and special features; the BMW has an aerodynamic form, alloy wheels and a spoiler package as optional extras, while the Cadillac may have a cigar humidor, wine cooler and Sensurround TV built in.

Finally, the producer attempts to 'augment' (= increase, amplify) the buyer's sense of benefit by stressing the additional post-purchase value of the good; BMW has free service for the first three years and Cadillac has a 24-hour breakdown service including towing, repairs, and replacement vehicle.

HIGHER LEVEL

---

45. See www.rolex.com and *Wristwatches,* pp. 350–61; Brunner, Gisbert L. and Pfeiffer-Belli, Christian, Germany, 1999, ISBN 3-8290-0660-8.

46. Kotler, Philip, *Marketing management,* Prentice-Hall International Editions, 1988, sixth edition, ISBN 0-13-556267-8.

Storytime: Sex, drugs and rock 'n' roll

I bet the heading caught your eye. Unfortunately the story is about legal prescription drugs, and while there's a little bit of rock 'n' roll, there's no sex. That was just a marketing ploy to get you to read this.

A friend of mine (who understandably gets and alias here; Anders) works for one of the largest pharmaceutical companies in the world as a product specialist and marketer. Anders is responsible for a number of products in a large geographic region in the prescription drug market. His job is to work with the hospitals and physicians in informing them about new drugs, getting feedback and so on. He told me anumber of eye-opening stories about how he and other pharmaceutical companies worked in marketing. Most of the work involved keeping in touch with doctorsworking in the fields where Anders portfolio of prescription drugs would be used. Anders would do field trips weeks at a time in order to meet with doctors working in hostpitals and clinics. They would have lunch or dinner and chat abotu any developments pertaining to the various products for which Anders was responsible.

Every once in a while Anders would get 30 or 40 'valued' customers together and have a 'conference', i.e. meetings which somehow always involved taking cruise ships or sailing boats to destinations with really nice hotels which strangely enough were always on the beach front. There was entertainment, free meals, drinks on the house and many cultural activities were scheduled. The evenings were full of rock 'n' roll. Somewhere in all this there might have been a meeting or two, but let's not get caught up in details.

All the above is on the border of being illegal, as it is absolutely forbidden in Sweden for doctors to accept any form of gratuity (= hand-out or bonus) for prescribing Firm A' s drug rather than Firm B's. Yet most of the major pharmaceutical companies engage in these marketing activities. In point of fact, I remember Anders having to put in a great deal of overtime to reschedule a weekend conference he had been planning for weeks as it turned out that the majority of doctors were going to be away on another conference sponsored by a competitor. No wonder the hospital queues are so long here in Sweden!

The issue of 'sponsorship' by large pharmaceutical companies costs the taxpayer inestimable millions extra each year since many of the drugs which doctors prescribe will have much cheaper generic (= standardised, non-branded) alternatives. There is now increasing pressure from consumer groups here in Sweden to put through legislation making it mandatory for doctors to prescribe the lowest-cost alternative.

Branding and advertising

In a manner of speaking, brands originated during the middle ages when guilds (= associations for craftsmen) forced craftsmen to put a trade mark on their products in order to guarantee a certain level of quality for the consumer – and probably to keep out unwanted competitors! Oligopolistic firms of today put great effort into dividing up the market and focusing the marketing mix on specific target segments. Volvo sells cars using the 'safety' argument; Toyota is 'reliable and economical'; while BMW uses 'performance' – these marketing efforts serve to differentiate the products and at the same time limit the degree of head-to-head competition.

Marketing and advertising is very costly. Famous-brand companies will pay millions for a 30-second TV commercial during, say, the Academy Awards. These costs can actually serve to create barriers for firms which seek to enter the market – knowing how difficult it will be to compete with high-profile brands which have had years to enhance brand loyalty amongst customers. The marketing costs serve to create a 'one-and-only', 'high-quality' and/or 'luxury' image for the good. It must, however, be continuously upheld in order for the producer to exact a premium price for its products.

An increasingly common method of advertising is product placement in films by making sure that the product is clearly visible in a scene or two. In actual fact, sometimes the product takes on a roll central to the film! Just look at the most successful series of movies ever, the James Bond movies. How many products can you think of which have been firmly associated with Bond? Aston Martin and BMW in cars; Stolichnaya and Absolut Vodka in drinks; and Rolex, Breitling, Seiko and Omega in watches since no James Bond movie would be complete without the wristwatch gadgetry supplied by 'Q'.

'Well Moneypenny, I must be off. So many ~~women~~ evil-doers and so little time!'

'What's in a name!?' goes an old saying. The answer in connection with branding is 'A lot!' Brands have become increasingly valuable assets for firms. For example, Interbrand – a renowned branding consultancy firm – values the above-mentioned Rolex brand at close to $5 billion. The top three global names in term of brand value in 2008 were Coca-Cola ($66.6 billion), Microsoft ($59 billion) and IBM ($59 billion).[47]

Joke: 'Clint Eastwood toilet paper'

Picture a large grocery store with aisle upon aisle of goods. There are hundreds of different brands in every possible product category. Along comes a very well-dressed Indian gentleman who is evidently a good comparison shopper and very cost-conscious.

He walks along with the shopping cart taking great care to compare prices of all the goods. He gets to the tissue and toilet paper section, and once again compares the prices very carefully. After a few minutes, with a puzzled look, he finally calls a young employee who has been busy price-tagging goods on shelves. 'Excuse me young man. Would you please explain to me what this 'Generic' means. I have seen it on many goods and start to wonder.'

'Yes, with pleasure sir. Generic is something which we sell under a 'no-brand' policy. It means that we can sell a standard product – the toilet paper you're holding - at a lower price that the branded goods.'

'Ah, I see! Well, this toilet paper is certainly much cheaper than all the rest. I will take the no-name brand. Thank you for your assistance.'

Off goes the Indian gentleman … only to return the next day holding a roll of toilet paper in one hand. He looks purposefully around the store until he spots the young man who assisted him the day before. 'Ah, young man! You remember me, yes? Good. I have a name for the 'no name' toilet paper. Yes indeed. Very appropriate name. You should call it 'Clint Eastwood toilet paper'. It's rough. It's tough. And it doesn't take any crap out of Indians.'

And yet the small survive

In view of the ongoing process where (global) oligopolies arise, how do so many small firms manage to remain? Part of the answer is to be found in human nature. People tend to feel comfortable with the close and familiar, so a local fast food place will have its place in spite of any number of international chains. It also makes it easier to get additional service, say in repairs or follow-up service – anyone who's bought a bicycle knows the value of local service! Another reason for small scale success is that many services do not easily benefit from scale, for example haircuts, shoe repairs and garden services. Finally, local tastes, customs and preferences make large scale 'streamlining' more difficult for large firms and also give small/local firms an edge in quickly adapting to changes in local tastes. In short, it is a challenge for firms to be both global and local.

47. See http://www.interbrand.com/best_global_brands.aspx.

HIGHER LEVEL

Theory of contestable markets ©IBO 2003

What if there were no entry barriers to speak of so that incumbent (= existing) firms always faced the threat of the oligopoly turning into a competitive market? There is increasing evidence that many oligopolies operate in markets where entry and exit barriers are low. Theoretically, outside firms could use a 'hit and run' strategy by entering markets which show abnormal profits and leaving if/when the profits fade. How would then existing oligopoly firms act in order do dissuade this type of activity?

Assumptions

The theory of **contestable markets** is based on assumptions very close to those for oligopolies. Firms are profit maximisers; there is perfect knowledge/information; and goods can be homogeneous or differentiated. However, there are four assumptions which distinguish a contestable market from others.

1. There can be *one* firm with total market power (monopoly) *or many firms* which have limited market power.

2. The market is characterised by *competition – not collusion*. Thus the ability to effectively block market entry by way of colluding is not an option for incumbent firms.

3. There are *no significant barriers to entry*. Outside firms can therefore contest (= challenge) incumbent firms' market domination, threatening to steal some of their abnormal profits.

4. There are *zero exit barriers*. An important assumption of the contestable market is that no exit barriers exist. An exit barrier is when the firm experiences unrecoverable costs upon leaving the market, so called 'sunk costs'. Such costs can be considerable since a firm entering a market will have any number of start-up costs which it cannot regain upon leaving the market; advertising and marketing costs, insurance, acquiring of permits to run a business, capital which cannot be used in other sectors and therefore has no residual value, etc.[48]

An oligopoly portraying the above characteristics would be contestable, as nothing would prevent firms from challenging exiting firms' market dominance. This is the main theme of contestable market theory, that the model of oligopoly neglects the possibility of **potential market entry**[49]. Oligopoly theory focuses on competition in the market while contestable market theory focuses on competition for the market. If abnormal profit exists then other firms can easily enter the market by lowering their price, which would inevitably lead to a PCM outcome. They could then leave the market when abnormal profits dried up since there are no barriers to exit – a hit-and-run market strategy. Incumbent firms earning a normal profit would have their market share – and power – eroded by newcomers.

The theory of contestability posits that incumbent firms will act in a manner so as to remove the incentive for firms to enter by setting price and output at zero profit level. In other words, the mere threat of entry will force incumbent firms to act as if the market were perfectly competitive. Figure 2.3.43 on page 211 shows how a perfectly contestable market comprised of four firms results in a competitive outcome on the market. Each of the four firms has an equal share of the market, producing Q_0 and total market output is Q_{EQ}. At any price higher than P_{EQ} there would be an abnormal profit to be had, since average revenue would be higher than average costs for all firms. The threat of market entry forces incumbents to adjust to what would be a de facto competitive outcome, where no abnormal profits are being made and therefore there is no incentive for outsiders to enter the market. In the long run, the market price settles where AR = AR and only *normal profits* can be made.

Finally, the issue of efficiency. Since incumbents have a degree of price- and output-setting power – contrary to a PCM – they will adjust to the optimal level of efficiency. Each firm will be producing at an output level where average costs are minimised and the price is equal to marginal costs. This tells us that there is both *productive efficiency* (output at AC_{min}) and *allocative efficiency* (P [AR] = MC).

---

48. My favourite in-class example of sunk (literally!) costs is the monumental (again, literally!) screw up in trying to dig an 8.5 km tunnel through a mountain in my home country of Sweden. The Hallandsås tunnel between Ängelholm and Halmstad in southwestern Sweden was started in 1992 and supposed to be finished by 1997/98. By 2008 less than 60% of the tunnel was finished and it is estimated to be finished in 2015 (19 years late) and some 300% costlier than originally estimated. It was clearly evident after the first years that costs would skyrocket – so why continue? Well, what do you do with *half* a tunnel?! I suppose we could rent it to the French for mushroom farming…

49. 'Contestable' means (here) 'challengeable'; potential entrants challenge the dominance of incumbent firms.

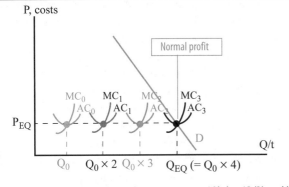

In a perfectly contestable market, any firm operating at an AC below AR (D) would make an abnormal profit. Each firm produces the amount **Q₀**, resulting in market output of **Q$_{EQ}$** and price of **P$_{EQ}$**.

Firms adjust output to most efficient level at market price:
- Output is at **AC$_{min}$** and there is **productive efficiency**.
- **P (AR) = MC** and thus firms are **allocatively efficient**.

Figure 2.3.43 *Normal profit and loss in monopoly*

POP QUIZ 2.3.9   OLIGOPOLY

1   Explain why non-price competition is such a strong element in oligopoly markets.

2   How can game theory and the kinked demand curve help to explain why there is a tendency towards price rigidity in oligopolies?

3   Explain how a cartel might ultimately fail due to cheating. (Try to illustrate your answer with diagrams!)

4   Explain how it is possible for small firms to survive right alongside oligopoly firms operating in the same market.

5   'Oligopolistic firms never actually compete with each other!' Why might this statement be true?

6   Is it true that only a competitive market will be both allocatively and productively efficient? Use diagrams to support your answer.

Price discrimination ©IBO 2003

When I was a young man and frequently out being naughty, I was often infuriated by a policy of discrimination found in discos and clubs where men paid an entrance fee and women did not. It was not until many years later that I understood the underlying economic logic in the price-setting: more women mean more men, and since men apparently have a more inelastic demand for clubbing (and for women?) they can be charged more than women. I said I understand it – I still don't like it. Perhaps it is a good eye-opener as my feelings might be something similar to those that women have endured for ages. Just a thought!

Definition ©IBO 2003

Price discrimination means that different people will be willing to pay different prices for the same good. The next time you take a really cheap flight or bus/train trip, try to get into a conversation with a well-dressed individual sitting in the waiting lounge. If it turns out that this is a businessperson on a business trip, tell him/her that you are an economics student and that you are writing about pricing policies of airlines/buses/railroads. Ask what he/she paid for the ticket – I wager that it will be a considerably higher price than yours! The businessperson has been subjected to **price discrimination**, since the airline/bus company has sold the same basic good at different prices to different consumer groups; a business person who is willing/able to pay a relatively high price and a student with higher price sensitivity for tickets[50].

One of the most inventive forms of price discrimination I have heard of in later years came from my friend Glenn. He runs a ju-jitsu dojo (= gym) together with Mike – who is a true entrepreneur! The dojo faced the same profit issues as other gyms; fluctuating demand and therefore highly uncertain revenues. Glenn and Mike's solution was as brilliant as it was simple: charge differently for old and new students.

> **Price discriminating**: When firms actively adjust the price of a good according to the willingness/ability (e.g. according to the price elasticity of demand) of different consumers to pay for it, the firm is price discriminating.

50. Be prepared for some anger. Many people do not realise the extent to which they have been discriminated against. A fellow passenger once caused quite a scene when he found out that I paid less than 10% of what he had paid.

Firms operating in perfectly competitive markets are price-takers and therefore lack pricing power. A firm with pricing power, e.g. a monopoly, can set any price, within the confines of demand, as it is operating behind entry barriers of some sort. Thus far we have assumed single-pricing strategies in our models, yet nothing prohibits a firm from charging *different* prices for a good. Economic theory identifies three main ways to price discriminate:

1. **First-degree price discrimination;** the firm charges whatever the market demand will bear. Auctions and 'haggling' at open markets are a form of price discrimination, as each good goes to the highest bidder.

2. **Second-degree price discrimination:** the firm sells at quantity discounts or 'tiered markdowns'. For example, many publishing houses will have different prices on school textbooks depending on the quantity ordered. The first 30 copies cost $25 per book, the second thirty $22 per book, and any order above 60 receives a 15% discount.

3. **Third-degree price discrimination:** the firm separates the market into distinct groups or segments and sells the good at different prices. The disco club and flight ticket examples fall into this category – as does most price discrimination. We will deal solely with third-degree price discrimination here.

Reasons for price discrimination

©IBO 2003

There are three main reasons (plus one 'Outside the box') why firms would have an incentive to price discriminate:

1. The most obvious reason for price discrimination is that selling a good at different prices will serve to *increase profits*. This is intuitively obvious; a firm that has market power can increase profits by selling the good at the highest possible price according to consumers' willingness to pay. The firm might also use price discrimination to cut prices in order to force competitors out of the market (predatory pricing) or in order to penetrate a new market.

2. Firms might also think in long-run terms, and price discriminate in order to *capture a future market*, for example by letting students purchase magazine subscriptions at a lower rate, the firm can look forward to higher future subscriptions – at the normal subscription rate. An export firm selling at a lower price abroad is very common and such practice is often vilified (= spoken ill of). This form of discrimination helps exporting firms attain economies of scale and strengthen competitiveness. In addition to the above pecuniary (= financial) motives, one should not disregard the goodwill firms can earn by letting certain groups benefit from lower prices; senior-citizen discounts on buses; student access to educational material on the Internet; free parking for handicapped, etc.

3. All the above examples arise from the private sphere, yet a good many examples of price discrimination arise in the arena of *public and merit goods*. Public utilities can charge lower rates to firms than households in order to provide competitive infrastructure for industries. Price discrimination can also help public monopolies to cover costs in high cost areas, for example by discriminating in railroad tickets the additional costs of providing train services to rural areas can be covered. A frequently used form of public price discrimination is based on concepts of fairness, where it is considered beneficial to society that all groups have equal access to goods. Such discrimination is often based on *income*; high income earners could pay more for municipal child care and schooling than lower income households.

4. Finally, as an 'outside the box' issue, it is possible for a price-discriminating firm to supply a good where a single-price market simply would not exist, due to high average costs. Discrimination can also allow a public monopoly such as a utility service to produce at an even *higher output level than the break-even* level of output (i.e. beyond the point where
AC = AR).

APPLIED ECONOMICS:
Innovative price discrimination

One of the most inventive forms of price discrimination I have heard of in later years came from my friend Glenn. He runs a ju-jitsu dojo (= gym) together with Mike – who is a true entrepreneur! The dojo faced the same profit issues as other gyms; fluctuating demand and therefore highly uncertain revenues. Glenn and Mike's solution was as brilliant as it was simple; charge differently for old and new students.

The basic idea is to charge an entry-level price which never changes! A new student in 2003 would pay SEK 2,000 (about $250 at 2003 exchange rates) for a year-long membership, while students who joined the club in 1999 continue to pay the membership fee they started with. The SEK 2,000 fee will never change as long as the student continues to be a member. However, as soon as a member leaves the club and doesn't pay that year's membership fee, he/she will start all over again if/when a new membership is bought. Thus, a student who entered in 1999 would still pay SEK 1,800 in 2003, but by leaving the club during 2003, he/she would pay the (higher) entry-level fee upon rejoining in 2005.

This is quite brilliant. It provides an incentive for students to remain in the club which diminishes dropout behaviour. The club will keep more of its students and have a much better grasp of future costs and revenue.

Necessary conditions for the practice of price discrimination ©IBO 2003

There are any number of ways for a firm to price discriminate. The most common are:

1. **Time:** airline tickets are subject to 'X weeks in advance' and movie theatres have different rates for different times of the day. Electricity, squash court rental and fishing licences will all be fairly easy to divide into 'peak' and 'off-peak' groups of demand.

2. **Age:** apart from previous examples, there are under-12 discounts for cinema tickets, amusement parks and air travel[51]; while senior-citizen discounts are often available for such services as haircuts.

3. **Income:** lawyers often price discriminate for their services according to income as do prostitutes and private tutors[52]; health care and college tuition are also often cases where different income groups pay different prices.

4. **Gender:** the aforementioned discrimination of nightclubs against men is one example. Other

examples – against *women* – would be haircuts and personal hygiene products.[53]

Preconditions for successful price discrimination

There are three preconditions for successful price discrimination.

1. The first is that the firm must be able to identify *different distinct groups* of consumers. As an extension of this, the groups must have distinct differences in their price elasticities of demand. Otherwise the firm would be unable to charge different prices in the first place.

2. The second requirement is for the firm to be in a *position of market power*, i.e. be able to set prices, which excludes the possibility of price discrimination in a perfectly competitive market as firms operating under such circumstances will not have pricing power. I will use a monopoly to illustrate the effects of discriminatory pricing.

3. The final and rather obvious condition is that the firm must be able to *limit the effects of arbitrage* – i.e. reselling. If I could get one of my students to buy my airline and cinema tickets at student-discount prices I would. This must be rendered impossible by the producer in order to be able to charge some groups higher prices. Thus, airline tickets have the travellers' names on them which must match their passports, while the student-discount cinema ticket can only be used upon showing a valid student ID. Basically, firms must be able to keep the different groups separate in order for the discriminatory scheme to function. This doesn't necessarily have to involve complicated administration in separating the groups, since there are often built-in segmenting walls, for example when an international firm sells services and price discriminates between countries.

Figure 2.3.44 on page 214 shows how a price-discriminating monopoly arrives at the profitmax price and output for the two market segments I and II, each with its own PED. The sum of MR ($MR_I + MR_{II}$) for each segment equals total market MR, and profitmax output at MC = MR is 40,000 units. The differing

---

51. Notice that airline tickets are used as an example in many methods of price discrimination. I strongly suspect that the confusion as to what an airline ticket actually costs is most intentional. Airlines simply don't want price transparency as this would lead to price competition. They want us confused, and by using several layers of discriminatory pricing, airlines increase our search costs of finding correct price information. Yet the only thing I want to hear is 'Smoking or non-smoking, Sir?'

52. I love putting these two professions in the same bracket. Guaranteed to yank a few chains in the halls of learning.

53. Yes, I looked this up. It seems that women's PED for products dealing with personal cleanliness and appearance is lower than men's! It works for me: I shocked my students and colleagues in an interview in the school paper by commenting on how shampoo and dish-washing liquid were perfectly substitutable for me. Since dish-washing liquid is cheaper I use that to wash my hair.

elasticities of demand in market segments will set two different prices; $7 in market I and $5 in market II. (Note that the diagrams only illustrate how output and

price is set – not the amount of profit. This is shown in Figure 2.3.45 on page 214 – A price discriminating monopoly.)

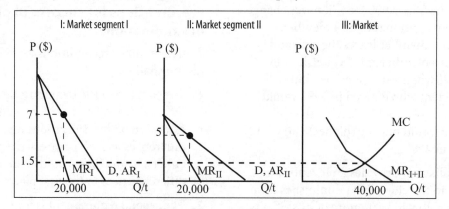

Figure 2.3.44 *Price discrimination – duo-price monopoly*

Possible advantages to either the producer or the consumer ©IBO 2003

Now we look at how producers and consumers can stand to gain and/or lose by the process of price discrimination. Assume a monopoly firm setting a profitmax price and output, shown in Figure 2.3.45. (Please compare this to Figure 2.3.44 above, as it builds on those figures.) The single-price monopoly is making an abnormal profit of $120,000 ($3 × 40,000 units) at the profitmax point of output. Now, assume that the firm is able to identify two distinct groups having different demand and sets the highest possible

price for half of total output. Diagram II of Figure 2.3.45 shows that these 20,000 units could be sold at a price of $7. Now, here's the tricky bit; as output has not changed there is no change in costs! This means that average costs are the same, $2, having been set by the original output of 40,000 units. Therefore the element of abnormal profit per unit goes from $3 to $5, bringing the profit for the higher-priced batch to $100,000. Adding the profit from the lower-priced batch ($3 × 20,000 = $60,000) brings the total abnormal profit up to $160,000. The net addition to abnormal profit by price discriminating is $40,000, shown by the square in diagram II.

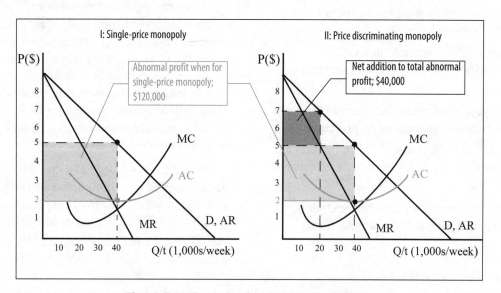

Figure 2.3.45 *A price discriminating monopoly*

A little depth:
Further price discrimination

Let's continue one step further. Say that the firm manages to divide the market into four segments, where each group can be priced according to its demand, shown in Figure 2.3.46. The highest-demand group will pay $8 for 10,000 units; the second-highest pays $7 for 10,000 units and so on. The addition to total abnormal profit by further price discrimination (going from two prices to four prices) is $20,000, shown by the two grey squares in diagram III. By dividing the market into four price groups, the firm makes a total abnormal profit of $180,000.

Winners and losers

The advantages to the producer are obvious; higher total profits. As an extension of this, a producer would be able block market entry by setting output at the break-even point (AC = AR) and make up for this by selling 'portions' of total output at discriminating prices – the producer would still be able to make an abnormal profit in spite of producing at break-even point. One can say that the abnormal profits gained by price discrimination serve to pay for an amount of goods sold at break-even cost. This will dissuade potential entrants as it will be most difficult to match the incumbent's price.

Consumers stand to both lose and gain from price discrimination. Some groups will benefit from lower prices while others will 'subsidise' the winners. Clearly consumers would lose if competition fell due to predatory pricing by the price discriminator, but again, abnormal profits allow the firm increased funding to plough back into the business in the form of **R&D**, resulting in new products and improved quality. Yet the main objection by consumers is probably the transfer of income to the producers, since the overall picture is that consumer expenditure increases but not necessarily the quantity consumed. (Outside the syllabus: The transfer, or 'capture' of consumer surplus by the producer clearly shows the redistribution effects.) On an international scale, there is a bit more conclusive evidence of consumer loss, since multinational companies often price discriminate on a country-wide basis owing to the fact of pure geographical barriers to arbitrage. This helps explain why – ceteris paribus – international firms often set the price higher in high-income countries than in low-income countries, for example, medicines, paperback books and services.

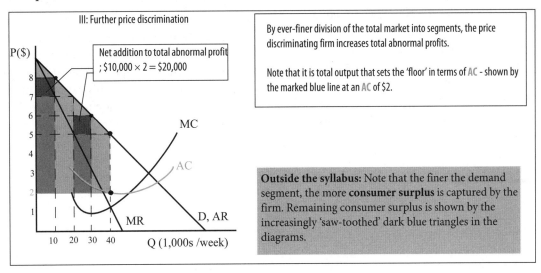

Figure 2.3.46 *Normal profit and loss in monopoly*

A little depth:
Possible redistribution gains

Price discrimination is often practiced by publicly owned monopolies, such as mail service, telecommunications and railroad travel. Price discrimination stands to benefit consumers by enabling a monopolistic firm to break even – or even earn a profit – from no

n-economically viable activity which would normally not be undertaken.

The aim of public monopolies is often to provide a societally optimal level of output rather than a profitmax level. The monopoly could seek simply to break even in terms of profit and set output where average costs equal average revenue – 70,000 units in Figure 2.3.47.

However, posit that installing telephone lines, railroad tracks and postal routes to outlying rural districts comes at a very high marginal cost. Should these members of society pay for this or should society as a whole pay? If an economy chooses the latter – as many in fact do – then the social benefits of supplying all areas are considered to outweigh the costs. Yet price discrimination can actually enable the public monopoly to cover the higher costs.

Assume that the public health service monopoly wishes to provide all areas in the country with equal amounts of health care hours. Initial total quantity provided is 70 million hours per year, but an additional 10 million hours of health care is needed to give what is considered uniform health coverage throughout the country. Producing 80 million hours of health care will cause average costs to exceed average revenue, resulting in a loss of $80 million (grey area in

the diagram) at an hourly rate of $2. The monopoly can make up for this loss by charging higher rates for certain groups, such as rates based on income or higher rates for non-essential (cosmetic) surgery.

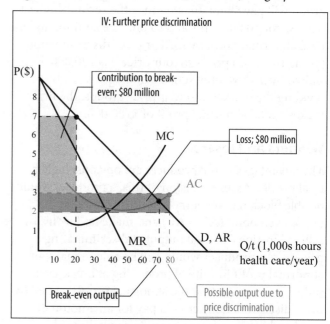

Figure 2.3.47 *Publicly owned monopoly*

The diagram illustrates a possible (highly idealised – see "Mermaidomics" on page 183!) outcome, where discrimination- pricing at $7 per hour adds a contribution of $80 million, resulting in a break-even outcome for the monopoly. One can say that the 25% of the population paying a higher price have subsidised the lower cost of health care for the remaining 75%. The discriminating monopolist has benefited society.

Outside the box:
Turning loss into profit

One possible advantage to society due to price discrimination is the possibility of producing a good where normally no firm would be willing or able to supply it. No firm would produce in a market where AC was higher than the profitmax price. Figure 2.3.48 illustrates the price of round trip travel by car on the bridge between Denmark and Sweden; at the profitmax (= lossmin!) output of 4,000 units the demand curve renders a maximum price of SEK 500 – but the **average cost is SEK 550**. It is impossible to make a profit – the loss is SEK 200,000.

A price discriminating firm could counteract the loss by setting output at profitmax and then discriminating against consumer groups A and B by, for example, setting a higher price for peak-time travel. 4,000 units are produced at an AC of SEK 550. 2,000 units are sold to **group A**; the total loss is SEK 50 × 2,000 = SEK 100,000.

The remaining 2,000 units are sold to **Group B,** e.g. people willing to pay a higher peak-time price – at a price of 700. (Remember that total output sets the 'floor' for AC!) The profit per unit of the units sold to Group B is SEK 150, giving a total of **SEK 300,000** as a contribution towards making up for the loss of SEK 200,000. In the final outcome, **total net abnormal profit** is the total profit contribution minus the total loss: **SEK 300,000** – SEK 200,000 = SEK 100,000.

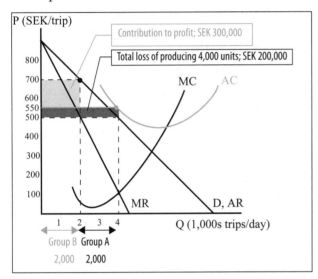

Figure 2.3.48 *Loss-making monopoly: Öresund bridge*

POP QUIZ 2.3.10   PRICE DISCRIMINATION

1   A firm charges a higher price for its product on a market due to higher storage costs. Why is this not price discrimination?

2   What difficulties would arise for firms trying to price discriminate on sales made over the Internet?

3   How does the possibility of arbitrage (reselling) affect a firm's ability to price discriminate?

4   Outside the syllabus! Assume that a firm could perfectly price discriminate, i.e. set a separate price along every possible point on the demand curve. Where would profitmax be? What would happen to consumer surplus?

5   Explain how a society might actually benefit from price discrimination. Account for both 'winners' and 'losers'.

Preparing for exams

Short answer questions (10 marks each)

1 What will happen to output and price when a profit maximising monopolist maximises revenue? Use a diagram in your answer.

2 Explain how diminishing returns differ from diminishing returns to scale.

3 How might a firm in an oligopolistic market attempt to increase market share?

4 How do economists differ from accountants in the use of the term 'profit'?

5 Explain how 'normal profit' and 'abnormal profit' differ.

6 A monopoly is broken into a number of competitive parts. Predict the changes in output and price which are likely to take place.

7 Why might an oligopoly be reluctant to change its price?

8 Discuss reasons why a monopoly could produce more output at a lower price than a competitive market.

9 Why might a PCM firm be willing to run at a loss in the short run?

10 Explain the difference between 'productive' and 'allocative' ('economic') efficiency.

11 Explain how consumers might benefit from the existence of monopolies.

12 Explain how/why profits from a monopoly are likely to be different from those in monopolistic competition.

13 In talking with three fellow passengers on a train, you discover that you have all paid different prices for the same journey. Explain how this could be.

Extended response questions (25 marks each)

1 a Why do so many international markets tend towards oligopolist structure? (10 marks)

   b What are the possible consequences of this? (15 marks)

2 a Explain what 'economies of scale' are and why they have become increasingly common in later years. (10 marks)

   b In spite of this, many small firms still exist. What possible reasons do you see for their success? (15 marks)

3 a What main features are found in oligopolies? (10 marks)

   b Explain how oligopolies can work both for and against consumers. (15 marks)

4 a What are the main assumptions made in the model of perfect competition and contestable markets? (10 marks)

   b Examine the relevance of the above assumptions in explaining market outcome in terms of quantity, price and efficiency. (15 marks)

5 a What is a 'natural monopoly' and how could it be superior to a competitive market in providing goods? (10 marks)

   b Explain why goods provided by natural monopolies are often publicly owned. (15 marks)

Market failure

2.4

CONTENTS

MARKET FAILURE ©IBO 2003

We have expounded on how markets succeed in both the production and distribution of goods – and how the price function ultimately creates a market clearing. Recall that when quantity supplied equals quantity demanded, the market is in equilibrium and there is optimal resource allocation – a Pareto-optimum. Should – for some reason – the market not achieve this equilibrium then the market has failed.

Reasons for market failure ©IBO 2003

Our premise in dealing with a free and competitive market is that the three main actors in the market – firms, consumers and owners of factors of production – will act in their own self-interest, i.e. all three groups will attempt to optimise their returns. Firms will maximise profits; consumers their utility and factor owners their return. In accordance with standard economic theory, allowing a 'free' market to reign will produce the best possible outcome in terms of resource allocation. This is the Smithian world of the 'invisible hand'; billions of individual transactions would together create a system where the **right** goods were produced in the **right** amounts. It is in defining 'right' that the concept of market failure arises, specifically when resources are not used in the best possible option.

> **Market failure:** When the price mechanism fails to allocate resources towards the socially optimal amount, i.e. there is sub-optimal resource allocation, one speaks of market failure; there is a non-Pareto outcome.

Markets are very efficient in deciding which goods to produce and how much to produce (see *price mechanism* in Section 2.1), but it is quite feasible that not all costs and/or benefits are taken into account or that imperfect competition puts the market price higher than the marginal cost. *Social* efficiency arises when the **marginal social benefits (MSB or demand)** in the production/consumption of goods are equal to the **marginal social costs (MSC or supply)**. Once again, 'marginal' indicates the *addition* to total costs or benefits in producing/consuming one more unit. There are three reasons why the market mechanism fails:

1. the existence of **externalities** (e.g. pollution)
2. **overprovision and underprovision** (tobacco and health care)
3. **imperfect competition** (i.e. monopolies).

Positive and negative externalities, with appropriate diagrams ©IBO 2003

Externalities arise whenever the market clearing price creates benefits or inflicts costs on a *third party*, i.e. a party other than the consumer or producer. In both cases, negative and positive externalities, the *signalling function* fails to correctly portray the *real* costs and *real* benefits to firms and consumers, resulting in overproduction or underproduction of goods at the wrong price. The market has failed to optimally allocate resources.

An easy way to get an immediate grip on the concept of externalities is to just think for a minute or two about the following two questions. Have you ever consumed a good where others (who didn't pay for it!) also received benefits from your consumption? And have you ever consumed a good where your consumption had a negative effect on others? I warrant that your answer is 'yes' in both cases; how about perfume and deodorant as an answer to the first question and cigars and noisy motorcycles as an example of the second? In both examples, your personal consumption has had effects on others – external effects which we call **externalities** (or 'spill-over' effects).

Marginal social benefits (MSB) and Marginal private benefits (MPB)

In addressing the issues of positive externalities, we use two new terms – marginal *private* benefits (MPB) and marginal *social* benefits (MSB).

- The downward sloping *MPB curve* in Figure 2.4.1 on page 222 shows how the marginal private benefits to the private individual (the consumer) fall with increased consumption. This is, of course, the *marginal utility* previously shown by the demand curve.
- When the marginal social benefit (MSB) is greater than the marginal private benefit (MPB) there are *positive externalities* (or 'spill-over' effects), e.g. positive effects for third parties. This is shown by the double-edged arrows between the MSB and MPB curves in the diagram I: **MPB + positive externality = MSB**.
- The *marginal social benefit* of a good shows the marginal utility of society as a whole in consuming a good. The **MSB curve** is the *demand curve* (**MPB**) plus positive externalities.

221

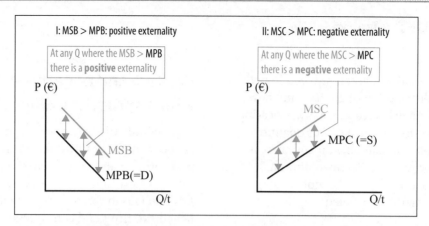

Figure 2.4.1 *MSB/MPB and MSC/MPC: externalities*

Marginal private costs (MPC) and Marginal social costs (MSC)

For negative externalities, see diagram II in Figure 2.4.1, we use the terms marginal *social* costs (MSC) and marginal *private* costs (MPC).

- The upward sloping **MPC curve** shows how firms' costs rise as output rises. (HL will recognise this from theory of the firm.) The marginal private cost is basically the *supply curve*.

- If there are costs to third parties – for example, pollution – then one speaks of negative externalities ('negative spill-over effects'). The double-edged arrows show the extent of the negative externalities at any given output. **MPC + negative externalities = MSC.**

- The *marginal social cost* of a good shows the marginal cost of society as a whole in providing a good. The **MSC curve** is the *supply curve* (**MPC**) plus negative externalities.

Positive externalities

A positive externality arises when the social benefit of consuming another unit, i.e. the marginal social benefit (MSB), is greater than the marginal private benefit (MPB). My employer, a private school here in Mexico, provides me with access to the gym and weight-lifting room free of charge. I have even been provided with my own boxing bag to work out my sizeable aggressions on and was invited to help redesign the gym together with my housey Rob the PE teacher.[1] I, and a good deal of research, claim that the *benefits to society outweigh my personal benefits* since my improved health will enable me to work harder and more efficiently and my sick days will decrease due to improved resistance to illness. There are benefits all

around: I personally will enjoy better health; the health care system will benefit from me becoming less of a burden; the school benefits from my increased productivity – and the economy as a whole benefits from increased output and tax monies. My consumption of gym time has positive effects on others.

> **Positive externalities:** A positive externality is a benefit arising for third parties (non-users and non-producers) from the production and/or consumption of a good which neither the firm nor consumer has paid for. Positive externalities arise whenever **MSB > MPB**.

This is not 'Never-Never Land' economics. Many employers are increasingly aware of the benefits of making sports and physical activities available to employees. So, while the employer pays *private* costs for the gym and the employee receives *private* benefits of staying fit, the additional benefits to society as a whole encompass benefits which are not paid-for by either the firm or the consumer. These benefits are *positive externalities* since others – so called third parties – benefit from gym consumption.

Diagrammatic illustration of positive externalities

Assume a new hospital is being built where the social benefits of providing additional health care are estimated as being greater than the total costs (both 'financial' and 'societal' costs) of building and running the hospital. Figure 2.4.2 on page 223 illustrates the cost/benefit issues arising when there are social benefits in excess of the purely private costs. At the price of P_0, the quantity provided by market forces (Q_0) is less than the societally optimal level of $Q_{soc\ opt}$. The resulting market failure has two key aspects:

---

1. I suspect that my colleagues signed a petition to Rob – it was too easy to get the school to foot the bill.

1. *The extent of the positive externality*: As we have thus far assumed that the goods provided are in accordance with a competitive outcome, output is set where MPB = MPC, or, as you have become accustomed to it 'supply equals demand'. Basically, as there are societal benefits arising from consumption which are not paid for by consumers, there is a marginal social benefit at each level of demand; this is the MSB curve parallel to the MPB curve. This is the external benefit of consumption at any given level of output. At equilibrium output of Q_0 of health care, the positive externality (MSB ⇔ MPB) is shown by the double-ended arrow. This illustrates that there are social benefits in consuming more hours of health care – the MSB curve shows that if all the social benefits are included in the marginal private benefits the *actual* demand curve is to the right.

2. *The potential welfare gain (or 'welfare loss')*: Note that the MSC curve is drawn assuming that all private costs are accounted for and that no external costs are levied on society. Since the social benefits are greater than the private benefits at all points of output between Q_0 and $Q_{soc\ opt}$, any increase in output between these two points would increase societal welfare. This is actually a societal waste, or a potential welfare gain, and is shown by the blue triangle; every additional unit between Q_0 and

$Q_{soc\ opt}$ renders a higher societal benefit than societal cost. Thus, in terms of optimal societal allocation of resources, too little of the good is supplied on the market; Q_0 is supplied rather than the societal optimum level of $Q_{soc\ opt}$.

It is worth noting that if users could account for all the benefits they would be willing to pay a higher price for the additional output. This would be $P_{soc\ opt}$ in Figure 2.4.2. To summarise, since the market has failed to produce at the point where the *real* costs are equal to the *real* benefits, the market has failed. Allocative efficiency can be attained by increasing output of the good.

Any number of privately produced and consumed goods will have positive spill-over effects on society. *Consumption* of goods such as milk, inoculations and gym memberships will result in better health and increased benefits to society. *Production* can also lead to positive externalities; for example, increased production of solar panels will benefit society in reduced emissions of carbon dioxide; aqua-farming will reduce pressure on heavily depleted stocks of fish and shrimp; and medicines will benefit any number of non-consumers in helping to limit the spread of infectious diseases. As shall be duly noted, many of the goods linked to positive externalities are in fact goods which are supplied by public monies such as education, health care, theatres and libraries to name but a few.

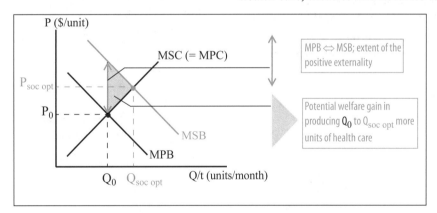

Figure 2.4.2 *Positive externalities of health care*

Negative externalities

> *I know the human being and fish can coexist peacefully.* – George W. Bush

Conversely, when the marginal private costs (MPC) are outweighed by marginal social costs (MSC) then there is a **negative externality**. A good which renders higher marginal social costs than private costs is an example of overproduction/consumption; the production of coal-powered electricity causes emissions of sulfur and nitrogen dioxide which ultimately cause acid rain

which kills forests and fish. Here, the market has underestimated the *true* costs of the good to society and produced too much of it.

Negative externalities: A negative externality is a burden/cost endured by third parties arising from the production/consumption of the good. Negative externalities arise when the **MSC > MPC**.

Every year for over 25 years I have returned to my fishing paradise in Helsingland, middle Sweden, where my friends Östen, Musen and I have fished since pre-teenagerdom. Every year when I return, I have the same heart-in-throat experience of wondering whether the beautiful little brook-trout have finally succumbed to increasing pollution – primarily acid rain. You see, the middle part of Sweden is along a thermal weather path where a goodly proportion of emissions from Germany's industrial centre (Ruhrgebiet surrounding Köln) ultimately land. Sulfur and nitrogen oxides emitted in Germany ultimately land as weak solutions of sulfuric and nitric acid in Swedish lakes and streams. This lowers the pH-values of the water and can rapidly kill off entire populations of trout and the insects upon which they feed.[2]

Therefore, when I drive the 850 kilometres north in my German VW Polo, listening to CDs manufactured by the German firm TDK, and subsequently pitch my German VauDe tent by the river, I will *not* be paying the full price of these goods since the real cost – the social costs – are considerably higher! Even the people who have never had the thrill of stalking trout with a 9-foot fly-rod would seriously oppose measures to keep a natural strain of trout alive. Why? Because the cost would be … well, incalculable. How does one measure the loss of a sub-species?! Yes, one could measure the value of trout streams in purely monetary terms such as tourism and fishing license revenues, but there are numerous intangible benefits which, while impossible to calculate, are most evident; 'a living natural environment' sums it up. As Ronald Coase, one of the world's leading economists and Nobel Laureate in 1991 has put it: 'The question to be decided is: is the value of the fish lost greater than the value of the product which contamination of the stream makes possible?'[3]

Priceless! (Kölån, Helsingland, Sweden, July 2008)

The negative effects of pollution are shown in Figure 2.4.3. Using my fishing example, a tent-maker in Germany using Teflon[4] coatings does not include the costs of dying ecosystems in Sweden in the cost picture when focusing on maximising profits. Any level of output will have external effects on third parties – Swedish-American-Ecuadorian fly-fishing economics teachers on well deserved holidays for example. Output will be set at Q_0 (where MPC = MSB) rather than at the societal optimum of MSC = MSB. This overproduction of goods causes external costs to society – which will not be reflected either in the firms' costs or the prices paid by consumers.

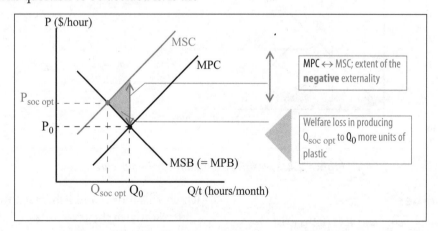

Figure 2.4.3 *Negative externalities of plastic production*

---

2. Local municipalities and fishing clubs combat this by dumping large amounts of limestone in source lakes and feeder-streams in order to raise the pH value.

3. Coase, Ronald, 'The Problem of Social Cost', *Journal of Law and Economics,* October 1960, p. 3.

4. Teflon contains perfluorinated chemicals (PCOs) which accumulate in protein and can build up to high levels in both humans and wildlife. Recent studies suggest PCOs are linked to birth defects, developmental problems, liver damage and affect the neuroendocrine system. (I am *way* out of my depth here and had to look this up … so you better ask your biology teacher.)

1. *The extent of the negative externality*: The external costs to society – dead fish and very sad fly-fishermen – at Q_0 are shown as the vertical distance in Figure 2.4.3 on page 224 between the marginal private costs and the marginal social costs: MPC ⇔ MSC.

2. *Welfare loss*: The shaded triangle in Figure 2.4.3 shows how the MSC is higher than the MSB for any unit of output produced between $Q_{soc\ opt}$ and Q_0. This is the welfare loss (burden) to society in producing these units.

The MSB is assumed to be the same as the MPB, i.e. all benefits to society are accounted for by the private benefits. Price and output is set where private costs equal private benefits. Since third parties suffer from this, there are negative externalities arising from consumption. (Social costs = private costs + external 'spill-over' costs.)

Please note that the in examples used, acid rain, carcinogens and particulates, will naturally have numerous negative externalities other than for us fishermen. I remember when one could walk around hundreds of statues littering the grounds of the famous Acropolis in Athens. Returning some 30 years later, I found that most of them have been moved indoors. While this might in part be due to the risks of theft and vandalism, it is often simply to protect the invaluable antiquities from the highly damaging acid rain and air-born particulates resulting from heavy traffic and industries – which have eroded this priceless cultural heritage more in the past 40 years than the preceding 2,000 years!

Warning!
'Externality' and 'welfare triangles'

Frequently students fail to differentiate sufficiently between 'extent of the externality' and the 'welfare triangles'. The externality shows the net benefit/cost to society in the consumption of the good. The triangles show how the external effects result in misallocation; a potential welfare gain or welfare loss. I also urge you to 'pull out the arrows and triangles' as I have done in the illustrations in order to make it easier on your examiner.

The concept of externalities can be applied quite broadly. A new building which blocks your view confers a loss of utility on you – and thus you, as a third party, will bear the cost of lost viewing pleasure. This is a negative externality for society. A new building which enhances your viewing pleasure will of course bring society positive externalities. It goes without saying that one ultimately stands on a pedestal of normative judgement in assessing external costs and benefits; a free pop concert in the park will bring both depending on one's preferences. It is obvious, however, that there are some costs which are more objectively observable. An example is a World Bank study in 2000 which attempted to assess the social costs of air pollution in developing countries.[5] The study showed that air pollution could be linked to the premature death of over 500,000 people each year, costing some 2% of GDP in health care and lost output.

Short-term and long-term environmental concerns and sustainable development ©IBO 2003

A far greater threat to overall wellbeing is the possibility that environmental externalities ultimately make it evermore difficult to sustain output increases over time. In the short run, the production of goods will cause environmental damage such as air-borne pollution and toxicity in rivers and will often use non-renewable resources. The basic issue is not *whether* growth is detrimental to the environment and uses limited resources, but rather to *what degree* this is sustainable in the long run. A country with a real growth rate of 2% per year will have doubled its income in 35 years. This could have serious implications for total use of non-renewable resources such as oil and coal. Most economists would agree that a great deal of output uses resources which are irreplaceable in the short run and that the ability to increase long-run output is contingent upon improved technology and production methods.

Consider energy sources as one example of the short term versus the long term. Any form of energy using fossil fuels (oil, natural gas, coal) will have severe repercussions to the environment. Burning fossil fuels means increased soot and particulates, carbon dioxide/monoxide which contributes to the *greenhouse effect* and thus global warming. Nuclear energy on the other hand, is possibly the cleanest form of economically viable energy forms in existence at present – in the short run. The long-run hazards of dealing with the

---

5. See http://www.worldbank.org/cleanair/global/topics/health_imp.htm.

nuclear waste which have lethal half-lives of thousands of years are inestimable – and put quite a burden on generations as yet unborn. The issue is in fact far more complex when viewed from an economic perspective, since it is a fallacy to believe that the ideal quantity of pollution would be zero. This perspective fails to consider that this 'Utopian' state of being will have severe opportunity costs in itself, such as far less available energy at higher cost.

Inter-temporal opportunity costs

Let's apply the concept of **inter-temporal** ('between two time periods') opportunity costs to the question of environmental issues. If society desires present output and growth, then it will in all likelihood see pollution, soil degradation and deforestation as a cost. However, in focusing on future availability of clean air, ample soil and forests, then society will forgo an amount of present output. Play now and pay later – or vice versa?! Quite frankly, this issue has been answered in a rather negative way in many of the rich industrialised countries; forests, minerals, land and oil were severely depleted during the initial phases of development throughout the 18th to 20th centuries. This in fact created a great deal of the present wealth in developed countries and highlights the conflict of interests today in less developed countries (LDCs). How far should these countries go in limiting their use of natural resources in order to sustain future levels of output – knowing full well that this limits present growth and present levels of living standards? There are also arguments supporting present use of resources in order to attain technological advances which would enable us to use fewer resources in the future.

Sustainable development

The issue centres on the question of whether economic growth and use of natural resources in order to increase living standards is sustainable. One of the major shortcomings in dealing with the environmental impact and **sustainable development** is that far too often it is assumed that the term 'sustainable' is well defined. It isn't. Nor are there any agreed-upon objectives for achieving it.

Pessimistically speaking…: The basic definition of sustainable development is that present use of resources in satisfying needs in an economy should not lessen or limit future generations' use of resources in satisfying needs.[6] This definition is slippery at best. Any action taken by a developing society today *will* have an impact on future output and *will* involve using limited non-renewable resources such as minerals and oil. Furthermore, it is a common (and faulty) assumption that when the production of a good impacts negatively on the environment, the production should be banned. This is not an economic analysis since many of the goods whose production pollutes will also have benefits to society – cars for example. Economics aims to assess the **net** marginal benefits, which entails taking into account additional external costs and benefits in setting output and price. Basically, economists provide a way of looking at socially acceptable levels of pollution. In this harshest of lights, it is clear that it is impossible not to adversely affect future generations' use of non-renewables to some extent.

Optimistically speaking…: On the other hand, improved technology and production methods have enabled more developed countries (MDCs) to substantially increase output whilst lowering the use of natural resources. In many cases, such as oil, copper and coal, available 'years left at present consumption-rates' of these finite natural resources have actually increased in spite of population increases and depletion of known reserves. This is a reflection of how relative scarcity and the price mechanism leads to productivity increases and the search for substitutes; the cost of telecommunications has plummeted due to increasing use of computers and also the replacement of copper wires with optic cables made of fibreglass – that is to say, sand! Therefore, while the pure physical availability of many resources is diminishing, one can argue that improved technology/efficiency in production means that we are providing the next generation with a better production base than we ourselves have.

The debate on development, growth and sustainability is fierce and multifaceted. Many environmental groups claim that present consumption and production is impossible in the long run and even that our world will not survive if developing countries were to follow the same growth and consumption path as present-day MDCs. 'Imagine the same ratio of cars and Freon-using refrigerators in China as in the USA!' is a common argument. Countering this is the above argument on how production in MDCs is increasingly efficient and the environmental costs progressively lower. Therefore increasing the income in developing countries will enable a transfer of technology from richer countries and ever improving output-to-pollution ratios.

---

6. The concept was initially used in the aforementioned (United Nations) *Brundtland Report* from 1987.

Environmental Kuznets curve

The complexity in trying to analyse the costs and benefits involved in growth and development has received a good deal of attention. Recent studies and increasingly clear data indicate correlation between economic growth and environmental degradation, primarily airborne pollutants.[7] Note that I did not use 'positive' or 'negative' correlation. The reason is simple; at low levels of income an increase in national income will be associated with increasing environmental costs (positive correlation between growth and pollution), while at some point along the growth curve increasing income will show improvements in the environment (negative correlation).[8] Figure 2.4.4 shows how increasing per capita GDP is correlated to a decrease in environmental degradation.

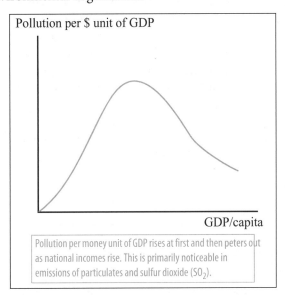

Pollution per $ unit of GDP

GDP/capita

Pollution per money unit of GDP rises at first and then peters out as national incomes rise. This is primarily noticeable in emissions of particulates and sulfur dioxide (SO_2).

Figure 2.4.4 *Environmental Kuznets curve; growth and environmental impact*

At low levels of income the amount of pollution is relatively nominal and increases as incomes rise. However, as per capita incomes rises the relative intensity of pollution (= pollution per unit of output) in the economy falls, as technological improvements take place and environmental standards are raised. The reasoning is graspable at an intuitive level; when people become wealthier they are more willing to pay for a cleaner and healthier environment. In actual fact, they would demand it, and increased income provides the resources necessary to clean up the environment. Unfortunately, the curve in Figure 2.4.4 has not been shown to apply to the main greenhouse gas, CO_2, which solidifies this as one of the major environmental issues to address.

POP QUIZ 2.4.1   EXTERNALITIES AND SUSTAINABILITY

1   Using diagrams, explain how economic activity can negatively impact on society. Use both consumption activities and production activities in your examples.

2   What would be the main difficulties in assessing external costs and benefits?

3   Given that all economies are to some degree reliant on finite resources – for example, oil – explain how it is possible for the present generation to leave the next at least as well off in terms of being able to meet their own needs.

Lack of public goods ©IBO 2003

Well, it's getting late and I dearly want to head up the hill to Toni and Pati for tacos, beer, TV news and football. I could walk but hey, this is Mexico, so I'll put on my manta ray cowboy boots, get in my car and drive up. Here's where the concept of **public goods** comes in: I will be using the *public roads* to drive home on – guided by *streetlights* and *road signs* galore. I will studiously avoid any and all contact with the corrupt Mexican *police*. The underlined examples above are goods which would all be **underprovided** or not provided at all by a competitive market.[9]

Public goods

Imagine if, in driving home, I had to stop and pay a fee for road use (which is actually becoming increasingly common) and then had to put a few coins into coin-operated street-lights and coin-operated road-signs along the way. (I was about to say something about

---

7.   See, for example, the 'Environmental Sustainability Index' put together by the World Economic Forum's Global Leaders for Tomorrow Environment Task Force, The *Yale Center* for Environmental Law and Policy, and the *Columbia University Center* for International Earth Science Information Network (CIESIN); http://www.ciesin.org.

8.   Alan Kreuger and Gene Grossman of Princeton University estimate that the turning point (in terms of GDP/cap) is around USD5,000 – roughly where the Czechs are now. By the time per capita income is at USD 8,000, all environment indicators show improvement. See *Economic Growth and the Environment, National Bureau of Economic Research*, NBER working paper W4634, February 1994. See also *World Bank, Policy*, research working papers 1992; no. WPS 904. World development report by Shafik.

9.   Once again, note that economists use the term 'goods' as an umbrella; it covers tangible goods such as guns and butter but also services such as health care and banking. Public and merit goods are, in fact, often services.

having to pay the police on the way – but of course that is exactly what one does here in Mexico.) The common denominator here is that the thought of paying for one's actual 'unit' use of the goods outlined here borders on the preposterous – not to mention impossible.

Roads, street-lights, road signs, police service and public broadcasting are all examples of **public goods**; they are 'publicly' available (as opposed to 'pay per usage'). Be careful in your use of this term! It is one of many unfortunate examples of how economists have corrupted the common use of a word and created a very definite subject-specific term. When economists use the term public goods they are referring to something quite specific – a good which by its very nature is impossible to charge for on a user-pays basis. A most treasured example of public goods are *ideas* – pasteurising milk for example, using coal/gas/uranium as a source of energy, and all forms of advances in farming technology – noting, of course, that the development of the horse- or oxen-drawn plough didn't run into the highly debated current practice of patenting genetically modified organisms. The two main traits – prerequisites, actually – of a public good are **non-excludability** and **non-rivalry**.

Non-rivalry

By putting on my manta ray boots to go up to Toni's, I *hindered others* from consumption of the good, which is an example of *rivalry* – my use of my boots bars others from use. My boots, car and MP3 player are examples of rivalry in consumption, since my use decreases the availability of the good for others. A public good, by contrast, does not have this element since the good can be used simultaneously by other people. My use of the road, road signs, police force, and streetlights does not reduce available consumption to others. Thus public goods are subject to (varying degrees of) *non-rivalry*, meaning that one person's use does not diminish the availability of the good for others. 'Get off of my cloud' by the Rolling Stones is actually far more meaningful than 'Get out from under my streetlight'![10]

Non-excludability

What about hindering someone from using the good in the *first* place? Yes, this is actually the definition of private goods; once the good has been provided, the provider must be able to *exclude* you from use – in order to be able to charge you. Thus the provider can exclude non-payers from use, just like the boots, car and MP3 player. This highlights precisely the problem with goods such as roads, road signs, and street lights; once they have been provided they can be used by anyone – payers and non-payers alike! This means that there is an element of *non-excludability* built into some goods, and this is the second prerequisite of a pure public good; once provided, one cannot exclude anyone from using it. This is also known as the **'free rider'** problem and should be well known amongst students who have ever done a group paper where three students did all the work and the fourth was a useless slacker. The term 'free rider' is actually taken from public transport, where the provision of a bus service would be 'free' for those who didn't pay the fare yet provided for by those who did. Hence 'free rider'.

> **Public goods:** A public good is distinguished by high positive externalities but also non-rivalry (my use does not diminish your use) and non-excludability (non-payers cannot be excluded once provided) in provision. It is very difficult to charge individual users is thus often provided by public monies.

The incentive for public provision

There is a very noticeable common denominator amongst the examples of public goods above, namely that they are in fact considered of such importance that they are supplied! There are in other words goods which cannot really be charged for – much less limited to users only – yet are provided for in virtually every modern society. Why? How? The answer to the first question is by now self-evident: any good which is considered to be of such obvious gain to society – roads, lighthouses, drainage systems, water filtration, electricity grids, military and civil defence, air traffic control, police force, judiciary system, etc. will ultimately be both desired and supplied somehow. The remaining question *How?* must enable potential suppliers to be able to provide the good economically in spite of not being able to charge for its use. This would exclude the private (free market) sector immediately.

---

10. But there's no way I'm not going to tell the following little story! My friend Toni lives in a 'gated community', e.g. an area behind gates where you have to show ID to get in. After some heated discussion in the community about who was paying for the streetlights or not, the community leaders assigned streetlights! Anyone who didn't pay their bill found themselves on a very dark street. Another favourite example in economics bites the dust …

The answer is **taxation** and **public sector provision** of the good. Everybody pays since everybody benefits. End of story. As everyone is reaping the benefits of consumption it is only fair that everyone 'pull a straw from the stack' and help pay for it.

On a rhetorical note, one must include a few weighty objections to the concept of a *pure* public good. Anyone who's been stuck in gridlock in the outer city access roads is well aware that your use does, in fact, diminish my use – something that any number of drivers in Athens will gladly attest to! The same goes for getting hold of a police officer to investigate a break-in to one's garage at the same time the community is swamped by either football hooligans, a rock festival or anti-globalisation demonstrators. It is also evident that increasingly sophisticated pay-per-use systems allow communities to charge for the use of inner-city roads and access routes. In truth, there are very few examples of goods which would fulfil the criterion of non-rivalry and non-excludability to 100%.

Underprovision of merit goods

©IBO 2003

The basic issue of a **merit good** is that it is meritorious (Did I tell you to 'taste the term' yet? Oh, right.) to society as a whole. One can define a merit good as one where the consumption of the good is highly beneficial to society yet would be gravely underconsumed by the individual, i.e. the MSB > MPB. Some classic examples are **education, health insurance** and **pension schemes**.

> **Merit good**: A merit good is a good where individual consumption benefits others in society, e.g. there are positive externalities. It is commonly underconsumed/underprovided due to consumers underestimating or ignoring the societal benefits. Examples include health care and education.

So, why would we not be inclined to consume 'enough' (as defined by the societally optimal level of MSB = MSC) of these goods – especially when economics shows us how society as a whole receives positive external effects? Why would people *underconsume* IB physics or French lessons and health care? Simple, the short-sightedness and self-interest of the individual cannot foresee how consumption of Newtonian physics and TBC vaccinations will

ultimately benefit oneself, or others. Two main reasons exist fro the underconsumption of merit goods:

1. *Consumers ignore the benefits to others*: The inability to see how personal consumption spills over and benefits other societal members is perhaps one of the largest obstacles in people consuming the socially optimal quantity. The existence of *positive externalities* in itself means that the good would be underconsumed and therefore underprovided.

2. *Consumers ignore their own future benefits*: Another explanation for underconsumption can be found in what economists call '**time inconsistent behaviour**'. This arises when the benefits to the user/consumer are far in the future while the costs are immediate. In such situations, people are not inclined to give the benefits enough weight in weighing the costs and benefits. Giving up present enjoyment in order to learn French would increase possible future benefits in travel and employment possibilities – but how many would actually think along these lines?![11]

Health care and pensions

Let's use two classic examples of merit goods; **health care** and **pensions** – both have strong elements of positive externalities and time inconsistent behaviour. Most European countries have relatively advanced publicly funded health care and pension systems rather than a system based on households paying to a private health insurance or pension fund. The reason is that most European governments have a strong element of social-welfare woven into the ideological policy base regardless of political hue. Europeans have long since considered it wasteful and harmful for the health care system to be based on private contributions. Simply put, people in their 20s to 50s would not give health problems (resulting from aging and hard work, perhaps) and retirement benefits enough thought and would thus have a strong propensity to neglect putting aside income for *possible* ill-health and *future* old-age. ('Live fast, die young and leave a beautiful corpse', and all that.[12])

The lack of adequate health-care will ultimately lead to illness – and thus to sick-leave and loss of possible output. The private individual loses good health and income. Society loses both the output, income and tax revenue which could have been generated through

---

11. One of my favourite examples of time-inconsistent behaviour was pointed out by one of my students. In the movie *Bridget Jones's Diary* there's the scene where she writes; 'Monday 28th of April. Gym visits, zero. Number of gym visits so far this year; 1. Cost of gym membership per year; £370.'
12. Credo set in stone by actor James Dean.

health care. As for pensions, it has been proven that people on lower incomes have a far more marked tendency to neglect pension fund payments, and thus will ultimately suffer from considerable declines in income when they retire. The *underconsumption* of both these merit goods will lower both life expectancy and the quality of life. Both represent a societal cost which European governments have long considered too high to bear and therefore use tax revenue to fund them and many other social/welfare goods.

Education

One final example, just for you! *Education* is considered one of the most vital merit goods, as it increases not only de facto output (by increasing the efficiency of labour) but also future *possible* output (by providing the basis for scientific research, development and innovation). This is a good which is grossly undervalued in many richer countries with tax-funded schooling, probably since we have become so used to not paying the actual cost of provision. I had the nasty habit of telling my Swedish public school students that roughly only one out of 20 of them would be sitting in class if they had to pay the actual cost of an IB education. The thought-provoking thing is that it is not so much a lack of ability to pay, rather than a lack of propensity that would preclude the other 19 from joining classes. We are disinclined to pay for something when we cannot see the benefits of consumption. Putting it harshly, as I am prone to do, one could say that the inability of the average 16-year old to assess the value of education will harm not only the individual student in the long run, but also society in the guise of geriatric economic teachers who look to well-padded societal coffers for help to the bathroom in old age. This social service is provided by tax revenue. Tax revenue cometh from economic activity – which is enhanced by education![13]

So who provides the goods?

I should add a final note on the provision of public and merit goods. It is a common error amongst students that these goods are always produced by some form of national or municipal government. Not so. You must distinguish between 'provision' and 'production'. In most countries public/merit goods are provided for

(here 'paid for') by government yet many countries have extensive tendering systems whereby private firms compete for government contracts. Tax money indeed *provides* the good – but it is *produced* by the lowest bidder.

In any case, all societies must deal with some sort of public provision of goods and thus with an element of planning in the economic system. Even if the society is based on an American model, where there is a far larger element of personal payment into health and pension funds than in Europe one must have a degree of public health and social security. Again, politics must decide this at the behest of economics and other social sciences. Note that it is virtually impossible to define which goods are actually merit goods on the basis of economic reasoning alone. The societal attitude that certain goods are desirable is in fact a political decision. Not all societies consider ballet, evening courses in carpentry or martial arts to be goods which should be provided by public monies. The political decisions herein help to characterise merit goods and help to fulfil the objective of *redistributing incomes*, since poorer groups gain access to goods often provided by progressive income taxes.[14]

Over provision of demerit goods

©IBO 2003

Here's the one you've all been waiting for: drugs. Nothing quite like quaffing a few pints whilst puffing on a sizable Havana cigar.[15] Oh, you were perhaps thinking of *illegal* types of mind-altering substances, say cocaine and LSD. We'll get to those, but for the time being I shall deal with the more conventional (and in western countries, socially acceptable) substances alcohol and tobacco.

It is often said by my more socially aware colleagues, that if cigarettes and alcohol were previously unknown and then invented tomorrow, they would immediately be banned and severe sanctions for selling and consumption would be imposed! They are quite right, to the extent that a lawsuit in Florida against American tobacco companies in 2000 resulted in a ruling that $US145 billion (145,000,000,000) be awarded to smokers (in Florida alone!) for health

---

13. We're back to self-interest as a motivator. Maybe this should be my strongest incentive to be as good a teacher as possible; the thought that someday the nurse who helps me to the toilet in my old age will be provided by tax revenue generated by my own students. Please make sure the nurse is equipped with a sense of humour and a cigar-lighter. Don't worry about the nurse's age, gender or looks. I'll be far beyond remembering why this would be of any possible interest to me.

14. A progressive income tax means that the proportion of tax (i.e. average percentage) increases as income rises. Higher income = higher average percentage tax paid.

15. These are, of course, **complement goods**.

damage.[16] While this might seem a trifle on the excessive side, no-one can possibly deny over 50 years of research showing very high correlation between smoking and various types of cancer, lung disease and premature death. Alcohol might well be even more costly for society. Not only do we have to contend with the severe health damage to individuals but also with the loss of labour skills and output resulting from inebriation, hangover, alcohol related disease, and, of course, premature death.

Author and victim – he'll no doubt sue me in 20 years if I'm still alive.[17]

Both tobacco and alcohol are demerit goods, since users either ignore or do not realise the full costs of consumption – both to themselves and third parties. Both goods show the characteristics of the individual consumer not being able to see how his/her consumption patterns negatively affects society. Indeed, when it comes to alcohol and illegal drugs, a case can be made for judging many individual consumers as seemingly incapable of making a correct decision even in terms of their own self-interest!

> Demerit good: A good which has negative externalities and where users do not realise – or ignore – the costs to themselves and the societal costs inflicted on third parties. Common examples are tobacco and alcohol.

Abuse of monopoly power ©IBO 2003

As earlier stated; when the market provides the correct amount of a good at the right price, then the basic economic problem has been successfully addressed and resource allocation is optimal. Thus, supply equals demand and (HL students only) marginal cost equals price (or AR). As soon as this is not the case, the market fails. This would be the case for firms operating under conditions of *imperfect competition* (monopoly, oligopoly and monopolistic competition) whereby the firm(s) would be in a position to gain at the expense of the consumer. A firm wielding monopoly power, in being threatened by few – if any – viable substitutes on the market, will to a certain extent have the ability to set output and price without consideration of potential rivals. In having this power, the monopolist will certainly have an incentive to lower costs by lowering output, and subsequently set the price as high as possible in order to maximise profits.

This is shown in Figure 2.4.5 on page 232. Assume that there are no externalities present and that the monopoly supply and perfectly competitive market (PCM) supply curves would be identical with the MSC curve. The competitive market would produce an output of Q_{PCM} at a price of P_{PCM}. A monopoly, on the other hand, would be prone to increase the price and lower output in order to find the 'greatest distance between price and costs', i.e. maximise profit. When the monopolist raises the price to P_{mon}, the quantity on the market will fall to Q_{mon}. The monopoly has created a market failure since MSB ≠ MSB. The triangle shows that each unit of output between Q_{mon} and Q_{PCM} has a higher marginal social benefit than marginal social cost. (Outside the syllabus: alternatively, the net loss of consumer and supplier surplus.) This is the *deadweight loss*.

---

16. *The Economist*, 20 July 2000.

17. Before I start getting hate mail, the story goes something like this: Summer of 2008 I was back in Sweden for a quick visit to Guy and his family – basically my adopted family. His (my) sister Monica had adopted two wonderful Korean lads and standing on the lawn of Musen and Pernilla's house it was time for a picture with Uncle Matt. I'm not too comfortable with children and the discussion prior to the picture went something like this: 'Matt! Picture time – get in there with the kids!' 'Em, I'm smoking a cigar.' 'So put it down!' 'I'm busy! It's a good cigar …' Someone tossed me an infant … and before I knew it, Toni the bendejo snapped a picture.

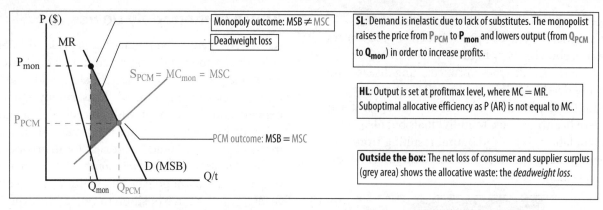

Figure 2.4.5 *Market failure due to imperfect competition (monopoly)*

Imperfect competition is perhaps the most common form of market failure, owing to the strong growth of oligopolies and monopolistic competition in the past 20 or so years. Imperfectly competitive firms – primarily monopolies – can use an assortment of practices which result in market failure. The monopoly can enter new markets by setting low predatory prices which could force other firms out of the market, which would lower competition and give the monopolist more power. The monopoly firm could also set prices at a low level to dissuade any potential entrants from attempting to gain a foothold in the market. Monopolies can restrict market access and competitive markets in many other ways, for example by buying up rivals; owning/controlling vital raw materials; refusing to sell to retail outlets which do not observe a minimum price set by the monopoly; setting different prices on different markets (price discrimination) and

finally by simply being able to disregard market demand to a certain degree, since few substitutes are available.

Note that monopolies and near-monopolies can use their market power in many different ways. Firms can attempt to control the market by price fixing (collusion); division of the market in order to limit head-on competition between powerful firms; limiting market entry by withholding access to raw materials or suppliers; forcing suppliers and buyers into disadvantageous contracts; and discriminating against consumers by charging different prices in different locations. All of this serves to enhance the (near-) monopolist's profit at the expense of the consumer and ultimately leads to higher prices and lower output than would be the case in a competitive market.

A little depth for HL:
How a monopoly might *lower* negative externalities

As previously shown in theory of the firm (see Section 2.3), it is theoretically likely that a profit maximising monopoly firm will set a higher price and lower output than a perfectly competitive firm. This would normally result in sub-optimal allocative efficiency (and a dead-weight loss) since the price (AR) would be higher than MC. (See Figure 2.3.33 on page 190.)

However, let us assume that the monopoly is producing a good for which the negative externalities are considerable, for example a major tobacco firm wielding monopoly power. The good inflicts costs to society in increased sick days and falling productivity, increasing health costs, etc. This is shown in the diagram I as the negative externality: $MPC \Leftrightarrow MSC$.

Assuming (as was done in Section 2.3 in comparing the PCM with a monopoly) that the sum of PCM firms'

individual cost curves (MPC in Figure 2.4.6 on page 233, diagram I) would be the same as the MC curve for the monopoly (MC_{mon}), then the MPC is the same as the MC_{mon}. This would render a competitive market output of Q_{PCM} and a price of P_{PCM}, and a negative externality (double-ended arrow in diagram).

The monopoly tobacco company, on the other hand, would base the output/price decision on a different MC = MR point. Diagram II shows the MC = MR point where the monopolist would set output, and the higher monopoly price of P_{mon} and a lower output level of Q_{mon}. Since this coincides with the optimal output and price ($Q_{soc\ opt}$ and P_{opt}) when the negative externalities are taken into account, the monopoly is actually more allocatively efficient than the competitive market.

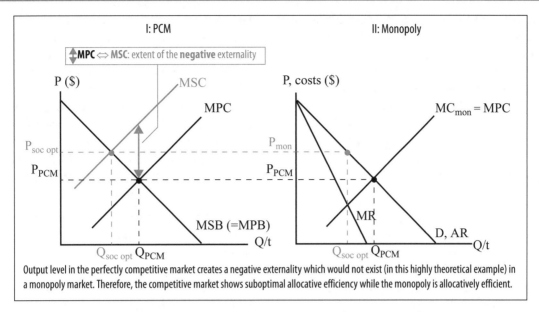

Figure 2.4.6 *Lower negative externalities due to monopoly*

Possible government responses ©IBO 2003

The debate on government involvement (or intervention) is an almost philosophical question. It is often about the choice – and thus trade-off – of public interest/gains versus the freedom/costs of the individual. In implementing the control functions designed to limit market failures, society has basically answered the question of whether government involvement is warranted or not. Society – often in the form of our elected governments – is deemed necessary to correct a number of market imperfections.

Legislation ©IBO 2003

Legislation is perhaps the oldest form of market intervention. By passing laws which limit the behaviour of firms, society can try to limit the impact of market imperfections and resulting societal losses. Legislation attempts to correct market failures by influencing both supply and demand for goods. Here is a (far from extensive) list of legislative methods common to many countries.

Ban

The most obvious form of legislative control is simply to **ban** production and/or consumption of certain goods which are connected to negative externalities. A ban will be used when the **net** marginal social benefit is

negative at all output levels, i.e. when no amount of the good on the market adds to social wellbeing. For example, the consumption – and even possession – of any number of drugs has been judged to fulfil this criterion and are thus illegal with severe penalties often attached.[18] Other examples of goods which have been banned in many countries are DDT (a highly toxic insecticide), asbestos (highly carcinogenic mineral used as fire-resistant insulation) and, increasingly, car engines which use leaded gasoline. Most of my generation (and gender) would like to include rap music!

Influencing production and consumption

Often legislation is less extreme and seeks instead to limit production and consumption by imposing restrictions on sales and use (see Figure 2.4.7 on page 236). More and more countries impose severe restrictions on smoking in public places (see "Storytime: The New York smoking ban" on page 64) to limit the effects of secondary smoke inhalation. Accordingly, any number of laws seek to limit access to tobacco; opening hours; restricting sales licences; age requirements; etc. In addition to this, government seeks to limit demand by decreeing that all tobacco products must have clear warning labels on each package, such as 'Smoking kills'. Legislation is also used

---

18. Possession of hard drugs such as opium can result in the death penalty in Malaysia, for example.

to force producers and consumers to produce/consume certain goods which have positive externalities, for example, car manufacturers are forced to attain certain minimum safety standards and consumers are commonly bound by law to use seat-belts. You should have no trouble in thinking of any number of goods which are subject to quite a few regulations and laws which govern their existence on the market.[19]

Regulation of externalities

In order to lower overall environmental impact, many countries set increasingly tight limits on pollutants and emissions. This means that externalities are kept in check by using penalties to dissuade firms from polluting. In order to uphold the law, for example the original *Clean Air Act* (USA 1955), a regulatory body is often formed, in this case the Environmental Protection Agency (EPA) in the US. The regulations can cover both the extent/degree of pollution (such as setting standards for parts-per-million for particulate emissions) and the production process itself (forcing firms to install water and air filters). Such regulatory agencies can be given wide-ranging legal powers to prevent pollution and environmental damage, from simple fines to plant closure. Increasingly, firms can be held accountable to the extent where managers risk prison sentences for disregarding environment laws.

Regulating competition

Virtually all industrialised countries have a body of law regulating anti-competitive behaviour. Legislation presupposes that oligopolies and monopolies will not act in the best interest of the public and should therefore be forced to circumscribe their activities. Governments seek to limit the effects of imperfect competition by way of limiting the degree to which firms can control markets. Limiting market power is often the objective of monopoly laws and **anti-trust** ('trust' being an older term for cartel) legislation and is frequently upheld by regulatory agencies, e.g. *anti-trust laws* and/or **Competition Commissions** which monitor and regulate market abuses outlined in the section on monopoly/oligopoly abuse.

Activities considered to be anti-competitive within the European Union (EU) carry penalties such as fines of up to 10% of total revenue. This is carried out and surveyed by the European Commission, which also has the power to stop mergers which may be considered to be harmful to competition. It is notable how differently countries regard the threat of monopolies, for example one can compare EU regulations with USA's anti-trust

laws outlined in the *Sherman Act* from 1890. In the EU, a firm can be fined for 'misuse of monopoly power', which is to say when a firm having over 25% of the EU market uses its power to limit competition in some way. In the USA this would be, per definition, impossible, since American anti-trust legislation outlaws monopolies in the first place and firms deemed monopolistic are forcibly broken up into separate (competing) firms. This is why Microsoft is being subjected to an ongoing inquiry to determine whether or not it is in fact a monopoly.

All the possible legislative moves above have some downsides. A ban could create and perpetuate black markets – where government control would be even smaller! All forms of legislation will need to be backed up by government action and will ultimately cost taxpayers. Harsh regulation of production can drive up costs and thus prices, leading to loss of both competitiveness and output. Finally, regulating agencies have often been criticised for being 'paper tigers' in not standing up to powerful lobby groups or failing to bring offenders up on charges.

Direct provision of merit and public goods ©IBO 2003

Merit goods, which have clear benefits for non-users, will be underprovided for in the competitive market since users cannot see how their use benefits others – or themselves in the long run. When it comes to the provision of goods which are difficult or impossible to charge for, the private sphere will simply not provide them. This is the case with public goods, which by their very nature of non-rivalry and non-excludability make such goods impossible to provide privately. One way of correcting these market failures is simply for government (local/regional/national) to step in and provide the good.

Merit goods

A *merit good* is a good where there are positive externalities to such an extent that society deems the good to be *underprovided* by free market forces. Subsequently the good is also underconsumed, since consumers lack sufficient information to consume the 'correct' amount. As previously explained, merit goods such as education, health care and pensions are considered highly beneficial to society and are therefore in many countries supplied by public monies. It is viewed as socially beneficial for more of the good

---

19. Most of my students, having seen my temper at one point or another, are now strong advocates of a total ban on handguns.

to be produced and consumed than would be supplied by a competitive market.

Let's use education as an example. Most consumers (students) would hardly be inclined to pay the full cost of education since they would not take into account future personal benefits. Nor would the person enjoying (?!) economics lessons be the only beneficiary of consumption since society at large will ultimately gain from a better educated labour force. The presence of large positive externalities moves many countries to provide the goods directly by running state schools.[20] (In fact, few, if any, schools are able to survive on purely private tuition, and most private schools will be subsidised in some way by grants and contributions from private firms, ex-students or governments.)

Public goods

Public goods also come with large positive externalities, yet with the troublesome attachment of being very difficult to charge users for. As outlined earlier, few goods could be considered to be pure public goods. Roads can be toll-roads (= 'pay per use') and police services can be unavailable at peak times which means that the non-rivalry and non-excludability criteria are not met. Examples of *pure* public goods would perhaps be defence, air traffic control and lighthouses.

Since the private benefits would be very small (or non-existent) compared to the public benefits, competitive markets would fail quite massively here. The good would simply not be provided in many cases and the social welfare losses would be very large. This is probably why the debate on whether public goods should be supplied by public monies is much more subdued. In fact, virtually all countries have a degree of government supply of public goods. It seems that there is broad agreement that lighthouses come with sizable social benefits – such as not having an oil tanker grounded on a holiday beach or the nesting ground of a seal population. And seriously, can you see air traffic control demanding that an off-course aeroplane outside of Washington pay a fee in order to be brought in safely?

What is potentially contentious is the *quantity* to provide since there is no market mechanism to gauge demand. The market fails to achieve optimal resource allocation and so society must make up for it. This is another example of how the planning element cannot ever be completely discarded – all economies must have a mixture of private and public it seems. Yet, once again, it is quite common for public goods to be supplied (as in *produced*) by private firms which have been contracted by government. Municipal government pays private mountaineers to dynamite overhanging snow-shelves in the Vorarlberg alps in Austria to avoid avalanches while on the other side of the earth the central government in Laos – one of the world's last centrally planned communist states – pays a private Swedish company to build 600 kilometres of road, Highway 8[21].

Taxation ©IBO 2003

One way of creating an 'improved' market is to use market forces to *internalise* the externality, i.e. intervene in such a way so as to make hidden costs visible and burden those responsible for them in some way (see "Extension of property rights" on page 241). One of the most common ways to bring external costs back into the fold of the market place is to levy an indirect tax on goods which have negative externalities. Commonly, such goods are associated with external costs in production, such as circuit boards where ozone-depleting chlorofluorocarbons (CFCs) are used in the manufacturing process. However, many negative externalities arise also from the consumption of goods such as petrol and cigarettes. In any case, taxing the good via expenditure is the basis of an incentive-based solution to distortions arising due to market failure.

The cardinal rule of taxes on expenditure (see Section 2.1) is: 'When you want less of a good, put a tax on it'. Figure 2.4.7 on page 236 exemplifies a good which creates a negative externality; $MSC > MPC$ and output is Q_0 rather than the allocatively efficient level of $Q_{soc\ opt}$. (figure grossly exaggerated for clarity.) In order to correct this market failure, the government imposes a (unit) tax of, shown by the double-ended black arrow between the MPC_0 curve and the MSC curve. (Note how we assume that the 'money' cost of smoking or such can be estimated correctly. In fact, this would be virtually impossible in reality, as assigning a money cost to loss of quality of life would be both highly subjective and arbitrary.) The tax serves

---

20. Again, be wary of confusing 'provision' with 'supplied by'. Many countries increasingly rely on various forms of 'school vouchers' where consumers (parents/students) can spend their allotment on the school of their choice. Thus, it is possible for a student to be educated by a private facility using public money.

21. Apparently Japanese firms have been contracted to build the bridges across some 15 rivers. Unfortunately, while many stretches of road have been completed, **none** of the bridges have been built! This might be a good example of when central planning/provision might be superior to private.

to shift the MPC_0 curve left to MPC + tax, which lowers the quantity demanded to Q_1. The results are a) lower externalities, and b) lower welfare loss to society.

In taxing the production/consumption of the good, the real costs have been brought forward and now burden those who are responsible for the externalities. Note that taxes can be imposed on either the consumer or the producer, such as a tax per pack of cigarettes or a pollution tax on emissions by firms. Both forms serve to *internalise* the externality. Smokers will bear more of

the real cost of their habit while in pollution cases it is an example of the 'polluters pay principle', which acts as a disincentive to producers to continue to pollute. Additionally, in a best-cast scenario, the government might divert tax revenue to those directly affected by the initial externalities, such as using road taxes to build sound barriers and plant trees between major roads and housing areas. This would help to correct the inequity of third parties paying a cost which rightly belongs to users/providers.

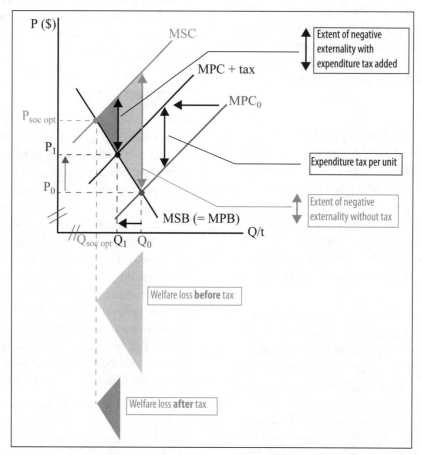

Figure 2.4.7 *Taxing away negative externalities*

Subsidies ©IBO 2003

As looked at previously, a subsidy is a way for governments to increase the output of certain goods. Many societies subsidise goods whose consumption/production are considered to have positive effects, such as any number of countries in Africa which subsidise maize meal which is a food staple. Other instances are when goods are subsidised due to the fact that users cannot see the future benefits or the benefits to third parties. Milk is frequently subsidised as the health benefits are large. Research in cancer receives government monies in most countries. In all these cases, the government has made a choice to intervene

in a market in order to increase output/consumption of the good.

Figure 2.4.8 on page 237 shows the effect of a subsidy on goods with positive externalities. The subsidy lowers producers' (marginal) costs, shifting the **MSC** (= MPC = supply) curve to the right; $MSC_{+\,subsidy}$. As government aims to maximise social benefits, the subsidy is set at the same amount as the positive externality. (This is a bit of wishful thinking, as it would be almost impossible to accurately gauge the amount.) This shifts the MSC (supply) curve to the right, setting output at the optimal level in terms of social benefit, $Q_{soc\,opt}$. What the government is doing, in effect, is setting output at the level where MSC =

MPB yet allowing consumers to enjoy a lower price than $P_{soc\ opt}$ by funding the difference; this is the total cost of the subsidy, shown by the black double-ended arrow ($P_1 \times P_{soc\ opt}$) times $Q_{soc\ opt}$.

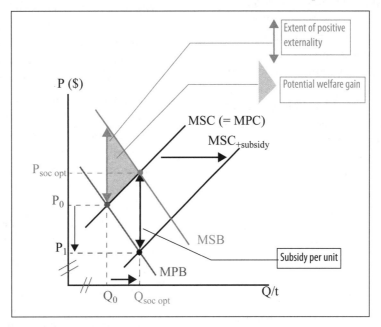

Figure 2.4.8 *Subsidising goods with positive externalities*

Examples of subsidised goods

It bears repeating that the costs to government in the form of funding the subsidies are considered to be less than the possible benefits – otherwise the subsidy would not exist. In other words, there is a **net social benefit** in increasing production/consumption of the good, the problem being that the private sector would not take care of the additional output without the incentive and cost-cutting effects of subsidies. There are many examples of goods subsidised by governments – often without consumers knowing it. Dental care for the under-16s, basic foodstuffs such as rice or milk, and local sporting events are common examples of subsidised goods. Yet there are a number of goods which increasingly come under the scrutiny of government officials 'subsidy microscope'. Such goods are often subject to purchasing subsidies (often by lowering value-added taxes or other indirect taxes). For example, a number of countries offer lower road taxes for owners of hybrid cars which run on both petrol and batteries. In a similar vein, some governments offer tax deductions for house owners who install solar panels and/or additional insulation.

My favourite example of late is the Danish government's persistent subsidising of wind generators over the past 30 years, starting just after the first 'oil crisis' in 1973. Subsidies were basically of three types: direct producer subsidies to the firms making the windmills; higher than market price was paid to windmill-generated power; and tax benefits to consumers who bought windmills (often local neighbourhoods and villages). By 1986 there were more than 2,500 windmills in the country producing 1.5% of electricity; in 2001 wind power accounted for 13%; and by 2003, 20% of total electricity consumption.[22] Denmark is now the largest producer of windmills in the world and the windmills comprise one of the country's largest export industries on a market growing at 28% per year (albeit from a very low initial level) and employing about 25,000 people. It now seems clear that this vibrant and growing industry would in all likelihood not be where it is today if government monies had not continuously supported it. As a result, the larger windmills during the 1980s and 1990s became more than 120 times more efficient and the price of wind power went down by some 80% over the course of the same time period.[23] Most of the price cut occurred between 1998 and 2003, when the price per kilowatt-hour of electricity dropped by half – which is close to the cost of gas-powered electricity.

22. *Business Week,* 'Denmark Inherits the Wind', 30 April 2001.
23. *Business Week,* 'A strong tailwind for wind power', 3 March 2003 and *The Economist,* 'Maybe this time', 8 March 2001.

Tradable permits ©IBO 2003

While this might sound like the medieval custom of sinners buying indulgences, a permit to pollute is slightly different – but almost as contentious (= debatable, controversial). This highly market-based solution to pollution is the establishment of programs wherein a government regulatory agency sets a ceiling on total emissions and then emits tradable '**pollution permits**' to offending firms. A tradable permit scheme essentially means that government decides the 'acceptable' level of pollution and then issues credits or allowances to firms and fines firms which pollute more than their permits allow. The permits are allowed to be resold to other firms, which in theory – and in practice in some cases – creates both an incentive to clean up production and a disincentive to exceed the limits imposed.

How tradable permits work

Consider a market comprised of ten firms, producing a market total of 100,000 widgets and also emitting a total of 1,000 tonnes of *greenhouse gases* (**GHG**, mainly carbon dioxide, ozone, methane, chlorofluorocarbons and nitrous oxide). Let us for the sake of simplicity say that this comprises the sum of externalities, which means that each widget has an external cost to society of 10 kilograms of GHG per widget (1,000 tonnes of GHG / 100,000 widgets). The government sets a ceiling of 500 tonnes of GHG and initially simply allocates 50 one-tonne pollution permits to each firm. Assuming that this would also halve market output, 50,000 widgets would be produced. What happens next depends largely on how efficient each individual firm is in producing widgets, but here is a possible scenario:

1. Say that the three *most polluting firms* (= most inefficient firms) can only produce 1,000 widgets each when limited to 50 tonnes of GHG emissions and would have to invest so much in new filtering technology in order to produce more that it simply wouldn't be worth it. These high-polluting firms leave the market but hold permits allowing for the emission of 150 tonnes of GHG which they will not use. Total market output of widgets is now 47,000.

2. The three exiting firms will sell the permits on the open market, the question being what will set the market price? Simple; the foregone profits of firms not using the permits will set the floor while the highest bidders, which will be the *most efficient firms*, will set the ceiling – since these firms will be able to produce the most widgets per tonne of GHG

and thus be willing to pay the most for the permits. (Keep in mind that the market price for widgets will rise as three firms have left the market.) Say that five of the remaining firms are producing half of their previous output and are marginally efficient, i.e. they have no incentive to buy additional permits. They produce 25,000 of the market total of 47,000.

3. Consider now that the final two firms, YellowFirm and GreenFirm, are also the most efficient firms and are bidding for the extra 150 tonne allotment. YellowFirm is producing 10,000 widgets with its 50 permits and estimates that it can produce an additional 20,000 widgets with the additional 150 permits up for sale. (Note that the additional 150 permits does not mean that the firm can increase output by 30,000 units! This is of course due to increasing marginal costs.) At the going market price of €10 per widget, YellowFirm's additional revenue of €200,000 (€10 times 20,000 more units) would cover all additional costs – both production costs and permit costs – if the price of the permits were maximally €500 each.

4. GreenFirm is producing 12,000 widgets and could produce an additional 30,000 widgets with the 150 permits. The marginal revenue of €300,000 would cover all additional costs even if the cost of the permits were as high as €510 each.

5. GreenFirm wins the bidding war, and after taking on Nikki (my shrink in the ex-pat community here) as chief negotiator, pays €501 per permit.[24] The final outcome is that the five non-bidding firms produce 25,000 widgets; YellowFirm produces 10,000; and GreenFirm 42,000. The **sum output total of 77,000 widgets** results in **500 tonnes of GHG**, or unit external costs of **6.5 kilograms of GHG per widget**.

6. The short-run result is that pollutants contributing to the green house effect have decreased by 50% while output has decreased by proportionately less, namely 23%.

7. It might appear that a polluting firm would have no real incentive to lower pollution levels once the permits have been purchased. This is faulty economic reasoning, as the firm has resources (money) tied up in the permits and thus incurs an opportunity cost. In the long run there will be an incentive for firms to increase efficiency and lower emissions in order to free resources by selling the permits. Put more bluntly; any new production method or technology which can save a polluting

---

24. Woe betide the hotelier or restaurateur who tries to do a number on her!

firm one tonne of pollution at a lower cost than buying a permit on the pollution market will be attractive. It will also enable firms to sell off unneeded permits and free up funds for other investment. (See Case study: "CO_2 permits and the Clean Air Act (USA)" on page 240).

Incentives Rule OK!

One question is whether the issued permits can be purchased by anyone on the market or whether the market is limited to firms only. Wouldn't there be an incentive for environmental groups to raise money in order to buy up as many permits as possible?! In fact, this is exactly what has happened to a certain extent in the US; environment groups have been most active in trying to get people to buy up permits and limit overall pollution levels.[25] This will ultimately reduce the amount of permits on the market, limiting overall allowance of pollutants over time. In theory, the secondary effects would be that polluting firms would have an incentive to become ever-more efficient, since the environmental groups would ultimately affect demand and drive up the market price of pollution permits. In the end, only the most efficient firms would be likely to buy additional permits since the price would be prohibitive for firms unable to get a high enough marginal rate of return, i.e. 'widgets per tonne of pollution', for the permits. There would also be an increase in R&D to find alternative, cleaner, production methods.

Advantages of tradable permits

There are a number of **advantages** to a system of tradable permits. The main advantage is that there is a built-in mechanism of incentives to force firms to lower pollution levels. The opportunity costs of having potential investment tied up in non-yielding permits, plus the added incentive of being able to sell the permits will influence firms to become more efficient. The additional effect of environmental groups using this market based system to permanently remove permits from the market will ultimately have the effect of driving up permit prices, making it evermore costly for firms to pollute. There is also the effect outlined in the example above, where the permits ultimately wind up with the most efficient producers, giving the highest output per measure of externality. Finally, the system is less costly for the regulating body, since setting the

initial levels of pollution will only have to be followed up by surveillance of emissions rather than a continuous reassessment of the extent of the pollution.

Disadvantages of tradable permits

The system does have a number of **disadvantages**, however. Many environmental groups feel that the market based system sends the wrong signal to both producers and consumers, in that there are 'permissible' or 'non-harmful' levels of pollution. The system might simply mislead society into believing that pollution is decreasing when in fact it is not – only the pollution per *unit*. It is also feasible that heavy polluters buying up ever-cheaper permits due to the diligence of firms cleaning up their act might actually perpetuate the very pollution the permits attempt to reduce. And, quite frankly, most economists seem to favour the appealing simplicity and straightforwardness of emission taxes.

---

25. Feel in the mood to do some good?! Just go to www.cleanairconservancy.com and you can help to retire a few hundred kilograms of sulfur dioxide. They claim that more than 7 billion pound weight– 3.18 billion kilograms – of SO_X, NO_X and CO_2 emissions have been prevented by this 'retirement program'. Why not present your economics/ environmental systems teacher with few permits for his/her birthday?!

Case study: CO_2 permits and the Clean Air Act (USA)

The first widescale example of a tradable permit program was the American Clean Air Act in its amended (= updated) version from 1990, where sulfur dioxide (SO_2 emissions (which together with nitrous oxide (NO_X) are the main contributor to acid rain) were capped and permits subsequently sold to firms.

The plan, implemented by President George Bush (Sr.) was hotly debated at the time but quickly became something of an example to other countries and other areas of the environment. The purpose was to control SO_2 and NO_X emissions in the long run by a 'ratchet-down' effect; the tradable permits would induce firms to lower pollution levels over time in order to become more profitable. As pollution decreased, permits were to be resold or even taken off the market, which would continuously lower possible emission levels for firms.

When the law was passed in 1990, SO_2 emissions were above 10 million tonnes and the cap set by government was a maximum of 8.7 million tonnes by 1995. Permits were then issued by the Environmental Protection Agency (EPA) which allowed one tonne of SO_2 emissions per permit and year and allotted on the basis of previous use of fuel. Any excess pollution met with a fine of USD2,000 per tonne and also meant that the firm's cap for the following year was reduced by an equal amount. However, if a firm did not use its allotment during the year, it could be saved and either sold or used during the next year. The EPA still holds annual auctions for SO_2 permits, which have historically sold for between USD 100 and 200.

The results thus far seem promising. Many of the most offending firms (primarily public utilities in the energy market) invested on a grand scale to decrease the level of pollutants – so grand in fact, that the pay-off of the one-off fixed costs led to much lower costs of reducing each additional tonne of SO_2. As costs for lowering pollution fell, so did the price of permits.

By 1995 the emissions of SO_2 had fallen by almost 50% – far below the minimum required level. The EPA estimates that the purely monetary savings to consumers was between USD400 to 600 million annually while Resources for the Future (RFF, a non-government think tank based in Washington) reckons that the system saved USD1 billion annually over the use of 'traditional' methods to curb pollution.

The most intriguing effect, perhaps, has been the ability of environmental groups to buy up permits, e.g. remove them permanently from the market, as the market price of the permits fell. In other words, there is a self-reinforcing feedback loop, where increased efficiency lowers demand for permits, which then lowers the price and enables environmental groups to buy more permits – which then forces firms to become more efficient, etc.

I must mention an interesting side-effect. It has become quite common – trendy even – for power firms to donate (!) permits to worthy causes, i.e. environmental groups.

(Sources: White House Conference on Climate Change October 6, 1997; *The Effects of Title 5 of the Clean Air Act Amendments of 1990*, p. 61, March 1997, published by the Energy Information Administration; Perloff for excellent case study on SO_2 in US p. 623)

Extension of property rights ©IBO 2003

If a cyclist scrapes your car you will in all likelihood be reimbursed (= compensated) by the cyclist – or his/her insurance company. This is because the **property right** to your car is firmly established and so is the link to the harm being done, i.e. your demand for compensation can be directed easily at the offending entity. Now try going to the local power plant with a demand for compensation due to damage to the paint on your car resulting from soot and particle emissions from the burning of coal and oil. Even worse, try getting satisfaction from a polluting firm situated in another part of the world! In either case, the problem is that there are no clearly defined property rights.

> **Extension of property rights**: Extending property rights means there is an explicit right of use of an asset or resource. Ownership – and thus responsibility – is granted, creating an incentive for owners to take into consideration all costs, i.e. externalities. In this way private costs are brought closer to social costs and firms are more inclined to limit total costs in line with a profit incentive. The externality is in this way internalised by bringing external costs into a market-based framework.

Internalising externalities

A possible solution is to extend property rights by granting distinct ownership rights to those who are affected. This is another way of **internalising** externalities; any damages to private property create a basis for claims on the offending party. By doing so, the externality is brought into the fold of the market mechanism since previously unattributed costs have been made clear and responsibility is assigned. In the case above, citizens suffering from prematurely rusting cars would have the right to claim from the polluting firm and the firm would pay for property damages. In the case of air/river/noise pollution we will get market failures and thus externalities since nobody owns any of these objects. One way to correct the failure would be to establish firm private ownership of them and thus allow owners to collect damages. Yet again, collecting damages in a situation where the offending firm is far away and cannot be directly connected to the car owners' loss of property is almost impossible. I didn't choose this example arbitrarily, as I simply wish to show that in many situations it is impossible to allocate and much less enforce property rights. However, let us look at two simplified examples of how an extension of property rights might be successfully implemented.

The Beach – how to exert pressure on offending firms

Imagine a beautiful beach in the summer vacation paradise of your choice. Sand, cloudless 32 degrees and nice breeze, crystalline azure blue water … no, wait, isn't that raw sewage pouring out into the bay?! Yech! And the sand resembles used kitty-litter upon closer examination. No wonder the tourists are at the beach front restaurants and cafés instead. Or rather, are not. It seems that the pollution has driven off a good many tourists and the restaurants and cafés are not as full as they once were. This is a clear case where other parties – manufacturing industries, households, hotels, etc. have inflicted damage on others who have a clear interest in clean beaches; the beach front businesses.

A possible solution here is to grant property rights to all businesses along the beachfront. Give each business a granted right to a section of beach front and allow the businesses to extend into sun-chair rentals, windsurfing schools, diving classes and the like. This creates an incentive for the businesses to clean up the beach as they compete for tourists. It will also induce them to put pressure on the offending polluters since the externality is damaging their property and thus in effect harming their profits. One could expect the beach businesses to act towards either implementing new legislation on sewage or demanding that existing suchlike is enforced. It is conceivable that the community acts to charge households and industries for increased water purification and/or increase taxes in order to build cleaning plants, since the costs of the externalities such as loss of tourism profits and tax revenues will be made apparent by the new property owners.

The River Runs Through It – how to get offending firms to exert pressure on themselves

What if a factory upstream from where I fish trout were to release effluent into the river causing the trout population to decline over time? This would be quite a blow to the thousands of fishermen who regularly return to the stream. They would bear the external costs of the factory's activity.

A possibility is to extend the property rights of the firm to encompass the entire river! Say that the municipality were to grant the firm sole entrepreneurial rights along the river – river rafting, fishing, camping – you name it. The decision the firm would face is whether the river is more valuable clean or dirty; in other words, would the marginal revenue of all the river sports activities be greater than the marginal costs involved in reducing pollution to acceptable levels? This solution would of course only be considered if the answer were 'yes', and therefore the firm would be able to add to total earnings by keeping the river clean. In creating a framework where the party responsible for a negative externality (cost) must take them into account, the externality has been brought into a market framework, i.e. internalised. However, it is quite possible that the original property right owners – say fishing clubs – might simply have to pay the firm to limit pollution.

Examples of property rights

It should be noted that the concept of expanding property rights is quite wide. Many examples involve granting sufferers the right to litigate (= take legal action, sue) against offenders. For example, many cases of lung cancer have been brought within the legal jurisdiction (= responsibility) of firms which produced asbestos in the 1960s – firms will have to compensate these workers as the workers' ownership of factors of production (= their own labour) has been harmed. The workers' damaged property will have to be paid for by

the offender – the firm. A most notable case of late, is the class action suit (where many people who have been injured get together and sue a company as one) against the Swiss/Swedish multinational engineering company, ASEA Brown Boveri (ABB).[26] When ABB bought the American company Combustion Engineering in 1989, it also took over all of the American company's liabilities – even in terms of previous employees who claim damages from dealing with asbestos. ABB is expected to pay more than USD1.2 billion in settlements for claims and total costs together with legal fees could run into the billions.[27]

While assigning property rights encounters any number of problems, such as who should pay whom and how much, there is a market-based appeal to the system. There is no need for extensive regulatory bodies which monitor and estimate the extent and cost of the externalities. This is instead done by the relevant parties; the offending firms and the third party sufferers. In setting out well-defined property rights (which is obviously the tricky part!) the offender and victim will be able to arrive at equitable compensation which optimises resource allocation and minimises environmental damage.

A little depth:
The tragedy of the commons

Every once in a while, history and the coining of a phrase has wide applicability and usefulness for a wider audience. Such a phrase is the 'tragedy of the commons', which refers to land set aside by villagers in the 17th century which was to be owned by everyone, i.e. community-owned pastures. This common (where 'commons' comes from) land was freely available to all who wished to use it for grazing cattle. The indistinct property rights ultimately resulted in a 'Do it to others before they do it to you' attitude.

Villagers would try to avoid overgrazing on their (privately) held land in order to keep it as high-yielding as possible. This, of course, did not extend to the commons. The self-interest of individual farmers did not extend to land which had no designated owner. It is basically a type of Prisoners' dilemma where putting another cow on the pasture is 'cheating' on the total

possible gains for others – compliance would be to limit one's use to increase everyone's overall gain. Thus the common land was subject to hard use and ultimately suffered from continuous overuse – abuse even. Overgrazing, poor drainage, lack of fencing all contributed to lower the carrying capacity of the land to the point where it became virtually useless; a squandered resource.

This failure was due to lack of private incentives and ownership. As many other examples have arisen over time, any case where inadequate or non-existent maintenance of public domain has been referred to by economists as a 'tragedy of the commons'. Overfishing in international waters and overuse of antibiotics (creating resistant strains of diseases) are good examples of how this tragedy is reprised on a much larger scale.

---

26. An attempt to sue McDonald's for causing obesity was tossed out of court in the US in 2003.
27. See http://www.forbes.com/2003/01/17/0117autonewsscan01.html and http://www.corpwatch.org/news/PND.jsp?articleid=1888.

Advertising to encourage or discourage consumption ©IBO 2003

We were driving on the highway outside of Windhoek, Namibia when a most eye-catching sign appeared by the side of the road. Apart from the less-than-subtle sign itself, which read 'Drink kills', there was an additional extra to really drive the point home, so to speak. A smashed-up car had been wrapped around one of the poles holding the billboard up. A most effective message. Another ad we saw frequently in Namibia was an AIDS poster where a young lady says, 'My boyfriend said that using a condom takes all the fun out of it. Boy did I have fun proving him wrong!'

The objective is to alter peoples' behaviour. Educating and informing citizens of both possible costs of use or the benefits of use can change market demand and thereby correct overconsumption and underconsumption of goods.

The diagrams in Figure 2.4.9 show how advertising and public announcing can help correct market failures.

- *Decreasing demand for goods with negative externalities*: For alcohol – and the highly non-complementary good driving – the issue is to get consumption down by advertising negative aspects of consumption. Anti-drinking campaigns hope to decrease demand (MSB_0 to MSB_1 in diagram I) and move consumption levels towards the social optimum at $Q_{soc\ opt}$.

- *Increasing demand for goods with positive externalities*: For condoms there are high external social benefits – not only does the private individual benefit from protection but society at large benefits from the decrease in the spread of sexually transmitted diseases (STDs). The aim, obviously, is to get people to consume more of the good in order that society benefits from lower spread of venereal diseases – not to mention the societal costs of unwanted children, and in many LDCs, population growth.[28] Government information campaigns aimed at persuading people to use condoms would hopefully increase demand (MPB_0 to MPB_1 in diagram II) and move consumption towards the societally optimal point at $Q_{soc\ opt}$.

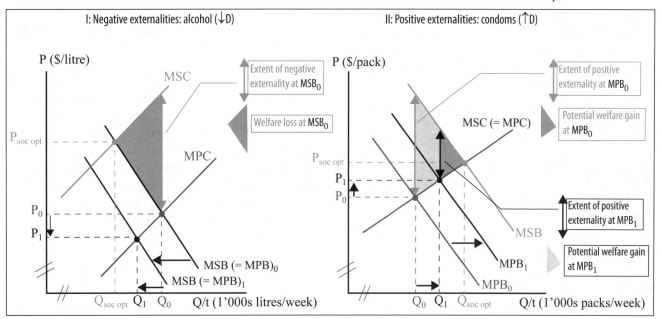

Figure 2.4.9 *Changing demand to decrease externalities*

There are many examples of how societies use persuasive and/or informative advertising to change citizens' behaviour in order to limit externalities. Warning labels on cigarettes are perhaps the most widely recognised example, yet there is any number of

rather ingenious attempts to influence our behaviour. Schools are visited by government and non-profit organisations which inform students of the dangers of drugs, alcohol and other substance abuse. Many cities use advertising campaigns to get more people on

---

28. I fully realise that my use of condoms as an example in a textbook aimed at 16–19 year olds will cause a few hiccups of shock in some cultures but I offer no apologies. The issue of HIV/AIDS has moved far beyond the niceties and confines of morality and/or cultural relativity (ask your TOK teacher) and boils down to saving lives. The 0.06 mm of latex might make the difference between life and death. Talk about marginal benefits …

bicycles in order to lower inner-city congestion and pollution. Municipalities send households information brochures on recycling centres. Here in Mexico I was staggered by the numerous murals (= wall paintings) in rural areas sponsored by the federal government to get people to use mosquito nets against dengue fever.[29] The list is long and you will have little difficulty in finding numerous examples simply by looking around you on your way to school.

International co-operation among governments ©IBO 2003

It should come as no surprise that most of the possible solutions above involve a great many problems of implementation due to the simple fact that externalities know no borders. Drug use, for example, is an international problem since user countries are often not the same as producer countries, making clear that any real solution will involve attacking not only use but supply. In pollution, there are massive difficulties in getting a country to pay for externalities inflicted upon the domestic economy of another. In all, these issues require extensive arrangements in cooperation which is why there are an increasing number of international agencies involved in information-sharing, monitoring and assessment. In dealing with negative externalities on a global basis, there are a number of difficulties involved. Here are the main issues:

Accountability: Clearly it would be rather difficult to assign 'pollution portions' to different countries. A country which suffers from acid rain resulting from emission in another country will have a most difficult burden of proof in showing who the culprit is. Just how much of the acid rain falling in Belgium is the result of factories in France?

Cost estimation: Once again, one of the basic problems in ascribing costs to negative externalities is setting appropriate costs. Most of us would react if we were asked to put a 'price' on a loved one, and correctly pricing the environment runs into similar subjective and normative problems. How would one estimate the loss of biodiversity in lakes in terms of money?

Method: There is great debate as to which methods are the most efficient. While the US argues that market-

based systems such as pollution permits are the most efficient way to lower overall pollution levels, there has been widespread criticism from environmental groups that neither taxes nor permits squarely address the root of the problem. It is often pointed out that (due to time lags in cause and effect) we have not yet seen the total results of emissions, for example, that even if every industry in the world shut down tomorrow, global warming would continue for a number of years.

Trade-offs: The OECD estimates that CO_2 emissions – accounting for 60% of greenhouse gases – will increase by roughly 33% by the year 2020. This could have severe repercussions when countries try to strike a balance between growth and environmental impact, as the opportunity cost of lowering CO_2 will mean lower growth rates.

Loss of competitive edge: Stricter legislation on the environment will drive up production costs for firms. There will be a clear incentive for countries to accept laxer environmental legislation in order to remain internationally competitive and keep both growth high and unemployment low.[30]

Multilateral environmental agreements (MEAs)

The above notwithstanding, the fact remains that it is in everyone's interest to lower environmental damage in the world. Clearly, any long-term solution must involve all the contributing and affected countries and have clear mutual benefits. To this end a number of organisations, often under the collective umbrella of the United Nations (UN), have worked to create international environment treaties and agreements. An increasing number of **multilateral environmental agreements** (multilateral meaning that a number of countries are involved rather than an agreement between two countries), so-called **MEAs**, have been implemented in the past decade and more are subject to ongoing negotiations. MEAs cover topics ranging from trade in endangered species and hardwood to regulations on the use of chlorofluorocarbons (CFCs) and emission caps on CO_2. I conclude this section with a short list (as in 'far from conclusive') of some of the organisations involved and two of the most noticeable MEAs – one relative success and one major disappointment.[31]

---

29. Dengue fever (pronounced 'den-gee') is caused by a mosquito borne virus similar in geographical spread to malaria. While seldom fatal, the aches, pains and fevers associated with dengue are quite severe. My father had both dengue and malaria – and claimed that dengue made malaria seem 'like a boy scout picnic'.

30. There has even been some speculation that countries would even compete in having the poorest environmental standards in order to attract foreign manufacturing companies. This is the 'race to the bottom' effect which many environmentalists have long predicted. As yet, there is little – if any – evidence of this happening. More on this in Section 4.2.

31. See an extensive list at http://www.greenyearbook.org/agree or http://www.unep.ch/conventions/geclist.htm.

Organisations/conferences

There are numerous international organisations dealing with environmental issues, a most incomplete list being:

The United Nations Intergovernmental Panel on Climate Change (IPCC)

This UN panel of scientists and researchers has been one of the main bodies in environment control and standards in the international community. The IPCC is responsible for disseminating the latest relevant research on climate change in order to provide other (UN and other) organisations with up to date information as a basis for decision making.

The United Nations Framework Convention on Climate Change (UNFCCC)

The IPCC was instrumental in the 1992 **Rio Convention** which established the UNFCCC. This convention had 186 signatory countries by 2002 (almost all UN members) which have all agreed to work towards a common goal of stabilising and ultimately limiting greenhouse gases (GHG) which contribute to global warming. The UNFCCC provided the 1996 report which provided the basis for the 1997 **Kyoto Protocol**.

The United Nations Environment Program (UNEP) and United Nations Conference on Environment and Development (UNCED)

One hundred and seventy-eight countries gathered at the first UNCED meeting (otherwise known as 'Earth Summit') in 1992 to agree on, amongst other things, a plan to implement sustainable development in accordance with the Brundtland Report submitted in 1987. The result was 'Agenda 21', a blueprint for attaining sustainable development over the coming decades. A second 'Earth Summit' was held in 2002.

Agreements

The Montreal Protocol

In 1987 a total of 41 countries (12 acting under the EEC – now the EU) signed an agreement to severely limit and phase out the use of substances that deplete the ozone layer. These original signatory countries accounted together for over 80% of total ozone depleting emissions when the agreement came into effect in 1990. Since then, other countries have joined, whereby 185 have now ratified the agreement. The primary method has been to set strict (and legally binding) caps on emissions of ozone depleting substances such as chlorofluorocarbons used in refrigeration and aerosols. These chemicals have been phased out and replaced with ozone friendly substances. According to recent research, the agreement has been a success, with levels of harmful chemicals falling and ozone levels actually slowly recovering.[32]

The Kyoto Protocol

The UNFCCC (see above) provided the basis for the 1997 agreement on limiting greenhouse gases (GHG). The Kyoto treaty was partially modelled on the success of the Montreal Protocol, but has been something of a failure so far. The scheme calls for industrialised countries to reduce their emissions of GHG by an average of 5.2% from the 1990 level over the period 2008–12, using a mixture of emissions trading and mechanisms to earn 'emission credits'. The Kyoto Protocol would come into force when *ratified* (= formally signed, a binding agreement) by no fewer than 55 countries which together accounted for no less than **55% of global GHG** emissions in 1990. During the initial phase, developing countries are exempt from emission curbs.

These signatory countries accounted for 44.2% of CO_2 emissions, leaving 10.8 percentage points left before the agreement could come into effect. Only five industrialised countries initially refused to ratify the agreement, amongst others the USA and Russia, who together account for half of global GHG emissions. By February 2005, after Russian ratification, the necessary 55% of 'GHG contributions' had been reached and the Kyoto Protocol came into effect.[33] At the time of writing, December 2008, 185 nations (comprising 63.7% of emissions) have ratified the treaty. Notably, the world's largest emitter of GHG, USA, has still refused to ratify the agreement claiming that it would be too costly for US industries and that notable contributors to global emissions (China and India) are largely exempt from the agreement.

The Kyoto debate: The pro et con debate has been high-pitched and very politicised. *Proponents* of the Kyoto Protocol refer to the proposal as a first step of many and the only truly global attempt to diminish possibly the greatest threat to our world. Supporters of the treaty point out that the USA accounts for 4% of the world population but emits 33% of the GHG (1990 values), which would make the treaty close to futile

---

32. See http://www.unep.org/ozone/pdf/execsumm-sap2002.pdf. and http://worldbank.org/montrealprotocol.
33. See http://UNFCCCc.int/kyoto.

even if all other countries were to ratify. It is pointed out that since the present industrialised nations have caused over 80% of present GHG and are the only nations which have the economic and technological ability to clean up their act, the brunt of the burden of GHG cuts should go to them rather than spreading responsibility 'evenly' by including developing countries which are not the culprits. Environmental groups have frequently stressed how strong business links and lobby groups in America have been instrumental in shaping US environmental policy – Greenpeace goes so far as to say that President Bush is 'really being led by ExxonMobil'.[34]

Opponents of the protocol point to the heavy economic burden that implementation would bring to the USA, the world's largest economy; a reduction in emissions of an initial 7% resulting in the long run of some 35% to 40% overall reductions from 1990 levels during 2008 to 2012 at enormous costs in terms of global GDP – the OECD estimates the total cost to be 2% of OECD countries' GDP by 2050. In addition to this, there seems to be little evidence that world GHG emissions are able to be kept within Kyoto limits for the foreseeable future. There is also an argument that the Kyoto Protocol will in effect only delay a rise in global temperature by a meagre 6 years during the coming century – the 0.15°C rise in temperature estimated to result in the year 2100 will instead arrive in 2106 if Kyoto is implemented and carry a price tag of a 2% to 4% reduction in GDP.[35] US officials are quick to point out that most developing nations – primarily China and India – are to a large extent exempt from the Kyoto protocol, but are quickly catching up with industrialised countries in terms of GHG emissions, which would mean that the most efficient producers would be harnessed while the most inefficient would be exempt from the treaty. Finally, one could mention that research is inconclusive as to whether ongoing

global warming is *primarily* man-made or part of a larger general climate pattern.[36]

The future of the Kyoto Protocol: The Kyoto agreement is a first step in an ongoing process aimed at reducing GHG. It expires in 2012 and in December 2009 signatory nations will meet in Copenhagen to assess the results and also decide the next round of GHG emission caps. A main issue is whether the main 'carbon-culprit', USA, will ratify. A new president and a majority of Democrats in the US Congress seem to support ratification – yet there will in all likelihood not be sufficient time for the new administration to push through support by December of 2009. Another issue is the extent to which developing nations will be bound by the same rules of capping as developed nations.

POP QUIZ 2.4.2   DEALING WITH EXTERNALITIES

1 Why are public goods underprovided by the market mechanism and how is this problem often solved?

2 What are possible solutions to negative externalities?

3 How might governments attempt to address the problem of underconsumption of merit goods?

4 How might the extension of property rights diminish negative externalities?

5 Why would the most efficient firms be willing to pay the most on a market for tradable pollution permits?

6 Why are international agreements so vital in dealing with negative externalities such as pollution?

---

34. See http://www.greenpeace.org.au/climate/government/kyoto/index.html.
35. Lomborg, pp. 302–05.
36. You are going to have to read up on this on your own. The more I read on the subject of global warming, the more confused I get.

MACRECONOMICS

3

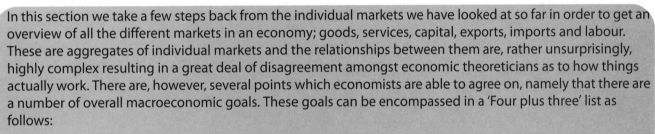

In this section we take a few steps back from the individual markets we have looked at so far in order to get an overview of all the different markets in an economy; goods, services, capital, exports, imports and labour. These are aggregates of individual markets and the relationships between them are, rather unsurprisingly, highly complex resulting in a great deal of disagreement amongst economic theoreticians as to how things actually work. There are, however, several points which economists are able to agree on, namely that there are a number of overall macroeconomic goals. These goals can be encompassed in a 'Four plus three' list as follows:

Growth – defined as the increase in gross national product (GDP) or gross national product (GNP) and measured in money terms

Price stability – defined as a stable incremental increase in the price level (inflation) and measured by the consumer price index (CPI) and the GDP deflator.

Low levels of unemployment – defined as the number of people, out of the total available workforce, who do not have jobs and given as a percentage value

External equilibrium – defined as stable exchange rates and balance between imports and exports (this is the focus of Section 4).

In addition to the above four mainstream goals, economists increasingly bring up issues to be found within the following captions:

Environmental concerns – often defined as economic growth in compliance with 'non-depleting' and 'non-degenerative' resource use and measured using various environmental indicators of pollution over time

Distribution of income – defined as how well income is spread between the richest and poorest sections of the population

Productivity of factors – defined as the output per unit of input (factors of production) and often measured by labour productivity indices and capital use per money value of output.

All the above are subject to a variety of government policies aimed at achieving the goals or targets. The problem is that it is impossible to achieve all of the goals at once. In fact, virtually every macroeconomic goal will conflict with at least one other goal. A simple illustration is when an economy experiences increased output (the growth goal) this often leads to inflation (making the price stability goal more difficult) and possibly an environmental burden (conflicting with the environment concerns goal). As we shall see in Section 3.5, these conflicting goals will create numerous trade-offs for governments which in turn adds to an already heated theoretical and political debate.

Measuring national income

3.1

CONTENTS

MEASURING NATIONAL INCOME ©IBO 2003

At the heart of macroeconomics is **aggregate** economic activity. Economic activity in an economy is commonly measured by gross domestic product (GDP) and gross national product (GNP). There are a number of uses for these figures and we will look at several in the following section. What we need to do initially is lay down the basics of what national income is and how it is computed.

> **National income:** National income is the real money value of the sum total of all final goods and services produced in an economy during a given time period – usually one year. This give the identity of expenditure ≡ output ≡ income, in money terms. As income is measured as an amount between periods, it is a **flow concept**.

Warning!

National income

There is an unfortunate overlapping of key terms here. While the term 'national income' is commonly used by economists to refer to GDP calculated by any of the three methods below, there is a highly specific usage of the term meaning 'net national product'. I have decided to use the term only in its widest sense, i.e. for GDP, and specify clearly when using it to convey net national product.

Circular flow of income ©IBO 2003

I usually introduce this keystone macroeconomic illustration by pulling a few coins out of my pocket (and as I never seem to have any money I mostly have to borrow them from one of my people) and 'buying something' off the table of a student. For example, a time management calendar (my people are scarily well organised) for 100 Swedish Crowns (SEK). This simple transaction illustrates the entire macro model in one fell swoop. I have spent SEK 100 (= expenditure, E) on a good valued at SEK 100 (= output, O) and the student has received the SEK 100 as a payment for his/her output (= income, Y). Assuming a two-person economy as above, we see that total **expenditure** equals **income** (in money terms) which equals **output**. As a result of how we define expenditure, income and

output in national income accounting, the three flows resulting from the simple economic transaction above are per definition **identities**, i.e. E ≡ O ≡ Y. We have now measured economic activity by assigning a monetary value to it, the SEK 100 paid for the calendar. On a wider scale, national income is simply the sum of all such transactions taking place during a given period of time.

The circular flow in a simple two-sector economy

Let us expand the scale of our economy a bit and assume that it is comprised of households and firms – no financial institutions, government or other countries exist. The flows involved are shown in Figure 3.1.1 on page 250. Firms create the output (O) which is consumed by households – this is expenditure (E). (Note that since only a household sector exists, all expenditure (E) is, in fact, consumption expenditure (C).) Households are the actual owners of production factors and rent these out to firms for which an income is received (Y). (It is imperative that you view firms as separate entities which are owned by households! Ownership is either directly or via shares in the company. In other words, while the firm is responsible for producing goods and services, the buildings, machines and labour is supplied by households to firms for a price.) National income is thus a flow concept since we are measuring how much money is passing through the system during a given amount of time (normally one year) to handle all the economic transactions.

In order to drive home the point that expenditure, income and output are indeed the same flows measured in different ways, I have compared the model to a closed-circuit heating system. (Yes, I know I'm being childish.) Picture a furnace in the basement of a house which heats water (see Figure 3.1.1 on page 250) and forces a flow of hot water through a piping system and a heating radiator in a room above. The system is a closed circuit – no water can leak and no additional water can be injected. Therefore, no matter where one puts a 'probe' to measure the flow of water per unit of time the amount would be the same. Just think of a river which has narrow and wide sections. The same amount of water per minute flows by regardless of width – assuming that there are no tributaries (= in-flowing streams) or seepage into the ground.

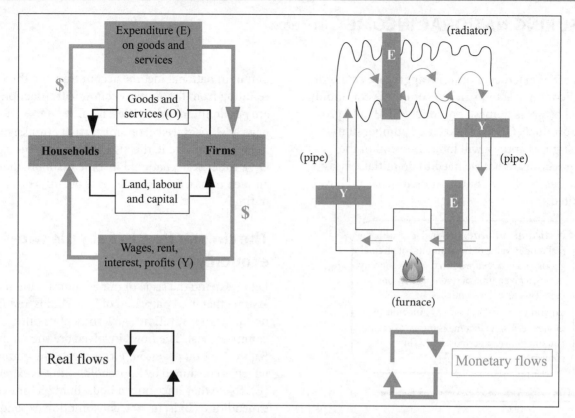

Figure 3.1.1 *Circular flow in a simple economy*

The flows in the simple circular flow in Figure 3.1.1 match each other since we are making a number of assumptions in this simple model: there are no taxes, savings or imports so households cannot do anything but spend their income. Also, there are no exports, government spending or investment, which means that firms cannot sell their goods/services anywhere but to domestic households. This provides an uninterrupted flow since there are no financial leakages or injections into the system. The model also shows that there are two parallel flows in operation. One flow (inner black circular flow arrows in Figure 3.1.1) shows a **real flow**; land/labour/capital from households to firms corresponding to the output going from firms to households. The **monetary flow** (outer blue circular flow arrows) shows how households are rewarded with wages, rent, interest and profits (Y) from firms while firms are on the receiving end of households' expenditure (E).

Adding financial institutions, government and a foreign sector

We now relax the above assumptions and include other parts of the economy making the model more realistic. Let's follow the monetary flow of income through the system and see what happens. Starting at Y income in Figure 3.1.2 on page 251, a household receives an income of, say, $100. The household will not spend all of this on output from domestic firms:

- A portion of the income flow will go to the government coffers as **tax** (T)
- Some will go to financial institutions (e.g. banks) as **savings** (S)
- And some of the remaining income will be spent on goods produced in other economies, i.e. expenditure on **imports** (M).

Assuming that households pay $25 in tax, save $10 and use $15 on imports, then there are $50 left for domestic consumption (C). In other words, out of an income of $100 there has been a **leakage** (L) of $50 out of the system.

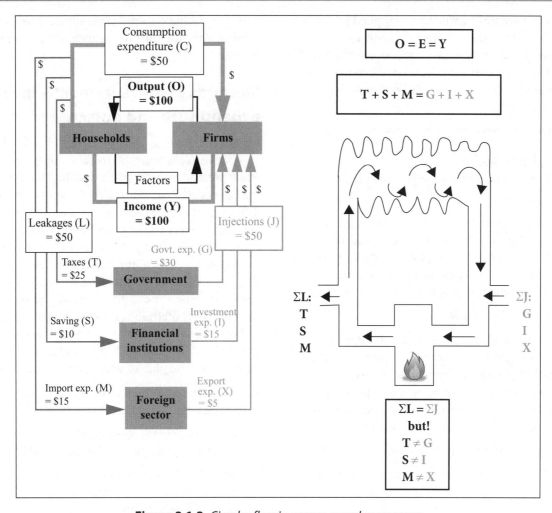

Figure 3.1.2 *Circular flow in a more complex economy*

What happens to this 50? Simple, it flows in from other sectors in the model. These inflows are called **injections** (J). (Referring again to the radiator model, there *has* to be an inflow of 50 or the water pressure will not be enough to keep the flow up.)

- The taxes (T) will provide governments with funds needed for hospitals, defence, etc. the public sector. This is **government expenditure** (G) which flows back into the system, i.e. to the firms providing these goods.
- Households' savings will provide financial institutions with loanable funds which firms use for **investment expenditure** (I).
- And finally, there will be expenditure from the foreign sector which is an inflow of **export expenditure** (X) from abroad.

To continue with the example of the missing 50, posit that government spending is 30, investment is 15 and exports 5. This gives a total inflow of 50, i.e. **total injections are equal to total leakages**, since it is a

definitional impossibility for more money to be pumped into the system than ultimately flows out. In the final calculation, the money value of injections must equal leakages. The money value of output must equal total expenditure, which in turn is the same as income.

The circular flow model thus renders two sets of identities:

$$O \equiv E \equiv Y \text{ and } \Sigma J = \Sigma L$$

It is worthwhile to warn of a common error concerning injections and leakages. While it is quite apparent and perhaps even logically obvious that each leakage has a mirror image or counterpart, this most assuredly does not mean that the values will be identical. The 25 money units of household taxes paid in the example above resulted in government spending of 30, i.e. G > T, an all too frequent occurrence unfortunately[1]. This overspending is enabled by the government taking loans which are provided by financial institutions … and these funds are supplied

---

1. This is the government budget deficit, and causes government to borrow creating government debt. More later.

by depositors' incomes ... which are supplied by firms and so on. Therefore taxes are not the same as government spending; savings do not necessarily equal investment, and imports are not equal to exports. It is instead the sum of these inflows and outflows that must be the same.

A little depth:
Algebraic method of proving that
$\Sigma J = \Sigma L$

Regarding the flows in diagram I of Figure 3.1.2 on page 251 (circular flow in a more complex economy) it is clear that the income received by households goes to tax, saving, imports (consumption of non-domestic goods) and domestic consumption. Thus:

$$Y = T + S + M + C$$

Now look at the right-hand side of the circular flow model. The very same firms which are paying for the use of households' factors of production are on the receiving end themselves; consumption expenditure, government expenditure, investment expenditure, and export expenditure flow to the firms. We get:

$$E = G + I + X + C$$

And since Y = E, putting both sides together gives us:

$$T + S + M + C = G + I + X + C$$

... and subtracting C on both sides gives us:

$$T + S + M = G + I + X$$

... which is nothing else than:

$$\Sigma L = \Sigma J.$$

Transfer payments

You might have noticed that certain flows are missing in the circular flow model. Most governments have provisions to aid household incomes via some form of social welfare system, or social safety net: social security payments to low-income households; housing allowances; student grants for university education, etc. In addition to government transfers, certain economic transactions between households are missing in the circular flow model, such as payments for used goods and gifts of money. It is important to understand that all the above **transfer payments** are *not* included in government spending. This money has already been accounted for in the national income accounts and does not represent additional expenditure, so adding it anew to the flow of G would be to double count it. The

basic rule is that only the expenditure flows which have a **corresponding output** are included in national income.

Methods of measurement – income, expenditure and output ©IBO 2003

An electrician once took upon himself to explain to me – in between his bouts of drinking my beer and coffee while pretending to install a washing machine – how the flow of electricity through the wires resulted in different measurements such as ohms, watts and amperes. I never understood it, but it seemed clear enough that final output of electricity could be calculated by using a number of different parameters – all of which had very specific meaning. Calculating output/income/expenditure is much the same since each different method results in identical values. The rest of Section 3.1 will show different ways of calculating GDP and subsequent adjustments to this base figure. The plan of attack here is in four steps:

1. Compute the money value of aggregate output during a year, i.e. gross domestic product, GDP.

2. Adjust for the use of foreign factors of production to arrive at gross national product, GNP.

3. Subtract depreciation of capital (often called capital consumption) to show net addition to GNP, net national product, NNP.

4. Take into consideration changes in the price level to show real output, real national income; GDP_{real} and GNP_{real}.

Three ways of calculating GDP

Starting with computing GDP, the three methods of calculating GDP at factor cost are as follows:

1. *Factor income method of accounting*

Adding up total payments for use of factors of production paid to households is commonly divided into four flows of payments: income from employment (wages) and income from self-employment (wages and profits); income to firms (profits); rents; and interest. These four correspond to the four factors of production: labour, entrepreneurs, land and capital.

The easiest way to exemplify income accounting is to use some actual figures. The 2001 national income accounts for Ireland will be used for all three methods, starting off with the figures for **factor incomes** in Table 3.1.1 on page 253.

In all three accounting methods I shall comment briefly on the posts and figures compiled in the accounts.[2]

Table 3.1.1 *Gross domestic product in Ireland 2001 – (factor) income method of accounting*

Factor income	Amount (millions of €)
Employment income (wages)	47,090
Self-employment income (wages + profit)	10,903
Rental income	6,181
Private/public gross profits (profit)	26,290
Interest	11,619
Total domestic income	
less stock appreciation	218
statistical discrepancy	569
GDP at factor cost	**102,869**

- **Employment income** is readily understandable; it is the flow of payments to providers of labour for their services, called either wages or salaries.

- **Self-employment income** is the income generated by own businesses. It is accounted for and contains a profit element since an owner-operated business will generate a value-added element which goes to paying the owner's wages.

- **Rental income** is generated when owners of land, housing and property receive payments for other economic agents' use.

- Private and public **profits** are commonly separated in the accounts, but I have lumped them together here since the concept is the same; surpluses created by firms which are then paid back to the owners. This can be done directly (in small companies) or indirectly via dividends (= payouts) to shareholders.

- **Interest** in national income accounts is the bank interest earned by households. Households' deposits are used by firms and the *payment* for the loans is the interest paid to households. (It is in fact *net* interest since households' interest payments are deducted.)

- In assembling all the millions of figures comprising the national accounts, one tries to be as true to real output as possible. This can be tricky when dealing with the money values of goods since – as we shall see – price increases will distort (inflate) real output figures. We deduct **stock appreciation** in order to use a truer value since unsold goods and half-finished products lying in warehouses for lengthy periods would be given a higher value when added to the GDP figures than when originally produced. For example, a firm produces 100 widgets in June and stocks them at a list price of AUD5 each, at a total value of AUD500. During the time these goods sit on the firm's shelf waiting to be sold, the price level increases by 5% and when the firm's annual report is filed the firm can list the unsold stock as an asset worth AUD525 since inflation has added an additional AUD25. However, the real contribution is only the original AUD500 and the stock appreciation must be deducted.

- The final figure is then adjusted for a **statistical discrepancy**, which is basically assessed by comparing the values in all three methods and adding/subtracting an error component arrived at by comparing to an average based on all three accounting methods.

The compiled figures give us **GDP at factor cost**, which means that the final figure is to the furthest possible extent based on real use of factors of production which will compute with real expenditure figures in the next method of GDP accounting.

2. *Expenditure method of accounting*

The basic accounting premise here is that all expenditure flows from economic agents (households, firms, government, and foreigners) constitute total expenditure and thus income. Basically, this method of accounting looks at total spending during a period of time and divides the spenders up into groups in order to follow the flows and see who is spending on what. Total expenditure in an economy becomes the sum of consumption expenditure (C), investment expenditure (I), government expenditure (G), export expenditure (X) minus the import expenditure (-M). While you skim through Irish expenditure in Table 3.1.2 on page 254, try to figure out why we subtract imports from GDP.

---

2. The official figures for national income vary enormously in Official Accounts from country to country and can be immensely difficult to plough through. I owe a large debt of gratitude to Margaret Power at the Central Statistics Office of Ireland (An Phríomh-Oifig Staidrimh in Gaelic) for assistance in putting the following figures together for me.

Table 3.1.2 *Gross domestic product in Ireland 2001 -
expenditure method of accounting*

Expenditure type	Amount (millions of €)
Household consumption (C)	55,202
Total private expenditure on capital (plus physical change in stocks) (I)	27,461
Government expenditure (G)	15,413
Exports (X)	112,938
Imports (-M)	-95,702
less taxes on expenditure	-14,572
plus subsidies	2,697
statistical discrepancy	-569
GDP at factor cost	102,869

- **Consumption** measures the amount of personal money spent on goods and services during the year. Consumption is often divided into **durables** (cars, refrigerators, etc.), **non-durables** (beer and Donegal tweed) and **services** (such as car repairs, hotel stays and banking).

- **Investment** is firms' expenditure on capital goods such as machines, equipment and factories, often referred to as **fixed capital formation**.

The total figure on investment also includes changes in stocks, **circulating capital**, since any unsold goods produced in the time period are part of inventory and still represent output even though they have not been sold. Unsold and unfinished goods are accounted as expenditure by the firm. Say a firm produces €100,000 worth of widgets but sells only €90,000 worth. If we counted only the expenditure the firm has received then actual periodic output would be underestimated by the additional widgets valued at €10,000 now in the firm's warehouse. This addition to stock must therefore be included in the accounts. Similarly, had inventory fallen by €10,000 then €10,000 must be subtracted, since total expenditure exceeds the actual amount produced in the time period. Circulating capital also includes the elements of completed work in long-term projects, **works in progress**, such as airports and roads.

- Governments build roads, hire more teachers and buy fighter aircraft from domestic firms. This is simply your tax money buying goods and services – **government spending**. Since it is far easier to

account for the market price of a jet fighter than 100,000 school hours, many services are estimated at the cost of provision rather than market prices.

- If an Irish company sells €1 million worth of knitwear but domestic expenditure for this good is only €900,000, then there would be a discrepancy between the value of expenditure and output, i.e. E ≠ O. This explains why **export expenditure** – foreigners' spending on Irish goods – is added, since we are estimating the total expenditure on goods produced in the country.

- In adherence with this, any expenditure by Irish on non-domestic goods must be deducted. This **import expenditure** does not represent any domestic output and represents a flow of money out of the system. Often one sees the term 'net exports' used, which is the product of export revenue minus import expenditure.

- We now arrive at **GDP at market prices**, which must be adjusted for two systematic inconsistencies – taxes and subsidies. Since we are measuring expenditure, most goods will include a proportion of indirect (expenditure) taxes, such as value-added taxes (VAT) and excise duties. Since these taxes do not have any corresponding output they must be subtracted. Subsidies skew the figures in the opposite manner, since the value of subsidies lowers the final market price below the actual factor cost. Therefore subsidies must be added on.

After adjusting for statistical errors once again, we arrive at **GDP at factor cost**, which is the same value as in the income method used earlier. These two methods show the flip sides of the coin, as income in an economy must equal expenditure, which in one of the most common formulaic expressions is:

$$Y = C + I + G + X - M.$$

We now finish with the method used to calculate the physical output in money terms.

3. *Output method of accounting*

In calculating GDP using money values of total output one must be aware of the possibility of *double counting*, i.e. take measures not to count the same good twice. The issue of double-counting is important enough to warrant a brief example. Let's follow a product, peat for gardening, through the process of manufacturing to final purchasing at an Irish gardening store. Assume at the initial end of the chain a landowner in County Cavan who has a few thousand acres of prime peat bog and at the other end of the chain a consumer who walks in to the flower shop to buy a bag of garden earth.[3] To simplify the example, we will assume that there are only four stages in the transaction chain:

Stage I: The landowner, Paddy, sells the unprocessed raw bog – stripping rights – to Paddy, at the Soggy Bottom Peat Company for €10,000.

Stage II: Paddy at the Soggy Bottom Peat Company then cuts out cross sections of peat and dries it and sells it for €30,000 to …

Stage III:Paddy and Paddy at The Leprechaun Garden Boyos, a garden wholesaler. The peat is carefully bagged and labelled with 'Gnome-approved' stickers and sold for €250,000 to …

Stage IV:Paddy's Gardening Emporium, which, after sticking on labels reading 'Made from Gnome-friendly Irish peat!' are sold during the year for €10 apiece, totalling €500,000 in retail sales. It is quite possible that some of the customers are named Siobhan (pronounced Shevaun).

Trick question: What is the total value of **final output**, i.e. GDP, in this economy? If your initial impulse is to start adding the value of output at each stage, i.e. €10,000 plus €30,000, etc. then stop immediately and read on instead. Adding the output at each stage of production is exactly what we are trying to avoid, since we would be double-counting values at every stage. Figure 3.1.3 on page 256 shows how the initial output of peat bog sold for €10,000 is purchased by the peat company and sold on for €30,000. The value of output at Stage I is €10,000 and at Stage II €30,000. However, the original €10,000 has been included in the output value of €30,000 at Stage II when it is sold on to the garden wholesaler. This €10,000 must be deducted in order to see the value of output which is linked solely to the Soggy Bottom Peat Company, i.e. the value-added of €20,000. And so it continues on up the chain. Each consecutive stage buys the output of the previous link in the chain and adds value before selling it on. Total final value of output is the €500,000 paid at retail level by consumers, which is identical to the **sum of all value-added** through the chain: €10,000 + 20,000 + 220,000 + 250,000 = €500,000.

Calculating GDP using the output method is commonly done by collecting the figures on value-added for firms. In actual fact, it is virtually impossible to measure output by attempting to count final output in every industry. Imagine an economy comprised of three firms: an iron mine, a tool firm and a building firm. The iron goes to the tool firm. The tools go to building firm … and the building firm uses the tool to build a shed for the iron mine! Oh, and the mine buys tools from the tool firm. So, how does one calculate final output of each firm without double counting? The answer is, one summarizes total output value (equivalent to total sales revenue) for each firm and deducts the costs of factor use. This shows how much value each firm has added and Table 3.1.3 shows how GDP is arrived at using this method.

Table 3.1.3 *Gross domestic product in Ireland 2001 – output method of accounting*

Output type	Amount (millions of €)
Agriculture, forestry, fishing	4,003
Electricity, gas, water	1,329
Construction	8,085
Manufacturing	32,715
Transport, communications	6,014
Wholesale & retail trade	8,728
Banking, finance, insurance	8,478
Other services	22,789
Public administration, defence	4,032
Health care, education	9,991
Total	
less adjustment for	
financial services	-3,863
statistical discrepancy	569
GDP at factor cost	102,869

---

3.   I've received a few emails from students who had no idea what peat is. It is basically decomposing vegetable matter (early precursor of coal) formed over millions of years and often found in marshy wetlands. It can be used for building material, fuel and garden soil.

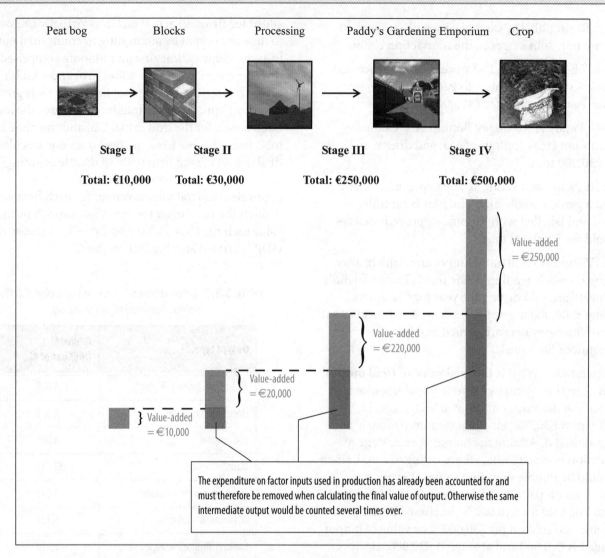

Peat bog   Blocks   Processing   Paddy's Gardening Emporium   Crop

Stage I   Stage II   Stage III   Stage IV

Total: €10,000   Total: €30,000   Total: €250,000   Total: €500,000

Value-added = €250,000

Value-added = €220,000

Value-added = €20,000

Value-added = €10,000

The expenditure on factor inputs used in production has already been accounted for and must therefore be removed when calculating the final value of output. Otherwise the same intermediate output would be counted several times over.

Figure 3.1.3 *Value-added in output method*

The methodology is fairly straightforward. Value-added from all the various sectors comprising the economy are summed up and adjusted for financial services (which are interest payments that must be discounted in order to avoid double counting) and a statistical discrepancy. We get the same value of GDP as in the previous two cases.

Finally, the importance of avoiding double counting brings me to one of the most common misuses of economic principles, namely the insistence of a good many laymen and even well-regarded economists in comparing the revenue of multinational companies (MNCs) with the *national income* of selected countries. This muddled and rather misguided comparison is ostensibly an attempt to show the power of MNCs in comparison with – and often put in terms of 'at the expense of' – less developed countries. (I will return to this in Section 5.5 "Outside the box: Getting the facts

straight on comparing MNCs to countries" on page 610.)

POP QUIZ 3.1.1   GDP ACCOUNTING METHODS

1 Explain why the value of final output must be equal to the sum of value-added.

2 Why do we deduct transfer payments when calculating GDP?

3 Calculate GDP from the following figures:

Consumer expenditure = €15 bn
General government final consumption = €8 bn
Gross domestic investment = €6 bn
Value of total exports = €3 bn
Value of total imports = €4.5 bn
Capital consumption (depreciation) = €2.5 bn

Distinction between ...

'*In all things, be precise*.' I have no idea who said that but it stuck. It also makes sense, especially when dealing with concepts which have a great many general uses and also has subject specific meaning, such as national income. The following headings try to straighten out a few question marks.

National and domestic

As usual, one can go a long way by simply 'tasting' the terms. We have so far computed the flow of income and expenditure created within a country, GDP, where the 'domestic' part should give you a clue. GDP is the output created within the economy using *domestic* factors of production. However, not all of this output is created by domestic companies since there will be a proportion of foreign-owned enterprises operating within the economy. In addition to this, domestic companies will hold foreign assets in the form of subsidiaries and joint-owned companies abroad. Both will lead to in-flows and out-flows of income (profits, wages, interest and rents) in each country. A country will receive income from property held abroad (subsidiaries and wholly owned businesses) and will pay property income abroad. By taking into account this **net property income from abroad** to and from the foreign sector, we get **gross national product**, GNP.

> **Gross national product (GNP)**: **GDP** is an account of the money value of goods and services produced within an economy, regardless of domestic or foreign ownership of the firms. **GNP** takes into account foreign ownership in the economy and domestic ownership of firms abroad by adding on net property income from abroad.
>
> GDP + property income *from* abroad – property income *paid* abroad = **GNP**
>
> or
>
> GDP + net property income *from* abroad = **GNP**

Net property income from abroad

Let me exemplify[4] property income flows using a country with which Ireland has a large degree of economic integration, USA. Figure 3.1.4 on page 258

illustrates how property income flows would affect the US and Ireland:

- **USA:** An American company, Dell Computers, runs a subsidiary company in Ireland and repatriates (= brings back to the fatherland) total income of USD150 million. Ireland's Allied Irish Banks (AIB) has offices in America and the US sees a remittance of USD100 million to AIB's headquarters in Ireland. Assuming these to be the only international firms in both countries, the US now has a net property income of USD 50 million.

- **Ireland:** Correspondingly, Irish holdings of foreign property in the US generate property income from abroad of USD100 million while US property in Ireland has generated an income of USD150 million paid abroad to the US. The net property income from abroad is USD -50 million for Ireland. (I am disregarding exchange rates.)

GNP for Ireland

The simple illustration above shows that one country's inflows of property income are the other country's outflows. (In other words, the sum of global net property income from abroad must per definition equal zero.) The example illustrates why Irish GDP is in fact greater than GNP. When negative net property income from abroad is deducted from GDP, GNP will be smaller. After putting GDP into market prices[5], the figures for the Irish economy are:

Gross domestic product (Note: market prices) €114,744 million

Net property income from abroad €-18,295 million

Equals: Gross national product (Market prices) €96,448 million

(Source: http://www.bea.doc.gov/bea)

It becomes clear that gross domestic product is larger than gross national product by some €18 billion, an indication of the relative weight of multinational companies operating in Ireland aiming to take advantage of a well-educated work force, low corporate taxes and excellent Guinness. This situation mirrors the GNP figures of the counterpart country, USA, where GNP is much higher than GDP due to massive foreign ownership abroad and incoming property income in excess of that paid abroad.

---

4. 'Using an example isn't another way to teach, it is the only way to teach.' quote from Albert Einstein
5. We add on taxes and deduct subsidies, then adjust the figures for European Community taxes and subsidies to arrive at GDP at market prices. This is outside the syllabus.

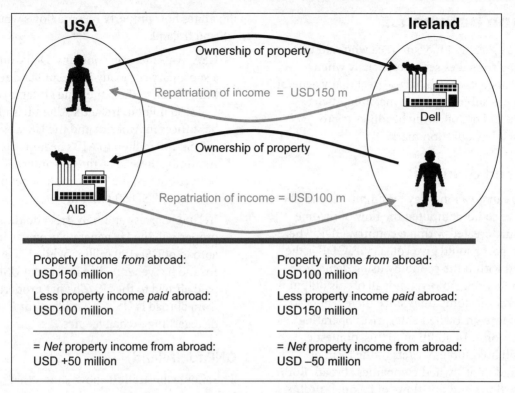

Figure 3.1.4 *Property income flows (US and Ireland)*

What other countries that would have very little property income from abroad, i.e. negative net property income from abroad? Well, frequently it is countries ... hang on, you figure it out! Here's a representative country as a clue: this country is famous for reggae, calypso music, Rastafarians and Blue Mountain coffee[6], and had a GNP of USD 6 billion in 1999 while GDP was USD 6.2 billion. (And no, reggae and rastas have nothing to do with why GDP is larger than GNP.) Have you figured it out? This is a *developing country*, Jamaica, where foreign companies will remit income at a greater rate than repatriated incomes. There are simply not that many Jamaican international companies operating abroad. Thus, it is the case that LDCs often have larger GNP than GDP.

To summarize:

- Gross **domestic** product means 'produced within a country's boundaries'. These are goods resulting from home-based assets – regardless of whether they are owned domestically or by foreigners. GDP is thus delineated by country boundaries; 'where (produced) – not who (owns)!'

- Gross **national** product on the other hand, means 'produced using a given country's factors' –

regardless of where. GNP deals with ownership originating in a certain country: 'who (owns) – not where (produced)!' In the next section, we will look a little closer at the question of which measurement constitutes the best indicator of economic performance.[7]

Gross and net national product

©IBO 2003

Noticed how a can of olives will read 'Net weight 500 grams' on a 750 gram jar? Correct, 1/3 of the content is water. 'Gross' and 'net' in national income accounting has nothing to do with olives but with the net increase in capital during a year. A standard issue Webster's dictionary covers both these examples since 'net' is defined as 'without deductions'. Olives are 500 grams dry weight after deducting water, but what does one deduct from GNP? Simple: one subtracts the value of 'worn-out' and 'used up' capital which has taken place during the year, i.e. the **depreciation** (sometimes called *capital consumption*), to obtain the net national product.

---

6. And also famous for being where yours truly as a 7 year old tried to burn down the English Priory School. My old man was holding a diplomatic passport which is probably the only reason I didn't do some serious prison time.

7. By now you should know that the answer will start with 'It depends. Assume the following...'

Net national product: To account for net national product, NNP (or net national income, NNY), one deducts from gross national product (GNP) the total value of depreciation taken place during the time period accounted for. Thus:

GNP – depreciation (capital consumption) = NNP

This is another area where I resort to childishness in class in trying to explain the analytical importance of adapting national income values to show net addition to capital. I use my classroom to explain how expenditure on capital is not necessarily 'more capital' but quite often 'replacement capital'. Every year a number of new desks are purchased but not all of them are for new students since a good many desks need to be replaced – having been subjected to too many students holding both artistic ambitions and sharp instruments. If 120 new desks are purchased in a year, yet 100 of them are replacing worn out desks then the net increase in capital, i.e. net investment, is 20 desks.

The desk example is much the same as in an economy, where firms' capital wears out and needs to be replaced. Now, it would clearly be impossible to accurately estimate the wear and tear on machines and such: different machines will have different lifespans and some companies will continue to use old machines and repair them rather than buy new ones. The element of depreciation, or capital consumption, is therefore an estimate which is often based on the write-off values used by firms in their balance sheets.

An example: a single-firm economy

Assume an economy with a single widget firm which buys machines every year over a period of five years. Each machine has *a lifespan of four years* according to accounting rules (which vary enormously in different countries), which means that *one fourth* of any new machine will 'wear out' – depreciate – during a year. Table 3.1.4 shows fictitious GDP, GNP (the firm has a subsidiary abroad) and finally the depreciation of capital resulting in **NNP**.

Table 3.1.4 *Going from GNP to NNP*

Year	1	2	3	4	5
Event in firm	machine #1	machine #2	machine #3	machine #4	machine #5
	= €100,000	= €200,000	= €40,000	= €80,000	= €160,000
Gross investment	€100,000	€200,000	€40,000	€80,000	€160,000
Depreciation #1 (1/5 of €100,000 per year)	€25,000	€25,000	€25,000	€25,000	0
Depreciation #2 (1/5 of €100,000 per year)	0	€50,000	€50,000	€50,000	€50,000
Depreciation #3-5 (1/5 per year)	0	0	€10,000	€30,000	€70,000
Total depreciation	€25,000	€75,000	€85,000	€105,000	€120,000
Total output (GDP)	€2 m	€2.5 m	€2.4 m	€3.5 m	€4 m
Net property income	€400,000	€300,000	€350,000	€200,000	€250,000
GNP	€2.4 m	€2.8 m	€2.75 m	€3.7 m	€4.25 m
Less depreciation	- €25,000	- €75,000	- €85,000	- €105,000	- €120,000
NNP	€2.375 m	€2.725 m	€2.665 m	€3.595 m	€4.13 m

The figures in Table 3.1.4 tell us a bit more about the economy in question. We can see that while there is an amount of investment every year, some of it is simply replacing old and worn out machines – in fact, during year 3 the gross investment doesn't keep up with depreciation leading to a de facto decrease in total

capital in the economy. You see, if a country is simply replacing worn-out machinery, then the income figures will be somewhat misleading as the total gross investment (which shows up in the accounts as investment expenditure) has not added to the overall capital stock of the economy. Such a status quo in terms of capital growth can have grave repercussions for a country's future output capabilities, as explained in Section 1 using PPFs. Researchers and analysts therefore commonly wish to know to what extent an economy is adding to capital as this says a great deal about growth capabilities. In fact, most economists would probably refer to net national product when gauging a country's progress in terms of *future* output capability. The main problem with NNP is the difficulty in correctly assessing depreciation.

Accounting for Ireland's net national product is a simple matter of **deducting total capital consumption** from GDP. This is shown in Table 3.1.5.

Table 3.1.5 *GDP, GNP and NNY in Ireland, 2001 (millions of € at current year values)*

1	Gross national product (Note: market prices)	96,448
2	Less: Consumption of fixed capital	-11,619
3	Equals: Net national income (Market prices)	84,829

(Source: *National Income and Expenditure 2002*, Irish Central Statistics Office, http://www.cso.ie)

Nominal and real income   ©IBO 2003

As GDP is comprised of millions of different goods it would be virtually impossible to measure it in actual quantities of the goods produced which is why it is put in *money* terms. The problem with using money as a measurement is, of course, that the value of money continuously changes – there is *inflation*. One unit of a currency does not buy the same amount of goods if prices have increased. And since we measure GDP using money terms, the value of output has been inflated by the increase in prices because output is calculated by taking the quantity times the price for all units of output.

Understanding the difference between real and nominal is very important in economics. Generally speaking, economists tend to avoid nominal values since real values tell us so much more. The term 'nominal' means 'face value' or 'money sticker price', while 'real' is a way of comparing the nominal (face) value with a given **base value** to see what the actual change is. Putting nominal values into real terms is also known as using *constant prices*, i.e. output valued at a price level of a given, base, year.

If output in 2000 is 100 widgets at a value of €50 then *nominal* output is €5,000. Now, if we call the year 2000 our **base year** (or period) then this is the period

we will refer to when comparing all other values. This means that the **base** year nominal value is also a real value, since all coming output values will be put in terms of base year prices. So, if 110 widgets are produced in the next time period at a value of €55, nominal output would be €6,050, which is an increase of 21%. Yet clearly real output has only increased by an additional 10 widgets, i.e. 10%. What we must do is *deflate* the nominal value by removing the inflationary element in order to show real output in the second time period. This is shown later in the section "Consumer Price Index (CPI)" on page 261.

As an illustrative exercise, ask your parents – or even better, your grandparents – whether they find things expensive today. I wager they will say yes. You see, they are intuitively comparing today's prices with what they were accustomed to maybe 20 or even 40 years ago! If a bagful of groceries cost $20 in 1980 and an identical bag cost $60 in 2000 then inflation has caused the bag to increase in price threefold. It does *not* mean that the bag is three times bigger! It means that since one needs $60 (in 2000) to buy what one only needed $20 to buy in 1980, the real value of the $60 is actually $20; $60 in the year 2000 has a real value of $20 in constant 1980 prices. Now ask your parents if they are poorer! If it also turns out that prices have indeed increased by 200% but their incomes have increased by 300% then their real incomes have increased, since they can actually buy more things for their wages.

> **Real and nominal income: Nominal national income** is expressed in the current prices of the output period and thus contains an element of inflation. **Real national income** is the nominal value put into base year (or constant) prices to allow real comparisons of output over time. The formula for deflating nominal GDP is:
>
> $$GDP_{real} = \frac{GDP_{nom} \text{ of year meaured}}{\text{Price index of year measured}} \times 100$$

Using the formula above and applying it to my example of your parents' income (GDP_{nom} in the formula) would show that real income is arrived at by adjusting their nominal wages by the price index. If the price level went from 100 to 300 (an increase of 200%) and their income went from €5,000 to €20,000 (an increase of 300%), then real income has gone from €5,000 to €6,666 during the time period ([€20,000/300] × 100 = €6,666.6), a 33.3% increase. Another way of putting it is that your parents can buy 33% more goods than 20 years earlier.

Consumer Price Index (CPI)

The basis for deflating nominal values into real values is an index showing price changes. The most commonly used price index is the Consumer Price Index (CPI). This index series is basically arrived at by following an 'identical basket of goods' in a country over time in order to show the change in the overall price level. Figure 3.1.5 follows such a basket in Ireland over a period of six years. The CPI, which is a stock concept, is measured in December each year. Its start date was 1995. This is the *base year*, i.e. the year all coming index values (e.g. the price of the basket) will be compared with. The formula for concocting a price index is to divide the nominal price of the basket of goods with the price at base year values:

$$\text{CPI at } t_0 = \frac{P_{basket} \text{ in } t_n}{P_{basket} \text{ in } t_0} \times 100 \text{ where } t_n \text{ is the year}$$

being looked at t_0 is the base year for values, i.e. the original price of the basket.

This is usually where a few of my people start to freak out, thinking that it's all so incredibly complicated. Wrong. If I can get it, you can! Just imagine that a basket containing Guinness, mutton, crab paté and potatoes increases in price from €50 to €55. Now, slip these figures into the formula above. Clearly the price has increased by 10% or – indexed – from 100 to 110. Now add a few more goods to the basket …

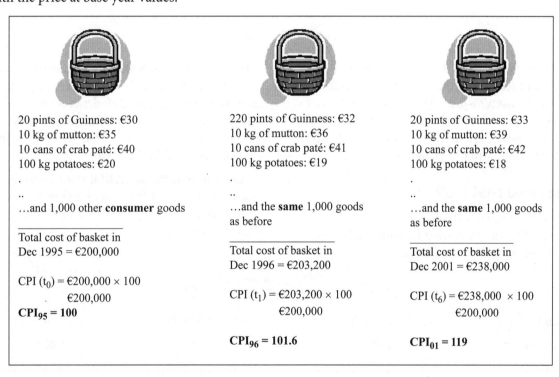

20 pints of Guinness: €30
10 kg of mutton: €35
10 cans of crab paté: €40
100 kg potatoes: €20
.
..
…and 1,000 other **consumer** goods
_____
Total cost of basket in
Dec 1995 = €200,000

CPI (t₀) = €200,000 × 100
            €200,000
CPI₉₅ = 100

220 pints of Guinness: €32
10 kg of mutton: €36
10 cans of crab paté: €41
100 kg potatoes: €19
.
..
…and the **same** 1,000 goods as before
_____
Total cost of basket in
Dec 1996 = €203,200

CPI (t₁) = €203,200 × 100
            €200,000
CPI₉₆ = 101.6

20 pints of Guinness: €33
10 kg of mutton: €39
10 cans of crab paté: €42
100 kg potatoes: €18
.
..
…and the **same** 1,000 goods as before
_____
Total cost of basket in
Dec 2001 = €238,000

CPI (t₆) = €238,000 × 100
            €200,000
CPI₀₁ = 119

Figure 3.1.5 *The basket of goods: CPI calculation for Ireland*

The CPI is amassed by having a representative basket of consumer goods over time to show overall price changes in a country. Every country's 'basket' will have different goods in varying quantities, but the basic methodology is the same. The base year is 1995 in Figure 3.1.5, rendering a CPI value of 100. Summing the total cost of the basket at consecutive points in time shows that the price level has increased to 101.6 during the first year, or a 1.6% increase. Over the entire six-year period the price level went from 100 to 119, a 19% increase in the price of the basket, e.g. the *average* price level has gone up by almost a fifth.

POP QUIZ 3.1.2   CONSUMER PRICE INDEX

1   What can you say about inflation by looking at the CPI above? Is the rate increasing or decreasing?

2   What has happened to the real price of Guinness during the six years?

3   What has happened to the real and nominal price of potatoes during the period?

GDP deflator – a better overall indicator of the price level

While the CPI is the most commonly referred-to measure of inflation, it is too narrow for general use in macroeconomic models. This is alleviated by using another index of the price level, the **GDP deflator**, which includes *all goods accounted for in GDP*. Since the CPI only includes consumer goods, many important prices are left out, notably those for investment goods, government goods and exported goods. The GDP deflator is calculated using the same basic principles as in the CPI, but includes prices on all these types of goods in the economy rather than just consumption goods. It is this wider definition of the price level we use to arrive at real GDP and real GNP. So, let us assume that in factoring in price changes for I, G and X we get the following GDP deflator series:

Dec 1995 ($t0$)	Dec 1996 ($t1$)	Dec 2001 ($t2$)
CPI (t_0) = 100	CPI (t_1) = 102	CPI (t_2) = 119
... plus I, G and X goods = **GDP deflator 1995: 100**	... plus I, G and X goods = **GDP deflator 1996: 102**	... plus I, G and X goods = **GDP deflator 2001: 128.5**

Figure 3.1.6 *The GDP deflator*

The GDP deflator shows that the average price level of all goods and services in the Irish economy has increased by almost 30% during the period 1995 to 2001, far more than the 19% shown by the CPI. Keep in mind that our 'basket' is a representation of the *average* change in price rather than a change in *all* prices!

Nominal and real GDP

Polishing off the example above, Ireland had the following GDP figures in current (i.e. nominal) values: 1995 = €52,641 m, 1996 = €58,080 m and 2001 = €114,744 m. Notice that national income looks to have more than doubled in a six-year period! However, by using the GDP deflator series in Figure 3.1.6 to deflate these figures, we remove the 'pumped up' component, which is to say the inflation element included in the nominal figures.

Deflating nominal GDP is done by using essentially the same formula as before, but using the **GDP deflator** as the general price index rather than the CPI (see Figure 3.1.7):

$$GDP_{nom} = \frac{GDP_{nom} \text{ of the year}}{GDP \text{ deflator}} \times 100$$

Nominal GDP:	year 1995 = €52,641 m	1996 = €58,090 m	2001 = €114,744 m
GDP deflator:	100	102	128.5
Real GDP:	year 1995 = €52,641 m	1996 = €58,090 m	2001 = €114,744 m

Figure 3.1.7 *GDP deflator calculation*

Adjusting the current (nominal) values for the increase in general price level ([GDP$_{nom}$ at year measured/CPI at year measured] × 100) we get the real GDP figures shown in Table 3.1.6 and Figure 3.1.8 on page 263. This is the 'shrinking balloon effect' of deflating nominal values into real values.[8]

After adjusting the nominal figures for inflation and thus putting them into base year values, we see how a portion of nominal GDP was in fact comprised of increasing prices rather than increasing output. After deflating these values we get a GDP series showing output in constant year 1995 prices. This is real GDP in terms of base year values of output.

Table 3.1.6 *Nominal and real GDP in Ireland, 2001 (millions of € at constant 1995 values)*

1	Nominal GDP (market prices)	114,744
2	Deflated using GDP deflator (index)	128.5
3	Equals: Real GDP (market prices)	89,320

(Source: *National Income and Expenditure 2002*, Irish Central Statistics Office, http://www.cso.ie)

8. I have rounded the figures a bit.

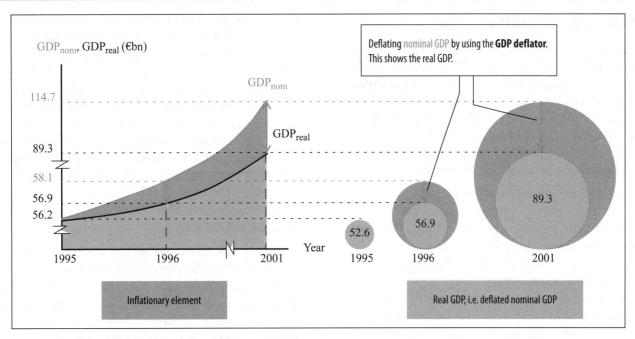

Figure 3.1.8 *'Pricking the balloon': deflating nominal GDP in Ireland 1995–2001*

In summary, real Irish national income increased by almost 70% during the period 1996–2001, which is less than the over 100% which nominal income suggests, but still one of the highest growth rates in the industrialised world during this period. Just imagine that you were an average Irishman and that your personal income kept pace with the real GDP – you would be able to buy 70% more goods with your income. And since price indexes have a marked tendency to understate real output by not taking into account quality increases and availability of substitutes, real GDP in all probability increased by more than 70%.

Real growth rate: In a similar vein, if one wants to see **real growth rates**, i.e. the real increase in output, then we must adjust for changes in prices. For example, the US had a nominal GDP of USD 10,082 billion in 2001 and USD 10,445 billion in 2002, giving a growth rate of 3.6% during the year 2002.[9] However, as prices rose during the same period by 1.23% we need to adjust the GDP figure for inflation. The real growth rate, i.e. the **actual increase** in the amount of goods and services produced, is 2.47% (3.7% to 1.23%).[10]

POP QUIZ 3.1.3   NOMINAL AND REAL VALUES FOR USA IN 2000

The table below shows GDP, GNP and NNP in the USA (billions of constant 1996 USD) for the year 2000.

1	Gross domestic product	9,824.60
2	Real gross domestic product	9,191.40
3	Gross national product	9,848.00
4	Real gross national product	9,216.20
5	Net national product	8,619.10
	Real net national product	7,994.40

(Sources: http://www.oecd.org/dataoecd/48/4/2371304.pdf and http://www.bea.doc.gov)

1 How much have prices increased in America between 1996 and 2000?

2 Has real net investment taken place in 2000?

---

9.   As a little Trivial Knowledge Tidbit, real GDP in the USA was USD 311 billion in 1900 which means the economy had grown by some 3,258% by the year 2000. See http://www.eh.net

10.   This is an approximation. In actual fact, the correct value will be slightly lower: 2.35%. The method is to deflate the new value of nominal GDP by the index of price change using 2001 as base year: GDPnom/price index gives 103.7/101.23 = 1.02349, i.e. real GDP has grown by 2.35%.

Total and per capita ©IBO 2003

National income is also often put into terms of 'average income per person', which is nothing other than GDP divided by the population. This is **income per capita** (= GDP or GNP per head). Irish nominal GDP in 2001 was €114,744 million, and dividing by the population gives €29,889 – this is Irish GDP per capita. Figure 3.1.9 and Table 3.1.7 on page 265 follow the Irish figures used throughout this section.

Real income per capita in Ireland went from €22,211 in 2000 to €23,266 per capita in 2001. This means that real per capita growth in Ireland for this period was 4.3% compared to 6.2% real growth for the economy as a whole. This way of adjusting growth figures to take into account a changing population gives a better overall picture of economic growth. Just imagine trying to compare growth rates of two countries where both countries have 5% growth rates but where one country has a stagnant (= unchanging) population while the other has a 5% increase in population. As a single indicator of economic wellbeing, real GDP is probably the 'least bad' measurement – yet we will adjust in further in the next section.

I offer you a piece of advice here: *beware of averages*! Bill Gates did a world tour in 2003 of developing countries in furtherance of the Gates Foundation. Find a picture of Gates sitting with a few hundred villagers and then calculate the average income of the group! See my point? The lesson is simple: the more divergence between the maximum and minimum values, the weaker the arithmetic average is. Whether looking at real or nominal GDP or GNP per capita it is essential to keep in mind that income distribution can be such that a small proportion of the population accounts for most of the income. This doesn't show in per capita GDP/GNP figures.

Finally, I should comment on my having mostly used wealthy countries' statistics in this section. This has been quite intentional. I intend to use a bit of shock therapy in the sections on development and use a few figures from developing nations which will show a sharp contrast to many of the values used above. In the meantime, why don't you get out a map of the world and mark out the rich economies? Try to define 'rich' before you start marking.

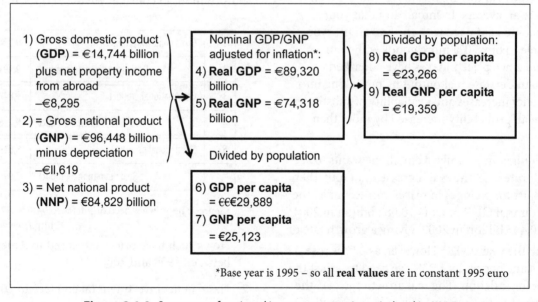

Figure 3.1.9 *Summary of national income accounting – Ireland in 2001*

Table 3.1.7 *National income accounting: Ireland 1995–2002*

Description	1995	1996	1997	1998	1999	2000	2001	2002*
Gross Domestic Product at Constant (1995) market prices (millions €)	52,641	56,891	63,201	68,663	76,410	84,113	89,320	95,499
Per head of population (€)								
GDP at current market prices	14,618	16,018	18,335	20,929	23,929	27,157	29,889	33,021
GNP at current market prices	12,967	14,215	16,138	18,397	20,473	23,262	25,123	26,405
GNI at current market prices	13,236	14,615	16,476	18,681	20,132	23,491	25,392	26,727
Net national product at factor cost	9,947	10,986	12,379	14,125	15,449	17,281	19,004	19,635
GDP at constant (1995) market prices	14,618	15,690	17,263	18,553	20,403	22,211	23,266	24,381
GNP at constant (1995) market prices	12,967	13,882	15,086	16,090	17,336	18,899	19,359	18,986
GNI at constant (1995) market prices	13,236	14,251	15,390	16,370	17,606	19,162	19,630	19,355

(Source: *National Income and Expenditure 2002*, Central Statistics Office of Ireland. Published August 2003)

POP QUIZ 3.1.4   NATIONAL INCOME ACCOUNTING

1 Why might an LDC have higher GDP than GNP? Why might Singapore?

2 What is the sum of **global** net property income from abroad?

3 A Volkswagen Polo cost SEK (Swedish Crowns) 65,000 in 1985 and SEK113,000 in 2000. CPI in 1985 was 154 and 258 in January 2000. What is the **real price** of the Polo in 1985 and 2000 respectively using 1980 as the base year? Is there any weakness in comparing prices like this?

4 A country has the following figures:

   GDP = 600
   property income paid abroad = 120
   net property income from abroad = 30
   capital consumption = 60

What are the values of GNP and NNY?

5 Let us say that in 1987 the CPI is 220 and the same year nominal GDP is €600 bn. In 1999 the CPI is 330 and nominal GDP is €900 bn. How has this country fared in terms of real output (= real GDP)?

6 Over a 10-year period, the following happens: GNP (nominal) increases by 25%, population remains unchanged and CPI goes from 150 to 200. How has this affected nominal GNP per capita and real GNP per capita?

7 Refer to the figures below. During which period does the rate of inflation fall **first**?

	1972	1973	1974	1975	1976
Prices	97	105	106	105	103
Wages	100	105	110	112	109

8 Explain how 'double counting' can occur in calculating national income, and how measuring 'value-added' can overcome this problem.

9 GDP figures for a country are as follows:

   USD 200 bn in 1989
   USD 230 bn in 1990
   USD 260 bn in 1991

What are the growth rates? Are they rising, falling or constant during this period?

10 Over a period of time, the GDP index in an economy goes from 100 to 120 while the population index goes from 100 to 130. What could be deduced from this regarding the average national income? What is missing be able to comment on the change in **real** income?

Introduction to development

3.2

CONTENTS

INTRODUCTION TO DEVELOPMENT

While the previous section focused on the quantitative measurements of the progression of a nation's economy, this section deals more with the qualitative aspects of economic and social welfare. In looking at things from this perspective we will in fact be laying bare a number of weaknesses in income figures and thus subjecting our national income measurements to some weighty criticism.

Definitions of economic growth and economic development

©IBO 2003

Economic growth, as outlined both in Section 1 and Section 3.1, is the increase in real GDP or GNP from one time period to the next. Economic growth is a quantitative variable and lends itself rather easily to comparisons both between countries and over time. Table 3.2.1 shows the average growth rates for the world's regions during the past two decades.

Table 3.2.1 *Increase in GDP for world's regions, 1980–2000*

Region	1980–85	1985–90	1990–2000
Developed market economy countries	2.5	3.7	2.4
Developing countries and territories	3	4.5	4.8
Countries in Eastern Europe	3.1	1.5	-2.3*

* Note that there was actually *negative* growth in Eastern Europe during the 1990s. See Section 1.

(Source: *UNCTAD handbook of statistics 2002*, p. 347)

The table above shows economic growth for developing countries, but having said this one must be careful not to confuse the issue with **economic development**. Usage of the term 'economic development' has undergone something of a revolution in the past 30 years. It originally referred to the process by which an economy would shift from a primarily agricultural output to one with a larger proportion of secondary goods, i.e. a process of industrialisation. In this context, the development process was almost entirely an economic reform process, encompassing GDP/GNP increases which outstrip both inflation and population increases – resulting in real per capita growth. One can say that growth has been used as a narrow definition of development.

Growth rates have evidently varied a great deal between regions and over time. (See Table 3.2.1 which shows world growth during the past 20 years.) Note that while developing countries have had consistently higher growth rates during the past two decades, they started at a far lower level than the developed world in terms of de facto GDP. Simple maths says that an increase in GDP of USD 0.5 billion in a small economy will show a far higher growth rate than a USD 0.5 billion increase in a large economy. As an example, the corresponding GDP figures for one of the world's poorest countries, Ghana, was USD 5.3 billion in 2001 and 5.8 in 2002, giving a growth rate of 9.3% – a growth figure which any American president of the past 50 years could only dream of. However, the de facto (= in effect, actual) increase in Ghana's GDP of USD 0.5 billion would be the equivalent of a 0.00005 percentage increase in America's GDP during the same year. One must therefore take great care when dealing with absolute and comparative increases.

During the latter part of the 1960s, the view of development in purely economic terms was increasingly seen as insufficient. The failure in many developing nations to show how increasing income 'trickled down' to broader layers of society indicated that simply measuring growth – however 'real per capita' it was – in fact was highly inadequate for showing true development in terms of an overall increase in the standard of living and quality of life for citizens. Developing countries which showed that unchanging portions of the populace were not partaking of income increases and enjoying greater economic equality and employment opportunities could not be considered to have developed. The concept of economic development was therefore broadened to portray not only economic growth, but also a reduction in *poverty*, income *inequality* and *unemployment*.

> **Economic growth and economic development**: **Economic growth** is the increase in real national income during a time period, usually one year. **Economic development** is a wider concept, adding to the above definition the overall aims of the reduction of poverty, income inequality and unemployment. Growth is a quantitative concept while development is a qualitative (and thus normative) concept.

Differences in the definitions of the two concepts ©IBO 2003

So, economic growth is computational by nature, i.e. a matter of defining output and adding up the numbers, while economic development is more complex since it involves looking at several aspects of society rather than simple numeric values of national income. Clearly development is desirable and thus it is normative in nature where 'the more the better'. One can say that economic development as a concept takes into account the questions of *what* and *who*: what is being produced and who is getting it? Addressing these two questions using figures for poverty levels, unemployment levels and distribution of income provides a basic way of outlining economic development since all three are closely linked to the creation and sharing of national output.

Why growth is not the same as development

The following questions can illustrate the issue: In an economy where real **GDP per capita** has increased without affecting the poorest 25% or 50% of the population at all, has the economy developed? And does economic development take place if, during economic growth, a large proportion of the population is unable to meet basic needs for food, shelter and sanitation? Does economic development take place when long-term unemployment increases in a growing economy due to an increase in productivity? If economic growth is fuelled by a few wealthy land owners producing primary goods for the foreign export market rather than for the domestic market, and the profits are reinvested abroad, can one speak of economic development?

Most development economists answer 'no' to all the above. (But I hope you also realise that I am being a bit provocative!) By bringing into economics a *social dimension* of the dispersion of output and income, e.g.

value judgements on what is socially desirable, the definition of economic development has undergone a radical change. Economists now incorporate 'income equality' into economic theory and put forward suggestions aimed at alleviating poverty and increasing income distribution. This is done without a great deal of reflection on normative issues involved – yet, as we shall see in Section 5.4, pure economic arguments are increasingly put forward in support of development.

Simply put, economic growth which does not enhance the **living standards** of a broader measure of the population is defined as sub-optimal in developmental terms; widening income gaps between rich and poor are bad while narrower gaps are good. This includes effective allocation of labour resources in keeping unemployment low and also a 'fair' system of taxation and social benefits to even-out income gaps. It was seen quite clearly during the 1970s that growth did not measure up to these development criteria since income gains were often not distributed across a wider section of society.

A spectrum of growth and development

Figure 3.2.1 on page 269 illustrates how the concept of development is successively widened. From a narrow definition of real GDP/GNP per capita, economic development expands the conceptual framework to include people's access to the benefits of growth; employment and a share of the output increase. By adding on a number of socioeconomic indicators/ measurements, development as a concept went from the measurement of pure economic welfare to what we now attempt to measure by using an array of variables. 'Wider' development (note: my own choice of words) encompasses any number things which enable people to enjoy richer lives:

- **Political freedoms** such as voting rights and equality under a rule of law
- **Access to education** and a choice in careers
- **Social freedom** of free time – and having choices of cultural activities to fill this time
- **Societal independence** in terms of freedom of indebtedness and/or indentured (= contracted) labour service.

Ultimately, a high level of development is primarily *enabling* and *empowering*. It enables personal freedoms and choice and empowers people to make these choices.

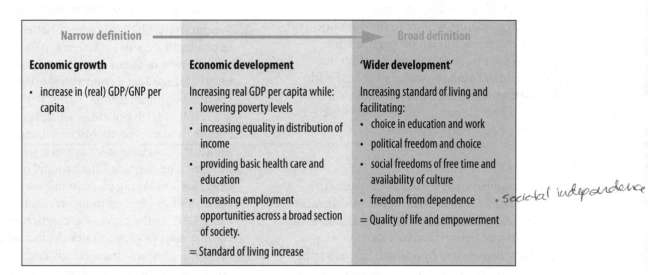

Narrow definition ➡ Broad definition		
Economic growth	**Economic development**	**'Wider development'**
• increase in (real) GDP/GNP per capita	Increasing real GDP per capita while: • lowering poverty levels • increasing equality in distribution of income • providing basic health care and education • increasing employment opportunities across a broad section of society. = Standard of living increase	Increasing standard of living and facilitating: • choice in education and work • political freedom and choice • social freedoms of free time and availability of culture • freedom from dependence • *societal independence* = Quality of life and empowerment

Figure 3.2.1 *Growth and development spectrum*

The progression in Figure 3.2.1 is my own version and builds strongly upon the work of Nobel Laureate Amartya Sen who helped develop the Human Development Index (HDI)[1]. As I have stated earlier, development is hard to define and the table above is an attempt to start from a basic agreed-upon basis – growth – and widen the definitional span in stages. Whereas pure economic development stresses such elements as the existence of jobs, a viable workforce and a taxable income base, development stresses the wider context of an *enabling function*. It enables people to enjoy the wider benefits of life outside meeting the basic necessities of food and shelter. Figure 3.2.1 shows how the concept of development has progressed from being equated with economic growth to the far wider definition of development. It should be noted that a number of additional variables shall be included in the wider definition of development in Section 5.3.

One final 'however'. While few economists would **equate** growth with development, few would deny the **link** between the two. There is clear positive correlation between GDP per capita and development, leading to the proposition that growth is a prerequisite (= basic requirement) for development. While this might seem a contentious statement, it is in fact increasingly incorporated as a mainstream notion. As such, The World Development Report in 2001/2002 establishes the reduction of poverty as a main goal and economic growth as means to this end.[2] The hotly debated – and to my knowledge, as yet unresolved – issue herein is whether growth has thus far led to

greater or less income inequality in LDCs. This too will be subject to scrutiny in Section 5.2.

Gross Domestic Product versus Gross National Product as measures of growth ©IBO 2003

There are limitations in using any measure of national income as a measure of growth, since both inflation and population growth will eat away at any nominal total value. Any measure based on money will be misleading – and any measure which disregards the size of the country will further weaken any claim as to growth rates. That is why, as above, nominal figures are put into constant (real) terms and often adjusted for population to show per capita income.

GDP versus GNP in measuring growth

However, let us disregard the issues of real and per capita and focus on the usefulness of Gross Domestic Product (GDP) and Gross National Product (GNP) as *growth measurements*. The issue is once again 'It depends ...'

GNP

GNP has traditionally been the main measure of economic activity, since most industrialised countries have a net inflow of foreign property income from abroad earned by domestically owned factors of production. Since this repatriated property income is

---

1. *Development as freedom*, pp. 5–11and also a very accessible account in Todaro, pp. 14–24.
2. See http://www.worldbank.org/poverty/wdrpoverty/report/index.htm.

created by domestic firms – albeit by foreign hands – there would in all likelihood be an overall improvement in economic welfare in the domestic economy. The incoming foreign property income creates a base for reinvestment, induces additional consumption and of course provides a tax base with which domestic government can even out income inequalities and provide public/merit goods which further enhance production capabilities.

GDP

Increasingly, however, *GDP* is used as the prime measure of economic activity. One of the world's most famous economists, Paul Krugman, Nobel Laureate in 2008, points out that living standards are overwhelmingly determined by domestic factors rather than international.[3] If one is looking at purely domestic aspects of economic growth, such as use of labour (employment) factors, then **GDP** is more suitable. This is because it is largely irrelevant who *owns* the firms in terms of overall increase in domestic production. Two issues stand out:

1. **Unemployment**. There is a far straighter link between the trend in *unemployment* and *GDP* than unemployment and GNP. As we saw earlier, Ireland's GDP is greater than GNP due to the large element of foreign direct investment coming into the country – yet Ireland has had amongst the lowest levels of unemployment and highest levels of personal consumption gains in the EU during the 1990s. The growth rate of Ireland has also been outstanding during the 1980s and 1990s – once again keeping in mind that proportional increases are seemingly very large when the initial values are low and that Ireland was one of Western Europe's poorest countries in the 1970s. Two brief statistics to convey this: in 2002, foreign firms in Ireland accounted for 47% of all employment in manufacturing jobs and 16% of GDP.

It is estimated that Ireland produces some 40% of all packaged software sold in Europe.[4] This is why comparing Ireland's GNP with a country which has a large number of MNCs, say Switzerland, would distort reality since actual economic activity within

the two countries would favour the country with large elements of property income from abroad.

2. **Productivity**. GDP growth is a better measurement of productivity, since *efficiency gains* – the effectiveness of factor use – in an economy are mostly accrued on a countrywide basis rather than specific by (international) firms. Irish productivity is a result of Irish policies – whatever 'corporate culture' is imported via Microsoft and other multinational companies operating within the borders. The ongoing international integration (e.g. *globalisation*) taking place in industrialised countries has resulted in increasing preference for using GDP as the main single indicator for comparisons of growth rates. As industrialised economies become increasingly connected via cross-border ownership of factors such as land and capital, it becomes increasingly difficult to compare economic growth, since GNP has an increasing proportion of non-domestic activity factored in.

Limitations of using GDP as a measure to compare welfare between countries ©IBO 2003

> *I have observed that we all get the same amount of ice. The rich get it in the summertime and the poor get it in the winter.* – Bat Masterson[5]

It is extremely important to understand the uses of growth and GDP figures and also the limitations. The figures are useful for assessing how well the economy is using resources and how the economic system compares to other countries. The figures are also invaluable in showing possible government policies and future government tax revenue and thus how well pensions, schooling and infrastructure will be covered. Having said this, it is vital to realise that GDP and growth figures do not show how the environment is impacted, whether the increased wealth has been relatively evenly distributed, whether people can actually buy more goods for their money or whether general welfare in the society has increased correspondingly. Taken together, one should always try to use a critical eye and 'look behind' the actual numbers.

---

3. *Pop internationalists*, p. 9.
4. *Sunday Post*, 14 July 2002, http://archives.tcm.ie/businesspost/2002/07/14/story324113.asp.
5. Legendary gunfighter in the 'Old American West'.

Comparison in a single country over time

There are a number of criticisms levelled against GDP figures when they are used to show growth **within** a country over time. Three main points emerge:

1. **Money values and population change.** We have shown how changes in price levels and population can skew income figures and how this can be dealt with by putting all figures in constant and/or per capita values. However, there is still quite often a bias.

2. **Quality and substitution bias.** Which goods are included in the basket which is compared over time? Price indexes frequently *overestimate inflation* and thus underestimate real output growth over time due to the fact that when aggregate demand changes permanently over time there has been a shift to other, superior, goods; *substitutes*. This causes an overestimation of the price level since a downshift in production of goods on the way to becoming obsolete (= outdated) reduces the possibility of benefits of scale and keeps costs and prices higher than for new goods not yet included in the basket. Similarly, GDP figures cannot estimate the *increased quality* of new goods, for example the fact that newer cars need less service and maintenance and use less fuel. Thus, there is a bias in overestimating actual price increases by underestimating the quality of new goods substituting old goods.

3. **Errors and/or changes in accounting methods.** Imagine the hundreds of millions of figures entering into the overall calculation of national income during a year – there are bound to be both *accounting errors* and time lags in assessing all the data. It is also often the case that older data is less comparable with newer, due to different methods of accounting.

Comparing GDP between countries

In addition to the above, a number of weaknesses in national income figures become apparent when different countries are compared. These include (but are not limited to):

- **Composition of output.** Perhaps the main criticism of GDP as a measure of welfare is that however accurate the figures are for output, the final GDP figure does not show what is being produced – we're back to a 'guns or butter' problem. The Soviet Union of the 1930s put great effort into competing with the west in terms of output and growth in order to show the superiority of the centrally planned system. Going by official output figures the USSR won the race, but what the figures do not show is that the Soviets put the majority of resources into producing capital goods – and never really got around to providing for the wants and needs of its citizens in terms of consumer goods. A country with double-digit growth rates and empty shelves is something of an anomaly but quite possible, which is also often the case in times of major conflicts when armaments account for economic growth which in no way represents an increase in the standard of living.

- **Composition of expenditure.** In a vein similar to the above, national income figures are often skewed by the simple fact that different countries will have different expenditure patterns. The cold and icy Nordic countries spend a sizable proportion of their income on heating homes and offices – but this doesn't mean a higher standard of living than in temperate climate. Comparing Finland's GDP figures with Bermuda's could get tricky indeed.

- **Distribution of income.** All per capita national income figures are **averages** and therefore neglect how income is distributed amongst citizens. The third richest country in the world, the USA, had a per capita GDP of USD 35,200 in 2000 while the second richest, Norway, had USD 37,200.[6] Yet the highest 10% of all income earners in America accounted for 30.5% of national income – and at the same time the country had some 30 million people living below the official poverty line.[7] In Norway, on the other hand, 21.8% of income went to the richest 10% – thereby accounting for one third less than the USA's richest upper deciles.

(A somewhat lengthy parenthesis: An 'upper middle income' country according to the World Bank's World Development Report has a per capita GNP of between USD 3,031 and USD 9,360, which puts Mexico, Botswana, Malaysia, Lebanon in this category. However, the poorest 20% in Mexico and Malaysia account for 3.5% and 4.5% respectively of income whereas the richest 20% for 57.4% and 54.3%[8] (see "Lorenz curve" on page 382). Focusing on income figures and growth rates disregards the fact that a good many countries in the developing world have experienced increasing gaps between

---

6. National Accounts of OECD countries, Main aggregates, Volume 1, updated version from 2003.
7. *Poverty in the United States*, US Census Bureau 2000, p. 3.

rich and poor – and all to often the poor have become poorer in absolute terms, not only in relative terms.[9])

- **Unaccounted-for activity.** Statistical inaccuracies will be enhanced by the fact that a portion of economic activity will be hidden. *Parallel markets* for goods and labour are notable examples of a type of *systematic error* since real output is consistently under-reported. The large element of barter and non-money economic activity in LDCs will lead to consistent under-reporting of real output figures. More developed countries will also have a large section of unreported activity, but in this case primarily due to tax avoidance and evasion of labour laws. Point in fact – according to an unpublished report by the European Union in 1998, underground economic activity is estimated at between 7% and 16% of total GDP for member nations and employs between 10 and 28 million people.[10] Another shocking figure of recent date is from Russia, where pure criminal activity accounts for close to 50% of Russia's total economic activity, according to the Financial Monitoring Committee in January 2003.[11]

Take note, however, that 'unaccounted-for' does not necessarily entail 'illegal', as in illegal goods and operations or tax evasion. It can consist of other hidden activity, such as the goodly portion of all economic activity which is simply not accounted for on definitional grounds and causes GDP figures to be consistently underestimated – for instance, own home repairs and training a local youth football team in your spare time.

- **Exchange rates distortions:** Since the comparison of different countries' GDP must be put into some form of common language, a single currency is used, often the USD. In doing this, the market exchange rates for different currencies are used – with the unfortunate side-effect of grossly underestimating average incomes of low-cost countries when *purchasing power* is taken into account. See "PPP – some real-life figures (2006)" on page 274.

- **Externalities and environmental damage.** GDP figures do not show soil erosion, air pollution, land degradation, deforestation, depleted natural reserves of resources or the often monumental

disruptions to values and traditions as a result of large scale economic growth in a relatively brief period of time.

In spite of the heavy criticism levied above, GDP per capita adjusted for purchasing power (see next section) is still the best 'single' indicator of development available. There is relatively clear positive correlation between most standard of living indicators and economic growth – the problem being that it is very difficult to see which comes first, i.e. there is a causality problem.

Allowing for differences in purchasing power when comparing welfare between countries ©IBO 2003

We were sitting outside having a cold beer at a nice restaurant in Oshakati, Namibia in November 2002: Anna, Per, myself and John Shamhula – our fearless guide/nanny. John was curious about Sweden and asked many questions about our lives there and I think we all were amazed not at how different we were but how alike we were! At one point John asked me, 'How much would this beer cost in your country?' He held up his half-litre stein for emphasis. After some quick head counting based on an exchange rate of one Swedish Crown (SEK) to 0.9 Namibian dollars (NAD) and a few murmurs of agreement from the colleagues I said 'About NAD 40 at a place like this. Now you know why we think that NAD 5 for a large beer here is so cheap!'

John got furious – and loud: 'Forty dollars for a beer?! For ONE beer?! This … this … this is CRIMINAL! These people are thieves! They should … they should be *punished*! Punished most severely!' What John disregarded, brilliant mathematician that he was, was that translating Swedish crowns into Namibian dollars meant that a great deal was lost in translation; **while SEK 1 was equal to NAD 0.9 according to the exchange rate** (or NAD 1 = SEK 1.1) you could buy a great deal more for 100 SEK, i.e. NAD 90, in Namibia than in Sweden. The exchange rate made my Namibian colleagues look very poor in comparison as the differences in price levels did not show in the **purchasing power** of each currency.[12]

8. All income distribution figures are taken from the World Bank's 2002 World Development Indicators, www.worldbank.org/poverty/data/2 8wdi2002.pdf. No income distribution figures are available for Botswana or Lebanon.

9. See http://www.worldbank.org/poverty/data/2_8wdi2002.pdf.

10. National Center For Policy Analysis, *Friday, 4 September 1998*, Brief Analysis No. 278 – http://www.ncpa.org/ba/ba278.html.

11. English version of *Pravda* – http://english.pravda.ru/politics/2003/01/23/42448.html.

A simple purchasing power example

The trick is to convert the two currencies in some way to show the relative power for each citizen in his/her own country. What we did, sitting there in the restaurant trying to cool John down, was to figure out how many beers you could buy for an average teaching salary (see Table 3.2.2).

Table 3.2.2 *Teachers' salaries and purchasing power*

Country	Average monthly salary for a teacher	Price of a 0.5 litre beer	Beers per salary
Sweden	SEK 18,000	SEK45	400
Namibia	NAD 2,000	NAD5	400

In other words, the exchange rate grossly distorted (underestimated) the actual purchasing power of Namibian teachers. Since the average Swedish teacher earns nine times as much as the Namibian teacher, one might be led to assume that the Swede can buy nine times as much. This is clearly not the case, at least for beer, since the half-litre stein costs nine times as much in Sweden. In other words, the purchasing power of Namibian and Swedish teachers in terms of beer is identical!

The 'beer exchange rate' would give the Namibian and the Swede the same quantity of beer in the other's country; the 'beer exchange rate' at purchasing power parity would be when SEK18,000 = NAD 2,000, i.e. SEK 1 = NAD 0.055 or **NAD 1 = SEK 18**. Since we were getting sixteen times this amount (by getting NAD 0.9 for each SEK) when we changed money at the banks, the exchange rate was stacked highly in our favour in terms of purchasing power.

A purchasing-power adjusted exchange rate

Clearly one must take purchasing power into account when comparing incomes in countries. The NAD 2,000 earned by my Namibian colleagues is hardly fit for comparison with the 18,000 earned by my Swedish colleagues since the values in no way capture real purchasing power. Let us build a slightly more extensive example, including other goods for income earners in the two countries. The procedure is only a trifle more complex than above. Assume a standard basket of goods in each country containing five identical goods and we will get a basis for constructing a purchasing power parity (PPP) exchange rate.

Sweden	Namibia
100 litres of petrol: SEK 1,000	100 litres of petrol: NAD 300
100 km in a taxi: SEK 1,400	100 km in a taxi: NAD 150
Night in a hotel: SEK 800	Night in a hotel: NAD 200
100 beers at a pub: SEK 4,500	100 beers at a pub: NAD 500
Meal in a good restaurant: SEK 500	Meal in a good restaurant: NAD 150
100 litres of milk: SEK 800	100 litres of milk: NAD 250
Total cost of basket in SEK: 9,000	Total cost of basket in NAD: 1,550

De facto exchange rate: SEK 1 = NAD 0.9
Implied exchange rate at perfect purchasing power parity: SEK 9,000 = NAD 1,550. This would give a PPP exchange rate of SEK 1 = NAD 0.17 or NAD 1 = SEK 5.8.

Figure 3.2.2 *A basket of goods in Sweden and Namibia*

The fictitious example in Figure 3.2.2 shows that in order to compare incomes between a citizen of Namibia and a citizen of Sweden, one must adjust income figures to show the purchasing power of income rather than simply using official exchange rates. In doing so, one gets a far more accurate method of comparing the incomes of two different countries, since the PPP calculations show that a Swedish teacher would be able to buy two domestic baskets while the Namibian teacher would get 1.3 baskets. In other words, while the Swedish teacher's income is still higher than the Namibian's even based on purchasing parity, there has been a marked evening-out effect since the official exchange rate shows how the Swede's exchange rate-based income is 8.2 times higher than the Namibian's.

---

12.   While this will probably guarantee that I never get another job at an international school, I'm going to tell the story of how I was hired here at my school in Mexico. During the job interview with the headmaster, there was a brief silence in the conversation and the headmaster asked, 'Well, do *you* have any questions?!' 'Yes indeed', I replied. 'What does a beer cost in a restaurant in Mexico?' There was a long pause. I could hear the line of thinking: 'This guy's nuts, possibly alcoholic …' To the head's credit, I was given an answer and quickly figured out that the offered salary increased my purchasing power (well, for beer at least) by a factor of three. I use restaurant prices for beer as my PPP indicator since the good is domestically produced, contains an element of service costs and is heavily taxed. It turns out to be a pretty good indicator of relative purchasing power. My soon-to-be boss happily conceded the point and hired me, yet still has doubts about my sanity. My colleague in the economics department doesn't touch alcohol so I figure between the two of use we've got on average *one* normal economist – which might be a contradiction in terms.

PPP – some real-life figures (2006)

The UNDP does a purchasing power calculation for all countries every year by putting all the world's GDP figures into a common currency, the US dollar, and adjusting the figures to show what these dollars would buy a citizen in a given country. These PPP adjusted figures are more frequently used instead of exchange rate based figures. Table 3.2.3 shows the GDP per capita in US dollars at both current exchange rates and adjusted for PPP for selected countries in 2006.

Table 3.2.3 *GDP per capita 2006 in US dollars, at current prices and PPP US dollars*

Rank	Country	GDP per capita at current exchange rates	GDP per capita adjusted for PPP
5	Ireland	51,920	40,823
7	Sweden	43,291	34,056
8	Japan	34,200	31,951
10	Switzerland	52,014	37,396
15	United States	43,366	43,968
87	Jamaica	3,844	6,409
94	China	2,137	4,682
129	Namibia	3,389	4,819
169	Ethiopia	164	700
179	Sierra Leone	288	630
Developing countries		4,572	5,282
OECD countries*		30,879	29,197

* The Organisation of Economic Co-operation and Development (OECD) is comprised of the 30 wealthiest industrialised countries in the world.

(Sources: The GDP/capita values are at http://data.un.org and http://hdrstats.undp.org/indicators. The PPP values are at UNDP, www.undp.org)

Overestimation of GDP in MDCs – underestimation in LDCs

In adjusting GDP figures to assess the purchasing power of citizens in each country, some remarkable patterns emerge. Two of the notoriously most expensive countries in the world, Japan and Switzerland, have significantly lower purchasing power than national income figures would indicate. Simply put, rich countries' GDP figures are often *overestimated*

using conventional exchange rate methods, while developing countries show the opposite. It is often the case that the price level in LDCs is much lower than in developed countries – which means that the domestic LDC currency will go a lot further at home than in an (expensive) MDC. Using PPP methodology to compare GDP will render higher per capita income for LDCs than only using an exchange rate to convert the figures.

Hence, Japan's GDP per capita is 6.5% lower when PPP prices are taken into consideration while Namibia's turns out to be 42% higher. Switzerland's per capita income adjusted for purchasing power is 28% lower than the exchange rate based figures while Ethiopia's is more than four times higher. Another comparison shows that, as a percentage of USA's GDP per capita, average income in China is not 4.9% of the USA's but rather 10.6% when PPP is used instead of the foreign exchange rate.

Finally, I have chosen the countries in Table 3.2.3 based primarily on countries I have used as examples so far. They are in a *ranking* order as can be seen in the far-left column. You might at this point wonder what the ranking means. Ponder this before reading the next chapter.

Alternative methods of measurement ©IBO 2003

Once again, the main problem in outlining welfare in developmental terms is solving the problem of measuring what in effect cannot be objectively measured. In order to overcome this problem, economists have tried to construct measurements based on relatively quantifiable and identifiable variables which can be used to show relative living standards and overall human welfare. The discussion on measuring development has so far been limited to national income, which is too limited in scope to be used as the only indicator. Here are a few other common development indicators:

- the 'distance' between the richest 10% and poorest 10% in society
- amount of medical doctors per 1,000 inhabitants – and average travel time to a hospital

- how many in a population have access to clean water and sanitation
- average daily caloric intake per person
- road miles and other transportation networks in km per capita
- telephones/computers/internet access per 1,000 inhabitants
- infant mortality rates measured by infant deaths per 1,000 newborns
- percentage of under-14s active in the labour force
- amount spent on public education as a percentage of the national budget or GDP
- GDP/GNP adjusted for economic 'bads' such as pollutant levels and environmental damage and the addition of non-money activities such as barter
- adjusting income figures to show long-run sustainability by factoring in the depreciation of **environmental capital**, e.g. natural resources.

The advantage of any of the above is that they are all *measurable* in purely quantifiable terms. The disadvantage is that no single indicator will suffice to show overall development. The solution is often to create a composite (= multiple, combined) index where a number of different variables are used together and indexed in order to make comparisons possible. The most commonly used index for development levels is the *Human Development Index*, the HDI.

The Human Development Index (HDI)

A common failing in our strange science is the implicit notion that for something to be truly definable it must be measurable. While this is not quite true, it is often helpful to have a set of objective standards which can be applied to different phenomena in order to compare them. The Human Development Index is an attempt to create a way to rank countries according to their degree of development using three different easily measurable variables and then composing the results in a single value. It is published annually in the Human Development Report from the United Nations Development Programme (UNDP). The variables used are:

1. *Life expectancy* at birth
2. *Adult literacy* together with enrolment in education
3. *GDP per capita* adjusted for purchasing power. These variables are put together in a **composite index** where 1.00 is the highest attainable value. This is the ranking used in Table 3.2.4.

A selection of HDI values

The three measurements have not been chosen arbitrarily. Life expectancy will be highly correlated to health care, freedom from warfare/armed strife, availability of food and shelter, and so on. Literacy and enrolment in school is strongly linked to a country's ability to produce goods and services and to its level of democracy – both of which in turn means higher income and more equal distribution of income. GDP per capita is an indicator of the country's general standard of living. One could say that the variables have been chosen in order to provide at least a rough estimate of the ability of citizens to lead long, healthy, and productive lives.

Table 3.2.4 *A selection of countries' ratings in the HDI, 2006 (HDI rank, country, HDI value)*

HDI Ranking	Country	HDI value
1	Norway	0.942
2	Sweden	0.941
3	Canada	0.940
4	Belgium	0.939
5	Australia	0.939
80	Ukraine	0.748
81	Georgia	0.748
82	Peru	0.747
83	Grenada	0.747
84	Maldives	0.743
169	Burkina Faso	0.325
170	Mozambique	0.322
171	Burundi	0.313
172	Niger	0.277
173	Sierra Leone	0.275

(Source: Human Development Report 2007/8, UNDP, at http://hdr.undp.org/reports)

The values in Table 3.2.4 can be interpreted as showing the level of possible development attained by a country. Thus, 0.968 in Norway means that the Norwegians are 3.2% short of maximum potential human development while Burundi has achieved 38.2% of its potential. Take care in interpreting the figures literally. The values are in fact far more useful for measuring countries' development levels relative to one another. It is also wise to regard the HDI values more as *indicators* of political/economic/social strength rather than as values in a gauge. In the words of the UNDP in 1995:

> It is not a measure of wellbeing. Nor is it a measure of happiness. Instead, it is a measure of empowerment.

Weaknesses of the HDI

As in all constructs of this type, there are a number of weaknesses built-in to the HDI. Many of the figures used are notoriously unreliable due to inadequate statistical material. For example, many births and deaths take place outside hospitals in many LDCs and do not become part of official statistics. Enrolment in school does not necessarily mean that the child is actually in school full days or even at all – far too many families are dependent on sons and daughters working the family land. Finally, GDP per capita is perhaps one of the easiest variables to criticise. Many countries have flourishing parallel markets where goods and services are traded rather than purchased with money, or where goods are purchased without the troublesome burden of notifying the tax authorities. This means that there is a goodly portion of unaccounted-for output – which means that GDP figures will in reality be higher than the official figures. Other countries, notably the previous centrally planned (communist) economies of Eastern Europe and the Soviet Union, had intentionally inflated output values for political reasons – to such an extent that many research institutions in the west would largely disregard official figures and do their own calculations.

The Human Development Report 2002 (published every year by the United Nations Development Programme) states that:

> *Politics matter for human development. Reducing poverty depends as much on whether poor people have political power as on their opportunities for economic progress. Democracy has proven to be the system of governance most capable of mediating and preventing conflict and of securing and sustaining wellbeing. By expanding people's choices about how and by whom they are governed, democracy brings principles of participation and accountability to the process of human development.[13]*

Other composite indices

While the Human Development Index is the most widely used index of development, the UN uses additional development indices as complements. The **Human Poverty Index** measures the percentage of a population which does not meet specific (target) levels of economic and living standard indicators. The index's target values are the percentage of people not expected to reach the age of 40; percentage of illiterate adults, and people who fail to attain decent living standards as measured by the percentage of underweight children and percentage of people not having access to safe water and health service.

Taking into account the fact that most societies still have a heavy social bias in favour of half the population means that the indices above need to be adjusted in some way for gender. The **Gender-related development index** (GDI) attempts to adjust for gender inequality by lowering the HDI values in accordance with how unequal the society is in terms of gender. The **Gender Empowerment Measure** (GEM) is an additional measure which shows the ability and extent to which women take part in social and political life. It highlights how inequalities arise in terms of the opportunities for women in selected areas.

I often try to get my people to come up with their own welfare indicators – my request being that any variables used must be most specific, measurable and of course ultimately relevant in terms of development. Some of the more interesting suggestions I have received are: crime levels on a per capita basis and the percentage of population in prison; percentage of income spent on amusements such as movies, eating out and holidays; percentage of citizens in low income/education brackets holding public office; and finally, a rather scary measure, namely the number of labour hours lost due to workers attending funerals.[14] I leave it to you to discuss how/why these variables would be linked to development – and also to point out the inherent (= built-in) weaknesses in them.

Problems of measuring development ©IBO 2003

As can be seen throughout this section, development is far from a universally agreed-upon measurement and can have a number of broad meanings in different contexts. Perhaps the only point of agreement amongst economists is that no single measure will suffice to

13. *Human Development Report* 2002, p.1.
14. This was put forward by a South African student. Do a panda (= look it up) and figure out why.

either define or measure development. Instead, one often outlines a set of criteria in order to arrive at some agreed-upon common ground – giving a semblance of objectivism in the use of measurements of development. However, it should be noted that simply by using the term 'development' we are in fact leaning heavily on a value judgement, i.e. that development is something to strive toward ('good') while lack of development is to be avoided ('bad'). In reality things are not always that simple as many people in 'newly developed' areas would tell you. As my friend Anna Collins-Falk points out – after spending almost 20 years working for development projects in Africa and Southeast Asia – it is not always that someone (e.g. development organisations) actually *asks* the local people what they want …

In any case, the task of measuring development will come up against many obstacles. We have covered most of the measurement problems already, both in this section and in Section 3.1. This section concludes with a compilation of the main problems in measuring development, most of which can be put within two headings: **definitional** problems and **accounting/ measurability** problems.

Definitional problems

This section concludes with a compilation of the main problems in measuring development, most of which can be put within two headings: **definitional** problems and **accounting/measurability** problems.

- **Growth** is not development, as shown in some depth earlier. Simply focusing on economic development disregards any number of social indicators which are increasingly regarded as essential in measuring the overall wellbeing of citizens. Social indicators such as longevity, literacy and democracy attempt to adjust for this problem, yet there is as yet no agreed-upon all-encompassing definition of development. The definitional problems in outlining development give us perhaps the greatest measurement difficulties, since it becomes so hard to pin down quantitative variables in what is evidently a qualitative area of study.

- Another tricky definitional issue is the concept of **poverty**. Unsurprisingly enough, poverty is directly correlated to average income and income distribution in an economy; the lower the average income and/or the more uneven the distribution, the higher the poverty levels. Poverty is highly

normative and no form of international comparison really works.

- *Relative poverty* is the result of uneven income distribution, where the lowest income earners are compared to other groups. This definition is of course highly normative and will vary greatly between different countries, depending on income levels and also upon how 'poverty' is defined. 'Relative' in its definitional context of poverty means that the poverty bar will be set according to domestic norms. Thus, a poor person in Iceland – shown in recurring surveys to have the highest perceived quality of life in the world – would have a king's ransom as a monthly income according to a squatter on the outskirts of Mexico City. This makes it essentially impossible – and pointless – to compare different countries in terms of poverty levels.

- The alternative is to use a definition of *absolute poverty*, which is commonly defined as a level of income or consumption falling below the minimum level required to meet basic needs, creating a 'poverty line' allowing between-country comparison. In an attempt to at least have some standardized bar of poverty whereby different countries could be compared more objectively using a common unit, the World Bank has set *international poverty lines* at $US1 and $US2 per day in purchasing power parity terms. Using the more common 'one $US a day' as a lower limit, the World Bank estimates that 1.2 billion people (23% of the population in LDCs) in the world could be defined as living in absolute poverty in 1999.[15] Setting the bar at $US2 the number increases to 2.8 billion people. The problem in using this absolute measure is that what is considered 'minimum level required' will vary over time and in different societies, so even the absolute poverty line will change – something the World Bank carefully points out.[16]

- Finally, the field of development is rife (= common) with a number of additional key concepts which are either very broadly used and/or subject to the same **normative limitations** as above. Using terms such as 'equitable' or 'inequitable' distribution of income/ resources clearly means that one has drawn a normative line somewhere. Just imagine two societies: Society A consists of 1 million people where 980,000 people are well off and 20,000 are

---

15. http://www.worldbank.org/poverty/mission/up2.htm.
16. IBID (See also the full text of the 2001 WDR on Poverty at http://www.worldbank.org/poverty/wdrpoverty/report/index.htm.

living in poverty and Society B of 2 million people where 30,000 live in poverty. Which society is 'best' in terms of income distribution? Well, if you use 'amount of poor people' then A is preferable. If you use 'percentage living in poverty' then B is likely to be preferable. Now, assume a third society, C, consisting of 30,000 people where 29,999 lived in poverty. Using 'amount of poor people' to define 'best' would point to Society C being preferable to both A and B. Of course my example is hideously exaggerated, but the point is that positive economics runs into some severe obstacles in development.

Accounting and measurability problems

Poor statistics of lagging and unreliable quality, black markets, parallel markets, unaccounted-for income, (barter and subsistence level agriculture), etc. mean that averages do not show distribution and exchange rates do not show PPP.

- Poor **statistical reliability** and quality. Many countries do not have the wherewithal to compile accurate statistics on growth and development, and the time involved in collecting data and processing it will cause lags in data series. This is immediately evident when looking through official statistics for a number of countries and the problem is frequently noted by institutions such as the UNDP and the World Bank.

- Accounting for income as an element in overall development gives a number of **weaknesses of GDP/GNP figures** as observed earlier in this section; black markets, barter economies and non-market activity such as subsistence farming are not shown and will skew (= slant) any national income figures.

- In accounting for and using indicators of development there are a number of **negative side effects** which are difficult to factor-in to the wider

development picture. Negative externalities such as pollution are difficult to measure as are environmental impacts such as deforestation. (See Section 5.2).

- Many **other indicators** of societal wellbeing are conspicuously absent. For example, personal safety issues such as robbery, assault and other crime are not included in any of the most commonly used development indices.[17] None of the measurements used above show, for example, how many people are allowed to vote freely in elections; availability of culture and free time; level of corruption necessary in dealing with government officials; freedom of education, movement and choice for women; access to information and free media; lack of crime …

It suddenly strikes me how daunting (= scary) the above list of problems in measuring/assessing development looks. I assure you this was not my intention and I urge you not to stare yourself blind at it but rather put effort into constructing your own reasonably solid definition of development – and then outline variables that are strongly indicative of the concept. As long as you use and have a solid grasp of a number of key development indicators, such as might be found in the HDI, you will be able to use the concept of development with relative comfort.

POP QUIZ 3.2.1   GROWTH AND DEVELOPMENT

1 Why might GDP per capita not be a particularly good measure of the standard of living in a country?

2 Outline the difficulties in defining and measuring development.

3 Why do economists favour the use of composite indices when measuring development?

4 Finally, suggest alternative components one might put into a composite index, such as the HDI, in order to show relative development levels in countries.

---

17. At the risk of getting targeted for 'sanction with extreme prejudice' by the Mexican Tourism Board, I must tell the following enlightening story. Like all private schools in Latin America, I have several students in my class from rather wealthy families. One day a very good student stayed behind class here at my school in Mexico and since the IA deadline was that lesson I simply waited for the 'my computer ate my homework' excuse. 'Em, Matt, I need an extension …' I replied, truthfully, that I simply don't do extensions. Tears welled up in the student's eyes. 'I know … but my sister has just been kidnapped …' The deadline was extended. (The sister is safe!)

Macroeconomic models

3.3

CONTENTS

MACROECONOMIC MODELS ©IBO 2003

It's the economy stupid!
– Campaign slogan for Bill Clinton dreamt up by his advisor James Carville

In our circular flow model, national income was viewed as a flow through the system measured in three different ways: output, income and expenditure. Our basic model is the AS-AD model, meaning aggregate supply and aggregate demand. 'Aggregate' means total or combined and refers to all goods and services produced and purchased in an economy. In the aggregate supply and demand model we focus on **expenditure** and **output** flows to describe changes in national **income** – measured as GDP. Additionally, the model is used to analyse and illustrate other key elements in the macro environment:

- Changes in economic activity – the business cycle – and effects on inflation and unemployment
- The macro effects of government policies aimed at growth, full employment, price stability and external equilibrium (exchange rates and trade balance).

Aggregate demand – components

©IBO 2003

Aggregate demand is the sum of total *planned* expenditure for a given price level by households, firms, government and foreign sector during a period of time. The components of aggregate demand have been covered in Section 3.1 in the expenditure method of GDP accounting:

- Consumption expenditure (*C* in the formula below): households' spending on goods and services
- Investment expenditure (*I*): firms' expenditure on capital goods such as machines and factories – this is an addition to the capital stock of the economy (do *not* confuse investment with 'buying shares' – this is in fact a form of saving)

  - *Gross* investment is when firms increase spending on capital goods due to an increase in demand for their goods
  - *Net* investment occurs when firms replace worn out capital (also known as replacement investment)

- Government spending (*G*): government spending goes to health care, defence, roads, etc. It is assumed to be unlinked ('exogenous' in econ-speak) to the

price level, e.g. determined by political decisions at local, regional and national level. (Transfer payments such as unemployment benefits and student grants are *not* included in government spending.)

- Export revenue (*X*): spending on domestic goods by foreign firms, households and governments
- Import expenditure (*-M*): expenditure on foreign goods by domestic firms, households and firms (note that this component must be deducted since foreign goods and services are not part of GDP)

Aggregate demand is the sum of expenditure components, which gives us:

$$AD = C + I + G + X - M$$

It is worthwhile noting at this early stage the italicized 'planned'. In the previous circular flow model all expenditure was de facto (= actual, realised) GDP, since all output also represented expenditure and income – it would be impossible for expenditure to exceed output. In the aggregate demand/supply model we attempt to show a more dynamic and realistic view of the macroeconomic world by showing what happens when planned expenditure increases at a different pace than de facto output, e.g. inflation is brought into the picture.

The aggregate demand in an economy is dependent on a great many influences, which is to say that the individual components of aggregate demand are influenced by a great array of underlying variables. And similar to the previous case of (simple) supply and demand, a model is built to show the relationship between price and quantity but since we are dealing with all goods and all prices we have to expand the model a bit.

Similarities to simple demand

Let us point out a few basic similarities to the simple demand curve in order for you to have something to hook your learning curve on to – all the while keeping in mind that aggregate supply and demand models are far more complex since we are dealing with all goods and services rather than a single good.

1. The aggregate demand curve is downward-sloping, which shows *negative correlation* between the price

level (measured by the GDP deflator) and real output (measured by real GDP). This is quite similar to the simple supply and demand model. However, note that it is impossible to use 'quantity' on the *x*-axis when dealing with the aggregate since there is a slight difference between paper clips, nuclear submarines and deep-sea oil rigs. To overcome this, we use the inflation-adjusted *monetary* value of aggregate output, e.g. *real* GDP.

2. The pattern of correlation shows that a fall in the average price level (GDP deflator) will lead to a movement along the aggregate demand curve, i.e. an increase in real GDP at a given price level. Didn't we just forget something?

3. Yes, that all other influences on aggregate demand are assumed to be held constant, i.e. **ceteris paribus**. Once again our model is based on the concept that the pattern of correlation will hold true only if all other variables are left unchanged. (See *Shifting the aggregate demand curve* following.)

The aggregate demand curve

Figure 3.3.1 shows the relationship between aggregate demand (AD) and the average price level. The AD curve shows the connection between the price level and real GDP. The GDP deflator puts the price level into constant (real) prices (here, 1995) and the four points, *A*, *B*, *C* and *D*, show how the quantity demanded of real GDP increases as the price level falls. If we were still dealing with simple demand, say video films or bicycles, we would explain this by saying that there is an *income effect* (lower prices mean that people have more spending power) and a *substitution effect* (people change consumption habits and switch to other goods). Both of these effects are in fact present in the downward slope of the aggregate demand curve but there is a greater level of complexity when dealing with the aggregate.

The AD curve in Figure 3.3.1 shows the relationship between the price level (measured by the GDP deflator) and real GDP (constant values). The AD curve is downward sloping for three reasons:

1. **Real income effect**: when the price level falls, real income rises.

2. **Real balance effect**: a fall in the price level means that the opportunity cost of saving increases, so households and firms lower saving levels and increase expenditure.

3. **International substitution effect**: lower prices – *ceteris paribus* – will increase exports and decrease imports.

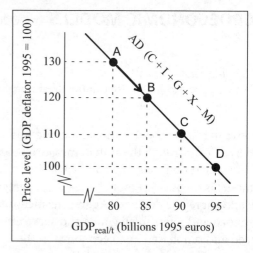

Figure 3.3.1 *Basic aggregate demand model*

Why the aggregate demand curve slopes downward

It is most important to keep in mind that in drawing the curve we are assuming *ceteris paribus*, so only the price level changes. Other macro variables such as interest rates, income for trade partners, domestic incomes, inflation, etc. *remain the same*. The income and substitution effects from the simple demand model are discernable in the three main reasons for a downward sloping aggregate demand curve:

1. **Real income effect:** A fall in the general price level means that real income has increased, assuming, as we are, that all else remains the same. In this case, we are assuming that the amount of money flowing around the system – the nominal quantity of money has not changed and neither have wages – therefore people will increase their planned expenditure and quantity demanded of real GDP will rise. Referring to Figure 3.3.1, if the price level goes from 130 to 120, the quantity demanded of real output will increase from 80 billion to 85 billion. This would move us along the aggregate demand curve from point **A** to point **B**.

The aggregate demand/supply model is based on real output which means that GDP is based on *real* values of money in terms of purchasing power. A fall in the price level means that the purchasing power of any given quantity of money increases, resulting in a de facto increase in real incomes. We are in essence positing that the larger the amount of real money in the economy, the higher the quantity of goods and services – real GDP – will be demanded.

In economic short-hand:

$$\Delta\downarrow\text{price level} \rightarrow \Delta\uparrow Y_{real} \rightarrow \Delta\uparrow C \rightarrow \Delta\uparrow Q_{AD}$$

2. **Real balance effect**: Another way of looking at the downward slope of aggregate demand is that both households and firms try to strike a *balance* between planned *present* and *future* investment/consumption. Future investment/consumption are to a large extent the savings of the present. When households and firms save they are in fact putting off present expenditure to the future. The balance between present expenditure and future expenditure is disrupted when the price level changes, since lower price levels mean that firms' and households' savings are worth more in *real* terms. (This is analogous (= similar) to the real income effect above.)

A fall in the price level means that firms and households can save less but still retain a satisfactory level of future consumption/investment. With less being saved, consumption and investment expenditure rises, leading to a movement from A to B in Figure 3.3.1 on page 282. This is an example of the **inter-temporal substitution effect**. Again, don't be alarmed by the term 'inter-temporal'. It simply means between ('inter') times ('temporal') and deals with how households and firms might substitute planned future consumption/investment by bringing some of it to the present. Since the opportunity cost of decreasing present saving has gone down – due to the fall in the price level and the increase in real savings – firms and households will be able to increase consumption and investment sooner rather than later.

In economic shorthand:

$\Delta\downarrow$price level $\rightarrow \Delta\uparrow$value real savings
$\rightarrow \Delta\uparrow$potential *future* C & I
$\rightarrow \Delta\downarrow$opportunity cost of *present* C & I
$\rightarrow \Delta\uparrow$C & I $\rightarrow \Delta\uparrow Q_{AD}$

3. **International substitution effect**: Two components of domestic aggregate demand deal with the foreign sector, namely exports and imports. Assume an open economy and that the domestic price level falls *relative* to trade partners'[1]. Domestic firms and households will substitute some of their expenditure on imported goods for domestic goods; import expenditure will decrease. (Since imports are a minus value in aggregate demand, lower import expenditure will increase aggregate demand.) Conversely, a lower price level – assuming *ceteris paribus*, i.e. the exchange rate and

price level in trading countries remains the same – will lead to increased quantity demanded from our export sector. This means that **net exports** (X – M) increase, leading to an increase in quantity demanded of real output – a movement from **A** to **B** in Figure 3.3.1.

In economic shorthand:

$\Delta\downarrow$domestic price level $\rightarrow \Delta\uparrow$*relative* $P_M \rightarrow \Delta\downarrow M$
$\rightarrow \Delta\uparrow Q_{AD}$

and

$\Delta\downarrow$domestic price level $\rightarrow \Delta\downarrow$*relative* $P_X \rightarrow \Delta\uparrow X \rightarrow$
$\Delta\uparrow Q_{AD}$

Warning!
Macroeconomic models: Confusing a change in price level with a change in interest rates

A strong influence in aggregate demand is the rate of interest, i.e. the 'price' one pays for borrowing money – alternatively, the 'return' one receives for keeping money in the bank. The *interest rate is positively linked to the price level*, i.e. when the price level goes up, so do interest rates. This is because lenders (creditors, e.g. banks) will want to retain the real rate of interest being paid to them by debtors (= borrowers, e.g. firms and households), and higher inflation means that banks will have to raise the interest demanded from households and firms in order for future incoming interest flows to the bank to have at least the same value in *real* money terms as when the loan was taken. Another reason is that when the price level rises, firms and households will have to increase their borrowing (= demand for loans increases) in order to retain consumption and investment levels – the interest rises (= price of loans) rises. So:

$$\Delta\uparrow \text{price level} \rightarrow \uparrow r \text{ (interest)}$$

and conversely,

$$\Delta\downarrow \text{price level} \rightarrow \Delta\downarrow r$$

Assume now the economy is at point A on the aggregate demand curve in Figure 3.3.1 on page 282 and that the price level falls. This will lead to a *fall in interest rates*, as explained above.

The lower the interest rate, the lower the opportunity cost of consumption and investment since households and firms forgo less interest on their

---

1. Inserting 'relative' here is rather important. If trade partners' average prices increase by 5% and domestic prices increase by 3% then domestic prices have fallen *relative* to trade partners'.

savings. Households and firms will now be inclined to increase their expenditure. Another way of looking at this is that since the interest rate has fallen, expenditure on items funded by credit – firms' expenditure on capital and households' purchases of durable goods such as cars and furniture – will increase. There is a movement along the aggregate demand curve from point A to point B. We get:

$$\Delta\downarrow \text{price level} \rightarrow \Delta\downarrow r \rightarrow \Delta\downarrow S \rightarrow \Delta\uparrow C \,\&\, I \rightarrow \Delta\uparrow Q_{AD}$$

Now, here's the warning! In the example given, it is the *price level that has changed*, which, in turn, affected interest rates and thus consumption and investment. This is an increase in quantity demanded of real GDP, i.e. a *movement along* the aggregate demand curve. However, as shall be seen in Section 3.4, an increase or decrease in interest rates will cause, respectively, a decrease or increase in aggregate demand – that is to say, a *shift in the aggregate demand curve*. Whether there is a movement along or shift in aggregate demand depends on which variable has initially changed in the economy. A change in the price level – *ceteris paribus* – leads to an increase in quantity demanded of real GDP. If interest rates change for any other reason, say that the central bank lowers the rates, there will be a shift in the aggregate demand curve.

In summary:

- Δ**price level** $\rightarrow \Delta r \rightarrow \Delta C \,\&\, I \rightarrow \Delta Q_{AD}$
  = *movement along* AD curve
- Δ**r** $\rightarrow \Delta C \,\&\, I \rightarrow \Delta AD$ = *shift of* AD curve

---

Finally, a few words on government spending. Have you noticed how government expenditure (G) has been noticeably lacking in this initial 'movement along' phase? That is because we are basing the pattern of aggregate demand on the premise that government expenditure is an **exogenous** (= originating outside, as in the **exo**skeleton of insects) **variable** in the model. Government spending is basically a *political* decision, and therefore considered to lie outside the influence of the price level. And while government expenditure is most definitely part of aggregate demand, we assume in the model that it is uncorrelated to the price level.

1   Explain how the variables interest, inflation and consumption are inter-linked.

2   Which component of aggregate demand is assumed to be independent of the price level? Explain why.

3   Why is it possible for a change in interest rates to be linked to both a movement along and shift of the aggregate demand curve?

4   How does the international substitution effect help create a downward sloping AD curve?

Aggregate supply ©IBO 2003

The aggregate supply curve shows the ability and propensity of firms to put goods on the market, or the relationship between the price level and real output. In the short run, the higher the price level, the more goods firms will be able and willing to supply – the short-run aggregate supply curve will thus show positive correlation between the price level and real national income. In the long run, it is not as simple, since there is great deal of controversy in the theoretical divide between two broad schools of thought.

Short-run supply ©IBO 2003

Production takes place because suppliers anticipate revenue and profit from coming sales. Costs, on the other hand, rise simultaneously with suppliers' increase in output. Suppliers run a risk of not receiving revenue enough to match costs, since they cannot predict future prices. Therefore, should real profits exceed expected profits suppliers will have an incentive to increase output, which strongly suggests an upward sloping aggregate supply curve. Assuming that the prices of all factors of production (e.g. wage rates, raw material prices, price of capital, etc.) remain constant, then suppliers will indeed increase output when the price level rises.

This is portrayed in Figure 3.3.2 on page 285 as the upward-sloping portion of the *short-run aggregate supply* (SRAS) curve. The aggregate supply of an economy in the short run is based on the notion of fixed factor prices and availability, e.g. the constraints are similar to those used in Section 2.1, that is to say, that all else remains constant – the *ceteris paribus* assumption.

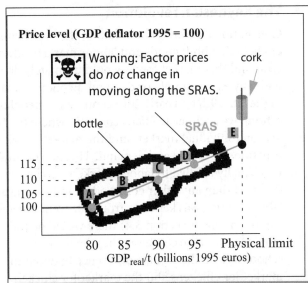

- Higher market prices will induce suppliers to increase output. The AS curve is drawn under the assumption that prices of **factor inputs do not change** in the short run, so a higher price level means larger profit margins for firms. Thus the price level and output are positively correlated.

- The upward slope of AS also shows how firms experience **diminishing returns** (as existing fixed factors are ever increasingly utilised) and **increasing scarcity** of variable factors. Both serve to create **bottlenecks** in production (shown by the shadowed bottle in the figure).

- When it becomes impossible to increase output in the short run, the **physical limit** of the economy's capacity is reached and real GDP is no longer correlated to the price level. An increase in the price level simply means a general rise in prices without any increase in output (shown by the corked portion of the SRAS curve).

Higher Level: What holds true for a single firm will in this particular case hold true for the aggregate, namely that increased output will result in higher **marginal costs** – the sum of MC curves for individual firms will give us the SRAS curve for the economy as a whole. This helps explain the relatively high elasticity of aggregate supply in the short run.

Figure 3.3.2 *Short-run aggregate supply (SRAS)*

Let's look at the three sections of the SRAS curve in Figure 3.3.2 in turn:

- **Horizontal section**: The horizontal portion of the short-run aggregate supply curve shows output when the economy is in severe recession, or *depression*. Output can increase without an increase in price, i.e. short-run aggregate supply is horizontal and therefore uncorrelated to the price level. Firms can increase production regardless of the price level since there is:

  ■ High unemployment and thus abundant labour and inability to bid up wages – no cost pressure on firms due to increasing wages

  ■ Excess capacity in firms, which enables them to increase output without incurring higher (marginal) costs

  ■ Low demand in the economy which makes firms unwilling/unable to raise their prices

- **Upward sloping section**: At an output beyond 80 billion (point **A** and beyond on the short-run aggregate supply curve) firms will increase output in accordance with a rise in final prices (= market prices) but will start to encounter *diminishing returns* and *supply constraints*.

  ■ Fixed factors of production such as machines, assembly lines and factory space will not increase during the short run; *diminishing returns* set in.

  ■ Adding to this is the increased *scarcity of factors* as

output increases in the short run, leading to *bottlenecks* – supply constraints – in production; increased scarcity of skilled labour, transportation, delivery and availability of raw materials will all serve to limit firms' ability to put more goods on the market. (Remember, factor prices do not change, so increasing production costs are the result of overtime, increasing maintenance costs of machines, search costs for ever scarcer raw materials, etc.)

  ■ As firms' costs increase there must be an incentive of higher (final) prices for firms to be willing and able to increase output. Points **A** through **E** show the positive correlation between the price level and real GDP.

(The bottle in the diagram is my incredibly childish way of showing that the upward slope is due to bottlenecks in supply and *not* higher factor prices.)

- **Vertical section**: The vertical portion of the short-run aggregate supply curve (beyond **E**) illustrates how the economy ultimately hits the output capacity ceiling. This is the *physical limit* of firms' short-run output capacity. Up to **point E** the economy is able to increase output by paying workers overtime, hiring ever more labour and pushing capital to the limit. At some point (here **E** in the diagram) workers will be reluctant to work overtime, additional labour will be unavailable, and firms will be unwilling to drive machines into the ground without major overhauls (= repairs and maintenance). The inducement of higher final prices will not increase output in firms no matter what the profit margins are, so the short-run aggregate supply curve becomes vertical – or completely inelastic.

(The cork is a silly illustration showing that no more 'flow', e.g. output, is possible at any point beyond E.)

A final technical note: I have drawn the shape of the short-run aggregate supply curve (SRAS) in Figure 3.3.2 on page 285 partially to show the historical link to Keynesian theory (see below) and partially to illustrate the issue of how an economy will show increasing difficulties in increasing output due to supply bottlenecks. In the continuation, I will confine the range of the short-run aggregate supply curve to the upward-sloping section, e.g. points **A** to **E**. It is within the span of the upward-sloping section that all short-run analysis will take place and the horizontal and vertical sections add little in terms of analytical value. This is also in keeping with what has become standard mainstream usage of short-run aggregate supply curves.

Long-run supply (Keynesian versus neoclassical approach) ©IBO 2003

I live on an Aztec lookout hill here in Mexico City at 2,300 metres above sea level – and the shore line is some 400 kilometres away. If one were to take all the books written about John Maynard Keynes and dump them into the sea, I'd have beachfront property and Al Gore would be howling, 'I told you so!' However, books on Keynes are of high marginal social benefit, so book-dumping would be a major loss.[2] In any case, *macroeconomics* – as a specific field of economics – was basically invented by Keynes (see "Celebrity bubble: John Maynard Keynes (1883–1946)" on page 290) during the 1920s and 1930s. In order to understand the 'competing' schools of thought on the subject of demand-side or supply-side, it is necessary to briefly look at the historical background of macroeconomics and trace the strong theoretical and ideological differences which come to a point in the dispute over the shape of the long-run aggregate supply curve.

The Keynesian revolution

Conventional economic wisdom in the pre-Keynesian era held that both goods and labour markets ultimately clear and that market forces would ultimately do away with any excess supply or demand. Economic analysis in the late 19th and early 20th century, the **neoclassical school**, was primarily *microeconomic*, where the focus was on individual markets and the market clearing functions of supply and demand. This line of thinking was equally applied to labour markets; labour was no different than any other commodity and as long as the labour market was kept free from interventionist forces (more on this in Section 3.4) there would be full employment. One could say that the neoclassical school sees no discernible difference between the market for chickens and the market for chicken pluckers. In other words, the labour market would always tend towards equilibrium in the long run.

The Great Depression of the 1930s and prolonged mass unemployment was viewed by neoclassical theory as the result of market interventionist and anti-competitive forces such as trade unions which kept wages above market clearing levels. As long as wage rates responded to market forces and were flexible the labour force would adapt to wage changes. According to the predominant view, unemployment was 'voluntary' to the extent that labourers were not willing to accept jobs at the going wage rate. See Section 3.5 for a full explanation of voluntary/involuntary unemployment and 'downward stickiness'.

This view came under scrutiny and subsequent challenge during the 1930s, especially when unemployment rates hit hitherto unseen levels – over 15% in Great Britain and 25% in the US – in the early 1930s and remained high. Two simultaneous – and largely unrelated – schools of thought developed; one in Sweden and one in England. The Swedish School, later known as the 'Stockholm School' evolved primarily from the work of Gunnar Myrdal and Bertil Ohlin (later a Nobel laureate) while in England it was Keynes who was the prime instigator.[3] The basic position taken in this new line of theory was that the drawn-out depression where high unemployment and stagnant (or falling) output levels existed for such long periods could neither be explained nor solved by the predominant theory of the day.

---

2. Don't worry, I'm waiting for global warming and melting ice caps to take care of things nicely.

3. *Makroekonomi – teori, politik och institutioner*, Klas Fregert & Lars Jonung, Studentlitteratur 2003, pp. 105–120 (The authors point out that the Swedes' very similar theory predated Keynes by a few years and posit that had Myrdal, Ohlin and others not written in Swedish we could very well have been talking about Stockholmian theory rather than Keynesian theory today.)

Keynes addressed the issue squarely in his 1936 magnum opus, *The General Theory of Employment, Interest and Money*, which did for economics what Newton's *Principia Mathematica* did for physics – with pretty much the same amount of formulae. With customary elegance laced with not so small a touch of snide disdain, he wondered why the neoclassical economists 'were apparently unmoved by the lack of correspondence between the results of their theory and the facts of observation'.[4] Quite evidently, it was pointed out, the labour markets had not cleared and that in fact it was highly doubtful that this could be accomplished by lowering wages. In fact, the contrary was more likely: lower wages would worsen the situation by lowering demand and creating additional unemployment. The solution was instead to *increase incomes* and *create demand*. Keynes was basically proposing that 'market stability' under a 'laissez faire' economic system was a contradiction in terms and the solution was for governments to intervene. Since the labour market evidently was unable to do away with massive 'excess labour' and create **full employment**, it was left to government to take an active and even pro-active part in creating jobs. While we today don't find anything at all unusual about this proposition, this no doubt sounded like trying to put out a fire with gasoline to the policy makers of the time.

Keynesian critique of neoclassical thinking

'The real difficulty in changing any enterprise lies not in developing new ideas, but in escaping from the old ones.' The origins of Keynesian theory are squarely rooted in the seeming failures of depression era economic thinking which did not seem to be able to deal with stagnant growth and high unemployment. Here are the main points of Keynes's criticism of the neoclassical view:

- Markets are inherently (= essentially) unstable and do not necessarily clear. It is quite possible for labour markets to render high levels of unemployment even in the long run. Keynes harshly criticised neoclassical thinking for **fallacy of composition**; simply because individual markets might clear does not mean that this holds true for the aggregate. Lowering wages might well increase the demand for – and amount of – labourers in one industry but not in *all* industries.

- Wages are '**downward sticky**', i.e. labourers/unions are most unwilling to accept cuts in wage rates. This

adds to labour market disequilibrium by keeping wages above market clearing level. Real wages simply do not fall enough to completely clear the market and restore full employment. (Revise 'minimum price' in Section 2.1.)

- Since **labour markets are imperfect**, non-interventionist policies do not help unemployment and in fact may serve to keep unemployment rates high over long periods of time.

The strength in Keynes's work lay in his predisposition for hands-on applicability. While his work was heavily based in mathematics – he was, in fact, a mathematician by education – he was clearly focused on practical solutions. The logical conclusion to the criticism of prevailing neoclassical thought was that there is merit in **government intervention** to help create market equilibrium. Fiscal policies such as increased government spending can help achieve full employment by increasing aggregate demand. According to traditional Keynesian theory, disequilibrium on the labour market is primarily due to lack of demand for labour – this is *demand deficient unemployment* – and can be remedied by increasing aggregate demand and therefore increasing the demand for labour. (Remember 'derived demand'?!) While 'pre-Keynesian' thought accepted Say's Law of 'supply creating its own demand'[5], meaning that there could never be a permanent glut in supply (and thus deficiency in demand), Keynes vehemently disagreed and one might well imagine him reversing the order – 'demand creates its own supply'.

The Keynesian aggregate supply curve – 'In the long run we are dead'

I bet the caption caught your eye. You will understand it in a moment. Figure 3.3.3 on page 288 shows the Keynesian aggregate supply curves which ranges from a horizontal portion, a 'trade-off' portion, to a vertical portion. (Note that the *y*-axis reads 'Price level' rather than 'GDP deflator', which will be the case in all diagrams when referring to 'P_0, P_1' rather than actual index values.)

The 'traditional Keynesian' aggregate supply curve, AS, shows three possible ranges of output:

- **Horizontal portion**: The depression range of mass unemployment (up to Y_0) follows the course of the previous aggregate supply curve, where output increases without an increase in the price level. The

4.   'The General Theory of Employment, Interest and Money', p. 33, from *Collected Writings of John Maynard Keynes, Vol. 7 - The General Theory, 1973,* edited by Donald Moggridge, London: Macmillan for the Royal Economic Society
5.   Jean-Baptiste Say, famous French *laissez faire* advocate and neoclassical economist, (1776–1832)

horizontal portion of the 'inverted-L' shaped curve shows that income can increase to Y_0 without a rise in the price level. This is based on:

- Keynes's premise of *downward stickiness of labour*. Since labourers/unions are unwilling to accept lower wages (this is the 'downward stickiness of labour prices' part[6]) during a period of demand deficiency and resulting unemployment, a situation of high unemployment may persist in the long run.

- Due to the *abundance* – excess supply – *of labour* and other factors at low income levels, labourers will be highly reluctant to bid up wages even as output increases. Imagine that output increases from any output level up to Y_1 with the ensuing increase in demand for labour. Both newly hired and existing workers would not be in a position to bid up wages since there are thousands waiting in line for their jobs. Thus it is possible to increase output without creating upward pressure on wages and final prices, resulting in a horizontal aggregate supply curve.

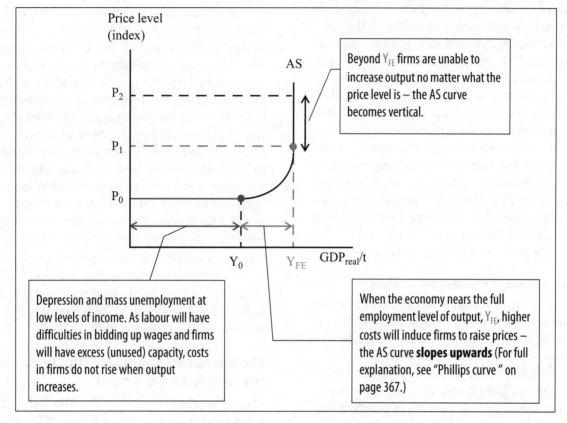

Figure 3.3.3 *Keynesian aggregate supply*

- **Trade-off portion**: At Y_0 the economy is moving closer to the full employment level of output and firms are responding to higher final prices for their goods and services. This middle range portrays the correlation between a higher price level and increasing real output (explained earlier) leading the aggregate supply curve to be upward-sloping. This range, Y_0 to Y_{FE}, illustrates two important points.

  - The first is that aggregate supply will increase only when firms are able to enjoy higher final prices for their output and thus cover additional costs arising from bottlenecks in supply.

- This portion highlights one of the most important policy debates in economics; the apparent *trade-off between unemployment and inflation*. Recall that one of the key conclusions of Keynesian theory is that markets are imperfect and thus government intervention is necessary in order to create labour market clearing and thus full employment. The middle-range of the aggregate supply curve indicates that governments will face a macroeconomic opportunity cost issue.

---

6. I often explain 'downward sticky' by referring to good and bad wines. It's easy to get used to good wines – and most difficult to move back down on the quality list once one is used to the good stuff.

Increased government spending (which stimulates AD) might result in lower unemployment at the cost of a higher price level, i.e. inflation. This trade-off between inflation and unemployment is a central subject of Section 3.5, the Phillips curve.

- **Vertical portion**: The vertical range of AS at Y_{FE} and beyond is the same as the physical limit illustrated earlier (see Figure 3.3.3 on page 288) where firms simply cannot increase output whatever the incentives of final prices. The complete price inelasticity of supply beyond point Y_{FE} illustrates the effect of evermore scarce factors of production and thus increasing output constraints. This is the *full employment level of output*, Y_{FE}. Firms will not be able to hire additional labour and no increase in output is possible as the aggregate supply curve is vertical. Any increase in aggregate demand will be purely inflationary.

SR and LR

We finish where we began, where we all die. Have you noticed an inconsistency between the current syllabus heading and the curves in Figure 3.3.3 on page 288 "Keynesian aggregate supply"? Ponder before you read on. Did you see it? The heading reads '*long-run aggregate supply*' but the curve in the diagram is labelled 'aggregate supply'. This is completely in line with Keynesian reasoning on aggregate output, where it may take years, or even decades for labour markets to clear, during which the economy can remain at an equilibrium below full employment – since there is nothing inherent in the economic system to move the economy out of depression.

The Keynesian prescription of increased government spending during recession/depression to stimulate the economy ('priming the pump' as it was known during Keynes's time) serves to increase output and rectify disequilibrium on the labour market. In taking care of the short run, the long run will take care of itself, so to speak. So, while it might be possible in the *long run* for real wages to fall enough to create full employment without government intervention … in the long run we are all dead.

For the record:

Aggregate supply according to 'Keynesians' and Keynes

There is no end of confusion as to what Keynes actually did or did not say. Much of what is considered to be 'traditional Keynesianism' was in fact the result of followers of Keynes rather than the master's own work. Part of the confusion apparently arises from the fact that Keynes was by training a mathematician rather than an economist, leading him to use mathematical formulae for his illustrations, rather than diagrams (against the express recommendations of his famous teacher, Alfred Marshall, to whom Keynes lovingly referred as 'an absurd old man'). Most of the

diagrammatical work was done by others, primarily the economists (and Nobel laureates) Paul Samuelson and Sir John Hicks. In any case, while Keynesian theory has commonly utilised diagram II in Figure 3.3.4, it is in fact highly likely that Keynes himself accepted the standard neoclassical theory of an upward-sloping aggregate supply curve (diagram III) given his assumption of constant nominal wage rates making it possible for firms to increase output when final prices of goods increase since real wage rates will have effectively fallen.

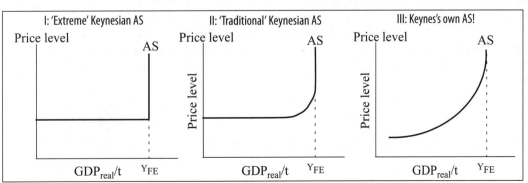

Figure 3.3.4 *Aggregate supply according to Keynesians and Keynes*

CELEBRITY BUBBLE: JOHN MAYNARD KEYNES (1883–1946)

John Maynard Keynes (rhymes with 'rains' and Keynesian rhymes with 'rains-ian' – whatever else you might hear) was in all probability one of the most brilliant and gifted people ever to walk the face of the earth. Luckily, he also became one of the most influential. What else can you say about someone who basically 'slipped' into economics and thereby created a new science? Who, according to legend, made his fortune by reading the morning paper in bed every morning and then placing a call to his stockbroker? Who had a heavy hand in creating several of the most influential international agreements in the post-WWII period? Who ... I give up. It is impossible to fit the gigantic figure of Mr Keynes into a few hundred words. Here are a few basic biographical notes topped off by five books well worth reading.

Victorian in upbringing and Old School to the hilt, Keynes displayed brilliance from the first. At 14 he won a scholarship to Eton and went on to King's College at Cambridge. There he studied mathematics but was begged by the famous Alfred Marshall to become an economist. Instead, he went to India for two years as a civil servant, after passing the civil service examination with the second highest marks – his lowest marks being in economics: 'I evidently knew more about Economy than my examiners.'

Having accomplished little in India other than getting a pedigreed bull sent to Bombay, as he later remarked, he returned to Cambridge where he taught and also ran the prestigious Economic Journal. *He became a part of the group of artists and intellectuals know as the Bloomsbury Group, including Leonard and Virginia Woolf, E. M. Forster, and Lytton Strachey with whom he had one of several homosexual affairs.*

He speculated in shares and bonds, making the considerable fortune of some £500,000 in current values. He ran the Cambridge theatre and managed the restaurant – plotting food receipts against what was currently playing to see which plays could be linked to increased demand for food. He married a famous Russian ballerina, Lydia Lopokov. In between all this he reshaped the world.

He joined the Treasury at the outbreak of WWI and acted as an advisor during the Versailles negotiations at the end of the war – only to return in disgust at the terms imposed on an impoverished Germany and subsequently to write his first major piece 'The Economic Consequences of the Peace on the economic consequences of the Versailles Peace Treaty', in which he basically predicted WWII. In 1934 he visited President Roosevelt in Washington and saw the ongoing New Deal of public sector job creation – and urged Roosevelt to extend the program.

*In a letter to George Bernard Shaw in 1935, Keynes wrote that 'I believe myself to be writing a book on economic theory which will largely revolutionize ... the way the world thinks about economic problems'. * He was right – the following year he published* The General Theory of Employment, Interest and Money. *This incredibly dry and theoretically intimidating work would turn economic theory on end, create the field of macroeconomics, and shape economic policy for the entire post-WWII period.*

In spite of his failing health he was England's chief negotiator during the famous Bretton Woods conference in 1944. He was instrumental in building post-war institutions for economic stability and cooperation, notably the IMF, the GATT (now the World Trade Organisation, WTO), the World Bank, and constructing the fixed exchange rate system that lasted from 1945 until the early 1970s.

His main regret in life was that he had not drunk enough champagne.

(*Source:* The Worldly Philosophers, *pp. 249–87*)

Recommended reading:

1.   *The Worldly Philosophers*, Robert L Heilbroner, Simon & Schuster, 1986 (6th ed.), ISBN 0-671-63482-8
2.   *Essays on John Maynard Keynes*, Milo Keynes, Cambridge University Press, 1975, ISBN 0-521-20534-4
3.   *John Maynard Keynes: Hopes Betrayed 1883–1920*, Robert Skidelsky, 1992, ISBN 033357379X (US Edition: ISBN 014023554X)
4.   *John Maynard Keynes: The Economist as Saviour 1920-1937*, Robert Skidelsky, 1994, ISBN 0333584996 (US Edition: ISBN 0140238069)
5.   *John Maynard Keynes: Fighting for Britain 1937-1946* (published in the United States as Fighting for Freedom), Robert Skidelsky, 2001, ISBN 0333779711 (US Edition: ISBN 0142001678)
* I wrote something similar to my editor recently.

The monetarist/neoclassical view of long-run aggregate supply

The Keynesian view of aggregate supply dominated economic thinking and policies throughout the 1950s and 1960s whereupon a counterview arose which took as its base the neoclassical premise of perfectly functioning markets. This was the **monetarist school** of thought initially put forward by Milton Friedman (see "Celebrity bubble: Milton Friedman (1912–2006)" on page 293) which would also spawn a number of similar schools of thought, primarily the neoclassical and supply-side schools (see "A little depth: Neoclassical, monetarist, new classical, supply-side" on page 293).[7] The monetarist line of reasoning took issue with a number of key Keynesian assumptions:

Monetarist criticism of Keynesian AS

1.   The starting point for the monetarist school was that 'people are not fooled by having more money'. In other words, as income increases when moving along the short-run aggregate supply curve people would realise that the higher price level would hollow out their – unchanged – wages. Labourers in the monetarist/neoclassical view thus do not suffer from *money illusion* but are well aware of the negative effects of a higher price level on *real wages*.

2.   This view ('neoclassical' from now on) therefore strongly disagreed with the Keynesian assumption that wage rates would remain unchanged in the long run. Wages are market based and therefore highly flexible. Workers' **inflationary expectations** (see Section 3.5) would force them to use their bargaining power to bid up wages when the price level increased in order to retain their purchasing power.

3.   Since higher wages 'eat up the distance' between the final price firms get for their goods and the costs of producing them, the short-run aggregate supply curve will shift to the left when wage levels in the economy are bid up. (This is no different from saying that an increase in factor prices lowers supply, i.e. aggregate supply.) Thus there will be a **separate short-run aggregate supply curve** for every wage rate.

---

7.   There are a number of distinctions between these schools, but I will limit myself to using 'monetarist' or 'neoclassical', since the nuances are too far beyond the scope of the syllabus.

Neoclassical LRAS

Putting the above into points in Figure 3.3.5, we get a long-run aggregate supply curve showing that real GDP is independent of the price level.

- **A to B**: In the neoclassical model any increase in the price level accompanying an increase output, A to B in the diagram, will result in higher wages for workers who act to at least retain (if not increase) real wages.

- **B to C**: The increase in factor prices, e.g. labour costs, shifts short-run aggregate supply from $SRAS_0$ to $SRAS_1$ and the economy returns to Y_0 at a higher price level, shown by C.

- **C to E**: The long-run aggregate supply curve shows how firms' costs adapt to changes in final prices. For example, if the price level increases by 5% and wages and other factor prices also increase by 5% then real factor costs and real wages have not changed. This means that there is in fact no increase in the real price level and therefore no real inducement for an increase in output. Further movements along $SRAS_1$ will result in the same thing, moving the economy from point C to D to E via a new short-run aggregate supply curve.

- **LRAS and full employment**: The resulting vertical LRAS curve shows the economy's long-run potential GDP. At this level of output there is full employment – Y_{FE}. (Strong warning here: this does

not mean 'zero unemployment' but the '*natural* rate of unemployment' as we shall see.)

Looking at it in the reverse order, starting at point E, consider how a fall in output prices at a given money wage rate would increase the real wage rate and therefore increase the supply of labour and cause an excess supply of labour. Since wages are flexible they will quickly decrease and restore equilibrium on the labour market – and the lower real wage rate would increase aggregate supply from SRAS2 to SRAS1, moving the economy from point E to point C in the diagram. The long-run aggregate supply curve is thus uncorrelated to a change in the price level.

LRAS versus physical limit

It is most important that you do not confuse long-run aggregate supply with the physical limit outlined earlier. The LRAS curve shows potential real output in the long run, which is the same as the full employment level. It is possible for real output to exceed this point in the short run – according to most, but not all, classically orientated economists – just as it is possible for real GDP to be less than potential output. The key is in understanding that 'potential' in this context indicates the long-run capacity of firms in the economy to remain at a certain output level before having to adjust to changes in factor markets. So while firms can physically produce beyond Y_{FE} in Figure 3.3.5 (diagram II), increasing factor prices will force them back to the output level on the long-run aggregate supply curve.

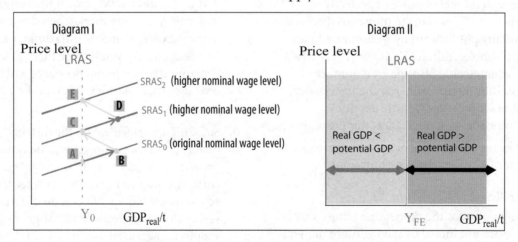

Figure 3.3.5 *Monetarist/neoclassical LRAS*

CELEBRITY BUBBLE: MILTON FRIEDMAN (1912–2006)

Milton Friedman is perhaps one of the foremost representatives amongst economists advocating limited government intervention. His close to 40 years of research and teaching at the University of Chicago made him the pivotal figure in what is now known as the 'Chicago School', which is based on free markets and stable money supply being the optimal method of attaining macroeconomic growth and stability. He is also the most famous economist of today, and the central figure in the monetarist school.

His work has mostly focused on price theory, where the core theme is how individual market prices are set. His theoretical direction took its vantage point in the neoclassical centrepiece quantity theory of money – which proposes that price levels and inflation are primarily dependent on the money supply. His books Studies in the Quantity Theory of Money *from 1956 and* Monetary History of the United States *(co-authored by Anna Schwartz) argued that increased monetary growth would not in the long run increase real output but only the price level – which set the stage for monetary theory …*

… during the 1970s as much of what Friedman had predicted seemed to come true. The early and mid 1970s was a period of high inflation and low – or falling – growth, so called 'stagflation' or 'slumpflation'. This was the period where the Phillips curve relationship seemingly broke down (see Section 3.5) and Friedman put forward the expectations augmented Phillips curve – which ultimately resulted in the New Classical concept of a natural rate of unemployment and the long-run supply curve.

Friedman has been an informal economic advisor to the American presidents Nixon and Reagan and won enough awards to fill two more pages – but one can assume that his winning of the Nobel Prize in economics in 1976 is worth mentioning. While he has always been controversial, there is no denying his enormous impact on economic theory. Indeed, economic policy too, as the entire Reagan and Thatcher 'epochs' of the 1980s was heavily influenced by Friedman's work.

 A little depth:
Neoclassical, monetarist, new classical, supply-side

I recall when Coca-Cola in the mid-1980s decided to change the taste ever so slightly. There was massive outrage amongst consumers in the US and the Coca-Cola Company finally had to reinstate the original Coke along side newer versions. I don't recall how many versions there were for a while, but it was something like 'Classic Coke', 'New Coke', 'New Classic Coke', and perhaps even 'Old New Classic Coke'. I am reminded of this every time the issue of neoclassical theory arises, since there are many confusing (very similar) labels here. Below is an attempt to put the different main schools of economic thought into a timeline perspective.

Classical side	Keynesian side
Late 1800s — **Neoclassical school**: • focus on microeconomics; labour is like any other commodity • all markets clear in LR • unemployment will tend towards equilibrium level in LR	
1930s	**Keynesian, neo-Keynesian school**: • markets are imperfect and do not necessarily clear
1940s & 1950s	• price of labour is 'downward sticky'; high unemployment possible even in LR
1960s — **Monetarism**: • based on neoclassical economics • workers do not suffer from 'money illusion' • the LRAS curve is vertical • focus on supply-side; microeconomic adjustments • focus on monetary policy, i.e. controlling the supply of real money; quantity theory of money • supply-side orientated and non-interventionist • unemployment is voluntary	• unemployment is primarily cyclical or demand deficient • focus on demand side; interventionist policies necessary • unemployment and inflation rates show a trade-off • primary macroeconomic instrument; fiscal policies
1980s — **New Classical school** • 'extreme monetarism'; markets adapt almost instantaneously • macro environment governed by people's 'rational expectations' **Supply-side school**: • 'spin-off' from monetarism focusing on long-run growth • macro policies should aim to create market conditions at micro level; increase labour mobility, remove market imperfections • focus on incentives; lower taxes, reduce social benefits, privatisation • see 'Thatcherism' and 'Reaganomics' during 1980s	

POP QUIZ 3.3.2 AGGREGATE SUPPLY

1 How/why can an economy be in equilibrium at less than full employment according to Keynes?

2 Explain how the difference between an increase in final prices (of goods) and factor prices create an upward sloping aggregate supply curve.

3 What was the main criticism put forward in the 'Keynesian revolution'?

4 Why might there be unemployment at the equilibrium level of income according to Keynes?

5 The monetarist school in its turn put forward criticism of Keynesian assumptions. Explain how this led to a short-run aggregate supply curve and a vertical long-run aggregate supply curve.

6 'The physical output limit is not the same as long-run aggregate supply.' Explain.

Equilibrium level of national income ©IBO 2003

In later years, there has been a degree of broad consensus on the short-run aggregate supply curve, in that it is in all likelihood upward-sloping. Just as in the simple supply and demand model, equilibrium occurs when aggregate supply equals aggregate demand, i.e. when planned expenditure (quantity of real GDP demanded) equals planned output (quantity of real GDP supplied) in an economy.

Consensus view – and continued disagreement

The consensus view is limited to the short run, since there is still stark disagreement between the two broad schools of thought – Keynesian and neoclassical – as to the shape of the long-run aggregate supply curve.

Consensus

The diagrams in Figure 3.3.6 illustrate the issue. Diagram I shows the broad consensus on the 'middle range' along a short-run aggregate supply curve. When quantity demanded of real GDP equals quantity supplied then macroeconomic equilibrium is attained. This occurs when real GDP is 90 billion at a price level of 110. (Note that I am using the values of the GDP inflator used in Figure 3.3.1 on page 282 and Figure 3.3.2 on page 285.)

Disagreement

The debate has become less heated in later years, but the core division remains. Diagram II in Figure 3.3.6 shows the line of continued disagreement between the two schools.

- The *neoclassical school* sees long-run equilibrium where the economy operates at full employment – commonly referred to as the natural rate of unemployment (explained below). This is the intersection where the aggregate demand curve cuts the long-run aggregate supply curve. As will be shown in Section 3.4, neoclassical theory posits that a shift in the aggregate demand curve will ultimately result in a shift in the short-run aggregate supply curve, returning the economy to the long-run equilibrium along the LRAS curve.

- This is contested by the *Keynesian body of theory*, which rejects the notion that labour market equilibrium – and thus full employment – must necessarily be attained in the long run. Since wages are downward sticky, not everyone on the labour market will accept lower real wages which means that there can be *less* than full employment at equilibrium output. In the Keynesian model, the aggregate supply curve (note the second GDP-axis) shows that there can well be long-run equilibrium at below the full employment level of output, Y'_{FE}.

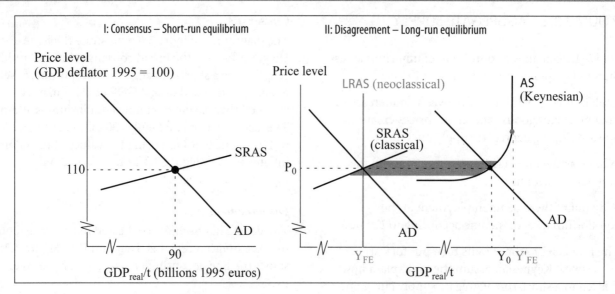

Figure 3.3.6 *Short-run and long-run equilibrium*

The span of the AS-AD model

While there are other macroeconomic models, the AS-AD model is a rather neat way of showing how planned expenditure in the economy influences output and the price level. Note how the model illustrates *all three flows in the circular flow model*: SRAS = **output**, AD = **expenditure** and real GDP shows **income**. The price level can illustrate inflationary pressure. There is also a strong implicit reference to the labour market, in that the LRAS curve is based on the full employment level of national income. In the remainder of this book, I will use the consensus or neoclassical versions as the standard model and the Keynesian version only when warranted by a discussion on different policies and possible outcomes.

Full employment level of national output ©IBO 2003

The long-run aggregate supply curve has thus far been explained as the level of potential output in an economy in the long run. This output level is known as **general equilibrium** – all factor markets and goods markets have cleared. It is also the *full employment* level of output since all available labourers willing and able to accept jobs are employed at the going wage rate. Figure 3.3.7 illustrates the long-run macroeconomic equilibrium.

The point of intersection between aggregate demand and short-run aggregate supply also intersects with long-run aggregate supply. At this point output equals the full employment level. **Full employment** is defined as the level of unemployment in an economy existing when supply of labour equals demand for

labour, i.e. when the labour market has cleared. As the market for labour is intimately connected to output the demand for labour will be derived from planned output and planned expenditure. Those without jobs at full employment level on the labour market are 'between jobs', and since there will always be a portion of the total available work force seeking employment, full employment renders a *'natural' rate of unemployment* (see also Section 3.5).

Strong economic forces will be enacted in a situation where the economy is operating above or below the full employment level of output of Y_{FE} in Figure 3.3.7. As the neoclassical AS-AD model assumes that labour markets function perfectly, any disequilibrium in the labour market will be short term so when markets clear the economy will be at full employment no matter what the price level in the economy is. Keep in mind that the neoclassical view is that labour markets function perfectly so any disequilibrium (unemployment) in the labour market will be short term only.

One question begging to be addressed is how we arrive at the point we call potential output in the first place. Good question. I don't have an answer. Unfortunately, nobody else does either. In fact, it is impossible to precisely set down potential output in an economy and the LRAS curve must be viewed as a theoretical assumption put in place to aid us in our analysis. So while there is theoretical merit in *assuming* that potential output is unrelated to the price level and thus vertical, the actual position of long-run aggregate supply must be *estimated*. I will touch upon this in the chapter on business cycles further on in this section.

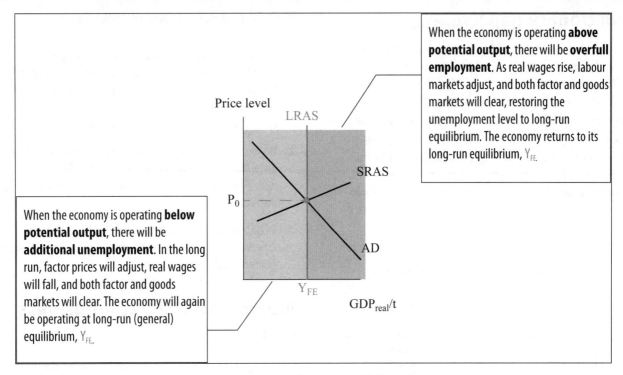

When the economy is operating **above potential output**, there will be **overfull employment**. As real wages rise, labour markets adjust, and both factor and goods markets will clear, restoring the unemployment level to long-run equilibrium. The economy returns to its long-run equilibrium, Y_{FE}.

When the economy is operating **below potential output**, there will be **additional unemployment**. In the long run, factor prices will adjust, real wages will fall, and both factor and goods markets will clear. The economy will again be operating at long-run (general) equilibrium, Y_{FE}.

Figure 3.3.7 *National income and full employment*

Inflationary gap ©IBO 2003

One of the 'strong economic forces' referred to above is of course inflationary pressure. Inflation is rather carefully defined in economics, and means a *sustained rise in the general price level*. Since the macroeconomic environment is most dynamic over time, price levels will be continually adjusting to economic activity. In fact, 'long run' in our AS-AD model doesn't really mean 'the point where the economy will wind up ultimately' but rather 'the level around which economic activity will hover over the longer term'. In other words, it is highly unlikely that the economy will be at general equilibrium for any length of time since there is always an ongoing process of adjustment *towards* the long-run output level – not *at* the long-run output level.

We shall look at two scenarios where there is short-run equilibrium creating pressure towards long-run equilibrium. The first example is when the short-run equilibrium is above potential output levels and the full employment level of real GDP. Figure 3.3.8 shows such a situation where output is at Y_0 – which is above the full-employment equilibrium at Y_{FE}. Since real GDP exceeds potential GDP, there is inflationary pressure created by this gap between de facto and potential output. The distance between Y_0 and Y_{FE} is the *inflationary gap* in the economy.

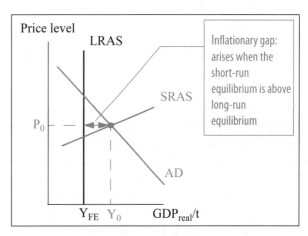

Inflationary gap: arises when the short-run equilibrium is above long-run equilibrium

Figure 3.3.8 *Inflationary gap*

While nothing has been said (as yet) about how the economy portrayed in Figure 3.3.8 arrived at this inflationary gap, in reality there is in fact a narrow range of options. Either the aggregate supply curve or the aggregate demand curve has shifted to the right – or both. It is also possible that potential output has decreased due to natural disasters or the like. The question is really what happens *after* this point? This is a very central issue in macroeconomics and deals once again with the theoretical rift between Keynesian and neoclassical economists. This is a main theme in Section 3.4.

Deflationary gap ©IBO 2003

When output is below the long-run output level there will be downward pressure on the price level, i.e. *deflationary* pressure. Figure 3.3.9 shows how the short-run equilibrium of Y_0 is below the full employment level, Y_{FE}, and thus potential long-run aggregate supply. This is the **deflationary gap** (also known as the **recessionary gap**) and shows that the economy is either experiencing a recession (see *Business Cycle* following) or that the economy's long-run potential is outstripping (= exceeding) the short-run increase in real GDP.

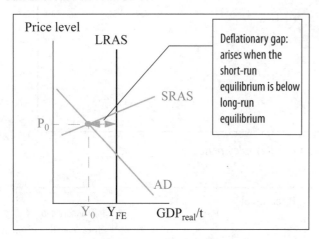

Figure 3.3.9 *Deflationary gap*

Referring to an inflationary/deflationary gap is a bit like going through simple supply and demand curves one at a time. It doesn't really mean anything until put into context, i.e. utilised in an economic analysis as an illustration. The most important thing for now is that you understand the central issue in using the neo-classical model, namely that economic forces arising during short-run equilibrium will assert themselves and seek to restore long-run equilibrium at Y_{FE}. In concluding this section in the next chapter, the AS-AD model is put into the wider context of variations in economic activity over a longer time period portrayed by the business cycle.

POP QUIZ 3.3.3 EQUILIBRIUM OUTPUT

1 What is the likely outcome, according to the neoclassical school, of the situation portrayed in Figure 3.3.8 on page 297? Let us assume that it is either a shift in aggregate supply *or* aggregate demand and not a mixture of both.

2 If you were the minister of finance and head of government of the economy in the situation described in question **1**, what policies would you consider enacting?

3 What indirect relationship can be seen in the AS-AD model other than that between output and price level?

Illustrating the trade/business cycle ©IBO 2003

> *Economists have forecast nine out of the last five recessions.* – Unknown.

The observation that economic activity varies over time is not a new discovery. I always find it fitting irony that in many Germanic languages the word for cyclical variations in the business cycle is *Konjunktur*, derived from the Roman word *conjugare* – 'to bend, bring together, align' – which was used in Roman times to explain planetary alignments in astrology. Rulers and the ruled have for centuries known that general prosperity fluctuated between 'good times' and 'bad times' and there have always been attempts to explain and predict the economic future. Perhaps the most interesting of these, mentioned earlier, was a proposal by William Jevons (one of the original neoclassical economists from the late 1800s) that the fluctuations in the economy were caused by sunspots.[8]

While economists today seldom use planetary alignments (or the entrails of geese and dogs) to predict business activity, I am not entirely certain that we are much better at predictions than the Roman fortune-tellers and astrologers – as economists were then called. Economists today have as yet to construct a method for accurately predicting the sequences of economic expansion and contraction, but not for want of trying. What we refer to as the business cycles (or trade cycle) is the *aggregate of economic activity* over a longish period of time, and economists use a number

---

8.   This is actually not as zany as it may sound. Jevons saw distinct correlation between the periodicity of sunspots and the duration of the business cycle. He hypothesized that sunspot activity caused changes in the earth's weather cycle, and that this then affected crops and thus the entire agrarian economy. Unfortunately, it was discovered that the calculations of sunspot activity were in error and their length did not actually match the business cycle. Back to the drawing board.

of variables in trying to map out the changes. The most common variable used and correlated to time is real GDP. Business cycle theory then looks for the causes of business cycles and of possible responses by policy makers. We will look at several possibilities herein, but first let's examine the basic cyclical variation through the lens of the AS-AD model more closely.

Aggregate supply/demand and the business cycle

The diagram series in Figure 3.3.10 on page 299 is a continuation of Figure 3.3.8 and Figure 3.3.9 on page 298 (inflationary and deflationary gap, respectively).

- **Deflationary gap:** Point A of diagram I in Figure 3.3.10 on page 299, shows that real GDP, Y_0, is below the long-run potential, $\mathbf{Y_{FE}}$. This is illustrated as a deflationary gap in diagram II. A deflationary gap is often characterised by falling inflation rates (or falling prices) and increased unemployment (called *cyclical* unemployment).

- **General equilibrium:** Over the next time period (note that t_0 is a *point* in time and t_0 to t_1 is a *period* of time) aggregate demand increases, bringing short-run AD and AS in line with long-run

potential at Y_{FE} at point B in diagram I. As aggregate demand rises between t_0 and t_1, unemployment decreases and settles at the full employment level and real GDP increases from Y_0 to Y_1/Y_{FE}. General equilibrium is achieved (AD = SRAS = LRAS) as seen in diagram III.

- **Inflationary gap:** Aggregate demand continues to increase during the next period, (t_1 to t_2), resulting in real GDP of Y_2 at point C and an inflationary gap shown in diagram IV. Unemployment decreases below the full employment level. Inflationary gaps are associated with, well, inflationary pressure.

- **Points D and E** are real output levels when the AD trend is reversed, in other words when aggregate demand is falling over the time period t_2 to t_4.

In moving from point A to point E in Figure 3.3.10 a cycle is completed. Please note that the series is only an *illustration* and a rather simplistic one at that. I am trying to explain the basic business cycle – not reality! I have in this respect made two highly simplifying assumptions: 1) real potential GDP has not changed over the cycle and 2) only aggregate demand changes during the cyclical phases which is rather unrealistic. If you can answer Pop Quiz 3.3.4 question 1 below correctly then you are well on your way to understanding this.

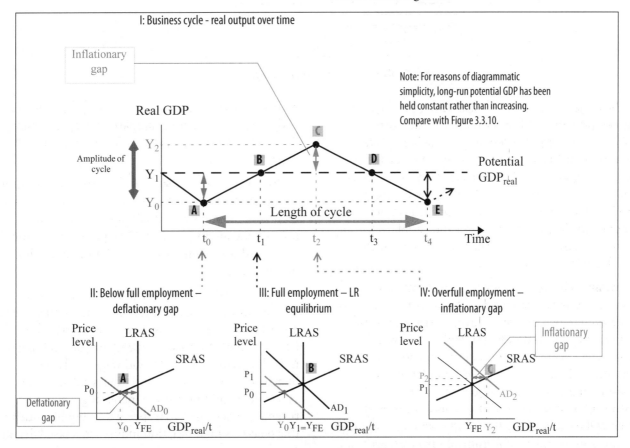

Figure 3.3.10 *Inflationary and deflationary gaps and the business cycle*

POP QUIZ 3.3.4   AS-AD AND BUSINESS CYCLE

1 Explain how the economy has moved from point D at t_3 to point E at t_4 using only the SRAS curve.

2 Think! Say that real GDP at point **B** is US$50 billion and the GDP deflator is 100. At point **D**, the GDP deflator is 110. What is nominal GDP? Is it actually possible for prices to rise between points **C** and **D**?

The business cycle – troughs and peaks

There should be no difficulties for you in finding your way through Figure 3.3.11 on page 300. The difference now is that the long-run trend (potential real GDP) is upward sloping, which is far more in keeping with empirical evidence which suggests a long-run trend of around 1.5 to 3.5% yearly growth. (Yet note that the cycles are highly stylised.) The cycle is discernible as recurring expansions and contractions. Economic activity – measured by real GDP – at its lowest point is called a '**trough**', followed by '**recovery**', '**boom**' and '**peak**'. When economic activity slows and then falls over a period of time, one speaks of '**recession**'. When the bottom of the cycle is reached once more a cycle has been completed – which is also measured as the time periods from peak to peak.

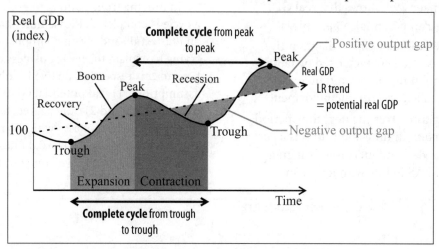

Figure 3.3.11 *Business cycle*

The cycle in Figure 3.3.11 also shows the difference between potential and actual output in the **output gaps**. The output gap is defined as actual real GDP minus potential GDP, and one therefore speaks of negative output gaps when de facto real GDP is lower than potential and positive output gaps when real GDP is higher than long-run potential. Over the cycle, the components of aggregate demand and variables within the main macro objectives will be affected in many ways. Here is a general outline.

Trough: This phase is marked by overall low economic activity (compared with earlier periods) and increased unemployment, as firms lower output and workers are made redundant (= laid off). Lower incomes will decrease consumption expenditure in the economy and there will be low (-er) inflationary pressure. In general, the period is one of low consumption, low investment and also low imports which will be affected by the fall in both consumption and investment. Lower government tax revenues

coupled with high transfer payments (unemployment and social benefits, for example) often lead to budget deficits for governments (see "Fiscal policy" on page 313).

Recovery: When the economy picks up, i.e. output increases due to demand and/or supply variables, GDP increases, unemployment falls and consumption, investment and imports rise. The period is commonly associated with an increase in inflation and rising interest rates.

Boom/peak: When growth rates increase over shorter time periods, the economy can 'overheat'. Firms are nearing capacity, labour markets are tight (i.e. labour is becoming scarce due to output levels beyond the full employment level) and wage levels are increasing and so feeding inflation. Consumption, investment and imports are increasing – as are tax revenues. There are often speculative bubbles during this phase, as high inflation induces increased demand and subsequent speculation for items considered to be good value-retainers – land, property and shares are examples herein.

Recession: When, for any number of reasons, economic activity abates (= grows less) to the point where real GDP actually falls, one speaks of recession. Firms will lower investment and output while seeking to rid themselves of labour no longer needed. Households will be affected by rising unemployment and decrease consumption and thereby also imports. Government tax revenues fall and transfer payments rise. Inflation rates decrease as do interest rates. (In fact there might be deflation – falling prices.)

> **Inflation, deflation, recession**:
> **Inflation** is defined as a sustained general increase in the average price level and measured by the change in CPI.
>
> **Deflation** is a sustained general decrease in the average price level.
>
> **Recession** is when an economy experiences two consecutive quarters (six months) of falling real GDP.

Other effects of the business cycle

In addition to the above, a good many **other factors** in the economy will be affected during cyclical variations in economic activity:

- Excess capacity in firms will increase during recessions and vice versa.
- The rate of technological change will be affected by changes in investment.

- Housing prices will be affected by changes in household wealth and interest rates.
- The stock market will be strongly linked to business activity and the expectations of households and firms.
- Exchange rates and trade balances will be affected due to differences between the business cycles of trade partners.
- Changes in tax revenues and transfer payments could affect the borrowing requirements of government and create budget deficits and government debt.
- And finally, there will be noticeable **links** between a number of other variables such as the amount of overtime worked, productivity gains, wage levels, crime levels, drug abuse and other social indicators and hundreds of other variables in a very long list.[9]

Causes of cyclical variations seen in the business cycle

Perhaps the main question in business cycle economics is what causes the changes in economic activity. The simple answer is that there is no single dominant theory able to explain the fluctuations fully. A rather unsatisfactory answer is that when aggregate demand or aggregate supply change, then GDP is affected and so too is the business cycle. A far more complex – and imprecise – answer deals with the array of *underlying variables* which in turn influence the components of aggregate demand and the influences on aggregate supply. We will cover some of the main cyclical variables in using the AS-AD model in Section 3.4.

Outside the box:
Economics and politics revisited in a political business cycle

I hate to admit it but there is, of course, a strong connection between political decisions and policy making and the economy.[10] There are two prime reasons for this, the first being that there is a 'left–right' divide in the use of macroeconomic theory. The **political left** has strong leanings towards Keynesian policies, where economic equilibrium is considered to

be unattainable without government intervention, i.e. demand-side policies aimed at adjusting aggregate demand. The **political right** supports the neoclassical view, where markets are best left alone and government policies are instead aimed at creating the conditions for increased long-run output by supply-side measures. Quite naturally, changes in (the ideological base of)

---

9.   Some of the best extended essays I have supervised have aimed at finding 'undiscovered' variables that show correlation to long-run changes in GDP shown in the business cycle. My favourite thus far: consumption of chocolate and the business cycle!

10. My students know me well enough not to try to discuss politics with me since I simply find it incredibly boring. Sometimes a student from another class (inevitably of politically active hard-left or hard-right type) will corner me, wishing to discuss the latest fiscal policies in this or that country. The last time this happened I pretty much cut the poor fellow off in mid-sentence with the comment 'politicians using economics are like monkeys using the TV remote control. They both see cause and effect but never understand it'. My students hurriedly came over and saved us from each other.

governments will result in changes in economic policy, which in turn will have great influence on taxes, government spending, interest rates, etc. all of which will affect short-run and long-run output.

Another reason for looking at the possibility of a political business cycle is the somewhat cynical proposition that incumbent (= in office, sitting) politicians will enact economic policies that will get them re-elected. This notion has turned out to have a degree of foundation in reality, where researchers have plotted changes in government spending against the term in office. For example, in the US there is evidence

suggesting that sitting presidents enact budgetary measures – such as government spending and/or tax cuts – aimed at 'priming' the economy with confidence. One strong indicator of such consumer/investor confidence is the stock market, which normally precedes an upswing in economic activity. This is a key **leading indicator**. Since 1951, the third year of an American president's four-year term has shown an average 18% increase in the stock market, indicating that there is indeed an element in the business cycle that is politically motivated.[11]

Measuring the waves

As I've said earlier, I have to watch my posterior around my people or they'll shoot it off with a few rounds of rather sharp questions. Two questions I invariably get at this stage show not only insight but an intuitive feel for economic relationships; how do we know where the long-run aggregate supply curve is; and what does the potential real GDP trend line look like over longer periods of time? The answer is that it is impossible to set a precise value for the LRAS curve. In answering the second question we also address the first; potential GDP is an estimate based on the **long-run trend** of output in the economy. In calculating the trend, we also have a value of long-run aggregate supply. Putting things brashly, we know that the LRAS curve is vertical but not its actual position along the GDP-axis in the AS-AD model.

A trend over time can be calculated by adapting a trend line which removes cyclical variations to a series of GDP values over time. Without beating you over the head with mathematical computations – that is best left to your maths teacher – the method basically takes GDP values and plots them over a given time period. Then a line of best fit is adapted to give the long-run trend line.[12] One of the main goals in business cycle research is identifying key turning points, i.e. the troughs and peaks, over the longer term, in order to adjust monetary and fiscal policies correctly. This has met with limited success so far and economics is still far better at predicting where we've *been* (on the business cycle) than where we *are* – or indeed, where we are *heading*.

The business cycle in Sweden 1980–2000

Figure 3.3.12 on page 303 exemplifies how real output over a given time period has been adapted to show the trend for potential GDP. Based on 20 years of real GDP values for Sweden, where the trend line has been adapted in order to remove cyclical variations, basically, the sum of the positive and negative output gaps should be zero. Over the 20 year period, real GDP in Sweden increased from SEK1,350 billion to SEK1,900 billion. This shows that long-run potential output during the time period has grown by some 40%, and, solving the equation (X = average growth rate); $1,350 \times X^{20}$ and 1,900 gives a yearly average increase of real GDP of 1.723%. This is significantly lower than the average growth rate of 2.75% for other developed countries during the same time period.[13]

The trend method used above comes with a most noticeable weakness attached, namely that the trend for any given economy will differ depending on **which time period** is used to calculate it. The trend in Sweden based on the period 1980 to 2000 was 1.7%, but other figures show that in the 50-year period prior to 2000 the average yearly increase was closer to 2.8%. The trend over a five, ten or even one hundred year period will be different than the trend based on the past twenty years. (See for example, Table 3.2.1 on page 267, for average national income growth over different time periods.) Therefore the long-run trend can be most subjective depending on the time period and will not be constant over time – thus we have a problem in setting a correct trend line since it will vary over the longer and shorter time series used in the calculation of

---

11. *International Herald Tribune*, 'Third year's charm for stocks', 22 May 2003.
12. In fact, the trend will often be exponential since the 'interest upon interest' effect exists. The trend line is therefore in most cases a log value against the y-axis. Pester your math teacher for details. Don't give him/her my email address.

the trend. In conclusion to the above, while I have not addressed any additional methods in assessing long-run potential output, the fact remains that since we cannot agree on what time period the long-run trend should be based on – 'how long the long run is' – there will be no conclusive way to set the waterline and agree on how high the waves and how deep the swells are.

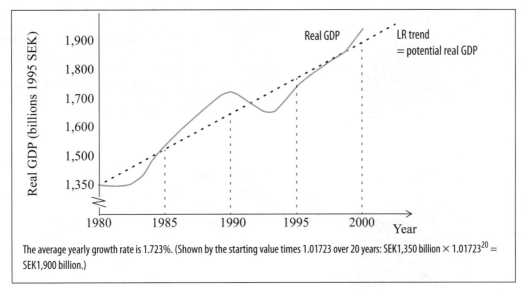

The average yearly growth rate is 1.723%. (Shown by the starting value times 1.01723 over 20 years: SEK1,350 billion $\times$ 1.01723^{20} = SEK1,900 billion.)

(Source: *Makroekonomi*, Fregert & Jonung, pp. 252–55)

Figure 3.3.12 *Cyclical variations and GDP trend in Sweden 1980–2000*

The importance of business cycles

The long phase of strong growth and relatively benign recessionary phases in the US between 1945 and 1970 led to the suggestion (primarily by American economists) that the business cycle was 'dead' – or at least badly beaten and coughing blood. Pretty much the same argument was put forward during the latter part of the latest expansionary period – the 'IT boom' of the 1990s. I venture to say that in both cases, the reports of the demise of the business cycle were grossly exaggerated.[14] Studying business cycles has great importance for the improvement of economic policy. Extreme fluctuations are very damaging to the economy for several reasons.

- First and foremost, swings in the economy lead to great *unpredictability* for firms and households, making it difficult for firms to plan both input and output and adding insecurity to households.

- Cyclical variations can also create excessive swings in business activity and heighten *social costs*, primarily by inducing firms to increase investment during upturns, which builds in redundant capacity during downturns, which increases unemployment.

- Governments are also affected by any and all *unplanned changes in tax revenues* and social spending needs, and since both are built-in to the government budget a volatile business cycle adds an unneeded degree of uncertainty in setting a budget for the coming fiscal year.

13. *UNCTAD handbook of statistics 2002*, p. 347.
14. Misquoting Samuel Langhorne Clemens (aka Mark Twain). This was his famous quip when he read his own obituary in the newspaper.

A little depth:
Predicting cyclical variations in the business cycle

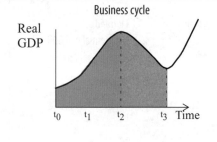

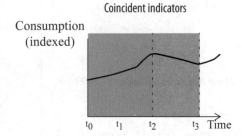

Business cycle

A key element in studying the cyclical variations in economic activity is finding variables that show correlation with the business cycle. To this aim, a number of indicators have been noticed to 'shadow' changes in real GDP. For example, unemployment falls during a recovery (called counter-cyclical variables) while consumption increases during the same period (pro-cyclical). Three main groups of indicators have been identified showing to coincide, lag and precede changes in real output.

Coincident indicators

A coincident variable is broadly in line – in terms of a time line – with the business cycle. Industrial production, investment, consumption and imports are all examples of pro-cyclical coincident indicators.

Lagging indicators

Inflation and interest rates are pro-cyclical and lagging, as are housing prices and number of bankruptcies. Unemployment is counter-cyclical and rather markedly lagging, since employers do not want to lay-off workers and delay this as long as possible. Thus unemployment levels can lag output changes by as long as 12 to 18 months.

Leading indicators

Perhaps the most closely watched of all indicators of economic activity are those that seem to precede changes in real output, since such variables would have strong predictive value. Key indicators (all pro-cyclical) are inventory levels (as firms build up stocks in anticipation of increased demand), stock market index, new car sales, consumer confidence (survey-based), initial claims for unemployment benefits, price of raw materials and new orders levels to firms. These are often weighted, indexed and used to construct a composite index of leading indicators which is closely followed by firms and policy makers alike. (Note the element of 'nonsense correlation' (see page 6) herein. Increased sales of new cars do not cause GDP to increase, but serve instead as an indicator of far more complex undercurrents in the economy, say 'warm fuzzy feelings' in households causing people to have confidence in the economy and subsequently go for the 'big ticket items' such as new cars.)

Figure 3.3.13 *Cyclical variations in the business cycle*

Many economists would therefore agree that the most desirable macro state in the long run is a *steady increase* in real GDP with minimal fluctuations – but there is wide disagreement as to both the causes and solutions of business cycle fluctuations. As the next section will show, there is a great divide between proponents of Keynesian and neoclassical theory on the subject of economic policies aimed at evening out the business cycle while enhancing growth in the long run.

POP QUIZ 3.3.5   BUSINESS CYCLE

1 How would the main macro objectives be affected over different phases of the business cycle?

2 Depict all four stages of the business cycle using the AD-AS model.

3 Explain why an output gap can be inflationary.

4 Here's a tricky one. Assume that the labour demand for nurses is not directly linked to changes in economic activity. Why might nurses still receive higher wages in an economic boom period?

5 Say that firms in an economy have increased investment a great deal during an 'overheated' period and that the economy suddenly moves into recession. How might this increase in capital worsen unemployment and also delay a movement back to full employment when the economy starts to recover?

6 Suppose that you write your extended essay over a period of five years – which many of my people unfortunately attempt. Your essay poses the question of whether there is correlation between business confidence and the business cycle. Your method is that you ask 100 firms the same question every quarter: 'Do you feel more or less confident about the future than three months ago?' You build a 'business confidence index' based on the answers and plot this out over the business cycle of the five-year period you are studying. What type of correlation would you expect? See "Measuring the waves" on page 302 for guidance.

7 Why is understanding the business cycle so important for economic policy makers?

Demand-side and supply-side policies

3.4

CONTENTS

DEMAND-SIDE AND SUPPLY-SIDE POLICIES ©IBO 2003

Economics is the only field in which two people can share a Nobel Prize for saying opposing things.
– Specifically, Gunnar Myrdal (demand side, Sweden) and Friedrich Hayek (supply side, Austria/Britain/US) shared one in 1974.

Shifts in the aggregate demand curve/demand-side policies

©IBO 2003

In the previous chapter we looked at the AS-AD model and outlined the link to the business cycle. In this section we will look at the main variables causing aggregate demand to increase or decrease. Then the focus is on how governments can use various policies in order to stimulate or lower aggregate demand.

Shifting the aggregate demand curve

Some basic revision; aggregate demand shows planned expenditure in the economy and is comprised of consumption (C), investment (I), government spending (G), export expenditure (X) and minus import expenditure (-M). Figure 3.4.1 shows how a change in one or more of these components will affect aggregate demand in the economy:

- $\Delta\uparrow AD$ (AD_0 to AD_1) [$Q_{AS}\uparrow$] →
  $\Delta\uparrow Y$ (Y_0 to Y_1) & $\Delta\uparrow$ price level (P_0 to P_1)
- $\Delta\downarrow AD$ (AD_0 to AD_2) [$Q_{AS}\downarrow$] →
  $\Delta\downarrow Y$ (Y_0 to Y_2) & $\Delta\downarrow$ price level (P_0 to P_2)

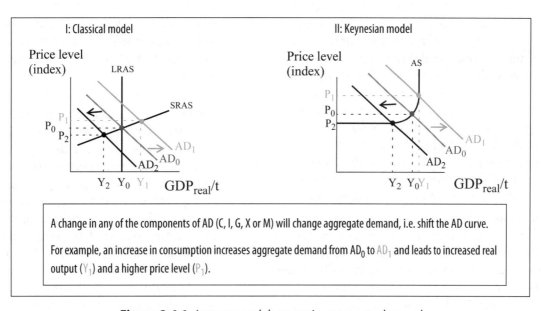

A change in any of the components of AD (C, I, G, X or M) will change aggregate demand, i.e. shift the AD curve.

For example, an increase in consumption increases aggregate demand from AD_0 to AD_1 and leads to increased real output (Y_1) and a higher price level (P_1).

Figure 3.4.1 *Increase and decrease in aggregate demand*

While the neoclassical AS-AD model will be used as the standard here, I have included the Keynesian model as contrast in order to show the implications for economic policy later on. The focus at this stage is on the causes of changes in aggregate demand. The rule of thumb is that in order for aggregate demand to shift, there must be a change in one of the components of aggregate demand. Anything which affects the components of aggregate demand other than the price level will cause the AD curve to shift in the AS-AD model. This gives a great number of possibilities as you can imagine, so the rendition below is limited to four

main headings: **expectations, international issues, fiscal policies** and **monetary policies**.

Change in AD: Expectations

This is not at the top of the list by accident. The expectations of households, firms and financial institutions are perhaps the most powerful overriding forces in change in aggregate demand. This is why it is so difficult to predict such changes, since so many psychological minutiae (= details) enter into the computations. The main expectations-based variables are:

- **Inflationary expectations**: Assuming *ceteris paribus*, the expectation of a higher rate of future inflation will lead to increased present consumption. This is based in opportunity cost thinking of households, since buying in the future – when the real value of money has fallen – means foregone consumption possibilities for households. One can also say that people will choose to hold more of their wealth in real assets (cars, housing, furniture) rather than money assets which are expected to erode ever quicker due to the expected rise in inflation.

  - $\Delta\uparrow$inflation expectations $\rightarrow \Delta\uparrow C \rightarrow \Delta\uparrow AD$
    or
    $\Delta\downarrow$inflation expectations $\rightarrow \Delta\downarrow C \rightarrow \Delta\downarrow AD$

- **Wealth and income expectations**: An increase in *perceived wealth* will increase households' consumption, since an increase in perceived wealth represents an increase in total savings. Please be aware that there is a difference between *perceived wealth* and *de facto (actual) wealth* in terms of money. While households holding assets such as property or shares might experience that they are wealthier during a property or stock market boom this is not the same as a de facto increase in monetary wealth, since it is not at all certain that these assets can or will be converted (liquidated) into money at market prices. The effect is instead analogous with the real balance explained earlier. If households feel that future consumption possibilities represented by the perceived value of present assets have risen then present saving can be decreased, leading to an increase in consumption.

  Expectations of higher *income* work in the same direction. If households expect their incomes to rise – perhaps due to successful union negotiations or increased demand on the labour market – then they will react by increasing present consumption. Conversely, every time I almost get fired there's a 'blip' in the McGee planned household expenditure. I am no different from other citizens, in that the prospect of becoming unemployed – or simply reading in the papers about increasing unemployment in the economy – will lead to lower consumption when the image of 'hard times' rears its ugly head.

  - $\Delta\uparrow$perceived wealth $\rightarrow \Delta\downarrow S$ & $\Delta\uparrow C \rightarrow \Delta\uparrow AD$
    or
    $\Delta\downarrow$perceived wealth $\rightarrow \Delta\uparrow S$ & $\Delta\downarrow C \rightarrow \Delta\downarrow AD$

  - $\Delta\uparrow$expected income $\rightarrow \Delta\uparrow C \rightarrow \Delta\uparrow AD$
    or
    $\Delta\downarrow$expected income $\rightarrow \Delta\downarrow C \rightarrow \Delta\downarrow AD$

- **Profit and revenue expectations**: Firms rely a great deal on expected expenditure in the economy for their planned investment. When firms expect future profits to rise they will be more willing to invest in the present. Accordingly, new technology which might serve to increase productivity and quickly regain investment costs will add to firms' willingness to invest. This was one of the reasons for the massive increase in Information Technology spending in the US during the latter part of the 1990s.

  - $\Delta\uparrow$profit expectations $\rightarrow \Delta\uparrow I \rightarrow \Delta\uparrow AD$
    or
    $\Delta\downarrow$profit expectations $\rightarrow \Delta\downarrow I \rightarrow \Delta\downarrow AD$

- **Policy expectations**: All the main actors on the macro scene will adjust their behaviour when possible changes in government policies appear on the horizon. For example, the mere rumour of proposed interest rates hikes can cause a change in expenditure patterns when firms and households advance investment and consumption in order to avoid higher loan burdens in the future. An expectation of higher profit and income taxes will induce firms and households to cut back on expenditure in anticipation of falling net profits and incomes.

- **Overall positive/negative outlook**: I don't know of any mainstream economic term which covers this, so I often simply refer to the 'warm fuzzy feelings' of citizens in an economy. This 'feel good – feel bad' element should not be underestimated! How many times have you made up for a bad week by going out and spending a bit of money on movies, dinner or shoes? Or the opposite: rewarding yourself after a particularly good week by going to the movies, a restaurant or buying new shoes?! Exactly, your consumption increased in both cases in spite of diametrically opposing feelings. On a macro scale of things, there is a strong element in our consumption habits arising from the basic hopes, fears, joys and sadness of the 'societal organism', as I often call it.

  As an example, just consider the attacks on the World Trade Center in the US on 11 September 2001 which caused a decrease in already declining economic activity – both in the US and the world. Insecurity, lack of confidence, fear and overall negative expectations served to lower households' consumption plans and also firms' investment. There was also a strong negative impact on trade, i.e. an *external shock* to aggregate demand.

Finally, it should be noted that there is often an element of a 'self-fulfilling prophecy' or **self-reinforcing feedback loop** in aggregate demand. This is frequently found in the *expectations element* of households and firms. If enough people expect a certain event or series of events to take place, their very actions might cause it to happen. For example, if households experience that the price level is falling and expect the trend to continue they might put off consumption in anticipation of lower future prices. In other words, they will cause aggregate demand to fall and thereby create the very situation they expected; deflation. This is what happened in Japan during the end of the 1990s and proved to be a most difficult situation to counter. The resulting so called *liquidity trap* will be explained in Section 3.5.

Change in AD: International issues

As Section 4 will show, no economy is an island. Well, not literally, but in terms of being unconnected to other countries via trade and investment. There are three basic factors affecting an economy's aggregate demand due to international variables: exchange rates, trading partners' income and relative prices of trade partners. A fourth factor is, of course, barriers to trade such as import taxes (tariffs) and other restrictions, but assume for the time being that no trade barriers exist. I will exemplify with two trade countries, Argentina and USA. Assume that there is only one good, beef, and that it makes up a major proportion of each country's GDP.

- **Exchange rates**: If the value of the domestic currency falls then imports will be more expensive for domestic households/firms – just as export goods will become cheaper for foreign households/firms.

  Assume that the Argentine peso (ARS) is at an exchange rate of US$0.32 for one ARS (or USD1 = ARS3.125) and that a kilogram of beef costs USD10 in America and ARS31.25 in Argentina.

  The price – in terms of the exchange rate and not purchasing power – is the same in both countries at this exchange rate: ARS 31.25/3.125 = USD10.

  Now posit that the Argentinean peso depreciates (falls) to ARS 1 = USD0.30 (or USD1 = ARS3.33):

  - The Americans experience that Argentinian beef has fallen in price and now need only USD9.38 (ARS 31.25/3.33) to buy the pesos necessary to buy a kilogram of Argentinian beef.

  - The Argentines, conversely, will see how the price of American beef has risen to ARS 33.3 per kilogram. *Ceteris paribus*, one can expect

Argentina's exports of beef to increase and the imports of American beef to decrease. Both variables are forces in increasing aggregate demand. (Note that this is a shift in aggregate demand not a movement along! It is the price of the **exchange rate** which has changed – not the domestic Argentine price level.)

- $\Delta\downarrow$exchange rate $\rightarrow \Delta\uparrow$X & $\Delta\downarrow$M$\rightarrow \Delta\uparrow$AD
  or
  $\Delta\uparrow$exchange rate $\rightarrow \Delta\downarrow$X & $\Delta\uparrow$M$\rightarrow \Delta\downarrow$AD

- **Trading partners' income**: Posit instead that the exchange rate remains the same (along with everything else) but instead American incomes rise faster than Argentinian income. This will lead to increased consumption in America and as some of the goods consumed come from abroad, some of the increased consumption expenditure will go to Argentinian goods, which increases aggregate demand in Argentina.

  - $\Delta\uparrow$trade partners' Y $\rightarrow \Delta\uparrow$X $\rightarrow \Delta\uparrow$AD
    or
    $\Delta\downarrow$trade partners' Y $\rightarrow \Delta\downarrow$X $\rightarrow \Delta\downarrow$AD

- **Relative prices**: Finally, still assuming ceteris paribus, what if the price level in America increases more rapidly than in Argentina, i.e. that *relative prices* swerve in favour of Argentine goods? Exactly: there would be an increased demand for Argentinian beef and therefore increased exports to the US. And, since US goods have become dearer across the board for Argentinians, imports from the US will fall. Both cause aggregate demand to increase in Argentina.

  - $\Delta\uparrow$trade partners' price level $\rightarrow \Delta\uparrow$X & $\Delta\downarrow$M $\rightarrow \Delta\uparrow$AD
    or
    $\Delta\downarrow$trade partners' price level $\rightarrow \Delta\downarrow$X & $\Delta\uparrow$M $\rightarrow \Delta\downarrow$AD

APPLIED ECONOMICS:
Exporting people

One international issue in AD terms that is often overlooked is the fact that countries in fact export labour. Working here in Mexico and sending money back to Sweden means that Sweden has exported an economics teacher. These remittances (money sent back to the home country) can account for a sizeable portion of aggregate demand.

There is an estimated 10 to 12 million migrant workers from Mexico working in the US and most of them have strong ties to their families back home. The remittances sent back to Mexico are the third largest export post (after manufactures and oil) in Mexico, accounting for 2.9% of GDP[1]. Total remittances in 2006 rose to a record USD23.1 billion – after rising at an average of 15% per year for a decade. In some of the poorer Mexican states these remittances account for up to 16% of GDP (GSP really – gross state product).[2]

During the winter of 2008–09 I continuously brought up the 'contagion effect' of falling US output and the effects on Mexico. 'When the US catches cold, Mexico gets pneumonia!' Basically, when US aggregate demand falls fewer workers are needed building houses, picking fruit, working on highways, etc. As Mexican migrant workers – often illegal immigrants – lose their jobs, there is less money available to be sent back home. As this decreases Mexican household income, there will be immediate negative effects on AD in Mexico.

I don't need to read *The Economist* (see for example, 'Remittances to Mexico – The end of the American dream', 11 December 2008) to see the results of a more than 4% drop in remittances during 2008. I see it primarily in house building which comes to a sudden stop. This has become a rather poignant (= moving, sad) economic indicator in my 'economic analysis by running around'. I see weekly on my long runs how increasing numbers of houses have boarded up sections in progress. Hacking my way through Spanish, I've asked (rather rudely really, but the Mexicans are such wonderfully open and hospitable people that I always get not only an answer but a soft drink and fruit!) home builders what the deal is. The answer is always a variant of '… ah, señor, the problems in Estados Unidos …'

I will return to this issue in Section 4.2 and include a few barbed (= sarcastic) comments on the very questionable economic benefits of building a wall along the US–Mexican border to stop illegal immigration.

Change in AD: Demand-side policies

The two remaining influences on aggregate demand have been put here, under demand side policies, in order that their connection to political intentions and the business cycle may be made clearer. *Monetary* and *fiscal* policies, conducted by the government and

Central Bank respectively, have a major impact on aggregate demand and the business cycle.

Fiscal policy

Governments can influence aggregate demand in the economy by using taxes (T) and/or government spending (G).

An increase in **income taxes** lowers the households' disposable income which in turn lowers consumption and aggregate demand. Increased **expenditure taxes**, e.g. VAT, have the same effect due to the decrease in real income.

- $\Delta{\uparrow}T \rightarrow \Delta{\downarrow}C \rightarrow \Delta{\downarrow}AD$
  or
  $\Delta{\downarrow}T \rightarrow \Delta{\uparrow}C \rightarrow \Delta{\uparrow}AD$

Since the government has the power to adjust government spending – which is a component of aggregate demand – this will have a direct impact on total expenditure in the economy. A boost in **government spending** will lead to an increase in aggregate demand and vice versa.

- $\Delta{\uparrow}G \rightarrow \Delta{\uparrow}AD$
  or
  $\Delta{\downarrow}G \rightarrow \Delta{\downarrow}AD$

Monetary policy

Monetary policy is in the hands of the Central Bank (or national bank) and involves adjusting **interest rates** (r) – either directly or indirectly (see "Interest rates as a tool of monetary policy" on page 317). *'Tight' monetary policy*, here an increase in interest rates (r), has a two-fold effect:

1. The opportunity cost of consumption rises since there is more interest foregone by keeping money in the bank.

2. The cost of servicing loans (the interest payments) increases.

The compounded effect of an increase in interest rates will be that saving (S) increases and borrowing decreases. Both lead to a decrease in investment (I) and consumption (C) – these are components of aggregate demand in the economy. Conversely, 'loose' monetary policy of lowering interest rates will have a stimulatory effect on aggregate demand.

- $\Delta{\uparrow}r \rightarrow \Delta{\uparrow}S \ \& \ \Delta{\downarrow}I \ \& \ \Delta{\downarrow}C \rightarrow \Delta{\downarrow}AD$
  or
  $\Delta{\downarrow}r \rightarrow \Delta{\downarrow}S \ \& \ \Delta{\uparrow}I \ \& \ \Delta{\uparrow}C \rightarrow \Delta{\uparrow}AD$

---

1. See http://www.ifad.org/events/remittances/maps/latin.htm.
2. See http://www.dallasfed.org/research/swe/2007/swe0704b.cfm.

Demand management and the business cycle

Figure 3.4.2 illustrates how the government can influence economic activity by using fiscal and monetary policies. This 'cutting the peaks and filling the troughs' (Figure 3.4.2, diagram I) by way of adjusting aggregate demand is commonly undertaken in order to cool down an *overheating economy* (at around t_0 and beyond) and to pull the economy up out of *recession* (at around t_1 and beyond). Using fiscal and monetary policies to adjust aggregate demand and even-out business cycle fluctuations is often referred to as *fine tuning*. It was the main form of economic control exercised by governments during the 1950s and 1960s in industrialised market economies. It has largely fallen from use as a 'fine tuner' due to the problems associated with implementation – see further on.

- **Cooling the economy**: When real GDP increases beyond the long-run trend of potential GDP (t_0 in the business cycle diagram) there are negative influences on several of the main macro objectives,

such as rising *inflation* and possibly a *trade deficit* (exports < imports). The government can try to countermand this by **contractionary policies**:

- **Fiscal policies**: Government can lower government spending and increase various taxes in order to reduce consumption and/or investment. As C and I are components of aggregate demand, the AD curve decreases from AD_0 to AD_1 in diagram II.

- **Monetary policies**: The Central Bank can increase interest rates. Higher interest lowers consumption and investment and hence decreases aggregate demand. This is illustrated in diagram II by the shift from AD_0 to AD_1.

If successful, the contractionary policies will serve to keep the economy in line with long-run potential real GDP, shown by the blue line's lower amplitude around the trend line in diagram I.

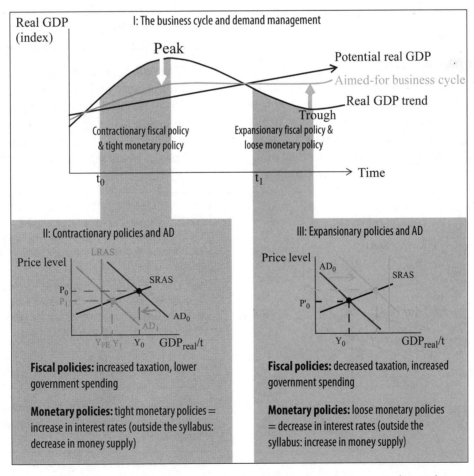

Figure 3.4.2 *Demand management, business cycle and aggregate demand*

- **Stimulating the economy**: An economy in recession will warrant stimulatory demand management policies, **expansionary policies**:

  - **Fiscal policies**: When the economy is operating below potential GDP and moving into recession, around t_1 in Figure 3.4.2 on page 311, diagram I, government can lower taxes and/or increase government spending. Lowering income taxes would increase consumption and government spending is an AD component. Aggregate demand increases from AD_0 to AD_1 in diagram III.

  - **Monetary policies**: The Central Bank can implement loose monetary policy by lowering interest rates. Investment becomes cheaper for firms and increases. Households can increase their borrowing for consumption goods and consumption increases. The AD shifts right in diagram III, from AD_0 to AD_1.

Both policies stimulate aggregate demand. The economy moves closer to the long-run equilibrium – *the aimed-for business cycle* shown in Figure 3.4.2, diagram I.

Short run versus long run

Coming up next, a **Most Important Diagram**, as my upcoming bestseller *Economics According to Winnie the Pooh* will read. Central to the neoclassical view is that demand management is relatively ineffective in the long run. Figure 3.4.3 shows the long-run effect of expansionary demand management – increasing

government spending and/or lowering interest rates – with the economy initially at full employment level of output, point A.

A to B: The increase in aggregate demand due to fiscal/monetary stimulation increases aggregate demand from AD_0 to AD_1. Real income increases from Y_{FE} to Y_1 and the price level rises from P_0 to P_1. Since wage levels and factor prices are assumed to remain constant during the short run, the short-run supply curve does not shift. Instead firms experience higher costs due to bottlenecks and scarcer factors.

B to C: The short-run effect is an inflationary gap at point B. In line with derived demand effects on factors, this will result in ever scarcer factors of production, e.g. capital, raw material and labour – and the increase in the price level from P_0 to P_1 will lead to a hollowing-out of wages for workers. Factor prices will ultimately be forced upwards as firms bid on available factors and workers will demand higher wages to make up for lost real purchasing power. Short-run aggregate supply will decrease in the long run, shown by the shift from $SRAS_0$ to $SRAS_1$. The economy has returned to the full employment level of output, Y_{FE}, but at a higher price level, P_2. This is point C in the diagram.

The A-B-C series in Figure 3.4.3 once again shows the importance of the long-run aggregate supply in the neoclassical AS-AD model. Any point of short-run equilibrium below or above the long-run potential – shown by the LRAS curve in the model – will ultimately be corrected as factor markets clear.

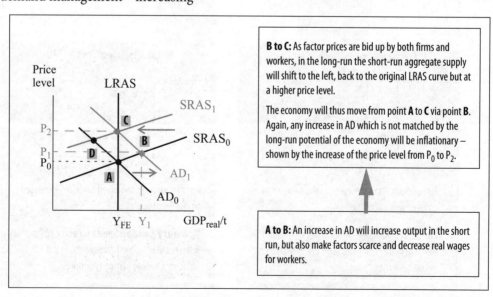

B to C: As factor prices are bid up by both firms and workers, in the long-run the short-run aggregate supply will shift to the left, back to the original LRAS curve but at a higher price level.

The economy will thus move from point **A** to **C** via point **B**. Again, any increase in AD which is not matched by the long-run potential of the economy will be inflationary – shown by the increase of the price level from P_0 to P_2.

A to B: An increase in AD will increase output in the short run, but also make factors scarce and decrease real wages for workers.

Figure 3.4.3 *Neoclassical view of LR effects of stimulating AD*

A fall in AD – point C to D to A: I briefly illustrate the neoclassical view of the long run by assuming that the economy is initially in equilibrium at point C, and that aggregate demand instead has decreased, shifting aggregate demand from AD_1 to AD_0 moving the economy to point D and a resulting deflationary gap. As firms lower prices in accordance with falling demand, the gap between (falling) final output prices and wage prices narrows, this in fact means higher relative labour prices for firms. Firms respond by demanding less labour and as the labour market responds, labour prices fall – which enables firms to increase output and increase short-run aggregate supply. This increases the short-run aggregate supply from $SRAS_1$ to $SRAS_0$ bringing the economy back to general long-run equilibrium at point A.

Overview of demand management

The four mainstream macro objectives and possible monetary and fiscal policy responses to various stages in the business cycle are given in Table 3.4.1. Notice that any use of monetary and fiscal policies aimed at demand management will have noticeable trade-offs, where adjusting aggregate demand in order to achieve a particular macro objective will have negative effects on some other objective. As mentioned in Section 3.1, it is quite evident that many of the macro objectives are very difficult to attain simultaneously, leading to conflicts and opportunity costs for the economy.

Table 3.4.1 *Macro variables and possible policy responses*

Macro objectives	Overheating economy (inflationary gap)	Recessionary economy (deflationary gap)
1. High/stable growth	High growth rate	Falling growth rate or negative growth
2. Stable prices, i.e. low inflation rate	High or increasing inflation rate	Low(-er) inflation rate, possibly deflation
3. Low level of unemployment	Low unemployment	Increasing/high unemployment
4. Trade balance (X = M)	M often larger than X; trade deficit	M falling; possible trade surplus
Possible **fiscal** policies	$\uparrow$T, $\downarrow$G/transfer payments	$\downarrow$T &/or $\uparrow$G/transfer payments
Possible **monetary** policies	Tight monetary policy; $\downarrow$Sm, $\uparrow$r	Loose monetary policy; $\uparrow$Sm, $\downarrow$r
Positive effects of policies	Lower inflation, relieves pressure on tight labour market, possible improvement in trade balance	Decrease in unemployment, increased output (or slower negative growth), societal benefits
Negative effects of policies	Growth rate falls back, lower investment can harm long-run potential growth	Inflationary pressure, increase in imports might cause trade deficit

Fiscal policy ©IBO 2003

It has been my experience that a good many students have only the vaguest notion of what a *government budget* is and since this and related concepts are central to fiscal policies, a brief description is essential.

The government budget

Just like you might make a list for expected inflows of money and planned spending for the coming semester, governments must do the same. (And, just like you, governments often spend more than they receive.) A government budget is basically an outline or proposal of all government spending, transfer payments and tax receipts for the coming fiscal year.[3] The budget lists all incoming **tax receipts** and other inflows and also all outlays for **government spending**. It is worth noting that both the composition and amount of spending is quite politically motivated, in fact, the budget is often something of a political agenda in itself since it mirrors ideologically motivated spending, for instance on defence and social safety nets.

---

3. A 'fiscal' year, as opposed to a calendar year, is a **chosen time period** for 'making ends meet' and can run from August to August, May to May or any other 12 month period. The fiscal year often coincides with the deadline for parliament/congress accepting the budget.

Figure 3.4.4 is a highly stylised illustration of a government budget – and the large illustration is also heavily idealised since it portrays a perfectly balanced budget. (Note that I have not bothered to include currency units.) When government receipts exceed expenditure there is a budget surplus – when expenditure exceeds receipts a budget deficit. This is shown in the two smaller figures, which in a Peter Pan (= highly imaginary) economic cycle *balance out*. The surplus during a boom period is used to fund deficit

spending during a recessionary period. In reality, government spending often exceeds receipts over a substantial portion of the business cycle and the government is forced to *borrow* in order to finance the deficit. The sum of this borrowing over time, known as the national debt, can severely hamper (= hinder, obstruct) future fiscal freedom of governments. The debt owed to foreign banks or governments is known as external or foreign debt.

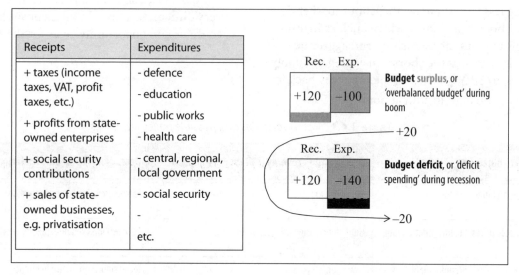

Figure 3.4.4 *Government surplus and deficit (over a cycle)*

> **Government budget, surplus, deficit, national debt, foreign debt:**
> The **government budget** is a fiscal policy instrument and political intention comprising government spending (based on receipts) for a fiscal year.
>
> • When government receipts are higher than spending there is a budget **surplus**.
> • When government spending exceeds receipts there is a budget **deficit**.
> • The sum of deficits minus surpluses over time equals the **national debt**.
> • The portion of the national debt which is owed to foreign banks/governments is the **foreign debt** (or **external debt**).

Built-in safety nets and active policies

One of my many childish allegories is that the economy is like a sailing ship and I inflict this on my students as the need arises. Like right now. Picture a ship sailing along on the seas. Waves and wind exert forces on the ship's direction and stability and may force the ship towards reefs and rocks. The stability and direction of the ship is set by two primary forces; the keel and ballast which serve to *automatically* stabilise the ship,

and the rudder – which in the hands of the captain and at his *discretion* (= will, choice, freedom) can also be used to help stabilise the ship and plot a chosen course. Fiscal policy is divided along these lines, and is commonly grouped into **automatic stabilisers** and **discretionary fiscal policy**.

Automatic stabilisers – the 'keel' and 'ballast'

When the economy starts to 'heat up', a number of stabilising effects will automatically kick in – mechanisms which are built-in to the economic system and social welfare system.

• Government spending in the form of **social benefits** is one such stabiliser. An increase in economic activity and GDP will see lower unemployment levels and serve to lower the need for social benefit payments such as unemployment benefits, income-based housing allowance and so forth. This lowers disposable income for households on the receiving end of benefits.
• The other stabiliser, **taxes**, influences net income (income after tax) of households and therefore their consumption. Most countries have some element of *progressive* income taxation, meaning that the percentage paid in income tax increases when gross

personal income rises. When household incomes rise during a boom period, around t_0 in Figure 3.4.5 on page 315 diagram I, either due to overtime, new jobs or wage increases, many wage earners will move into higher income brackets and thus pay a larger proportion of their take-home pay in tax.

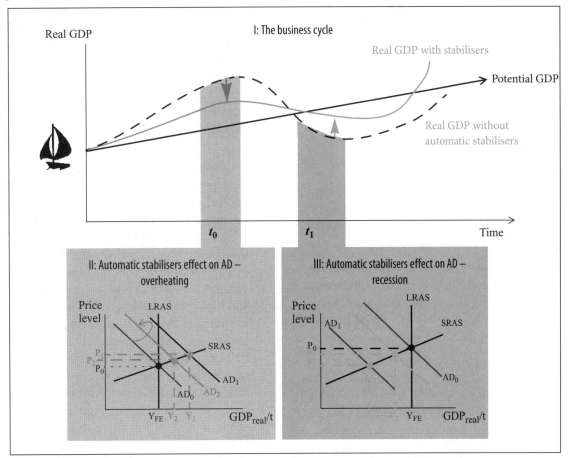

Figure 3.4.5 *Business cycle and the effect of automatic stabilisers on AD*

Taken together in the macro environment, lower social benefits and higher proportionality of taxes paid both serve to lower net disposable income in the economy and therefore consumption. Since both social benefits and progressive income taxes are built into the economic and social system, the braking effect on aggregate demand, shown by the downward readjustment from AD_1 to AD_2 in diagram II, is automatic. The effect is that aggregate demand falls less than otherwise would be the case, cutting the peak of the business cycle.

During **recession**, around t_1 in diagram I, the effect of automatic stabilisers helps dampen the fall in economic activity.

- When incomes fall and unemployment rises, falling marginal tax rates mean that tax burdens on households will decrease. This stimulates consumption.
- Lower AD and lower real GDP is associated with increased unemployment. Hence unemployment

and social benefits will also increase in the economy. This has a positive effect on household spending which helps to limit the decrease in aggregate demand. This can help lessen the severity of a downturn/recession.

This is shown by the upward readjustment from AD_1 to AD_2 in diagram III. (Remember: unemployment benefits and transfer payments are *not* included as elements of GDP, as this would cause double counting. However, since these transfer payments help to bolster aggregate demand, there is a positive **effect** on GDP.)

The effect of automatic stabilisers over time is that the swings in economic activity, the amplitude of real GDP cycles, are somewhat milder than without, shown by the blue cycle in Figure 3.4.5, diagram I. Note that automatic fiscal stabilisers do not **solve** recessions or overheating but merely lessen the impact of them somewhat.

315

> Recession - revisited and criticised: A number of my colleagues adamantly (= stubbornly) claim that the textbook definition of a recession ('two falling quarters of real GDP') is not only unrealistic but highly out of date. There is merit in this view. The NBER (National Bureau of Economic Research – a very powerful US non-profit organisation where, amongst 16 other Nobel Laureates, Milton Friedman has submitted research) uses key monthly indicators of economic output, including employment, industrial production, real personal income, and wholesale and retail sales to determine when economic growth has turned negative, rather than relying solely on two quarterly declines in GDP.

Discretionary fiscal policy – the 'rudder'

The automatic stabilising effect of taxes and social benefits are enhanced by the intentional adjustments of government spending and/or changing taxes, known collectively as *discretionary fiscal policies* as they are 'at the discretion' of government.

During a *recession*, the government increases spending on roads, education and such, and this has the effect of increasing aggregate demand – of which government expenditure is a component – and taxes can also be adjusted downwards in order to increase disposable income and induce increase consumption. This is called **expansionary fiscal policy**.

- When the economy shows signs of *overheating*, government can cut back on spending and increase taxes in order to lower aggregate demand. The aim is once again to even-out the business cycle, as in Figure 3.4.5 on page 315, bringing cyclical variations closer to the long-term trend. (The extent to which this actually works is hotly debated and we will look at this briefly in "Strengths and weaknesses of these policies" on page 328.) These are **contractionary fiscal policies**.

Fiscal policy was the main instrument used during the 1950s and 1960s to influence aggregate demand, where Keynesian theory prescribed using government spending as a 'rudder' to adjust the economy. According to the Keynesian view of demand management during the 20-year period following the Second World War, the focus should be on lowering unemployment. Deficit spending could be used during recessions as a way of increasing output/growth and thereby increased employment. The aim was to use 'good times' to even out 'bad times'. Government surpluses created by low(-er) government spending and higher tax receipts during booms were to be used to stimulate the economy during recessions, thus evening-out the business cycle and creating long-run stability. During the 1970s, a number of things – most noticeably increasing government debt and both high inflation and high unemployment – caused many governments to abandon attempts to fine tune the economy and look at alternative policies, most noticeably supply-side measures. We will return to this after looking at an additional method of demand management, namely monetary policy.

Case study: **Fiscal policy in the USA**

The Bush administration implemented a number of tax breaks during 2002 and 2003 to stimulate aggregate demand. Two examples of this expansionary fiscal policy had a large impact during the fall of 2003: the '**tax credit cheques**' sent to higher income households with children, and **tax allowances to firms** allowing them to write off more of their investment expenditure and thus save money.

The child tax credit involved $US13.7 billion in tax credits to households, which was strategically done during the 'back to school' period. This guaranteed that the lion's share of the tax return would be spent by these households on clothing and books for their children returning to school for the new semester. This one-off consumption effect of fiscal policy accounted for a substantial proportion of the 5% soar in the US economy (at a yearly rate) during the fall. The tax allowance granted to firms meant that any investment before the end of 2004 would allow firms to deduct more from their pre-tax profit and thereby lower total profit (corporate) tax. This was an incentive for firms to bring forward future investment plans, which subsequently increased aggregate demand during 2003.[a]

It would appear that these policies had taken effect by the fall of 2003, as real GDP grew at an annualised rate of 8.2% during the third quarter (July–September) – the largest gain in 19 years. This boost in investment by 21% (fixed investment) and consumption (which accounts for 70% of GDP increase) of 6.9% surpassed even the most optimistic predictions.

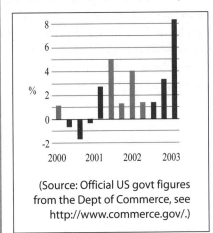

(Source: Official US govt figures from the Dept of Commerce, see http://www.commerce.gov/.)

The growth during the second half of 2003 reflects a most Keynesian demand-side approach in stimulating the American economy – something a number of economic commentators have pointed out. Deficit spending has increased the government deficit from 3% of GDP in 2000 to 6% during 2003. In line with standard economic theory, there has also been an overall increase in the price level of some 1.8% during the third quarter. However, at the time of writing (January 2004) this has not had a noticeable impact on unemployment which remains (historically) high at around 6%.

---

a. Official US government site at http://www.bea.gov/bea/newsrel/gdp303f.htm, *USA Today* at http://www.usatoday.com/money/economy/gdp/2003-10-30-gdp_x.htm, *International Herald Tribune Tax credit checks...* 4–5 October 2003, p. 11 and *Business Week: Business Turns On The Tap*, 17 November 2003.

Interest rates as a tool of monetary policy ©IBO 2003

If you have five dollars and Chuck Norris has five dollars, Chuck Norris has more money than you. – Anonymous

If you lend someone $100 and get it back in a year, has it cost you anything? 'Inflation would mean that the real value of the $100 is less' you might reply. OK, but what if we assume that inflation during the year was zero? Of course you would still incur a cost; the

opportunity cost of not having access to the $100. You make up for this opportunity cost by charging interest.[4]

Real interest: Assuming that your next-best option is estimated at a money value of $5, then you would charge and interest rate of (at least) 5% ($100 × 5% = $5). If we now assume that there indeed is a steady rate of inflation, say 5%, what would you do? Correct, you would charge a *higher* rate of interest (the **real interest rate**), 10.25%[5], since receiving $105 in a year's time when the price level has gone from 100 (indexed at the time of the loan) to 105 means that the $105 you get back is worth only $100 in real terms.

> **Real interest rate**: If nominal interest is eaten up by inflation then there has been an opportunity loss for the lender. It is therefore more relevant, once again, to focus on real values rather than nominal. The real interest rate is the nominal rate minus inflation:
>
> $$r_{real} = r_{nominal} - \text{inflation}.$$

Interest rates and the Central Bank

The above iteration on real interest rates shows one of the major influences on the rate of interest – inflation. However, interest rates in an economy are also used to adjust economic activity since both consumption and investment are highly correlated to interest levels. This makes the relationship between interest and inflation somewhat tricky since cause and effect works both ways – an increase in inflation causes interest rates to rise, yet an increase in the interest rate is used as a monetary tool in order to reduce inflation. Interest rates are in fact the key tool in monetary policy and managed by the Central Bank. There are a number of functions of the Central Bank and three are central to the monetary policy dealt with here:

1. To implement **monetary policy** through goals set by government (often in the form of inflation targets), involving setting interest rates and the supply of money.

2. To be the '**lender of last resort**', i.e. seeing to it that commercial banks' need for cash is met. This is done at an interest rate known as the **discount rate**[6] which is a key in setting market interest rates. (See Figure 3.4.6.)

3. To **regulate commercial bank lending**, an example of which is setting minimum levels of cash which commercial banks must keep on hand, so called '**minimum reserve requirements**'.

Figure 3.4.6 on page 319 illustrates how a Central Bank can influence market interest rates. Let's follow a simple lending flow by assuming that there is only one commercial bank which is lending to households and firms at an interest rate (the 'price of money') of 7%. Now, commercial banks make a profit by having as much of their money assets in turnover as possible, i.e. they want to lend as much money as possible. In order to have loanable funds available, commercial banks offer households and firms an incentive; a return on deposited money, i.e. an interest rate. In the example below, the interest rate received is 2%. The banks basically make their money by borrowing money from you and your business at 2% interest and then lending it to your neighbour and her business for 7% – the five percentage points being the banks' profit margin.

---

4. During an 'Open House Day' at school, I gave a lecture on economics to the parents of my students. I brought up the issue of opportunity cost and interest. The next day one of my people, Jakob, came back with a bottle of Polish vodka (Zubrowka, my favourite) as a thank-you gift from his mother. He wasn't too pleased about things: 'Thanks a lot Matt. My mum's now charging me interest on money she lent me to buy a computer.'
5. Since you want to have $105 in **real** terms, you must charge an interest rate that gives you $110.25, i.e. 10.25%.
6. There is a most confusing array of different terms and forms of interest that central banks charge commercial banks for loans. I will simply use 'discount rate'.

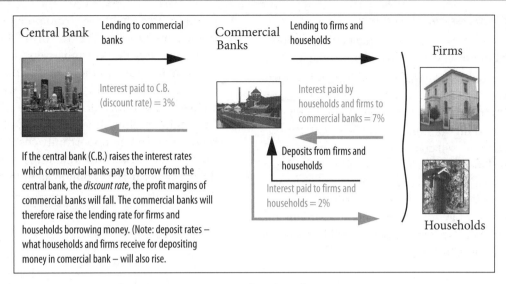

Figure 3.4.6 *Central Bank and interest rates*

Dampening an overheating economy

Now, say that the economy shows signs of overheating, i.e. that the rate of inflation exceeds a predetermined ceiling rate of inflation set by the Central Bank. The Central Bank, implementing **tight monetary policy**, raises the discount rate to 3.5% whereby commercial banks immediately respond by raising their lending rates to households and firms – since the commercial banks will now pay a higher 'price' for borrowing from the Central Bank. (In effect, the Central Bank has hereby **decreased the supply of money** since commercial banks are less willing to increase lending levels. See "Outside the box: Supply and demand for money" on page 321.) The deposit rate will also increase, since banks will be competing for households' and firms' deposits. Assume that the commercial banks

increase the lending rate to 7.5% and the deposit rate to 2.5%.

Two forces will cause a decrease in aggregate demand:

1. Firstly, the opportunity cost of investment and consumption will increase due to a higher rate of interest received by money deposited by firms and households. Savings will therefore increase, causing a decrease in investment and consumption.

2. Secondly, the increased cost of borrowing money will lead firms to hold back on investment and households to decrease consumption. Taken together, lower levels of investment and consumption will decrease aggregate demand, or, to be more correct, decrease the rate of increase in aggregate demand, as shown in Figure 3.4.7, diagram I.

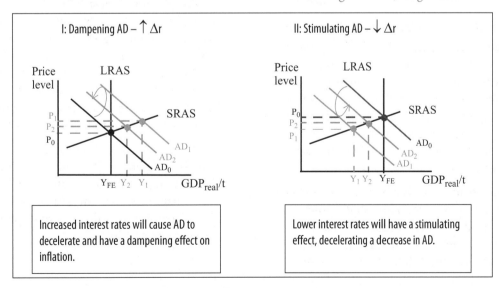

Figure 3.4.7 *Demand management using interest rates*

Stimulating a recessionary economy

When inflation shows signs of falling below the floor of a targeted interest corridor, the Central Bank will implement *loose monetary policy*[7], seeking to stimulate the economy. The Central Bank decreases the discount rate from 3% to, say, 2.5%. Commercial banks now have cheaper credit on money borrowed from the Central Bank, and will compete with each other by lowering the lending rates for firms and households. If commercial bank rates fall to 6.5% there will be a lower opportunity cost associated with investment and consumption – so savings will fall and investment and consumption will rise. This causes the fall in aggregate demand to decelerate, shown in Figure 3.4.7 diagram II.

Note how the effect of an increase or decrease in interest rates is illustrated in Figure 3.4.7 diagrams I and II as an 'increase/decrease in the rate of decrease' or 'acceleration/deceleration' in aggregate demand rather than using a single aggregate demand curve that shifts to the left. This is not by accident. The reasoning is that monetary policy is often very 'forward looking' and seeks to countermand inflation that has not set in yet. Central Banks attempt to steer the economy – or rather, inflation – by looking forward in time and estimating what inflation *will* look like. Interest rates are in effect used to countermand excessive changes in aggregate demand before they happen. This is because there are significant *time lags* in operation: it takes between two and six quarters before interest rates actually affect inflation and up to two years before the full effects on aggregate demand hit. This is why so much effort is put into predicting future output fluctuations in business cycles.

The relationship between interest and investment

While it is not *directly* part of the syllabus, a most useful theoretical concept in understanding underlying forces connecting interest rates with aggregate demand (and also aggregate supply as shall be seen) is the downward sloping demand for investment, called the **investment schedule** (= demand curve for investment). Lower interest rates induce firms to increase investment for two reasons.

1. **Opportunity cost issue:** When the interest rate falls, a number of investment opportunities previously considered unprofitable are suddenly profitable. For example, assume that firms in an economy have only two options for their retained

profit (= profit held over from previous years) – put it in the bank or invest it in the firm. Now, say that firms in an economy itemize and assess all possible investment opportunities and that the current market interest rate is 7%. Any investment which does not yield a rate of return of 7% or more will be put in the bank, since an investment yielding, say, 6.5% will render the firm an opportunity cost (loss) of 0.5%. Figure 3.4.8 shows how total investment demand during the year is €10 billion at an interest rate of 7%.

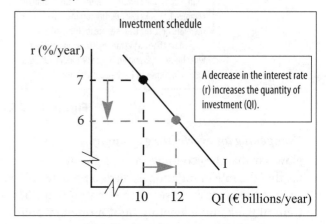

Figure 3.4.8 *Interest rates and quantity of investment*

Say that the economy slows down and the Central Bank loosens monetary policy and interest rates fall (as outlined earlier) from 7% to 6%. Investment options that were previously considered unprofitable suddenly become more attractive; what firm would leave money in the bank at 6.5% interest when an investment opportunity yields 6.9% – or even 6.55%! Firms will therefore increase investment when the opportunity cost of investment (interest being the alternative) falls.

2. **Cost of investment:** Not all investment is funded internally, i.e. by held-over profits accumulated within the firm. A great deal of the funding for investment comes from banks and other financial institutions in the form of loans. When the interest rate falls, the cost of servicing debt (paying interest on loans) goes down and firms will be willing to take on more debt in order to invest.

The lower rate of interest in this example causes total investment in the economy to increase from €10 billion per year to €12 billion per year. The inverse relationship between interest and quantity of investment is thus a downward sloping curve, the investment schedule.

---

7. Many of my non-native English speakers struggle with the words 'loose' (= slack, movable) and 'lose' (= drop, misplace) – all too frequently mixing them up. One of my colleagues at the Oxford Study Courses has experienced the same thing and came up with 'I keep *loose* change in my pocket so I don't *lose* it.'

Outside the box:
Supply and demand for money

The **demand for money** does not show 'how much money we want'. It shows the propensity of firms and households to want to hold their assets in liquid form (e.g. money) rather than in non-monetary forms such as machinery, cars, shares, property, etc. The 'price' of money is the rate of interest and the demand curve for money (also known as the 'liquidity preference schedule') is downward sloping, signifying that the lower the interest rate the higher the quantity of money will be demanded.

The narrow definition of the money supply is the total amount of notes and coins circulating in the economy plus the balances held by commercial banks. The **supply of money** is assumed to be vertical (here) in that it is exogenous – created outside the system and set by monetary policy. The complete interest inelasticity of the money supply is based on the simplifying (and rather unrealistic) assumption that the supply of money is totally controlled by the Central Bank's monetary policy. Figure 3.4.9 on page 322 diagram I shows how the supply of money (**Sm**) and demand for money (**Dm**) create an equilibrium interest rate of r_0 and **Qm**.

Change in demand for money: Just like demand for goods and services, when any other variable changes other than the price (here, interest rate) the demand curve will shift (diagram II). A rise in incomes, GDPr, would increase the demand for money from Dm_0 to Dm_2 and interest rates would rise from r_0 to r_2. A fall in income would cause the opposite. People's positive expectations of future values of non-monetary assets such as shares and government bonds (see "Open market operations" below) would cause the demand for money to fall, since households would move out of holding liquid assets in order to hold shares or bonds. A decrease in the demand for money causes interest rates to fall.

Change the supply of money: While interest rates are the main instrument in monetary policy, Central Banks can use several other instruments to influence the supply of money and thereby the rate of interest. The Central Bank commonly has a monopoly on printing money, and thereby total control over the amount of outstanding notes and coins, i.e. it is possible to 'print money' (which the Central Bank

technically then lends to the government) in order to fund government spending. The three most common methods for controlling the supply of money are *discount rate* changes, *open market operations*, and *direct controls* on lending.

Discount rate: As described earlier, the discount rate is the Central Bank's rate of lending to commercial banks. An increase in the **discount rate** reduces the willingness of commercial banks to borrow from the Central Bank and thus limits their ability to lend money, which serves to lower the amount of loans. This decreases the money supply (Sm_0 to Sm_2 in diagram III above) and drives up interest rates (r_0 to r_2).

Open market operations: The Central Bank can conduct open market operations on the financial market much like any other financial institution. It can issue government debt, IOUs[8], in the form of interest-bearing bills and bonds (collectively known as government securities). When the government sells securities, they can be purchased by both the financial and non-financial sector (firms, households and other governments). When these securities are purchased, the money supply is decreased (diagram III) since funds in terms of cash are 'soaked up' from the market (Sm_0 to Sm_2) – the rate of interest increases from r_0 to r_2. If instead the Central Bank instead buys (back) securities on the open market, there is an increase in the supply of money (Sm_0 to Sm_1) and a fall in the rate of interest (r_0 to r_1).

Direct controls on banks' lending: In its capacity of regulatory body for the financial sector, the Central Bank sets certain limits on the amount of outstanding loans (= total loans given to households and firms) banks are allowed to have, some form of reserve requirement. A reserve requirement of 5% means that a bank which has maximised its lending capacity and has €100 million in deposits must keep €5 million in cash reserves. If the Central Bank wishes to decrease the supply of money, the reserve requirement can be increased, say to 6%, whereby the bank in the example will have to limit new loans until it once again has the minimum requirement of cash on hand. An increase in reserve requirements will decrease the supply of

---

8. An IOU is a layman's (= normal person's) term. It is a bill of debt issued by the lender (creditor) and signed by the borrower (debtor). The debtor now owes money and the creditor has a piece of paper verifying this which basically says, 'I owe you' = 'IOU'.

money (Sm$_0$ to Sm$_2$ in diagram III) and increase interest rates from r$_0$ to r$_2$. A decrease in reserve requirements will enable banks to increase lending,

which increases the money supply and lowers the rate of interest.

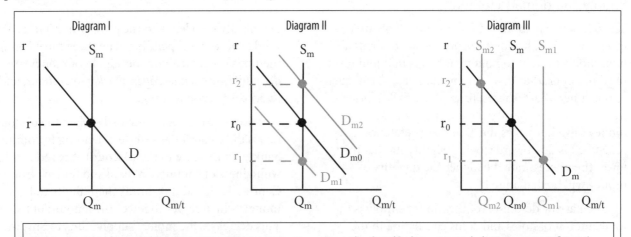

Changing the supply of money: While interest rates are the main instrument in monetary policy, Central Banks can use several other instruments to influence the supply of money and thereby the rate of interest. The Central Bank commonly has a monopoly on printing money, and thereby total control over the amount of outstanding notes and coins, i.e. it is possible to 'print money' (which the Central Bank technically then lends to the government) in order to fund government spending. The three most common methods for controlling the supply of money are discount rate changes, open market operations, and direct controls on lending.

Figure 3.4.9 *Supply and demand for money and interest rates*

Final notes on money supply and interest: The causal relationship between the money supply and interest rates is extremely complicated. It is impossible to set a precise supply of money and very difficult to foresee the extent to which interest rates will change as a result of adjusting money supply. Also, while basic economic theory stipulates that a change in the supply of money causes a change in interest rates, there is heavy empirical evidence of a stronger reverse causal flow, i.e. that a change in interest rates causes a change in the supply of money. Point in fact, Central Banks increasingly use the rate of interest to adjust the supply of money rather than the reverse. While this is clearly outside the boundaries of your syllabus, it is well worth noting that Central Banks can set the money supply (and let interest rates adapt) or set interest rates (and allow the supply of money to adapt) – but it cannot set *both* the rate of interest *and* the supply of money.

You might have noticed how I have used the plural form mostly – interest rates. This is not sloppiness on my part as there are a good many different interest rates: mortgage rates for housing; short-term rates from banks; government rates on bills, bonds; repo rates and discount rates. I have a list of some 50 different interest-bearing instruments, all of which will be *interdependent*. You see, while interest rates will most definitely vary (primarily short-term and long-term rates), there will be very noticeable *co-movement in all the different market rates* offered. If the Central Bank raises one of its interest rate forms, then there will be concomitant (= associated) upward movement amongst all other interest forms on the market. I bring this up in order that you do not get confused when you are confronted by the myriad (= multitude) of different rates flickering by in the media.

Exchange rate policies

Although it is a main theme of Section 4.6, I cannot help but briefly bring up the subject of how monetary policy can affect a country's exchange rate and thus the domestic economy. Consider an economy operating in equilibrium beyond the full employment level of output, i.e. where there is an *inflationary gap*. The Central Bank can use monetary policy as outlined above to increase the interest rate and lower

consumption and investment in the economy, which exerts downward pressure on aggregate demand. There will be an additional dampening effect on aggregate demand arising from the effect on the exchange rate of the domestic currency. In other words, increased interest rates and the international substitution effect (see Section 3.3) will help to create additional disinflationary pressure on the domestic economy.

> **Disinflation**: Disinflation occurs when government and/or central bank policies decrease the rate of inflation. Do not confuse this with deflation which is a decrease in the price level! Disinflation means that the yearly inflation rate falls, say from 5% to 4.5%.

Say the Central Bank of Japan (Bank of Japan, BOJ) raises interest rates. Foreign firms, financial institutions, investors/speculators and governments will see that by readjusting a portion of their foreign currency holdings in their international portfolio of assets (which is comprised of foreign assets such as currencies, shares and securities) and buying yen (¥), an increased rate of return is possible. This, naturally, assumes *ceteris paribus* in that all other countries' interest rates are left unchanged.

- The *demand for yen will rise*, since foreigners will have to first purchase yen to deposit in Japanese banks.

- This increases demand for the yen which *drives up the value of the yen*. (The price of the yen is put in terms of other currencies, say the US dollar.) Thus the yen increases in value vis-à-vis other currencies, it **appreciates**.

- The effect on the Japanese economy is two-fold:

  - Japanese *exports become more expensive* on the foreign goods market since foreigners now have to use more of their domestic currency to buy yen.

  - Japanese *imports on the other hand will increase*, seeing as how Japanese consumers get more foreign currency with which to buy foreign goods they will substitute some domestic goods with foreign.

Decreased export revenue and increased import expenditure in Japan will cause aggregate demand to decrease and have a disinflationary effect on the Japanese economy.

The mechanisms linking monetary policy to the exchange rate and exports/imports are frequently employed by central banks to adjust aggregate demand. Since a decrease in interest rates puts downward pressure on the exchange rate, export dependent countries have often used interest rates to decrease the exchange rate and increase demand for their export goods. While this might sound relatively straightforward, there are a number of negative effects arising in an economy experiencing a falling exchange rate. These are the looked at in Section 4.6.

POP QUIZ 3.4.1   DEMAND-SIDE POLICIES

1   Explain how inflationary expectations in households might influence aggregate demand.

2   How are the variables *M*, *Y*, *CPI* and transfer payments commonly affected during a recession?

3   Explain how fiscal policy might be used in an economy showing increasing inflation.

4   Draw four separate AS-AD diagrams (and perhaps supporting diagrams) showing the effects of:

   a   lower income taxes

   b   increased interest rates

   c   increased supply of money

   d   higher exchange rate.

5   Explain why an increase in aggregate demand caused by increased government spending might not increase real output in the long run. Use the AS-AD model in your answer.

6   'The government raised interest rates today in response to a fiscal stimulus package presented by the Central Bank.' What's wrong with this picture? Look carefully.

7   Why might aggregate demand fall as a result of falling property prices? Why might a decrease in aggregate demand result in falling property prices?

8   Canada and Mexico are trade partners. If Canada's inflation rate increases at a faster rate than Mexico's, *ceteris paribus*, how might one expect aggregate demand to be affected in each country?

9   A tricky one: in an economy the interest rate falls from 9% to 7% and at the same time the rate of inflation falls from 8% to 5%. Explain why borrowers might in fact not be better off.

10 Explain how the Central Bank could reduce the rate of inflation in the economy.

11 Using the AS-AD model, illustrate the American economy during the autumn of 2003 based on the "Fiscal policy in the USA" on page 317.

12 Using the same case study, try to explain why unemployment has not fallen in spite of the remarkable increase in aggregate demand.

13 Thinking ahead to Section 4 (trade): Assume that a decrease in the exchange rate (depreciation) has shown to have a positive influence on aggregate demand in an economy due to a rise in export revenue and/or a decrease in import spending. Might the inverse be true also, e.g. might increased national income instead affect a country's exchange rate?

Shifts in the aggregate supply curve/supply-side policies ©IBO 2003

I've talked to you on a number of occasions about the economic problems our nation faces, and I am prepared to tell you it's in a hell of a mess … we're not connected to the press room yet, are we? – Ronald Reagan

The upward sloping aggregate supply curve has been explained earlier as the correlation between the price level (of final goods) and the willingness/ability of producers to put goods on the market – assuming *ceteris paribus*. Any change in the underlying variables which affect the willingness/ability of producers to produce, will affect aggregate supply at all price levels, i.e. the aggregate supply curve will shift. This is identical to simple supply and demand analysis, but the AS-AD model distinguishes between shifts in the short and long-run aggregate supply curves.

Shifting the short-run aggregate supply curve

The short-run aggregate supply curve in the AS-AD model will shift when production costs for firms change. Three specific short-run influences can be identified:

1. **Price of labour**: An increase in wage rates will mean higher production costs for firms and shift the short-run aggregate supply curve to the left, from $SRAS_0$ to $SRAS_2$ in Figure 3.4.10 diagram I.

This will result in lower output, Y_2, and a higher price level, P_2. A decrease in the wage rate will naturally have the opposite effect.

2. **Price of inputs**: Changes in other factor markets, e.g. the markets for raw material, capital and components will have effects on the cost picture of industrial firms. For example, a decrease in the price of steel will enable producers of cars, houses and washing machines, etc. to increase output at all price levels. This is shown by a shift in short-run aggregate supply from $SRAS_0$ to $SRAS_1$, increasing output to Y_1 and lowering the price level to P_1.

3. **Taxation and legislation**: There are a variety of taxes levied on production which increase costs for firms. Labour taxes (a percentage on wages paid by employers which go to social security contributions, pensions and such) add to overall labour costs. Profit taxes (or corporate taxes) deny firms money that could be used for investment. Environmental taxes on emissions add to firms' costs. Legislation on minimum wage rates, overtime regulation, work hours, etc. also add to the total cost picture of firms. Increased taxes on labour, etc. and stricter regulatory legislation will shift short-run aggregate supply to the left, from $SRAS_0$ to $SRAS_2$, while lower taxes and looser legislation will shift the short-run aggregate supply curve to the right, from $SRAS_0$ to $SRAS_1$.

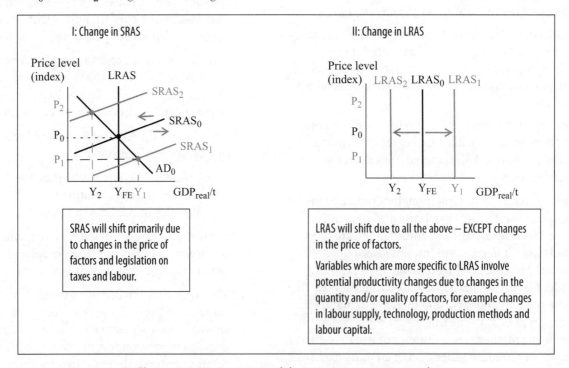

Figure 3.4.10 *Increase and decrease in aggregate supply*

Shifting the long-run aggregate supply curve

A number of other influences will affect short-run aggregate supply, mainly improved technology, increased labour capital, improvements in production processes and other general efficiency gains. However, these are more **long-run influences** since the introduction of new technology, production methods and improvements in the labour force are incremental (= 'bit by bit') and permanent. Long-run aggregate supply – again, representing long-run potential output – will be affected by changes in the *quality* and/or *quantity* of factors of production. However, long-run aggregate supply will *not* be affected by a change in the *price* of factors, since the model is built on the assumption that factor prices will adjust to any increase in the price of final output. The long-run aggregate supply curve is vertical for this very reason; it shows potential output regardless of price level. Recall how demand-side economics is viewed as solely inflationary in the long run – points A to B to C in Figure 3.4.11 diagram I– since factor price will be bid up to ultimately match final output prices, bringing the economy back to the full employment level of output, Y_{FE}.

Supply-side economists favour policies aimed at creating the basic economic conditions for long-run increases in output, where **long-run aggregate supply increases** over time allowing aggregate demand to increase without creating only inflationary pressure. This is shown in Figure 3.4.11 diagram II, where the shift of the long-run aggregate supply curve from $LRAS'_0$ to $LRAS'2$ increases real (potential) output while keeping the economy in long-run equilibrium.

The increase in long-run aggregate supply allows for increased demand without creating harmful inflation rates which would decrease short-run aggregate supply – the economy moves along via points A', B' and C', whereas *potential* (the full employment level of output) output increases over time, from Y'_0 to Y'_2. The major variables affecting long-run aggregate supply are to be found in increased investment, research and development (see "Supply-side example – Nokia" on page 327), new technology, improved production methods, increased labour pool, improved labour quality due to training/education, more efficient use of raw materials, increase in infrastructure (roads, electricity grids, telecommunications, etc.), and labour and tax incentives implemented by government.

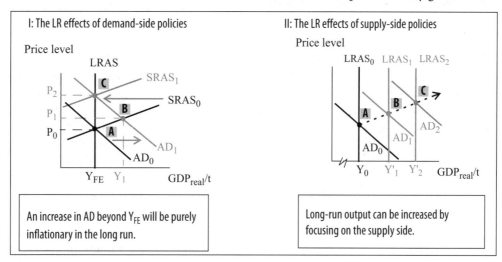

Figure 3.4.11 *Neoclassical view of demand-side and supply-side policies*

Supply-side policies

Supply-side economics arose out of the same mould as the monetarist/neoclassical school during the 1980s and focuses on policies which enhance the long-run output potential in the economy by way of creating well-functioning factor markets and incentives for both producers and labourers. Supply-side policies are in essence **microeconomic** policies, since the policies target specific markets such as the labour or capital market. Supply-side policies are highly market orientated, aiming to 'liberate' markets which are

hindered from clearing due to various forms of market 'impurities' such as labour legislation and government intervention. I have collected the various supply-side policies under three main rubrics: *labour, capital* and *competition.*

1. **Labour:** Supply-side economics in labour markets centre on increasing labour mobility – both in terms of geography location, industry and 'time between jobs' – by increasing the incentives of firms to hire and labourers to accept jobs. The basic ideal is to increase the supply and overall quality of

labour while creating mechanisms for well-functioning labour markets. The following points are often put forward:

- Change labour laws and make it easier for firms to hire and fire, reducing search costs and risks for firms while decreasing between-job time for labourers.

- Education and retraining schemes will increase the quality of labour, e.g. labour capital and increase the speed by which redundant labour can be reallocated. Such schemes can be encouraged by giving tax breaks to firms which implement them.

- Reducing/abolishing regional support schemes in order to highlight differences in regional unemployment levels and thus encourage people to move to new jobs in other regions.

- Cutting back on social welfare/unemployment benefits in order to encourage people to accept jobs by increasing the opportunity costs of unemployment.

- Reducing union power – say, by making sympathy strikes illegal and making collective bargaining harder – to reduce wage stickiness.

- Abolish minimum wages to allow market forces to set wages.

- Decrease marginal tax rates on income as an incentive for labourers to work more and decrease labour taxes in order to decrease labour costs for firms.

2. **Capital:** By increasing both the quality and quantity of capital, supply-side economics aims to increase the long-run aggregate supply:

- Tax breaks/deductions to firms for (re-) investment will stimulate investment expenditure.

- Lower taxes on dividends (a share of company profits paid to shareholders) can increase investment funding for firms since more people will be willing to buy shares.

- Lower profit (corporate) taxes encourage further investment by firms.

3. **Competition:** Finally, supply-side economists point to the importance of competition in an economy as an overriding element in increasing long-run aggregate supply:

- Privatisation of government-run businesses and deregulation of markets are staple supply-side measures in increasing competitive forces in an economy.

- Grant subsidies or tax reductions for firms funding R&D centres.

- Encourage entrepreneurship by granting tax relief and creating beneficial funding schemes for start-ups/new firms.

- Trade liberalisation – reducing tariffs (import tariffs) and other barriers to free trade – and free capital flows (easier foreign investment) are policies often put forward by supply-siders.

The main theme in supply policies is that market forces are far better at creating output in the long run than government intervention in the form of demand management. *Sustainable* – long run – increases in GDP can only be increased, according to this neoclassically orientated view, by increasing long-run aggregate supply. Allowing firms to make a profit under competitive forces and creating conditions for factor markets to clear will shift the long-run aggregate supply curve and therefore decrease the natural rate of unemployment.

Supply-side in the 1980s: It will come as no surprise that supply-side advocates are found primarily to the political right. The highest profiled proponents of supply-side economics were British Prime Minister Margaret Thatcher (1979–90) and US President Ronald Reagan (1981–89). Thatcher's government set out on a markedly supply-side programme of privatisation and deregulation during the early 1980s when Britain was in severe recession. Trade union power was successively diminished, income taxes and marginal tax rates were drastically lowered and state owned enterprises were privatised. The policies of Reagan (later dubbed 'Reaganomics') during the first half of the 1980s were similar: taxes were cut, government expenditure was slashed (creating large budget deficits and government debt) and government agencies downsized, and implemented tight monetary policy to curb inflation. Reagan also increased military spending enormously which, together with some of the largest tax cuts in American history, increased demand and helped bring the US out of the severe recession of 1981. Critics of the Reagan/Thatcher economic regimens maintain that the social suffering of the supply-side reforms – such as marked increases in unemployment initially, increased income inequality, cutbacks in government programs and deteriorating social welfare nets – were excessive. While the final outcomes of both the Reagan and Thatcher eras remain highly debated, there is no doubt that in both cases severe inflation was brought under control and that productivity gains produced growth rates which were some of the highest in the industrialised world. The period also ushered in a more broad-based acceptance for 'rightist' policies based on supply-side measures. In fact, most western economies implemented various forms of supply-side measures during the 1990s.

Case study: Supply-side example – Nokia

The Finnish telecommunications giant, Nokia, became a champion of Finland's economy and major growth engine by clearly focusing on **research and development** (R&D). The company was worried about being too dependent on the USSR and therefore set up the National Technology Agency in 1982 in order to finance spending on research. R&D rose from 1.1% of GDP in 1982 to 3.4% in 2002. The company spends USD3.5 billion a year on R&D and universities have aimed courses at supplying the high-tech industries' needs. By the late 1990s, in Finland, growth was at 5% and unemployment had been cut in half. Nokia – an ex-tyre and rubber-wear maker – became the world's leading mobile phone producer and now accounts for some 20% of Finland's exports. The massive telecom investments, research and university funding resulted in numerous spin-off firms which greatly powered the Finnish economy. This is a 'growth dividend' from R&D.[a]

a. 'The Nokia Economy', *Business Week*, 17 November 2003.

 A little depth and a warning!
A major distinction between simple S/D and AS-AD

All too often students see the similarities between simple demand (e.g. demand for a single product) and aggregate demand (e.g. the sum of all product markets) and draw the conclusion that – as in the simple supply and demand model – aggregate demand does not influence aggregate supply. This is in fact erroneous, since it is quite possible that the investment component of aggregate demand indeed will serve to cause a change in aggregate supply over time. Figure 3.4.12 illustrates an economy initially in long-run equilibrium, point A.

- Investment increases and AD shifts from AD_0 to AD_1, taking the economy from point A to point B.

- In due course, the effects of increased capital will increase productivity, causing aggregate supply to increase from $SRAS_0$ to $SRAS_1$ – point C.

- The increase in productivity and output capability causes LRAS to increase from $LRAS_0$ to $LRAS_1$, creating a new long-run equilibrium at YFE_1.

This is a case where a change in a component of aggregate demand, *investment expenditure*, can directly influence both aggregate demand and aggregate supply over time. Another possibility is that lowering income taxes at first increases aggregate demand due to larger disposable incomes and increased consumption, which the serves to increase aggregate supply in the long run when households' incentives to work more kick in.

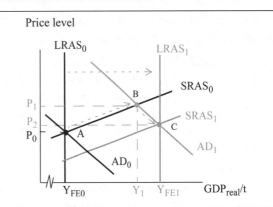

This is a case where a change in a component of aggregate demand, investment expenditure, can directly influence both aggregate demand and aggregate supply over time. Another possibility is that lowering income taxes at first increases aggregate demand due to larger disposable incomes and increased consumption, which the serves to increase aggregate supply in the long run when households' incentives to work more kick in.

Figure 3.4.12 *How AD can shift SRAS*

POP QUIZ 3.4.2   SUPPLY-SIDE ISSUES

1 Show in a diagram how in SR inflation could rise and output fall. What might cause this?

2 Why do neoclassical economists claim that demand-side policies do not increase real long-run output? Illustrate your answer with a suitable diagram.

3 Explain how supply-side policies can be applied to the labour market.

4 What would the supply-side effects be of an increase in:

a income taxes

b tax breaks for small businesses

c fewer subsidies to 'sunset industries' (industries experiencing permanent decline in demand for their goods) in regions with high unemployment rates?

Strengths and weaknesses of these policies ©IBO 2003

> *Predictions are rather hard to make – especially about the future.* – An observation credited to Niels Bohr.

Advantages of demand-side policies

The theoretical benefits of demand management have pretty much been outlined above:

- **Macro goals**: By adjusting monetary and fiscal policies, it is possible to influence the level of economic activity and therefore output, unemployment, inflation and the trade balance. In other words, demand management gives politicians tools to achieve the macroeconomic goals of society.

- **Stability**: Built-in fiscal stabilisers – automatic stabilisers – help even out the economic cycles and create stability and predictability in the economy, while evening-out some of the excesses/surpluses in productive capacity over time.

- **Government goals**: Discretionary fiscal policies in turn allow governments to steer the economy in line with both consensus views of economic goals and ideological underpinnings and ideals of social/economic welfare. Full employment increases living standards while tax rates, unemployment benefits and government spending all help in improving social welfare systems and redistributing incomes in the economy. Note that the concepts such as

'fairness' and 'equality' are *not* entirely normative. There are in fact a good many sound economic arguments underlining social redistribution by way of taxes and transfer payments, in that a great many economic and social costs show strong positive correlation to increased inequality of income and wealth; crime, alcoholism and drug abuse are notable examples. This is a subject of Section 3.6.

- **The Keynesian multiplier**: Keynesian economics also stresses the element of self-perpetuation is stimulating aggregate demand via fiscal policy during recessionary periods – the **multiplier effect** (HL, see below). The effect is built into the Keynesian model and shows how the net final effect of increased government spending or lower taxes is increased over successive 'rounds' in the economy. For example, if government spending increases by £10 billion – say, to build roads and other infrastructure – then jobs will be created and unemployment will fall. It doesn't stop there; many of those who have been unemployed for some time will have pent-up consumption demands, so they will spend most of their wages. This spending will in turn create more demand, which creates more jobs, which lowers unemployment, etc. Thus, according to Keynesians, a major benefit of demand-side economics is that there is a 'leverage' effect of using fiscal stimulation, since the final increase in national income is greater than initial budget costs; $\Delta\uparrow Y_{final} > \Delta\uparrow G_{initial}$ (or $\Delta\uparrow Y_{final} > \Delta\downarrow T_{initial}$). The increase in national income will ultimately pad government tax coffers and help to make up for possible deficit spending done in the first place.

Weaknesses of demand management

Keynesian demand management was virtually unchallenged as the macroeconomic method of choice during the 1950s and 1960s. High growth rates and low unemployment seemed to justify demand management policies. However, during the early 1970s, a number of weaknesses of demand management became evident.

- The business cycles were often erratic and 'untamed' or even aggravated by demand management policies –there were increasing indications of *politically* inclined business cycles over the course of changes in governments.

- *Inflation* rose to hitherto unseen levels and budget deficits grew since government spending during recessionary periods was evermore seldom made up for during booms.

- This increased government *indebtedness* led to most debilitating exchange rate problems (see Section 4.6). Increasingly open economies meant that government spending and/or lower taxes would not have the same multiplicative effect on the domestic economy, as an increased proportion of disposable income gains flowed out of the country to buy imports.

These main weaknesses in using demand management to control the economy are given below under three headings:

- Trade-off problems
- Time lags and exacerbation of the cycle
- Neoclassical economists' critique of demand management.

Difficulties in attaining macro objectives – trade-off problems

The purpose of fiscal and monetary policies is of course to control the swings in the business cycle and achieve macro objectives. This has been illustrated earlier (see Figure 3.4.2 on page 311) let's now look at the possible opportunity costs – *trade-offs* – that arise as a result.

- **Growth and inflation:** High growth and low unemployment are key macroeconomic goals. Governments can use expansionary fiscal policy to stimulate the economy where there is below full employment. See "Fiscal policy in the USA" on page 317 earlier. The aim of these tax measures is to stimulate consumer spending and investment spending and increase aggregate demand. This creates inflationary pressure which results in higher final prices and a *trade-off* between growth and inflation in the short run. (Note that price stability does not imply zero inflation but low and steady inflation.)

- **Budget and unemployment**: When unemployment rises the government can decrease taxes and/or increase government spending in order to increase aggregate demand. Since stimulatory fiscal measures are often undertaken during recessions, they often result in **deficit spending**, resulting in a trade-off between a balanced budget and unemployment levels.

- **Growth and trade balance**: In stimulating the economy, incomes increase and for reasons explained earlier imports will also increase due to the propensity of citizens to import goods and

services. An economy experiencing a *trade deficit* (or, more correctly, a *current account deficit*, see Section 4.5) might use fiscal policy to adjust the trade imbalance. Since high growth rates are associated with both increased inflation and increased imports, tighter fiscal policy could be instigated to counter both inflation and trade imbalance. The contractionary policies would thus lower growth in order to lower import expenditure. A government will have difficulty in keeping the trade balance in equilibrium while stimulating domestic growth and employment – something that the US has noticed for all but one of the past 20 years.

- **Interest rates and exchange rate**: Finally, there is both a domestic and foreign sector trade-off arising from monetary policy. When the Central Bank decreases interest rates in order to stimulate the economy, there will be downward pressure on the *exchange rate* as foreign investors/speculators pull some of their funds out of the country in order to place them elsewhere at a relatively better rate of interest. This will lower demand for the currency and thus the price of the currency falls – which is nothing other than the exchange rate. The Central Bank therefore cannot set the domestic currency's value to other currencies and still freely use monetary policy as a demand-management tool. This was a main argument for European Union opponents of the single currency, the euro, since monetary policy would in effect be taken out of domestic hands and surrendered to the European Central Bank (ECB) in Frankfurt.[9]

Five possible **macroeconomic trade-offs** emerge from the discussion above:

A. Growth ⇔ price stability
B. Unemployment ⇔ price stability
C. Unemployment ⇔ balanced budget
D. Growth ⇔ trade balance
E. Domestic monetary policy (interest rate) freedom ⇔ stable (or fixed) exchange rate.

Time lags and exacerbation of the business cycle

In trying to attain these goals, governments can actually make things worse by exacerbating (= worsening, intensifying) the business cycle. It is possible that attempts to fine-tune the economy result in 'stop-go' cycles, where the economy frequently moves between boom and recession. Neoclassical

---

9. Frankfurt **am Main** – not the other Frankfurt.

economists are quick to point out that fiscal stabilisation policies often come as 'pouring gasoline on a growing fire and water on dying embers', i.e. that foreseeing correct demand management policy is virtually impossible due to time lags.[10] There are a number of possible lags built into the macroeconomic system, all of which make it most difficult to steer – 'fine tune' – the economy.

Lags in fiscal policies

Identification lags arise simply because it is always difficult to see where you are on the business cycle, i.e. the depth of a boom/recession and the length. In Figure 3.4.13 the recognition stage when contractionary policies should be instigated is at point I.

It will take time for the political and administrative process to result in actual policy decisions, leading to *decision and implementation lags*. Say that the government decides to tighten fiscal policy to deflate the overheating economy at point II.

It will still take time before the effects of higher taxes and/or lower government spending actually has an impact on the economy. *Effect and impact lags* are possibly the most heavily weighted of all three, since the resulting change in aggregate demand might deflate

an already contracting economy. This is shown by point III in the diagram, where tighter fiscal policies kick in and lower real GDP at a faster rate than would otherwise be the case.

The exaggerated cyclical effect resulting from contractionary policies in Figure 3.4.13 continues in the next stage of recession. The identification lag (IV) is followed by an implementation lag (V) and an inflationary policy that takes effect at point VI, where the economy has already started to recover. The effects of these reflationary lags are like 'pouring gasoline' on a growing fire, once again causing GDP to increase more acutely than otherwise. The effect over an entire cycle is that real GDP fluctuates more than would otherwise be the case.

Lags in monetary policies

Not all lags and concomitant difficulties in correctly timing contractionary and expansionary policies arise due to fiscal policies. There are notable **lags in monetary policy** also, pointing to at least two quarters before interest rate changes take effect – and often as long as six quarters. The English central bank, the Bank of England, estimates that it takes at least four quarters for a change in interest rates to affect inflation and over two years before maximum impact is reached.

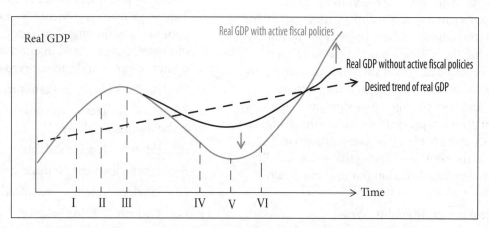

Figure 3.4.13 *How lags can exacerbate fluctuations in the business cycle*

---

10. A famous allegory of economists' attempts to predict/control the business cycle is that it's like trying to drive a car where all the windows are blacked out and you try to steer by looking in the rear view mirror. In addition to this, the accelerator (throttle) and brakes are very sluggish and therefore slow to react, leading to time lags between putting your foot on them and the reaction of the car. Finally, the car has exceptionally good shock absorbers so that you cannot feel whether you are going up or down. Now try to keep between the lines. No, don't try this at home kids.

Neoclassical economists' critique of demand management

This subject could fill an entire book on its own. Come to think of it, it has filled *hundreds* of books. However, I will limit the discussion here to three main points of criticism central to the supply-side reaction against demand management.

Inflation versus long-run growth

Classical economics points to the *stagflationary* (= rising inflation and low/falling GDP) demand-side period of the 1970s and the period of price stability and growth of the supply-side 1980s. Demand-side policies ultimately failed quite drastically in balancing budgets over a cycle, as deficit spending during recessions was never countered during boom periods. Demand-side policies therefore have their place in combating inflation, not in increasing output, according to the neoclassical view. Neoclassical economists put heavy emphasis on using supply-side policies rather than demand-side policies to increase long-run growth. (See Figure 3.4.3 on page 312 to see how demand-side policies are considered, ultimately, inflationary.) This viewpoint has to a certain degree become mainstream and most economists would agree today that there is merit in using an element of supply-side policies in order to lower unemployment in the long run.

Demand-side policies lessen market efficiency

Another basic premise of the neoclassical school is the inter-temporal opportunity cost issue of demand management, where demand-side policies focusing on alleviating unemployment will have far greater long-run costs when inflationary pressure not only dissolves any short-run gains in income, but where resources are squandered (= wasted) on inefficient government spending. The interventionist leaning of demand management distorts factor markets and inhibits market clearing. The neoclassical school prescribes the use of production incentives such as lowering corporate taxes and labour incentives such as decreasing income taxes and lowering social/

unemployment benefits. The short-run social and economic costs of these policies would be more than compensated for by increased long-run output and full employment levels. One could say that neoclassical economists are inclined to let the golden eggs hatch and produce more geese rather than using the golden eggs.

People's expectations are rational

A key component of neoclassical economic thought is that people are rational and well-informed economic agents. When people see that the real value of their income has been eroded due to inflation, they will know that 'the rules have changed' and act accordingly; when government policies aimed at stimulating the economy are implemented, rational economic behaviour will expect inflation to rise and real income to fall.[11] The solution is of course to increase nominal wages in order to at least remain at purchasing power status quo. The expansionary effects on aggregate demand are thus negated by the higher factor prices and decreased aggregate supply. See Figure 3.4.3 on page 312 for diagrammatical illustration.[12]

Weaknesses in supply-side policies / Keynesian critique of the neoclassical school

Many of the weaknesses of supply-side policies put forward deal with the negative side-effects on society. The list of supply-side policies given is ample indication of the possible effects on households comprised of low-income earners, people with only basic education, and older workers who would have difficulty switching jobs. These 'grin-and-bear-it-policies', as Keynes called them, can be compounded as follows.

Incentive function of tax cuts is limited

While most economists accept that positive correlation exists between marginal income tax rates – the tax paid on the 'last' money earned – and the supply of labour, studies show a rather weak link. For example, the large tax cuts given in the US during the Reagan

---

11. An early version of the expectations argument was put forward by the classical economist **David Ricardo** (1772–1823), and came to be known as '**Ricardian equivalence**'. Ricardo posited that households were forward-looking and would react to any decrease in present government spending by lowering their consumption – having seen through the policy and realising that any deficit and increased borrowing resulting from lower government tax receipts would, ultimately, have to be paid for by increased taxation. Since people were rational, they would put aside money in order to meet future increased taxation by saving the increase in disposable income rather than spending it. The net effect of government's lowering of taxes would be nil. Ricardian equivalence has often been used as an argument against demand management by several modern-day new-classical and monetarist economists. Look up new-classical economist (and 1995 Nobel laureate) Robert Lucas, for example.
12. I *told* you it was a Very Important Diagram!

administration are estimated to have increased labour supply by between 0.4% and 0.9%.[13] Another argument put forward by supply-sider is that reductions in taxes and social benefits have a strong incentives effect and therefore increase productivity in the economy. This has been strongly contested by many Keynesian economists who point to the fact that labour productivity growth was virtually the same in the ten years before and after Reagan's supply-side measures. Critics of supply-side measures do acknowledge that cuts in taxes which affect output, such as profit and labour taxes, have had some measure of success in supply-side terms. However, they hasten to add that such policies take a long time to affect the economy – 10 years or more – during which time there are considerable opportunity costs involved, such as …

Social costs

Demand management has often been used as a 'buffer' (= shock absorber) against alarming unemployment rates in various industrial sectors and geographical areas. Targeted increases in government spending, transfer payments and social programs have been used both in increasing aggregate demand and in 'social engineering', i.e. spreading wealth and curtailing income inequalities. Supply-side tax cuts have tended not only to increase **budget deficits** but also to starve the government sector of funds, which can lead to negative effects for poorer households when transfer payments and social programs diminish. Therefore governments run the risk of increasing **unemployment** in the short run since the supply-side policies will initially have the effect of lowering aggregate demand, causing great economic and social loss during the time it takes for the supply-side policies to take effect. The long-run effect is increased **inequality in income distribution**, something that one of the most vocal Keynesians, Paul Krugman[14], has pointed out in America, simply stating that 'Reaganomics made things worse, pushing millions of people … over the poverty line'[15]. Critics also point out that diminishing the size of government and its spending is not only difficult and politically dangerous but can have negative effects on the long-run potential of the economy. Cost cutting in schools, health care and social programs proves to be economically foolish as it will adversely affect the long-run potential of the economy.

Imperfectly functioning markets

Keynesian economists generally view markets as imperfectly functioning mechanisms, where intervention by government is seen as well motivated and necessary to correct some of the more glaring market failures. **Disequilibrium unemployment,** i.e. employment rates below full employment – is seen as the result of demand deficiency (see Section 3.5) and wage stickiness rather than the neoclassical view that market impediments simply do not allow labour prices to fall. In this manner, Keynesians argue that while the labour market *might* ultimately clear and return the economy to full employment, there would be considerable economic loss in the time being as factors lay idle and output was below potential. The correction of demand-insufficiency in the economy lies in the hands of government interventionism and demand management.

Finally, a few words on the alluring – and erroneous – conclusion that economists of demand-side cut are against all forms of supply-side policies. In fact, one of the areas of consensus in economic policy today is that supply-side policies indeed increase long-run aggregate supply. However, it is in the *choice* of supply-side policies that disagreement is still to be found. neoclassical economists favour policies based on **free markets and incentives**, such as lower taxes and privatisation. Keynesian economists prefer supply-side policies of **interventionist type**, such as government funding of worker recruitment/education and retraining centres.

POP QUIZ 3.4.3   WEAKNESSES OF ECONOMIC POLICIES

1   Why might there be conflicts between several of the macroeconomic goals?

2   Explain one of these conflicts in terms of a trade-off.

3   How might fiscal policy actually serve to increase the amplitude of the business cycle?

4   Explain how neoclassical/monetarist economists use 'rational expectations' to criticise demand-side policies.

5   Why do you think Keynes referred to classical policies during recessions in terms of people in the economy having to 'grin and bear it'?

---

13. Abel & Bernanke, p. 578.
14. Nobel Laureate in economics, 2008.
15. 1993 article by *Krugman*, published at http://www.pkarchive.org/economy/ConservativeMirage.html.

HIGHER LEVEL EXTENSION TOPICS

Q: How many Keynesian economists does it take to change a light bulb?

A: All. Because then you will generate employment, more consumption and shifting aggregate demand.

Multiplier ©IBO 2003

The multiplier is a key component of Keynesian theory, and shows the possibility of a given increase in injections, i.e. government spending, investment and exports, increasing aggregate demand by more than the initial value. This is quite logical at an intuitive level since an increase in, say, investment might create employment opportunities in firms producing capital, whereupon newly hired labourers will receive income which is used for consumption – which increases demand for goods and ultimately more capital to produce the goods.

Keynes posited that the main influence on consumption was income, or rather that **consumption was a function of income**. Given that households have a **marginal propensity to consume**, an initial increase in aggregate demand caused by an increase in injections (investment, government spending and exports) would cause increased flows in the economy leading to larger final aggregate demand and national income.

I will use the circular flow model to illustrate how there might be a multiplicative effect of an initial increase in government spending. Assume an open economy comprised of firms, households, financial institutions, government and foreign sector. An increase in any of the aggregate demand components will mean a larger flow around the system, in other words, an increase in aggregate demand. The theory of the multiplier states that an increase in injections of €100 will cause final national income to increase by *more* than €100 – depending on the value of the multiplier. The question here is *how much* aggregate demand will ultimately increase due to a change in injections, i.e. what is the value of the multiplier.

Posit that government wishes to implement expansionary fiscal policies and increases government expenditure by €50 billion.

Round 1: This initial expenditure, round 1 in Figure 3.4.14 on page 334, increases output by €50 billion which flows to households in the form of wages/rent/interest/profit.

Round 2: In round 2, households will use this income in two ways. A portion will go to taxes, imports and savings – this is a leakage out of the system – and a portion will go to consumption. Assume that €10 billion – 20% – leaks out of the circular flow in this manner and that the rest goes to consumption expenditure, i.e. €40 billion (€50 to €10 in leakages) of households' increase in income goes right back into the system. In this manner, national income increases by an additional €40 billion. The initial government expenditure of €50 billion has now caused a total increase of €90 billion.

Round 3: The €40 billion worth of additional output is once again transferred to households in the form of wages/interest/rents/profits, and after 20% of this (€8 billion) leaks out via taxes, imports and savings, the remaining €32 billion is injected into the economy as consumption expenditure in the third round. National income Swill now have increased by €122 billion as each successive round adds more to the flow in the system. Note, however, that each consecutive round adds ever less to national income; this is the leakage effect where 20% of each new round is going to taxes, imports and savings and is therefore withdrawn from the system.

The multiplicative effect shows how much final expenditure will be as a result of an initial increase in injections. This gives us a ratio, $\Delta Y / \Delta J$, which is the value of the multiplier. In the example here, if the government primes the economy by increasing government spending by €50 billion and aggregate demand as a result ultimately increases by €250 billion, then the initial injection has **multiplied by a factor of 5**, i.e. $250/50 billion.

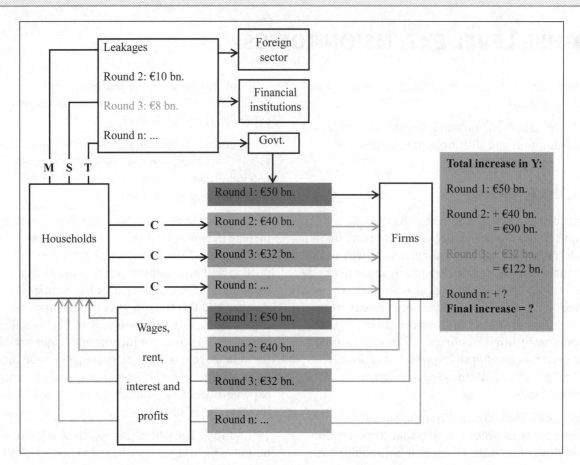

Figure 3.4.14 *The multiplier in the circular flow*

Calculation of multiplier ©IBO 2003

The value of €250 billion in the previous example was not pulled from a hat, but calculated using the formula for the multiplier – which is actually fairly straightforward, but let's go through it one step at a time.

Marginal propensity to consume (MPC)

In the Keynesian model, households' **marginal propensity to consume**, MPC, is the proportion of any increase in income used for domestic consumption. The MPC is the change in consumption over the change in income: $\Delta C/\Delta Y$.

This proportion of increased consumption in the example is 0.8 (i.e. 80% of any increase in household income goes to consumption), which is the *marginal propensity to consume*. In the first round in Figure 3.4.14, the increase in income (Y) of €50 billion in government spending resulted in an increase in consumption (C) of €40 billion.

$$MPC = \frac{\Delta C}{\Delta Y} = \frac{40 \text{ billion}}{50 \text{ billion}} = 0.8$$

Marginal propensity to leak (MPL)

Correspondingly, the 0.2 proportion which does not go to consumption – *savings*, *taxes* and *imports* – is leaking out of the system. This proportion of a change in income which does not return to the system in the form of consumption is the **marginal propensity to leak**, MPL, which is comprised of the marginal propensity to **save** (**MPS**), the marginal propensity to **import** (**MPM**) and the marginal propensity to **tax** (**MPT**).[16]

$$MPS = \frac{\Delta S}{\Delta Y} \quad MPM = \frac{\Delta M}{\Delta Y} \quad MPT = \frac{\Delta T}{\Delta Y}$$

Let us assume that out of the €50 billion increase in income, households save €2 billion (4%), use €3 billion (6%) for imports and have to pay €5 billion in tax (10%).

---

16. You don't need to be Werner von Braun (a rocket scientist) to realise that the sum of the marginal propensity to consume and the marginal propensity to leak must always equal one. This makes perfect sense, since any increase in household income will either be used for domestic consumption or savings/taxes/imports. Thus, MPC + MPL = 1, and 1 – MPC = MPL.

HIGHER LEVEL

$$MPS = \frac{\Delta 2}{\Delta 50} \quad MPM = \frac{\Delta 3}{\Delta 50} \quad MPT = \frac{\Delta 5}{\Delta 50}$$

$$MPL = 0.04 + 0.06 + 0.1 \rightarrow MPL = 0.2$$

$$MPL = \frac{\Delta S + \Delta M + \Delta T}{\Delta Y} \rightarrow \frac{10 \text{ billion}}{50 \text{ billion}} = 0.2$$

Summing up so far:

- Households' increase in consumption due to an increase in income is the marginal propensity to consume: $MPC = \frac{\Delta C}{\Delta Y}$. In the example given, the **MPC is 0.8.**

- The remaining 0.2 is a leakage out of the system. The marginal propensity to leak is comprised of saving (MPS), import expenditure (MPM) and taxes (MPT). The sum of leakage propensities is MPS + MPM + MPM. In the example, the **MPL is 0.2.**

- Basically, any increase in income can go only two ways – consumption or savings/imports/taxes. Thus, the sum of the marginal propensity to consume and the marginal propensity to leak equals 1. **MPC + MPL = 1.**

Keynesian multiplier (*k*)

Finally, we arrive at how to calculate the actual multiplier, *k* (for Keynesian naturally). The initial injection of €50 billion in government spending will reverberate within the flow, with each successive round giving a smaller and smaller increase in consumption – €40 billion in the first round, €32 billion in the second, and so on. The final increase in national income is given by:
initial change in income times k.

The formula for the Keynesian multiplier is

$k = \frac{1}{MPL}$ or $k = \frac{1}{(1 - MPC)}$. Yes, the denominator is of course the same in both versions, e.g. the MPL = 1 – MPC.

Version 1:

$$k = \frac{1}{MPL} \rightarrow \frac{1}{0.2} = 5$$

Version 2:

$$k = \frac{1}{1 - MPC} \rightarrow \frac{1}{1 - 0.8} = 5$$

J – injection (here, government spending)
k – the value of the multiplier
MPC – marginal propensity to consume $\frac{\Delta C}{\Delta Y}$
MPL – marginal propensity to leak

Δinitial J × *k* = Δfinal Y

thus, €50 billion × 5 = €250 billion

The initial increase of €50 billion in government spending led to an ultimate increase in national income of €250 billion, giving a multiplier of 5. This value of *k* is very high and depends on the low level of leakages – 0.2 – out of the system during each round. If we instead apply a more realistic leakage component, say a total leakage of 0.4, then the multiplicative effect (*k*) will be $\frac{1}{0.4}$, i.e. a value of 2.5 rather than 5. This is in keeping with the formulae above: **the higher the leakages** (taxes, imports and saving) **the lower the multiplicative effect** of any given increase in government, investment or export expenditure. This is the same as saying that the higher the marginal propensity of households to consume, the higher the value of the multiplier. By affecting the marginal propensity to withdraw (leak), government can enhance the multiplicative effects in the economy: lower interest rates will lower the MPS; lower income taxes will lower the MPT, and barriers to trade will lower the MPM. Any and all of these actions would theoretically lower the MPL – *ceteris paribus* – and thus increase the value of the multiplier, *k*, which would increase the effects of policies aimed at influencing aggregate demand.

Evaluation of the multiplier: There is an obvious appeal of the multiplier in demand management since a government will theoretically be able to calculate a larger final increase in GDP than initial government spending. In fact, governments have counted on multiplicative effects in utilising demand-side fiscal policies in order to achieve balanced budgets – in spite of deficit spending – over a business cycle. The multiplicative increase in income has been factored-in when deficit spending and/or reduced taxation has been undertaken. This brings us to an additional reason for the reduced influence and therefore use of fiscal policies during the 1970s and 1980s, namely the **increased openness** and ease of trade between countries. Lower barriers to trade such as tariffs and quotas, plus deregulation of financial markets increased the ability of households to consume goods from abroad. Increasingly goods and services could be purchased via import, which meant that any given increase in stimulatory government spending would be withdrawn from the domestic flow of economic activity. The *increase in the marginal propensity to import,* i.e. leakage, meant a corresponding fall in the value of the multiplier, hence a decrease in the effectiveness of fiscal policies aimed at creating a multiplicative effect by way of increasing disposable income.

HIGHER LEVEL

Accelerator model ©IBO 2003

The **accelerator model** is very similar to the multiplier – in fact, they are assumed in traditional Keynesian theory to work hand-in-glove. The accelerator theory of investment assumes that firms' past output levels form the basis for expectations of future needs for capital. In other words, *investment* is assumed to be primarily *linked to changes in demand for output* rather than to a change in interest rates. Firms experiencing an increase in demand will need to increase total capital, i.e. there will be a net addition to capital. If output is growing at a constant rate, firms will also increase their capital spending at a constant rate, while an increase in growth will cause firms to increase desired investment levels.

Assume that a firm producing bottles for the soft drink industry bases capital expenditure on previous output levels. Furthermore, that one machine is needed for each million bottles produced and that for two years demand has been 20 million bottles per year. Thus, the firm has need for 20 machines – and since the machines last for 10 years there has been no net investment (i.e. no increase in capital) for two years. (Of course, there will be replacement investment to make up for worn out machines. Since the machines last for 10 years, and the firm has 20 machines, 2 machines will have to be replaced each year.)

Table 3.4.2 shows the progression for the first two years of constant demand and then what happens when demand increases and falls over the course of the following eight years.

Since demand has remained steady for the first two years, the firm can remain at appropriate output levels simply by replacement investment of the two machines which wear out annually – net investment years 2 and 3 is zero, seen in column 3 in Table 3.4.2. During the next period, years 3 and 4, sales increase and the firm needs to add to capital. The increase in demand of 10% – from 20 million bottles to 22 million bottles and then 24 million – means that the bottle company needs an additional two machines each year. **Gross investment therefore increases** from 2 to 4 (column 4), an increase of 100%, and net investment increases from zero to 2. In other words, as a consequence of an increase in demand of 10%, gross investment has doubled. This is the accelerator effect of an increase in aggregate demand, which incidentally also helps to explain why fluctuations in business cycles can be so erratic and sudden; the compounded (= enhanced) effect on aggregate demand due to investment will accentuate the fluctuations. This works in the other direction also, as we shall see.

Table 3.4.2 *The acceleration model of investment*

Time		(1) Yearly sales of bottles	(2) Desired number of machines (column 1 / 1,000,000)	(3) Net investment (= change in column 2)	(4) Gross investment (column 3 plus 2 machines every year)
Steady sales	Year 1	20,000,000	20	0	2
	Year 2	20,000,000	20	0	2
Rising sales	Year 3	22,000,000	22	2	4
	Year 4	24,000,000	24	2	4
Levelling sales	Year 5	25,000,000	25	1	3
	Year 6	25,000,000	25	0	2
Falling sales	Year 7	23,000,000	23	-2	0
	Year 8	21,000,000	21	-2	0
Levelling sales	Year 9	20,000,000	20	-1	1
	Year 10	20,000,000	20	0	2

During year 5, sales increase less, to 25 million bottles, and net and gross investment falls – as it does the next year when sales level off at 25 million bottles. The emphasis here is that it is not necessary for de facto sales to decline in order for investment to fall! It is enough that the *rate of increase of sales decreases to affect gross investment*. During years 7 and 8, the fall in demand/sales will result in the firm not replacing worn out machinery at all, seeing as the capital stock is too high for required output of 23 million and then 21 million bottles. There will be *negative net investment* of –2 and zero gross investment each of these years. Demand levels off at 20 million bottles during years 9 and 10, when gross investment climbs back to initial start-of-cycle levels of two machines per year and zero net addition to capital stock.

Drawing direct parallels to the macro economy, a number of important points can be illustrated by the example above.

- Firstly, investment expenditure is both highly connected to aggregate demand and also far more volatile (= sensitive) than demand changes. Investment changes far more than the change in demand, which serves to increase the **fluctuations** in a business cycle. (See "Measuring the waves" on page 302.)

- Secondly, once output starts to rise, it must continue to rise at the same rate in order for investment to remain constant, i.e. a slower growth rate will cause a decline in investment. Conversely, a higher growth rate will lead to increases in investment. Again, the effect of the accelerator is that it enhances relatively mild changes in demand and increases business cycle amplitude.

- Thirdly, it is possible for investment to virtually collapse due to a relatively small decrease in demand – just look at year 7, where a decline in sales of 8% (-2 m/25 m) leads to *zero* gross investment and *negative* net investment.

Evaluation of the accelerator: There are a number of weaknesses with the accelerator theory. Nowhere is it written that firms cannot adjust output by increasing the use of labour rather than capital – either by overtime or new hiring. In addition to this, many businesses operate on excess capacity levels in order to be able to manage demand surges over shorter time periods, and may decide that an upswing in business activity is temporary and not worth increasing investment. Finally, there are many time-lag issues involved which would cause the link between aggregate demand and addition to capital stock to be rather hard to finger. Therefore the extent to which the multiplier effect works in concert with the accelerator is still rather unclear.

'Crowding out' ©IBO 2003

There are basically three ways government can fund increased government spending during a fiscal year; printing money, raising taxes, and borrowing from its citizens. Printing money is relatively straightforward and most economists would agree that this indeed raises output at least in the short run. Most would also agree that raising taxes to fund spending has a relatively minor effect on aggregate demand. Instead, the disagreement has centred on whether government spending *funded by borrowing* will bring about an increase in aggregate demand or not.

The argument goes as follows: Assume that the government borrows money (by issuing government securities, i.e. bills and/or bonds) in order to fund government spending in line with demand-side fiscal policies. The increase in government borrowing increases the demand for loanable funds which drives up interest rates and causes investment expenditure to fall. Thus, the potential increase in aggregate demand due to government spending is negated – crowded out – by the increase in interest rates and concomitant fall in investment, hence the name crowding out. The concept has frequently been used as another neoclassical/monetarist argument against fiscal policies.

> Crowding out: When government expenditure is financed by increased government borrowing, interest rates may be driven up. This might cause a decrease in investment in the private sector as firms scale back on capital expenditure. The increase in government expenditure and borrowing has 'crowded out' an amount of investment.

Assumptions: However (this is economics – there is *always* a 'however'), there are a couple of weighty assumptions involved in claiming that government borrowing would crowd out investment.

1. Firstly, the economy has to be operating **at or above the full employment** level of output in order for complete crowding out to take place.

2. Secondly, **real borrowing** has to take place. The government's increased borrowing from either households or the financial sector cannot be compensated by pumping additional money out into the market via the printing press.

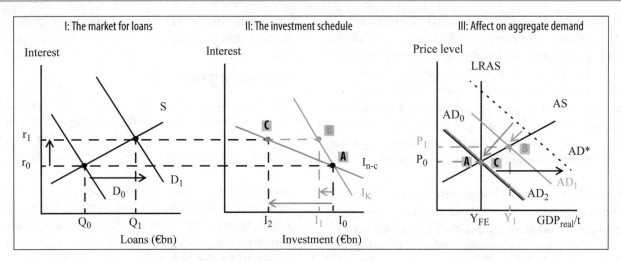

Figure 3.4.15 *Crowding out – Keynesian and neoclassical view*

Figure 3.4.15 shows how the crowding out mechanism works.

1.   Assume that the economy is operating at the full employment level of output, Y_{FE} in diagram III, and that government increases government spending by way of increasing its borrowing on the open market. The increase in government spending increases aggregate demand from AD_0 to AD^*, but …

2.   … the increase in demand for loanable funds (diagram I) caused by government borrowing will drive up the interest rate from r_0 to r_1, which in turn decreases investment …

3.   … shown in the two different investment schedules in diagram II. This has a *contractionary* effect on aggregate demand: AD_1 or AD_2 in diagram III. The movement from **A** to **B** or **A** to **C** in diagrams II and III are two of a number of possibilities.

Summing up in economic shorthand:
$G \rightarrow D_{loanable\ funds} \rightarrow r \rightarrow I \rightarrow AD$ … the increase in government spending drives up interest rates which crowds out investment.

Keynesian view – partial crowding out: One possibility is that there is a *degree of crowding out* due to increased government borrowing, and that aggregate demand does not fall completely back to its original position, AD_0, but to AD_1 in diagram III. The economy moves from **A** to **B**.

Neoclassical view – complete or near-complete crowding out: The increase in government spending aims to increase aggregate demand from AD_0 to AD^*, but since there has been *real borrowing* in order to fund the increase in government spending, the increase in the interest rate concomitantly decreases investment – shown by the shift of aggregate demand from AD^*

back to AD_2. The stimulatory effect of government spending is thus entirely eradicated by a decrease in private sector borrowing and thus lower investment levels. There is *complete crowding out* and the economy moves from **A** to **C**.

Evaluation of crowding out: The question of crowding out is largely one of degree. Most economists would agree that there is some crowding out when government borrows money to fund additional spending, but there is a great deal of contention as to the extent to which investment funding is affected.

- **Keynesians** traditionally largely disregarded any possible crowding out effects, operating as they were under the assumption that investment levels were largely unaffected by interest rates. Modern-day Keynesians accept a *degree* of crowding out, but still regard investment demand as relatively inelastic, shown in diagram II as I_K. The decrease in investment from I_0 to I_1 does not entirely negate the effects of fiscal stimulation. Hence the Keynesian theory does not disregard the potential stimulatory effects of fiscal policy funded by government borrowing.

- **Neoclassical economists/monetarists** on the other hand claim that complete – or near-complete – crowding out will indeed occur (as long as there is *real borrowing* taking place) since the demand for investment is highly responsive to changes in interest rates. The inelastic investment schedule of the neoclassical/monetarist school, I_{n-c} in diagram II, causes a far greater decrease in private sector investment, from I_0 to I_2. In the example here, complete crowding out takes place. The results are well in line with the neoclassical view that fiscal policy squanders resources by diverting funds from the private sector to government.

POP QUIZ 3.4.4   MULTIPLIER, ACCELERATOR AND CROWDING OUT

1   In an economy, equilibrium *Y* rises by 25 billion as a result of an initial investment of 10 billion. What is the value of the *marginal propensity to consume* (MPC)?

2   If government spending increases by 10 billion and the *marginal propensity to consume* (MPC) is 0.5, what will the final increase in national output be?

3   How will an increase in the *marginal propensity to save* (MPS) affect the multiplier?

4   Looking ahead: How might the creation of a common market (see Section 4.3) affect individual countries' ability to rely on multiplicative effects in using fiscal policies to stimulate the domestic economy?

5   How might the accelerator model help to explain fluctuations in the business cycle?

6   Why might an increase in government spending 'crowd out' a degree of investment expenditure?

7   Explain how the neoclassical/monetarist view of crowding out strengthens this school's view on the ineffectiveness of fiscal demand management policies.

HIGHER LEVEL

Preparing for exams

Short answer questions (10 marks each)

1   Explain the link between the rate of interest and inflation.

2   Using the AD-AS model, explain how an increase in government spending would affect an economy.

3   Why might stimulatory fiscal policy have no (long run) effect on national income?

4   Why is it so difficult for government to achieve all macro objectives simultaneously?

5   Explain how automatic (fiscal) stabilisers may help to lower fluctuations in the business cycle.

6   How might monetary policy be used to influence economic activity?

7   How might a country's central bank use monetary policy to stimulate domestic aggregate demand via exchange rates?

[HL only]

8   How might an accurate value for the multiplier aid a government in setting fiscal policy?

9   Explain 'crowding out' and why it may be considered important for policy makers.

Extended response questions (25 marks each)

1   a   Carefully distinguish between 'demand-side' policies and 'supply-side' policies. (10 marks)

   b   What are the main weaknesses of using demand-side policies? (15 marks)

2   a   Why is investment so important in an economy? (10 marks)

   b   Explain the role governments can play in supporting investment levels in the economy. (15 marks)

3   a   Outline and briefly explain the main macroeconomic objectives of governments. (10 marks)

   b   Critically examine one of these objectives, and explain why it should be considered the most important of them all. (15 marks)

Unemployment and inflation

3.5

UNEMPLOYMENT AND INFLATION

The first panacea for a mismanaged nation is inflation of the currency; the second is war. Both bring a temporary prosperity; both bring a permanent ruin. But both are the refuge of political and economic opportunists.
– Ernest Hemingway.

Full employment ©IBO 2003

The concept of **full employment** has so far been used in conjunction with the long-run aggregate supply curve, where long-run potential output is also the full employment level of output. Full employment does not mean that there is 'zero **unemployment**' but rather that all of the people willing and able to work have jobs at the going wage rate. Putting things simply – initially – full employment is the quantity of the total labour force employed when the labour market is in equilibrium. Figure 3.5.1 illustrates this, where the demand for labour and supply of labour at the real wage level W_0 creates full employment at **FE**.[1]

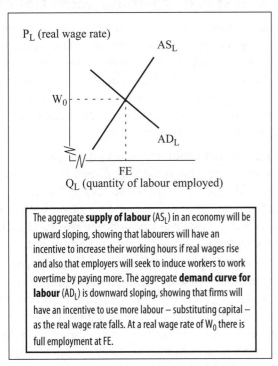

The aggregate **supply of labour** (AS_L) in an economy will be upward sloping, showing that labourers will have an incentive to increase their working hours if real wages rise and also that employers will seek to induce workers to work overtime by paying more. The aggregate **demand curve for labour** (AD_L) is downward sloping, showing that firms will have an incentive to use more labour – substituting capital – as the real wage rate falls. At a real wage rate of W_0 there is full employment at FE.

Figure 3.5.1 *Labour market*

The concept of full employment deals with the sum total of all labour markets, the *aggregate supply/demand for labour*, AS_L and AD_L in Figure 3.5.1. Since employment (and thus unemployment) is a stock concept, at any given point in time there will be people between jobs and entering/leaving the labour market. It is likely that a number of individual labour markets, say dentists, have an excess of demand while there is an excess supply for computer programmers. Full employment therefore does not mean 'everyone has a job', but that in total the supply of labour equals demand. This is why full employment is defined as equilibrium on the *total* labour market rather than individual labour markets.

Underemployment ©IBO 2003

An initial weakness of the concept of full employment is the simple fact that any number of people who are technically employed will in fact be working part time or in odd jobs and therefore in effect are suffering from **underemployment**.

- **Women**, for example, are often caught in an underemployment trap due to traditional roles of child care, while many might be looking for close to full-time employment. As the children grow up women often have difficulty finding increased work hours.

- People working **part-time**, such as handymen and odd-jobbers will frequently be underemployed over the course of the year, since such labour demand is highly varied.

- Finally, **developing countries** often have high levels of underemployment since rural households and families will soak up a good deal of what otherwise would be counted as unemployment. This has been accentuated by high levels of population growth which add to the labour force and lower the productivity of labour.

---

1. We deal solely with **real** values. Real wages are average wage levels in the economy adjusted for inflation, i.e. set in base year values.

> **Full employment, unemployment and underemployment:**
>
> - **Full employment** is when there is equilibrium on the aggregate labour market, i.e. the total number of hours demanded by firms corresponds to the total number of hours supplied by households at the going real wage rate.
>
> - **Unemployment** is the number of people in the labour force, e.g. able and willing to work – not holding a job. It is usually expressed as a percentage, for example, 400,000 unemployed out of a total labour force of 5,000,000 is 8% unemployment.
>
> - **Underemployment** is when people who are offering their services on the labour market can not find full time work.

Unemployment ©IBO 2003

Newlan's Truism: An 'acceptable' level of unemployment means that the government economist to whom it is acceptable still has a job.

Unemployment rate ©IBO 2003

A recession is when your neighbour is out of work. A depression is when you are out of work.
– Harry Truman

Defining and then measuring the unemployment rate looks straightforward and simple. Take the number of unemployed people at a given point in time in an economy and divide the amount by the work force. This seemingly simple stock concept comes with quite a few 'howevers', but let's start off with a basic example. Figure 3.5.2 shows the unemployment figures in Canada in December 2008.[2]

Out of a total of 26.92 million citizens, the Canadian labour force is just over 18 million workers, or 67.8% of the population – also known as the *participation rate*.[3]

So who are the other 8.68 million Canadians in Figure 3.5.2 who are not either felling pine trees (for lumber) or sticking taps into maple trees (to make delicious maple syrup)? Well, the labour force is defined as those **above the age of 16 who are considered to be economically active**, i.e. are either seeking employment or have employment. This

excludes a number of people other than under-16s such as military personnel, retirees, parents on child leave, people with disabilities, and perhaps students, those who do not want to work, people in government retraining programmes. It depends on how both the numerator (unemployed) and denominator (labour force) are defined and measured – and this differs between countries.

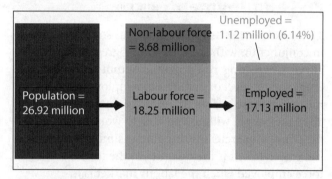

Figure 3.5.2 *Canadian population, labour force and unemployment, 2008*

Weaknesses in unemployment figures

Be careful in comparing official unemployment rates for different countries! Each country will have their own methodology for defining the labour force – and also those considered to be unemployed. The problems arising in trying to correctly estimate the rate of unemployment are of two main types: *definitional* problems and *accounting* problems.

- **Definitional problems** arise in defining, for example, whether those with disabilities and long-term illnesses, unemployed workers close to retirement age and those who no longer bother to seek work (known as **discouraged workers**) should be counted as part of the labour force or not.

- **Accounting problems** arise when unemployment figures are primarily based on those who have registered as seeking employment at employment agencies and those receiving unemployment benefits (claimant count). There could be a large number of people who in reality are unemployed but are 'hidden' in job training schemes, youth employment/training programs and people who are not even part of the formal economy.

One way to deal with the problems of definition of and accounting for unemployment is by standardizing the measurements and then doing a survey of the population. This is what the International Labour

---

2. Official government figures at http://www.statcan.ca/english/Pgdb/labor20a.htm.
3. I note with interest that in updating these figures from the previous edition where figures for 2003 were used, that while the population has increased from 25.25 to 26.9 million and the labour force 17.2 to 18.25 million, the participation rate is *identical* at 67.8%.

Organisation (**ILO**) does. The results are commonly used for international comparisons. The ILO defines unemployment as people who are without a job (= work less than one hour a week), have actively sought employment in the past four weeks and are able to start a new job within two weeks.[4] A cross-section

representing the entire country is then surveyed via forms and interviews, whereupon the results are statistically organised to show the total unemployment rate. The Organisation of Economic Cooperation and Development (OECD) uses the ILO standard, giving the unemployment rates shown in Figure 3.5.3.

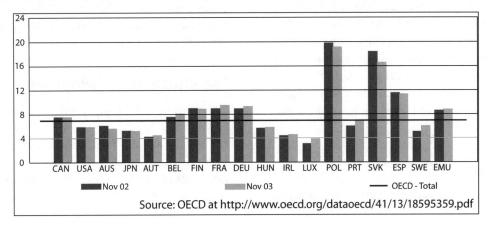

Source: OECD at http://www.oecd.org/dataoecd/41/13/18595359.pdf

Figure 3.5.3 *Unemployment rates*

Costs of unemployment ©IBO 2003

Having high levels of employment is perhaps the foremost macro objective since unemployment is strongly associated with societal costs. While many of these costs are naturally primarily felt by the unemployed themselves – primarily loss of income and living standards – a good many costs are inflicted on society. The costs of unemployment are often put in terms of economic and social costs – which, of course, overlap each other.

Economic costs

There are numerous economic costs involved in having people unemployed:

- Perhaps the most intuitive cost of unemployment is the **loss of output** in the economy resulting from idle factors of production. While these costs might be relatively lenient in the short run, in the long run there will be a number of negative aspects which arise.

- Lower income in the economy will diminish the **tax base** and decrease income tax receipts for government.

- This will put an additional burden on the budget which would in all probability already be under

pressure due to **increased transfer payments** in the form of unemployment and social benefits.

- The use of government funds in this manner might mean **opportunity costs** in the form of less money available for schools, health care and roads. Or even if the government keeps planned government spending constant it might borrow money to fund deficit spending which could **crowd out** private investment [HL concept]. Government might instead increase taxes to make up for the loss of tax receipts, in which case there will be a burden on the tax payer.

- Longer periods of high employment also make it **difficult for labour market entrants** (e.g. young people looking for initial employment) to get into the market, since employers will have the 'pick of the crop' and naturally look to the experienced workers first. Finally, long-term unemployment will inevitably erode the skills and abilities of experienced workers (deskilling) and reduce the economy's ability to get back on its feet later on.

Social costs

The above highlights the allocative waste involved in unemployment; labour and labour capital is a most valuable resource in improving living standards in an economy. These economic costs quite naturally glide

---

4. My experience in Mexico re the ILO definition: it ain't working! One of my students, Ximena, did a brilliant extended essay on actual unemployment in Acapulco, a tourist resort city on the west coast. Since so many labourers are employed in the tourism industry and often rely on occasional odd jobs, the official rate of unemployment is around 2%. In reality the figure is closer to 25%. The results were stark illustration of the weaknesses in unemployment figures.

into social costs. I often tell my students to ask their parents how they identify themselves, i.e. how they see themselves 'from the outside'. Is it 'Jan the parent', 'Jan the doctor', 'Jan the fly-fisherman', etc. Odds are in favour of people identifying themselves in terms of *occupation*, here, 'Jan the doctor'. Modern societies (frequently in the form of parents) often put heavy emphasis on 'getting a job and being able to support yourself' and career-building. I recall a story about an upper-level manager in Japan who was laid-off during a recession and couldn't face letting his family, friends and neighbours find out – so he continued to get up at 6:00 in the morning to 'go to work', i.e. sit in the park and read the papers.[5] In many societies there is enormous social stigma (= dishonour) attached to being unemployed.[6]

The social effects are perhaps even more damaging than the economic effects – and this is not touchy-feely-economics, but a hard-line view of economic realities. Just ask yourself who will be the most productive/constructive member of the community; a proud, committed, confidant and dignified person – or someone with low self-image and little sense of self-worth. Yes, it is actually that simple: being unemployed is highly value-laden and will damage those who are subjected to it for longer time periods and by extension this will damage society. Macroeconomic studies consistently show correlation between unemployment rates and domestic violence, crime, drug and alcohol abuse, broken families and mistreated children, and general mental and 'spiritual' (for lack of a better word) ill health leading to higher suicide rates and depression – all of which are quite evidently economically sub-optimal.[7]

Types of unemployment ©IBO 2003

Since unemployment is a stock concept the level will change continuously as people enter and leave the labour force. An increase or decrease in population, school-leavers, and people simply returning to the job market after illness or paternity/maternity leave will serve to increase/decrease the size of the labour pool. Conversely, assuming a constant labour force, there

will be people from the labour force gaining and losing jobs for any number of reasons, so if more people gain jobs than lose jobs unemployment will fall. This ongoing process of inflows and outflows into the labour market and available jobs will necessarily mean a degree of unemployment will always exist at any given point in time. This is called *equilibrium unemployment* and consists of three main types: **structural**, **frictional** and **seasonal** unemployment.

Structural unemployment ©IBO 2003

The most difficult type of unemployment to deal with is when it is 'built-in' to society by forces inherent to the economy itself. Structural unemployment is basically the mismatch of available labour skills and the demands of the economy. The main forces affecting unemployment levels here are *labour mobility*, *declining* ('sunset') *industries* and job redundancies resulting from *technological advances* in production. Any changes of these variables will give rise to structural unemployment since labour is configured to match certain demands in the labour market. There will be job losses when labour demands change, often resulting in very painful long-run unemployment for large numbers of workers. Structural unemployment is one of the most serious macroeconomic problems facing nations today, and three (often overlapping) types of structural unemployment can be identified.

1. **Regional unemployment** happens when a main industry in a region suffers from permanent loss of jobs, such as the fishing industry along the Norwegian coast (caused by depleted fish stocks); the steel industry in North America's so-called 'Rust Belt' (caused by increased global competitiveness), and coal mining in the Yorkshire region of England.

2. Very similar, and indeed often arising simultaneously, is **sectoral unemployment**. This is when a specific sector of the economy suffers from lengthy and often permanent decline. Industries producing horse-drawn buggies, mechanical adding machines and typewriters, and slide rules were all once commonplace but are now largely relegated to being part of history. In each case, skilled labour was made redundant.

---

5.   A couple of my Japanese students, Buddha and Shota, read this and commented: 'Well, yes, of course. Eh?' Oh well, at least they bring me sake.

6.   I recommend the film *Falling down* by Robert Altman for a most illustrative case in point.

7.   I was invited out to dinner by parents the other night. The father and I sat after dinner puffing cigars, drinking Cognac and discussing the ongoing plight of the world economy (January 2008). This man is a rather powerful individual in the business world and heavily in the know. I mean, several times during the course of conversation there were snippets like '... and I told [Mexican President] Calderon that ...' He, as I, spoke anxiously about the increase in very nasty criminality that will doubtlessly ensue when the full force of falling national income and rising unemployment hits Mexico. He is in fact getting ready to leave the country for fear of his family's safety.

3. In 1811 and 1812, during the first part of the Industrial Revolution, there was a great number of violent attacks on weaving machines in the Lancashire and Yorkshire districts of England. Men and women in the weaving industry destroyed textile machines that were replacing their labour during this transformation of English economy and society.[8] This violent reaction was to ongoing **technological unemployment**, where new technology in textiles shifted the entire manufacturing base from labour intensive manufacturing to capital intensive. This is a continuous process in economies, since ever-improving technology will increase output per labourer and in many cases create large-scale redundancies amongst professional groups. As one of many possible examples, just think of how computer technology has vastly increased the capacity of putting together a newspaper – thousands of highly trained professional typesetters were made redundant within a few years.

Frictional unemployment ©IBO 2003

Labourers leaving/losing one job will mostly set out to find another. This is frictional (or **search**) unemployment and is mostly short term. The speed with which job seekers are able to find new employment depends on their work skills and education, plus the needs of the labour market. In addition to these market forces, there are a number of 'interventionist' variables which will affect the ability/willingness of employers to hire and labourers to accept jobs. For example, if labour law makes it difficult for employers to lay off workers then there will be greater care – and time spent – in hiring new workers. If unemployment benefits are high, the unemployed will have relatively low incentives in looking for jobs. (See *Supply-side policies* in Section 3.4.) In addition to this, the availability and efficiency of job centres and unemployment agencies will affect time between jobs.

Seasonal unemployment ©IBO 2003

Waiters in holiday resorts, ski instructors and construction workers on North Sea oil platforms will all have to deal with longer periods of inactivity, giving rise to varying patterns of seasonal unemployment. Other than these workers finding backup jobs in off-

seasons, there is little to be done about this type of unemployment. This type of unemployment will often overlap regional unemployment.

> **Structural, frictional and seasonal unemployment:**
>
> - **Structural unemployment** is 'built into the very fabric' of society – labour immobility, declining industries and technological advances all contribute to structural unemployment. Three sub-types within structural unemployment are **regional**, **sectoral** and **technological** unemployment.
> - When workers are between jobs and actively seeking employment, one speaks of **frictional unemployment**. (Also known as search unemployment.)
> - Workers who are unemployed in industries subject to 'off-seasons' such as tourism are **seasonally unemployed**.

Full employment revisited: why we are different from chickens

Chickens rarely – if ever – volunteer their services on the food market.[9] Labour is a little different from the market for chickens (or any other good, of course) in that the 'good' on offer (e.g. labour) has a mind of its own and will therefore *cause its own supply*. In other words, there will be a difference between the total *potential* supply of labour – the labour force – and the *actual* supply of labour. While the illustration of the market for chickens simply shows the supply and demand at any given price, it is far more interesting when one is illustrating the labour market to show *how many* chic ... eh, labourers are *not* part of supply. The difference between the people supplying their labour and the total labour force is of course unemployment.

Equilibrium unemployment – the natural rate of unemployment

Figure 3.5.4 on page 346, diagrams I and II illustrate how *structural*, *frictional* and *seasonal* unemployment together make up the natural rate of unemployment. The aggregate supply of labour, AS_L, shows the quantity of labour supplied at any given wage level, while the total labour force, TLF, shows the potential amount of labour available if everyone who offered

---

8. These became known as 'Luddites' in reference to a fictitious 'General Ludd' that the workers professed to follow. Today the term Luddite is used rather derogatorily as someone who is 'techno-phobic' and 'backward striving'.
9. But the genetic modifiers are probably working on it. Kamikaze chickens, coming up.

their services had a job. (Think of the AS_L curve as the *job acceptance curve* – it shows the willingness of labourers to accept a job at a given real wage rate.) The TLF curve is upward sloping since higher wages would induce more people to enter the labour force, for example recent retirees and discouraged workers who would find it increasingly worth their while to offer their labour on the market. Notice that the TLF curve is steeper than the ASL curve, indicating that as the real wage rate increases, ever fewer people will spend time unemployed so the distance between the two curves decreases.

The curves don't meet since there will always be someone unwilling to accept a job no matter what the wage level.[10] In Figure 3.5.4 diagram I, the *labour market is in equilibrium* at the full employment level, FE. At the going wage rate of W^*, there will still be a number of people in the labour force who are unemployed; the *structurally unemployed* (U_0), the *frictionally unemployed* (U_1) and the *seasonally unemployed* (U_2). The sum of unemployment at the

market clearing real wage level W^* is $FE \Leftrightarrow U^*$. This is the equilibrium level of unemployment.

Figure 3.5.4 diagram II (note: different scale) shows the sum of the three unemployment types. Structural, frictional and seasonal unemployment together make up voluntary unemployment. I know that this sounds ludicrous and perhaps even derogatory (= insulting), but the term simply implies that for one reason or another, a portion of the available labour force doesn't perceive the opportunity cost ratio incentives (i.e. the opportunity cost of unemployment compared with the opportunity cost of working) as strong enough to accept jobs. The structurally unemployed could re-educate themselves; the frictionally unemployed could accept any job while they seek employment, and the seasonally unemployed could see to it that they had alternatives in the off-season. A proportion, e.g. percentage, of the total labour force which chooses not to accept jobs at the going wage rate will exist at any wage level, thus the percentage of voluntarily unemployed is also the **natural rate of unemployment.**

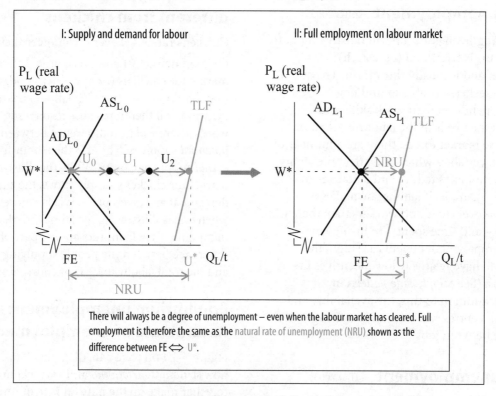

Figure 3.5.4 *Supply and demand for labour – full employment*

---

10. His name is Lars Swahn. I went to university with him.

I know all the terminology gets confusing, so allow me to do the definitions via another syllogism:

1. If everyone in the labour force who wants a job at the going wage rate has a job, there is **full employment**.

2. Since these people accept the real wage rate, AS_L equals AD_L and the labour market is in equilibrium. Any existing unemployment is thus **equilibrium unemployment**.

3. Anyone who has not accepted the real wage rate has done so voluntarily and is **voluntarily unemployed**.

4. Since there is *always* an element of voluntary unemployment in the economy, it is **natural**. The percentage of workers voluntarily unemployed is the **natural rate of unemployment**.

Hence:
Full employment = equilibrium unemployment = voluntary unemployment = natural rate of unemployment

Cyclical/demand-deficient unemployment ©IBO 2003

When unemployment exceeds the rate at which the labour market is in equilibrium, there is disequilibrium unemployment. Economic theory identifies two main reasons for disequilibrium unemployment and the debate is frequently rather high pitched and politicised.

- The *Keynesian/demand-side view* is that disequilibrium unemployment is caused by too little demand in the economy.

- The *neoclassical/supply-side view* is that disequilibrium unemployment is caused by market imperfections such as minimum wages and strong unions.

We start off by looking at cyclical (or demand-deficient) unemployment. In this view, unemployment is strongly linked to phases in the business cycle, as the demand for labour is derived from the demand for goods and services. This is known as cyclical unemployment since it is connected to cyclical variations of economic activity. When total unemployment is higher than the full unemployment rate there is a *cyclical addition* to total unemployment caused by relatively low aggregate demand.

Diagram I in Figure 3.5.5 on page 348 utilises the aggregate demand and aggregate supply curves for labour to illustrate how a change in the demand for labour during a recessionary period causes *disequilibrium* on the labour market, i.e. a degree of **involuntary unemployment**. The decrease in the demand for labour from AD_{L0} to AD_{L1} adds $U_0 \Leftrightarrow FE$ unemployment to the previous (full employment rate) $FE \Leftrightarrow U^*$ shown in diagram II. The question you should now be asking yourself is *why* the real wage rate doesn't fall to W_1 and create a new equilibrium level of unemployment lower than the rate at W^*.

Here's a clue: cyclical/demand deficient unemployment is also known as **Keynesian unemployment**! Recall that Keynesian economics views markets as imperfectly functioning in general, and that labour markets specifically suffer from downward stickiness. The concept of cyclical unemployment, in accordance with Keynesian assumptions, means that real wages will not fall in the short run and the market will be in disequilibrium. In other words, since labourers will be highly unlikely to accept lower wages (and firms will also be reluctant to lower them) the real wage rate will remain at W^* and create an excess supply of labour at the going wage rate. While the labour market might ultimately clear, the proportion of people not accepting jobs at lower rates might last for some time, with unemployment rates above the market clearing level of W_1.

Cyclical (or demand deficient or Keynesian) unemployment: Cyclical unemployment is the addition to equilibrium unemployment (full employment) resulting from a contractionary economy. Since the demand for labour is largely derived from the demand for goods and services, a fall in aggregate demand (and/or aggregate supply) during a recessionary period will decrease the demand for labour. The term derives its name from the cyclical variations in economic activity.

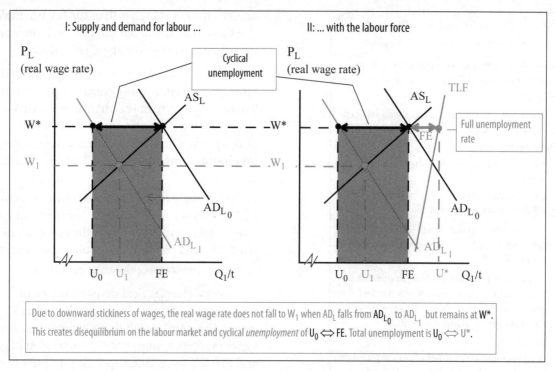

I: Supply and demand for labour ...

II: ... with the labour force

Due to downward stickiness of wages, the real wage rate does not fall to W_1 when AD_L falls from AD_{L_0} to AD_{L_1} but remains at **W***. This creates disequilibrium on the labour market and cyclical *unemployment* of $U_0 \Leftrightarrow FE$. Total unemployment is $U_0 \Leftrightarrow U^*$.

Figure 3.5.5 *Cyclical/demand-deficient unemployment*

Warning!
Using labour market diagrams

Here are a few common mistakes you will want to avoid – plus a few comments on my labour market diagrams:

- A common error in using labour diagrams is to mislabel the axes. Quite frequently in the stress of an exam students will use 'AD' rather than 'AD_L'.

- Another common error is to put 'P' on the P-axis rather than the correct 'P_L' or 'Real wage rate'.

- Include relevant assumptions! Here, you should include whether you are assuming real wages to be downward sticky or not.

Here are my comments on my use of diagrams to illustrate unemployment:

I know of no secondary school textbook which consistently uses the TLF curve in diagrams seeking to illustrate changes in AS_L or AD_L. Commonly, textbooks briefly explain labour market equilibrium, e.g. the natural rate of unemployment, and then use a rather simplistic diagram omitting the TLF curve. My question is invariably: 'Right, can you see the quantity of unemployment?' Well, no. A shift in AD_L shows the change in people who have jobs, not the number of labourers who do not have jobs. Thus, I have decided to retain the TLF curve in all diagrams.

*I am telling you the above simply to point out that you will **not** be penalised in your exams or IA by using the more common version without the TLF curve.*

Aggregate demand and demand for labour

The relationship between aggregate demand and the demand for labour should be fairly clear cut – a rise in aggregate demand will lead to an increase in the demand for labour and vice versa. Figure 3.5.6 on page 349 diagrams I–III show how a decrease in

aggregate demand during a recession will affect the aggregate labour market.

- During a recession (blue section in diagram I) aggregate demand falls which is shown in diagram II as a decrease in aggregate demand from AD_0 to AD_1.

- This will cause a decrease ultimately (remember that there are lags to take into consideration) in the demand for labour, shown by the decrease in the aggregate demand curve for labour from AD_{L_0} to AD_{L_1} in diagram III.

- This creates a cyclical addition to unemployment of $U_1 \Leftrightarrow FE$ – cyclical unemployment – increasing total unemployment from $FE \Leftrightarrow U^*$ to $U_1 \Leftrightarrow U^*$ in diagram III.

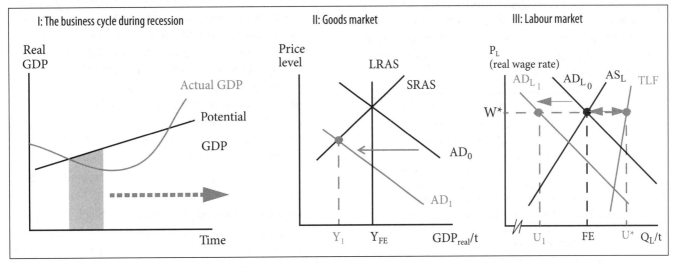

Figure 3.5.6 *Cyclical unemployment*

Outside the box:
The kinked supply curve for labour

The effect of wages being perfectly downward sticky has virtually the same effect as a **minimum wage**. (See Section 2.1 on minimum prices.) A decrease in the aggregate demand for labour from AD_{L_0} to AD_{L_1} does not clear the market since the real wage rate remains at W^* (see Figure 3.5.7). In effect, this creates a **kinked supply curve** for labour.

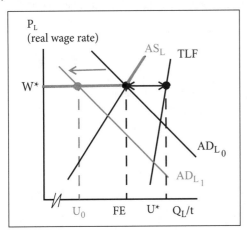

Figure 3.5.7 *The kinked supply curve for labour in cyclical unemployment*

Real wage unemployment ©IBO 2003

By now you will need some revision. Here are three introductory points to real wage unemployment:

1. *Disequilibrium unemployment* – for example, where unemployment exceeds the *equilibrium* or *natural* rate of unemployment – can be explained by a decrease in economic activity which leads to a decrease in the aggregate demand for labour. Since wages are 'downward sticky' the labour market does not clear and the addition to total unemployment is called cyclical or demand-deficient unemployment. This is the Keynesian/demand-side view of disequilibrium unemployment.

2. There is another way to view disequilibrium unemployment, namely that the labour market does not clear at the real wage rate. This is known as **real wage unemployment**. In short, the real wage rate is too high. The real wage is too high since there are 'labour market impurities' or 'rigidities' disallowing the market to clear. For example, minimum wage legislation and union bargaining power helps keep wages too high resulting in non-market clearing real wages. This is the neoclassical view. Here's another clue: real wage unemployment is also known as **classical unemployment**. Classical theory views labour markets as not entirely dissimilar to the market for goods such as, em, chickens.

3. The difference between cyclical and real wage unemployment is worlds apart – since the former is based on Keynesian premises and the latter on neoclassical – but you'd have a hard time discovering these differences by simply looking at the labour market diagrams. You see, the difference lies not so much in the fact that there *is* an excess of labour supply at a given wage rate but in *why there* is disequilibrium unemployment – and *what should be done* about it.

> **Real wage (or 'classical') unemployment**: Real wage unemployment is the neoclassical view that any addition to equilibrium unemployment is due to labour market imperfections such as minimum wage, union bargaining power, high social and unemployment benefits and other labour market rigidities. These imperfections keep real wages too high and disallow market clearing, leading to increased unemployment.

The neoclassical view

Figure 3.5.8 is virtually the same as in the diagram showing demand-deficient unemployment. Real wage rates (W_0) are such that the market has not cleared, creating disequilibrium unemployment of $U_0 \Leftrightarrow U_1$. Why is there disequilibrium unemployment in the economy according to real wage theory?

According to neoclassical views, when the real wage rate is above market equilibrium wage, W^*, there will be more labourers willing to accept jobs than there is demand from firms. More labourers are willing to accept a job (e.g. there is a movement along the AS_L curve) at W_0 but there is less demand from firms,

shown by the quantity demanded for labour at U_0. There is now more labour willing to take jobs than there are offers of jobs.

- **Voluntary unemployment**: The blue arrows show *voluntary unemployment* at both W^* and W_0. Neoclassical theory regards voluntary unemployment as the result of people not being *willing* to accept available jobs at the going wage rate for various reasons. This is the same as saying that labourers not accepting jobs at W^* are searching for jobs (frictionally unemployed), are unwilling to move (regionally unemployed) or cannot find jobs matching their skills (technological unemployment), etc. $FE \Leftrightarrow U^*$ and $U_2 \Leftrightarrow U_1$ show the quantity of voluntary unemployment at the different real wage levels.

- **Involuntary unemployment**: The black double-edged arrow shows the amount of *involuntary* unemployment. At a real wage of W_0 there are more workers now willing to accept jobs than at a wage level of W^*. However, the quantity of labour demanded at W_0 is less than at W^*. The unemployment arising between U_0 and U_2 is therefore involuntary.

According to the neoclassical view, disequilibrium unemployment (e.g. unemployment above the natural rate) exists because labour market forces have not been able to clear the market by lowering the real wage rate sufficiently. In Figure 3.5.8, the wage rate of W_0 is above the market clearing rate of W^*, creating real wage unemployment of $U_0 \Leftrightarrow U_2$. Total unemployment is above what would be the level of unemployment if the labour market cleared at a wage rate of W^*.

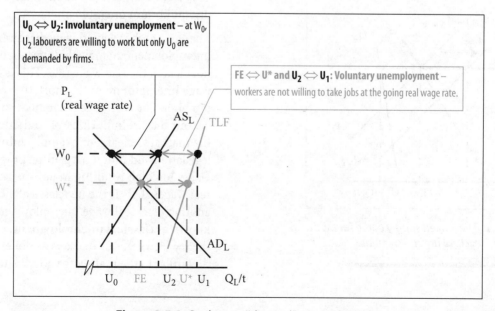

Figure 3.5.8 *Real wage ('classical') unemployment*

How is the real wage rate set at above market clearing level (W* in Figure 3.5.8 on page 350) and why can it remain there? The neoclassical side gives three main reasons:

1. One main reason is that the government might have instigated *minimum wage legislation* which sets the price of labour higher than the labour market would.

2. Another common argument is that social welfare states might have *social/unemployment benefits* which would decrease the propensity of people in the labour force to accept wages below a certain rate. High unemployment benefits mean that the opportunity cost of remaining unemployed is relatively low – labourers lack incentives to take jobs at the going real wage rate.

3. *Trade union power* might serve the same purpose; by successful bargaining of wages, wages are bid up above equilibrium level. (Note that the concept of downward sticky wages is relevant here too.)

All in all, these three factors are considered to build in market imperfections and hinder the labour market from clearing. The result is higher levels of unemployment.

Measures to deal with unemployment ©IBO 2003

We have now covered two possible ways of explaining disequilibrium unemployment.[11] There are also two broad methods used to attack the problem: from the *interventionist* side and the *market-side* of the labour market. Interventionist solutions involve increasing the demand for labour via fiscal and monetary stimulation of aggregate demand. The market approach utilises primarily labour supply solutions aimed at increasing the ability/willingness of workers to accept jobs or the ability/willingness of firms to offer employment.

Interventionist solutions on the demand side

By now you should be reasonably comfortable with the concept of demand management policies aimed at adjusting economic activity over business cycles. A key goal in such policies is of course full employment, and both fiscal and monetary policies are used in furtherance of this. These traditional demand-side policies have been increasingly complemented by other government policies and incentives aimed at increasing labour mobility in order to decrease structural

unemployment. Figure 3.5.9 shows how labour demand is stimulated by **demand-side policies**.

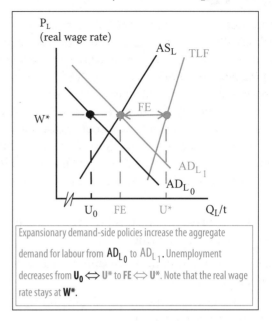

Figure 3.5.9 *Demand-side intervention – increasing the AD$_L$*

Demand management policies to decrease disequilibrium unemployment are rooted in traditional Keynesian views of wage and factor price rigidity: markets are not perfect and even the most 'perfect' market will take time to clear. The resulting social and economic costs of unemployment were argued to be unacceptable for many governments during the post-World War Two period to the 1970s when demand-side economics was in its heyday. Figure 3.5.9 shows a demand-side approach to cyclical unemployment. Active fiscal policies such as increased government spending plus perhaps looser monetary policy increases aggregate demand to stimulate the economy. As increased consumption and investment take place – together with possible multiplicative effects – there will be an increased demand for labour.

The increase in labour demand, shown by the shift of AD$_{L_0}$ to AD$_{L_1}$, decreases the rate of employment from U$_0 \Leftrightarrow$ U* to FE $\Leftrightarrow$ U* – which in this case is assumed to be the full unemployment. Once again it should be noted that the diagram is only an illustration, and a most simplistic one at that. There is in fact no possible way for governments to correctly gauge the amount of fiscal/monetary stimulus necessary to achieve full employment.

---

11. Note that unemployment also increases when the labour force increases, e.g. a population increase, immigration, deterioration in pensions forcing retirees to look for jobs, increased numbers of school-leavers, etc.

Interventionist solutions on the supply side

Supply-side policies are not the sole domain of neoclassically orientated free-market policies, yet care should be made to distinguish *market*-based policies from *interventionist* ones. The 1980s and 1990s saw increasing use of government empowerment to influence the supply side of the economy. Generally speaking, governments intervened on factor markets by trying to enhance the attractiveness and availability of labour, i.e. the supply of labour, which also had the secondary effect of increased demand for labour over time.

Typically, **governments can intervene on the supply side** in the following ways:

- government/community run *training and skills projects* for labour
- extensive government online job and information *centres and hiring agencies*
- *grants/subsidies* to employers hiring youths, older workers and long-term unemployed
- various forms of *regional incentives* aimed at reallocating labour from depressed areas to areas in need of labour, for example free train fare to job interviews and financial help in moving to another region
- entrepreneurial incentives such as *soft loans* and subsidised rent for start-up companies and R&D loans
- *tax incentives* to firms which invest in education/training amongst employees risking redundancy

Basically, any government policy causing an increase in labour market participation increases the supply of labour. Figure 3.5.10 shows how various forms of *interventionist supply-side policies* – notably education, (re-) training and greater labour mobility – increase the aggregate supply of labour.

By increasing the skills base of labour, decreasing the search costs of both employers and job searchers and creating incentives for increased labour mobility, there will be an increase in the aggregate supply of labour, shown in Figure 3.5.10 as the shift in the aggregate supply of labour from AS_{L_0} to AS_{L_1}.[12] Assuming that wages adjust relatively quickly, i.e.

no downward stickiness of wages, the real wage rate falls to W^* and unemployment decreases from $U_0 \Leftrightarrow U_1$ to $FE \Leftrightarrow U^*$ – the natural rate of unemployment (NRU).

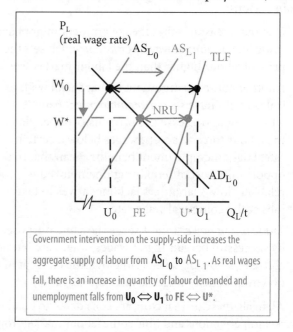

Government intervention on the supply-side increases the aggregate supply of labour from AS_{L_0} to AS_{L_1}. As real wages fall, there is an increase in quantity of labour demanded and unemployment falls from $U_0 \Leftrightarrow U_1$ to $FE \Leftrightarrow U^*$.

Figure 3.5.10 *Intervention on the supply side*

Market solutions

The market approach to disequilibrium is of course supply-side policies. Such neoclassically based policies assume disequilibrium unemployment to be real wage unemployment. Supply-side labour policies can be summed up as 'any policy which increases the propensity of labourers to accept jobs'. One can distinguish between policies aimed at *removing market imperfections* and policies aimed at *decreasing the natural rate of unemployment*.

Removing labour market imperfections

Flip back to Section 3.4 and supply-side issues, specifically concerning minimum wages and union power. By lowering *union power*, lowering *taxes on labour*, and decreasing *minimum wages* it is possible to reduce the influence of labour market imperfections which diminish the ability of the market to clear. If successful, the real wage rate will conform to labour market forces and lower the wage rate from W_0 to W^* (see Figure 3.5.11 on page 353) decreasing total unemployment from $U_0 \Leftrightarrow U_1$ to the natural rate of unemployment of $FE \Leftrightarrow U^*$.

---

12. It is highly plausible (= believable) that these same policies, together with hiring incentives for firms, might ultimately also result in an increase in *demand* for labour.

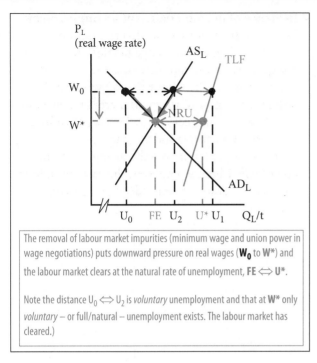

The removal of labour market impurities (minimum wage and union power in wage negotiations) puts downward pressure on real wages (W_0 to W^*) and the labour market clears at the natural rate of unemployment, $FE \Leftrightarrow U^*$.

Note the distance $U_0 \Leftrightarrow U_2$ is *voluntary* unemployment and that at W^* only *voluntary* – or full/natural – unemployment exists. The labour market has cleared.)

Figure 3.5.11 *Removing labour market imperfections*

Decreasing the natural rate of unemployment

Other supply-side policies for labour aim to reduce labour market rigidities and increase the supply of labour by increasing the overall propensity of labourers to accept jobs. Assume an economy in labour market equilibrium with a natural rate of unemployment of $FE_0 \Leftrightarrow U^*_0$ (see Figure 3.5.12). By implementing various *supply-side measures* the aggregate supply for labour increases, i.e. more people in the labour force are willing to supply their labour to the market at all real wage levels. This is shown in as a shift in aggregate supply of labour from ASL_0 to ASL_1, which lowers the natural rate of unemployment from $FE_0 \Leftrightarrow U^*_0$ to $FE_1 \Leftrightarrow U^*_1$.

Such policies, commonly referred to as **structural reforms**, often include:

- *lowering social/unemployment benefits* in order to persuade labourers to accept jobs (since lower benefits increase the opportunity costs of remaining unemployed)

- *lowering income taxes* to induce increased labour hours and create an incentive for those in the labour force to accept jobs

- *increasing overall labour flexibility* by reforming labour market legislation, for example by making it easier to hire/fire labourers and lowering mandatory severance pay

- using *retraining and education* schemes to enable labourers to decrease time spent between jobs and to improve reallocation of labour from declining industries to growth industries.

The overall aim of market solutions to unemployment is to alleviate supply and demand mismatches, i.e. to improve labour allocation. Proponents of market solutions point to the US and Great Britain as examples of how long-run unemployment rates fell markedly during and after the Reagan and Thatcher reforms of the 1980s. Figure 3.5.13 on page 354 illustrates how the natural rate of unemployment has fallen in the US during the last two decades of the 20th century.[13]

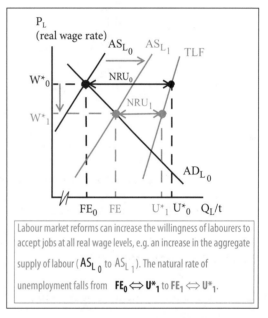

Labour market reforms can increase the willingness of labourers to accept jobs at all real wage levels, e.g. an increase in the aggregate supply of labour ($AS_{L 0}$ to $AS_{L 1}$). The natural rate of unemployment falls from $FE_0 \Leftrightarrow U^*_1$ to $FE_1 \Leftrightarrow U^*_1$.

Figure 3.5.12 *Decreasing the NRU*

Criticism of supply-side policies for labour: In spite of the values in Figure 3.5.13 being estimates, few critics of supply-side policies would dispute that long-term unemployment rates have dropped substantially in the US and Britain during the 1980s and 1990s. Instead, criticism is levied at a number of noticeable weaknesses of supply side policies. Perhaps foremost is the implicit assertion that disequilibrium unemployment is primarily the result of labourers not being willing to accept jobs. Many economists would take issue with the strict categorisation of what is to be considered voluntary and/or frictional unemployment; a skilled piano builder can hardly be 'unwilling' or 'voluntarily unemployed' for failing to accept an available job waiting tables.

---

13. Corresponding graphs for Great Britain during the same time period are strikingly similar.

Critics of supply-side labour market policies furthermore assert that:

- **Social costs**: Lowering social/unemployment benefits and reducing minimum wages will have the severest effect on the low wage earners and increase income inequalities in society. Supply-side policies also take far longer to have an effect on the economy than demand-side policies.

- **Limited impact of marginal tax rates**: Studies indicate that there is little effect on labour supply due to decreases in marginal income tax rates.

- **Evidence of demand deficient unemployment**: Finally, observers are quick to criticise the neoclassical view that a large portion of disequilibrium unemployment is the result of 'mismatches' in the labour market which in fact implies that employers would increase their search for labour during recessions. This is belied by the fact that job postings and 'help wanted' advertisements fall markedly during economic downturns which strengthens the case for at least some of the employment indeed being demand deficient.

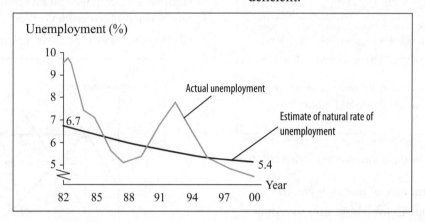

Figure 3.5.13 *The estimated natural rate of unemployment in the US, 1982–2000*

(Source: *US Regional Business Cycle and the natural rate of unemployment*, Howard J. Wall and Gylfi Zo'ga at the Federal Reserve Bank of St. Louis; http://research.stlouisfed.org)

POP QUIZ 3.5.1   UNEMPLOYMENT

1   Why might underemployment be high in a developing country?

2   Why might two countries with exactly the same population size and exactly the same amount of people holding jobs have different rates of unemployment?

3   A number of American firms are now able to manufacture perfect diamonds! Explain what type(s) of unemployment might result from this.

4   'Arguably, those who are frictionally unemployed are voluntarily unemployed.' Discuss.

5   What is the main difference in the neoclassical and Keynesian viewpoint on the causes of unemployment?

6   Draw a diagram illustrating the effects on the labour market when new labour-saving technology is widely implemented in an economy.

7   What are the possible outcomes of removing a minimum wage policy?

8   Use a diagram to explain the effects of supply-side policies on the labour market.

Inflation ©IBO 2003

Inflation is when you pay fifteen dollars for the ten-dollar haircut you used to get for five dollars when you had hair. – Sam Ewing, author

Definition of inflation ©IBO 2003

Consider two possible events in an economy:

- the price of agricultural goods rises due to a bad harvest
- the price of all consumer goods rises due to an increase in VAT.

Neither of these will technically constitute inflation since the change in the price level either only affects certain goods or occurs 'one-off'.

> **Inflation:** Inflation is defined as a *consistent increase in the general (i.e. average) price level.* Thus the entire basket of goods represented in the consumer price index (CPI) or GDP deflator will be persistently affected.

Inflation shows the change in the price level between two time periods: this is the *rate of inflation*. For example, a change in the consumer price index (CPI) from 108 to 112 means that the 'speed' of price increase is 112/108, i.e. a 3.7% rate of inflation. Frequently it is necessary to subdivide the term into various types of inflation.

- **Creeping inflation** would be 'moderate' and involve a change in prices of a few percent per year. Most OECD countries showed inflation rates of this magnitude during 2003 – between 1% and 6%.[14]
- **Hyperinflation** is a situation where inflation hits triple-digits, for example when inflation in Brazil peaked at over 2500% during the early 1990s.[15]
- Economists often find it useful to exclude goods which are notoriously volatile, such as oil and agricultural goods, in which case one refers to **core inflation**.
- When the overall consumer price index is adjusted by removing household costs for housing loans – mortgage costs – and/or various forms of indirect (expenditure) taxes, one has a measurement of inflation referred to as **underlying inflation**.

Inflation decreases the ability of money to function as in 'money units per unit of output'. Modern economies are highly dependent on a functioning monetary system. The basic **function of money** is to provide the economic system with a *medium of exchange* in order to make transactions between actors on the market easier. Another key function of money is as a *store of value*, since it can be put aside and used later – which a bit more difficult with goods which have limited shelf lives such as carrots or piglets. This allows firms and households to *defer payments* over time. Finally, money is a most valuable *unit of account*, i.e. the value of goods and services can be put into a common unit so one doesn't have to continuously calculate the correct market ratio of carrots to piglets. Inflation – and especially hyperinflation – diminishes the functions of money and inflicts numerous costs on society.

This is what happens when 3 kg of paper money buys one roll of toilet paper. Taken on the South African side of the Zimbabwean border at Beitbridge. The annual inflation rate in Zimbabwe in November 2008 was 89,700,000,000,000,000,000,000%. I'm not making this up – heck, I can't even pronounce this figure! (– from a Zimbabwean colleague)

Definition of deflation

Deflation is strictly speaking the opposite; a persistent fall in the general price level. However, the term is often used a bit more loosely to convey downward pressure on prices due to a decline in economic activity, e.g. a 'deflationary gap'.

---

14. *OECD in figures*, 2003 edition, see http://www.oecd.org.
15. IMF working paper, WP/01/50, *High inflation and Real Wages*, Benedikt Braumann, 2001.

Deflation: When the price level, determined by the CPI or the GDP deflator, falls consistently during a time period, there is deflation, or negative inflation.

A concept confusingly similar to that of deflation is **disinflation**, which is a fall in the *rate* of inflation, i.e. when inflation drops from say 7% per year to 3% per year. Disinflation occurs either when aggregate supply increases faster than aggregate demand – benign (= good) – or when aggregate demand falls faster than aggregate supply – malign (= bad) disinflation. An example of disinflation would be China during the latter 1990s and an example of deflation would be Japan (see below) during the same time period.

Costs of inflation and deflation

©IBO 2003

Inflation has the effect of eroding the value of money, which can inflict serious damage on an economy if inflation is high enough. Yet too low an inflation level runs the risk of turning into deflation – which most economists consider a far worse a problem. Finding the 'Goldilocks rate'[16] of inflation is an almost magical feat.

Costs of inflation

Say that your retired grandmother gives you a gift of £100 pounds which you immediately put into a bank account, which in turn the bank immediately lends to your brother. During the next year prices rise by 20%; who in the family is a winner and who is a loser? Ponder this as you read on.

Redistribution effects of inflation

Vulnerable groups such as pensioners, households dependent on social security benefits, stand to lose a great deal when inflation rates are high since they are often on **fixed incomes**. (See Case study: "In real life – Effects of inflation in Russia after 1991" on page 43'.) Even if these incomes are indexed to inflation rates, there will be time lags which will have adverse effects on purchasing power. In addition to this, workers in weak positions will not be able to bid up wages as much as workers in strong bargaining positions.

Two other groups which stand to lose real income due to inflation are **lenders and savers**. Inflation has the tendency to decrease the distance between inflation and interest – the real interest rate – which will lower real returns for lenders. Similarly, savers will see how the real value increase in their savings will go down as it is eaten away by inflation and therefore diminishes future real purchasing power. On the other hand, borrowers will gain at the expense of savers and lenders, since inflation will also serve to erode the real debt of the original loan. Basically, income has been redistributed from lenders and savers to borrowers.[17]

Finally, the **financially strong** will suffer far less than the weak. The wealthy will have access to more and better information and thus the ability to cope with inflation by finding assets which are relatively secure in value-retention, such as land and other fixed assets.

Negative effects on growth

Inflation causes an increase in interest rates and will therefore have a negative effect on **investment and output**, both of which will adversely affect **employment rates**. neoclassical and monetarist economists are quick to point to this particular effect of inflation.

Behavioural distortions in the economy

Inflation (and increasing rates of inflation) affects the 'view' of firms seeking to maximise returns on investment since the ratio between future profitability and the cost of loans is distorted when price levels increase. (Keynes, in keeping with his philosophical preference to be 'vaguely right rather than precisely wrong', referred to firms' expectations as the '*animal spirits*' of firms' investment plans.) Inflation also affects factor prices differently from final output prices, which adds further variables and thus complications to investment plans. Anything which causes **insecurity and lack of predictability** in firms' futures will serve to make them more cautious.

In addition to investment, consumption plans are often affected by inflation. Households have an incentive to increase consumption of durable goods if future inflation is expected to rise, which can actually create higher inflation rates. This is a macro force which to a certain extent can actually countermand falling investment in firms.

---

16. That is, not too hot and not too cold. You know, the porridge …

17. I know a good many people who bought houses in the early 1970s and are overjoyed at what high inflation rates did to their real debt over the next 20 years.

'Shoe leather' and 'menu' costs

Stable prices give the economy an element of transparency, in that firms and households can – within margins – safely foresee changes in prices and interest rates and plan accordingly. High inflation rates decrease the certainty in knowing correct (or at least fair) market prices for factors and goods, leading firms and households to spend more time searching for the best prices on the market. The time spent analysing the market yields opportunity costs in productivity – this is a '**shoe leather cost**', i.e. the cost of walking around comparing prices.

Higher inflation also means that businesses will have to continuously change their prices in order to keep up to date on the price level. Catalogues, price lists, price labels, vending machines, etc. will all have to be adjusted continuously in order to avoid losses in real terms. These '**menu costs**' for firms can be quite considerable when inflation hits double digits.

Possible breakdown of the monetary economy

All the examples of how inflation damages the economy are in fact illustrations of how the functions of money wear down. In an economy with *hyperinflation* it is possible for the entire monetary system to collapse. For example, in Bolivia during 1985, the rate of inflation (at an annualised rate) soared to 11,750%![18] Now, ask yourself this: 'Would I want to hold on to money when it will be worth 0.84% of its present value in one year's time?'[19] No, you will want to get rid of your Bolivianos as quickly as possible since every day you spend with cash in your pocket means an opportunity cost in terms of what it will buy you. The solution is to get something *tangible* for your cash such as consumer durables – or another currency. Since everyone else is thinking the same thing, inflation will be driven even further by increasing demand for goods but decreasing demand for the domestic currency. The result is a breakdown in the system since money becomes virtually worthless. People will spend enormous amounts of time tracking down the best prices and ultimately simply resort to bartering.

This process is incredibly time-consuming and allocatively wasteful since **barter** involves high search costs for all parties in finding someone with *co-wants*; if you have piglets and need tomatoes then you have to find someone who not only has tomatoes but also wants a few piglets. This shows the importance of the transactions function of money. The breakdown of the functions of money will cause massive disruptions to the government sector, since households and firms will have an incentive to put off tax-paying for as long as possible. This can cause severe cash flow problems for governments needing money with which to keep public services going.

Exchange rates, trade and inflation

Finally, inflation is strongly linked to the *external value of the currency*, i.e. the value of the domestic currency in terms of other currencies, which is the **exchange rate**. When domestic inflation is higher than in countries with which trade is done, there is a tendency for the value of the domestic currency to fall. The reason is that a higher domestic price level will make domestic goods less competitive internationally. As foreign demand for domestic goods falls, the derived demand for the domestic currency (which foreigners need to buy goods) will also fall – as will the price of the domestic currency, which is non other than the exchange rate. To use the Bolivian example again, the Bolivian currency (the peso, until 1987) had an exchange rate in 1980–81 of 25 pesos to the US dollar – or 1 peso = 4 US cents. The official rate towards the end of the hyperinflation in 1985 was 75,000 Bolivian pesos per US dollar, while the black market value was over one million pesos per dollar – that's 0.0001 US cents per peso![20] (In other words, the *external value* of the Bolivian peso – measured in terms of the US dollar – went from 4 US cents to 0.0001 cent. The peso depreciated (= fell in value) by 99.9975%.)

As Section 4.6 will show, the exchange rate in its turn is strongly linked to trade. A fall in the price of the domestic currency – ceteris paribus – will mean that domestic goods are relatively cheaper for foreigners to buy, since they will get more domestic currency for their foreign currency. Correspondingly, domestic consumers/firms will find foreign goods more expensive, so imports will fall. Thus, a fall in the exchange rate of the domestic currency can increase export revenue and decrease import expenditure.

---

18. Abel & Bernanke, *Macroeconomics,* 4th edition, Addison Wesley Longman 2001, pp. 459–61.
19. The purchasing power of one Boliviano after one year of inflation at 11,750% is calculated as 1/[inflation/100]+1. At 50% inflation your Boliviano would be worth 1/[50/100]+1 = 0.666…, or 66.6% of the original value. At an inflation rate of 17,750 one Boliviano will be worth 1/[11,750/100]+1 = 0.0084, or 0.84%.
20. *Federal Research Division of the Library of Congress* at http://countrystudies.us/bolivia/49.htm.

POP QUIZ 3.5.2   INFLATIONARY SURVIVAL QUIZ FOR TRAVELLERS

Picture yourself in Turkey: wonderfully hospitable people; fabulous food and drink; azure water at 27°C, some of the finest remnants of ancient civilizations in the world, and manufacturers of hand-woven oriental carpets of the highest quality. You spend a week in Turkey under the following premises: inflation is running at over 100% per year and the exchange rate for the Turkish lira is falling measurably and continuously every day.

1   How do you think restaurants and bars catering to tourists deal with the menu costs of changing all their prices daily?

2   There are foreign exchange offices everywhere. What is the most sensible way to manage your foreign exchange activities?

3   You buy a beautiful silk carpet for 2,500,000,000 lira – which is the equivalent of $2,000 at the time of purchase. Should you pay in cash or use a credit card?

4   Turkey is home to two of the ancient Seven Wonders of the World. Which? (This has absolutely nothing to do with economics but it's definitely cool.)

Costs of deflation

Deflation can be good, bad, and pretty darned ugly. Economists commonly differentiate between two types:

- **Good or benign deflation**: This is caused by an *increase in aggregate supply*. Diagram I in Figure 3.5.14 shows how the price level falls when short-run aggregate supply outpaces demand; the price level falls from P_0 to P_1. Such deflation might result from increasing productivity and cannot be considered harmful since the economy is growing and real incomes are increasing. In reality, **disinflation** (falling inflation *rates*) has become the norm in industrialised countries, where average inflation was 5% during the 1980s but had fallen to around 2% by the end of the 1990s.[21]

- **Bad, or malignant deflation**: However, if the price level falls due to a *decrease in aggregate demand*, as in diagram II, there can be serious and long-lasting negative consequences for the economy – *malignant* deflation. An economy experiencing a recessionary period that becomes protracted might cause households and firms to decrease consumption and investment to ride out the bad times and wait for the good times. This can actually prolong the recessionary period when households and firms decrease expenditure in favour of saving. Remember, a fall in the price level will increase the value of money. If households expect prices to continue to fall they will put off expensive purchases in order to get more for their money. This fall in aggregate demand can therefore confirm firms' beliefs that less investment is necessary (HL – see *accelerator model* in Section 3.4) which together with the decrease in consumption can become self-reinforcing in the economy.

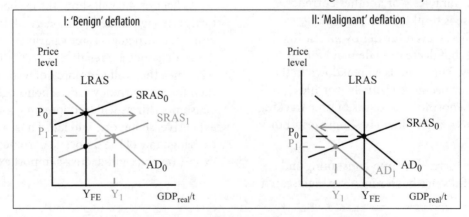

Figure 3.5.14 *'Benign' and 'malignant' deflation*

21. *IHT*, 'A new economic era – a global shift to deflation', 22 May 2003.

One might say that *malignant deflation* cures inflation something like lung cancer cures smoking, and I dare say that most economists would agree that deflation is a far greater threat to economic stability and growth than inflation. The self-reinforcing loop – known as a **deflationary spiral** – created by falling prices → expectations of falling prices → lower aggregate demand → falling prices, etc. is a most powerful force for fiscal and monetary policy to overcome. In fact, many textbooks use the Great Depression of the 1930s to describe the effects of continuously falling aggregate demand and resultant deflation. As prices, expenditure, output and incomes fall there will be increasing unemployment which further dampens aggregate demand and can quite possibly become permanent as some sectors fold and others see permanent reductions in demand. This might lead to a higher natural rate of unemployment.

It seems that deflation, once it becomes entrenched (= deeply rooted) cannot be dealt with easily. The 'trick' is to *create inflation by increasing the inflationary expectations* of households and firms, but the severity of the situation seems to resist standard monetary and fiscal policies. The solutions offered can therefore be at the extremist end of policy making, where common suggestions involve some or all of the following: quickly lowering interest rates (see **liquidity trap** in the case study below) as soon as prices show a tendency to fall; very publicly announcing that the Central Bank has increased the target rate of inflation; large scale purchasing of bonds to create additional liquidity on the market; depreciating/devaluing the currency to increase exports; and printing 'funny money', i.e. printing consumption certificates which can only be used for consumption and then sending them to households in order to boost consumption and aggregate demand.[22]

Case study: **Deflation – the ten-year sunset in Japan**

The Land of The Rising Sun, Japan, was the envy of an astonished world during the 1960s, 1970s and 1980s due to its fantastic growth rates and low inflation and unemployment. GDP grew at an average of over 6% during the period 1960 to 1990 with unemployment rates hovering around 2%. Yet during the beginning of the 1990s, Japan was to become a case study in the difficulties in getting out of malignant deflation. The

background is to be found in the property price bubble of the late 1980s where property speculation and loose monetary policy led to alarming levels of property prices. (For example, the classic story is that the land on which the Imperial Palace in Tokyo stood was at one point valued at more than the entire American state of California!).

*W*hen property prices started falling in 1990 a goodly proportion of the loans taken by speculators could not be serviced, and this created a severe lack of loanable funds – which in turn had a negative effect on investment. In spite of falling interest rates, Japan has experienced falling prices, e.g. deflation, and stagnant or falling GDP during most of the period from 1995 to 2003.

22. In fact, Milton Friedman's tongue-in-cheek suggestion for solving deflation was for the government to print money and fly around in helicopters and unload the bills on a happy citizenry – the bills would be time-limited in order to induce consumption rather than saving. This was actually attempted – without helicopters – during the deflationary crisis in Japan.

The Central Bank, the Bank of Japan, loosened monetary policy to the point where interest rates were virtually zero during the period 1997 to 2003. This is explained by some – but definitely not all – economists as being a classic example of the **liquidity trap**. When interest is zero and the economy continues to shrink, the Central Bank basically 'runs out of ammunition' and there are few monetary policy tools left since it is impossible to lower interest rates and stimulate the economy. In addition, recall that real interest is nominal interest minus inflation. Thus, if **nominal interest is zero and inflation is below zero**, there is a **negative rate of real interest**. The repercussions are as astounding as they are simple:

- Negative real interest means that money increases in value even when you stick it in your mattress (or futon, in Japan). For example, Japan had inflation of –1% (or deflation of 1%) during 2002 while nominal interest was zero. Thus sticking money in a futon actually meant a real interest of 1% over a year. Negative real interest is therefore a disincentive to spend money.

- Monetary policy becomes ineffective since it is impossible to lower interest rates below zero. This would mean that banks would pay borrowers to take on debt!

- Corporate and household debt rises when prices fall, since a fall in prices increases the negative real interest rate. This is a major disincentive to firms and households in taking on debt to fund investment and consumption.

In labour markets, firms will need to increase productivity or cut wage costs in order to stay competitive, since falling final prices mean that profit margins are squeezed. In reality, firms will not be able to lower wages and will resort to laying-off workers. The reason is that when inflation is 6% a firm can accomplish real wage cuts of 4% by offering an increase of 2% nominal. To achieve the same effect when inflation is zero the firm would have to cut nominal wages by 4%! This is not practically feasible in most countries, wherefore deflationary pressure inevitably leads to sizable lay-offs.

During the 1990s, the Japanese government also lowered taxes and increased government spending to the point where government debt exceeded national income by some 60% – the highest ratio of government debt to GDP in the industrialised world. The limits of fiscal policy in Japan show how the propensity to save can countermand a possible multiplicative effect of fiscal policy. The Japanese are a most frugal and careful people when it comes to saving; for most of the 1970s and 1980s the Japanese saved 15% to 20% of disposable income – twice that of the US. While the savings rate fell to below 10% during the 1990s, it was still high enough to have a severely limiting effect on tax reductions and increased government spending. In fact, in a fit of desperation the government issued time-limited 'spending certificates' valued at over USD 5 billion in 1998 to induce some spending and inflationary pressure in the economy. The result? Households used the certificates to **replace** money-based consumption and **save more**! In other words, there was little or no impact on aggregate demand. Neither fiscal nor monetary policy has been able to draw Japan out of what in effect seems to be a deflationary spiral.

POP QUIZ 3.5.3   INFLATION AND DEFLATION

1 Explain how an economist would regard an increase in cigarette taxes in terms of inflation.

2 How might the functions of money be put out of order during inflation?

3 Why might you, the student, stand to lose due to inflation?

4 Using a supply and demand diagram for your home currency, explain why double-digit inflation will have a negative effect on your exchange rate, i.e. cause your currency to fall in value.

5 Why might deflation in fact be considered 'good' for an economy?

6 Outside the box question: Draw a demand curve for investment (investment schedule) showing how the quantity of investment is totally unaffected by a decrease in the interest rate below 0.25%.

Causes of inflation ©IBO 2003

Having a little inflation is like being a little pregnant – inflation feeds on itself and quickly passes the 'little' mark. – Dian Cohen, economics communication consultant

Two main causes of inflation are Keynesian in origin: *cost push* inflation arising from higher factor costs to firms, and *demand-pull* inflation which arises when aggregate demand in the economy outstrips available aggregate supply. A third, neoclassical/monetarist view, posits that inflation is demand-pull in nature, but that it is the underlying variable of *increased money supply* which is the root cause.

Cost push ©IBO 2003

An increase in factor costs on a macro scale can cause prices to rise due to the increase in costs. This causes **cost-push inflation** and is frequently associated with 'one-off' increases in price level, known as *supply-side shocks*. There are a number of possible causes of cost-push inflation: *ages* rising faster than productivity gains in the economy; a fall in the *exchange rate* driving up the price of imported raw materials and components, or an increase in *factor prices*, say the price of oil. All of these will shift aggregate supply to the left, shown in Figure 3.5.15 diagram I.

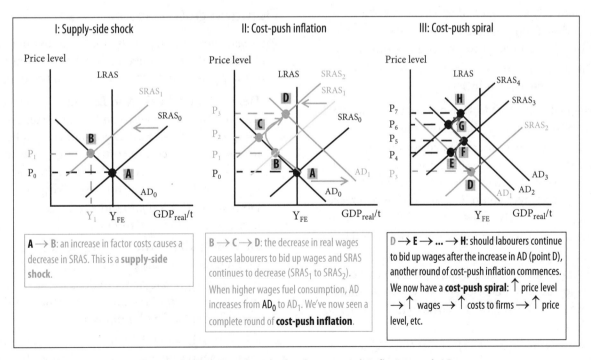

Figure 3.5.15 *Supply-side shock, cost-push inflation and AD_0*

- **Supply-side shock, A to B**: The price increase in key factors of production shifts the short-run aggregate supply curve from $SRAS_0$ to $SRAS_1$ (see Figure 3.5.15 on page 361, diagram I) which increases the price level from P_0 to P_1. This combination of a fall in output and inflation is known as **stagflation** (i.e. *stag*nating and in*flation*ary economy). [*Note: many textbooks and teachers use diagram I to illustrate cost-push inflation. This is perfectly acceptable!*]

- **Cost-push inflation, A to D**: Technically speaking, the supply-side shock illustrated in diagram I does not comprise inflation, since it is a one-off increase rather than consistent. One could say that the supply shock sets the scene for cost-push inflation:

  - When labourers realise that real wages have fallen due to a higher price level, individual wage bargaining and unions will *drive up wages* to regain lost purchasing power.

  - The higher cost of labour will shift aggregate supply even further to the left, from $SRAS_1$ to $SRAS_2$ in diagram II. The price level rises from P_1 to P_2.

  - Ultimately, the increase in wages (perhaps accompanied by expansionary policies in order to countermand increased unemployment) increases consumption and increases aggregate demand from AD_0 to AD_1. The increased spending (and possible expansionary policies) move the economy towards equilibrium at Y_{FE} but at a higher price level. We have now had a round of **cost-push inflation**.

- **Cost-push spiral, D to H**: Now, consider that final prices have risen to P_3 (now continued in diagram III) due to increased consumption and fiscal stimuli. Real wages have once again fallen due to the effects of inflation. Another period of bidding-up wages could lead to a further decrease in aggregate supply, shown by the shift from $SRAS_2$ to $SRAS_3$, and another round of cost-push inflation.

  Diagram III shows how successive shifts in SRAS and AD create an upward spiral, known as a **cost-push spiral** or **wage-price spiral**. The basic effect is: ↑price level → ↑wages → ↑costs to firms → ↑price level, etc.

The 1970s cost-push spiral: The most (in-) famous of supply-side shocks occurred during 1973 and 1994 when OPEC managed to force oil prices upwards by 300%, the first **oil crisis**. (See "APPLIED ECONOMICS: We're on a highway to hell!" on page 123 and "Long-run Phillips curve" on page 368.) Oil is vital to production since it provides energy, transportation, compounds for plastics, etc. and when the price of oil quadrupled, firms' costs increased greatly, causing a severe supply shock and stagflation in most industrialised countries. When stagflation hit industrial countries, many responded by stimulatory policies which drove prices higher and resulted in cost-push inflation. Many countries saw repeated rounds of higher costs and wages which led to cost-push spirals.

The effect on the global economy was tremendous, with falling output levels and rising unemployment in most of the world. It also spelled the end of *pure* Keynesian demand-side policies (see long-run Phillips curve following). As a most illuminating final footnote, recently declassified documents (December 2003) in Great Britain paint a illustrative picture of just how serious the oil crisis was regarded by the president of the US in 1973–74, Richard Nixon. In a copy of a report sent to British Prime Minister Edward Heath (12 December 1973), Nixon put forward serious plans for the military occupation of Saudi Arabia, Kuwait and Abu Dhabi.[23] Perhaps the world is lucky that Nixon was restricted by the Watergate scandal around the same time.

Demand pull ©IBO 2003

Aggregate demand might rise for a number of reasons such as stimulatory monetary/fiscal policies, greater consumer confidence, 'animal spirits' of firms, etc.

- **Demand-side shock, A to B**: When aggregate demand increases swiftly in the short run due to, say, greater demand for exports, there will be a *demand-side shock* and concomitant (= associated) increase in the price level, shown in Figure 3.5.16 on page 363, diagram I shift from AD_0 to AD_1. [*And again, this is a perfectly acceptable way to illustrate demand-pull inflation!*]

- **Demand-pull inflation, A to D**: Once again, the initial increase in the price level (P_0 to P_1) due to increased aggregate demand does not mean inflation *per definition*, but might rather set the stage for demand-pull inflation.

  - Diagram II shows how *inflationary expectations* cause aggregate demand to feed on itself, as the spending plans of firms and households increase in *anticipation* of higher future prices. Aggregate

23. *IHT*, 'US considered seizing Arab oil fields', 2 January 2004, p. 5.

demand increases further, from AD_1 to AD_2, and the price level increases to P_2.

- This is unsustainable in the long run, since higher final prices cause labourers to suffer real wage loss, and subsequently they start to bid up wages.

- This results in higher labour costs for firms and a decrease in aggregate supply from $SRAS_0$ to $SRAS_1$. The economy has moved towards long-run equilibrium (Y_{FE}) but at a higher price level, P_3. The original shift in AD sets off a round of

demand-pull inflation where aggregate demand increases beyond long-run potential output.

- **Demand pull spiral, D to H**: If aggregate demand continues to rise – due to continued expectations of high inflation – then the economy can expect a process where prices increase → labour adjusts by bidding up wages → and firms scale back on production due to lower margins between input prices (e.g. labour costs) and final output prices. This is a demand-pull spiral, as illustrated in Figure 3.5.16 diagram III.

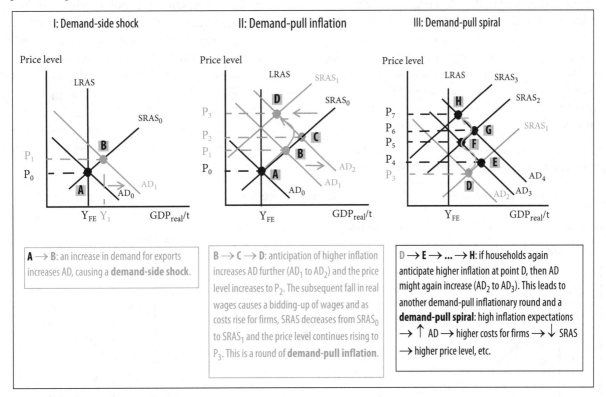

Figure 3.5.16 *Demand-side shock, demand-pull inflation and demand-pull spiral*

Excess monetary growth ©IBO 2003

Assume an economy with only one firm, which produces 1,000 widgets per year at a price of $1 per widget. Additionally, the supply of money is $1,000. Assuming all widgets are sold, what is national income? Easy: it's $1,000 – the same amount spent (E) and earned (Y) on output (O).

- What if the supply of money doubled to $2,000 but output remained the same? Quickly check Section 3.1 "Nominal and real income" on page 260 to realise that nominal national income will increase but *real income will remain the same*. Assuming that the additional $1,000 flows around the economy at the same rate as the original $1,000,

we can also fairly safely assume that the price of widgets goes from $1 to $2 – the price level has doubled.

- However, what if the ability of the firm to produce widgets also increases during the time period, say that new technology and production methods enables the firm to produce twice as many widgets at the same cost as before? Assuming that all are sold and that, once again, people use their notes and coins at the same rate as before, the price of widgets will remain at $1, and real income will double to $2,000.

The above is a highly simplified and, of course, exaggerated example of how excess money supply causes demand-pull inflation.[24] neoclassical/

---

24. For more depth on this outside the syllabus (and this book) – look up 'quantity theory of money' and/or 'the Fisher equation'.

monetarist economists view inflation as primarily *demand-driven* and caused by an increase in the supply of money (i.e. monetary growth) above and beyond the long-run ability of the economy to increase the supply of goods. In simple terms, **if the increase in the supply of money is above productivity gains the result will be inflation**. The mechanism herein can be explained by the *monetary transmission mechanism*.

The monetary transmission mechanism

Monetarists view inflation as primarily caused by demand-pull, often phrased as 'too much money chasing too few goods'. One of the pillars of monetary theory is the overriding importance attached to the supply of money in the economy. Monetarists view the demand for money as relatively inelastic, so an increase in the supply of money will have a large impact on firms' investment and households' consumption via falling interest rates.

The series of diagrams in Figure 3.5.17 illustrate how an increase in the supply of money and lower

interest rates feed through to an increase in investment and aggregate demand in the short run.

- Diagram I: Increasing the supply of money from Sm_0 to Sm_1 forces interest rates down from r_0 to r_1.

- Diagram II: Lower interest rates induce an increase in investment, which is shown by the movement along the investment schedule. Investment increases from I_0 to I_1.

- Diagram III: The increase in investment causes an increase in aggregate demand; AD_0 to AD_1. This is the **transmission mechanism**, where an increase in the supply of money is 'transmitted' to an increase in real output. (There is also a direct link between the lower interest rate and greater *household expenditure* which also fuels aggregate demand.)

- In summary: $\uparrow\Delta Sm \rightarrow \downarrow\Delta r \rightarrow \uparrow\Delta I$ and $\uparrow\Delta C \rightarrow \uparrow\Delta AD$ and $\uparrow\Delta$ inflation. The resulting inflation caused by increased money supply can thus be viewed as 'too much money chasing too few goods'.

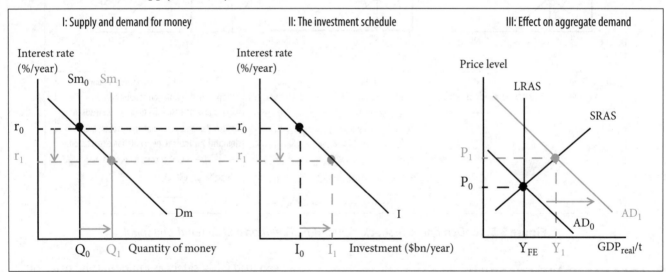

Figure 3.5.17 *The transmission mechanism*

The neoclassical view of money-driven inflation – LR effects

It is important to realise that monetarist theory views any increase in money that is *not matched by an increase in real potential output* (LRAS) as being solely inflationary in the long run. As the increase in AD has pushed output beyond LRAS, the increase in real GDP shown in Figure 3.5.17 diagram III will not last, since wages will rise to match labour demand. This serves to

increase costs for firms and thus push the AS curve to the left as in Figure 3.5.18 on page 365. Output returns to the full employment level of output, Y_{FE}, but at a higher price level.

Milton Friedman coined a main monetarist article of faith by stating that 'inflation is always and everywhere a monetary phenomenon'.[25]

---

25. One of my many cheeky students, Ms O'Connor, once sent me a picture of two machines; one had numerous dials, knobs, levers, wires, connections, scales and indicators on it while the other machine had a single button, 'On-Off'. The first machine was labelled 'Woman' and the second 'Man'. I often think of monetarist policy as a 'Man' machine, since all the various forms of fiscal policies are basically replaced with a single knob labelled 'Money: More ⇔ Less'.

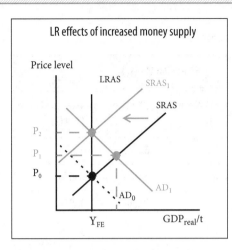

Figure 3.5.18 *The LR effects of increased money supply*

While I am oversimplifying, the basic idea of steering the economy primarily by regulating the money supply is in keeping with neoclassical theory since it advocates minimum government intervention in favour of a few simple rules and guidelines such as the Central Bank openly setting target rates of monetary growth and allowing the economy to adapt in terms of inflation and output. Alternatively, the Bank can set inflation ceilings and then adjust money supply to keep inflation under control. A common 'rule of thumb' is that monetary policy should be tightened when nominal interest rates are lower than nominal GDP growth and vice versa.

POP QUIZ 3.5.4   CAUSES OF INFLATION

1. Why might governments in high inflation countries actually gain from the effects of inflation? Hint; governments issue bills and bonds to borrow money.

2. An economy 'imports' inflation due to the increase in price of irreplaceable raw materials. Unions push for higher wages to counter the cost of living increase and … now what? Use a diagram to explore possible outcomes.

3. Over a five-year period, the following changes are noted in an economy:

Time period	Increase in money supply	Inflation	Real GDP growth
t_1	7.0%	6%	4%
t_2	10.5%	6.5%	2.8%
t_3	18.4%	8.5%	1.4%
t_4	9.6%	11.5%	-0.8%
t_5	9.0%	10.5%	-1.5%

Use the viewpoint of a neoclassical/monetarist economist to explain the pattern of inflation rates and growth during the five-year period.

HIGHER LEVEL EXTENSION TOPICS

This section delves deeper into the causes of inflation and the debate on the trade-off between inflation and unemployment. And while I in no way wish to put a burden on SL students, I would strongly urge you to study the simple (= short run) Phillips curve on page 367, as it is of immeasurable help in understanding some of the basic policy trade-offs faced by governments.

Methods of measuring inflation

©IBO 2003

We have dealt with the basic methodology in measuring inflation in "Nominal and real income" on page 260. The Irish economy was used to build an example of a consumer price index (CPI) and a GDP deflator. The weakness in the method used was that both baskets of goods totally **disregarded the relative importance** of different goods. Some goods are more important than others, for example, housing will be a major consumption item for households and electricity for firms. Knitting needles and paper clips won't. What one must do to make a price index more applicable is to weight the goods in the basket in a manner that reflects their relative importance; rent for housing should have a far heavier weight than knitting needles in households' expenditure patterns just as electricity over paper clips in firms. Table 3.5.1 on page 366 shows a weighted basket of consumer goods using the same goods and values as in Section 3.1 for comparison. Note that the same basic methodology is applied when constructing a broader measure of inflation such as the GDP deflator.

Table 3.5.1 *Weighted consumer price index (CPI)*

Base year (t$_0$)	Unweighted CPI (t$_1$)	Weighted CPI (t$_1$)			
		% of income spent on good	(1) Weight	(2) Price	Effect on CPI (1) x (2)
20 pints of Guinness: €30	20 pints of Guinness: €32	20%	0.2	6.70%	1.34%
10 kg of mutton: €35	10 kg of mutton: €36	30%	0.3	2.90%	0.87%
10 cans of crab pâté: €40	10 cans of crab pâté: €45	10%	0.1	12.50%	1.25%
100 kg potatoes: €20	100 kg potatoes: €21	40%	0.4	5%	2.00%
Total cost of basket = €125	Total cost of basket in next time period = €134	100%	1		Total: 5.46%
$CPIt_0 = \dfrac{125}{125} \times 100$	$CPIt_1 = \dfrac{134}{125} \times 100$	Weighted CPI shows an increase in the price level from 100 to 105.46. $CPIt_1$ (weighted) = **105.5**			

By assigning weights to the various goods in a basket of consumption goods it is possible to get a better picture of how price changes affect households. In Table 3.5.1 it is evident that the 12.5% price increase in crab pâté does not affect households as much as the 5% increase in potato prices. This is exactly the purpose of weighting an index, since all methods for measuring inflation are estimates aimed at showing how the average household (or firm when using GDP deflator) is affected. In the example above, the inflation rate of 5.5% in the weighted index is more accurate than a rate of 7.2% as the case is in the un-weighted price index. Using weights to show which goods are more important as proportion of total spending more correctly illustrates the impact on households. All countries use a weighting system of some kind when calculating indices such as the CPI and the GDP deflator. What varies between countries are of course the weights; goose-down jacket will not have the same relative importance for Finns and Algerians, just as Mongolians will hardly have the same weight for Guinness as the Irish (but they might actually have similar weights for lamb and mutton).

Problems of the methods of measuring inflation ©IBO 2003

Perhaps the most important limitation of using the CPI to measure inflation is that the index values are **averages**. Different households will not be equally affected by inflation caused by large price increases in certain goods. For example, households on lower incomes will spend proportionately more on food than high income households, so an increase in foodstuffs will affect low income households more. Another weakness dealing with averages is that not all goods will show the same rate of price increase. Taken together, one could say that every household – indeed, every person – in the economy will have an individual rate of inflation. In addition to this, there are three general *bias problems* in the CPI which weaken the actual values in the index:

1. **Quality and novelty bias:** Products improve over time – some of them quite considerably. The first hand-held computer I purchased in 1998 cost $US500, had a black and white screen and 2 megabytes of memory. My next one, in 2003, cost $US400, has 65,000 colours and close to 150 megabytes of memory – plus a number of features not even dreamt of when I bought the first one. The one I bought in December 2008 … forget it. The information will be obsolete (= out of date) by the time this leaves the printer. Anyhow, this ongoing process of continuous improvement and innovation often grossly overestimates inflation since the enhanced value of better products is not taken into account in the CPI.

2. **Substitution bias:** The CPI does not adequately take into account that consumers will substitute expensive goods with lower-priced alternatives over time. The time lag between when increasingly substituted goods are also taken out or replaced in the CPI basket will overestimate inflation.

3. **Weight and content bias:** Another way in which the CPI overestimates inflation due to time lags arises when goods become obsolete. The CPI basket needs to represent household spending and since

consumption patterns change over time the contents in the basket need to change. If there is a lag in adjusting the basket to consumption patterns then the basket will incorrectly measure and weight items in the basket thereby skewing inflation measurements. In the other direction, if the goods and weights are changed often then the CPI might be comparing increasingly different baskets of goods over time, which would weaken the value of lengthy inflation series.

Phillips curve ©IBO 2003

A study conducted by Professor Phillips in 1958 showed a strong relationship between two of the most looked-at macroeconomic variables, unemployment and wage rates. The study, which covered the time period 1861 to 1957 in the UK, showed a clear *negative correlation* between the two variables. The relationship

was to have great importance for further economic models after being slightly altered to show instead the relationship between **inflation and unemployment**.

Short-run Phillips curve ©IBO 2003

Figure 3.5.19 diagram I shows Phillips's original curve. Diagram II illustrates what ultimately became the graph we now refer to as the Phillips curve. Professor Phillips plotted all the wage and unemployment values for the UK over an almost 100 year period and based his line of best fit on the values. Wage increases were shown to have strong statistical correlation to decreases in unemployment. As wage increases ultimately feed through to the overall price level, a subsequent relationship between wage rates and inflation was found to hold steady. This provided the empirical and theoretical foundation for what became the **Phillips curve** where higher inflation rates are associated with lower levels of unemployment.

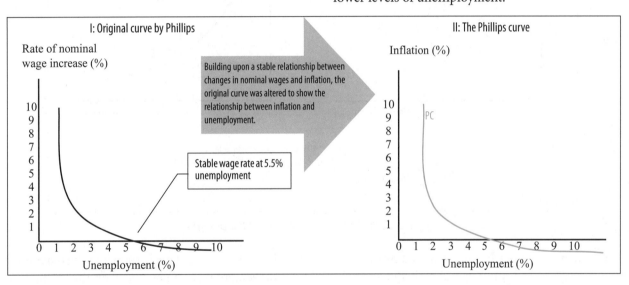

Figure 3.5.19 *The Phillips curve*

The relationship between inflation and unemployment was subsequently found to hold broadly true in other countries during the 1950s and 1960s. One rather remarkable fit of the Phillips curve to actual values was the period between 1960 and 1969 in the US, shown in Figure 3.5.20.

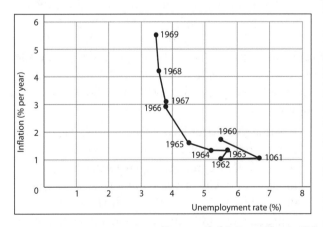

(Source: Abel & Bernanke, p. 435)

Figure 3.5.20 *Inflation and unemployment in the US, 1960–69*

HIGHER LEVEL

Aggregate demand and the Phillips curve

Having provided strong empirical evidence of correlation between inflation and unemployment, the results were incorporated into economic theory of the time by a number of notable economists.[26] A main conclusion based on the trade-off was that while governments could apparently never fully conquer unemployment, there was at least an available choice for policy makers. The view that the Phillips curve showed a *stable relationship* between the price level (inflation) and unemployment had stark implications

for economic policy. It provided governments with a 'menu' of possible policy goals shown by points A, B and C along the Phillips curve in Figure 3.5.21 diagram II, where each level of unemployment/inflation would have its own specific opportunity cost. In simple terms, any given policy goal concerning aimed-for unemployment would have a trade-off in terms of inflation and vice versa. Lowering unemployment from U_0 to U_1 (via, for example, expansionary fiscal policies – AD_0 to AD_1 in diagram I) would entail the costs of higher inflation rates, i_0 to i_1. This is point A to B in both diagrams.

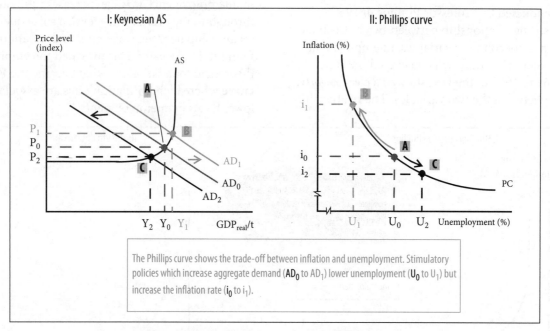

The Phillips curve shows the trade-off between inflation and unemployment. Stimulatory policies which increase aggregate demand (AD_0 to AD_1) lower unemployment (U_0 to U_1) but increase the inflation rate (i_0 to i_1).

Figure 3.5.21 *The AS curve and the Phillips curve*

The evidence and conclusions rendered by the Phillips curve fit nicely into Keynesian theory since each point along the Phillips curve represented a macroeconomic equilibrium in line with the view of how the aggregate supply curve was constructed. Figure 3.5.21 diagram I shows how the 'inverted L' aggregate supply curve was adapted to show the trade-off. Each point along the Phillips curve in diagram II has a corresponding movement along the aggregate supply curve.

- Assume that prices have been increasing at a stable rate at an output of Y_0 (diagram I) and U_0 (diagram II) whereupon *expansionary fiscal/monetary* policies are used to increase aggregate demand from AD_0 to AD_1. The increase in aggregate demand will increase national income from Y_0 to Y_1, and lower unemployment from U_0 to

U_1 (diagram II). This is shown in the diagram as a movement from point A to B on the Phillips curve, which shows that the cost of these expansionary policies is an *increase in inflation* from i_0 to i_1.

- Conversely, fiscal/monetary *contractionary policies* would decrease aggregate demand, AD_0 to AD_2, resulting in a lower rate of inflation, i_2, but a higher level of unemployment at U_2. This is shown by the movement from point A to C in diagrams I and II.

Long-run Phillips curve ©IBO 2003

During the 1950s and 1960s governments, in line with demand management policies, used the Phillips curve trade-off as a premise in setting economic policies aimed at fine-tuning the economy. It was often easier to accept higher inflation rates than high unemployment,

---

26. Primarily Paul Samuelson and Robert Solow in 1960. Both became Nobel laureates in economics.

which contributed to rising inflation in many countries during the latter part of the 1960s. To make a simple point, the stable relationship between inflation and unemployment broke down in industrialised countries during the early 1970s. Figure 3.5.22 illustrates how the stable relationship between inflation and unemployment in the US apparently ceased to exist.[27] (Compare with Figure 3.5.20 on page 367.)

Notice in Figure 3.5.22 how the most noticeable 'breakdown' occurs from 1973 onwards, where inflation doubled in 1974, unemployment almost doubled by 1975 – and both continued to spiral outwards for the rest of the decade. The primary cause, you have no doubt already guessed, is to be found in the **first oil crisis in 1973–74** and the next one in 1979–80. Diagrams I–III in Figure 3.5.23 are based on the values given in Figure 3.5.22 and serve as an illustration of what happened.

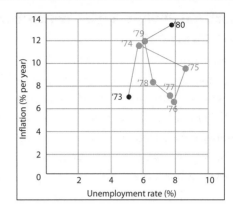

(Source: US Dept of Labor, Bureau of Labor statistics at ftp://ftp.bls.gov/pub/suppl/empsit.cpseea1.txt and http://stats.bls.gov/cpi/home.htm#data)

Figure 3.5.22 *Inflation and unemployment in the US, 1970–80*

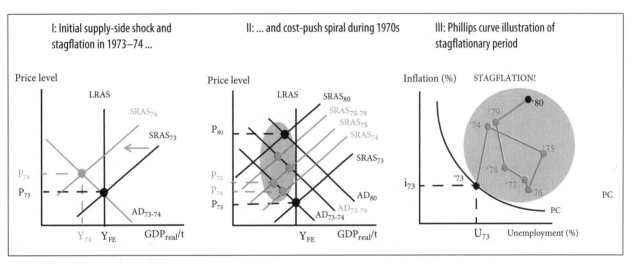

Figure 3.5.23 *Supply-side shock, cost-push inflation and stagflation*

- The initial supply-side shock in 1973–74 (diagram I) caused inflation to rise from 6.2% in 1973 to 11% in 1974, while unemployment increased from 4.9% to 5.6% (and to 8.5% in 1975).

- Consecutive periods of demand-side policies, bidding up of wages and thus increasing costs for firms (diagram II) resulted in cost-push inflation of between 5.5% and 13.5% annually, and unemployment levels hovering between 6% and 9%.

- Diagram III illustrates this process in an 'outward bound spiral' in terms of the Phillips curve, where it is quite evident that the relationship between

inflation and unemployment has collapsed, resulting in **stagflation**.

The breakdown of the relationship depicted in the Phillips curve is a rare example of when economic theory precedes real events. During the latter part of the 1960s, two economists, Milton Friedman and Edmund Phelps, came to the conclusion that the *Phillips curve trade-off could only work in the short run* and thus that the stable relationship depicted could not last. The Friedman–Phelps proposition from the 1960s turned from theory-based prediction to empirically based 'truism' during the stagflationary period of the 1970s and early 1980s.

HIGHER LEVEL

---

27. My defence in continuing to use US figures is that they are highly representative of what happened in most countries during the 1970s and 1980s and that a great deal of what we now call mainstream theory has its origin amongst American economists and US data.

The short-run Phillips curve – criticism of neoclassical school

Assume an economy in equilibrium at Y_0 in Figure 3.5.24 diagram I where the natural rate of unemployment is U_0 and yearly inflation is i_0, diagram I. Aggregate demand increases from AD_0 to AD_1, and the economy moves from Y_0 to Y_1. In moving from Y_0 to Y_1, inflation is actually eroding real wages, since the rate of inflation has increased from i_0 to i_1, shown in diagram II. Say that labourers have negotiated for wage increases of 3% for the coming time period but that inflation during the time period turned out to be 3.5%. This means a real wage loss of 0.5%. If workers are unaware of this fact, then they suffer from **money illusion** (i.e. that the nominal wage increase is real) and will ultimately adjust demand and spending to real wages. Aggregate demand will fall back to AD_0 and deflationary pressure will lower inflation and increase unemployment. Thus the economy would move from point B (in diagram II) along the short-run Phillips curve back to i_0 and U_0 at point A.

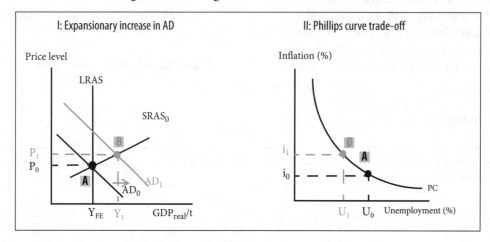

Figure 3.5.24 *What Friedman/Phelps reacted to*

Labourers do not suffer from 'money illusion'

It was precisely the above scenario that Friedman and Phelps opposed. According to their neoclassical/monetarist view, labourers do not suffer from money illusion and will therefore *adapt* to changing inflation rates by altering their **inflationary expectations**.[28] As pointed out in "The monetarist/neoclassical view of long-run aggregate supply" on page 291, economic agents (producers and consumers) act strongly upon expectations.

A silly parallel: Getting your breakfast together in the morning, you will open cupboards and drawers where you expect to find things and your actions are based on expectations which in turn have been strengthened by past experiences; the bread is *always* in the right-hand cupboard. If your mum/maid/spouse one day changes where everything is kept you will quickly adapt depending on how quickly your brain wakes up in the morning. 'Ah, it's now kept in the bread bin by the stove!' Next morning you go for the bread bin. You will act similarly in your wage demands if you expect inflation rates to increase, e.g. you will demand higher wages if you expect your real wages to have deteriorated by an increase in inflation.

The short-run Phillips curve is similar in that the curve is based on the inflationary expectations of firms and households. Expected inflation is based on previous inflation rates, and the short-run Phillips curve governs a time frame where the expected inflation rate does not change, i.e. where the inflation rate has been such that firms and households assume that the current time period will have a predictable and thus *anticipated* rate of inflation. This means that when labourers engage in wage negotiations in order to at least retain real wages, the premise will be that inflation for the coming period is a known constant.

The expectations-augmented Phillips curve (LR Phillips curve)

Assume an economy operating at full employment and at a natural rate of unemployment of 5% and where inflation has held steady at 3% for a longish period. Labourers' inflationary expectations render a short-run Phillips curve of $SRPC_1$ (see diagram I of Figure 3.5.25 on page 371) based on an expected

---

28. This is why the theory is referred to as 'expectations augmented'; augmented means 'enhanced' or 'supplemented'. In other words, economic agents' behaviour is **augmented by inflationary expectations**.

inflation rate (i^e in the diagram) of 3%. If inflation is indeed 3% then anticipated (expected) inflation is the same as de facto inflation and labourers and firms will have correctly increased both output and factor prices to market clearing levels. In other words, an increase in aggregate demand has been matched by a decrease in aggregate supply so that the economy remains at the natural rate of unemployment and prices have risen by the anticipated 3%. This is point A in diagrams I and II.

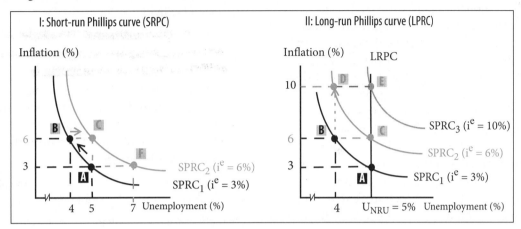

Figure 3.5.25 *Short-run and long-run Phillips curve*

Posit instead that firms/labourers anticipate 3% inflation but that government considers a doubling of inflation (to 6%) a reasonable cost of lowering unemployment by one percentage point. By **stimulating aggregate demand** (say by lowering interest rates), firms will increase output to meet the increase in demand and also start to hire more workers. In Figure 3.5.25:

- **A to B:** The decrease in unemployment moves the economy from point A to point B along the SRPC$_1$ in diagram I. Since de facto inflation now exceeds anticipated inflation, and workers' wages are fixed for the short term, firms will be able to increase their profit margins since final output prices have risen but nominal wages are unchanged. Note that wage rates and wage increases were set when both employers and labourers anticipated 3% inflation!

  ▪ Now, government has achieved its aim of lowering unemployment to 4%, but since *labourers do not suffer from money illusion*, point B is not a long-run equilibrium point. In due course labourers and unions **adjust inflationary expectations to 6%** and will bid up wages to compensate for loss of real income. This will result in higher production costs and dissolve the previous real increase in profits for firms.

- **B to C:** As real costs become apparent to firms, they will cut output and *decrease their demand for labour*. Simultaneously, labourers who initially offered themselves on the labour market under the illusion that real wages were higher than turned out will withdraw from the labour market. This will cause

both markets – goods and labour – to clear, leading to point C where the economy is once again in equilibrium and unemployment has increased to the *natural rate of unemployment*. Economic agents now operate under inflationary expectations of 6%, i.e. along a new short-run Phillips curve, SRPC$_2$ (i^e = 6%).

If no further stimulatory action is taken the economy will remain at full output and the natural rate of unemployment at point C, now shown in Figure 3.5.25 diagram II, at a 6% rate of inflation. Diagram II shows a number of **short-run Phillips curves**, each based on specific rates of expected inflation. At each new level of inflationary expectations, equilibrium is restored when unemployment matches the natural rate of 5%, i.e. points A, C and E along the long-run Phillips curve LRPC. If workers continuously adjust inflationary expectations upward in accordance with stimulatory policies, the short-run Phillips curve will move ever outward/upward. The only way for demand side measures to once again reduce unemployment is for government to 'fool' workers again, e.g. by using even more fiscal/monetary stimulation.

The **long-run Phillips curve** indicates that to keep unemployment *below* the natural rate, ever higher inflation rates will be necessary to keep a degree of money illusion present by continuous monetary expansion and/or fiscal stimulus. This is indicated in diagram II as the dotted arrow leading upwards from point B with 6% inflation to point D with 10% inflation.

What if **deflationary monetary policies** are implemented in order to deal with inflation? Assume that at point C in diagram I of Figure 3.5.25 on page 371, contractionary monetary policies are implemented, thereby reducing aggregate demand. Assume the tight monetary policy is effective and decreases de facto inflation to 3%. This means that households/firms have overestimated inflation. Firms' real costs rise since wages levels were based on the premise of 6% inflation and aggregate supply will slow more than aggregate demand, leading to layoffs and increased unemployment. The economy is at point F in diagram I and assuming that the inflation rate remains constant over the next time period, households and firms will ultimately adapt inflationary expectations to the actual rate of 3%. Labourers will lower wage demands enabling the labour market to clear and the economy returns to equilibrium at point A. While this may sound relatively straightforward, keep in mind that the 'journey' from point C to point A entails passing by point F, marked by the considerable social costs of two additional percentage points of unemployment for an indeterminate time period.

Natural rate of unemployment

©IBO 2003

The conclusion of the expectations augmented Phillips curve is that there is **no trade-off in the long run** between inflation and unemployment. Attempts to reduce the rate of unemployment by demand side measures will fail in the long run since each successive stimulatory package aimed at *permanently* reducing unemployment would ultimately lead the economy back to its natural state but at a higher price level. There would be a separate Phillips curve for each anticipated level of inflation, rendering a **vertical long-run Phillips curve** most similar to the long-run aggregate supply curve. In fact, strictly speaking, they portray the same issue; any stimulatory measure to the economy which does not have a foundation in real (potential) output will not increase output or lower unemployment in the long run.

The congruence (= correspondence) between the AS-AD model and the long-run Phillips curve is shown in Figure 3.5.26 on page 373, diagrams I–IV, in an attempt to put the pieces together for you while illustrating the natural rate of unemployment.[29] In following the iteration in Figure 3.5.26, keep in mind the following points:

- When the labour market is in equilibrium then only structural, frictional and seasonal unemployment exist.
- As this unemployment exists even though the labour market has cleared, it is the *natural rate of unemployment*.
- In the long-run market forces tend to move unemployment levels towards market clearing, e.g. the natural rate of unemployment.
- If the economy is at the natural rate of unemployment then the economy must be in long-run equilibrium, which is to say that AD = LRAS. This is of course the level of output at the natural rate of unemployment – Y_{NRU}.

Diagram I in Figure 3.5.26 shows how an economy is initially moving along at a rate where inflation is correctly anticipated, $SRPC_0$ (i^e = low) in diagram II. The resulting rate of inflation is i_0, e.g. point A in diagrams II and IV. This *general equilibrium* renders the natural rate of unemployment.

- **A to B:** If government now stimulates aggregate demand (AD_0 to AD_1, diagram I) there will be *unanticipated* inflation resulting from the demand side shock. This is shown by a movement along the initial short-run Phillips curve $SRPC_0$ (in accordance with earlier arguments) and the economy moves from point A to B.
  - The change is illustrated further in diagram III (unemployment falls to U_1) and diagram IV (increasing rate of inflation).
- **B to C:** As labourers do not suffer from money illusion, they bid up wages in adjustment to higher inflationary expectations. The increase in labour costs for firms causes aggregate supply to decrease to $SRAS_1$ and point C in diagram I. Jobs are lost while the economy experiences yet another increase in the rate of inflation before returning to the natural rate of unemployment at Y_{NRU}.
- Diagram II shows how a new short-run Phillips curve, $SRPC_0$ (i^e = high), is formed at an anticipated inflation rate of i_2. Diagram III shows how unemployment has returned to U_{NRU} at point C. Diagram IV illustrates how inflation now progresses at a higher rate, i_2.

The progression from point A to B to C in Figure 3.5.26 explains the neoclassical view of how the economy will always tend towards the natural rate of

---

29. I use these diagrams with grateful acknowledgement to Professor Klas Fregert and Associate Professor Lars Jonung at Lund University.

unemployment in the long run. The vertical long-run Phillips curve tells policy makers that there is no long-run trade-off between inflation and unemployment. If the aim is to decrease unemployment below the natural rate of unemployment in the *long run*, then the appropriate policy action is supply-side policy.

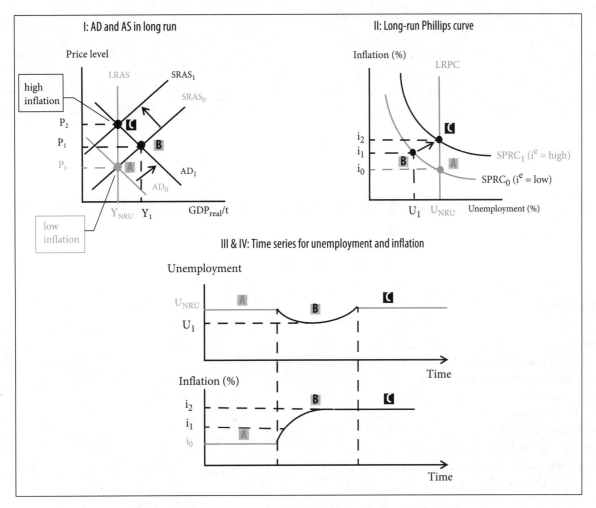

Figure 3.5.26 *AS-AD model and natural rate of unemployment*

POP QUIZ 3.5.5 INFLATION AND THE PHILLIPS CURVE

1 Why are goods in the CPI weighted?

2 What are the main weaknesses of using the CPI as a measure of inflation?

3 How does 'money illusion' help to explain the trade-off shown by the Phillips curve?

4 Illustrate how increased inflationary expectations would lead to higher inflation.

5 Using the long-run Phillips curve, explain how demand side policies would be unable to decrease the natural rate of unemployment.

6 How might supply-side policies affect the natural rate of unemployment?

Distribution of income

3.6

CONTENTS

DISTRIBUTION OF INCOME ©IBO 2003

Pecunia not olet. ('Money does not smell.')[1]

Equity

As outlined in Section 3.3, governments use taxes to fund government spending and to steer the economy using fiscal policies. Section 2.6 brought up how taxes can be used to discourage production and consumption of goods yielding negative externalities and how government monies could be used to increase production/consumption of goods having positive externalities. A third main area in the use of taxation is to create a more socially acceptable, or 'fair', distribution of resources, i.e. wealth and income.

One of my favourite baiting-games I play with younger students is to claim that there is nothing wrong with a society where people starve alongside the extremely rich. I sometimes refer to the gap in wealth and income to be found in, say, Brazil, and claim that this is perfectly acceptable in terms of economics. We have, after all, solved the basic economic problem of who gets what – we allow income and wealth to decide. I do this towards the end of class in order to make my escape and avoid the inevitable screaming and general outrage. I make sure that the whiteboard is full so that they are preoccupied as I sneak out. When the students have cooled down a bit, usually after a few days, I carefully distinguish between 'equity' and 'equality'. **Equity** in economics is a concept meaning 'fairness' and 'justice', for example, that everybody should have the same **right** to work, own property and start a company – regardless of gender, ethnicity, etc. whereas **equality** would entail that everyone would have the same **ability** to work, own property and start a company.

Economics must often deal with the questions of equity:

- Should the rich be taxed proportionately more than the poor and middle-class?
- Is it better to tax consumption (value-added taxes, VAT, for example, or income (taxes on profits and dividends)?
- To what extent should the socially/economically disadvantaged be given additional resources at the

expense of the economically advantaged, i.e. transfers of income and wealth aimed at evening out income disparities?

- What about the viewpoint of the wealthy? Is it not an economic fact that the goods and services we desire are better furthered by self interest and the profit motives of firms? Is it more economically efficient to *increase* output rather than *redistribute* it? Should not governments try to create a favourable environment for firms and a framework for enterprise in order to increase the cake from which all subsequent taxes and income transfers will be sliced? Wouldn't society ultimately gain if the incentives to produce (say via low corporate taxes) were enhanced?

The above examples are but a small portion of a recurring debate within both economics and politics, dealing with the desirability and efficiency of government intervention in matters of equity. We have returned to the issues outlined in production possibility curves earlier, but now with a slightly more ideological and thus political flavour. The appealing simplicity of 'invest now in order to produce more in the future' must be appended by realism: it is not at all certain that any part of 'more' will be distributed equitably or evenly. Our basic economic problem is not so basic after all. If output were to grow by 50% and go to 0.1% of the population then we would certainly face some sort of sharp societal reaction – from protest lists to burning tyres in front of parliament. Most countries will have a redistribution system built into government policy, which evens out income differentials to a certain extent. Governments can redistribute income in three basic ways; *taxation*, *transfer payments* and *goods* and *services in kind*.

A good tax – Smith again

An American saying pounded into me by generations of hard-headed McGees is that only two things are for certain: death and taxes.[2] Most of my forebears would thus have looked upon the heading 'A good tax' as an oxymoron (= contradiction in terms). In any case,

---

1. Quote by the Roman emperor Vespasian (9–79 AD, emperor 69–79 AD) in defence of his plan to put a tax on using public urinals.
2. I thought this was amusing until I discovered that many countries in fact have death or funeral taxes.

taxation of citizens has been a source of heavy debate, disagreement and even civil war for thousands of years. Adam Smith laid down the 'canons (= standards, rules) of taxation' in his magnum opus *The Wealth of Nations*. According to Smith, taxes should have four main characteristics:

1. **Certainty** – those paying should know how much they are paying.
2. **Convenience** – they should be easy to collect.
3. **Economy** – they should be cheap to collect relative to their yield, i.e. 'cost-efficient'.
4. **Equity** – the sacrifice should be equally felt by those being taxed.

Another issue is of course that the overall effects of taxation should not be counterproductive in terms of the goals of economic policies – see automatic stabilisers in "Fiscal policy" on page 313. Smith was referring to both efficiency and equity, where the cost of collecting the tax deals with efficiency and the ability to pay deals with equity.

Horizontal and vertical equity

Equity in tax terms means 'fairness' of the taxes levied, i.e. that the sacrifice or burden should be felt equally amongst those paying. **Horizontal equity** is 'treating equals equal', for example, when IB students get the same amount of time to complete their exams, or workers of equal experience and training are paid the same. This concept of 'equality for equals' would also apply in tax levies, where two people having the same income should pay the same tax.

Vertical equity involves 'treating different people differently' in order to enhance 'fairness'. Continuing with the examples given above; a student with a writing disability can be granted the right to 15 extra minutes in exams and minority groups can be given preferential treatment in job applications. In both these examples, the different treatment of different people can help to even out inequities. In applying vertical equity to taxes, less tax would be paid by low income earners while more tax would be paid by high income households. You no doubt realise that any form of the term 'equity' is highly normative in nature.

Direct taxation ©IBO 2003

When a wage earner receives his/her wages, *income tax* has for the most part already been deducted. Other taxes which are levied directly on individual incomes are taxes on profits, interest received, capital gains taxes (on income earned by selling property or shares) and

dividends from the ownership of shares. Other economic agents, e.g. firms, pay *corporate taxes* (often called profit taxes), and *labour taxes*. In each of these cases, the tax is clearly distinguishable and goes directly from the taxpayer to the tax office; these are direct taxes. (Refer to "PED and taxation" on page 128.)

Direct taxes on income are associated with two main economic effects.

1. The first is the **redistribution effect**, whereby income tax is collected and then redistributed to other (less fortunate) members of society. Note that this is not only in the form of money (see "Transfer payments" on page 379) but also in the form of health care, education and road networks ('benefits in kind' below).
2. The second effect is the possibility of a **disincentives effect**, when taxes on income increase at higher income levels, workers might not view additional working hours as worthwhile. It is also possible that an unemployed person gets a job and incurs a net loss of disposable income when income tax is paid at the same time as various social benefits disappear – this is a form of *poverty trap* for low income households. In addition, there is the possibility of a **black labour market** when increasing tax levels create an incentive for workers to avoid taxes by not reporting income to the tax office.

> Direct taxes: Direct taxes are levied on economic agents' income, wealth or property. Firms pay profit tax and labour tax. Households pay income tax, capital gains tax and property tax.

Indirect taxation ©IBO 2003

One of the snappier comebacks by one of my students in high-tax Sweden was a retort to my inevitable chastisement 'My tax money paid for that!' when pupils complained about the school lunch. 'My tax money paid for it too! Oh, and also for your salary.' Cheekiness aside, the point is well taken; a good deal of government tax revenue is comprised of taxes on expenditure such as value added taxes (**VAT**), specific taxes commonly levied on petrol and alcohol (**excise duties**) and import taxes (**tariffs**). All of these are indirect taxes, since economic exchanges such as consumption/expenditure rather than individuals are taxed.

Indirect taxes: Indirect taxes are levied on consumption and expenditure. Value-added tax, excise duties (special taxes on tobacco and alcohol) and tariffs (taxes on imports) are examples of indirect taxes.

WARNING! Many students confuse tariffs with excise duties. Perhaps it is because 'duties' is so easily associated to 'Duty free'! Whatever the origin of the confusion, an excise duty is a tax on 'bads', e.g. alcohol, tobacco and petrol. Oh, one of my American students informed me that there is often an excise duty on gambling in the US. I looked it up – he's quite right.)

Indirect taxes affect supply which implies that market equilibrium is negatively affected: the supply curve for the good shifts left. While the case is often that this causes a misallocation of resources (and deadweight loss), we have also seen that in fact taxes might serve to decrease negative externalities and therefore instead increase allocative efficiency (see Section 2.4). An issue worthy of notice here is whether a tax on a good having negative externalities should be designated to cover only its own costs or not. For example, many countries have road taxes which contribute to government tax receipts far in excess of what is subsequently paid for building and renovating roads. A strong case can be made by car owners that they are paying more than their fare share of taxes, since any surplus receipts will benefit those who do not own cars. The counter-argument is that road usage is strongly associated with negative externalities such as pollution and noise, so the additional tax is an adequate disincentive for road use.

Progressive taxation ©IBO 2003

Direct taxation has one clear advantage over indirect taxes, namely that a direct tax can be adjusted to conform to societal views on equity. Income tax rates can be adjusted to each person's ability to pay, i.e. adjusted to income. A progressive tax on income means that higher income will result in a higher percentage of tax paid, i.e. an increasing proportion of income goes to tax. Most countries will have a systematic increase in the proportion (= percentage) of income tax paid as income rises, since this is virtually the only way in which income can be redistributed – by 'taking from the rich and giving to the poor'. Commonly in income tax systems, there is a minimum income level where no tax is paid, whereupon the marginal tax – the tax paid on the last money earned – increases.

For example, say that income tax on the first 2,000 is zero but 15% on any income above this. Earning 3,000 would mean that income tax would be paid only on the additional 1,000 – the amount exceeding the threshold of 2,000. This is the *marginal tax rate*. Tax at an income of 3,000 would be 1,000 × 0.15 = 150. (Take heed! The *average tax* on income is of course total tax paid over total income, i.e. 150/3,000 = 5%.)

The progressive taxation element in this method of income taxation is that higher income brackets will mean higher percentage tax paid. Continuing with the example, say that the tax rate progressively increases to 20% for income above 5,000 but below 10,000, and that a person's income increases from 5,000 to 7,000. The *marginal tax* on the 2,000 above the 5,000 tax bracket is 400 while the *average tax* paid will be 3,000 × 0.15 + 2,000 × 0.2 = 850. The tax rate then increases at every higher income bracket. This is illustrated in the upward sloping progressive curve in Figure 3.6.1, where the marginal tax rate is, of course, the slope of the curve.

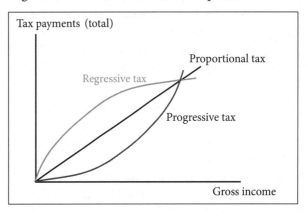

Figure 3.6.1 *Progressive, proportional and regressive taxes*

Proportional taxation ©IBO 2003

A proportional tax is exactly what it sounds like – a percentage of income paid in tax. Since the percentage is unchanged at higher income levels, there is no marginal tax effect and any rise in income will add to total tax payment at a constant rate, so average tax rate is unchanged. In other words, the proportional tax curve will have a constant slope, as illustrated in Figure 3.6.1. Capital gains, corporate profits and dividends are types of income which are frequently taxed on a proportional basis.

Regressive taxation ©IBO 2003

Just as indirect taxes can be 'flat rate' – such as unit taxes on wine – direct taxation can consist of a fixed sum which does not change as income rises, which means that average taxes paid fall as income rises. A

regressive tax means that the average proportion of tax paid on income or profit falls as income/profit increases. For example, a yearly business registration tax of £1,000 for a small corner shop with £20,000 in profit means 5% average tax. For Imperial Tobacco Group PLC, the £423 million in profit in 2002[3] would mean that the registration tax is on average 0.00023%. Since the average tax payment as a proportion of income is falling, the regressive tax curve will become successively shallower, shown in Figure 3.6.1.

Another regressive effect of taxation is that lower income groups are often hit harder by *indirect taxes* than higher income groups. Alcohol, tobacco and petrol are all major contributors to total government tax revenues and contain a large element of **flat-rate tax** (excise duty). The regressive element herein is when low income earners pay the same tax as high income earners; the former are spending a greater proportion of income on the goods than the latter. In fact, value added taxes are arguably regressive since a 10% sales tax on a £100 purchase constitutes a far larger part of income for a person earning £12,000 than for someone earning £120,000. One could say that this lowers the effectiveness of any intended redistribution effects of the tax. See Table 3.6.1.

I frequently put forward scathing comments on how corrupt police here in Mexico are in fact a system of regressive taxation. When police stop drivers for real or made-up offences, they have a 'price list' of fines at the ready (they can draw that list faster than Wyatt Earp could pull his six-shooter). They then make clear how much time, effort and inconvenience it will be for the driver to have to go through the motions of paying the official fine – often claiming that they will also have to confiscate the vehicle. They are waiting for the driver to say, 'So, how can you help me officer?!' A common bribe ('mordida' – roughly 'little bite') is 200 Mexican pesos, about USD18. This is four days' earnings for about 40 million people here in Mexico and about 25 minutes for an expatriate IB teacher. In other words, a flat-rate bribe will hit Benito the day labourer far harder than Graham the IB coordinator. Oh yes, before I forget: the State of Mexico toughened the driving laws two years ago, increasing the number of possible violations while driving. My Mexican friends rather fatalistically called the harsher legislation a tax raise. I called it the cheapest possible form of pay increase for the police – it gives the police more power to extort bribes and the government pays nothing.

> **Progressive, proportional and regressive taxes:**
>
> **Progressive tax** means that the percentage of tax paid increases as income rises – a larger proportion of income goes to tax as income rises.
>
> When the percentage paid is the same no matter what income level, the tax is **proportional** – the same proportion of income goes to tax regardless of income.
>
> A tax that is the same amount of money (flat rate) regardless of income is a **regressive tax** – a decreasing proportion of income goes to tax as income rises.

Table 3.6.1 *Summary of income taxes*

	Tax payments on an income of:					
	£ 10,000		£ 50,000		£ 200,000	
	Tax paid (£)	Average (%)	Tax paid (£)	Average (%)	Tax paid (£)	Average (%)
Regressive tax (flat rate £1,500)	£1,500	15%	£1,500	3%	£1,500	0.75%
Proportional tax (15%)	£1,500	15%	£7,500	15%	£30,000	15%
Progressive tax (average rates of 15%, 20%, 30%)	£1,500	15%	£10,000	20%	£60,000	30%

---

3. Annual report Imperial Tobacco PLC at http://www.imperial-tobacco.com.

And justice for all ...

All taxes will in some way lead to market distortions, since they lead to a decrease in supply and concomitant decrease in quantity demanded. Taxes on labour lead to higher costs for firms and an increase in unemployment; indirect taxes lead to less goods being consumed; corporate taxes lead to fewer new firms and less investment; and capital gains tax reduces incentives and lowers economic activity. However, the economic argument in favour of enduring these distortions is that the allocative losses can be made up for by the overall redistribution gains to society in terms of public and merit goods. Governments use tax receipts to provide goods which are beneficial to all of society. For example, the efficiency loss in firms due to labour taxes are offset by productivity gains arising from a well-educated work force, and the relatively small decrease in consumption arising due to high marginal taxes on the richest 1% can be offset by welfare gains when the taxes are redistributed to poorer groups.

It gets trickier when governments have to decide which tax creates the fairest outcome. Indirect taxes have the advantage of being simple and easy to collect, but have the disadvantage of levying a heavier burden on the poor than the rich. For example, a unit tax of 2 per litre of alcoholic beverage will have a far greater real income effect on Otto Normalverbraucher[4] purchasing a six-pack of beer for €3 than it will have on Countess Antoinette du la Monet[5] buying a bottle of 1966 Chateau Neuf du Pape for €150. In effect, a flat-rate tax expenditure tax will have strong regressive tax effects on poorer groups.

As for income taxes, where is it written that higher income must lead to higher proportion of tax – when in fact a proportional tax already means that higher income leads to more tax payments?! The argument for progressive income taxes ('higher income = higher percentage tax') is highly normative, in that there is an evening-out effect of incomes which is 'fair' to society in general. Increased income equality also has economic benefits, such as lower crime rates and inner city regeneration which, of course, benefits everyone. Quite naturally, the well-off point out that between one third and half of all income tax receipts in developed countries come from the top 5% income earners – the implication being that this is 'more than their fair

share'. Another common argument put forward by the affluent is that progressive taxes are a major disincentive for people to push themselves, being in fact a 'punitive tax' on achievement, hard work and entrepreneurial spirit.

Transfer payments ©IBO 2003

Societies often find it necessary and prudent to provide benefits for certain groups of citizens. Social (welfare) benefit systems which redistribute income via cash **transfer payments** exist in most countries in some form. Students will receive grants and soft loans; retired people receive pensions and additional health care monies; low-income households and single parents (far too often one and the same) receive supplemental housing allowance and welfare payments, and unemployed people receive unemployment benefits and perhaps travel contributions for job seeking.

The other main form of societal redistribution is **services in kind** – merit goods such as health care and education. Since these goods would be both underprovided and thus under-consumed on a free market, it would be the poorer groups who would suffer the most. By using government (tax) monies to provide these goods on a general basis of not-for-profit, total economic welfare is increased.

Yet another trade-off?

Notice the question mark in the above heading and prepare yourself for another of my 'No, there is no answer' paragraphs. Redistributing income has a double-edged price tag of administrative costs to government and allocative losses to society. Redistribution has been likened to attempting to transfer water from one bucket to another.[6] A portion of the water – income – will invariably be lost in the process, i.e. there will be costs associated with administration and economic efficiency. The taxes on economic endeavours such as labour and investment also render opportunity costs in the form of forgone ... labour and investment. This argument thus puts forward that attempting to improve social welfare by increasing equity will render a social cost in terms of greater inefficiency in the use of resources which leads to a loss of income.

---

4. German for 'Joe Average'.
5. Pronounced 'de Money'.
6. Expressed by the famous economist Arthur Okun in his book *Equality and Efficiency: The Big Trade-off*, Washington DC, Brookings Institution, 1975.

The basic question here is whether the costs to society of trying to increase equity are counterproductive in terms of economic growth. The trade-off, according to this line of reasoning, is between growth in total income and growth in income equality. In the final analysis, a good many studies show that there is indeed a trade-off – increased income inequality is 'pro-growth'. However, a good many studies show the reverse, i.e. that greater inequality leads to lower growth! And for my final trick; a recent study by the OECD showed 'no evidence that the level of income inequality affects GDP one way or another.'[7] I told you there would be no answer.

HIGHER LEVEL EXTENSION TOPICS

Laffer curve ©IBO 2003

Well, of course, when you cut taxes, government revenues go up. Why couldn't I see that before? – *Time* Magazine columnist Michael Kinsley's first words (according to his editor) upon waking up from brain surgery.

A question which ultimately arises when dealing with taxes is what happens if tax rates are changed. This question is similar to the issue of price elasticity of demand and what happens to quantity demanded when the price changes. A famous supply-side economist during the Reagan administration in America, Arthur Laffer, suggested that it is quite possible/probable that in some cases a decrease in the tax rate would lead to an increase in tax revenue.[8]

The supply of labour for an individual

Allow me to explain the Laffer curve from a vantage point outside the syllabus, using the *individual supply of labour curve*. Figure 3.6.2 suggests that two conflicting forces are at work when people decide whether to work more for higher wages since the real wage rate and labour hours are positively correlated up to W_0 but then become negatively correlated. The *substitution* and *income effect* can explain this.

- **Substitution effect on individual labour supply**: The *substitution effect* means that a worker will be willing to substitute free time with work when the rewards (real wages) outweigh the opportunity costs (giving up free time). Thus the *substitution effect is positive* – higher real wages lead to more hours of work.

- **Income effect on individual labour supply**: At the same time, there is a negative *income effect*, since higher income means the individual has to put in fewer hours for the same money. The *income effect will therefore be negative* – higher real wages lead to fewer hours of work.

- **The 'backward bending' curve**: The supply curve is positively correlated to wage levels at first and then become negative correlated.

  - At low levels of income the substitution effect will outweigh the income effect and higher wages will lead to more hours worked.

  - However, at some point the opportunity cost of working additional hours will catch up with the labourer and the additional money will simply not be worth giving up free time for; the opportunity cost of labour will be too high. That is wage level W_0, when the income effect outweighs the substitution effect and the individual supply of labour curve, $S_{L_{ind}}$, bends backwards.

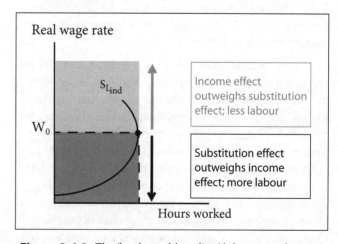

Figure 3.6.2 *The 'backward-bending' labour supply curve for an individual*

---

7. 'OECD Economic Studies No. 35, 2002/2' at http://www.oecd.org/dataoecd/42/33/22023319.pdf.

8. Laffer apparently drew the original curve on a cocktail napkin at a Washington restaurant on 4 December 1974, to explain things to a journalist, Jude Wanniski of *The Wall Street Journal* and future American Vice President Dick Cheney. See http://www.fortune.com/fortune/articles/0,15114,447776,00.html.

The 'inverted U' of Laffer

Figure 3.6.3 shows the **Laffer curve**, which illustrates the marginal tax effect on income and thus tax revenues; if the tax rate is higher than t*, lowering income tax will increase tax revenue, while a tax rate below t* means that tax revenue will increase if tax is increased.

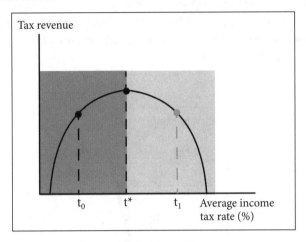

Figure 3.6.3 *The Laffer curve*

The argument supported by the Laffer curve is that high income taxes distort labour markets and lead to a socially sub-optimal level of labour hours and thus tax revenue. Continuing with the terminology used to explain the individual supply of labour above, a cut in the tax rate will mean an increase in real disposable income. Will people then increase their labour hours? Yes, according to supply-side economists, since this view asserts that the substitution effect is stronger than the income effect and therefore workers will have an incentive to work more. If a worker is earning 20,000 a year and paying 30% tax, then total tax revenue is 6,000. Say that the tax rate is lowered to 27% and that this induces the worker to increase his/her hours, increasing gross wages to 23,000. This would result in total tax revenue of 6,210. Referring to the Laffer curve in Figure 3.6.4 on page 382, if the income tax rate is above **t*** then total tax revenue will increase if the tax rate is lowered.

Optimal tax rate?

The Laffer curve suggests that there is an *optimal* tax rate in terms of optimising total tax revenue. Naturally, tax revenue is zero at a tax rate of zero and would be zero at a tax rate of over 100% since one would basically have to pay the government to work. Tax revenue will be collected in between these two extreme values and the general shape of the curve is hardly up for debate. The problem is in finding the point where taxes can be optimised to yield the highest revenue. I venture to say that while Laffer himself suggested that big governments and thus big taxes would in all likelihood be to the right of point **t*** and would benefit from lowering taxes, most economists would read purely empirical evidence to the effect that *high income* countries lie somewhere to the left of point **t***.

I cannot help mentioning a rather interesting example from Russia which seems to offer a degree of support for the Laffer curve. In 2001, President Putin introduced a flat rate income tax of 13% – down from over 30% – and during the first two years of the new (entirely non-progressive) tax rates income tax payments more than doubled government tax revenues. The tax enjoys seeming widespread support from Russians, to the extent that a survey showed more people in favour of a flat-rate tax than a progressive tax.[9] On a more frivolous note, the Italian prime minister, Silvio Berlusconi, was quoted in February 2004 as saying: 'If reasonable taxes are demanded, no one thinks about avoiding paying them. But if you ask 50% or more … I consider myself morally justified to do everything I can to avoid paying them.'[10]

Lorenz curve and Gini coefficient
©IBO 2003

One of the many controversial areas in economics is the issue of income inequality *within* societies (often over a time period) and *between* societies. Media coverage commonly puts this in terms of a 'gap between rich and poor', or 'inequality in country X'. For example, an article in the *International Herald Tribune* states that in 2000 the richest 1% of Americans had more after-tax income than the bottom 40%, representing 15.5% of total national income – triple the level that this group had 20 years earlier.[11] Another article, in *Time* Magazine, points out that in 2003 the wealthiest 1% of Americans accounted for 40% of total wealth (note, not income) while the corresponding

9. *Business Week*, 26 May 2003, 'From each according to…oh, never mind'.

10. *Time* Magazine, 1 March 2004, p. 17 (I must mention that the Italian budget deficit at the time of writing [January 2009] is circa 2.5% of GDP and that total national debt is 104% of GDP – the third highest in the world. See http://www.reuters.com/article/bondsNews/idUSLO27400220081125).

11. *International Herald Tribune*, 'US rich get richer, and poor poorer, data shows', 25 September 2003. (During 2005 the top 1% of USA's richest people earned 21.2% of total income. *Wall Street Journal* in October 2007, quoted in http://www.privataaffarer.se/newsText.asp?src=pa&a=23038).

HIGHER LEVEL

value in the UK was 18%.[12] Table 3.6.2 on page 383 shows a simple and graspable way to compare inequality within and between countries, namely the **Lorenz curve**.

Lorenz curve

In Figure 3.6.4 diagram I the *y*-axis shows the cumulative (= collective, summed-up) percentage of total income and the *x*-axis shows the cumulative percentage of all wage earners. The 45 degree line is the line of perfect equality, i.e. a country where 1% of income goes to 1% of wage earners, 2% of income goes to 2% of wage earners and so forth along the line. The upward-sloping curve is a Lorenz curve, in this case showing that income distribution is rather uneven. The farther away the Lorenz curve is from the line of perfect equality, the more unequal the income distribution. In the example above, the bottom 20% (the first quintile) of wage earners accounts for just 2.8% of total income; the second quintile accounts for 6.4% of income (9.2% to 2.8%); and skipping the next two, the top quintile of wage earners accounts for 61.1% of all income.

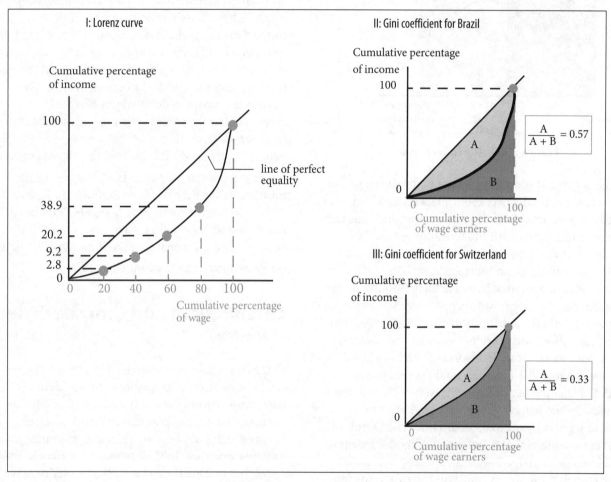

Figure 3.6.4 *Lorenz curves*

Gini coefficient

How far removed from reality is this example? Well, actually, I have just described Brazil, notoriously one of the most unequal societies in the world. Now, if we wish to compare income distribution in Brazil with other countries (or indeed, Brazilian income distribution over time), we can calculate the so-called **Gini coefficient**, which is a value of the 'distance' of the curve from the 45-degree perfect equality line. This is calculated by taking the ratio between area A and A + B (diagrams II and III in Figure 3.6.4).

If income were perfectly distributed then the Gini coefficient would be 0. If one wage earner accounted for 100% of income, the coefficient would be 1. The *higher* the Gini coefficient, the more *unequally* income is distributed. According to the World Bank in 2007,

---

12. *Time* Magazine, 17 November 2003, p. 22 (Official US government figures at the US Census Bureau show clearly that income inequality has been increasing from 1947 to 2007. See http://www.census.gov/hhes/www/income/histinc/f04.html.).

Brazil had a Gini coefficient of 0.57 while Switzerland had 0.33. Table 3.6.2 shows these and a few other Gini coefficients for comparison.

The Gini coefficient is a most convenient way of summarizing the degree of income inequality in a country, lending readily available figures for comparison. It is immediately apparent that Brazil is indeed a most unequal country in terms of income distribution, rendering a Gini coefficient of 0.57. I have included three of the richest countries in the world as a contrast. It should come as no surprise that Sweden's fair-minded egalitarian philosophy and high tax rates results in one of the lowest Gini coefficients in the world – 0.25. The country which probably has the most uneven distribution of income in the world is Namibia, with an estimated Gini coefficient of 0.7. Data from a population census taken in 1994 pointed to the richest 7,000 people (out of a population of 1.4 million) having the total income of the poorest 800,000.

Table 3.6.2 *Gini coefficients, selected countries*

Country [year of survey]	Gini coefficient	Percentage share of income		Kuznets ratio [(2) / (1)]
		Lowest quintile (1)	Highest quintile (2)	
Brazil [2004](see diagram)	0.57	2.8%	61.1%	21,8
Honduras [2003]	0.56	3.4%	58.3%	17.1
Jamaica [2004]	0.38	5.3%	51.6%	9.7
Sweden [2000]	0.25	9.1%	36.6%	4.0
Switzerland [2000] (see diagram)	0.33	7.6%	41.3%	5.4
Luxembourg [2002]	0.27	9.4%	36.5%	3,9

(Sources: World Development indicators 2007, at World Bank, at http://siteresources.worldbank.org)

At the other end of the scale, the country with the lowest Gini coefficient in the world seems to be Denmark at 0.247. Keep in mind that the Gini coefficient only measures the *relative* distribution of income and not poverty levels. There are also a few weaknesses with the Gini coefficient:

- It is quite possible that two countries with entirely different income distributions have the same Gini value.

- Also, the shape of the curve gives information only on total distribution and not on the relationship between the richest and poorest segments (see "The Kuznets ratio" on page 384).

- Finally, a country with a high Gini coefficient might in fact have a generally high standard of living in low-income groups – just as it is equally possible for a country with a low Gini coefficient to have widespread poverty across most income groups.

HIGHER LEVEL

the Kuznets ratio and Kuznets curve

The Kuznets ratio

I have included three additional Outside the box columns in Table 3.6.2 on page 383 to show the Kuznets ratio, originating with economist Simon Kuznets. This ratio of inequality is a measurement of the 'span' or 'distance' between the richest and poorest segments in a society. Taking the proportion of income going to the highest earning 20% – quintile – and dividing it by the proportion going to the poorest quintile gives an indication of the gap between the richest and poorest portions of society. The higher the value of the Kuznets ratio, the greater the distance between rich and poor, e.g. the higher the value the more unequal the income distribution. By this measure, in Table 3.6.2, Honduras is more unequal than Brazil in terms of income whereas the Gini coefficient indicated the reverse. Sweden still comes out near the top with a ratio of 3.6.

The Kuznets curve

Another highly controversial and thus infinitely more famous concept put forward by Kuznets is that there is correlation between economic growth and income distribution. He posited that during initial stages of economic growth the distribution of income would worsen, i.e. the rich would gain proportionately more of the increased income than the poor. During later unspecified stages of growth the distribution of income would improve, i.e. the gap between rich and poor would narrow. Plotting income against income distribution (measured by the Gini coefficient) gives an inverted 'U', known as the Kuznets curve, where growth in per capita income results initially in worsening income distribution, i.e. a higher Gini coefficient (see Figure 3.6.5). At some unspecified level of income, correlation will reverse and income distributions will improve.

The Kuznets curve has been fiercely debated for over 40 years now. The proposition that income distribution would at first widen and then narrow was widely studied and by the 1970s had broad acceptance. Yet a good many later empirical studies show little evidence of either positive or negative systematic relationships between per capita growth and income distribution.

The controversy continues unabated around a curve which Kuznets himself claims was '5% empirical, 95% speculation'!

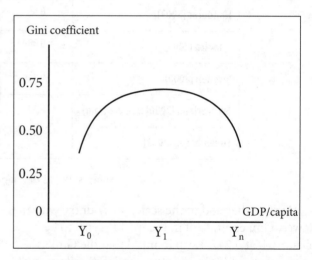

Figure 3.6.5 *Kuznets' inverted 'U' curve*

Preparing for exams

Short answer questions (10 marks each)

1 Why might there be unemployment at the equilibrium level of income?

2 Discuss whether inflation or deflation is the more serious problem for an economy.

3 Explain what the 'natural rate of unemployment' is.

4 Explain how an unexpectedly large increase in the price of oil might affect a non oil exporting country.

5 What are the economic and social costs of high inflation levels?

6 Discuss the merits of supply-side policies aimed at reducing unemployment.

7 Explain how unemployment could be 'voluntary' or 'involuntary'.

8 The government of a less developed country decides to reduce the extent of income and wealth inequality. What methods could the government use to achieve its goal?

[HL only]

9 How could knowledge of the shape of the Phillips curve benefit governments?

Extended response questions (25 marks each)

1 a What are the main causes of unemployment? (10 marks)

  b How might governments lower the natural rate of unemployment? (15 marks)

2 a Examine whether full employment is possible to attain. (10 marks)

  b What possible social and economic costs might arise in trying to attain full employment? (15 marks)

3 a What are the causes of inflation? (10 marks)

  b Explain how monetary and fiscal policies can be used to alleviate (= lessen) different types of inflation. (15 marks)

4 a How could government change its tax system in order to shift more of the overall tax burden from the poor to the rich? (10 marks)

  b Analyse why the government might wish to do this and the possible effects of the tax changes. (15 marks)

[HL only]

5 a Is there a trade-off between inflation and unemployment? (10 marks)

  b What are the implications of your answer in terms of economic policies aimed at growth? (15 marks)

INTERNATIONAL ECONOMICS

4

International issues are amongst the most controversial and divisive in economics but I dare say that the majority of economists agree that trade and international exchange has been one of the most beneficial economic endeavours in humankind. Most economists view trade – more specifically free and fair trade – as one of the prime determinants of increased living standards in the world. Trade is good. Yet in spite of the benefits of trade having time and again proven to far outweigh costs, a good many interest groups will look upon my statement as highly political and therefore inappropriate to put into a school textbook.

However, my defence of the statement 'Trade is good' is not founded in a political standpoint but an economic standpoint whereas a good deal of the anti-trade rhetoric supporting statements such as 'Trade creates unemployment' is often erroneous and indeed sometimes nothing else but cheap political point-winning. A good deal of this section and the next will attempt to define 'good' in as measurable economic terms as possible. Then I leave it to you, the economist, to deliberate whether the statement is normative or positive – and right or wrong.

The core of international economics is comprised of issues which arise when independent nations interact in order to conduct economic transactions such as trade and foreign investment. The topics looked at here centre on the reasons for and benefits of trade; why protectionism exists; trade patterns and economic integration; the balance of payments and exchange rates, and the terms under which nations trade.

Reasons for trade

4.1

CONTENTS

REASONS FOR TRADE ©IBO 2003

'No nation was ever ruined by trade.' – Benjamin Franklin

On the shelves around me here in my office/classroom in Mexico as I write this sentence one finds a bowl of bananas (Mexico), a thermos of coffee (Colombia/Kenya/Nicaragua), cigars (Cuba) and sugar (Denmark) – basically all the major food groups needed by writers. I also have a mobile phone, two computers, a hand-held computer, a USB memory stick and about 150 books on economics. With the exception of the bananas and my manta ray boots[1], very little has actually been produced in Mexico, yet here I am, happily eating a banana and sipping sweet coffee in anticipation of my evening cigar.[2] At the same time, my editor in Australia, Marcia, is using silver from Mexican mines to frame her 'Economics Textbook of the Year' award. This must mean that someone in Tegucigalpa, Honduras, is walking to work wearing a pair of kangaroo skin boots – since my bananas didn't come from Australia but Honduras. In effect, the Mexicans sent silver to the Australians in exchange for boots, and used the Australian boots to trade for Honduran bananas. No, wait: the Aussies used Australian dollars (AUD) to buy Mexican pesos (MXN) with which they then bought silver; the Mexicans used the Australian dollars to buy Honduran Lempira (HNL) and then bananas, and the Hondurans exchanged the Lempira to get Australian dollars and R. M. Williams boots.

Now each country has a pile of foreign currency to be used at will. Mexicans on their way to The Great Barrier Reef in Australia can get some AUD at the airport in Toluca; a Honduran steel business can buy MXN at the bank in order to purchase steel rolling machines from ArcelorMital in Mexico; and when Marcia gets fed up with editing silly footnotes in economics textbooks she can buy HNL at the exchange office to import goods from Honduras and start a *Things Honduran* shop in Cunnamulla. This is an example of, respectively, trade in services, capital and goods.

Ek Chuah, God of Trade, Tulum, Mexico (circa 5th century AD)

Differences in factor endowments
©IBO 2003

The triangle of trade above shows a most basic economic fact that is all too often lost in the debate; the only way Mexicans can visit the Great Barrier Reef is by trading some silver. (Or rather, since most tourists don't produce silver themselves, they will use a domestic 'silver certificate' – MXN – which Australians will accept in order to buy silver and boots from Mexico.) Why do we trade instead of producing everything domestically?

Simple: growing bananas in my home country of Sweden would be only slightly more ludicrous than having herds of kangaroos in Kiruna in northern Sweden.[3] In a similar vein, the cigars on my desk are from Cuba but could just as easily have come from Nicaragua, Mexico, the Dominican Republic or 20 other countries. In fact, increasingly, my cigars *are* from Mexico and Honduras – but none of them are from Sweden, Norway or Finland.

---

1. You think I'm joking, right? I'm not. People often ask me why I've come to Mexico. Simple: it's one of the few places one gets to wear cowboy boots without going to a Halloween party. I have boots made from armadillo, ostrich, crocodile, lizard and manta ray. To general outrage amongst my students I told them I intend to put in an order for the USD1,000 *whale* skin boots. 'Why?' they asked. 'Well, I've got to get the order in before we run out of whales!' Eventually they figured out I was yanking their chains and didn't beat me up.
2. And, in all likelihood, a tequila. I've got about 15 bottles of booze on my classroom shelf – presents from happy students and their parents. Yes, my boss knows. His smiling comment was 'Matt, *everyone* knows. Just put a visible mark on the levels of the bottles so I don't see students staggering out of your classroom.' Why am I so lucky with bosses and not wives?
3. But times they are a'changin'! On my way to work in southern Sweden a few years ago, I almost ran into an ostrich (!) on the road. It is apparently economically profitable in Sweden to farm ostriches domestically. Or is this globalisation – like the ostrich – run amok? Whatever; get taller fences.

Swedish ballbearings and Honduran bananas

You get the picture. Part of the answer lies in each country's **factor endowment** (= 'gift') in land, i.e. soil and climate – labour and capital. Honduras is perfect for banana cultivation and has abundant labour; Sweden has a 500-year history of producing industrial steel and invented the ball bearing; and Australia has kangaroos. The argument just put forward is easy to understand; each country has an abundance of certain factors of production which the others do not. This is the simple argument. A slightly more advanced argument is that the trading which takes place in different goods arises from a difference in the *relative* factor endowment of land in each country. Sweden could (and indeed *did*) grow tobacco and manufacture cigars, but would give up a great deal of resources in doing so, thus forgoing a great many SKF ball bearings which could be used to pay for an even higher quantity of Honduran cigars.

Countries are differently endowed with the factors labour and capital and will therefore have different cost ratios in the use of these factors; the higher the relative abundance of labour compared to capital, the lower the labour costs. Honduras has far more labour relative to capital while Sweden has the reverse situation. This is reflected in the domestic cost ratios for capital; Sweden is a most technologically advanced nation with very high labour costs while Honduras is a developing nation with low labour costs. The cost of using labour – relative to capital – will be much higher in Sweden than in Honduras. Honduras will therefore be far more likely to utilise labour in its production than capital and vice versa in Sweden.

Some 292 individual manufacturing steps are involved in making a good cigar – and almost all of them are done by hand.[4] The average cost of labour in Sweden is roughly 15 times that of Honduras[5] so you can imagine why cigars are manufactured in Honduras rather than Sweden. The conclusion is that countries will produce and thus export goods in which they are relatively well endowed with appropriate factors, since the goods will be produced relatively cheaply using abundant factors. Capital-intensive production will take place in countries with high capital-to-labour ratios: Sweden produces ball bearings, aeroplanes and nuclear reactors whereas Honduras produces cigars, textiles and bananas. The gains for each country arise when trade takes place and each country can consume more than would be possible on a purely domestic market. (See "The gains from specialisation and trade" on page 399.)

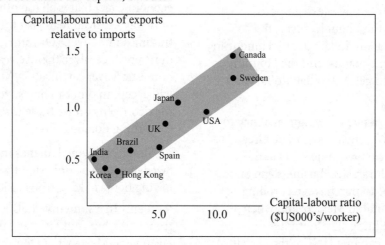

(Source: Begg et al, pp. 580–81)

Figure 4.1.1 *Capital-labour ratios relative to exports*

There is substance in the conclusion that countries with high capital-to-labour ratios will have relatively capital intensive exports, and Figure 4.1.1 shows the correlation between relative factor endowments in capital/labour and type of exports. The *x*-axis measures total amount of capital per labourer (in $US1,000 per worker), where a higher value means a higher relative abundance of capital. The *y*-axis shows how capital intensive exports are relative to imports, i.e. a value of 0.5 means that the imports of a country use half as much capital in their production as exports. A higher *y*-value means more capital intensive exports in relation to imports. The positive correlation affirms to a certain extent the conclusion that resource endowment indeed influences exports.

---

4. *Cigarren*, p. 113.
5. International Labour Organization at http://www.ilo.org.

Variety and quality of goods

©IBO 2003

Why is it then that so much trade takes place between countries with similar factor endowments?! The ball bearings in the previous example could just as soon be produced in any of the three which would mean that Swedish, Honduran and Australian ball bearings could be exported and co-exist on each of the countries' shelves. Germany and France share a common border and make thousands of similar products; France makes Sabatiér kitchen knives and Renault cars while Germany makes Zwilling Henkel kitchen knives and VW cars, for example. Why would France produce cars for export and then use the money to import cars from Germany? Resource endowment can hardly explain it and labour costs are over 60% higher in Germany than in France![6]

Consumer preference theory and **non-price theories of trade** (similar to non-price theories done by HL in Section 3.3) suggest that consumers desire *choice* and *diversity* of products, and the theory of non-price competition adds that consumers are willing to pay a premium for this benefit. Branded goods such as Adidas shoes (Germany), Toyota automobiles (Japan) and Nokia phones (Finland) will be sold in countries which might well have domestic producers of the same goods, i.e. close substitutes. But a pair of Adidas is not the same as a pair of Brookes; a Toyota is not the same as an Audi; and a Nokia phone is not the same as a Sony-Ericsson. Firms continuously attempt to enhance their products' non-homogeneity via marketing, so such goods are all competing for our 'allegiance to a brand and the intangible benefits for the consumer that go with that consumption. Whatever the underlying reasons, it is quite clear that most of the growth in trade deals with *intra-industry trade* (= trade in same-industry goods), which now comprises between 60% and 70% of all trade in North America and in the EU.[7]

Greater choice enhances consumer sovereignty which together with increased (or freer) trade ultimately leads to greater *competition*. When firms can operate on domestic markets behind trade barriers the result is that foreign potential rival firms are kept out.

These *entry barriers* (HL may wish to review theory of the firm here) create a situation of protective comfort wherein domestic firms have the power to keep prices higher and quantity/quality lower than in a case where free trade exists. (**HL**: In other words, there is a distinct possibility that both productive and allocative efficiency is sub-optimal.)

In being forced to compete with more firms producing similar goods, the probable outcome is that quality and quantity will increase while prices drop. Firms will seek to hold on to market shares by enhancing products and keeping ahead in innovation. They will also have the incentive to take the step abroad in terms of both new markets and possible production facilities. Unsurprisingly, there is also ample evidence that countries with highly competitive home markets become successful exporters on the international market. In fact, a famous business theoretician, Michael Porter, suggests that smaller countries such as Holland and Sweden could not have become so successful internationally without having domestic firms to hone their competitive skills against.

Gains from specialisation ©IBO 2003

Trade is a transaction where two parties exchange goods and both feel better off – or as John Mill put it as early as in 1821: 'The benefit which is derived from exchanging one commodity for another, arises, in all cases, from the commodity *received*, not the commodity *given*.'[8] Two main features of trade that I try to put across to my students at an early stage are:

1. Trade has nothing to do with country borders.

2. If a voluntary exchange takes place, then both parties have benefited, i.e. a 'win–win' situation rather than 'win–lose'.[9]

Trade is an economic activity that takes place between villagers in the village; between the villages in the countryside; and between the city and the countryside. I don't produce cigars or boots but I am an enthusiastic consumer of both. The way I am able to do this is by specialising in something I do reasonably well; warp young fragile minds with economics. The

6. *Globalization, growth and poverty*, World Bank, 2002, p. 45.
7. OECD, 'The European Union's trade policies and their economic effects', Economics Department working papers no. 194, 1998.
8. Quoted from *Globalisation – Making sense of an integrating world*, p. 74.
9. One of my favourite in-class tricks in IB1 is to take of my watch – usually a rather pricey Rolex, Blancpain or Panerai – and 'trade' it with someone wearing a cheap digital watch – lately my IB2 student Hardrock. 'So, Hardrock, is there a winner and a loser?!' General howls of glee at the old man's loss and the student's gain. I then ask if anyone saw a gun or physical threat involved. Quieting down, the students then start to realise that if the transaction is free and voluntary we BOTH win! I seem to feel better off with the cheap watch and Hardrock feels better off with the Rolex. Hardrock has increased his total utility and so have I. Win-win. (There *was* almost some physical violence when he tried to sneak out after class with my watch on his wrist!)

value placed on this earns me 'cigar/boot' certificates – which other producers ('specialists') accept as payment. Whether these producers are domestic or foreign is really beside the point.[10] Just view the economy as a firm or village, where tasks are allocated according to what each person does best and division of labour is utilised. Now expand this to include a neighbouring country. Adam Smith said it brilliantly in *Wealth of Nations*: 'The division of labour is limited only by the extent of the market.'[11] Drawing a line in the sand and sticking different flags on either side does not diminish the validity of Smith's statement. Trade gives producers a larger arena and the possibility of being manufactured within *scale economies* while consumers enjoy a far greater range of goods.

Consumption gains

Few, if any, of the present high income countries in the world would be where they are today without trade. It would be impossible for any single country to produce all the goods desired using domestic resources alone. Perhaps you are holding a ballpoint pen in your hand as you read this. Imagine the countless chemicals and materials that went into making such a simple (?) instrument: oil to produce plastic and dye, the many compounds in the ink, the chromium and steel for the nib (= point), etc. Furthermore, consider all the machines involved in producing the raw materials ... and the machines to make the machines that produce raw materials ... I venture to claim that few economies could produce a simple ball point pen based *entirely* on domestic resources. A single person would not live long enough to be able to produce the pen all alone. The solution is **specialisation and trade**.

'Impossible!'

A simple example: Capital and consumption goods

Let me exemplify possible gains in consumption due to trade by assuming two economies, 'Capitalia' and 'Consumentia', where domestic production is divided into capital goods and consumer goods in Figure 4.1.2 on page 393. Furthermore we assume that no trade barriers exist, no benefits of scale and that both economies are maximally efficient, e.g. on the PPF, and thus are able to move *along* the PPF. We also assume that there is initially no trade with the other country so that everything that is consumed is also produced domestically. The economies can produce and consume anywhere along the PPFs, in accordance with our assumptions.

- Capitalia starts out at point A (diagram I), producing and consuming 100 units of capital goods and 75 units of consumer goods; Consumentia is at point D (diagram II) producing/consuming 75 units of capital and 100 units of consumer goods. (I use 'units' here in a most general sense.)

- Posit now that each country were to *specialise* in the production of one good (and *which* good is something HL will look at in a moment). Capitalia specialises 100% in producing capital goods, point B, and Consumentia puts 100% of its resources into producing consumer goods, point E; Capitalia would have no books, shoes, or Clint Eastwood films, while Consumentian farmers would be harvesting wheat and drilling for water using fingernails and sharp sticks.

---

10. I remember attending one of my first trade lectures at university where the professor continuously used the term 'international trade'. I found this rather tautological, similar to the usage of *Speiserestaurant* (literally 'Eating Restaurant') in German-speaking countries. Actually, the professor was simply being most correct in his use of economic terminology since goods are in fact traded both domestically and internationally.
11. Husted & Melvin, *International Economics*, p. 57.

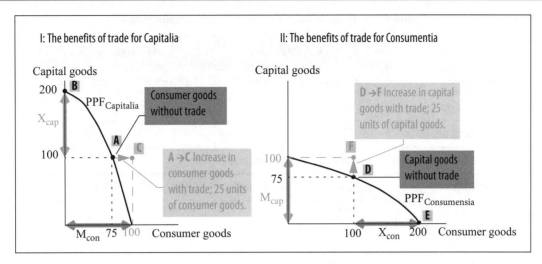

Figure 4.1.2 *Benefits of trade for Capitalia and Consumentia*

This is of course where trade comes in (see Figure 4.1.2):

- Capitalia's **domestic demand** for capital goods is 100 units, and therefore it has 100 units with which to trade for consumption goods – shown by the X_{cap} (export of capital goods) and blue double-arrow in diagram I. (Note that if Capitalia 'gave up' those 100 units of capital on a closed domestic market, the liberated resources could be put into the production of consumer goods and the economy would be back at point A; production and consumption would be comprised of 100 units of capital goods and 75 units of consumer goods.)

- So, after lengthy negotiations, Capitalia manages to get rather a good deal on its capital goods; 1 unit of consumption goods for 1 unit of capital. (This is known as the *terms of trade*, see Section 4.8.) Trading the surplus 100 units of capital returns to the citizens of Capitalia 100 units of consumer goods for domestic use – shown by the grey arrow at M_{con} (imports of consumer goods). (Hopefully the import package contains at least the most essential Eastwood masterpieces.)

- Capitalia is now at point C, and the gains from trade are quite evident in the distance between points A and C. Opening up the economy to trade has benefited the domestic economy by 25

additional units of consumer goods and the economy is able to consume *outside* its PPF.

- Consumentia has exported 100 units of consumer goods (X_{con} in diagram II) and imported 100 units of capital goods (M_{cap}) – 25 units more than it would have received in trading domestically. Consumentia moves from point D to point F outside the PPF. This win-win situation is summarised in Table 4.1.1 on page 394.

Is this example of the gains of trade a far-fetched notion, taken from the outskirts of abstract economic theory? Absolutely not! Just imagine Switzerland and Ecuador; each country consumes both watches and bananas. Now picture each country trying to go it alone … The gist of this trade example is that both countries are able to consume outside their PPF. By specialising in capital and trading with a consumer goods specialising country, Capitalia can consume more consumer goods – via imports – than could be produced within a closed domestic economy. The increased consumption means that there is a *welfare gain in society* as more wants are satisfied. As icing on the cake, it is quite possible that increased specialisation for both trading partners will enable them to shift their PPFs outwards over time, e.g. there would be *productivity* gains.

Table 4.1.1 *Gains of trade for Capitalia and Consumentia*

	Capitalia		Consumentia	
Pre-trade...	Capital goods	Cons. Goods	Capital goods	Cons. Goods
...production	100	75	75	100
...consumption	100	75	75	100
'World' output = 175 units of capital goods & 175 units of consumption goods				
Post-trade...	Capital goods	Cons. Goods	Capital goods	Cons. Goods
...production	200	0	0	200
...consumption	100	100	100	100
'World' output = 200 units of capital goods & 200 units of consumption goods				

Productivity gains

An addendum to the *static* gains (of trade) shown in the above trade example is the long-run issue of the effects of specialisation. It is fairly safe to assume that an economy focused on a relatively narrow range of goods would over a period of time 'move up the learning curve', i.e. enjoy the benefits of increased *productivity* due to experience and innovations in production. These forms of *dynamic gains* (of trade) – i.e. gains of a reinforcing nature over time – are portrayed in Figure 4.1.3, where the initial PPF over time 'pivots' in favour of capital.

Even assuming that the quantity of factors of production do not increase (remember, Capitalia is exporting 50% of its capital), the qualitative aspects such as improved technology and production methodology will most assuredly increase the productive potential of an economy specialising in capital. Even a country which has little in the way of domestic resources will benefit from specialisation due to ultimately hitting *economies of scale*, i.e. where the costs per unit (average costs) fall considerably as output increases. Just think of Japan and its specialisation in, amongst other areas, automobiles for the past 40 years. The production cost of each car has

fallen in inflation adjusted terms throughout the time period. The Japanese have quite clearly shown that specialisation indeed increases productivity and lowers average costs over time.

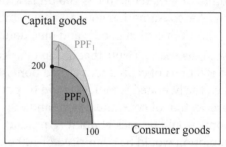

Figure 4.1.3 *Possible dynamic gains*

Open markets, increased trade, increasing specialisation and benefits of scale all help to explain the astounding increase in the proportion of goods manufactured solely for export purposes. Figure 4.1.4 on page 395 illustrates how more and more of what is produced is subsequently sold on foreign markets; in the past 50 years world (real) GDP has increased by 500% while exports have increased by over 1,600% – over three times as much. During this period, the ratio of exports to GDP in the world rose from 7% to 15%.[12]

---

12. 'Globalisation', p. 72.

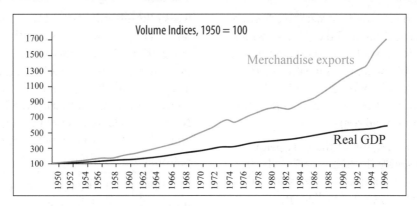

Volume Indices, 1950 = 100

(Source: 'Open markets matter...', OECD, October 1999)

Figure 4.1.4 *Trends in World merchandise exports and GDP*

The graphs above have a remarkably powerful message attached, once you start to think about it. Any export must mean corresponding imports. As the increase in exports/imports far outstrips the increase in real GDP, then an ever-increasing proportion of world consumption expenditure – and therefore corresponding income – comes from trade. The powerful message is that the largest increase in world trade which the world has ever known coincides with the highest rate of increase in livings standards in human history – the past 50 years. This makes it very difficult indeed to claim anything other than that trade adds to income and resulting prosperity and welfare. If a country does well it will not 'harm' other countries it trades with – it will instead benefit them with more/cheaper/better goods. International trade is not a zero-sum game.[13]

Political gains ©IBO 2003

A day will come when we will see these two huge groups, the United States of America and the United States of Europe, standing face to face, clasping hands across the seas, exchanging their products, their business, their industry. – Victor Hugo.

Just as Adam Smith claimed, integration and larger markets have meant economic growth. Not only via benefits of scale, but by the transfer of technology, new ideas and production methods. Trade and the many associated activities are ultimately conducted by **people**; foreign workers, companies and ownership will all add to trading nations' fixed and labour capital

as people exchange ideas and interact to become more efficient. In this process, there will naturally be clashes of cultures, norms and traditions, but also learning, understanding, acceptance and interdependence. People who are dependent on each other are highly unlikely to wage war against each other.[14] This is not a novel insight but something that nations have been aware of for centuries. Perhaps Guy Tozzoli, a famous trade and peace advocate who founded the World Trade Centers Association with members in over 100 countries, put it best: 'When you're promoting business, you're promoting peace. Because when I understand your aims and your culture, I don't have any reason to declare war on you, and instead we work together. If we're doing business together, we're not going to fight each other because if I owe you money, you're not going to shoot me.'[15]

Peace dividend – the EU

The prospect of a 'peace dividend in trade' was in fact one of the founding arguments in creating what was to become the **European Union**. Three devastating wars had been fought on European soil in the 75 years between 1870 and 1945, all three of which involved French-German antagonism. The immediate post-WWII years saw the disintegration of former alliances and – perhaps most notably – the welcoming by the US of previous arch-enemy Germany into the 'western' fold as a bulwark against 'communist aggression'. French fears of a revitalised Germany and further destructive hostilities led a most remarkable Frenchmen, Jean Monnet, to put forward a plan of

---

13. Paul Krugman's *'Pop internationalism'* is highly recommended reading on the lighter side of economics, where a number of most compelling arguments in support of win-win trade possibilities are given. I also recommend anything written by Naomi Klein for the other (frequently factually erroneous and dismally flawed) side of the story – after you've studied trade economics!

14. A trivial anecdote of the effects of economic integration is that there has never been a war between two countries that have McDonald's. Nor has there ever been a war between two democracies.

15. 'Let There Be Peace, and Trade', *The New York Times*, 21 June 1998.

economic integration to an equally remarkable French foreign minister, Robert Schuman. Like all plans which have reshaped the world, it was both visionary and firmly practical; the ultimate goal was for Europe to be united under a common economic union – but both men realised that this was a long-term goal and could only be attained in many small steps.

The first step was the creation of the **European Coal and Steel Community** (ECSC) in 1951, which established far-reaching reductions in tariffs and other barriers to trade in coal and steel. The 'Original Six' signatory countries were France, Germany, Italy, Belgium, Netherlands and Luxembourg. Why coal and steel?! Simple; these are two of the main ingredients – aside from stupidity, greed and xenophobia – of war. The heavy industrial base of coal and steel were strongly linked to domestic military industries and by integrating two of the main military adversaries, France and Germany, the aim was to create an economic disincentive for conflict. The economic integration of the Original Six continued with the signing of the Treaty of Rome in 1957 whereupon the European Economic Community (EEC) was created the following year. In 1993 the EEC became the European Union in furtherance of continued economic, political and monetary integration.

By 1995 there were 15 member countries, increasing to 25 by 2004 and comprising the majority of the European population. Did the original plan work? Simply put, yes. While I once again warn against far-reaching conclusions and the risk of nonsense correlation, the evidence of the past 50 years suggests that the plan has worked brilliantly; not one single armed conflict has erupted between any of the member nations (other than internal conflicts such as those in Northern Ireland and the Basque country) and 72% of all trade in 2002 in member countries was inter-regional EU bound trade.[16]

Other politically sensitive 'hot spots' have noticeably cooled down in the past decade or so. China – US relations have improved vastly as both become increasingly interdependent in matters of trade and even one of the most inflamed conflicts in Asia, the Indian-Pakistan conflict over Kashmir, has seen relatively successful rounds of high level negotiations aimed at peace through trade.

An additional area where trade has proven highly beneficial to economies is within development. There is increasing evidence that open economies and increased trade has the highest rate of return of all development strategies. In 2003, Horst Köhler and James Wolfensohn (then Managing Director of the IMF and president of the World Bank, respectively) put it most explicitly; 'Expanding trade by collectively reducing barriers [to trade] is the most powerful tool that countries, working together, can deploy to reduce poverty and raise living standards.'[17]

HIGHER LEVEL EXTENSION TOPICS

Absolute and comparative advantage

One of the legends floating around amongst economists is that Nobel laureate Paul Samuelson was once challenged by the sceptical mathematician Stanislaw Ulam to come up with one single proposition or theory in economics which was not either trivial or impossible to prove in reality. Samuelson went away, brooded, and came back with his reply: comparative advantage. 'That it is logically true need not be argued before a mathematician; that it is not trivial is attested by the thousands of important and intelligent men who have never been able to grasp the doctrine for themselves or to believe it after it was explained to them.'[18]

Absolute and comparative advantage (numerical and diagrammatic representations) ©IBO 2003

Nations trade simply because it is more economically efficient to have some goods made abroad and then trade for them. If code for computer programs is increasingly being done in India by American firms rather than in the US, then it simply means that

16. *International Trade Statisics 2003*, World Trade Organisation, table 9, p. 16.
17. Horst Köhler (Managing Director IMF) and James Wolfensohn (president World Bank), *The Financial Times*, 12 December 2003, or see online version at http://www.imf.org/external/np/vc/2003/121003.htm.
18. 'Defending free trade', Arvind Panagaria, *Economic Times, 22* November 2000.

America is getting it done cheaper than domestically. American consumers gain and India benefits from higher incomes. America will ultimately have to export other things in order to be able to import, since no one will sell goods to the US unless they find something worthy of their US dollars.

Absolute advantage

When a country can produce goods at a lower cost, i.e. using fewer resources, than another country it has an absolute advantage. Another way of putting it is that a country has an absolute advantage if the unit of output per unit of input is higher than another country's. A simple example using two countries, 'Orangia' and 'Textilia' is shown in Table 4.1.2:

Table 4.1.2 *Orangia and Textilia*

	Oranges	Cloth
Orangia	1,200	1,200
Textilia	500	1,000

Orangia's resources (= factor endowment) enables it to produce 1,200 units of oranges or 1,200 units of cloth; the same resources enable Textilia to produce 500 or 1,000 units. Clearly Orangia is more efficient as it can produce more of both goods than Textilia. The intuitive conclusion suggests that there is no incentive for trade to take place – Orangia cannot possible benefit from trading with Textilia. Therefore, most of those who insist on opposing trade as a method of increasing overall wellbeing make a classic beginners mistake by confusing absolute advantage with *comparative* advantage, commonly phrased as 'If a country is disadvantaged in all production then it cannot benefit from trade'. This is a very common statement, but most erroneous as shall be seen.

Comparative advantage

The concept of absolute advantage is quite straightforward and understandable at an almost intuitive level. The more challenging issues arise in explaining how a country with an absolute advantage might still benefit from trade. Even though Orangia has an absolute advantage in production of the goods, Textilia actually *gives up fewer resources* in the production of cloth than Orangia. In core economic terms, Textilia's *opportunity costs* in the production of cloth are lower than Orangia's. Textilia has a comparative advantage in the production of cloth.

> **Absolute and comparative advantage**:
> Using David Ricardo's classic example: when country X can produce more wine and cloth than country Y using the same amount of resources, then country X has an **absolute advantage**.
>
> When country X has a higher opportunity cost (in terms of foregone production of cloth) in the production of 1 unit of wine, then country Y has a **comparative advantage** in the production of wine.

Let's use an example close to home: Imagine that you and a classmate are given the task of doing a 15 minute presentation in economics in front of the class. Odds are you would divide the labour so that each one does what he/she is best at, say illustrations on overheads or writing the script. If one of you happens to be better at *both* then the task becomes finding where the other is *least disadvantaged* – and still divide the labour. In other words, the one who is worse at both illustrations and writing will at least have a *comparative* advantage in one of the two. This simple example is understood by every brother and sister who have been given a set of chores to do together, and for all the seeming complexity of the coming example it still boils down to the basic issue of the 'weaker' partner doing the tasks in which he/she is least disadvantaged.

The theory of comparative advantage was set down in the early 1800s by the famous English economist David Ricardo, who understood that while the concept of absolute advantage was very powerful in its argumentation for free trade, it was too limited to have general applicability and acceptability in the real world. In reality many countries are better than others in the production of any number of goods, so Ricardo set forth to show that even one country having an absolute disadvantage in many goods could be mutually beneficial to both countries when trade takes place.

That is the focus of the remainder of this chapter, where an example of comparative advantage will be done in three steps: 1) Set down relevant assumptions and outline production possibilities for two countries; 2) establish cost ratios and terms of trade, i.e. an exchange rate; 3) and finally, we use the cost ratios to show how specialisation and trade will allow each country to consume outside its PPF.

Assumptions and PPFs

As before, we assume that there are only two economies, Orangia and Textilia, and two goods, oranges and cloth. Again we assume that economies can attain maximum potential output – full employment exists – and move along the production possibility frontier, but that no economies of scale exist. We will also assume that costs are *constant* – this is not absolutely necessary but it makes the example easier to follow. Finally, we assume that neither trade barriers nor transport costs exist. Diagrams I–III in Figure 4.1.5 show the situation facing the two countries:

- Initially there is no trade between them, whereby Orangia produces/consumes 800 tonnes of oranges and 400 tonnes of cloth (point **A** in diagram I)

- Textilia produces/consumes 250 tonnes of oranges and 500 tonnes of cloth (point **B** in diagram II).

- Diagram III shows each country's PPF in relation to the other, where it is evident that Orangia has an *absolute advantage* in the production of both goods, since Orangia can produce more of both goods using any given amount of factors. However, you will notice how the *PPFs are divergent*, which is central to your understanding of comparative advantage.

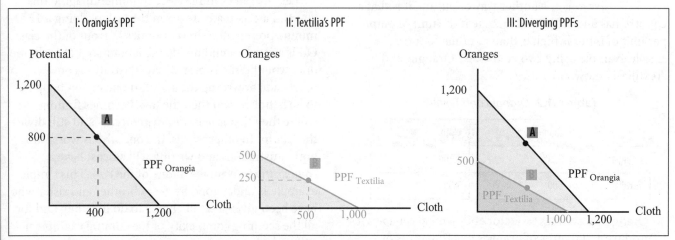

Figure 4.1.5 *PPFs and opportunity costs for Orangia and Textilia (tonnes/yr)*

Cost ratios and terms of trade

The theory of comparative advantage states that, ceteris paribus, if a country has a comparative advantage then there are gains to be made in trade. Are there comparative advantages shown in diagram III in

Figure 4.1.5? Go back and reread the definitions of absolute and comparative advantage and apply them to Table 4.1.3.

Table 4.1.3 *Opportunity costs in Orangia and Textilia*

	Potential output (1,000s tonnes)		Opportunity costs (in terms of the other good; producing 1 unit of oranges in Textilia means foregoing 2 units of cloth)	
	Oranges	**Cloth**	**Oranges**	**Cloth**
Orangia	1,200	1,200	1	1
Textilia	500	1,000	2	0.5

Clearly the answer is 'yes', since Textilia – which is absolutely disadvantaged since Orangia can produce more of both goods – has a lower opportunity cost in the production of cloth than Orangia. Textilia foregoes 0.5 tonnes of oranges in producing 1 tonne of cloth whereas Orangia foregoes 1 tonne of oranges in producing a tonne of cloth. **Textilia has a comparative advantage in cloth** while **Orangia has a comparative advantage in oranges**.[19]

---

19. Yes, I know, …it's not like the silly made-up names don't give it away…

A little depth:
Constructing cost ratios to show possible terms of trade

By putting the opportunity costs shown in the PPFs (see Figure 4.1.5 on page 398 and Table 4.1.3 on page 398) into **cost ratio** terms, we can construct diagrams II and III in Figure 4.1.6.

- Cost ratios:

  ▪ The cost ratio for cloth in Textilia is 1:0.5 (diagram II) e.g. 1 tonne of cloth means foregoing 0.5 tonnes of oranges. Textilia's cost ratio for oranges (diagram III) is 1:1 one tonne of oranges has an opportunity cost of one tonne of cloth.

  ▪ The cost ratio for oranges in Orangia is 1:1 for both goods.

- Textilia *has a comparative advantage in cloth*, since each tonne of cloth costs 0.5 tonnes of oranges whereas Orangia's cost of a tonne of cloth is 1 tonne of oranges.

- Orangia *has a comparative advantage in oranges*, since each tonne of oranges costs 1 tonne of cloth whereas Textilia's cost of a tonne of oranges is 2 tonnes of cloth.

- The **terms of trade** (diagrams II and III) are shown as the grey areas in between the diverging cost ratios.

- Textilia can trade domestically at a rate of 1 tonne of cloth for 0.5 tonnes of oranges, diagram II, and would therefore be willing to trade with Orangia if the return – imports! – were *more than 0.5 tonnes of imported oranges* for each tonne of exported cloth.

- Orangia, in turn, would pay 1 tonne of oranges for each unit of cloth produced domestically, and would trade if it *paid less than 1 tonne of exported oranges* for each tonne of imported cloth.

- The terms of trade will lie somewhere between 1 unit of cloth = 0.5 to 1 unit of oranges (diagram II). Alternatively, 1 unit of oranges = 1 to 2 units of cloth (diagram III).

The conclusion is that it is possible for Orangia to receive more cloth for each tonne of oranges produced by way of trading with Textilia. Equally, it is possible for Textilia to pay less than 2 units of cloth for each tonne of oranges and the citizens of Textilia will be able to consume more oranges for each unit of cloth foregone. Win–win.

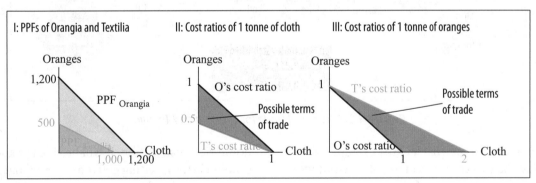

Figure 4.1.6 *PPFs and cost ratios for Orangia and Textilia*

The gains from specialisation and trade

Let's assume that both countries specialise completely, and then look at the issue of trade, terms of trade and the consequent gains from trade. (I shall look at these issues from the point of view of Orangia in order to stress that even the country with an absolute advantage in both goods can gain from specialisation and trade.)

- **Orangia** now has 1,200 tonnes of oranges which could have been traded domestically at the ratios of 1 tonne of cloth for each tonne of oranges. The trade incentive is that the *Orangians will trade if they can get more than one tonne of cloth* per tonne of oranges. (When 'trade negotiations' take place with Textilia the object is to make it worth the while for citizens of Textilia; they too must gain.)

- **Textilia**, having specialised 100% in cloth, has 1,000 tonnes of cloth where 1 tonne of cloth could have been traded domestically for 0.5 tonnes of oranges, i.e. each tonne of oranges costs Textilia (as in opportunity costs) 2 tonnes of cloth. *If Textilia can pay less than 2 tonnes of cloth* for each tonne of oranges there will be an incentive to trade. Figure 4.1.7 shows each country's menu of alternatives and preferences.

Orangia is completely specialised in oranges, with domestic trade possible at 1:1 for cloth. If the terms under which Orangia can trade oranges for imported cloth – **the terms of trade** – are better than this ratio, trade will take place:

- The more cloth Orangia receives for each unit of oranges, the better the terms of trade are for

Orangia. This is shown in the columns on the left in Figure 4.1.7, where increasing quantities of imported cloth per exported tonne of oranges represents improving terms of trade.

- Textilia, totally specialised in cloth, will have the reverse situation (expressed in payment per tonne of oranges from Orangia), and will not give up more than 2 tonnes of cloth for 1 unit of oranges, since this is the domestic trade-off. Textilia's terms of trade will improve if it can pay, i.e. export, less than 2 tonnes of cloth in payment of each tonne of imported oranges. The two columns on the right show Textilia's improving terms of trade.

- The terms of trade will lie somewhere in between 1 tonne of oranges for 1 tonne of cloth, to 1 tonne of oranges to 2 tonnes of cloth. We have now firmly established that *since cost ratios differ, there are benefits to be had by specialisation and subsequent trade.*

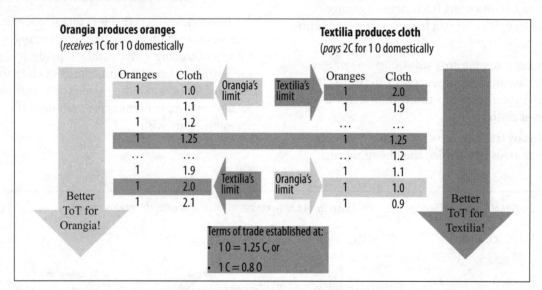

Figure 4.1.7 *Terms of trade for Orangia and Textilia*

Let us polish this somewhat lengthy example off by assuming that the two countries arrive at an **equitable trade ratio (= terms of trade) of 1 tonne of oranges to 1.25 tonnes of cloth** (alternatively, 1 tonne of cloth for 0.8 tonnes of oranges).[20] Assuming furthermore that Textilia wishes to remain at 500 tonnes of cloth in

domestic consumption, it will be able to export 500 tonnes of cloth, getting 400 tonnes of oranges. Orangia, having specialised in oranges, exports 400 tonnes of oranges in order to import 500 tonnes of cloth. The results of this trade are illustrated in diagrams I and II, Figure 4.1.8 on page 401.

---

20. Quite naturally, terms of trade are not 'negotiated' or 'arrived at'. Terms of trade **evolve** over time in accordance with each country's demand for imports (i.e. relative preferences) and supply/price of domestic goods.

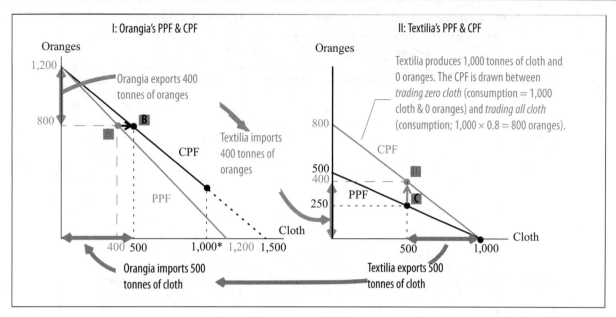

Figure 4.1.8 *PPFs and CPFs for Orangia and Textilia*

POP QUIZ 4.1.1   COMPARATIVE ADVANTAGE

1   Why is the CPF for Orangia dotted at cloth consumption levels between 1,000 and 1,500 tonnes?

2   What would be the value on the *y*-axis for Orangia at 1,000 tonnes of cloth?

3   What happens to Orangia's and Textilia's terms of trade if Orangia's CPF were to 'swivel outward', say to 1,200 tonnes of oranges (*y*-axis) to 1,800 tonnes of cloth (*x*-axis)? (See Figure 4.1.7 on page 400 for guidance.)

Win-win outside the PPF

If Orangia gave up the 400 tonnes of oranges domestically (i.e. a closed economy with no trade), these factors of production would enable the production of 400 tones of cloth whereby Orangia would be at **A** in diagram I, Figure 4.1.8. By specialising in oranges and trading the 400 tonnes of

oranges at a rate of 1:1.25 with the 'cloth-specialist', Textilia, Orangia is able to increase consumption of cloth to 500 tonnes, point B.

Similarly, Textilia's export of 500 tonnes of cloth enables it to import 400 tonnes of oranges – 150 tonnes more than could have been produced using solely domestic resources – and moves from point C to point D. Both countries now have *consumption possibility frontiers* (CPFs) lying outside their production possibility frontiers. Note that each CPF is drawn to display the different levels of consumption that are possible for each country based on an 'exchange rate' of 1 tonne of oranges = 1.25 tonnes of cloth. Textilia could consume at any point along its CPF between 1,000 tonnes of cloth and zero oranges if it doesn't trade; or up to 800 tonnes of oranges and zero cloth if it exports all cloth produced. (A change in the 'exchange rate' – terms of trade – will of course change the slope of each country's CPF.) Table 4.1.4 on page 402 sums up the win-win trade outcome.

Table 4.1.4 *Increase in total production and consumption in Orangia and Textilia*

No trade	Orangia		Textilia		Closed economies' 'World totals'
	Production	Consumption	Production	Consumption	
Oranges	800	800	250	250	1,050 tonnes oranges
Cloth	400	400	500	500	900 tonnes cloth

Trade	Orangia		Textilia		Open economies' 'World totals'
	Production	Consumption	Production	Consumption	
Oranges	1,200	800	0	400	1,200 tonnes oranges
Cloth	0	500	1,000	500	1,000 tonnes cloth
	Exports: 400 tonnes oranges	Imports: 500 tonnes cloth	Exports: 500 tonnes cloth	Imports: 400 tonnes oranges	

The example shows how differing opportunity cost ratios between countries create comparative advantages. When these advantages are used by reallocating resources and specialising, both countries can consume outside their production possibility frontiers while total output increases. Table 4.1.4 shows that total 'world' output has increased from 1,050 tonnes of oranges and 900 tonnes of cloth to, respectively, 1,200 and 1,000 tonnes. Herein lies the argumentative power of the theory of comparative advantage: **more is produced using the same amount of resources and both parties can increase total consumption.**

Opportunity cost ©IBO 2003

Opportunity costs in connection with production possibility frontiers have been dealt with in some depth above and also in Section 1. The key point in respect to trade is to realise that comparative advantage arises only when countries' **PPFs are divergent**, i.e. when the **opportunity cost ratios differ** between countries. If cost ratios in producing the two goods are identical in country A and country B, there can be no gain for either country in specialising and trading – at least not in terms of quantity. Figure 4.1.9 on page 403, diagrams I to III shows three possibilities between Portugal and Spain in the production of wine and wool. Which of these diagrams shows an incentive for trade in accordance with the theory of comparative advantage? (Answer in footnote below.[21])

21. **Answer**: diagrams I and III show that quantitative gains in consumption are possible since the opportunity cost ratios for Spain and Portugal are different. Diagram II is not conductive to trade according to the theory of comparative advantage since each country has identical opportunity cost ratios and neither can benefit (quantitatively) by trading with the other.

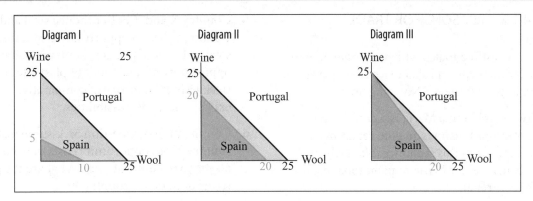

Figure 4.1.9 *PPFs for Portugal and Spain*

Limitations of the theory of comparative advantage ©IBO 2003

Does the theory of comparative advantage stand up to the test of reality? Well, yes, albeit a 'yes' with some notable qualifications (= conditions):

- Quite evidently no country will **specialise completely** as in our model, which lowers the possible specialisation gains and thus the amount available for trade. This will naturally limit the extent to which the consumption possibility frontier lies outside the production possibility frontier.

- The theory of comparative advantage is based on the **premise of product homogeneity**, which, in the light of increased non-price competition in the trade of similar goods, is not explained by different opportunity costs between trade partners. It is theoretically possible that two countries with identical domestic cost ratios for goods X and Y still trade since consumers in both countries wish to have a greater range of goods.

- The assumption of **zero transport costs is unrealistic** – especially for bulky goods with low value-added such as empty plastic containers and iron ore. For such goods the proportion of transport costs to total production costs will be very high, which might negate any comparative advantages of trade.

- Another assumption subject to criticism is that there are **no barriers to trade**. This is perhaps one of the strongest prevalent forces against the comparative advantages of countries.

- The model used here is based on **constant opportunity costs**, which are highly unlikely in the real world – however, as pointed out earlier, constant costs were assumed to make the example easier to follow and a 'convex' production possibility frontier could in fact have been used.

- The theory also neglects to incorporate the significant **benefits of scale** that have been shown to exist, thus failing to explain the very large increase in trade between similar economies, primarily OECD countries. However, as shown earlier in Section 2.3, economies of scale *support* our conclusion that specialisation leads to lower average costs which in fact strengthens the argument of international specialisation benefits.

- Finally, the theory of comparative advantage does not deal with **income distribution** within countries. Trade will create both winners and losers in terms of domestic income; sectors competing with relatively cheap imports will see incomes fall while export sectors will show increased income. Whether the winners' gains outweigh the losers' losses is a most complex question, dealing once again with the vagaries of fairness. Most economists would prefer to view income distributions aspects and trade benefits as separate issues and look at distributional effects in the light of domestic policy rather than trade policy.

The objections listed can in some cases carry considerable weight, yet the strength of the now over 200-year-old theory of comparative advantage lies primarily in illuminating a *basic principle* which has been empirically shown to hold true; trade depends primarily on comparative rather than absolute advantage. Studies confirm that it is often the case that countries which are less productive in all industries (i.e. have an absolute disadvantage in all areas) than another country will still be able to export goods in which they are relatively competitive.[22]

---

22. See, for example, *International Economics,* Krugman & Obstfeld, pp. 23–34.

HIGHER LEVEL

POP QUIZ 4.1.2   REASONS FOR TRADE

1 You enter a wrestling match with an opponent who is 20% faster than you and also twice as strong as you. Explain your strategy. (No going home.)

2 Assume two neighbours: Maria is a professional house painter and Johann is an auto repair man. Using concepts from this section, explain why it would be beneficial for Maria to paint Johann's house while he repairs her car.

3 Look up Jamaica and Iceland in a World Factbook and then use trade theory to explain why Jamaica is one of the world's largest exporters of bauxite and Iceland is a major producer of aluminium. Use the same reasoning to explain how Icelanders can consume far more bananas than are imported! (Eh, the aluminium issue is not related to the banana issue.)

4 Explain why a worker at the Nissan car plant in Japan might drive a Ford.

5 Country X and Y both produce steel and plastic. Country X has an opportunity cost ratio of 1 unit of steel to 1 unit of plastic; country Y has an opportunity cost of 1 unit of plastic to 0.5 units of steel. Using the theory of comparative advantage, explain the trade possibilities.

6 Continuation of Question 5: Assume instead that country Y has opportunity costs of 0.5 units of plastic to 0.5 units of steel. What are the possible terms of trade for country Y?

7 Why do economists generally regard the theory of comparative advantage as a very strong argument in favour of trade?

8 Can a country benefit from trade even though it has higher production costs per unit of output in all goods than other countries?

9 How might a country improve its comparative advantage?

10 How might exporters view a worsening of the terms of trade? How about consumers?

Free trade and protectionism

4.2

CONTENTS

FREE TRADE AND PROTECTIONISM ©IBO 2003

When goods can't cross borders, armies will. – Frédéric Bastiat

Trade has been shown both historically and theoretically to have multiple and resounding economic and social benefits. Global trade is growing at roughly twice the pace of global output – which means that more and more of what we produce is exported and what we consume is imported. In spite of this, there are many barriers to trade between countries arising from various protectionist policies. It is worth commenting on the fact that protectionism is almost solely the result of *government* policies (sometimes under pressure from domestic industries) and not due to decisions made by *people* buying the goods. Most protectionist measures are also against the expressed recommendations of economists.

The main reason for this lies in the seeming inability of economists and various interest/lobby groups to see eye-to-eye. Economists estimate the societal value of trade through the looking glass of the 'benefits of consumption' which in essence views *increased imports as the benefits of exports*; more exports facilitate increased imports.[1] A more common view amongst interest/lobby groups, ostensibly acting on behalf of industries/labourers, is that *exports are the gain and imports the costs*; more exports generate more income and employment.

This section attempts to address the main reasons for limiting trade and whether the costs of this outweigh free trade. HL students are recommended to revise the incidences of taxes/subsidies, resource allocation in context with consumer/supplier surplus, and long-run average costs.

Definition of free trade ©IBO 2003

It's fortunate for me that my writing desk is in Mexico and not in the US, since my weekly tally of Cuban cigars would *have* to be replaced by cigars from other nations – regardless of my personal preferences. This is due to the **trade embargo** that America has on imports of Cuban goods. A ban, such as it is, is of course the most extreme version of a trade barrier, but a good many other barriers serve to decrease trade. Totally free trade does not exist anywhere, let us set that straight from the outset. Military goods, plutonium

and coca leaves will be subject to rigorous trade limitations for example. Even mainstream goods and services such as textiles or fruit will be subjected to a number of more or less obvious trade barriers – in fact, it seems that Hong Kong is the only country in the world which has no taxes whatsoever on imports.

Free trade is when countries can exchange goods and services unhindered by any form of market intervention which disadvantages a country in selling its goods on a foreign market. Anything which increases the costs or reduces market accessibility for foreign firms relative to domestic firms constitutes a barrier to trade. For example:

- *Import taxes* add to foreign firms' costs while *subsidies* lower domestic firms' costs – both actions serve to shift relative prices in favour of domestic firms.

- When domestic economies *limit import licenses* and/or impose *import quotas* on foreign firms, the effect is that foreign firms' access to the market is restricted. Thus, if a Norwegian firm experiences any disadvantages in getting its frozen haddock to London (other than pure transaction costs such as foreign exchange commissions and transport costs) which a firm in England does not, then there are barriers to trade.

In short, only when a foreign producer can sell goods in another market under the same conditions as their domestic rivals, can one speak of free trade.

> **Free trade**: Free trade is the total absence of any form of intrusion or barrier in the flow of goods and services between countries which disadvantages foreign firms in favour of domestic firms. Free trade means that the only additional disadvantages experienced by a firm on a foreign market arise due to transaction costs such as foreign exchange costs, transportation costs and poorer market knowledge and closeness to foreign markets. Protectionism can be widely regarded as any form of action taken by a country whereby the price of domestic goods become more favourable relative to imported goods.

---

1. Keynes put it brilliantly, as usual: 'Imports are receipts and exports are payments. How as a nation can we expect to better ourselves by diminishing our receipts? Is there anything a tariff can do, which an earthquake could not do better?' Taken from Husted & Melvin, p. 201.

Types of protectionism ©IBO 2003

Protectionism is commonly divided into *tariff* and *non-tariff barriers*, where the former is basically a tax on imports and the latter is any of dozens of other possible barriers to trade, notable examples of which are quotas, subsidies to domestic producers and various forms of regulatory rules on imported goods.

Tariffs ©IBO 2003

When the European Union (EU) puts a 140% tax on imported sugar – notoriously one of the most protected goods in the EU – but not domestic sugar, it has imposed a tariff. A tariff can be an *ad valorem* tariff based on the import price as the sugar example, or a *specific* (unit) tariff, e.g. the $US 2.36 on a bottle of wine entering the US.[2] While tariffs are by far the most common form of trade barrier, the average tariff rates in the world have fallen drastically in the past 70 years, from over 40% in the 1940s to less than 4% today. This doesn't really mean that there is less protectionism today but rather that highly visible trade barriers such as tariffs have to a great extent been replaced by less obvious barriers.

> **Tariff:** A tariff is a tax levied on imported goods. The tariff can be both an ad valorem tax, e.g. a percentage of the import price, or a specific tax, e.g. a tax based on a measurable unit such as tonnes or bottles.

How a tariff works

Assume an economy which goes through three stages; an initial stage of zero trade followed by perfectly free trade and finally a tariff. Figure 4.2.1 on page 409, diagrams I to III, illustrate what would happen to a fictitious economy producing and consuming oranges.

- In diagram I, the country is consuming only what it produces, i.e. it is a closed economy and produces/consumes Q_0 tonnes of oranges at P_0 per tonne.

- When the economy opens its doors to foreign competition, diagram II, it will face a horizontal world supply curve (we drop the assumption of 'only two countries in the world' so world supply will to all intents and purposes be infinite) of S_{world}. The world price of oranges, P_1, is lower than the domestic price of P_0 leading consumers to increase their quantity demanded to Q_{D1} at a market equilibrium of S_{world}/D. (Note that we are assuming that domestic and foreign oranges are perfectly substitutable.) Observe that the effect of an open economy on *domestic output/consumption of oranges* is negative; S_{dom} shows that domestic producers are competitive up to Q_{S1} where after foreign producers are able to undercut domestic suppliers along the horizontal world supply curve S_{world}. This open economy will now have domestic consumption at Q_{D1} and domestic output at Q_{S1}. The difference is made up of imports of $Q_{S1} \Leftrightarrow Q_{D1}$. This is the free trade equilibrium.

- Now, if a tariff of $P_1 \rightarrow P_2$ is levied on imported oranges, shown by the arrow in diagram III, the world supply curve shifts from S_{world} to $S_{world + tariff}$, increasing the price on the domestic market from P_1 to P_2. This will have the effect of encouraging/enabling increased domestic production in a manner similar to that of a minimum price (see Section 2.1). Domestic producers replace $Q_{S1} \Leftrightarrow Q_{S2}$ tonnes of imported oranges with domestic, which shows how the tariff protects domestic producers by raising the price of imported oranges. The increase in the domestic price of oranges also has the effect of decreasing the quantity demanded from Q_{D1} to Q_{D2}. The combination of a higher price level and lower demand achieves the purpose of lowering imports and raising domestic production.

---

2. United States Dept of Agriculture at http://www.fas.usda.gov/info/agexporter/1997/August%201997/uswine2.html.

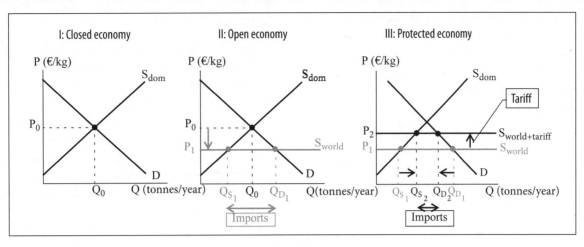

Figure 4.2.1 *Tariffs and domestic output/Q_{D_1}*

The effects of a tariff

There are other issues involved in the imposition of tariffs. Figure 4.2.2 shows – now using fictitious figures for clarity – how the tariff will have both **transfer effects** on society and also **costs to society** in the form of waste. Domestic suppliers are able to increase their output from 500 tonnes of oranges to 600 tonnes while imports fall from 400 tonnes to 200 tonnes. Foreign producers' revenue diminishes to area E after having lost revenue in areas F and G. The grey trapezium of A+B+C+D shows how consumers lose by paying a higher price for less quantity consumed; consumers could be consuming 900 tonnes of oranges at a price of €1 per kg but are instead paying €1.2 per kg for 800 tonnes per year. (HL will recognise this as a loss of **consumer surplus**.)

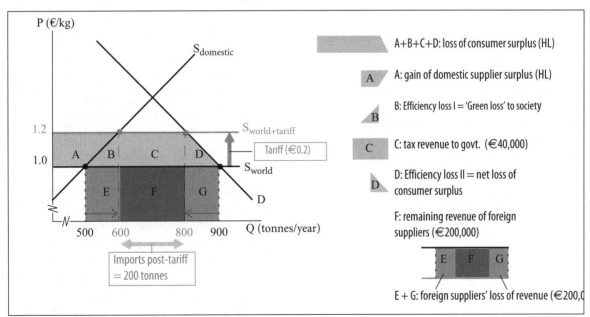

Figure 4.2.2 *Effects of a tariff on oranges*

Not all of the area A+B+C+D in Figure 4.2.2 is a *net* loss to society since parts of it represent a **transfer** to other parts of society. Another childish example: Picture that you lose your wallet in the forest and it contains €100; the wind blows open the wallet and spreads €90 to other happy members of the forest community while €10 is never found. Society as a whole has lost only the €10 since your loss of €90 has been offset by others' gain.

In our trade example, the domestic economy is made up of three players; consumers, domestic suppliers and government.

- *Area A*: A loss to consumers which is offset by a gain to one of the other two players means that society is in fact equally well off. Thus area A shows how domestic firms benefit from selling more at a higher price (HL: the increase in *supplier surplus*.)

- *Area C:* Area C is the gain to government from additional *tax receipts* of the tariff times imports; 200 tonnes at 20 cents per kg = €40,000.

- *Areas B and D:* Areas B and D represent the net reduction in overall economic welfare; the **net societal loss**.

  - Area B shows the cost to society of production being taken over by relatively inefficient producers; at all levels of output between 500 and 600 tonnes, foreign producers could have produced oranges at a lower cost. The triangle shows the extra resources used by society in producing domestically rather than importing from more efficient foreign producers at the world price. This can be labelled a 'green' loss since it is wasteful to allocate productive resources to areas best left to others.

  - Area D shows the loss of consumer benefits which have not been transferred to others in society (e.g. domestic firms and government).

Taken together, areas B and D constitute a pure allocative waste to society called a deadweight loss (which HL will recognise from Section 2.3, "Theory of the firm").

The loss of consumer benefits and the allocative losses arising due to the imposition of a tariff are one of the strongest arguments in favour of free trade. In effect, tariffs serve to penalise domestic consumers in favour of domestic producers – in effect subsidising more inefficient production by transferring additional income from consumers to domestic firms. However, there are possible offsetting gains to the domestic economy arising from tariffs and general protectionism, such as safety, environmental and employment issues. We will look into some of these issues below.

Quotas ©IBO 2003

We now turn to other forms of trade barriers, i.e. *non-tariff barriers*. A common method to protect the domestic economy is by setting actual quantitative limits on the amount of imports, a quota.

This form of non-tariff barrier has the effect of raising the domestic price of the good just as a tariff, but has different transfer effects – the wallet contents are found by different forest citizens. Figure 4.2.3 on page 411 shows how the domestic economy imposes a limit on imports of oranges rather than imposing a tariff. (To make the comparison with tariffs easier, assume that a quota of 200 tonnes is set.) When foreign suppliers are confronted with a quota that halves the quantity they are allowed to sell to another country, simple supply and demand analysis suggests that the highest possible price will be charged. The maximum price foreign suppliers can charge for the 200 tonnes of oranges is €1.2. Since foreign suppliers raise the price in order to receive the highest possible price on their goods, the market price is forced upwards and domestic suppliers increase supply from 500 to 600 tonnes per year.

> **Import quotas:** A quota is a quantitative (physical) limit on imports set by the importing country. The effect of a quota is that domestic suppliers will replace some of the imports at a higher than world market price. Foreign suppliers will have an incentive to raise the price of their goods, thus making a windfall gain.

Again there are societal transfers and net efficiency losses. Figure 4.2.3 outlines these as previously demonstrated with tariffs. The main difference between tariffs and quotas is within the issue of which societal members will benefit from the difference between the import price of €1 and the new price of €1.2 resulting from protectionism. Area **C** does not go to government tax coffers as in the case of tariffs, but into the pockets of foreign suppliers. This unexpected increase in revenue is known as a **windfall gain**, and partially offsets the loss of revenue shown by areas **F** and **G**. (Another difference is that an increase in domestic demand will have completely different effects on domestic output and foreign imports. Under tariff protection, an increase in domestic demand will be met by an increase in exports whereas under a quota system the increase in demand will induce domestic suppliers to fill the increased demand.)

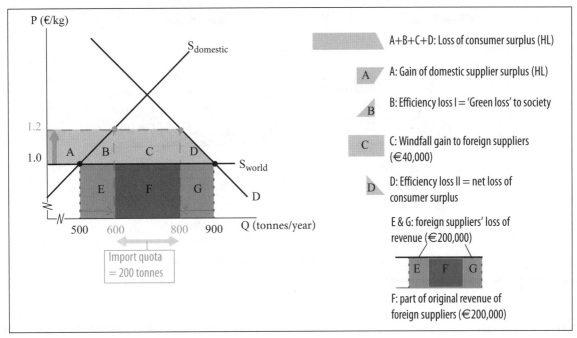

Figure 4.2.3 *Effects of an import quota for oranges*

Again there are societal transfers and net efficiency losses. Figure 4.2.3 outlines these as previously demonstrated with tariffs. The main difference between tariffs and quotas is within the issue of which societal members will benefit from the difference between the import price of €1 and the new price of €1.2 resulting from protectionism. Area **C** does not go to government tax coffers as in the case of tariffs, but into the pockets of foreign suppliers. This unexpected increase in revenue is known as a **windfall gain**, and partially offsets the loss of revenue shown by areas **F** and **G**. (Another difference is that an increase in domestic demand will have completely different effects on domestic output and foreign imports. Under tariff protection, an increase in domestic demand will be met by an increase in exports whereas under a quota system the increase in demand will induce domestic suppliers to fill the increased demand.)

Outside the box:
Price elasticity of demand and quotas

Supply and demand curves are seldom '45° lines' such as have been used above for quotas. It is in fact quite possible for the price elasticities of demand and supply to be such that foreign producers' windfall gain is larger or smaller than shown previously. There will also be a difference in total final output and consumption of the good depending on price elasticities. Figure 4.2.4 on page 412, diagrams I and II, illustrate two possible outcomes of the effects of a quota on a good due to different demand elasticities.

- Using the same starting figures as above, diagram I shows how a good with few substitutes – a good with low price-elasticity of demand – will enable foreign firms to earn a larger windfall gain. Setting the highest possible price for the 200 units at £1.5 renders a windfall gain of €100,000 (€0.5 → 200,000 kg), helping to offset the revenue loss of €200,000 (€1→50,000 kg + €1→50,000 kg). As one would expect, total consumption falls less than in the previous example, from 900 tonnes to 850 tonnes rather than to 800 tonnes, while domestic output increases to 6.5 tonnes rather than to 6 tonnes.

- A good with high price elasticity of demand, diagram II, shows how foreign producers have less manoeuvrability in setting a higher price. A price sensitive good will mean a proportionately larger decrease in quantity demanded than the increase in price. In this case quantity decreases from 900 tonnes to 750 tonnes, and a smaller proportional increase in price than in diagram I, from €1 to €1.2. The windfall gain is €40,000 (€0.2 → 200,000 kg) but the loss of revenue is still €200,000. Unsurprisingly, the fall in total consumption is greater for an elastic good than for an inelastic good and the increase in domestic output is less for an inelastic good.

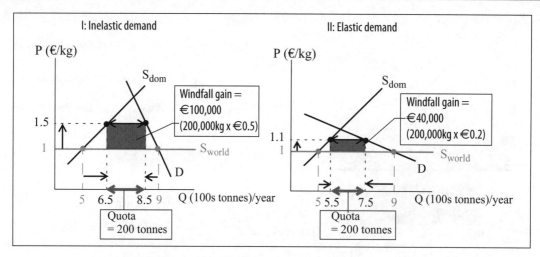

Figure 4.2.4 *Quotas and price elasticity of demand (PED)*

Subsidies ©IBO 2003

Any action by government which lowers the ratio of domestic prices to import prices (in other words *raises the relative price of imports* or *lowers the relative price of domestic goods*) will serve as a barrier to trade. Therefore, when domestic producers receive direct payments for production or *indirect* production incentives such as tax breaks or low-interest loans, the effect is that of a subsidy. A subsidy lowers the production costs (HL: marginal costs) for domestic producers and enables them to be more competitive with foreign producers.

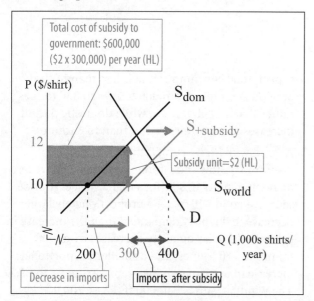

Figure 4.2.5 *Effects of a subsidy on cotton T-shirts*

Figure 4.2.5 shows how a subsidy going to domestic producers affects the market for cotton T-shirts in an economy. Initially the domestic economy is producing 200,000 T-shirts and importing 200,000 T-shirts,

enabling domestic consumption of 400,000 T-shirts at a price of $10. When the government subsidises domestic production at $2 per T-shirt, domestic suppliers are able to increase supply from 200,000 to 300,000. This is shown by the shift of the domestic supply curve from S_{dom} to $S_{+subsidy}$. (HL: note that the entire incidence of the subsidy goes to domestic suppliers.) The subsidy allows domestic producers to capture market share from foreign producers who are now left with one quarter of the market rather than half.

Subsidies can take other forms, two of the more noticeable being export subsidies and guaranteed price schemes. An **export subsidy** is a direct payment to domestic producers that operates on the international market. The subsidy serves to lower production costs and make domestic producers more competitive internationally. This mechanism enables domestic firms to sell on foreign markets at prices below production costs – which is known as dumping and is absolutely forbidden under WTO rules. (See "Anti-dumping" on page 426.) A **guaranteed price scheme** can be considered a subsidy since a minimum price is created and the excess supply can be 'dumped' on the international market via export subsidies. (See "Outside the box: Minimum price scheme in the EU and dumping on developing countries" on page 427.)

Voluntary Export Restraints (VERs)

©IBO 2003

Since the 1970s, the World Trade Organisation (WTO) has implemented explicit restrictions on member countries as to which forms of trade barriers are legitimate. New tariffs and quotas became increasingly uncommon during the 1980s and 1990s but the de facto effects on free trade were less than to be expected as countries increasingly sought out new methods to limit foreign competition. A rather cunning method used primarily in the 1980s, mainly by the UK and the US, was to get powerful export nations – notably Japan at the time – to 'voluntarily' limit exports. This situation, when exporters rather than importers impose quotas, is known as a **voluntary export restraint**, VER, and has exactly the same effect as a quota. Such *bilateral* (= between two countries) agreements are reached by high level negotiating between governments, often as the result of political pressure channelled through powerful lobby groups such as the automobile and steel industries.

> **Voluntary export restraint (VER):** A voluntary export restraint (VER) is when a foreign producer voluntarily limits the quantity of exports to another country, often as the result of political pressure from the importing country.

It doesn't take a great deal of imagination to realise that the joy with which exporting countries voluntarily limit exports is, well, like when one visits the dentist; one does it in order to avoid even worse pain in the future. Commonly, an importing nation would call for trade negotiations and ask that the exporting nation limit its exports. This is done in the true spirit of Teddy Roosevelt's basic credo: 'Talk softly and carry a big stick'. In other words, whatever the diplomatic sugar-coated phraseology, the implication is that if the 'offending' exporting country does not impose its own quotas, the importing nation will impose trade restrictions of far heavier calibre.

Example of VERs: Japanese car exports to the US in the 1980s

In the case of Japan's self-imposed quotas limiting auto exports to the US during the first half of the 1980s, the repercussions of the two oil crises had given Japan a strong competitive edge in the manufacture of small fuel efficient and low cost cars. As Japanese car makers dramatically increased their market share at the expense of US manufacturers, political pressure and intense lobbying for protectionist measures resulted ultimately in a request by the US government for Japan to voluntarily limit the exports of cars to the US. In 1981 the first agreement was reached, whereupon

Japanese auto makers agreed to lower exports from 1.8 to 1.62 million cars. Successive renewed agreements continued until 1985.[3]

Did the VER on cars have the effect predicted by the quota diagram above? Succinctly put; yes. Japanese imports decreased by 3% while Japanese car prices rose by close to 20% between 1980 and 1981. The price of American cars increased by 11% to 14% (depending on size) during the same period. An additional effect was that countries which were not subjected to voluntary export restraints were able to increase their exports to the US.[4] As a final footnote, the WTO has outlawed VERs since 1995, giving nations 8 years to phase out any existing agreements. Thus, as you are reading this, VERs should no longer officially exist.

Administrative obstacles ©IBO 2003

When my mother and father moved to Austria in the late 1980s they made the mistake of bringing a foreign car with them. It took more time and money to comply with Austrian rules on headlights, colour of blinkers, ground clearance, etc. than was worth it. This is but one example of national legislation which in fact acts to create – unintentionally for the most part – barriers to trade. When foreign auto producers have to spend time forcing through *administrative red tape* the delay adds to overall costs. **Administrative barriers** take on many forms, such as the restriction of foreign ownership; licensing rules; excessive documentation on place of origin; extensive testing of new products (very common for pharmaceuticals) and translation of all documentation into the language of the importing country are but a few examples.

It is also quite possible that *international developments* increase existing barriers or create new ones, such as more stringent security controls at all points of entrance to a country such as airports and shipping ports. Increasingly, in these times of worries over international terrorism, the International Maritime Organisation (IMO – a UN agency) has increased security demands on many ports around the world. Instituting such safeguards as fenced off and guarded port areas, security codes and baggage checks for all personnel and visitors to the port and security cameras will inevitably add to delays in shipping and increased costs for shipped goods.[5]

---

3. Krugman & Obstfeld, pp. 201–05.
4. Husted & Melvin, pp. 186–89.
5. Sydsvenska Dagbladet; *Säkerheten I hamnarna höjs*, Friday 12 March 2004.

It is notably easy to implement intentional administrative barriers; a classic example of such was when France decreed in 1982 that all imported (e.g. Japanese) videocassette recorders had to clear customs at a tiny customs house in Poitiers – far from any and all major ports and points of entry to the country. This backlogged the imported VCRs (not 'Very Cunning Restrictions' but 'Video Cassette Recorders') tremendously and limited the imports to a trickle – giving domestic producers time to 'catch up'.

Health and safety standards ©IBO 2003

An extension of administrative barriers is when domestic legislation decrees that imported products must meet certain health and safety criteria. When I was writing a final paper at university, I visited a large Swedish knife manufacturer, Krång Johan Ericsson, which sold knives all over the world. One of the managers told of how the company was in the final stages of getting approval from the US Food and Drug Administration (US FDA) for a series of ergonomic butcher knives for American slaughterhouses. The company had already spent over two years and shipped countless prototypes of the knives to the US to be subjected to successive rounds of testing prior to approval for use in the food industry. The process was very costly for the knife firm and the only problem was apparently that the handles contained certain chemicals necessary to give the knife handles a good grip and the FDA demanded with absolute certainty that there would be no leakage into the meat.

There are literally thousands of sets of standards which countries impose on products in the interest of public health and safety, which all serve to increase costs to importers and/or limit the physical access to the market. Here are a few examples of such standards: Moped manufacturers in the EU will face varying speed limits and the engines will have to be accordingly modified to reduce top speeds; legislation on content labelling will vary greatly in different countries and force manufacturers to print a variety of different labels; certain food additives, colouring and preservatives will be outlawed in some countries; bans on advertising goods such as alcohol and tobacco are increasingly common; and fireworks will face numerous safety regulations as to size and to whom they may be sold.

Misuse of health and safety concerns?

Perhaps the most famous example of health standards which limit trade is the EU ban on all beef containing growth hormones which was implemented in 1989. This has had the effect of a de facto ban on American beef, since virtually all US cattle are treated with growth hormones. Successive American administrations have all claimed that the EU policy is clearly in violation of WTO rules of free trade, since no conclusive evidence exists that growth hormones in any way endanger the health of beef eaters. The WTO, which is the mediator in such disputes, ruled in favour of the US in 2003 yet the EU has as yet not complied. The Americans retaliated with tariffs on $US100 million worth of EU agricultural goods and the ensuing tit-for-tat retaliatory 'tariff game' between the world's two major traders came close to escalating to a trade war.

In March 2008, the WTO again criticised the EU ban on beef from hormone-treated cattle as scientifically unjustified. US Trade Representative Susan Schwab applauded the WTO restatement: 'The findings confirm the principle that measures imposed for health reasons must be based on science.'[6] Another, perhaps equally famous, example of the EU – US trade conflict is the EU restriction on imports of genetically modified (GM) produce such as soybeans and corn. This issue, like that of beef, has yet to be resolved.

---

6. The UN Mission to the EU. See http://useu.usmission.gov/Dossiers/Beef_Hormones/Mar3108_WTO_Dispute_Panel.asp.

Outside the box:
Spurious (= fake) health and safety concerns

It is historically clear that a number of regulations ostensibly part of a health and safety code can be considered covert (= hidden, concealed) trade barriers. The *Reinheitsgebot* – purity laws – in Germany regulated what could be used to make beer and had the effect of banning most imports. This restricted access was lifted in 1990 in line with the increasingly integrated market of the EU.

Italy had a similar experience when previously banned imported pasta – made from the wrong kind of wheat – gained access to the Italian market at the same time. France has banned imported barbecues as 'unsafe'; Belgium has laws demanding extensive labelling on imported foodstuffs; Japan previously 'inspected' imported tulip bulbs by slicing them open (!) and still has a safety inspection on every single imported car – at a cost to the importer of several thousand US dollars; and Canada takes an average of twice the amount of time to approve new US pharmaceuticals than the notoriously tough US FDA.[7]

My personal favourite regulation which in fact was a covert trade barrier was the EU ruling on camel cheese imported from Mauritania; the EU Commission ruled that while the low-cholesterol high-protein cheese was indeed healthy, basic sanitary requirements dictated that the cheese could only be imported if the camels were milked by machine. What the EU ruling failed to take into consideration was that the camels were owned and milked by *desert nomads*.[8] Let me get this straight; the camels should carry electrical milking machines around in the desert? Talk about the final straw …

Environmental standards ©IBO 2003

As trade growth continues unabated, it is increasingly common for countries to demand that imported goods meet with domestic environmental standards. For example, the US – with California at the forefront – has implemented a number of laws governing emission standards and fuel consumption on cars, which any and all imported cars have to conform to. This forces non-US auto manufacturers to adapt engine performance to fit the American market, adding to costs. Another example was the ban on aluminium cans and certain non-reusable plastic containers in Denmark during the 1980s in favour of re-usable glass bottles which were considered environmentally friendly.[9] A number of European producers of soft drinks and beer lodged numerous complaints with the European Commission (the administrative power of the EU) since this posed a trade barrier on their exports to Denmark. Their case was strengthened by the fact that Danish producers continued to export beverages in cans to other EU countries, and the ban has since been rescinded by the Danish government.

Increasingly in our ever-integrating world, environmental standards are set not so much to meet domestic demands but to set global standards for environmentally acceptable production. This has arisen in partial response to increasing developed nation outsourcing of production to developing countries where environmental standards can be noticeably lacking. This is the '**race to the bottom**' argument, which argues that negative externalities such as pollution, diminishing forests and encroachment of wildlife are 'exported', in a manner of speaking, to poorer countries in order that firms in rich countries might avoid increased costs of strict domestic environmental policies. To countermand this, a number of countries have implemented environmental standards which limit – or ban – imports of goods which do not meet certain criteria.

> **Environmental standards as trade barriers:** Environmental standards are government rules and regulations on production methods, product content and environmental impact of use. These are forms of protectionism since they can force costly product alterations on foreign suppliers.

---

7. See the official EU site at http://europa.eu.int/comm/internal_market/en/goods/infr/602.htm and the Independent Canadian public policy institute, The Fraser Institute at: http://oldfraser.lexi.net/publications/forum/2002/02/section_06.html.
8. *Businessworld*, 'Don't say Cheese', 30 December 2002.
9. A number of studies show in fact that aluminium cans have less environmental impact than glass bottles since cans use less energy in (re-)production, cleaning and transportation than glass bottles.

Increasingly in our ever-integrating world, environmental standards are set not so much to meet domestic demands but to set global standards for environmentally acceptable production. This has arisen in partial response to increasing developed nation outsourcing of production to developing countries where environmental standards can be noticeably lacking. This is the **'race to the bottom'** argument, which argues that negative externalities such as pollution, diminishing forests and encroachment of wildlife are 'exported', in a manner of speaking, to poorer countries in order that firms in rich countries might avoid increased costs of strict domestic environmental policies. To countermand this, a number of countries have implemented environmental standards which limit – or ban – imports of goods which do not meet certain criteria.

The debate on environmental standards

The issue of using environmental arguments in trade is highly contentious (= controversial), as it is incredibly difficult to distinguish between commendable environmentalism and contrived trade barriers. The WTO has a number of articles which specifically allow for measures which are 'necessary to protect human, animal or plant life or health' *provided* the measures do not constitute 'an arbitrary or unjustifiable discrimination between countries where the same conditions prevail or a disguised restriction on international trade'.[10] For example, the US imposed a ban on tuna fish imports caught using methods known to kill a large number of dolphins and another ban on shrimp from several Asian countries that used nets which also trapped turtles; the WTO ruled both bans illegal to general outrage amongst environmental groups.

Other environmental arguments are much less contentious, such as the restrictions on imports of certain hardwoods from rainforests in many OECD countries, where a range of certification procedures are in place to see to it that goods made of hardwood come from plantations rather than rainforests. Perhaps one of the most well known examples of how environmental standards have been beneficial is that virtually all developed countries have long since banned goods either containing or made using chlorofluorocarbons (CFCs).[11] Taken as a whole, many administrative, health/safety and environmental standards are sometimes referred to as covert trade barriers. This does not mean that the barriers are necessarily intentional but that differing standards disadvantage foreign producers. Yet it bears repeating that the line between legitimate and contrived barriers of these types is blurred and subject to continuous debate and international litigation.

Other forms of trade barriers

There are a number of barriers to trade not mentioned above. I include three additional brief points below so that you can widen your scope in searching for good articles to use in internal assessment.

- **Currencies and exchange rates:** Exchange rate fluctuations will create uncertainty for exporters and importers, leading perhaps to less trade. Commissions (service charges) on foreign exchange transactions also create barriers. Many countries also have strict controls on the amount of currency which can be traded and by whom. A country can also devalue its currency (i.e. lower the exchange rate, which is the 'price' of the domestic currency) thereby making imports more expensive and domestic goods cheaper relative to imports.

- **Government favouritism in procurement:** Government agencies will frequently be required to favour domestic industries. Look closely at the brand of cars you see used for official functions in countries which have domestic auto production.

- **Nationalism:** Persuasive advertising slogans and campaigns such as 'Buy American/French/Italian…' can skew demand away from imports which might be both better and cheaper.

---

10. McCulloch et al, *Trade liberalisation and poverty: A handbook*, p. 327 and Article XX of GATT 1994.
11. Legrain, *Open world – the truth about globalization*, pp. 241–53.

POP QUIZ 4.2.1   TARIFF AND NON-TARIFF BARRIERS TO TRADE

1   Using a diagram, explain how tariffs create both 'winners' and 'losers'. Explain the net allocative result according to economic theory.

2   A government imposing a tariff is choosing between putting the tariff on a good with low domestic price elasticity of demand or a good with high domestic price elasticity of supply. Explain possible arguments in favour of each.

3   A government wishes to increase domestic output of a good without decreasing domestic consumers' welfare and is choosing between imposing a tariff, a quota or a domestic subsidy on a good. What would you recommend here?

4   In Switzerland, gold is defined as having a minimum content of 75% gold (18 carat). Some countries have 110 volts while others have 220 volts. Germany does not allow winter tyres with metal studs. Which of these examples represent a barrier to trade?

Arguments for protectionism

©IBO 2003

Standard economic theory states that protectionism generally creates losers amongst foreign import firms and domestic consumers; winners amongst domestic firms; possible gains to government in the form of tax receipts; and overall allocative losses for society. Thus far, most economists' conclusion would be that costs outweigh the gains of protectionism, which merits asking why there are so many avoidable barriers to trade still in place. A follow-up question must address the issue of whether there are in fact trade barriers which carry net societal gains, i.e. where the benefits are greater than the costs. While there are no clear cut answers to any of these questions, a number of arguments can be put forward in defence of protectionist measures. There is strong disparity amongst economists on the degree of validity of virtually all these arguments, so in some cases I will include a *pro and con* addendum.

Infant industry argument   ©IBO 2003

The infant industry argument was put forward almost 200 years ago and is thus one of the longest standing arguments in favour of protectionism. Suppose that a country has potential comparative advantage in the production of a good, but is competing on an international market where global benefits of scale exists and the market is mainly comprised by entrenched firms from technologically advanced countries. A small 'infant' firm in an industry on the domestic market would have little chance of successfully competing against the larger international firms which have enormous advantages in size, market share, production knowledge, etc. Meeting the international firms (which have far lower average costs) in head-on competition is hardly doable, whereby some form of intermediate (= transitional, temporary) protection can be warranted. This is the **infant industry argument** for trade barriers, which prescribes reducing price and or cost differences between small domestic firms and international firms. Commonly a mix of tariffs, import quotas and/or subsidies are used to protect the infant industry, allowing these firms to move along the learning curve and ultimately be able to employ comparative advantages and compete with older and more experienced foreign producers.

> **Infant industry barriers**: When there are possible comparative advantages to be had in an undeveloped domestic industry, trade barriers can be erected to protect these 'infant' industries from far more efficient producers. The aim of *infant industry barriers* to trade is to give domestic industries time to move along the learning curve and ultimately lower costs enough to be competitive with imports.
>
> (HL: The protection allows smaller industries to increase output and ultimately move along the long-run average cost curve as benefits of scale are realised.)

Infant industries and less developed countries (LDCs)

The argument is frequently – if not always today – put forward in the context of developing countries competing on international markets ruled by firms from developed countries. When a less developed country (LDC) initially cannot utilise its possible comparative advantage in, say, manufacturing then tariffs can be used to raise domestic market prices and allow domestic firms to cover their costs, which are higher than international producers'. A subsidy to domestic producers would have the effect of lowering domestic production costs. In both cases the domestic firms become more competitive and increase their output, enabling the industry time to 'grow up' under the cover of temporary protectionism. When the LDC becomes increasingly efficient and competitive, the tariffs/subsidies are gradually reduced to free-trade levels.

Figure 4.2.6 on page 418, diagram I, shows how an LDC can protect a potential domestic industry by imposing trade barriers. The domestic supply curve shows how domestic LDC production initially is zero, since the free trade world price is lower than potential domestic price at all domestic supply levels. LDC

consumers consume (= import) Q_{D0} goods at the world price, P_W. In setting a tariff of $P_W \Leftrightarrow P_{W+T}$, the domestic price level rises to P_{W+T} and Q_S domestic goods can be produced in competition with the world price while total imports fall by $Q_{D1} \Leftrightarrow Q_{D0}$.

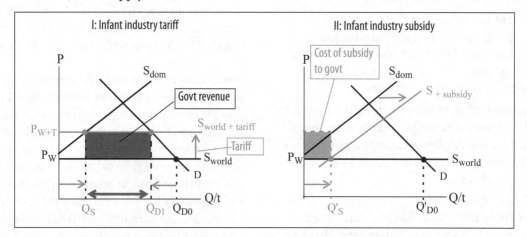

Figure 4.2.6 *Infant industry barriers to trade*

A **subsidy** to domestic suppliers, diagram II above, has similar domestic *quantitative* effects as a tariff but entirely different costs/benefits and therefore a different allocative outcome. Domestic output increases from zero to Q'_S as before. However, domestic consumers do not lose out by having to pay a higher price for less quantity (HL: consumer surplus is unchanged) which means that domestic production adapts to the international price rather than raising it. Finally, the government does not receive tax revenue but in fact has to shoulder the entire cost (incidence) of the subsidy, which HL should easily recognise as the blue area in the diagram. Developing countries frequently make use of tariffs rather than subsidies in protecting infant industries, as the cost of the subsidies can be prohibitive.

Pro and con in infant industry arguments

Pro: It should be pointed out immediately that the three major industrialised nations, US, Japan and Germany, all had high trade barriers in their initial stages of industrialisation. There is a case to be made in that the *dynamic gains* to the domestic economy – the 'spin-off effects' of moving along the learning curve such as increased know how, technological advancement, etc. ultimately provides benefits which outweigh such intermediate costs as higher prices and lower consumption. There has also been some justification for adopting infant industry protections using market failure arguments; the domestic capital markets in many LDCs have simply lacked viable financial institutions and funds to finance investment

in industries with potential domestic comparative advantages. Thus there is an *economic argument* in support of infant industry protectionism if the social benefits (comparative advantage, increased knowledge/technology, improved workforce) are greater than the losses (deadweight losses due to higher prices and misallocation).

Con: There are, however, few absolute successes in using infant industry protection according to most economic analyses. The criteria for 'absolute successes' would be that the protectionist measures were indeed *temporary* and have *benefits which exceed the costs* to society. Historically, few tariffs and subsidies implemented in line with the infant industry argument became anything like 'temporary' but in fact became permanent for longer periods – often at the behest of (large and often monopolistic) domestic suppliers fearing competition. High tariffs and/or domestic subsidies all too often create comfort zones where even inefficient domestic firms can stay in business. As for costs and benefits, governments have been noticeably poor in picking winning industries to protect and support. For example, India was long one of the most protectionist countries in the world, and had almost impenetrable barriers on imported cars. Yet when the country introduced sweeping changes to foreign trade policy in 1991, following in the footsteps of China ten years earlier, India became a major exporter in entirely different areas, noticeably textiles, leather goods and more recently Internet-based services such as call-back centres.

Efforts of a developing country to diversify ©IBO 2003

A major barrier for developing nations is the dependence on basic commodities such as minerals and agricultural goods. This has in many respects 'trapped' such countries into producing and exporting primary goods with low value-added content. And since the price of such goods has fallen continuously for the past 50 years, developing countries have seen a decline in their *terms of trade*; they have to sell increasing quantities of raw materials and agricultural goods in order to buy any given amount of imported manufactured – secondary – goods.

The new and the old in Chile – an economic success story

Hence, as an extension of the infant industry argument above, a developing country might implement trade barriers to offer temporary protection to manufacturing industries such as textiles and components for electrical appliances where abundant labour gives a potential comparative advantage. Such targeted (= strategically directed) barriers can help alleviate dependency on a narrow range of goods by broadening the production base, thereby improving the country's terms of trade and perhaps lessening the severity of global recessions. Another point in favour of infant-industry protectionism is that multinational companies have had many years to attain large economies of scale and could in effect undercut prices in fledgling industries in LDCs – hindering the diversification process out of basic commodities into higher value-added goods.

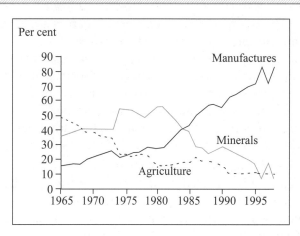

(Source: World Bank: *Globalization, growth and poverty: Building an inclusive world economy*, p. 32)

Figure 4.2.7 *Shares in merchandise exports in developing country exports*

While it is most difficult to assess possible positive correlation between targeted trade barriers and the increasing diversification in developing countries, the fact is that in the past 25 years developing countries representing over 3 billion people have increasingly moved up the 'value-added chain', moving from 25% of exports in 1980 to 80% in 1998, shown in Figure 4.2.7 It should be noted that the World Bank mostly attributes this diversification to increased liberalisation of trade and capital flows rather than targeted protectionism in developing countries.[12]

Protection of employment ©IBO 2003

The employment protection argument is probably the most controversial argument for protection. It is certainly the most divisive amongst economists, where views range from 'partially viable' to 'absolutely erroneous'. The basic argument in implementing trade barriers in reference to unemployment is that traditional/large industries which are subjected to increased foreign competition will cause *structural unemployment*. When comparative advantage ratios shift as foreign competitors become increasingly proficient in certain industries, governments often resort to protectionist measures in order to preserve jobs – or at least delay a decline in what becomes a 'sunset industry'. A large proportion of the trade barriers of the past 20 years fall within this argument; steel, cars and cotton in the US; sugar, wine and ship building in the EU; and agricultural goods and textiles – to some extent – in all developed countries.[13]

---

12. World Bank: *Globalization, growth and poverty: Building an inclusive world economy*, pp. 31–35.
13. Again, Hong Kong being the exception.

The argument often enjoys broad support amongst both citizens and government officials, since cheap foreign imports and concomitant loss of jobs is an easy connection to make and the perceived societal benefits are clear. Anyone who has seen the effects of massive layoffs in a staple industry, such as in Northern England during the mine closures in the early 1980s will easily understand the appeal of softening the blow by restricting foreign competition.[14] Increasingly the argument is extended to limit 'the exportation of jobs' to low cost labour countries resulting from the increased ease with which firms can move capital. (See "Globalisation" on page 439.) When firms such as Flextronics (a component manufacturer for mobile phones) shut down entire factories in the EU and moved production to China in order to take advantage of lower labour costs, the resulting sectoral unemployment inflicted severe social and economic costs on the job exporting country. In light of this, it would appear that protectionism is indeed warranted.

Pro and con in employment argument

The employment argument has limited validity at best and is seriously flawed and fallacious at worst:

Pro: The argument can have *limited validity* when protectionism is used to grant domestic industries *temporary* relief from debilitating (= devastating) foreign competition in order to grant time for domestic product and factor markets to clear and reallocate factors to other industries. This reasoning is often applied in the case of important domestic industries that are in a state of permanent decline, so-called *sunset industries*. Protectionist policies might also be complemented by various labour market policies such as retraining and education to facilitate a smoother transition period. However, such policies have a tendency to become entrenched and therefore long run, leading to numerous negative effects, primarily higher prices of goods and efficiency/competitive losses.

Con: Economists claiming that the infant industry argument is *seriously flawed* commonly put forward the following three points:

1. Recall that in order to import one must export. No country will be able to buy imports 'on credit' in the long run. When the world's number two cotton producer, the US, protects domestic cotton growers from imports from the number one cotton producer, China, the effect is to limit Chinese ability to buy Caterpillar bulldozers – increasing unemployment in this other US industry. This is a classic example of the **fallacy of composition** in economic argumentation; what is good for one industry is not necessarily good for *all* industries. Protecting cotton jobs in the US thus comes with a triple price tag: 1) The protectionism is often in the form of subsidies which cost taxpayers via government funds; 2) Textile firms pay a higher price for cotton and consumers pay a higher price for cotton goods; 3) And jobs lost in road machinery manufacturing inflict additional economic and social costs.

Official US statistics show overwhelming evidence that US trade with China is indeed not a one way street: exports of iron, steel and copper from the US to China increased by over 100% from 2002 to 2003. During the period 1997 to 2003, Chinese exports to the US increased from $US65.8 billion to $US163.3 billion, which is an increase of 148%. During the same period, US exports to China went from $US12.8 billion to $US28.4 billion, an increase of 122%.[15]

2. Protectionism might save jobs in domestic production but *jobs will be lost in the import sector*, where people are employed in wholesaling, retailing and servicing imported goods. During the past 20 years in the US, during the most trade-expansive and open period in US history, 40 million *more* jobs were created than lost; strong indicative evidence supporting the economic truism that trade creates rather than destroys jobs.[16]

3. Protecting the domestic economy from cheap foreign labour is perhaps the most erroneous and misleading argument of them all and is almost always advanced by rich countries in reference to poor countries.[17] The main fallacy of this argument is the assumption of a '**lump sum**' (= fixed amount) of available employment opportunities and that cheap foreign imports remove employment opportunities

---

14. Recommended movies: *Brassed Off*, *The Full Monty* and *Billy Elliot*.

15. US International Trade Commission, US Department of Commerce at The US-China Business Council: http://www.uschina.org/statistics/tradetable.html.

16. Horst Köhler, Managing Director of the International Monetary Fund and James Wolfensohn, President of The World Bank, 'We can trade up to a better world', *Financial Times*, 12 December 2003.

17. I hate to say it, but even Albert Einstein fell for it. Quote: '*If two factories produce the same sort of goods, other things being equal, that factory will be able to produce them more cheaply which employs fewer workmen, i.e. makes the individual worker work as long and as hard as human nature permits. From this it follows inevitably that, with methods of production as they are today, only a portion of the available labour can be used.*'

for domestic labourers.[18] In fact, the opposite has continuously shown to be true, where increased openness, trade and competition has been met in rich countries with rising productivity and thus higher wages. While this evolution has indeed created periods of labour redundancies and unemployment, higher real wages have triggered increased demand for a multitude of other products over the past 20 to 30 years. This has primarily increased the demand for **services**, many of which cannot be imported and therefore are supplied domestically. So while manufacturing jobs in the US fell from just under 21 million to under 20 million between 1970 and 2000, over 50 million new jobs were created in services during the same period.[19]

A little depth:
The wall: Mexico–US border

I must have broken some sort of record the other week when I gave my IB1s homework they truly enjoyed and did with enthusiasm. I brought up the so-called Tortilla Wall being erected between the border of the US and Mexico which was reaching a length of 1,000 kilometres during January 2009. My request was simple: 'Look up some facts on the very inflamed issue of Mexican immigration to the US and answer one basic question; is the US doing the right thing in putting a great amount of resources into keeping Mexicans from entering the US?' I had two qualifications: 1) 'The right thing' had to be clearly defined in cost-benefit terms, e.g. whether the contributions of US Mexicans outweighed the costs. 2) Argumentation must be along economic lines rather than political or moral lines.

I was bombarded with data (and a few off-colour comments) together with a most resounding and general conclusion: the increasing anti-immigration sentiments, laws and barriers are not in the US's best interests. Here are a few of the points my students came up with:

- The Mexicans indeed have an advantage in cheap labour – this is in fact a comparative advantage. It is not 'cheating' or 'unfair competition'. If the same labour is willing/able to work for lower wages in the US, Americans benefit hugely in having basic services and jobs done in low skilled markets.

- Many of the jobs filled by Mexican immigrants would be unfilled by Americans.

- The circa 11 million Mexicans in the US account for roughly 5% of the total labour force:

  ■ The Mexicans contribute about USD635 billion to the US economy (2003 estimate) which is 5% of GDP.

  ■ The illegal proportion of Mexicans working in the US (circa 5.3 million) contribute USD220 billion to the US economy, that is, 2% of GDP.

  ■ This USD220 billion represents some 20% of Mexico's GDP.

- Hispanics living and working in the US also stimulate demand – the purchasing power of Hispanics in the US in 2005 was estimated at USD736 billion in 2005. By 2010 this will be the equivalent of over 9% of US GDP.

- The US labour force is on the verge of shrinking. The growth in the labour force has fallen from 5% per year to less than 1% per year. Without immigration the US labour force would decline. As Americans are living longer and more pensioners will need to be cared for, immigrants are in fact a vital resource for US living standards.

- The majority of Mexican immigrants are in the peak working age, the average immigrant being 34 years old. Most of the jobs taken by these immigrants will require minimal training and education. This is going on at the same time as Americans are getting university degrees in increasing numbers and will be highly reluctant to take the low-paying jobs now filled by immigrants.

- The final point made by several of my students in line with my prerequisites for the task, is that in the *Economic Report of the President, 2005*, a cost-benefit analysis revealed that immigrants are *net*

18. An anecdote herein is the story of a trade economist visiting China in the 1970s and seeing how hundreds of road workers were using shovels. He suggested that a few bulldozers and other road machines would do the job far more efficiently. His horrified host replied that this would create enormous unemployment. The economist subsequently suggested that if the aim was employment creation the shovels might be replaced with spoons. (Taken from *Defending Free Trade, Arvind Panagariya; Economic Times*, 22 November 2000).

19. As a percentage of employment, manufacturing jobs have gone from over 26% to under 15% during the 30 year period, while services increased their share to 72% in 2000. See US Bureau of Labour Statistics at www.bls.gov/fis/fls/flslforc.pdf.

contributors to the US economy. The net present value of all future tax payments of immigrants exceeds the costs of the social services they are expected to use during their time in the US by USD80,000 per person on average.

None of the above paints a picture of 'Mexicans stealing American jobs'. The faulty logic is a classic case of the 'lump-sum of labour fallacy'; there is not a 'given' amount of work to do so an increase in the labour force does NOT mean 'less work available for everyone'. Goods markets expand with labour markets and this has been going on for hundreds of years. Building barriers against the most valuable resource economies have – human beings – will not 'save jobs'.

(Sources: www.cis.org; www.ime.gob.mx/investigaciones; www.pewhispanic.org; www.immigrationpolicy.org; 'The Economic Logic of Illegal Immigration', at Council of Foreign Relations, http://www.cfr.org/content/publications/attachments/ImmigrationCSR26.pdf)

Case study: India and offshoring

If you live in America and at some point need to call and check the line of credit on your credit card, chances are that you will be met on the phone by a very polite and well-educated young person speaking excellent English with a most enchanting lilting accent – Indian English. Increasingly jobs which can utilise ever lower-cost information technology – the Internet and related computer technologies – are being outsourced (= production is moved to outside firms) to firms outside the US which can supply labour at a fraction of US labour costs. Commonly referred to as offshoring, this process of allocating increasingly qualified jobs to other countries has become a serious source of controversy in countries which have long been considered technologically driven.

If a software engineer in the US earning an average of $US150,000 a year can be replaced by equally competent engineers in India who earn $US20,000 a year then there is clearly an economic incentive for US firms to do so.[a] On 24 March 2004 I ran a check on Google, the Internet search site, using the words 'outsourcing', 'India', 'jobs', 'unemployment', 'US', and got over 400,000 US hits. This indicates the scope of the intense debate going on in the US on how domestic US jobs are being lost to overseas suppliers.

Here are a few examples of jobs which increasingly are moving to India from the US:

- Jobs in computer programming can just as easily be done in India as in Silicon Valley, using the Internet to send program code back to the mother company in the US. For example, IBM announced in December 2003 that 5,000 programming jobs were being relocated to India.[b]

- Back office services such as insurance services, credit card services, online computer support and other customer services are being outsourced to India at an accelerating rate. Also, data compilation, accounting procedures and paying wages to employees are being done in India for firms such as American Express, Microsoft and GE Capital.[c]

- Reading X-rays, health charts and analysing medical data is another area which India excels in due to a wealth of well-educated doctors and specialists and the ease with which these files can be sent via the Internet.

---

a.   'Exporting jobs is not free trade - Rethinking protectionism', *New York Times*, 7 January 2004.
b.   *E-commerce Times* online at http://www.ecommercetimes.com/perl/story/32396.html.
c.   'The remote future', *The Economist*, 19 February 2004.

Increasing calls for protectionist measures have arisen in the US during the early 2000s. Proponents of such measures point to the loss of some 2.7 million US jobs in the three years since the mild economic downturn in 2001. Additional nourishment for their argument is found in estimates pointing to the 'jobless recovery' lacking some 7 million additional jobs which would be the case for a normal recovery phase of the business cycle. It is pointed out that increasingly it is not low-cost, labour intensive jobs that are being lost to foreign competition, but highly qualified professionals with university degrees that are being replaced by foreign labour. This is exacerbated by the fact that it is much easier and cheaper to outsource service jobs than manufacturing jobs, since there is little capital investment involved in the transfer.

Increasing calls for protectionist measures have arisen in the US during the early 2000s. Proponents of such measures point to the loss of some 2.7 million US jobs in the three years since the mild economic downturn in 2001. Additional nourishment for their argument is found in estimates pointing to the 'jobless recovery' lacking some 7 million additional jobs which would be the case for a normal recovery phase of the business cycle. It is pointed out that increasingly it is not low-cost, labour intensive jobs that are being lost to foreign competition, but highly qualified professionals with university degrees that are being replaced by foreign labour. This is exacerbated by the fact that it is much easier and cheaper to outsource service jobs than manufacturing jobs, since there is little capital investment involved in the transfer.

Commentators in opposition to the above line of reasoning point out that outsourcing is nothing new and in fact has been a strong element throughout the vibrant economy of the 1990s where some 24 million new jobs were created in spite of the globalisation of the job market. The 2.7 million jobs lost are accredited cyclical rather than structural unemployment resulting from an overheated job market in the late 1990s. Opponents to protectionist measures on outsourcing jobs build their arguments primarily on the general economic validity of comparative advantage; if a good can be produced at less cost abroad than at home, both countries will benefit. To support this argument, it is pointed out that firms outsourcing to India – 'traitors', in the words of presidential candidate Senator John Kerry – in fact caused less than 1% of total unemployment during the 1990s and furthermore that economic activity and increasing incomes in India have boosted demand for American exports to India. American exports to India thus grew by some 8% during 2002, passing the $US4 billion mark for the first time ever.[d] A further argument against the perceived ills of outsourcing is that the lower production costs in Information Technology (IT) lowered hardware prices by some 30% in the US during the 1990s. This spread of technology and increasingly lower costs of IT hardware have added an estimated $US230 billion to American GDP between 1995 and 2002, adding 0.3 percentage points to yearly growth due to increased productivity.[e] Outsourcing has saved Americans some $US8 billion in financial services over between 1999 and 2003.[f]

By 2004, it seemed that the protectionists have met with a measure of success, as a ban on the outsourcing of federal government jobs was imposed in February, and several US states are considering similar legislation banning state government outsourcing to foreign countries. India's foreign minister has vehemently criticised this course of action as '… doing more damage to your [US] economy.'[g]

d. 'Smile, these are good times. Truly.', *The Economist*, 11 March 2004.
e. *Globalization of IT Services and White Collar Jobs: The Next Wave of Productivity Growth*, Catherine L. Mann, International Economics Policy Brief, Institute of International Economics 2003.
f. 'Leader in outsourcing a victim of backlash', *International Herald Tribune*, 23 March 2004.
g. 'India slams US ban on outsourcing jobs', UPS Int'l in *The Washington Times*, 2 February 2004 and 'Proposed Pennsylvania Legislation Would Discourage Outsourcing', *The Miami Herald*, 19 March 2004.

Source of government revenue

©IBO 2003

Two centuries ago, the largest share of government revenue came from tariffs. These customs duties were easy to control since points of access (i.e. ports) were limited, and also easy to collect as the goods had to pass customs warehouses before being distributed. Today, however, modern administrative systems, well functioning census bureaus and efficient tax offices allow other forms of taxes, such as income taxes, to form the brunt of government tax revenue.

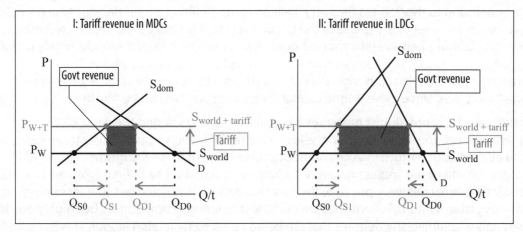

Figure 4.2.8 *Tariff revenues for manufactured goods in MDCs and LDCs*

Noticeably different in this respect are developing countries, where domestic production in many cases will not provide viable substitutes for imported goods – primarily manufactured goods (secondary goods) with higher value-added content. The contrast in levying tariffs on such imports is shown in Figure 4.2.8, diagrams I and II, which show how the government in a more developed country (MDC) will have less to gain from tariffs than an LDC.

- An **MDC**, diagram I, will have a high level of industrialisation, intra-industry trade and therefore viable domestic substitutes, which means that both domestic supply and demand will be relatively elastic.

- The situation in an **LDC** (diagram II) is often the opposite – a low proportion of intra-industry trade, relatively low level of industrialisation compared to MDCs and negligible domestic substitutes with resulting demand inelasticity.

The imposition of a tariff will have a greater impact on tax receipts in an LDC than an MDC – shown by the size of the grey area in the two diagrams. The above helps to explain why average tariff rates in developed countries are less than 5% while developing countries have an average tariff of roughly 20%.[20]

Additionally, the formal economy in LDCs is frequently relatively small and the informal economy does not comprise a taxable base. Tariff revenues in developing countries therefore make up a far larger portion of tax receipts and general government revenues. The United Nations Conference on Trade and Development (UNCTAD) estimates that close to 18% of all government revenues and over 20% of total tax receipts come from import duties in developing countries. Corresponding figures for developed countries are less than 4% of both government revenues and tax receipts.[21] Understandably, a developing country government lacking a distinct domestic tax base, a well functioning tax/administrative system, and thus a steady inflow of tax receipts will be quite dependent on tariffs. Unfortunately, some 70% of this tariff revenue comes from other developing countries.[22]

Strategic arguments ©IBO 2003

Referring to any number of conflicts and wars, I often claim that the only thing that goes up faster than anti-aircraft turrets in a country entering a war are trade barriers – both in the form of coastal mines and forced embargoes put in place by enemies and their allies. A

20. Hertel, Thomas W & Martin, Will, *Would developing countries gain from inclusion of manufactures in the WTO negotiations?* Geneva (WTO) 1999, (WTO/World Bank Conference on Developing Countries' in a Millennium Round, 20–21 September 1999), see http://www.itd.org/wb/hertel.doc and Environmental Working Group (EWG); an independent US organisation monitoring subsidies, at http://www.ewg.org.

21. *Tariffs, Taxes and Electronic Commerce: Revenue Implications for Developing Countries,* Susanne Teltshcer at UNCTAD, 2000.

22. Hertel & Martin, ibid.

country which has specialised greatly will have difficulties in getting hold of traded goods during times of conflict, resulting in any number of goods – for example food and clothing – having to be produced domestically in order for the war-time economy to function.

This non-economic argument has a degree of general validity, where pure military goods will naturally have the strongest argument in favour of domestic production and protectionism since no

country will want to be dependent on potential enemies for the supply of vital military goods. It is this 'self-sufficiency' argument which has led a number of smaller countries to become exporters of military goods; in order to gain benefits of scale, military suppliers will sell to foreign countries – and not uncommonly receive domestic export subsidies in direct support. This lowers the average cost of goods produced for the domestic market and the export revenue can even help cover some of these costs.

Case study: Pulling the wool over taxpayers' eyes

Even in the arena of valid strategic protectionism there can be spurious (= false) arguments. For example, during the Second World War and the Korean War, America had to import fibres to manufacture its military uniforms. In order to become completely self-reliant in this sector, the American Congress declared wool to be a strategic material and therefore enacted the **National Wool Act** in 1954. This was basically a system of subsidies which granted producers a certain payment for every pound of wool produced. Although of little strategic value, this also included **mohair**. Have you ever heard of mohair? How about Angora? When I asked my people, several of them thought the former was a hairstyle and the latter some sort of rabbit. Close but not quite. Mohair is a type of wool which comes from Angora goats and the wool was (previously) used in aforementioned US military uniforms. While wool and mohair were 'declassified' as strategic materials in 1960, the cost of subsidising these materials – 80% of which was exported – was $US156 billion between 1995 and 2002, with the top ten percent of recipients receiving 82% of the subsidies. The subsidies were reinstated in the $US180 billion 2002 Farm Security Act encompassing 2002–2012, which passed the US Congress in 2002.[a]

---

a.   EWG at http://www.ewg.org/farm/regiondetail.php?fips=00000&summlevel=2 and also CBS News at http://www.cbsnews.com/stories/2002/05/13/politics/main508765.shtml.

Means to overcome a balance of payments disequilibrium ©IBO 2003

Traditionally, most of Australia's imports come from overseas. – Keppel Enderbery, former cabinet minister in Australia[23]

The balance of payments

The **balance of payments** is an account of all the monetary dealings a country has with other countries and basically accounts for all money flows across the border during a period of time. The balance of payments is comprised of two parts; the current

account and the capital account. The **current account** shows export revenue and import expenditure while the **capital account** shows money in- and outflows resulting from foreign investment and loans. Leaving further details to Section 4.5, a balance of payments disequilibrium refers to a situation where export revenue for a country is less than import expenditure. This is known as a **trade deficit**, shown in Figure 4.2.9 on page 426, where export revenue is $400 million and import expenditure is $500 million. Disregarding other money flows (for example arising from services and transports) there is a current account deficit, i.e. a balance of payments disequilibrium.

---

23. Quoted from Perloff, p. 295.

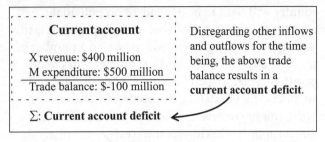

Current account	Disregarding other inflows and outflows for the time being, the above trade balance results in a **current account deficit**.
X revenue: $400 million	
M expenditure: $500 million	
Trade balance: $-100 million	

Σ: **Current account deficit** ⟵

Figure 4.2.9 *The current account*

Protectionism and the balance of payments

The results of protectionist measures in the balance of payments are shown in Figure 4.2.10, diagrams I and II.

Tariff: A tariff is an *expenditure switching* policy, i.e. an amount of domestic expenditure will be diverted away from imports (diagram I). A tariff increases the price of imported goods, shifting the S_{world} curve upwards to $S_{world+tariff}$. The result is that domestic suppliers increase their output from Qs_0 to Qs_1 and imports fall by the sum of $Qs_0 \Leftrightarrow Qs_1$ and $Q_{D1} \Leftrightarrow Q_{D0}$.

Subsidy: Similarly, domestic subsidies (diagram II) will increase domestic supply from S_{dom} to $S_{dom + subsidy}$, resulting in a decrease in imports of $Q's_0 \Leftrightarrow Q's_1$. The decrease in total spending on imports – the grey areas in both diagrams – improves the trade balance and thus improves the current account in the balance of payments.

Important note: A decrease in import expenditure does not necessarily mean a current account surplus (e.g. that export revenue is larger than import expenditure). The decrease in net money outflows on current account can mean a lower negative value, i.e. a *lower current account deficit*.)

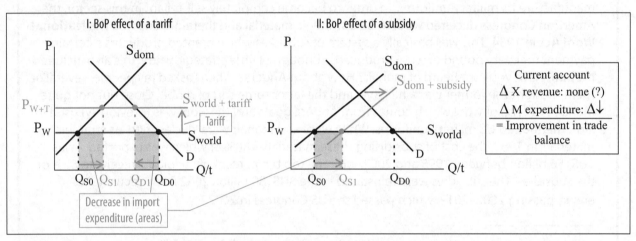

Figure 4.2.10 *Trade barriers and balance of payments*

Notice the question mark after '**X revenue: none**' in the current account illustration. As pointed out previously, a country's export revenues enable imports – when a domestic tariff or non-tariff barrier limits trade partners' income, a possible result is that the trade partners reduce imports. It is also possible, or even likely, that countries on the receiving end of protectionist policies retaliate in kind – in much the same way that the Great Depression of the 1930s was exacerbated. Such 'reciprocal' or 'retaliatory' trade barriers are often the result of beggar-my-neighbour policies.[24] It is therefore a distinct possibility that the improvement in the current account will be eroded in the longer term. The frequency and debilitating effects of such tit-for-tat protectionism led the WTO in 1995 to outlaw the practice of balance of payments readjustment using tariffs. Yet, as Section 4.7 will show, it is still possible to use exchange rate adjustments to similar effect.

Anti-dumping ©IBO 2003

When domestic suppliers sell goods abroad at below domestic production costs (HL: below *marginal* cost – assuming a competitive market) or domestic market equilibrium price one says that dumping takes place. While it is possible that firms might do so in order to get rid of excess goods, use excess production capacity or capture market share by driving out rivals (so called 'predatory pricing'), dumping far more commonly arises due to export subsidies. (See "Outside the box: Minimum price scheme in the EU and dumping on developing countries" on page 427.)

---

24. Beggar-my-neighbour policies are any type of protectionist foreign trade policy where domestic output and jobs are 'saved' by limiting goods exported by others, i.e. at another country's expense. Tariffs, quotas and currency devaluations are common examples.

Problems arising in setting anti-dumping tariffs

The WTO allows for anti-dumping tariffs to offset an unfair price differential and thus trade advantage of foreign firms. Two immediate problems arise in setting anti-dumping tariffs:

1. It is most difficult – in some cases impossible – to correctly **assess the production costs** of firms accused of dumping. Often these difficulties arise from the fact that there are subsidies given to firms in the dumping country which are immensely difficult to accurately account for.

2. As a result of the above, it is common to use the domestic market price of the country of origin to determine whether dumping is taking place. This creates a problem for firms which are simply **adapting to local market prices** in furtherance of gaining market share.

A good number of countries consider dumping as an unfair trade practice and so too do WTO rules; offending imports can be taxed to bring the import price up to what is considered the correct market price in the importing country. Therefore anti-dumping tariffs are allowed by the WTO, resulting in accusations of unfair trade barriers by the countries accused of dumping. And since all anti-dumping tariffs must be instigated by an official complaint to the domestic regulatory body by firms in an industry, the counter-argument of the country being dumped upon is that domestic industries are simply being protected from unfair competition. Many of the disagreements herein are due to the difficulties in assessing whether dumping is in fact taking place, since it is so difficult to evaluate the actual costs of production in the exporting country. This creates one of the major obstacles to free trade; since real dumping is so difficult to pinpoint and prove one way or another, countries can slap anti-dumping measures on goods much like any other tariff. Anti-dumping tariffs are also easy to defend politically using the argument of 'fairness' in trade.[25]

> **Dumping and anti-dumping tariffs:**
> When a country's firms sell goods below production cost – and more widely defined, below the domestic price level – the goods are being **dumped** on the importing country. When the importing country taxes these imported goods to reflect the 'true' cost of production one speaks of an **anti-dumping tariff**.
>
> (Note: HL should use '…below the marginal cost….')

Outside the box:
Minimum price scheme in the EU and dumping on developing countries

By now you have seen what might be considered a bias in the arguments for and against protectionism, yet once again, allow me to state that this bias is based on *economic* rather than *emotional* reasoning. However, adopting a somewhat emotional stance, it is very difficult not to become rather cynical in looking at the effects of dumping goods on developing markets and I shall only partially restrain myself.

Just imagine that you walked into a shop and had to pay for each good twice; firstly you would pay a flat rate fee to producers whether you bought the good or not and secondly you would pay an actual price for the good at two to three times the market price. Additionally, the flat rate fee would destroy more efficient producers in (poor) foreign lands, causing increased poverty. A measly portion of this unnecessary increase in poverty might cost you a *third* time when your government provides aid money to the country whose potential export livelihood has been destroyed. This is pretty much how developed country agricultural export subsidies work, and often confuses my people who find it difficult to conceive how subsidies could serve to *increase* the market price rather than lower it. Well, it confuses me too…

Roughly $55 billion – 43.5% of the entire €126.5 billion EU budget – was spent on the Common Agricultural Policy's (CAP) subsidies and various price support schemes in 2007.[26] The CAP accounts for roughly 42% of all agricultural support and 85% of the entire world's agricultural subsidies.[27] Let's look at how subsidies to tomato farmers in the EU have affected markets in West Africa. Diagrams I and II in

---

25. Anti-dumping duties have in fact been referred to as 'ordinary protection with a great public relations programme'. See McCulloch, *Trade liberalization and poverty*, p. 295.

26. See http://ec.europa.eu/budget/reform/library/contributions/p/20080415_P_42.pdf.

27. OECD report, number 46, August/September 2003 and Heritage Foundation at http://www.heritage.org/Research/TradeandForeignAid/BG1686.cfm.

Figure 4.2.11 illustrate the effects of a price support (i.e. a minimum price) scheme coupled to an export subsidy.

Diagram I shows that with free trade, the EU would be a net importer of $Q_1 \Leftrightarrow Q_2$ at P_{world_0}. When a minimum price is set at P_{min}, EU output increases and the resulting excess of $Q_D \Leftrightarrow Q_S$ would normally be purchased by the EU at a cost of $P_{min} \Leftrightarrow P_{world_0} \times Q_S \Leftrightarrow Q_D$ and subsequently

stockpiled.[28] However, agricultural producers in the EU are instead given an *export subsidy* of $P_{min} \Leftrightarrow P_{world_0}$, enabling EU farmers to sell the surplus in other – for the most part developing – countries at (and often below!) the world price. Since EU farmers receive P_{world_0} for the excess created by the minimum price, the cost to the EU is the blue area shown between P_{min} and P_{world_0}.

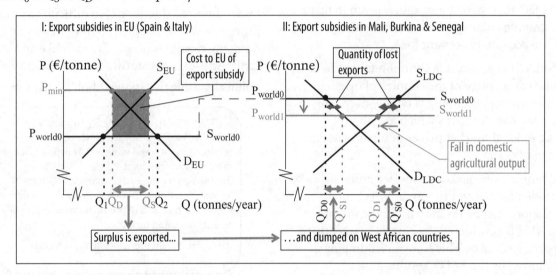

Figure 4.2.11 *Export subsidies on agricultural goods and dumping*

West African countries will have a number of advantages in producing tomatoes, being liberally endowed with the factors land and labour. Therefore, the world price of tomatoes will be higher than domestic market equilibrium and an exportable surplus will result, shown in diagram II as $Q'_{D_0} \Leftrightarrow Q'_{S_0}$. When the excess of $Q_D \Leftrightarrow Q_S$ (diagram I) is dumped on such countries as Mali, Burkina Faso and Senegal in Western Africa, the result is to depress the domestic market for tomatoes in these countries. 'Depress', shown in diagram II as the decrease in the world price from S_{world_0} to S_{world_1}, in this case means:

- That the EU is a large enough supplier on the global market to *force world prices downwards* from P_{world_0} to P_{world_1}.

- That Mali, Burkina Faso and Senegal are *less competitive* on the world market due to the decrease in the world price, and *lose exports* of $Q'_{D_0} \Leftrightarrow Q'_{S_1}$ and $Q'_{D_1} \Leftrightarrow Q'_{S_0}$.

In addition to the three points above, EU citizens will pay a far higher price for their tomatoes and tomato paste than is necessary; diagram I shows that EU consumption could be taking place at Q_2 and a price of P_{world_0} rather than at Q_D and P_{min}. When more efficient foreign producers of tomatoes lose market share as a direct result of trade barriers, it doesn't take a diagram to arrive at the conclusion that the combined costs of higher prices and taxpayer dues for EU citizens outweigh the benefits to domestic producers. This example is equally applicable to a great number of agricultural goods in the EU, tomato subsidies being but part of total agricultural subsidies. Milk, beef, sugar, grain, wine and olive oil are other notable produce which cost billions of euros in subsidies while raising the prices for EU citizens. Out of thousands of possible examples, I must mention that milk costs 76% and sugar 200% more than it should in the EU and that almost 50% of EU farmers' revenues for wheat come from CAP support.[29]

---

28. Note that it will be necessary for the EU to implement import restrictions, notably quotas and/or tariffs, in order to dissuade importers from buying the goods at a cheaper world price and selling it at the higher domestic price.

29. The Food and Agricultural Organisation at http://www.fao.org/DOCREP/003/X8731e/x8731e13.htm and the European non-government organisation Eurostep at http://www.eurostep.org/pubs/position/coherence/cap.htm.

Personal final comment: If you are reading this paragraph, it means that my editor trusts that you students can spot the difference between substantiated facts and the author's opinions. The *facts* are that the EU support schemes and export subsidies inflict upon EU taxpayers the cost of the subsidies and higher prices of agricultural goods, while destroying the livelihoods of thousands of impoverished citizens in developing countries around the world. My *personal* opinion is that those responsible for keeping the CAP policies in place are doing so in contradiction to the public commitments to human rights of their respective countries.

Anti-dumping tariffs in the EU and US

Easy to use, difficult to prove/disprove, allowed by the WTO and largely supported politically. One would think that anti-dumping measures would be a dream come true for protectionism and that the use of anti-dumping duties would be one of the more common methods of protectionism as more visible barriers such as tariffs are continuously lowered. Yes, this is exactly what has happened. Anti-dumping tariffs have increased enormously in the past 30 years, serving to replace some of the earlier (visible) tariffs. In fact, anti-dumping is now the protectionist method of choice. Between 1987 and 1997, close to 2,000 anti-dumping investigations (at the behest of domestic industries) were initiated – 37% of them by the US and EU alone. Studies show that anti-dumping tariffs are applied far more frequently than any reasonable economic analysis would warrant.[30]

One very high-profile round of dispute in international trade concerned the US imposition in 2001 of up to 30% anti-dumping tariffs on steel which the EU violently protested and which the WTO concomitantly found to be illegal in 2004, allowing the EU to impose retaliatory tariffs of $2.2 billion on US goods from March 2004 onwards. In December 2003, President Bush averted what started to look alarmingly like an all-out trade war by rescinding the tariffs.[31]

During the onset of the world financial/liquidity crisis in 2007, the WTO organisation reported a surge in anti-dumping investigations. During the first half of 2008, there was a 39% increase in initiations (e.g. anti-dumping complaints) by WTO members for the WTO to investigate alleged dumping. Turkey, USA, India and the EU were the top initiators.[32]

You will have noticed the strong bias in my use of examples, where anti-dumping policies involving the US and EU make up the lion's share. This is in no way accidental; the US and EU together accounted for over 51% of all existing anti-dumping regulations in place in 1996 – with the US at 311 separate anti-dumping rules in place versus the EU's 153.[33] As for the success of anti-dumping regulations imposed, 71% of anti-dumping claims in the EU and 80% of those in the US succeeded between 1980 and 1997. I must say that I was most surprised at how anti-dumping policies in the US *overwhelmingly* surpassed all other countries in the world and a few minutes of investigation provided the answer; two US laws – one from 1916 and one from 2000 – grant US firms not only the right to lodge complaints about dumping but also grants these American firms the proceeds of fines levied on firms found guilty of dumping. In other words, there is a massive incentive for domestic US firms to file grievances of being dumped upon by foreign firms. The WTO has ruled that the US legislation is in violation of trade rules but there has as yet been no compliance by the US.

---

30. McCulloch, *Trade liberalization and poverty*, p. 293.

31. BBC News at http://news.bbc.co.uk/1/hi/business/3291537.stm.

32. WTO: 2008 PRESS RELEASES. Press/542. 20 October 2008, 'Secretariat reports surge in new anti-dumping investigations'; see www.wto.org.

33. *Globalization*, p. 77.

POP QUIZ 4.2.2 ARGUMENTS FOR PROTECTIONISM

1 Compare the costs and benefits of using tariffs and subsidies as a method of protecting domestic industries.

2 Why might the 'infant industry argument' be considered a viable trade argument?

3 Criticise the argument that trade barriers can save domestic jobs.

4 Explain how a non-economic barrier to trade can limit imports.

5 When might protectionism be labelled a 'beggar-my-neighbour' policy?

6 Explain how trade barriers might be used to adjust the balance of payments.

Arguments against protectionism

©IBO 2003

The remainder of this chapter is partially a reiteration of the counter-arguments put forth above using real world examples to back up economic theory. Most of the arguments against protectionism centre on efficiency losses and higher prices, i.e. the allocative and welfare losses to society. Perhaps the most obvious example of damages inflicted on society by implementing trade barriers is the Great Depression in the 1930s. When US President Hoover signed the Smoot-Hawley tariff bill in 1930 in order to protect American jobs, average American tariffs increased to 53%. Most economists agree that this worsened a world economy already in serious trouble. The US was even then the world's largest importer and the bill severely hampered income in exporting nations – many of which were in desperate need of US dollars to pay off war debts. The bill sparked massive retaliatory tariffs from over 25 countries, setting off a tit-for-tat escalation of trade barriers. By 1933 world trade had fallen by approximately 25% and industrial output by 32%. The bill had no positive effect on American unemployment – 3 million people in the US were jobless in 1930 and 13 million by 1933.[34] Figure 4.2.12

shows how world trade shrank over the five-year period between 1929 and 1933.

As a more recent example, it has been calculated by the World Bank in 2001 that the welfare loss due to developed countries' trade barriers was $US43.1 billion in developing countries and $US65.1 billion in developed countries in 1995.[35] Two years later the World Bank estimated that highly realistic reductions in trade barriers could increase global income by somewhere between $US290 and $US520 billion a year – with considerably more than half of the boost in income going to developing countries. Successful tariff reductions could take some 140 million people above the poverty line by 2015 claims the Bank.[36] This is a rather serious indictment against recent surges in protectionism in developed countries.

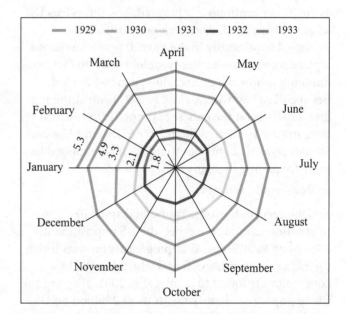

(Source: League of Nations World Economic Survey, 1932–33)

Figure 4.2.12 *Spiderweb of protectionism – world trade 1929–33 ($bn)*

At the time of writing (February 2009) there are some very frightening events unfolding in the international trade arena with the US at the forefront. The ongoing financial/liquidity crisis is causing old-fashioned job-saving protectionism of the 1930s type to rear its ugly head. A G20 meeting[37] in November 2008 resulted in promises not to raise existing or

---

34. *A world without walls*, Mike Moore, p. 27; National Center for Policy Analysis at http://www.ncpa.org/oped/bartlett/oct2999.html; and Canadian Dept. of Foreign Affairs and International Trade at http://www.dfait-maeci.gc.ca/ciw-cdm/wto1-en.asp.

35. World Bank: World Development Indicators at http://www.worldbank.org/data/wdi2001/pdfs/globallinks.pdf.

36. 'The Cancun challenge', *The Economist*, 4 September 2003.

37. The G20 is comprised of the eight largest industrialised countries plus eleven smaller industrialised countries and emerging market nations. See http://www.g20.org/about_index.aspx.

implement any new trade barriers – within a week both India and Russia raised tariffs on, respectively, cars and steel.[38]

In the US, the current trend is falling trade, increased import restrictions, and very distasteful elements of misguided patriotism: 'Buy American' addendums are being included in economic stimulus bills. One such bill passing through the US House of Representatives in January 2009 was a USD825 billion stimulus package which included a requirement that only US steel be used in any public works projects. A study by the Peterson Institute for International Economics estimates that this would create about 1,000 new jobs but cost the US far more in lost jobs due to retaliatory measures by other countries.[39] The European Union (EU) very quickly warned the US that the Buy American provisions would be in possible violation of WTO rules.

Inefficiency of resource allocation

©IBO 2003

The Multi-island Olive Grove

A few years ago on my Greek island, Sifnos, I hitched a ride with a very pleasant Greek gentleman in his 40s who was driving his jeep off to a rather remote spot. I tagged along and after 20 minutes of rough-riding on what essentially were donkey paths, we arrived at a cul-de-sac on a slope overlooking the sea. The Greek gentleman got out and started putting on rubberised overalls (it was 40°C in the shade!) and a backpack that looked like, well, a vacuum cleaner with a nasty spray nozzle attached – something right out of 'Ghostbusters'. He was on his way down to spray his newly planted olive trees and since he lived in Athens he came out only once a year and gave them a really good spraying – thus the heavy protective gear. It turned out that he had a number of plots on various islands where he had a few hundred olive trees.

Standing discretely upwind of him and his toxic backpack, I asked if it really made economic sense to have bits of land all over the Aegean Sea – especially for olives for which there was such a mountain of excess already. He laughed uproariously and then explained how olives were subsidised by the *tree*, not *per kilogram* of actual olives produced. It turned out that he had taken bank loans and bought up a bunch of out-of-the-way plots on various islands in order to

plant as many olive trees before impending changes in subsidy rules went into effect. The subsidies he collected for each tree more than made up the costs of servicing his loans and visiting various land plots for a yearly spraying of insecticide. He looked to pay off his loans in about 20 years, by which time he would be the owner of quite a few hectares of land. Not once did he mention actual olive or olive oil production.

Sub-optimal resource allocation

The above story is a somewhat extreme illustration of the often horrendous wastefulness and downright misuse of resources resulting from trade barriers – in this case subsidies. Recall that optimal resource allocation is using limited factors of production to create the best possible outcome for society – 'best' being defined as the point rendering the highest output at the lowest cost. No waste is present, i.e. no goods would be made without them being in demand. As such, when supply equals demand, the market has cleared and there is optimal allocative efficiency. At any other level of output, resource allocation will be sub-optimal.

When we enlarge the concept of 'society' to include trade partners, it is evident that any form of intervention in open markets in international trade will result in allocative losses. Refer to "How a tariff works" on page 408 and Figure 4.2.3 on page 411, the effects of an import quota for oranges, to see that tariffs and quotas both serve to put less efficient domestic resources to use rather than foreign. Trade barriers always mean that a portion of goods are being produced by suppliers which are not the most efficient – which means that resources are being squandered, leading to misallocation.

Other costs of trade barriers

In addition to being directly wasteful, tariffs and quotas have other economic costs attached, such as administration, enforcement and regulation costs. Thousands of civil servants are needed to process applications and send out payments. For example, in preparation for joining the EU in May 2004, the Polish bureaucracy expressed concern in having to hire an additional 4,000 workers simply to administrate the sending of payments to eligible farmers. As for the costs of enforcement, one could mention the costs of sending police officers out to olive groves to count olive trees as I've seen done in Spain.

---

38. 'Fare well, free trade', *The Economist,* 18 December 2008.
39. Dan DiMicco, chief executive of Nucor (a large US steel manufacturer) dismissed the report as 'complete garbage'. (See, for example, 'Steel-state lawmakers vow to save 'Buy American', *International Herald Tribune,* 4 February 2009.

Subsidies to domestic industries not only cost taxpayers billions every year but seriously distort production and reallocate resources to far less efficient producers. Subsidies are often used in conjunction with quotas and minimum price schemes – which serve to increase prices for domestic consumers rather than lower them, as seen in "Outside the box: Minimum price scheme in the EU and dumping on developing countries" on page 427. When more efficient foreign producers are disadvantaged by such trade barriers, the protectionist policies will have the effect of increasing domestic costs and/or domestic prices. In either case, the domestic economy moves away from the market clearing price with resultant sub-optimal resource allocation.

Storytime: Illuminating story by Frédéric Bastiat

One of the sharpest pens ever to slash a 'Z' across the chest of proponents of trade barriers was held by the brilliant French satirist Frédéric Bastiat (1801–51). Writing during the time of prevailing mercantilist trade philosophy, he used the protectionists' own arguments to drive his point home. By extending and exaggerating arguments in favour of trade barriers he was able to reach the most absurd but logical conclusions. His most famous text is a fictitious petition by French candle makers who demand protection from foreign competition. Here is an excerpt of that text:

We are suffering from the ruinous competition of a rival who apparently works under conditions so far superior to our own for the production of light that he is flooding the domestic market with it at an incredibly low price; for the moment he appears, our sales cease, all the consumers turn to him, and a branch of French industry whose ramifications are innumerable is all at once reduced to complete stagnation.

This rival, which is none other than the sun, is waging war on us so mercilessly we suspect he is being stirred up against us by perfidious Albion [= the lying British] particularly because he has for that haughty island a respect that he does not show for us.

We ask you to be so good as to pass a law requiring the closing of all windows, dormers, skylights, inside and outside shutters, curtains, casements, bull's-eyes, deadlights, and blinds -- in short, all openings, holes, chinks, and fissures through which the light of the sun is wont to enter houses, to the detriment of the fair industries with which, we are proud to say, we have endowed the country, a country that cannot, without betraying ingratitude, abandon us today to so unequal a combat. Be good enough, honourable deputies, to take our request seriously, and do not reject it without at least hearing the reasons that we have to advance in its support.

First, if you shut off as much as possible all access to natural light, and thereby create a need for artificial light, what industry in France will not ultimately be encouraged?

If France consumes more tallow, there will have to be more cattle and sheep, and, consequently, we shall see an increase in cleared fields, meat, wool, leather, and especially manure, the basis of all agricultural wealth.

If France consumes more oil, we shall see an expansion in the cultivation of the poppy, the olive, and rapeseed. These rich yet soil-exhausting plants will come at just the right time to enable us to put to profitable use the increased fertility that the breeding of cattle will impart to the land.

Our moors will be covered with resinous trees. Numerous swarms of bees will gather from our mountains the perfumed treasures that today waste their fragrance, like the flowers from which they emanate. Thus, there is not one branch of agriculture that would not undergo a great expansion.

The same holds true of shipping. Thousands of vessels will engage in whaling, and in a short time we shall have a fleet capable of upholding the honour of France and of gratifying the patriotic aspirations of the undersigned petitioners, chandlers, etc.

………………..[shortened]………………..

We anticipate your objections, gentlemen; but there is not a single one of them that you have not picked up from the musty old books of the advocates of free trade. We defy you to utter a word against us that will not instantly rebound against yourselves and the principle behind all your policy.

Will you tell us that, though we may gain by this protection, France will not gain at all, because the consumer will bear the expense?

(Source: http://bastiat.org/en/petition.html)

Outside the box:

Food for thought

- One of my students told the story of her family farm which received EU subsidies to plant rapeseed. The subsidies were granted on how many hectares were planted. (Note: 'planted' – not 'produced'.) In due course an EU inspector came by, counted the acreage, and left. Some time later the subsidy cheque arrived in the mail. Since thousands of other farmers around Europe were getting the same subsidy, the market had fallen through the floor and it was evidently far too costly to harvest and attempt to sell it on the market. Accordingly, entire fields of rapeseed were ploughed back into the ground as fertilizer, in order to grow another round of subsidised crops.

- The distribution of funds in the CAP is highly uneven; about 20% of EU farms receive approximately 70% of the payments and support. The main beneficiaries of agricultural subsidies in the EU are French farmers, who receive over $US10 billion annually – close to 20% of the entire EU budget.[40] This skewed distribution of subsidies is mirrored in the US, where two-thirds of farm subsidies are received by 10% of total recipients – many of them large multinational companies.[41]

- The United States Department of Agriculture (USDA) estimated in 2001 that the total cost to the American taxpayer in granting every single full-time farmer in the US a social safety net at a minimum of 185% of the national poverty level of income ($US32,652 for a family of four in 2001) would be slightly more than $US4 billion. Contrast this figure with the $US29.8 billion that was spent on American crop subsidy programs in 2000.[42]

- Total cotton subsidies in the US during 2001 were $US3.4 billion. This went to 25,000 cotton farmers, which is equal to $US136,000 per farmer – over four times the average income in the US. It costs 68 cents to produce a bale of cotton in the US – three times more than in, for example, Burkina Faso.[43]

This is horrendously inefficient. Basically, we could take all the money used for agricultural protectionism in developed countries and buy a small island, say Manhattan or Crete, and put all the farmers of the developed world there. The fall in agricultural output would be made up for by imports from the developing world. With the money saved, we would simply pay the developed country farmers to remain on the island and not get involved in agriculture. We could probably pay them more than they were earning by farming. Thus, farmers get more money, citizens' tax burden and food/textile bills fall, and developing countries will increase their incomes by hundreds of billions of US dollars thereby enabling them to buy many of the innovative new products invented by entrepreneurial ex-farmers in Manhattan and Crete. Sound like a plan?

 Storytime: First-class cows

The total cost of agricultural subsidies in the 29 OECD countries in 1999 was $US361 billion. This was enough to send all 56 million OECD cows 1.2 times around the world on first class flights. If the cows were willing to accept business class, each bovine traveller would have $US2,800 in pocket money left over to spend at the tax-free shops along the way.[a] And we worry about cows being mad.

a. Taken from *Till världskapitalismens försvar,* Norberg, p. 141.

40. 'The EU Common Agricultural Policy', *The Guardian*, 26 June 2003, and 'EU Common Agricultural Policy', *Reuters*, 26 June 2003.
41. 'How Farm Subsidies Became America's Largest Corporate Welfare Program', Brian Riedl; *Backgrounder* 1520, 25 February 2002 at http://www.heritage.org/Research/Budget/BG1520.cfm.
42. 'A Safety Net for Farm Households', U.S. Department of Agriculture, *Agriculture Outlook*, January-February 2000, pp. 19-24.
43. 'A great yarn', *The Economist,* December 18 2003; and 'Brazil case may break stalemate on trade', *IHT,* 24 January 2004.

Costs of long-run reliance on protectionist methods ©IBO 2003

When countries implement barriers to trade in accordance with any of the above arguments, there is seldom an 'Expiration date' attached. All too often, protectionist measures become long-lived and virtually permanent. Apart from the direct monetary costs to governments/taxpayers and the allocative losses, there are a number of **dynamic efficiency costs** which arise behind protectionist walls. Many of these costs are similar to those that might arise in monopolies – and indeed trade barriers create monopoly outcomes in domestic markets on a macro scale. The long-run costs of industries dependent on protectionism are summarised in three points:

- **Misallocation costs:** Trade barriers cannot in the long run save non-competitive (sunset) industries from competition. By imposing tariffs on imports and/or subsidising domestic firms, the government is simply delaying a process of reallocation at great cost to society in terms of alternative output. Protectionism creates overproduction – often at higher prices to consumers – and inhibits inefficient firms from reallocating resources to other sectors.

- **Disincentive costs:** When domestic firms come to rely on protectionism, the propensity to improve productivity is diminished. Ultimately other – non protected countries – will increase productivity and lower production costs to the point where they will be competitive even facing a tariff. Additionally, protected industries will have a lower level of research and development (R&D) spending and technological innovation due to lack of international competition. The secondary effects are that industries in non-protected industries will ultimately have higher costs compared to foreign firms, losing competitive edge and furthering the productivity gap between domestic and foreign firms.

- **Forward linkage effects:** When imported raw materials and components become more costly for firms using these inputs, the production cost moves forward down the line towards end-users. For example, when a tariff is put on steel, there is an increase in the price of steel and therefore an increase in the cost of producing trucks → costs for transportation firms rise → cost of shipping Widgets rises → price of Widgets rises.

- The forward linkage effects of protectionism can in fact *cost* jobs rather than *save* them. When manufacturers of cars, washing machines and refrigerators lose customers – both domestically and abroad – there will be layoffs. Several studies in the US have shown how tariffs on imported steel would save steel jobs *at the expense* of jobs in steel consuming industries. Steel consumers outnumber steel producers by 40 to 1 and each steel job saved would cost between 8 and 10 jobs elsewhere down the line of manufacturing.[44]

Increased prices of goods and services to consumers ©IBO 2003

No matter how one slices the cake, one piece will fall on the floor; every form of protectionism has a price tag which is ultimately borne by consumers/taxpayers/citizens. Tariffs and quotas cost consumers via increased domestic prices directly, and subsidies indirectly via taxes. Philippe Legrain, an economist and free trade advocate, estimates that American citizens have paid about $US174 billion in total for steel protection between 1969 and 1999 – $US151 in higher steel prices plus an additional $US23 billion in taxes for steel subsidies.[45]

Another extreme example is in textiles and clothing, where the cost of protectionism (tariffs, quotas and subsidies) to American consumers is estimated at $US24 billion annually, preventing the loss of 170,000 jobs – a cost to US taxpayers of $US140,000 per textile job.[46]

While the most obvious examples of how protectionism raises consumer prices on both domestic and imported goods are to be found in tariffs and quotas (refer again to "How a tariff works " on page 408 and Figure 4.2.3 on page 411, the effects of an import quota for oranges), many other forms of protectionism render the same outcome. When domestic suppliers can rely on various forms of administrative, technical and legislative barriers to imports, there will be a strong incentive for domestic firms to increase their profit margins by heavy mark-ups (= price increases) on retail sales. My personality being such that I am prone to opening eggs with a sledgehammer, I will exemplify using possibly the most extreme example: Japan. The domestic price in

---

44. See 'Romancing big steel', *The Economist,* 14 February 2002; and *A world without walls,* Mike Moore, p. 30.
45. *Open World...,* Legrain, p. 34.
46. Irwin, p. 93.

Japan (over and above world market price) for rice is 734%. Allowing for a reasonable profit for an importer, the average Japanese family is thus spending close to seven times more on this staple food than is necessary. Similarly, the Japanese above-world-market price on wheat is 477% and on radios and televisions 607%. Guess what the tariff level on these goods is. Zero percent. For a number of other goods, the above-world-market price is considerably higher than the tariff, for example, tee and coffee prices are 718% higher yet tariff levels are 12%. The above world market-price on cosmetics is 661% (2% tariff) and on gasoline 229% (5.5% tariff). The estimated total cost of protection to Japanese consumers is an estimated $US110 billion a year – 3.8% of national income.[47]

CAP – The ~~Catastrophic~~ Common Agricultural Policy

One of the most hotly debated elements within the European Union's common market is the system of agricultural policies operating under the Common Agricultural Policy, the CAP. The CAP was implemented in 1962 in order to guarantee a minimum level of income to farmers and secure the availability of agricultural produce. The CAP has increasingly come under fire primarily for three reasons.

Firstly, it is **allocatively inefficient**, by creating incentives for EU producers to overproduce goods – many of which can be produced more cost efficiently elsewhere. There is growing agreement within the EU that the system has become too large and cumbersome to be efficient – and far too costly.

Secondly, the system inflicts large **welfare losses** on society via higher prices and decreased consumption, as consumers basically pay twice for agricultural goods in many cases; once via taxes and then via higher prices kept artificially aloft. Costing some $US46 billion per year – half the annual EU budget – and going to the 4% of the labour force which is involved in farming, the result for EU citizens is a 44% increase in food prices.

Thirdly, the system's staunch protectionist practices are **destroying markets in developing countries** – primarily northern Africa. It is widely acknowledged that the EU position on agricultural support severely hampers the ongoing WTO talks, the Doha Round, which aims to limit protectionist measures which damage developing countries.[48]

Thus, in an EU agricultural summit in Luxembourg, June 2002, Franz Fischler, the EU farm commissioner proposed a series of far-reaching, even radical, reforms which met with massive resistance – primarily from the French who are the largest single benefactor of agricultural subsidies. The final somewhat watered down result was primarily the de-linking of subsidies from output levels in order to reduce excess supply, and reducing a number of subsidies. The proposals should take place starting in 2005 and be fully implemented (France having been granted exceptions) by 2007.[49]

The cost effect of protected imports on export competitiveness ©IBO 2003

It is quite possible that domestic production suffers from increasing costs and thus decreased competitiveness due to protectionism. There are two ways this can happen.

Firstly, there is the **forward linkage effect** given above, where higher domestic production costs will hamper the domestic economy's ability to compete on international markets. An economics adage from the US in the 1980s read; 'A tax on Nippon Steel is a tax on General Motors!' What happened was that the steel industry in America lobbied for tariffs on cheap imported steel from Japan. When such tariffs were in place, domestic American suppliers were able to increase their prices of steel – which increased the cost of producing automobiles in America. Guess what consumers around the world did? Yes; they increased their purchases of Japanese *cars*. The forward linkage effect of higher input prices due to tariffs cost the US economy far more in loss of both domestic and foreign sales of cars than was gained by slapping tariffs on imported steel. In extreme cases, the production cost disadvantage will lead firms to *relocate* production outside protectionist walls, i.e. to another country. For example, high US tariffs on sugar – a key ingredient – caused one of America's largest food producers, Kraft, to move production of the classic LifeSavers candy from the US to Canada.[50]

Secondly, the protectionist policies **shield domestic producers from competition** which lowers there ability to compete with more open economies which are forced to forever enhance productivity, improve products and innovate. Domestic suppliers

---

47. Perloff, p. 300.
48. *Freedom, Development, Free Trade and Global Governance,* Cambridge University Press 2003, p. 181.
49. *Bästa jordbrukspolitiken – ingen, Dagens Nyheter,* 31 March 2003; and International Centre for Trade and Sustainable Development at http://www.ictsd.org/weekly/03-07-03/story1.htm.
50. *A world without walls,* Mike Moore, p. 47.

allowed to lead 'the quiet life' sheltered behind protectionist walls will have a marked tendency to increase prices domestically and this abnormal profit will ultimately build in inefficiency. Lack of competitive forces will also create a degree of R&D lethargy and unwillingness to invest in new

technology. Taken together, domestic firms will see a continued erosion of cost advantages towards foreign firms under the false comfort provided by trade barriers, as competing firms in free-trade economies continuously strive to become more efficient, cut costs and gain scale benefits.

Outside the box:
Final rumination on trade barriers

In light of the considerable economic and welfare costs involved in trade barriers, it seems to be something of a lunacy to have so many forms of protectionism in place. Few of the arguments upholding protectionist policies are regarded by economists as viable in terms of economic welfare, so why are countries given to imposing tariffs, quotas and many other forms of barriers? Even better, why are so many obviously senseless policies implemented by very sensible policy makers? Quite frankly, I really don't know – and it's something to which I've given considerable thought and study.

In a dark moment I think: Domestic firms, labour groups and other groups have a vested interest in protecting themselves from foreign competition. These groups are well organised and have strong well-funded lobby groups which have long since been able to sway politicians in their favour in spite of the fact that these groups are in a minority. Populism, vote-winning and simply staying in power are powerful incentives for politicians to listen to anti-trade slogans, which ultimately has resulted in an 'anti-trade litany' which few dare to dispute – at least in public. Furthermore, history has shown how easy it is to gain political power by pandering to the unfortunate undertows of xenophobia (= fear of foreigners/ things foreign) and nationalism.

I also wonder if the media is not propagating the myth of 'harmful trade' by exploiting peoples' fear and ignorance. It takes 10 seconds to put forward the argument that jobs are being lost to foreign countries and that domestic citizens will be worse off. This provides a wonderful 20-second sound-bite on TV and a splashy newspaper-selling headline that 12-year-olds can understand. Explaining the theory of comparative advantage, on the other hand, takes time and some real intellectual effort to grasp and accept – and doesn't make much of a story either in terms of sensationalism. So when television stations set programming, the 30 minutes of evening news will give 45 seconds to the

story '1,500 jobs lost to Poland/China/Vietnam' while 'How everyone ultimately gains from trade' will not get the minimum two hours of TV network time needed to explain it.

In a bright moment I think: Most of us ordinary people quietly vote for trade every time we add to our marginal utility in selecting from a wide variety of imported goods and for us the benefits are quite evident. There's a wonderful Swedish adage; *Hälsan tiger still*, which is a bit tricky to translate but in essence reads 'Health lies quietly still'. The millions of consumers around the world who see immense increases in their standard of living and quality of life due to trade will have little need to manifest this in media proclamations or 'Thankful Consumers for Trade' organisations. They have stated their case with their wallets.

I then posit that most of the anti-trade and anti-globalisation rhetoric has its origin in various interest groups who stand to be disadvantaged by trade, such as people losing jobs when firms move abroad and firms that lose revenue and market share to foreign competitors. I wonder if a great deal of the vocal anti-trade protests in fact aren't simply due to well organised and well funded interest groups voicing opinions which a vast majority of people wouldn't actually sympathise with given the opportunity to seriously weigh the pros and cons of trade. Perhaps protectionist tendencies are allowed to get a strong foothold in trade policy simply because a silent majority is not voicing an opinion.

In my brightest moment I think: Thank God for my students and colleagues around the world! What better way to set a few shocking wrongs to right than by a sound education in economics. Please, study hard; get excellent grades; go to university and then get into a position of power where you can influence society for the better. Oh, and pay lots of taxes so that my colleagues and I get ample public/merit goods and pensions. I figure we deserve it.

Preparing for exams

Short answer questions (10 marks each)

1 How might a country improve its comparative advantage by producing manufactured goods?

2 Explain how a country might use trade barriers in order to improve the current account in the balance of payments.

3 'Trade is much freer today since tariffs have fallen drastically in the past 50 years.' Discuss this statement.

4 Explain why subsidies to domestic firms act as a trade barrier.

5 How can trade barriers for agricultural goods in developed countries affect developing countries?

6 What factors might influence the competitiveness of a firm operating in export markets?

7 Use a diagram to illustrate how a tariff causes resource misallocation.

Extended response questions (25 marks each)

1 a What is meant by 'dumping'? (10 marks)

   b Why have anti-dumping tariffs become so common and how might manufacturers in low cost countries defend themselves against dumping accusations? (15 marks)

2 a What are the possible advantages of free trade? (10 marks)

   b In light of these advantages, why do so many barriers to trade exist? (15 marks)

3 a Identify the ways in which an economy can limit imports. (10 marks)

   b Argument for and against such policies. (15 marks)

4 a Distinguish between the terms of trade and the balance of trade for a country. (10 marks)

   b How might a country use trade barriers and the exchange rate to affect both the terms of trade and the balance of trade. (15 marks)

Economic integration

4.3

CONTENTS

ECONOMIC INTEGRATION ©IBO 2003

This section looks into the various ways in which economies – which is to say countries/firms/institutions/people – join together and become interdependent, i.e. economic integration. This process is nothing new historically, but the speed and breadth of integration has increased tremendously during the past 30 or so years.

Globalisation ©IBO 2003

Globalisation is when a European telecommunications firm builds a plant in Indonesia to manufacture components for products assembled in the same firm's Korglobalisean subsidiary for sale in the US. As firms around the world increasingly look for new markets and lower cost manufacturing, the world is ever more woven together. Globalisation is also the 'fruits' of the above integration in production; the toothpaste and soft-drink selection on the shelves of your local supermarket will in many cases be the same as those on the shelves of your IB schoolmates all over the world. Many of you will work for foreign companies and often as not in foreign countries as well. Globalisation is also when your savings go into shares registered on stock markets around the world and your state pension benefits come from international stock market funds as well. In short, your income, consumption and saving will have taken on a much wider macro definition as flows of profits, spending and saving increasingly arise due to trade and international investment.

A commonly used 'key indicator' of the level of globalisation is the extent to which firms set up subsidiaries and manufacturing companies abroad. This form of direct ownership and control is called **foreign direct investment** (FDI) and increased dramatically during the last two decades of the 20th century. Figure 4.3.1 illustrates how FDI flows worldwide have increased by a factor of 25.

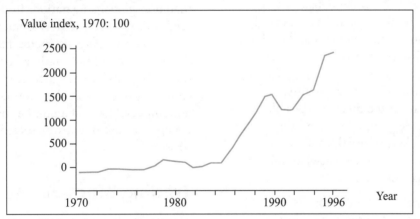

(Source: UNCTAD (1997), World Investment Report (selected years), Geneva UNCTAD)

Figure 4.3.1 *Global trends in foreign direct investment (FDI)*

Globalisation is essentially the ability of people, firms, organisations and institutions to operate on a global basis. It is therefore not a 'thing' but rather a process. As barriers to *trade* are slowly eradicated there will be increased movement of goods and changing tastes in different countries.[1] When *immigration, tax* and *labour* laws increasingly enable citizens of economically integrated regions such as the EU to work, study and collect social benefits in other member countries, there is increased movement of people. Removing *restrictions on capital flows* means that both firms and citizens can seek out the highest rate of return on savings and investment. Taken together, globalisation involves not only the spread of goods, technology, investment and labour, but also ideas, customs, tastes, and preferences.

---

1. During a stint of teaching at the Oxford Study Courses in 2004, I asked my British colleagues if we could go out and have a traditional English meal. We did – Indian curry. Ah, that sly British sense of humour.

> **Globalisation:** Globalisation involves the spread of economic, social and cultural ideas across the world, and the growing uniformity between different places that results from this spread. It has come about as a result of the increased integration of national economies through the rapid growth of international trade, investment and capital flows, made possible by rapid improvements in technology.

'Globalization' or 'globalisation'?! Two broad sides of globalisation

Few terms from economics evoke such powerful and mixed emotions today as the term 'globalisation'. Even the spelling is value-laden; using a 'Z' – globalization – in accordance with American spelling has become something of a statement in itself, as many debaters and commentators focus on the dominance of US multinational companies on the global market. In fact, Mike Moore, ex-Director General of the World Trade Organisation (WTO) and staunch free-trade advocate, points out that anti-globalisation is often synonymous with anti-Americanism.[2] The wider debate is about whether globalisation is good, bad or just plain ugly. The demonstrations in Seattle 1999 set the stage for a series of loud – and all-too-often violent – protests against increasing globalisation; Gothenburg, Genoa, Prague, Davos to name a few. While the different groups of protesters are far too diverse to be able to lump together as a single group, there are a number of points which broadly characterise the anti-globalisation 'movement' and the somewhat quieter opposing 'pro-globalisation' camp.

Anti-globalisation: On the anti-globalisation side, a good deal of the rhetoric focuses on how large *multinational companies* (MNCs) are increasingly powerful entities which can freely move capital, production and profits in pursuit of the highest possible rate of return. International firms can easily move operations to low-cost labour countries, which have beneficial (= low) taxes on company profits. Furthermore, MNCs have an incentive to place subsidiaries in countries with lax or non-existent *environmental and labour standards*, resulting in the exploitation of labour in such countries. The result of this global freedom of movement empowers MNCs at the expense of local consumer and political interests.

The famous American consumer advocate and anti-globalisationist, Ralph Nader, has characterised globalisation as 'a subordination of human rights, [and] democracy rights to the imperatives of global trade and investment'.[3]

Pro-globalisation: Globalisation creates jobs and enables *increased income* while *spreading knowledge* and *technology* in the process. The assertion that global companies are becoming as powerful as governments is highly exaggerated since governments make laws which firms must abide by – all the while being subject to media and consumer scrutiny. There is little empirical evidence that multinational companies relocate to countries with the lowest labour, tax and environmental standards and even less evidence that developing countries compete with each other in a 'race to the bottom'. On the contrary, there is strong evidence that inward flows of foreign investment to developing countries can be linked to improved working conditions, higher wages and increased tax revenues for host countries. Countries which have opened up to *foreign investment* – China, South Korea and India for example – have been more successful than non-globalising nations in terms of both economic growth and development. As for *environmental concerns*, increasing integration within the framework of international organisations such as the WTO in its role as a mediator in international trade conflicts (for example the US versus Mexico tuna/dolphin case) has put a number of issues on the table which can subsequently be solved via international treaties.

Trading blocs ©IBO 2003

A most visible aspect of the ongoing process of economic integration in the world today is the many different trading blocs which have arisen over the past 30 to 40 years. The WTO had 324 **Regional Trade Agreements** (**RTAs**) registered in 2008, and the expectation is close to 400 by 210.[4] The enormous impact of these RTAs can be seen in the increasing proportion of intra-regional trade taking place. In 2002, the two largest RTAs, EU and NAFTA, accounted for more than one-third of the world's exports, shown in Table 4.3.1 on page 441.

---

2. Moore, p. 20.
3. Moore, p. 63.
4. *International Trade Statistics*, WTO 2007, and http://www.wto.org/english/tratop_e/region_e/region_e.htm.

Table 4.3.1 *Intra-regional trade of major regional trade agreements (RTAs), 2002*

Billion $, %	Intra-trade	
RTA	Value	Share in World exports
EU (15)	1509	24.1
NAFTA (3)	626	10.0
AFTA (10)	97	1.6
CEFTA (7)	19	0.3
MERCOSUR (4)	10	0.2
ANDEAN (5)	5	0.1
Total	**2266**	**36.3**

(Source: *International Trade Statistics*, table 9, WTO 2003, p. 16)

Overview of economic integration

Integration is more of a process than a final stage. Table 4.3.2 illustrates six stages of increasing economic integration. I include a few examples of each stage, going into further depth in stages II to IV below.

Table 4.3.2 *Stages of integration*

Stage	I: Preferential trading area	II: Free trade area	III: Customs union	IV: Common market	V: Economic & monetary union	VI: Full integration
Type of agreement	Reduced tariff levels for selected countries	Zero tariffs on selected goods. Each country keeps its own tariffs towards non-members	Zero tariffs on goods between members and a common tariff towards other countries	Free movement of goods, services, capital and labour between members	Fixed exchange rates or single currency.	Harmonisation of tax laws, social systems, and federative/ 'supranational' state
Example	Lomé /Cotonou Agreement between the EU and African, Caribbean and Pacific (ACP) countries	North American Free Trade Agreement – NAFTA	EEC (EU) prior to 1993	European Union (EU)	European Monetary Union (EMU) in the EU	For example, the German and US federal system
Difference from previous stage	Tariffs are selectively lowered	Tariffs are removed rather than lowered	Setting of a common external tariff (CET)	The 'four freedoms' of movement above result in convergence in taxes, laws and social welfare systems	Convergence in monetary and fiscal policies. (16 EMU members of the EU 27)	Centralised economic, political and legislative power of government

Free trade areas (FTAs) ©IBO 2003

When a group of countries sign an agreement whereby tariffs and quotas are removed between signatories, i.e. member countries, while keeping individual tariffs/quotas towards non-members in place, a **free trade area** has been constructed. While seemingly a straightforward method to encourage and increase trade, the proliferation of FTAs has resulted in a number of criticisms of the subsequent *exclusion of non-members* – notably from developing countries which frequently are disadvantaged.

> **Free trade area**: A free trade area arises when a group of countries remove tariffs and quotas between themselves, while retaining the right to set tariffs/quotas towards non-members.

Figure 4.3.2 shows the progression of three countries, **A**, **B** and **C**. (To simplify, we assume that the same tariff level is applied to *all* goods entering each country.) Notice that while all three countries have different tariff levels towards each other and the 'outside world', each country has the same rate for all countries. Country A has a tariff of 7% on goods

coming from B, C and other countries; Country B has a 9% tariff and C a 5% tariff. This is in keeping with one of the key rules of the *World Trade Organisation's* (WTO) policy of non-discrimination, notably manifested in the MFN – the **most favoured nation clause** (= legal paragraph), which states that any WTO member (153 nations in December 2008) which lowers a tariff for another country on certain goods must grant all other member nations the same tariff as the most favoured nation. Thus, in setting a 5% tariff on goods from Country A, Country C has had to set a maximum 5% tariff towards all other countries.

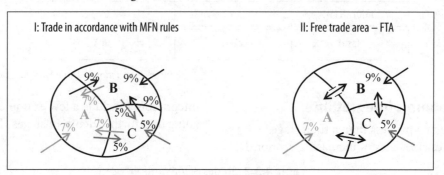

Figure 4.3.2 *Constructing a free trade area – FTA*

In forming a free trade area, the three countries remove tariffs and quotas between themselves – but retain the right to set individual external tariffs towards non-members. (Note that the WTO rules allow for such exceptions from the general rule of non-discrimination.[5]) Figure 4.3.2 diagram II illustrates how trade flows freely between members yet each of the three FTA members keep the same external tariff.

Implications of a FTA

There are several implications of this arrangement:

- Firstly, there will be an incentive to trade more within the FTA and as a result **increase intra-FTA trade**.

- Secondly, governments of member countries are likely to experience a **reduction in tariff revenues** when overall trade flows increasingly are between non-tariff countries within the FTA.

- Thirdly, there will be an **increase in economic welfare** amongst members as prices of goods fall and efficiency losses are reduced.

- Fourthly, a larger tariff-free market can create long run **dynamic benefits** arising from larger markets

and increased competition, such as benefits of scale and spread of technology.

- Fifthly, countries outside the FTA might in fact be more efficient in the production of certain goods but these **non-members will be disadvantaged by the tariffs**, which would results in a degree of misallocation. (HL: See "Trade diversion" on page 449.)

Local content requirements (rules of origin)

Ever used a friend's membership card in a video rental chain to get a better deal on renting a film? This is similar to the problem which faces members of a FTA; there is an incentive for producers outside the FTA (see Figure 4.3.2 diagram II) to avoid the highest tariffs by bringing in goods via **Country C** and then re-exporting to **Countries A** and **B** (also known as trade deflection).

Say that cars produced outside the FTA are destined for **Country B** but are brought in via **Country C** in order to pay 5% tariffs rather than 9%. A $US15,000 car would then cost $US15,750 in **Country B** rather than $US16,350 when paying the full 9% tariff in Country B (discounting additional profit margins and

---

5. This is in all probability due to the difficulties arising in a rather tricky issue: If Countries A and B create some form of political/legal entity, e.g. a 'United States of A-B', then trade becomes a domestic issue and not subject to WTO regulation. The tricky issue is how to define a political or legal entity?! The WTO leaves this alone by allowing countries to establish FTAs which in fact are highly discriminatory towards other WTO countries.

administrative/transport costs). **Country C** would gain tariff revenue at **Country B**'s expense. The response by FTA members is to put a **tariff on goods which are re-exported** – commonly so that the final price of the good equals what would have been the case if the normal tariff rate of the destination country had been applied. Thus, the solution in this example is to put a re-export tariff of 3.8% on all cars coming into **Country C** from **Country B**. ($US15,750 × 1.038 = $US16,350.)

However, recall that goods are tariff-free if they are *produced within* the FTA! Non-FTA firms will respond to re-export taxes by setting up simple assembly plants in Country C and then importing the cars in pieces and large components. The car is then 'manufactured' in Country C and avoids re-export duties when exported to Countries A and B. Thus the FTA will have to implement yet another set of rules, **local content rules**, which set a minimum requirement on the value-added of final goods within the FTA. For example, NAFTA (see below) has a requirement that 62.5% of the content of any automobile sold in the US from Mexico must come from within the FTA.[6]

As free trade areas become increasingly common, there is talk of 'fortress Europe', 'walled-in North America', etc. When countries join RTAs there is a risk of international trade in fact becoming regional, with increasingly complex bilateral trade agreements between RTAs becoming the norm. There is increasing debate as to whether RTAs act as 'hubs' in creating global free trade or if they serve to undermine the intentions of the WTO in creating truly free trade in the world. Part of the discussion inevitably deals with foreign direct investment, as exporting countries which face regional trade barriers have increasingly responded by exporting factories, i.e. *foreign direct investment* – rather than the goods themselves in order to tunnel under RTA tariff walls.

A little depth:
Other Regional Economic Associations (REAs)

- **APEC** – Asia-Pacific Economic Cooperation: One of the largest RTAs in the world and potentially the largest FTA, comprising 21 member countries – from wealthy countries such as Japan, US, Canada and Australia to developing countries such as Chile, Peru, Indonesia and Vietnam. As yet APEC has not totally dismantled tariffs and quotas, but the aim is to have made the step to a fully-fledged FTA by 2010. The countries in APEC will together account for some 60% of world output.
(See http://www.apecsec.org.)

- **ASEAN** – Association of South East Asian Nations: This 10 member organisation overlaps APEC as many of the members belong to both. ASEAN is primarily comprised of developing countries – Cambodia, Indonesia, Thailand and Vietnam to name a few. Tariff levels have been preferentially lowered between members and the aim is to create a complete free trade area, the Asian Free Trade Area – AFTA, for the original six countries by 2010 and by 2015 for the remaining four.
(See http://aseansec.org.)

- **MERCOSUR**: This South American customs union consists of 10 countries; the founding four members Argentina, Brazil, Uruguay, Paraguay; Venezuela (pending ratification [= confirmation] for full membership) and associate members Bolivia, Chile, Columbia, Ecuador and Peru. A common external tariff was implemented for most goods in 1995. Trade has increased a great deal between members as a result of tariff reductions but also highlighted the results of decreasing trade between members and non-members.
(See http://www.mercosur.org.)

---

6. NAFTA articles, article 403 at http://www.nafta-sec-alena.org/DefaultSite/legal/index_e.aspx?articleid=116#A403.

Case study: The North American Free Trade Agreement

There are few examples which highlight the issues of Regional Trade Agreements in starker colours than the **North American Free Trade Agreement**[a], between Mexico, USA and Canada which was created in 1994. The area has over 360 million citizens and over $US1 trillion in GDP – both figures roughly the same as the EU's. As for the level of economic integration, tariffs between Canada and the US were successively removed by 2000, but complete free trade with Mexico will not take place until 2009 – primarily due to the two northern members fears of their agricultural markets being flooded by cheap Mexican produce.

The creation and results of NAFTA are under continuous debate. Initial – and continuing – **opposition to the treaty** came from both left and right, environmentalists and 'smoke stack' industries, and even pro- and anti-globalisation groups. Perhaps the most memorable criticism was put forward in 1993 by then presidential hopeful Ross Perot, who claimed that the free trade agreement would result in a 'giant sucking sound' as jobs left the US in favour of far cheaper labour in Mexico. In addition to the loss of jobs, the poor of Mexico would inevitably be exploited while poor environmental standards there would attract high-polluting firms in an environmental race to the bottom. **Proponents** stated pretty much the opposite: jobs would instead be created in the US and Canada while consumers would benefit greatly as each member country exploited comparative advantages. Workers in Mexico would benefit from increased incomes and improved working conditions and overall intra-FTA trade would increase economic growth and development while decreasing poverty levels. Inward flows of FDI to Mexico would enable better use of resources and create positive technological and knowledge spin-off effects.

The outcome of the first decade is a mixed bag indeed and figures can support both sides pretty much equally. Proponents of NAFTA point to Mexico's 225% increase in exports and that this accounted for more than 50% of Mexico's real GDP growth during the first 10 years. Trade between the countries has more than doubled in the same period, from $US306 billion to $US621 billion. The 'giant sucking sound' was never heard in America, as US exports to Mexico and Canada went from $US142 billion to $US 263 billion and US manufacturing output increased by 44% from 1994 to 2000.

In addition, Americans in manufacturing increased their real wages at twice the rate during NAFTA's first 10 years than they had during the preceding decade. Mexico's real GDP per capita would have been an estimated 4% to 5% lower without NAFTA by 2002 and there is little evidence of any adverse effects on Mexican working conditions or wages – in fact, wages are considerably higher in sectors exposed to export markets.

On the other hand, point out NAFTA's detractors, there has been no net addition of US jobs to speak of and in fact there has been a net loss of 110,000 US manufacturing jobs per year between 1994 and 2000. And while growth in the US and Canada has been impressive, Mexico has had several periods of zero and even declining growth, notably in 1994/95 and again in 2001 – real wages in Mexico took over 8 years to recover from the mid-1990s economic crisis. American opponents of NAFTA point to the over 170% increase in FDI in Mexico and over 430% in Canada during the 1990s to show how firms are relocating production outside of the US which will cost more jobs in the long run. As for economic growth, both the US and Mexico have experienced widening gaps in income between the poorest and richest 10% of the population, with an estimated 15 to 25% of the increased inequality resulting directly from increased trade. Finally, there has been growing discontent amongst the rural poor in Mexico, as small scale farmers are marginalised due to the increase in agri-business orientated agriculture and large imports of American corn.

The plan of bringing about a Free Trade Area of the Americas (FTAA) encompassing NAFTA and 31 countries from South America and the Caribbean has been debated since 1994 and is still being debated 14 years later. At the time of writing, February 2008, the official website no longer exists.

---

a. See NAFTA homepage at http://www.nafta-sec-alena.org; The *Fraser Institute* at http://oldfraser.lexi.net/public; Free Trade Area of the Americas (FTAA) at http://www.ftaa-alca.org; Free trade on trial, *The Economist,* 30 December 2003; *NAFTA: Positive for Mexico but not enough,* World Bank at http://web.worldbank.org/WBSITE/EXTERNAL/TOPICS/TRADE/; Jeffrey J. Schott, *Prospects for Free Trade in the Americas, Institute for International Economics,* 2001 at www.iie.org.6.

Customs unions ©IBO 2003

When a stage of economic integration is adopted by which a *common external tariff* (CET) is set for member countries, a **customs union** has been created. These unified tariff levels solve the problem of re-exports, since any one country in the union will have the same tariff on goods coming from non-member countries. The CET also creates a need for far greater convergence, since different tax rates on goods need to be harmonised across the board. Thus, one could say that free trade areas are politically uncomplicated and administratively complex (due to re-export and rules of origin agreements), customs unions are administratively simpler but more politically complex.

> **Customs union**: A regional economic association where tariffs and quotas have been eliminated and common external tariffs and quotas are applied to member countries.

The tariff effects of a customs union are shown in Figure 4.3.3 on page 446 diagrams I and II. Positing that our fictitious FTA moves to this next step of economic integration, the three countries A, B and C agree on a *common outer tariff* towards non-members – here an average of the three tariff rates. This stage is best exemplified by the **EU** – the **EEC** prior to 1995, which came into being in 1958; the 1957 **Treaty of Rome** spelt out the phased elimination of all tariffs and quotas within the union and identical such barriers outwards. This was completed by 1987. (See Case study: "Brief history of the European Union (EU)" on page 448.)

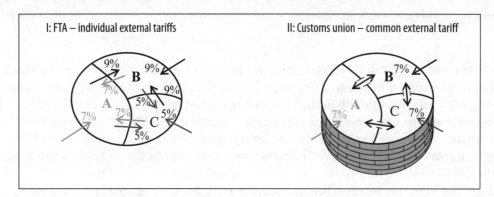

Figure 4.3.3 *From a free trade area to a customs union*

Figure 4.3.3 illustrates once again how *trade might both increase and be diverted*; Country C will see increased trade with fellow members – but possibly at the expense of diminished imports of lower cost goods from trade partners who previously met tariffs of 5% but now meet a 7% tariff (diagram II). (HL will study this **trade creation** and **trade diversion** in greater depth.) A customs union is somewhat like an 'infant common market' or 'common market lite', in that all goods and services may be moved freely between member states free of tariffs and quotas.

Note that there is no textbook definition of a customs union or a common market. Yet a clear distinction can be made here; a customs union may be said to deal with the obliteration of visible trade barriers on goods and services but not on technical, environmental and other 'invisible' barriers. Another notable difference would be that a customs union would have limited freedom of movement for capital and labour while a common market would have total freedom of factors of production.

Common markets ©IBO 2003

When countries agree on moving towards market integration, eliminating not only visible trade barriers on goods, but all hindrances in the flow of goods, services, investment, labour and other factors, a common market is established. A common market is complex and entails far greater depth in integration; economic integration is added on to by social, legal and political integration. The as yet only example of a common market is the European Union, dealt with in Case study: "Brief history of the European Union (EU)" on page 448.

> **Common market**: A common market is established when countries agree to move towards market integration, eliminating not only visible trade barriers on goods, but all hindrances in the flow of goods, services, investment, labour and other factors. A common market is complex and entails far greater depth in integration; economic integration is added on to by social, legal and political integration. As yet, the only example of a common market is the European Union.

Implications of a common market

The world's closest version of a common market, the EEC, was expanded during the 1970s, 1980s and 1990s, reaching 15 members by 1995 when the shift towards a common market was signified by a change of name to the **European Union** (EU). By this time a de facto common market (or single market) – in accordance with the four points above – had largely been in effect for two years. Figure 4.3.4 on page 447 diagram I illustrates how, to all intents and purposes, member countries now comprise a single unified market for all forms of economic activity.

The impact on trade and economic integration is quite considerable. The EU has stated this most clearly in the '**Four Basic Freedoms**' of the free movement of goods, services, people and capital within the single market. **People** can move to other member countries to work, study or simply live. **Goods** can be bought and sold without hindrances across national borders as can **services**. **Firms** can operate freely across borders and **capital** can be transferred without restrictions.

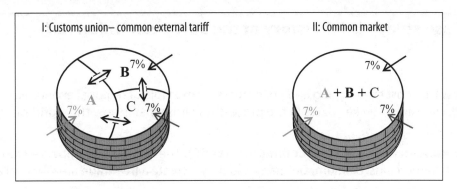

Figure 4.3.4 *From a customs union to a common market*

A common market and further integration

While there is – once again – no absolute definition etched in stone, a common market will ultimately have to implement several features of cooperative economic policies:

- **Factors of production** will be free to move across country borders, as will wages, profits and other **incomes**. A common market will therefore move towards broad scale conversion in **labour laws**, **competition legislation** and **financial rules**. For example, EU competition laws regulating mergers and monopolies are inserted into each country's national legislation and in fact take precedence over domestic legislation.

- **Non-tariff barriers** are removed which necessitates far-reaching cooperation in technical/health/safety/environmental **standards**. Product specifications, certification and technical standards are increasingly brought into a common line. The EU **mutual recognition rule** thus states that any product and/or production which is accepted in one EU country must be accepted in all.

- **Taxes** on labour, income, goods and profits must ultimately be coordinated in order to hinder tax evasion, avoid large scale arbitrage (= reselling) of goods due to VAT differentials, and to limit regional unemployment arising when firms relocate to countries with more beneficial taxes. The EU has harmonised a good number of taxes, for example, VAT is paid only once, in the country of final consumption. From 2005, citizens working in another EU country will get their income figures registered in the home country's tax authorities.

Benefits and costs of a common market

There are many benefits of a common market:

- **Less market distortion** as tariffs are removed and therefore increased **consumer welfare.**

- Increased **competition** and improved **resource allocation.**

- Freer flow of factors will **spread technology** and ideas.

- Increased trade and the possibility of **scale economies** arising from larger markets.

- Increased **labour mobility.**

- And finally, there is a possible '**peace and stability dividend**' arising from diverse cultures becoming closer and interdependent.

There are, of course, several costs or disadvantages:

- Increased harmonisation inevitably leads to far deeper political cooperation where centralised policy making leads to a **loss of domestic political and economic sovereignty**.

- A larger market and free movement of capital creates a foundation for mergers between firms and **possible monopoly and oligopoly** markets.

- The free flow of goods and the harmonisation of certain taxes – say, on alcohol and tobacco – makes it very difficult for a country to run purely **domestic social policies** designed to lower the social costs of such goods.

- Countries with strict **environmental rules and labour legislation** might see standards lowered due to the harmonisation of rules and regulations.

Case study: Brief history of the European Union (EU)

The EU is now the most far-reaching and encompassing example of regional economic integration in the world. Here are a few key dates in the process towards what is now the world's largest common market:

1952 The European Coal and Steel Community (ECSC): The founding members – France, Luxembourg, Netherlands, Belgium, Germany and Italy – create a free trade area for coal and steel.

1957 The Treaty of Rome: The ECSC countries integrated further by signing the 1957 Treaty of Rome which created the **European Economic Community** in 1958. This **customs union** had the expressed intention of creating a common market in the near future. The original six members were joined by a succession of countries during the last 30 years of the 20th century, totalling 15 members by 1995: the original six plus United Kingdom, Ireland, Denmark, Spain, Portugal, Greece, Sweden, Austria and Finland.

1962 The Common Agricultural Policy: A co-ordinated system of price schemes and subsidies designed to guarantee food production.

1992 Treaty of Maastricht: The treaty outlined increased cooperation in defence, social and judicial issues. The name was changed to **European Union** to mark further inter-governmental cooperation and the shift to a fully-fledged common market. This formally completed the **Single Market** and also set a timetable for implementing the **European Monetary Union (EMU)** and a common currency, the **euro**, which subsequently came into effect on the 1 January 2002. All but four EU members – Sweden, Denmark and the UK – joined.

Increased economic and political integration necessitated increased cooperation in the setting and implementation of policies. **Convergence in monetary and fiscal policies** (for Euro members), common policies in agriculture, competition legislation and environment are but a few examples herein. The EU now acts as under signer in areas of trade and aid, and is moving towards common policies in matters of foreign policy and security issues. The often heated debate amongst members arises primarily over concerns of whether the EU is moving towards some form of federation, e.g. 'The United States of Europe' and the possible loss of national sovereignty.

2004 EU expansion: On 1 May 2004, the EU underwent its largest expansion ever, as ten new countries joined: Estonia, Latvia, Lithuania, Poland, The Czech Republic, Cyprus, Hungary, Malta, The Slovak Republic and Slovenia.[a] In 2007 Bulgaria and Romania joined, bringing total membership to its current 27 members. There will, however, be varying degrees of phasing-in for the ascension countries before they are fully integrated as 'equals' by in the EU.[b] This is primarily due to the considerable differences in economic performance and fears amongst the EU 15 of increased budget burdens for agriculture and social programs, and that goods and labour markets will be swamped by the lower cost newcomers.

Maps and up-to-data information can be found at: http://www.eurunion.org/legislat/agd2000/agd2000.htm.

---

a. EWG at http://www.ewg.org/farm/regiondetail.php?fips=00000&summlevel=2 and also CBS News at http://www.cbsnews.com/stories/2002/05/13/politics/main508765.shtml.

POP QUIZ 4.3.1   ECONOMIC INTEGRATION

1 Why might there be both winners and losers due to globalisation?

2 What are the possible negative effects for a country joining a free trade area?

3 What other regulations are necessary for countries entering into a free trade area?

4 What is the main difference between a free trade area and a customs union?

5 Explain why a common market involves more political and economic cooperation than a customs union.

HIGHER LEVEL EXTENSION TOPICS

Trade creation and trade diversion ©IBO 2003

There are a number of additional consequences arising due to economic integration. Countries can both gain (*trade creation*) and lose (*trade diversion*) when relative prices are changed due to regional economic integration.

Trade creation

In joining a customs union, the removal of tariffs between members serves to increase the volume of trade between members, thereby creating trade. **Trade creation** takes place when domestic consumers in member countries import more goods from other members as import prices fall due to the removal of tariffs and quotas – production will shift to lower cost producers. Initial positive effects are the increase in consumer welfare resulting from more goods and lower prices, while *long-run* (dynamic) effects include enhanced comparative advantage and increasing specialisation – leading to increasing real incomes and increased trade with non-members. In effect there is a possible expansion in world trade due to a RTA.

For example, consider that Japan can produce DVD players domestically and supply them at a price of $US120. Assume that Korea can sell them to Japanese consumers for $US100 and China for $US95 but that Japan levies a 30% tariff on imported players, bringing the price of imported DVD players to $US130 for Korean players and $US123.5 for Chinese players. Consumers in Japan would predominantly buy domestically produced DVD players.

Now, if Japan and Korea were to form a customs union and tariffs were eliminated, imported DVD players from Korea ($US100) would replace Japanese VCRs ($US120). Since the price goes down from $US120 to $US100 there will be an increase in Japanese consumption and Korean production. This in itself shows *trade creation*, and assuming further that Japan has goods which can be produced at a lower cost than Korea, resources will be accordingly reallocated in order to meet increased Korean demand. (The outcome is similar to that shown in Figure 4.1.2 on page 393, "Benefits of trade for Capitalia and Consumentia", where two countries which specialise in certain goods are able to consume outside their production possibility frontiers.[7])

> **Trade creation:** When intra-RTA trade increases and production is moved from higher-cost producers outside the RTA to lower-cost producers within the RTA due to the removal of trade barriers there is trade creation. Increased incomes resulting from specialisation and benefits of scale can further this by creating increased demand for imports from non-members.

Trade diversion

However, say the initial tariff in Japan was lower, 20%. Japan would then instead be importing DVD players from China and selling them for $US114 ($US95 plus 20% tariff) rather than buying domestically at $US120 or importing them from Korea at a market price of $US120 ($US100 plus 20% tariff). The outcome in creating a customs union between Japan and Korea would be quite different from the previous example.

---

7. You should be aware of the fact that *comparative* advantages are more likely to arise than absolute advantages.

The tariff-free Korean DVD players at $US100 would *divert* trade from the more cost-efficient Chinese players produced for $US95 but sold in Japan at $US108 inclusive of a (discriminatory) 20% tariff. In other words, *lower cost imports from outside the union have been replaced by higher cost imports from within the union*, which is trade diversion. In spite of Japanese consumers benefiting from lower DVD player prices and increased consumption, trade flows have been diverted away from the country with a trade advantage, namely China. The example of trade diversion shows that it is not entirely certain that preferential tariff reductions always increase economic efficiency and welfare, since tariffs in the customs union discriminate against non-members. In summary, trade diversion is allocatively suboptimal as resources are diverted away from more efficient suppliers which have a comparative advantage.

> Trade diversion: When a FTA/customs union is created and tariff differentials between members and non-members result in trade flows being diverted towards higher cost producers outside the union, trade diversion has taken place.

Examples of trade creation and trade diversion

In reality, RTAs have *both* trade creation and trade diversion effects. The EU has resulted in considerable trade creation in that intra-EU trade is estimated to be double the level that would be the case without economic integration – where over 50% of the expansion in trade by EU members has been in intra-industry trade. During the first ten years of NAFTA, Mexico's exports grew threefold and per capita income rose by 24% - making it the ninth largest economy in the world.[8] MERCOSUR likewise saw a tripling of intra-FTA trade – within the first four years of inception in 1991.[9] Taken together, numerous statistical studies show that RTAs indeed create trade.

However, all three RTAs above have also resulted in varying degrees of trade diversion. For example, EU agricultural subsidies, tariffs and quotas for sugar block out far less costly production in developing countries, adding some 200% to EU sugar prices. (This diversion of trade to higher-cost producers is augmented by the fact that the EU does not use sugar cane but sugar beets which adds over 50% to the production costs of sugar.)[10] The evidence in NAFTA is strikingly confusing, where studies show a range of 'no trade diversion whatsoever' to 'NAFTA has been primarily trade diverting', yet strong indicative evidence shows that North American imports of textiles from Asia decreased significantly.[11] Perhaps the clearest picture of trade diversion due to preferential tariffs in RTAs is to be found in MERCOSUR, where a preliminary report by the World Bank showed strong evidence that consumers in the FTA were forced into buying more expensive intra-FTA goods rather than cheaper non-member goods which carried high tariffs.[12]

---

8. 'Was NAFTA worth it?', *Business Week,* 22 December 2003.

9. Krugman & Obstfeld, p. 244.

10. 'The Great Sugar Scam', Briefing paper by Oxfam, 2002, p. 2–5.

11. *An Econometric Analysis of Trade Diversion under NAFTA*, Kyoji Fukao and Toshihiro Okuba, University of Michigan, 2002, pp. 3–5, 11.

12. Krugman & Obstfeld, p. 245. The authors point out that the original report leaked to the press and created a 'firestorm of protest' from MERCOSUR member governments and the final report was a watered-down version.

WAY outside the box:
Diagrammatical illustration of trade creation and trade diversion

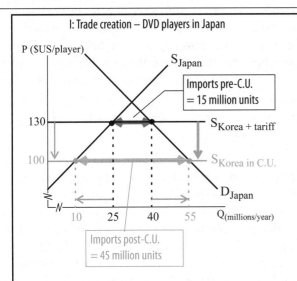

I: Trade creation – DVD players in Japan

Imports pre-C.U. = 15 million units

Imports post-C.U. = 45 million units

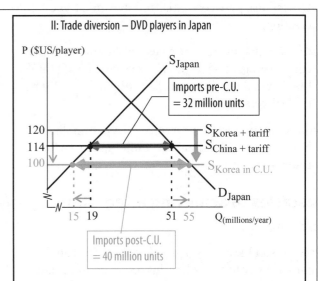

II: Trade diversion – DVD players in Japan

Imports pre-C.U. = 32 million units

Imports post-C.U. = 40 million units

Using the previous example where the Japanese *tariff is 30%*, when Japan enter into a customs union (C.U. in the diagrams) with Korea, DVD players from Korea will be more price competitive than the $US120 for Japanese players. As the tariff is removed, Korean DVD players fall in price from $130 to $US100. Imports from Korea will increase from the initial 15 million units at $S_{Korea+\ tariff}$ to 45 million units at $S_{Korea\ in\ C.U.}$. The customs union has resulted in **trade creation** of 30 million additional units from a lower-cost importer.

Assuming *tariffs of 20%* on both Korean and Chinese goods, the domestic Japanese price of $US120 would be undercut by Chinese DVD players at $US114 ($US95 plus 20%), shown by the black supply curve $S_{China\ +\ tariff}$. The Korean players are not competitive at $US120 ($US100 plus 20%), shown by the grey supply curve $S_{Korea\ +\ tariff}$.

Japan thus initially imports 32 million units from China at a price of $US114. Upon entering into a customs union with Korea, inter-union tariffs on imported DVD players are eliminated (shown by the shift of $S_{Korea+\ tariff}$ to $S_{Korea\ in\ C.U.}$) and Korean DVD players are now sold in Japan for $US100 – below the Chinese-plus-tariff price level of $US114.

Japanese consumers increase imports of DVD players from 32 million to 40 million units while the market price falls from $US114 to $US100. Yet since China's exports have been taken over by Korean manufacturers, there has been a **diversion of trade** away from the most cost-efficient supplier (China, at a production cost of $95) to *less efficient* suppliers (Korea, at a production cost of $100) within the customs union.

Figure 4.3.5 *Trade creation and trade diversion*

HIGHER LEVEL

POP QUIZ 4.3.2   TRADE CREATION AND TRADE DIVERSION

1 Explain how firms and consumers might benefit from the construction of a free trade area.

2 Distinguish between initial and dynamic trade creation.

3 Assume that in creating a customs union, member countries agree on a common external tariff that is lower for all goods than before. Might there still be trade diversion?

4 Some economists have termed FTAs 'stumbling blocks for trade' rather than 'building blocks for trade'. Explain.

Obstacles to achieving integration

©IBO 2003

Every person I know from an EU country has an indignant story to tell of how his or her country had to give up, adjust or somehow change a traditional good; beer in the Netherlands, sausage in Austria…or the technical definition of a cucumber in Portugal. Ever more interdependence between regional economic area members makes it increasingly necessary to have common policies and broad harmonisation of legislation in both economic and social areas. Quite naturally, this process has met with considerable suspicion and resistance from both citizens and policy makers alike within RTA countries.[13]

Reluctance to surrender political sovereignty

©IBO 2003

> *Hell hath no fury like a bureaucrat scorned.* – Milton Friedman

The famous British philosopher John Locke claimed that legislators do not have the right to transfer legislative powers into the hands of others, since their power has been delegated (= entrusted) to them by the people. Resistance to integration arises when countries have to give up a degree of self-government and abide by new rules created by a foreign institution. At the centre of the debate is the issue of whether de-democratisation takes place; can a *supranational* (= members grant power to an outside institution) body

in fact claim **democratic legitimacy**? When countries increase economic integration by establishing a RTA, increasing goods flows will create a need for rules on a variety of issues; from re-export tariffs and rules of origin in a FTA, coordinated taxes and labour laws in a customs union/ common market, to decreased freedom in setting monetary policies in a single currency area with a Central Bank which governs member states. Sovereignty is in this manner 'never lost, but only reallocated'. When a state's sovereignty is reduced, the important question raised is where the sovereignty goes.'[14] Three areas illuminate a few core issues of countries' reluctance to cede (= give up) political sovereignty:

Legislation: Different laws evolve over time in different countries, and there will be resistance to giving up a degree of legislative power to 'supranational' institutions. The current best example of this is within the EU; when EU members agree to be governed by legislation put forward by the **EU Commission** (which is not elected by EU citizens) and undersigned by the EU Parliament (elected by about one third of EU citizens eligible to vote), member states have in fact given up a degree of self-rule. The degree of supranational legislation in the EU is considerable; EU law to a large extent has precedence over national laws in areas such as competition and labour – and any new legislation in member states must not contradict existing EU legislation. Perhaps nowhere has resistance to further integration been stronger than in the case of the **European Monetary Union** (see below) and the ongoing attempts to draft an *EU constitution* regulating the division of sovereignty between member states and the EU Parliament/Commission.

Taxation: When countries form a RTA there is a tendency for cross-border expenditure to increase (assuming geographical closeness) and prices will tend to even-out. It becomes difficult to maintain highly differentiated taxes on *goods*, as freedom of imports will allow consumers to buy goods across the border. Integration on an EU scale means that *factors* also become increasingly mobile. Thus, a RTA member with high taxes on income would risk losing human capital – often the most well-educated and mobile – to other member states, i.e. a 'brain drain'. Similarly, lower taxes on labour, profits and capital gains will attract investment and can ultimately force a country to lower

---

13. A number of economists point to the **internal dynamics** of economic integration, where an initial degree of integration leads to a next step; a FTA will result in cooperation in tariffs, re-export duties and VAT. A base is thus created for additional integration such as harmonisation of standards and policies governing factor mobility between members. The step towards political and not just economic integration is therefore rather short.

14. *Sovereignty, economic integration, and the world trade organisation*, Susan Hainsworth, D. Jur. Candidate York University, 1996, in *Osgoode Hall Law Journal* [VOL. 33 NO. 3], p. 588.

taxes in order to avoid large scale loss of technological expertise and employment opportunities.

Social policies: The loss of domestic sovereignty in the above can have serious consequences for the social policies of a country. A decline in investment, production, consumption and employment due to factors shifting to other countries basically means that the domestic tax base is 'exported' to a certain extent. The loss of tax revenue and concomitant lowering of social spending due to downward adjustment of tax levels is only part of the issue. The other part is of course that taxes on alcohol, cigarettes and pollution commonly are applied to limit negative externalities, and lower taxes (and increased availability of 'bads' such as alcohol and tobacco) will not sit well with countries which have used taxes and government monopolies as a method of limiting consumption in order to increase societal welfare.[15] I order my cigars via the internet from Spain – which has the lowest taxes on tobacco in the EU – and there is little the Swedish government can do about it. No wonder Spain's total tax revenue from cigarette tax – as a percentage of total tax receipts – is three times that of Sweden's![16]

Reluctance to surrender economic sovereignty ©IBO 2003

Countries in a free trade area surrender tariff revenues and the ability to set quotas which benefit domestic industries. This loss of economic sovereignty is accentuated when the FTA moves towards a *customs union*; external tariffs might cause trade diversion (see above) while increased trade within the union can diminish a member's ability to 'save jobs' by curtailing imports. Increased factor mobility within the next step,

a *common market*, means that any given member country will find it more difficult to keep markedly different tax rates and will also decrease the efficiency of domestic unemployment policies, as firms/capital can be moved to the most advantageous countries.

Finally, a **monetary union** creates a single central bank which severely limits the degree to which a country can use monetary policies to manage its domestic economy.

Having one currency means that interest rates have to converge in member countries, as it will be impossible for different countries to have separate interest rates. This puts the responsibility of monetary policy in the hands of a common central bank rather than in individual member countries' central banks. It is therefore impossible for an individual member to pursue domestic monetary policy. If the economies in the monetary union are not in line along the business cycle, the loss of monetary policy power will be felt by countries needing to adjust interest rates - in order to stimulate/deflate the economy – but unable to do so.

It is thus understandable that fierce political resistance to regional economic areas arises when a degree of decision-making power is put into the hands of non-elected administrators and bureaucrats. When RTA institutions are empowered to make decisions in the interests of overriding goals rather than individual member countries in the trade area, there will naturally be a feeling of *disempowerment* amongst citizens and elected officials in member countries. The most far-reaching form of economic integration to date between separate countries is the **European Monetary Union**, which HL will look at in greater depth in Section 4.6.

---

15. Just in the news: the EU commission is reportedly going to propose that the age limit on purchasing fireworks should be lowered to 12 for all EU countries. This has created quite a stir in several EU countries which have very strict age and purchasing limits on such goods. The Swedes – inventors of automobile safety belts and bicycle helmets – are spitting blood.
16. 'Economics of tobacco for the EU region', Regional Report (EU), June 2001.

Storytime: Alco-lemmings

Sweden, Norway and Finland notoriously have amongst the highest taxes on alcohol in the world – and all three sell alcohol through state-owned monopolies. When Sweden and Finland joined the EU in 1995, both countries were granted a few years 'reprieve' from having to fully adopt the virtually limitless quotas allowed for personal consumption.

This has resulted in a kind of 'Domino Theory of Alco-Lemmings' where people flock en masse to the nearest country with lower alcohol taxes: the Norwegians (non-EU but with far-reaching local free trade agreements with other Nordic countries in place since the 1960s) go to Sweden to stock up; the Swedes go to Denmark; the Danes go to Germany; and the Germans ... stay home and count money and tax revenues I suppose.

*Living here in Helsingborg, a 20 minute ferry from Helsingör (you know, Hamlet) in Denmark, I have enjoyed the show immensely. Thousands of Swedes from hundreds of kilometres away take the ferry across to Denmark to buy (primarily) beer – which costs $US1.7 per bottle in Sweden at the Systembolaget (state-run monopoly) and $US0.50 at any local store in Denmark. One can rent a sturdy beer cart for about $US10 at the ferry station in Helsingborg and whip over Öresund Sound[a] for another $US7 – which is made up for in the purchase of one case of fine Danish beer. But the Swedes don't buy a single case – they buy **several** cases! This lemming train of alcohol of course means that arbitrage is rampant and with each new increase in the amount Swedes were allowed to bring back, the distance from which it became economically viable (and legal!) to drive to Helsingborg/Helsinör in the south increased. In fact, the tabloids publish figures for regions on how much a citizen would have to buy in order to make a trip to Denmark viable.*

By 2004, the Danes, Swedes and the Finns were allowed to bring in the same amount as other EU countries[b], in addition to which the three Baltic states entering the EU on the 1 May 2004 had alcohol prices which were lower than black market prices in the Nordic countries. Guess what? The Swedes adapted by incrementally lowering taxes on wine and beer and the Danes and Finns suddenly lowered alcohol taxes by over 40% during 2003/04. The Swedes then seriously considered lowering alcohol taxes even more as sales of alcohol domestically went down by some 20% to 25% and the loss of tax revenue is considered a serious problem. This 'exportation' of an important tax base and increased consumption of demerit goods illustrates how difficult it can be for countries to have different social and economic policies within a single market. More alarmingly, alcohol consumption is higher than ever in modern times, and while such figures are notoriously difficult to estimate, studies point to a 20% to 30% increase – and perhaps half of all alcohol consumed is brought in via personal imports. Nordic governments are gravely concerned over the increased availability of low-price alcohol to teenagers, and the increasing ease of bringing in alcohol via 'booze cruises' to new EU members such as the Baltic States and Poland.

a. Renamed *Ölesund* by local wit, literally 'Beery Sound'.

b. Basically, there is no limit – as long as one can prove that the alcohol is for personal consumption. Uh-huh; 'But officer, my son is getting married and we're holding a four-day fete for two hundred guests. Here's the guest list.'

c. Official protocol from the Swedish Parliament, 9 December 2003, at http://www.riksdagen.se/debatt/200304/prot/45/sam/45SAM.ASP.

POP QUIZ 4.3.3   ECONOMIC INTEGRATION

1   What democratic issues might arise due to the formation of a regional economic association?

2   Explain why a customs union leads to increased political co-operation.

3   Why does a common currency lead to a loss of domestic monetary policy?

World Trade Organisation

4.4

CONTENTS

WORLD TRADE ORGANISATION ©IBO 2003

As the average age in the agricultural sector is so high (above 60) we are just waiting for them to die off.
– Chief Economist of the WTO, Patrick Low, when asked by one of my former students, Eric Blomquist, what the WTO was planning to do about the problem of agricultural subsidies and the CAP

A colleague and I got caught in a demonstration in Malmö (one of southern Sweden's largest cities) a few years ago. Thousands of young people were out screaming slogans and occupying public squares. The police had arrived in force which subsequently fuelled stone throwing and some violence. I'll never forget my colleague's awed spontaneous comment: 'Is the WTO holding a meeting in town?!' How did a seemingly well-intentioned free-trade organisation get such a bad reputation?

Background to the WTO

The WTO was born as the General Agreement on Tariffs and trade – GATT – in a hotel in **Bretton Woods**, New Hampshire in 1944, along with its 'sisters' the International Monetary Fund (IMF), the World Bank, and an exchange rate system subsequently known as the Bretton Woods system. The intention of the Bretton Woods conference was to create post WWII systems and organisations which would lead to greater economic stability and increased trade around the world. Thus, in 1947, 23 nations signed the **General Agreement on Tariffs and Trade (GATT)**, which obligated members to commit themselves to trade under non-discrimination rules (the most favoured nation clause) and reduce tariffs on goods.

There were eight successive lengthy negotiations, called 'rounds', between 1947 and 1979, and by the seventh, the Tokyo Round, average tariffs had fallen from over 40% to 4.7%. The next round, the Uruguay Round, lasted from 1986 to 1993 and the 117 members expanded talks to include goods which had previously not been tabled for discussion, namely non-tariff barriers, agricultural/textile goods, investment, and intellectual property rights (e.g. patent and trademark rights). The Uruguay Round also replaced GATT with the **WTO on 1 January 1995**, giving the new organisation greater power and responsibility in international trade matters. The current round of negotiations started in 2001 in Doha, Qatar, and the 142 members agreed that it was time to put development firmly on the table. The **Doha Development Agenda**, as it became known, put the main emphasis on environmental and developmental issues in trade.

The WTO today

The headquarters of the WTO[1] is situated in Geneva, Switzerland. Some 600 administrators – bureaucrats – work there full time for the now 153 member strong organisation which accounts for over 95% of global trade. Over 30 additional countries are applying to join. It is headed by director-general Pacal Lamy from France, and had a budget of $US185 million in 2008.[2] All WTO agreements are both outlined and ratified (= signed) by member governments – thus far by consensus rather than majority vote. 600 administrators with a budget less than the 2,600 strong International Monetary Fund uses for travel expenses – hardly a threat to world prosperity, democracy and justice. Or do the demonstrators have a point?

Aims of the WTO ©IBO 2003

The function of the WTO is to create a global free trade environment by eliminating trade barriers and facilitating an arena in which to settle disputes. While GATT dealt primarily with eliminating visible trade barriers on goods, the WTO has increasingly cast a wider free trade net, which now focuses on invisible trade barriers such as dumping and subsidies. Another aspect of the WTO's increased sphere of action is that not only goods are dealt with, but issues such as industry standards, labour rules and intellectual property.

---

1. See excellent overview at http://www.wto.org.
2. I simply must complement the WTO for its incredible homepage. The site is clear, easy to use, has excellent sources – and is incredibly open in terms of 'who's paying the bill and what are they getting for their money'.

Guidelines and principles of the WTO

The WTO[3] sets out five specific objectives in the multilateral trade system:

1. **Non-discrimination:** All agreements between members are based on treating other members equally, most prominently exemplified by the **most favoured nation clause**, MFN (see Section 4.3).[4] Any trade agreement for any good extended to one country must be granted for all members – exceptions are as mentioned earlier REAs but developing nations are allowed certain exceptions also.

2. **Freeing trade through negotiation/mediation:** The successive rounds focused on tariffs and quotas, but increasingly include non-tariff barriers and services. The WTO has considerably more power than GATT as an open market forum for multilateral negotiations and through its power as **mediator in trade conflicts** and its ability to enforce its verdicts.

3. **Stable trade environment:** The WTO aims to create a stable and predictable trade environment by setting **binding rules on maximum tariffs** and by demanding **openness and accountability** in trade policies in member countries.

4. **Fair competition:** The WTO does allow certain barriers such as anti-dumping tariffs and bans on hazardous goods, so while free trade is so far only a goal, the rules and regulations governing WTO members attempt to create a framework for a 'level playing field' in terms of competition.

5. **Development:** It has been recognised by the WTO that while freer trade has often contributed to development, a good many of the poor member countries – about three quarters of WTO members – will face transitional difficulties in fully implementing reductions in trade barriers to designated levels. The poorest countries have thus been **granted extensions of current policies** and **special consideration**.

The five points above are a bit dry, but basically show how the WTO is based on the principles of **non-discrimination**, **equality** in rules and **fairness** in competition aimed at freeing trade between member states.

A little depth:
Making the Rounds

When the Uruguay Round was finally completed after seven years of negotiations, the agreement continued along the lines of tariff reductions and liberalising trade. However, there were also some considerable changes in the scope of what was to become WTO authority. This was partially due to increasing globalisation and the need to set down rules for ever freer movement of **capital**. Another reason for broader WTO agreements was that **services** were growing far faster than manufactured goods – now making up about 3/5 of world output but only 1/5 of world trade. Finally, there was growing realisation that developing countries had been largely unaffected positively in that two of the main export commodities from developing nations had been left out of the discussion – **agriculture and textiles**. Thus, four main areas stand out.[5]

The Uruguay Round (1979–93)

1. The agreement aims to establish rules on international capital flows and foreign investment along the lines of non-discrimination. This is the **Trade-related Investment Measures (TRIM)**.

2. Trade in services received recognition and preliminary regulation in the **General Agreement in Trade in Services (GATS)**.

3. Intellectual property rights – patents, logotypes, trademarks, etc. were reinforced internationally via the **Trade-related Intellectual Property agreement (TRIP)**.

4. Perhaps the most noticeable achievement of the Round was to at least address the areas which GATT had avoided for so many years; agriculture and textiles. Both of these goods have been fiercely protected by developed countries, costing

---

3. *Understanding the WTO*, September 2003, downloadable at www.wto.org.

4. This is a bit like having a birthday party when you were a kid and you had to invite *all* your classmates rather than just the ones you liked. My mother tried this – once – when I was seven; 'Matthew, if you don't invite Johnny, there will be no party!' There was no party. I just didn't like him. (The following year we did have a party – with a more discriminating guest list.)

5. See *Understanding the WTO*, WTO 2003, pp. 23–46; Irwin, pp. 179–95; and also Todaro, pp. 583–87.

developing countries an estimated $US24 billion per year in potential export earnings in textiles alone, and close to $US40 billion in total. **Agricultural** tariffs were reduced (by some 35%) in all member countries by 2005, limits on export subsidies were imposed (and ultimately abolished together with voluntary export restraints in 2005), and the total volume of agricultural subsidies cut by 21%. In textiles, the **multi-fibre agreement (MFA)**, notoriously one of the most convoluted and complex systems of quotas and export restraints ever to obstruct international trade with developing nations, was scrapped in 2005.[6]

The Doha Round – the Development Agenda (2001–?)

The ninth WTO Round began in November 2001 in Doha, Qatar. The agenda was to continue along the lines outlined in the Uruguay Round, with particular emphasis on development – thus the name **Doha Development Agenda**. The development issues listed for negotiation primarily outlined the obligations of developed countries to continue to lower – and in some cases eradicate – all forms of trade barriers on agricultural goods and textiles outlined in the Uruguay Round. A successful completion of the Round would mean some $US300 billion in increased income in poor countries, pulling over 140 million people out of poverty, according to the World Bank.[7] The Doha Round was to be concluded by 31 December 2004.

To be blunt, the Doha Round has thus far been a massive failure. During the Ministerial Conference (the higher level negotiations of WTO members) at **Cancun**, Mexico, in September 2003 the talks broke down and it seemed that the distance between developing and developed countries was wider than ever. Staunch EU, US and Japanese resistance to tariff and export subsidy reductions was met by the formation of an alliance of 21 developing nations – G21 – which further polarised the positions of countries supposedly negotiating. The meeting ended when the chairman prematurely closed negotiations, and delegates have since then pretty much blamed everyone else for the failure.

A less heated but no more successful outcome were the **Geneva** negotiations in July 2008. One of the key issues was a proposal of a Special Safeguard Mechanism (SSM), originally proposed by the so-called G33 – a group of developing countries cooperating in trade issues. The SSM allows developing countries to impose special tariffs on key agricultural goods under certain conditions – e.g. unexpected decreases in world prices and huge increases in imports. This was the pivotal point of disagreement and arose between India which had the SSM as a key demand, and the US (a large exporter of agricultural goods) which opposed the SSM. It is at the time of writing (February 2009) highly unlikely that the Round will be completed during 2009.

Success and failure viewed from different perspectives ©IBO 2003

The main difference between WTO and its predecessor GATT, is that the WTO is an organisation based on establishing set rules by which members must abide while GATT was basically a series of inter-governmental trade agreements. In essence, the main weakness of GATT was that there was no formal authority to back up trade agreements. The WTO on the other hand has the power to act as judge in dispute settlements. And while the WTO does not directly impose sanctions or penalties, it can **allow injured countries to impose penalties** on a member found guilty of illegal tariffs and such.

The WTO is the only true worldwide trade organisation, and in sketching an outline of the 'successes and failures' of the WTO, I came upon a somewhat surprising pattern, namely that economists and free-trade advocates generally regard the WTO's successes as outweighing the failures while 'global opinion' voiced through any number of anti-globalisation non-government organisations (NGOs) take a predominantly opposite stance. I fully realise the danger in sweeping generalisations like this and I use the two captions below rather tongue-in-cheek, to represent the different perspectives of the WTO record.

---

6. *The Economist*, 'The WTO under fire', 18 September 2003.
7. Op. cit.

The economist/free-trade view

...what we actually achieved at Doha was a significant breakthrough.[8,9] – Mike Moore, former Director-General of the WTO (1999–2002)

Supporters of the WTO point out that 600 bureaucrats, two-thirds working as translators, with an annual budget one-fourth of the World Wide Fund for Nature (WWF – one of many vocal NGO critics) do not quite qualify as an evil conspiracy attempting to rule the world. Nor has any reason been put forward why 2.5 million members of Greenpeace should have anywhere near the influence on the WTO as the Indian trade delegate elected by 600 million voters in India. The success of the WTO is primarily in its capacity as a **democratic forum for discussion and a medium of same-rules** for both large and small countries.

- **Representation:** The WTO is far more accountable to its members than most NGOs, and is in fact more *democratic* than most of the NGOs, since every member has an equal vote and all decisions are made by consensus, giving each country a **veto** on decisions. Countries apply for membership and all agreements are undersigned by duly elected representatives of each country.

- **Pro-poor:** The WTO has increasingly put forward developing country issues - the Doha Development Agenda is a case in point. Rules and representation will allow developing countries to negotiate more equitable terms of trade and thus join in the economic success evidenced in increasingly **free-market** countries such as China and India.

- **Equality:** The WTO does not pander to individual lobby efforts – that is done at national level. Thus the WTO acts to **protect smaller members** from strong domestic groups such as US steel and European farmers.

- **Dispute settlement:** Any country in the WTO can appeal to the WTO for a binding ruling by an independent panel. If country A accuses country B of illegal trade barriers and wins, the WTO can rule that country A can impose **reciprocal trade sanctions** (= punishment) on country B. The WTO cannot itself impose sanctions.

- **Developing countries:** The WTO now includes a good many developing countries – over three quarters of the members in fact. This provides poor countries with a solid **negotiating base** for rectifying some of the highly unjust trade barriers erected by rich countries. Developing countries stand to gain far more from lower trade barriers than developed countries.

- **Trade barriers:** The WTO has been **largely successful**; tariffs have come down considerably; non-tariff barriers are decreasing and becoming increasingly outlawed. The result is that world trade has increased 20-fold and living standards and output are higher than ever. The Uruguay Round has added an estimated 0.74% to real incomes on a global basis.[10]

However, there are a number of points where the WTO has failed, according to the economist/free-trade view:

- It allows **RTAs such as NAFTA and the EU**. Such regional exceptions to the WTO policies of non-discrimination and equal treatment for all, undermines global efforts to create a level playing field in trade.

- **Subsidies and export subsidies** have changed little during the time since the Uruguay Round was completed. The main issue of rich developing countries' enormous subsidies to domestic farmers still remains unsolved.

- There are still noticeably higher trade barriers on goods which are the most important to developing countries, i.e. **agricultural goods and textiles**. The continued breakdowns of negotiations in the Doha Round are a case in point.

The grassroots/anti-globalist/NGO view

The World Trade Organisation is carrying out a slow-motion coup d'état over democratic governance worldwide.[11]

The detractors of the WTO[12] often take a standpoint where the organisation is a non-democratic and non-transparent tool of rich countries and multinational companies, where poor countries and the environment are victims.

---

8. See, for example, Legrain, pp. 174–210; Irwin, pp. 179–224; Wallach & Sforza, passim.
9. Moore, p. 175.
10. Salvatore, p. 286.
11. *Five Years of Reasons to Resist Corporate Globalization*, Wallach & Sforza, The WTO, p. 13.
12. See Irwin, pp. 179–224; Wallach & Sforza, passim; Global Trade Watch at http://www.tradewatchoz.org/newissues/index.html; Global Exchange at http://www.globalexchange.org/.

- **Undemocratic power:** The WTO transfers power from national assemblies to an organisation which is squarely in the hands of **unaccountable corporate interests** aimed at increasing profit via increased trade. Since WTO rules are binding for signatory countries, national laws will have to adapt to WTO regulations.

- **Race to the bottom:** Freer **mobility of capital** will encourage poor countries to attract foreign investors by lowering standards on labour and environment.

- **Investment and intellectual property:** Allowing multinationals to freely allocate investment around the world further weakens the position of poor countries, as they increasingly become dependent on foreign firms. Granting global intellectual property rights to big business around the world (see TRIPs on page 458) in pharmaceuticals and crop varieties would cause thousands of deaths in developing nations, as poor people could not afford monopoly prices on medicines and seed grains.

  > More stringent protection for patents will increase the costs of technology transfer. Developing countries will lose approximately $40bn a year in the form of increased license payments to Northern-based TNCs, with the USA capturing around one-half of the total. Behind the complex arguments about intellectual-property rights, the TRIPs agreement is an act of institutionalized fraud, sanctioned by WTO rules. – Read more at http://www.maketradefair.com.

- **Environment:** The WTO puts **free trade over environment**, by allowing countries to file complaints against rules devised to protect the environment and plant/animal species. For example, when the US imposed strict rules on clean gasoline, Venezuela and Brazil complained that this more stringent regulation in effect was a trade barrier to their exports of gasoline. The WTO ruled in favour of Venezuela/Brazil and the US softened its regulations.

- **Labour standards:** The WTO has not implemented safeguards on labour standards, allowing multinational companies the ability to **exploit labour** in low labour countries.

- **Public health:** In insisting that countries allow free trade, the WTO forces countries to relax regulations on public health which could be considered trade barriers, allowing **imports of harmful goods**. For example, the EU ban on American beef containing trace elements of artificial hormones was deemed illegal by the WTO. (The EU has thus far ignored the WTO ruling.)

Both sides have a number of weighty arguments and it is virtually impossible to assess the final outcome in terms of net benefits. Most of the arguments put forward are non-economic arguments and are properly dealt with in the arena of democratic institutions. The issues which can be dealt with in economics are often very difficult to summarise, such as the problem of when a ban on a certain good due to health/safety reasons is a valid concern or simply hidden protectionism. I should mention that a good many commentators feel that some issues, such as labour standards and child labour, should not be dealt with by the WTO.

Balance of payments

4.5

CONTENTS

BALANCE OF PAYMENTS ©IBO 2003

Nothing, however, can be more absurd than this whole doctrine of the balance of trade, upon which, not only these restraints, but almost all the other regulations of commerce are founded. – Adam Smith[1]

If you have an income of £100 during a given time period and expenditure of £90, then by the end of the period you have increased your *net* holdings, i.e. your net assets have increased. If, however, you spend £110 then the £10 which did not flow in during the time period must come from somewhere; loans from a friend or the selling of your economics textbook. In any case, the 'overspending' means that your *net* assets have decreased.

The balance of payments works pretty much as above but for entire countries. It is a record of a country's money inflows and outflows to and from the foreign sector during a period of time. Inflows can consist of export revenues while corresponding outflows would consist of payments for imports. Other in- and outflows could be investment flows from/to other countries. In essence, the balance of payments accounts for a country's income flows, investment flows and asset base in dealing with the foreign sector. The balance of payments categorizes these flows into two components; the **current account** and the **capital account**.

> **Balance of payments:** The balance of payments is a record of all inflows and outflows of money in a country arising from economic activity with foreign countries during a given time period. The balance of payments consists of the **current account** and **capital account**.

Warning!
Balance of payments ≠ government budget

For some reason students commonly confuse the government budget with the balance of payments – and thus a budget deficit with a current account deficit. I urge you to study both concepts *side by side* and focus on understanding the differences between the two; the budget deals with a) tax receipts (T) and b) government spending (G). The **balance of payments** deals with a) trade (X and M) and b) investment flows (I) and other flows of money in net foreign assets. Confusing the two concepts is just the

sort of woofley (= my own made-up word for vague, obtuse, garbled) thinking which will cost you marks in your IB exams.

Here's the section game plan:

1. The balance of payments will be outlined in a basic overview.

2. Each individual component will be explained using the Irish balance of payments for 2003. (Refer back to Ireland and national income accounting in Section 4.1.)

3. I will finish by 'playing around' with a few examples to give you a feel for how international money flows affect the balance of payments.

If you are satisfied with a grade 4 or 5 in economics, feel free to skip part 2. However, if you are aiming for a 6 or 7, I strongly recommend getting a firm grip on all issues arising within the balance of payments, as almost every international trade issue touches upon this very central concept.

Overview of the balance of payments

The balance of payments in Figure 4.5.1 on page 464 has been slightly simplified but shows the basic inflows and outflows an economy will experience.

The current account is a country's record of all money flows arising from economic activity with foreign countries. The fictitious example shows that export revenue (+100 – shown by an 'inward' arrow) is less than import expenditure (-110 – 'outward' arrow); there is a net outflow of money, i.e. a **trade deficit** of –€10. The remaining points show *net values*, i.e. the balance of inflows and outflows of money. These are comprised of various 'invisibles' such as services, investment income and transfers such as foreign aid payments. In total there is a net outflow of €5 million, a **current account deficit**, which essentially means that this economy has spent more on imported goods and

---

1. Adam Smith in *Wealth of Nations*; quoted from Irwin, p. 90.

services from other countries than it has earned from exports of goods and services.

> **Current account:** The current account shows all money flows to and from a country arising from exports and imports of goods and services, plus transfers of income (repatriated profits, interest and dividends) and other net transfers (workers abroad sending money home, government 'membership' fees to UN/EU, development aid).

The other side of the balance of payments shows how the country has *financed* the €5 million. This is the capital account which shows all other forms of money flows. Broadly speaking, the capital account tallies (= counts) investment and savings flows between the domestic economy and foreign countries and in this case must show *net inflows* which make up for the net outflow of €5 million in the current account. The net outflow of €5 million in the current account must be made up for by €5 million in inward flows from investment, saving and loans from other countries. The initial cardinal rule here is that the sum of the current account and capital account is always zero!

Current account balance + capital account balance = zero!

> **Capital account:** The capital account is the mirror image of the current account, showing how capital transfers flow to and from other countries. The capital account shows the change in net foreign assets of a country due to foreign direct investment (FDI), portfolio investment (shares, bills, bonds), currency flows, loans, and deposits.
>
> A current account deficit means that there must be a net inflow in capital account, e.g. a capital account surplus. Basically the capital account surplus shows how the import expenditure exceeding export revenues has been financed.

Hint from Hollywood. I loved the movie *Jerry McGuire*, and often refer to the scene where Jerry (Tom Cruise) is screaming into the phone, '*Show me the money!*' That is what should be ringing in your ears as you try to hack your way through the figures in the balance of payments, as we are **following the flows of money** and nothing else. Far too many students get confused by the '+' (credit) and '–' (debit) signs in current account, all too often looking at a '+' value as 'goods coming into the country' (i.e. imports) rather than correctly establishing that a '+' is a *payment for exports.* Another common error is regarding '+' values as 'good' and '–' values as 'bad'.

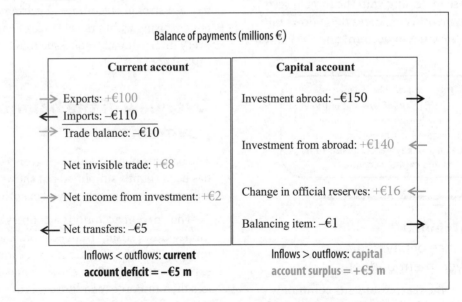

Balance of payments (millions €)	
Current account	**Capital account**
Exports: +€100	Investment abroad: –€150
Imports: –€110	
Trade balance: –€10	Investment from abroad: +€140
Net invisible trade: +€8	
Net income from investment: +€2	Change in official reserves: +€16
Net transfers: –€5	Balancing item: –€1
Inflows < outflows: **current account deficit = –€5 m**	Inflows > outflows: capital account surplus = +€5 m

Figure 4.5.1 *Simplified overview of balance of payments*

Current account ©IBO 2003

Moving on to a bit more depth, Figure 4.5.2 on page 465 gives the balance of payments for Ireland in 2003. The current account has been subdivided into two main components: The **visible trade balance** [3] comprised of merchandise exports [1] and imports [2];

and the **invisible trade balance** [7] which in turn is comprised of net flows in services [4], income [5] and transfers [6]. Please note that the balance of payments is a 'snapshot picture' of total flows which have occurred *during a time period*, e.g. a year.

Current account	Capital account
Merchandise exports: +77,586 [1] Merchandise imports: – 45,478 [2] <hr> Visible trade balance = +32,108 [3] +/– Net trade in services: –12,652 [4] +/– Net flows of income: –22,701 [5] (Generated by repatriated incomes, profits, interest, and dividends) +/– Net transfers: +1,022 [6] (Govt. monies to EU/UN/IMF, etc. foreign workers sending money home, student grants paid/received abroad, development aid paid/received) <hr> **Invisible trade balance = –34,331** [7] **Current account balance= –2,223** [8]	*Net* capital flow in assets and liabilities towards other countries, e.g.: • *Net* investment abroad (direct and portfolio): –136,440 [9] • *Net* incoming investment (direct and portfolio): +115,048 [10] <hr> **Investment balance: –21,392** [11] • Other *net* financial flows abroad (deposits, speculation, loans to foreigners): –50,508 [12] • Other *net* financial inflows (deposits, speculation, loans from abroad): +71,587 [13] <hr> **Balance of other financial flows: +21,079** [14] • *Net* change in foreign reserves (note that "+" actually means reserves have fallen): +1,770 [15] • Balancing item (i.e. statistical discrepancy or error): +766 [16] <hr> **Capital account balance = +2,223** [17]

(Source: Central Statistics Office of Ireland at http://www.cso.ie/publications/finance/bop.pdf)

Figure 4.5.2 *The balance of payments for Ireland, 2003 (millions €)*

Balance of trade ©IBO 2003

When an Irish good is sold to a foreigner, goods flow out and money flows in, while goods from abroad sold in Ireland create money outflows. One calls an inflow a **credit** in current account and an outflow a **debit**. (I will use credit and debit initially, so that you recognise the terms in other literature, but will thereafter confine myself to the use of 'inflow' and 'outflow'.)

Exports: When my Irish friend Joe Collins in Cambodia gets homesick for Ireland and his wife goes down to the local liquor store in Phnom Penh for a bottle of Irish whisky, the effect is to **credit** (+) the Irish current account in merchandise exports [1]. When the Collins family goes home to Ireland and visits his father's pub, there will also be a credit in Irish exports since Joe lives and earns money in Cambodia rather than Ireland.[2]

Imports: When Joe's father, Michael, buys foreign beers for the pub in Ireland, there is a **debit** (-) in the Irish current account in merchandise imports [2].

Adding up all the other millions of visible trade transactions with the foreign sector during 2003, i.e.

the sum total of exports [1] minus the sum total of imports [2] we get a visible trade balance [3] of over €32 million. This is a (visible) trade surplus. Basically, the Irish have earned more from exports of goods than they have spent on imported goods.

> Visible trade balance: The sum of visible export revenue minus the sum of visible import expenditure equals the (visible) trade balance. A negative value is called a **trade deficit** while a positive value is a **trade surplus**.

Invisible balance ©IBO 2003

The same principles as in the examples in merchandise trade above hold true for trade in *services* and other invisible (i.e. intangible) goods. The invisible trade balance is comprised of a variety of flows arising when money passes a border for reasons other than for the payment of merchandise.

• *Tourism/services*: Tourist services are exported whenever they are being bought by foreign money, for example, when Uwe from Germany stays at O'Leary's Bed and Breakfast in Adare or when

---

2. In actual fact, Joe gets a rather good price on food and drink there.

Hiroshi from Japan takes a boat trip in Dingle Bay to see Fungi the dolphin. Other services are when Ireland's Allied Irish Banks (AIB) sells financial services in New York, or when Ryan Air sells flights to French people – both will entail service export income for Ireland. Conversely, when Irish people buy foreign services there will be an outward flow of income – an import of services – in the Irish balance of payments. The net sum of these flows is a **net import of services** [3] of €12.6 billion.

- **Flow of incomes generated abroad:** Irish economic activity abroad will generate foreign earnings. When these are *repatriated* (= brought home to the mother country)[3] the Irish current account is credited.

  ■ When Irish firms make a **profit** abroad and repatriate it, there is an inflow of money. A foreign firm in Ireland repatriating profits is of course an outflow in current account.

  ■ This is also the case when Irish savings abroad generate incomes which are repatriated, such as **dividends** from foreign shares and **interest payments** on foreign bank accounts and bills/bonds. Naturally, there will be outflows from Ireland as foreigners repatriate incomes generated by their ownership of Irish capital.

  The net sum of these outflows is shown by the **net outflow** of income [5] of €22.7 million in Figure 4.5.2 on page 465.

- **Net transfers:** Ireland will have a number of additional money flows which are recorded in the current account.

  ■ For example, if my friend Joe in Sweden sends some of his income home to his parents every month, this **remittance** is shown as an inflow in the invisibles section of the Irish current account. Basically, Ireland has exported labour in the form of an IB math/physics teacher. (See "Applied economics: 'Migratory cash'" below.)

  ■ Other inflows to Ireland are **farm subsidies** from the EU and **project grants** from various international organisations.

  ■ Naturally Ireland will also have an outflow of transfers: **government dues** to the EU and UN; **grants to Irish students** overseas; **aid monies** paid directly and indirectly to recipient countries, etc.

The **net inflow** of these transfers [6] was just over €1 billion in 2003.

> **Invisible trade balance:** The net sum of the trade in invisibles, e.g. services, incomes and transfers, equals the invisible trade balance.

The current account balance

The sum of the visible trade balance [3] and the invisible trade balance [7] shows the net inflows and outflows of money to Ireland during 2003, the current account balance. Ireland shows a net outflow of €2.2 billion during the year, in other words a **current account deficit**. I shall comment on these figures at the end of this chapter, but I recommend that you go back and revise gross national income accounting in Section 3.1. Try to figure out why Ireland has a current account deficit. Focus on [5] in the balance of payments above. (The answer is in "Putting the pieces together: Comments on the Irish balance of payments" on page 469.)

> **Current account balance:** The sum of the visible and invisible trade balances equals the current account balance in the balance of payments. A positive value means there is a current account **surplus** while a negative value indicates a current account **deficit**.

Applied economics: 'Migratory cash'

Total remittances in the world in 2006 were close to USD300 billion – an 83% increase over five years where some USD240 billion of the total goes to developing countries. For developing countries this represents close to one third of all financial flows. Figure 4.5.3 on page 467 shows the top ten recipients and sources of workers' remittances from abroad during 2006. It is clear that monies sent home by citizens working abroad can have a colossal effect on the current account in the balance of payments. For example, the $US27 billion going to India represents over 3% of India's GDP and 37% of total net invisibles in India's current account. In the US, the world's largest importer of foreign labour, the $US42.2 billion leaving the country as remittances constitutes close to 5% of the *total* USD856 billion current account deficit of 2006.[4]

---

3. I've always wondered if 're*patriate* to the *mother* country' is a contradiction in terms.

4. International Organization for Migration at http://www.iom.int/jahia/Jahia/about-migration; Migration News at http://migration.ucdavis.edu; World Bank at http://siteresources.worldbank.org/INTPROSPECTS/Resources/334934-1199807908806/Top10.pdf; Bureau of Economic Analysis (BEA) at http://www.bea.gov/newsreleases/international/transactions/transnewsrelease.htm.

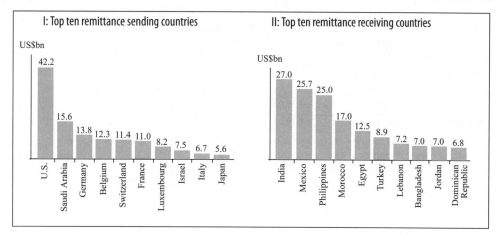

(Source: World Bank, 2008 Remittance Handbook, Top Ten)

Figure 4.5.3 *Top ten foreign remittances in selected countries (2006)*

Capital account ©IBO 2003

In keeping with my rather sad habit of using childishness to get the message across, consider that an account of your income, spending and asset flows during a month are as follows:

Income:	£90 (+)	Sold a music CD: £20 (+)
Spending:	£120 (–)	Loan from a friend: £10 (+)
Overspending:	–£30	Net decrease in assets to fund spending: +£30

What has happened during the month is that you have spent £30 more (£120 on 'imports') than you have earned (£90 in 'exports'). The only way you can balance this *deficit* is by either borrowing from someone or selling some of your assets. By selling off a CD you have decreased your asset holdings by £20, and by taking a loan you have given someone a legitimate claim on £10 worth of your remaining assets. The **reduction in your net assets** has financed the spending which exceeded your income.

However, what if you earned more than you spent?

Income:	£90 (+)	Bought 65,000 shares in AIG: £5 (–)
Spending:	£80 (–)	Loan to a friend: £5 (–)
Underspending:	+£10	Net increase in assets: –£10

Using less childish economic terminology now; as your 'export earnings' (income in the figure above) are larger than your 'import expenditure' (spending above) by £10, you have a *current account surplus*. You used this money to buy shares and lend money to a friend. As you now have £5 worth of shares and a £5 claim on someone else's assets, your *net* assets have increased by

£10 – a *capital account deficit*. The trick here is that you must readjust your thinking a bit when looking at the minus and plus signs in the capital account:

- A plus sign (inflow) in the capital account means that money has flowed into your economy but that you have *decreased your foreign asset base*.
- A minus sign (outflow) in the capital account therefore means that you have *increased* your net foreign assets.

Back to the Irish balance of payments; capital account

Isn't it irritating when textbooks refer to figures or diagrams 5 or 6 pages away?! That is why I have cut in the Irish 2003 capital account again in Figure 4.5.4 on page 468. Recall that Ireland had a current account deficit of €2.2 billion during 2003, i.e. a net outflow. The capital account below shows where that 'additional' €2.2 billion came from – in effect, which assets foreigners are buying in Ireland. It is important to realise that all the values given in the capital account are *net values* and that total inflows and outflows over the course of 2003 were hundreds of times larger.

Net investment: Investment abroad is either *direct* investment or indirect investment. An Irish company building a plant or buying an existing factory in Germany entails *direct* investment. If an Irish company/resident buys German shares, bills or bonds, one speaks of *portfolio* investment. The €136 billion net outflow from Ireland [9] means that Irish firms/residents have increased their foreign holdings, while the net inflow of €115 billion [10] means that foreigners have increased their holdings of Irish assets. The investment balance of –€21 billion [11] tells us that Ireland has *increased* its net foreign investment holdings.

```
Net capital flow in assets and liabilities towards other countries, e.g.:
Net investment abroad (direct and portfolio): -136,440          [9]
Net incoming investment (direct and portfolio): +115,048        [10]
Investment balance: -21,392                                     [11]
Other net financial flows abroad (deposits, speculation, loans to foreigners): -50,508[12]
Other net financial inflows (deposits, speculation, loans from abroad): +71,587   [13]
Balance of other financial flows: +21,079                       [14]
Net change in foreign reserves (note that '+' actually means reserves have fallen): +1,770   [15]
Balancing item (i.e. statistical discrepancy or error): +766    [16]
Capital account balance = +2,223                                [17]
```

Figure 4.5.4 *The capital account for Ireland, 2003 (€millions)*

Other financial flows: The Irish will deposit some of their savings in foreign banks; Irish banks will lend money to foreigners; and Irish financial institutions will place short-term monies abroad in order to earn a higher rate of interest, or simply speculate that a certain currency will increase in value. The €50 billion in financial outflows [12] signifies an increase in short-term foreign assets for the Irish, and the €71 billion in outflows [13] is an increase in Ireland's short-term liabilities to foreigners. The balance in financial inflows of +€21 billion shows an *increase in foreigners' short-term holdings* in Ireland.

Foreign reserves: All countries' central banks hold an amount of foreign currencies and, traditionally, gold. The positive value of €1.77 billion [15] means – rather confusingly – that reserves at the Bank of Ireland have *fallen* by this amount. Somewhat simplified, foreign currencies have been used to buy up euros, shown in the balance of payments as an inflow of money. In any case, using a positive value in the capital account to show a *decrease in foreign reserves* is in keeping with the argument that a net inflow means that domestic holdings of foreign assets have fallen.

Balancing item: The millions of daily money transactions between Ireland and other countries is an almost impossible task to precisely account for. There will be statistical errors, time lags in accounting, and a number of money flows which simply will not show up due to tax/tariff avoidance, parallel markets and illegal trade. Since the balance of payments must always balance, a **balancing item** ('the bit missing') of €766 million [16] has been added into the capital account.

The capital account balance

The current account deficit has to be made up for by other money inflows. The 'mirror image' of the −€2.2 billion current account deficit has been financed by a **capital account surplus** of +€2.2 billion [17].

> **Capital account balance:** The sum of all investment and financial flows to and from a country during a time period, e.g. the change in net foreign assets, is given in the capital account in the balance of payments. A positive value shows a capital account surplus and a negative value shows a capital account deficit.

Putting the pieces together: Comments on the Irish balance of payments

Now, did you go back and revise Section 3.1 with special notice to GDP methodology? Right; GDP minus net property income from abroad equals GNP. In 2001 Irish GDP was larger than GNP and the same holds true for 2003. Let us see why this is relevant for the Irish balance of payments. First off, notice that while there is a considerable *visible trade surplus* of over €32 billion, the current account in total shows a deficit of –€2.2 billion. The main reason is to be found in the **net outflows of income in the invisible trade accounts**.

Background: Ireland has attracted a great deal of foreign direct investment (FDI) over the past 20 years by granting firms tax holidays – initial periods during which foreign firms pay no taxes on profits – of up to 10 years, and ultimately a low 12.5% corporate tax rate. In addition to this, Ireland has strong historical/cultural ties with the US and an abundant, young, well-educated English-speaking workforce. This attracted FDI in massive amounts and US multinational companies (MNCs) accounted for 16% of Ireland's GDP by 1995.[a] By 1998, Irish GDP at PPP had gone from less than 65% of the EU average to over 100% of the EU average.[b]

Analysis of balance of payments: The over 1,100 foreign companies operating in Ireland will generate a great deal of profit which will be repatriated abroad. (This was clearly evident in the figures in Section 3.1 where **net property income from abroad** was negative in 2000; €18.295 million.) The same holds true for 2003, where Ireland has seen a net outward flow of income; foreign companies operating in Ireland have withdrawn –€22,701 million more than Irish companies repatriated from abroad.

Positive value of net property income from abroad = net inflows of income in current account

It should therefore come as no surprise that a country such as Ireland which attracts a large amount of FDI might: 1) have **greater GDP than GNP** because of 2) a **large outflow of repatriated profits** in the current account of balance of payments.

---

a. *Worldwide Capital Shares and Rates of Return to Corporate Capital: Evidence from U.S. Multinationals,* Mihir A. Desai, Harvard University and NBER, November 2001.

b. *Taxation and foreign direct investment in Ireland,* Brendan Walsh, 2001. This is an update of Stabilisation and Adjustment in a Small, Open Economy: Ireland, 1979–95; Oxford Review of Economic Policy 12, 3. (October): 74–86.

Is a current account deficit bad for a country?

This is a good question and one which is vociferously (= loudly) debated amongst economists and in the media. In simple terms the answer is no, not always. A more balanced answer is that since a current account deficit means a capital account surplus, it depends on *why* money is coming in on capital account and *what* the money is being used for. In Ireland's case, the current account deficit has evidently been largely financed by the willingness of other countries to invest in Ireland, and the Irish economy has benefited enormously from the foreign investment inflows; growth rates have been the highest and unemployment rates the lowest in the EU for years. Generally speaking, as long as a current account deficit is made up by *investment* inflows on capital account there is little cause for worry in the short to medium term.

It is when *loans* and *speculative monies* flow in on capital account to fuel *consumption* that harmful effects will show, as the country is in effect living beyond its means and will someday have to pay back loans.[5] There are also long run considerations. For example, should foreign companies start pulling out of Ireland – to invest in the new low-cost EU states for example – then there could be serious repercussions for the Irish economy. We will return to this issue in Section 4.7.

---

5. It's a bit like a household borrowing money. If the money goes to rebuilding the porch and repairing the roof, then the house will be worth more in the future, e.g. there is a return on the spending. Hence, there is no harm in borrowing money. If, however, the borrowed money goes to pay for Christmas presents… go figure.

Outside the box:
Humans are from Venus, economists from Mars

A question that all students of balance of payment accounts ultimately ask themselves is of course 'Do we trade with Mars'? This is a good question, posed by several high-ranking economists.[6] Here's why the question arises …

Assume only two countries, A and B, who trade with each other: one country's outflows on balance of payments would be the other country's inflows. A's exports would be B's imports; B's FDI would flow out of the capital account and into A's capital account, etc.

What would the *sum* of both countries current account be?! Yes, zero. Adding 190 more countries doesn't change this; the sum of the world's current accounts (or capital accounts) must be zero.

It turns out, however, that the world has been running a *current account deficit* for over 25 years, and since we in fact do not trade with other planets, there must be another explanation. Think before you check the answer in the footnote.[7]

Playing around with a few examples

I finish this chapter by giving a few schematic examples of balance of payments flows between two countries. Let's look at the Irish and Australian economies which are now happily trading goods and service instead of prisoners and colonial taxes.[8] Assuming that the two countries only trade with each other, here is a selection of economic transactions taking place between the two economies during a few months (using country-neutral 'dollars'):

1. A distiller in Ballyragget, Ireland, sells $2,500 worth of 'Top o' The Mornin' whiskey to a pub in Cootamundra, Australia.

2. Goanna-Mick from Meekathurra, Australia, on vacation in County Mayo, Ireland, rents a cottage overlooking lots of sheep in Ballyhaunis for a week at $2,000.

3. Mrs Power from Ballydehob, Ireland, puts $6,000 into starting a subsidiary legal firm in Sydney, Australia.

4. Bruce from Kingoonya, Australia, is prolonging adolescence at university in Galway, Ireland. He receives a $3,000 student grant from an unwitting municipal council back home.

5. Sean from Ballyroan, Ireland, buys shares in the Areyonga Shipyard for $3,500. (Sean really needs to get a good map of Australia.)

6. Alice from Three Springs, Australia, puts $6,500 into a bank account in Ballycanew, Ireland.

7. Mrs Power in Ballydehob, Ireland (from [3] above), repatriates $500 in profits from her first customer – an Irish descendant out on bail – in Sydney.

8. Bush Tucker International Delicatessen in Bulgroo, Australia, sells $5,000 worth of sliced baby koala and pickled platypus nibbles to the local Greenpeace chapter in Ballyconnell, Ireland.

These international flows of money between the two countries are shown in Figure 4.5.5 on page 471. Following the flows, it is clear that any outflow of money from Ireland leads to a corresponding inflow to Australia, and vice versa. Irish exports of whiskey and services are inflows to the visible and invisible trade balances in the Irish current account – which are of course outflows in the Australian trade balances in the Australian current account. Irish investment in Australia gives outflows of money in the Irish capital account and concurrent inflows to the Australian current account.

---

6. See for example, Abel and Bernanke, p. 177.

7. The most likely explanation is that a portion of interest, profits and dividends earned abroad simply are not reported at the receiving end (inflow into current account) in order to evade taxes. However, the funds will frequently be registered in the country **sending** the money (outflow from current account). This systematically *understates* the current account inflows in many countries, leading to a 'global current account deficit.'

8. Thousands of Irish 'troublemakers' and convicts were evicted from Ireland and sent as forced colonisers to Australia in the 19th century. This popular export commodity has resulted in tens of thousands of present-day Irish descendants in Australia with names like my Australian editor; 'McAuliffe' (which in fact reads, 'son of Olaf', which means he is actually a Scandinavian descendant!).

Ireland has a current account surplus of $3,000 and thus a corresponding capital account deficit. Once again, do not be confused by the negative value in the Irish capital account! An outflow here means that Ireland has increased its net foreign assets; Ireland has increased holdings in Australia more than Australians have increased holdings in Ireland. Australia has a current account deficit, concomitantly. The $3,000 worth of imports in excess of export revenue has apparently been funded by an inflow of investment money from Ireland.

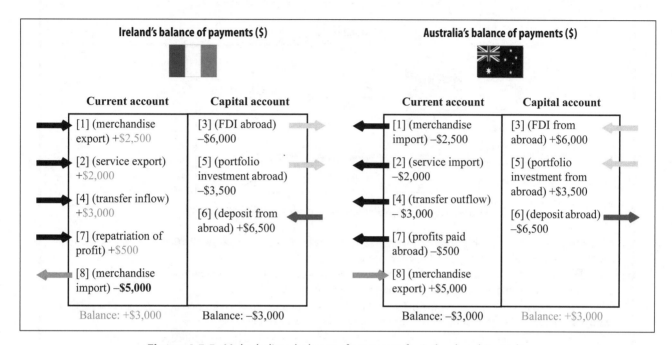

Figure 4.5.5 *Make-believe balance of payments for Ireland and Australia*

Exam tip: Balance of payments diamond

As shall be shown in the remaining Section 4 chapters, the balance of payments will have an effect on other macro variables, primarily exchange rates, aggregate demand and the terms of trade. But it doesn't stop there - said macro variables will in turn influence the balance of payments! And finally, the macro variables will influence *each other*. It's a big can of worms basically but I shall attempt to give you a few examples. Figure 4.5.6 illustrates the 'multi-causal' nature of macro variables that are linked to the balance of payments (BoP in the figure).

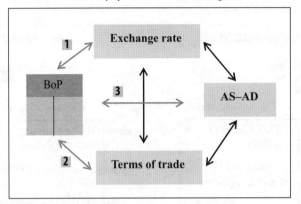

Figure 4.5.6 *The BoP diamond – dual causality all around*

There are three arrows for each box and two directions, giving a total of 24 possible examples (if both current and capital account are used). I shall confine this to the following six:

1 A) A depreciation of the home currency would make exports cheaper (rise in exports) and imports dearer (fall in imports). This would improve the balance of trade in current account.

  B) Increased exports would improve the balance of trade in current account, and the increased demand for exports would increase the demand for the home currency and cause an appreciation.

2 A) A decrease in demand for exports in current account would cause demand for the home currency to decrease. This lowers the price of exports and worsens the terms of trade.

  B) A decrease in the terms of trade by way of lower export prices would cause an increase in exports and improve the current account in balance of payments.

3 A) If AD in the home economy rises there would be an increase in domestic income and inflation (relative to trade partners' inflation). Rising relative inflation means exports would decrease. Both rising domestic income and inflation would cause imports to increase. This affects the current account negatively.

  B) An increase in exports and/or decrease in imports would improve current account and also have a positive effect on aggregate demand, as both imports and exports are AD components.

POP QUIZ 4.5.1 BALANCE OF PAYMENTS

1 A firm in Argentina sells $US250,000 worth of beef to Canada and then the firm buys $US50,000 worth of machines for slaughterhouses from Brazil. What is the *net effect* on each country's balance of payments due to these two transactions?

2 What is the result of a country's capital account balance minus the invisible trade balance?

3 We have the following figures in the balance of payments (billions) for a country; exports = €340, imports = €380, net invisibles = + €50, net financial flows = - €120. What is the current account balance?

4 'The US current account deficit is increasing all the time and it's China's fault – they are stealing our jobs.' This oft-heard statement provides you with a clue as to the state of China's current account. Explain.

5 How would a visit to Thailand by Italian IB students affect both countries' balance of payments?

6 Explain how a capital account surplus in Kenya might create jobs and increase national income.

7 Why might a country have a persistent current account deficit for many years?

8 In preparation for the next section: How might South Korea's current account be affected if the exchange rate for the Korean won were to fall? (i.e. the 'price' of the won decreases.)

Exchange rates

4.6

CONTENTS

EXCHANGE RATES

Introduction

This can be done the hard way or the easy way. I am going to pick the latter. An exchange rate between two currencies is very similar to two goods illustrated by a production possibility frontier (PPF); the cost of one currency is always in terms of the other. If one American dollar (USD) gets you 0.77 euros (€), then the **exchange rate for the US dollar is €0.77**, i.e. the price of the dollar is €0.77. If the US dollar also gets you 0.69 British pounds (£) then the exchange rate for the dollar is £0.69. Thus, **USD1 = €0.77 = £0.69**.

In the examples using a PPF, when 1 unit of cloth had an opportunity cost of 2 units of oranges, then the opportunity cost of 1 unit of oranges was 0.5 units of cloth. Similarly, if USD1 = €0.77, then €1 = USD1.3 (1 / 0.77). Thus, using the same figures as above, the **exchange rate for the euro becomes €1 = USD1.3 = £0.89**. Table 4.6.1 shows the exchange rates for a few major currencies. The exchange rates for each currency are given in columns, i.e. USD1 costs 90.42 Japanese yen (¥), or 1.16 Swiss francs (SFR).

Table 4.6.1 *Selection of exchange rates for major currencies (February 2009)*

Currency 6 May 2004	U.S. Dollar (USD)	Yen (¥)	Euro (€)	U.K. Pound (£)	Swiss Franc (SFR)
U.S. Dollar (USD)	1	0.0111	1.287	1.45	1.86
Yen (¥)	90.42	1	116.41	131.06	77.95
Euro (€)	0.776	0.0086	1	1.123	0.67
U.K. Pound (£)	0.69	0.0076	0.888	1	0.59
Swiss Franc (SFR)	1.16	0.0128	1.49	1.68	1

(Source: http://finance.yahoo.com/m3?u – an excellent site for up-to-the-minute exchange rates which also plots out five year trends.)

Exchange rate: The exchange rate is the **price of a currency expressed in terms of another currency**. Thus the exchange rate for the US dollar can be expressed in the amount of British pounds, euro or Mexican pesos needed to buy one dollar. (The exchange rate can also be expressed as the price of a currency against a 'basket' of other currencies.) Note that when we refer to the 'exchange rate for the dollar' we use the price of the US dollar in terms of, say, pounds. The exchange rate for the pound would naturally be expressed as the price of pounds in another currency – here, US dollars. Thus, £1 = USD1.45 and USD1 = £0.69.

The foreign exchange market

Currencies are bought and sold on a *foreign exchange market*. The demand for a currency is a function of three main variables.:

1. **The demand for other countries' goods and services:** When European tourists visit the US they will need US dollars and European citizens wanting more US goods will be met by European importers increasing their demand for US dollars in order to buy US goods. (Note that these transactions for which EU citizens need dollars correspond to the **current account**.)

2. **The demand for FDI and portfolio investment in another country:** Firms setting up subsidiaries abroad will need foreign exchange, and citizens, firms and investment houses in the US wanting to buy shares, bills/bonds or deposit money in European banks will need euros.

3. **Speculative demand:** When international speculators such as fund management firms and other financial institutions believe that the euro will

appreciate, they will buy euros in order to make a gain in selling them when the euro rate rises.

There are thus a number of 'players' on the foreign exchange market. *People* and *export/import firms* will buy currencies from banks and foreign exchange offices to conduct international transactions. *Foreign exchange brokers* – currency traders – will in turn be used by banks to supply needed currencies and to cash-in unneeded currencies. Finally, the *central banks* of trading countries might intervene on the currency market by drawing upon (or adding to) the foreign reserves in order to adjust the exchange rate. Keep this straight; all of the players on the market can influence the price of the currency – as long as they are powerful enough!

The market for a currency is just like any other market – but far more efficient and much faster. (In fact, the international foreign exchange market could well be the most perfectly competitive market of them all: abundant information via low-cost computer links; homogenous goods; low barriers to entry; and many buyers and sellers.) People, firms and importers, etc. in different countries will have a demand for foreign goods and foreign investment. Currency traders and banks will want to 'sell' as much currency as possible as they make money on the transaction via commissions – which is a service charge.[1] The foreign exchange

market is simply a mechanism to put the two parties in contact with each other. Back to supply and demand.

Supply and demand again – a tale of two currency markets

I will limit the discussion to two currencies, the euro and the US dollar, in order to make things a bit simpler and to impress upon you that since the price of the euro is in terms of the US dollar –and vice versa – then the activities in one market will affect the other market. (Note that we are assuming that the exchange rate is operating under market forces; i.e. a **floating exchange rate**.)

> **Floating exchange rate:** A floating exchange rate is when a currency's price (in terms of other currencies) is totally determined by market forces, e.g. supply and demand for the currency.

The supply curve for euros is upward sloping (diagram I in Figure 4.6.1) since a higher price for the euro – *ceteris paribus* – would enable European citizens to buy more American goods, and in doing so more euros would be available on the US market. The demand curve is downward sloping to indicate that Americans will buy more euros when they get more euros – and thus goods – for their US dollars.

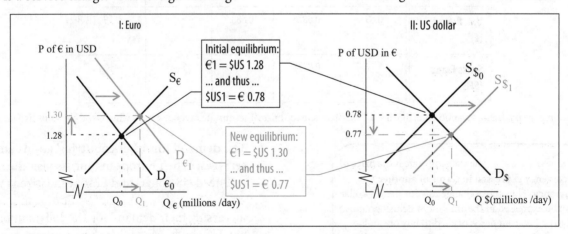

Figure 4.6.1 *The exchange rates for the euro and the US dollar*

Diagram I in Figure 4.6.1 above shows how an initial equilibrium in the exchange rate for the euro is set at USD1.28. This gives an exchange rate for the US dollar of €0.82, shown in diagram II. Say that there is increased American demand for European goods or an increase in American tourists to Europe:

- **Euro**: the demand for euros will increase from D_{ϵ_0} to D_{ϵ_1} in diagram I, and the **exchange rate for euros will rise** (appreciate – see further on) from USD1.28 to USD1.30.
- **USD**: As more dollars would flow into foreign exchange offices to buy the euro, the supply of US

---

1. Note that a 'No commission!' sign on a foreign exchange office simply means that there will be a larger margin between buy and sell rates. For example, an American tourist in Rome might get €75 for $US100 – but an Italian leaving for the US would get less than $US100 in exchange for €75. The foreign exchange office lives on the difference as a profit.

dollars would increase. This is shown in diagram II, where the supply of US dollars increases from S€₀ to S$₁, and the **exchange rate for the US dollar falls** (depreciates) from €0.78 to €0.77. The new exchange rate for the USD is naturally the inverse of the price of the euro (1/1.30).

Please note that I use two diagrams simply to illustrate the 'price of one in terms of the other', and the shifts in demand and supply for a currency in *two markets* – the euro market and the US dollar market. In the remainder of this chapter, I will illustrate using one currency at a time.

Warning!
Supply/demand for money and the exchange rate

Students frequently confuse the supply and demand for money with the foreign exchange market. Any given currency will have an internal value and an external value.

- The **internal value** shows how much can be purchased domestically, i.e. the real purchasing power of money within the economy. Any change in the internal value is caused by domestic price changes, e.g. inflation.

- The exchange rate shows the **external value** of one's domestic currency, i.e. what can be purchased in other countries – after first buying other countries' currencies. The external value of the currency is therefore broadly determined by two factors; the price of other currencies needed to buy foreign goods and the price level in other countries.

While there is indeed a strong connection between the supply of money and the exchange rate, it is … … way, way, way outside the syllabus. An increase in the money supply in Britain could lead to inflation via the transmission mechanism (see Section 3.5). As prices in Britain rise relative to other countries, British imports will rise. This in turn will mean that more foreign currencies will be bought with the British pound which increases the supply of pounds on the foreign exchange rate market. So yes, a change in the supply of money does affect the supply of a currency and the exchange rate.

POP QUIZ 4.6.1   INTRODUCTION TO EXCHANGE RATES

1   The exchange rate for the US dollar is 7.5 Swedish Crowns (SEK). What is the exchange rate for the SEK?

2   What will happen to the exchange rate for the Japanese yen if more tourists visit Japan?

3   What will be the effect on the Japanese exchange rate if Japanese imports rise?

4   Farawayistan places a large quantity of embassy personnel in Nearistan. These personnel buy lots of goods and services from Nearistani firms. Explain what will happen on the foreign exchange markets in terms of Faraway dollars and Neari pounds.

Fixed exchange rates ©IBO 2003

In the foreign exchange market examples used thus far, we have assumed that the exchange rate is established by market forces of supply and demand. When a group of two or more countries instead intentionally keep their exchange rate constant, a fixed exchange rate has been established. Typically, countries in a fixed exchange rates regime (= system or mechanism) use the central bank to intervene on the foreign exchange market in order to keep the exchange rate within a narrow band – much like the mechanism used in a buffer stock scheme (see Section 2.1).

> **Fixed exchange rate:** A fixed exchange rate links a currency to others within a narrow band, or 'corridor'. The central bank keeps the currency fixed in the short run by *buying/selling its own currency* on the foreign exchange market, and by *increasing/decreasing the interest rate*.

The central bank can affect the exchange rate in the **short run** by *buying or selling its own currency* on the foreign exchange market, and by adjusting the *interest rate* to influence investors'/speculator's demand for the currency.

In the **long run**, governments might intervene using *fiscal policies*, *supply-side measures* and *protectionism* to adjust national income in order to increase or decrease exports and citizens' propensity to import. Changes in exports would affect the demand for the home currency, as outlined in Figure 4.6.1 on page 476, while a change in imports would affect the supply of the home currency (see Section 4.7).

A little depth:
History of fixed exchange rates

The Gold Standard: There have been a number of types of fixed exchange rate regimes, the purest form – and most rigid – being the Gold Standard of the late 19th and early 20th century. In this system, each country's currency was based on the value of gold and each note issued was backed up by gold in the central bank's reserves. Since all currencies under the gold standard were locked into the price of gold at a certain rate, each currency was fixed to the others. The gold standard was disused during the First World War, made a brief return during the 1920s and was finally abandoned during the 1930s.

The Bretton Woods exchange rate system: Similar to the gold standard, the post-WWII Bretton Woods system linked currencies to each other by 'anchoring' them to the US dollar rather than gold, which is why the system was also known as the **Dollar Standard**. Countries set a par value of their currency against the US dollar and thus all currencies within the system were fixed against each other and allowed to move within a narrow band (see Figure 4.6.2 on page 479). The US dollar was in turn linked to gold at 1/35 ounces per dollar (USD35 per ounce). In order to give the system some flexibility, countries were allowed to readjust their exchange rates when pressure was so strong on a currency that the central bank could not in the long run keep the rate within the band. Thus if England was consistently running a current account deficit and thereby 'flooding' the exchange market with pounds, the Bank of England would ultimately run out of foreign currency reserves with which to buy up the pound and keep the rate. Such a **fundamental disequilibrium** could be solved by downward realignment (*devaluation* – see further on), e.g. lowering the exchange rate for the pound.

The possibility of *realignment* in the Bretton Woods system meant in fact that countries had pegged their currencies to the US dollar. The system was therefore in fact an **adjustable peg regime**, since countries could re-peg their currencies in the long run when economic fundamentals such as current account deficits so dictated. The Bretton Woods system broke down during 1971/72 as inflation and frequent repegging by a number of countries, meant that to all intents and purposes, the currencies were now floating rather than fixed. What finally crashed the system was an overvalued dollar, which meant increasing current account deficits in the US, and ultimately **declining US reserves of gold**. There were simply too many dollars floating around in the world for the US treasury to be able to guarantee the outstanding dollars with gold.

How a fixed exchange rate works

In the **short to medium term**, a fixed exchange regime is upheld by keeping the exchange rate within a narrow band by central bank intervention. Using the Bretton Woods system as an example, diagrams I and II in Figure 4.6.2 on page 479 illustrate how Britain's central bank, the Bank of England, pegged the pound to the dollar at an exchange rate of USD2.8.

In order to maintain the fixed exchange rate, the Bank of England would use the foreign reserves to buy and sell the pound on a day-to-day basis:

- **Keeping the pound down:** Diagram I shows how the long-run goal of an exchange rate of USD2.8 to the pound is kept at **point A**, at $S_{\pounds_0}$ and $D_{\pounds_0}$. The pound was allowed to fluctuate within a narrow band of 2 US cents up or down which the pound had to remain within. An increased demand for the pound, $D_{\pounds_0}$, which threatened to put the exchange rate above the ceiling, USD2.84 at point C, would be met by *intervention selling* of the pound by the Bank of England.[2] This would increase the supply of pounds on the foreign exchange market, $S_{\pounds_0}$ to $S_{\pounds_1}$, and bring the exchange rate for the pound back down within the upper limit of the band at point D – USD2.82 per pound.

- **Keeping the pound up:** In the same way, when the exchange rate for the pound fell below the lower limit, say to point C' at USD2.76 per pound, $S'_{\pounds_2}$ and $D'_{\pounds_0}$ in diagram II, the Bank of England would intervene and *buy pounds* using foreign

---

2. In effect, the Bank of England buys up US dollars with the pound.

currencies (e.g. US dollars) from the foreign reserves. This increased the demand for the pound, $D'\varepsilon_0$ to $D'\varepsilon_1$ bringing the exchange rate

back up to the lower limit of USD2.78 per pound at **point D'**. In essence, the English central bank used US dollars to buy back its own currency.[3]

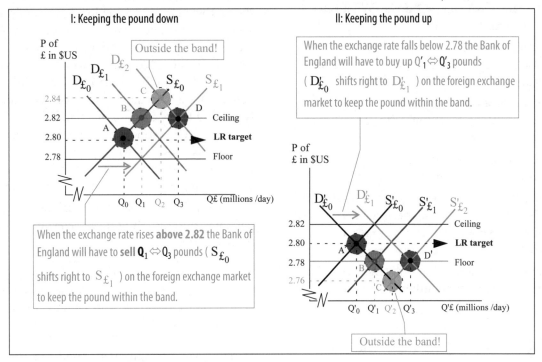

Figure 4.6.2 *Fixed exchange rate – the Bretton Woods system*

A little depth:
Other exchange rate tools available to central banks

Central banks are not limited to buying and selling their currencies in order to influence the exchange rate. There are two other alternatives in the short run:

1. The central bank can **change the interest rate**. If the central bank wishes to increase the exchange rate, the interest rate could be raised. This would influence the demand for the home currency as foreign investors/speculators would see a higher rate of return in holding the currency - demand for the home currency would rise.

2. The central bank could borrow from the **International Monetary Fund**, the **IMF** (see Section 5.5). The IMF was created at the Bretton Woods conference for precisely this purpose; to aid countries having difficulty in keeping a stable exchange rate. When a country's currency falls, and

the central bank runs out of foreign exchange to buy up the home currency, the central bank can **borrow funds from the IMF** to get over the crisis.

In addition to the short-run exchange rate policies above, a country might have to resort to more **fundamental adjustments** if the home currency showed signs of long-run weakness. The currency could be repegged at a lower exchange rate; the government could implement **deflationary policies** to reduce import demand and thus the demand for other currencies; **protectionist measures** could also lower imports; and various **supply-side policies** could increase the long-run competitiveness of the economy and thereby increase demand for the home currency. See Section 4.7, expenditure-switching and expenditure-reducing policies.

---

3. Perhaps this helps clarify the confusing issue of how a **minus value** in the **foreign reserves in capital account** (Section 4.5) means that in fact the **foreign reserves have increased**. When the Bank of England buys foreign currency, pounds flow out of England (minus value in the capital account) and now the Bank of England has increased its holding of foreign currencies.

POP QUIZ 4.6.2   FIXED EXCHANGE RATES

1   The Chinese government pegs the yuan to the US dollar at a rate of 8.3 yuan = 1 dollar. What is the exchange rate for the yuan?

2   Assume that the Bank of China will allow a fluctuation of the yuan of 2% up or down. Between which values will the yuan be allowed to move?

3   The yuan becomes stronger on the market and looks like exceeding the ceiling of the peg. What does the Bank of China do?

4   How does the Bank of China's action in question **3** affect the balance of payments in China?

5   Say that the Chinese start to import massively from the US. How would this affect the exchange rate and how might the Bank of China have to react ultimately?

6   If the Bank of China runs out of foreign reserves, is there any other way it can influence the exchange rate?

Floating exchange rates ©IBO 2003

While a fixed exchange rate means that currencies are, well, fixed against each other, a floating exchange rate means that currencies … um, float. OK, let me try one more time; in every country I ever lived in as a child – around twelve I believe – children have played marbles. People, I was the marble KING. Man I took the game seriously! What I didn't win on the playing field I would make up for by keeping track of the marble market and engaging in some heavy-duty arbitrage[4]. Five 'swirlies' for 1 'cleary', 4 'clearies' for one 'steely' (= large steel ball from a ball-bearing) would be the rate of exchange rate in one group of players while in another group I might find that 4 'swirlies' would get me 1 'cleary' and 3 'clearies' 1 'steely'.

Acting as a marble-trader, I would buy 'clearies' at a rate of 4 'swirlies' and re-sell on the other market to get 5 'clearies' – and then repeat the process. Sometimes I got burned when I had swamped the market for 'clearies' and got left holding a goodly number of 'clearies' at an exchange rate of 3 'swirlies'. Or when some new kid showed up (whose mother worked for an aircraft company) and unloaded a bucket of 'steelies' on the market – destroying the value of my hoard of 'steelies'. Such is life.

A floating exchange rate system is very similar to the marble market; market forces of supply and demand set the rate, or price, of a currency. A currency 'floats' amongst the other currencies on the market and the price is set in accordance with the mechanisms of supply and demand outlined earlier. In short, the demand for a currency is a derived demand. It is **fundamentally** based on the demand for goods, services and investments in other countries. There is also **speculation** in currency – which is perhaps the main **short-run** determinant of exchange rates – which is based on the predictions/hopes/fears of currency speculators 'betting' on changes in exchange rates.[5] We will look more closely at these determinants further on in this section.

> **Floating exchange rate**: A floating exchange rate is when a currency's price (in terms of other currencies) is totally determined by market forces, e.g. supply and demand for the currency.

The main difference between the marble and currency market is the degree of *perfect information* available on foreign exchange markets. Currency traders will not be able to enjoy large differences in rates between the currencies in different parts of the world for any length of time – commonly measured in minutes rather than days. The currency market never sleeps. From Japan to London via New York, there will always be 24-hour trading taking place. Note that a pure, or completely free, exchange rate regime is almost unheard of, since central banks have a tendency to intervene ultimately to correct what is considered to be disequilibrium in a floating exchange rate. This is called a **managed float** – or more commonly, a **dirty float**. The latter infers that 'impure' market forces – central bank interventions – are present. For example, Japan has amassed considerable foreign reserves (primarily US dollars) by using yen to purchase other currencies (US dollars, etc.) on the foreign exchange market in order to keep the yen at a favourably low exchange rate level in order to boost export competitiveness.

---

4.   Arbitrage refers to the process of seeking out price differences in different markets and reselling; buying cheap and selling dear.

5.   Notice that very small changes in exchange rate margins can lead to *astounding* profits if large enough numbers are used. For example, if a speculator feels that the euro will fall (depreciate) by 0.1% against the Swiss Franc (SFR) by tomorrow, he/she might borrow €50 million overnight and immediately buy Swiss Francs at an exchange rate of €1= SFR 1.551 (SFR1 = €0.6447). The speculator now has SFR 77.55 million. When/if the euro does depreciate by 0.1%, the speculator cashes in his/her SFR and gets €50,004,240 (€1 = 1.5508 or SFR1 = 0.6448). Disregarding the interest the speculator will pay on the EURO loan, an overnight profit of €4,240 is a tidy sum for five minutes work on the phone and computer terminal.

Outside the box:

Trade weighted exchange rate

The exchange rate method thus far applied is in fact a bilateral exchange rate, i.e. the rate between two countries only. This neglects the total effect – the effective exchange rate – when taking into account other countries with which trade takes place. Therefore currency values are often expressed in an index, where the relative importance of trade done with various countries is taken into consideration. By putting the exchange rate in terms of a 'basket' of currencies, one can see the average change in the price of the currency. The currencies are assigned weights depending on how much trade is done with that country.

Example: Assume that Britain trades entirely with three currency areas: Euroland, the US and Japan (see Table 4.6.2). A trade weighted exchange rate is composed by weighting the British pound in terms of the amount of trade done with the three currencies, and indexing them over a period of time:

Table 4.6.2 *TWI – Comparing currencies*

Currency	Trade weight	Price of £ 2003	Price of £ 2004	Percentage changes in exchange rate Unweighted	Percentage changes in exchange rate Weighted
	0.6	1.4	1.45	3.50%	2.10%
USD	0.3	1.62	1.85	14.20%	4.30%
Japan	0.1	190	200	+5.2%	0.50%
				Average: +7.6%	Trade weighted: +6.9%
					TWI 2003 = 100 TWI 2004 = 106.9

A simple average shows that the exchange rate for the pound has increased by 7.6%, but by using weights which show the trade patterns of Britain the pound has increased by 6.9%. This trade weighted index (TWI above) is a far more meaningful value of the pound's rate of exchange than a simple average of the change in different currencies.

Managed exchange rates ©IBO 2003

Completely fixed exchange rates create a problem of **inflexibility**, since economies will have different fundamentals such as growth rates and inflation rates. In the long run, it could be very costly for a country with a weakening currency to defend its link to other currencies, for example by running down the foreign reserves and dampening the domestic economy by raising interest rates (thereby reducing imports and the supply of the home currency).

For this reason, fixed exchange rate regimes are largely a thing of the past. The most common form of exchange rate regimes is a floating exchange rate system (see further on) where the price of a currency is determined by the forces of supply and demand. In between the two 'extremes' of a fixed and floating regime, one finds a managed exchange rate regime and a pegged system. A managed float means that the government and central bank allow the currency to float freely but will intervene at times to either raise or lower the exchange rate. A pegged system is a form of fixed exchange rate where a country unilaterally (= one side only) pegs its exchange rate against another currency.

> **Managed and pegged exchange rate system**: When a country allows a currency to float freely but intervenes in order to adjust the exchange rate, one speaks of a **managed** exchange rate regime. It is sometimes referred to as a 'dirty float'. An example is the Singapore dollar.
>
> When a country adjusts the price of its currency in order to fix it against that of another, it is known as a **pegged exchange** rate regime.

Managed exchange rate regime: the Singapore dollar (SGD)

The Singapore dollar (SGD) has been managed against an undisclosed basket of currencies since 1981. The central bank of Singapore, the Monetary Authority of Singapore (MAS), allows the SGD to float within a 'band' and allows the exchange rate to move up and down within this band. The MAS uses the same policy tools outlined earlier; buying and selling the SGD and adjusting the interest rate. (Refer back to Figure 4.6.2 on page 479, "Fixed exchange rate – the Bretton Woods system" for diagrammatic illustration of how central bank intervention affects supply and demand for a currency.)

- *A movement above the band*: Should the exchange rate for the SGD tend towards a level above the

band (P_{high} in Figure 4.6.3) then the central bank of Singapore can:

- Sell the SGD in order to increase the supply of the SGD …

- … and/or lower interest rates to decrease demand for the SGD.

- *A movement below the band*: When the exchange rate tends towards a level below the band (P_{low}) then the central bank can:

- Buy the SGD (using the foreign currency reserves) in order to increase demand for the SGD …

- … and/or raise interest rates to increase demand for the SGD.

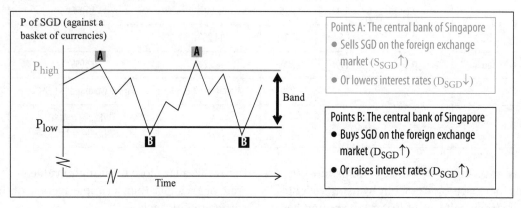

Figure 4.6.3 *A managed exchange rate – the SGD*

It is worth mentioning that few countries have a *completely* floating exchange rate. There are strong political and economic reasons for a government to intervene on the foreign exchange market in order to bolster or weaken the exchange rate. For example, during October 2008 the Mexican central bank sold off some USD15 billion in order to halt a falling peso exchange rate. Most countries will at one point intervene in order to stabilise the exchange rate. In fact, perhaps the only major currency which has not been subjected to interventionist buying by the home country central bank during the past 30 years is the US dollar. This policy of 'benign neglect' has been a cornerstone of US exchange rate policy since the early 1970s under President Nixon.

Pegged exchange rate regime: the Chinese yuan (1995 to 2005)

The Chinese yuan was pegged to the US dollar since between 1995 and 2005 at a rate of USD1 = CNY8.3, giving an exchange rate for the yuan of USD0.12048. Figure 4.6.4 on page 483 shows how the pegged rate for the yuan was managed.

When the exchange rate exceeded the ceiling of USD 0.12082 per yuan, points A, the Chinese central bank sold yuan (e.g. bought USDs) in order to increase the supply of yuan and lower the exchange rate. When the rate fell below the floor level of USD0.12024 per yuan, points B, the central bank would buy yuan (with foreign currencies, primarily the USD) which increased the demand for yuan and caused the exchange rate for the yuan to rise.

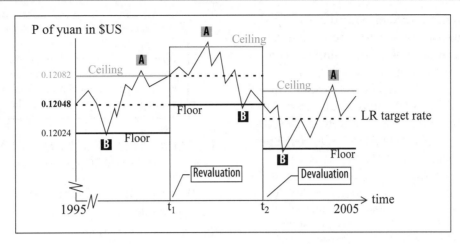

Figure 4.6.4 *Exchange rate for the yuan in USD, 2003–04*

If there was a **fundamental** upward movement in the yuan, i.e. the managed rate (ceiling) was below the long-run rate the market sets, the Chinese central bank could realign the currency by **revaluating** the yuan. This is shown in Figure 4.6.4 at t_1, where a revaluation moves the managed exchange rate corridor upwards. Conversely, a fundamental overvaluation of the yuan, shown at t_2, might cause the central bank of China to **devalue** the currency, rather than continue to bolster the yuan by massive purchasing of yuan and running down the foreign reserves.

The yuan fluctuated very little between 1995 and 2005 – less than 0.2%. During the first years of 2000 there was increasing international pressure on China to **revalue** the yuan in order for major trade countries (read: USA) to be able to compete with Chinese goods. In 2005 China dropped the peg to the US dollar but adopted a peg towards a wider basket of currencies. By the end of 2008, the yuan had appreciated by over 20% against the US dollar.

Storytime: Stalinist exchange rate mechanism

A popular story amongst historians tells of how the Minister of Finance in the Soviet Union was asked by Stalin to advise him in setting an exchange rate for the rouble. The Minister had a thick file which he leafed through during his meeting as he put forward his case for an exchange rate of $US1 to 14 roubles. This apparently displeased Stalin as it made the rouble look inferior, so he leaned over and drew a line through the '1'. This established the exchange rate of the rouble at $US1 to 4 roubles.

Distinction between depreciation and devaluation ©IBO 2003

Devaluing the currency is like wetting the bed; at first it feels warm and comfy, but ultimately turns cold and uncomfortable.[6]

It is important that you have a firm grasp of the economic terminology used to describe fluctuations in exchange rates. Try to work the following terms into your active vocabulary.

Depreciation: When the exchange rate (expressed in terms of another currency or a trade weighted basket of currencies) for a freely floating currency falls, then the currency has depreciated. During 2003 the US dollar fell by 12% (against an average of the seven currencies used by America's main trading partners), i.e. the dollar became an average of 12% cheaper for America's trade partners and visitors to the US.[7] Since the US dollar is a *floating currency*, one says that the dollar has depreciated – it has fallen in value compared to another currency, or basket of currencies.

---

6. Assar Lindbeck, famous Swedish economist.
7. US government site at http://www.bea.gov/bea/newsrel/transnewsrelease.htm.

Devaluation: When a fixed or pegged currency is realigned by the government to a lower exchange rate, the currency has been devalued. For example, when Venezuela readjusted the Venezuelan Bolivar in February 2004, amidst a degree of fiscal turmoil, the Bolivar fell from a peg of 1,598 Bolivars per US dollar to 1,918 per dollar – which means the exchange rate for the Bolivar went from USD0.00062 to USD0.00052 per Bolivar. This is a devaluation of 16.1%.

> **Depreciation and devaluation:** A fall in the price of a floating currency against another currency (or basket of currencies) means the currency has depreciated. When a fixed or pegged currency is realigned to a lower value, the currency has been devalued.

Appreciation and revaluation

©IBO 2003

Appreciation: When the market value of a freely floating currency increases, i.e. the **market price has increased**, the currency has appreciated. This can be caused by a decrease in the supply of the currency and/or an increase in demand for it. For example, the Indonesian rupiah went up by over 25% against the US dollar in the 18 months between January 2002 and July 2003. (Note that one could well say that the US dollar has depreciated against the Indonesian rupiah.) This was due to controls on foreign exchange imposed by government and an increasing demand for Indonesian exports.

Revaluation: Naturally, a government which is operating a pegged exchange rate regime can re-peg its currency at a higher exchange rate, in which case the currency has been revalued. This was the case in aforementioned Venezuela in February 2003, when the case was exactly the opposite; the Bolivar was adjusted upwards (repegged) from USD0.00052 to USD0.00062 per Bolivar, a revaluation of 19%.

> **Appreciation and revaluation:** When the exchange rate of a freely floating currency rises, the currency has appreciated. When the government/central bank of a country running a fixed or pegged exchange rate regime repegs a fixed/pegged currency at a higher rate, the currency has been revalued.

POP QUIZ 4.6.3   FLOATING AND MANAGED EXCHANGE RATES

1 Why is the demand for a currency so evidently a **derived** demand?

2 What is a 'dirty float'?

3 How does a country succeed in keeping its currency pegged to another currency?

4 The Hong Kong dollar (HKD) is pegged to the US dollar and the US dollar appreciates. What happens to the HKD compared to:

 a the US dollar

 b other currencies?

Effects on exchange rates

The exchange rate will be affected by a good many factors, and this section will deal with the main determinants of the exchange rate. Note that two important assumptions must be made: 1) The currency in question (the US dollar) is not only floating but also freely floating – there is no intervention by the US central bank; 2) Each of the determinants below is operating under the ceteris paribus conditions – a change in interest rates is not accompanied by a change in another variable. Note that the US currency in Figure 4.6.5 on page 486 is priced using a *trade weighted index* (TWI), see "Outside the box: Trade weighted exchange rate" on page 481), i.e. an average price of the US dollar in terms of the main American trade partners' currencies.

A little depth:
The never-ending story of exchange rates and demand

Refer to "Exam tip: Balance of payments diamond" on page 472. Any change in the exchange rate will naturally have an effect on the demand for goods, services and investments. For example, an increase in demand for US goods will cause an appreciation of the US dollar. Ultimately, this might lead to a decrease in US exports as it has become more expensive for non-US residents – relative to other countries – to buy US

goods. This contributes to exchange rate fluctuations over time. Thus: Demand for US exports ↑→ demand for $US ↑→ x∆ for $US ↑ … and a higher price of the $US ultimately causes demand for US exports to fall → demand for $US ↓ → x∆ for $US ↓ → demand for US exports rises, etc.

Putting the pieces together: CPED and exchange rates

Perhaps the best example of how international firms will need to keep an eye on cross-price elasticity, is the foreign exchange market, where the price of currencies –the exchange rate – is set. Every day, thousands … eh, that's millions of buying and selling actions set the exchange rate for the Japanese yen. Every visiting businessman and tourist in Kyoto will increase the demand for the yen just as every Toyota purchased by Americans or Spaniards will increase the demand for yen. This is derived demand – I would avoid using the term 'complement goods' here – and there is a positive relationship between the demand for Japanese goods/services and the demand for the Yen! It also works in the opposite direction; a rise in the Japanese exchange rate (i.e. a rise in the price of the yen) will lower demand for Japanese exports. As Japan is one of the world's major exporters, don't you think Japanese businesses will keep a close eye on the price of the yen? Of course they will, knowing that if the yen rises in value, the American will have to use more dollars to buy the yen in order to buy the Toyota Land Cruiser and demand will fall.

Trade flow ©IBO 2003

When American exports increase, there will be an increased demand for the dollar as importers in other countries will need more dollars to buy the American goods. The same goes for services and tourism; more banking services and tourism mean greater demand for the dollar.

- **Increased exports** will increase the demand for the dollar, shown by the shift in the demand curve from $D\$_0$ to $D\$_1$ in Figure 4.6.5 on page 486, and subsequently an appreciation of the dollar from 100 to 104.

  $\Delta\uparrow$US exports → $\Delta\uparrow$demand for USD → appreciation of the USD

- An **increase in imports** and/or and increase in American tourism abroad means that more dollars will be traded to purchase imports and buy tourist services. This **increases the supply of dollars** on the market – $S\$_0$ to $S\$_2$ – and the US dollar depreciates from 100 to 96.

  $\Delta\downarrow$US exports → $\Delta\uparrow$supply of USD → depreciation of the USD

Capital flows/interest rate changes

©IBO 2003

One of the main reasons for the phenomenal appreciation of the US dollar during the 1990s was that it was so attractive for foreign firms to invest in the US. Strong growth, high profits and a dynamic and innovative environment attracted billions of investment yen/euro/British pounds. In order to build a plant in the US or buy American shares, one must first buy US dollars; demand for dollars increases and the dollar will appreciate.

- Posit then that one of the following happens: profits in US companies rise; US corporate taxes are lowered; US productivity increases; or legislation is limiting foreign ownership in the US is scrapped. Any of these will affect FDI and portfolio investment from abroad positively as investment conditions and returns on investment have improved. As foreigners' demand for setting up firms and buying American shares goes up, the demand for the US dollar will increase. Hence, increased foreign investment demand in the US will cause the dollar to appreciate.

  $\Delta\uparrow$Inflows of investment to US → $\Delta\uparrow$demand for USD → US dollar appreciates

- Conversely, when American firms set up factories abroad and US investors increase their holdings of European/Japanese bills, bonds and shares, Americans will have to buy other currencies in order to make these exchanges. The supply of the US dollar will increase, which in turn will lower the exchange rate of the dollar in countries receiving FDI/portfolio inflows.

  $\Delta\uparrow$US investment abroad → $\Delta\uparrow$supply of USD → US dollar depreciates

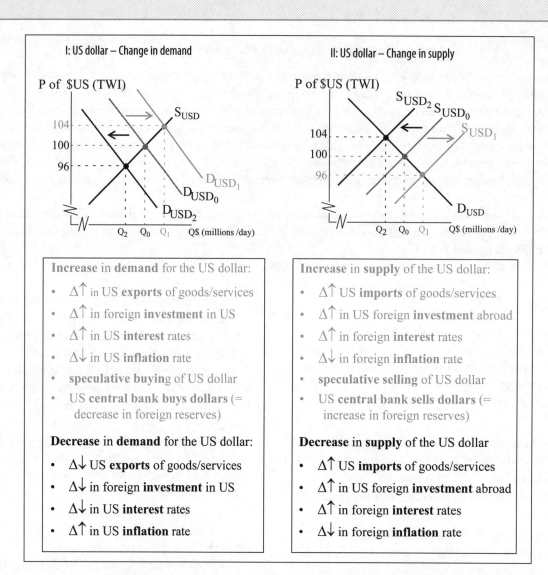

Figure 4.6.5 *Variables affecting the exchange rate for the US dollar*

Inflation ©IBO 2003

Keep in mind our assumption of *ceteris paribus*, as it means that a change in the macro environment in the US means a *relative* change. If inflation during a time period is 5% in the US and 3% in trade partners' economies, the US relative rate of inflation has increased.

- *Increase in relative inflation*: When the rate of inflation in the US increases *relative* to that of trading partners, US goods and services become comparatively more expensive and **US exports will fall** as will demand for the US dollar. There will also be an **increase in imports** to the US (as foreign prices are relatively lower) which means that more dollars will be traded for other currencies and the supply of the US dollar will increase – which also helps to lower the exchange rate for the dollar.

$\Delta\uparrow$ relative inflation in US
$\rightarrow\Delta\downarrow$ demand for US exports and $\Delta\uparrow$ US demand for imports
$\rightarrow\Delta\downarrow$ demand for US dollar and $\Delta\uparrow$ supply of US dollar
$\rightarrow$ USD depreciates

- *Decrease in relative inflation*: In the same way, a lower relative rate of inflation in the US would therefore mean an *increase in demand for US goods* and dollars. There would also be a *decrease in US imports* and decreased supply of dollars

$\Delta\downarrow$ relative inflation in US
$\rightarrow \Delta\uparrow$ demand for US exports and $\Delta\downarrow$ US demand for imports
$\rightarrow\Delta\uparrow$ demand for US dollar and $\Delta\downarrow$ supply of US dollar
$\rightarrow$ USD appreciates.

Speculation ©IBO 2003

Financial investors and speculators around the globe keep trillions of yen, US dollars, euros, Swiss francs, etc. as part of their portfolios. They often 'live on the edge' by buying and selling large amounts of currencies for very short periods of time – often hours. The actions of speculators are based on **expectations** of future (as in hours or days away) currency movements. Speculation is the central determinant in exchange rate fluctuations, as the 'herd behaviour' of speculators often leads to a self-fulfilling prophecy; if one ~~large wildebeest~~ international currency trader believes that

the US dollar will depreciate and starts selling dollars, others might follow. What happens then is that large scale selling of the dollar creates the very situation foreseen; a fall in the dollar due to an increase in the supply of dollars and the dollar depreciates.

- Speculative belief that the US dollar will *depreciate* → US dollar is sold → Δ↑ supply of the US dollar → the USD depreciates.
- Speculative belief that the US dollar will *appreciate* → US dollar is bought → Δ↑ demand for the US dollar → the USD appreciates.

Case study: Speculation – How George Soros cracked the British pound in 1992

1. The English pound was linked to the precursor to the euro, via the European Exchange Rate Mechanism, **ERM** (a fixed exchange rate system between several EU countries), in 1992.

2. As the **pound was fixed**, monetary policy was limited in domestic scope since the Bank of England used the interest rate to adjust the exchange rate.

3. The benchmark currency that all ERM countries followed was the German Deutschmark, DM. This is where asymmetry comes in – Germany was in a different position entirely from that of the rest of Europe. Europe was wallowing in low growth, high unemployment and recession (and thus desperately needed to lower interest rates). Germany had just reunified and was spending trillions on the restructuring of Eastern Germany, which had forced up interest rates in Germany.

4. **Germany feared inflation** (remember the 1923 hyperinflation!) and thus raised interest rates to keep its economy from overheating.

5. So, the **pound was weakening** vis-a-vis the DM and the British government was using currency reserves to defend the pound, e.g. **using the foreign reserves to buy pounds**. The currency speculators on the foreign exchange market considered the pound overvalued and there were whispers of England leaving the ERM – which of course the government vehemently denied.

The scene was thus set for a currency crisis!

6. The world's most famous currency speculator, George Soros decided not only to use the impending crisis but to create it! [a]

7. Soros's Quantum Fund quietly established large lines of credit and borrowed $US15 billion USD worth of English pounds which he could convert into US dollars at will.

8. In essence, Soros's fund started quietly **exchanging the borrowed pounds for US dollars** (or other currencies). After a while this exchanging had to get **NOISY**!

9. Soros therefore started a high-profile media attack on the pound; he gave interviews and made other very ostentatious statements as to how the pound would soon have to be **devalued – or leave the fixed exchange rate** system.

a. *The Return of Depression Economics*, Paul Krugman, pp. 121 ff.

10. It worked! Within weeks, the Bank of England had spent some **50 billion US dollars defending the pound** but there was still massive downward pressure on the pound. By the beginning of September the Bank of England had raised interest rates drastically, but this was politically impossible to sustain in a recessionary economy. By mid-September, **the pound left the ERM and was allowed to float**, which it still does.

11. Soros sold back his dollars to the BoE at a lower exchange rate, paid off all his loans denominated in pounds, and made about 1 billion US dollars.

Did Soros create the devaluation?! Well, no, probably not. There was too much pressure on the pound and too many actors that considered the pound to be weak. He did, however, accelerate the issue by his actions.

Did Soros screw the Brits? Well, he **did** cost the British taxpayer about $US50 billion for the defence of the pound, and also humiliated the government of John Major (remember him?). However, the devaluation did not cause an economic crisis – quite the opposite, in fact. The devaluation freed the Bank of England of its shackles to the ERM and allowed interest rates to be cut to stimulate the economy. The lower exchange rate also boosted British exports. Within three years, the British economy was booming way beyond the rest of the EU zone and had amongst the lowest unemployment figures in the OECD. A happy ending, thus.

Use of foreign currency reserves

©IBO 2003

Governments can intervene on the foreign currency market via the foreign currency reserves[8] held in the central bank. The US dollar is a floating currency and the US government and central bank have for over 30 years had a policy of non-intervention, called 'benign neglect'. However, between mid-2001 and the end of 2003, the US dollar depreciated by over 11% in trade weighted terms and over 30% against the euro.[9] This worried US firms which have seen how foreign investors decreased financial flows to the US. The US central bank (often referred to as the 'Fed' – as in Federal Reserve Bank) could counteract the dollar's depreciation by using the foreign currency reserves to **buy the US dollar**. This would increase the demand for US dollars and help prop up the dollar exchange rate. (Recall also that this action decreases the foreign reserves and creates an inflow into the US capital account in balance of payments.)

- US dollar depreciates 'too much' → US central bank intervenes by buying the US dollar → demand for US dollar ↑ → price of USD↑ (decrease in US foreign reserves and inflow to US capital account)

- US dollar appreciates 'too much' → US central bank intervenes by selling the US dollar → supply of the US dollar ↑ → price of USD↓ (decrease in US foreign reserves & inflow to US capital account).

Outside the box:
Other determinants of the exchange rate

Change in national income: Interconnected and integrated countries will naturally influence each other. As has been pointed out, when incomes rise there is an increase in spending in households. Some of this spending will of course be on imports. Thus, an increase in national income in the US will increase imports and increase the supply of the US dollar. An increase in national income in Mexico, one of America's main trading partners, will naturally mean increased exports for the US and an increase in demand for US dollars. (HL: the higher the marginal propensity to import – MPM – the more imports will increase when national income rises, and vice versa.)

---

8. I should mention that the US dollar accounted for over 60% of total foreign reserves held around the world in 2008.
9. 'The incredible falling dollar', *Business Week*, 22 December 2003.

Deficits and debt: Another strong influence on the **long-run trend** of exchange rates is the level of the **budget deficit** and increasing **government debt**. Large budget deficits and increasing debt in the US between 2001 and 2003 have made foreign investors wary, since there is a risk that the government might be forced to raise taxes and cut government spending – both of

which would decrease aggregate demand and lower profits for firms, reducing inward FDI and portfolio investment and in turn lowering demand for the currency. It also created an incentive for US investors to place more of their holdings abroad, which increases the supply of the US dollar. In summary, the US dollar depreciates.

High and low exchange rates – more trade-offs

It is clear that governments often intervene on the foreign exchange market in order to adjust the exchange rate. A question that arises is of course 'Why?' One often reads about how the exchange rate is 'too high' or 'too low' and that domestic firms and/or government feel that intervention is justified or necessary. Exchange rates clearly have numerous economic consequences and the iteration below brings up some of the more evident effects on an economy. Please note that the headings below have quotation marks around 'Too high' and 'Too low' – the reason is that there is no absolute definition of the *correct* exchange rate.

Exchange rate is 'too high'

Positive effects of 'overvalued' currency:

- *Importers* will win since they will pay less for imported goods and receive their revenues in domestic currency. This could also well have beneficial effects on the domestic *inflation* rate since competitive forces will cause importers to pass on some of their cost savings to consumers.

- *Firms* which rely to a large extent on imported raw materials, components and other factors of production will see their costs go down. This can in fact make them more competitive on the international market.

- *Households* will see that imports and trips abroad will be cheaper in terms of the quantity of domestic currency needed to buy imports and travel abroad.

- A *government* which has a large external (foreign) debt would see that the debt servicing (amortisation and interest payments) would be easier.

- Export firms in a country with a strong currency might be forced to become more *efficient* in order to be able to compete on international markets.

Negative effects of 'overvalued' currency:

- The *current account* in the balance of payments can be adversely affected if the strong currency leads to increased import expenditure and/or decreased export revenue. There has been clear correlation between a stronger dollar and the US current account deficit.

- A strongly export-orientated country, for example China, would fear the effects of a higher exchange rate on *growth* and *unemployment*. The official figures show that exports account for 37% of GDP and one can well imagine the effects on domestic growth and unemployment due to a strong currency.[10]

- Domestic firms which have large *foreign investments* will see that profits decline when they are repatriated.

Exchange rate is 'too low'

Positive effects of 'undervalued' currency:

- Naturally the positive effects of an 'undervalued' currency are something of a 'mirror image' of the negative effects given above: A weaker currency lowers the price of exports and will benefit exporters and domestic industry; as the price of exports has fallen and the price of imports has risen there will be a positive effect on the balance of payments (HL: see the Marshall–Lerner and J-curve in Section 4.7.); jobs will be created in export industries; countries with a high proportion of exports in relation to GDP will see growth; and international firms repatriating profits will enjoy greater returns in terms of domestic currency.

Negative effects of 'undervalued' currency:

- An 'undervalued' currency will have the following effects: Importers and firms reliant on imported factors of production will see costs rise; households will cut back on imported goods and foreign travel;

---

10. The official figure of "37% of GDP" should be taken with scepticism. There are some serious studies showing that the official figures are seriously inflated and the real value lies closer to 10%.

and governments with a high proportion of foreign debt will see how debt servicing becomes dearer.

- A country with a 'low' or 'undervalued' exchange rate will in all likelihood experience *inflation*. There are two contributing causes:

  - A strong exporting nation will experience rising aggregate demand and *demand-pull* inflation.

  - A nation with a high volume of (HL: relatively price inelastic) imported factors of production will see increased expenditure on imported factors. This will decrease aggregate supply and thus contribute to *cost-push* inflation.

POP QUIZ 4.6.4 EXCHANGE RATE DETERMINANTS

1 European tastes switch in favour of East Asian culture and goods. What would happen on the foreign exchange market for the euro?

2 Britain grants 'tax holidays' for foreign firms. How would this affect the exchange rate for the British pound?

3 Korea manages to keep its inflation rate lower than that of its trading partners. How might this affect the Korean won?

4 The European Central Bank (ECB) considers the exchange rate for the EURO to be too low. What actions can be taken?

5 Here's a tricky one: Using a S/D diagram for the Swiss franc, show how a remittance of profits to Switzerland by Swiss firms in Germany would affect the value of the Swiss franc.

HIGHER LEVEL EXTENSION TOPICS

Relative advantages and disadvantages of fixed and floating rates

Like in so many other areas in economics, there are a number of trade-offs in choosing a certain exchange rate regime over another. Experience tells us that in choosing fixed over floating exchange rates, countries will both gain and lose. There is no perfect system of exchange rates.

Fixed exchange rates

Advantages of a fixed exchange rate

- *Predictability and certainty:* Fixed exchange rates make it easier for importers and exporters to calculate earnings. Costs, revenues and profit margins are clear and *predictable*. This creates an incentive for firms to invest and households to engage in entrepreneurial activity.

- *Exchange rate stability encourages trade:* When exporters and importers can be sure of tomorrow's exchange rate and future profits, it is easier to plan business. International stability in exchange rates lowers barriers to partaking in international trade and thus *increases trade*. However, there is limited merit in the argument that stable exchange rates create trade, as the increase in global trade has in fact increased faster since the breakdown of the Bretton Woods system in 1971–72.

- *Fiscal/monetary discipline domestically:* This has been one of the main arguments in favour of fixed exchange rates. Recall that inflation and government deficits exert downward pressure on the exchange rate. Since the central bank will have to use limited foreign reserves to adjust the exchange rate, governments in fixed exchange rate regimes will keep inflation and deficits to a minimum in order to avoid depleting the reserves. This *limits expansionary fiscal and monetary policies*.

Another aspect of the discipline issue is that countries within a fixed exchange rate system will not be able to run up large current account deficits in the long term. Stimulating aggregate demand leads to increased imports and inflation – both of which will create net outflows in current account. A current account deficit means that more domestic currency is hitting the international market which will exert a downward force on the exchange rate.

- *Less risk of speculation:* Mainstream economic theory holds that since the exchange rate is fixed there would be *little or no element of speculation* in currencies, since there is little movement in the rates. In reality, most of the currency crises of the post-Bretton Woods period have been the result of speculative attacks on pegged currencies which were considered overvalued. (Refer to Case study: "Speculation – How George Soros cracked the British pound in 1992" on page 487.)

Disadvantages of a fixed exchange rate

- *Loss of domestic monetary policy freedom:* When a country commits to keeping a certain exchange rate, the central bank will have *limited freedom in setting interest rates* in order to influence the domestic economy. Interest is one of the tools which a central bank can use to keep a peg towards another currency, since higher interest rates attract foreign funds and thus increased demand for the domestic currency. Since the priority of the central bank must be to keep the exchange rate steady there is little room to set interest rates in order to stimulate or deflate the domestic economy via aggregate demand. There is a *trade-off* between having a fixed exchange rate and being able to set domestic monetary policy – which in extension means a trade-off between exchange rate stability and unemployment.

- *Need of large foreign reserves ('war chest'):* In order to maintain a fixed exchange rate, the central bank will need *ample foreign reserves* for market intervention. Even if this 'war chest' is never used, there must be reserves enough to dissuade speculators from attacking the currency.

- *Possibility of increased unemployment:* If a country runs the risk of continued current account deficits, subsequent downward pressure on the currency will create an incentive to raise interest rates to increase demand for the domestic currency. Government spending might also be cut to decrease imports. Both these policies will have *contractionary effects* on aggregate demand and thus employment.

- *Possibility of 'imported inflation':* When prices rise in trade partner economies relative to the domestic economy, there is a risk that firms and households will simply have to pay more for imported materials and goods, creating *inflation*.

Floating exchange rates

Advantages of a floating exchange rate

- *The balance of payments automatically adjusts:* When a country runs a current account deficit, the supply of the domestic currency will increase on the foreign exchange market which in turn will lower the exchange rate. Thus, imports will become more expensive and exports relatively cheaper – the *current account will be self-correcting.*

- *No large foreign reserves necessary:* The central bank will *not need to intervene* by buying/ selling its domestic currency. This means that a large foreign reserve is not needed.

- *Freedom in domestic/monetary policies:* Not having to focus on setting interest rates to achieve a given exchange rate means that the central bank is *free to use monetary policy* to pursue domestic goals of growth and unemployment. This is perhaps the central argument for floating exchange rates.

- *Reduced speculation:* Floating currencies are intensely traded by the minute around the world. The availability of information to all traders limits the degree to which one trader will have information that others don't. The past thirty years have shown how floating currencies in fact *do not create speculative crises* – something the famous economist James Tobin noted a few years ago.[11]

- *Less risk of imported inflation:* If trade partners' inflation rates rise relative to domestic inflation, then the domestic economy's goods become relatively cheaper. Hence there will be an increased demand for the domestic currency and an appreciation of the domestic currency. An appreciation of the domestic currency means that *import prices fall* – or at least do not rise as much as in the other countries. Thus there is less risk of importing inflation.

Disadvantages of a floating exchange rate

- *Instability and lack of predictability:* Firms often lock international deals far in advance of payment. Not knowing what the actual cost is going to be – due to exchange rate fluctuations – *can deter international trade* and investment. (However, most firms actually set a given exchange rate for future payment, called hedging.)

- *Lack of monetary/fiscal discipline:* Since governments are not forced to keep the exchange rate steady, there is less incentive for governments

---

11. Interview in *Radio Australia*, 17 November 1998.

to keep *budget deficits and inflation* under control. Basically, government can pursue domestic expansionary/ inflationary policies in the knowledge that the depreciation of the currency might serve to automatically adjust any resulting current account deficit in the longer term. However…

- *Loss of competitiveness and efficiency:* …there might be a *loss of competitiveness* over time since the domestic economy increasingly relies on depreciation to remain internationally competitive rather that being forced to innovate and increase productivity.

Advantages and disadvantages of single currencies/monetary integration ©IBO 2003

The Treaty of Maastricht in 1992 clearly stated the EU's movement towards monetary integration; the **European Economic and Monetary Union (EMU)**. In 1999 the EURO technically came into being and during 2001 EU currencies (from all 15 EU members except UK, Denmark, Sweden and Greece[12]) were 'locked' in place in exchange rate terms. A European Central Bank (ECB) took over the task of setting and implementing monetary policies for all EMU countries. On 1 January 2002 euro notes and coins were issued. This project created one of the largest shifts in economic power in history. By 2009 there were 16 country members of the EMU.[13]

The European and Economic Monetary Union (EMU)

In order for each country wishing to join to be eligible, a set of criteria had to be met to ensure that EMU members were not too far apart from each other in macroeconomic terms, i.e. the economies were to *converge*. Each member had to adjust domestic fiscal and monetary policies in order to fulfil the following five criteria.

Convergence criteria

The intention of the convergence criteria[14] is to ensure that economic performance in all member countries

are in roughly the same phase along the business cycle. This is absolutely necessary since the single currency would entail a common monetary policy and to a certain extent a limit on the use of purely domestic fiscal policy for individual EMU countries.

1. **Inflation** can be no more than 1.5 percentage points above the average inflation of the three countries with lowest inflation.

2. **Interest rates** have to be within 2 percentage points of the average of the three countries with lowest interest rates.

3. A maximum **budget deficit** of 3% of GDP.

4. **Exchange rates** have to be kept within a narrow band for 2–3 years prior to joining.

5. The **national debt** must be lower than 60% of GDP.

Effects on monetary and fiscal policy

Monetary policy: Having a single currency means that two EMU countries cannot have different rates of interest. Just as a single country will have a single monetary policy and thus one interest rate for all regions in the country, a common currency area must have the same system. For example, consider that Belgium had a 4% interest rate while the Netherlands had 5%; savers would simply put their money into Dutch banks and borrow from Belgian banks – and if the rate differential were wider it might even be possible to borrow at a lower rate in one country and deposit it for a higher rate in another country! This means that individual interest rates in EMU countries are set by a common bank, the European Central Bank, and *member countries forego domestic monetary policy*.

Fiscal policy: In order to keep EMU members roughly in line on the business cycle, key economic indicators must move in relative concert. To enable this – or 'force' it, according to opponents of the EMU – a set of rules were laid down in a **Stability and Growth Pact**, (SGP) similar to the convergence criteria above. The main element in the pact is that members must keep budget deficits within an upper limit of 3% of GDP. To keep countries in line, penalties of up to 0.5% of GDP can be levied on countries exceeding this limit. This can severely limit a member country's ability to fund expansionary fiscal policies.

---

12. Greece was allowed to join in 2001. I was there – great party!
13. Members as of January 2009 were: Germany, France, Italy, Spain, Netherlands, Belgium, Austria, Finland, Greece, Ireland, Portugal, Slovenia, Slovakia, Malta, Luxembourg and Cyprus.
14. See the full text at http://www.eurotreaties.com/emupact.html and http://europa.eu.int/comm/economy_finance/about/activities/sgp/sgp_en.htm.

HIGHER LEVEL

Benefits of the EMU

The overall benefits of a common currency centre on the benefits of economic integration looked at in Section 4.3: [15]

- *Trade creation*: Having a single currency will facilitate increased trade flows amongst member countries. Consumers will also enjoy greater *price transparency*, since a common currency unit enables consumers to compare prices, which will increase trade flows and lead to…

- …*greater competition*: When households have greater choice in substitutes, firms will have to increase *efficiency* and/or improve products.

- *Benefits of scale*: Increased trade and larger markets will enable firms to *lower average costs* and benefit from scale economies.

- *Lower transaction costs:* Firms dealing in foreign currencies would not have *commission costs* or the risks of dealing with exchange rates.

- *Inter-union and non-union investment:* Increased *predictability and reliability* in dealing with same-currency countries might cause members to invest within rather than outside member countries. Non-EMU foreign direct investment (FDI) and portfolio funds might also be attracted to a market based on a currency which is quickly becoming a competitor to the US dollar – in fact, over 50 countries have pegged their currencies to the euro[16].

Costs of the EMU

There are considerable economic costs associated with a 'one size fits all' monetary policy:

- *Loss of domestic monetary policy:* There will naturally be differences in economic activity and inflation in different countries, so-called '**economic asymmetry**'. While the ECB sets interest rates based on average (expected) inflation in EMU countries, there can be large differences between individual countries. For example, while inflation in EMU countries was an average of 1.6% (annualised) in 2004, there was increasing divergence amongst member countries; Germany, Finland and Austria had 1.0% to 1.2% inflation rates while Portugal, Greece and Ireland had inflation rates between 2.9% and 3.5%.[17] Clearly, the former three might wish to employ lower interest rates in order to stimulate

growth, while the latter three countries might then suffer from increased inflation. None of the countries have the option of reducing or increasing interest rates, having surrendered monetary policy to the ECB.

- *Restrictions on domestic fiscal policy:* The de facto limits on EMU members' domestic use of fiscal policy have been likened to a '*fiscal straitjacket*' as there is clearly a boundary to deficit spending during recessions. It did not take long before an EMU member, Portugal in 2002, exceeded the 3% limit, and by 2003 it was clear that half the members of EMU would break the 3% rule during 2004 – with Germany, France, Portugal, and the Netherlands as 'repeat offenders'.[18] While the European Commission has issued public warnings to offenders, no penalties have as yet been imposed on any EMU country.

- *Regional unemployment:* A single currency works well when factor mobility is high; a depressed area will have outward movement of labour and capital towards areas with better employment and investment opportunities. In the US, for example, over 50 million Americans moved during the last three decades of the 20th century. Labour mobility in EMU countries seems to be rather low, perhaps because of language, cultural and remaining bureaucratic barriers. Since regions (or countries) have limitations on using reflationary monetary policies the aforementioned asymmetry in the EMU can create wide divergence in unemployment rates. So while the EURO zone average in 2008 was 7.5% unemployment, Austria had 3.8% while Slovakia and Spain had 9.6 and 11.3 respectively.[19]

Purchasing power parity theory

©IBO 2003

Recall from Section 3.2 that purchasing power parity exists when an identical basket of goods costs the same in two countries at a given exchange rate; at an exchange rate of USD1 = €0.80 a bundle of goods costing USD100 in the US would cost €80 in the EU. Assuming perfect flows of goods, money and information between trading nations, domestic consumers will detect *price differentials* and act upon them.

15. See: http://library.thinkquest.org/19110/english/advantag/advantag.html.
16. EU homepage at http://europa.eu.int/scadplus/leg/en/lvb/l25063.htm.
17. *Eurostat, Euro-indicators*, news release no 39/2004, 17 March 2004 at http://europa.eu.int/comm/eurostat/Public.
18. BBC at http://news.bbc.co.uk/2/hi/business/3607933.stm.
19. *Eurostat, Euro-indicators* at http://europa.eu.int/comm/eurostat/Public.

If the bundle of goods costs less in EMU countries, Americans would buy more goods from 'Euroland' which would drive up demand for the EURO. Ultimately the EURO would appreciate and the price differentials would be eradicated, resulting in an exchange rate where the bundle of goods is the same price in the US as it is in 'Euroland'. The theory of purchasing power parity thus predicts that exchange rates will ultimately even-out to *reflect changes in inflation* in trading countries. In other words, in the *long run* PPP will ultimately be restored via the exchange rate.

> **Purchasing power parity (PPP) theory:** The theory of purchasing power parity states that exchange rates will in the long run adjust to different inflation rates in countries, leading to equilibrium where a given amount of home currency traded for a foreign currency will buy an equally-sized bundle of goods. The theory is used as a possible explanation of long run influences on the exchange rate.

Arbitrage (reselling) and the law of one price

Assume that two countries, side by side – let's use USA and Canada, for didactical (= educational) reasons explained further on – with no trade barriers; no transactions costs; no transport costs; homogenous goods; identical expenditure taxes; and a floating exchange rate. Americans can buy a kilogram[20] of flour for US$2 dollars domestically. Canadians can buy a kilogram of flour for $3 Canadian (CAD) domestically. The exchange rate is USD1 = CAD2, or CAD1 = USD0.5. What do you think will happen?! Well, two things: 1) Americans will cross over to Canada to buy flour, seeing as how the USD2 they pay at home would get them CAD4 and then 1.33 kilograms of flour; 2) there would be *arbitrage*, as enterprising people in Canada would buy flour domestically and sell it in US for *just under* USD2 per kilogram.

What ultimately must happen should not come as any great shock to a student who has come this far in economics. Increased demand for the Canadian dollar will cause the **CAD to appreciate**. Also, the traders from Canada will exchange their US dollars earned in the US for Canadian dollars back home – thereby increasing the supply of USD and causing a **depreciation of the USD**. (Or, in terms you are perhaps more familiar with, increased US imports will increase the supply of the USD on the foreign exchange market.)

Demand for Canadian flour will cease and arbitrage activities will end when the exchange rate between the two countries is such that **the price is the same in both countries** – the law of one price. This happens at an exchange rate where 1 kilogram of flour in US = USD2 = CAD3 = 1 kilogram of flour in Canada. Thus 2 US dollars equals 3 Canadian dollars, i.e. an **exchange rate of 1USD = CAD1.5**, or 1CAD = USD0.66.[21] This is the exchange rate at which purchasing power parity exists.

> **The law of one price:** Assuming that there are no market imperfections, two homogenous goods must ultimately have the **same price** on a market.

The law of one price and PPP theory

What would happen in the US/Canada example if inflation rates were to differ soon after the purchasing power parity exchange rate of USD1 = CAD1.5 had been set? Say that **inflation in USA was 10%** and zero in Canada – 1 kilogram of flour would cost USD2.2 in the US but still CAD3 in Canada. If the exchange rate remained unchanged Americans would get more flour for their money in Canada and arbitrage would be conducted again – the US would *import* more flour. This would continue until a new exchange rate existed which again gave citizens from both countries purchasing power parity. This new exchange rate would be when 1 kilogram of flour in US = USD2.2 = CAD3 = 1 kilogram of flour in Canada. Thus 2.2 US dollars equals 3 Canadian dollars, i.e. a **new exchange rate of 1USD = CAD1.36**, or CAD1 = USD0.73 has been established.

The **Canadian dollar has appreciated by 10%** and the **US dollar has depreciated by 10%**.[22] This is in line with purchasing power parity theory which predicts that the exchange rates will fall in a country with higher relative inflation and offset differences in purchasing power.

---

20. Yes, I know that the Americans and Canadians use pounds, but I'm too old to learn a new system.
21. Note that we are assuming that the domestic prices in both countries do not change!
22. The Canadian dollar goes from USD0.66 to USD0.73 – an appreciation of (0.73 – 0.66) / 0.66 = +10.6%. The US dollar goes from CAD1.5 to CAD1.36 – a depreciation of (1.36 – 1.5) / 1.36= -10.3%.

Evidence of purchasing power parity affecting exchange rates

While there is some evidence that exchange rates in the long run show some adjustment to purchasing power, there are far too many exceptions abounding to be able to draw general conclusions. The limitations set by the assumptions of the theory would appear to be quite strong.

- Many goods are like ill-mannered infants and saké (Japanese rice wine); they simply don't travel well – e.g. services such as restaurant meals and cinema tickets are **not exportable** and many goods will have high transport costs and also meet high trade barriers.

- Goods are **not homogenous** and thus price differences will exist which show consumer preferences.

- In addition, **expenditure taxes** can vary considerably between countries and international firms will indulge in **price discrimination** whenever possible.

Point in fact, a survey of the most integrated single market in the world, the European Union, showed that prices of cinema tickets varied by 170% between lowest and highest prices in the EU.[23] Another example is Switzerland, which is surrounded by five countries (including Liechtenstein) and has relatively open borders towards its EU neighbours – yet it is one of the notoriously most expensive countries in the world, where a basket of goods costs an average 40% than the OECD average. These are but a few examples of how purchasing power parity theory comes up a bit short in predicting that exchange rates will adjust and eventually even-out prices.

IN THE NEWS:
Purchasing power of loonies in Canada

No, don't get upset and think I am having a go at the Canadians. I am referring to the Canadian dollar which is affectionately known as the 'loonie' due to the aquatic bird, the loon, which adorns the Canadian one-dollar coin. During 2007 the Canadian dollar appreciated by some 19% and by October it was at parity with the US dollar, e.g. CAD1 = USD1 – for the first time in 31 years. This created quite a stir amongst Canadian shoppers and the concept of PPP quickly made its way into the daily vocabulary.

Real duck and Canadian dollar.

'I'm worth one dollar!'

Canadians quickly noticed that a dollar in Canada would buy far less than a dollar in the US. For example, *The Age of Turbulence* by former chairman of the Federal Reserve Bank Alan Greenspan had a price of CAD26.45 in Canada but only USD20.99 in the US. A Toyota Avalon was priced at CAD41,000 in Ottawa but USD31,000 just an hours drive south of the US border. The Bank of Montreal calculated that the price of a random basket of goods was an average of 24% higher in Canada than in the US.

The strong Canadian dollar had immediate effects on shopping trips, where Canadians would head south and stock up on goods in the US. Naturally the increased imports hit domestic Canadian merchants hard and there were even attempts by large automobile manufacturers to bar the selling of cars in the US to Canadian citizens. Canadian exporters also felt the results of the higher exchange rate as foreign sales fell and profits repatriated from subsidiaries abroad meant less when converted to Canadian dollars.

Was the rise in the Canadian dollar justified or 'too high'? Good question. According to the OECD, the PPP value of the Canadian dollar should have been 81 US cents. Thus, the loonie was overvalued by some

---

23. 'The flaw of one price', *The Economist*, 16 October 2003.

23%. Was the outcome in line with PPP theory? Well, yes; after hovering at around CAD1 to USD1 between November 2007 and August 2008, the loonie started to fall, and then fell like a paralysed, well, loon. By November 2008, the Canadian dollar was at the estimated PPP value of 80 US cents to the Canadian dollar and has fluctuated around this level up to the time of writing in February 2009.

However, there are a goodly number of other variables which have affected the exchange rate – primarily the fact that the US dollar has noticeably strengthened during the global financial/credit crisis of 2008. Two reasons stand out: 1) As the US economy reeled in recession with rising unemployment and falling GDP, imports decreased drastically. This decreased the supply of US dollars on the foreign exchange market. 2) International capital is 'cowardly' and in time of crisis it will do like a loon in a storm out on the lake – seek shelter on the biggest rock possible. The US is a big rock. When investors/speculators seek shelter they buy US government securities and this increases the demand for the US dollar.

Preparing for exams

Short answer questions (10 marks each)

1 Using a suitable diagram, explain how a change in a country's imports and exports can affect the exchange rate.

2 Why might a country have difficulty in attaining full employment whilst keeping a current account surplus?

3 [HL Only] Using a diagram, explain how a country can peg (fix) its currency to another currency.

4 Explain why a country's currency might appreciate.

5 Analyse the possible effects of speculation on exchange rates.

6 The central bank in a country raises interest rates. How might this affect this country's currency and balance of payments?

Extended response questions (25 marks each)

1 a Examine the factors that influence a country's exchange rate. (10 marks)

  b How might a change in the exchange rate affect the domestic economy of the country? (15 marks)

2 a Explain the difference between a floating and managed exchange rate. (10 marks)

  b Discuss the advantages and disadvantages of having a managed exchange rate regime. (15 marks)

3 a Account for the difficulties of establishing a common currency amongst 10 countries. (10 marks)

  b Discuss the costs and benefits of establishing a common currency. (15 marks)

Balance of payments problems

4.7

CONTENTS

BALANCE OF PAYMENTS PROBLEMS ©IBO 2003

The balance of payments together with exchange rates, monetary and fiscal policies is like a collection of string kept in a bag: there are a lot of loose ends and every piece of string is somehow connected to all the others. This section attempts to tie up a few loose ends by showing how the balance of payments will affect exchange rates and domestic policies – and that exchange rates and domestic policies will also affect the balance of payments! Once again, causality is indeed a two-way street. Please refer back to the "Exam tip: Balance of payments diamond" on page 472.

Consequences of a current account deficit or surplus ©IBO 2003

A country running a current account deficit will of course have a corresponding capital account surplus – the country is in effect selling domestic assets to the foreign sector. A current account surplus means a capital account deficit, e.g. net foreign assets have increased. However, it is far too simple to label a current account *deficit* as 'bad' or harmful and a current account *surplus* 'good' or beneficial; it depends on *why* there is an imbalance.

Current account deficit

When a country's net outflow on current account is greater than net inflows, the country is in some way making up for this in the *capital account*. There are two broad ways in which a current account deficit is covered; loans from abroad or investment from abroad. There are several possible *negative effects* of current account deficits – capital account surpluses – in the long run for a net **debtor nation**.

Negative effects of current account deficit

• Perhaps the most immediate and visible effect of a current account deficit is the effect it has on the **exchange rate**. Since a current account deficit means larger import expenditure than export revenue, there will be downward pressure on the exchange rate. Two forces are at work:

  ■ The export expenditure means that the domestic consumers are changing domestic currency to buy foreign currency. This *increases the supply of the home currency* and causes a depreciation.

  ■ If the current account deficit is also due to lower levels of exports, then the *demand for the domestic*

currency would be decreasing. This also puts downward pressure on the exchange rate.

• Borrowing from abroad means that the loans will ultimately have to be repaid with interest. Continuous current account deficits will be looked upon harshly by the international business and financial community, and ultimately the **ability to pay off foreign debts** might be questioned. Wary investors might choose to avoid a weak economy and this will result in less demand for the home currency as fewer investors/loan-givers are willing to risk putting assets into the country, putting downward pressure on the currency. In case the home currency depreciates, the debtor nation could suffer a severe shock as **debt servicing** becomes more costly. The home country will have to offer even higher interest to foreign lenders – which together with a depreciated currency can make future debt payments a serious issue. It also puts the domestic economy somewhat at the mercy of international business cycles and interest rates – something a good many developing countries learned the hard way during the 1970s and 1980s.

• The domestic economy might be forced into **raising interest rates** in order to attract continued foreign (portfolio) investment and keep a desired exchange rate. In essence, the domestic economy is letting foreign firms fund domestic investment. Ultimately, the sales of domestic assets to foreigners will cause outflows in the form of **repatriated profits** and dividends – which could in fact intensify the current account deficit. Also, the increase in interest rates will have a **contractionary effect** on the domestic economy.

• The incoming funds on capital account might be due to **speculative inflows** – in which case the recipient country could be in for some serious trouble when these inflows cease. See Case study: "Southeast Asian crisis of 1997–98" on page 501.

• Finally, there is always the **risk that foreign capital starts to exit**. If inflows of FDI and portfolio investment seek other markets, then the home country can find itself in the situation where domestic unemployment rises as capital leaves. There might also be a significant reduction in imports. This is something that the Irish became painfully aware of during the credit crisis of 2008–09.

Maybe not so bad?

On the other hand, a current account deficit allows a country to enjoy greater consumption than production – even though it might be on borrowed money. If the deficit is relatively short-lived, a few years or so, then there would be little economic damage – quite the opposite if the inflows in capital account are partially used for investment.

Even **long-run current account deficits** may have relatively little impact on the domestic economy. A good many countries have run current account deficits for many years in a row without any seeming ill effects. A main reason is that while a current account deficit of hundreds of millions of dollars/euros sounds ominous, it must be related to the countries' fundamental ability to pay the money back, i.e. the size of national income. For example, the US, which has now broken every record in the book concerning current account deficits, had a current account deficit of $US435 billion in 2000 and $US417 in 2001. Putting this in relation to US GDP, the deficit was 4.4% of GDP in 2000 and 4.1% in 2001.[1] While this indeed is a considerable deficit, causing the US to become the world's largest net debtor nation, it did not threaten to 'collapse' the US economy in any way. As long as the borrowed funds goes

towards investment, the debt will be paid by future generations of Americans which have been able to enjoy higher living standards using the loans.

The US current account deficit – world-class debtors!

Figure 4.7.1 shows that, in fact, the US ran a current account deficit for virtually 26 years between 1982 and 2008 – with the exception of 1991. Basically, foreign investors considered the risks smaller, and the returns greater, in investing in the vibrant and innovative US economy than at home. In other words, foreign capital flows have benefited the US economy by creating funds for investment which served to lower unemployment and increase GDP considerably during the 1990s.

The US current account deficit bottomed out in 2006 at around USD875 billion – 7% of GDP. In testimony before the US Budget Committee in 2007, the Peterson Institute for International Economics put forward the view that the deficit was 'clearly unsustainable.'[2] It was pointed out that any form of 'overspending' means that one has to in some way finance the debt. To uphold such a current account deficit the US had to attract foreign capital to the tune of close to USD4 billion … every working day!

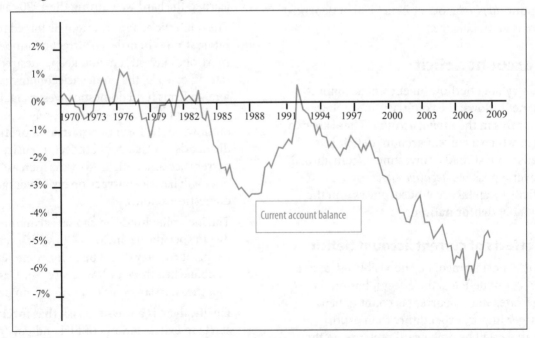

(Source: US Bureau of Economic Analysis)

Figure 4.7.1 *US current account deficit 1970–2008*

---

1. Official US government figures at http://www.bea.gov/bea/dn2/gpoc.htm#1994–2001.
2. "The Current Account Deficit and the US Economy", by C. Fred Bergsten, Peterson Institute for International Economics, Testimony before the Budget Committee of the United States Senate, 1 February 2007. (See http://www.iie.com/publications/papers/paper.cfm?ResearchID=705.)

Current account surplus

A current account surplus means that there is a net outflow in capital account, i.e. the home country's net foreign assets have increased. There will be a number of gains for such a net *creditor nation*:

- The foreign assets can be viewed as another form of saving for the home country which will enable increased **future consumption**.

- Capital will flow to countries with a higher rate of return than the home country. This enhances **resource allocation and increases profits** for domestic firms.

- The increase in foreign holdings will in time **generate income** in the form of profits, interest received, and dividends. (Inflows in current account.)

In spite of these there are several **possible disadvantages** in having sustained current account surpluses:

- **Current consumption** possibilities for the home country decrease as resources are diverted abroad.

- A current account surplus means that there is a degree of **diverting investment** from the domestic to the foreign market. This could lead to a loss of jobs (yet this is highly contentious), skills and technology gains.

- There will be a degree of **tax loss**, as a portion of tax bases – investment, output and wages – will be taxed outside the home country.

- There is also a **political element** in running continuous current account surpluses for many years. This was a main ingredient in trade friction between the US and Japan during the 1980s, and between the US and China during the 2000s. Guess which of these countries were running large current account surpluses? [3]

General external equilibrium

The link between equilibrium in the balance of payments and equilibrium in the exchange rate is very strong. The two concepts are technically two sides of the same coin; when there is no pressure on the exchange rate to change, there will theoretically be a balance of payments equilibrium. If the value of exports – expressed in a currency – is equal to the value of imports, then there will be no excess demand or supply for the currency. Should the home economy become more efficient and thus more internationally competitive, exports will rise and so too will the demand for the home currency. Naturally, the opposite holds true.

In reality, however, a currency can easily appreciate for lengthy periods while consistent current account deficits rise. This is primarily due to investment and speculative demand for the home currency. We have looked at the former so now let us have a look at how general disequilibrium can arise due to speculation in the case study below.

 Case study: Southeast Asian crisis of 1997–98

By 1997, the situation in Asia was basically the following: The 'Tiger' economies (Thailand, Taiwan, South Korea, Hong Kong, Malaysia, Indonesia, Singapore) were growing at an annualised rate of between 5% and 12%. Massive FDI was pouring in from OECD countries, primarily EU countries and Japan, (USA at a lower level) as the successful resolution of the Mexican economic crisis in 1995 plus the fall/death of communism (and thus the threat of a 'take over' of private property) made investment in LDC's safe. The Third world, or developing nations, was redubbed 'Emerging Markets' by the Marketing Babble Section of Very Large American Investment Firms. *The flow of private funds from Europe and Japan to developing nations increased by about 400% during the period 1990 to 1997!*

---

3.   China and Japan. The all too common view was that China has been growing at the United States' expense. See a good high level debate at http://www.cfr.org/publication/11631/.

The **bubble-baht**:

This is how funds got from Japan/Europe to Thailand (where the crisis started):

A) A **Japanese bank would make a loan to a Thai finance company** – which is an institution that acts as a 'go-between' for foreign capital.

B) The finance company then had Yen which it would lend to a local real estate developer (= construction firm). However, **the developer needed baht**, (= Thai currency) not yen, to pay the construction crew/land, etc. The developer would go to the foreign exchange and buy baht.

C) Result: the demand for the baht increased and thus the **baht appreciated**.

D) Now, the central bank of Thailand had committed itself to maintaining a **stable (= pegged) exchange rate to the USD**. To offset the increase in demand for the baht, the central bank had to increase the supply of baht, i.e. print more baht. The result now was that the Thai central bank had larger currency reserves and the money supply increased.

E) Credit was now easy, **investment soared and foreign investment and monies** (speculative now!) **continued to pour in**.

Why didn't the Thai government simply abandon the peg to the USD and let the baht assume a higher exchange rate? Answer: because this would have damaged Thai exports.

F) Thailand started to see a larger and increasing current account deficit – remember, FDI and other inflows of currency on capital account necessarily entail a deficit on current account. Is a large current account deficit necessarily evil? It depends on what the inflow on capital account is used for …

G) In the case of Thailand (and indeed Indonesia) a good deal of the foreign funds were **lent to high-risk projects** with very questionable securities. Basically, the finance company that borrowed the yen in the first place, was nothing more than an institution run by a relative/friend of the government! This is where '**crony-capitalism**' comes in.

H) Foreign investors and lenders (= banks) to the finance company, would not ask for the normal securities of such loans – the company was, after all, **run by the nephew/friend/schoolmate** of the minister of finance. How risky could the loan be?!

I) So, the nephew would get a low interest loan from abroad and then lend the money to his friend the real estate developer who's planning a new Mega Tower. If the Tower was successful, everybody wins. If the Tower is a total disaster (= no renters/buyers) then the taxpayer will lose as the finance company will be bailed out by Uncle Finance Minister: 'Heads, I win; tails, you taxpayers lose.' **Now we have a speculative bubble economy!**

J) Ultimately, firms started incurring losses; finance companies and real estate companies started to go bankrupt. Foreign investor confidence started to decline and less money flowed in. The baht started to lose value.

K) The **government had two alternatives**:

1) **Protect the baht** by reducing the supply of baht and raising interest rates. The Thai government waited (as this would cost them foreign reserves and the interest rise would hurt the already ailing economy) and the market started to regard the baht as soon to leave the peg to the USD. But as long as the exchange rate remained, one could borrow baht and in ANTICIPATION of the baht being devalued! That's what the market did; borrowed baht and exchanged these **immediately** for USDs, thereby increasing the supply of baht even more!

2) **Let the currency float** and accept a lower exchange rate ... and the Thai government still waited – as this would have meant that hundreds of domestic firms already in trouble would have to pay far more baht to service foreign debt in US dollars! So the government defended the baht – and failed. Ultimately, the peg to the US dollar was abandoned and the baht fell by 50% in a few months taking the Indonesian rupiah, Malaysian ringit, Korean won and Hong Kong dollar with it.

The devaluation thus caused a string of devaluations in Southeast Asia. As the Thai **foreign currency reserves** – the 'war chest' – were depleted, the only option left to keep an element of foreign confidence in the baht was to raise the interest rates and reduce the supply of baht. This further aggravated an economy under severe recessionary pressures.

This was the 1997 '**meltdown**' of Southeast Asian economies. It was basically caused by speculation and resulting bad debt, and furthered by lack of liquidity, high interest rates and economies in deep recession. Again, we are dealing with economic basics; **expectations and confidence**. The financial crisis can be seen as a negative self-reinforcing loop – a vicious circle; loss of confidence in Asian economies → currency values plummet, interest rates rise and Asian economies suffer from recessionary pressure → financial problems for Asian banks/firms/households → loss of confidence in the Asian economy, etc.

Current account deficit: methods of correction ©IBO 2003

While there is no general *rule* stating that a current account deficit is harmful to the economy, many countries have considered this to be a form of balance of payments disequilibrium and thus something to be dealt with using various policies. When a country shows an alarming current account deficit – and there is little agreement as to what 'alarming' means – there are a number of economic policies which might be used to alleviate the situation.

Short-run policies invariably intervene on the market in such a way as to lower the ratio of the price of domestic goods to imported goods. One possibility is to 'manage' the *exchange rate* (see below) in order to make domestic goods cheaper for foreigners. Another method is of course *protectionism*; if domestic goods are subsidised and/or tariffs levied on imports then import spending will fall and improve the current account. Contractionary policies aimed at reducing overall demand, e.g. aggregate demand, serve to lower overall expenditure, which includes imported goods.

Long-run policies commonly focus on enhancing domestic competitive abilities, i.e. increasing productivity, increasing R&D and introducing innovation, improvements in quality and the like. These are looked at under *supply-side policies* further on.

Managed changes in exchange rates

©IBO 2003

A country operating under a managed currency regime, e.g. a pegged exchange rate system, can **devalue its currency** in order to alleviate a persistent current account deficit. By pegging the home currency at a lower exchange rate, the relative price of domestic goods falls. (Recall that a lower price does not necessarily mean more revenue! A fall in export prices might actually mean that while export **volume** increases, export **revenue** does not. HL, see "Marshall–Lerner condition" on page 507.)

Improvement in the current account due to devaluation

Say that Singapore devalued the Singapore dollar (SGD) from 0.67 US dollars per SGD to 0.60 (or from SGD1.5 to the US dollar to SGD1.67 per dollar). A coat costing 500 Singapore dollars in Singapore will cost ... 1,000 Singapore dollars in Singapore – but Americans will not have to hand over $US335 (0.67 × 500) to buy the SGD500. The exchange rate has fallen, so the SGD500 will cost 300 US dollars (0.60 × 500) as will the SGD500 coat.

Conversely, a USD120 American toolkit which previously cost SGD180 (120 × 1.5) for Singapore to import will now cost SGD200 (120 × 1.67). The devaluation will cause 1) export volumes to increase and thus *export revenue to increase*; 2) import volumes to decrease and *import spending to decrease*. This will **improve the Chinese current account** in the balance of payments. It would also lead to the opposite for the US and no doubt a political firestorm of American protests.

- Devaluation $\rightarrow P_X\downarrow \rightarrow$ X volume$\uparrow \rightarrow$ **X revenue** $\uparrow$ (HL: assuming PED for exports > 1)
- Devaluation $\rightarrow P_M \uparrow \rightarrow$ M volume$\downarrow \rightarrow$ **M spending**$\downarrow$ (HL: assuming PED for imports > 1)

Improvement in the current account due to managed depreciation

The same basic outcome is possible in a floating exchange rate regime, which would of course then be a *depreciation* rather than a devaluation of the currency. The central bank of a country operating under a floating exchange rate system could sell home currency on the foreign exchange market in order to increase supply and lower the exchange rate. This is illustrated in the case study on Japan below.

Case study: How to spend a few trillion yen

Japan has had something of a world record in currency intervention during the first years of the 21st century. During 2003, the Bank of Japan, BoJ, spent over 20 trillion yen – $US190 billion – in currency market interventions buying up foreign currencies, primarily the US dollar. Figure 4.7.2 illustrates how BoJ purchasing of foreign currencies increases the supply of yen on the market, thus lowering the exchange rate.

The reasoning of the Japanese government is that a falling dollar has severely affected Japanese exports and threatened what might be an export-led tentative crawl out of deflation. However, this type of 'beggar thy neighbour' trade policy is seldom without political repercussions. During a G7[a] meeting in February 2004, European ministers of finance expressed their dissatisfaction with the Japanese interventions which left EU nations bearing too much of the cost of the depreciation of the US dollar.

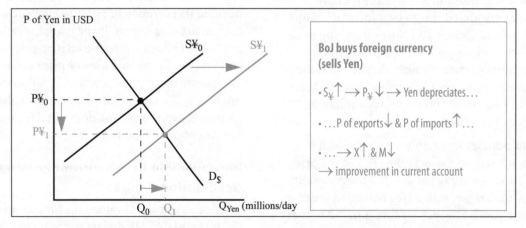

Figure 4.7.2 *Managing the yen and the effects on the Japanese balance of payments*

A question to see whether you've been paying attention: Why hasn't the BoJ lowered interest rates to help depreciate the yen? Reread "Deflation – the ten-year sunset in Japan" on page 359 for a clue.

a. G7 is the Group of Seven, consisting of the largest economies in the world: USA, France, Canada, Germany, Italy, Japan and Britain.

Protectionism/expenditure-switching policies ©IBO 2003

Recall that protectionism can be broadly defined as any policy where the ratio of the price of domestic goods to imported goods falls, i.e. imports become relatively more expensive. Devaluation and interventionist depreciation both serve to decrease the home country's demand for imports, which means that demand for goods is *diverted* from imports towards domestic goods. This *substitution effect* is known as expenditure switching. Another method – now illegal for WTO members to use – is the use of tariffs and quotas to limit imports and force home citizens to consume domestic goods.

> **Expenditure-switching policies**: Policies which divert – substitute – domestic expenditure away from imports towards domestically produced goods are expenditure-switching policies. Trade barriers and/or intentionally lowering the exchange rate (devaluation or depreciation) are examples of such policies.

While devaluation and tariffs work well in countries which have a high propensity to import, the former is a bit like opening eggs with a katana (Japanese long-sword) while the latter is more like using a sledgehammer. In other words, countries increasingly consider such methods a trifle heavy-handed, and while the egg won't fight back, expenditure switching policies frequently invite **retaliatory protectionism** and **reciprocal devaluations**.

Reduction in aggregate demand/ expenditure-reducing policies ©IBO 2003

Household spending is greatly influenced by income, which of course means that a degree of income will be spent on imports. An overall reduction in aggregate demand will lower incomes and *reduce imports*. Therefore, deflationary fiscal and monetary policies can be implemented in order to adjust a current account deficit by reducing imports – this is an expenditure-reducing policy. (HL will recall from Section 3.4 that the marginal propensity to import – MPM – is defined as the change in imports over a change in income: M/Y = MPM. The higher the MPM, the larger the effect on current account will be due to an expenditure reducing policy.)

> **Expenditure-reducing policies**: Contractionary policies such as increased interest rates and/or decreased government spending will cause a decrease in aggregate demand and a general reduction in expenditure (national income). Overall lower expenditure levels will also decrease the demand for imports.

It is worth noting that there is also an expenditure-switching element in deflating an economy. Lower relative inflation might cause home citizens to substitute imports with domestic goods. It is also possible that a reduction in aggregate demand lowers inflation (relative to trade partners) and thus further improves the current account by increasing demand for exports.

By lowering aggregate demand in order to improve the current account, there will be secondary negative effects on *employment and growth* in the economy. The use of deflationary policies to correct a current account deficit once again illustrates conflicts which arise in macro issues, i.e. the possibility of a trade-off in accomplishing both macro goals of high growth/employment and external balance. (See also "Difficulties in attaining macro objectives – trade-off problems" on page 329.)

Change in supply-side policies to increase competitiveness ©IBO 2003

There are a number of policies which will increase long run aggregate supply by increasing the ability and propensity of firms to produce and labourers to supply. (See section 3.4 for review of supply-side policies.) By reducing labour costs, adding to labour skills (human capital), creating incentives for investment in technology and generally increasing productivity, a country can increase its international competitiveness. This would ultimately increase imports and also divert some spending towards domestic goods rather than imports. The problem is that such supply-side policies commonly take several years to implement and even longer before the effects are visible in the balance of payments.

Case study: **The falling dollar**

'*Good news! The dollar is down*' proclaimed *Business Week* in a headline dated 26 May 2003. After running increasingly worrying current account deficits since the mid-1990s – a record-breaking 5% of GDP in 2003 – the US dollar started to fall during 2001. This did not come as any great shock to the majority of economic spectators. Three variables contributed to the fall; 1) a massive outflow of US dollars to pay for imports; 2) a weakened US economy no longer attracted the same degree of foreign investment demand for the US dollar; and 3) the lowest US interest rates in over 20 years dissuaded foreign portfolio investment to a certain extent. Between November 2000 and January 2004, the US dollar fell by over 30% against the EURO and 11% in trade weighted terms.

This was good news for a number of US firms on export markets. It benefited not only US firms which export goods, but also US multinationals earning profits in other currencies, since the repatriated profits rendered more US dollars. This might explain why the current account deficit did in fact not breach the 6% of GDP barrier during 2003 predicted by many observers as late as in the summer of 2003. (Yet **intervention purchasing** of US dollars by both China and Japan – with whom the US runs sizable trade deficits – has limited the total effect on US imports and exports of a weaker dollar.)

However, there is always a downside to every economic issue. The depreciation of the dollar has increased costs severely for US firms which are either importing goods for domestic reselling or whose products contain a large proportion of imported components. Another side-effect has been that oil exporting countries, with OPEC at the forefront, have raised the price of oil to 13 year highs in order to make up for revenue losses arising from being paid in US dollars.

Consequences of a capital account deficit or surplus ©IBO 2003

This has been largely dealt with previously, seeing as how the effects of a deficit or surplus in the capital account are largely a mirror image of a corresponding surplus or deficit in the current account.

Capital account deficit

A capital account deficit in effect means that the country has increased its net holdings of property, capital and financial assets abroad. These outflows of money will ultimately create profits and returns which will flow into the current account. One disadvantage of this increased foreign wealth is the possibility of a currency appreciation in the long run due to a current account surplus. It is also possible that outflows in capital account deprive the home economy of investment funds and negate growth and employment opportunities.

Capital account surplus

When the capital account shows a surplus, the economy is receiving net money inflows – which are matched by outflows for imports in current account. In effect, other countries are funding the home economy's imports to a certain extent. There is little need for a country to worry about these net capital account inflows if it is short term or if most of the funds are being used for investment rather than consumption. It is when sizeable sums of money are being borrowed from abroad to fuel consumption for longer periods that a capital account surplus can become a threat to the home economy. Debts have to be repaid; the exchange rate might fall due to negative expectations from foreign investors; interest rates might rise to keep speculative flows coming; and foreign capital might start to leave the country causing lower growth and increased unemployment.

POP QUIZ 4.7.1   BALANCE OF PAYMENTS AND EXCHANGE RATES

1   How will the current account be affected if a country supports its exchange rate so that it is above the free market equilibrium?

2   Why might a country raise interest rates in order to sustain a current account deficit?

3   What are the possible long run benefits of a current account surplus?

4   Which measures imposed by a country to reduce a current account deficit would be described as 'expenditure switching'?

5   Why might an increase in personal income tax in an economy improve the current account in balance of payments?

6   Say a government wished to improve a current account deficit immediately; would you recommend devaluation or supply-side policies? Explain your choice.

HIGHER LEVEL EXTENSION TOPICS

This HL section looks into the effects of devaluation on exports and imports. I beg you once again to keep in mind the distinctions between export **price**; export **volume**, and export **revenue**.

Marshall–Lerner condition   ©IBO 2003

The effects of a devaluation appear relatively straightforward; a devaluation of the currency will lower the price of exports and increase the price of imports, which in turn will increase the volume of exports and decrease the volume of imports. However, the degree to which export *revenue* and import *spending* is affected – and thus the current account – depends on the price elasticity of demand for exports and imports.

Choose a pair of baskets ...

The series of diagrams in Figure 4.7.3 show a number of possibilities arising from devaluation. **Most important note here:** the diagrams are simply a method to explain how different elasticities will affect export revenue and import spending. I have taken great liberty (known as cheating) in my use of economic concepts by stating that a change in the exchange rate will cause a **movement along** the demand curve for both exports and imports. The connection between the exchange rate (which is in effect home's price of exports and imports relative to trade partners) is in fact a good deal more complex than this. I am using the demand curves **only to explain/illustrate** the effects of price elasticity of demand on exports and imports. I recommend that you do NOT use them in internal assessment or exams.

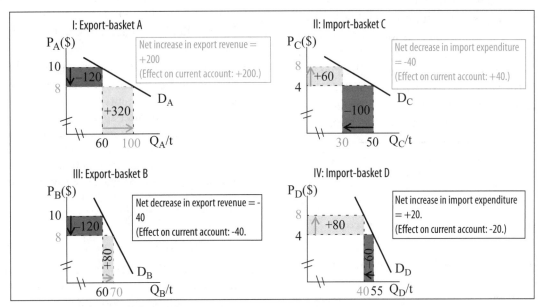

Figure 4.7.3 *Devaluation and the possible effects on current account*

Note that each diagram assumes that 'price' is not for a single good but an *average* price of a basket of export and import goods. For export goods which are price elastic, the result of a devaluation is to increase export revenue, as shown for **export-basket A**, where lower average export prices result in a loss of export revenue of $120 and a gain of $320. The relatively high price elasticity of demand for this country's export goods results in a *net increase in export revenue of 200*. In raising the price of imports, devaluation will also affect total import spending. Assuming that imports are also relatively price elastic, as in **import-basket C**, there will be a net decrease in import spending of $40.

Summing up, if the country in question has an average price elasticity of demand for exports as in basket A, and average price elasticity of demand for imports as in basket C, there will be a net increase in the current account improvement of 240. However, if the combinations of average price elasticities for export- and import-baskets change then there are other possibilities:

- Export basket A and import basket D: current account balance *increases* by 180
- Export basket B and import basket D: current account balance *decreases* by 60
- Export basket B and import basket C: *no change* to current account balance

These examples show that for a devaluation to be considered successful, certain conditions of price elasticities must be upheld. It is possible for the current account to improve even when either exports or imports are demand inelastic. The Marshall–Lerner condition summarises this in stating that devaluation will improve the current account as long as the sum of the price elasticity of demand for exports plus the price elasticity of demand for imports is greater than one. Conversely, if the sum of price elasticities of demand for exports and imports is less than one, a *revaluation* of the currency will improve the current account.

Marshall–Lerner condition: If the sum of the price elasticities of demand for exports and imports is greater than one, a devaluation will improve current account in the balance of payments. Thus:

*De*valuation $\rightarrow$ $PED_X + PED_M > 1$ $\rightarrow$ current account improves

*Re*valuation $\rightarrow$ $PED_X + PED_M < 1$ $\rightarrow$ current account improves

J-curve ©IBO 2003

The conclusion that a devaluation leads to an increase in net export revenue is generally valid. However, depending on how quickly households, importers and exporters respond to the de facto change in relative prices, *there might initially be a worsening* in the current account. There are three main reasons why this might be the case.

1. The Marshall-Lerner condition may not be upheld as the price elasticities for exports and imports are likely to be **relatively inelastic in the short run**. It will take time for firms importing raw materials and components to find alternative sources, so a devaluation will in fact worsen the balance of payments as firms in the short run continue to purchase imported factors of production at higher import prices.

2. Firms are **locked into contracts** for months in advance. An importer with a contract in foreign currency to be paid six months down the road will have to pay more to fulfil the contract after a devaluation. Similarly, exporters contracted in foreign currency will receive less in home currency. Both cases will cause the current account to worsen.

3. It takes time for both firms and consumers to adjust to the fact that relative prices have changed and thereby **change expenditure habits**.

Figure 4.7.4 on page 509 shows the J-curve effect of a devaluation:

- t_0 to t_1: A current account deficit is countered by a *devaluation at t_0* whereupon there is an initial worsening up to point t_1 as households and firms have difficulties in adjusting to the new exchange rate in the short run.

- t_1 to t_2: Ultimately, domestic firms will find alternative (lower cost) sources of factor inputs and long run commitments (contracts) will end, households will alter spending habits more in favour of domestic goods, and foreign trade partners will increase their purchases of goods and services of the country which has devalued. Taken together, import expenditure is falling and export revenue is rising so the current account starts to improve. At t_2 the current account is back to pre-devaluation level.

- t_2 **and beyond**: Beyond t_2 the balance of payments shows a smaller current account deficit than per-devaluation and at t_3 the balance of payments is in perfect equilibrium. Beyond t_3 the current account moves into surplus. (The portion of the net export curve between points t_1 and t_3 show the 'J' portion of the J-curve.)

HIGHER LEVEL

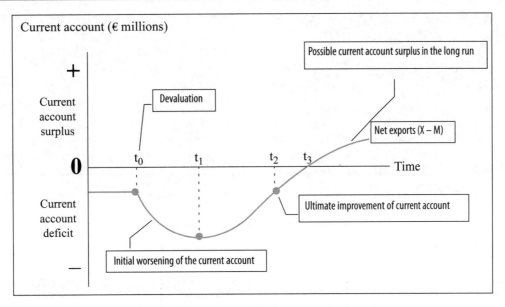

Figure 4.7.4 *J-curve effect on current account*

POP QUIZ 4.7.2   MARSHALL–LERNER CONDITION AND J-CURVE

1   A country's price elasticity of demand for imports is 1.3 and for exports 0.5. The country operates under a fixed exchange rate regime and desperately wants to correct a severe current account deficit. What do you recommend?

2   Is upholding the Marshall–Lerner condition an example of expenditure-switching or expenditure-reducing?

3   Is it possible to have a J-curve effect even in the short run when the Marshall-Lerner condition is upheld?

Terms of trade

4.8

CONTENTS

TERMS OF TRADE ©IBO 2003

Definition of terms of trade

©IBO 2003

Getting four rather than three 'clearies' (see marble story previously) for your 'steely' is naturally preferable – as is getting more units of cloth for every exported unit of oranges (see trade example in Section 3.1). This is commonly known as the commodity or barter terms of trade, as one is using the concept of pure trade without using money.

In adding in a price dimension, the terms of trade will be expressed as the *ratio* of export prices to import prices. For example, assume that Finland and Russia trade only two goods, mobile phones (Finland) and caviar (Russia). One mobile phone costs $US300 and one hectogram (= 0.1 kilogram) of caviar costs $US100. The Finnish terms of trade are $US300/$US100, i.e. 3, which means that one mobile phone will buy 3 hectograms of Russian caviar. You are probably wondering if the exchange rate enters into the equation and the answer is yes, it most assuredly does as we shall see.

> Terms of trade: The amount of export goods needed to purchase a given amount of import goods is the (barter) terms of trade. Using a currency (common to both countries), the terms of trade is the ratio of export prices to import prices, e.g. the price of exports over the price of imports.

Consequences of a change in the terms of trade for a country's balance of payments and domestic economy ©IBO 2003

In reality, traded goods will be priced in terms of domestic currencies so the terms of trade will be expressed as a ratio between the price of exports and imports. Anything which changes the ratio of export prices to import prices will affect a country's terms of trade. Since each country has both a good and a currency – and both the goods and the currencies have prices – then a change in either one will affect the terms of trade.

Causes of a change in the terms of trade

The main causes of a change in terms of trade are price changes on the market for goods, changes in the exchange rate and changes in variables linked to AS-AD. (Refer back to Section 4.5 and the 'balance of payments diamond' in Figure 4.5.6 on page 472.) Let us look at two countries, Namibia and Denmark, and two goods produced in each country; salt and Bang & Olufsen (B&O) headphones respectively. Assuming they trade only theses goods with each other.

Effects on the terms of trade due to market forces

Any change in the price of one good – salt or earphones – will mean that the price of imports for the other country changes, assuming ceteris paribus:

- *Demand for B&O earphones*: Say that B&O develop a new revolutionary headphone for the very popular iPods. The increase in demand for the B&O earphones would drive up the price and mean that Denmark will have to export fewer earphones in order to import any given amount of salt from Namibia. *Denmark's terms of trade have improved* while Namibia's terms of trade have worsened.

- *Supply of salt in Namibia*: If Namibia develops improved methods of extracting salt from seawater then the supply of salt will increase driving down the price. More salt will have to be exported to import any given quantity of B&O earphones. The Namibian terms of trade have worsened.

Effects on terms of trade due to exchange rates

Naturally the Namibians don't buy Danish earphones using the Danish crown but the Namibian dollar. Any change in the exchange rate will mean that there will be a change in the relative price of exports in terms of imports for each country.

- *Exchange rate for the Namibian dollar (NAD)*: If the NAD appreciates then the price of Namibia's exports will rise in relation to Danish imports and the Namibian terms of trade improve.

- *Exchange rate for the Danish Crown (DKK)*: If the DKK depreciates then the price of Danish exports will fall against the Namibian imports – the Danish terms of trade worsen.

Effects on terms of trade due to changes in AS and AD

Both aggregate demand and aggregate supply will have an impact on the terms of trade, since both AD and AS will have an impact on inflation and income.

- *Increase in AD in Denmark*: An increase in AD in Denmark and resulting demand-pull inflation will also drive up the price of goods exported – here, earphones. This would improve Denmark's terms of trade. (Note that we are in fact saying that *relative* inflation in Denmark has risen.)

- *Increase in AS in Namibia*: An increase in AS would have a deflationary effect on the Namibian economy and the fall in (relative) inflation would also cause export prices of salt to fall. The Namibian terms of trade worsen.

- *Increase in LRAS*: A main long run variable affecting the terms of trade is the gain in productivity in an economy. If Namibia experiences increased productivity relative to its trade partner Denmark then the price of Namibian exports will fall compared to the price of Danish imports.

Summing up terms of trade

Figure 4.8.1 illustrates a 'terms of trade gauge (= measure)' for Namibia and Denmark. As outlined above, there are ultimately three elements which make up the terms of trade for a country; 1) the exchange rate; 2) the price of exports and; 3) the price of imports. A change in any one variable – ceteris paribus – will affect the terms of trade (ToT in the figure).

Initially Namibian salt fetches a price of 1,000 Namibian dollars (NAD) per tonne and Danish B&O headphones cost 900 Danish crowns (DKK). The 'gauges' in Figure 4.8.1 (within the dotted box) show an initial exchange rate of DKK0.9 = NAD1, or DKK1 = NAD 1.11. In other words, *one tonne of salt equals one pair of Danish headphones* at the current exchange rate. Now we can play around with the gauges a bit.

- *Depreciation of the Danish Crown*: A depreciation of the Danish Crown (DKK) from 1.11 Namibian dollars (NAD) to 1.05 ('A' in Figure 4.8.1) will cause Denmark's terms of trade to deteriorate, as Denmark will have to sell more headphones in order to get the Namibian dollars necessary to buy a given quantity of salt. Note that in this two-country example, Denmark's deterioration of the terms of trade amounts to an improvement in Namibia's terms of trade.

- *Appreciation of the Namibian Dollar*: Similarly, an appreciation of the Namibian dollar ('B') will enable Namibian exports to be traded for an increased amount of Danish imports, which is an improvement in the Namibian terms of trade.

- *Fall in the world market price for salt*: Should the market price for salt fall ('C') then Namibia's terms of trade will have deteriorated, since more salt will have to be sold to buy each pair of headphones.

- *Increase in the price of headphones*: This is the same outcome as when the price of Denmark's headphones rises ('D').

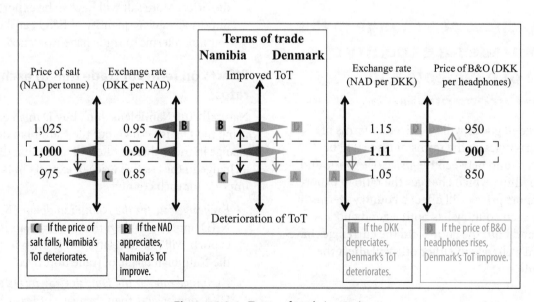

Figure 4.8.1 *Terms of trade 'gauge'*

Effects of an improvement in the terms of trade

It is all too common to fall into the trap of regarding 'improvement in the terms of trade' as generally beneficial. This is an erroneous conclusion since the terms of trade is simply a **ratio** between the price of exports and the price of imports and tells us nothing about the effects of a change in the ratio. The fact is that there are a number of outcomes of a change in the terms of trade in both the balance of payments and the macro environment in general.

Good: Perhaps the most obvious effect is that a country which has improved its terms of trade will be able to consume more imports and thus experience a general increase in *living standards*. Another effect of being able to get more for domestic goods is that *external debt servicing* (i.e. paying off loans and interest) will be easier. Firms will also be able to *import cheaper raw materials* and capital, which can enhance competitiveness.

Improved terms of trade can also improve the **current account** in the balance of payments. If exports are relatively *inelastic*, an improvement in the terms of trade can increase export revenue and improve the current account, since the relative increase in price will be greater than the relative fall in the quantity of export goods sold. The same holds true if imports are demand inelastic; import spending would decrease. (To better understand the effects of relative export and import prices on current account, perhaps SL students should have a look at the HL extension, Figure 4.7.3 "Devaluation and the possible effects on current account" on page 507.)

Bad: As you may have guessed, if exports are demand elastic then an improvement in the terms of trade will cause export revenue to fall – just as import spending would rise if the demand for imports is relatively elastic. Both would have a *negative effect on the balance of payments*. A decrease in export revenue and/or an increase in import spending could lower national income and adversely affect employment.

Effects of a deterioration of the terms of trade

Good: A decrease in the price of exports relative to the price of imports will lead to an *improvement in current account* if the price elasticity of demand for exports is *elastic*. If the demand for exports is also price elastic then export revenue will increase and also improve the current account balance. Increased demand for exports and/or decreased demand for imports will increase *aggregate demand* and perhaps increase job opportunities.

Bad: Higher prices of foreign goods will not only lower consumption possibilities for households, but increase foreign debt burdens and make imported factors dearer. A deterioration of the terms of trade will have a negative effect on the current account if the demand for export goods is price inelastic, as total export revenues will fall. Inelastic demand for imports will also be negative for the current account, as total import spending will rise.

Ugly: See terms of trade for developing countries below.

The significance of deteriorating terms of trade for developing countries

©IBO 2003

Developing countries are for the most part highly dependent on a few commodities (primary goods) for export earnings. In fact, 62 out of 141 developing countries depended on non-oil commodities for over 50% of all export earnings in 2000 – and if oil is included, the number rises to 95.[1] Increasing supply and in many cases falling demand for commodities has resulted in continuously falling commodity prices over the past 40 years. Some commodity categories have in fact fallen by more than 50% as Figure 4.8.2 on page 514 shows.

Falling commodity prices have severely worsened the terms under which developing nations trade.

Figure 4.8.3 on page 514 shows how the terms of trade (indexed at base year 1986) have fallen by 25% since the mid-1980s.

---

1. UNCTAD report, TD/B/50/CRP.3, 10 October 2003, p. 3.

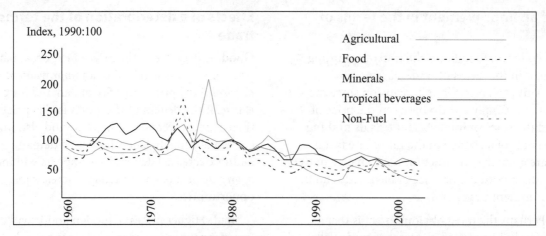

(Source: UNCTAD, 'Escaping the poverty trap', The least developed countries report, 2002, p. 138.)

Figure 4.8.2 *Commodity prices over the past 40 years*

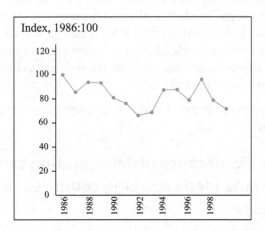

(Source: UNCTAD, 'Escaping the poverty trap', The least developed countries report, 2002, p. 139.)

Figure 4.8.3 *Terms of trade in developing countries, 1986–99*

Let us summarise a key point on deterioration of the terms of trade of developing countries in conjunction with the current account. Falling commodity prices lead to a decrease in the terms of trade for LDCs. As the price elasticity of demand for commodities is low there is a decrease in export revenue and a worsening of the current account.

In economic shorthand: Δ↓price of commodities → Δ↓ terms of trade (low PED for exports) → Δ↓ export revenue → Δ↓ current account.

The results of falling terms of trade for developing countries are almost always negative:

- Higher costs of **debt servicing** as a greater quantity of exports are necessary to earn a given amount of foreign currency with which to repay foreign debt.

- **Current account deficits** often lead to increased borrowing – which in turn increases the debt burden.

- Falling commodity prices often encourage producers in developing countries to **increase production of commodities** – which further depresses the world price of the commodity.

- Deteriorating terms of trade **reduce much-needed imports** such as capital, intermediate products in production, and fuel. All are needed to industrialise and increase value-added output.

Less developed countries – which have a comparative advantage in primary production – will in all likelihood see their terms of trade decline even further in the near future due to increased capacity and low price elasticity of demand for primary goods. This is done in greater depth in Section 5.3.

POP QUIZ 4.8.1   TERMS OF TRADE

1   How would a depreciation of the Canadian dollar affect USA and Mexico's terms of trade?

2   How might a deterioration of a country's terms of trade lead to inflation?

3   Why might an improvement of the terms of trade have negative effects for an economy?

4   How have deteriorating terms of trade affected the majority of less developed countries during the past 40 years.

HIGHER LEVEL EXTENSION TOPICS

Measurement of terms of trade

©IBO 2003

The terms of trade for two goods is the price of the exported good over the price of the imported good. As there are thousands of goods being traded, the easiest way to measure the terms of trade for a country is by indexing the values (similar to the method used in creating a consumer price index in Section 3.5, HL extension). The average prices of export goods and import goods are calculated using weighted indices, whereupon the average price of exports is divided by the average price of imports at a given point in time. For ease of use, the average prices are commonly indexed.

> **Terms of trade index:** The terms of trade index is the (indexed) average price of exports over the (indexed) average price of imports. A decrease in the terms of trade index shows a deterioration of the terms of trade.
>
> Index of ToT
>
> $= \dfrac{\text{Index of the average price of exports}}{\text{Index of the average price of imports}} \times 100$

The base year value of the terms of trade index would of course have a value of 100, e.g. both the average price of exports and imports would be indexed at 100. An increase in the average price of exports relative to the average price of imports will render a higher index value and thus improved terms of trade: a lower index value means that the terms of trade have deteriorated. Thus if the terms of trade go from 105 to 112, the terms of trade have improved. The index in Figure 4.8.3 on page 514 shows how the terms of trade have deteriorated an average 25% for developing countries over a 12-year period.

Causes of changes in a country's terms of trade in the short-run and long-run

©IBO 2003

The terms of trade change over time. In the short run, a number of influences will cause a change in the terms of trade:

- Perhaps the most obvious influence on the terms of trade is a change in the exchange rate. Depreciation of the home currency worsens the terms of trade

while depreciation of trade partners' currencies improves home's terms of trade.

- Increased demand for a country's exports will improve the terms of trade – due to both the exchange rate effect and the price effect on export goods. Increased supply of export goods will lower the terms of trade – especially goods which are demand inelastic.
- It is possible to intentionally alter the terms of trade by the use of trade barriers, intervention purchasing/selling of the home currency and devaluation.
- A booming economy can attract investment funds and cause the currency to appreciate and thus the terms of trade to increase. It is also possible that demand pull inflation causes depreciation and a deterioration of the terms of trade.

In the **long run**, there are a number of fundamental factors which will have an impact on the terms of trade:

- Increased investment and **supply-side policies** which increase long run aggregate supply can lower domestic prices relative to trade partners. Increased productivity would have the same effect.
- Increased world supply and market 'gluts' can depress the market for a country's exports. This happened to a number of coffee producing nations during the 1980s and 1990s.
- Increasing incomes will shift demand towards secondary and tertiary goods with higher **income elasticities**, increasing the terms of trade for industrialised countries and decreasing the terms of trade for countries dependent on exports of primary goods.
- **International Commodity Agreements** (ICAs – see Sections 2.1 and 5.5) can use buffer stocks and pricing agreements to keep prices at a desired level.
- **Purchasing power parity** theory (see Section 4.6) predicts that exchange rates will ultimately adjust to different inflation rates in trading countries. Since the terms of trade are strongly linked to exchange rates, PPP adjustment of exchange rates will naturally affect the terms of trade.

Elasticity of demand for imports and exports ©IBO 2003

We have dealt with the issue of elasticities in conjunction with exports and imports in some depth already, more specifically in Section 4.7. Let me summarise with a few examples of how different price elasticities of demand for traded goods can affect the **price**, **terms of trade** and the **balance of payments**.

Price elasticity of demand and price fluctuations

As shown in "APPLIED ECONOMICS: Commodity price fluctuations" on page 127, primary good prices will fluctuate a great deal more than prices for secondary goods.

Figure 4.8.4 illustrates how changes in the supply will cause different price fluctuations for primary and secondary goods. Demand for primary goods is more inelastic than demand for secondary goods, as primary goods have fewer substitutes. A disruption, 'shock', in supply such as a poor harvest/flooding (primary goods) or disruptions in the supply of factor inputs (secondary goods) shifts the supply curve from S_0 to S_2. A good season or improved technology shifts supply from S_0 to S_1. The outcome of decreased or increased supply is of course fluctuations in price, but far more for primary goods than for secondary goods.

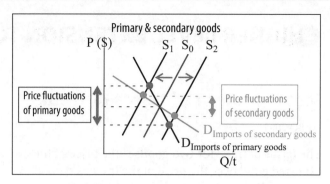

Figure 4.8.4 *Price elasticity of demand and price fluctuations*

Price elasticity of demand, terms of trade and balance of payments

The commodity price index in "APPLIED ECONOMICS: Commodity price fluctuations" on page 127 shows that the price of primary goods has fallen drastically during the past 40 years. Diagrams I and II in Figure 4.8.5 illustrate how the terms of trade for commodity exporters have deteriorated over time; increased supply of both primary and secondary goods has lowered prices over time, but due to low price inelasticity of demand, the price of primary goods has fallen from 100 to 60 – more than that of secondary goods which have fallen from 100 to 80. As the *relative* price of primary goods fallen more than that of secondary goods, primary good exporters have had a worsening in their terms of trade.

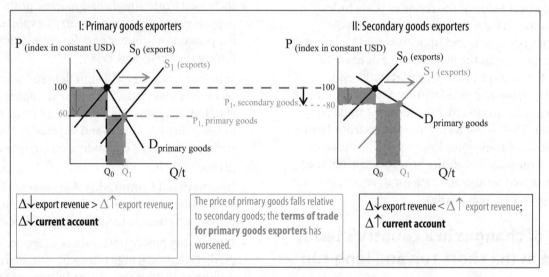

Figure 4.8.5 *Price elasticity of demand and terms of trade*

The price elasticity of demand mechanism illustrated for imports in diagrams I and II in Figure 4.8.5 has further consequences for countries dependent on a narrow range of primary goods for export earnings, namely the negative impact on the *balance of payments*. Diagram I shows how an increase in the supply of primary goods exports lowers net export revenue (the revenue gain is less than the revenue loss) while the same increase in supply for secondary goods increases net export revenue. This will have a negative effect on the current account for primary goods exporters but a positive effect on the current account for secondary goods exports.

Preparing for exams

Short answer questions (10 marks each)

1 'A current account deficit damages the domestic economy.' Discuss.

2 Explain how a country which is experiencing a 'boom' in the domestic economy might see the current account go into a deficit.

3 How might a country's exchange rate influence the balance of payments?

4 How might deteriorating terms of trade improve the current account in the balance of payments?

5 'An appreciation of the exchange rate is always beneficial to an economy.' Discuss.

6 **[HL Only]** Why might a devaluation of a country's currency not necessarily improve the current account in the short run?

Extended response questions (25 marks each)

1 a What problems might arise for a country running a current account deficit? (10 marks)

  b How might the deficit be reduced? (15 marks)

2 a Distinguish between the 'terms of trade' and the 'balance of trade'. (10 marks)

  b How might both be affected by a fall in the country's exchange rate? (15 marks)

3 a Explain how a country might have a consistent current account deficit for longer periods. (10 marks)

  b Is this necessarily a serious problem? (15 marks)

[HL Only]

4 a Explain how a floating exchange rate works and the variables which affect the rate. (10 marks)

  b Why might exchange rates ultimately reflect the relative prices of traded goods in trading countries? (15 marks)

'How does it feel to be amongst the richest five per cent of humans ever to walk the face of the earth?' is the question I ultimately ask all my people. My intention is not to create guilt or bad conscience but simply to make them aware of the monumental gulf between haves and have-nots; ability and disability; freedom and confinement; choice and lack of options; and wealthy and poor. I grew up in most privileged circumstances in a number of developing countries in the Caribbean and South America. I was surrounded by servants, diplomats and expatriates at home – and kids on the street who lived in another universe. I knew that there was a gulf separating us but I never really understood why. I still don't.

The answer might lie in education but how then do you explain the situation of Russia? Or it might lie in natural resource endowment but then you look at the Democratic Republic of Congo. How about technology – oh yes, both India and Pakistan can split atoms now. What I am trying to get across is that development issues have been studied for some 70 years as a specific field, and as yet no absolute or generally applicable solutions have arisen. Thus, while this section looks at the problems facing developing countries and some of the possible solutions, there are no patented 'keys' or '12-step programs' available. Issues pertaining to development have been looked at in Sections 1 and 3.2 and this final section delves deeper into this core syllabus area. Development issues are not 'last' by order of importance, but by order of application: the preceding sections are the basis for being able to study development issues.

Students in IB economics are therefore rather lucky in having so much revision built-in, yet I would urge you to revise elasticities, production possibility frontiers and barriers to trade. Development economics is something of a trap for many students, who all too frequently fall into a habit of using normative thinking and loosely linked anecdotes rather than clear economic terminology and theory. I have seen good students fall several grade points on tests in development economics simply because they used sweeping normative statements in their analyses which were not backed up by mainstream economic theory and terminology.

Sources of economic growth and/or development

5.1

CONTENTS

SOURCES OF ECONOMIC GROWTH AND/OR DEVELOPMENT

Success is a science. If you have the conditions, you get the result. – Oscar Wilde

Classification of countries

There is a most confusing and even somewhat contradictory array of terms used in development economics to classify countries. One of the standard ways of classifying the world was 'First World' (rich countries), 'Second World' (planned/command economies) and 'Third World' (poor countries). As the Second World no longer exists as an identifiable entity, the classification is pretty much obsolete (= outdated).

Another common division is the 'North–South' division, where rich countries lie in the north and poor in the south. What about Australia, New Zealand and Singapore? Then it gets even trickier when one speaks of 'industrialised' versus 'industrialising' countries; Russia is most definitely an industrialised country but has seen average income fall drastically – around 30% –

between 1990 and 2001 and has had an average growth rate of -0.1 per cent between 1990 and 2005.[1] In addition, you will often see references to '**newly industrialised countries**', NICs, which is perhaps even more wide of the mark as the term often includes Korea, Thailand and Hong Kong – which have been rather industrialised since the 1960s.

The distinctions are academic rather than useful. I will limit myself to using 'developing country' and 'developed country' or 'less developed country' (LDC) and 'more developed country' (MDC).[2] In some specific cases, reference will be made to high, low and middle income countries (see Table 5.1.1) in accordance with the United Nations Development Program (UNDP) classifications taken from the annual Human Development Report (HDR).

Table 5.1.1 *UNDP classification of countries*

High income countries (GNP/capita over $US9,266 in 2000)	Middle income countries (GNP/capita of $US756–9,265 in 2000)	Low income countries (GNP/capita of $US75 or less in 2000)
35 countries	79 countries	59 countries
Australia	Algeria	Angola
Canada	Bolivia	Cambodia
Denmark	Ecuador	Haiti
Ireland	Honduras	Indonesia
Japan	Russian Federation of States	Nepal
USA	Turkey	Ukraine

(Source: *HDR 2002*, p. 270)

---

1. *HDR 2003*, p. 53, and *HDR 2007/2008* at http://hdrstats.undp.org/indicators/135.html.
2. One can normatively say that a developing country is one which has several of the following characteristics: poor health care; low productivity and GDP per capita; poor standard of living; lack of capital, and a dependency on agricultural produce and raw materials. In this characterisation, approximately 135 of the poorest countries in the world are developing countries. It is worthy of notice that there will be very large differences between these countries, from dictatorships to democracies and from countries suffering recurring famines to countries which are industrialised export nations.

Natural factors: the quality and/or quantity of land or raw materials

©IBO 2003

Clearly arable land, abundant forests, plentiful water, and any one of thousands of other land resources are linked to a country's ability to satisfy its citizen's needs and wants. Different countries are differently endowed with such natural factors: Canada has the world's largest freshwater supply while Namibia has one of the largest reserves of uranium in the world. Natural factors can to a certain extent explain development. England's abundant coal and iron helped bring about a technical revolution which enabled them to become the richest country in the world by 1900. Another country of some fame in this respect is **Iceland**, whose 240,000 inhabitants enjoy one of the highest standards of living in the world. Natural hot springs provide plentiful cheap energy and the island is surrounded by one of the largest fish stocks in the world.

On the other hand, the oil reserves of **Saudi Arabia** are estimated to account for one-third of all known reserves, yet the country ranks 55th in the Human Development Index (see "The Human Development Index (HDI)" on page 275). **Nigeria** has oil, virgin rainforests filled with hardwoods, tin, iron, coal, palm oil trees, cotton, bananas, peanuts (called 'groundnuts' by the British) … and a good deal more. How does Nigeria measure up on the HDI? The country is one of the poorest in the world and had an HDI value of 0.499 in 2008, placing Nigeria at 154th place of 179 countries included in the index.[3] The 'Asian Tigers' Hong Kong, Taiwan, South Korea and Singapore have nowhere near the natural factor endowments of Nigeria but are now amongst the riches countries in the world.

> **Natural factors of production:** Natural factors consist of a country's endowments (= gifts) in natural resources, such as minerals, forests, arable land for agriculture, plant and animal diversity, etc.

So while natural resources are vital in both economic growth and development, they in no way explain the whole story. A good many poor countries have abundant natural resources and are still in early development stages. While commodity production can be a vital source of income in the short term in LDCs, it is highly unlikely that primary industries such as mining, agriculture and fishing can fuel development

in the long run. Increasingly the focus has been on **human factors** in production rather than pure natural resources.

Human factors: the quantity and/or quality of human resources

©IBO 2003

> *If India can turn into a fast-growth economy, it will be the first developing nation that used its brainpower, not natural resources or the raw muscle of factory labour, as the catalyst.[4]*

Growth of human resources

The growth/development potential resulting from human factors of production can be narrowly defined as more and/or better labourers. Both serve to shift the PPF outwards (see Section 1). Population growth adds to overall potential output – whether it is a matter of more people being born or immigration. However, overall economic growth resulting from an increase in population does not necessarily mean that average incomes rise. In fact, a majority of the 40 or so **least** developed countries saw GDP per capita decline in the 25-year period between 1975 and 2000.[5]

Yet this should not detract one from the simple fact that people are a *resource* and that more resources adds to potential. Demographic changes can render amazing outcomes in a very short period of time. Ireland was one of the poorest countries in the EU in 1980 but had 50% of the population under 25 years of age. This large group of young people contributed greatly to making Ireland one of the riches in the EU 20 years later. India is in a similar situation, with a large young person to dependant ratio, and a number of economists now talk about a 'window of development opportunity' for India in the next 20 years.

Increase in the quality of human resources

The quality of the working population – the human capital – is the result of knowledge, skills, education and training. Human capital also results from health care, as this adds to productive capabilities in a country. Most economists would agree that education/knowledge and health care are central factors in potential growth and development. The benefits of enhancing human resources – *investment* in human

3.   *HDR 2008*, http://hdrstats.undp.org/2008/countries/country_fact_sheets/cty_fs_NGA.html.
4.   'The Rise Of India', *Business Week*, 8 December 2003.
5.   *HDR 2002*, pp. 192–93.

resources rather – go far beyond economic growth. A short-list of positive effects resulting from investment in human capital would have both economic and social benefits:

- **Economic benefits** would be higher productivity in the economy; increased labour mobility as more people would be attractive on the job market; more dynamism as a result of entrepreneurial spirit; and better use of finite resources.

- **Social benefits** include better health and longer lives; greater participation and democratisation in local and municipal issues; better opportunities for women in choosing their own lives, and the ability to partake in a wider range of cultural offerings.

Again, the above is a short-list. It is almost impossible to quantify and assess the benefits of human capital investment, but there are a number of strong indications. Table 5.1.2 shows the comparative literacy rates, life expectancies and real GDP in purchasing power parity for six countries over a 45-year period.

This selection of countries in Table 5.1.2 does not enable far-reaching conclusions. It is mostly an example of how education comes hand-in-glove with development. Life expectancy and real GDP per capita (PPP USD) were similar in India, China and Indonesia in 1960.[6] Over the next 45 years both China and Indonesia pulled ahead in literacy, life expectancy and GDP per capita. An even greater increase in life expectancy and GDP per capita was recorded by South Korea where per capita income increased 1300% during the period.

While one must realise that the figures do not show whether education and health care *caused* growth or vice versa, the *correspondence* between growth/development and investment in human capital is clear. An in-depth study on this correlation by the World Bank in 1993 suggested that one of the main factors in the strong economic development in East Asia was that a significant proportion of resources went towards basic education.[7]

> **Human factors and human capital**:
> Human resources – labour – comprise the skills, knowledge, experience, education and health of the population which makes up the labour pool. Investment in these areas, often called social investment, increases human capital.

Table 5.1.2 *Comparisons in human development, selected countries (2006)*

Country (HDI value/rank)	Life expectancy (years)		Adult literacy (% of population)		Real GDP per capita (PPP$)	
	1960	2006	1960	2006	1960	2006
India (0.609/132)	44	64.1	34	65.2	617	2,489
Botswana (0.664/126)	45.5	48.9	41	82.1	474	12,744
Indonesia (0.726/109)	41.2	70.1	54	91	490	3,455
China (0.762/94)	47.1	72.7	..	93	723	4,682
Thailand (0.786/81)	52.3	70	60	93.9	985	7,613
South Korea (0.928/25)	53.9	78.2	88	98.5	690	22,985

(Source: Composed from *HDI 2008* at http://hdr.undp.org/en/statistics/)

---

6. In the previous edition I used Botswana as an example and the time span was 1960 t0 1993. Botswana's life expectancy in 1993 was 65.2 years. By 2006 life expectancy had fallen to 48.9 according to the UN figures used here (39 years according to USAID.) A decrease in life expectancy of 25% over a period of 13 years?! Look it up and tell me why this has happened.

7. World Bank: *The East Asian Miracle' Economic Growth and Public Policy*, Oxford University Press 1993.

Case study: The driest country in the world – Namibia

Namibia is noticeably lacking in a most precious natural resource – water. Just under 2 million people live in a country which is almost four times the size of the UK and has 60 million people. This gives you a clue. Most of Namibia is desert, with the Namib Desert along the coast to the west, and the Kalahari to the east. Rainfall in most of the country is erratic and sparse.

Namibia does have several resources upon which it depends; diamonds, copper, uranium, gold, lead, tin, lithium, cadmium, zinc, salt, vanadium, natural gas, hydropower (in the far north) and fish. There are suspected reserves of oil, and coal.

However only around 1% of the land is actually arable and some 50% of foodstuffs are imported, the majority from South Africa. And while mining accounts for 20% of GDP, only 3% of the population are employed in the mining sector.

There is of course one more natural resource; elephants, rhinos and wildebeest. Thousands of tourists come every year to visit Etosha National Park to drive around on dirt tracks looking at the magnificent wildlife. And while the Namibians are acutely aware of the potential revenue in increased tourism, the problem is that already low water tables are being depleted even now. It simply wouldn't be feasible to accommodate larger numbers of tourists in the long run.

It turns out that the water tables being used are the result of rains which fell hundreds of years ago and simply cannot be replenished at current consumption rates. Most of the scant rain that falls evaporates before it can sink down into the table. So deep water drilling is not really an option for the long term. Desalination plants (where seawater is de-salted) are a possibility – but the Atlantic is some 500 kilometres away from where people live and where tourists want to visit. A pipeline is simply not economically feasible.

The water issue is going to have serious implications for future growth and prosperity in Namibia and will constrain growth. The mining industry is a major consumer and the availability of water limits potential production in several sites. Even foreign direct investment in Namibia is constrained by the water issue. For example, an Indian textile firm was to set up a production site outside of the capital, Windhoek, during 2003. The Namibian government was most keen on attracting this FDI and went to great lengths to provide adequate infrastructure for production. There was, however, a great deal of debate about the appropriateness of this particular factory, as the textile industry is a very heavy user of water.

Physical capital and technological factors: the quantity and/or quality of physical capital ©IBO 2003

Physical capital

Man-made factors of production are collectively known as physical capital. You have encountered this numerous times in this book as *investment* or an *increase in capital stock*. Machinery and factories are directly involved in production, while roads and communications are necessary 'backbones' of production, e.g. **infrastructure**. Any accumulation of capital will enable increased output in the future –

recall that there is an **opportunity cost** in the form of other goods forsaken in the short term (see Table 5.1.2 on page 523).

> **Physical capital:** An increase in investment means that physical capital has increased. Examples are factories, machinery and roads. The accumulation of capital increases a country's capital stock.

Sustained growth in an economy will necessitate increased capital stock, which means that there must be continuous (net) investment taking place. This often leads to a most difficult 'chicken or egg' problem for LDCs, since savings are needed for investment, income is needed to create the basis for saving, and investment is necessary to increase income. So which comes first? See Section 5.3 for a non-answer.

Technological factors

The basic definition of technology as applied to economic development is simply 'method of production', so a man-pulled plough is one form of technology and a tractor another. New technology is any new and improved *technique* in production which increases output per unit of input, and technological progress will increase output and growth over time. New grain types and improvements in irrigation techniques; innovation in solar cells, and mechanisation in garment production are all examples of technological improvements.

In summing up, economic growth is a **function** of land, labour, capital and efficiency. Any increase in the amount or improvement in quality will enable higher output. Note that investment can come with an assortment of price tags attached. The most obvious is the trade-off between consumption and investment, i.e. the **opportunity cost** of present consumption. This can be felt rather harshly in LDCs which might have little choice but to use resources for present needs – they simply cannot afford to wait. Ponder what 'afford to wait' means until Section 5.5.

Another issue is the **appropriateness** of the technology in question. While increasing availability and use of capital will have many positive effects such as the spread of technological knowledge and capabilities in developing countries, there can be negative side effects due to the labour-saving element in technological progress. Technology which makes a few hundred workers redundant might have far higher societal costs than economic benefits. In addition, advanced machinery needs to be installed, maintained and repaired – all of which often involve imported parts and expertise which will need to be paid for in scarce foreign currencies. It is therefore argued that using abundant relatively cheap labour often results in higher overall social benefits than imported labour-saving capital.

Land, labour and capital again

Figure 5.1.1 is pretty much a reprise of the production possibility frontier issues illustrated in Section 1. Bundling together human and capital investment on the *y*-axis, an economy can increase potential output in the long run by incurring the opportunity cost (sacrifice) of present consumption. This is shown by the movement from A to B, and the shift of the production possibility frontier from PPF$_{SR}$ to PPF$_{LR}$. Point C is – possibly – a new level of total output.

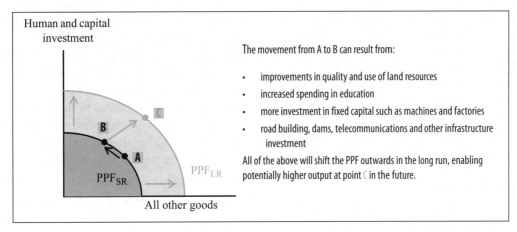

Figure 5.1.1 *PPFs and investment*

Institutional factors that contribute to development

Institutions do not necessarily mean a physical building or place. Instead, the concept is broadly a set of rules and norms which come together under organisations. The institutions in the captions below are often considered the *result* of a developed and well-

functioning economy, but increasingly the flip-side of the correlation coin is pointed out: these institutions play an integral part in the *process* of development.

Banking system

A banking system has one basic purpose: to **provide liquidity** (money) on the capital and goods markets. The system does so by offering a return to depositors and setting a price for borrowers – interest. In this manner, banks function as a means of putting potential entrepreneurs in contact with the individual savings of others. A bank thus facilitates (= makes possible) finance and the efficient allocation of funds by supplying a system for savings and investment.

Functions of a banking system

In acting as a conduit (= channel) for investment, a modern banking system provides a number of vital services in a money-based economy:

- Banks provide a system for **payment services** which is central to a market system involving supply chains of wholesalers and retailers.
- Banks enable entrepreneurs to get access to **start-up capital**. Few businesses are started using household savings alone. Banks allow entrepreneurs to realise their business ideas by borrowing against future profits. The cost of the loans – interest – is spread out over a period of time, enabling the entrepreneur to use capital now and pay for it later.
- An efficient banking system allows **profitable business** ventures to blossom, thereby allocating venture capital efficiently.

Development banks

As efficient domestic banking systems have been noticeably lacking in many LDCs, funding for small and medium domestic enterprises has also been unavailable. Much of the funding came from foreign banks and went to large enterprises which could put up sufficient collateral (= security for loans). In answer to this gap in liquidity, a number of development banks have arisen in developing countries to supply long-term loans. Much of the money has in turn been supplied by loans and aid monies from international development organisations and domestic governments.

Group lending schemes

Yet the development banks still leave a considerable gap in credit availability to small scale farmers and local traders, as development banks often will not bother with loans of a few hundred – or even a few thousand – US dollars. It is simply far more time-consuming and costly to administrate 1,000 loans of USD200 than two loans of USD100,000. This credit gap is increasingly being filled by small-scale credit organisations called **group lending schemes**.

Dr Muhammad Yunus
– founder of Grameen Rural Bank and

Like all really good ideas, it is astoundingly simple. A group of five borrowers band together and collectively borrow a sum of money from a development bank or other financial institution. Each member of the group is given part of the total loan and has an obligation to the group to repay his or her loan – but the entire group is responsible for the loan ultimately being repaid. There are two major benefits of the system: 1) the group can borrow enough money to make it worth a bank's while; 2) internal pressure within the lending group induces members to pay their debts and interest on time. One of the most notable successes of a group lending scheme is the **Grameen Rural Bank** in Bangladesh, started in 1976. Individuals can borrow as little as USD100 within the group. This has enabled thousands of poor people to gain access to desperately needed capital to fund small but life-supporting business ventures, such as buying cloth for producing clothing. It also turns out that over 90% of the borrowers are women and that default rates (= non-payments of loans) are less than 1%.[8] We will return to this form of 'micro-lending' in Section 5.4.

Education system ©IBO 2003

One of the highest rates of return in both economic growth and development issues is undoubtedly to be found in education. Every country in what we now call the developed world experienced the brunt of growth and development once primary education had been established. In fact, one of the world's most famous development economists, Nobel laureate Amartya Sen, points out that Japan as early as 1870 had higher literacy rates than Europe – allowing rapid transition to

---

8. 'From tiny acorns', *The Economist* 10 December 1998, and http://www.grameen-info.org/.

an industrialised power 50 years later. Sen points out that the 'miracle' economies of East Asia had similar levels of literacy.[9] (See Table 5.1.2 on page 523.)

The benefits of education are, as noted in Section 2.4, both **private** and **social**. The element of merit good in education is very high, which to a large extent ends the discussion on 'private or public provision' in developing countries. The societal return in education investment is so high that a majority of developing countries strive to spend as large a portion of government funds as possible on the education sector. For example, Kenya and Malawi, with GDP per capita under USD1,000 in 2003, directed more than 20% of total government expenditure towards education.[10]

Private and social benefits of education

- An individual stands to benefit in increased lifetime *earnings*, higher *productivity* and better *jobs*. Studies show that each additional year of education increases individual output by 4–7%, while increasing lifetime earnings by 10–20%.[11] The benefits to society are **growth** and an *expanded tax base*.

- In addition to the economic benefits, being able to read and write will greatly expand the **quality of life** for a person who is able to take an active part in society via media. This is put most directly by Amartya Sen, development economist and Nobel laureate, in that the personal benefits of education 'exceed its role as human capital in commodity production'. Education enables people to read, communicate, form serious opinions and ultimately argue their case. This furthers political participation and studies show strong links between education and political stability/democracy.

- Individuals' **health** will improve due to knowledge in sanitation and how to prevent transmissible diseases, amongst them HIV/AIDS. The particularly gruesome figures on the spread of HIV amongst young people lends particular weight here; the World Bank estimates that 15 to 24-year-olds account for 60% of all new HIV infections in developing countries.[12] Education improves health care simply by enabling people to read food and medicine labels, pamphlets on health care and family planning and so forth. The Swedish author Henning Mankell who spends most of his time in Africa puts it rather bluntly: 'All the statistics available are clear – it's the ones who can read that have the lowest prevalence of AIDS'.[13]

- There are few areas in development studies where the correlation between two variables is as strong as that which is shown between increased education of women and falling birth rates.[14] Education greatly **empowers women** in giving them an opportunity to provide for themselves. They will have safer and healthier pregnancies, and will provide better nutrition and living conditions for their children. Increased financial independence is perhaps the best overall form of population control, and evidence shows that women who are allowed a secondary education have significantly lower birth rates than women who are uneducated.

- Education renders **economic benefits** such as growth and increased tax revenues in the long run – allowing increased social spending on public and merit goods so vital to society. **Social benefits** are improved health, lower death rates and birth rates, and political/democratic stability. Table 5.1.3 on page 528 shows illiteracy rates for the 10 most populated countries in the world in contrast to the three largest/richest economies in the world. Yes, there is still a lot of work to do.

---

9. *Development as freedom*, Amartya Sen, p. 41.
10. *HDR 2003*, table 9, p. 268.
11. 'Teach a child – transform a nation', *Basic Education Coalition* report using UNDP, World Bank and UESCO statistical material, pp. 7–8.
12. 'Teach a child – transform a nation', p. 15.
13. Jag dör men minnet lever vidare, Henning Mankell, p. 59.
14. Todaro, pp. 279–85.

Table 5.1.3 *Illiteracy rates – most populated countries in the world*

Country	Adult Illiteracy Rate (%), 2008		Secondary School Enrolment Rate (%), 2003	Student-Teacher Ratio, Primary Schooling, 2000
	Females	Males		
China	13.5	4.9	55	22
India	52.2	26.6	44	40
Indonesia	13.2	6	48	22
Brazil	11.2	11.6	71	26
Pakistan	64.6	35.9	30	44
Bangladesh	59.2	46.1	43	57
Nigeria	39.9	21.8	30	34
Mexico	9.8	6.8	60	27
Vietnam	13.1	6.1	62	*na
Philippines	6.4	8.4	53	35
U.S.	**	**	88	15
Japan	**	**	100	20
Germany	**	**	88	15

** no data available (Source: World Bank, *World Development Indicators 2003* and *HDR* at http://hdrstats.undp.org/indicators/)

Storytime: Brightest Africa

My long-standing habit of going off for long runs wherever I am in the world caused a good deal of amusement and not a little worry among my colleagues during our time in Namibia. The first time out running I lost track of time and the sun went down. Man, when the sun goes down in the Namibian bush it gets dark; no warning, no long period of dusk, just pitch black nothing. Naturally I got myself severely lost – I mean, how do you know where you came from when you can only see a few feet ahead. After getting instructions from some highly amused local people, I got home three hours late and was chastised by worried colleagues and forbidden to run later than 16:00.

On one of these late afternoon runs way out in the desert/bush, I was hailed by a 'Hellooooooooo!' which I barely heard through AC/DC in the earphones. In the distance was a waving person who, upon running closer, I discovered was a very pretty young girl in a school uniform flashing a brilliant smile. She was on her way home from school, and in one hand she had a bag with books and groceries and in the other hand her shoes. She was barefoot.

We had a nice chat the way one can with neat young people in Namibia. She was most polite and very open and laughing. This is why I was able to ask a somewhat rude question; 'Why aren't you wearing your shoes?'

Her answer is the reason I am wasting space here. She said, 'Oh no, these are for school only! It is most important to be proper in school. When I finish school I will be able to get a job and then I will wear my shoes when I take the bus to work.'

I wish all my IB students had walked a few miles in her shoes.

Health care ©IBO 2003

A common characteristic of many LDCs is that health care is lacking, poor or simply non-existent. Few LDCs spend the 5% or more of GDP on public health care that high-income countries do; medium income countries average 2.7% and low-income countries 2.1%. This gives per capita spending of USD1,061, USD194 and USD38 in these country groupings respectively.[15] The outcomes in terms of life expectancy and infant mortality rates are clearly seen in Table 5.1.4.

Education and health care have been shown to be strongly interlinked and **self-reinforcing**. Estimates by the World Bank indicate that a 10% rise in primary school education is associated with an average 10.8 month increase in life expectancy.[16] Better educated people will earn more money and lead longer, healthier lives. This will increase national income and improve tax bases which, in turn, creates more funds for social spending on education and health care. The

problem is another *Catch-22*[17], since income and tax bases are needed to provide the health care which … can create income and tax bases.

The difference between developing and developed countries in health spending is staggering, with high income countries spending an average of USD2,700 per person and year on health care. Middle income countries spend USD115 and low-income countries USD21 per year.[18] This has led the **World Health Organisation**, WHO, to calculate not only the impact of premature death, but the average healthy lifespan a person can expect in a given country. Table 5.1.5 on page 530 shows the expected time span a person can expect to live in full health. The values are calculated by adjusting life expectancy figures to disability caused by disease, injuries and lack of care. The average of 39 healthy years of living to be expected in Sub-Saharan Africa would be an estimated 6 years higher in 2000 had it not been for HIV/AIDS – and without malaria and tuberculosis, close to nine years longer.

Table 5.1.4 *Life expectancy and infant mortality rates (selected countries)*

HDI Rank	Country	Life expectancy at birth (years)		Infant mortality rate (per 1,000 live births)		Under-five mortality rate (per 1,000 live births)	
		1970–75	2000–05	1970	2001	1970	2001
High human development							
1	Norway	74.4	78.9	13	4	15	4
2	Iceland	74.3	79.8	13	3	14	4
3	Sweden	74.7	80.1	11	3	15	3
4	Australia	71.7	79.2	17	6	20	6
5	Netherlands	74.0	78.3	13	5	15	6
Medium human development							
76	Kazakhstan	64.4	66.3	..	61	..	76
77	Suriname	64.0	71.1	51	26	68	32
78	Jamaica	69.0	75.7	49	17	64	20
79	Oman	52.1	72.4	126	12	200	13
80	St. Vincent & the Grenadines	61.6	74.1	..	22	..	25

15. *HDR 2003*, p. 98 (note, PPP dollars).
16. 'Teach a child – transform a nation', p. 8.
17. A now idiomatic expression from the novel of the same name by Joseph Heller; 'a no-win situation' or 'a double bind'.
18. *WDR 2004*, p. 257.

Table 5.1.4 *Life expectancy and infant mortality rates (selected countries) (cont.)*

Low human development							
167	Congo, Dem. Rep.	45.8	41.8	148	129	245	205
168	Central African Rep.	43.0	39.5	149	115	248	180
169	Ethiopia	41.8	45.5	160	116	239	172
170	Mozambique	41.1	38.1	163	125	278	197
171	Burundi	43.9	40.9	138	114	233	190

(Source: *HDR 2003*, pp. 262–65)

Table 5.1.5 *Healthy life expectancy at birth, 2000 (by region)*

Region	Years
Africa	41.4
Northern Africa	57.3
Sub-saharan Africa	38.7
Asia*	55.5
Eastern Asia	60.9
South-Central Asia	51.8
South-Eastern Asia	55.8
Western Asia	50.8
Latin America and the Caribbean	58.0
Oceania†	49.6
Developing Countries	53.6
Developed Countries	66.1
World	56.0

*.   excludes Japan
†.   excludes Australia and New Zealand

(Source: *HDR 2003*, p. 195)

Storytime: Maria – In memoriam

This is a story that I'd actually rather not tell but Rob the housey and I agree that it should be told.

When I moved here to Mexico in 2006 I was incredibly lucky to get the fantastic Maria as my housekeeper. She had been taking care of the expatriate teachers here on Expat Row for some 30 years and was a legend. In fact, there were several mutterings of discontent from colleagues who had been waiting in line to take on Maria when she instead agreed to work for me.

Standing at 148 centimetres, Maria was a powerhouse of energy, kindness and attention to details that I didn't even realise existed. For example, the first week she worked for me I was taking an after-run shower and Maria knocked on the door to enquire if I might speed it up a bit. Perplexed and sporting a towel around my waist I opened the bathroom door to ask what was going on. Totally ignoring the half-naked economics teacher dripping water on the floor, she waltzed in and starting taking the shower curtain down. 'Why?' I asked. 'Señor, I must wash the shower curtain of course!' Wash a shower curtain? You can do that?

When I moved into a shared house with Rob the amazing PE teacher in 2007 she took care of everything. I mean everything. I had just returned home from working at the Oxford Study Courses and was looking forward to having a week's vacation with my lady friend – only to discover that the repairs to the new house had not been done and there was a huge pile of boxes and clothing lying in the living room. Rob was off doing whatever Welsh people do in Wales. Maria noticed how frustrated I was in losing my vacation to deal with the mess of moving: 'Mateo, off you go! Take Patricia to the beach. Eat a lot of Mexican food – you are so thin! I will take care of things.'

I came back ten days later to find that Maria had moved all our things from two houses, supervised the rebuilding of floors, stood over handymen and made them redo thresholds which were not up to her standards, had rooms repainted, hung loads of pictures on the walls, moved all our clothing into our rooms (neatly washed and pressed), cowed the school gardeners into taking care of the garden and basically turned a house into a home for two very messy guys who need 16 months to change a light bulb and can let dishes pile up until the mould takes on life and washes them.

We adored Maria! We made it very clear to her and anyone who knocked that 'La Jefa' (The Boss) was Maria – we lived there but she ran the household. One day I came home after school to find Rob sitting outside on the steps with tears in his eyes. 'What's happened?!' I asked. 'Maria just died …'

She had complained of aching joints and difficulties in breathing. Then she had been admitted to hospital and was away for a week. Much of that week was spent seeing various local physicians who all had different diagnoses. She had spent several nights lying on a cot in the hallway of a hospital because no beds were available. To this day we expatriate teachers are not quite sure what killed her. Probably a combination of pneumonia and an arthritic affliction, but again, nobody seems to know. She was 48 years old – one year older than I as these lines are written.

What we all knew was that this would most assuredly not have happened to one of us expatriate teachers! With a ratio of less than one teaching hour to one full days' work for Maria, our incomes and very generous health benefits put us at a level of health care which few of our Mexican hosts can match. Rob and I also agreed that the chances of something similar happening in England or Sweden are virtually nonexistent. One of my students summed it up very succinctly when I said the same thing in class re development and health care: 'Matt, it's simple. Rich people don't die of pneumonia.'

The global killers

Out of a horrendously long list, the following three diseases are the top killers in the world:

- **Tuberculosis:** A bacterial infection disease carried by about 2 billion people, whereof 7 to 8 million fall ill each year. Death toll: 3 million per year.

- **Malaria:** This mosquito-borne parasite affects millions of people around the world, primarily in developing countries. Many malarial strains are now immune to the common treatment drugs. Death toll: 2 million per year.

- **Hepatitis B:** A blood-spread virus, often via sex and intravenous drug use. Chronic sufferers worldwide estimated at 200 million people. Death toll: 1 million per year.

A brief comment on the worst of them all: HIV/AIDS

I took pictures but I will never put them in print. Having stumbled across a burial ground way out in the bush on one of my runs in Namibia, a few of the colleagues wanted to see it. Per, Pär, Lars-Göran and I drove out and spent 15 very quiet minutes looking at grave markers – or, as often as not, the lack of markers. Quite a few very small graves there. Quite a few very young people buried there. Quite a few with recent markers. You know why.

The statistics on HIV/AIDS are perhaps the most chilling reading available. It is now the number one killer of working age people in developing countries – and it is going to get worse. An estimated 22 million have died so far and over 13 million orphans have been left behind. Over 42 million people are infected worldwide. In several Sub-Saharan countries – such as aforementioned Namibia – more than 20% of the population is infected and the proportion is still growing.

You don't need any more statistics; you are hopefully bombarded with them by your teachers. But here's one you could look up: What is the probability of getting infected with HIV by having unprotected sex? What is the probability when using a condom? Think of it in terms of 0.07 millimetres of latex or possible death. Have a good look at Figure 5.1.2. Feel lucky?

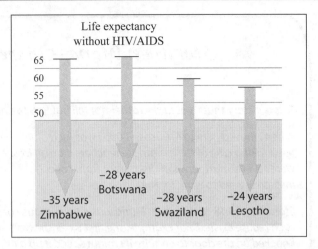

(Source: *HDR 2003*, p. 43)

Figure 5.1.2 *Decline in life expectancy due to HIV/AIDS, selected countries*

Infrastructure ©IBO 2003

When economists use the term infrastructure, they are referring to the 'internal skeleton' which holds an economy upright and moving. Infrastructure provides the basis for an economy to function, and consists of the system of road networks, telecommunications networks, sewage facilities, water supply, electricity and power sources, financial/education/health system, public transportation networks and ports/harbours or other international points of trade access.

Infrastructure is vital to a well-functioning economy and the effects of investment here are hard to overestimate. It allows all the factors of production in a country to be productively utilised: labourers can get to their jobs; produce can be transported to urban areas from rural areas; power, water and information so vital to firms can be transported, and increases the level of competition in an economy. Keeping in mind that the sum of infrastructural components is far greater than the individual parts, here are a few specific examples of how key elements of infrastructure affect the development process[19]:

- Improved infrastructure lowers transportation times and costs[20] which can be up to 40% higher in LDCs (as a percentage of GDP) than in MDCs. Good infrastructure thus has a large impact on national income and reduces poverty. World Bank studies show that the increase in investment in

---

19. http://web.worldbank.org/WBSITE/EXTERNAL/NEWS/0,,contentMDK:20127296~menuPK:34480~pagePK:34370~theSitePK: 4607,00.html.

20. A reporter for the *The Economist* wrote about travelling with a lorry transporting Guinness in Cameroon. The 500 km journey took four days and arrived with one-third of the brew missing – bribes to 'robber-cops' at road blocks. (See 'Trucking in Cameroon', 19 December 2002.)

infrastructure in LDCs in the 1990s reduced poverty levels by as much as 2% in low-income countries.

- Poor water and sanitation facilities result in around 4 billion cases of diarrhoeal diseases every year – causing between 1 and 2 million deaths. **Clean water and basic sewer systems** would reduce deaths and enhance health tremendously – a conservative estimate puts an eightfold increase in benefits to society for every US dollar spent here.[21] Child mortality has been shown to have fallen by 55% owing to access to clean water and the WHO estimates that some 80% of all diseases and a third of all deaths in LDCs are caused by lack of adequate drinking water and sanitation facilities.

- Adequate **roads** enable fresh produce to reach markets. Roads allow capital assets to be transported to remote areas which need resources,

such as for the building of dams for power plants. Roads also help to get children to school – an especially significant increase in girls' school attendance has been observed.

- There are external effects of adequate infrastructure, namely the ability of LDCs to attract **foreign direct investment**. Firms which are willing and able to invest abroad are primarily interested in keeping costs down, quality of goods up – and making a good rate of return. Poor infrastructure in LDCs helps explain why close to 90% of all FDI takes place between developed countries.

Table 5.1.6 ranks a number of countries according to GDP per capita (PPP USD) from lowest to highest. The level of infrastructure, measured by four variables, is a clear indicator of relative wealth but also implies the potential for countries' future output and growth.

Table 5.1.6 *Infrastructure and GDP per capita (PPP USD)*

	Telephone mainlines per 1000 persons	Paved roads, % of total	% of population with access to safe water, 1995	Irrigated land % of cropland 1994–96
Mozambique	4	19	9	3.4
Tanzania	3	4	49	4.6
India	19	46	85	32.0
Jamaica	140	71	93	14.0
Romania	167	51	62	31.4
Brazil	107	9	69	4.9
South Africa	107	42	59	8.1
Chile	180	14	91	32.6
New Zealand	486	58	90	8.9
Spain	403	99	99	17.7
Singapore	543	97	100	na
United States	644	61	100	12.0

(Source: *WDR* 1997)

---

21. 'The stuff of life', *The Economist*, 15 May 2004.

Political stability ©IBO 2003

Imagine trying to work efficiently in a company where the leadership changed every year; where rules were altered continuously or were simply paper products which had no applicability in reality; where disputes were settled by whom one knew in power rather than by equal rules for all; where people got fired arbitrarily, and where orders, contracts and shipments vis-à-vis other firms were honoured only part of the time.[22] Now put the same board of directors in charge of a country.

Most – but far from all – economists would agree that developing nations will need a larger element of planning than developed nations. And while there is debate as to whether a democratic system (South Africa) is more efficient than an authoritarian system (Singapore), economists generally agree on the empirical evidence showing that development is more likely to take place when basic political foundations for the rule of the land are in place. There are three broad aspects of **political stability** which help foster the development process:

1. *Implementation of policies and long-term goals:* Stable governments will be more prone to plan for the future, formulate long-term goals, and implement them. It is also easier for countries with political stability to attract foreign investment and aid.

2. *Rule of law:* Stability helps in setting down and upholding laws which govern property rights, competition laws, and starting businesses – all of which aid in economic growth.

3. *System of power transfer:* Whatever the level of autocracy/theocracy/democracy, a system of governance which has shown stability over time will probably have a lower degree of social disruption such as civil war and armed conflicts.

The last aspect warrants a final comment. *Political instability and conflict* go hand-in-glove; internal wars and conflicts, ethnic divisions and violence are both **causes** and **effects** of instability. The correlation between conflict and development is very clear: high levels or frequency of conflict are strongly correlated with low human development. Of all countries experiencing conflict since 1990 we find:[23]

- Nine out of ten of the lowest HDI countries
- Seven out of ten of the lowest GDP per capita countries
- Nine out of ten countries with the highest infant mortality rates
- Eight of the ten countries with the lowest primary school enrolment ratios.

POP QUIZ 5.1.1   SOURCES OF GROWTH AND DEVELOPMENT

1 Explain the difficulties arising when one attempts to clearly categorise countries along 'developmental' lines.

2 'Natural factors of production are absolutely essential for a country's prosperity!' Discuss this statement. Refer to real examples.

3 In this chapter, many of the 'factors which contribute to development' have been illustrated using the HDI in various tables. Why is the HDI an appropriate measure for illustrating these factors?

4 Use Figure 5.1.1 on page 525 to plot a curve showing the correlation between the HDI and refugees. Comment.

---

22. I think I just described a school I've worked for.
23. *HDR* 2005, p. 154.

Consequences of growth

5.2

CONSEQUENCES OF GROWTH ©IBO 2003

Read the contents list on the previous page. Now take a close look at Figure 5.2.1. Your economist knee-jerk reaction should be to ask about a number of other variables which are *not* included in the diagram. Each dot represents a country and a number of other effects of increased growth will have occurred such as particulate pollution, changes in income distribution and/or deforestation. In other words, the variables income and development shown in the diagram do not show the *negative consequences* of growth.

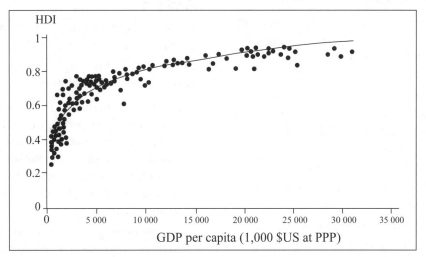

(Source: Norberg, p. 68)

Figure 5.2.1 *Growth and development*

Externalities ©IBO 2003

Recall that any consumption and/or production which levies costs or benefits on a third party is an externality. Growth will come with such a price tag attached: water and air pollution; traffic noise and congestion; encroachment of wildlife areas; and thousands of other negative results which are the unintended consequence of growth. Economic theory has increasingly sought to include these consequences in tallying up the costs and benefits of economic growth and development. The World Bank's World Development Report (WDR) in 2003 states that a 3% growth rate in the world will quadruple global GDP by 2050.

The other side of an increase in incomes: pollution and traffic

An example of how income growth affects the demand for goods which have high income elasticities is the growth of car ownership in Mexico. Income elasticity of cars is approximately 2 and the average yearly increase in income in Mexico was 3.4% between 1973 and 1998. During the 1990s, the amount of private vehicles had increased by 30% leading to recurring traffic gridlock and pollution[1].

In later years, there has been another most pronounced shift from secondary to tertiary goods. Western Europe together with North America account for nearly half the world's GDP.[2] As incomes increase in wealthy countries there is an increased demand for services – at a faster rate than for primary and secondary goods.

Population growth and the environment

Even with **constant** population growth rates, population increases will put additional burdens on the environment. Most estimates of population growth indicate that around 2 billion people will be added to the current global population of 6 billion within the next 50 years – almost all of it in developing countries[3] (see Figure 5.2.2 on page 538). This will put an immense strain on our resources and the natural

---

1. 'All jammed up', *The Economist*, 3 September 1998; and *The World Economy, A millennial perspective*, OECD, table A2-e, p. 197.
2. *The World Economy, A millennial perspective*, OECD, table 3-2c, p. 127.
3. WDR 2003, chapter 1, p. 1.

environment, adding to an already alarming list of externalities:[4]

- *Air*: Greenhouse gases will continue to grow unabated if there is no large scale movement away from the burning of fossil fuels. Seven economies account for 70% of global CO_2 emissions – the US alone, with 4% of the world's population, accounts for 25% of the CO_2 emissions.[5]

- *Water*: There is a real risk that fresh water becomes increasingly scarce in a world where one-third of the population already experiences chronic shortages of drinkable water.

- *Land*: Soil degradation – such as erosion and increased salt content – has already affected close to 2 million hectares of land since 1950 – 320,000 hectares virtually irreversibly.

- *Forests*: One-fifth of tropical forests have been cleared since 1950, which often results in increased desertification (= spread of deserts).

- *Fish stocks*: Over 70% of the world's fish stocks are exploited to the point of carrying capacity – or simply overexploited.

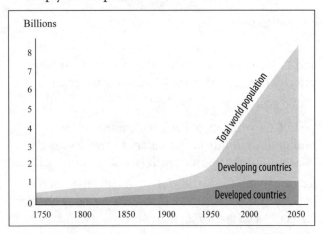

(Source: *Beyond economic growth*, World Bank 2000, p. 16)

Figure 5.2.2 *World population, 1750–2050*

It isn't difficult to see that growth in the three-quarters of the world considered developing will have a considerable impact on the environment if they follow the same path as the developed world. In China, which has averaged some of the highest growth rates of the 1990s, air pollution has reached levels in Beijing and Shanghai which make these two cities the dirtiest in the world. The attraction of jobs and cultural opportunities has led to mass urbanisation and 'mega-cities' such as Mexico City, where population has exceeded 15 million.[6] Urban growth puts additional pressure on infrastructure such as water and sanitation, while inner-city congestion is forcing a number of cities to limit cars.

And yet ...

Global population is expected to peak at 9 to 10 billion people by 2100 – some 20 to 30% lower than predicted in the 1960s.[7] It is worth noting that are also many *positive externalities* of growth.

- Back roads in distant rural areas built by timber companies give people the ability to commute and get produce to market. (This is clearly evident in the northern Scandinavian forests, where timber roads from the growth period in the 1800s still enable thousands of people to live in the countryside and commute to jobs.)

- An increasing number of firms in high-growth regions will have free medical care, education and housing schemes for employees as a policy of enhancing labour capital.

- Growth in information technology centres in India has created a need for – and thus supply of – improved infrastructure such as electricity grids and phone lines which have benefited the region in general.

- Globalisation and trade will spread new technologies – many of which will be far more ecologically sound than older production methods.

There is also evidence that growth – ultimately – has *positive* effects on the environment. While the evidence is very unclear (since there are so many other variables to take into consideration other than income) as to whether growth in poor countries can be tied to environmental improvement, it is quite clear that wealthy countries have seen significant improvement in a number of areas.[8] When people get richer, they *demand* for and can *pay* for a cleaner environment. As incomes increase there are resources available to clean the environment – just witness the improvements over the past 30 or so years; London's air is far better and the Baltic Sea far cleaner than one generation ago.

---

4. These are figures from the WDR 2003, chapter 1, pp. 1–5, and it should be noted that they are not uncontested. See for example, *The sceptical environmentalist* by Björn Lomborg (op cit).
5. 'Globalization, Growth and Poverty', World Bank report 2002.
6. During the three years I've been here in Mexico City I have seen population estimates of 15 million to 25 million. Nobody really knows.
7. *WDR 2003*, chapter 1, p. 4.
8. Op cit. World Bank 2002, p. 130 ff.

Technology enables efficiency – more widgets at less pollution – and wealth means that people start to demand other things, like a view unobstructed by garbage; enjoying clean air and fishable lakes, etc. Wealth, technology and disutility then feed off each other. When people get richer they have the 'luxury' of wanting a liveable environment and caring about environmental issues. Technology enables something to be done about it. Wealth allows them to pay for it.[9]

Furthermore, while evidence is not conclusive on environmental performance related to growth in developing countries *specifically*, the OECD has shown broad positive correlation between growth and income in countries *generally*. Figure 5.2.3 shows that positive correlation between income and environmental performance (a composite index of a number of environmental measures) can be seen for a range of countries. Other evidence – put forward by the World Bank – suggests that growth which is primarily trade-based has not created 'pollution havens' due to multinational companies seeking out countries with low environmental standards.[10]

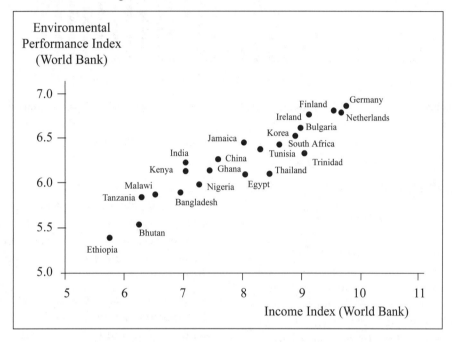

(Source: *Open markets matter*, OECD policy brief, October 1999, p. 9)

Figure 5.2.3 *General correlation between income and environment*

Poverty is, arguably, a worse threat to the environment than growth.[11] Poor people living on ever lower-yielding land will be forced to use marginal resources for survival. They know full well that the depletion and destruction of natural resources worsen future living standards but simply do not have a choice. Poverty also leads to population growth as children are needed for labour to work on land suffering with diminishing returns. Children also provide a 'social security net' in a society where there is scant availability of pensions, health benefits and social security benefits. The forces of increasing numbers of people living off depleting resources create yet another vicious cycle: poverty → population growth → lower productivity and land yields per capita → poverty. Lifting people out of poverty is increasingly viewed as the most effective way of improving the environment.

9. I just needed to look out my window back home in Sweden, at Öresund, the strait between Sweden and Denmark, for a good example. Just 25 years ago, raw sewage went straight into the sea. The strait was so polluted that swimming bans were commonplace, fish stocks were severely depleted, and the bottom of the sea was predicted to be unable to sustain life by the year 2000. By late May of every year, my IB2s were down post-exam frolicking on the beach and the heartier specimens were jumping in the water (14°C) – while sports fishermen cast for wild salmon and sea-trout. The wealthy citizens of Sweden and Denmark simply cleaned up their act – and the sea – by installing waste removal plants and implementing strict legislation on pollution. They were able to do this as they were *wealthy* and could afford the cleaning technology.

10. 'Economic man, cleaner planet', *The Economist*, 27 September 2001.

11. See, for example, Moore, p. 89 and Legrain, p. 244.

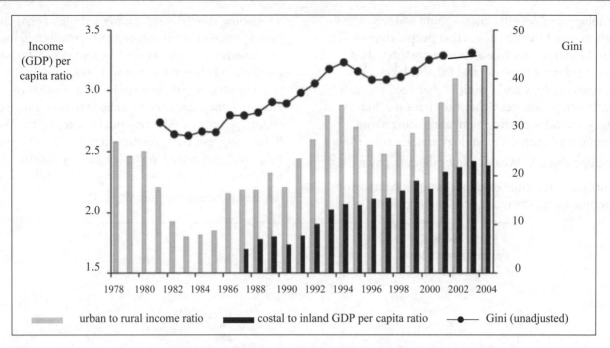

Figure 5.2.4 *Income inequality in China (1978–2004)*

Income distribution ©IBO 2003

A society can be Pareto optimal and still be perfectly disgusting. – Amartya Sen

Just as there is bitter debate about whether global income distribution is worsening, i.e. whether the gap between rich and poor countries is widening – there is inconclusive evidence as to income distribution within countries. (HL students might want to revise the HL extension topics in Section 3.6.) 'Inconclusive' here actually means 'confusing' as the following two captions show.

'**Inequality of income *increases* due to growth**': Looking at the effect of growth on income distribution within an economy, there is evidence suggesting that income inequality increases when national income rises – at least initially.[12] Inequality in some of the largest economies – for example Britain, the US and China – has risen over the past 30 years if consideration of populations is factored in. Using the most extreme example, China's growth rate of circa 9% annually between 1990 and 2008 has caused rather alarming income inequality rates; it has been estimated by the World Bank that urban average household income was some 3.4 times higher than rural average

income.[13] The rate of change in the disparity in income in within China is amongst the highest in the world, shown in Figure 5.2.4. It is clearly noticeable that income inequality has increased considerably during the period of rapid economic growth which started in the beginning of the 1980s.

'**No general conclusions on growth and income distribution can be drawn**': There is a great deal more evidence in favour of this conclusion. Both the UNDP and the World Bank agree that 'the available data show *no stable relationship between growth and inequality.* [Italics are mine.] On average, income inequality within countries has neither decreased nor increased over the last 30 years.'[14] Figure 5.2.5 on page 541 illustrates this quite clearly.

One pattern that does emerge, although I would be most careful in drawing extensive conclusions, is that the general inequality in income distribution is lower in developed countries than in developing countries. Table 5.2.1 on page 541 shows the share of total income of the richest and poorest proportions of populations in a number of countries. The inequality issue in comparing high, medium and low human development countries is most pronounced when the upper and lower 10% are used as a comparison.

---

12. See a rather famous report by *Sala-i-Martin* at http://papers.nber.org/papers/w8904.pdf.
13. 'Rising Income Inequality in China: A race to the top', Policy research paper 4700, World Bank, 2008.
14. World Bank at http://www.worldbank.org/poverty/data/trends/inequal.htm.

Table 5.2.1 *Distribution of income, selected countries*

HDI Rank	Country	Survey year	Share of income or consumption			
			Poorest 10%	Poorest 20%	Richest 20%	Richest 10%
High Human Development						
1	Norway	1995	4.1	9.7	35.8	21.8
2	Sweden	1992	3.7	9.6	34.5	20.1
3	Canada	1994	2.8	7.5	39.3	23.8
4	Belgium	1996	3.2	8.3	37.3	23.0
5	Australia	1994	2.0	5.9	41.3	24.5
Medium Human Development						
54	Mexico	1998	1.3	3.5	57.4	41.7
59	Malaysia	1997	1.7	4.4	54.3	38.4
60	Russian Federation	1998	1.7	4.4	53.7	38.7
124	India	1997	3.5	8.1	46.1	33.5
125	Swaziland	1994	1.0	2.7	64.4	50.2
Low Human Development						
151	Tanzania	1993	2.8	6.8	45.5	30.0
152	Mauritania	1995	2.5	6.4	44.1	28.4
153	Zambia	1998	1.1	3.3	56.6	41.0
154	Senegal	1995	2.6	6.4	48.2	33.5

(Source: *HDR 2002*, pp. 192–97)

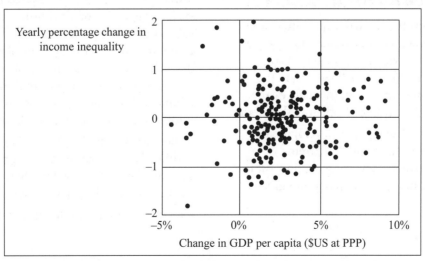

(Source: Dollar, David & Kraay, Aart, 'Growth is good for the poor', World Bank, March 2000 (working paper), http://www.worldbank.org/research/growth/pdfiles/growthgoodforpoor.pdf)

Figure 5.2.5 *Correlation between growth and income inequality*

The world in a champagne glass

The Gini coefficient (HL concept) for the world has remained very constant at 0.67 since the 1970s. The Human Development Report of 2005 illustrates the disparities in income between the rich world and the poor world by computing the richest 20% against the poorest 20% of the world's population. The average income of the top 20% is roughly 50 times higher than the average of the poorest 20%. The 'champagne glass' illustration (see Figure 5.2.6) shows that the top 20% accounts for 75% of world income. The bottom 40% – the 'stem' of the glass – accounts for 5% of world income. The bottom 20% account for 1.5%.[15]

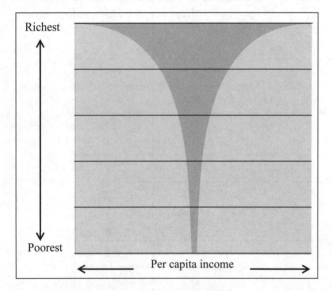

(Source: *HDR 2005*, p. 37)

Figure 5.2.6 *World income distributed by percentiles of the population, 2000*

But what about a reversed sequence?

So, no clear indications that growth causes increased income inequality. However, what about looking at a reversed causal flow, i.e. whether growth is in some way affected by existing inequality levels? Here the evidence is a trifle more conclusive. Inequality can be shown to have a negative effect on both growth and the reduction of poverty.[16] The Human Development Report of 2005 puts it rather bluntly: 'Extreme inequality is not just bad for poverty reduction – it is also bad for growth. Long-run efficiency and greater

equity can be complementary.'[17] There are three contributing reasons for this correlation:

1. Relative income equality allows for a greater **sharing of societal resources** and indicates the existence of some form of redistribution system. Increased income will therefore be 'spread' via taxes to societal goods such as health care and education – which in turn is pro-growth. The 'Asian Tigers' have often been referred to as examples herein.

2. Given a larger proportion of poor people in the economy, fewer will have the ability and collateral to be **qualified as borrowers**. Poor people simply cannot borrow against future earnings. This stifles economic activity.

3. High income inequality often results in small but **powerful elites** uninterested in 'fairness' in tax rates and redistributive mechanisms. Social spending as a percentage of GDP is therefore often lower.

4. Gross inequality – both in terms of income, gender-based policies or regions – leads to a larger section of society lacking **access to education**. As has been pointed out earlier, education is a very strong development driver.[18]

5. Inequality will disadvantage rural poor and lead to weak participation in various forms of **democratic institutions** – which undermines the development of democracy and also to internal conflicts over, for example, natural resources.

Growth and poverty

The evidence concerning growth and poverty reduction is much clearer. Increased national income lowers poverty levels – measured in absolute terms such as the USD1 or USD2 (in constant values, i.e. real values) a day line. While there is debate on whether the **number** of people living in absolute poverty has declined over the past couple of decades, virtually all evidence points to the **proportion** of absolutely poor falling quite considerably. The proportion of **absolute poor** in the world (USD1 per day measured in constant values) went from 28% in 1987 to 24% in 1998.[19] In another, longer term study, the proportion of absolutely poor (in a wider USD2 per day measure in constant values) is shown to have fallen from just over 40% in 1970 to just under 20% in 1998.[20] The sharpest

---

15. *HDR 2005*, p. 36.

16. *HDR 1996* and World Bank at http://www.worldbank.org/poverty/data/trends/inequal.htm.

17. *HDR 2005*, p. 53.

18. *HDR 2005*, pp. 51–59.

19. Todaro, p.221.

20. Sala-i-Martin at http://papers.nber.org/papers/w8904.pdf and 'Economic Trends', *Business Week*, 17 June 2002.

fall in poverty has been in high growth countries, notably Vietnam, China and India, shown in Figure 5.2.7.

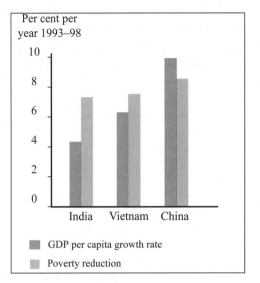

Per cent per year 1993–98

(Source: 'Globalization, Growth and Poverty', World Bank report 2002, p. 6)

Figure 5.2.7 *Growth and poverty reduction*

There is also the question of whether growth in fact serves to benefit the poor in a society, i.e. whether economic growth reduces general poverty levels. A recent and widely quoted/debated study shows that growth is indeed 'pro-poor'. An increase in average incomes of 1% will indeed render a 1% increase in income for the poor also.[21]

Sustainability ©IBO 2003

None of the environmental effects listed under the caption *Population growth and environment* above are consistent with **sustainable** growth. Sustainable growth entails output increases which do not limit future output potential by running down available resources. (See 'The Brundtland Report' on page 11.) One of the world's most eminent development economists, Michael Todaro, puts this rather eloquently in stating that from an economist's point of view, a development course is sustainable 'if and only if the stock of overall capital assets remains constant or rises over time'.[22]

As stated earlier, the concept of sustainable growth/development is not universally agreed upon and a number of interpretations are possible. Yet the basic issue is graspable; an economic system which does not utilise resources at or below the rate at which these resources regenerate will ultimately collapse.[23] In any case, a far more relevant issue than that of definitions is whether development enhances or reduces potential natural assets.

Growth: trade-off or pay-off?

Poverty means that people will use whatever resources are available simply to stay alive. Virgin forests in South America will be slashed and burned to make farmland available[24]; rapidly diminishing patches of forest in North Africa will be cut for firewood and charcoal to cook and provide heat; ever more low-yielding lands will come under increasing strain due to population growth amongst the poorest peoples, and a thousand other examples. The question that arises is whether increased economic growth will lighten the environmental burden in developing countries or whether this growth will accelerate environmental degradation.

There is no resoundingly clear answer. To make matters even more confusing, consider that the 1 billion richest people in the world use close to 80% of the world's energy and account for close to half of CO_2 emissions – the main green house gas emissions. At the other end of the spectrum, some 1.3 billion people are living so close to the edge that they are forced to misuse limited resources in order to make it in the short run. Somewhere in the middle are the transitional economies which are using outdated and inefficient capital and infrastructure in production but simply do not have the funds to upgrade to more efficient methods. None of these three qualifies as 'sustainable'.

There are a number of views on how best to address the issue of sustainability. One view is that it could be possible to grow now and pay (back) the environmental debt later. The ultimate **pay-off** in running up an environmental bill would hopefully be the ability to restore damage done. In other words, focus on economic growth in order to accumulate the resources to deal with the harmful effects later on. Another view would be that growth indeed involves a

21. *Growth is good for the poor*, David Dollar and Aart Kraay, World Bank 2000 (see www.worldbank.org/research).
22. Todaro, p. 465.
23. With it goes civilization.
24. Just today, Rob the housey and I bribed two of the hombres who work around the school to chop down a 200-year-old eucalyptus tree. We're cold and need some firewood. Worth about $1,000, we paid 100 pesos (= USD7.5) and a bottle of wine. Mexico has *severe* penalties for cutting down trees – I mean draconian. I bet you could get off easier in killing a cop than chopping down a mango tree. Em, in case there is a Mexican cop out there who can actually read, this is a completely made-up story!

trade-off rather than a pay-off and that better-off countries will ultimately have to lower consumption in order to create room for poorer countries to grow.

Economists and environmentalists have attempted to show the relationship between national income and environmentally sustainable growth levels, i.e. some form of GDP-to-environment index. One version,

Figure 5.2.8, is the **Environmental Sustainability Index** (ESI) which measures over 20 different environmental components and summarises this in an index. While in no way conclusive, plotting the ESI values for 117 countries against GDP per capita (USD at PPP) gives an **indication** that higher levels of income are indicative of improved sustainability.

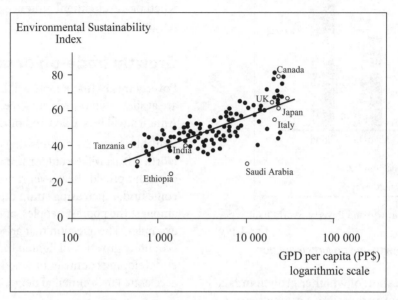

(Source: Lomborg, p. 33. See also *World Development Indicators 2000,* World Bank; Center for International Earth Science Information Network at Columbia University at http://ciesin.columbia.edu/indicators/ESI/))

Figure 5.2.8 *GDP per capita and sustainability, 2001*

 Case study: China and the side-effects of economic growth

China's phenomenal growth rate of just under 8% annually during the 1990s and the first years of the 2000s has had an incredible impact on Chinese society. Yet two highly noticeable side-effects of economic growth are increasingly worrisome; income distribution and environmental degradation.

Income distribution: Before China's market reforms of the early 1980s the planned economic system provided jobs, housing and social benefits and while incomes were low there was 'equality in poverty'. The market reforms created a surge in exports and a boom for export industries. By the mid-1990s, it became apparent that previously unheard of levels of poverty had arisen, where 9% of urban citizens lived below the official poverty line – up to 60% in areas where sunset industries folded. By 1999, according to official Chinese statistics, average urban incomes were 2.65 times higher than average rural incomes – up from 1.7 times in 1984.

At the upper end of the incomes scale, there were some 3 million millionaires by 2000 and the richest 20% of urban households accounted for 42% of income. The poorest 20% of households accounts for 6.5% of income. A common measure of income distribution (done at HL in Section 3.6) is the Gini coefficient, where a value of 0 says that income is perfectly distributed while a value of 1 means that one person accounts for all national income in a country. Thus, the higher the value, the more unequal the distribution of income. In 1978 the Gini coefficient was 0.21 for rural areas and 0.16 in urban areas. By 1999 the (official) values were 0.34 and 0.29 respectively, indicating a dramatic increase in income inequality.

Environment: Rising industrial needs now put factories at 2/3 of total use of coal and China supplies 3/4 of its energy by burning coal. The results are clearly visible – albeit not the horizon in many rural areas. China is now one of the most polluted countries in the world in terms of air pollution in general and particulates more specifically. Adding to this is higher incomes and thus the increasing use of automobiles – many of which are manufactured domestically and do not adhere to modern emission standards. Domestic cars are several times more polluting than imported cars. The World Bank estimates that some 174,000 deaths a year are directly attributable to air pollution in urban areas. The World Health Organisation (WHO) states that 15 of the 20 most polluted cities in the world are now Chinese.
(Have a look at http://www.wri.org/wr-98-99/prc2air.htm#levels for a few additional statistics.)

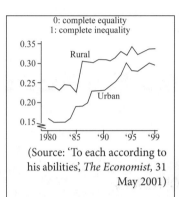

(Source: 'To each according to his abilities', *The Economist*, 31 May 2001)

Figure 5.2.9 *Gini coefficients for income inequality in China*

I can't finish this case study without mentioning the $US25 billion Three Gorges Dam being built on the Yangtze river, set to be completed by 2009. The hydroelectric plant will produce 18.2 gigawatts of much-needed energy for China's growing economy. Apart from the forced removal of 1.2 million people living in the area to be flooded, this clean and renewable energy source has some severe environmental downsides: The over 600 kilometre long dam will cover thousands of latrines, millions of tonnes of rubbish, and flood disused mines full of waste products – in addition to which several billion tonnes of waste water from industries upstream will continue to flow into the river. This will in effect create the world's largest sewer according to one of many environmentally concerned critics of the project. There is also the possibility that diminished water flows into the sea 200 km downstream can cause sea water to flow backwards and contaminate fresh water tables. A number of experts also question the economic validity of the project, pointing out that the thousands of tonnes of silt flowing through the turbines will quickly clog up the system and cause extensive down-times in the hydroelectric plant and severely limit the lifespan of the turbines.

POP QUIZ 5.2.1   CONSEQUENCES OF GROWTH

1   Why might increased growth in some respects lead to negative development?

2   Explain why there seems to be positive correlation between economic growth and improvements in the environment?

3   Is it possible to run down the 'capital stock' of the world and still leave future output potential unchanged?

Barriers to economic development

5.3

CONTENTS

BARRIERS TO ECONOMIC DEVELOPMENT ©IBO 2003

My father told the story of how he moved to yet another island in the Caribbean and went down to a hole-in-the-wall store to get a case of soft drinks for us kids. The lady behind the counter put the case of soda on the counter and, bottles being scarce for the local bottling plant, asked for the empties in return. My father explained that he had just moved to the island and hadn't yet accrued any empty bottles. The shopkeeper subsequently refused to sell any soft drinks unless an equal amount of empties were part of the exchange. My father's final response to this *Catch-22*[1] situation was 'How do you get into the game?!'

The virtuous cycle of development

A good many *Catch-22*s arise in development issues as shall be seen. Figure 5.3.1 illustrates how various preconditions for human development are linked to forces which enable economic grow – a **virtuous circle** of growth and development. As looked at in Section 5.1 there are a number of sources which enable economic growth, such as investment in human capital and infrastructure. This, in turn, will enhance productivity and growth – which in turn creates improved *conditions* for development.

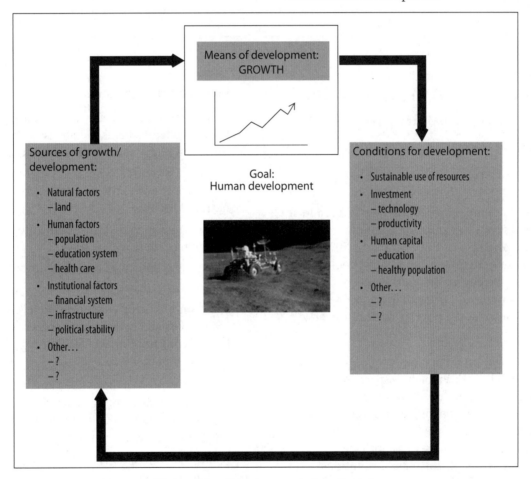

Figure 5.3.1 *Development's virtuous circle*

It should be noted that Figure 5.3.1 is indeed optimistic and perhaps even a trifle misleading. The UNDP has conducted numerous studies on the links between growth and development, and while indeed the links are strong and self-reinforcing, they are not automatic. In other words there is no evidence to support that growth **inevitably** leads to development, but that increased national income must be 'translated'

---

1. The phrase was coined by Joseph Heller in the book *Catch-22*. The main character wanted to get out of the military service by declaring that he was insane. The military psychologist explained that this was fine but for Paragraph 22 which said that if you **wanted** to get out of the armed forces you couldn't be insane. This was the catch (= trap, vicious circle), that is, Catch-22.

(UNDPs choice of words) into development by sound policies and well-functioning institutions and infrastructure.[2] Table 5.3.1 illustrates that while there is a most discernable link between growth and poverty

reduction, there are a number of populous exceptions, i.e. Latin America/Caribbean and Middle East/North Africa.

Table 5.3.1 *Links between economic growth and poverty*

Region	Growth in the 1990s (annual growth in per capita income, %)	Poverty Reduction in the 1990s (% point reduction)
East Asia & the Pacific	6.4	14.9
South Asia	3.3	8.4
Latin America & the Caribbean	1.6	-0.1
Middle East & North Africa	1.0	-0.1
Sub-Saharan Africa	-0.4	-1.6
Central & Eastern Europe & the CIS	-1.9	-13.5

(Source: *HDR 2003*, p. 41)

Poverty cycle: low incomes → low savings → low investment → low incomes ©IBO 2003

Perhaps the most obvious indicator of lack of development is **poverty**. The UN Millennium Goals of 2000[3] set down a number of development goals, and at the top of the list was to reduce the amount of people living on less than $US1 (at PPP) per day by 50% by the year 2015. There were close to 1.2 billion people living below this absolute poverty line at the time of the Millennium Summit, and many of them face a predicament known as the **poverty cycle** or **poverty trap**.[4]

Poor people will have a notably low propensity to save, as there will be little enough to spare after basic necessities have been purchased. In other words, savings will have a very high opportunity cost in the form of foregone – vital – consumption. Recall that investment is the mirror image of saving (see Section 3.1) and that banks/financial institutions facilitate this flow of funds from households to firms. Economic theory posits that households' willingness to put aside present consumption in order to increase future consumption is based on income levels. The cycle of poverty is thus:

Low savings in developing countries results in …

- … scarcity of investment funds – the investment funds needed by firms to increase output and build infrastructure – and **low investment,** …

- … which is central to a country's output potential, will hamper economic growth, e.g. result in **low national income** …

- … and since income provides the proportion used for savings, there will be **low** …

The cycle is enhanced by two additional forces:

1. Firms' investment plans are to a certain extent based on predicted **consumption** levels by households and investment by other firms. A low level of consumption will feed through to continued low investment levels.

2. Low investment (in both fixed and human capital) will stifle **productivity** gains in the economy and keep real wages low. This too will exert a negative force on incomes and consumption.

Figure 5.3.2 on page 549 is like a merry-go-round from hell; you can jump on anywhere. But there are ways for developing countries to get off the negative cycle, for example by creating sound financial institutions and attracting foreign investment. Unfortunately, these and other possible solutions

---

2. See *HDR 1996*, chapter 3 passim and *HDR 2003*, p. 17.
3. See complete list at http://www.un.org/millenniumgoals/.
4. See, for example, the *HDR 2003*, p. 41.

require working governments, political stability, and the rule of law – some or all of which are noticeably lacking in many developing countries.

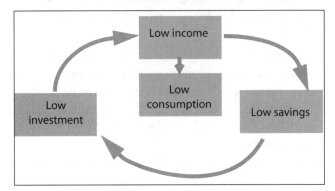

Figure 5.3.2 *The poverty cycle*

Criticism of the 'poverty trap'

One of the most critical economists dealing with development issues is William Easterly (see, for example, his scathingly critical book *The White Man's Burden*) and he is quite scornful of what he calls the 'poverty trap legend'. He finds little correlation between poverty levels and low growth over the period 1975 to 2001 and puts forward three main points of criticism[5]:

1. While many developing countries indeed showed stagnant and even negative growth during the period, there is little evidence linking low incomes to low growth. The poorest countries' growth rates did not significantly differ from middle-income countries between 1980 and 2001.

2. Some 11 countries out of the 28 poorest countries in 1975 were not amongst the lowest income countries in 1950 – again belying a clear link between low income levels and poor growth performance.

3. There is much stronger statistical evidence that in fact poor government causes low growth rather than initial poverty; '… stagnation of the poorest countries appears to have more to do with awful governments than with a poverty trap …'[6]

On the other hand …

One of the world's most famous economists, Jeffrey Sachs, head and co-founder of the UN's Millennium Project, takes an entirely different stance. He identifies six key factors where the cycle of poverty → low investment → low income has severe anti-developmental effects[7]:

- Low level of *human capital* due to poor health care and education will lower productivity
- Low level of *business capital* – machinery needed in agriculture, transportation and industry – decreases potential output
- Insufficient *infrastructure* such as roads, railways, ports, telecoms, etc. limit commerce and the ability of firms to get goods to markets
- Poor or declining *natural capital* – arable land and healthy soils, for example – provide a basis for basic human needs in developing countries
- *Public* and *institutional capital* such as a functioning and fair legal system and commercial law enables peaceful and reliable economic transactions. It also decreases parallel markets.
- *Knowledge capital* – scientific and technological know-how not only raises productivity but 'creates value' for future generations of entrepreneurs.

Outside the box:
How investment can be greater than savings

Before you read on, go back and revise the circular flow of income in Section 3.1. Notice that the sum of injections equals the sum of leakages, i.e. T + S + M = G + I + X. Now go back and revise the balance of payments, paying particular attention to how a country might have a current account deficit, i.e. X < M. Recall that a current account deficit is not 'bad' depending on where the inflows in capital account are coming from.

Now, assume that an economy has a perfectly balanced budget, in other words that government spending equals tax revenues: G = T. Now, what if savings are less than total investment in the economy? Say that total savings are $US500 million and total investment is $US600 million:

$$T + 500 + M = G + 600 + X$$

Since the government budget is perfectly balanced, we can strike T and G on each side:

$$500 + M = 600 + X$$

Now, skipping all the stuff you will pester your maths teacher with, we can see that imports are going to have to exceed exports by $US100 million. And this should be enough for you, but I'll slam in the final nail: X – M = net exports, which means that there is a current account deficit of $US10 million.

5. Easterly, *The White Man's Burden*, pp. 40–52.
6. Easterly, p. 43.
7. Sachs, pp. 244–45.

549

Consequently, there is a net inflow of $US100 million on capital account, which explains how the country has just been able to finance $US100 million over and above domestic savings. This helps to illustrate the importance of developing countries being able to attract foreign investment.

Institutional and political factors ©IBO 2003

Keep the 'virtuous circle' (see page 547) in mind as we turn to look at a number of hindrances to a human development flow. As we shall see, the issues in development are quite complex owing to the fact that so many conditions necessary for economic growth and improved living standards hinge upon foundations that are all too often lacking. Better institutions, such as legal systems and bureaucracies, have been shown to have resounding effects on national income. For example, some estimates show that per capita incomes may be raised by 2 per cent per year if property rights and competition laws are established.[8] This has been increasingly recognised, in fact, the 2002 annual World Development Report from the World Bank devotes a goodly portion of the report to institutions which grant important market mechanisms such as the rule of law and property rights.

Ineffective taxation structure ©IBO 2003

I saw Russian tax collection a few years ago live on TV. It went something like this: 'OK, everyone got their Kevlar vests on? Good. Helmets? Stun grenades? Ammunition? Right, Oleg, get the battering ram over here … here we GO!' When a country has to resort to extremes like this to collect taxes, there is clearly something wrong with the tax system. In Russia's case the problem seems to have been a poor system of accountability and rampant parallel markets – close to 50% of all economic activity was at one point estimated to be non-taxed. In addition to this, a good portion of the parallel market activity was also for illegal goods such as narcotics and guns. Such economic activity doesn't lend itself easily to honest income tax returns and many people will not even be registered with the tax authorities.

In general, developing countries face some overwhelming challenges in putting together an efficient tax system:

- Much of the economic activity is in **informal markets** such as produce markets and small enterprises which are largely unaccounted for. As most of this income is parallel to the official markets, the tax base will be most difficult to account for.

- Governments in LDCs often set **low profit taxes** to act as incentives to domestic firms and to facilitate inflows of FDI. Also, foreign firms are frequently offered tax holidays to attract FDI.

- Multinationals can often **avoid taxes** by overpricing intermediate goods which are purchased from subsidiaries in low tax countries outside the LDC. By increasing costs on paper, the final 'visible' profit can be lowered and profit taxes with it. This practice is called **transfer pricing**.

The problems above deal with **direct** taxation, i.e. income and profit taxes. Aggravating the difficulties herein is simply the cost of implementing a functioning tax system. A census will have to be taken; records kept, referenced and indexed; administrators of adequate education and skills will have to be employed, and the gathering of taxes will have to be enforced. Taken together, this explains why the majority of taxes in LDCs are collected via **indirect taxes** such as expenditure (VAT) and import taxes, as shown in Table 5.3.2 on page 551. Note: figures do not add up to 100 since other taxes have not been included. (See also Figure 4.2.8 on page 424.)

Taxes are needed in order for governments to provide **merit and public goods** such as education and roads – not to mention **welfare systems** such as social security and pension funds. The lack of tax bases due to informal markets and weak tax administration causes governments in developing countries to often overspend and run up deficits. It also means that existing taxes often have a *regressive effect* since flat rate taxation will mean less as a proportion of income for the rich than for the poor.

---

8. *WDR 2002*, p. 42.

Table 5.3.2 *Tax revenues in developing countries*

Group averages	Income taxes as % of revenue	Social Security Taxes as a % of revenue	Sales Taxes as a % of revenue	Trade Taxes as a % of revenue
Lower-middle income	18	4	36	10
Upper-Middle Income	19	21	38	4
Non-OECD high income	13	6	31	1
OECD	32	22	28	0

(Source: *Tax policy in developing countries*, Christopher Heady, OECD 2002, p. 19)

Lack of property rights ©IBO 2003

The first and chief design of every system of government is to maintain justice: to prevent the members of society from encroaching on one another's property, or seizing what is not their own. The design here is to give each one the secure and peaceable possession of his own property. – Adam Smith[9]

Property rights means that **ownership** or **legal rights of use** have been established by law. I own my car and apartment and can therefore use them as I see fit. Property rights enable people to use property as a means of:

- *Securing an income:* land and buildings can be rented out or even sold to make a profit.
- *Collateral to take loans:* few young couples starting out in life would be able to own homes if the property being purchased could not be used as collateral (= security) for the loan.

In addition to the two points above, ownership provides an incentive to both improve the property and to use it in the best possible way. The situation is no different around the world; if the land upon which one lives or the house upon it is not deeded (= written down in official records) then there will be less incentive to improve the land and virtually no possibility of using it as collateral to start a business.

The basic problem when the institution of civil ownership and property rights is weak is that business activity will suffer from the *lack of investment*, since property cannot be used for collateral. Lack of property

rights also *lowers entrepreneurial incentives* and reduces the propensity of farmers living on 'customary land'. In Africa, for example, less than 10% of all land is formally owned and in several countries the land is allotted by central government – which can also reallocate the land to others. Simply not knowing whether the land one is working on might be sub-divided and shared with others is a powerful disincentive for improving land and enhancing capital by building walls against erosion, digging wells to carry over into the dry season, and planting trees to bind topsoil.

A majority of people in developing counties are directly dependent on the land for their survival, yet around 500 million people do not have property rights to this land.[10] These tenant farmers and agricultural labourers will not be able to sell land or pass on land to the next generation, which means that there is will be little in the way of capital investment or land improvements which would be able to increase there livelihood. This also has sizable negative implications for environment issues such as overgrazing and soil erosion.[11]

It is often the poorest segments in developing countries which lose out the most in a society where property rights are weakly established. While the wealthy can use political contacts and influence to secure resources, the poor do not have this option. For example, the time and cost involved in getting a permit to set up a small shop can be overwhelming for poor people in many developing countries, involving grappling with bureaucracy and bribery at various

---

9. Adam Smith, *Wealth of Nations*, quoted from Policy Analysis No. 482, 7 August 2003, Cato Institute.
10. *HDR 2003*, p. 81.
11. Here on Expat Street in Mexico City the property rights to both water and electricity are notoriously hazy! The crazy jumble of wires and pipes between our houses, school property and the workers' area means that nobody is quite sure who is paying for whose use of water and electricity. It's a situation leading to allocative waste: if one doesn't really know whether the water bill represents only one's household use, there is an incentive to overuse water thinking that 'somebody else will pick up part of the bill'. This yanked my chain enough for me to actually remove the handle from all the outdoor taps (faucets).

stages. As often as not the outcome is that the business is not started – or becomes a part of the parallel

economy. In either case, growth is stunted and potential tax bases are destroyed.

 CELEBRITY BUBBLE: HERNANDO DE SOTO

One of the strongest voices in support of establishing basic and systematic property rights is the Peruvian economist Hernando de Soto. He tells of how he illustrated the difficulties involved in simple start-ups by using a couple of university students to set up a small garment factory in Lima, Peru. By the time the permits for the two sewing machines were obtained, 289 days had gone by and the procedures had cost 31 times the average monthly wage.* De Soto's subsequent studies showed that 90% of Peruvian small manufactures were part of the parallel market – as was over half of the market for groceries and 60% of the fishing fleet (one of the world's largest). de Soto sums up the results of lack of property rights as follows:

*As it is difficult for poor people to get the rights and titles to land and homes registered, there will be a large section of the economy which is not part of the **tax base**, as these people will not pay property or housing taxes.*

*Nor will poor people be able to use this land and capital as collateral, since they do not have **deeds or title** to their assets. No bank will accept a 'squatters' shack' as security for a loan which makes it impossible for asset-backed loans to fund investment.*

*Poor people are sitting on an enormous stock of **unused capital**; 'dead capital'. The estimated value of this is approximately $US9 trillion in developing countries around the world.*

De Soto has written a number of best-selling books, the most noted of which is The Mystery of Capital. As his writing is noticeably free-market, he has received roses from the right (for example, Milton Friedman) and lashes from the left (almost any article written on him in the English Guardian *will do).*

It is also clear in any number of studies, that stronger legislation concerning property rights has a marked effect on the development process when it empowers women. Women have a higher propensity than men to save and invest in the family. Children to women with own incomes will be better fed and cared for resulting in lower infant mortality and higher survival rates. These children will also have a better chance to get a basic education – and will be taught by their mothers.[12] With increased status and economic independence come political participation and the ability to influence not only policies and legislation but also the norms and attitudes which stifle women's ability to become entrepreneurs and run businesses.

Political instability ©IBO 2003

A liberal democracy is a system whereby the rulers get votes from the poor and money from the rich while promising to protect each from the other. – Kevin McGee, brother and cynic

The quote above is a bit unfair to my dear brother as he well realises the virtues of a society based on the rule of law. He, as I, has lived through a number of uprisings, revolutions, and military dictatorships in, respectively, Jamaica, Panama and Greece. I'll never forget landing in well organised and egalitarian (= equal, classless) Sweden, where things were so … um, *ordentlig* – roughly meaning neat/tidy/organised. Everything and everybody does exactly what is expected and it would drive anyone from my current home country of Mexico absolutely crazy.

---

12. See *WDR 2003* chapter 4 pp. 71–72 and *HDR 2003* p. 80 ff, for example.

The basics of political stability

But my point in using Sweden as an example is that there is a system and it *works*; there are rules which apply to everybody and countless institutions which make sure that civil, political and legal rights are upheld.[13] When good governance and social stability are lacking the results are to be seen in newspapers everyday: persecution of the weak; corruption and unjustifiable expropriation of other's property, and simple chaos resulting from conflicts and all-out war. Weak governments are also amongst the most oppressive and nepotistic (= favouritism towards family and friends) since force is needed to hold down the general population and favouritism is used to court favour of the powerful.[14] Political instability often arises due to the absence of one or all of the following.

Rule of law: The rule of law prohibits the oppression of the weak by the strong. A good system of law is one where the rules apply equally and to all – rulers and ruled alike. The rule of law will provide stability and reliability since citizens will be able to rely on fair treatment in the system. This is particularly important in matters concerning the protection of property rights and competition, since both are necessary for economic growth. Figure 5.3.3 shows that there is very high positive correlation between strong rule of law and national income (the higher the index value on the *x*-axis, the stronger the rule of law).

Legal institutions: There must be a functioning police, judicial, and penal system where police act on authority limited by law; cases are tried and rulings are based upon law so as to exclude arbitrary rulings, and those who are convicted of crimes have the right to appeal their case. Moreover, courts must be accessible, open and free for all in order to guarantee public oversight. Other institutions will be highly complementary, for example land registration offices and patent offices to protect intellectual property rights.

Democratic institutions: People who have the right to elect their rulers commonly become better 'subjects' or simply citizens. Rules and regulations which govern our actions are far easier to abide by if one has been allowed to participate in the legislative process – however indirectly. A free and fair electoral process which gives equal voting rights to all is common to virtually all developed countries.[15] Open and transparent government institutions must also have an external system of checks and balances; freedom of expression, organisation and press. Democracy, as a 'soft' or humanitarian system of rule, has been proven to be strongly pro-growth – perhaps simply because democracy allows and encourages ideas, enterprise and social responsibility. Bad rulers don't survive elections in a democracy and it bears repeating that there has never been a famine in a democratic country.[16]

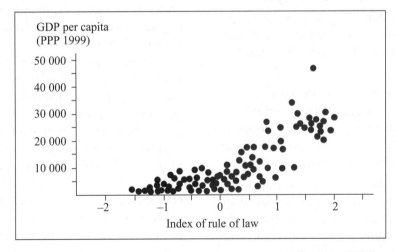

(Source: *WDR 2003*, p. 43)

Figure 5.3.3 *Rule of law and national income*

---

13. It is no accident that the only Swedish word – other than smorgasbord ('smörgåsbord' in fact) – to make it into the English dictionary is *ombudsman*! No, ABBA is *not* in the dictionary.

14. Recommended reading on some of the most horrific results of weak governments: *The State of Africa* by Marin Meredith.

15. The jury is still out on Singapore.

16. See Sen, chapter 6.

The results of political instability

Political instability means that society is laced with **insecurity** and **fear**. What is the incentive to plant and build fences on land you don't own, when there is a very real risk that marauding gangs – supported by the government's blind eye – come by to 'tax' you? What if civil unrest keeps you ever-ready to flee to the next province or country? Or that your chances of prosperity, and even survival, depend on being a member of the right tribe or clan – the one in power at the moment?

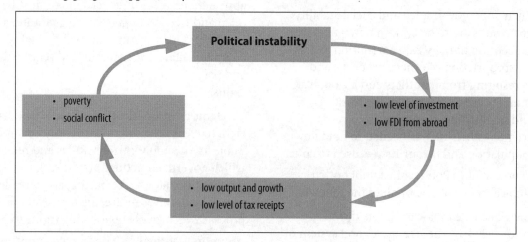

Figure 5.3.4 *Political instability and development*

The results are painfully obvious (see Figure 5.3.4). Economic activity will be very low as will both domestic and foreign investment. The effect is perhaps more serious in case of the latter, as foreign firms would be able to provide much needed injections of capital to developing countries – not to mention the transfer of knowledge and technology. There is understandable reluctance to invest in a country which cannot guarantee the safety of personnel, capital or profits.[17] The absence of this vital growth mechanism leads to yet another vicious cycle, this time of political instability → low investment → poverty → political instability.

Political instability goes a long way in explaining the plight of Africa during the past 30 years. One-third of all countries in the continent were involved in armed conflicts – most of them civil conflicts – and all of these nations will be found in the bottom third of the Human Development Index.[18] Investment in Africa, both domestic and foreign, is the lowest in the world, and an estimated 40% of the continent's wealth is held abroad. It is the only continent to grow poorer between the late 1980s and early 2000s. One bright light is Botswana which has had stable governance during the same period, giving it one of the highest per capita growth rates in the world during the past 30 years.[19]

Corruption ©IBO 2003

Closely linked to the rule of law is corruption, found at many levels and in many guises in administrative systems and government offices which are supposedly controlled by rules and regulations. Anyone who has been stopped by a police officer and fined for some made-up offence has seen the result of corruption first hand. Or a mother who has to pay extra for the doctor's secretary to make an appointment; a builder who needs to grease the palms of several layers of bureaucrats responsible for permits; or when important documents have been 'mislaid' only to magically surface once a gratuity (= supplemental bonus, e.g. bribe) has been paid. Less petty examples of corruption are when government officials 'skim off the top' and keep government tax funds for themselves, and often transfer the monies to banks abroad – this is another form of **capital flight**. These and many other forms of bribery and betrayal of peoples' trust constitute **corruption**, which is when people acting in an official capacity of trust and responsibility misuse their position for private gain. In keeping with my propensity to call an ace of spades an ace of spades, it is theft.

17. The issue of crime, corruption and lack of clarity in the legal system is something frequently discussed by many of the expatriate parents in my school in Mexico. During the international financial/liquidity crisis of 2008/09 I spoke to several parents who were going to be relocated to other – safer – countries as the crisis exacerbated (= intensified) into violent crime.

18. 'Coping with conflict', *The Economist*, 15 January 2004.

19. 'First get the basics right', *The Economist*, 15 January 2004.

Corruption and development

Corruption is both the **cause and effect** of poor governance and corruption levels are far higher in developing countries than in developed. Lack of good governance creates fertile ground for corruption, as the mechanisms to enforce proper institutional behaviour are all too often missing. Lack of democracy, little transparency in government institutions and a media which is pro-government or simply state controlled will all yield poor public insight into misdoings and advance corruption. This in turn will reinforce corruption in the system.

A yearly index of corruption by *Transparency International*, a non-government organisation, shows that there is clear correlation between development and corruption. Figure 5.3.5 shows that development, measured by the HDI, indeed renders higher transparency – the higher the level of societal transparency (e.g. lower corruption) the higher the HDI value.

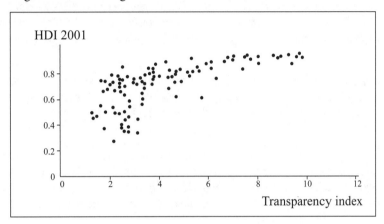

(Source: *The Challenge of Poor Governance and Corruption 2003*, Susan Rose-Ackerman at The Copenhagen Consensus, see www.copenhagenconsensus.com)

Figure 5.3.5 *Corruption index and the HDI 2003*

The causes of corruption

So why does corruption arise and what promotes it? A number of clear causal variables can be identified:

- *Complicated and extensive regulations*: When there are many licenses, permits and other legal documents necessary in, say, starting a business or opening a shop, the authorities will have a form of monopoly power to hinder entrepreneurs. If there are several papers needed and several stamps necessary to start a business, there is a clear incentive for bureaucrats to 'lose' papers or simply withhold stamps in order to get a bribe. There is also an incentive for the applicant to want to speed up the process.

- *Taxation system*: Unclear and complex tax laws mean that honest citizens will spend a great deal of time and money on filling in income tax forms correctly. Why not just 'pay' the tax inspector to fill in the forms?

- *Discretionary power*: When officials in public office have unlimited decision-making power, say in granting land rights for building hotels, then there will be a clear incentive for building contractors to pay a bribe to get favourable terms for the use of private land, so-called zoning laws. There is also an incentive to bribe public officials to get attractive contracts such as building municipal housing.

- *Bureaucracy*: Large bureaucracies with poor and unclear decision-making systems will inevitably lead to politically motivated hiring, e.g. nepotism, cronyism, and other forms of favouritism. Close relations between bureaucrats creates the conditions necessary for corruption.

Nasty storytime: Corruption in Mexico

Living here in Mexico has indeed been … educational. The contrast between Sweden and Mexico is basically like moving between planets; every step on new soil could be either a magnificent discovery or a life-threatening situation. You never know until it's too late.

By now you have probably noticed how I never fail to take a bite out of the Mexican police whenever possible and there is a very simple explanation; while corruption in Mexico is rampant throughout every institution in society, it is the police one meets the most. Basically, the police are robbers with the legal right to carry weapons and are universally despised and held in utter contempt by virtually every Mexican I have ever spoken to. In Sweden one ran to the police for help. Here, you run from the police to avoid getting threatened and robbed.

- *Car + foreigner = target! We extranjeros (= foreigners) stand out here in Mexico like … a diamond in a goat's ~~ass~~ navel. Driving a car is like carrying a sign saying 'Victim here! Get it while it's hot!' Every teacher and student at school has a story to tell. Here is a small selection of Robocop ('robo' is robbery in Spanish) stories I've collected:*

  - *During the October break numerous colleagues went off for some sun and sand in Acapulco. Without exception, every single one of them had been singled out by corrupt police. The most common form of robbery by the police was to claim that a red light had been ignored. 'This is a very serious offence señor, but allow me to help you …' Average palm-greaser: MXN400 (approximately USD30).*

  - *One colleague drove down to the local supermarket and forgot his licence. The police stopped him and gave him a choice; having the car impounded and paying MXN500 a day while the '… papers were cleared to release the car …' or a MXN1400 'fine' on the spot. You are wondering how long it would take for the paperwork to be done, right? Apparently about 3 weeks – at a 'parking fee' of five hundred pesos per day.*

  - *Dave and I went downtown to buy some mountain climbing boots and parked the car on a side street. We came back 45 minutes later to find the car gone. A very helpful gentleman explained that the police saw us get out of the car, called a tow-truck and had our car taken away. We finally found the car impound. The police were basically holding the car ransom! MXN1,000 later we drove off.*

  - *A colleague went of the road and totalled his car. Within 10 minutes there were six (!) police cars there. There was no offer of help or ambulance but a very real and nasty threat; prison or MXN12,000 '… for damage to government property …' What damage? The scrape along a containment wall along the road.*

- *Mexican police and kidnappings: Mexico has been estimated to have three to four kidnappings a day - a higher frequency than Iraq. Long suspected links between the rather prosperous (and growing!) kidnapping industry and higher ranking police officers came to light clearly in August of 2008 when the son of one of Mexico's richest men, Fernando Marti, was kidnapped and killed – even though the family had not notified the police and paid millions in ransom. A federal officer was arrested under suspicion of organising the police road block which enabled the kidnappers to extract Marti. It's a scene taken right out of the movie* Man on fire.

- *Disarming the police: There is a clear link between the notoriously violent and powerful Mexican drug cartels and corrupt police. In January 2007, the new Mexican president, Felipe Calderon, sent some 3,000 military (!) troops to Tijuana – a major transit city for drugs close to the US border. At the same time he disarmed the Tijuana police force which is notorious for its ties to the cartels. What happened? Well, apart from the police resorting to slingshots or refusing to patrol, the crime rate fell! The governor himself reported a fall in kidnappings and murders and claimed an overall fall in crime of 14% since the disarming. Mexican citizens were basically cheering in the streets – not only because of the noticeable fall in violent crime, but because they had never felt safer.*

The effects of corruption

There are a number of direct links between corruption and economic/social performance in developing countries:[20]

- Corruption **discourages investment** and thus growth. Foreign companies tend to avoid countries where the costs of doing business are high and risky due to corruption, in addition to which they are increasingly unwilling to 'play the baksheesh (bribe) game' on account of increased shareholder pressure and demands on operational openness. For example, the consultant firm PriceWaterhouseCoopers estimates that Russia loses close to $US10 billion per year in foreign investment due to corruption and a fragile legal system.[21] Paolo Mauro from the IMF has calculated that a country improving its corruption rating from 6 to 10 (10 being the least corrupt) investment can be expected to rise by an average of 4 percentage points and increase GDP per capita growth rates by 0.5%.[22]

- When firms are committed to doing business by bribery there is going to be a larger degree of 'hidden bookkeeping' and **tax evasion**.

- When countries are run by dictatorships, or an elite group, there will often be '**crony capitalism**', where attractive government contracts and soft loans go to family members or trusted friends. This has often led to highly inefficient use of government funds.

- Bribery in effect is **another tax** on doing business and the poor are hit the hardest since piecemeal bribery will have a much larger effect on those with small incomes. The real tax in the form of bribery is thus a regressive tax. An increase in the corruption index by one point (10 point scale) has been estimated to be equivalent to a 5% increase in the tax rate and decrease foreign direct investment by 8%.[23]

- Corruption has a tendency to distort government policies and skew public funds away from areas rendering general social benefits. Highly corrupt countries tend to **under-spend in human capital** goods such as education and health care. For example, a parliamentary committee in the Philippines in 2002 estimated that corruption cost close to $US2 billion annually – double the monies allocated to the education budget.[24] **Environment** issues also tend to rate poorly in corrupt societies as officials accept bribes not to enforce environmental laws. **Crime rates** are high due to ineffective and corrupt law officials.

- Corruption breeds **distrust** and scepticism towards government agencies and makes it harder to implement democratic reforms, as those who hold power will seek to uphold a system which empowers them.

- When corruption results in misuse of funds and capital flight the country can suffer from an **increase in the burden of debt**.

Surveys continuously indicate that citizens in developing countries view the problem of corruption as a very serious problem, as Figure 5.3.6 on page 558 clearly shows. Strengthening government institutions in legal, administrative and democratic areas is a key factor in coming to grips with what in effect is a loop of corruption → poor governance → corruption. In increasing the ability of institutions to function as intended, it is possible to create a basis for implementing many of the developmental goals spoken of here, such as the collection of taxes, issuing of permits for businesses, pension schemes and social nets, etc.

20. See the excellent paper on corruption by Susan Rose-Ackerman, 'The Challenge of Poor Governance and Corruption' at www.copenhagenconsensus.com.

21. *Global Agenda Magazine* at http://www.globalagendamagazine.com/2003/petereigen.asp.

22. Paulo Mauro, 'Corruption: Causes, Consequences, and Agenda for Further Research', at http://www.worldbank.org/fandd/english/0398/articles/010398.htm.

23. ibid.

24. 'Mugabe Stands Out Among the Politically Corrupt, While Banks and Energy Sector Top Dirty Business Deals Uncovered in 2002', Transparency International press release, 17 December 2002.

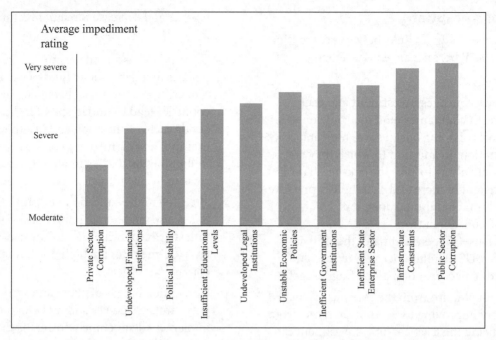

(Source: *Corruption and Integrity Improvement Initiatives in Developing Countries*, UNDP, at
http://magnet.undp.org/Docs/efa/corruption.htm)

Figure 5.3.6 *Views on severity of development impediments (obstacles) in LDCs*

Unequal distribution of income

©IBO 2003

Trickle-down economics is the idea that if you feed the horse enough oats eventually some will pass through to the road for the sparrows. – J.K. Galbraith

While economic growth cannot be conclusively shown to influence income distribution, the opposite holds broadly true; low levels of income inequality can be shown to have beneficial effects on growth – see Section 5.2. In addition, highly unequal distribution of income commonly has a number of general adverse effects on human development:

- High income inequality is strongly associated with high poverty levels. A study by the International Monetary Fund (IMF) shows that **absolute poverty can be decreased** if economic growth takes place under conditions of increasing (or at least unchanging) income equality.[25]

- When there is gross discrepancy between the rich and poor, **crime levels** are measurably higher. This will have a far greater effect on the poor than on the rich.

- Inequality leads to **sub-optimal economic performance**. At high levels of income inequality,

savings will be low and therefore so will investment, since poor people will save a significantly lower proportion of income. While the rich might save more in absolute terms, the proportion will be small. Additionally, a large proportion of expenditure in upper-income groups will be spent on imported luxuries, which does not fuel domestic production. There will also be a proportion of **capital flight**.

- High inequality enables the rich to control and exploit the political and economic system by favouritism and crony capitalism. Such economic activity does not focus on 'fairness' in taxes or redistribution of income via transfer payments and public/merit goods. In effect, the poor are neglected and development suffers.[26]

It appears that inequality in income distribution is something which is quite stable in many countries over time. This belies the theory of '**trickle down**' **economics**, which advocated a 'traditional path' of free market conditions benefiting the well-to-do section of society in the belief that the incentives to produce and profit would generate income which would ultimately trickle down to the poor. I should mention that this theory has been largely discredited.

---

25. 'Tax Policy for Developing Countries', International Monetary Fund, March 2001 at http://www.imf.org/external/pubs/ft/issues/issues27/.

26. See, for example, *HDR 2003* p. 16.

Formal and informal markets ©IBO 2003

When economists speak of **formal markets**, they are referring to markets which are part of the system which acts within the boundaries of the institutions of competitive rules, tax regulations and overall legislative frameworks. All activities are within legislative guidelines and recorded in some way: minimum wages and labour taxes are paid; expenditure taxes such as VAT are registered, and social welfare contributions are paid.

Why informal markets arise

The **informal sector** – sometimes referred to as the *unofficial economy* – is composed of two (often overlapping) parts in developing economies:

1. **Subsistence agriculture** and manufacturing of tools and clothing for the household.

2. **Parallel markets** for goods which vary from cottage manufacturers of cloth and agricultural produce to drugs, weapons and prostitution. To be blunt, there is even trade in human beings – slavery – in parts of northern Africa and Asia.

Do not be fooled into underestimating informal markets; in developing countries the informal sector is a most important element in creating jobs and output. The informal sector comprises between 25% and 40% of all economic activity.[27]

The mechanisms behind informal markets are simple: market activity will arise parallel to formal markets due to complex, costly and **overly-formalised regulation** and **hazy property rights**. Add to this a weak system of administration/regulation/supervision and an almost inevitable result is a large informal economy. Developing countries are often **dual economies**; there is a formal and informal sector side-by-side. Any number of countries will have a most astonishing difference between the two, with highly industrialised and technologically advanced urban areas just a few kilometres from rural people living off the land and trading goods with others.

Results of informal markets

The informal market can be termed a 'natural' market as it arises in answer to the different needs of people looking to satisfy different wants. The success in this is of course that each transaction facilitates the satisfaction of needs; for cassava, wooden bowls or home-made satellite dishes.[28] The informal market allows economic activity to take place that would otherwise be lost due to weak institutions and therefore in fact increases **allocative efficiency** since there would otherwise be very little in the way of markets.

However, there are a number of notable economics costs associated with informal markets:

- **Loss of income/output** in the economy. The formal economy will have difficulty in growing due to the **'unfair' competition** from an informal economy which is not paying taxes – and the informal economy will have severe restraints in moving towards and becoming part of the formalised economy due to lack of access to capital.

- An economy which has a large informal section will provide a **poor tax base** and limit potential tax revenue for the government – and set limits to merit/public goods and transfer payments.

- People working in the informal sector will have little or no **social security** or social welfare benefits.

- The poor who operate businesses within informal markets will have **little protection** from the law. Nor will they be able to insure their goods or enforce contractual agreements in a court of law. This puts both their assets and often their physical wellbeing in the hands of corrupt officials and gangs providing 'protection'. The payments for both amount to a business tax for which they receive no societal goods in kind.

In order to reduce the size of informal market activity the opportunity cost ratios between illegality and legality must be changed. In other words, the **benefits** in registering a business and paying fees/taxes **must outweigh the costs**. While it is in no way an easy task, economists have increasingly put forward suggestions of: better paid tax collectors with incentive-based wages to reduce corruption, reforms in legislation making it easier and cheaper to start and run businesses, and simplified tax systems shifted towards easy-to-collect tax bases.

---

27. World Bank at http://wbln0018.worldbank.org/HDNet/HDdocs.nsf/0/3d876a6c6f40389d85256a7100589c85?OpenDocument&ExpandSection=2.

28. True! I've seen such dishes made of aluminium cans cut open and joined together. Very cool indeed.

29. A 'mordida' is, literally, a 'little bite', e.g. a bribe to the police. It is one of the most well-organised systems in Mexico, where illegal businesses pay a daily 'rate' of approximately MXN50 (USD4) to the police to be left alone.

Lack of infrastructure ©IBO 2003

Just imagine a group of villagers whose livelihoods depend on selling agricultural goods. The simple lack of basic infrastructure such as roads and telecommunications means they will lose out on a number of counts:

1. They will have difficulties in getting the goods to central markets.

2. They will pay a higher price for goods in the village which have incurred transport costs.

3. Goods which villagers cannot bring to market themselves will be sold at lower prices to wholesalers who will be advantaged by the villagers' lack of knowledge of market prices.

4. Villagers willing to make the effort of bringing their goods to an urban market might face low demand or increased supply and end up selling their goods at a loss – a phone call to check market prices might have saved them the trouble.

While the example above might seem a bit simplistic, one must realise that similar situations face millions of people around the world everyday, and getting a good price for produce can be the difference between being able to send one's children to school or not. In a wider context, the network of roads, communication, electricity and gas, health care and education, water and sanitation, etc. all enable economic activity and exchange. As pointed out in Section 5.1, good infrastructure is absolutely vital for transportation, production, attracting investment and generally improving the standard of living for citizens. There are additional negative repercussions in having low levels of infrastructure in developing countries:

- Lack of seaports, airports and transportation networks will **increase the costs of trade**. For example, Africa has far fewer railroad tracks than Asia which serves to double the cost of African rail freight. Air freight is four times as much.[30]

- People will naturally flock to areas where it is possible to find schooling, housing and health care. This **urbanisation** has created enormous inner-city problems in many countries, putting additional pressure on already overburdened water supplies, roads and sewers.

- There are a great number of positive **self-reinforcing effects** in infrastructure. Poor access to basic education and resulting low literacy rates means that other types of infrastructure will not have maximum societal rates of return. For example, a study in Vietnam showed that an irrigation scheme would have greater net economic benefits if all grown-ups had a full primary education.[31]

A summary of the relationships between institutional and political barriers is shown in Figure 5.3.7 on page 561.

---

30. 'Globalization, growth and poverty', WB report 2002, chapter 2, p. 40.
31. *WDR 2001*, chapter 5, p. 78.

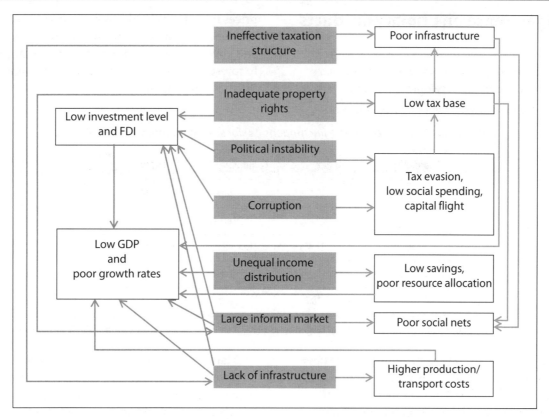

Figure 5.3.7 *Summary of institutional/political barriers*

POP QUIZ 5.3.1   INSTITUTIONAL BARRIERS TO DEVELOPMENT

1   Explain how an inefficient tax system weakens the ability of a country to develop.

2   Why would property rights help to solve the problems of a poor tax base?

3   Explain why the rule of law and good legal institutions might have positive effects on foreign investment.

4   'Bribery as a way of doing business is a regressive tax.' Explain.

5   How can corruption increase the debt burden of a developing country?

6   How do informal markets influence the ability of a country to provide merit and public goods?

International trade barriers

©IBO 2003

The UN has estimated that trade barriers which limit access of developing countries to markets in the developed world mean an annual loss of export revenue more than twice that of all aid monies received in 2000.[32] The world has increasingly moved towards trade liberalisation in many areas **except** those which most concern developing countries – basic commodities, agricultural goods and textiles. It has been estimated by the World Bank that the elimination of tariffs would primarily benefit developing countries – gains of some USD500 billion by 2015 would lift some 300 million people above the poverty line. It bears mentioning that most of the gain would come from developing countries removing their own barriers to trade.[33,34]

---

32. Todaro, p. 492.

33. World Bank, 'Global Economic Prospects (2002)', p. 168.

34. For more information on the ongoing issue of increasing food prices and how MDCs perpetuate the problem with subsidies, see http:/ /www.imf.org/external/np/exr/faq/ffpfaqs.htm.

Overdependence on primary products

©IBO 2003

The link between dependence on exporting primary products and low human development is well established.[35] The short-run volatility of commodity prices makes it difficult for producers to plan output and foresee income – thus making both tax revenues and government investment in infrastructure difficult to foresee. Table 5.3.3 shows just how severe these fluctuations can be.

Table 5.3.3 *Average yearly price fluctuations (%) for selected commodities 1986–1999*

Commodity	Index	Commodity	Index
Coffee	25.5%	Jute	18.1%
Sugar	22.4%	Cocoa	17.7%
Poultry	21.4%	Groundnut oil	16.2%
Rubber	18.7%	Butter	16.1%
Palm oil	18.7	Cotton	15.9

(Source: Food and Agricultural Organisation (FAO) at http://www.fao.org/DOCREP/005/Y3733E/y3733e0d.htm)

Over the long run average **commodity prices have fallen continuously** in real terms for over 150 years (see "APPLIED ECONOMICS: Commodity price fluctuations" on page 127). As exports in developing countries – primarily the least developed countries – make up for a large proportion of GDP (see Table 5.3.4 on page 563) such nations will be most vulnerable to world market prices for commodities.

Developing countries which rely on a few commodities for the brunt of export revenue have faced some rather serious problems in the last few decades:

- As much of developing countries' exports goes to developed countries, **recessions** in developed countries have had severe negative effects on the demand for primary goods.

- Many of the primary products exported to developed countries are used as raw material in manufacturing. As production became more efficient and more and more substitutes were found, **demand for primary goods has fallen** in some cases.

- Since the income elasticity of demand for primary goods is low, the growth in developed countries has resulted in slow growth in demand for primary goods. This has continuously worsened the **terms of trade** for developing countries (see "Consequences of adverse terms of trade" on page 563).

- The slow growth of exports and national income has in many countries meant that **per capita incomes have fallen**.

---

35. See, for example, 'The least developed countries report 2002', UNCTAD, p. 137.

Table 5.3.4 *Trade as a percentage of GDP and composition of exports*

HDI Class	Imports of goods & services (% of GDP)		Exports of goods & services (% of GDP)		Primary exports (% of exports)		Manufactured exports (% of exports)	
	1990	2000	1990	2000	1990	2000	1990	2000
Developing countries	26	32	26	34	38	28	60	71
Least developed countries	23	31	14	22	..	..	..	..
Arab states	39	29	40	40	81	81	20	19
East Asia & Pacific	40	51	41	56	24	13	75	86
Latin America & Caribbean	12	18	14	17	66	51	34	48
South Asia	15	19	11	18	..	40	71	58
Sub-Saharan Africa	26	33	27	32	..	57	..	36
Central and Eastern Europe & CIS	25	41	25	49	..	42	..	52
OECD	18	21	18	21	20	15	78	81
High income OECD	18	20	18	20	19	16	78	81
High human development	20	22	20	22	20	16	78	82
Medium human development	19	27	20	30	49	40	48	58
Low human development	24	28	20	24	..	69	..	32
High Income	19	21	19	22	19	15	78	82
Middle income	20	29	21	32	43	35	54	63
Low income	20	28	17	28	..	45	..	53
World	20	22	20	23	24	20	73	77

(Source: *HDR 2002*, p. 201)

Consequences of adverse terms of trade ©IBO 2003

In Section 4.8 we looked at how the **terms of trade** are dependent on the price of exports and the price of imports. Looking at how the price of primary goods has fallen continuously for many years, it is little wonder that the terms of trade for primary goods exporters has deteriorated also. In fact, the terms of trade for primary goods producers have been falling since the 1880s.[36] Adjusting prices to inflation yields even worse figures; the Food and Agricultural Organisation (FAO) estimates that the *real* price of agricultural goods fell by 50% between 1980 and

1999.[37] Historical evidence points to a continuous fall in primary goods prices relative to secondary goods which means that primary goods exporters have seen their terms of trade steadily decline.

A good many developing countries are dependant on three or four primary goods for the better part of export revenue (see Table 5.3.4) and the results of **falling terms of trade for developing countries** are almost always negative:

- Higher costs of **debt servicing** as a greater quantity of exports are necessary to earn a given amount of foreign currency with which to repay foreign debt.

---

36. Cypher & Dietz, pp. 86 and 180.
37. FAO at http://www.fao.org/DOCREP/005/Y3733E/y3733e0d.htmp.

- Falling export revenue can cause **current account deficits** – which have sometimes forced countries to increase borrowing – which in turn increases the **debt burden**.

- Deteriorating terms of trade **reduce much-needed imports** such as capital, intermediate products in production, and fuel. All are needed to industrialise and increase value-added output.

- When the market for legal crops falls through the floor, **illegal crops** such as coca become very attractive to poor farmers. This tragic example of **producer substitutes** can be seen in several South American countries.

- When developing countries' terms of trade falls continuously, there is an incentive to make up for this by increasing output and **exporting more**. The long run effect of this – other than having to pay more for any given amount of imports – is that supply of the commodity increases and helps lower

prices further. Between 1986 and 1999, non-fuel exporters of commodities saw the average price of exports fall by 12%, export volume increase by 43% – while the amount of imports that they could buy for total export revenue (i.e. price × volume) increased by only 2%. In other words, the 2% increase in imports costs 43% more in exports.[38]

Yet another negative cycle: the terms of trade, balance of payments and exchange rate

Developing countries dependent on primary goods for export revenue face the possibility of a 'loop' arising from falling commodity prices, illustrated in Figure 5.3.8. A fall in the price of export commodities leads to a deterioration in the terms of trade → low PED for exports → export revenue falls → current account worsens → exchange rate depreciates → fall in the price of exports …

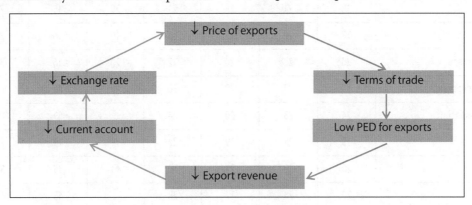

Figure 5.3.8 *Adverse cycle of falling terms of trade*

Consequences of a narrow range of exports ©IBO 2003

It is evident that dependency on a few commodities for export revenues has been damaging for many of the poorest countries in the world, and the link between dependency on a small basket of export goods and absolute poverty is very strong.[39] In 1999, 79% of the

people living on less than $US1 a day in the poorest countries in the world (*least* developed countries) were dependent on a few export commodities.[40] Table 5.3.5 on page 565 shows five developing countries which all have more than 40% of export earnings originating from *one single agricultural commodity* and over 50% coming from three commodities.[41]

38. 'Least developed countries report', UNCTAD 2002, p. 140.

39. 'Least developed countries report', UNCTAD 2002, p. 101.

40. http://www.unctad.org/Templates/webflyer.asp?docid=2451&intItemID=2079&lang=1.

41. Notice that **cash crops** (i.e. crops which are grown for the single purpose of exportation) such as tea, tobacco and coffee make up virtually all of the commodity exports in these five countries.

Table 5.3.5 *High dependency on commodities, selected countries*

Country/ territory	Export earnings of top single agricultural export commodity				Export earnings of top three agricultural export commodities		
	Percentage share in		Earnings as a percentage of GDP (1998)	Commodity	Percentage share in		Commodities
	Total merchandise exports	Total agricultural exports			Total merchandise exports	Total agricultural exports	
Burundi	75	83	7.2	Coffee (green)	89	99	Coffee (green); tea; sugar refined
Guinea-Bissau	48	91	6.3	Cashew nuts	51	98	Cashew nuts; cotton; palm oil
Sao Tome and Principe	69	97	16.9	Cocoa beans	70	100	Cocoa beans; coffee (green); copra
Ethiopia	62	69	5.4	Coffee (green)	75	84	Coffee; dry-salted sheepskin; crude org. mat.
Malawi	59	74	23.8	Tobacco leaves	70	87	Tobacco leaves; tea, sugar

(Source: FAO at http://www.fao.org/DOCREP/005/Y3733E/y3733e0d.htm)

The outcome for a country such as shown in Table 5.3.5 is **dependency** and **vulnerability**:

- While 'a narrow range' does not imply that all developing countries are exporting the same type of commodities, a number of the same goods are in fact produced in many countries since they have a comparative advantage in these goods – which makes it difficult for low income countries with inadequate capital markets **to diversify** into other industries.

- The difficulties in moving up in the scale of value-added production are made worse by the fact that most developed countries which import the developing countries primary goods (around three quarters of all LDC exports of primary goods) will have **differentiated tariffs** on processed goods. (See "Protectionism in international trade " on page 566.)

- Small scale farmers supplying global markets with their produce are often price takers without benefit of **market knowledge**. Intermediate buyers can set prices low in order to increase profit margins and this pricing power severely limits farmers' ability to get a fair market price. The most vulnerable producers in such uneven negotiations are small farmers which make up the majority of output, for example coffee, which is grown in some 70 countries where family farms make up about 70% of output. Oxfam reckons that Ugandan coffee farmers get about 2.5% of the retail price in the UK while one of the world's largest producers, Nestlé, has a 26 to 30% profit margin on instant coffee.[42]

- Agricultural production is directed towards the export sector rather than the domestic sector. This has frequently been **linked to foreign debt** and non-convertible currencies; in order to service foreign loans the country focuses on producing cash crops for hard currency in order to pay off interest and amortise loans. Fertile lands are used for debt repayment rather than food production.

- Low PED and PES for primary goods means that changes in demand/supply will inevitably result in price volatility, e.g. large changes in price. Such **export earnings instability** makes it difficult for producers to plan future output since revenue streams are so unforeseeable. This hampers investment in primary production and lowers growth rates.

---

42. 'Europe and the coffee crisis', Oxfam 2003 at http://www.oxfam.org/eng/pdfs/pp030226_EUcoffee10.pdf.

Protectionism in international trade

©IBO 2003

There is growing evidence that it is the developing countries *not* taking part in global trade which have been worst at lowering poverty levels. There is also increasing realisation that rich countries hold many of the keys necessary to improve trade for developing countries which export primary goods, textiles and simple manufactures. Section 4.2 showed how developing countries' potential exports are affected by *tariffs*, *quotas* and *subsidies*; domestic producers are advantaged by government intervention which raises import prices and/or lowers domestic producers' costs. Section 4.3 brought up the problem of *regional trade areas* (RTAs) which are allowed to promote intra-association tariff reductions without observing the most favoured nation clause of the WTO – in effect locking out non-members from market access. Let us look at two other development issues in trade barriers:

- *Higher effective tariffs on the poor*: While the Uruguay Round of trade talks established that developed countries would successively lower tariffs towards developing countries, there have been limited effects as yet. The World Bank estimates that the poorest countries have gained the least since their exports are precisely the goods where protectionism is the highest; agriculture and textiles. This means that while average tariffs in developed countries might have fallen considerably, the *effective* (trade weighted) *average* tariff on countries exporting agricultural goods and textiles is still far higher than for manufactures. Poor people – broadly defined as those living under $US2 a day – dependent on these goods thus face more than double the tariff wall of developed countries.[43]

- *Tariff escalation*: Developing countries often face higher tariffs on goods which have higher proportions of **value-added**, i.e. a tariff on cocoa will have lower tariffs than on cocoa butter or chocolate. For example, raw ('green') coffee entering the EU has no tariff while coffee that has been processed in some way, e.g. roasted and/or ground, faces 7.5% to 9.0% tariffs.[44] This method of **tariff escalation** reduces the demand for processed goods and inhibits developing countries' ability to move from low to high value-added. Figure 5.3.9 illustrates how average tariff rates for agricultural products and textiles in a developed country, Canada, are higher when imported goods have a higher element of value-added.

The tariff escalation mechanism slows down the process of **diversifying** into processing industries, limits the **accumulation of skills and capital**, slows **export growth** since basic commodity prices are continuously falling, and perpetuates primary goods exporters' **vulnerability** to global price fluctuations.

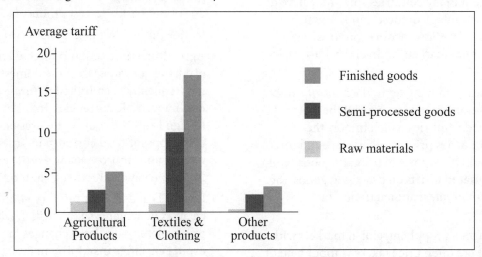

(Source: 'Market Access for Developing Countries' Exports', IMF and the World Bank 2001, p. 24)

Figure 5.3.9 *Tariff escalation in Canada, 2000*

---

43. *Global Economic Prospects and the developing countries*, World Bank 2002, p. 57.

44. *Government Actions to Support Coffee Producers – An Investigation of Possible Measures from the European Union Side, Germán Calfat Institute for Development Policy and Management*, University of Antwerp, Belgium 2002, p. 19. (Note that these tariffs do not apply to countries in the Association of Coffee Producing Countries, ACPC.)

POP QUIZ 5.3.2 TRADE BARRIERS TO DEVELOPMENT

1 Prices of commodities continue to fall. Explain why using price elasticities.

2 Why have the terms of trade moved against a number of developing countries for decades?

3 What are the consequences of deteriorating terms of trade for developing countries?

4 Exporting a narrow range of goods increases a country's vulnerability. Explain.

5 Why is there an incentive for developed countries to have differentiated tariffs on goods with different levels of value-added?

International financial barriers

©IBO 2003

Development economists stress the importance of developing countries having access to financial markets in order to increase investment. In particular, to have access to *foreign* capital, since domestic savings and institutions are often unable to provide adequate funds. Unfortunately, many of the poorest countries are still suffering from what became known as the **debt crisis** of the 1980s, and servicing *foreign debt* will have to be done using hard currencies such as the dollar or yen, which mostly must be obtained via exports. Adding to the problems of finding investment sources is the fact that large amounts of money have been placed in foreign banks rather than funding domestic investment and consumption, so-called capital flight.

Indebtedness ©IBO 2003

Total debt in developing countries went from $US68 billion in 1970 to approximately $US2.3 trillion in 2002 – an increase of over 3,000%.[45] Within this there is a group of most **heavily indebted poor countries** (the 41 **HIPC** countries of which 32 are African) accounting for close to $US190 billion of debt in 1998–99, which sounds proportionately little until one realises that this represented over 400% of total exports by 1999.[46] How did so many developing countries end up with such amounts of clearly unsustainable debt?

The oil crises revisited – the origin of the debt crisis

The debt crisis in developing countries became all too clear in the 1980s and had its origin in the quadrupling of the price of oil in 1973–74 and resulting supply shocks around the world. (See "APPLIED ECONOMICS: We're on a highway to hell!" on page 123 and Section 3.5.) Oil is paid for in US dollars and the massive increase in revenues for OPEC and other oil producing nations resulting from higher oil prices flowed into commercial banks in developed countries. The deposits of petrodollars in commercial banks – primarily in the US and Europe – increased almost tenfold between 1973 and 1974. This increase in loanable funds must be seen in the light of two additional factors:

1. The **Bretton Woods system** of fixed exchange rates had broken down. Countries were thus free to set interest rates to pursue domestic macro policies in setting interest rates.

2. The oil crisis resulted in a worldwide **recession in 1974/75**. The recession was unusual as it was **inflationary** due to the supply-side shock of increased oil prices.

There was a large increase in loanable funds and low demand for loans in developed countries. Commercial banks looked for alternative borrowers and the scene was set for a surge in lending to developing countries – countries are low risk as the do not go bankrupt like firms. In addition, *real* interest rates were very low due to high inflation and also due to the fact that developing countries relaxed credit in order to stimulate demand. Accordingly, debt in developing countries increased by over 22% annually between 1975 and 1980, going from a total of $US180 billion to $US500 billion.[47]

When oil prices once again rose drastically in 1979–80, there was a shift in monetary and fiscal policies in the developed world, primarily in the US. The newly elected American president Ronald Reagan lowered taxes and ran up large budget deficits which were covered by loans – which of course drove up interest rates and the exchange rate for the US dollar. Interest rates skyrocketed both in the US and other developed nations also due to deflationary policies aimed at coming to grips with high inflation. The results were nothing short of disastrous for developing countries:

---

45. IMF at http://www.imf.org/external/np/exr/ib/2000/092300.htm; Intergovernmental Group of 24 at http://www.g24.org/losertab.pdf; Todaro, p. 608.
46. *World Economic Outlook*, IMF 2000, chapter 4, p. 141.
47. *World Economic Outlook*, IMF 2000, chapter 4, p. 139 and http://www.imf.org/external/np/exr/ib/2000/092300.htm.

- As a large proportion of developing countries' debt was **denominated in US dollars**, debt servicing (i.e. paying off the loan – amortising – and paying the interest) became ever more burdensome. More export revenue was needed to pay off debt.

- The loans in commercial banks were at market rates and often variable. The increase in interest rates thus increased the **cost of the loans**.

- A large portion of the borrowed funds going to developing countries bounced right back to bank accounts in developed countries. This is known as **capital flight**, and is looked at below.

- Continuously **falling commodity prices** hurt exports and many developing countries went into recession, which further decreased their ability to service loans. When Mexico defaulted (= declared itself unable to amortise and pay interest) in 1982, the **debt crisis** was established as fact.

Effects of overindebtedness

> *… foreign aid is necessary to enable underdeveloped countries to service the subsidized loans … [taken] under earlier foreign aid agreements.* – Lord Peter Bauer

Again, it must be pointed out that taking on debt is not necessarily a bad thing for developing countries. Borrowed funds are a way of filling the finance gap, i.e. the gap between domestic savings and investment needs. Foreign loans are one method of providing this finance, but when the debt is beyond the country's capacity to service the debt in the long run, the results can be devastating.

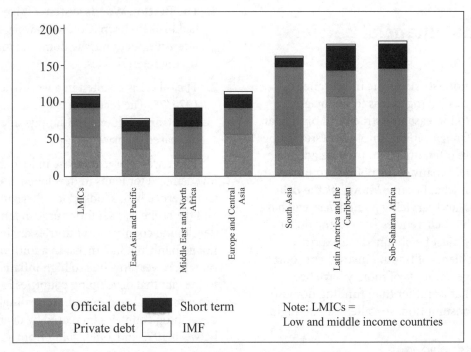

(Source: *Global Economic Prospects and the developing countries*, World Bank 2002, p. 19)

Figure 5.3.10 *Total foreign debt in developing countries as a percentage of exports 2000*

Debt has shown to have some major anti-developmental effects:

- *Diversion of funds*: Since the largest proportion of loans in developing countries have been taken by governments, *official debt* in Figure 5.3.10,[48] large **debts divert much-needed funds for roads, health care and education** to debt servicing (e.g. payments on the loan itself plus interest). When debt servicing amounts to 20% of total government expenditure

while 13% is spent on education and 6% on health, the opportunity costs of large debt becomes obvious. This is in fact the case in some 30 least developed countries.[49] In addition, aid monies from abroad supposedly going towards development – and often immediate relief – are all too frequently used to pay off debt. Africa is estimated to spend four times more on debt servicing than on health care.

---

48. While debt is often put in terms of the percentage of total debt to GDP, it is more meaningful to put debt ratios in terms of debt as a percentage of debt to exports. This is simply due to the fact that many developing countries will have to earn foreign currencies to pay off external debt.

49. See, for example, 'IMF World Economic Outlook 2000', p. 143.

- *Further debt:* Many developing countries found themselves locked into a 'perpetual debt mechanism' in the 1980s, when governments took on additional debt to service old debts. Many governments simply hoped that additional debt would buy some time for exports to increase and thereby be able to service additional loans.

- *Harsh domestic macro policies*: When countries get a reputation as '**bad borrowers**' they will find it increasingly difficult to get loans from private sources – and when they are able to procure loans they will pay a higher interest rate as a risk premium. The other alternative has often been to **refinance loans** (renegotiate loans at lower interest and/or longer amortisation periods) with the IMF as a guarantee of 'good fiscal and monetary conduct' on the part of the developing country. 'Good conduct' often meant that the debtor LDC would have to submit to a number of strict policy guidelines of fiscal austerity (decrease government spending and/or increase taxes) and monetary tightening (increase interest rates). The **severe conditionality** imposed by such **IMF stabilisation**

policies have been criticised for the anti-developmental effects of decreased government spending and the deflationary effects of higher interest rates. We return to this issue in Section 5.5.

Non-convertible currencies ©IBO 2003

The exchange rate examples used in Section 4 had one thing in common; the currencies could be freely exchanged on the foreign exchange market. This is not always the case in developing countries, for a variety of reasons. Most developing countries have fixed exchange rates, i.e. the domestic currency is pegged to another at an **official rate** that is higher than the **market rate** would be, i.e. the domestic currency is overvalued.

Official and market rates for a currency

Hmmmm, 'excess demand' and 'controls and rationing' for a currency. Does this remind you of something? Yes, parallel market activity will rise – in this case a parallel rate (black market rate) for foreign currency will arise.

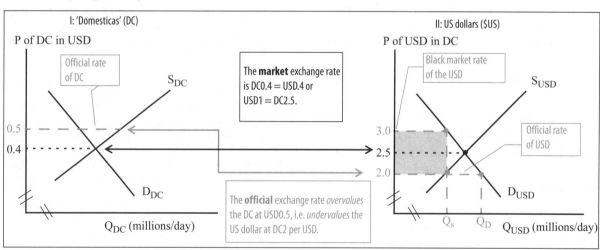

Figure 5.3.11 *The exchange rates for the 'Domestica' and the US dollar*

Diagram II in Figure 5.3.11 illustrates the outcome of an overvalued exchange rate in a fictitious developing country, using 'domesticas' (DC) as the domestic currency. (NOTE: diagram I is simply to help you in identifying how a currency is overvalued, yet it is diagram II – the market for US dollars –that illustrates the issue of a parallel exchange rate.) The market rate for the domestica, diagram I, would be at 40 US cents to the US dollar but **the rate has been officially set at a higher exchange rate** of one domestica = 50 US cents. Diagram II – for the US dollar – shows how the official exchange rate has set the price of the dollar too low, at a rate of 2 domesticas

rather that the free market rate of 2.5 domesticas to the US dollar.

In other words, the official exchange rate overvaluation of the domestic currency has the same effect as a *maximum price* on foreign currency. Since such a country will not have the foreign reserves necessary to buy up excess domesticas in order to establish the rate at a higher level, there is **excess demand** of US dollars, $Q_S \Leftrightarrow Q_D$ and a potential parallel market for the US dollar, shown by the blue rectangle, resulting in a *black market exchange rate* of DC3 to the US dollar. While increasingly uncommon, many countries dealt with this overvaluation of the domestic currency by imposing exchange controls and limits on foreign exchange.[50]

Now, do you think that international foreign currency traders will accept such market shenanigans (= trickery, nonsense, foolery) activities? Not a chance. The foreign currency market won't touch such currencies with a 5-metre barge pole. Even countries which are not *intentionally* trying to keep the domestic currency overvalued often have limited tradeability on the foreign exchange markets, as foreign countries will not be prone to trade with currencies for which there are parallel markets. For example, try trading in your birr (Ethiopia), kip (Laos) or gopik (Azerbaijan) at a foreign exchange office in the EU. These currencies will in most cases not be accepted – or even forbidden to be used – outside the country of origin and are therefore considered **non-convertible**.

Effects of currency non-convertibility

There are a number of side-effects for a country whose currency is not accepted in other countries, none of them good:

- Currencies facilitate trade, investment and all the other possible economic exchanges going on between countries. An LDC with a non-convertible currency adds to the risks and costs of foreign firms doing business and will **limit trade** and incoming **foreign investment**.

- Exporters in countries with non-convertible currencies will commonly have to exchange a portion or all of their foreign export earnings – at the **official** exchange rate. What this amounts to is in effect an **export tax** on domestic producers.

- Black markets for currency will **distort prices** and **waste resources** as time and effort goes into avoiding official rates and withholding monies from taxation. It has also been amply demonstrated that a fixed exchange rate in the hands of a corrupt and autocratic regime gives many opportunities for those in power to line their own pockets: the dictator simply forces traders to hand over valuable foreign currencies in exchange for highly overvalued domestic currency. I simply *must* point out that such rulers will have a printing press in the basement!

Capital flight ©IBO 2003

When firms, governments and individuals transfer money to deposits and other financial assets abroad in order to avoid currency risks and low rates of return on savings and investment, one speaks of **capital flight**. Many of my people fall into the erroneous trap of believing all capital flight to be either illegal or the result of illegal economic activity. While this is certainly all too often the case, it is equally common that people in developing countries simply seek out safety and higher returns by keeping their earnings in another – often developed – country.

Causes of capital flight

The main reasons why capital has flowed out from developing countries is simply that money is 'cowardly', i.e. risk adverse and prone to avoiding anything resembling insecurity, and that economic agents will seek to maximise their returns. This gives us three main causes of capital flight:

1. **Corruption and lack of controls:** In a country where there are **poor civil checks and balances** in the form of democratic and legal institutions, the ability of those in power to embezzle (= steal) government funds and foreign loans increases. The rest is, tragically, human nature.

2. **Avoiding insecurity:** When corruption, lawlessness and **general instability** spreads through an economy, those who are able to will have strong incentives to put their funds somewhere safe.

3. **Inadequate policies: Exchange rate misalignment** and high levels of **debt** have been found to be two major factors in capital flight.[51] People/firms/ financial institutions will act in accordance with points 1) and 2) above. When institutions providing stability are lacking then it will be easier for those in power to appropriate foreign exchange earnings – and this creates an incentive for others to get their assets out of harm's way.

4. **Financial deregulation:** Capital markets have become increasingly efficient on a global scale due to **deregulation**, which has simply made capital flight easier.

---

50. In some extreme cases it is illegal for citizens to possess foreign currency, thereby forcing traders to hand over foreign hard currencies at a low rate.
51. *Globalisation, growth and poverty*, World Bank report 2002, Chapter 2, p. 41.

Effects of capital flight

When large amounts of money leave a developing country, there are some very strong anti-developmental effects (see Figure 5.3.12):

- A horrendously large portion of the **foreign debt** accrued via loans and aid money in developing countries has fled to undisclosed bank accounts in countries with strict non-disclosure policies such as Switzerland and the Cayman Islands. When foreign loans meant for development efforts are appropriated by government officials and put in personal foreign accounts, the effects are twofold: 1) The development projects do not take place, and 2) the money goes to *personal* use – but the debt is accrued for the *country* as a whole. Billions of current debt in developing countries was taken on by corrupt and dictatorial governments in the 1970s and 1980s but there is very little to show for it in terms of schools, housing and infrastructure.[52]

- Capital flight in developing countries **undermines the domestic economy** by denying the domestic capital markets funds for investment. This also weakens financial institutions in developing countries which perpetuates a cycle of capital outflow. For example, the World Bank estimates that by the end of the 1990s 40% of African wealth was held abroad.[53] *The Economist* reckons that around 80 cents of every dollar lent to Africa between 1970 and 1996 was placed abroad the same year it was lent.[54] Capital flight is in reality a most tragic form of participation in globalisation in non-globalised and marginalised LDCs.

- Capital flight weakens the willingness of international **donors and aid agencies** to provide funds – both as loans and aid money. **Foreign investors** will naturally also be wary of investing in countries where a proportion of both investment monies and revenues will have a tendency to wind up in foreign accounts.

It has been estimated that developing countries lost between USD858 billion and USD1 trillion to capital flight during 2006.[55] That's a lot of school books.

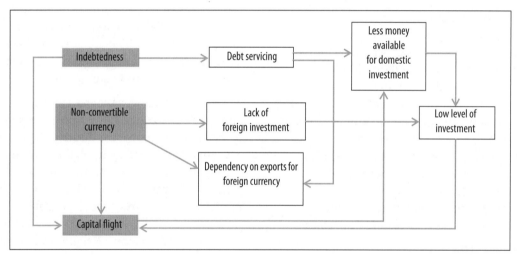

Figure 5.3.12 *Financial weaknesses and development*

POP QUIZ 5.3.3   FINANCIAL BARRIERS TO DEVELOPMENT

1 Explain the connection between the oil crises in the 1970s and increasing debt burdens in developing countries.

2 Why might a developing country in fact have two exchange rates?

3 How does a non-convertible currency create a barrier for development?

4 'Capital flight hurts the poor far more than the rich.' Comment on this statement.

52. See *HDR 2003*, p. 152.
53. 'Globalization, growth and poverty', WB report 2002, Chapter 2, p. 40.
54. 'An addictive lullaby', *The Economist*, 15 January 2004.
55. 'Illicit Financial Flows from Developing Countries: 2002–2006', Executive Report from Global Financial Integrity (see www.gfip.org).

Social and cultural factors acting as barriers ©IBO 2003

One popular – and now largely discounted – theory of economic prosperity and growth was put forward by the famous sociologist Max Weber in the early 20th century. He posited that the success of liberal capitalism had its primary roots in the protestant work ethic – something that equally successful catholic countries in Europe rather belie. Another popular theory, of later date, puts forward that the Confucian ethics in East Asia can help explain the powerful economic growth seen in the last 30 or so years. Whatever the case may be, it is clear that social and cultural factors indeed do influence economic and development performance while it is equally clear that great care should be taken in attributing too large a degree of influence. There are simply too many exceptions in the world to make generalisations about which social and cultural elements are best suited to modern (or 'western' if you will) economic systems of growth and development.

At this point I must point out the difficulties in writing about social and cultural as barriers to development. Looking at other cultures in terms of how well they facilitate growth and development is naturally done from the viewpoint of one's **own** culture. Such a 'top-down' or 'Eurocentric' viewpoint necessarily looks at the issues from the vantage point of a developed country supported by industrialisation and liberal democracy. Nowhere will **cultural bias** be more present than here, and I have been suitably warned by very knowledgeable development experts that one is on very shaky ground indeed in attempting to show that factors such as religion and tradition act as hinders to development *per se*.[56]

It is instead more appropriate – and justified – to look at how social and cultural factors **facilitate development** by adapting to change; providing rights and enabling citizens to partake in a developing society; and providing social stability. Growth and development bring change – in fact, both terms strongly imply change. Social customs, traditions and culture are all woven into the fabric of every society and form a 'template' (= pattern or model) for human behaviour. Such factors in turn affect not only the stability of society, but the ability and propensity to adapt and change. Furthermore, domestic cultural/ ethnic/ religious differences within countries frequently confine various groups to poverty and also

underpin conflicts and civil unrest – all of which hinder human and economic development.

Finally, it must be pointed out that much of the failure in development efforts in conjunction with social and cultural factors is due to **lack of consideration** of existing indigenous structures rather than the inability of indigenous social structures to be used in the development process. Getting local cooperation and using existing social structures is pretty much common sense. When a village or tribal council is not only participatory but **influential** then indeed change will take place. This mindset is now firmly a part of mainstream economic theory and has been adapted by virtually all development cooperation organisations.

Religion ©IBO 2003

A view that is sometimes advanced is that **religion** as a system of **beliefs** and **values** will often play a central role in society and rapid change might come into conflict with these. Thus, religions as **institutions** often emphasize continuity, tradition and adherence to patterns of social behaviour, and as such can create 'drag' on changes which are often implemented in developing societies. This view is largely anecdotal and little evidence seems to support it.

What does show is that religious persecution and conflict will have a negative impact on society and growth. When people are **disadvantaged and marginalised** due to their religion, the effect is to block these people from a large part of the development process. The caste system in India, for example, perpetrates a system where the casteless – 'untouchables' – have long since in effect been barred from many occupations. Religious **wars and conflicts** are different from any other conflict only in the nature of the cause – one sees the same destruction of lives and property, refugees and waste of resources as in other wars. The fact that Sudan is one of the poorest countries in the world is not entirely unrelated to an over 30 year civil war partially involving two religious groups, Muslims and Christians.

Culture and tradition ©IBO 2003

Cultural attitudes are some of the most enduring elements in a changing world – something I am sure all young people would say about their parents. **Culture** is an umbrella concept which covers a great deal. It is the evolution of a set of unwritten rules of conduct and

---

56. My cultural-anthropologist friend Anna Collins-Falk has spent over 20 years working for development agencies around the world. I am most indebted to her for taking time out of her Ph.D. work and play-time with Maya to help me.

ways of doing things, but also a broader concept of language and patterns of behaviour. **Tradition** is a continuation of culture, in that traditions in societies are part of the overall makeup of culture.

Culture and traditions are basically ways to pass on a way of life and to provide continuity. In this respect, it is possible that cultural values and traditions might affect development in obstructing change. Many of the **institutions** we have spoken of such as legal systems, the rule of law and democratic rights are noticeably western (in search of a better phrase) but this doesn't mean that such institutions are absent in non-western countries in general or developing countries specifically. Instead there are different cultural institutions; tribal councils and chieftains instead of written laws and courts; communal land instead of individual properties; and hereditary titles rather than elected representatives. Implementing a 'modern' or 'western' institutional framework will quite naturally lead to fierce resistance from those with vested interests and power.

There are other – largely anecdotal – examples of how cultural objections come into play in development. Implementing development plans based on foreign concepts of **property rights** can often run into resistance. For example, attempting to create competitive and entrepreneurial forces in agriculture has sometimes been met by broad confusion in countries which cannot imagine owning land **personally**. Other cultures are horrified at the thought of selling land rather than passing it on to the children. Cultures can also inhibit such things as **sex education** and thereby increase the spread of HIV/AIDS. In many countries discussions of sexual issues such as homosexuality and the use of condoms has been taboo (= forbidden). Countries which have made forceful efforts to change attitudes and encourage openness in discussion, such as Uganda, are the ones which have combated the spread of sexually transmitted diseases most efficiently.

Gender issues ©IBO 2003

In 2000, representatives of 191 countries met under the UN flag to set out an ambitious agenda for development – the **Millennium Development Goals**.

Eight major goals were agreed upon, most of which are to be accomplished by 2015. One of the goals is the promotion of gender equality and the empowerment of women – but it is made quite clear that this must underline all other goals since viewing any other goal, such as poverty reduction or providing universal education 'without promoting gender equality will both raise the costs and decrease the likelihood of achieving the other goals.'[57]

While 'gender' in fact implies both male and female, it is commonly women who are subjected to the many forms of prejudice and bias, and I limit the discussion to gender inequality pertaining to women. Gender issues play a pivotal role in human development for two reasons:

1. Development is defined as a broad, across-the-board increase in living standards and independence. Clearly, when half the population is excluded in several respects, such as legal rights and access to education, there is limited development scope. Therefore, gender equality is a measure of development in its own right.

2. Gender equality is a **facilitator of development**. For example, virtually all studies show that women's education reduces child mortality, increases growth and improves health.[58]

Education: About two thirds of the children which do not go to school are girls, for the simple reason that poor households have calculated a poor rate of return on educating girls. This is erroneous, as there is ample evidence that investment in the education of girls is a most cost-effective way of development – perhaps the most cost-effective way. Education enables women to take more control of their lives by having the opportunity to get jobs. Better educated women marry later, which lowers birth rates and increases the survival rate of children. Female education is basically an investment that raises national income – and national income will in turn lead to more gender equality in education and elsewhere.[59] In fact, an estimated 0.4% to 0.9% of the difference in growth rates between East Asia and Sub Saharan Africa, South Asia plus the Middle East is due to gender inequality in education in the latter three areas.[60]

57. *Millennium Development Goals – A look through a gender lens*, UNDP 2003.

58. See excellent overview in 'Does Gender Inequality Reduce Growth and Development?', World Bank Development Research Group November 1999, p. 1.

59. 'Gender Inequality, Income, and Growth; Are Good Times Good for Women?', World Bank Development Research Group, May 1999, p. 21.

60. See summary in 'Does Gender Inequality Reduce Growth and Development?', World Bank Development Research Group, November 1999.

Legal rights: There are large differences between men's and women's right to own and inherit property in many developing countries. Having access to the family plot of land does not always mean that women will also have ownership or control of the land, as discriminatory laws, customs and practices are all too common. In not having basic property rights, women are in a most vulnerable position – they have low 'bargaining power' within the household. Women become dependent on men and will have little say in how resources are used. So while women in many developing countries shoulder most of the household chores and the tending of land for home produce, they are often unable to get credit for small investments or use the proceeds from selling excess produce.

Health care: Gender inequality in health care is abundantly clear in the statistics on child mortality for male and female children in a goodly portion of the developing world (China and South Asia) – more male than female children survive. Social and cultural norms favour sons, which has led to selective abortion, neglect of female children and outright infanticide (= killing of infants). Amartya Sen, the famous Indian development economist and Nobel Laureate, famously asks, 'Where are the missing 100 million women in India and China?!'[61] In addition to access to health care, it is clear that gender inequality in schooling and employment increases the spread of HIV/AIDS, as women are so often powerless within the home and unable to deny the men sex.[62]

The sum of the above is that gender inequality disenables women from partaking in education, civil rights and health care. Furthermore it limits their ability to participate in economic, social and political structures. This in turn will have detrimental effects on the health care and education of children – which in turn will lower future national income and negate development.

Illustrating 'de-development' using a PPF

It is all too often the case in the developing world that both the quality and quantity of production factors *deteriorate* as well. Imagine the change in both actual and potential production in a country plagued by

earthquakes, desertification, war, AIDS, flooding, etc. and that all of this is compounded by a marked lack of all the infrastructural institutions necessary to deal with the disasters – poor emergency health care, few rescue teams, insufficient transport systems, etc. For example, it is estimated that the loss of GNP in Nicaragua attributable to hurricane Mitch which hit in 1998, was roughly $US4.36 billion. In addition to this, there were 5,000 dead, 8,000 missing and over one million people homeless – out of a total population of 6 million where two thirds live in subsistence level poverty.[63]

The (in-?) famous Björn Lomborg, author of *The Skeptical Environmentalist*, got a group of very distinguished economists together in Copenhagen in May 2004 to prioritise the world's greatest problems.[64] The unanimous outcome was that the HIV/AIDS pandemic is the number one issue. I will use this to portray the overwhelming task facing primarily Sub-Saharan Africa, India and China. It is estimated that by 2010 there will be some 46 million people infected in these areas if drastic – and expensive – measures are not taken immediately.[65] Figure 5.3.13 represents a country where the spread of HIV/AIDS has reached 10% of the population (a conservative figure for many areas in Sub-Saharan Africa) and how this affects the economy.

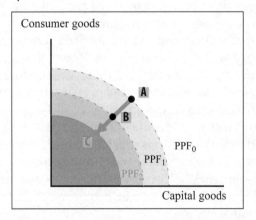

Figure 5.3.13 *'De-development' due to HIV/AIDS*

The effects on an economy suffering from a cataclysmic disease such as HIV/AIDS will have an immediate effect on the economy. According to the 2007 World Development Report, HIV/AIDS might reduce economic growth by close to 20%.[66] Firstly, it

---

61. *Development as freedom*, Amartya Sen, pp. 104– 07.
62. 'Engendering development' (summary), World Bank Policy Research Report 2001, p. 9.
63. See http://globalization.about.com.
64. See http://www.copenhagenconsensus.com and http://www.lomborg.com.
65. *IHT*, 6 July 2002, p. 2.
66. World Development Report 2007, overview, p. 3.

affects the main labour sector of the country, as the disease is spread primarily amongst the young and sexually active. Thus the main factor of production in an LDC economy, labour, is severely weakened. One can also expect a great many labour hours lost as people stay home to care for sick and dying loved ones. The result is that the economy will shrink, i.e. output will fall – moving the economy from **point A** to **point B** and shifting the PPF inwards, from PPF_0 to PPF_1, in Figure 5.3.13 on page 574.

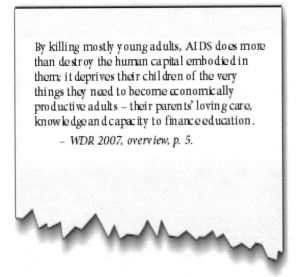

By killing mostly young adults, AIDS does more than destroy the human capital embodied in them; it deprives their children of the very things they need to become economically productive adults – their parents' loving care, knowledge and capacity to finance education.

– WDR 2007, overview, p. 5.

Secondly, the ill and dying will become an immense strain on already inadequate health care systems in many LDCs. This means that there will be an incredible toll on the public purse and a strain on government budgets even further, shifting the PPF inward again, from PPF_1 to PPF_2. Basically, the question will boil down to horrific choices such as 'Shall we close schools to care for the dying or not?' A self-perpetuating circle is created when output falls: incomes fall → tax revenues fall → fewer resources to hospitals, schooling, infrastructure → future actual and potential output falls → incomes fall, etc. all over again.

Thirdly, an increasing number of mothers pass the disease on to their children, which explicitly intensifies the problem of future labour. Simply put, there will be fewer and fewer young people entering the labour market to produce goods for society – and also provide a tax base needed to take care of the funds so desperately needed in health care. This means that the PPF shifts even further to the left from PPF_2. We now see that **potential output is lower than initial de facto output**. This is, unfortunately, not too wild a scenario in reality.

Growth and development strategies

5.4

CONTENTS

GROWTH AND DEVELOPMENT STRATEGIES ©IBO 2003

For every problem there is a solution that is simple, direct and wrong. – H. L. Menken

Harrod–Domar growth model

©IBO 2003

I have been told by a number of development people, as we economists tend to focus a great deal on investment's influence on economic activity, that there is something of an 'investment – savings bias' when we view development strategies. The Harrod–Domar model (named after the two economists who developed the theory) is a case in point, and was actually developed in the 1930s to help explain short-run business cycles and only later adapted to explain long-run economic growth.

Assumptions of the model

The basic model assumes a **closed economy** and an **absence of a government** sector, i.e. there are no exports, imports, government spending or taxes. Therefore all investment must come from domestic savings in order to fund investment since the sum of leakages (S) must equal the sum of injections (I). The model also assumes **no depreciation** of existing capital, so that all investment is **net investment**, i.e. an increase in the capital stock. While the underlying derivation of the model will give you a headache (see "Outside the box: Algebraic base of the Harrod–Domar model" on page 578), the basic logic is very simple; for economic growth to take place, economies must both save and invest. The more saving in a country, the higher the growth rate.

Savings, investment and growth

The theory states that **saving**, **investment** and **productivity of capital** are the central variables in attaining growth, or basically that saving → investment and technological efficiency → growth, which in turn provides income enabling further saving. The growth rate of an economy is determined by the increase in net investment, and the increase in capital is in turn dependent on two variables:

1. The **savings ratio**, **s**, and the level of saving. Assuming saving (S) to be a proportion (s) of national income (Y), then s × Y = S. The higher the ratio of savings, the more out of national income will be saved.

2. The *productivity* of capital in the economy, which is the **capital-output ratio**, **k**. For example, if it takes 10 dollars of capital to produce 2 dollars of output, then the capital-output ratio is 10/2, i.e. 5.

The Harrod–Domar model states that the rate of economic growth, g, is *positively dependent* on the **saving ratio** (s) and *negatively dependent* on the **capital-output ratio** (k).

The Harrod–Domar model is stated as $g = \dfrac{s}{k}$.

> **Harrod–Domar model:** Economic growth depends on saving to fuel investment and economic growth. The **growth rate** $(\Delta Y / Y)$ is given by the ratio between **savings ratio** and the **capital-output ratio**.
>
> Thus: $g = \dfrac{s}{k}$ or $\dfrac{\Delta Y}{Y} = \dfrac{s}{k}$
>
> An increase in the savings ratio: $s\uparrow \rightarrow g\uparrow$
>
> A decrease in the capital-output ratio: $k\downarrow \rightarrow g\uparrow$

Implications of the Harrod–Domar model

Assuming that a country has a saving ratio of 8% and a capital-output ratio of 4, then the growth rate is given by 8% / 4 = 2%. In assuming that there is no foreign sector (and thus that investment cannot be funded via foreign investment) and no government sector, there are two basic ways for growth to occur:

1. An **increase** in the **savings ratio**, ceteris paribus, will yield a higher growth rate. For example, if in the example above, the savings ratio were to increase from 8% to 10%, then growth would increase from 2% (8% / 4) to 2.5% (10% / 4).

2. An **increase** in the (marginal) **productivity of capital** will increase the rate of growth, since the amount of capital needed for each dollar increase in output will fall. So, if instead the capital-output ratio were to *fall* from 4 to 2, then the growth rate would increase from 2% to 4% (8% / 2).

The implications for policy-makers is clear: increase saving and/or increase in the efficiency of capital, i.e. decrease the capital-output ratio. This is a very 'linear' view of development thinking, where one step leads to another in a progressive manner until development takes place. The model was appealing due to its relative simplicity and the fact that it presented clear-cut problems to be dealt with. Since low domestic saving levels in developing countries created a gap between desired levels to fund investment and availability of saving, the solution could be found in aid money and loans from abroad. By filling the savings gap, countries could increase investment levels and attain higher growth rates in order to develop.

Critique of the Harrod–Domar model

The model was influential in the development thinking during the late 1940s and 1950s, and indeed, still influences economic policy and planning today. Yet, according to Evsey Domar, one of the authors, the theory was originally intended to help explain short-run business cycles and never intended to be used as a tool to provide 'an empirically meaningful rate of growth'.[1] This is in line with evidence, as the model has been shown to have neither general application nor success in reality.[2] Three major points of criticism are put forward:

- The main reason for the failure of this growth model, is that while investment is an important precondition for growth, it is by no means **sufficient** in itself in creating growth. The focus on capital neglected the fact that **human capital** is vital in being able to use the machines and technology to its potential. Issues such as infrastructure, institutional capacity and political stability must also be addressed.

- Filling the savings gap (e.g. when domestic savings are less than investment) via loans can lead to very large **foreign debt**. Also, both the foreign loans and domestic savings were subject to **capital flight**, which hampered investment.

- Capital, like all factors, runs into **diminishing returns**. Many countries have had significantly rising investment rates over long periods during which GDP actually fell. This does not support the model's claim that an increase in investment leads to growth.

Outside the box:
Algebraic base of the Harrod–Domar model

Saving must be equal to investment, and since **saving is a proportion**, **s**, of national income, Y, we get:

$S = I$ [1] and so $s \times Y = S$ [2]

which means that $s \times Y = I$ [3]

Since there is **no depreciation**, all investment is an **increase in the capital stock**, **K**.

$$K = I \qquad [4]$$

If each existing dollar value of output needed 5 dollars of capital to produce it, there is a capital-output ratio of 5. If only 3 dollars of capital is needed for each dollar value of output, then the capital-output ratio is 3. Assuming a ratio of 5, an increase in net investment, K, of 100 would increase national income by 20. Denoting the **capital-output ratio** as **k**, we have:

$$k = \frac{K}{Y} \quad [5] \quad \text{and} \quad k = \frac{\Delta K}{\Delta Y} \quad [6]$$

which is the same as $\Delta Y = \frac{\Delta K}{k}$ [7]

which, using an output ratio of 5, reads: 'An **increase in investment** of 100 (K) will give an **increase in national income** (Y) of 20, since the **capital-output ratio** (k) is 5:1.' Total capital stock is thus a proportion of income, i.e. $K = k \times Y$ [8].

Combining [4] and [6] then: $I = K = k \times Y$ [9]

Combining the last part of [9] with [1] and [2] gives:

$$\underbrace{k \times \Delta Y}_{\text{investment}} = \underbrace{s \times Y}_{\text{saving}} \qquad [10]$$

Dividing both sides of equation [10] by Y gives:

$$\frac{k \times \Delta Y}{Y} = \frac{s \times Y}{Y} = s \quad [11]$$

Taking $\frac{k \times \Delta Y}{Y} = s$ and rearranging it gives:

The left-hand side of the equation, $\frac{\Delta Y}{Y}$, is of course, the change in national income, i.e. **growth**, and this is the **Harrod–Domar growth equation**.

$$g = \frac{\Delta Y}{Y} = \frac{s}{k}$$

1. *The Ghost of Financing Gap – How the Harrod-Domar model Still Haunts Development Economics*, William Esterly at the World Bank, 1997, p. 2.

2. In fact, Evsey Domar later largely disavowed his 1946 article which formed part of the basis of the model. See *The Ghost of Financing Gap – How the Harrod–Domar model Still Haunts Development Economics*, William Easterly at the World Bank, 1997, p. 2 (see http://www.worldbank.org).

Structural change/dual sector model ©IBO 2003

Models dealing with structural change focus on how developing countries will undergo structural changes in moving from primary to secondary and tertiary production. This is often referred to as a transformation from a 'traditional' sector to a 'modern' sector. Developing countries will have a large rural economy based on subsistence agriculture and a growing urban sector with secondary and tertiary industries, i.e. a **dual economy**.

Two related issues arise here:

1. Increasing **industrialisation** and productivity will enable increased agricultural output and …

2. … result in **migration** from rural areas to urban – industrialised – areas.

> **Structural change/dual sector model:**
> The structural change school of development thought views economic development as the progressive move from an economy based primarily on agriculture to a capitalist-based **industrialised** economy. The transformation from traditional to modern sector will be closely linked to **rural-urban migration**.

The Lewis model

One of the earliest and most influential models of structural change was put forward by 1979 Nobel Laureate Sir W. Arthur **Lewis** in 1954 and developed during subsequent years. There are three basic assumptions of a developing economy in this model:

1. Two distinct parts of the economy are present side-by-side; a **traditional sector** comprised of primarily agriculture, and a **modern sector** comprised of industries in a capitalist system.

2. **Productivity** in the traditional sector is very low owing to the fact that underemployment is very high – many people will be working land that needs far fewer people to produce the same amount of output. The abundance of labour results in extremely low increase in output when another labourer is added – this is the **marginal productivity of labour**. The marginal productivity of labour is in fact assumed to equal zero. People can leave the land without agricultural output falling, giving a *large surplus pool of labour* available from the traditional sector.

3. The modern sector is found in urban sectors, and is based on industrial output such as processed goods and manufactures. There the **productivity is growing** and firms' profits are assumed to be largely reinvested. Thus there is *increasing demand for labour.*

The conclusions put forward are simple. A large surplus pool of labour in the traditional sector and increasing demand for labour in the modern sector; people will have an incentive to move to the modern, urban, sector. A key point here is that this *migration will not yield opportunity costs* in terms of agricultural output, since the assumption of zero marginal productivity of rural labour means that rural migrants will not lower agricultural output. Thus, marginal workers who are either unemployed or underemployed can be transferred to the modern – higher productivity – sector in urban areas. The emergence of a high productivity modern sector would create conditions for economic growth since:

- **Higher productivity** would lead to higher wages amongst workers in the modern sector. Since low income earners will have a low rate of saving, increased income would *increase the saving rate* and enable **increased investment**.

- Increased **investment** – both from increased saving and due to profits being ploughed back in to the business – would speed the transformation of the economy as more and more workers would be employed in the modern sector. This view, that economic development stems largely from **capital accumulation,** is central to the theory – which indeed builds upon the line of reasoning put forward by the Harrod–Domar model.

- Ultimately in the traditional sector, the **supply of surplus labour will fall** and wages there too will start to rise, since both sectors will now be competing for labour.

Critique of the Lewis model

The Lewis model was a dominant development view in the 1960s and has its strength in trying to find a solution to the saving-investment-income cycle by looking at industrialisation and capitalism as a possibility.[3] The model has some severe limitations, when looked at from the point of view of developing countries' situation in the past 30 years:

---

3. Note: **not** capitalism as an **ideology**! Lewis made very clear that he was largely indifferent to whether capitalism was state directed or private.

- Perhaps the main criticism is that the assumption of **zero marginal productivity of labour** is simply too unrealistic.

- The main weakness is that urban job creation has been far lower than predicted by Lewis and urban **unemployment** is in fact frequently very high.

- In spite of this, there has been **massive rural-urban migration** and **wage differentials** between urban and rural areas remain high.

- Another criticism is that investment in fact does not always create jobs but has been shown to **destroy jobs** as well, when capital intensive, rather than labour intensive production, comes into play.

- A good deal of the earnings of firms has been subject to **capital flight** rather than being ploughed back into domestic investment opportunities.

The Todaro model

While not technically a dual-economy model, the renowned development economist Michael **Todaro** has put forward a model which tries to explain why there is such heavy **migration to urban areas** in spite of the fact that all evidence shows how urban unemployment is very high.

Todaro looks at the **opportunity cost** and **opportunity gain** issues involved in the choice between staying in the **rural sector** and moving to the **urban sector**. Posit that you simply **expect** your wages to be higher in the city – would you move? It would of course depend on how strong your expectations were and the difference in wages. It's a bit like a lottery: if one stands a chance of winning a great deal one might be prepared to pay a higher price for the lottery ticket. So too, reasons Todaro, will people function: as long as the expected wages in urban areas are considerably higher – or just **assumed** to be considerably higher – people will flock to urban areas. The possible gains of employment and good wages make up for the high costs of moving.

Todaro posits therefore that a **rational decision** could be made to move to an urban area as long as the expected earnings are higher than the costs of moving. The expected earnings of migration are not only wages, but the benefits of health care, opportunities and the 'bright lights/big city' atmosphere. These possible gains must be weighed against the costs of moving, such as the money costs of transport, breaking up from family and home, loss of crops and land, and the risk of simply not finding a job.

POP QUIZ 5.4.1   GROWTH MODELS

1 An economy wishes to achieve a growth rate of 3% and has a saving rate of 9%. According to the Harrod–Domar model, what must the capital-output ratio be for this growth to be achieved?

2 How would an improved level of technology in an economy affect the capital-output ratio?

3 What are the possible negative consequences in filling in an investment-saving gap via the foreign sector?

4 Explain why the Lewis model assumes that the availability of labour is limitless during an initial stage of growth.

5 Why does the Lewis model foresee that wage differences between the traditional sector and the modern sector would ultimately be zero?

Types of aid   ©IBO 2003

There are a number of ways for developed countries to assist developing countries, many of which are along the lines of 'win-win', such as trade, FDI and development loans (see Figure 5.4.1). There are also any number of organisations which seek to help by way of development assistance, a somewhat less value-laden term for aid. This chapter looks at some of the various ways in which people, organisations and governments assist in the development process.

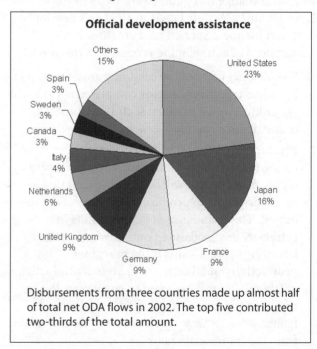

Disbursements from three countries made up almost half of total net ODA flows in 2002. The top five contributed two-thirds of the total amount.

(Source: World Bank, World Development Indicators, 2004)

Figure 5.4.1 *Overview of official development assistance (ODA) – largest net donors, 2002*

A few statistics on aid – comparative eye-openers

At the time of writing, March 2009, the world is in severe economic crisis and every government in the developed world is putting together 'rescue packages' to save financial institutions and/or stimulate domestic economies via government spending. The US president Obama has put through a USD787 billion 'rescue package' to combat rapidly rising unemployment and falling GDP. Allow me to put these billions into a bit of perspective.

Aid and income

Looking at the issue of development aid with an initial 'wide-angle' lens, **official development assistance**, ODA, from the 28 major donor countries in the OECD

decreased by 14% between 1990 and 2000 in real per capita terms.[4] ODA comprises a major portion of total inflows in the poorest countries, for example, total ODA for Sub-Saharan Africa is a staggering 90% of net capital inflows.[5] This happened during a time period where per capita national income in donor countries increased substantially, as illustrated in Figure 5.4.2.

In dollar terms (2000 values) total ODA in 2000 was USD54 billion, or 0.14% of GNP. Total ODA for the top 22 donor countries represented 0.22% of GNP for the donor countries – down from 0.33% ten years earlier.[6]

In dollar terms (2000 values) total ODA in 2000 was USD54 billion, or 0.14% of GNP. Total ODA for the top 22 donor countries represented 0.22% of GNP for the donor countries – down from 0.33% ten years earlier.[7]

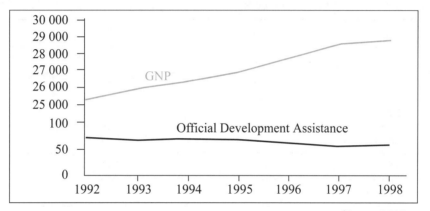

(Source: WDR 2001, p. 190)

Figure 5.4.2 *Per capita GNP and ODA for donor countries 1992–98*

Aid and agricultural subsidies

Figure 5.4.3 diagrams I and II compare the USD54 billion with agricultural subsidies in OECD countries. Comments are sadly superfluous.

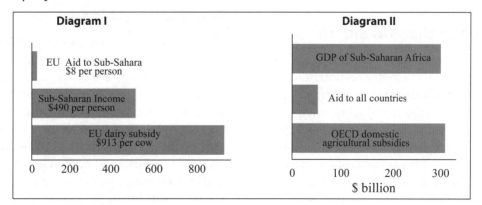

(Source: *HDR 2003* pp. 155–56)

Figure 5.4.3 *Aid and agricultural subsidies 2000 and 2001*

4. *HDR 2002*, table 15, p. 202.

5. *HDR 2005*, Occasional Paper 'Assessing rhetoric and reality in the predictability of aid', p. 3 at http://hdr.undp.org/en/reports/global/hdr2005/papers/HDR2005_Ruth_Vargas_Hill_25.pdf.

6. See OECD at http://www.oecd.org/dataoecd/42/61/31504039.pdf.

7. See OECD at http://www.oecd.org/dataoecd/42/61/31504039.pdf.

Aid and military spending

I can't remember where I read it, but there's a great and poignant (= moving) quote on the 'guns or butter' issue in developing countries: 'There never seem to be enough trucks to transport food to famine stricken areas – but somehow there are always trucks available to transport arms.' I don't need to spend 45 minutes

going through data from UNHCR to know the sad truth of this. On the donor side, the pattern is depressingly similar for some of the richest and most powerful countries in the world, where military spending as a ratio of ODA in extreme cases goes from 10:1 (Italy) to over 25:1 (USA).[8] Table 5.4.1 shows the top military spenders in 2007.

Table 5.4.1 *Top military and ODA spenders 2007*

Country	In $US Billions		Military spending as % of GNI	ODA as % of GNI
	Military spending	ODA		
US	547	21.7	4.3	0.16
UK	59.7	9.92	2.6	0.36
China	58.3	unavailable	2.6	unavailable
France	53.6	9.94	2.5	0.39
Japan	43.6	7.69	0.9	0.17
Norway	4.9	3.72	1.6	0.95
Sweden	5.2	4.33	1.4	0.93
Luxembourg	319 million	365 million	1.1	0.90
Netherlands	9.8	6.21	1.5	0.81
Denmark	3.6	2.56	1.3	0.81
Total	**$786.109**	**$66.435**	**19.8%**	**5.48%**

(Source: *Military spending and Finance for Development*, Nicola Winter, International Peace Bureau, 2008, p. 12)

If one looks at the US, military spending is 26.8 times higher than official aid as a percentage of gross national income. France, a distant second, spends 6.4 times more of national income on the military than ODA.

Bilateral and multilateral aid ©IBO 2003

Bilateral is literally 'two sides', so in the case of aid it is one country giving support to another country directly. **Bilateral aid** is commonly done via direct money support, shipments of machines and tools, emergency aid such as food, medicines and temporary housing, and experts who are sent to help in building dams or setting up road projects. Bilateral aid is often targeted at countries due to political considerations and/or historical ties – see below.

Conversely, multilateral means 'many sides'. When the World Health Organisation, UNESCO[9] (both UN agencies) and the World Bank disburse funds which

come from donor countries one speaks of **multilateral aid**. A multilateral organisation is thus allocating funds rather than the country providing the funds.

Grant aid, soft loans ©IBO 2003

There is a somewhat bewildering variety of terms for aid – basically it's another umbrella concept (e.g. 'covers a lot of different concepts'). Aid can be defined as any non-commercial and non-military flow of funds to a developing country. **Grant aid** is a 'gift' of money, goods, capital, etc. for which there is **no reciprocal agreement** or strings attached. When money is lent on favourable terms, i.e. at interest lower than market rates and/or with longer amortisation periods – then one speaks of **soft loans**. Such loans are frequently managed by the International Bank for Reconstruction and Development (IBRD) – more commonly known as the World Bank – and other national development banks.

8. Sachs, *The End of Poverty*, p. 330.
9. United Nations Educational, Scientific and Cultural Organisation.

Official aid ©IBO 2003

Official aid, often referred to as **official development assistance** (ODA) is the sum of bilateral and multilateral aid, thus comprising all aid forms not coming from charities such as Oxfam and religious organisations. The United Nations (UN) has a target aid objective that wealthy donor countries should donate a minimum of 0.7% of GNP per year. Figure 5.4.4 shows a selection of the wealthiest

countries in the world – few of which meet the UN aid target. In fact, only five countries have fulfilled the UN objective: Luxembourg, the Netherlands, Norway, Sweden and Denmark. Another notable item is that while US aid is the highest aid contribution in (absolute) money terms, it is the proportionately least amount of all. Japan as number two in absolute terms is third from last in relative terms.

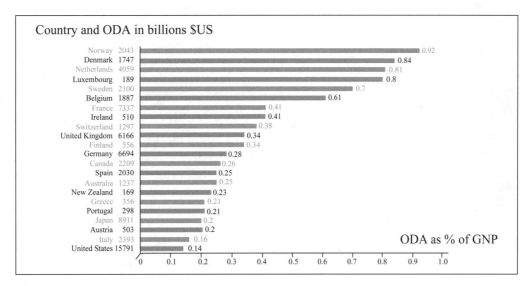

(Source: OECD statistics at http://www.oecd.org/dataoecd/42/61/31504039.pdf)

Figure 5.4.4 *Official development assistance 2003 (ODA)*

Tied aid ©IBO 2003

There is a simple method for tackling the waste of money associated with tied aid: stop it in 2006. – Human Development Report 2005, p. 9)

Bilateral aid is frequently in the form of **reciprocal agreements** between donor and recipient countries, known as **tied aid**. It's a bit like 'I'll scratch your back if you scratch mine', but more along the lines of 'We would be happy to help your country build a new airport – oh, and incidentally, you might also be in the market for some very nice fighter jets that my country happens to produce!' OK, I'm being facetious again, but this is in fact pretty much what happened when Sweden offered a few hundred million US dollars in assistance to South Africa in the 1990s. You didn't think SAAB only made safe/ugly cars did you?

Tied aid is in fact seldom as nasty as I've portrayed it (see Figure 5.4.5), but I can resist anything except temptation.[10] Most tied aid is in fact simply a form of agreement between donor and recipient nations, where loans or direct money to the recipient is to be used on goods and services from the donor country. Since the donor country sees an increase in exports and the aid is disbursed, one might say that something of a win–win outcome is possible. It depends, for the most part, on what kinds of strings are attached and where the aid is going – as in all cases of aid. One major criticism of tied aid is that the **cost of the reciprocal goods** and services purchased by the developing country can be far higher than when purchased on a competitive market. The OECD estimates that the average cost of such tied-aid goods is 20% to 25% higher.[11] The UNDP estimated that yearly losses due to tied aid amount to between USD5 to USD7 billion – enough to fund primary education in all developing countries.[12]

---

10. ... and misquotations. This was of course said by Oscar Wilde.

11. See http://www.oecd.org/document/44/0,2340,fr_2649_201185_1915628_119690_1_1_1,00.html.

12. *UDR* 2005, p. 119.

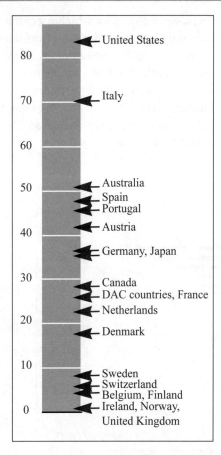

(Source: *HDR 2005*, p. 102)

Figure 5.4.5 *Tied aid as a percentage of total ODA (2002–03)*

Export-led growth/outward-oriented strategies ©IBO 2003

One option which a number of developing countries have chosen is to concentrate on producing goods specifically aimed at export markets. Generally, such a strategy involves focusing on industrialisation and opening the economy by moving towards free (-r) trade and free (-r) capital flows from abroad. Countries such as South Korea, Singapore, Hong Kong, Taiwan (the 'Asian Tiger' economies) and Malaysia have shown phenomenal growth rates since the 1960s – over 7% on average during the past 40 years compared to 2% to 3% for the US and Europe – most of which is attributable to strong export-led/outward-oriented policies. India and China have had growth rates of between 6 and 9% during the 1990s due to increased liberalisation in trade and investment flows.

Characteristics of outward-oriented strategies

These **newly industrialised countries, NICs**, are of course very diverse and have great differences in trade policies and levels of government intervention. Yet there are a number of broad characteristics of countries which have adopted an outward strategy:

- In order for increased trade to take place, **trade barriers are lowered** on goods and services. Yet one should take care in claiming that all barriers for all goods have been lowered in outward oriented countries. In fact, several of the Tiger Economies have been rather protectionist initially, targeting certain central industries for **infant industry protection**. For example, during a period of extreme growth in the mid-1980s, average protection rates in the Tiger Economies was still 24%.[13]

- **Capital markets** are opened and regulations on capital flows are relaxed. This facilitates inward portfolio and direct investment by foreign firms – often multinationals. All of the NICs have been open to inward investment flows and attracted a great deal of direct investment from foreign multinational companies.

- In most cases there has been a focus on goods which are **labour intensive** in manufacturing, such as shoes, leather goods and apparel, i.e. the economy has concentrated on goods for which there is a **competitive advantage**.

- **Government involvement** has been notably strong – contrary to many beliefs on the 'free market' content of the NICs. (Do not confuse 'laissez faire' with market-based policies. Both Korea, Singapore, Taiwan and Japan have been strongly market-based economies but with a notoriously strong element of government planning.) A variety of government policies have supported investment and industries: production and export subsidies to key industries; land grants; soft loans; and generous tax write-offs for profits ploughed back into investment. Thus it should be noted that while there is indeed correlation between trade and economic growth, there is wide disagreement as to which came first. Several economists conclude that the success of Asian outward oriented countries in trade might well be primarily the result of **interventionist policies** and strong **saving**, **investment** and focus on **education**.

There are numerous other export-promoting methods which developing countries can apply. For example, the currency can be kept artificially low to promote exports

---

13. Krugman & Obstfeld, p. 268.

and deflect imports, tariffs on much needed factor imports can be removed, and the establishment of 'free trade zones' and industrial parks for export firms.

Reasons for outward-oriented strategies

A glance at the size of Hong Kong, Singapore and Taiwan provides a clue as to why an outward oriented strategy of growth was adopted; small populations and therefore **small domestic markets**. Yet even Korea, with its 46 million people, had a mere fraction of the potential markets available when the US and Europe were included. From Adam Smith onward, economists have pointed out that market size matters. Here are a few notable points on how an outward oriented strategy can benefit a country:

- *Increase in export revenue*: Increased exports as seen in the NICs have had an immense impact on the domestic economy. Exports grew at an average rate of between 8% and 20% between the 1960s and 2000 in the NICs, and most of the exports are manufactures.[14] This has been a tremendous boon to the domestic economies – for example, the proportion of exports to GDP in Korea went from just 2.4% in 1962 to 42% in 1999.[15]

- *Benefits of scale*: When the size of the market increases due to open markets, then it becomes possible for small countries to establish economically viable plant sizes to compete internationally. Longer production runs, better use of resources and the spreading of fixed costs are examples of how the **average costs fall** for firms increasing the scale of operation.

Figure 5.4.6 on page 585 shows how average costs in an industry continuously fall as scale benefits rise. As the industry **output increases faster than additional costs**, the average cost of each unit falls. This renders the long run average cost (LRAC) curve shown in the diagram. A developing country at point **A** will not be able to compete with international – foreign – competitors, so it must seek to move towards point **C** in order to have an export competitive price. In order to initially move towards point B, the country might subsidise its industries and/or impose trade barriers on imports. This is the classic **infant industry argument** in support of an outward-oriented policy.

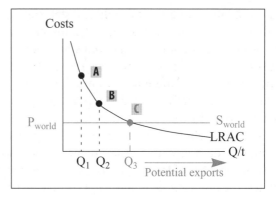

Figure 5.4.6 *Falling long run average costs (LRAC) in an industry*

- *Increased competition*: When a country competes internationally, there will be far more incentive for domestic suppliers to increase efficiency and produce quality goods, rendering dynamic gains over time.

- *Additional resources*: An outward-oriented country stands to benefit not only from increased exports but from increased imports, i.e. raw material, components and intermediary goods needed in production. About two-thirds of all manufacturing output is sold as inputs to other firms, which means that access to global networks of suppliers lowers production costs.

- *Technology transfers*: In addition to this, there is technological transfer, both in the form of capital and in the form of knowledge and experience imparted by foreign firms' direct investment inflows.

Successes or failures?

The relative success or failure of outward oriented policies is part of the globalisation issue and thus subject to a heated debate. I would, however, dare say that the majority of economists would judge outward-orientation a success on the whole. For example, Ghana had roughly the same GDP per capita as South Korea in the 1960s, and by 1996 Korea had joined the 'rich man's club', the OECD, having increased per capita income by a factor of 9.[16] The figures for the other Asian Tigers are similar and relative late-comers have also shows strong growth: China had 8% to 10% growth rates during most of the 1980s and 1990s and India's growth has been around 7%. Both countries have seen this growth after large-scale reforms to increase openness and remove policies which hampered trade – China in the early 1980s and India some 10 years later.

---

14. *World Development Indicators*, World Bank 2002.
15. Legrain, p. 69.
16. Norberg, p. 62.

It would be wonderful if I could just stop right here, but there is, of course, another side. A number of issues have been raised in opposition to outward oriented policies, many of which you will have studied in Section 4: **low wage and environmental policies** might be intentionally set by developing countries in order to attract foreign investment, leading to exploitation of labour and environmental degradation; dependency on multinational companies could lead to the empowerment of foreign businesses over **domestic policies**; the domestic economy for a strongly export oriented country would be **dependent** on international business cycles, and **speculative inflows** can have devastating effects on the economy such as the 1997 Asian Crisis (see Case study: "Southeast Asian crisis of 1997–98" on page 501).

Yet perhaps the main problem is simply that developing countries opening up to trade will initially be far from competitive, and opening their economies along the lines of free trade will **threaten domestic output** and employment as very efficient foreign suppliers enter the market. For this reason, many economists consider that there is merit in limited – infant industry – trade barriers. There is also scant supporting evidence that what works in one country will inevitably work in another. Once again, the relative success or failure of a development strategy does not stand alone but depends on all the other factors which enable development. Korea and Singapore were remarkably successful because the tax revenues from growth were to a large extent immediately poured back

into **education**. In addition to this were high saving rates which contributed to investment; a relatively high rate of initial literacy; and political stability – all of which were noticeably lacking in a number of other developing countries.

Import-substitution/inward-oriented strategies/protectionism

©IBO 2003

During the 1950s and 1960s a number of countries attempted to industrialise by substituting imported goods with domestically produced goods. The basic strategy of **import-substitution** is to implement barriers to imports, e.g. tariffs, while perhaps also encouraging domestic producers with subsidies. (This of course requires that there are government funds available.) The rationale is that increased demand for domestic goods will move domestic industries along a learning curve so that they can ultimately compete on equal ground with foreign firms.

Diagrams I and II in Figure 5.4.7 show the range of possibilities for a developing country implementing import restrictions (or protectionist policies) as a step in inward oriented policies. Diagram I illustrates how a **tariff** can reduce imports and increase domestic output. Domestic output is initially zero and imports are Q_{D_0}; a tariff of $S_{world+tariff}$ will lower imports to $Q_S \Leftrightarrow Q_{D_1}$. Domestic production increases accordingly to Q_S.

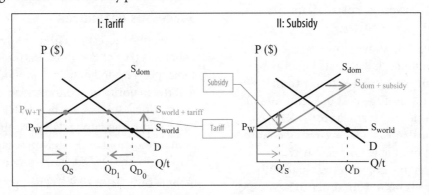

Figure 5.4.7 *Tariff and subsidy possibilities in import-substitution*

It is also possible that tariff protection is mixed with a degree of domestic subsidies. Diagram II in Figure 5.4.7 illustrates how a subsidy increases domestic output from zero to Q's. Note that this solution results in the same increase in domestic output as the tariff rate in diagram I, but that the increase in domestic production due to a subsidy does not increase the market price.

Whatever protectionist mix government ultimately decides on, the aim is to increase output to the point where benefits of scale arise, i.e. where unit costs fall due to larger production scale. This is illustrated in Figure 5.4.6 on page 585, as a movement along the long-run average cost curve (LRAC). When the domestic industry becomes competitive at an international level, point C, tariffs and other barriers can be successively removed as the industry can now stand on its own feet.

As the outward-oriented industrial development strategy is often based on infant industry trade barriers allowing firms to achieve scale economies behind protectionist walls, inward oriented policies might be expected to function better in countries with **large inner markets**, such as China and India. Indeed, these two countries had inward-oriented strategies for decades but abandoned this path in the 1980s and 1990s respectively. The growth rates of these two countries – which make up over half of the population in the developing world – escalated considerably after opening up to trade. For example, 30 years of inward orientation in India between 1950 and 1980 rendered an average per capita growth rate of around 1.5% per year – a rate that has been beaten by a factor of 3 during *any single year* since 1992 when trade liberalisation policies took effect. By 2004, India's economy had doubled in real terms.[17]

Failure of import-substitution

There is a great deal of controversy concerning the degree to which outward oriented policies are the main source of the growth differences. A frequently referred-to example is that, during the 1950s, Korea and India had very similar per capita incomes yet in the following two decades Korea grew at a far faster pace – and the other three Asian Tigers (Taiwan, Singapore and Hong Kong) grew even faster than Korea. The conclusion is that the outward-oriented policies of the Asian Tigers have been far more efficient in terms of growth than India's strongly inward oriented policies up to the 1990s. Yet some economists attribute considerable weight to the protectionist and government interventionist policies of the Tigers.[18] There was also a strong *political* element in many developing countries' choice between inward and outward-orientation; many developing countries wished to prove their independence from western – often colonial – powers.

Whatever the actual cause of the growth differences between outward-oriented countries and inward oriented countries, the fact remains that most countries that pursued the latter **failed to achieve substantial growth or development**:[19]

- The main failing was probably due to **lack of competition**. Domestic firms produced high-priced and shoddy goods – which did little for the domestic economy and even less for potential exports. Nor have governments been particularly adept at choosing the right industries to protect and subsidise. India's 'National Champions' of domestic industry have been competitive failures in almost every case.

- Import restrictions were often far **lower on capital goods**, since these were needed in domestic production. This limited the creation of employment and thus income which could fuel consumption and saving/investment. This also countermands the entire foundation of **comparative advantage**, as goods which are labour intensive will be disadvantaged when use of capital is favoured by government policy. Additionally, capital is often imported, as are components for upkeep/renovation/repairs and labour skills required for assembly and service – all of which will burden the **current account** in the balance of payments.

- Another factor was pure outright **corruption**; protected economies will unerringly create smuggling, tax evasion and bribery.

- A great deal of industrial output is used as inputs in other industries. By levying tariffs on imports needed for production, costs will rise for domestic producers; this is the **forward linkage effect**.

All the above contribute to slow growth and low proportion of exports relative to GDP. For example, Brazil has had a notable policy of promoting domestic production by curtailing imports, and has seen how exports have remained pretty much unchanged (around 7% of GDP) between 1970 and 1998.[20] However, it is worth noting that the line between an import-substitution and export led strategy is very fine when you consider that a good many outward oriented countries implemented infant industry trade barriers and export subsidies. What stands out is that countries which focused on import substitution as a **main** strategy of growth in most cases opted out in the 1980s and 1990s, in order to put emphasis on markedly outward-oriented policies.

---

17. See http://in.rediff.com/money/2004/jan/24wef1.htm.
18. See, for example, Todaro & Smith, pp. 620–53.
19. See, for example, 'Once more into the breach: economic growth and global integration', Center for Global Development, Working paper no 34, December 2002, p. 33.
20. Irwin, pp. 76–78. It should be noted that Brazil in fact has had a markedly outward oriented strategy for **primary goods** – which have fallen drastically in price and thus not enabled an increase in export revenue.

POP QUIZ 5.4.2   DEVELOPMENT AID

1   What is the main difference between bilateral and multilateral aid?

2   Why might a developing country actually be disadvantaged by tied aid?

3   'An outward-oriented strategy means that a country moves towards free trade.' Discuss this statement.

4   Why might an export-oriented strategy appeal to smaller countries?

5   Why was the strategy of import-substitution generally abandoned in most developing countries in the 1980s and 1990s?

Commercial loans ©IBO 2003

Commercial loans provide liquidity to the business sector by transferring savings. As such, commercial loans are a most valuable element in economies based on a market/capitalist system of production. The availability of credit via commercial banks is often overlooked, but has received increasing attention in development economics.

Commercial loans and development

Foreign banks primarily cater to **international firms** and **large domestic enterprises** in developing countries. In addition, domestic banks in will often be operating under a situation of severe shortage of loanable funds and therefore also focus on medium to large firms. The lack of credit for start-up firms and potential entrepreneurs has a negative effect on growth, income and thus saving – which is needed to recycle the loan carousel. There is increasing evidence that the presence of foreign banks in developing countries in fact helps to create a sounder investment infrastructure, by providing an increased asset base in the domestic financial infrastructure, and better practices.[21]

The weaknesses of commercial lending institutions in developing countries will limit the amount of available credit on the official markets. Poor people who need a small loan to buy a mule or a small community looking to install a water pump will not be serviced by the major banks. This gap in capital flows often drives the poorest and therefore most vulnerable people into the arms of loan sharks (illegal money lenders) who for the most part charge absolutely horrendous interest rates of between 10 to 20% ... per **day**. This strengthens the gap between the formal and informal markets and perpetuates a **dual economy**.

To fully understand the significance of private-sector lending, it is necessary to look at how commercial banks fit into the overall **macro** structure of a modern economy, and how the lack of banks in developing countries is so detrimental to economic growth and development. This is done in the next section.

Micro-credit schemes ©IBO 2003

A method of financing small scale projects and thus supplying liquidity to the millions of people with scant assets in developing countries is **micro-credit schemes**. The most famous example is the **Grameen Bank** in Bangladesh which serves poor people – primarily women – who establish small credit groups of five people which together are responsible for the loans. By 2004, around 12 million women in Bangladesh were borrowers of some USD1.2 billion and the bank has a loan recovery rate of 90%.[22] Due to the success, clearly evident in the 1980s, the idea took off during the 1990s and similar schemes are now to be found all over the developing world.

The typical 'Grameen Bank Replication', as they are often called, targets the poorest groups in society – people who would normally not qualify for loans at a bank. The approach is unlike normal banking business; bank workers spend a great deal of time in rural communities informing people of the program and taking applications. The entire idea rests on the **group pressure** arising within the credit groups, as no collateral is offered by the borrowers. Credit groups that qualify can then borrow small sums of money – usually less than USD100 – which is then repaid on a weekly basis. Interest rates are commonly 2% to 3% per month which is higher than commercial banks but considerably lower than loan sharks' rates. The percentage goes to pay the wages of the community bank workers and no more.[23]

A number of micro-credit schemes other that Grameen Bank Replications operate along similar lines, often under the hat of non-government organisations (NGOs) and credit unions. Increasingly, the 'bank branches' of these NGOs have become self-

---

21. 'Globalization, growth and poverty', World Bank 2002, p. 73 ff.

22. 'World Bank praises Bangladesh for its progress in past 20 years', *Indian Times* 12 April 2004.

23. See the Global Development Research Center at http://www.gdrc.org/icm/inspire/gb-choice.html, and also OneWorld at www.oneworld.net.

sustaining rather than as previously relying on donor funds and concessions. The success of the micro-credit schemes rests in part on the fact that the majority of loans are aimed at women, the logic being that women are most likely to spend the money on strengthening the family by using the money for food, education and health care. Another aspect is that a good many women are capable of providing for their families once they have some initial start-up capital and are highly committed to repaying loans in order to have access to future loans.

While micro-credit is in no way a 'miracle cure' for poverty, it has shown to be a most cost-efficient method of getting entrepreneurial spirit out of the bottle. It is also allocatively efficient – who better than the poor themselves will know where best to use USD20? Micro-credit enables those without assets to have access to small amounts of credit which can make a great difference to impoverished people only too willing to work their way out of poverty. Have a look at a few success stories at the Global Development Research Center: http://www.gdrc.org/icm/human/human-angle.html.

Fair trade organisations ©IBO 2003

Fair trade organisations can be loosely defined as alternatives to the prevalent world trading system – and I use the term 'loosely' advisedly, since definitions vary somewhat. The general idea is that developing countries' producers are to a large extent poor people who do not get a 'fair' price for their produce. Instead, the brunt of the profits goes to middle-men along the supply chain towards the consumers in developed countries. Fair trade according to these organisations will often encompass three basic points:

1. Producers should get a **'fair' price** for their product. This is frequently defined as a minimum wage or at least a 'liveable' wage enabling basic foodstuffs, education and housing. One of the original fair trade organisations, **Oxfam**, has outlined a fair trade **floor** price for coffee of USD1.26 per pound, which is 3 to 4 times as much as the international system would give them.[24]

2. The organisation of the supply-chain cuts out most of the middle-men. The basic idea is for the producer to get a larger share of the **final consumer price** – not for the final price to be higher.

3. There is a focus on **environmental sustainability** and **labour rights** in many of the fair trade organisations. Organic production is emphasized and encouraged and many of the labelling schemes include such guarantees. A fair trade organisation will commonly undersign the principles of labour rights set out by the International Labour Organisation, ILO, such as rules on child labour and the right to organise labour unions.

The idea of fair trade thus goes beyond simple price structures and profit margins, as there is clearly an element of ethical and ecological ambition in both production and purchasing. This is incorporated in the brand imaging of the product. Consumers should be able to identify and trust products which are labelled as fair trade goods. The Fairtrade Labelling Organisations International is an umbrella group which gathers a number of national organisations under each countries' fair trade labels, for example, TransFair in Austria, Canada and Germany, Max Havelaar in Belgium, France and Norway, and Fairtrade Foundations in the UK and Ireland.[25]

The main products supported by free trade organisations are primarily to be found in cash crop commodities, e.g. coffee, tea, sugar and cocoa. Manufactured goods include textiles, furniture and jewellery. There is scant statistical material available, but the Fair Trade Federation estimates that 0.1% of all international trade (USD400) is sold under fair trade conditions outlined above.[26]

Foreign direct investment ©IBO 2003

Foreign direct investment is undertaken by **multinational companies**[27], defined as companies that have production in several countries – and the debate on both foreign direct investment and multinational companies rages on undiminished. (See "Globalisation" on page 439). The main bone of contention is whether multinational companies are pro- or anti-developmental. This issue will be looked at in some depth in the next section. Here the focus is on the *extent* of foreign direct investment, the *reasons* for it, and the *importance* of these capital flows for less developed countries.

---

24. See http://www.oxfamamerica.org/campaigncoffee/art3391.html.

25. An excellent overview is available at http://en.wikipedia.org/wiki/Fair_trade.

26. See http://www.fairtradefederation.com/ab_facts.html.

27. Also known as multinational enterprises, multinational corporations, transnational corporations, and a few other variants. These terms are subject to fads basically, and seem to have the life expectancy of my marriages.

Overview of global FDI

A number of factors combined during the 1980s and 1990s to dramatically increase the flows of foreign capital to developing countries. The switch from inward oriented to outward oriented strategies invited more foreign capital. The GATT rounds lowered tariffs and increased trade, which in turn encouraged multinational companies to seek lower cost opportunities for production, and decreased regulation on capital flows enabled them to set up subsidiaries abroad. The increase in free trade areas provided an incentive for international firms to 'tunnel under' tariff walls by establishing production and sales networks within the FTA barriers. Finally, one should not underestimate the effects of the demise of the Soviet Union and the end of the cold war in the early 1990s, as this cut off a great deal of politically motivated US and Soviet aid which in turn prompted more countries to look at foreign direct investment (FDI) as an alternative.

The amount of foreign owned capital in less developed countries doubled between the early 1970s and 1998, amounting to 22% of GDP. Figure 5.4.8 shows how foreign direct investment increased dramatically after 1990, while official aid declined before peaking towards the end of the 1990s.

The top 12 receiving countries, such as China, India, Mexico and Brazil, account for most of the inward flows of foreign direct investment, and the 'triad' of the US, EU and Japan account for most of the outward flows, about 82%. Over 60,000 multinational companies invested over 1.24 trillion abroad in 2000, with a little over a fifth of this going to less developed countries. The top 30 countries – mainly industrialised countries – account for 95% of world FDI inflows and 99% of outflows, and the US alone holds one-third of all foreign assets in the world.[28] Sub-Saharan Africa received 1.2% of **all** flows to developing countries in 1998.[29] Taken together, these statistics give a rather strong indication of the highly unequal distribution of foreign direct investment.

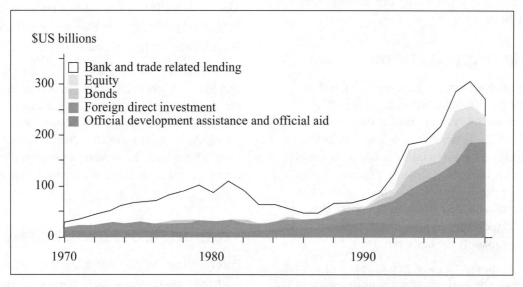

(Source: 'Globalization, growth and poverty', World Bank 2002, p. 42)

Figure 5.4.8 *Total net flows of capital to LDCs 1970–98*

Reasons for FDI

There are a number of compelling reasons for firms to invest in other countries, and it should be noted that such reasons deal with revenue and profit – not development. Firms are not in business to create welfare and equality but to make money for owners and shareholders. So while it is increasingly common for multinational firms to adopt a stance of 'corporate citizenship' and 'corporate social responsibility', this is

for the most part simply good marketing in the face of increasing opposition to multinational corporations. I am not being cynical or playing down any of the positive aspects arising from FDI and/or multinational companies, but simply pointing out that the aims of firms are not the same as those of development institutions.

---

28. *World investment report 2001*; UNCTAD, pp. 9, 12 and 95.
29. *WDR 2001*, p. 190.

Firms investing directly abroad stand to gain on a number of counts: *Niederlassungen*

- By setting up subsidiaries abroad, multinational companies gain access to **lower cost factors** of production, primarily raw materials and labour.

- Companies which sell internationally will also be able to better **monitor consumer tastes** and preferences in order to adapt their wares internationally.

- Setting up both production and sales units within free trade areas will enable companies to **avoid tariffs** and other trade barriers.

- There are **logistical reasons** sometimes. A country well placed geographically can be used as a central supplier for surrounding regions.

- **Lower taxes** on labour, capital and profits will attract foreign direct investment.

- Firms producing environmentally hazardous goods might seek out countries with **low environmental standards** (a textbook argument largely refuted by empirical evidence.)

The importance of FDI in developing countries

Total capital flows to less developed countries grew throughout the 1990s but the composition of these flows changed dramatically, as Figure 5.4.8 on page 590 shows. Official flows decreased by more than 50% and private capital flows are now the major source of inflows to developing countries. These flows of foreign capital can considerable impact on developing countries. While the results of FDI are contentious, the following points illustrate the *potential* benefits of foreign direct investment in less developed countries:

- Perhaps the main benefit of foreign direct investment for a developing country is that the **investment gap** between savings potential and investment need can be filled. This can be linked to the Harrod–Domar theory of growth, where a desired growth rate (g) can be attained by increasing the ratio between the proportion of GDP going to saving (s) and the capital-output ratio (k), i.e. g = s / k. If the aim is a growth rate of 6% and the capital-output ratio is 3, then a savings ratio of 18% of GDP is needed. If the domestic saving ratio is only 10%, foreign direct investment can help fill the gap.

- FDI provides a 'one off' **increase in foreign currency** when the investment takes place, and can contribute to **export earnings** of foreign currencies.

Unfortunately, there are often successive outflows from host countries as profits are repatriated back to headquarters in a developed country.

- Foreign firms create jobs and **provide tax revenue** for host governments in less developed countries. Labour, income and profit taxes will all contribute to much-needed spending on infrastructure, health care and education.

- Increased economic activity will have **secondary effects** on the host economy, as local parts manufacturers, builders, service providers, etc. are needed. Additionally, the increase in incomes for workers will fuel demand for other goods and help generate an increase in aggregate demand. (HL should recognise these *multiplicative effects*.)

- The presence of highly efficient multinationals can have a stimulatory effect on **competition** and therefore efficiency in developing countries, ultimately pushing down costs for domestic firms and improving resource allocation. There are also scale benefits to be considered. Yet a number of worrying effects of multinationals are evident and will be looked at in the next section.

- Foreign direct investment to a developing country is often not a simple transfer of money, equipment and managers, but a **transfer of technology, knowledge and skills**. By increasing the level of sophistication in the use of technology, a developing country will ultimately increase its technological level though training programs and 'learning by doing'. Skilled labour from abroad can educate local workers and help ease a skill-constraint found in many less developed countries.

Many of the possibilities above will of course not present themselves to all recipient countries and there is considerable scope for criticism. Yet the World Bank has found that while there are indeed a number of cautionary notes within the field of FDI, there is increasingly strong evidence of the **positive growth effects** of FDI inflows. Point in fact: FDI in developing countries would appear to have a much stronger effect on economic growth than the overall level of investment. In other words, **foreign** investment seems to have a greater effect on growth than **domestic investment**. Instead, other domestic factors such as education and infrastructure seem to have a greater impact on growth than domestic investment.[30] (See Section 5.5 under 'Multinational corporations' for discussion on the negative effects of FDI and multinational companies.)

---

30. 'Globalization, growth and poverty', World Bank 2002, p. 43.

Outside the box:
The marginalisation of Africa

While most other developing areas in the world have seen an increase in FDI inflows during the latter part of the 1990s, Africa was the exception, receiving less than 1% of all FDI during 2000.[31] Africa – and primarily Sub-Saharan Africa – has been a notable outsider in the ongoing process of globalisation. One wonders why. The World Bank asks the same question in its report from 2002, 'Globalization, growth and poverty' and considers three views:[32]

1. They have been unable to use their **comparative advantage** in abundant labour due to poor infrastructure, weak institutions, low education levels and political instability. This 'Join the Club' view[33] puts forward that when these issues start to be resolved, Africa will join in the ongoing process of global integration called globalisation.

2. Another view is that yes, Africa hasn't joined the club – and might well in fact have '**missed the boat**'. Even if the institutional, infrastructural and political problems were largely solved, the fact is that globalised production patterns are becoming more set by the day and abundant African labour simply might not be needed.

The third view takes a standpoint that many African countries suffer from a basic **geographic disadvantage**. Malaria and a number of other diseases limit tourism, as do harsh climates and lack of water in many instances. Huge distances and many landlocked countries with poor transportation networks and communications infrastructure have a resounding impact on trade and the costs of doing business.

Sustainable development ©IBO 2003

Whether growth and development are sustainable in the long run is one of the most daunting issues we face. The World Bank has long since recognised this and the annual World Development Reports of 1993 and 2003 are devoted to this topic. The core questions can be put in economic terms by first positing the following:

- Growth and development are based on using resources. Some of these resources are **renewable** and **expandable**, such as human resources. Other resources are **limited** and/or **non-renewable**, trees and land as an example of the former and oil as an example of the latter. A third group, **capital**, is a combination of the two.

- These resources are complementary and to a certain extent **substitutable**; capital use and improved technology can increase output for any given use of limited/non-renewable resources.

During early stages of development, the present-day developed countries drew heavily on limited and non-renewable resources. In later stages, fixed and human capital replaced an increasing amount of these limited resource, i.e. wealthy countries increased output for any given amount of input. For example, the world produced twice the money value of output per unit of energy input in 1992 compared to 20 years earlier.[34] These efficiency gains are to a large extent the result of human knowledge and technology.

The sustainability dilemma

Providing growth to growing populations while maintaining future output potential and maintaining our environment and natural resources will be quite a balancing act. Sustainability will depend on the mix of our use of resources and human/fixed capital, and on the speed with which we are able to increase our *efficiency* in use of resources. Two to three billion more people will join us in the next 50 years and output will quadruple to 140 trillion.[35] The following questions are at the heart of the **sustainability dilemma**:

- Since the billion people in wealthy developed countries consume 70% of the world's resources and are a major contributor to environmental degradation, what will happen if developing countries follow the same development path as developed countries?

---

31. World investment report 2001, UNCTAD, page XIV.
32. 'Globalization, growth and poverty', World Bank 2002, page 38 ff.
33. The report's words – not mine.
34. Lomborg, p. 126.
35. *WDR 2003*, p. 8.

- The poorest billion people also have severe environmental impact as they often have no choice but to use limited resources in an unsustainably manner. The solution here is poverty alleviation – but the problem of sustainability in growth remains.

- Can efficiency in the use of renewable resources increase at a pace that will keep up with growth of incomes and population? What about non-renewable resources; can they be used at sustainable rates and/or can we find viable substitutes?

- Can economic growth and prosperity in both developing and developed regions be sustained given the considerable externalities visible in terms of urban overload and inner city congestion?

Sustainable development paths

The whole aim of practical politics is to keep the populace alarmed – and hence clamorous to be led to safety – by menacing it with an endless series of hobgoblins, all of them imaginary. – H. L. Mencken

No, I haven't provided any answers – and nobody really can, as yet. The quote above is a bit of a 'chain yanker' directed towards the numerous environmental organisations which have been predicting doom and gloom for some 40-odd years now. Hard-line environmental groups claim that we will have to fundamentally change our consumption and production habits: travel less, trade less, and simply adjust our mouths to a given food parcel. Optimists and technophiles set high hopes on the ingenuity of people to ultimately come up with solutions: the cry of the doomsayers in the 1960s and 1970s that we would be fighting for air, water, food and oil by the year 2000 has been proven false.[36]

The entire issue of sustainability is often put into a 'development' context, which in fact becomes something of a contradiction in terms. Externalities such as pollution, global warming and depleted fish stocks are common to *all* countries. In summing up the concerns of a sustainable development path in the future, The World Bank outlines several 'responsibilities' for:[37]

Developing countries: Strengthen **institutions** such as governance, rule of law and banks to enable a virtuous cycle of income → saving → investment. There must be a strong focus on **social investment** such as infrastructure and education, and it must be as broadly accessible to all as possible. All **institutional reform** must be transparent and those in charge must be openly accountable.

Developed countries: The key for developed nations is to enable poverty reduction by providing invaluable transfers of aid, knowledge, capital, and technology in order that developing countries may increase the speed of development. In lowering poverty levels and increasing general incomes, the burden on land and resources will lighten.

Developed countries can **increase aid** and direct it more efficiently by focusing on **public goods** and infrastructure. Wealthy countries could **increase debt reduction** for the countries most heavily in debt – which are also the poorest for the most part. **Removing barriers to trade** on agricultural and textile products would be enormously beneficial to developing countries; over USD20 billion a year in increased income. Finally, developed countries can increase the **transfer of technology** to developing countries. This includes improvements in grain varieties and farming methods and new **medicines**/vaccines.

Joint responsibilities: Basically there needs to be broad-based agreement on a number of **institutions** and **rules** which govern developed and developing countries alike. Three main areas need to be addressed:

1. **Trade** rules need to by carefully outlined, and the inequity of developed country subsidies must be solved.

2. Environmental agreements must be reached which deal with the **global** problem of **negative externalities**.

3. Rules governing the protection of **international property rights** in areas such as medicines, genetically engineered crops and technology.

The 'sustainable path' is one which includes poor people and developing countries since it is simply not feasible for one fifth of the world's population to go it alone. Returning to my 'hard-line' view of development, rich countries are not 'helping the poor' but actually helping themselves – this is in essence the self-interest argument again. Developing countries are in this respect not a **subject** to render aid to but a **partner** with which to cooperate.

---

36. Read anything by Rachel Carson, Lester Brown or Paul Ehrlich. Then refresh yourself with anything by Björn Lomborg, Ronald Bailey or Indur Goklany.

37. *WDR 2003*, pp. 193–96.

POP QUIZ 5.4.3   LOANS, FDI AND SUSTAINABILITY

1   Why is the availability of domestic credit – in the form of commercial loans – important to an economy?

2   The 1990s saw a colossal increase in foreign direct investment flows to developing countries; explain why this happened.

3   What are the incentives for an international firm to set up a subsidiary in another country?

4   Explain why foreign direct investment in a developing country might have positive secondary economic effects in the recipient economy.

5   Why is poverty such a threat to sustainability in the developing world?

Evaluation of growth and development strategies

5.5

CONTENTS

EVALUATION OF GROWTH AND DEVELOPMENT STRATEGIES ©IBO 2003

Evaluation of aid, trade and markets in terms of achieving growth and/or development

©IBO 2003

This final section looks at several growth/development strategies and organisations and attempts to assess them in terms of development. It is impossible to state, however, than one particular strategy works better than another, since there are large differences between the countries involved and also since the relative success or failure of any given strategy is so heavily dependent on many other variables. There is no 'single best' strategy, but rather a range of connected options which may or may not work. There is also an unfortunate propensity towards development fads which come and go: *structural change models* in the 1950s, *inward orientation* in the 1960s, *free trade market liberalism* of the 1980s, and possibly *sustainable development* of the 1990s.

Aid and trade ©IBO 2003

> *Aid without trade is a lullaby – a song you sing to children to get them to sleep.* – Uganda's president Yoweri Museveni[1]

Foreign aid

When children in America go door to door during Halloween, they say 'Trick or treat!?' (= 'Give me some candy or we play a trick on you.'); when Vikings met other ships the line was 'Trade or plunder?!' It seems that all too often developed countries have met the plight of developing countries with 'Trade on our terms or aid on our terms?' Many economists claim that *fair and free trade* would in fact lessen the need for aid, and that there is a greater return on addressing trade issues such as barriers to trade in developed countries. A counter-position is that many developing countries are in much too weak a position to be able to compete on completely free trade terms and that domestic industries in developing countries would suffer from highly efficient multinational companies' oligopolistic – and even monopolistic – positions of power. Somewhere in between these two positions one finds a degree of consensus in that one does not exclude the

other; aid can be channelled towards institutions, infrastructure and knowledge/technology transfers which both complement and enhance increased trade.

It is important to define foreign aid in rather strict terms. Loans from the World Bank and military aid are frequently associated with aid. In fact, these lie outside the boundaries of what is considered aid, since they are not **concessionary**. Foreign aid consists of outright grants (donor aid), soft loans and tied aid. This is mostly undertaken by official aid agencies, multilateral aid agencies and non-government organisations (see below). Also, while some literature includes debt relief, i.e. writing off debilitating loans for heavily indebted poor countries – I exclude this from the discussion below and give it a heading of its own further on.

The aid debate

Few observers – economists or otherwise – would be willing to condemn aid across the board (see 'A little depth: Views of development economists' further on). Yet a number of questions persist as to the efficiency and desirability of aid.

1. Is aid going to those most in need or is aid given primarily for other considerations, e.g. for **political**, **military** and **self-interest** reasons? It is evident that donor countries allocate aid primarily to countries with which there are previous – often colonial – ties, and also where there are strong strategic arguments supporting aid.[2] For example, the world's largest donor nation, the US, focused aid on Southeast Asia to create a defence against communism in the 1960s. Later shifts in aid were directly caused by changes in American considerations to strategic and political policies: South America in the 1970s and 1980s, Middle Eastern countries during the 1990s, and noticeably towards Islamic countries which might support global terrorism during the 2000s. All too often, aid serves to prolong bad government.[3]

2. To what extent **does aid actually reach developing countries**, much less the people? All too often, mismanagement, corruption and capital flight have wasted aid funds and even served to prop up dictatorial regimes in developing countries.[4]

---

1. *The Economist*, 'An addictive lullaby', 15 January 2004.
2. *WDR 2001*, Chapter 11, p. 190.
3. *Assessing aid – What works, what doesn't and why*, World Bank study 1998, p. 49.

3. To what extent **does aid actually increase the wellbeing** and living standards of people in developing countries? Critics quickly point out that there is little correlation between the amount of aid and growth or development. On the other hand, there are a number of economic arguments for aid. In helping developing countries to close the gap between saving and investment, developing countries can be aided by creating better fundamental conditions for growth and better living standards. This in turn can potentially lead to **mutually** beneficial trade and commerce arising between developed and developing countries. Additionally, one can argue that increased aid might help diminish conflicts and wars which have plagued the developing world for decades.

4. Has there been 'too much' aid? Donors increasingly suffer from aid '**saturation**' or '**fatigue**'. Aid sceptics argue that many countries simply do not have the capacity to absorb aid efficiently and that lack of infrastructure will cause aid monies to quickly run into diminishing returns. Adding to this, aid failures of the past might lead to a tightening of the purse strings as donor countries see squandered resources, corruption and failure to develop in many deserving areas which are competing for aid.[5]

Arguments for aid

Aid is of course a wide term. It covers a span between soft loans for long-term investment in infrastructure to short-term emergency relief for famines and natural disasters. Any discussion revolving around 'pro et con' must of course take this into consideration. There are a number of arguments in favour of aid which can be considered generally valid:

- **Aid and government spending:** Developing countries derive great benefits by being able to increase education, health and infrastructure and aid can help. As pointed out in "Institutional and political factors" on page 550 there is frequently a gap between the need to provide public and merit goods and the tax bases required to fulfil such needs. Aid can help fill this gap – in fact, aid represented 10% or more of all GDP in 21 African countries in 1997, and cutting this aid would have had most damaging effects on tax receipts and government spending.[6]

- **Aid and technology/capital:** Foreign currency can help developing countries to import the capital and technology necessary for economic growth. This is often coupled with direct technical and training assistance from the donor.

- **Aid and aggregate demand:** Aid can help create demand pull conditions and stimulate aggregate demand and investment. Aid to the low-income developing countries averaged 2.7% of GNP in 2002 – and some of the poorest countries in the world had aid proportions close to 50% of GDP.[7]

Criticisms of aid

A number of criticisms have been put forward from both developed and less developed countries. Aid has a large number of vociferous critics,[8] and as this debate has been ongoing since the Marshall Plan in the late 1940s, the list below is in no way complete.

- **Poor economic efficiency:** The most vocal critics claim that aid in effect is largely inefficient and therefore wasteful. Far too much aid does not have development per se in mind, but is the result of geopolitical considerations aimed at supporting friendly countries and allies. Many observers have also been highly critical of the amounts of money squandered on large 'status' projects such as airports and government buildings, and also of the simple fact that too much money is lost to capital flight, corruption and bureaucracy. For example, in 1993, the World Bank estimated that official development aid **giving** amounted to $US56.7 billion, while ODA **received** was $US45.1 billion – the rest was apparently sucked up in high administrative and overhead costs of disbursing aid monies.[9] Another example is Zambia, where The World Bank in 2001 estimated that if Zambia had used its aid efficiently between 1961 and 1994, the country would have a per capita GDP of $US20,000 rather than $US600.[10]

---

4.   An absolutely blistering account of aid mismanagement is to be found in a rather shocking book from the late 1980s: *Lords of poverty* by Graham Hancock. Recommended reading, but severely depressing.

5.   See, for example, *HDR 2005*, p. 96.

6.   *Taxation and tax reforms in developing countries: Illustrations from sub-Saharan Africa*, Development Studies and Human Rights, C. Michelsen Institute, 2003, p. ix.

7.   World Development Indicators 2005, table 6.10.

8.   One of the staunchest opponents of aid, (Lord) Peter Bauer, argues that developing countries were pretty much invented by foreign aid. A most memorable (?) quote of his was that aid is 'an excellent method for transferring money from poor people in rich countries to rich people in poor countries.' Quoted from *The Economist*, 'A voice for the poor', 2 May 2002.

9.   *HDR 1993*, pp. 172–74 and 203; *WDR 1993*, pp. 238–39.

10. *WDR 2001*, p. 192.

- Another issue is **tied aid** – criticised in Section 5.4 – which is vociferously (= loudly) condemned in the Human Development Report 2005 for its wastefulness. In fact, the UK banned all tied aid in 2002 and some 12 additional OECD countries are also well on this path.

- **Zero – or even negative! – correlation between aid and growth in the poorest countries:** Some of the harshest criticisms – and hence also some of the more debated – levelled at aid look at the dismal performance of the poorest nations' growth rates in relation to aid received. In a rather blistering critique of aid's inability to foster economic growth, development economist William Easterly found that there was strong evidence of negative correlation between aid and growth (see Figure 5.5.1).[11]

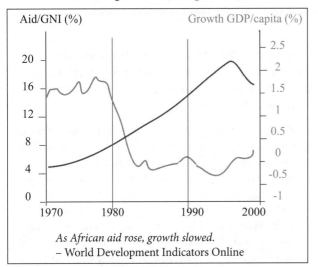

As African aid rose, growth slowed.
– World Development Indicators Online

(Source: http://news.bbc.co.uk/2/hi/science/nature/4209956.stm and Easterly, p. 46)

Figure 5.5.1 *Aid and growth in Africa, 1970–2000*

- **Aid diminishes local investment:** Aid can actually worsen the domestic production base in an economy by replacing domestic saving and investment (HL: a form of 'crowding out'). Later research points out that aid has not closed the financing gap between saving and investment which was the claim earlier.[12] Additionally, aid in the form of money can increase imports and worsen the current account balance, while direct food aid has in several cases destroyed domestic market

fundamentals by lowering the price of domestic crops and thus removing the incentives function of supply.

- **Control of monies:** The everlasting question is 'Who decides where the money goes'? Donor countries, as stated above, frequently have strong political and economic motives in recipient countries. (For example, 6% of US bilateral aid in 2002 went to Israel. Similarly, 10% of UK bilateral aid went to India and 11% of France's went to Côte d'Ivoire.[13] Get yourself a good history book and figure out why.) In addition to this bias, donor countries will want some form of control over where the money goes. On the other hand, recipient countries might rightfully claim that they best know how to allocate funds. As an extension of this, there are numerous examples of how poor coordination between development agencies has resulted in mixed goals between donors and recipients, leading to inefficient use of funds and poor resource allocation.[14]

- **Aid doesn't reach the neediest:** Often it is countries which have relatively good institutions and infrastructure which receive the majority of aid, and most aid flows to a relatively limited area. It turns out that only a fraction of these flows reaches the poorest segments of the population. The UNDP estimates that official aid misses around 20% of the poorest people and that even non-government organisations specifically targeting the poorest communities might miss 5% to 10%.[15]

- **Aid helps to support evil regimes:** Another argument frequently put forward is that aid going to undemocratic and corrupt regimes aids bad governments in continuing to exercise power.

- **Debt relief:** Finally, there is the issue of **debt relief** as a form of aid. The debt relief granted to a number of heavily indebted poor countries (HIPCs) is an initiative aimed at alleviating poverty and the burden of debt in some of the world's poorest countries. Between 1989 and 1997, debt relief for 41 HIPCs amounted to $US33 billion.[16] An initial criticism of this procedure is that it gives no control whatsoever to countries writing off debt as to how

---

11. William Easterly, 'The White Man's Burden', pp. 42– 45. Again I warn of drawing erroneous conclusions as to causality! So does Easterly, e.g. that the increase in aid is most likely due to the fall in growth rates. Yet he does allow for the distinct possibility that aid has not done much in the way of *stopping a decline* in per capita growth rates over the past 30 years in Africa.
12. *WDR 2001*, p. 192.
13. World Bank, World Development Indicators 2004.
14. See, for example, *WDR 2001*, p. 192.
15. *HDR 1993*, p. 96.
16. *WDR 2001*, p. 203.

funds which do not go towards debt servicing will be used. A recent criticism is also that debt write-offs during the 1990s have in fact had little or no effect on growth or development in the poorest countries. And while there is a good deal of support globally for the effort, a number of commentators have expressed worries that writing off debt might in fact lead to wrongful behaviour in the future. Debt relief might create a situation known as 'moral hazard', which means that if the government in a developing country sees that there is a possibility of debts being written off, there is an incentive for overborrowing.[17]

Good policies + good institutions + aid = growth(?)

While there is no conclusive outcome in the aid debate, a number of indications point to the fact that aid indeed has had some notable successes in countries which have strong basic institutions and sound economic policies. This is not surprising and really only strengthens was has been previously said: development is a process involving multiple and simultaneous variables. Aid monies will only be effectively used when there is/are: a functioning financial systems, e.g. **banks**; sound **macro policies** resulting in price stability and balanced budgets; **aid agendas** based on needs rather than grandiose development schemes; **good governance** based on openness and accountability, and efficient administrative institutions under the **rule of law** which minimise corruption and theft.[18]

Note from a famous economist: Jeffrey Sachs

Delving into the issue of whether aid 'works' or not is a bit like fly-fishing; the more one learns the less one understands. During the collection of sources and outlining of this updated version, I was increasingly confused by the wide range of views on development aid by some very notable economists. The most acrimonious (= hostile) debate ranged between Professor Jeffrey Sachs (author of *The End of Poverty*) and William Easterly (author of *The White Man's Burden – Why the West's efforts to aid the rest have done so much ill and so little good*). Read the titles – guess which side these two stand on!

Easterly basically claims that there is little indication that the majority of aid money over the past 50 years – some USD2.3 trillion – shows little in the way of development for the recipient countries. In some 380 well-annotated pages, Easterly builds an argument that the well-intentioned 'planners' of development aid have wasted huge amounts of resources with little to show for it. In summary: aid is ineffective.

Sachs, who ran the UN Millennium Project between 2002 and 2006, is a strong advocate of massive scaling-up of aid. He very clearly points out that the aid money from the world amounted to USD12 per person a year to Africa and that net aid to Africa from the largest economy in the world, USA, amounts to, wait for it, 6 cents per African. In other words, there is little to show for aid since there is little to show in aid.

Rather vaingloriously (= boastfully, or self-aggrandising) I wrote to Professor Sachs and asked him about the 'Does aid work?' debate. He very kindly answered. Here is his response:

As I am sure that you would gather, I find the debate a bit wearisome, because there is no such thing as 'aid' in general, but only aid for specific purposes. There are bad ways to do things and good ways to do things, including the provision of development assistance. The real question is 'Can aid be properly managed (with high likelihood) to provide useful and important results?' not 'Has 'aid' worked or not worked?' The latter question is too broad and in some ways silly.

I would like to remind you that after a slashing attack on aid for more than 300 pages, Easterly actually writes the following:

Put the focus back where it belongs: get the poorest people in the world such obvious goods as vaccines, the antibiotics, the food supplements, the improved seeds, the fertilizer, the roads, the bore holes, the water pipes, the textbooks, and the nurses. This is not making the poor dependent on handouts; it is giving the poorest people the health, the nutrition, education, and other inputs that raise the payoff to their own efforts to better their lives. (The White Man's Burden, p. 368-69).

That's approximately what I've been recommending for years. Where's the real debate?

---

17. *WDR 2001*, p. 203.

18. *Assessing aid – What works, what doesn't and why*, World Bank study 1998, pp. 2–6; and *The Economist*, 'An addictive lullaby', 15 January 2004. (It should be noted that a follow up report using later years for data failed to show convincing results that aid indeed promoted growth and development in 'good policy environments'.)

The trade debate

The debate on the merits of trade follows the issues outlined in Section 4.2 and 5.4. To recapitulate:

- Many developing countries are caught in producing and exporting **primary goods** which have low price and income elasticities of demand. Thus their terms of trade have been falling as the relative price of these commodity exports has fallen continuously for decades.

- Many **barriers to trade** still remain in developed countries for precisely the goods which less developed countries have a comparative advantage in, primarily agricultural goods and textiles.

- While **free and fair trade** is generally advocated as a method for developing countries to increase income, there are risks involved in removing trade barriers in developing countries, notably the harmful effects on domestic production and employment as a result of highly efficient foreign competitors; loss of tariff revenue which makes up a large portion of government tax receipts, and a developing country with strong outward-orientation could be highly vulnerable to international business cycles.

The trade advocates say ...

Proponents of trade as a major development driver point out that highly successful newly industrialised countries (NICs) have followed strongly export-oriented paths based on producing according to comparative advantages. The Asian Tiger economies, and more recently China and India are commonly referred to examples. A great many in-depth studies by the World Bank, OECD and the WTO show strong indicative evidence that successful integration into global trade flows is **strongly pro-growth and pro-developmental**.[19] Figure 5.5.2 illustrates that increasingly outward-oriented countries have not only only outpaced other countries but are also pro-poor, in that the poorest 20% of the population enjoys the strongest relative income growth.

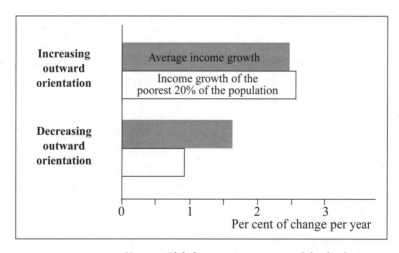

(Source: *Global economic prospects and the developing countries*, World Bank 2001, p. 44)

Figure 5.5.2 *Export-orientation and pro-poor growth*

However, as more *trade-cautious* commentators point out, income growth in fast growth countries is not evenly spread and has led to increasing **income inequality** – primarily between urban and rural citizens. There are also negative externalities such as very high **pollution** levels in some cases, China being a case in point. In addition, there are no guarantees that the success formulas of the NICs can be transferred to any and all other developing countries. Finally, there is no evidence whatsoever that trade liberalisation has had any effect on **poverty reduction** in the **least** developed countries – in fact, there is more evidence that rapid and thorough trade liberalisation has resulted in increased poverty in the short run.[20]

Perhaps the main hindrance for developing countries is the fact that **effective tariffs** in place in developed countries are still very high – one estimate points to an average effective tariff rate (when all trade barriers are combined into a single effective tariff) of 34% in the US, 100% in the EU and 230% in Japan.[21]

---

19. See, for example, *Global economic prospects and the developing countries*, World Bank 2001, chapter 2.
20. 'The least developed countries report 2002', UNCTAD, pp. 117–19.
21. 'Trading up: trade policy and global poverty', Center for Global Development brief, September 2003, p. 2.

So while the importation of manufactured goods from developing countries to developed countries has indeed risen in the past decade, the total value of manufactured goods exported from developing countries still only accounted for 1.6% of OECD countries' combined output in the mid 1990s.[22] In fact, total output from the developing world accounts for only 5% of world output.[23] And, as illustrated in Figure 5.5.3, developing countries made up less than 20% of total OECD imports in 1995.

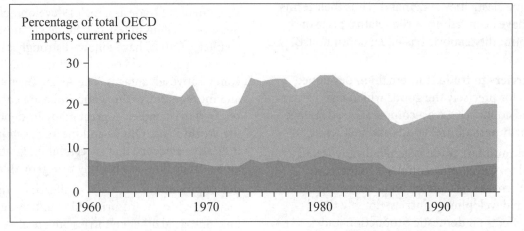

(Source: OECD policy brief October 1999, p. 5)

Figure 5.5.3 *Imports to OECD countries from low, middle and high income countries*

Interventionist and market-led strategies ©IBO 2003

The period between the end of the Second World War and the beginning of the 1980s was marked by heavy **government intervention** in virtually all developing countries. During the course of the 1980s there was a general shift towards market strategies based on neoclassical thinking. Much of this gained momentum during the period of accelerating globalisation during the 1990s.

Interventionist strategies and planning

Governments adopted planning during the 30-year post-war period for a number of reasons. In part the Keynesian view of interventionism was adopted and the mixed economy was a reference point in all mainstream economics. There was also heavy emphasis on growth models such as the **Harrod–Domar model** from Section 5.4, and governments in developing countries used such **aggregate growth models** to estimate and influence saving and investment in the economy. Government intervention was also considered necessary to **maximise social benefits** of development and **minimise negative externalities**. Free markets at an early development stage were considered non-viable, as investment and output would not yield the optimal societal results such as employment and equality in income distribution. Government ownership of key industries and control of assets were therefore all part of the high degree of planning. In conjunction with the externalities argument, the issue of **positive externalities** arising from societal goods such as education and health care were considered of central importance to development and would be underprovided for by market forces – an argument that has strong foundations in economic theory. Finally, there was broad consensus that development was far too important an issue to be left to market forces, and that this in itself justified a high level of government involvement.

Scepticism towards the market mechanism and the belief that government intervention could be used to correct market failures and provide growth led to extensive state planning and control of production assets. This was also combined in many cases with **import-substitution strategies** and **nationalised industries**. Other common elements of interventionism were **central pricing policies** on many goods; **limited financial freedom** in order to ensure that government-sponsored industries received the brunt of financing; an **increasing government sector**, and **overvalued exchange rates** to enable cheaper imports of capital goods. A good deal of the government intervention was rather heavy-handed. For example, land was sometimes forcibly taken by

22. OECD policy brief October 1999, p. 5.
23. 'Grinding the poor', *The Economist*, 27 September 2001.

government and then allocated according to a central plan; agricultural produce prices were often set centrally and farmers were forced to sell at lower-than-market rates, and rural economies were often distinctly disadvantaged in taxes and subsidies in comparison with urban areas.

The abandonment of interventionist policies

It looked good in theory, but was generally a failure. By the end of the 1970s it was becoming increasingly obvious that countries which had implemented market-oriented strategies were growing at a far higher rate. Several key reasons for the limited success of interventionist methods prior to the 1980s stand out.[24]

- Perhaps the main reason is that government intervention requires a **framework of administration and control** that simply didn't exist in most of the developing countries at that particular stage. Inefficient bureaucracies, poorly educated staff, and very little in the way of monitoring progress or control do not make large scale and detailed development planning programs readily applicable.

- As governments increased in size and tax revenues did not increase proportionately, large and increasing **government deficits** became the norm. This helped fuel replacement funding of government spending via loans from abroad. (See "The oil crises revisited – the origin of the debt crisis" on page 567.)

- The increase in foreign loans together with imports financed by an overvalued currency caused significant **current account deficits** in most developing countries.

Market-led strategies – a neoclassical shift

The beginning of the 1980s saw the emergence of neoclassical theory, primarily in Reagan's America and Thatcher's Britain (see Section 3.4 and supply-side policies for example). Growth had been shown to be far stronger in economies which had a higher degree of market forces which were not controlled or limited by government intervention. The seeming failure of interventionist policies in developing countries helped shift many governments towards **market liberalisation**

policies and increased outward orientation. Some or all of the following market-oriented reforms were implemented to some degree in developing countries during the 1980s and 1990s.

- **Encouragement of foreign direct investment** has been a marked element in the market process in many countries, as is allowing foreigners to own property. Vietnam's 'doi moi' (renewal) policy starting in 1988 had a central (planned!) theme of attracting foreign companies. When President Clinton did a little 'doi moi' of his own in 1994 by lifting the trade embargo the US had in place with Vietnam, there was a surge of American FDI from the US to Vietnam. The capital stock in Vietnam rose from 3.6% of GDP in 1990 to 55.6% by 1999.[25] Poverty reduction was such that while three-quarters of the population lived on less than one US dollar a day [26] in 1988, the figure was 37% by 1998[27].

- **Privatisation of land and capital** was a key element in forming economies based on market structures. In China, for example, what was possibly the largest single push of privatisation put most of the land in private hands by the beginning of the 1980s. The results were remarkable; agricultural output increased by an average of close to 8% per year enabling a country which 20 years earlier saw millions of famine fatalities now had an exportable excess of produce. The increase in income brought some 500 million people in China out of extreme poverty – which the World Bank refers to as the largest and fastest decrease in poverty in history.

- Many of the policies implemented were part of a general macroeconomic **structural adjustment programme**. This was a process recommended by the World Bank and the International Monetary Fund aimed at restoring general macro equilibrium in the economy.[28] (And was to receive a large amount of criticism during the 1980s and 1990s – see further on.) The goal of structural adjustment was to restore *balance of payments* and government *budget balances*, reduce *inflation*, stabilise *exchange rates*, and generally create conditions for long-term economic growth. This meant that the public sector in many developing countries was considerably reduced while inefficient state enterprises were

24. For a rather scathing review of interventionist planning in development, see *The White Man's Burden*, by William Eastery, chapter 1.
25. *Foreign direct investment in Vietnam: an overview*, N.J. Freeman, Visiting Professor, National Economics University Business School, Hanoi, September 2002, p. 17.
26. Norborg, p. 41.
27. Legrain, p. 54.
28. The strongly market-oriented view of development policy by the World Bank and IMF during the 1980s and 1990s became known the 'Washington Consensus' – as both of these institutions are based in Washington.

privatised. This was often accompanied by a removal – or at least reduction – in central price-setting which had distorted market prices.

Success and failure of market-led strategies

The three points above should be most recognisable to you; this is a 'freeing the market' process which is very similar to supply-side policies. Did they work in developing countries? Sorry people, the answer is 'yes – and no'. Yes, market-led strategies have increased incomes and lowered poverty levels (generally) in some cases, most notably in the Tiger Economies, China, India, Malaysia, Mexico and Vietnam. In other cases, notably Argentina, Brazil, and many of the transition economies in former Eastern Europe, the results have been mixed – as have the degree of market orientation, according to some scholars – and have not met with the success seen primarily in Asia. A third group must pretty much be characterised as dismally failing, and the majority of these countries are to be found in Sub-Saharan Africa.

However: It bears repeating that a number of the 'non-interventionist' market-oriented economies mentioned above were in fact to a lesser or greater extent steered by *government micro-management policies*. Entire industries in Korea, Singapore and Malaysia all had very powerful government institutional backing and support during the 1960s and 1970s. It was made abundantly clear – via subsidies, tax breaks, protectionism and what not – to certain key businesses that the focus was on cooperation between firms and a focus on exports rather that on domestic competition and import substitution. There have also been strict limits to foreign direct investment inflows in some cases, notably Korea and Taiwan. This illustrates how difficult it is to draw general conclusions as to the *general* superiority of market-led and outward-oriented strategies. Some economists view the East Asian 'miracle' as proof of the validity of the free-market argument, while others would view the success as simply as good open market policies combined with skilful government intervention.

The question is *why* some countries have succeeded and others have failed. This is of course the 24-carat question and is at the heart of the debate concerning interventionist versus market liberalisation. There is some consensus, according to notable development economist Michael Todaro, in that successful market-orientation does not miraculously pop up in a vacuum.[29] A market system is not 'a lack of governance and rules' but quite the opposite. For a market

economy to function, a number of requirements need to be met, notably along the **infrastructural/institutional lines** outlined earlier, e.g. financial system, legal institutions, rule of law, communications networks, etc. There is also strong correlation between investment in education and the effectiveness of free-market orientation. Once again it seems to come down to having a basic institutional/socioeconomic framework in place before growth and development models based on market orientation can take permanent root.

The role of international financial institutions ©IBO 2003

The structural adjustments which developing countries undertook during the 1980s had the side-effect of making two international organisations, the International Monetary Fund and the World Bank, household names – or (in-)famous at the least. The proliferation of non-government organisations, NGOs, during the 1980s and 1990s was in part a response to what many people felt was a dominance of official 'top-down' institutions. NGO activity and growth can also be attributed to the growing fear that the increase in the size and amount of multinational companies around the world would empower international corporations at the expense of citizens in developed and developing countries alike. The growth of multinational companies, in turn, was partially a result of continuing international financial deregulation during the early 1980s in line with free market thinking, and the shift towards outward-oriented policies in many less developed countries.

The International Monetary Fund (IMF)

©IBO 2003

The main IMF prescription has been budgetary belt tightening for patients much too poor to own belts. – Jeffrey Sachs (*The End of Poverty*, p. 74)

The 45-nation Bretton Woods conference in July, 1944, created four institutions which were intended to increase stability in the post-war period: the fixed exchange rate system which became known as the Bretton Woods system; the General Agreement on Tariffs and Trade (GATT) which became the World Trade Organisation (WTO) in 1995; the International Monetary Fund (IMF) and the World Bank. The **International Monetary Fund**, with headquarters in Washington DC, came into effect with 39 members in 1945 and is based on membership. Member countries

---

29. Todaro, p. 696 ff.

pay what in effect is an annual membership due to the IMF, which is based on the size of each country's economy. The size of the membership dues control members' voting rights unlike, for example, the WTO where each country has equal voting rights. The US has by far the largest percentage of votes (17%), then Japan and Germany (6% each) and France (5%).[30]

Original purpose of the IMF

The membership dues create a jointly owned fund which can be used to stabilise currencies which had difficulties in keeping the fixed exchange rate created at Bretton Woods. In acting as an overseer of the fixed exchange system, the IMF had two primary functions: firstly to **monitor the balance of payments** in member countries to detect signs of fundamental disequilibrium, and secondly to **intervene on behalf of countries** which showed serious balance of payments problems and downward pressure on their currencies.

Recall from Sections 4.5 and 4.6 that a current account deficit puts downward pressure on the exchange rate, so in a fixed exchange rate system the currency would become overvalued. In order to restore credibility to the currency, a country would need to borrow foreign currency in order to bolster the value of its own currency. By allowing countries to borrow from the fund (*inflow* on capital account in the balance of payments) the IMF would enable countries to get through periods of current account deficits (*outflow* in current account) without having to devalue their currency. The IMF was basically to act as an **international lender of last resort** to the countries which were part of the Bretton Woods fixed exchange rate system.

Thus the IMF was to act as a guarantor of international exchange rate stability by enabling countries to borrow from a pool of funds collectively owned by members – a bit like an insurance company which is owned by a cooperative of insurance buyers. During the early 1970s, the Bretton Woods exchange rate system broke down (see Section 4.6) and the following decade was marked by international instability and oil crises, stagflation, increasing current account deficits in developing countries and the debt crisis. All of this contributed to a considerable shift in the role of the IMF.

Role of the IMF from the 1980s forward

Developing nations which had fallen into severe debt problems by the end of the 1980s also had severe government and current account deficits, together with high inflation and low growth. The IMF played a central role during the **debt crisis of the 1980s** by acting as go-between for deeply indebted countries and creditors in developed countries. The IMF enabled indebted countries which were unable to service loans to **reschedule** their debts, i.e. take on further loans under longer time periods to meet current loan payments. Commonly, the creditor nation or commercial bank would work out an agreement with the debtor nation and the IMF. No country was willing to default on IMF loans as this would pretty much lock the country out of future loans and IMF assistance, so the rescheduling was made possible by the IMF in its capacity as guarantor against default (= non-payment of loans). In essence, having the IMF involved in the process lent creditor countries credibility, enabling future loans from banks and international institutions. The IMF did not indulge in 'free lending' in any way – on the contrary, countries which needed to borrow from the fund were subject to a number of very strictly imposed conditions by the IMF. This is the (in...) famous **IMF conditionality**, where a debtor would have to implement a 'package' of macroeconomic policies in order to meet IMF approval and the cooperation of the creditor bank.

The objective of the IMF is still focused on upholding currency stability/convertibility, and the supervision of policies to influence balance of payments problems. And while the IMF is adamant that it is **not an aid agency or development bank**, during the 1980s and 1990s the IMF continued to act as a major creditor and greatly extended the lending operation to developing countries. The IMF now consists of 185 members (March 2009) and as one the world's largest creditors to developing nations has increasingly adopted a role in development in addition to the role of international monetary/financial stability and cooperation. It is in this capacity that such harsh criticism has been directed at the IMF in later years.

IMF stabilisation policies

A country which needs to reschedule debt and/or take on new loans from the IMF will meet a number of strict conditions imposed on the debtor nation. IMF loan conditionality comes in the form of so-called **stabilisation policies**, aimed at correcting fundamental macroeconomic problems. Generally, a stabilisation package imposed by the IMF aims to resolve balance of payments difficulties, contribute to sustainable growth and thus allow the debtor nation to

---

30. See http://www.imf.org/external/np/sec/memdir/members.htm.

repay the loan. These policies are strongly **market-oriented** and typically contain most of the following:

- Forms of currency market intervention, such as foreign exchange controls and intentionally overvalued exchange rates must be eradicated, and a freely convertible currency must be established. This facilitates increased exports and decreased imports, which in turn improves the **balance of payments**.

- **Inflation** must be combated, which often involves raising interest rates and decreasing government spending.

- The decrease in government spending is often complemented by an increase in taxation in order to balance the **government budget**.

- Limits on foreign direct investment must be curtailed to **increase FDI** inflows.

- A number of **supply-side policies** are often demanded by the IMF, such as the removal of minimum wages, doing away with minimum price schemes and other market distortions, cutting of subsidies on many goods, and privatising state owned enterprises.

- While it is not put in the form of a demand, the IMF encourages the removal of **trade barriers**.

The harshness of these policies has been defended by stating that sooner or later they will have to be done, and the later such policies are implemented, the more severe they will be for debtors. Countries which come to the IMF for assistance are in deep financial trouble already and will face fiscal hardship any which way one looks at it. The IMF provides loans which enable the country to adjust the economy quicker and with less pain than otherwise would be the case.

Criticism of the IMF

The stabilisation policies above serve as **strong indicators** of economic improvements in an economy for other potential creditors, e.g. commercial banks, enabling a country to get further loans outside the IMF. In other words, financial institutions see IMF involvement as a 'seal of approval' for loans, giving the IMF in fact a far more powerful role than solely a lender. As one consequence of this power, few organisations of latter days have come under such harsh scrutiny and disapproval as the IMF. The criticism has come from within and outside the IMF, from left and right, and from developing and less developed countries. While it is clearly impossible to

include an in-depth study of all of these points here, the following four captions cover the main points of discontent. The first two represent a 'grassroots/anti-globalisation/anti-capitalism' view and the last two a 'neo-liberal/capitalist/conservative' point of view.

- *Stabilisation policies are anti-developmental*: The harshest criticism has been whether the 'medicine' prescribed by the IMF in fact does not make the patient worse off. The harsh demands of stabilisation policies will have serious effects on development: Trade liberalisation destroys domestic markets and leads to **unemployment**; high interest rates **stifle investment**; cuts in government spending have devastating effects on much-needed **education**, **infrastructure** and **welfare programs**; reduction of food subsidies will affect the poorest groups the most; and increased inward FDI and market deregulation often creates **monopolies** due to poor competition rules and oversight.

- *The IMF is non-democratic and run according to rich country interests*: The Managing Director of the IMF is always from Europe and the richest seven countries (the G7) can in effect block all proposals which require a qualified majority vote of 75%. The US alone has more votes than all of Africa together.[31] The harshness of stabilisation policies is always inflicted on poor countries and never on rich countries, and policies which require developing countries to lower trade barriers will serve the interests of developed countries rather than developing countries.

- *IMF lending leads to moral hazard*: The IMF crisis loans are simply reworded 'bailouts' which serve to perpetuate bad loans and bad debtor countries. When countries realise that poor debt service can lead to further loans to reschedule debt and/or possible write-off of debt, there is less incentive to behave in a morally responsible manner. Thus there is moral hazard.

- *IMF lending works poorly – if at all*: In far too many cases, IMF loans show poor results. Debtors have often failed to implement necessary reforms so the taxpayers of large IMF countries foot the bill. Brazil has received over USD53 billion in IMF loans since 1958, which has done little to open up the economy and implement market reforms. Argentina, the third largest IMF debtor, has implemented limited structural reform, and has had little increase in real per capita GDP in the last 30 years.[32]

---

31. See http://www.imf.org/external/np/sec/memdir/members.htm.

The World Bank ©IBO 2003

The World Bank is often called a 'sister organisation' to the IMF. Created at the same time and housed in Washington, it too has 184 member countries whose voting rights are contingent upon economic size. Contrary to the IMF, the World Bank is indeed an outright **development organisation** created initially to deal with the reconstruction of war-torn Europe, which is fact is indicated by the bank's original name – the **International Bank for Reconstruction and Development (IBRD)**. Together with the **International Development Association (IDA)**, which was created in 1960, we have the grouping commonly referred to as the World Bank.

The overriding purpose of the World Bank is to create the groundwork for social and economic development by providing funds in the form of loans. It is an investment bank in reality, acting as go-between for investors and loan recipients, and is thus one of the world's largest borrowers on capital markets. The World Bank is owned by the 184 member nations and has offices in over 100 countries. The two institutions of the World Bank have the same general goals but have slightly different responsibilities.

IBRD: During the post-WWII period, the IBRD was focused on reconstructing the economies by financing infrastructure. During the 1950s the IBRD became increasingly involved in helping developing countries with finance by diverting deposits from developed countries to developing countries via loans. The IBRD sells bonds on the world market and then re-lends the money to developing countries. The loans from the IBRD are on commercial terms or near-commercial terms, and there is strong emphasis on the debtors ability to service loans – in fact, the IBRD has run at a profit since 1948. Thus, in a most similar fashion to the IMF, the IBRD has since the early 1980s demanded that debtor countries implement **structural adjustment programmes**, primarily open-market reforms and the removal of trade barriers as itemised under IMF stabilisation policies above.

IDA: The IDA is the **concessional** lending arm of the World Bank, and lends only to the poorest countries (with a GNP per capita below $US865 mostly) which would not be able to borrow at IBRD rates or meet the demands of adjustment programmes. The IDA is basically a provider of **soft loans**, i.e. loans at less than market rates and with very favourable terms of debt servicing. Commonly, IDA loans are interest free, and have longer payback periods – often 35 to 40 years.[33] In contrast to the IBRD, the IDA receives most of its funding via donor contributions from member countries.

In addition to financing loans, the World Bank has increasingly expanded operations to a wider field of development than pure economic development. It is one of the major sources of development statistics and research, and the yearly **World Development Report** is highly regarded as one of the most important compilations of development statistics. The Bank also provides development assistance, technical support and education in over 100 countries via local branch offices.

And the critics say ...

The criticism of the World Bank follows the same lines as for the IMF: the consequences of **conditionality** in borrowing from the Bank are very negative for the poorest parts of developing countries. Fiscal austerity (severity) imposed by World Bank officials has been shown to have clear anti-developmental effects on the poor. In fact, the UNDP's Human Development Report has shown clearly that the Human Development Index (HDI) has fallen in a number of countries which have implemented structural adjustment programmes in order to qualify for World Bank loans.[34]

Harsher – and perhaps more ideologically tainted – criticism comes from many NGOs operating in development. It is pointed out that the World Bank is clearly run by the richest countries, with a strong American presence, for example, every president of the World Bank Group[35] has been an American, and the US has over 16% of the voting rights while China and India – accounting for one third of the world's population – each have 2.8%.[36] Critics on the neo-liberal, free-market side claim that a good third and possibly half of all World Bank projects are failures.

Perhaps the heaviest criticism comes from **Joseph Stiglitz**, ex-chief economist at the World Bank and

---

32. Report from the Heritage Foundation, a US liberal think-tank, at http://www.heritage.org/Research/InternationalOrganizations/bg1689.cfm.
33. See an excellent overview of both the World Bank and the IMF at http://www.imf.org/external/pubs/ft/exrp/differ/differ.htm.
34. *HDR 1990* in Todaro, p. 631.
35. There are **five** institutions in what is called the **World Bank** *Group*: The IBRD, IDA, the International Finance Corporation, the Multilateral Investment Guarantee Agency, and the International Centre for Settlement of Investment Disputes.
36. See World Bank at http://web.worldbank.org/WBSITE/EXTERNAL/EXTABOUTUS.

Nobel Laureate, who has harshly accused the World Bank for wrongful policies and basic incompetence over many years. His main point is that the structural adjustment policies have been so obviously damaging for many years, but have not led to fundamental shifts in World Bank methodology and practice[37]. Stiglitz has pointed out that countries which opted out of World Bank loans due to the harshness of conditionality, e.g. Malaysia in the late 1990s, have frequently fared far better than countries which took the loans and subsequently applied the market liberalisation policies prescribed by World Bank structural adjustment demands.

Private sector banks ©IBO 2003

Commercial banks have a number of central functions in an economy. They act as '**brokers**' between savers and investors by attracting savings and then lending this on to businesses. In this capacity, commercial banks will also *assess investment* risks and allocate funds according to risk and perceived profitability. This helps to efficiently allocate capital. By bundling the savings of many people, banks also help to *spread the risks* of savers by allocating funds to a wide variety of investments. Finally, it is the function of commercial banks to act as an extension or 'signal' for the *monetary policies* of central banks by implementing tight or lose credit.

The costs of an underdeveloped banking system

The institution of commercial banking in developing countries is noticeable weak in many cases, and will have strong anti-development effects on the economy for a variety of reasons:

- Perhaps the main weakness is simply the **lack of loanable funds** available in domestic banks. This is perpetuated by the fact that many prospective borrowers will not have an asset base to use as collateral for loans. This can take on ludicrous proportions; in Russia a bank had a meagre $US2 million in loanable funds which could be borrowed as long as collateral was a sufficiently liquid asset, such as cash.[38]

- A large proportion of bank assets in developing countries are in fact owned and **controlled by foreign banks**.[39] Commonly, the banks in developing countries are subsidiaries of developed countries' banks, and will be more focused on external transfers of funds than on domestic risk assessment and lending.

- This will serve to **weaken the monetary policy** of the central bank, since foreign banks will often deal in foreign currencies. In addition, overvaluation of the domestic currency will create a parallel currency market which is under limited government control. The link between official monetary policies – described in "The monetary transmission mechanism" on page 364 – and overall investment demand is thus often far weaker in developing countries than in developed countries.

Non-government organisations (NGOs) ©IBO 2003

A non-government organisation, or NGO, is a voluntary organisation which is funded by contributions rather than government funds. These organisations span not only the globe but a wide range of more or less special interests. Examples of some of the larger include Oxfam, the World Wildlife Fund for nature (WWF), Christian Aid, Greenpeace, the Red Cross/Crescent, and around 38,000 others. Some 30,000 of these NGOs were created during the 1990s.[40] The phenomenal increase in NGOs during the 1990s of course coincides with the ability of a small number of people with special interests to reach an enormous number of people around the world via the Internet.

The proliferation of NGOs has had considerable positive impact on development issues and policies over the past decades, and their influence is growing. A number of benefits can be seen for development in this:

- Many NGOs conduct and **publish studies** which bring to light a number of issues which might otherwise be sidelined. Oxfam reports are increasingly used as a reference on the effects of trade barriers in developing countries.

- The ability of NGOs to coordinate efforts across country borders makes them a force to be reckoned with as **pressure groups** towards government policies and the activities of multinational companies.

37. 'A plague of finance', *The Economist*, 27 September 2001.
38. I'm not joking: see 'Too much trouble', 8 January 1998.
39. 'Globalization, growth and poverty', World Bank 2002, p. 98.
40. Legrain, p. 202.

- Many of the development NGOs operate in developing countries; setting up irrigation projects, operating field hospitals, delivering emergency aid relief and so forth. The fact that most of these NGOs are **politically unaffiliated** means that local people are more prone to trust them, which gives them wider margins to operate in and increases the efficiency of development projects.

- The vast majority of people working for NGOs are volunteers. Many are from developed countries and will **share their experiences** at home, helping to spread hard-earned and first-hand knowledge of development issues.

Yet there are a few negative aspects of NGOs. I have several friends who are long-standing members of Greenpeace and other environmental NGOs while I also have friends who are card-carrying members of conservative democratic parties. Guess which of them get invitations to elect leadership and/or to speak out at conventions to set policy guidelines? Correct, NGOs are often run by a non-elected clique or core of dedicated leaders surrounded by a much larger group of supporters and contributors. Some sharp criticism of the **lack of democracy and accountability** in many NGOs has been put forward – notably by officials at the receiving end of NGO hostility. The former Director-General of the World Trade Organisation, Mike Moore, and Philippe Legrain (also formerly WTO), pose a number of barbed questions:[41]

- Why don't NGOs go the traditional democratic route of ballot boxes and elections? Is this due to the realisation that **broad support** is in fact simply lacking?

- Why should special-interest groups consisting of **unelected** people and representing a very small minority be granted a seat at international conferences together with duly elected democratic representatives? Is it reasonable that 2.5 million members of Greenpeace can make demands on international issues with the same weight as the Indian parliament which is elected by 600 million voters?

- Why do many NGOs seem to be exempt from **transparency** demands such as open financial statements and meeting protocols? Especially when many of these NGOs themselves have criticised official and multilateral development organisations and multinational companies of operating behind closed doors.

Multinational corporations/ transnational corporations (MNCs/TNCs) ©IBO 2003

In looking at foreign direct investment in Section 5.4, the issue of **multinational companies** (MNCs) showed a somewhat biased view in favour of foreign direct investment (FDI). In fact, I have simply left the negative aspects for this section. The controversies over multinationals and FDI arise on two basic levels; the ideological and the functional.

- The **ideological split** arises over the question of whether free market private enterprises are good or bad for development in general.

  - **Proponents** of foreign direct investment and multinational companies are primarily of the free-trade/liberal school.

  - **Opponents** of multinational companies look at the power relationship between developing countries and view multinational companies as a threat to the cultural/political/ social/economic identity and strength of developing nations.

- The **functional split** deals with the pro-developmental aspect of foreign direct investment and multinational companies.

  - **Proponents** of foreign direct investment view the transferral of capital in accordance with classical economics; capital will seek out the highest rate of return and allocate resources efficiently, whereby developing countries will benefit from increased investment, jobs and output. This is pro-developmental.

  - The **opponents** would counter that foreign direct investment in less developed countries in fact empowers the already powerful companies and the rich countries in which they are based. Multinational companies benefit the few and widen inequality gaps, and are able to exploit low labour-cost countries while diverting profits homeward rather than reinvesting them in the host country.

While FDI and multinational companies clearly can benefit developing countries (see Section 5.4), there are a number of points of criticism which most definitely deserve notice:

- Multinationals are not prone to reinvest profits. Thus the initial investment will be countered in the long run by outflows of profit, and **adversely effect the current account** in balance of payments.

---

41. Moore, p. 187 ff and Legrain p. 202 ff.

- It is quite possible that multinational presence **forces local firms out of business** as these smaller firms will not be able to compete with the larger rival. This could in fact **lower** total saving in the economy due to the loss of jobs and income.

- It can be argued that **heavy capital** use by multinational companies is **inappropriate** for developing countries, as such production will not be labour intensive enough to have an impact on unemployment. Furthermore, capital will create future demand for imports such as spare parts and specialised labour for maintenance and renovation.

- Multinationals have also been accused of using monopoly power to create demand for **inappropriate products** aimed, via heavy marketing, at a relatively small clique of well-to-do people.

- Multinationals are of such **economic power** that they in effect have **considerable leverage** in getting good terms from developing countries which desperately need capital inflows and employment opportunities provided by multinational companies which set up subsidiaries. If tax concessions are granted, there will be less of an improvement on the developing country's **tax base** and tax receipts.

The debate is far from over. The next decade will surely show results that both prove and disprove both sides. Hopefully the heat and divergence of commentators' opinions will diminish, allowing for a more level-headed analysis of the outcome. I bring my own straw to the stack, by scaling away one of the most common but largely irrelevant – and erroneous – points put forward within the issue of multinational companies' power. This is done in "Outside the box: Getting the facts straight on comparing MNCs to countries" below.

Outside the box:
Getting the facts straight on comparing MNCs to countries

You might want to revise national income accounting before reading this. Specifically, you will need to have a firm grasp of the output method of assessing GDP and the **importance of avoiding double-counting** (see Section 3.1). When you have done so, you will be able to grasp a fundamental economic fallacy that is put forward all too often.

You see, the inability or rather lack of propensity of a number of economists, NGOs and anti-globalists to understand the error in double-counting has led to a most common and seriously flawed comparison, where *total revenues* of large multinational firms are *compared to the GDP* of developing nations. This comparison is something like comparing apples and … wildebeest, yet amazingly enough has been done by a number of very well-educated and knowledgeable people. Quite frankly, **too** well educated not to know that what they are doing is erroneous, which means that they are being deceitful rather than ignorant – a far scarier offence.

These apparently well-meaning but rather woofley[42] commentators often state that multinational companies are becoming more powerful than governments. This is either heavily inferred or explicitly stated. This outrageous off-hand use of economics usually includes a list of countries and multinational companies, such as in Table 5.5.1 on page 611. The accompanying text would then read something like 'The size of many multinationals now exceeds the total income of many countries', and continue with a line of reasoning that ExxonMobile, with total sales of USD217 billion in 2001, has more economic power than Angola, Ecuador, Finland and Sierra Leone put together – which had a combined national output of USD153 billion in 2001.

What an amazing fact! What utter nonsense.

---

42. You will have noticed my use of 'woofle', or 'woofley' by now. You will not find woofle in the dictionary as I have made it up. It is a composite term like stagflation (**stag**nant + in**flation**). **Woofle** is comprised of *woolly* (as in hazy or imprecise) and *waffle* (meaning nonsense or rubbish). I figure that if enough of us economists use the term, we can get it into the Oxford dictionary. However, you heard it here first: Woofle ©.

Table 5.5.1 *Largest US companies by sales compared to GDP of selected countries 2001*

Company	Sales (= revenue) (billion $US)	Profit (billion $US)	Country	GDP (billion $US at current values)
Wal-Mart	217.8	6.6	Angola	8.9
ExxonMobil	187.5	15.1	Ecuador	21
General Motors	177.2	0.601	Finland	121
Ford Motor Co.	162.4	-5.4	Greece	117
General Electric	125.9	14.1	Sierra Leone	0.75

(Sources: *Forbes* Fortune 500, at http://www.forbes.com/finance/lists, and United Nations Statistics Division at http://unstats.un.org/unsd/)

Let's have a closer look at the issue. Assume a small country which has three large firms that produce all output in the economy: Megafirm, Superfirm and Maxifirm. Say that Megafirm sells USD100 worth of goods to Superfirm (illustrated in Table 5.5.1, Table 5.5.2 and Figure 5.5.4 on page 612), which Superfirm then uses as intermediate goods in the production of USD400 worth of goods sold to Maxifirm in round 2. Stop and calculate total revenue and total output: when Superfirm sells goods to Maxifirm, revenue is USD400, but total output is only USD300 as the USD100 dollars worth of goods used as factor inputs by Superfirm **must be deducted to avoid double counting**! The same holds true as these intermediate goods – factor inputs – flow around the production system during rounds 3 to 5. Total revenue will of course be higher than total output value during each round.

Table 5.5.2 *Revenue and value-added in an economy ($US)*

Rounds of selling and buying in a simple economy	Total revenue	Total output (value-added) at each stage = contribution to GDP
Round 1: Megafirm sells goods to Superfirm for $100	$100	$100
Round 2: Superfirm sells goods to Maxifirm for $400	$400	$300 ($400 – $100)
Round 3: Maxifirm sells goods to Megafirm for $1,000	$1,000	$600 ($1,000 – $400)
Round 4: Megafirm sells goods to Superfirm for $2,000	$2,000	$1,000 ($2,000 – $1,000)
Round 5: Superfirm sells goods to Maxifirm for $4,000	$4,000	$2,000 ($4,000 – $2,000)
Round 6: Maxifirm sells goods to final consumer for $8,000	$8,000	$4,000 ($8,000 – $4,000)
Sum totals:	$15,500	$8,000 (= **GDP**)

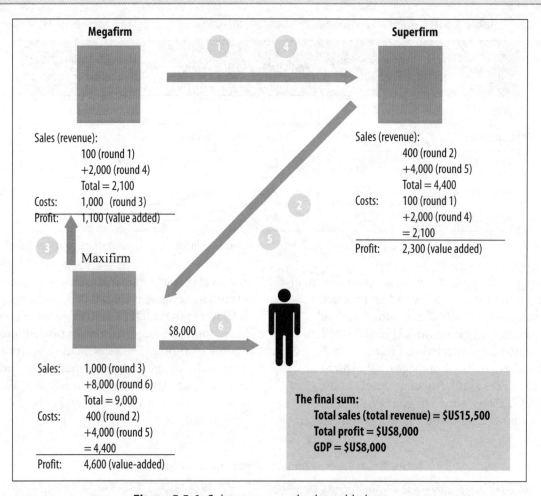

Figure 5.5.4 *Sales revenue and value-added output*

This is exactly what happens in real economies. A large portion of output is used as inputs in other firms. When Maxifirm ultimately produces an **USD8,000 widget** which is sold to an end user in round 6, the final sale is the same as the sum of value-added, i.e. a **GDP of USD8,000**. Now here's the interesting part: if you look at the profit and loss statement of each firm, you will discover that summing up **each firms' *profit* gives exactly the same value as *GDP*!** Total revenue is entirely dissimilar to de facto output value. Bluntly put, one simply *cannot* compare total sales (revenue) of firms with the total value of output. Total revenue includes all the costs of inputs and value added – while GDP is only the value added.

Now go back and look at Table 5.5.1 on page 611 and spot the flawed reasoning in comparing total sales and GDP. The appropriate – but still rather meaningless – comparison would be **between companies' profits and GDP.**[43] It then turns out that ExxonMobil in fact is considerably smaller in 'economic power' than both Ecuador and Finland. Ford Motor Company ran a loss in 2001. In other words, the 'Ford economy' was in fact smaller than Sierra Leone – one of the poorest countries in the world.

43. Note that in reality there will not be a **perfect** match between corporate profits, value added and GDP. Firms will have additional costs and income other than those associated purely with the sales of goods. Profits and GDP are the **closest** comparisons one can make in a silly exercise which compares companies to countries.

Commodity agreements ©IBO 2003

When commodity producers commit themselves to pricing or output agreements to regulate the market, one speaks of a commodity agreement – or an international **commodity agreement**, **ICA**, as commonly referred to (see "Commodity agreements" on page 99). Most developing countries are to some extent dependent on commodities, and when 77 developing countries created the United Nations Conference on Trade and Development – UNCTAD – in 1964, commodity agreements were amongst the top items on the agenda and UNCTAD became the overseer of international commodity agreements. Commodity agreements have two main goals:

1. **Reduce price fluctuations and set output levels:** Commodities such as coffee and copper are notoriously unstable in price, as low demand and supply elasticities create relatively large changes in price when demand and/or supply changes. A commodity agreement between suppliers can help to even out price fluctuations by using **buffer stocks** (see Section 2.1), setting output targets and allocating production quotas.

2. **Raise the long-run price level:** Falling commodity prices have caused the terms of trade in developing countries to deteriorate continuously. By limiting overexpansion of supply, the aim is to counteract the long-term decline in price and compensate for poor terms of trade and declining national income.

With the exception of oil, commodity agreements have generally been unsuccessful in limiting the decline of commodity prices and increasing revenues for developing countries.[44] The cost of upholding the scheme often proves economically unsustainable since the success of market intervention via buffer stocks and quotas is based on **temporary** fluctuations in demand and supply. Commodity prices, on the other hand, have declined continuously for many years. The commodity agreements for tin, sugar, cocoa and coffee all collapsed in the mid-1980s, as did the rubber cartel in 1999. It is once again all too clear that developing countries which are dependent on a narrow range of commodities for export earnings will face considerable challenges.

...THE END...

Final word from John Shamhula

During the last week of May 2004, *The Economist* sponsored a five-day conference on development in Copenhagen, Denmark. Under the chairmanship of Björn Lomborg, author of *The Sceptical Environmentalist* and director of Denmark's Environmental Assessment Institute, the 'Copenhagen Consensus' gathered a group of leading economists to address one issue: Which are the most urgent problems in the world to solve? At number one, the answer was unanimous: HIV/AIDS.

In November 2002, on a study trip through Namibia, my colleagues and I met many different people from all walks of life. Ultimately, I asked the same question: 'If you had the power to put limitless resources into solving one single issue in your country, which would it be?' Let us hear how my Namibian friend and colleague, John Shamhula answered this question late one quiet night sitting in the garden with my Swedish friends Anna and Per:

'The main problem is the HIV/AIDS virus. If we can get the African countries to the level of richer countries, we can do something. If we can create development and understanding for every Namibian person to say 'Yes, this is a serious problem', then we can be able to stop this virus, to fit in all Namibian people. Really there cannot be any other way.

'That's the problem: we cannot be open like you people. Really, I like the way you Swedish people are so open, you can tell the truth about such things which is really not the case for the Namibian people.

---

44. See, for example, Todaro & Smith, pp. 623–24.

'But HIV, really that's the main problem. I have seen, I believe, three infected teachers in the last term at school and one passed away. If I look at a young person, 27 to 28 years old, this person still has many contributions to the country. But HIV will end that person's life perhaps. And this is where the teacher must be a source of information to young people in the community. We must be a role model … if not an example to people in the community. Like this, we are educating the entire nation.

'Many men have affairs with young women because the girls are uneducated and the man simply has a job and some money. If the girls could just understand … but many times of course the girls feel that they must be with this man because they themselves do not have anything for survival. She might go with him, but it is because of 20 Namibian dollars only. That sex will not be safe because they will not use condoms. The effects are a spread of infections … many young girls.

'To your students, I say you must come up with treatments and solutions to this problem. In Namibia maybe we can just stop the spread or at least minimise the spread. But what I'd like to say to them [your students] is to educate themselves and others. That's my issue as a Namibian person.'

'If I could solve anything … actually, it is a most difficult question, only being in a classroom as a teacher. As a teacher, you are leading the nation … yes really, for teachers the most important thing is to educate the young ones, at least to go on to better education to help development. If I could be given a chance then I will further my studies.

Preparing for exams

Short answer questions (10 marks each)

1 Why is human capital so important in the development process?

2 What barriers to economic growth can be explained using the Harrod-Domar model?

3 Why might economic growth not be compatible with sustainable development?

4 What are the possible negative consequences of economic growth in a developing country?

5 Distinguish between the various forms of aid received by developing countries.

6 Evaluate the role of multinational companies in helping developing countries to achieve economic growth/development.

7 Explain how many developing countries became burdened with severe debt problems in the 1980s.

8 How have falling commodity prices affected many developing countries?

9 Discuss whether economic growth leads to an improvement of the environment.

10 Why are so many developing countries 'dual sector' economies?

11 Describe the 'poverty cycle' and suggest how a developing country can break the cycle.

12 Explain the importance of well-established property rights in the process of development.

13 Distinguish between 'growth' and 'development'.

14 Describe stabilisation policies as outlined by the International Monetary Fund (IMF).

15 Outline the possible negative effects of import-substitution policies.

16 Discuss whether the success of newly industrialised countries – such as the 'Asian Tiger economies' – is solely the result of outward oriented policies.

Extended response questions (25 marks each)

1 a How might one measure differences in living standards between less developed and developed countries? (10 marks)

 b How might developed countries assist less developed countries to increase their living standards? (15 marks)

2 a Outline the main features of outward-oriented and inward-oriented development strategies. (10 marks)

 b Explain which of the two strategies is most likely to lead to development. (15 marks)

3 a What are the various forms of aid a developing country might receive? (10 marks)

 b Compare aid and trade as the most effective means of development. (15 marks)

4 a Explain how developing countries can acquire investment funds for development. (10 marks)

 b Evaluate the role of multinational companies (multinational enterprises) in investment and development. (15 marks)

5 a Explain three major barriers to development experienced by developing countries. (10 marks)

 b What strategies might developing countries adopt in order to overcome these barriers? (15 marks)

6 a Explain how a developing country can have growth without development. (10 marks)

 b Evaluate import-substitutions as a method of achieving growth and development. (15 marks)

7 a Outline the benefits of increased openness in trade. (10 marks)

 b Critically assess the claim that developing countries will benefit from increased trade liberalisation. (15 marks)

8 a Explain how foreign aid might help in the development process of a developing country. (10 marks)

 b Critically examine the claim that 'Trade is better than aid' in the development process. (15 marks)

9 a Distinguish between interventionist and market-led strategies of development. (10 marks)

 b Evaluate the effectiveness of each approach. (15 marks)

10a Examine the role of foreign direct investment (FDI) for developing countries. (10 marks)

 b Evaluate whether foreign direct investment is more important than aid in attaining growth/development. (15 marks)

EXAMINATION NOTES, ANSWERS AND BIBLIOGRAPHY

These notes are offered to assist students and their teachers.

The definitive rulings on all these issues are disseminated by the IBO via their syllabus documents and subsequent clarifications.

Candidates and teachers are strongly advised to make sure that they are familiar with these documents.

Examination notes

I.   GRADES

The IB final grade is comprised of two parts; an externally assessed component consisting of three test papers, and an internal assessment component consisting of a portfolio of four written commentaries on economic issues which are graded by the individual teacher. The final grade breaks down as follows:

Higher level

External assessment (exam papers; 80% of total grade)

Paper 1 (1 hour) 20% of final grade

This paper consists of 4 extended-response questions, which are based on all 5 syllabus sections. Candidates choose one of the four.

Paper 2 (1 hour) 20% of final grade

This paper consists of 6 short-answer questions, which are based on all 5 syllabus sections. Candidates choose 3 of the 6.

Paper 3 (2 hours) 40% of final grade

This paper consists of 5 data-response questions, which are based on all 5 syllabus sections. Candidates choose 3 of the 5.

Internal assessment (portfolio of 4 commentaries; 20% of total grade)

A portfolio of 4 commentaries is handed in to the teacher over the 2 year IB course. Each commentary is between 650 – 750 words in length, and focuses on issues from at least 3 of the 5 sections in the IB economics syllabus.

Standard level

External assessment (exam papers; 75% of total grade)

Paper 1 (1 hour) 25% of final grade

This paper consists of 4 extended-response questions, which are based on all 5 syllabus sections. Candidates choose one of the four.

Paper 2 (2 hours) 50% of final grade

This paper consists of 5 data-response questions, which are based on all 5 syllabus sections. Candidates choose 3 of the 5.

Internal assessment (portfolio of 4 commentaries; 25% of total grade)

A portfolio of 4 commentaries is handed in to the teacher over the two-year IB course. Each commentary is between 650–750 words in length, and focuses on issues from at least 3 of the 5 sections in the IB economics syllabus.

II.   COMMAND TERMS IN IB QUESTIONS

All three types of written papers will contain a variety of key examination terms and phrases. It is vital that students understand the distinctions between these command terms, in order that the questions may be squarely addressed.

Command terms

Account for	Explain a specific case or situation using sound economic reasoning. For example, 'Account for the rise of supply-side policies during the 1980s'.
Analyse	Analyse means breaking the question down into specific parts in order to look at them point by point. Relevant assumptions and definitions should be included. This entails understanding the central issues involved in order that you may apply correct terms/concepts/models to the parts. For example, 'Analyse the effects of implementing a value-added tax on a good'.
Analyse the extent	This is an extension of 'analyse', asking that some form of judgement be rendered. For example, 'Analyse the extent to which a value-added tax can increase government tax revenues'.

Assess	Analyse an issue/problem by outlining component parts and then weighing the relative importance or magnitude of different possible outcomes. The command term indicates that some form of reasoning and conclusion must be included. For example, 'Assess the impact of a minimum wage on the labour market'.	Evaluate	Similar to 'discuss' above, this command term asks for different views to be clearly outlined and then weighed against each other in economic terms. Evidence in favour of different arguments/standpoints should be given and discussed. A conclusion must be included which is clearly based on evidence brought up in the discussion. For example, 'Evaluate the success of planned economies in solving the basic economic problem'. (A basic ingredient in the answer would of course be to contrast the planned system with the market system).
Calculate	Use mathematics to arrive at a specific answer. For example, 'Calculate the savings ratio needed according to the Harrod–Domar model, when a growth rate of 8% is desired and the capital-output ratio is 2'.		
Compare/contrast	Describe various situations and show similarities and differences between them. For example, 'Compare the performance of countries which have utilised outward-oriented development policies to those which have utilised inward-oriented strategies'.	Examine	Separate the issue/problem into component parts, and look at each one separately in order to make clear certain features. For example, 'Examine the possible side effects of rapid economic growth based primarily on heavy industry'.
Critically analyse	Analyse a situation/problem and then evaluate the outcome using economic terminology. Economic assessment should be used, which means that definitions such as suboptimal resource allocation or negative externalities should be included as assessment criteria. For example, 'Critically analyse the impact of imposing tariffs on goods'.	Explain	Basically, 'make clear', by outlining assumptions and definitions, and then describing component parts of the issue. For example, 'Explain how taxes may be used by governments to redistribute incomes in a country'.
		Identify	Separate or outline a distinctive feature or key component in an issue. For example, 'Identify the main causes of unemployment'.
Define	Give a precise meaning of a word/term/concept. For example, 'Define marginal revenue'. When a formula is possible; use it!	Suggest	Offer possible ideas, interpretations, or alternatives to a given scenario. For example, 'Suggest reasons why a country might be forced to lower income taxes'.
Describe	Give an account of an issue/problem by outlining the relevant parts in detail. For example, 'Describe the benefits of a free trade area'.		
Discuss	Consider different aspects of an issue or problem, by comparing different views or arguments. The views should be stated neutrally but a balanced conclusion is often necessary. For example, 'Discuss whether tariffs are more costly than domestic subsidies. (Note; one should take care to include relevant terms, e.g. 'costly').	Summarise	Put forward the main points or arguments in a given field of questioning. For example, 'Summarise the arguments against economic integration in common markets'.
		To what extent?	This command term requires a background analysis which results in an evaluation of different outcomes or results. For example, 'To what extent should supply-side policies be used to control inflation?'
Distinguish	Make clear the difference between two things by identifying distinguishing characteristics. For example, 'Distinguish between GDP and GNP'.	What?	This asks for clarification of an issue/problem – often by clearly contrasting one issue with another. For example, 'What are the main types of development aid?'

III. ATTACKING IB QUESTIONS

While I in *no way* will attempt to take over the job of your teacher, a few tips on writing exam papers are probably in order. Just keep in mind that writing exam papers is a skill and must be practised. No matter how good you are in economics, if you can't convey your message clearly in print, your grades will suffer.

General tips

- Read the question! It is astounding how many students actually neglect to carefully read what is asked for, and instead make up their own minds what the question is about.

- Re-read the question occasionally as you write to make sure you haven't strayed away from the core issues.

- Scribble notes on the side of the question paper, and underline key terms. This will help you to focus on the main issue and not get side-tracked.

- Re-read the question.

- Set up a brief plan of writing. I recommend to my people that they use the following steps:

  Brainstorm; make quick notes of all the possible terms/theories/concepts, etc. which might deal with the question

  Organise; decide which points you will use and in which order you will use them

  Define/assume; it is often necessary to include key assumptions and definitions in order to adequately answer the question

  Exemplify; it is often useful to refer to specific examples in order to clearly illustrate your line of reasoning

  Diagrams; it is absolutely imperative that you illustrate your iteration with numbered, clear and well labelled diagrams which are then referred to in the written part of your answer.

  ### (B-O-D-E-D)

- Get a watch and put it on the desk in front of you during exams. Never spend more than the allotted time per question, i.e. 20 minutes per short answer question and/or 40 minutes per data response question.

- Use the first few minutes to brainstorm and organise. This is time will spent, as it helps you to focus on the key issues in the question.

- Use relevant main-stream diagrams when possible. Don't toss them in, but use them properly by referring to them in your body of text. Diagrams

should be used to support and illustrate well-articulated text, not replace it.

- Make sure that all diagrams, figures and tables you use are numbered. This makes it easier for you to refer to them in the text.

- Re-read the question so as not to go off-track!

- Neatly label all axes, curves, price/quantity changes, etc. Refer to these in the text, i.e. 'As illustrated in diagram 1, an increase in demand from D_0 to D_1 causes the price to increase from P_0 to P_1 …'

- If you use any form of calculations, make sure that your line of reasoning is clear and easy to follow. If you make a simple calculating error, the examiner will at least realise that your method is correct.

- Structure your answer by using a few headings and blank spaces between paragraphs.

- Make the examiners life easier by underlining key concepts used.

- Re-read the question!

- If the question is of a type requiring you to take a stance or arrive at a conclusion, make sure that this is clear in your iteration.

- Leave 5 cm of space at the bottom of each page so, when you edit, you are able to add in things which you forgot.

- Make sure that pages and questions are numbered and in consecutive order.

- Keep an eye on the time!

- Re-read the question!

Basically your answers should address the question squarely using good solid economic terminology and theory. Your answer should try to make life as easy as possible for the examiner, by being clear, legible and neat. Too many students seem to think that examiners will desperately try to decipher illegible handwriting and woofley commentary. They won't.

Short answer questions (HL only, 10 marks each)

Short answer questions should be addressed in 20 minutes, neither more nor less. You get 6 questions and must choose 3 of them. Read through them carefully, decide which ones you will do, and then stick to them. Don't spend time on a question only to decide that you would do better on another. Use 5 minutes and notepaper to outline a BODED methodology and then get cracking.

Many students find short answer questions more stressful than essay-type questions, for the simple reason that they try to fit in essay length answers into

20 minutes. Don't fall into this trap. It's really down to good resource allocation; use the first five minutes to outline which concepts and models you will use and what your answer will be. Basic assumptions/ definitions together with proper economic terminology and clear diagrams which answer the question posed will get you good marks.

Extended response questions (25 marks each)

Extended response questions are basically essay questions divided into two parts, a) and b). The first part is worth 10 marks and the second part is worth 15 marks. You get four questions and are to choose one of them. Use your 5 minute reading time to read the questions carefully and decide which one you will address. Use 10 minutes to outline a BODED plan, carefully distinguishing between parts a) and b). Thus you should use approximately 20 minutes on part a) and 30 minutes on part b). I strongly recommend writing down start and finish times of each part when the exam begins, so you don't spend too much time on the part a).

Extended response questions test high order skills such as analytical, evaluative and critical capabilities. The command terms in part a) are often 'explain' or 'describe', while command terms in part b) are more in line with 'evaluate' or 'assess'. Keep this in mind as you address the first part so you don't address issues in part a) which are better left to part b).

Perhaps most importantly in extended response questions; divide the two parts clearly! Do NOT answer both parts in one large body of text. This is a common mistake and I've heard a number of examiners comment on how difficult it is for them to assess and therefore correct a two-part question which has been 'thrown together' in a single answer. The question you want to ask yourself is: 'Do I want to make things difficult for the person responsible for setting my grade?'

Data response questions (20 marks each)

Data response questions have a wide span, both in terms of the syllabus and the range of skills necessary to answer them. You have a choice of five questions and are to answer three – which means you are to spend 40 minutes on each question. Again, write down the start/ finish times for each question at the beginning of the exam, e.g. 12:03 → 12:43 → 13:23.

A data response question is a series of questions based on a newspaper article and/or various tables/ diagrams. The first two questions are of 'define/ describe/calculate' type and are worth 2 marks each. The next two questions are 'explain/outline' type and are worth 4 marks each. The last question is inevitably of the 'assess/evaluate/discuss' type, and is therefore worth 8 marks. The questions are linked to the data and/or article provided. Keep the following in mind:

- Having multiple questions of ascending levels of difficulty means that you should spend more time on higher-mark questions than lower mark. Examiners frequently comment on how students put lots of needless effort into lower-order questions, and get their two points in the first paragraph – while the rest of the answer is in 3 more paragraphs which get zero points. Basically, do not use more than 2 minutes per mark. Once you have answered the question, or run out of time, move on to the next.

- Refer to data or article content whenever possible. This does not mean using extensive quotes, but briefly underlining your answer by linking to a point in a diagram or facts given in the text.

IV. INTERNAL ASSESSMENT

The internally assessed component of the IB economics course allows the student to demonstrate knowledge and application of economic concepts. During the entire course, the student is to write four commentaries on newspaper/ magazine articles or Internet journals. Each commentary should:

- Explain the linkages between the article and economic theory from a focal syllabus section.

- Demonstrate economic insight into the implications of the extract, i.e. it should provide evidence of an ability to look at current events from the particular point of view of an economist.

- Basically show that you can explain and put into context the complexities of real life by way of using the language and symbols of an economist.

Requirements

- Each candidate is required to select 4 articles (extracts) and prepare 4 commentaries. The articles must be from four different sources. The four commentaries comprise a portfolio which will be graded as a whole, not as individual commentaries.

- Each of the four commentaries must be between 650 and 750 words. No more and no less. One word more or less gets you zero marks on criterion A. Everything but the coversheet and article is included in the word count, such as comments to diagrams, footnotes, etc.

- Students are not allowed to use articles that are older than six months before the start of the course. Nor may in-class articles issued by the teacher be used.
- The article should be in the working language of your school. Other languages are allowed if the student provides an exact translation of the article.
- The analysis must deal with economics – not business! Use the concepts, theories and models in the syllabus.

Format requirements

Each commentary heading on the first page must include the following: the student's name, class, title and date of article; the date the commentary was written; the commentary number; the source of the article; the article title; a word count; and syllabus section.

Three of the four commentaries must focus on concepts/theories/models from three different IB syllabus sections. Any diversion from this will render zero marks on criterion B.

All articles must be referenced, i.e. a source must be given. If the Internet is used to select the extract, then the above reference system must be used to identify the original source. Any reference to the Internet should also cite the Uniform Resource Locator (URL), e.g. http://curia.ucc.ie/info/net/acronyms/acro.html,

Grading criteria

The 4 scripts make up the Internal Assessment portfolio. Grades are given based on the portfolio as a whole. To attain higher marks, all criteria (A-E) must be shown in every single script. Again, the trick is finding a good article. The 4 commentaries making up the portfolio will be graded according to five criteria, the sum of which is 20 marks. Terms within quotation marks are official IB wordings:

Criterion A: 'Rubric requirements'. This deals with meeting the word limit and using economic theory from three different syllabus sections. (2 marks)

Criterion B: 'Organisation and presentation'. The assessment here is based on the range of sources (different for each article), organisation and presentation of scripts and portfolio and use and applicability of diagrams. (4 marks)

Criterion C: 'Use of economic terminology'. This criterion deals with how well you use the language and illustrations of an economist. Appropriateness, relevance and use of economic terms, concepts and language is the key here. Terms requiring definitions must be correctly defined. (5 marks)

Criterion D: 'Application and Analysis of economic concepts and theories'. This is applied economics; you must not only be familiar with economic language but also use it relevantly in order to link the complexities of reality to economic theory in an insightful manner. In other words, it is not enough to use economic terminology well – you have to apply it to the right things. (5 marks)

Criterion E: 'Evaluation'. This evaluates the extent to which you are able to constructively evaluate economic concepts and models used to analyse real-world contexts. (4 marks)

Tips for the student

- Avoid articles where the analysis is already done for you. You get no points for simple reiteration of someone else's analysis.
- Don't pick overly complicated issues – there's nothing wrong with applying your skills and economic knowledge to day-to-day issues, such as why the municipality wishes to make public swimming pools more available by lowering the price of admission.
- It is generally more fruitful to choose a relatively brief article (not too brief!) and build up a structure of economic arguments, rather than to choose a long article and comment generally on a few definitional points.
- Put some time and effort into finding and picking out articles – this is half the battle! Don't put off your search for articles until a few days before the deadline.
- It is helpful to the assessor if article sections which are discussed in the commentary are highlighted and numbered.

An example of how a commentary might look is given below. Far more extensive information is available in the Teacher Support Material, Economics Internal Assessment, which is sent to all IB schools.

COMMENTARY COVER

Economics commentary number 1/4 (HL)

Candidate name/number: Jim Henson/0666-0743   School code: 0743

Title of extract: "Big Bird on the FBI's most wanted list – interest rates soar"

Source of extract: *Financial Times*

Date of extract: 11 Aug. '0   Word count: 710 words

Hand-in date: 12 Sept. '04.

Syllabus sections relating to commentary: Sections 3.2 & 3.3

COMMENTARY

Name: Jim Henson   Hand-in date: 12 Sept. '04.

Class: IB1a   Source: Financial Times, 11 Aug. '04., p.12

School: Filbornaskolan, IB code 0734

Title: "Big Bird on James Bond's Most Wanted List…" Syllabus sections: 3.2 & 3.3

Word count: 710

EXTRACT:

BIG BIRD ON THE JAMES BOND'S MOST WANTED LIST – INTEREST RATES SOAR

Once again, the government has screwed up and left the rest of the nation turning slowly in the wind. True to the tradition of agency ineptitude blablablablablablablablablablabla

COMMENTARY

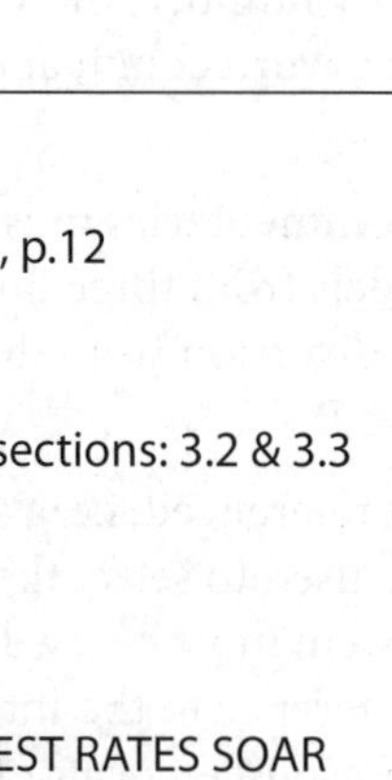

The main issue facing the American Federal Reserve (Fed) is whether or not the ensuing terror attacks against public figures are going to have a dampening effect on an already declining economy. The article brings up the issue of "pressure on prices" (see (*A*) above in highlight). According to the original Philips curve (fig. 1) blablablablablablabla….

Fig 1: Unempl.

As the interest rate rises, blablablabla blablablablablablablabla… on until you hit 650 to 750 words

V. EXTENDED ESSAY

Introductory comments on the extended essay

The extended essay allows students to delve deeper into economics by using economic theory in an area of research. The following brief outline of essay writing is in no way meant to be a complete step-by-step handbook, but rather a basic outline and general guide on essay methodology. Caroline and Maria (both 42 pointers!) have kindly allowed me to put their complete extended essays online at http://www.ibid.com.au. Both of these are excellent – and indeed received an 'A' – and give a general outline of what an economics essay is all about. Recommended reading.

The general outline of an extended essay

Past experience lends credence to the claim that the best way of learning a craft (for writing is indeed a craft!) is to actually **do** it. As this would be clearly impossible within the framework of an IB workload, I shall exemplify selected points by way of referring to – or quoting from a real extended essay on purchasing power parity in *Italics*.[1] This will hopefully illuminate the captions covering the bulk of this little extended essay section: abstract; introduction; purpose; method; body of text; and finally summary. The last part here deals with subjects not directly related to the above, i.e. more general technicalities such as footnotes (references), table of contents, bibliography, etc.

Title/ front page

See the IB criteria here. One always has a front page where the title, author, date and supervisor are clearly written. Artistry usually acceptable.

The abstract

An abstract gives a *Reader's Digest* version of the study, and is entered immediately after the cover page. (Note: not paginated). The purpose of the abstract is to give the reader a brief outline of the purpose of the essay, the research question, and the results of the study. There is a 400 word limit, so it is important to be brief and to the point.

> *Many economic studies have attempted to predict changes in the exchange rate. This study looks at the purchasing power parities (PPP) of different currencies by constructing an index based on a basket of IKEA furniture and then comparing PPP to actual exchange rates...//*
> *...the conclusion is that an IKEA index has a degree of relevance for exchange rate movements when there are large price differences between countries.*

The table of contents

Precedes the introduction. There are many ways and formats here, but each chapter and sub-chapter should be listed in order of appearance together with page numbers. (Note: not paginated).

The introduction

A good introduction has two main purposes: First, it should create interest in the subject. Second, it should present the topic at hand in such a manner that the reader sees the relevance of the subject as an economic issue. Remember, there is nothing wrong with using one's artistic license to grab the reader – as long as one keeps within the somewhat inflexible framework of proper research procedures.

I: INTRODUCTION

> *Every day people in every corner of the world try to predict exchange rate movements for different reasons...//...a very famous index of PPP is the Big Mac Index...//...*

The introduction should be brief and to the point. Present your broad outline of the topic and the reasons for studying it. This is often something totally lacking in EEs; the pupil puts forward a sound purpose and research question which simply 'is'. Nothing is said or implied as to whether the impending writing effort has any value whatsoever. Spend some time and effort on the title! The title should, again, be **short and poignant**. The IB is very strict on having a title that is closely linked to both the research question (= purpose) and the essay content. A little clarity here will go a long way indeed. In addition to this, the question should be returned to at times during the iteration in order to focus the writer and show intent of purpose throughout.

The purpose/research question

The introduction should flow smoothly into a more clearly stated field of study. Having a clearly stated research question in one's essay serves to further whittle down the scope of study and also helps the author in defining what sources and material will be of value.

> *With these two measurements, it should be possible to **see if an IKEA index, based on PPP, could possibly predict exchange rate movements.** Further issues that are going to be investigated are the weaknesses and limitations of an IKEA index...//...*

It is often praxis to clearly state one's purpose in the form of a **basic question** (and perhaps sub-questions therein) or a hypothesis to be verified or falsified. It mostly depends on the subject at hand, the writer's personal leanings and the scientific discipline itself. It is recommended that the question is highlighted in some way in order for it to stand out.

Other common ways to formulate a research question are to test the applicability/validity of a theory or model; build one's own model or theory based on primary statistics (quite difficult and time-consuming); and to describe an evolution/series of events/situation, etc. It is strongly advised that students avoid the

---

1. Please note that the captions and headings used here are not (NOT!) necessarily the same as you would use in your own essays. The discerning pupil should exercise his/her own judgement here.

alluring simplicity of writing a *completely* descriptive essay, as this all too often leads to garbled objectives, weak theoretical foundations and inherently hazy conclusions.

Almost equally important here, is to mention **what will not be a subject** for study! This is called 'stating the limitations' of the essay and clearly shows how any conclusions reached are subject to these limitations.

> *The investigation is comprised of prices of five different goods, from five different countries, ranging over a time span of ten years.*

The method

This is the part that really freaks people. First off let it be said that a brief description of how one has gone about writing the essay is **NOT A METHOD!** Method is the assembly of disparate tools one uses to answer the questions posed at the outset. The methodology is your **basic approach to the research question**. For example, conducting interviews as a research method is probably more fruitful in addressing the question 'Are consumers in America confident of the future?' than in answering the question, 'Do Norwegian gerbil populations change at rates positively correlated to temperature rises?' Simply speaking, method is comprised of the following three ingredients: **sources**; **theory/model**; and **compilation of the data** used.

One can say that any approach to answering the research question is viable as long as it is scientifically acceptable within the chosen discipline. Surveys, experiments, statistical compilations, etc. are all examples of acceptable methods. Again, the individual supervisor will assuage any worries you might have here.

1. **Sources**: These could be anything from newspaper articles to collecting data via extensive questionnaires:

   Primary sources: material gathered by yourself such as interviews and statistics, and also raw statistics compiled by institutions such as the central bank or the OECD.

   Written sources: books, articles, etc. – these are secondary sources.

   Verbal sources: interviews and the like.

   Note that one has to think about the **validity and reliability** of the sources one is using. The former deals with whether the source indeed can help answer the questions, the latter with the 'trustworthiness' of the source.

   > *The IKEA prices are found in the original IKEA catalogues for each of the five countries...//...the*

exchange rates are the average selling rates for respective years...

2. **Theory/model**: All models built have been based on more or less extensive studies by the founder. Naturally all theories have basic assumptions, limitations and levels of applicability. The author must include these! This is perhaps (?) a bit easier for those writing in the 'hard sciences' such as Biology and Physics – but how would I know?

   > *PPP states that identical goods, sold in two countries should have the same price after being adjusted to the exchange rate...//...according to the theory of PPP 100 Swedish Crowns (SEK) should buy the exact amount of IKEA furniture in any of the countries...//...the theory is built on a number of assumptions...*

3. **Compilation of data**: Basically, this means 'how I have gone about putting together the data I have amassed'. This is partially a question of legibility but also gives additional credence to the value of the theory in answering the questions posed.

   > *For each country the five goods are added to form a basket. The baskets for each country are identical and will be used to calculate the PPP rate of over-/undervaluation...*

At the end of the section on method, one should include **any weaknesses and limitations** that are inherent in the method and briefly discuss whether or not these weaknesses will skew the results and therefore conclusions. This is all part of academic humility and scientific honesty. One can also give a brief outline of the paper, or disposition, where one states the subsequent subjects to be brought up.

THE BODY OF TEXT

Avoid verbosity in general. Keep to the point without stooping to Hemingway-style taciturnity. Most important here is to make the essay easy to read and the line of thought easy to follow. A few notes:

Very often it helps to give some form of **background** to the subject in the first chapter.

Use simple yet appealing methods to **separate main headings from sub-headings**.

Use the **neutral form** of writing; i.e. use "...it could be said that..." rather than "...I think that..." or "...for me this means...". (Em, just as I have *not* done in this book).

'Air' the text body so as to make it **easier on the reader**. None of this Greenpeacing and tree-hugging; use some space!

Use charts, tables, diagrams and illustrations as needed. Note; do not use them *in place* of text but rather as an addendum or elaboration/ exemplification of the surrounding text.

Avoid blatant emotionalism! You are assumed to have donned the mantle of an aloof scientist and as such you have no use for anything even remotely resembling emotionalism. Avoid exclamatory, inflammatory or otherwise agitating invectives. A stance can be taken only in summation - and then only when the commentary is clearly that of the author and based exclusively on facts brought up earlier in the essay.

In general; be systematic! This will show that you are on-line in terms of both intention and content of your iteration. One cannot stress the virtues of neatness and clarity enough.

THE SUMMARY

This is where the results of the study are compiled. Very often writers start this section by briefly re-iterating the main topic/questions and how one has gone about answering it. Then one gives the conclusions.

Answer the questions posed! It is surprising how many budding scientists forget this simple task. One does not need to itemise all the questions posed in the introduction and then answer them piecemeal; use the flow of narrative to fit the compounded answers in neatly. This is also the only area in which you are allowed to insert your own remarks and comments; yet you must **never use any new material here!** One should in other words not need to have any footnotes (references) for the Summary.

> *...found that the IKEA index could predict mean reversion in the long run...*

One can also add a discussion on certain aspects of interest that arose in the body of text, such as whether or not a certain source has perhaps skewed the results or not. Also, this is the place to draw one's own conclusions.

> *...the most possible restriction for predicting exchange rates would be the fact that IKEA seems to attempt price strategies...*

BIBLIOGRAPHY

One **must** list all the sources (on a separate page) one has used in the essay. Again, this is up to the IB and your supervisor to iron out, but basically, be neat. Author, title, edition, date of issue, place of publication and publisher.

General technicalities (and a few words of paternal advice)

Here are a few additional points and FAQs that didn't fit neatly into the above captions:

References/footnotes: This seems to be a big problem for young writers - and many do not realise that references are part of the footnotes. The basic rule of thumb is to **add a reference to any statement/claim that cannot be considered to be general knowledge** in a footnote. One also adds footnotes in order to **elaborate on a marginal point in the body of text** such as whether a source can be considered valid or not. Basically, it is better to have one footnote too many than too few! Use common sense and see the examples in Italics above. There are about 15,678 different ways to include footnotes; ask your supervisor. In this author's humble opinion, footnotes should be **placed at the bottom of the page** - not at the very end of the essay. This simply makes it easier for the reader to find the notes.

Some advice here: As soon as you use a source when you are writing, add the page number and title of the book/newspaper in parentheses **immediately** after! This could save a lot of time later on when the supervisor asks you to add a footnote to a paragraph.

Quotations: One always uses quotation marks when excerpting verbatim from a text or interview. Any quotes are naturally endowed with a footnote. One should be very careful of including too many quotations as this weakens one's work rather than strengthening it.

Who is the reader: Basically you are writing for people in your field; yet this should in no way inhibit writing to a wider audience! If one has come to some really awesome conclusions then one might want to make the results known.... ('IB math teacher really a transvestite Celtic druid', might make a headline or two in the local paper).

Language: Note that good use of economic terminology and language always gets credit – even at the subliminal level of the Chief Examiner. Writing is not mechanics – it is an art!

Finding a subject: This is pretty much the only thing that supervisors cannot help you with. All we can do is help you in your **formulation** of the research question – we cannot find one for you. Base your choice of subject on what you are **interested in**, what you have **knowledge/experience** of and where you might have **good contacts** and/or **sources**. If all three are present, you have a winner. Get started early, here! Do not postpone this matter, as the earlier you decide on a broad issue, the faster you will hone down the scope to viable questions. This will make searching for relevant sources easier, too.

Acknowledgements: One might like to thank a number of people for being helpful in supplying information and such.

Appendices: This is optional and might include compilations of primary data, examples of important sources, questionnaires used, etc.

Finally:

Get started as early as possible! Use some of your holidays to compile your data/sources as this is probably the most time-consuming element of writing. Don't squander all holidays by way of adolescent hair-pulling and jumping about; there will be plenty of time for that later (during university). There is 100% correlation between students poncing around during the IB1/IB2 summer and getting poor grades on the EE.

Answers to Pop quizzes

SECTION 1

Pop quiz 1.1.1 On social science

1. 'Weaker' in this case means that social science often enables different and even contradictory interpretations of the results in studies.

2. The assumptions are necessary in order for the social scientist to be able to narrow a question down to a specific answerable subject as far as possible.

3. It is likely that the company data is biased – intentionally or not.

Pop quiz 1.1.2 Economics as a science

1. The actions of individual firms are within the field of *microeconomics*.

2. Growth, unemployment, price stability and the external balance are the main macro issues. Environmental issues, income distribution, development and productivity are other macro areas.

3. Micro deals with issues arising in specific firms or industries, while macro is the *aggregate* of all firms, households and economic activities arising between countries, e.g. trade.

Pop quiz 1.1.3 Positive, normative, ceteris paribus

1. This is an example of dual causality; increased GNP has been shown to affect development but the opposite also holds true, i.e. development provides the foundations for growth.

2. This is a normative statement; "...should raise taxes..." indicates a value-laden statement.

3. This is actually a positive statement! The speaker is not putting forward an opinion but telling us how others feel about an issue. Nothing normative has actually been said.

Pop quiz 1.1.4 Factors of production

1. Money simply *represents* economic goods, i.e. it is an indicator of the value of other goods.

2. The circular flow represents the factor markets (for example labour) and the market for goods and services.

3. An economist would say "Nonsense!". Scarcity is something that all societies must deal with.

Pop quiz 1.1.5 Utility

1. "...decrease."

2. Because of diminishing marginal utility, a spilled third pint will have less effect on total utility than the increase in total utility gained from buying the second pint.

3. The higher the marginal utility, the more one is willing to pay for a good. In other words, one is willing to bear a higher opportunity cost of foregone consumption of goods Y and Z if the marginal utility is high enough when purchasing good X.

Pop quiz 1.1.6 Opportunity costs

1. Not being able to earn money, holding a full time job or having lots of free time.

2. One has to rank the alternatives in order to find the *next best alternative* – which is of course the opportunity cost.

3. No, per definition, free goods cannot have opportunity costs.

4. No, all economic goods can be used in the production of something else. Hence there is an opportunity cost.

626

Pop quiz 1.1.7 More opportunity costs

1. The additional 1,000 tonnes of roses means sacrificing 500 units of guns.

2. Since we are on the PPF at both points, the assumption is that all resources – factors of production – are used to the maximum. Moving from point C to E simply reallocates labour, and unemployment would remain at zero.

3. Point X lies outside the boundaries of what is possible for Mirageville to produce given the *current* availability and efficiency of factors of production.

Pop quiz 1.1.8 PPFs

1. An 'outward-bending' PPF tells us that resources are not equally reapplicable, or not perfectly mobile, which is more realistic.

2. It shows that opportunity **costs** are rising since all factors of production are not equally efficient when **reallocated** to alternative production.

3. All countries will have limited resources and will thus have to make choices in what to produce, giving rise to opportunity costs in terms of foregone output.

Pop quiz 1.1.9 PPFs, growth and development

1. Information technology has had an enormous impact on efficiency in production. This will shift the PPF outwards, to the right.

2. Fewer available labour hours – as a result of earlier retirement – will shift the PPF left.

3. Specialisation increases efficiency and productivity, and shifts the PPF to the right.

4. Both the 'point' and the PPF shift right. Note that the point does not have to be *on* the PPF.

Pop quiz 1.1.10 Markets and their merits

1. The market economy lets consumers' desire for goods and producers' ability to meet those desires set market prices, respectively; demand and supply. What is produced, how it is produced, and who gets the good is decided by this market mechanism. A planned economy has government control over output and production methods and consumer demand has limited influence on the price or quantity of goods.

2. The more scarce a good, the higher the price, as willing buyers 'bid over' each other, forcing prices higher. Conversely, goods which are plentiful will generate competition amongst suppliers, decreasing the price.

3. Many goods such as roads are very difficult to charge for, and many goods such as education would be under-demanded. Thus suppliers would not supply such goods in sufficient quantity. Society values goods such as transportation and education very highly and will intervene in the market in order to supply them.

4. Education and health care are examples of goods which people would be unwilling to purchase in what society considers "sufficient amounts".

5. Property rights mean that one has ownership over production factors and the gains from commerce, e.g. the profits. This creates an incentive for entrepreneurs to conduct business.

Pop quiz 1.1.11 Prices, rationing and allocation

1. Money enables people to hold off on consumption by saving which allows investment, thus creating a modern capitalistic system. Barter means that people must have co-wants, and the search costs are high.

2. Basically, the high level of demand will force ticket prices upward, limiting the ability of a number of people to buy tickets. This *rations* tickets to those who are willing and able to pay the going market price.

3. …good resource allocation! The concert producers have evidently put resources into the wrong 'product', e.g. group, and are better off finding a group which will sell 40,000 tickets.

Pop quiz 1.1.12 Transitional economics

1. People on fixed incomes (students and pensioners) and those unable to shift their assets to good value retainers (primarily low income groups).

2. The level of national income during the Soviet era was in all likelihood highly *overestimated*, which means that the decline during the 1990s is somewhat exaggerated.

3. Financial institutions are needed in order to put savers in contact with borrowers, i.e. provide funds for investment in the economy.

SECTION 2

Pop quiz 2.1.1 Non-price determinants of demand

1. Demand for both tourism services – hotels and restaurants – and travel fell considerably. This is *exactly* what is happening here in Mexico as I write this (April 2009) due to the swine flu epidemic and fear of pandemic.

2. Decreased demand for air travel meant that the price was too high at existing supply. Airlines lowered prices (and decreased supply) accordingly.

3. Fish and beef can be considered substitutes for chicken. It is likely that demand for these two substitute goods will rise.

4. Bauxite is the raw material used in producing aluminium, thus there will be an increase in the (derived) demand for bauxite as more aluminium is needed to produce cars.

5. The statement is correct – but only up to the comma. You see, it works the other way around too! If the exchange rate (= price) of the EURO falls, it will be cheaper to tour Europe and demand for tourism in Europe will increase.

Pop quiz 2.1.2 'Quantity demanded' vs. 'demand'

1. The *law of demand* states that if the price of a good falls – ceteris paribus – a higher quantity will be demanded.

2. …shift the demand curve.

3. a) demand for oil will fall as less gasoline will be needed; b) a fall in the price of gasoline will not change demand but the *quantity demanded*; c) public transport is a substitute for using cars so demand for gasoline/oil should fall; d) increased use of solar power should lower its cost and price, thus decreasing demand for oil, which is a substitute.

Pop quiz 2.1.3 Market equilibrium

1. Equilibrium market price is where $Q_s = Q_d$, i.e. at a price of $6.

2. This would result in excess quantity demanded and a possible black market.

Pop quiz 2.1.4 Effect of changes in demand

1. The demand for bicycles would probably fall as it becomes cheaper to drive.

2. For example, demand for bicycles would increase if more cycle paths were built (= complement) or if the price of public transportation (= substitute) increased.

Pop quiz 2.1.5 Effect of changes in supply

1. Assuming that coffee and cocoa are substitutes, a fall in coffee prices will cause consumers to switch some of their consumption to coffee, and demand for cocoa would decrease.

2. If cocoa producers knew in advance that demand for cocoa was going to fall, they would decrease supply in order to avoid excess supply.

Pop quiz 2.1.6 Effect of a change in supply for one good on the price of another

1. As the price of good A has increased and demand for good B has decreased, these two goods could be *complements*.

Pop quiz 2.1.7 Supply and demand

1. The price of solar panels (e.g. the panels used to produce energy) rose dramatically. The cause was households' search for substitutes, one of which is solar power. As demand for solar power increased so too did the price of panels.

2. Re "Oil, maize and tortillas": How might the price of oil have affected the price of silicon? One of the main raw materials in the manufacturing of solar panels is silicon. Rising demand for photovoltaic solar panels increased demand for silicon, driving up prices.

3. Aha, you didn't look things up! Well, you would have figured out that since the price of silicon rose drastically and that silicon is a key factor input in computer chips the result was an increase in manufacturing costs for computer manufacturers. This decreased supply for computers.

4. The statement jumbles up cause and effect. The increase in demand will of course *create* an increase in the price of houses.

5. Productivity is the quantity of output per given unit of input (land, labour, capital) during any given time period. Agricultural land can become more productive due to improved grain varieties, better irrigation and increased use of pesticides/fertilizer, etc.

6. This is easily illustrated by shifting the supply curve left (out of season supply) and right (in season supply). The two equilibrium points show the extent of price fluctuation.

7. You will want to sell off property before prices fall – and your demand for buying new property will decrease. If other property speculators follow you, then you will in fact create precisely the situation you anticipated; a fall in property prices due to increased supply and decreased demand.

Answers to questions on Figure 2.1.30

1. Nothing! The market price would already be below the maximum price.

2. …lowest….// …much…// …high(-er)…// …more…

3. The excess demand would force the price upwards towards the market clearing level. Quantity supplied would increase and quantity demanded would decrease. The black market would disappear.

Answers to questions on Figure 2.1.33

1. The total purchasing cost to government is $P_{min} \times Q_D \Leftrightarrow Q_S$ and total government revenue if all this were sold at a price of P_{mkt} would be $P_{mkt} \times Q_D \Leftrightarrow Q_S$. The *final* (net) loss to government is therefore $P_{min} \times Q_D \Leftrightarrow Q_S$ *minus* $P_{mkt} \times Q_D \Leftrightarrow Q_S$.

2. Removing the minimum price would increase quantity demanded and decrease quantity supplied. This would save the government money; decrease revenue for farmers; and lower the price of grain for consumers.

3. The government could put higher consumption taxes on agricultural goods.

4. If the government buys up the excess supply created by a minimum price scheme, then this comes out of the taxpayers' pockets ultimately. The consumer then pays a higher price than the market equilibrium when purchasing the good.

Answers to questions on Figure 2.1.34

1. Nothing. The minimum price would remain.

2. Unemployment would fall.

3. The average wage rate (= price of labour) would decrease, quantity of labour demanded (Q_{LD}) would increase and Q_{LS} would decrease – unemployment would fall.

4. The demand for labour is derived from the demand for goods and services in an economy, so the demand for labour would increase.

Pop quiz 2.1.8 Maximum and minimum prices

1. See Figures 2.1.31 and 2.1.34 – there is misallocation of resources. A maximum price causes an excess of demand and a minimum price leads to an excess supply.

2. A maximum price set by government will create an excess in demand and possible black markets. Some form of rationing system and/or queuing system will be necessary.

3. See Figure 2.1.34 – the cost to government is $P_{min} \times Q_D \Leftrightarrow Q_S$. Note that other costs arise, such as administration and storage costs.

4. Farmers' income will increase by the increase in price ($P_{mkt} \Leftrightarrow P_{min}$) times the increase in quantity supplied ($Q_{mkt} \Leftrightarrow Q_s$). (A boomerang-shaped area.)

Pop quiz 2.1.9 Price support/buffer stock schemes

1. Government stockpiling would decrease supply and raise the market price – see 'minimum price scheme'.

2. A buffer stock scheme will have costs similar to those in a minimum price scheme, such as the costs of buying up excess supply, storage and administration.

Pop quiz 2.2.1 PED and 'slope'

1. The price inelastic good shows only the portion of the demand curve which is inelastic, while the other curve shows only the elastic portion of the demand curve.

Pop quiz 2.2.2 PED and cross price elasticity

1. As both price and quantity have increased for the complement good Y, the demand curve has shifted to the right. This is caused by a decrease in the price of complement good X.

2. Highly inelastic, i.e. a PED lower than 1.

3. The percentage decrease in quantity demanded is 10% due to an increase in price of 12.5%, yielding a PED of 0.8.

4. Apples and oranges are substitutes, while oranges and orange peelers are complements.

5. Demand for email will increase 150%.

Pop quiz 2.2.3 Income elasticity

1. a) demand falls; b) lower unemployment will mean rising (national) income and thus lower demand for inferior goods; c) a rise in the price level will mean that peoples' real income has fallen – demand for inferior goods would increase.

2. This could be either price elasticity or income elasticity of demand. -2 for PED would mean the good is normal, while -2 in terms of yED means the good is inferior.

3. No, income elasticity of demand can be positive at low levels of income and negative at high income levels – an inverted 'U' in a diagram with quantity and income on the axes.

Pop quiz 2.2.4 Price elasticity of supply

1. The first curve will start from the origin; the second from the price axis; and the third from the quantity axis.

2. Price elasticity of supply would increase.

3. PES is likely to be quite low.

Pop quiz 2.2.5 Elasticities

1. This is the "rectangular hyperbola" illustrated in Figure 2.2.21.

2. The more inelastic the demand curve, the higher the total tax revenue – see Figure 2.1.23 – since the quantity demanded will not decrease as much as for a good with high PED.

3. Yes, it makes sense if the price has decreased – and the starting price was lower than the unitary elastic price point on the demand curve.

4. ...the same...//...zero!

5. You would much prefer a unit tax, since this would be a very small proportion of the price of a very good (expensive) bottle of wine.

6. Dried goods can be stored and thus overstocked, enabling suppliers to put more on the market more quickly than fresh goods.

Answers to questions in Figure 2.2.31

1. The consumer. Low PED would decrease the price more than high PED, thus more of the incidence of the subsidy would go to the consumers.

2. The question reads "...*instead* of the subsidy...", thus the minimum price of €105 would intersect demand at 40,000 tonnes and S_0 at 60,000 tonnes. The repurchasing scheme would force government to spend €2.1 million. Calculation: €105 × 20,000 tonnes (e.g. P_{min} × excess supply) = €2,100,00.

3. An increase in demand will

- increase the price
- increase the quantity supplied, and hence...
- ...increase the total amount of subsidised wheat – total government expenditure on the subsidy would increase

Pop quiz 2.2.6 Incidence of taxes and subsidies

1. Inelastic demand will benefit consumers relatively more than producers. Staple foods which are important for poorer households are often subsidised. This is a form of income redistribution, as the subsidy will have a greater effect on low income families.

2. See Figure 2.2.33 Effects of an expenditure tax on nuclear power and coal power.

3. Both taxes and subsidies are forms of market intervention. It is possible that resource allocation is improved due to taxes and subsidies when there are negative and positive externalities (see Section 2.4). Reallocation effects will be greater when demand is price elastic.

4. These goods are highly demand inelastic and will therefore create large amounts of tax receipts, while the societal benefits are lower consumption.

Pop quiz 2.3.1 Cost theory

1. It depends on the profession or job. Labour would be a fixed cost when the staff is permanent (say, accountants) but variable when additional units are employed to meet changes in output (for example, labourers picking fruit).

2. The short run is defined by the time period where one or more factors of production are fixed. In the long run all factors are variable.

3. Average total cost (ATC) is £25. ATC is AVC plus AFC. To arrive at AFC one divides TFC by the quantity; £1,500,000 / 100,000 units = £15. Thus ATC is £10 + £15.

4. Economic costs show how resources could have been otherwise allocated, i.e. economists look at the *opportunity* costs.

Pop quiz 2.3.2 Short run and the firm

1. Diminishing returns will set in.

2. When total product increases at it highest rate, marginal product will be at maximum.

3. "...rise at a slower rate".

4. Again, diminishing returns set in. These are short-run concepts and thus not applicable to the long run.

5. There is a lag between changes in marginal and average costs as output increases. Marginal rates change faster than average rates.

6. MC = TC/ Q. £30,000/500 = £60.

7. Falling MP means that the MC per unit rises, since the *cost* of each additional unit of labour stays the same. Decreasing output per same-cost unit of labour means rising MC.

8. At low levels of output, the change in TFC will be spread over fewer units than at higher levels of output. Thus the ATC curve will shift further upwards at low levels of output.

9. MC will not change! (AC will rise more at low levels of output than at high output levels – the AC curve will 'roll' upwards.)

10. Both MC and AC curves shift upwards, i.e. both average marginal and average total costs increase.

Pop quiz 2.3.3 Long run and the firm

1. When fixed costs increase less than output, then LRAC falls. Spreading administrative and marketing costs; bulk-buying benefits; financial benefits, etc.

2. a) There is an incentive for firms to become larger in order to benefit from scale economies… b)…which means there is an incentive to merge with other firms(-s) … c)…which can lead to the emergence of a few powerful and large firms…d) which are increasingly global since home markets are too small for the firm to attain scale economies.

3. Use the unit cost picture (MC, AC) for diminishing returns and rising LRAC ('enveloping effect') to show possible diseconomies of scale.

4. Average costs show how well **all factors** of production are being used – both fixed and variable. Marginal costs only show the cost of producing the last unit.

Pop quiz 2.3.4 Revenue

1. When the price is also marginal revenue, we are dealing with a perfectly competitive firm – a price taker.

2. MR for a competitive firm is horizontal while it is downward sloping for a monopoly.

3. When TR is maximised in a monopoly, MR is zero. When MR turns negative, TR falls.

Pop quiz 2.3.5 More revenue

1. **Higher MC** ➔ lower output; **higher MR** ➔ increase in output.

2. Perhaps a LR strategy of capturing the market by setting the price at AC.

Answer to question on Figure 2.3.21

The individual firm will have a smaller part of a *larger* total market due to market entry by other firms.

Pop quiz 2.3.6 Perfect competition

1. Allocative efficiency is when P equals MC. Productive efficiency is when average costs are minimised, i.e. AC_{min}.

2. The firm will be a price-taker resulting in infinite demand for an individual firm on a perfectly competitive market.

3. As each firm produces at MC = MR in accordance with our profit maximising assumption and has a perfectly elastic MR/AR/demand curve, an increase in market demand will raise MR/AR/demand and the firm will increase output along the MC curve. Thus the sum of each firm's MC curve becomes the total market supply curve.

4. Marginal costs would increase – the MC curve would shift upwards. We are assuming that labour is a **variable** factor.

5. We are assuming no barriers to entry and perfect information. Any abnormal profit will attract market entry by other firms. This increases supply and therefore lowers the MR curve for firms making abnormal profits. Loss making firms would be forced to leave the market, decreasing market supply and raising MR for individual firms. In the long run, only normal profits are possible.

6. If MR is above AVC then the firm is covering at least some of the fixed costs. It may cost the firm more to leave the market as the fixed costs will still exist.

7. 12,000 units. Since we are assuming long run equilibrium, firm C's AC_{min} will be where MC = MR.

8. MR/AR for the individual firm will be higher and abnormal profits available so existing firms will increase output. However, this will attract other firms and over time the increase in supply will lower MR/AR. In the long run the market price will decrease – possibly to below the original price.

9. A lump-sum tax is basically a fixed cost; MC will remain unchanged but AC will 'roll' upwards.

Answer to question on Figure 2.3.29

The monopoly is not producing where P = MC so the firm is not allocatively efficient.

Answer to question on Figure 2.3.31

Neither of the monopoly firms are producing at the lowest possible cost per unit, i.e. the P is not equal to AC_{min}.

Answer to question on Figure 2.3.32

The firm must either seek to increase demand or decrease costs. (Note that increasing demand via marketing means that variable costs rise – this might offset any increase in demand.)

Pop quiz 2.3.7 Monopoly

1. The monopolist is a price-setter since there are market barriers to entry.

2. The monopolist will set output at MC = MR since it is assumed to be a profit maximiser. Price is then set at the highest possible demand point above MC = MR. The MC curve cannot cross the MR curve beyond the point where MR is zero – which is the unit elastic point on the demand curve. Thus the MC curve will only set price along the elastic portion of the demand curve. (Compare with diagrams in Figure 2.3.30.)

3. As in answer 2 above, output for a profit maximising monopoly will be below the point where MR cuts the Q-axis – which is the point of revenue maximising output. Going from profit maximising to revenue maximising output means that the firm increases output. (Compare with diagrams in Figure 2.3.30.)

4. Lower output to where MC = MR. This will increase profit.

5. Monopolies are commonly associated with higher prices and lower output than perfectly competitive markets. Possible exceptions are natural monopolies; price discrimination; and monopolies which apply break-even pricing (often public utilities).

6. Competitive firms would have a higher price than a natural monopoly. See Figure 2.3.36.

Pop quiz 2.3.8 Monopolistic competition

1. There are non-homogeneous goods, i.e. differentiated goods.

2. There are no barriers to entry, so existing firms will see profits 'stolen' by rivals which enter the market. In the long run, AR = AC.

3. A monopolistically competitive firm tries to 'stay ahead' by differentiating its products in some way. Consumers might be prepared to pay a premium for a certain brand or feature.

4. It is possible that monopolistic competition spurs innovation and leads to greater variety and choice of goods.

5. The monopolistically competitive firm is neither productively nor allocatively efficient; it does not operate where P = MC or where AC is minimised.

Pop quiz 2.3.9 Oligopoly

1. Firms are highly interdependent and will often avoid price competition since all firms stand to lose revenue and profit. Firms will instead compete by non-price methods.

2. Game theory helps explain why an oligopoly firm is reluctant to both raise and lower prices, as both actions might lose the firm revenue. See Prisoner's Dilemma.

3. A cartel is seldom legal and the agreement cannot be upheld in a court of law. there will be an incentive for cartel members to cheat, i.e. decrease the price and/or increase output in order to 'steal' customers from other members. When other members respond in kind in order to win back customers, the cartel breaks down.

4. Small firms will have specialised products – niche markets – which large firms do not find worthwhile to enter. Also, small local firms will have better knowledge of local tastes and be able to adapt quicker than large firms. Small firms also have long term relationships with local customers.

5. Non-price competition can mean that firms actually avoid head-on competition by differentiating products and aiming at different market segments.

6. No, not true; a contestable market will be both allocatively and productively efficient.

Pop quiz 2.3.10 Price discrimination

1. Price discrimination means that prices are altered according to what certain groups are willing to pay for the good, not due to differences in costs. This is clearly a case of price **differentiation**, where increased costs cause the firm to increase the price.

2. The Internet is global and price comparisons are very easy, which will make it difficult for firms to sell the same good at different prices – assuming low trade barriers and transport costs.

3. If reselling is easy then price discrimination becomes difficult, as firms cannot hinder a 'low-price' group from selling to a 'high price' group.

4. Profitmax output would still be at MC = MR. However, as the firm is a *perfect* price discriminating monopolist, the AR curve also becomes the MR curve. This is because there is no revenue lost as the monopolist sets another price. Thus monopoly output is where PCM output would be and the monopolist has captured all consumer surplus.

5. Winners would be students, pensioners and other groups with more elastic demand which pay a lower price than, for example, businessmen who have more inelastic demand. The benefit to society is increased output – and the possibility that goods which would otherwise not be provided now exist on the market. (See 'Outside the box; turning loss into profit'.) Losers are of course those who pay a higher price – aforementioned businessmen for example.

Pop quiz 2.4.1 Externalities and Sustainability

1. See Figure 2.4.3. An example of a negative externality in consumption would be cigarettes, while an example of a negative externality in production would be the production of electricity in coal fuelled power plants.

2. Externalities are difficult to both see and evaluate costs, since the third party effects are often unknown or un-attributable – especially *future* costs and benefits.

3. By increasing the availability of substitutes and/or improving efficiency in the use of such resources via technology.

Pop quiz 2.4.2 Dealing with externalities

1. Public goods are subject to non-rivalry and non-excludability, which means that such goods are virtually impossible to charge users for consumption. Private enterprise will not provide such goods for the most part. Since the positive externalities are so great, society – tax payer monies – often provide public goods.

2. Taxes on both consumption and production; bans; extension of property rights; and negative advertising.

3. Merit goods such as health care can be provided via direct production, provision via contracting to the private sector, or subsidies. Positive advertising might also be used.

4. By granting those who are affected by externalities the property rights, firms will face legal issues in damaging others' property and therefore have an incentive to reduce the externalities.

5. The most efficient firms will be willing to pay more for permits than less efficient firms, since their marginal costs are lower. The efficient firms will be able to produce the most output per unit of pollution allowed and will have an incentive to outbid less efficient firms for additional pollution permits.

6. Pollution knows no country boundaries. Green house gases emitted in the US, Europe and East Asia will affect South America, Africa and Oceania.

SECTION 3
Pop quiz 3.1.1 GDP accounting methods

1. The value of intermediate goods must be removed from the calculation of GDP, otherwise the same goods would be counted twice. Goods which are purchased by a firm as factor inputs are deducted from the firm's output – only the value-added is accounted for. The sum of all value-added in the economy is GDP.

2. Transfer payments are not included as they do not have a corresponding output. The income which enabled these transfers of money has already been accounted for.

3. €27.5 billion. Capital consumption is not included in accounting for GDP.

Pop quiz 3.1.2 Consumer price index

1. We can't say since the rate of inflation for the years in between 1996 and 2001 are missing.

2. The real price of Guinness has gone down. The real price of 20 pints in 2001 is €33/1.19 = €27.7 and the price in the base year was €30.

3. The real price of potatoes has fallen, as has the nominal price.

Pop quiz 3.1.3 Nominal and real values for USA in 2000

1. Since nominal GDP in 2000 is $US9,848 billion and real GDP in 2000 is $US9,216 billion, the GDP deflator can be calculated as; $(GDP_{nom} / GDP_{real}) \times 100$. This gives us $(9,848 / 9,216) \times 100 = 106.86$. The price level has increased by an average of 6.9%.

2. No way to answer since there is no *previous* year to compare with.

Pop quiz 3.1.4 National income accounting

1. An LDC might have higher net property income outflows than inflows due to having few multinational companies operating abroad, rendering higher GDP than GNP. Singapore has a number of multinationals, but is also very attractive for foreign direct investment inflows, which will lead to net property income paid abroad.

2. Technically speaking, zero. However, there will be discrepancies due to unaccounted flows of repatriated profits.

3. The real price in 1985 was SEK42,207 and in 2000 it was SEK43,798. The main weakness here is that the CPI does not take into account the technological improvements in the car.

4. GNP; 600 + 30 = 630. NNY; 630 – 60 = 570.

5. There has been no change in real GDP. In both years real GDP is €272,7 billion.

6. Nominal GNP per capita has increased by 25%. Real GNP has fallen by 6.25%, and as the population remains unchanged, so too has real GNP per capita.

7. The rate of inflation falls between 1973 and 1974. Note that the wage index is just there to confuse you.

8. Double counting occurs if intermediate goods between firms are counted twice; if $US150 worth of output contains raw materials and components purchased for $US110 from another firm, then counting both firms' output is double counting. Using the value-added method gives correct output, i.e. $US110 + $US40 = $US150.

9. Growth rates are falling; first period gives 15% growth and the second period 13%.

10. GDP per capita has fallen by 7.7%. We cannot figure out real GDP since the price level at both points in time is unknown.

Pop quiz 3.2.1 Growth and development

1. Many variables dealing with living standards are not shown: what is produced; distribution of income; purchasing power, etc.

2. Measuring development means that a good definition is necessary – which is the first difficulty, since such definitions inevitably become normative. Measurement difficulties arise since development is a qualitative variable rather than quantitative. The HDI attempts to overcome this by using a composite of variables.

3. Composite indexes are used since there is no *single* measure which covers the very wide span of development.

4. This is a very open field, and just the sort of thing your teacher will encourage you to discuss in class!

Pop quiz 3.3.1 Aggregate demand

1. There is causality in both directions. An increase in consumption might increase AD and cause inflation and rising interest rates. Conversely, an increase in interest rates will dampen consumption and AD and thus reduce inflationary pressure.

2. Government spending is independent of the price level. Governments decide whether to increase or decrease spending largely regardless of the price level. It is more a political decision.

3. An increase in the price level can cause an increase in interest rates, which in turn decreases investment and consumption – this is a movement *along* the AD curve. If, however, the interest rate increases, the AD will *shift* left, since investment and consumption will fall but a change in price is not the cause.

4. (Note that we are in fact dealing with *relative* prices, i.e. the increase in domestic prices in terms of foreign prices.) When domestic prices rise, people will substitute some domestic goods with foreign goods. This increases imports and decreases aggregate quantity demanded. Also, an increase in domestic prices will lead to a decrease in exports, which also decreases the aggregate quantity demanded.

Pop quiz 3.3.2 Aggregate supply

1. Markets are imperfect and do not necessarily clear. Thus it is quite possible for an economy to be in equilibrium in spite of high unemployment.

2. In drawing the AS curve, we assume factor prices to remain unchanged. If the price level rises, producers will be willing and able to put more goods on the market, seeing as how factor prices do not increase. Another reason is that increasing output means higher costs due to diminishing returns and bottlenecks in supply.

3. Keynes criticised neoclassical assumptions that factor markets will clear without any form of government intervention, and that equilibrium will be restored ultimately. Keynes argued that intervention by government is necessary to stimulate demand, e.g. 'prime the pump' of the economy.

4. Monetarists argued that people do not suffer from money illusion; they will bid up wages when AD and thus prices rise, shifting AS to the left. This creates a long run equilibrium output level, LRAS.

5. It is quite possible for output to exceed LRAS in the short run, since LRAS illustrates the long run potential of the economy. It is the *physical limit* which cannot be exceeded – just as it is impossible to produce outside the PPF.

Pop quiz 3.3.3 Equilibrium output

1. The higher price level of final output will cause labourers to bid up wages. This will shift AS to the left.

2. Perhaps one might consider raising interest rates or other policies which might dampen AD.

3. There is a strong connection between aggregate supply/demand and the labour market. The AS-AD model is thus linked to the concept of full employment.

Pop quiz 3.3.4 AS-AD and business cycle

1. SRAS has shifted left from an initial equilibrium.

2. At point D, real GDP must be the same as at point B, $US50 billion. If the GDP deflator is 110 at point D, then nominal GDP must be $US55. (GDP$_{real}$ x [GDP deflator / 100]). Yes, it is quite possible for the price level to rise between points C and D; a shift of SRAS to the left for example, will both decrease output and raise the price level.

Pop quiz 3.3.5 Business cycle

1. During a 'boom' period, one would expect lower unemployment and higher inflationary pressure, and the opposite during recession or downturn. The trade balance (exports minus imports) is rather unpredictable, yet imports often increase when incomes rise.

2. See Figure 3.3.11.

3. An increase in AD beyond long run capacity can cause inflationary pressure when, i.e. there is a positive output gap. (If SRAS shifts left from initial equilibrium, there will be inflation and a *negative* output gap.)

4. When the high level of economic activity creates a demand for labour, prices will rise and there could be a scarcity of labour. Nurses will be more prone to look at other jobs and be in a relative position of strength in bidding up nurses' wages.

5. High levels of capital will enable many producers to meet output needs with fewer labourers – both

during the recession and subsequent recovery. The 'shallow' recovery of 2001 – 2003 in the US can be attributed to the large build-up in IT capital during the late 1990s.

6. I wonder myself! One could expect positive and *lagging* correlation; an improving economy would make people feel better and more secure about the future – e.g. higher national income causes an increase in business confidence. However, one often finds that confidence is a good *lead* indicator; if firms feel more confident about future demand this feeds through to increased investment and new businesses – e.g. increased confidence leads to an increase in AD and national income.

7. The business cycle represents output and thus the potential standard of living available in the future. From a narrow perspective, understanding cyclical economic activity enables governments to correctly anticipate and adjust policies. In a wider perspective, studying business cycles can help us understand how to create an economy which provides stable (high) growth together with low inflation and unemployment.

Pop quiz 3.4.1 Demand-side policies

1. If households expect inflation to rise in the future, expenditure might be brought forward and cause an increase in AD. However, it is possible that since inflation "eats away" at the value of savings, households might in fact increase saving and thus decrease consumption which would then decrease AD. (See "real money balance effect".)

2. Imports tend to decrease during a recession as national income falls. Less overall expenditure on domestic goods tends to dampen inflation and thus the CPI will either fall (deflation) or increase at a slower rate (disinflation).

3. Government can decrease government spending and/or increase taxes to decrease AD and thus deflate an economy which shows signs of overheating.

4. a) AD shifts right; b) AD shifts left; c) AD shifts right; d) AD shifts left – a stronger domestic currency would make imports cheaper and increase imports and also make exports more expensive. Increased import spending and decreased export revenue would decrease AD. Supporting diagrams – outside the syllabus – would be the investment schedule to show the effects of interest on investment, and supply and demand for money in question c).

5. This is in accordance with classical views, where an increase in government spending might increase AD beyond LRAS. This will ultimately result in higher factor prices which will shift AS to the left. Output returns to long run equilibrium but at a higher price level. See Figure 3.4.3.

6. First of all, government is not responsible for monetary policy, nor is the central bank responsible for fiscal policy. It is also rather unlikely that one institution would implement policies in order to countermand policies employed by the other institution.

7. When property prices fall, people will feel less wealthy (wealth effect) and therefore tend to save more; and lower property prices will also mean that households will not be able to borrow as much using property as collateral. This will decrease planned consumption and AD. As for the reverse, a decrease in AD will lower national income and perhaps increase unemployment. This can decrease demand for major purchases such as property.

8. Canada might increase imports from Mexico, while Mexico decreases imports from Canada. AD will decrease in Canada and increase in Mexico.

9. The *real* interest rate has actually increased from 1% to 2% - i.e. doubled. Also, the value of real debt is not being "eaten away" to the same degree since the inflation rate has fallen.

10. The central bank can raise interest rates. Outside the syllabus: the central bank can decrease the money supply or increase reserve requirements for commercial banks. All three policies are contractionary (= decrease AD) since they will decrease borrowing by households and firms.

11. Shift AD to the right and link this to the 'tax refund' which increased household expenditure and the tax allowance to firms which increased investment.

12. A reasonable explanation is that US firms had a great deal of idle capacity and were able to meet the increase in AD without increased labour.

13. Two ways to answer this – both working in the "same direction":

a) Assume that Home Economy national income has increased due to an increase in aggregate demand. An increase in AD which is inflationary might cause other countries to decrease their purchases of goods from the Home Economy. Since the exchange rate to a large extent is determined by the demand for goods and services (derived demand), the *demand for the Home currency will*

decrease – and the exchange rate (i.e. the price of the Home currency in terms of other currencies) will fall. The Home currency depreciates.

b) An increase in Home Economy income will lead to an increase in import expenditure. As Home citizens/firms increase their imports, they will have to buy other currencies. This will increase the supply of the home currency on the Foreign Exchange market. An *increase in supply of Home currency* will cause a fall in the price – e.g. a depreciation of the Home currency.

Pop quiz 3.4.2 Supply-side issues

1. Shift AS to the left. This supply-side shock could result from higher prices of irreplaceable factor inputs, e.g. oil.

2. As people will realise that an AD which is inflationary actually lowers real incomes, they will act to regain lost income by bidding up wages. This shifts AS to the left. Classical economists claim that any stimulatory measures which move the economy beyond long run potential are solely inflationary in the long run. Use AS-AD model with LRAS curve.

3. Such policies include: lowering labour taxes; diminishing the ability of trade unions to keep wages high; lowering unemployment benefits; decreasing income taxes… Anything which increases the propensity of people to seek and accept jobs and/or the willingness of firms to hire more labour.

4. a) Less hours of labour offered on the labour market (AS); b) more start-up firms and increased investment in small firms (AS); c) This is a bit tricky. In the short run one would see a decrease in AS. However, in the long run, assuming 'negligible' rigidities in the labour market in general, a decrease in subsidies to declining industries would lead to a larger pool of labour and lower wages – which would entice firms to hire more labour, increasing AS.

Pop quiz 3.4.3 Weaknesses of economic policies

1. High growth/low unemployment can often be associated with increasing inflation, worsening of income distribution and increased imports and a trade deficit.

2. For example, when government stimulates the economy in order to decrease unemployment, the trade-off might be a higher inflation rate. (The government "trades-off" higher inflation for lower unemployment.)

3. Fiscal policy lags might cause an already slowing economy to decrease more, as deflationary policies kick in when the economy is already contracting.

4. Classical economists assume that people are rational in their expectations of future inflation. Expansionary fiscal policies (e.g. stimulating AD) would lead people to expect inflation and they would seek to increase wages to retain – or increase – real wages. This would decrease AS. Demand-side policies will thus have limited effect on real output in the long run.

5. Because labour markets are imperfect. It could take quite a long time for non-interventionist policies (talk about a contradiction in terms!) to clear the labour market. The unemployed would just have to "grin and bear it" while they waited for better times.

Pop quiz 3.4.4 Multiplier, accelerator and crowding out

1. We know that Y has increased by a factor of 2.5, which is k. As $k = 1 / (1 – MPC)$, MPC is 0.6.

2. National income will increase by a factor of 2, since $k = 1 / (1-0.5)$; €20 billion.

3. The value of k will fall.

4. A common market will enable households and firms in member countries to purchase goods from other members without hindrance, so an increase in government spending and/or a decrease in taxes will have less of a multiplicative effect, as more expenditure goes towards imports. In other words, a common market might increase the marginal propensity to leak/withdraw.

5. The accelerator model attempts to show how a change in income might result in even greater increases in investment. An increase in consumption of 2% would cause an even greater effect on AD if firms need to increase investment by 10% to meet this demand.

6. If real government borrowing takes place in order to stimulate the economy via government spending, then this increase in demand for loanable funds will drive up interest rates and crowd out other investment.

7. As the classical view is that complete – or near-complete – crowding out takes place, the effects of government borrowing and fiscal stimulation are negligible.

Pop quiz 3.5.1 Unemployment

1. Many rural farm labourers are in fact 'disguised' unemployed, as they cannot find full time jobs and thus remain on land which already has enough labour.

2. The proportion of working age populations – e.g. the total labour force – will be different. Also, the definition of the working age population might differ.

3. Demand for manufactured diamonds could lead to less demand for natural diamonds, lowering demand for labour in diamond mines. (It is unclear, however, whether people will accept manufactured diamonds as close substitutes to natural diamonds). This would be both sectoral and technological unemployment.

4. Assuming that the labour market is efficient, then people between jobs are 'looking around' for the best jobs and can be considered voluntarily unemployed.

5. The classical view is that disequilibrium unemployment arises due to labour market impurities, such as minimum wages and union bargaining power, which sets the real wage too high and disallows the market to clear. Keynesians view markets as naturally imperfect – primarily due to downward sticky wages – and that disequilibrium unemployment is the result of demand deficiency in the economy.

6. This would shift the AD_L curve to the left.

7. The real wage rate in the economy would ultimately decrease. Quantity of excess unemployment would fall and the labour market would move towards equilibrium at a lower overall rate of unemployment. (All of this is according to the classical view).

8. Supply-side policies aim to help the labour market to clear by removing impurities that keep the real wage rate above market clearing price. Illustration; Figure 3.5.11. Another possibility is to increase the aggregate supply of labour (ASL shifts right, Figure 3.5.12) by retraining and education programs (thus lowering the natural rate of unemployment.)

Pop quiz 3.5.2 Inflationary survival quiz for travellers

1. Note that the question reads "…catering to **tourists**…"! Turkish shop owners and restaurateurs will put the prices in a foreign currency such as the British pound or American dollar – and accept Turkish lira at the going daily rate.

2. Change as little as possible as late as possible. The lira you hold on to will lose value by the hour – and of course you will get more lira for your foreign currency tomorrow.

3. Credit card. Then hope that your account is not debited for a few days. The 2.5 million lira will then cost you less in your own currency as the lira falls in value.

4. The temple of Artemis (Greek goddess of hunting and nature) in Ephesus (near present Selcuk), and the tomb of king Mausolos, 4th century BC, at Halicarnassus (Bodrum).

Pop quiz 3.5.3 Inflation and deflation

1. This is not inflation since a specific tax is not a 'consistent and general' increase in the price level.

2. Money will not retain value, and its value as a medium of exchange will go down. It also becomes less useful as a unit of account and as a method of deferring payments.

3. You will lose because any grants or such you receive will be fixed and not move in line with inflation.

4. High inflation at home will lower foreigners' demand for the home goods and thus the currency – decreasing the price (= exchange rate) of the home currency.

5. When deflation is the result of increasing aggregate supply, national income increases and real earnings actually rise.

6. This is the 'liquidity trap' referred to in the case study on Japan. When the interest rate approaches zero, the investment schedule becomes infinitely elastic. No matter how much the interest rate is lowered beyond this point, investment remains unaffected.

Pop quiz 3.5.4 Causes of inflation

1. High inflation eats away at real debt! Governments borrow money from citizens, so high inflation will make the government debt burden lighter.

2. This is the start of a cost-push inflationary spiral. See Figure 3.5.15.

3. The neoclassical view would be along the lines of *excess money supply* and resulting demand pull inflation. The increase in the money supply will increase AD in the short run, and in the medium to long term cause households to adapt to higher expected inflation levels, which shifts AS to the left; a demand pull spiral increases the rate of inflation and lowers the growth rate. During t_4 and t_5, there is a tightening of monetary policy, and AD and output decrease – as does inflation after a lag of one period.

Pop quiz 3.5.5 Inflation and the Phillips curve

1. The weights take into account the relative importance of goods included in the CPI basket of goods in terms of the proportion of household expenditure.

2. The CPI does not show improvements in quality and function for goods. Also, due to changes in the weights of goods and content of the consumer basket, it becomes very difficult to compare average prices over longer time periods.

3. When people suffer from money illusion, they believe that more money means more spending power. An increase in AD which causes prices to increase will not cause labourers to demand higher wages, as they are 'fooled' by nominal rises in income from working overtime. This is shown by movements along the short-run Phillips curve.

4. According to the monetarist/classical school, people are rational in their behaviour. If people expect inflation to rise, they will try to minimise their real income losses by bidding up wages in order to at least retain real wages. This can be illustrated by a shift to the right of the short-run Phillips curve. (See Figure 3.5.26.)

5. Each short-run Phillips curve is drawn under the assumption of given inflationary expectations of households and firms. Demand-side policies would lead to higher inflationary expectations in households, which in turn would shift the short-run Phillips curve to the right. The economy would return to the natural rate of unemployment. (See Figure 3.5.26.)

6. Supply-side policies aim to shift the long-run Phillips curve to the left, i.e. decrease the natural rate of unemployment.

SECTION 4

Pop quiz 4.1.1 Comparative advantage

1. Because Textilia simply cannot produce more than 1,000 units of cloth.

2. The missing value is 400, since the 1,000 units of imported cloth would cost Orangia 800 tonnes of oranges.

3. Orangia's terms of trade would improve; instead of 1.25 units of imported cloth for each tonne of exported oranges, Orangia would receive 1.5 units of cloth. Subsequently, Textilia's terms of trade would worsen.

Pop quiz 4.1.2 Reasons for trade

1. You fight your opponent on speed, as you are less disadvantaged in this respect.

2. Maria will be able to paint the house quicker than Johann – and Johann will do a better job of repairing Maria's car. Each has an absolute advantage in her/his profession.

3. Jamaica is endowed with the natural resource bauxite, while Iceland has very cheap electrical power due to an abundance of geothermic energy needed to produce aluminium. As for bananas, the Icelanders grow bananas in greenhouses – again due to abundant energy.

4. Simple consumer preference explains why. Goods are seldom homogeneous and consumers enjoy having choices.

5. Country X will specialise in plastic (lower opportunity cost) and Y in steel. Trade can take place if country X receives one unit of steel for less than 2 units of plastic – and when country Y can get more than one unit of plastic for each unit of steel. The terms of trade lie between 1 steel = 2 plastic, or 1 plastic = 0.5 steel.

6. The cost ratios are identical, which negates the possibility of trade looked at from the point of view of comparative advantage.

7. Comparative advantage 'proves' that trade can benefit countries which are both absolutely advantaged and disadvantaged in the production of goods.

8. Yes, this is the comparative advantage argument of trade. Comparative advantage argues that differing opportunity cost ratios can be conducive to trade.

9. Increased productivity resulting from increased specialisation and/or improved technology will narrow the gap towards trade partners' PPFs.

10. The terms of trade is basically the price of exports compared to the price of imports. A decrease in the terms of trade means that export prices have fallen in relation to import prices. Exporters would see foreign demand for domestic goods increase and benefit from increased export sales. However, consumers would have to give up an increased amount of domestic goods in order to buy foreign goods.

Pop quiz 4.2.1 Tariff and non-tariff barriers to trade

1. See Figure 4.2.2. Winners are domestic producers (increased sales and revenue) and the government (tariff revenue). Losers are domestic consumers (higher price, less quantity) and foreign suppliers (fall in export revenue). Note the two allocative loss triangles, B and D.

2. A tariff on imported goods which have low PED will decrease imports less than goods with high PED but tariff revenue will be higher. Concomitantly, a tariff on goods with high PED will decrease imports more and thus have a greater positive effect on the trade balance (or current account). On the other hand, higher PED will render less government tariff revenue.

3. A subsidy to domestic producers, since this will increase domestic output without increasing the market price.

4. All are barriers to trade in one way or another, since these standards and regulations impose increased costs on foreign suppliers.

Pop quiz 4.2.2 Arguments for protectionism

1. The costs of tariffs are higher prices for consumers and lower quantity consumed (lower consumer surplus), plus efficiency losses to society. Gains of tariffs are increased domestic production and improved current account. The cost of subsidies is the government spending, while the benefits are increased domestic production without increasing the price for domestic consumers. In both cases, there is the possible benefit that protectionism allows infant industries to grow up. There is also the risk that the protectionist measures invite reciprocal protectionism from trading partners.

2. Since it is theoretically a temporary form of protectionism, infant industry trade barriers allow a country to exploit possible comparative advantages in the production of goods and ultimately achieve economies of scale.

3. Domestic jobs are also *lost* due to trade barriers, for example when importers and retail outlets do less business. Other criticisms are that barriers invite reciprocal protectionism; there are possible forward linkage effects in higher costs for domestic export industries; and that trade partners' fall in export revenue will decrease their demand for imported goods.

4. Domestic technical standards and various forms of legislation will levy additional costs on foreign producers who are forced to modify/alter products to comply with various rules and regulations.

5. A country which attempts to 'save' domestic jobs by way of imposing tariffs, quotas and devaluing the currency, will inflict damage on trade partners' exports.

6. A tariff, quota and subsidy will all increase domestic production and decrease imports. The decrease in imports might decrease import expenditure and thus improve the current account in the balance of payments. Subsidies might increase export revenue and therefore also improve current account.

Pop quiz 4.3.1 Economic integration

1. Increased trade is generally viewed as a 'win-win' situation, yet the increase in prosperity is by no means evenly spread. Losers will primarily be those labourers working in industries which face severe international competition. There are also – highly contestable – arguments put forward which centre on the unevenness of power between developing countries and foreign multinational firms which are able to exploit cheap labour, low taxes and poor environmental standards.

2. Possible loss of jobs as competition in certain industries increases, and the possibility that zero internal tariffs will redirect trade to less efficient producers within the FTA (HL: this is *trade diversion*).

3. Re-export tariffs and local content rules will need to be implemented in the FTA.

4. A FTA enables each member to set its own outward tariffs towards non-members, while a customs union means that there is a common outer tariff wall.

5. A common market will allow a range of freedoms in the mobility of goods, labour and capital, which will necessitate a degree of convergence in standards, taxes and labour legislation.

Pop quiz 4.3.2 HL: Trade creation and trade diversion

1. Consumers will gain due to increased competition, i.e. more choice, lower prices and improved quality. Firms stand to reap benefits of scale, adopt new technology and ideas, and increase their competitiveness towards non-members.

2. Initial gains can be seen when RTA members increase trade with each other. Dynamic gains are possible when increased specialisation, and improved comparative advantage allow members to increase non-RTA trade.

3. Yes indeed. It is in fact highly unlikely that all members of the customs union are more efficient than all non-member producers. Thus the zero tariff between members will still have a diverting effect on some more efficient producers outside the union.

4. A FTA creates trade within a limited membership, by which there might well be trade diversion when non-member countries' tariffs remain in place. When non-members have tariffs and other forms of trade barriers which FTA members do not, there is a tendency for outsiders to 'stumble' in trying to compete on equal terms.

Pop quiz 4.3.3 HL: Economic integration

1. When there is further integration within RTAs, i.e. a movement towards a customs union and beyond, there will be a need for member countries to coordinate legislation, taxes, import rules, etc. This might put a degree of authority into the hands of non-elected bureaucrats and administrators.

2. A customs union will have a common outer tariff, which will have to be agreed upon and upheld by all member states. Other issues are expenditure taxes within the union, as completely free trade in goods will naturally be an incentive for wide-scale arbitrage (= reselling) if there is great divergence in tax rates.

3. A common currency area will have monetary policies set by a single central bank. This sets interest rates across the single-currency area, thereby removing each individual members' ability to set interest rates. (This is often referred to as a "one size fits all" monetary policy.)

Pop quiz 4.5.1 Balance of payments

1. Argentina's current account: +$US250,000 – $US50,000 = net improvement in current account of $US200,000. Canada's current account: net outflow of $US250,000. Brazil's current account: net inflow of $US50,000.

2. The visible trade balance.

3. The current account balance is +€10 billion. (Net financial flows are in *capital* account.)

4. China has a current account surplus due to exports.

5. This would be an outflow in the invisible trade account in Italy, with corresponding inflows to Thailand's invisible account. (Tourism and services primarily.)

6. FDI inflows to Kenya (in the capital account) might create jobs and growth in Kenya.

7. If the inflows to capital account are investment flows rather than loans, a country might finance a current account deficit. The US has been a long-standing example of this situation.

8. A 'cheaper' Korean won would make Korean exports more attractive, and possibly increase export revenues. (HL: take heed of the Marshall–Lerner condition and possible J-curve effects!) Koreans would also have to pay more Korean won to buy foreign currencies and foreign goods, which might decrease import spending. This would improve the Korean current account.

Pop quiz 4.6.1 Introduction to exchange rates

1. The exchange rate for the Swedish crown – expressed in US dollars – is $US0.133, or 13.3 cents. (US$1 / SEK7.5)

2. The yen will be increasingly demanded, and the yen will appreciate.

3. Japanese imports will increase the supply of yen on the foreign exchange market, depreciating the yen.

4. The supply of Faraway dollars will increase, lowering Farawayistan's exchange rate.

Pop quiz 4.6.2 Fixed exchange rates

1. The exchange rate for yuan – in US dollars – is $US0.12048, or 12.048 cents.

2. The yuan will be allowed to move between and 0.11807 and 0.12289 US dollars.

3. The Bank sells yuan for foreign currencies. This increases the supply of yuan and lowers the price of the yuan.

4. There will be an outflow in capital account – and the foreign reserves have increased.

5. Increased Chinese imports will increase the supply of yuan and so cause downward pressure on the yuan. The Bank of China might have to intervene by buying up yuan with foreign currencies in order to increase demand for the yuan and keep the peg. (This is an inflow to the Chinese capital account in balance of payments.)

6. The Bank of China could raise interest rates to attract financial inflows (deposits).

Pop quiz 4.6.3 Floating and managed rates

1. The demand for a currency is basically dictated by what foreigners are able to do with another currency; buy goods/services and invest. Increased interest in a country's products and/or investment opportunities by foreigners will increase demand for the currency.

2. When governments intervene in the market for a floating currency, it is referred to as a 'dirty float'.

3. By buying and selling the home currency on the foreign exchange market, a country can influence the supply and demand for its currency. Other short-run options are to alter interest rates. In the long run the country might have to resort to supply-side policies in order to become more competitive.

4. If the HKD retains its peg to the US dollar, the HKD will also appreciate against other currencies.

Pop quiz 4.6.4 Exchange rate determinants

1. The supply of euros will increase and thus depreciate.

2. The British pound would appreciate, as more foreign firms move to invest in Britain. The increased demand for the pound would drive up the exchange rate.

3. A lower rate of inflation in Korea would alter relative prices in Korea's favour. This would increase demand for the Korean won. The won would appreciate.

4. The ECB can intervene by using foreign reserves to buy euros and thereby increase demand for the EURO.

5. The profits made by Swiss firms in Germany will be euros. Repatriating these euros to Switzerland and exchanging them for Swiss Francs (SFR) will increase demand for SFR. The SFR would appreciate.

Pop quiz 4.7.1 Balance of payments and exchange rates

1. The current account will be adversely affected, as exports become dearer and imports cheaper than what would be the case if the exchange rate floated freely.

2. In order to attract inflows from investors/speculators from abroad. (This is an inflow to capital account which finances the current account deficit.)

3. A current account surplus means that there is a net outflow in capital account. The country has increased foreign holdings, which will provide a stream of profits (in to current account) in the future.

4. Tariffs and other trade barriers, plus devaluation perhaps.

5. An increase in income tax would lower overall expenditure in the economy (expenditure-reducing policy, e.g. a decrease in AD) and in doing so lower import spending.

6. Devaluation, no doubt about it. Supply-side policies are long run policies. (Yet keep in mind that the current account might take some time to improve due to possible J-curve effects and/or Marshall-Lerner condition.)

Pop quiz 4.7.2 HL: Marshall-Lerner condition and J-curve

1. Devaluation, since the sum of PED for exports and imports is greater than 1.

2. It would primarily result in expenditure-switching.

3. Yes, since firms are locked into long term contracts and households will not adjust spending habits immediately.

Pop quiz 4.8.1 Terms of trade

1. Since both Mexico and the US have a great deal of trade with their NAFTA partner, Canada, a depreciation of the Canadian dollar will improve the two other countries' terms of trade. (Assuming, of course, ceteris paribus.)

2. Industries in a country which has low price elasticity for vital imported goods needed in domestic production would pass these increased costs on to consumers.

3. An improvement in the terms of trade might decrease export revenue. If the country is highly dependent on exports then there will be a noticeable negative impact on the economy.

4. Deteriorating terms of trade have made it more difficult to purchase vital imports such as intermediated goods and capital, and also made debt servicing of foreign debt far more costly.

SECTION 5

Pop quiz 5.1.1 Sources of growth and development

1. Development is simply such a wide concept and there are such wide differences between countries. There are any number of notable exceptions to the 'standard' divisions such as 'North-South', and 'First – Second – Third World', and 'developing country/LDC' covers some very disparate countries.

2. This would not appear to be generally valid, since there are a number of very notable exceptions – for example the Asian Tigers and Japan.

3. The HDI composite measure takes into account the ability of a country to provide its citizens with health care, education and economic growth. To a certain extent, the HDI points to the quality of other factors which are not included in the index; for example, high growth rates may indicate that property rights are established, or that basic infrastructure is in place.

4. There will be negative correlation. Look up Darfur.

Pop quiz 5.2.1 Consequences of growth

1. Growth often entails using limited natural resources and increasing negative externalities such as pollution.

2. Increased income enables countries to "clean up their act". It should be noted that countries which show positive correlation in this respect also have relatively equal income distribution.

3. Yes, by becoming more efficient in our use of finite resources.

Pop quiz 5.3.1 Institutional barriers to development

1. When less tax receipts are available to governments, infrastructure, merit and public goods will suffer.

2. Clear and enforced property rights create incentives for business start-ups and other economic activity, which in turn provides an increased tax base.

3. Foreign firms are risk adverse, and will be reluctant to invest in countries where additional costs and risks of doing business – such as bribery and corruption – are high.

4. Bribery will have a far larger impact on small firms and low income groups, as "set rates" of bribes will account for a larger percentage of revenue/income than for large firms and high income groups.

5. Corruption has all too often led to capital flight, as corrupt government officials transfer borrowed foreign funds to personal bank accounts abroad.

6. Informal markets hide large potential tax bases and decrease government tax receipts which could be used to provide merit and public goods.

Pop quiz 5.3.2 Trade barriers to development

1. As incomes increase in developed countries, the price of commodities rises far slower – or even falls – due to low income elasticity of demand for commodities. In addition, demand for commodities is often outpaced by an increase in supply; low price elasticity of demand will cause prices to fall.

2. As commodity prices fall, developing countries dependent on commodities for export revenue have seen their terms of trade fall. In many cases this forms a negative cycle of falling terms of trade falling export revenue falling exchange rates falling terms of trade. (See Figure 5.3.8).

3. Deteriorating terms of trade often increase a current account deficit in LDCs; increase the foreign debt burden; limit the availability of imports; and provide an incentive for developing countries to produce more of the good which has fallen in price – further increasing supply, lowering the price and thus causing the terms of trade to deteriorate further.

4. See table 5.3.5; a narrow range of exports invariably leads to dependency on foreign markets and frequently very powerful buyers. Decreased demand in consumer countries – for example due to increased use of substitutes or lower aggregate demand – will have a strong impact on the exporting country.

5. Differentiated tariffs – i.e. lower tariffs on goods with low value-added – helps provide developed countries with low-cost raw materials needed in production. Higher tariffs on higher value-added goods 'protects jobs and industries'.

Pop quiz 5.3.3 Financial barriers to development

1. Oil profits in oil producing nations were largely deposited in banks in developed countries, creating a surplus of loanable funds at a time when most of the world was in recession. In order to put these funds to work, commercial banks lent large amounts of money to developing countries at what were then (mid 1970s) favourable interest rates. As interest rates were raised in the early 1980s to combat high inflation, many developing countries were unable to service their foreign debt. Some countries relied for a time on new loans to enable debt servicing.

2. There might be an official exchange rate which intentionally sets the price of the domestic currency too high, and a lower unofficial (black market) rate.

3. It limits trade, foreign investment and creates conditions for capital flight. A non-convertible currency can also exacerbate a developing country's dependency on primary goods exports.

4. It is often the rich and powerful themselves who are responsible for the capital flight in the first place. The strong secondary effects are that these funds have very high developmental opportunity costs, as capital flight represents a loss of economic activity, tax receipts and merit/public/infrastructural goods.

Pop quiz 5.4.1 Growth models

1. The capital-output ratio must be at most 3.

2. The ratio would decrease, as more output would be possible per unit of capital employed.

3. It is possible that foreign debt increases, and/or that the current account deficit increases.

4. Since productivity in the traditional sector will be very low, and underemployment very high, large amounts of labour are available for a high-growth modern sector.

5. The surplus of labour in the traditional sector will ultimately fall, and wage levels there will start to rise as increasing labour scarcity raises wages. In the long run wages must even out between the two sectors.

Pop quiz 5.4.2 Development aid

1. Bilateral aid is given directly from the donor country to the recipient country.

2. The recipient country might in fact be getting a bad deal in not 'shopping around' for the reciprocal purchases on the open market.

3. The statement is not entirely true in a few notable cases, where outward oriented countries have erected infant industry barriers.

4. Smaller countries will have correspondingly small domestic markets. Outward orientation enables benefits of scale and a wider range of production.

5. Inward orientation failed to achieve economic growth in most cases. This was largely due to lack of competition in protected home markets, lack of imported materials needed for domestic production, and forward linkage effects on domestic output.

Pop quiz 5.4.3 Loans, FDI and sustainability

1. Institutions providing credit enable efficient resource allocation by putting savers in contact with borrowers. This facilitates investment.

2. Increasing outward orientation; decreasing barriers to trade; and the seeming success of countries partaking in globalisation all contributed to increased FDI flows.

3. A subsidiary might allow an international firm to: have access to low cost production factors; avoid trade barriers; avoid high labour and profit taxes; lower transportation costs; and adapt products to local market conditions.

4. Higher national income in the recipient country can create additional demand for domestically produced goods and services (HL: refer to multiplicative effects), creating businesses in sub-contracting and parts manufacturing, etc.

5. Poverty often forces people to misuse domestic resources simply to survive in the short run. A strategy of 'grow now and repay the environment later' may well become increasingly difficult.

Bibliography

ABEL, A.B. & BERNANKE, B.S., *Macroeconomics*, 4th ed. Addison Wesley Longman, 2001.

ANDERTON, A., *Economics*, 3rd ed. Causeway Press Ltd, 2000.

BEGG, D., FISCHER, S. & DORNBUSCH, R., *Economics*, 4th ed. McGraw-Hill Book Co, 1994.

CALDERISI, R., *The Trouble with Africa*, Palgrave Macmillan, 2006.

CYPHER, J.M. & DIETZ, J.L., *The Process of Economic Development*, Routledge, 1997.

The Economist: *Globalisation – Making sense of an integrating world*, Profile Books, 2001.

DESCHODT, E. & MORANE, P., *Cigarren* (Swedish version of French original), Replik AB, 1996.

DILLARD, Dudley: *Västeuropas och Förenta staternas ekonomiska historia*, Liber Förlag, 1985.

FISHMAN, T.C., *China Inc*, Simon & Schuster, 2006, ISBN-13: 978-0-7432-5752-9.

FREGERT, K. & JONUNG, L., *Makroekonomiteori, politik och institutioner*, Studentlitteratur, 2003.

Freedom, Development, Free Trade and Global Governance, Cambridge University Press, 2003.

GILLESPIE, A., *Advanced economics through diagrams*, Oxford Revision Guides, Oxford University Press, 2000.

GRAHAM, E.M., *Fighting the Wrong Enemy: Antiglobal Activists and Multinational Enterprise*, 2000, ISBN paper 0-88132-272-5, http://bookstore.iie.com/merchant.mvc?Screen=PROD&Product_Code=91.

HUSTED, S. & MELVIN, M., *International Economics*, 2nd ed. HarperCollins College Publishers, 1993.

IRWIN, D.A., *Free trade under fire*, Princeton University Press, 2002.

KOTLER, P., *Marketing management*, 6th ed. Prentice-Hall International Editions, 1988.

KRUGMAN, P., *Pop internationalists*, MIT, 1996.

KRUGMAN, P. & OBSTFELD, M., *International Economics – Theory and Policy*, 5th ed. Addison-Wesley Publishing Company, 2000.

LEGRAIN, P., *Open world: The truth about globalisation*, London, Abacus, 2002.

LOMBORG, B., *The skeptical environmentalist*, Cambridge University Press, 2001.

MANKELL, H., *Jag dör men minnet lever vidare*, Leopard Förlag, 2003.

MOGGRIDGE, D. (editor), *Collected Writings of John Maynard Keynes*, Vol. 7. 'The General of Employment, Interest and Money', MacMillan for the Royal Economic Society, 1973.

MOORE, M., *A world without walls*, Cambridge University Press, 2002.

NORBERG, J., *I kapitalismens försvar,* Author and Timbrå Förlag, 2001.

MCCOULLOGH, N., WINTERS, L.A. & CIRERA, X., *Trade Liberalisation and Poverty: A Handbook*, Centre for Economic Policy Research & UK Department for International Development, UK, 2002.

OECD: *Open markets matter – the benefits of trade and investment liberalisation*, policy brief, October, 1999.

OKUN, A., *Equality and Efficiency: The Big Trade-off*, Brookings Institution, 1975.

O'ROURKE, P.J., *Eat the rich*, Picador, 1998.

PARKIN, M., POWELL, M. & MATTHEWS, K., *Economics*, 3rd ed. Addison-Wesley Publishing Company, 1997).

PERLOFF, J.M., *Microeconomics*, 2nd ed. Addison-Wesley Publishing Company, 2001.

RAJAN, R.G. & ZINGALES, L., *Saving Capitalism from the Capitalists*, Random House, 2003.

REES, G. & SMITH, C., *Economic development*, 2nd ed. Macmillan Press Ltd, 1998.

ROYAL ECONOMIC SOCIETY, Essays in Biography, *The Collected Writings of John Maynard Keynes*, Vol.X, MacMillan Press Ltd, 1972.

SACHS, J., *The End of Poverty*, The Penguin Press, 2005.

SEN, A., *Development as freedom*, Oxford University Press, 1999.

SHIPMAN, A., *The Globalization Myth*, Cox & Wyman Ltd, 2002.

SLOMAN, J., *Economics*, 4th ed. Prentice Hall, 2000.

SMITH, A., *Wealth of Nations*, books I – III, first published 1776, Penguin, 1999.

TODARO, M.P. & SMITH, S.C., *Economic Development*, 8th ed. Addison Wesley, 2003.

WALLACH, L. & SFORZA, M., *The WTO, Five Years of Reasons to Resist Corporate Globalization*, Seven Stories Press, 1999.

WANNACOTT, P. & R., *Economics*, 4th ed. John Wiley & Sons, 1990.

WORLD BANK, *Globalization, growth and poverty: Building an inclusive world economy*, Oxford University Press, 2002.

WORLD BANK, *The East Asian Miracle, Economic Growth and Public Policy*, Oxford University Press, 1993.

WORLD COMMISSION ON ENVIRONMENT AND DEVELOPMENT (WCED), *Our common future,* Oxford University Press, 1987.

WTO, *International trade statistics 2003.*

Recommended reference books for your studies:

While it might not be something my editor wishes me to include, simple honesty and a personal bent towards education rather than money-making dictates that I at least comment on a few of the books I have used in teaching for the past years. Here are three books I wish I'd written.

1. Top of the list is **Alain Anderton's *Economics.*** Just the kind of book I wish I could write but unfortunately will never be able to. Anderton writes straight to the point; uses thousands of examples; has an immense battery of applied economics and statistics; and generally does an excellent job of explaining really tricky issues. One of the better A-level textbooks and my personal favourite.

2. **Michael Parkin et al's *Economics*** is at a somewhat higher level, but most of it is accessible to the HL student. I used Parkin's books in introductory economics at university and still refer to it. Excellent explanations, applied economics and most illuminating use of diagrams.

3. If you are marooned on a deserted island prior to your exams and only take three books with you, **Andrew Gillespie's *Advanced economics through diagrams*** should be one of them. Truly amazing how much he manages to fit in to just over 100 A4 size pages. Incredibly clear, well-commented and easily accessible diagrams cover most of the IB syllabus. The only book I actually recommend that my students buy – other than the one you are holding of course.

Index

population growth 537
portfolio investment 467, 485
positive correlation 6, 68
positive externalities 538
positive externality 222
positive statements 12
potential market entry 210
potential real output 292
potential welfare gain 223
poverty 277, 548
poverty cycle 548
poverty, absolute 277
poverty, international 277
poverty, relative 277
PPF 522
predatory pricing 212, 215, 426
price discrimination 211
price elasticity of demand 104
price elasticity of supply 119
price fluctuations 97
price level 7
price mechanism 40
price of related goods 71
price support 97, 428
price support scheme 95
price taker 165
price transparency 493
primary commodity 14
primary goods 14, 97, 122
primary products, dependence on exporting 562
private ownership 36
producer substitute 71
producer substitutes 121, 122
productive efficiency 179
productivity 394, 577
profit 15, 69, 253
profit (corporate) taxes 326
profit tax 129
profitmax condition 169
progressive income taxation 314
progressive income taxes 230
progressive tax 377
property 67
property rights 38, 172
proportion of income 111
proportional tax 377
protectionist measures 479
public goods 75, 194, 235
public ownership 36
public sector 36
purchasing economies 161
purchasing power 272
pure monopoly 54

Q

qualitative area of study 277
quality of factors of production 72
quantitative variable 277
quantity demanded 56
quota 410

R

R&D 194, 215
race to the bottom 415, 416
rationing mechanism 40
raw material 14
Reagan, Ronald 326
Reaganomics 294, 326
real balance effect 308
real flow 250
real growth rates 263
real income effect 282
real wage unemployment 349
reallocation 85
recession 299, 300
recessionary gap 297
recovery 299
redistribution effects 356, 376
regional support 326
Regional Trade Agreement (RTA) 440
regressive tax 378
relative poverty 277
religion 572
rent 15
rescheduling debts 605
research and development 327
research and developments 54
resources 14
retail price 136
revaluate 484
revenue 69, 125
Rio Convention 245
rule of law 534
rural-urban migration 580

S

Saudi Arabia 522
saver 356
savings 250
savings ratio 577
scarcity 13
scarcity of factors 72
Schuman, Robert 396
self-fulfilling prophecy 61, 309
self-interest 15
self-reinforcing feedback loop 66, 309
services 254